Contemporary Authors®

ISSN 0010-7468

Contemporary Authors®

A Bio-Bibliographical Guide to
Current Writers in Fiction, General Nonfiction,
Poetry, Journalism, Drama, Motion Pictures,
Television, and Other Fields

volume 247

BRADLEY UNIVERSITY LIBRARY

Contemporary Authors, Vol. 247

Project Editor
Amy Elisabeth Fuller

Editorial
Michelle Kazensky, Joshua Kondek, Lisa Kumar, Julie Mellors, Mary Ruby, Stephanie Taylor

Permissions
Margaret Gaston-Chamberlain, Lisa Kinkade, Tracie Richardson

Imaging and Multimedia
Lezlie Light

Composition and Electronic Capture
Gary Oudersluys

Manufacturing
Drew Kalasky

© 2006 Thomson Gale, a part of the Thomson Corporation.

Thomson and Star Logo are trademarks and Gale is a registered trademark used herein under license.

For more information, contact
Thomson Gale, Inc.
27500 Drake Rd.
Farmington Hills, MI 48331-3535
Or you can visit our internet site at
http://www.gale.com

ALL RIGHTS RESERVED
No part of this work covered by the copyright herein may be reproduced or used in any form or by any means—graphic, electronic, or mechanical, including photocopying, recording, taping, Web distribution, or information storage retrieval systems—without the written permission of the publisher.

This publication is a creative work fully protected by all applicable copyright laws, as well as by misappropriation, trade secret, unfair competition, and other applicable laws. The authors and editors of this work have added value to the underlying factual material herein through one or more of the following: unique and original selection, coordination, expression, arrangement, and classification of the information.

For permission to use material from the product, submit your request via the Web at http://www.gale-edit.com/permissions, or you may download our Permissions Request form and submit your request by fax or mail to:

Permissions Department
Thomson Gale
27500 Drake Rd.
Farmington Hills, MI 48331-3535
Permissions Hotline:
248-699-8006 or 800-877-4253, ext. 8006
Fax 248-699-8074 or 800-762-4058

Since this page cannot legibly accommodate all copyright notices, the acknowledgments constitute an extension of the copyright notice.

While every effort has been made to secure permission to reprint material and to ensure the reliability of the information presented in this publication, Thomson Gale neither guarantees the accuracy of the data contained herein nor assumes any responsibility for errors, omissions or discrepancies. Thomson Gale accepts no payment for listing; and inclusion in the publication of any organization, agency, institution, publication, service, or individual does not imply endorsement of the editors or publisher. Errors brought to the attention of the publisher and verified to the satisfaction of the publisher will be corrected in future editions.

LIBRARY OF CONGRESS CATALOG CARD NUMBER 62-52046

ISBN 0-7876-7876-7
ISSN 0010-7468

This title is also available as an e-book.
ISBN 1-4144-1007-7
Contact your Thomson Gale sales representative for ordering information.

Printed in the United States of America
10 9 8 7 6 5 4 3 2 1

Contents

Indexing note: All *Contemporary Authors* entries are indexed in the *Contemporary Authors* cumulative index, which is published separately and distributed twice a year.

As always, the most recent Contemporary Authors cumulative index continues to be the user's guide to the location of an individual author's listing.

REF
Z
1224
.C6
v.247

Preface

Contemporary Authors (*CA*) provides information on approximately 120,000 writers in a wide range of media, including:

- Current writers of fiction, nonfiction, poetry, and drama whose works have been issued by commercial publishers, risk publishers, or university presses (authors whose books have been published only by known vanity or author-subsidized firms are ordinarily not included)

- Prominent print and broadcast journalists, editors, photojournalists, syndicated cartoonists, graphic novelists, screenwriters, television scriptwriters, and other media people

- Notable international authors

- Literary greats of the early twentieth century whose works are popular in today's high school and college curriculums and continue to elicit critical attention

A *CA* listing entails no charge or obligation. Authors are included on the basis of the above criteria and their interest to *CA* users. Sources of potential listees include trade periodicals, publishers' catalogs, librarians, and other users of the series.

How to Get the Most out of *CA*: Use the Index

The key to locating an author's most recent entry is the *CA* cumulative index, which is published separately and distributed twice a year. It provides access to *all* entries in *CA* and *Contemporary Authors New Revision Series* (*CANR*). Always consult the latest index to find an author's most recent entry.

For the convenience of users, the *CA* cumulative index also includes references to all entries in these Thomson Gale literary series: *Authors and Artists for Young Adults, Authors in the News, Bestsellers, Black Literature Criticism, Black Literature Criticism Supplement, Black Writers, Children's Literature Review, Concise Dictionary of American Literary Biography, Concise Dictionary of British Literary Biography, Contemporary Authors Autobiography Series, Contemporary Authors Bibliographical Series, Contemporary Dramatists, Contemporary Literary Criticism, Contemporary Novelists, Contemporary Poets, Contemporary Popular Writers, Contemporary Southern Writers, Contemporary Women Poets, Dictionary of Literary Biography, Dictionary of Literary Biography Documentary Series, Dictionary of Literary Biography Yearbook, DISCovering Authors, DISCovering Authors: British, DISCovering Authors: Canadian, DISCovering Authors: Modules* (including modules for Dramatists, Most-Studied Authors, Multicultural Authors, Novelists, Poets, and Popular/ Genre Authors), *DISCovering Authors 3.0, Drama Criticism, Drama for Students, Feminist Writers, Hispanic Literature Criticism, Hispanic Writers, Junior DISCovering Authors, Major Authors and Illustrators for Children and Young Adults, Major 20th-Century Writers, Native North American Literature, Novels for Students, Poetry Criticism, Poetry for Students, Short Stories for Students, Short Story Criticism, Something about the Author, Something about the Author Autobiography Series, St. James Guide to Children's Writers, St. James Guide to Crime & Mystery Writers, St. James Guide to Fantasy Writers, St. James Guide to Horror, Ghost & Gothic Writers, St. James Guide to Science Fiction Writers, St. James Guide to Young Adult Writers, Twentieth-Century Literary Criticism, 20th Century Romance and Historical Writers, World Literature Criticism,* and *Yesterday's Authors of Books for Children.*

A Sample Index Entry:

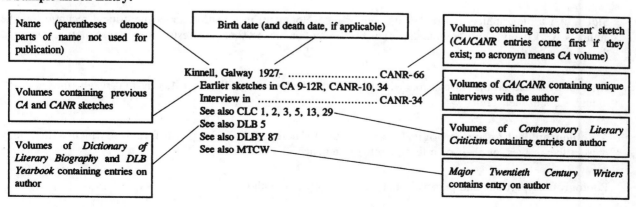

How Are Entries Compiled?

The editors make every effort to secure new information directly from the authors; listees' responses to our questionnaires and query letters provide most of the information featured in *CA*. For deceased writers, or those who fail to reply to requests for data, we consult other reliable biographical sources, such as those indexed in Thomson Gale's *Biography and Genealogy Master Index*, and bibliographical sources, including *National Union Catalog, LC MARC*, and *British National Bibliography*. Further details come from published interviews, feature stories, and book reviews, as well as information supplied by the authors' publishers and agents.

An asterisk (*) at the end of a sketch indicates that the listing has been compiled from secondary sources believed to be reliable but has not been personally verified for this edition by the author sketched.

What Kinds of Information Does An Entry Provide?

Sketches in *CA* contain the following biographical and bibliographical information:

- **Entry heading:** the most complete form of author's name, plus any pseudonyms or name variations used for writing

- **Personal information:** author's date and place of birth, family data, ethnicity, educational background, political and religious affiliations, and hobbies and leisure interests

- **Addresses:** author's home, office, or agent's addresses, plus e-mail and fax numbers, as available

- **Career summary:** name of employer, position, and dates held for each career post; resume of other vocational achievements; military service

- **Membership information:** professional, civic, and other association memberships and any official posts held

- **Awards and honors:** military and civic citations, major prizes and nominations, fellowships, grants, and honorary degrees

- **Writings:** a comprehensive, chronological list of titles, publishers, dates of original publication and revised editions, and production information for plays, television scripts, and screenplays

- **Adaptations:** a list of films, plays, and other media which have been adapted from the author's work

- **Work in progress:** current or planned projects, with dates of completion and/or publication, and expected publisher, when known

- **Sidelights:** a biographical portrait of the author's development; information about the critical reception of the author's works; revealing comments, often by the author, on personal interests, aspirations, motivations, and thoughts on writing

- **Interview:** a one-on-one discussion with authors conducted especially for *CA*, offering insight into authors' thoughts about their craft

- **Autobiographical essay:** an original essay written by noted authors for *CA*, a forum in which writers may present themselves, on their own terms, to their audience

- **Photographs:** portraits and personal photographs of notable authors

- **Biographical and critical sources:** a list of books and periodicals in which additional information on an author's life and/or writings appears

- **Obituary Notices** in *CA* provide date and place of birth as well as death information about authors whose full-length sketches appeared in the series before their deaths. The entries also summarize the authors' careers and writings and list other sources of biographical and death information.

Related Titles in the *CA* Series

Contemporary Authors Autobiography Series complements *CA* original and revised volumes with specially commissioned autobiographical essays by important current authors, illustrated with personal photographs they provide. Common topics include their motivations for writing, the people and experiences that shaped their careers, the rewards they derive from their work, and their impressions of the current literary scene.

Contemporary Authors Bibliographical Series surveys writings by and about important American authors since World War II. Each volume concentrates on a specific genre and features approximately ten writers; entries list works written by and about the author and contain a bibliographical essay discussing the merits and deficiencies of major critical and scholarly studies in detail.

Available in Electronic Formats

GaleNet. *CA* is available on a subscription basis through GaleNet, an online information resource that features an easy-to-use end-user interface, powerful search capabilities, and ease of access through the World-Wide Web. For more information, call 1-800-877-GALE.

Licensing. *CA* is available for licensing. The complete database is provided in a fielded format and is deliverable on such media as disk, CD-ROM, or tape. For more information, contact Thomson Gale's Business Development Group at 1-800-877-GALE, or visit us on our website at www.galegroup.com/bizdev.

Suggestions Are Welcome

The editors welcome comments and suggestions from users on any aspect of the *CA* series. If readers would like to recommend authors for inclusion in future volumes of the series, they are cordially invited to write the Editors at *Contemporary Authors*, Thomson Gale, 27500 Drake Rd., Farmington Hills, MI 48331-3535; or call at 1-248-699-4253; or fax at 1-248-699-8054.

Contemporary Authors Product Advisory Board

The editors of *Contemporary Authors* are dedicated to maintaining a high standard of excellence by publishing comprehensive, accurate, and highly readable entries on a wide array of writers. In addition to the quality of the content, the editors take pride in the graphic design of the series, which is intended to be orderly yet inviting, allowing readers to utilize the pages of *CA* easily and with efficiency. Despite the longevity of the *CA* print series, and the success of its format, we are mindful that the vitality of a literary reference product is dependent on its ability to serve its users over time. As literature, and attitudes about literature, constantly evolve, so do the reference needs of students, teachers, scholars, journalists, researchers, and book club members. To be certain that we continue to keep pace with the expectations of our customers, the editors of *CA* listen carefully to their comments regarding the value, utility, and quality of the series. Librarians, who have firsthand knowledge of the needs of library users, are a valuable resource for us. The *Contemporary Authors* Product Advisory Board, made up of school, public, and academic librarians, is a forum to promote focused feedback about *CA* on a regular basis. The six-member advisory board includes the following individuals, whom the editors wish to thank for sharing their expertise:

- **Anne M. Christensen,** Librarian II, Phoenix Public Library, Phoenix, Arizona.

- **Barbara C. Chumard,** Reference/Adult Services Librarian, Middletown Thrall Library, Middletown, New York.

- **Eva M. Davis,** Youth Department Manager, Ann Arbor District Library, Ann Arbor, Michigan.

- **Adam Janowski, Jr.,** Library Media Specialist, Naples High School Library Media Center, Naples, Florida.

- **Robert Reginald,** Head of Technical Services and Collection Development, California State University, San Bernadino, California.

- **Stephen Weiner,** Director, Maynard Public Library, Maynard, Massachusetts.

International Advisory Board

Well-represented among the 120,000 author entries published in *Contemporary Authors* are sketches on notable writers from many non-English-speaking countries. The primary criteria for inclusion of such authors has traditionally been the publication of at least onetitle in English, either as an original work or as a translation. However, the editors of *Contemporary Authors* came to observe that many important international writers were being overlooked due to a strict adherence to our inclusion criteria. In addition, writers who were publishing in languages other than English were not being covered in the traditional sources we used for identifying new listees. Intent on increasing our coverage of international authors, including those who write only in their native language and have not been translated into English, the editors enlisted the aid of a board of advisors, each of whom is an expert on the literature of a particular country or region. Among the countries we focused attention on are Mexico, Puerto Rico, Germany, Luxembourg, Belgium, the Netherlands, Norway, Sweden, Denmark, Finland, Taiwan, Singapore, Spain, Italy, South Africa, Israel, and Japan, as well as England, Scotland, Wales, Ireland, Australia, and New Zealand. The sixteen-member advisory board includes the following individuals, whom the editors wish to thank for sharing their expertise:

- **Lowell A. Bangerter,** Professor of German, University of Wyoming, Laramie, Wyoming.

- **Nancy E. Berg,** Associate Professor of Hebrew and Comparative Literature, Washington University, St. Louis, Missouri.

- **Frances Devlin-Glass,** Associate Professor, School of Literary and Communication Studies, Deakin University, Burwood, Victoria, Australia.

- **David William Foster,** Regent's Professor of Spanish, Interdisciplinary Humanities, and Women's Studies, Arizona State University, Tempe, Arizona.

- **Hosea Hirata,** Director of the Japanese Program, Associate Professor of Japanese, Tufts University, Medford, Massachusetts.

- **Jack Kolbert,** Professor Emeritus of French Literature, Susquehanna University, Selinsgrove, Pennsylvania.

- **Mark Libin,** Professor, University of Manitoba, Winnipeg, Manitoba, Canada.

- **C. S. Lim,** Professor, University of Malaya, Kuala Lumpur, Malaysia.

- **Eloy E. Merino,** Assistant Professor of Spanish, Northern Illinois University, DeKalb, Illinois.

- **Linda M. Rodríguez Guglielmoni,** Associate Professor, University of Puerto Rico—Mayagüez, Puerto Rico.

- **Sven Hakon Rossel,** Professor and Chair of Scandinavian Studies, University of Vienna, Vienna, Austria.

- **Steven R. Serafin,** Director, Writing Center, Hunter College of the City University of New York, New York City.

- **David Smyth,** Lecturer in Thai, School of Oriental and African Studies, University of London, England.

- **Ismail S. Talib,** Senior Lecturer, Department of English Language and Literature, National University of Singapore, Singapore.

- **Dionisio Viscarri,** Assistant Professor, Ohio State University, Columbus, Ohio.

- **Mark Williams,** Associate Professor, English Department, University of Canterbury, Christchurch, New Zealand.

CA Numbering System and Volume Update Chart

Occasionally questions arise about the *CA* numbering system and which volumes, if any, can be discarded. Despite numbers like "29-32R," "97-100" and "246," the entire *CA* print series consists of only 298 physical volumes with the publication of *CA* Volume 247. The following charts note changes in the numbering system and cover design, and indicate which volumes are essential for the most complete, up-to-date coverage.

CA First Revision
- 1-4R through 41-44R (11 books)
  Cover: Brown with black and gold trim.
  There will be no further First Revision volumes because revised entries are now being handled exclusively through the more efficient *New Revision Series* mentioned below.

CA Original Volumes
- 45-48 through 97-100 (14 books)
  Cover: Brown with black and gold trim.
  101 through 246 (146 books)
  Cover: Blue and black with orange bands.
  The same as previous *CA* original volumes but with a new, simplified numbering system and new cover design.

CA Permanent Series
- *CAP*-1 and *CAP*-2 (2 books)
  Cover: Brown with red and gold trim.
  There will be no further Permanent Series volumes because revised entries are now being handled exclusively through the more efficient *New Revision Series* mentioned below.

CA New Revision Series
- CANR-1 through CANR-152 (152 books)
  Cover: Blue and black with green bands.
  Includes only sketches requiring significant changes; **sketches are taken from any previously published CA, CAP, or CANR volume.**

If You Have:	You May Discard:
CA First Revision Volumes 1-4R through 41-44R and *CA Permanent Series* Volumes 1 and 2	*CA* Original Volumes 1, 2, 3, 4 Volumes 5-6 through 41-44
CA Original Volumes 45-48 through 97-100 and 101 through 247	**NONE:** These volumes will not be superseded by corresponding revised volumes. Individual entries from these and all other volumes appearing in the left column of this chart may be revised and included in the various volumes of the *New Revision Series*.
CA New Revision Series Volumes *CANR*-1 through *CANR*-152	**NONE:** The *New Revision Series* does not replace any single volume of *CA*. Instead, volumes of *CANR* include entries from many previous *CA* series volumes. All *New Revision Series* volumes must be retained for full coverage.

A Sampling of Authors and Media People Featured in This Volume

Maria Adelaide Amaral

Brazilian writer Amaral is primarily known as a playwright, but she has also published several novels and collaborated on many television screenplays. In addition, she has translated a number of English works into Portuguese. Several of Amaral's plays depict the socioeconomic conditions resulting from a period of dictatorship in Brazil. Amaral's play *Querida Mamãe* proved to be a great theatrical success. Amaral won her fourth Molière Prize and her second Mamembe Prize for it.

Pío Baroja

Baroja was considered one of the most prolific novelists of twentieth-century Spanish literature. He wrote over sixty novels during his lifetime, including several trilogies. Baroja's work typically describes the hypocrisy, poverty, and injustice that plague the lives of working-class people. In addition to fiction, Baroja also published numerous articles and essays on literary, social, and political themes. These articles have appeared in many of the widely read and influential newspapers of Latin America and Spain.

Linda Carroll

Author, therapist, and memoirist Carroll grew up as an adopted child in an affluent, but emotionally difficult, family setting. In *Her Mother's Daughter: A Memoir of the Mother I Never Knew and of My Daughter, Courtney Love,* Carroll tells the story of her own life, her search for her birth mother, and the tumultuous family connection between herself and her five children, one of whom is the controversial rock star Courtney Love.

Donovan

Donovan attained fame during the 1960s and 1970s. The singer-songwriter's music combines folk stylings, psychedelic influences, and a cheerful naivete. Donovan's hits, such as "Sunshine Superstar" and "Mellow Yellow," became classics of the flower-power era. Donovan has also written scores for films, worked on conceptual works, and was involved with the peace movement in Europe. He tells his life story in *The Autobiography of Donovan: The Hurdy Gurdy Man,* published in 2005.

Michael S. Glaser

Named the Poet Laureate for the State of Maryland in 2004, Glaser is respected for writing deceptively simple prose poems that are typically based on his own ordinary life experiences. He has published several poetry collections, including *A Lover's Eye* and *Being a Father.* His view of poetry is that it should serve as a medium for sharing experiences between people. After accepting the post of Maryland's poet laureate, Glaser planned to work with teachers around the state to include more poetry in the classroom.

Jean-Pierre Jeunet

Jeunet is a screenwriter who also directs all of his own works. Beginning his film-making career by working on short films, Jeunet ventured into feature-length film with 1991's *Delicatessen.* His most acclaimed effort to date is *Le Fabuleux destin d'Amélie Poulain,* released as simply *Amélie* in the United States. Jeunet has earned many honors for his work, including several awards from the British Academy of Film and Television Arts. He was named member of the Legion d'Honneur of France in 2006.

Heidi Eisenberg Murkoff

Murkoff collaborated with her mother, writer Arlene Eisenberg, and her sister, nurse Sandee Eisenberg Hathaway, to write a series of books for parents that began with the well known *What to Expect when You're Expecting.* The book informs new mothers on the physical, emotional, and psychological changes they can expect during pregnancy, as well as information about the development of the fetus. The book has been revised and reprinted several times. Murkoff and Eisenberg also founded The What to Expect Foundation, which promotes prenatal health for low-income women.

Elsa Triolet

French-émigré writer Triolet was a chronicler of her tumultuous times. In her novels she wrote about her childhood in Russia, her experiences with the French Resistance during World War II, and her disenchantment with politics during the postwar era. For several years she published theater reviews, and her translations of works by Russian poets and dramatists brought what would become classic works to wider audiences. She was also influential in journalism and was the wife of famous French poet and communist leader Louis Aragon. In 1945 Triolet won France's prestigious Prix Goncourt for *A Fine of Two Hundred Francs.*

A

* Indicates that a listing has been compiled from secondary sources believed to be reliable, but has not been personally verified for this edition by the author sketched.

ADAMS, Jessica 1964-

PERSONAL: Born July 25, 1964, in London, England. *Education:* Attended the Australian Film, Television and Radio School.

ADDRESSES: Home—Bellingen, Australia; Brighton, England. *Agent*—c/o Author Mail, Hodder Headline, 201 Kent St., Sydney, New South Wales 2000, Australia.

CAREER: Astrologer and writer. Has worked as a columnist for *Vogue, B, Cosmopolitan, Woman's Own,* and *Daily Telegraph;* trustee for War Child charity.

WRITINGS:

NOVELS

Single White E-Mail, Pan Macmillan (Sydney, New South Wales, Australia), 1998.
Tom, Dick, and Debbie Harry, Thomas Dunne Books (New York, NY), 2002.
Cool for Cats, Pan Macmillan (Sydney, New South Wales, Australia), 2003.
I'm a Believer, Thomas Dunne Books (New York, NY), 2004.
The Summer Psychic, Black Swan (London, England), 2005.

"MIND BODY SPIRIT" SERIES; NONFICTION

Astrology for Women, HarperCollins (Pymble, New South Wales, Australia), 1997.

The New Astrology for Women, HarperCollins (Pymble, New South Wales, Australia), 1998.
Fantasy Futures: The Amazing New Way to Predict Your Future . . . and Make It Happen, Penguin (Camberwell, Victoria, Australia), 2002.
(With Jelena Glisic and Anthea Paul) *21st Century Goddess: The Modern Girl's Guide to the Universe,* Allen & Unwin (Crows Nest, New South Wales, Australia), 2002.

"AMAZING YOU!" SERIES FOR YOUNG ADULTS

Psychic Power, Hodder Children's Books (Sydney, New South Wales, Australia), 2004.
Astrology, Hodder Children's Books (Sydney, New South Wales, Australia), 2004.

EDITOR; "NIGHT" SHORT STORY COLLECTIONS

(With Chris Manby and Fiona Walker) *Girls' Night In,* HarperCollins (London, England), 2000, Red Dress Ink (Buffalo, NY), 2004.
(With Chris Manby and Fiona Walker) *Girls' Night In: Gentlemen by Invitation,* Penguin (Camberwell, Victoria, Australia), 2001, also published as *Girls' Night Out/Boys' Night In,* HarperCollins (London, England), 2001.
(With others) *Big Night Out,* Penguin (Camberwell, Victoria, Australia), 2002.
(With Juliet Partridge and Nick Earls) *Kids' Night In: A Midnight Feast,* Puffin (Camberwell, Victoria, Australia), 2003.

Kids' Night In 2: A Feast of Stories, Puffin (Camberwell, Victoria, Australia), 2005.

(With Chris Manby and Fiona Walker) *Girls' Night In 4,* Penguin (Camberwell, Victoria, Australia), 2005.

(With Maggie Alderson, Imogen Edwards-Jones, and Chris Manby) *Ladies' Night,* HarperCollins (London, England), 2005.

Creator of the *Girls' Night In Journal* and author of "*Handbag Horoscopes,*" a series of twelve sign-specific astrology books.

ADAPTATIONS: Big Night Out was adapted as an audio book by Bolinda Publishing.

WORK IN PROGRESS: Astrobloke and *Astrobabe,* astrology books.

SIDELIGHTS: Author Jessica Adams told Yasmin Boland of the *Yasmin Boland* Web site that she became aware of her psychic abilities when she was eleven years old. When Adams saw her cat on her way home from school one afternoon, she later learned that it had been killed by a car earlier that morning. Adams began her career as a professional astrologer at the age of twenty-three and has since worked as a columnist on the subject for various magazines, including *Vogue* and *Cosmopolitan.* When asked in an interview posted on the *ChickLit* Web site where she gets her ideas for her books and columns, the author replied: "Most of my ideas are channelled to me from the spirit world, where there are lots of old authors and journalists knocking about who love nothing better than working with us on this side."

Adams wrote her first novel, *Single White E-Mail,* in 1998. In the story Victoria Shipworth strikes up an internet romance as a way to deal with her latest break up. As the relationship with the mysterious man progresses, other strange things concerning Victoria's friendships and career begin to occur. Sally Murphy, writing for *Aussiereviews.com,* called the novel "disarmingly accurate," and noted that the main character's "life is sad, funny and very real all at the same time."

Tom, Dick, and Debbie Harry followed *Single White E-Mail* and was Adams's first book to be published in the United States. The book features an ensemble cast of characters and outrageous situations; Richard (or Dick) marries Sarah, who is in love with his best friend, Tom. Dick's younger brother, Harry, has devoted his life to his Debbie Harry tribute band, and Dick's ex-wife, Bronte, is repeatedly contacted by the spirit of her dead horse. "If it seems a little much, it is—but the sheer lunacy is sort of fun," noted Tara Gelsomino in the *Romantic Times Book Club Online.* A contributor for *Kirkus Reviews* felt that Adams "weighs the story down with too much earnest relationship talk," but even so, there are "many honest laughs" throughout the novel.

In 2004 Adams published *I'm a Believer,* "a whimsical, poignant paranormal love story," according to a *Publishers Weekly* critic. The story tells of Mark Buckle, a junior-high science teacher, whose girlfriend Catherine is killed in a tragic car accident. After the funeral, Mark receives paranormal reminders of Catherine everywhere: their song is always on the radio, her perfume lingers in the air, and he hears her voice when no one else is around. Since the incidents are scientifically inexplicable, Mark reevaluates his beliefs about life and death and wonders where Catherine may be leading him. Although reviewers observed that the story did contain some flaws, they also pointed out many praiseworthy aspects. A *Kirkus Reviews* critic called the book "skillfully crafted and drolly amusing," but also pointed out that it "never quite manages to marry its twin strings of downbeat sarcasm and airy metaphysics." However, "it is a beautifully crafted, bittersweet, life-affirming story," wrote Carolyn Kubisz in *Booklist.*

In addition to her novels, Adams has written many nonfiction astrology books for both adults and teenagers. She has also served as coeditor of multiple short story collections, including *Girls' Night In, Big Night Out,* and *Kids' Night In: A Midnight Feast.* All of the profits from these collections are donated to War Child, an agency that offers relief to children victimized by war. Since 1999 the anthologies have raised over two and a half million dollars for the charity. As of 2005 the proceeds have also benefited No Strings, a charity that uses puppet shows to educate children in developing nations about important issues such as landmine safety and HIV/AIDS. In her interview with Boland, Adams commented on her charity work: "Without making a drama about it, I just think it's time to start giving back to the community. I think it's part of the law of the Universe."

BIOGRAPHICAL AND CRITICAL SOURCES:

PERIODICALS

Booklist, December 1, 2003, Carolyn Kubisz, review of *I'm a Believer*, p. 644.
Kirkus Reviews, May 15, 2002, review of *Tom, Dick, and Debbie Harry*, p. 676; December 1, 2003, review of *I'm a Believer*, p. 1369.
Library Journal, June 1, 2002, Karen Core, review of *Tom, Dick, and Debbie Harry*, p. 192.
Publishers Weekly, January 5, 2004, review of *I'm a Believer*, p. 39.

ONLINE

Allreaders.com, http://www.allreaders.com/ (March 13, 2006), Harriet Klausner, review of *I'm a Believer*.
Aussiereviews.com, http://www.aussiereviews.com/ (March 13, 2006), Sally Murphy, review of *Single White E-Mail*; (March 13, 2006), Sally Murphy, review of *Cool for Cats*.
ChickLit, http://www.chicklit.co.uk/ (March 13, 2006), interview with author.
Girls Night In Web site, http://www.girlsnightin.info (March 13, 2006).
Jessica Adams Home Page, http://www.jessicaadams.com (March 13, 2006).
Romantic Times Book Club Online, http://www.romantictimes.com/ (March 13, 2006), Tara Gelsomino, review of *Tom, Dick, and Debbie Harry*.
Yasmin Boland Web site, http://www.yasminboland.com/ (March 13, 2006), author interview and profile.*

*   *   *

AKBAR, Said Hyder 1984-

PERSONAL: Born 1984, in Peshawar, Afghanistan; immigrated to the United States c. 1985; became a naturalized U.S. citizen.

ADDRESSES: *Agent*—c/o Author Mail, Bloomsbury, 175 5th Ave., 3rd Fl., New York, NY, 10010.

CAREER: Writer and college student. Wadan Afghanistan (rebuilds Afghan schools and roads), founder and codirector.

WRITINGS:

(With Susan Burton) *Come Back to Afghanistan: A California Teenager's Story*, Bloomsbury (New York, NY), 2005.

SIDELIGHTS: Said Hyder Akbar was born in Afghanistan, grew up in California, and lived a typically American life. This changed abruptly after the September 11 terrorist attacks. In the aftermath of the attacks, Akbar's father sold his hip-hop clothing store and returned to Afghanistan, serving first as spokesman to Afghan president Hamid Karzai and then as the governor of a rural province. As a result, Akbar spent three successive summers in Afghanistan, starting at the age of seventeen. He worked with his father in the presidential palace and in his province, served as a translator for U.S. forces, and witnessed the interrogation of terrorists. He embraced Afghan culture, meeting relatives, eating and drinking the same food as the local people, and wearing Afghan clothing. He learned to shoot a gun, was ambushed, and visited Osama bin Laden's abandoned house.

Back in the United States, Akbar shared his experiences in radio stories for National Public Radio's program *This American Life* and later in his memoir *Come Back to Afghanistan: A California Teenager's Story*. Akbar wrote the book with *Harper's* magazine editor Susan Burton, who also helped him produce his radio segments. Reviewers had ample praise for the book. Joseph Di Prisco suggested in the *San Francisco Chronicle* that Akbar might well have a better grasp of the complexities of the Afghan situation than many older observers. Gillian Engberg, writing in *Booklist*, called the book "a wholly engrossing memoir that balances sophisticated political and social observations, . . . with irresistible flashes of teen enthusiasm."

BIOGRAPHICAL AND CRITICAL SOURCES:

BOOKS

Akbar, Said Hyder, and Susan Burton, *Come Back to Afghanistan: A California Teenager's Story*, Bloomsbury (New York, NY), 2005.

PERIODICALS

Booklist, September 1, 2005, Gillian Engberg, review of *Come Back to Afghanistan*, p. 46.

Entertainment Weekly, October 28, 2005, Michelle Kung, review of *Come Back to Afghanistan,* p. 93.

Kirkus Reviews, September 15, 2005, review of *Come Back to Afghanistan,* p. 1007.

San Francisco Chronicle, November 13, 2005, Joseph Di Prisco, review of *Come Back to Afghanistan.*

ONLINE

Bloomsbury Web site, http://www.bloomsbury.com/ (January 3, 2005), author profile.*

*   *   *

ALBER, Charles J.

PERSONAL: Male. *Education:* Indiana University, Ph.D., 1971.

ADDRESSES: Office—Department of Languages, Literatures, and Cultures, University of South Carolina, Columbia, SC 29208; fax: 803-777-0454. *E-mail*—alber@sc.edu.

CAREER: University of South Carolina, Columbia, director of the Chinese program.

WRITINGS:

(Translator) Vladimir Ivanovich Semanov, *Lu Hsuñ and His Predecessors* (translation of *Lu Sin'i ego predshestvenniki*), M.E. Sharpe (White Plains, NY), 1980.

Enduring the Revolution: Ding Ling and the Politics of Literature in Guomindang China, Praeger (Westport, CT), 2002.

Embracing the Lie: Ding Ling and the Politics of Literature in the People's Republic of China, Praeger (Westport, CT), 2004.

SIDELIGHTS: Charles J. Alber, a professor of Chinese studies, may be best known for his work on Ding Ling, a Chinese writer who lived from 1904 to 1986. Alber "probably knows more about [Ding] than any other Westerner," according to *Times Literary Supplement* contributor Jonathan Mirsky, and he chronicles her life for an English-speaking audience in two volumes. *Enduring the Revolution: Ding Ling and the Politics of Literature in Guomindang China* covers Ding's life and work from birth through 1949, and *Embracing the Lie: Ding Ling and the Politics of Literature in the People's Republic of China* examines the rest of her life. As Alber shows in his first volume, Ding was always a controversial author, writing stories that dealt explicitly with women's sexuality in the 1920s and daring to openly criticize the sexism of the Communist military leaders in the 1940s. As chronicled in *Embracing the Lie,* Ding briefly made her peace with the Communist authorities in the early 1950s and became a powerful member of the literary bureaucracy. However, she then spent much of the next twenty years branded as a right-wing traitor, which earned her beatings and time spent in prison and labor camps. After she was rehabilitated in the late 1970s, she chose to "embrace the lie" of the Communist Party line to attempt to ensure her continuing safety, a decision that Alber had trouble accepting. As he wrote in *Embracing the Lie,* "The tragedy of Ding Ling is that she traded her own integrity for legitimacy in the [Communist] Party. Except for self-satisfaction, if indeed there was any, there was little reward. . . . No reward can compensate for the loss of one's integrity; there is no honor in embracing a lie."

BIOGRAPHICAL AND CRITICAL SOURCES:

BOOKS

Alber, Charles J., *Embracing the Lie: Ding Ling and the Politics of Literature in the People's Republic of China,* Praeger (Westport, CT), 2004.

PERIODICALS

Times Literary Supplement, June 24, 2005, Jonathan Mirsky, review of *Embracing the Lie,* p. 24.

ONLINE

Department of Languages, Literatures, and Cultures, http://www.cas.sc.edu/ (February 22, 2006), "Chinese Program."

University of South Carolina Web site, http://www.sc.edu/ (February 22, 2006), "Languages, Literatures, and Cultures."*

*   *   *

ALDRIDGE, Sarah
    See MARCHANT, Anyda

*   *   *

ALEXANDER, Ann Field 1946-

PERSONAL: Born 1946.

ADDRESSES: Office—Mary Baldwin College, 108 North Jefferson St., Ste. 816, Roanoke, VA 24016. *E-mail*—aalexand@mbc.edu.

CAREER: Writer and educator. Mary Baldwin College, Roanoke, VA, professor of history, director of Roanoke Center, 1989—.

AWARDS, HONORS: Richard Slatten Award, 2002, for *Race Man: The Rise and Fall of the "Fighting Editor," John Mitchell Jr.*

WRITINGS:

Race Man: The Rise and Fall of the "Fighting Editor," John Mitchell Jr., University of Virginia Press (Charlottesville, VA), 2002.

SIDELIGHTS: Ann Field Alexander teaches courses on Virginia, Appalachia, and African-Americans. In 2002 Alexander published *Race Man: The Rise and Fall of the "Fighting Editor," John Mitchell Jr.* The book is a biography of black newspaper editor John Mitchell, Jr. who was born in 1863 (two years before the end of the Civil War). Mitchell's parents were slaves who worked in the house of a Richmond attorney. After graduating from high school, he went to work as a teacher in 1881, but he lost his job three years later when the Richmond school board fired all black teachers. Mitchell then became editor of the new

black-owned newspaper, the *Richmond Planet,* a post he held until his death in 1929. Mitchell subsequently used his post as editor to speak against the injustices of racial discrimination.

Scholars in the field welcomed Alexander's book as a fine addition to the body of work exploring race relations after the Civil War. Stephen Messer, reviewing the book for *History: Review of New Books,* observed that "specialists and generalists interested in African American history, the history of Richmond, the history of journalism, or southern biography will find this work rewarding." In addition, *Journalism History* contributor Ron Bishop noted that the biography "brilliantly details the events that motivated Mitchell."

BIOGRAPHICAL AND CRITICAL SOURCES:

PERIODICALS

New York Review of Books, July 15, 2004, Caleb Crain, review of *Race Man: The Rise and Fall of the "Fighting Editor," John Mitchell Jr.,* pp. 50-51.
Reference & Research Book News, May, 2003, review of *Race Man,* p. 58.
History: Review of New Books, spring, 2003, Stephen Messer, review of *Race Man,* p. 105.
Journalism History, fall, 2003, Ron Bishop, review of *Race Man,* p. 148.

*   *   *

ALLEN, John L. 1965-
    (John L. Allen, Jr.)

PERSONAL: Born 1965; married Shannon Allen. *Education:* Fort Hays State University, graduated 1989; University of Kansas, M.A.

ADDRESSES: Home—Rome, Italy. *Office*—National Catholic Reporter Publishing Company, 115 E. Armour Blvd., Kansas City, MO 64111-1203. *E-mail*—jallen@natcath.org.

CAREER: Journalist and writer. Formerly a high school teacher. *National Catholic Reporter,* opinion editor, 1997-2000, Rome correspondent, 2000—, author of "The Word from Rome" (weekly online column), 2001—. Contributor to the FOX News Channel; Vatican analyst for the Cable News Network (CNN), National Public Radio (NPR), and various European television networks.

WRITINGS:

Cardinal Ratzinger: The Vatican's Enforcer of the Faith, Continuum (New York, NY), 2000, published as *Pope Benedict XVI: A Biography of Joseph Ratzinger,* 2005, published as *Benedict XVI: Labourer in the Vineyard,* Continuum (London, England), 2005.

Conclave: The Politics, Personalities, and Process of the Next Papal Election, Image (New York, NY), 2002.

All the Pope's Men: The Inside Story of How the Vatican Really Thinks, Doubleday (New York, NY), 2004.

Opus Dei: The First Objective Look behind the Myths and Reality of the Most Controversial Force in the Catholic Church, Doubleday (New York, NY), 2005.

The Rise of Benedict XVI: The Inside Story of How the Pope Was Elected and Where He Will Take the Catholic Church, Doubleday (New York, NY), 2005.

Contributor to the *New York Times, Tablet, Jesus, Second Opinion, Nation, Miami Herald, Furche,* and *Irish Examiner.*

SIDELIGHTS: John L. Allen has earned a reputation as an expert on the behind-the-scenes political machinations within the Roman Catholic Church. This reputation is primarily built upon his print and online reporting for the *National Catholic Reporter,* a publication known for its liberal dissent to certain Church teachings, but Allen is also the author of numerous well-received books about the Catholic Church and the men who run it.

Allen's first book, *Cardinal Ratzinger: The Vatican's Enforcer of the Faith,* was published in 2000, the same year that Allen moved to Rome to cover the Vatican beat for the *National Catholic Reporter.* (After Cardinal Joseph Ratzinger became Pope Benedict XVI, the book was republished as *Pope Benedict XVI: A*

Biography of Joseph Ratzinger.) Allen presents "a cohesive, articulate biographical narrative," John-Leonard Berg wrote in *Library Journal,* and, as John P. Burgess noted in the *Christian Century,* "while Allen's style is journalistic, he is sensitive to theological questions."

Allen returned to writing about Ratzinger in 2005, after the cardinal was elected pope. He wrote *The Rise of Benedict XVI: The Inside Story of How the Pope Was Elected and Where He Will Take the Catholic Church* in under two weeks, beginning April 26, 2005 (exactly a week after Benedict XVI was elected pope) and finishing on May 7. Allen accomplished this feat by sequestering himself in a hotel in Paris and writing for sixteen hours a day, as he told *Publishers Weekly* interviewer Joe Tirella. The location was his wife's choice: "I told my wife, 'We can go anyplace in the world you want, because I'm not leaving the hotel room,'" he explained to Tirella. "Using his Vatican connections"—which included eight of the cardinals who were part of the voting—"Mr. Allen pieces together a credible scenario of the conclave," according to Chester Gillis in the *National Catholic Reporter.*

The Rise of Benedict XVI was not Allen's first book about the process of electing a new pope. In his 2002 title, *Conclave: The Politics, Personalities, and Process of the Next Papal Election,* Allen explains all aspects of naming a replacement for the then-aging Pope John Paul II, from the technicalities of conducting a conclave (the name for the process by which a new pope is elected) to the political factions within the College of Cardinals. Allen also lists and describes the top twenty contenders for the job and, helpfully for non-Catholics, explains exactly what the pope's job description entails. "*Conclave* fulfills its promise to offer us all we need to know about the next conclave," wrote *Conscience* reviewer Thomas Arens. The book is "timely, informative, and engaging," Berg similarly commented in another *Library Journal* review, and it provides a "popular and understandable" explanation of its topic. A *Publishers Weekly* critic described the book as "engagingly written" as well, and commended Allen for being "admirably objective" in his descriptions of the contenders for the job of pope.

Allen is also the author of *Opus Dei: The First Objective Look behind the Myths and Reality of the Most Controversial Force in the Catholic Church.* Opus Dei (the name means "Work of God") is a conservative, secretive group within the Catholic Church that is rumored to include many powerful figures, including American politicians. Although Opus Dei has found itself at the center of several conspiracy theories (most famously the one spelled out in the best-selling novel *The Da Vinci Code*), Allen finds the group to be much less dangerous. However, as John Jay Hughes noted in the *National Catholic Reporter,* "The book is no whitewash. Mr. Allen cites extensively from the Work's critics, including former members deeply hurt by Opus Dei." Unlike most authors who attempt to investigate Opus Dei, Allen was given near-complete access to both the group's members and to its archives, including financial records. While writing the book he conducted hundreds of hours of interviews with both current and former members of the organization and spent five days living in an Opus Dei house in Barcelona, Spain. The result is "balanced, even reporting" that is "most informative," concluded a *Publishers Weekly* critic.

BIOGRAPHICAL AND CRITICAL SOURCES:

PERIODICALS

America, October 11, 2004, John Jay Hughes, review of *All the Pope's Men: The Inside Story of How the Vatican Really Thinks,* p. 37.

Booklist, October 15, 2000, Steven Schroeder, review of *Cardinal Ratzinger: The Vatican's Enforcer of the Faith,* p. 392; June 1, 2005, Margaret Flanagan, review of *Conclave: The Politics, Personalities, and Process of the Next Papal Election,* p. 1647; October 1, 2005, Margaret Flanagan, review of *Opus Dei: An Objective Look behind the Myths and Realities of the Most Controversial Force in the Catholic Church,* p. 22.

Bookseller, May 13, 2005, "Rush Is on for Ratzinger," p. 12.

Catholic Insight, November, 2004, review of *All the Pope's Men,* p. 42.

Christian Century, May 9, 2001, John P. Burgess, review of *Cardinal Ratzinger,* p. 26.

Commonweal, November 3, 2000, Joseph A. Komonchak, "Dubious Demonizing," p. 31; December 3, 2004, Lawrence S. Cunningham, review of *All the Pope's Men,* p. 33.

Conscience, winter, 2002, Thomas Arens, review of *Conclave,* p. 46.

First Things, February, 2001, review of *Cardinal Ratzinger,* p. 55.

Kirkus Reviews, March 1, 2002, review of *Conclave,* p. 299; August 15, 2005, review of *Opus Dei,* p. 889.

Library Journal, November 1, 2000, Anna M. Donnelly, review of *Cardinal Ratzinger,* p. 87; May 1, 2002, John-Leonard Berg, review of *Conclave,* p. 105; July 1, 2005, John-Leonard Berg, review of *Pope Benedict XVI: A Biography of Joseph Ratzinger,* p. 85.

National Catholic Reporter, July 28, 2000, Tom Roberts, "John Goes to Rome; Teresa Moves Up," p. 2; November 3, 2000, Zachary Hayes, review of *Cardinal Ratzinger,* p. 31; April 5, 2002, Chester Gillis, review of *Conclave,* p. 19; December 26, 2003, "For the Inside Story," p. 2; July 16, 2004, "Catholics Must Create Dialogue Spaces on Key Issues, Says Reporter," p. 6; August 12, 2005, Chester Gillis, "New Pope, New Books," p. 18; October 21, 2005, John Jay Hughes, "The Facts and Fiction about Opus Dei: John Allen Investigates Secretive Organization Some Call a Cult," p. 20.

National Review, September 30, 2002, Michael Potemra, review of *Conclave,* p. 52.

Newsweek, December 22, 2003, Kenneth L. Woodward, "The Scoop on the Pope: This High-School Teacher Turned Journalist Speaks Italian and Dines with Cardinals. He's Got the Vatican Covered," p. 48.

Newsweek International, January 19, 2004, Kenneth L. Woodward and Robert Blair Kaiser, "An All-Seeing Outsider," p. 54.

Publishers Weekly, April 29, 2002, review of *Conclave,* p. 60; May 31, 2004, review of *All the Pope's Men,* p. 70; June 13, 2005, Joe Tirella, interview with Allen, p. 50, review of *The Rise of Benedict XVI: The Inside Story of How the Pope Was Elected and Where He Will Take the Catholic Church,* p. 53; July 11, 2005, review of *Opus Dei,* p. 84.

Washington Monthly, October-November, 2005, Paul Baumann, "Let There Be Light," p. 56.*

*   *   *

ALLEN, John L., Jr.
See ALLEN, John L.

ALTHEIDE, David L.

PERSONAL: Male. *Education:* Central Washington State College, B.A., 1967; University of Washington, N.D.E.A., 1969; University of California, San Diego, Ph.D., 1974.

ADDRESSES: Home—741 E. Granada Dr., Tempe, AZ 85281. *Office*—School of Justice and Social Inquiry, Arizona State University, Tempe, AZ 85287-0403; fax: 480-965-8187, 480-965-9199. *E-mail*—david. altheide@asu.edu.

CAREER: Southern Colorado State College, instructor, 1968-70, assistant professor, 1970-71, acting department chair, 1971; University of California, San Diego, teaching assistant, 1971-72; Grossmont College, San Diego, part-time instructor, 1971-72; Chapman College, San Diego, part-time instructor, 1972-73; San Diego State University, part-time instructor, 1972; Arizona State University, Tempe, visiting assistant professor, 1974-75, assistant professor, 1975-79, associate professor of sociology, 1979-92, associate professor in the Center for the Study of Justice, 1982-83, professor in the School of Justice Studies, 1983-90, Regents' Professor, 1990—, interim director, school of justice studies, 2000-01. University of Lund, Lund, Sweden, visiting professor of sociology, 1981; University of Lancaster, department of sociology, honorary research fellow, 1988; Lincoln Center for Applied Ethics, teaching fellow, 2002.

MEMBER: Society for the Study of Symbolic Interaction (vice president elect, 1989-90, president elect, 1993, president, 1994-95).

AWARDS, HONORS: Research fellowship, Television and Politics Study Program of the School of Public and International Affairs at George Washington University, 1981; grants from the Morrison Institute for Public Policy, 1984, the Kaltenbom Foundation, 1985; Charles Horton Cooley Award, Society for the Study of Symbolic Interactionism, 1985, for *Media Power,* and 2004, for *Creating Fear;* Premio Diego Fabbri Award, Ente dello Spettacolo (Italy), 1986, for *Creating Reality: How TV News Distorts Events;* Graduate College Distinguished Research Award, Arizona State University, 1990-91; Faculty Achievement Award, School of Justice Studies, 1994, 1996;

George Herbert Mead Award, Society for the Study of Symbolic Interaction, 2005, for career contributions; numerous research support grants from Arizona State University.

WRITINGS:

Creating Reality: How TV News Distorts Events, with an introduction by Arthur J. Vidich, Sage Publications (Beverly Hills, CA), 1976.
(With Robert P. Snow) *Media Logic,* Sage Publications (Beverly Hills, CA), 1979.
(With John M. Johnson) *Bureaucratic Propaganda,* Allyn & Bacon (Boston, MA), 1980.
Media Power, Sage Publications (Beverly Hills, CA), 1985.
(With Robert P. Snow) *Media Worlds in the Postjournalism Era,* Aldine de Gruyter (New York, NY), 1991.
An Ecology of Communication: Cultural Formats of Control, Aldine de Gruyter (New York, NY), 1995.
Qualitative Media Analysis, Sage Publications (Thousand Oaks, CA), 1996.
Creating Fear: News and the Construction of Crisis, Aldine de Gruyter (New York, NY), 2002.
Terrorism and the Politics of Fear, AltaMira Press (Lanham, MD), 2006.

Contributor to scholarly journals, including the *Sociological Quarterly, Symbolic Interaction,* and *Qualitative Inquiry.* Contributor of entries for encyclopedias, handbooks, and readers.

WORK IN PROGRESS: Research in mass communication, qualitative research methods, deviant behavior, propaganda and official information, and social control.

SIDELIGHTS: David L. Altheide has spent more than thirty years studying and writing about the media, propaganda, and other methods of mass communication. His research is conducted through qualitative research, including interviews, ethnology, and document and media analysis, generally using the symbolic interaction model of sociology. In lay terms, Altheide studies how the mass media operate and how the interaction of the media and those who consume the media's news stories shapes people's ideas about reality. This interaction generally results in Americans holding deeply flawed views about the world, as Altheide illustrates in such books as *Creating Reality: How TV News Distorts Events* and *Creating Fear: News and the Construction of Crisis.* In the latter title, Altheide discusses the shift in journalism towards stories that are designed to produce fear in their audience, such as stories about crime and how to protect oneself from criminals, and the negative effect that such stories have on society. He argues that the pervasive sense of fear caused by such stories was behind the popular "tough on crime" policies of recent years—policies which have led to an ever-increasing portion of the low-income and minority population being sent to prison for longer and longer terms. "Altheide provides a useful conceptual framework for making sense of the expansion of fear in contemporary societies," Frank Furedi remarked in the *American Journal of Sociology.* Writing in the *Journal of Sociology and Social Welfare,* Allan Brawley concluded that *Creating Fear* "is an accessible and articulate presentation of important research that is part of a large body of scholarship with which more social workers, social scientists, policymakers and media professionals should be familiar."

BIOGRAPHICAL AND CRITICAL SOURCES:

PERIODICALS

American Journal of Sociology, September, 2002, Frank Furedi, review of *Creating Fear: News and the Construction of Crisis,* p. 524.
Journal of Sociology and Social Welfare, June, 2003, Allan Brawley, review of *Creating Fear,* p. 179.
Social Forces, September, 1994, David L. Paletz, review of *Media Worlds in the Postjournalism Era,* p. 344.

ONLINE

Arizona State University Web site, http://www.asu.edu/ (February 22, 2006), "School of Justice and Social Inquiry."
David L. Altheide Home Page, http://www.public.asu.edu/~atdla (February 22, 2006).*

ALVTEGEN, Karin 1965-
(Karin Anna Alvtegen)

PERSONAL: Born June 8, 1965, in Huskvarna, Sweden; daughter of two teachers; married; children: two.

ADDRESSES: Home—Stockholm, Sweden. *Agent*—Salomonsson Agency, P.O. Box 2337, 103 18 Stockholm, Sweden.

CAREER: Writer.

AWARDS, HONORS: Glass Key award for best Scandinavian crime novel, 2000, and Silverpocket award, 2002, both for *Saknad;* Goldpocket award, 2004, for *Svek.*

WRITINGS:

NOVELS

Skuld, [Sweden], 1998, translation by Anna Paterson published as *Guilt,* Canongate (Edinburgh, Scotland), 2006.
Saknad, [Sweden], 2000, translation by Anna Paterson published as *Missing,* Canongate (Edinburgh, Scotland), 2003.
Svek, [Sweden], 2003, translation by Steven T. Murray published as *Betrayal,* Canongate (Edinburgh, Scotland), 2005.
Skam (title means "Shame"), [Sweden], 2005.

Alvtegen's works have been translated into more than twenty languages.

ADAPTATIONS: Missing was adapted by Jimmy Gardner as a film for SMG TV Productions.

SIDELIGHTS: Karin Alvtegen, niece of famous Swedish author Astrid Lindgren, is a best-selling author of thriller novels in her homeland of Sweden. Alvtegen never aspired to be an author until after a tragic occurrence in her family. In 1993 one of her two brothers, Magnus, died while mountain climbing. Stricken by the sudden realization of life's uncertainties, Alvtegen found herself paralyzed by frequent panic attacks for several years. "Then one morning," she related on her Web site, "I woke up with the beginning of a story in my head. I imagined someone being in the same state as me, but with the courage to break his own entrenchment." The idea inspired the character of Peter Brolin in her debut novel, *Skuld,* which was later translated as *Guilt.* Writing helped Alvtegen overcome her panic attacks by focusing on a goal. Since then, she has published several more novels that have been well received by reading audiences.

Guilt is about how, in a case of mistaken identity, Brolin is paid to deliver a package that contains something horrifying. Pursued by others who want the package, Brolin can only survive if he is able to face up to his own past. Other novels by Alvtegen have also tended to feature tormented protagonists, such as *Skam* ("Shame"), which is about a young girl whose zealously religious parents force her to suppress her own sexuality as well as the family's darkest secret, and *Saknad,* translated as *Missing,* which is about a homeless woman escaping her past only to find herself accused of murdering someone she does not even know. Writing in a *Spectator* review, Diana Hendry commented on how, in *Missing,* Alvtegen combines two main plots involving the crime and the protagonist Sibylla's coming-of-age struggles. Although Hendry felt that these elements "are skillfully woven together," she further commented that she "didn't emerge from the book knowing more about how it really feels to be homeless." On the other hand, Paul Richmond called *Missing* "a fine psychological mystery/thriller" in his *Reviewing the Evidence* online assessment. Contrary to Hendry, Richmond felt that "Alvtegen excels . . . in creating a haunting yet engaging character portrait of a homeless person."

BIOGRAPHICAL AND CRITICAL SOURCES:

PERIODICALS

Spectator, July 12, 2003, Diana Hendry, "Watching Panties Dry," review of *Missing,* p. 39.

ONLINE

Karin Alvtegen Home Page, http://www.karinalvtegen.com (January 21, 2006).

Reviewing the Evidence, http://www.reviewingthe evidence.com/ (October 1, 2003), Paul Richmond, review of *Missing.*

*   *   *

ALVTEGEN, Karin Anna
See ALVTEGEN, Karin

*   *   *

AMARAL, Maria Adelaide 1942-
(Maria Adelaide Almeida Santos de Amaral)

PERSONAL: Born July 1, 1942, in Porto, Portugal; brought to Brazil, c. 1954. *Education:* Faculdade de Comunicação Social Caásper Líbero, journalism degree, 1970.

ADDRESSES: Agent—Av. Jaguaré, 1485—Gerência de Apoio Editorial, São Paulo, Brazil 05346-902.

CAREER: Playwright, novelist, and television screenwriter. During early career, worked as a journalist; Editora Abril, São Paulo, Brazil, wrote for encyclopedias, 1970-86.

AWARDS, HONORS: Molière Prize, 1976, for *Bodas de Papel,* 1983, for *Chiquinha Gonzaga,* 1984, for *De Braços Abertos,* 1994, for *Querida Mamãe;* Ziembinsky Prize, 1976, for *Bodas de Papel;* Governador do Estado e da Associação dos Críticos de Arte for best national author, 1976, for *Bodas de Papel;* Serviço Nacional de Teatro Prize, 1977, for *A Resistência;* São Paulo Association of Theater Critics award, 1984, for *De Braços Abertos;* Mamembe Prize, 1984, for *De Braços Abertos,* 1994, for *Querida Mamãe.*

WRITINGS:

Luísa: Quase uma História de Amor (novel), Editora Nova Fronteira (Rio de Janeiro, Brazil), 1986.
Aos Meus Amigos: Romance, Editora Siciliano (São Paulo, Brazil), 1992.
Dercy: de Cabo a Rabo (biography), 2nd edition, Editora Globo (São Paulo, Brazil), 1994.

(Author of interview) *Maria Adelaide Amaral: depoimento em 18/03/96,* Fundação Memorial da América Latina (São Paulo, Brazil), 1996.

Coração Solitário (novel), 1997.

O Bruxo (novel), Editora Globo (São Paulo, Brazil), 2000.

STAGE PRODUCTIONS

Cemitério Sem Cruzes, 1978.

Bodas de Papel, first produced in São Paulo, Brazil, 1978, first produced in Rio de Janeiro, Brazil, 1980.

A Resistência, first produced in Rio de Janeiro, Brazil, 1979; produced in São Paulo, Brazil, 1980), Serviço Nacional de Teatro (Rio de Janeiro, Brazil), 1978.

Chiquinha Gonzaga, first produced in São Paulo, Brazil, 1983.

De Braços Abertos (based on her novel *Luísa: Quase uma História de Amor);* first produced in São Paulo, Brazil, 1984), Memórias Futuras Edições (Rio de Janeiro, Brazil), 1985.

(Adapter) Sophocles, *Electra,* first produced in São Paulo, Brazil, 1987.

Seja o que Deus Quiser, first produced in Rio de Janeiro, Brazil, 1987.

Uma Relação Tão Delicada, first produced in São Paulo, Brazil, 1989.

Viúva, first produced in production of *Solteira, Casada, Viúva, Desquitada,* in Rio de Janeiro, Brazil, 1993.

Para Tão Longo Amor, first produced in Porto, Portugal, 1993, produced in São Paul, Brazil, 1994.

Querida Mamãe, first produced in Rio de Janeiro, Brazil, 1994; produced in São Paulo, Brazil, 1995), Editora Brasiliense (São Paulo, Brazil), 1995.

Intensa Magia, first produced in Rio de Janeiro, Brazil, 1995; produced in São Paulo, Brazil, 1996), Caliban Editorial (São Paulo, Brazil), 1996.

Para Sempre, first produced in Curitiba, Brazil, 1997; produced in São Paulo, Brazil, 1997.

Inseparáveis, first produced in São Paulo, Brazil, 1997.

O Abre Alas, Editora Civilização Brasileira (Rio de Janeiro, Brazil), 2000.

Also author of play *Mademoiselle.*

TELEVISION SCREENPLAYS

(With Cassiano Gabus Mendes) *Meu Bem, Meu Mal,* Rede Globo de Televisão, 1990.

(With Silvio de Abreu) *Deus Nos Acuda,* Rede Globo de Televisão, 1992.

(With Cassiano Gabus Mendes) *O Mapa da Mina,* Rede Globo de Televisão, 1993.

(With Marcíllo Moraes) *Sonho Meu,* Rede Globo de Televisão, 1994.

(With Silvio de Abreu) *A Próxima Vítima,* Rede Globo de Televisão, 1995.

(Adapter) Cassiano Gabus Mendes, *Anjo Mau,* Rede Globo de Televisão, 1997–1998.

(Adapter) Dinah Silveira de Queiroz, *A Muralha,* Rede Globo de Televisão, 2000.

(Adapter) Eça de Queiroz, *Os Maias,* Rede Globo de Televisão, 2001.

SIDELIGHTS: Brazilian writer Maria Adelaide Amaral is primarily known as a playwright, but she has also published several novels and collaborated on many television screenplays, and she has translated a number of English works into Portuguese. Darlene Dalto noted in *JT* online that Amaral is one of the most important Brazilian authors writing today. While working for São Paulo publishers during the 1970s, Amaral wrote her first play, *A Resistência.* Finished in 1975, it would not be produced for the stage until 1979. Several of Amaral's plays from this period, such as *Bodas de Papel* ("Two-Year Wedding Anniversary"), depict the socioeconomic conditions resulting from a period of dictatorship in Brazil. David S. George commented in his *Flash and Crash Days: Brazilian Theater in the Postdictatorship Period* that "beginning in 1983 . . . the author propels her playwriting on the quest for female identity."

Amaral moved with her family from her native Portugal to Brazil when she was twelve years old. She was interested in writing at an early age, trying her hand at poetry and dreaming of becoming a theater critic. After working as a journalist for fifteen years, she found work writing encyclopedia entries for a publisher in São Paulo. According to Dalto, her fiction writing began during "a tense period at the publisher due to possible layoffs. . . . One night she went home and began writing without stopping, . . . about the situation she was living. She showed the result to Sábato Magaldi, with whom she worked at the time.

He read it and said, 'This is theater, and it's good.' That was all she needed to hear and hasn't stopped writing since." The result of this initial effort was the play *A Resistência.* First produced in 1979, it proved to be a box office hit. George remarked that "for the first time [since the dictatorship] the issues brought up by the play were being discussed openly; the characters were very familiar to the audience."

Another early play, *Bodas de Papel,* depicts a gathering at a wedding anniversary. The attendees belong to a new social class created by a short period of economic prosperity during the dictatorship that, according to George, led to "corruption on a mammoth scale and to the enrichment of a small group of people, government bureaucrats . . . and executives who often collaborated with the generals." He described how the play exposes an environment "filled with accusations, insults, painful truths, and humiliation. All the . . . rules of social courtesy are suspended. The women are secondary and decorative for the men, although the men accuse the women of being the cause of their problems."

In a play in which a woman is allowed considerable success, Amaral's musical *Chiquinha Gonzaga* is about "the life of one of the few women in the pantheon of Brazilian popular music and a seminal figure in the history of Brazilian feminism," explained George. In an interview with George, Amaral related that "the play was commissioned [by the Brazilian state labor agency] an extremely expensive production. I wanted to create a broad portrait of the period because when I did the research for the play I rediscovered Brazil, the nineteenth century, the history of Brazilian popular culture, especially Rio culture of the time. And the business about a totally forgotten career. No one knows who that woman was."

Based on her novel *Luísa: Quase uma História de Amor,* the 1984 play *De Braços Abertos* "performed stunningly at the box office, received universal acclaim from the critics, and won the São Paulo Association of Theater Critics award (for the play) and the Mambembe Prize (for the playwright)," reported George. He described *De Braços Abertos* as "a play about two characters, Luísa and Sérgio, who meet five years after their love affair has ended. Their relationship and subsequent search for individual identity are portrayed both in their conversation . . . and in flashbacks." He added that "there is no question that it has been

the most influential and successful play written by a woman in Brazil" in the twentieth century. Amaral told Dalto in *JT* that the former lovers in the play are her favorites because she identifies with them the most. Furthermore, she told George that the work "moved people, which is what I'm looking for. To affect people's lives, to help them think and make better decisions for themselves, to make their lives happier."

Amaral's more recent work *Querida Mamãe* is about a mother-daughter relationship that provides a way for the playwright to examine the theme of "the dynamics of relationships and families," according to George. The play explores "where those dynamics lead, where they break down, and how the stresses and fracture points are homologous to the larger society." A great theatrical success, *Querida Mamãe* offers more evidence of Amaral's staying power as a talented writer, winning her a fourth Molière Prize and her second Mamembe Prize.

BIOGRAPHICAL AND CRITICAL SOURCES:

BOOKS

George, David S., *Flash and Crash Days: Brazilian Theater in the Postdictatorship Period,* Garland Publishing (New York, NY), 2000.

ONLINE

Estado, http://www.estado.com.br/ (August 22, 2001), Haroldo Ceravolo Sereza, "Maria Adelaide Amaral Encontra Teatro de Saramago"; (August 23, 2001), Haroldo Ceravolo Sereza, "Nacionalismo atraphalha América Latina, diz Skármeta"; (August 31, 2001), Larissa Squeff, "Maria Adelaide Amaral Cria Roteiro para Walter Salles."
JT, http://www.jt.estado.com.br/ (February 28, 1999), Darlene Dalto, interview with Maria Adelaide Amaral.*

*   *   *

**AMARAL, Maria Adelaide Almeida Santos de
See AMARAL, Maria Adelaide**

AMIRY, Suad 1951-

PERSONAL: Born 1951, in Damascus, Syria; daughter of a Jordanian ambassador and a printing press operator; married Salim Tamari, c. 1981. *Education:* Degrees from American University of Beirut and University of Michigan; University of Edinburgh, Ph.D.

ADDRESSES: Home and office—P.O. Box 212, Ramallah, Al-sharafa, Palestine; fax: 02-240-69-86. *E-mail*—riwaq@palnet.com.

CAREER: RIWAQ Center for Architectural Conservation, Ramallah, Palestine, founder and director; Birzeit University, Ramallah, instructor, 1981—; deputy minister of culture in the Palestinian government, began 1996. Member of the Palestinian delegation to peace negotiations, 1991.

AWARDS, HONORS: Viareggio-Versilia Prize, Italy, for *Sharon and My Mother-in-Law.*

WRITINGS:

(With Vera Tamari) *The Palestinian Village Home,* British Museum Publications (London, England), 1989.

Traditional Floor Tiles in Palestine, illustrated by Lena Sobeh, Arabic translation by Taisir Hammad, RIWAQ (Ramallah, Palestine), 2000.

(With Rana Anani, Miya Jurundal, Elizabeth Hardin, Faras Rahhal, and Yara al-Sharif) *Imarat quraal-karasi: min tarikh al-iqta fi rif Filastin fial-qarnayn al-thamin ashar wa-al-tasi ashar* (title means *"Throne Village Architecture"*), RIWAQ (Ramallah, Palestine), 2003.

Kaputsino be-Ramallah: reshimot min ha-seger (title means "Cappucino in Ramallah: War Diaries"), Hebrew translation by Roni Meirshtain, Bavel (Tel Aviv, Israel), 2003.

(With Firas Rahhal) *Manatir: qusur al-mazari fi rif Filastin* (title means "Manatir: Agricultural Farmhouses in Rural Palestine"), RIWAQ (Ramallah, Palestine), 2003.

(Editor, with Mouhammad Hadid) *Earthquake in April,* 2003.

Sharon and My Mother-in-Law: Ramallah Diaries (memoir), Pantheon (New York, NY), 2004.

Sharon and My Mother-in-Law has been translated into numerous languages, including Italian and French.

SIDELIGHTS: Palestinian author Suad Amiry's first career was as an architect and preservationist of historic buildings. She has been teaching architecture at a Ramallah university for many years, and several of her books were on this subject. However, to Western audiences, Amiry is best known as the author of a very different type of book. *Sharon and My Mother-in-Law: Ramallah Diaries* began as a journal that Amiry kept and e-mails that she sent to her friends in 2002, when Israeli Prime Minister Ariel Sharon put Ramallah under a curfew for forty-three days. During this time, Amiry's ninety-two-year-old mother-in-law lived with Amiry's family for safety, a state of affairs that, Amiry writes, drove her nearly insane. In her introduction, she tells Sharon, "Perhaps one day I may forgive you for putting us under curfew for forty-two days, but I will never forgive you for obliging to have my mother-in-law with us for what seemed, then, more like forty-two years." Although the book deals with weighty geopolitical topics, it generally approaches them with humor. Amiry points out the absurdity of such situations as the time her dog had a passport to enter Jerusalem but she didn't (she convinces the Israeli border guard to allow her to enter the city as well, since the dog could clearly not drive into Jerusalem by herself), or her paranoia at being given a tacky plug-in model of Mecca by a neighbor—one of her first thoughts is to wonder if the knick-knack is bugged. Amiry's tale is "refreshingly different from any other writings on the Palestinian-Israeli conflict," Fred Rhodes remarked in the *Middle East. Booklist* reviewer Hazel Rochman also praised the book, calling it "laugh-out-loud funny," while *Library Journal* contributor Ethan Pullman concluded that *Sharon and My Mother-in-Law,* is "excellent for providing the Palestinian perspective on living in the West Bank through years of upheaval."

BIOGRAPHICAL AND CRITICAL SOURCES:

BOOKS

Amiry, Suad, *Sharon and My Mother-in-Law: Ramallah Diaries,* Pantheon (New York, NY), 2004.

PERIODICALS

Biography, fall, 2005, Nomi Morris, review of *Sharon and My Mother-in-Law,* p. 700.

Booklist, September 1, 2005, Hazel Rochman, review of *Sharon and My Mother-in-Law,* p. 46.

Economist (U.S.), August 6, 2005, "Where to Now? The Israeli-Palestinian Deadlock," p. 68.

Globe and Mail (Toronto, Ontario, Canada), September 17, 2005, Nomi Morris, review of *Sharon and My Mother-in-Law,* p. D18.

Library Journal, October 1, 2005, Ethan Pullman, review of *Sharon and My Mother-in-Law,* p. 95.

Middle East, February, 2005, Fred Rhodes, review of *Sharon and My Mother-in-Law,* p. 64.

Newsweek International, February 14, 2005, William Underhill, review of *Sharon and My Mother-in-Law,* p. 55.

Publishers Weekly, August 1, 2005, review of *Sharon and My Mother-in-Law,* p. 57.

ONLINE

Al-Jazeerah, http://www.aljazeerah.info/ (January 23, 2005), Genevieve Cora Fraser, "Suad Amiry's Book on Life in Palestine under Occupation Exposes Israeli Crazy-Makers."

Three Monkeys Online, http://www.threemonkeys online.com/ (February 22, 2006), Michael O'Connor, "The Human Side of Occupation: Suad Amiry, Author of *Sharon and My Mother-in-Law* in Interview."

RIWAQ Center for Architectural Conservation, http://www.riwaq.org/ (February 22, 2006).

Women for Palestine, http://www.womenforpalestine.com/ (February 22, 2006), "Suad Amiry."*

*   *   *

ANDERSON, Fil 1951-

PERSONAL: Born February 9, 1951, in Greenville, NC; son of William F. and Hazeline E. (a homemaker) Anderson; married June 5, 1976; wife's name Lucie K. (an educator); children: Meredith, Will, Lee. *Ethnicity:* "Caucasian." *Education:* University of North Carolina at Wilmington, M.A. (philosophy and religion), 1974; Fuller Theological Seminary, M.A. (theology), 1985; Shalem Institute for Spiritual Formation, certificate, 1995.

ADDRESSES: Office—Journey Resources, P.O. Box 9801, Greensboro, NC 27429. *Agent*—Kathryn Helmers, Kathryn Helmers Literary, 2263 Silent Rain Dr., Colorado Springs, CO 80919. *E-mail*—filanderson@ triad.rr.com.

CAREER: Writer. Young Life, Colorado Springs, CO, area and regional director and national director of training, between 1974 and 1999; Journey Resources, Greensboro, NC, executive director, 2000—.

WRITINGS:

Running on Empty: Contemplative Spirituality for Overachievers, WaterBrook Press (Colorado Springs, CO), 2004.

*   *   *

ANDERSON, Katharine

PERSONAL: Female. *Education:* McGill University, B.A. (with honors); University of Massachusetts, Amherst, M.A.; Northwestern University, Ph.D., 1994.

ADDRESSES: Office—303 Bethune College, York University, 4700 Keele St., Toronto, Ontario M3J 1P3, Canada. *E-mail*—kateya@yorku.ca.

CAREER: York University, Toronto, Ontario, Canada, associate professor in the science and society program.

AWARDS, HONORS: Faculty of Arts fellowship, York University, 2000-01; Massey College fellowship, 2005-06.

WRITINGS:

(Contributor) *Nineteenth Century Psychological Thought: The Transition from Philosophy to Science,* American Psychological Association (Washington, DC), 2001.

(Contributor) *Culture and Science in the Nineteenth Century Media,* Ashgate (London, England), 2004.

Predicting the Weather: Victorians and the Science of Meteorology, University of Chicago Press (Chicago, IL), 2005.

Contributor to scholarly journals, including the *British Journal for the History of Science* and *History of Science.*

WORK IN PROGRESS: Research in the history of modern science, especially meteorology and oceanography.

SIDELIGHTS: Katharine Anderson is a scholar of the interaction between science and lay society. In her first book, *Predicting the Weather: Victorians and the Science of Meteorology,* she examines both the development of weather forecasting as a science during the late nineteenth and early twentieth centuries and the public's reaction to the new, scientifically based but still frequently inaccurate weather predictions. As Anderson shows early in the book, both technological advances and social circumstances led to the founding of the British national weather service in 1854. The invention of the telegraph made it feasible to collect weather reports from all across the country and to send out predictions in a timely manner, but the fact that the British economy was so dependent on ocean-going ships was what made accurate weather forecasts such a government priority. The public, too, pressed for better predictions, and, according to Anderson, their demands were so intense that they led the head of the weather office to commit suicide. In addition to telling the story of the British weather service, Anderson also examines the debates sparked by the new science of meteorology, such as the question of how responsible scientists should be for their predictions. "Overall," Mace Bentley concluded in *Weatherwise,* "this is an excellent book, written in an accessible fashion with many interesting stories surrounding the trials and tribulations of pioneering scientists."

BIOGRAPHICAL AND CRITICAL SOURCES:

PERIODICALS

Science News, July 2, 2005, review of *Predicting the Weather: Victorians and the Science of Meteorology,* p. 15.

Weatherwise, January-February, 2006, Mace Bentley, review of *Predicting the Weather,* p. 60.

ONLINE

York University Web site, http://www.yorku.ca/ (February 22, 2006), author profile.*

* * *

ANDRESS, David 1969-
(David Robert Andress)

PERSONAL: Born 1969. *Education:* University of York, B.A. (with honors), 1990, D.Phil., 1995.

ADDRESSES: Office—University of Portsmouth, Milldam, Burnaby Rd., Portsmouth, Hampshire PO1 3AS, England. *E-mail*—david.andress@port.ac.uk.

CAREER: University of Portsmouth, Portsmouth, Hampshire, England, lecturer, 1994-99, senior lecturer, 1999-2002, principal lecturer in modern European history, 2002—. Member, Institute for Learning and Teaching in Higher Education.

MEMBER: Royal Historical Society (fellow).

AWARDS, HONORS: Institut des Hautes Études de la Sécurité Intérieure prize, 1996, for doctoral thesis; research grant, Humanities Research Board of the British Academy, 1999; grant for support of monograph publication, Scouloudi Foundation, 2000; overseas conference grants, British Academy, 2001, 2005.

WRITINGS:

French Society in Revolution, 1789-1799 ("New Frontiers in History" series), Manchester University Press (Manchester, England), 1999.
Massacre at the Champ de Mars: Popular Dissent and Political Culture in the French Revolution, Boydell Press (Rochester, NY), 2000.
The French Revolution and the People, Hambledon & London (New York, NY), 2004.

The Terror: Civil War in the French Revolution, Little, Brown (London, England), 2005, published as *The Terror: The Merciless War for Freedom in Revolutionary France,* Farrar, Straus (New York, NY), 2006.

Contributor of chapters to anthologies, including *History and Heritage: Consuming the Past in Contemporary Culture,* edited by J. Arnold, K. Davies, and S. Ditchfield, Donhead Publishing, 1998; *The French Experience from Republic to Monarchy, 1793-1824: New Dawns in Politics, Knowledge and Culture,* edited by M.F. Cross and D. Williams, Macmillan, 2000; *Language and Revolution: Making Modern Political Identities,* edited by I. Halfin, Frank Cass, 2002; *Enlightenment and Revolution: Essays in Honour of Norman Hampson,* edited by M. Crook, A. Forrest, and W. Doyle, Ashgate, 2004; and *Conspiracy and the French Revolution,* edited by P. Campbell, T. Kaiser, and M. Linton, Manchester University Press, in press. Contributor to scholarly periodicals, including *French Historical Studies* and *Cultural and Social History.* Member of the editorial board, *French Historian;* referee for *French Historical Studies* and *French History;* coeditor of the H-France scholarly e-mail discussion list.

WORK IN PROGRESS: A project about "melodramatic imagination" in late eighteenth-century France; a study of late eighteenth-century France, for Oxford University Press.

SIDELIGHTS: David Andress is a British historian who specializes in the history of the French Revolution. His first book, *French Society in Revolution, 1789-1799,* "is one of the better short treatments of the French Revolution," according to *History: Review of New Books* contributor Eric A. Arnold, Jr. In this title, Andress provides an overview of the historiography of the French Revolution, showing how both social historians and political culture historians evaluate the events of the conflict.

Andress's second book, *Massacre at the Champ de Mars: Popular Dissent and Political Culture in the French Revolution,* takes its title from an event that happened in Paris on July 17, 1791. On that date a group of republicans met on the Champ de Mars, a Paris street later to become the site of the Eiffel Tower, to draw up a petition. After a series of events that are

still hazy to historians, troops from the Paris National Guard fired into this crowd, killing up to fifty people. Despite the book's title, Andress is more concerned with the causes of and reactions to the massacre than to the mystery of what happened during the event itself. Specifically, he attempts to show that the republicans of July 17 were not merely members of the lower socioeconomic classes playing out a role assigned to them by the bourgeois leaders of the revolution, but instead were politically aware men and women acting of their own volition. "Discovering what the revolutionary crowd really thought, and just how politically sophisticated it was, is a fascinating—and ambitious—project," Munro Price remarked in the *English Historical Review.* "This is a nuanced, multilayered analysis from which scholars of the Revolution, particularly those interested in its early stage, will benefit," Michael P. Fitzsimmons wrote in a review for the *Journal of Modern History.* "Andress is to be congratulated for broadening our understanding of a pivotal event."

The Terror: The Merciless War for Freedom in Revolutionary France (originally published in Britain as *The Terror: Civil War in the French Revolution*) expands on the history covered in *Massacre at the Champs de Mars,* taking the story of the French Revolution from the attempted flight of King Louis XVI in 1791 through the coronation of Napoleon Bonaparte in 1804. These years included the Reign of Terror (1792-94), the period in which the French Revolution turned into a bloody and chaotic civil war in which countless people were killed on the suspicion of being counterrevolutionaries. The Terror has generally been considered by historians to be a dysfunctional display of paranoia and senseless violence, but Andress takes issue with this view. He argues that France was in a true state of civil war and that counterrevolution was a real and present danger, even if the mass murders of the Terror were a gross overreaction to the threat. This is "a bracing historical reassessment," concluded a *Publishers Weekly* critic, while a *Kirkus Reviews* contributor deemed the book a "meticulous, readable account of the French Revolution's poisonous politics." "Andress has managed, with high organisational skill and scholarly care, to weave together telling details of persons, places and events with convincingly articulated interpretive themes," Robert Stewart Castlereagh concluded in the *Spectator,* adding that "all the while the narrative unfolds in its dramatic intensity. His book is a tour de force."

BIOGRAPHICAL AND CRITICAL SOURCES:

PERIODICALS

Booklist, November 15, 2005, Gilbert Taylor, review of *The Terror: The Merciless War for Freedom in Revolutionary France*, p. 16.

Contemporary Review, October, 2005, review of *The Terror: The Civil War in the French Revolution*, p. 251.

English Historical Review, April, 2002, Munro Price, review of *Massacre at the Champ de Mars: Popular Dissent and Political Culture in the French Revolution*, p. 483.

History: Review of New Books, fall, 1999, Eric A. Arnold, Jr., review of *French Society in Revolution, 1789-1799*, p. 25; fall, 2004, review of *The French Revolution and the People*, p. 29.

Journal of Modern History, March, 2003, Michael P. Fitzsimmons, review of *Massacre at the Champ de Mars*, p. 169.

Journal of Social History, fall, 2002, Casey Harison, review of *Massacre at the Champ de Mars*, p. 200.

Kirkus Reviews, October 15, 2005, review of *The Terror*, p. 1118.

Publishers Weekly, September 5, 2005, review of *The Terror*, p. 42.

Spectator, August 6, 2005, Robert Stewart Castlereagh, "Protecting the Infant Republic," review of *The Terror*, p. 38.

Sunday Times (London, England), June 19, 2005, Andrew Roberts, review of *The Terror*.

ONLINE

David Andress Home Page, http://userweb.port.ac.uk/~andressd (January 19, 2006).

University of Portsmouth Web site, http://www.port.ac.uk/ (January 19, 2006), "Dr. David Andress."*

*   *   *

ANDRESS, David Robert
    See ANDRESS, David

ÂNGELO, Ivan 1936-

PERSONAL: Born February 4, 1936, in Barbacena, Minas Gerais, Brazil; son of Jesus Geraldo and Divina (Vianna) Ângelo; married; wife's name Angélica; children: Júlia.

ADDRESSES: Agent—c/o Author Mail, Dalkey Archive Press, ISU Campus 8905, Normal, IL 61790-8905.

CAREER: Cofounder, *Complemento*, Belo Horizonte, Brazil, beginning 1956; columnist and editor for newspapers in Belo Horizonte, 1958-64; *Jornal de Tarde*, São Paulo, Brazil, editor, 1965-68, managing editor, 1968-86, executive chief editor, 1986-96, editor of special projects, 1996-98, television columnist, 1998—.

AWARDS, HONORS: Literary Prize, City of Belo Horizonte, 1959, for the unedited manuscript of *Homem sofrendo no quarto*; Jabuti Prize, Câmara Brasileira Associação Paulista dos Criticos de Arte, 1986, for *A face horrível*; Best Children's Book, Associação Paulista dos Criticos de Arte, 1997, for *Pode me beijar se quiser*.

WRITINGS:

(With Silviano Santiago) *Duas faces* (short stories), Editôra Itatiaia (Belo Horizonte, Brazil), 1961.

A festa (novel), Vertente Editora (São Paulo, Brazil), 1976, translation by Thomas Colchie published as *The Celebration*, Avon Books (New York, NY), 1982.

A casa de vidro: Cinco histórias do Brasil (five novellas), Livraria Cultura Editora (São Paulo, Brazil), 1979, translation by Ellen Watson published as *The Tower of Glass*, Avon Books (New York, NY), 1986.

A face horrível (short stories), Editora Nova Fronteira (Rio de Janeiro, Brazil), 1986.

São Paulo, 1880-1990: 110 anos de industrializeção, Editora Três (São Paulo, Brazil), 1992.

Amor? (novella), Companhia das Letras (São Paulo, Brazil), 1995.

85 anos de cultura: História da sociedade de cultura artística, Studio Nobel (São Paulo, Brazil), 1998.

Verde, amarelo, bleu, blanc, rouge, DBA (São Paulo, Brazil), 1998.

Trabalho, superacão, coragem, pioneirismo, photographs by André Andrade and others, DBA (São Paulo, Brazil), 1999.

O comprador de aventuras e outras crônicas, Editora Atica (São Paulo, Brazil), 2000.

BASF 90 anos: uma histórias no Brasil, DBA (São Paulo, Brazil), 2001.

Also author of episodes of the television series *Séries Brasileiras,* Rede Globo de Televisão, 1981. Contributor to periodicals, including *Veja, Playboy, Itinerários, Correio Braziliense,* and *O Tempo.* Audiocassette recordings of the author reading from his books are available at the Library of Congress's Archive of Hispanic Literature on Tape, 1983, and the Instituto Moreira Salles, 1998.

FOR CHILDREN

O ladrão de sonhos, Editora Atica (São Paulo, Brazil), 1994.

Pode me beijar se quiser, Editora Atica (São Paulo, Brazil), 1994.

O vestido luminoso da princesa, Editora Moderna (São Paulo, Brazil), 1997.

História em ão e inha, Editora Moderna (São Paulo, Brazil), 1997.

(Translator) Kenneth Grahame, *O vento nos salqueros* (translation of *The Wind in the Willows*), Editora Moderna (São Paulo, Brazil), 1998.

SIDELIGHTS: Brazilian author Ivan Ângelo's literary activities began in 1956, when he cofounded the arts and cultural review *Complemento* with other young intellectuals. Two years later, he embarked on a journalism career as a columnist and editor. His novel *A festa* won the prestigious Jabuti Prize and was later translated into several languages; it was published in English as *The Celebration.* While continuing to write for adult readers, Ângelo has also published books for children, such as *Pode me beijar se quiser,* which won the Best Children's Book award from the Associação Paulista dos Criticos de Arte.

Ângelo's success as a writer did not come easily. The political environment in his native Brazil at the time favored censorship. Because of this, his *A festa,* which was written in 1963, was not published until 1976. In *A festa* the reader is presented with two very different sides of Brazilian society: one consists of young, liberal sophisticates who are preparing for the celebration of the title; and the other are the poor, starving immigrants from northern Brazil who riot at a train station. When a reporter is killed in the melee and the Department of Political and Social Order gets involved, these two worlds collide. Reviewers of the novel noted its experimental style. "Ângelo presents his events and characters through a variety of techniques and styles," observed Patrick Breslin in the *Washington Post,* "like a juggler showing all his tricks. He culls newspaper columns and political speeches for quotes that frame his story. . . . We hear one half of phone conversations, staccato interior monologues, an infant grappling with the first steps in constructing sentences."

The author's second book to be translated into English, *A casa de vidro: Cinco histórias do Brasil,* was published as *The Tower of Glass.* It contains five novellas that are tied together as commentaries on violence, corruption, poverty, and greed in Brazilian society. In the title story, a futuristic tale, Ângelo makes a statement about societal complacency when a prison's walls are replaced with glass. The populace is thus allowed to see the brutality that occurs within, but after a time they become used to it and ignore it. As John Gledson observed in his *Times Literary Supplement* review, the tale reveals "how even an apparent liberalization and removal of censorship can slowly create a sense of complicity and blockage, where the threat of violent intervention is never entirely absent." A *Publishers Weekly* critic, summarizing the impression of the other stories in the collection, stated: "Though thin on plot, they offer a vivid, street-level montage" of Brazil's poor, working classes, and authorities. Gledson concluded that "Ângelo's fiction is some of the most vivid and thoughtful to have come out of Latin America in recent years."

Ângelo's *A face horrível* is a collection of fourteen stories that updates and adds to his earlier collection, *Duas faces.* The "horrible side" referred to in the title is a comment on the "disturbing underside of surface reality," according to Nelson Vieira in a *World Literature Today* review. Vieira added: "With irony and humor, Ângelo compels his readers to face such unpleasantries as the ugly and repressive side of traditional roles, success stories under an authoritarian regime, police bureaucracy, single parenthood in a society of no divorce, and the lack of communication in marriage, love, and sex."

In an interview for the online *Klick Escritores,* the author described his reasons for writing: "I began because I had held a great number of injustices inside me, those that incite rebellion in children and in adolescents, and I was searching for a channel through which to speak out about them. . . . I realized that through those words I would be able to play with the mind of the reader, not simply playing with his emotions, not only revealing to him the oppressor or the oppressed dwelling within him, but also proposing to him a kind of text, calling into question the kind of text to which he had been accustomed."

BIOGRAPHICAL AND CRITICAL SOURCES:

PERIODICALS

Library Journal, December 15, 1981, Dru Dougherty, review of *The Celebration,* p. 2405.
Newsweek, July 12, 1982, Jim Miller, "A Barrage from Brazil," review of *The Celebration,* p. 71.
Publishers Weekly, November 27, 1981, review of *The Celebrarion,* p. 83; November 29, 1985, review of *The Tower of Glass,* p. 44.
Quill & Quire, March, 1982, Paul Stuewe, "Imports: Italian Folktales . . . Nouveau Cuisine . . . Giving Peace a Chance," review of *The Celebration,* p. 69.
Times Literary Supplement, February 27, 1987, John Gledson, "The Real, True S.O.B.," review of *The Tower of Glass,* p. 207.
Washington Post, April 4, 1982, Patrick Breslin, review of *The Celebration.*
World Literature Today, winter, 1987, Nelson H. Vieira, review of *A face horrível,* pp. 79-80.

ONLINE

Itaú Cultural, http://www.itaucultural.org.br/ (September 3, 2003), biographical information on Ivan Ângelo.
Klick Escritores, http://www.klickescritores.com.br/ (September 3, 2003), interview with Ivan Ângelo.*

ANTON, Maggie
(Margaret Antonofsky)

PERSONAL: Born Margaret Antonofsky, in Los Angeles, CA; married David Parkhurst; children: Emily and Ari. *Religion:* Jewish. *Hobbies and other interests:* Talmud study.

ADDRESSES: *Agent*—c/o Author Mail, Banot Press, 1413 Kenneth Rd., #280, Glendale, CA 91202. *E-mail*—author@rashisdaughters.com.

CAREER: Writer. Kaiser Permanente Biochemical Genetics Laboratory, clinical chemist.

AWARDS, HONORS: Best Book Award, *USABook News.com,* 2005, for *Rashi's Daughters, Book One: Joheved.*

WRITINGS:

Rashi's Daughters, Book One: Joheved, Banot Press (Glendale, CA), 2005.

WORK IN PROGRESS: *Rashi's Daughters, Book Two: Miriam.*

SIDELIGHTS: Maggie Anton became interested in Judaism after her marriage, when she and her husband David Parkhurst began attending synagogue and studying religious traditions. In the 1990s she joined a women's Talmud class and spent the next five years meeting weekly to discuss scriptures. Anton's children left home in 1997 and this gave her more time to devote to her studies. She started investigating the life of Rashi, a Jewish scholar who lived in France in the eleventh century. Rashi had no sons, only three daughters, and he broke with tradition by educating all of them in Jewish traditions.

After seven years of research, Anton began writing *Rashi's Daughters, Book One: Joheved.* The first volume of a planned trilogy focused on Rashi's eldest daughter, Joheved. Rashi notices that Joheved is brilliant and furnishes her with books so that she can study in secret. Joheved plays the traditional female roles of daughter, sister, and wife, caring for her grandmother and hiding her studies from her betrothed, but she also helps her father run his winery. Throughout, she is devoted to her faith.

The novel sold out of its first printing of 3,000 copies two months before publication, and a second printing sold rapidly. Anton has been pleased with the success of her novel, but claims a broader mission for her work. In an interview with Norm Goldman, editor of *BookPleasures.com,* she said, "I want to inspire more women and non-Orthodox Jews to study Talmud. I hope the short Talmud lessons in *Rashi's Daughters* will inspire them to do so."

BIOGRAPHICAL AND CRITICAL SOURCES:

PERIODICALS

Library Journal, October 1, 2005, Barbara Hoffert, review of *Rashi's Daughters, Book One: Joheved,* p. 46.
Small Press Bookwatch, June, 2005, review of *Rashi's Daughters, Book One.*

ONLINE

BookPleasures.com, http://bookpleasures.com/ (January 4, 2006), Norm Goldman, interview with Anton, and review of *Rashi's Daughters, Book One.*
Historical Fiction—TCM Reviews, http://tcm-ca.com/ (January 4, 2006), review of *Rashi's Daughters, Book One.*
Maggie Anton Home Page, http://rashisdaughters.com (January 26, 2006).
Romantic Times Book Club, http://www.romantic times.com/ (January 4, 2006), review of *Rashi's Daughters, Book One.**

*   *   *

ANTONOFSKY, Margaret
See ANTON, Maggie

*   *   *

ARATON, Harvey 1952-

PERSONAL: Born May 17, 1952, in New York, NY; married Beth Albert (a public relations executive); children: two sons. *Education:* City University of New York, graduated 1975.

ADDRESSES: Home—Montclair, NJ. *Agent*—c/o Author Mail, Free Press, 1230 Avenue of the Americas, New York, NY 10020.

CAREER: Staten Island Advance, Staten Island, NY, sports reporter, night sports editor, city side reporter, and copyboy, 1970-77; *New York Post,* New York, NY, sports reporter, 1977-83; *New York Daily News,* New York, sports reporter and columnist, c. 1983-91; *New York Times,* New York, sports reporter and national basketball columnist, beginning 1991, "Sports of the Times" columnist, 1994—. New York University, New York, instructor, 1987.

AWARDS, HONORS: Associated Press Sports Editors award, 1992, for enterprise reporting; Pulitzer Prize nomination, 1994; column writing award, Associated Press Sports Editors, 1997; column writing award, Women's Sports Foundation, 1998.

WRITINGS:

(With Filip Bondy) *The Selling of the Green: The Financial Rise and Moral Decline of the Boston Celtics,* HarperCollins (New York, NY), 1992.
(With Armen Keteyian and Martin F. Dardis) *Money Players: Days and Nights inside the New NBA,* Pocket Books (New York, NY), 1997.
Alive and Kicking: When Soccer Moms Take the Field and Change Their Lives Forever, Simon & Schuster (New York, NY), 2001.
Crashing the Borders: How Basketball Won the World and Lost Its Soul at Home, Free Press (New York, NY), 2005.

Contributor to periodicals, including the *New York Times Magazine, GQ, ESPN Magazine, Sport Magazine, Tennis Magazine,* and *Basketball Weekly.*

SIDELIGHTS: Sports journalist Harvey Araton gained considerable attention for one of his few works that is not about professional athletes: *Alive and Kicking: When Soccer Moms Take the Field and Change Their Lives Forever.* The book was inspired by the decision of Araton's wife, Beth Albert, and several other mothers from their area to begin playing in a competitive soccer league. Despite these women's busy lives and the fact that many of them had never played team sports in school, they practiced with dedication and played hard. In the process, Araton writes, they won the respect of their children, formed close friendships, supported each other through divorce and breast cancer, and discovered the joys of competition and teamwork. "These women experience the kind of solidarity that lifts us out of ourselves, the kind of which strong communities are made," Allison Pugh noted in the *New York Times Book Review.* Indeed, the players' community spirit extended beyond their own league: They organized an annual tournament that raised 50,000 dollars to fight breast cancer in its first year, and some of them became certified coaches of their children's soccer teams. The fact that Araton focuses on the impact that playing competitive sports has on these women's personal lives and on their families makes the book "more social history than a sports story," explained *Library Journal* reviewer John Maxymuk, but as Wes Lukowsky concluded in *Booklist, Alive and Kicking* "is a wonderful book by an insightful, empathetic author."

Araton's other books include *The Selling of the Green: The Financial Rise and Moral Decline of the Boston Celtics, Money Players: Days and Nights inside the New NBA,* and *Crashing the Borders: How Basketball Won the World and Lost Its Soul at Home.* All examine how such social problems as racism, greed, and socioeconomic class intrude on the sport of professional basketball. *The Selling of the Green* examines the Boston Celtic's decision to maintain an evenly balanced team, with six white and six black players, even though the National Basketball Association as a whole is almost three-quarters black. To Araton and his coauthor, Filip Bondy, this decision represents unconscionable pandering to white Bostonians (the vast majority of the Celtics' fans, despite the fact that Boston is a quarter black), who have long had a reputation for racism. The book is a "hard-hitting exposé," according to a *Publishers Weekly* critic.

Crashing the Borders, written in the wake of a brawl between Indiana Pacers players and Detroit Pistons fans in December 2004, illustrates how the quest for money has ruined basketball at all levels, with college programs selling out to the demands of television and young players tempted to drop out of college, or even high school, for a chance to turn professional. Yet despite the book's tone of despair, as a *Kirkus Reviews* contributor noted, its analysis of the social and economic factors behind basketball's decline make it "more than the usual lament for the good old days."

BIOGRAPHICAL AND CRITICAL SOURCES:

PERIODICALS

American Libraries, September, 2002, Bill Ott, review of *Alive and Kicking: When Soccer Moms Take the Field and Change Their Lives Forever,* p. 80.

Booklist, September 1, 2001, Wes Lukowsky, review of *Alive and Kicking,* p. 33; October 15, 2005, Wes Lukowsky, review of *Crashing the Borders: How Basketball Won the World and Lost Its Soul at Home,* p. 20.

Chicago Tribune, November 15, 2001, Bob Condor, "These Moms Are the Ones Who Are Driven."

Kirkus Reviews, October 1, 2005, review of *Crashing the Borders,* p. 1057.

Library Journal, September 1, 2001, John Maxymuk, review of *Alive and Kicking,* p. 189.

New York Times Book Review, July 6, 1997, Charles Salzberg, review of *Money Players: Days and Nights inside the New NBA,* p. 15; January 6, 2002, Allison Pugh, "Mom Was a Goalie: A Sportswriter Examines What Happens When Soccer Moms Take the Field for Themselves," p. 21.

Publishers Weekly, December 6, 1991, review of *The Selling of the Green: The Financial Rise and Moral Decline of the Boston Celtics,* p. 63; June 11, 2001, review of *Alive and Kicking,* p. 69.

Sports Illustrated, March 23, 1992, John Garrity, review of *The Selling of the Green,* p. 87.*

* * *

ARMSTRONG, Bob 1942-

PERSONAL: Born 1942.

ADDRESSES: Agent—c/o Author Mail, Carroll & Graf, 245 W. 17th St., 11th Fl., New York, NY 10011-5300.

CAREER: Writer. Has worked as a book salesman, DVD reviewer, and freelance writer; founder, Zen Escort Service. *Military service:* Served in the military during the Vietnam War.

WRITINGS:

Vanilla Slim: An Improbable Pimp in the Empire of Lust, Carroll & Graf (New York, NY), 2005.

Contributor to periodicals, including the *San Francisco Chronicle.*

SIDELIGHTS: After coming home from fighting in the Vietnam War, Bob Armstrong earned his living in a variety of ways. Among his occupations were traveling book salesman and freelance writer for the *San Francisco Chronicle* and adult magazines. Addicted to speed and other drugs, he then decided he needed to earn more money, and the idea came to him that he should become a pimp. Founding Zen Escort Services, Armstrong, a white man in his fifties at the time, easily located willing prostitutes by placing an advertisement in the *SF Weekly.* Calling himself Vanilla Slim— "Slim" in honor of a famous black pimp named Iceberg Slim, and "Vanilla" because he was white— Armstrong arranged the appointments and drove his girls to their waiting men; when they were done, he collected 150 dollars per hour and the girls kept 350. The easy money did not last long, however, and Armstrong soon found himself in prison, which is where his memoir, *Vanilla Slim: An Improbable Pimp in the Empire of Lust,* begins.

Reviewers of *Vanilla Slim* noted that Armstrong is obviously a well-read and intelligent person; however, many critics went on to complain that the author comes off as a very self-satisfied, egotistical man who never reveals whether or not he has a conscience about what he is doing. This mix results in some self-indulgent prose that critics often found unpalatable. *Baltimore City Paper* contributor Jessie Reeder, for example, commented that Armstrong "suffers from an inability to rein in his often-expository dialogue and the most nauseating of linguistic indulgences," adding that "it becomes clear that he is all too pleased with himself for being a Pimp Who Reads." Lincoln MacVeagh, writing for the *New York Press,* similarly observed, "The story of Vanilla Slim is essentially a comic one. It's the comeuppance of an aging blowhard, and in the right hands it could make for a witty novel. But the story isn't in the right hands. It's told by the blowhard, and Armstrong doesn't see himself as a clown." MacVeagh continued, "He has a nice eye for the absurdity of other people and as long as he's gazing outward he can be very entertaining." Nevertheless, a *Publishers Weekly* reviewer felt that "Armstrong offers funny, pungent lines interspersed with self-examining digressions, producing a funny read."

BIOGRAPHICAL AND CRITICAL SOURCES:

BOOKS

Armstrong, Bob, *Vanilla Slim: An Improbable Pimp in the Empire of Lust,* Carroll & Graf (New York, NY), 2006.

PERIODICALS

Kirkus Reviews, November 1, 2005, review of *Vanilla Slim,* p. 1167.
Publishers Weekly, October 10, 2005, review of *Vanilla Slim,* p. 46.

ONLINE

Baltimore City Paper Online, http://www.citypaper.com/ (February 8, 2006), Jessie Reeder, review of *Vanilla Slim.*
New York Press Online, http://www.nypress.com/ (March 1, 2006), Lincoln MacVeagh, "Pimp Mongering," review of *Vanilla Slim.*
Portland Mercury Online, http://www.portlandmercury.com/ (January 12, 2006), Scott Moore, review of *Vanilla Slim.**

*   *   *

**AROUET, François
See POLITZER, Georges**

*   *   *

ASHBY, Ruth

PERSONAL: Female.

ADDRESSES: Home—Huntington, NY. *Agent*—c/o Author Mail, William B. Eerdmans Publishing, 255 Jefferson Ave. S.E., Grand Rapids, MI 49503.

CAREER: Writer of children's books.

AWARDS, HONORS: Outstanding Science Trade Book selection, National Science Teachers Association/ Children's Book Council, 2004, for *Rocket Man.*

WRITINGS:

Quest for King Arthur, illustrated by Scott Caple, Bantam (New York, NY), 1988.

Sea Otters, Atheneum (New York, NY), 1990.

Tigers, Atheneum (New York, NY), 1990.

The Orangutan, Dillon Press (New York, NY), 1994.

(Editor, with Deborah Gore Ohrn) *Herstory: Women Who Changed the World,* Viking (New York, NY), 1995.

Elizabethan England, Benchmark Books (New York, NY), 1999.

T-Rex: Back to the Cretaceous, Scholastic (New York, NY), 2000.

Boss Tweed and Tammany Hall, Blackbirch Press (San Diego, CA), 2002.

Steve Case: America Online Pioneer, Twenty-first Century Books (Brookfield, CT), 2002.

Lincoln, Smart Apple Media (North Mankato, MN), 2003.

Lee vs. Grant: Great Battles of the Civil War, Smart Apple Media (North Mankato, MN), 2003.

The Outer Planets, Smart Apple Media (North Mankato, MN), 2003.

1800, Benchmark Books (New York, NY), 2003.

How the Solar System Was Formed, Smart Apple Media (North Mankato, MN), 2003.

Gettysburg, Smart Apple Media (North Mankato, MN), 2003.

Victorian England, Benchmark Books (New York, NY), 2003.

Fury on Horseback, Smart Apple Media (North Mankato, MN), 2003.

The Underground Railroad, Smart Apple Media (North Mankato, MN), 2003.

Extraordinary People, Smart Apple Media (North Mankato, MN), 2003.

The Earth and Its Moon, Smart Apple Media (North Mankato, MN), 2003.

(Editor) *The Letters of Elinore Pruitt Stewart, Woman Homesteader,* illustrated by Laszlo Kubinyi, Benchmark Books (New York, NY), 2004.

Rocket Man: The Mercury Adventure of John Glenn, Peachtree (Atlanta, GA), 2004.

The Diary of Sam Watkins, A Confederate Soldier, illustrated by Laszlo Kubinyi, Benchmark Books (New York, NY), 2004.

The Amazing Mr. Franklin; or, The Boy Who Read Everything, Peachtree (Atlanta, GA), 2004.

Pteranodon: The Life Story of a Pterosaur, illustrated by Phil Wilson, Abrams (New York, NY), 2005.

John and Abigail Adams, World Almanac Library (Milwaukee, WI), 2005.

James and Dolly Madison, World Almanac Library (Milwaukee, WI), 2005.

Ronald and Nancy Reagan, World Almanac Library (Milwaukee, WI), 2005.

George W. and Laura Bush, World Almanac Library (Milwaukee, WI), 2005.

George and Martha Washington, World Almanac Library (Milwaukee, WI), 2005.

Franklin and Eleanor Roosevelt, World Almanac Library (Milwaukee, WI), 2005.

John and Jacqueline Kennedy, World Almanac Library (Milwaukee, WI), 2005.

Bill and Hillary Rodham Clinton, World Almanac Library (Milwaukee, WI), 2005.

Woodrow and Edith Wilson, World Almanac Library (Milwaukee, WI), 2005.

Abraham and Mary Todd Lincoln, World Almanac Library (Milwaukee, WI), 2005.

Anne Frank: Young Diarist, Aladdin (New York, NY), 2005.

My Favorite Dinosaurs, illustrated by John Sibbick, Milk & Cookies, 2005.

Caedmon's Song, illustrated by Bill Slavin, W.B. Eerdmans (Grand Rapids, MI), 2006.

SIDELIGHTS: Ruth Ashby is a children's writer who focuses on nonfiction topics ranging from biology and paleontology to histories and biographies. She has also edited such volumes as *Herstory: Women Who Changed the World* and *The Letters of Elinore Pruitt Stewart, Woman Homesteader. Herstory* features short biographies of 120 of history's prominent women rulers, scientists, and athletes. According to a reviewer for *Publishers Weekly,* the "highly readable thumbnail sketches cover areas from literature to politics, fashion to aviation, music to science." A *Booklist* contributor noted that "women of all times, places, and professions are treated," and felt that the coeditors "admirably do justice to the topic and audience." Kristen Oravec, reviewing *The Letters of Elinore Pruitt Stewart* and another title for *School Library Journal,* commented that "the past comes strikingly to light in these first-person accounts."

Several of Ashby's original titles for young readers discuss dinosaurs. *T-Rex: Back to the Cretaceous,* a tie in for the IMAX film, follows the characters from the film while also providing trivia on Tyrannosaurus rex. "The author has constructed a book to appeal to dino-philes," wrote Patricia Manning in her *School Library Journal* review. *My Favorite Dinosaurs*, which covers various dinosaurs from different prehistoric eras, was considered "a browsing delight for dinosaur fans" by Todd Morning of *Booklist*. *Pteranodon: The Life Story of a Pterosaur* is an imagined day in the life of a pterosaur, based on scientific field studies of the albatross. Scientists theorize that the furry, flying dinosaur had similar habits to the modern day bird. "Dinosaur lovers will enjoy this handsomely illustrated picture book full of drama and speculation," quipped a contributor to *Kirkus Reviews*. Patricia Manning, writing for *School Library Journal*, noted that "the simple text includes . . . dramatic moments," and that the work is "an attractive and rewarding look at the possibilities in a long-lost life history."

Ashby has written a number of biographies on notable figures in U.S. history, including astronaut John Glenn, inventor and politician Benjamin Franklin, and several U.S. presidents and their wives. In *The Amazing Mr. Franklin; or, The Boy Who Read Everything*, Ashby offers a "lively narrative account," in the words of Carolyn Phelan in *Booklist*, describing Ashby's take on Franklin's varied career as a scientist, writer, politician, and inventor. Rebecca Sheridan, writing in *School Library Journal*, noted that "Ashby's clearly written narrative . . . flows smoothly and will hold the interest of children." *Rocket Man: The Mercury Adventure of John Glenn* recounts Glenn's childhood and his career that led to his becoming an astronaut, finally returning to space at age seventy-seven. "This book describes Glenn's life in a highly readable style," wrote Lana Miles in *School Library Journal*.

Ashby's series of titles about U.S. presidents and their first ladies includes short biographies that "are well designed and neatly tie together the lives of presidential couples," wrote Ilene Cooper in her *Booklist* review of *Bill and Hillary Rodham Clinton*. *School Library Journal* reviewer Janet Gillen, considering other titles in the series, deemed the books "readable, interesting, and accurate."

Along with biographies of famous Americans, Ashby has also penned fictionalized biographies of Anne Frank, whose diary has helped many young people to learn about the Holocaust, and Caedmon, the seventh-

century monk who is considered by many to be the first English poet. *Caedmon's Song* fills in imagined details of how a tongue-tied, disgruntled cowherd who hated poetry dreamed a hymn, leading him to become a monk so he could continue to create songs of praise. Ashby "creates a sympathetic protagonist, a man who is not ambitious but who, when the time is right, answers his calling," wrote Kara Schaff Dean in *School Library Journal*. "The episode is a significant one in our cultural history, and it's been many a year since any other version of it has been offered for young readers," noted a contributor to *Kirkus Reviews*. A *Publishers Weekly* critic considered the book an "accessible tale," and commented, "young readers will likely find the brief profile of a little-known figure intriguing."

BIOGRAPHICAL AND CRITICAL SOURCES:

PERIODICALS

Booklist, October 1, 1995, review of *Herstory: Women Who Changed the World*, p. 349; July, 2004, Carolyn Phelan, review of *The Amazing Mr. Franklin; or, The Boy Who Read Everything*, p. 1838; March 1, 2005, Ilene Cooper, review of *Bill and Hillary Rodham Clinton*, p. 1188; April 1, 2005, Todd Morning, review of *My Favorite Dinosaurs*, p. 1361.

Kirkus Reviews, March 15, 2005, review of *My Favorite Dinosaurs*, p. 347; June 1, 2005, review of *Pteranodon: The Life Story of a Pterosaur*, p. 632; December 15, 2005, review of *Caedmon's Song*, p. 1317.

Publishers Weekly, June 19, 1995, review of *Herstory*, p. 62; January 30, 2006, review of *Caedmon's Song*, p. 72.

School Library Journal, July, 1990, Ruth S. Vose, review of *Tigers*, p. 80; August, 1994, Helen Rosenberg, review of *The Orangutan*, p. 160; November, 1995, Maureen Connelly, review of *Herstory*, p. 133; January, 2001, Patricia Manning, review of *T-Rex: Back to the Cretaceous*, p. 113; February, 2003, Deborah Rothaug, review of *Extraordinary People*, p. 151; March, 2004, Kristen Oravec, review of *The Letters of Elinore Pruitt Stewart, Woman Homesteader*, p. 224; November, 2004, Rebecca Sheridan, review of *The Amazing Mr. Franklin*, p. 121; December, 2004, Lana Miles, review of *Rocket Man: The Mercury Adventure of John Glenn*, p. 156; April,

2005, Patricia Manning, review of *My Favorite Dinosaurs*, and Rita Soltan, review of *Anne Frank: Young Diarist,* p. 118; July, 2005, Patricia Manning, review of *Pteranodon*, p. 86; August, 2005, Janet Gillen, review of *Bill and Hillary Rodham Clinton* and others, p. 140; October, 2005, review of *My Favorite Dinosaurs,* p. S31; March, 2006, Kara Schaff Dean, review of *Caedmon's Song,* p. 206.

Voice of Youth Advocates, August, 1996, review of *Herstory,* p. 148; April, 2003, review of *Fury on Horseback,* p. 75.*

*   *   *

ATTALLAH, Naim 1931-
(Naim Ibrahim Attallah)

PERSONAL: Born May 1, 1931, in Haifa, Palestine (now Israel); immigrated to England, c. 1949; son of Ibrahim and Genevieve Attallah; married Maria Nykolyn (an interior decorator), 1957; children: one son. *Education:* Studied engineering at Battersea Polytechnic. *Hobbies and other interests:* Photography, cinema, theater, classical music, opera.

ADDRESSES: Home—25 Shepherd Market, London W1J 7PP, England. *Office*—Quartet Books, 27 Goodge St., London W1P 2LD, England. *E-mail*—nattallah@ aol.com.

CAREER: Publisher, film and theater producer, businessman, and author. During early career, worked as a power company steeplejack, a foreign exchange dealer, beginning 1957, and as a financial consultant, beginning 1966; director of companies, beginning 1969; Quartet Books (publishing house), London, England, publisher and owner, 1976—; also publisher and owner of The Women's Press, 1977—, and Robin Clark, 1980—; founder of magazines, including *Literary Review,* 1981-2001, *Wire,* 1984-2000, and *Oldie,* 1991-2001; owner, The Academy Club, 1989-97. Asprey, PLC, 1979-92, financial director and IT managing director, chief executive officer, 1992-95; managing director, Mappin & Webb, 1990-95; managing director, Watches of Switzerland, 1992-95; executive director, Garrard, 1990-95. Producer of stage plays, including (and copresenter of *Lyric*) *Happy End,* 1975, (presenter and producer of *Duke of York's*)

The Beastly Beatitudes of Balthazar B, 1981, and (as coproducer of *Mermaid*) *Trafford Tanzi,* 1982; film producer, including (with David Frost) *The Slipper and the Rose,* 1974, and (as executive producer) *Brimstone and Treacle,* 1982; producer and presenter of television documentaries. Perfume designer, including of Parfums Namara, a line of fragrances including Avant l'Amour and Après l'Amour, 1985, and l'Amour de Namara, 1990.

MEMBER: Royal Society of Authors (fellow), Beefsteak Club.

AWARDS, HONORS: M.A., University of Surrey, 1993; Retail Personality of the Year, UK Jewelry Awards, 1993.

WRITINGS:

NONFICTION

(Compiler) *Women* (interviews), Quartet Books (New York, NY), 1987.

Singular Encounters, Quartet Books (London, England), 1990.

Of a Certain Age (interviews with celebrities), Quartet Books (London, England), 1992.

More of a Certain Age, Quartet Books (London, England), 1993.

Speaking for the Oldie, Quartet Books (London, England), 1994.

Asking Questions: An Anthology of Encounters with Naim Attallah, Quartet Books (London, England), 1996.

A Woman a Week, Quartet Books (London, England), 1998.

In Conversation with Naim Attallah, Quartet Books (London, England), 1998.

Insights: An Anthology of Interviews, Quartet Books (London, England), 1999.

Dialogues (interviews), Quartet Books (London, England), 2000.

Old Ladies of Nazareth (memoir), Quartet Books (London, England), 2004.

The Boy in England (memoir), Quartet Books (London, England), 2005.

In Touch with His Roots (memoir), Quartet Books (London, England), 2006.

FICTION

A *Timeless Passion,* Quartet Books (London, England), 1995.
Tara & Claire, Quartet Books (London, England), 1996.

WORK IN PROGRESS: Two more memoirs.

SIDELIGHTS: Naim Attallah has had a colorful career as a publisher, film and stage producer, business executive, and even fragrance designer. Born in Palestine, he moved to England at the age of eighteen to study engineering. Deciding he did not enjoy the subject, and suffering from some financial problems, he dropped out of school and forged his own career. By the 1960s, he was making a very good living in banking, which he then leveraged into a successful publishing career; and by the 1980s he had ventured into stage and film productions, including the movie *Brimstone and Treacle,* starring Sting; he also began writing nonfiction, interview collections, and erotic novels. In London, he became known as a very charismatic personality whose publishing house Quartet Books sometimes offered titillating titles and held publishing parties featuring women dressed in lingerie serving drinks. In 2004, however, a scandal ensued when one of Attallah's former employees, Jennie Erdal, published *Ghostwriter: A Memoir.* In this book, Erdal declared that she had been Attallah's ghostwriter, penning his articles, working on his interviews, and authoring his novels. Attallah responded by denying Erdal's allegations, though he refused to sue her. "All the feminists would be up in arms, saying, 'Look what he's doing to that poor woman, he's trying to crush her!'" he explained to Samantha Conti in *W.*

With *Old Ladies of Nazareth* and *The Boy in England,* Attallah began a planned four-volume memoir about his childhood and rise to success in England. Describing the book as a "lyrical tale of powerful simplicity, which reads like a fable," a writer for *This Week in Palestine* praised the autobiography as a "poignant and touching autobiographical portrait" about Attallah's days in Haifa, where he was raised by his grandmother and great-aunt. In the *Spectator* critic Caroline Moorehead described it as "a charming tale, fluently told."

Continuing his story with *The Boy in England,* Attallah tells of a young man's adventures in a foreign country, where he mostly allows his hormones to take over, obsessing about sexual encounters for the most part. Although Moorehead complained of the author's use of the third person, she praised *The Boy in England* for its "pacy and eager" tone.

Attallah told *CA:* "I got interested in writing at the age of twelve. I wrote poetry in Arabic and ran a news sheet during the second world war, for sale to our entourage of family and friends.

"I was influenced as a boy by the writing of Pearl S. Buck about China, Ernest Hemingway, Oscar Wilde, Thomas Mann, and Stephen Zweig. Being French educated, I read the classics, Molière, Racine, Victor Hugo, and such modern writers like André Gide, Jean Cocteau, Jean Paul Sartre, and the Russian writer Maxim Gorki.

"I write long-hand, very old fashioned. Then I have it typed to be corrected. The most surprising thing I learned as a writer is once the flow is smooth and seems unending, don't stop. Carry on until you literally drop! My own favorite book, although small, is *Old Ladies of Nazareth.* Reliving my childhood with two wonderful old ladies who were to shape my future life."

BIOGRAPHICAL AND CRITICAL SOURCES:

BOOKS

Attallah, Naim, *Old Ladies of Nazareth,* Quartet Books (London, England), 2004.
Attallah, Naim, *The Boy in England,* Quartet Books (London, England), 2005.

PERIODICALS

Daily Telegraph (London, England), November 17, 2004, Anne Chisholm, "The Ghost Materializes," reviews of *Old Ladies of Nazareth* and *Ghosting.*
Guardian (Manchester, England), December 18, 2004, Blake Morrison, "Breaking Cover: Black Morrison Reads between the Lines of Jennie Erdal's *Ghosting* and Naim Attallah's *Old Ladies of Nazareth.*"

Spectator, April 30, 2005, Caroline Moorehead, "The Boy Done Good," review of *The Boy in England,* p. 41.

Times (London, England), December 17, 2004, Valerie Grove, "I Wrote Naim Attallah's Every Word," interview with Naim Attallah.

W, March, 2005, Samantha Conti, "War of the Words: London Mogul Naim Attallah Blasts Off at the Woman Who Says She Was His Longtime Ghostwriter," p. 340.

ONLINE

This Week in Palestine, http://www.thisweekinpalestine.com/ (March 2, 2006), review of *Old Ladies of Nazareth.*

*   *   *

ATTALLAH, Naim Ibrahim
    See ATTALLAH, Naim

*   *   *

AUSTIN, Dan 1971(?)-

PERSONAL: Born c. 1971; son of Dennis and Ann Austin. *Education:* Brigham Young University, earned film degree.

ADDRESSES: Home—Salt Lake City, UT. *Agent*—c/o Author Mail, Lyon's Press, 246 Goose Ln., P.O. Box 480, Guilford, CT 06437. *E-mail*—dan@truefans.com.

CAREER: During early career, worked as an advertising broadcast producer; currently a freelance filmmaker; director and producer of *The Pilgrimage of the True Jazz Fans,* 1997, and *True Fans,* 1999.

AWARDS, HONORS: People's Choice Award, Banff Film Festival, 1999, for *True Fans.*

WRITINGS:

(And director, editor, and producer) *The Pilgrimage of the True Jazz Fans* (screenplay), 1997.

Fourth Witness: The Mary Whitmer Story (screenplay), 1997.
The Strongest of Them All (screenplay), 1998.
(And director, editor, and producer) *True Fans* (screenplay), 1999.
True Fans: A Basketball Odyssey (based on Austin's screenplay), Lyon's Press (Guilford, CT), 2003.

Also creator of film *Last Game.*

WORK IN PROGRESS: True Fans Forever.

SIDELIGHTS: Dan Austin is a young filmmaker who first gained wide attention with his short documentary *True Fans,* a film he wrote, edited, directed, produced, and, with his brother and one of his friends, starred in. The film, which won an award at the 1999 Banff Film Festival, is about the three young men's bicycle trip from Venice, California, to the Basketball Hall of Fame in Springfield, Massachusetts. It is a kind of sequel to Austin's earlier film *The Pilgrimage of the True Jazz Fans,* his senior movie project at Brigham Young University that is about traveling to see the Utah Jazz play the Seattle Supersonics for a spot in the NBA playoffs. Taking a one-hundred-dollar professional ball with them, the companions traveled across the country on their bikes for ten dollars a day while filming *True Fans.* Along the way, they explained their mission to people who offered them assistance, such as room and board, to keep their expenses down. Austin asked those who helped them to sign their basketball, and by the time they reached Springfield the ball was covered with signatures. The ball is now kept at the Hall of Fame, and Austin took the footage they shot along the way and edited it down into a film.

Austin later adapted his experience into the book *True Fans: A Basketball Odyssey.* Some reviewers who enjoyed the movie were somewhat less enthusiastic about the book version. Noting how Austin often compares his experience to Jack Kerouac's—the author of the classic *On the Road*—critics felt this went too far. A *Publishers Weekly* contributor, for one, wrote that the author "doesn't quite succeed" in reaching the Kerouac standard, producing instead a "ho-hum travel journal." On the other hand, *Library Journal* contributor Boyd Childress commented that although "Austin may not rival Jack Kerouac . . . [*True Fans*] is a modern-day classic." Warning that this is not a sports book about basketball, Wes Lukowsky concluded in *Booklist* that "if one is out for laughs and a revealing look at average Americans, this is the right book."

BIOGRAPHICAL AND CRITICAL SOURCES:

PERIODICALS

Booklist, September 1, 2005, Wes Lukowsky, review of *True Fans: A Basketball Odyssey,* p. 50.
Kirkus Reviews, August 1, 2005, review of *True Fans,* p. 823.
Library Journal, September 1, 2005, Boyd Childress, review of *True Fans,* p. 150.
Publishers Weekly, August 1, 2005, review of *True Fans,* p. 57.

ONLINE

Lavin Agency Web site, http://www.thelavinagency. com/ (March 2, 2006), biographical information on Dan Austin.
True Fans Web site, http://www.truefans.net (March 2, 2006), biographical information on Dan Austin.*

*   *   *

AUTRY, Curt

PERSONAL: Male. *Education:* University of Oklahoma, degree in political science.

ADDRESSES: Home—Richmond, VA. *Agent*—c/o Author Mail, Poisoned Pen Press, 6962 E. 1st Ave., Ste. 103, Scottsdale, AZ 85251. *E-mail*—cautry@ nbc12.com.

CAREER: Broadcaster and author. Has worked as a broadcaster for KFOR-TV, Oklahoma City, OK, KTEN-TV, Dennison, TX, and WRAL-TV, Raleigh, NC; WWBT-TV, Richmond, VA, anchor for *Fox Richmond News at Ten,* 1994—.

AWARDS, HONORS: Emmy Award, for news anchoring and reporting; Best Summer Mysteries citation, *Boston Globe,* 2002, for *The Reunion.*

WRITINGS:

The Reunion (novel), Poisoned Pen Press (Scottsdale, AZ), 2002.

SIDELIGHTS: An Emmy Award-winning news anchorman, Curt Autry tried his hand at writing a thriller with his debut novel, *The Reunion.* The story combines historical and contemporary settings. During the early years of World War II, a German submarine is sunk off the coast of North Carolina. The crew is captured and spends the rest of the war as prisoners. Jumping ahead to modern times, the remaining members of the U-boat crew are planning a reunion to be held where their vessel sank. Unknown to them, a disturbed man named Joey DeMichael plans to set off a bomb at the event. His plot is discovered by Carolyn Baker, who accidentally learns about Joey while conducting research to find her biological parents. Although she tells the FBI about Joey's plans, nobody except Agent Martin Dunlevy believes her. The plot is further complicated when other parties plot to silence her for fear that Carolyn will uncover certain uncomfortable events from the past.

Reviewers of *The Reunion* found it to be an exciting tale that could easily be adapted as a successful film. However, the story is marred somewhat, according to critics, by too many subplots. A *Publishers Weekly* contributor praised the "strong suspense and action elements." A *Kirkus Reviews* writer reported that the author "writes with clarity and commendable attention to detail." Rex E. Klett concluded in the *Library Journal* that *The Reunion* contains "sturdy prose, rising tension, and plausible plotting."

BIOGRAPHICAL AND CRITICAL SOURCES:

PERIODICALS

Kirkus Reviews, May 15, 2002, review of *The Reunion,* p. 705.
Library Journal, July, 2002, Rex E. Klett, review of *The Reunion,* p. 126.
Publishers Weekly, June 10, 2002, review of *The Reunion,* p. 44.

B

BADRÉ, Frédéric 1965-

PERSONAL: Born May 6, 1965, in Versailles, France; son of Jean (a commercial airline pilot) and Colette (Azam) Badré; married Séverine Lèbre, September 14, 1996. *Education:* Attended Sorbonne, University of Paris, and École des Hautes Études en Sciences Sociales.

ADDRESSES: Agent—Éditions Grasset, 61 rue des Saint-Pères, 75006 Paris, France.

CAREER: Writer. *Ligne de Risque* (periodical), Paris, France, cofounder, 1997.

AWARDS, HONORS: Biography prize, French Academy, 1997.

WRITINGS:

Paulhan le juste, Grasset & Fasquelle (Paris, France), 1996.

Contributor to periodicals, including *Nouvelle Revue Française.*

SIDELIGHTS: Frédéric Badré told *CA:* "French literature no longer thrives; rather, it's in a coma. With the journal *Ligne de Risque,* my friends François Meyronnis and Yannick Haenel and I are trying to revive French literature. Although this might sound pretentious, it's not. It's a very serious endeavor. Jean Paul-

han interests me because during the twentieth century he was the greatest editor of a French journal. Since everything is to be started up again, it's important that I not choose the wrong model."

BIOGRAPHICAL AND CRITICAL SOURCES:

PERIODICALS

Journal of European Studies, March, 1997, John Flower, review of *Paulhan le juste,* p. 116.

*   *   *

BAILEY, Michael D. 1971-

PERSONAL: Born June 22, 1971, in Cleveland, OH. *Education:* Duke University, B.A., 1993; Northwestern University, Ph.D., 1998.

ADDRESSES: Office—Department of History, Iowa State University, Ames, IA 50011. *E-mail*—mdbailey@iastate.edu.

CAREER: St. Louis University, St. Louis, MO, visiting assistant professor of history, 2002-03; Iowa State University, Ames, assistant professor of history, 2003—. University of Pennsylvania, Mellon fellow in humanities, 2003-04.

MEMBER: American Historical Association, American Society of Church History, Medieval Academy of America.

WRITINGS:

Battling Demons: Heresy, Witchcraft, and Reform in the Late Middle Ages, Pennsylvania State University Press (University Park, PA), 2003.
A Historical Dictionary of Witchcraft, Scarecrow Press (Lanham, MD), 2003.

Contributor to periodicals, including *Historian, Church History, Speculum,* and *Mediaeval Studies.*

BIOGRAPHICAL AND CRITICAL SOURCES:

PERIODICALS

American Historical Review, December, 2003, review of *Battling Demons: Heresy, Witchcraft, and Reform in the Late Middle Ages,* p. 1510.
Church History, September, 2004, Alberto Ferreiro, review of *Battling Demons,* p. 691.
Journal of Religion, July, 2004, Armando Maggi, review of *Battling Demons,* p. 503.
Library Journal, March 1, 2004, Mimi Davis, review of *A Historical Dictionary of Witchcraft,* p.
Speculum, July, 2004, James Given, review of *Battling Demons,* p. 736.

*   *   *

BAKER, Raymond W. 1935-

PERSONAL: Born 1935. *Education:* Harvard Business School, M.B.A., 1960.

ADDRESSES: Office—Center for International Policy, 1717 Massachusetts Ave. N.W., Ste. 801, Washington, DC 20036.

CAREER: Investor, consultant, international businessperson, and writer. In private business, Africa, Latin America, Europe, and Asia, 1960-1996. Center for International Policy, Washington, DC, senior fellow; Brookings Institution, guest scholar. 1996—.

WRITINGS:

Capitalism's Achilles Heel: Dirty Money and How to Renew the Free-Market System, John Wiley & Sons (Hoboken, NJ), 2005.

SIDELIGHTS: An international businessman for forty years in over sixty countries, Raymond W. Baker frequently encountered corruption in the marketplace. In 2005 he put his wide knowledge of such practices as money laundering, fake transactions, fictitious pricing, and dummy corporations to use in his book, *Capitalism's Achilles Heel: Dirty Money and How to Renew the Free-Market System.* As Lewis I. Rice noted in the *Harvard Business School Alumni Bulletin Online,* this illegal flow of money worldwide "bolsters international crime and terrorism and contributes to global inequality and poverty."

Baker estimates in his book that 500 million dollars annually is drained from developing countries in these illegal schemes, worsening global poverty. Those who profit from these procedures include "terrorists, drug lords, and multinational corporate executives," wrote a contributor for *Reference & Research Book News.* Reviewing *Capitalism's Achilles Heel* in the *Dallas-Fort Worth Star-Telegram Online,* Cecil Johnson found the work "illuminating and disturbing," and further observed that Baker "advances the view that the transfer of dirty money all over the planet is one of the primary causes of world poverty and global instability and is undermining capitalism's underlying ideals." However, Baker, speaking with Rice, was optimistic that such practices could be stopped: "The illegalities I write about can be curtailed merely with the application of political will. It is not technically difficult to do. If we decide we want it to happen, it will happen."

BIOGRAPHICAL AND CRITICAL SOURCES:

PERIODICALS

Asia Times, September 24, 2005, Gary LaMoshi, "Follow the Money."
Bloomberg, July 11, 2005, James Pressley, "How the G-8 Can Help Africa—Choke $1 Tillion in Dirty Money."
Financial Times, August 10, 2005, Frank Partnoy, "Must Reads for Budding Fraudsters."
Japan Times, March 12, 2006, Jeff Kingston, "Money Laundering and Global Debt."
Little Trade, August, 2005, review of *Capitalism's Achilles Heel: Dirty Money and How to Renew the Free-Market System,* p. 56.

Reference & Research Book News, November, 2005, review of *Capitalism's Achilles Heel.*

ONLINE

Dallas-Fort Worth Star-Telegram Online, http://www. dfw.com/ (August 29, 2005), Cecil Johnson, "The Menace of Hijacked Capitalism," review of *Capitalism's Achilles Heel.*
Harvard Business School Alumni Bulletin Online, http://www.alumni.hbs.edu/ (March 27, 2006), "Q & A: Dirty Money: Raymond Baker Explores the Free Market's Demimonde"; (March 27, 2006), Lewis I. Rice, "The Deleterious Effects of Dirty Money."

*   *   *

BARBAS, Samantha

PERSONAL: Female. *Education:* University of California, Berkeley, Ph.D.

ADDRESSES: Agent—c/o Author Mail, University of California Press, 2120 Berkeley Way, Berkeley, CA 94704-1012. *E-mail*—barbas@chapman.edu.

CAREER: Arizona State University, Phoenix, instructor in interdisciplinary studies program; Chapman University, Orange, CA, assistant professor of history; University of California, Berkeley, visiting assistant professor of history.

AWARDS, HONORS: Excellence in Scholarship Award, Chapman University, 2005.

WRITINGS:

Movie Crazy: Fans, Stars, and the Cult of Celebrity, Palgrave (New York, NY), 2001.
The First Lady of Hollywood: A Biography of Louella Parsons, University of California Press (Berkeley, CA), 2005.

SIDELIGHTS: Samantha Barbas is a historian who studies the fan culture that has surrounded Hollywood from the beginning of the American film industry. Her first book, *Movie Crazy: Fans, Stars, and the Cult of Celebrity,* was described by *Library Journal* reviewer Carol J. Binkowski as "a unique film history with astute commentary." The book examines how audiences in the first half of the twentieth century attempted to turn themselves from passive consumers of movies into an active part of the film culture. As Barbas shows, moviegoers wrote millions of fan letters, sought to know the truth about stars' personal lives, conducted lively debates, and even organized themselves into clubs that actively publicized their chosen star and petitioned the studios to give him or her better roles. Critics praised the book. Barbas "does a nice job contextualizing movie star popularity in the midst of early-twentieth century social and cultural changes," George Potamianos noted in the *Journal of American History. Movie Crazy* is "a creative, accessible, and well-written book," Hiroshi Kitamura commented in *American Studies International.*

The original Hollywood gossip columnist is the subject of Barbas's second book, *The First Lady of Hollywood: A Biography of Louella Parsons.* This is the first biography of Parsons, whose famous columns, which appeared between 1915 and 1960, arguably launched the entire entertainment journalism industry. Although Parsons wrote her own autobiography, Barbas's thoroughly footnoted work shows that much of that book was fiction. *The First Lady of Hollywood* "is a terrific book about an unusual life," wrote a *Publishers Weekly* critic. *New York Times Book Review* contributor Mark Lewis termed it a "thoughtful biography."

BIOGRAPHICAL AND CRITICAL SOURCES:

PERIODICALS

American Studies International, October, 2002, Hiroshi Kitamura, review of *Movie Crazy: Fans, Stars, and the Cult of Celebrity,* p. 97.
Choice, March, 2006, review of *The First Lady of Hollywood: A Biography of Louella Parsons.*
Journal of American History, March, 2003, George Potamianos, review of *Movie Crazy,* p. 1563.
Library Journal, October 1, 2001, Carol J. Binkowski, review of *Movie Crazy,* p. 100; October 1, 2005, Carol J. Binkowski, review of *The First Lady of Hollywood,* p. 76.

New York Times Book Review, November 20, 2005, Mark Lewis, review of *The First Lady of Hollywood,* p. 24.

Publishers Weekly, October 8, 2001, review of *Movie Crazy,* p. 55; August 8, 2005, review of *The First Lady of Hollywood,* p. 224.

Variety, October 3, 2005, Beatrice Williams-Rude, review of *The First Lady of Hollywood.*

Wall Street Journal, October 18, 2005, Catherine Seipp, review of *The First Lady of Hollywood.*

* * *

BARNETT, Colleen A. 1925-

PERSONAL: Born February 22, 1925, in Green Bay, WI; daughter of Gerald (an attorney) and Mae (a homemaker; maiden name, Heney) Clifford; married John E. Barnett (an attorney), May 21, 1949 (died March 27, 2004); children: Jerome, David (deceased), Michael (deceased), Andrew, Catherine Barnett Wilson, James, Mary Marguerite, Thomas P.M., Edward. *Ethnicity:* "Irish." *Education:* University of Wisconsin—Madison, B.A., 1946, M.A., 1955, LL.D., 1990. *Politics:* "Democrat until recently, now independent." *Religion:* Catholic.

ADDRESSES: Agent—c/o Author Mail, Poisoned Pen Press, 6962 E. 1st Ave., Ste. 103, Scottsdale, AZ 85251. *E-mail*—barnett@mwt.net.

CAREER: Grant County Department of Social Services, Lancaster, WI, began as volunteer coordinator, became social work supervisor, between 1972 and 1987; Morrow Law Offices, Dodgeville, WI, attorney, 1990-97; Huebner and Associates, Richland Center, WI, mediator, 1998-2000; writer, 2000—. University of Wisconsin—Richland Center, instructor, 1996-2000. Southwestern Wisconsin Library Board, member; Boscobel Area Health Center, board member; Tri-State Health Planning, member.

WRITINGS:

Mystery Women: An Encyclopedia of Leading Women Characters in Mystery Fiction, Volume 1: *1860-1979,* Ravenstone Press (Manhattan, KS), 1997, revised edition, Poisoned Pen Press (Scottsdale, AZ), 2001, Volume 2: *1980-1989,* Poisoned Pen Press (Scottsdale, AZ), 2002, Volume 3: *1990-1999,* two volumes, Poisoned Pen Press (Scottsdale, AZ), 2003.

Contributor to periodicals.

WORK IN PROGRESS: Revising *Mystery Women: An Encyclopedia of Leading Women Characters in Mystery Fiction,* completion expected in 2008; research for a projected *Mystery Women,* Volume 4, 2010.

SIDELIGHTS: Colleen A. Barnett told *CA:* "My parents were readers, and I grew up in a house of books. Mysteries were favorites from my preteens, particularly those with independent young women. (Now I enjoy independent old women.) Through high school and college, I always made time for recreational reading."

"Writing was also important to me. I worked on grade-school and high-school newspapers. By my senior year, I was the managing editor of the *Daily Cardinal* at the University of Wisconsin—Madison. My stay in law school ended after three semesters when I met Navy veteran John Barnett, a fellow law student. John was ready to graduate, and we were both ready to marry. My law degree was put on hold for forty years. So was any serious writing, but I continued to read . . . at night after the children were asleep, whenever I could.

"My jobs as a volunteer coordinator and social work supervisor gave me many opportunities to write newspaper articles, newsletters, and speeches. They also sensitized me to the low self-images and ambitions of women with whom I became acquainted. When our youngest child was in college and I was unhappy with my job, my understanding husband suggested that I return to law school. I took the LSATs and began again, but I was reading and writing regularly.

"After graduation I worked as an attorney and a mediator, specializing in divorce and custody issues. I was impressed by the power of images, of how people are portrayed in the media, literature, and entertainment. Film critic Molly Haskell's book *From Reverence to*

Rape and Bobby Ann Mason's *The Girl Sleuth* helped me to focus. Two lines crossed: the impact of the images on young girls and women, how their expectations and goals were expanded or limited by what they read and saw; and the popularity of the mystery novel. I began by researching the earliest female protagonists I could find: through the British Library, the Congressional Library, civic and universities, and Elderhostel programs. My local library was a wonderful resource, bringing me books from all over the United States.

"Initially I was interested in patterns, how the books of a particular time reflected the role of women in society at that period. To get there I had to read the books, review them, and develop a biography of each female. I charted the changes in how women were portrayed and the world and national events that facilitated or reflected those changes: wars, depression or full employment, the right to vote, the Married Women's Acts, the Equal Employment Opportunity Act. It was thrilling work, and I wanted to share it. Thanks to my initial publisher of Volume 1 (Ravenstone Books) and Poisoned Pen Press, I could do that. Robert Rosenwald of Poisoned Pen Press said neither of us would make any money on the publications, but they were worth doing."

BIOGRAPHICAL AND CRITICAL SOURCES:

PERIODICALS

Booklist, May 1, 2004, Mary Ellen Quinn, review of *Mystery Women: An Encyclopedia of Leading Women Characters in Mystery Fiction,* p. 1494.
Library Journal, May 1, 1998, Denise Johnson, review of *Mystery Women,* p. 92.
Publishers Weekly, November 17, 2003, review of *Mystery Women,* p. 49.

*   *   *

BARNHART, David K. 1941-

PERSONAL: Born May 15, 1941, in Oak Park, IL; son of Clarence L.(a lexicographer) and Frances (Knox) Barnhart; married September 10, 1988; wife's name Hollis; children: William Clarence, Grant Marvel. *Education:* Syracuse University, B.A., 1964; New York University, graduate study, 1964-67. *Hobbies and other interests:* Canoeing, skiing.

ADDRESSES: Office—Lexik House Publishers, Hyde Park, NY 12538. *E-mail*—barnhart@highlands.com.

CAREER: Office of Clarence L. Barnhart, Bronxville, NY, editor, 1966-80; Lexik House Publishers, Hyde Park, NY, proprietor and lexicographer, 1980—. Commission on the English Language, board member, 1986; Southeastern New York Library Resources Council, member.

MEMBER: International Linguistic Association (president, 1985), Dictionary Society of North America, American Dialect Society, American Canoe Association (vice commodore, 1976), Yonkers Canoe Club (commodore, 1976).

AWARDS, HONORS: Payne Kretzmer Award, American Canoe Association, 1976 and 1977, both for *Canoe Sport.*

WRITINGS:

Barnhart Dictionary Companion Index, Lexik House Publishers (Hyde Park, NY), 1987.
Neo-Words, Macmillan (New York, NY), 1991.
(With Allan Metcalf) *America in So Many Words: Words That Have Shaped America,* Houghton Mifflin (Boston, MA), 1997.
The Barnhart New-Words Concordance, Lexik House Publishers (Hyde Park, NY), 2001.

Editor, *Barnhart Dictionary Companion,* 1982-93. Contributor to periodicals, including *American Speech, Dictionaries, Word,* and *Poughkeepsie Journal.* Also affiliated with the newsletter *Canoe Sport,* 1970s.

WORK IN PROGRESS: Research on new words and phrases in English.

BIOGRAPHICAL AND CRITICAL SOURCES:

PERIODICALS

Booklist, September 1, 1994, Sandy Whiteley, review of *The Barnhart New-Words Concordance,* p. 68; April, 1998, Mary Ellen Quinn, review of

America in So Many Words: Words That Have Shaped America, p. 1340; December 1, 1999, Bill Ott, review of *America in So Many Words,* p. 736.

Insight on the News, June 25, 2001, Stephen Goode, review of *America in So Many Words,* p. 4; February 18, 2003, Stephen Goode, review of *America in So Many Words,* p. 8.

Library Journal, December, 1997, Ilse Heidmann, review of *America in So Many Words,* p. 105.

*   *   *

BAROJA, Pío 1872-1956
(Pío Baroja y Nessi, Pío Baroja y Nessi)

PERSONAL: Name pronounced "*pee*-oh bah-*roh*-hah"; born December 28, 1872, in San Sebastián, Spain; died October 30, 1956, in Madrid, Spain; son of Serafín Baroja y Zornoza (a mining engineer) and Carmen Nessi y Goñi (a homemaker). *Education:* University of Valencia, M.D., 1891; University of Madrid, Ph.D., 1894.

CAREER: Physician and author. Also once worked as a bakery manager.

WRITINGS:

El tablado de arlequín, F. Sempere (Valencia, Spain), 1890.

La casa de Aizgorrí, novela en siete jornadas, B. Rodríguez Serra (Madrid, Spain), 1900.

Los amores tardíos, Caro Raggio (Madrid, Spain), 1900.

La ciudad de niebla, T. Nelson (London, England), 1900.

Camino de perfeccíon, Andueza (Madrid, Spain), 1901.

Idilios vascos, B. Rodriguez Serra (Madrid, Spain), 1901.

Tierra vasca (also see below), Renacimiento (Madrid, Spain), 1903.

Los últimos románticos, Sucesores de Hernando (Madrid, Spain), 1906.

Las tragedias grotescas, Sucesores de Hernando (Madrid, Spain), 1907.

La raza, R. Rojas (Madrid, Spain), 1908.

La dama errante, R. Rojas (Madrid, Spain), 1908.

El mundo es ansí, Renacimiento (Madrid, Spain), 1912.

El escuadrón del brigante, Renacimiento (Madrid, Spain), 1913.

El aprendíz del conspirador, Renacimiento (Madrid, Spain), 1913.

Los caminos del mundo, Renacimiento (Madrid, Spain), 1914.

Con la pluma y con el sabre; crónica de 1820 a 1823, Renacimiento (Madrid, Spain), 1915.

Los recursos de la astucia, Renacimiento (Madrid, Spain), 1915.

La ruta del aventurero, Renacimiento (Madrid, Spain), 1916.

La dama de Urtubi: novela inédita, [Madrid, Spain], 1916.

Nuevo tablado de Arlequín, Caro Raggio (Madrid, Spain), 1917.

La feria de los discretos, Fernando Fé (Madrid, Spain), 1900, translation by Jacob S. Fassett, Jr., published as *The City of the Discreet,* Knopf (New York, NY), 1917.

La veleta de Gastizar, Caro Raggio (Madrid, Spain), 1918.

Las horas solitarias: notas de un aprendíz de psicólogo, Caro Raggio (Madrid, Spain), 1918.

Los caudillos de 1830, Caro Raggio (Madrid, Spain), 1918.

El cura Santa Cruz y su partida, Caro Raggio (Madrid, Spain), 1918.

Páginas escogidas, Calleja (Madrid, Spain), 1918.

Idilios y fantasías, Caro Raggio (Madrid, Spain), 1918.

Aventuras, inventos y mixtificaciones de Silvestre Paradox (also see below), B. Rodriguez Serra (Madrid, Spain), 1900, reprinted, Caro Raggio (Madrid, Spain), 1919.

César ó nada, Renacimiento (Madrid, Spain), 1910, translation by Louis How published as *Caesar or Nothing,* Knopf (New York, NY), 1919.

La Isabelina, Caro Raggio (Madrid, Spain), 1919.

Momentum catastrophicum, Caro Raggio (Madrid, Spain), 1919.

La caverna del humorísmo, Caro Raggio (Madrid, Spain), 1919.

Cuentos, Caro Raggio (Madrid, Spain), 1919.

La lucha por la vida, Caro Raggio (Madrid, Spain), 1900, reprinted, 1920.

Juventud, egolatría, Caro Raggio (Madrid, Spain), 1917, translation by Jacob S. Fassett, Jr., and Frances L. Phillips published as *Youth and Egolatry,* Knopf (New York, NY), 1920.

Divagaciones apasionadas, Caro Raggio (Madrid, Spain), 1920.

Las figuras de cera, Caro Raggio (Madrid, Spain), 1920.

Los contrastes de la vida, Caro Raggio (Madrid, Spain), 1920.

La sensualidad pervertida: ensayos amorosos de un hombre ingénuo en una época de decadencia, Caro Raggio (Madrid, Spain), 1920.

Divagaciones sobre la cultura, Caro Raggio (Madrid, Spain), 1920.

La canóniga, Cosmópolis (Madrid, Spain), 1920.

Escuelas germánicas, retratos, medias figuras, Caro Raggio (Madrid, Spain), 1921.

El sabor de la venganza, Caro Raggio (Madrid, Spain), 1921.

Obras maestras de la pintura: escuela italianas, retratos, medias figuras, Caro Raggio (Madrid, Spain), 1921.

Las furias, Caro Raggio (Madrid, Spain), 1921.

El amor, el dandysmo y la intriga, Caro Raggio (Madrid, Spain), 1922.

La leyenda de Juan de Alzate, Caro Raggio (Madrid, Spain), 1922.

El árbol de la ciencia, Las Americas Publishing (New York, NY), 1900, translated as *The Tree of Knowledge,* Knopf (New York, NY), 1922.

La busca, Fernando Fé (Madrid, Spain), 1910, translation by Isaac Goldberg published as *The Quest,* Knopf (New York, NY), 1922.

Mala hierba, Fernando Fé (Madrid, Spain), 1900, translation by Isaac Goldberg published as *Weeds,* Knopf (New York, NY), 1923.

Crítica arbitraria (theater reviews), La Lectura (Madrid, Spain), 1924.

La nave de los locos, Caro Raggio (Madrid, Spain), 1925.

El mayorazgo de Labraz, Henrich (Barcelona, Spain), 1903, translation by Aubrey Fitz Gerald Bell published as *The Lord of Labraz,* Knopf (New York, NY), 1926.

El horroroso crimen de Peñaranda del Campo, La Novela Mundial (Madrid, Spain), 1926.

La casa del crímen, [Madrid, Spain], 1926.

Las máscaras sangrientas, Caro Raggio (Madrid, Spain), 1927.

Humano enigma, Caro Raggio (Madrid, Spain), 1928.

La senda dolorosa, Caro Raggio (Madrid, Spain), 1928.

El nocturno del Hermano Beltrán, Caro Raggio (Madrid, Spain), 1929.

Los pilotos de altura, Caro Raggio (Madrid, Spain), 1929.

Los confidentes audaces, Espasa Calpe (Madrid, Spain), 1931.

Aviraneta; o, La vida de un conspirador, Espasa Calpe (Madrid, Spain), 1931.

Intermedios, Espasa Calpe (Madrid, Spain), 1931.

El cabo de las tormentas, Espasa Calpe (Madrid, Spain), 1932.

La familia de Errotacho, Espasa Calpe (Madrid, Spain), 1932.

Los caminos del mundo, Espasa Calpe (Madrid, Spain), 1933.

Juan van Halen, el official aventurero, Espasa Calpe (Madrid, Spain), 1933.

Siluetas románticas y otras historias de pillos y de extravagantes, Espasa Calpe (Madrid, Spain), 1934.

Las noches del buen retiro, Espasa Calpe (Madrid, Spain), 1934.

Elizabide el vagabundo, Navarro y del Teso (San Sebastián, Spain), 1935.

Vitrina pintoresca, Espasa Calpe (Madrid, Spain), 1935.

El cura de Monleón, Espasa Calpe (Madrid, Spain), 1936.

Rapsodias, Espasa Calpe (Madrid, Spain), 1936.

Locuras de carnaval, Espasa Calpe (Madrid, Spain), 1937.

Tierra vasca: Zalacaín el aventurero: historia de las buenas andanzas y fortunas de Martin Zalacaín de Urbia, Espasa Calpe (Madrid, Spain), 1937.

Susana, B.I.M. (San Sebastián, Spain), 1938.

Ayer y hoy, Ercilla (Santiago de Chile, Chile), 1939.

Los judíos son unos corderos, Talleres Gráficos "La Mazorca" (Buenos Aires, Argentina), 1939.

Historias lejanas, Ercilla (Santiago de Chile, Chile), 1939.

El tesoro del holandés, Editorial Catolica-Española (Seville, Spain), 1939.

Laura; o, La soledad sin remedio, Editorial Sudamericana (Buenos Aires, Argentina), 1939.

Los espectros del Castillo y otras narraciones, Pal-las Bartrés (Barcelona, Spain), 1941.

Fantasías vascas, Espasa Calpe (Buenos Aires, Argentina), 1941.

Chopin y Jorge Sand, y otros ensayos, Pal-las Bartrés (Barcelona, Spain), 1941.

Las veleidades de la fortuna, Caro Raggio (Madrid, Spain), 1926, reprinted, Epasa Calpe Argentina (Buenos Aires, Argentina), 1942.

El diablo a bajo precio, Pal-las Bartrés (Barcelona, Spain), 1942.

El estanque verde, La Novela Actual (Madrid, Spain), 1943.

Pequeños ensayos, Editorial Sudamericana (Buenos Aires, Argentina), 1943.

El escritor según el y según los críticos, Biblioteca Nueva (Madrid, Spain), 1944.

Canciones del suburbio, Biblioteca Nueva (Madrid, Spain), 1944.

El puente de las animas, La Nave (Madrid, Spain), 1945.

El hotel del Cisne, Biblioteca Nueva (Madrid, Spain), 1946.

Obras completas, Biblioteca Nueva (Madrid, Spain), 1946.

Galería de tipos de la época, Biblioteca Nueva (Madrid, Spain), 1947.

Reportajes, Biblioteca Nueva (Madrid, Spain), 1948.

Los enigmáticos, Biblioteca Nueva (Madrid, Spain), 1948.

La intuición y el estilo, Biblioteca Nueva (Madrid, Spain), 1948.

Bagatelas de otoño, Biblioteca Nueva (Madrid, Spain), 1949.

Ciudades de Italia, Biblioteca Nueva (Madrid, Spain), 1949.

El cantor vagabundo: saturnales novela, Biblioteca Nueva (Madrid, Spain), 1950.

Tríptico, Editorial Sudamericana (Buenos Aires, Argentina), 1950.

La obsesión del misterio, Rollan (Madris, Spain), 1952.

Yan-Si-Pao; o, La esvástica de oro, Prensa Moderna (Madrid, Spain), 1928, reprinted, A. Aguado (Madrid, Spain), 1953.

Intermedio sentimental, A. Aguado (Madrid, Spain), 1953.

Los amores de Antonio y Cristina, [Madrid, Spain], 1953.

El país vasco, Ediciones Destino (Barcelona, Spain), 1953.

El capitán Mala Sombra, A. Aguado (Madrid, Spain), 1953.

El poeta y la princesa; o, El "cabaret" de la cotorra verde, A. Aguado (Madrid, Spain), 1953.

La obra de pello Yarza y algunas otras cosas, Espasa Calpe (Buenos Aires, Argentina), 1954.

Los contrabandístas vascos; Las hermanas Mac-Donald; Los amores de Antonio y Cristina; Los amores de un médico de aldea, Biblioteca Nueva (Madrid, Spain), 1954.

Paseos de un solitario; relatos sin ilación, Biblioteca Nueva (Madrid, Spain), 1955.

Memorias, Ediciones Minotauro (Madrid, Spain), 1955.

Mis mejores páginas, Editorial Mateu (Barcelona, Spain), 1961.

La decadencia de la cortesía, y otros ensayos, Ediciones Raid (Barcelona, Spain), 1956.

Las inquietudes de Shanti Andía, Renacimiento (Madrid, Spain), 1911, new edition, edited by Laurence Deane Bailiff and Maro Beath Jones, University of Chicago Press (Chicago, IL), 1930, translation by Anthony Kerrigan published as *The Restlessness of Shanti Andía, and Other Writings,* University of Michigan Press (Ann Arbor, MI), 1959, translation by Anthony and Elaine Kerrigan published as *The Restlessness of Shanti Andía, and Selected Stories* (includes "The Cabbages in the Cemetery" and "The Charcoal Maker"), New American Library of World Literature (New York, NY), 1962.

Pío Baroja: estudio y antología, Compañía Bibliográfica Española (Madrid, Spain), 1963.

Cuentos, Alianza Editorial (Madrid, Spain), 1966.

El gran torbellino del mundo, Caro Raggio (Madrid, Spain), 1926, published as *Agonías de nuestro tiempo: el gran torbellino del mundo,* Planeta (Barcelona, Spain), 1967.

Crónica escandalosa, Planeta (Barcelona, Spain), 1967.

Pío Baroja: antología, Coculsa (Madrid, Spain), 1969.

La venta de Mirambel, Espasa Calpe (Madrid, Spain), 1931, reprinted, Planeta (Barcelona, Spain), 1970.

Desde el principio hasta el fin, Espasa Calpe (Madrid, Spain), 1935, reprinted, Planeta (Barcelona, Spain), 1970.

Desde la última vuelta del camino: memorias, Planeta (Barcelona, Spain), 1970.

El mar (collection; includes "Las inquietudes de Shanti Andía" and "Los pilotos de altura"), Circulo de Lectores (Barcelona, Spain), 1970.

Un prince, 1939, reprinted, Losada (Buenos Aires, Argentina), 1972.

Escritos de juventud, edited by Manuel Longares, Editorial Cuadernos para el Diálogo (Madrid, Spain), 1972.

Hojas sueltas, Caro Raggio (Madrid, Spain), 1973.

Paisaje y paisanaje: artículos y ensayos, Talleres gráficos edigraf (Barcelona, Spain), 1973.

La selva oscura, Caro Raggio (Madrid, Spain), 1974.

La familia de Errotacho, Caro Raggio (Madrid, Spain), 1974.

Entretenimientos, Caro Raggio (Madrid, Spain), 1926, reprinted, 1976.

El caballero de Erláiz, La Nave (Madrid, Spain), 1943, reprinted, Caro Raggio (Madrid, Spain), 1976.

Allegro final, y otras cosas, A. Aguado (Madrid, Spain), 1957, reprinted, 1976.

Arlequín, mancébo de botica, o Los pretendientes de Colombina, Editorial Siglo XX (Madrid, Spain), 1976.

El dolor: estudio de psico-física, Real Academia de Medicina de Salamanca (Salamanca, Spain), 1980.

Final del siglo XIX y principios del XX, Biblioteca Nueva (Madrid, Spain), 1945, reprinted, Caro Raggio (Madrid, Spain), 1982.

Aurora roja, Fernando Fé (Madrid, Spain), 1904, translation by Isaac Goldberg published as *Red Dawn,* Knopf (New York, NY), 1924, reprinted, 1983.

Paradox, rey (also see below), Sucesores de Hernando (Madrid, Spain), 1906, translation by Nevill Barbour published as *Paradox, King,* Wishart (London, England), 1931, reprinted, 1983.

Mari Belcha y otros cuentos, Ediciones de la Torre (Madrid, Spain), 1988.

Personajes con oficio, Editorial Popular (Madrid, Spain), 1989.

Cuentos a contratiempos, Editorial Popular (Madrid, Spain), 1989.

El pasado, Fernando Fé (Madrid, Spain), 1905, reprinted, 1990.

Comunistas, judíos y demás ralea, Ediciones Reconquista (Valladolid, Spain), 1938, published as *Judíos, comunistas y demás ralea,* B.R.L. (Barcelona, Spain), 1993.

Itinerario sentimental: guía de Iztea, Iruña (Pamplona, Spain), 1995.

Zalacaín el aventurero (also see below), Ediciones Hispania, 1900, translation by James P. Diendl published as *Zalacaín the Adventurer: The History of the Good Fortune and Wanderings of Martin Zalacaín of Urbia,* Lost Coast Press (Fort Bragg, CA), 1997.

Cuentos de amor y muerte, Clan (Spain), 1997.

Cuentos de fantasmas, Acento (Madrid, Spain), 1997.

Vídas sombrías (title means "Somber Lives"), Antonio Marzo (Madrid, Spain), 1900, new edition, Biblioteca Nueva (Madrid, Spain), 1998.

Aquí París, [Madrid, Spain], 1955, reprinted, Caro Raggio (Madrid, Spain), 1998.

Epistolario (1933-1955), Edicions Vicent Llorens (Valencia, Spain), 1998.

Obras selectas, Espasa Calpe (Madrid, Spain), 1998.

Silvestre Paradox; y Paradox, rey, Consejería de Educación y Cultura, Comunidad de Madrid (Madrid, Spain), 1998.

Desde el exilio: los artículos inéditos publicados en la Nación de Buenos Aires, 1936-1943, Caro Raggio (Madrid, Spain), 1999.

El laberinto de las sirenas, Caro Raggio (Madrid, Spain), 1923, new edition, Tusquets Editores (Barcelona, Spain), 2000.

Opiniones y paradojas, edited by Miguel Sánchez-Ostiz, Caro Raggio (Madrid, Spain), 2000.

Libertad frente a sumisión: las colaboraciones periodísticas publicadas en España durante 1938, Caro Raggio (Madrid, Spain), 2001.

Los pilotos de altura, edited and with introduction and notes by Juan María Martín, illustrated by Tino Gatagán, Anaya (Madrid, Spain), 2002.

La estrella del capitán Chimista, Caro Raggio (Madrid, Spain), 1930, new edition edited and with notes and introduction by Juan María Martín, illustrated by Tino Gataán, Anaya (Madrid, Spain), 2003.

Baroja's works have been translated into many languages, including Basque, Chinese, Czechoslovakian, Dutch, English, Esperanto, French, German, Korean, and Russian.

SIDELIGHTS: Pío Baroja was considered one of the most prolific novelists of twentieth-century Spanish literature, writing over sixty novels during his lifetime, including several trilogies. His work belongs to the group of writers known as the "Grupo '98," whose members were concerned with the social problems that arose in early twentieth-century Spain due to political and colonial changes and to rapid industrialization. Baroja, however, did not think of himself as a member of that illustrious group of writers, which included such people as José Azorín, Benito Pérez Galdós, and Miguel de Unamuno.

The work of Baroja typically describes the hypocrisy, poverty, and injustice that plague the lives of working-class people. John Dos Passos commented in *Rosinante to the Road Again* that the scenes of Baroja's works are "dismal, ironic, the streets of towns where industrial life sits heavy on the neck of a race as little adapted to it as any in Europe. No one has ever described better the shaggy badlands and cabbage-patches round the edges of a city, where the debris of civilization piles up ramshackle suburbs in which starve and scheme all manner of human detritus."

Baroja was born in 1872 in the city of San Sebastián, located on the northern Basque coast of Spain. His father, a well-educated mining engineer, possessed an extensive personal library. He introduced Baroja, at a young age, to the world of literature. Throughout his life, Baroja included the works of Balzac, Dickens, Dostoevsky, and Poe among his personal favorites.

In 1887 Baroja began his medical studies at the University of Madrid. He continued his education at the University of Valencia, and four years later he earned a medical degree from that institution. In 1894, at the University of Madrid, Baroja presented his doctoral thesis on the psycho-physical aspects of pain. Upon the completion of his degree, Baroja practiced medicine in the town of Cestona for less than a year. From that brief period as a practicing physician, however, came the short story collection *Vídas sombrías.* Baroja then left Cestona and returned to Madrid, where he worked as the manager of his aunt's bakery and continued to write.

In 1899 Baroja traveled to Paris, where he became acquainted with important members of the literary world, including Oscar Wilde and the Spanish poets Antonio and Juan Machado. It was during this visit that he encountered the pessimistic philosophies of Nietzsche and Schopenhauer. Baroja returned to Spain with the resolve to devote himself completely to a literary career. Soon after, he published a collection of short stories titled *Vídas sombrías,* described as "a melancholy book, full of delicate feeling poetically expressed" by Beatrice P. Patt in her book titled *Pío Baroja.* These short stories came to the attention of the writer José Azorín, who was so moved by the work that he requested to meet Baroja. This meeting subsequently developed into a lifelong friendship between the two men.

Baroja showed more concern for the content of a piece rather than for following a particular stylized form, and it was well known that he wrote spontaneously and very rarely revised his work. His novels are filled with graphic "street" language, which Salvador de Madariaga, in *The Genius of Spain and Other Essays on Spanish Contemporary Literature,* stated was indicative of Baroja's "tendency to strike the world by saying unusually hard things in an unusually hard way." However, Madariaga also remarked that Baroja actually "gained a freer scope for the intensity and power of his vision" by ignoring the more socially polite, restrictive and traditional literary styles of language. As a result, the critic considered that Baroja's work "is a writing which for directness and simplicity has no rival in Spain."

Shortly after the publication of *Vídas sombrías,* the novel *La casa de Aizgorri, novela en siete jornadas* saw print. This book is part of the trilogy "Tierra vasca." The most popular and beloved novel of the trilogy is *Zalacaín el aventurero,* in which the hero Martín Zalacaín pursues the limits of his destiny. He is a man of action, not an intellectual, who is involved in many adventurous situations, often humorous, from smuggling to kidnapping to spying. He usually manages to escape a predicament only at the last possible moment. Sherman H. Eoff commented in *The Modern Spanish Novel: Comparative Essays Examining the Philosophical Impact of Science on Fiction* that although *Zalacaín el aventurero* is an adventure novel, one can sense Baroja's philosophical ideas "hovering over the whole like an invisible cloud."

Between 1904 and 1905 Baroja published his highly regarded trilogy "La lucha por la vida," consisting of the novels *La busca, Mala hierba,* and *Aurora roja.* The trilogy focuses on the problems of city life in modern times. Throughout these works, Baroja describes the effects of the advent of capitalism and industrialization on the underclass of Madrid. Patt observed that Baroja's attitude towards the masses in "La lucha por la vida" "is compassionate and humane, yet at the same time puritanical in its insistence on morality, work and steadfastness."

El árbol de la ciencia, a partially autobiographical novel, is generally regarded as the work that is most highly representative of Baroja's life and philosophy. Patt believed that it "is Baroja's most authentic novel," while Robert W. Hatton in *Hispania* called it "an extension of [Baroja's] own personality." *El árbol de la ciencia* is filled with characters based on people Baroja had known during his younger years. The chief protagonist, Andrés Hurtado, is a physician searching for the sense and meaning of life's injustices. He is unable to find either a satisfying love relationship or a meaningful life for himself, and he finally commits suicide.

Inspired by family stories about one of his distant relatives, Eugenio de Aviraneta, Baroja began to research the history of his relative's life and times. That research resulted in the twenty-two-volume "Las memorias de un hombre de acción." These historical novels, which were published between 1913 and 1935, depict the life of a romantic idealist who is actively engaged in the nineteenth-century Spanish war of independence against France.

Although Baroja was particularly fond of the genre of fiction, he also wrote in other genres as well. Throughout his life he published numerous articles and essays on literary, social, and political themes. These articles appeared in many of the widely read and influential newspapers of Latin America and Spain. As with his other work, in these articles Baroja remained individualistic and highly critical of the bureaucratic intricacies of Spanish politics. In July 1936, at the onset of the Spanish Civil War, Baroja was incarcerated as "an enemy of tradition." Luckily, a member of the army recognized the famous author and released him the following day. As a result of that incident, Baroja went into self-imposed exile in France and did not return to Spain until the end of the civil war.

BIOGRAPHICAL AND CRITICAL SOURCES:

BOOKS

Dictionary of Hispanic Biography, Thomson Gale (Detroit, MI), 1996.

Dos Passos, John, *Rosinante to the Road Again,* Doran (New York, NY), 1922.

Encyclopedia of World Biography, 2nd edition, Thomson Gale (Detroit, MI), 1998.

Encyclopedia of World Literature in the Twentieth Century, 3rd edition, St. James Press (Detroit, MI), 1999.

Eoff, Sherman H., *The Modern Spanish Novel: Comparative Essays Examining the Philosophical Impact of Science on Fiction,* New York University Press (New York, NY), 1961.

Hispanic Literature Criticism, Volume 1, Thomson Gale (Detroit, MI), 1994.

Madariaga, Salvador de, *The Genius of Spain and Other Essays on Spanish Contemporary Literature,* Oxford University Press (New York, NY), 1923.

Patt, Beatrice P., *Pío Baroja,* Twayne (New York, NY), 1971.

Twentieth-Century Literary Criticism, Volume 8, Thomson Gale (Detroit, MI), 1982.

PERIODICALS

Comparative Literature Studies, fall, 1984, Helga Stipa Madland, "Baroja's *Camino de perfeccion* and Schnitzler's *Lieutenant Gustl:* Fin de Siècle Madrid and Vienna," pp. 306-322.

Hispania, May, 1971, Robert W. Hatton, review of *El árbol de la ciencia,* p. 414; December, 1971, Evelyn Rugg, review of *El mundo es ansi,* pp. 987-988.

Library Journal, February 1, 1998, Jack Shreve, review of *Zalacain the Adventurer: The History of the Good Fortune and Wanderings of Martin Zalacain of Urbia,* p. 109.

Modern Language Journal, February, 1972, Jorge R. Ayora, review of *El mundo es ansi,* p. 102.

Modern Language Notes, March, 1987, Gonzalo Navajas, "La jerarquía, la letra y lo oral en *Paradox, rey,* de Pío Baroja," pp. 255-273.

Translation Review Supplement, July, 1998, review of *Zalacain the Adventurer,* p. 22.*

* * *

BAROJA Y NESSI, Pío
See BAROJA, Pío

* * *

BARRY, Michael 1948-
(Michael A. Barry)

PERSONAL: Born 1948, in New York, NY. *Education:* Princeton University, graduated, 1970; Cambridge University, diploma; McGill University, M.A.; École des Hautes Études en Sciences Sociales, Ph.D.

ADDRESSES: Office—Department of Near Eastern Studies, Princeton University, 110 Jones Hall, Princeton, NJ 08544. *E-mail*—mbarry@princeton.edu.

CAREER: Scholar, historian, educator. International Federation for Human Rights, Afghan affairs observer, 1979-85; Médecins du Monde, coordinating officer, Afghanistan, 1985-89; United Nations, consultant and humanitarian team leader, 1989-91; special envoy to

Dr. Bernard Kouchner, Kabul, Afghanistan, 1992-95; French government, advisor for education assistance programs, Kabul; Princeton University, Princeton, NJ, lecturer in Persian, 2004—; Metropolitan Museum of Art, New York, NY, chairman of the Department of Islamic Art.

AWARDS, HONORS: Six literary prizes from France and Iran; including Art History Medal, Académie Française, 1997, for French version of *Design and Color in Islamic Architecture: Eight Centuries of the Tile-Maker's Art;* Prix Fémina, 2002, for *Massoud;* and Book of the Year, Iranian government, 2002, for *Le Pavillon des sept princesses.*

WRITINGS:

(With others) *Design and Color in Islamic Architecture: Eight Centuries of the Tile-Maker's Art,* Vendome Press (New York, NY), 1996.
Le Pavillon des sept princesses (translation of *Seven Icons,* by Nizâmî Hafat Paykar), 2000.
Le Royaume de l'insolence: l'Afghanistan, 1504-2001, 3rd edition, Flammarion (Paris, France), 2002.
Massoud (biography), Audibert (Paris, France), 2002.
Figurative Art in Medieval Islam and the Riddle of Bihzad of Herat (1465-1535), Flammarion (Paris, France), 2004.
History of Modern Afghanistan, Cambridge University Press (New York, NY), 2006.

SIDELIGHTS: Near Eastern studies scholar Michael Barry was born in the United States but was also raised in Afghanistan and France. He graduated from Princeton University and studied in England, Canada, and France and spent the years from 1979 to 2001 working for humanitarian efforts in war-torn Afghanistan. According to his biography on the *Princeton University* Web site, "he has testified on Soviet human rights violations in Afghanistan before the U.S. Senate Foreign Relations Committee in December 1982, was received in private audience by Ronald Reagan in the White House to discuss the Soviet-Afghan war in January 1983, and was invited by the Norwegian Foreign Ministry to help organize the International Hearings on Afghanistan held in Oslo in March 1983."

Barry, who was named chairman of the of the Metropolitan Museum of Art's Department of Islamic Art, has written several books about Near Eastern art.

These volumes include *Design and Color in Islamic Architecture: Eight Centuries of the Tile-Maker's Art* and *Figurative Art in Medieval Islam and the Riddle of Bihzad of Herat (1465-1535).* In the latter, which includes more than 300 reproductions, Barry provides a history of Islamic figurative art from the eighth to the twelfth centuries and studies Persian miniatures, concentrating on the work of Bihzad, whom he considers a guild master. *Library Journal* contributor Martin Chasin wrote that "Barry is interested in the allegorical meanings of medieval Islamic painting and deciphers the visual symbols that pervade these works."

BIOGRAPHICAL AND CRITICAL SOURCES:

PERIODICALS

Library Journal, September 15, 2005, Martin Chasin, review of *Figurative Art in Medieval Islam and the Riddle of Bihzad of Herat (1465-1535),* p. 61.
Publishers Weekly, August 19, 1996, review of *Design and Color in Islamic Architecture: Eight Centuries of the Tile-Maker's Art,* p. 45.
Reference & Research Book News, August, 2005, review of *Figurative Art in Medieval Islam,* p. 221.

ONLINE

Princeton University Web site, http://www.princeton.edu/ (March 4, 2006), author biography.*

*   *   *

BARRY, Michael A.
   See BARRY, Michael

*   *   *

BAUERSCHMIDT, Frederick Christian 1961-

PERSONAL: Born September 21, 1961; married Maureen Sweeney (an immigration lawyer); children: Thomas, Sophia, Denis. *Education:* University of the South, B.A., 1984; Yale Divinity School, M.A.R., 1989; Duke University, Ph.D., 1996. *Religion:* Catholic.

ADDRESSES: Office—Department of Theology, Loyola College in Maryland, 4501 N. Charles St., Baltimore, MD 21210; fax: 410-617-2628. E-mail—fbauerschmidt@loyola.edu.

CAREER: Educator and writer. Duke University, Durham, NC, lecturer in religion, 1993; Loyola College, Baltimore, MD, assistant professor of theology, 1994-2000, associate professor, 2000—; Loyola International Nachbahr Huis, Leuven, Belgium, director, 2001-03. Katholieke Universiteit, Leuven, Belgium, visiting professor, 2001-03; Brazos Press, Grand Rapids, MI, editorial board member.

MEMBER: American Academy of Religion; Society for Catholic Liturgy.

AWARDS, HONORS: Departmental fellowship, Duke University, 1989; grants from Loyola College, 1995, 1999, 2004, 2005.

WRITINGS:

NONFICTION

Julian of Norwich and the Mystical Body Politic of Christ, University of Notre Dame Press (South Bend, IN), 1999.
Why the Mystics Matter Now, Sorin Books (Notre Dame, IN), 2003.
(Editor, with Jim Fodor) Aquinas in Dialogue: Thomas for the Twenty-first Century, Blackwell Publishers (Malden, MA), 2004.
Holy Teaching: Introducing the Summa Theologiae of St. Thomas Aquinas, Brazos Press (Grand Rapids, MI), 2005.

Coeditor of Modern Theology; member of editorial board for The Sign of Peace: Journal of the Catholic Peace Fellowship. Contributor to books, including American Catholic Traditions: Resources for Renewal, edited by Sandra Yocum Mize and William L. Portier, Orbis Books (Maryknoll, NY), 1997; Radical Orthodoxy: A New Theology, edited by John Milbank, Catherine Pickstock and Graham Ward, Routledge (London, England), 1999; The Blackwell Companion to Christian Ethics, edited by Stanley Hauerwas and Sam Wells, Basil Blackwell (Oxford, England), 2003; and

Reading John with St. Thomas Aquinas, edited by Matthew Levering and Michael Dauphinais, Catholic University of America Press (Washington, DC), 2005.

Also contributor to scholarly journals, including Nova et Vetera, Communio: International Catholic Review, Theology Today, New Blackfriars, South Atlantic Quarterly, Journal of Medieval and Early Modern Studies, Theology & Philosophy, and St. Luke's Journal of Theology.

WORK IN PROGRESS: Thomas Aquinas: Faith, Reason and Following Christ, for Oxford University Press; The Blackwell Introduction to Catholic Theology and The Blackwell Companion to Catholicism, both for Blackwell.

SIDELIGHTS: Frederick Christian Bauerschmidt, an author and professor, has spent his career researching and writing on the topic of religion and theology. A contributor to numerous books and journals, Bauerschmidt authored his first book, Julian of Norwich and the Mystical Body Politic of Christ, in 1999. Julian lived in religious confinement at the St. Julian Church in Norwich during the fourteenth century. A religious vision said to be sent to her from God inspired her work and legacy, A Revelation of Love. Bauerschmidt's book analyzes significant images contained in Julian's vision and relates them to current politics and community, affirming the value of her work in today's world. Bauerschmidt "reads Julian's text as a resource for dialogue between theology and social theory and practice . . . a startling claim to make about [the work of] a medieval female recluse," Joan M. Nuth stated in Theological Studies. Nuth went on to note that Bauerschmidt "succeeds admirably in supporting his thesis," and then commented: "I have nothing but praise for this uniformly excellent book."

Bauerschmidt's second book, Why the Mystics Matter Now, is a guide to the work of seven of the great Christian mystics, including Catherine of Sienna, Hildegard of Bingen, Ignatius of Loyola, Julian of Norwich, Meister Eckhart, Therese of Lisieux, and Thomas Merton. The volume introduces readers to the topic of mysticism and familiarizes them with its importance in both the past and present. Mary Bartholomew, reviewing the book for the Good Book Stall Web site, complemented the author's "deep understanding of his subject," calling the book "excellent."

Kevin Axe also praised the book in a review posted on the *Living Church Foundation* Web site: "Even if some of the seven [mystics] 'matter now' to some readers more than others, getting to know the topic and all seven is well worth the read."

In 2005 Bauerschmidt published *Holy Teaching: Introducing the Summa Theologiae of St. Thomas Aquinas.* St. Thomas Aquinas wrote the famous *Summa Theologiae,* or summary of theology, in order to create an overview of Christianity's teachings. Bauerschmidt's book explains the essential ideas of the *Summa Theologiae* in an attempt to improve its accessibility to all readers. Graham Christian pointed out in *Library Journal* that Bauerschmidt "approach[es] both Aquinas and the reader with respect." Although Timothy Renick, writing in the *Christian Century,* felt that "Bauerschmidt's presentation takes some getting used to," he concluded that "the reward is a lucid commentary."

BIOGRAPHICAL AND CRITICAL SOURCES:

BOOKS

Directory of American Scholars, 10th edition, Thomson Gale (Detroit, MI), 2002.

PERIODICALS

Christian Century, August 23, 2005, Timothy Renick, "Aquinas for Protestants: Second Chance for Thomas," p. 22.
Library Journal, July 1, 2005, Graham Christian, review of *Holy Teaching: Introducing the Summa Theologiae of St. Thomas Aquinas,* p. 88.
National Catholic Reporter, February 1, 2001, Arthur Jones, "Can Mystics Matter? Frederick Bauerschmidt Investigates Intersection of Christianity and Modernity—The Word Made Fresh: New Thinkers," p. 12.
Theological Studies, March, 2000, Joan M. Nuth, review of *Julian of Norwich and the Mystical Body Politic of Christ,* p. 153.

ONLINE

Loyola College in Maryland Web site, http://www. loyola.edu/ (March 15, 2006), author's curriculum vitae.

Good Book Stall, http://www.thegoodbookstall.org.uk/ (March 15, 2006), Mary Bartholomew, review of *Why the Mystics Matter Now.*
Living Church Foundation Web site, http://www. livingchurch.org/ (November 2, 2003), Kevin Axe, "Mystics: A Breed Apart, Yet Just Like Us."*

*   *   *

BEAHRS, Andrew 1973-

PERSONAL: Born 1973, in CT; married; wife's name Eli (a teacher); children: Erik. *Education:* Attended University of California at Berkeley; University of Virginia, M.S.; Spalding University, M.F.A. *Hobbies and other interests:* SCUBA diving, capoeira, playing the cello, bluegrass music.

ADDRESSES: Home—Berkeley, CA. *Agent*—c/o Author Mail, The Toby Press, 2 Great Pasture Rd., Danbury, CT 06810. *E-mail*—andrew@andrewbeahrs. com.

CAREER: Writer.

WRITINGS:

Strange Saint (novel), Toby Press (Danbury, CT), 2005.

WORK IN PROGRESS: A companion novel to *Strange Saint;* a novel about musical innovations in Paris around the time of the French Revolution.

SIDELIGHTS: An archeologist by training, Andrew Beahrs endeavored to write a first novel that uses some of his educational background, adding realism to his tale about the Pilgrims. Melode, the main character in *Strange Saint,* is enduring a life of servitude in England when she joins Adam, the son of a minister of the Saints—or Pilgrims—on a boat to the New World. Although she is falling in love with Adam, in his increasing religious fervor he soon rejects her. Melode subsequently has an affair with another man and becomes pregnant. Disgraced, she is thrown off the ship and left in Newfoundland, where she and her child face a new struggle just to survive. In a mixed blessing, she is rescued and makes her way to the new colony, where she finds herself a social reject among the pious Pilgrims. Although Mark Andre Singer commented in a *Library Journal* review that the heroine's views on sex were a bit hard to believe, the exciting plot in *Strange Saint* "smoothes out the occasional stylistic wrinkle." A *Publishers Weekly* contributor praised this "moving" story for its "sumptuous description and . . . period's language."

BIOGRAPHICAL AND CRITICAL SOURCES:

PERIODICALS

Library Journal, September 1, 2005, Mark Andre Singer, review of *Strange Saint*, p. 127.
Publishers Weekly, September 5, 2005, review of *Strange Saint*, p. 36.

ONLINE

Andrew Beahrs Home Page, http://www.andrew beahrs.com (February 1, 2006).
Word Museum, http://www.wordmuseum.com/ (February 1, 2006), Julie Failla Earhart, review of *Strange Saint.**

* * *

BEATTY, Terry

PERSONAL: Male. Married Wendi Lee (a writer); children: Beth.

ADDRESSES: Agent—c/o Author Mail, DC Comics, 1700 Broadway, New York, NY 10019. *E-mail*— terry@terrybeatty.com.

CAREER: Writer, comic book inker and illustrator, designer of model kits, commercial illustrator.

AWARDS, HONORS: Eisner awards, 1998, for *Batman and Robin Adventures: World's Finest,* and 1999, for *Batman: The Gotham Adventures.*

WRITINGS:

(Inker) Wendy Pini, *ElfQuest: Bedtime Stories,* Warp Graphics, 1994.
(Inker) Paul Dini, *The Official Comics Adaptation: Batman and Superman Adventures: World's Finest,* DC Comics (New York, NY), 1997.
(Inker) Max Allan Collins, *Johnny Dynamite,* Ait/ Planet Lar, 2003.

Inker of *Batman* for DC Comics, and for other publishers; inker for the comic book series *Ms. Tree's Thrilling Detective Adventures,* by Frank Miller.

SIDELIGHTS: Terry Beatty has inked *Batman* for DC Comics for many years, as well as working on projects for Marvel Comics and others. Ray Tate reviewed *Batman: Gotham Adventures* for *Silver Bullet Comic Books* online, writing that Beatty, "who seals all the art in his evocative inks, also uses his penciling opportunity to exude mood and atmosphere. He closes in on Bruce Wayne's eyes and tells the reader without words that nothing will stand in this man's way."

Beatty is married to the prolific author Wendi Lee, creator of the "Angela Matelli" mystery series, and the two have collaborated on a number of short stories that have been published in anthologies.

Beatty and Lee also worked together on *ElfQuest: Bedtime Stories,* a volume for young children that is based on the adult fantasy series. The elves tell the traditional stories, such as *Jack and the Beanstalk* and *Little Red Riding Hood,* while adding "fun, new twists to the familiar tales," commented *Booklist*'s Sally Estes.

BIOGRAPHICAL AND CRITICAL SOURCES:

PERIODICALS

Booklist, January 15, 1995, Sally Estes, review of *ElfQuest: Bedtime Stories*, p. 920.

ONLINE

Terry Beatty Home Page, http://www.terrybeatty.com (December 9, 2003).

Silver Bullet Comic Books, http://www.silverbullet comicbooks.com/ (December 9, 2003), Ray Tate, review of *Batman: Gotham Adventures.**

* * *

BEHLER, John L. 1943-2006
(John Luther Behler)

OBITUARY NOTICE— See index for *CA* sketch: Born June 28, 1943, in Allentown, PA; died of congestive heart failure, January 31, 2006, in Amawalk, NY. Herpetologist, museum curator, and author. A curator of herpetology at the Bronx Zoo, Behler was renowned for his successful efforts in saving turtle and alligator species in China. Since his boyhood, when he spent much of his time finding snakes and butterflies in his neighborhood, Behler was interested in wildlife. Completing a B.S. at the University of Miami, he then earned an M.Ed. in biological science at East Stroudsburg University. After finishing his studies, Behler taught briefly at William Smith College and Hobart College. In 1970, he was hired by the Wildlife Conservation Society, the organization that is also in charge of operations at the Bronx Zoo. Spending the rest of his career at the zoo, Behler worked to improve the reptile and amphibian exhibits, which now include over one hundred species—many of them rare or endangered—from around the world. He also conducted research in such countries as China and Madagascar. Three severe problems, he learned, were plaguing species of turtle and alligators in Asia: the pet trade, the food industry, and the traditional medicine industry. In China, turtles are a much-demanded delicacy, and by the 1990s the demand for turtles for food was still being sated by trapping the animals in the wild; reptiles were also killed to make various medicines. Behler warned that wild trapping would result in the extinction of many species of turtles, and he convinced the Chinese government to start captive breeding programs to raise turtles domestically for food. This did much to relieve the stress on the turtle populations, and Behler was hailed as a hero among conservationists. He also worked to save the Chinese alligator, which was almost extinct when he rescued several animals and brought them back to the Bronx zoo for breeding. In Madagascar, Behler conducted research to track the radiated tortoise, thus learning where they preferred to live and breed. Based on this information, he established a

protected reserve for them. In addition to his research and zoo work, Behler published several guides that are still widely read, including *Familiar Reptiles and Amphibians: North America* (1988) and *National Audubon Society First Field Guide: Reptiles* (1999).

OBITUARIES AND OTHER SOURCES:

PERIODICALS

New York Times, February 5, 2006, p. A25.

* * *

BEHLER, John Luther
See BEHLER, John L.

* * *

BENECKE, Mark 1970-

PERSONAL: Born 1970, in Rosenheim, Germany. *Education:* University of Cologne, B.S., 1994, Ph.D., 1997.

ADDRESSES: Office—International Forensic Research and Consulting, Postfach 250411, 50520 Cologne, Germany. *E-mail*—forensic@benecke.com.

CAREER: Office of the Chief Medical Examiner, New York, NY, forensic biologist, 1997-99; University of Cologne, Cologne, Germany, professor of zoology, 1999; International Forensic Research and Consulting, Cologne, Germany, 2000—. Visiting assistant professor, University of Medicine and Pharmacy, Ho Chi Minh City, Vietnam, 1999; Institute for Legal Medicine, Bogota, Colombia, 1999. Forensic entomology trainer, Police Academy of Germany, 1997, 1999. Scientific consultant at numerous universities and at the Federal Bureau of Investigation (FBI), Quantico, VA. Guest lecturer, Columbia University, John Jay College, University of Berlin, University of Bonn, University of Freiburg, and University of Konstanz. Scientific consultant, *Dracula Unearthed,* National Geographic Television.

MEMBER: International Academy of Legal Medicine, International Society of Forensic Genetics, American Academy of Forensic Sciences, German Society for Legal Medicine, German Zoological Society, Society of German Natural Scientists and Medical Doctors, Colombian Society for Legal Medicine, Linnean Society (fellow).

AWARDS, HONORS: Medal of honor, Association of the Criminal Police (Germany), 2002.

WRITINGS:

The Dream of Eternal Life: Biomedicine, Aging, and Immortality, translated by Rachel Rubenstein, Columbia University Press (New York, NY), 2002.

Murderous Methods: Using Forensic Science to Solve Lethal Crimes, translated by Karin Heusch, Columbia University Press (New York, NY), 2005.

Also author of *Scientists and Inventors,* 1997; *Forensic Biology,* 1999; *Criminal Cases of the 20th Century,* 2002; and *Handbuch Rechtsmedizin,* 2003. Coauthor, *Entomological Evidence,* 2000. Coeditor, *Annals of Improbable Research,* 1995—, and *Forensic Science International.* Contributor of articles to scholarly journals.

SIDELIGHTS: Mark Benecke earned a Ph.D. in the study of entomology, concentrating on the biological strains of certain genera of insects. His interests transcend the boundaries of that scientific endeavor, however. Since 1997 Benecke has traveled the globe lecturing and studying the uses of forensic science to solve murders, and the use of biomedical advances to slow the aging process. Benecke's two books, translated from the German, examine these topics in a style that is accessible to a general readership.

The Dream of Eternal Life: Biomedicine, Aging, and Immortality is in part a philosophical exploration of the inevitability of death and in part a description of ways in which scientific advances can prolong and enhance life. Benecke covers not only the probable ways in which biologists might extend the human lifespan—manipulating DNA and creating pharmaceu-

ticals to counter the effects of aging—but also the less plausible scenarios, including cryogenics. In *Booklist,* William Beatty called the book "thought-provoking." *Commonweal* contributor F. Gonzalez-Crussi concluded that Benecke's material "is interesting . . . and is framed in a concise, lucid language. Readers ought to find it informative and enjoyable." The reviewer concluded: "The impact of biotechnology on our lives is now of unprecedented magnitude, and public education on basic principles is urgent. Benecke contributes substantially to this end."

In *Murderous Methods: Using Forensic Science to Solve Lethal Crimes,* Benecke revisits some of the most notorious murder cases of the twentieth century and discusses how forensic evidence helped to incriminate such killers as Jeffrey Dahmer, German serial murderer Karl Denke, and the kidnapper of Charles Lindbergh's young son. Sidebars cover facts about violent death, facial reconstruction, and genetic fingerprinting. A critic for *Kirkus Reviews* noted: "This hodgepodge of crime stories is definitely not for the squeamish." *Library Journal* correspondent David Alperstein, in contrast, felt that the book would appeal to a wide readership because it "reads like true-crime literature."

BIOGRAPHICAL AND CRITICAL SOURCES:

PERIODICALS

Booklist, April 15, 2002, William Beatty, review of *The Dream of Eternal Life: Biomedicine, Aging, and Immortality,* p. 1370; October 15, 2005, Mike Tribby, review of *Murderous Methods: Using Forensic Science to Solve Lethal Crimes,* p. 8.

Commonweal, September 27, 2002, F. Gonzalez-Crussi, "Never Say Die," p. 24.

Kirkus Reviews, September 1, 2005, review of *Murderous Methods,* p. 949.

Library Journal, October 1, 2005, David Alperstein, review of *Murderous Methods,* p. 94.

Quarterly Review of Biology, December, 2002, Michael R. Rose, review of *The Dream of Eternal Life,* p. 483.

Publishers Weekly, September 19, 2005, review of *Murderous Methods,* p. 54.

Science News, May 18, 2002, Cait Goldberg, review of *The Dream of Eternal Life,* p. 319.

ONLINE

Mark Benecke Home Page, http://www.benecke.com (December 5, 2005).*

*   *   *

BENNETT, Robert W. 1941-

PERSONAL: Born March 30, 1941, in Chicago, IL; son of Lewis (an attorney) and Henrietta (a homemaker; maiden name, Schneider) Bennett; married Harriet Trop (a teacher), August 10, 1979; children: Ariana Trop. *Education:* Harvard University, B.A. (summa cum laude), 1962, LL.B. (cum laude), 1965; attended London School of Economics and Political Science, London, 1965-66. *Politics:* Independent. *Religion:* Jewish.

ADDRESSES: Home—2130 N. Racine, Chicago, IL 60614. *Office*—Northwestern University School of Law, 357 E. Chicago Ave., Chicago, IL 60611; fax: 312-503-5950. *E-mail*—r-bennett@law.northwestern. edu.

CAREER: Writer. Northwestern University School of Law, Chicago, IL, assistant professor, 1969-71, associate professor, 1971-74, professor, 1974-2002, Nathaniel L. Nathanson Professor of Law, 2002—, dean of law school, 1985-95. Visiting professor at University of Illinois, 1974, 1976, University of Virginia, 1976, University of Southern California, 1982-83, and Brooklyn Law School, 2004-05; European University Institute, visiting scholar, 1995-96. Professional arbitrator, 1974—; Center for Public Resources, Chicago Alternative Dispute Resolution, panel member, 1988—. Chicago Council of Lawyers, cofounder, member of board of directors, 1969-74, 1977-79, president, 1971-72; Illinois Attorney Disciplinary System, member of hearing board, 1973-75; American Bar Foundation, fellow, member of board of directors, 1986-95, president, 1992-94; National Association for the Advancement of Colored People, cochair of Legal Defense and Educational Fund, 1988-94; U.S. District Court for the Northern District of Illinois, member of civil justice reform act advisory committee, 1991-94; member of Special Commission on the Administration of Justice in Il-

linois and Illinois Task Force on Crime and Corrections, 1992-94; past consultant to Administrative Conference of the United States, U.S. Department of Justice, Federal Communications Commission, and other agencies. Commission to Revise Illinois Public Aid Code, member, 1978-80; Chicago Cable Television Study Commission, member, 1981-82; Chicago Council on Foreign Relations, member of Chicago Committee. George M. Pullman Educational Foundation, member of board of directors, 1986-96, 1997—; Appleseed Foundation, member of advisory council, 1996—; Chicago Appleseed Foundation, board member, 2002—.

MEMBER: American Law Institute, American Bar Association, Lawyers' Club of Chicago, Phi Beta Kappa.

AWARDS, HONORS: Knox fellow in England, 1965-66.

WRITINGS:

(With Arthur B. LaFrance, Milton R. Schroeder, and William E. Boyd) *Hornbook on Law of the Poor,* West Publishing (St. Paul, MN), 1973.
Representing the Audience in Broadcast Proceedings, Office of Communications, United Church of Christ (Cleveland, OH), 1974.
(Coauthor) *Harvard Child Health Project Report,* Volume 1: *Toward a Primary Medical Care System Responsive to Children's Needs,* Ballinger Publishing (Cambridge, MA), 1977.
Talking It Through: Puzzles of American Democracy, Cornell University Press (Ithaca, NY), 2003.

Contributor to books, including *The Burger Court: The Counter-Revolution That Wasn't,* edited by Vincent Blasi, Yale University Press (New Haven, CT), 1983. Contributor of articles and reviews to law journals and other periodicals, including *Judicature, Trial, Chicago Lawyer,* and *Constitutional Commentary.*

*   *   *

BENTOS, Carlos 1941-

PERSONAL: Born February 2, 1941, in Montevideo, Uruguay; immigrated to the United States, c. late 1960s; married and divorced twice. *Hobbies and other interests:* Fishing (licensed charter fishing captain).

ADDRESSES: Home—Annapolis, MD. *Agent*—c/o Author Mail, Tarcher Publicity, 375 Hudson St., New York, NY 10014.

CAREER: El Caribe (restaurant chain), Washington, DC, owner, 1974-c. 2000; Fathoms Grill, West Ocean City, MD, currently general manager and co-owner; commentator for Voice of America.

MEMBER: Ocean City (Light Tackle) Marlin Club (former president).

AWARDS, HONORS: Winner of over thirty fishing competitions, including White Marlin Open, 1996; also named Fisherman of the Year, Captain of the Year, Mate of the Year, and his ship was named Boat of the Year.

WRITINGS:

A Crew of One: The Odyssey of a Solo Marlin Fisherman, Jeremy P. Tarcher (New York, NY), 2002.

WORK IN PROGRESS: A book of poems in Spanish.

SIDELIGHTS: An immigrant Uruguayan who established a highly successful chain of restaurants in the Washington, DC, area and also became a radio commentator for *Voice of America,* Carlos Bentos is well known as a champion marlin fisherman. Having fished since he was a boy, he became passionate about sea fishing after moving to the American East Coast, where he bought a boat and became highly skilled at catching deep-sea fish. He writes about his lifelong relationship with the sea, his ship, and fishing in his debut work, *A Crew of One: The Odyssey of a Solo Marlin Fisherman.* The work relates memories of his life, along with tips on fishing and tales of his sailing experiences. Several reviewers maintained that it is best suited to audiences who are already fishing aficionados, "but landlubbers should glean some interesting tidbits," according to David Pitt in *Booklist.* A *Publishers Weekly* contributor considered the writing style to be merely "competent," however, *Library Journal* contributor Edwin B. Burgess remarked that Bentos "has an easy style" that forms "a pleasant and undemanding narrative." Despite some

reservations about the quality of the writing from other critics, Pitt concluded that *A Crew of One* is "a resonant autobiography."

BIOGRAPHICAL AND CRITICAL SOURCES:

BOOKS

Bentos, Carlos, *A Crew of One: The Odyssey of a Solo Marlin Fisherman,* Jeremy P. Tarcher (New York, NY), 2002.

PERIODICALS

Booklist, April 15, 2002, David Pitt, review of *A Crew of One,* p. 1373.
Kirkus Reviews, April 15, 2002, review of *A Crew of One,* p. 537.
Library Journal, May 1, 2002, Edwin B. Burgess, review of *A Crew of One,* p. 108.
Publishers Weekly, April 29, 2002, review of *A Crew of One,* p. 55.
Washington Post, May 20, 1997, Angus Phillips, "Solo at Sea, He's in a League of His Own"; July 29, 1999, Angus Phillips, "Middle-aged Man and the Sea."

ONLINE

Carlos Bentos Home Page, http://www.carlosbentos. com (January 18, 2006).*

*   *   *

BERGMAN, Susan 1957-2006

OBITUARY NOTICE— See index for *CA* sketch: Born 1957, in Bloomington, IN; died of brain cancer, January 1, 2006, in Barrington, IL. Author. Bergman was best known for her 1994 book, *Anonymity: The Secret Life of an American Family.* She was a 1979 graduate of Wheaton College, where she earned a degree in art, and in 1992 she completed a Ph.D. in literature at Northwestern University. Working variously as a teacher and lecturer at such universities as the University of Notre Dame, New York University, and

Northwestern, she also earned a living as a contributing editor to journals, such as the *North American Review*. Having been raised in a seemingly normal and stable household, Bergman discovered in 1983 that her father had contracted AIDS after leading a secret life as a homosexual. This shocking revelation led to much soul-searching, as well as the publication of *Anonymity*. Interestingly, her sister, actress Anne Heche, also had a lesbian affair with comedian and television host Ellen DeGeneres. Bergman would go on to edit *Martyrs: Contemporary Writers on Modern Lives of Faith* (1996), and in 2000 she cofounded the Web site PreviewPort, an electronic resource for writers and readers. She continued to write after learning she had cancer, to which she eventually would succumb. Her last book, the novel *Buried Life*, is scheduled to be published posthumously.

OBITUARIES AND OTHER SOURCES:

PERIODICALS

Chicago Tribune, January 2, 2006, Section 1, p. 11.
Los Angeles Times, January 4, 2006, p. B8.

*   *   *

BERL, Emmanuel 1892-1976

PERSONAL: Born August 2, 1892, in Vésinet, France; died September 22, 1976. *Education:* Sorbonne, graduated, 1913.

CAREER: Journalist and author. Editorial director, *Pierre Drieu la Rochelle* (weekly magazine), 1927, and *Marianne* (weekly newspaper), 1932-37; coeditor, *Pavé de Paris*, 1927, and *Les Derniers Jours*, 1937; government speech writer, 1940. *Military service:* French Army, 1914-17; served during World War I; received Military Cross.

AWARDS, HONORS: Grand Prix de Littérature, Académie Française, 1967; Marcel Proust Prize, 1975.

WRITINGS:

Recherches sur la nature de l'amour, Plon-Nourrit (Paris, France), 1923, translated by Fred Rothwell as *The Nature of Love*, Macmillan (New York, NY), 1924.

Méditation sur un amour défunt (novel), B. Grasset (Paris, France), 1925, reprinted, 1992.
Les Derniers jours (collection of articles), Editions J.-M. Place (Paris, France), 1927, reprinted, 1979.
La route no. 10 (novel), B. Grasset (Paris, France), 1927.
Mort de la pensée bourgeoise, B. Grasset (Paris, France), 1929, reprinted, R. Laffont (Paris, France), 1970.
Mort de la morale bourgeoise, Gallimard (Paris, France), 1929, reprinted, J.-J. Pauvert (Paris, France), 1965.
Le bourgeois et l'amour, Gallimard (Paris, France), 1931.
La politique et les partis, Rieder (Paris, France), 1932.
Discours aux Français, Gallimard (Paris, France), 1934.
Lignes de chance, Gallimard (Paris, France), 1934.
Le fameux rouleau compresseur, Gallimard (Paris, France), 1937.
Frère bourgeois, mourez-vous? Ding! Ding! Ding!, B. Grasset (Paris, France), 1938.
Histoire de l'Europe, Volume 1: *D'Atilla à Tamerlan*, Volume 2: *L'Europe classique*, Volume 3: *La crise révolutionnaire*, Gallimard (Paris, France), 1945, reprinted, 1973.
Les deux sources de l'art occidental, P. Cailler (Vésenaz-près-Genève, Switzerland), 1946.
Europe et Asie, Gallimard (Paris, France), 1946.
Structure et destin de l'Europe, Marguerat (Lucerne, Switzerland), 1946.
Prise de sang, R. Laffont (Paris, France), 1946.
De l'innocence, R. Julliard (Paris, France), 1947.
Traité sur la tolérance, Éditions du Cheval Ailé (Geneva, Switzerland), 1948.
La culture en péril, Table Ronde (Paris, France), 1948.
Destins de l'Occident, Table Ronde (Paris, France), 1948.
Sylvia (novel), Gallimard (Paris, France), 1952, reprinted, 1994.
(Editor) Voltaire, *Candide, ou l'optimisme*, Livre Club du Libraire (Paris, France), 1956.
Présence des morts (novel), Gallimard (Paris, France), 1956, reprinted, 1982.
La France irréelle, B. Grasset (Paris, France), 1957, reprinted, 1996.
Les impostures de l'histoire, B. Grasset (Paris, France), 1959.
(With Claude Arthaud) *Cent ans d'histoire de France*, edited by François Hébert-Stevens, Arthaud (Paris, France), 1962.

Rachel et autre grâces (novel), B. Grasset (Paris, France), 1965.

Le 9 thermidor, Hachette (Paris, France), 1965.

Le fin de la IIIe République, 10 juillet 1940, Gallimard (Paris, France), 1968.

Nasser tel qu'on le loue, Gallimard (Paris, France), 1968.

A contretemps, Gallimard (Paris, France), 1969.

Trois faces du sacré, B. Grasset (Paris, France), 1971.

Le virage, Gallimard (Paris, France), 1972.

A venir, Gallimard (Paris, France), 1974.

Regain au pays d'Auge, Livre de Poche (Paris, France), 1974.

(With Patrick Modiano) *Interrogatoire: suivi de Il fait beau, allons au cimetière,* Gallimard (Paris, France), 1976.

Essais, selected and edited by Bernard Morlino and Bernard de Fallois, Julliard (Paris, France), 1985.

(With Jean d'Ormesson) *Tant que vous penserez à moi* (interviews), B. Grasset (Paris, France), 1992.

Un Téléspectateur engagé, presented by Bernard Morlino, Editions François Bourin (Paris, France), 1993.

Also author of preface, *Histoires,* by Cornelius Tacitus, edited by Henri Jules Ernest Goelzer, Librairie Generale Française (Paris, France), 1963; and *Mélanges,* by Voltaire, edited by Jacques van den Heuvel, Gallimard (Paris, France), 1965.

SIDELIGHTS: A left-leaning journalist and author who spent most of his life in Paris, France, Emmanuel Berl was influenced early in his life with his experiences of the horrors of war. Having served in the French Army during World War I, he received the Military Cross and was discharged in 1917 because of a respiratory illness. During the 1920s and 1930s, he worked on several weekly magazines and newspapers in Paris, holding true to his pacifist and leftist beliefs, though his political ideology lay somewhere between capitalism and socialism. Among Berl's early books are the psychological novels *Méditation sur un amour défunt* and *La route no. 10.* Many of his other books are histories, essay collections, and political commentaries.

With the onset of World War II and the fall of France to Germany, Berl briefly worked as a speech writer for the Vichy government, which was set up by collaborationists. However, because he came from a Jewish family and because of his left-leaning politics and support for the Munich Peace Pact, he was forced to flee Paris and go into hiding. After the war, he became even more renowned as a writer, producing books on history, culture, and criticism. He also wrote several more novels, including *Sylvia* and *Rachel et autre grâces,* which are semiautobiographical works that draw on his Jewish past.

BIOGRAPHICAL AND CRITICAL SOURCES:

BOOKS

Kritzman, Lawrence D., editor, *Auschwitz and After,* Routledge (New York, NY), 1995, pp. 119-129.

PERIODICALS

RLA: Romance Language Annual, September, 1997, Kathleen W. Smith, "Bearing Witness: Modiano/Berl/Rembrandt," pp. 120-126.*

*   *   *

BERTOZZI, Nick

PERSONAL: Male.

ADDRESSES: Agent—c/o Author Mail, Alternative Comics, 503 N.W. 37th Ave., Gainesville, FL 32609-2204. *E-mail*—nbert@abac.com.

CAREER: Graphic artist, writer, comix creator, programmer. Worked in the marketing department of DC Comics, New York, NY.

AWARDS, HONORS: Xeric grant and Ignatz award, both 2000, both for *Boswash;* named Emerging Artist of 2002, *Comics Journal;* two Harvey awards, for best new series and best new talent, and an Ignatz award, for outstanding comic, all 2003, all for *Rubber Necker.*

WRITINGS:

Boswash (graphic story/map), Luxurious Comics, c. 2000.

The Masochists, Alternative Comics (Gainesville, FL), 2001.

Creator of mini and full-size comix series, including *The Incredible Drinking Buddies, Tranquilizer, Rubber Necker* and *The Salon* (online); contributor to anthologies, including *9-11: Emergency Relief,* Alternative Comics (Gainesville, FL), 2002; creator of strips, including "Beck" in *Spin* magazine and "Karmopolis, the Land of Cars," in *Nickelodeon* magazine.

WORK IN PROGRESS: Rubber Necker, The Salon, short stories.

SIDELIGHTS: Comix writer and artist Nick Bertozzi's work has earned him a string of awards and considerable praise, particularly for his "Rubber Necker" series.

Jesse Fuchs interviewed Bertozzi for *Alternative Comics,* asking him when he was first exposed to the genre, and Bertozzi answered that his father had read him *Zap Comix* before Bertozzi was old enough to read. "I read *Zap* by myself when I could read too," said Bertozzi. "I remember really liking Mr. Natural. Then, when I was eight or ten, I read a lot of *National Lampoon.* There was nudity in it, and I was always thrilled by that, as any little kid would be."

The adult Bertozzi worked in the marketing department of DC Comics and created his own minicomic, *The Incredible Drinking Buddies*—which he then took to full-size—as well as *Tranquilizer.* Bertozzi told Fuchs that he had been "exorcising the Crumb demon from when I was a kid. And then the *Comix 2000* piece actually got accepted, and I thought, finally somebody's paying attention to what I'm doing, and I did what I really wanted to. All the comics I was afraid to show to anybody because I thought they were too pretentious turned out to be the ones people actually liked! So that gave me the impetus to do *Boswash.*"

Bertozzi received a Xeric grant to create *Boswash,* an illustrated story printed on an accordian-style fold-out map. The folds mark the edges of the panels, which are laid out three to a column. The two-color format is not black and white, but rather blue and orange. The story is about a U.S. Army cartographer named Boswash who, at the end of the war with Mexico, disputes the location of the border of the two countries with his superior.

Greg McElhatton reviewed *Boswash* for *icomics* on-line, saying that this is "Bertozzi's best art yet. It's evolved into a clean line, with some really expressive faces. . . . The story itself is engrossing as well; you can feel Boswash's struggle, and by the time you've gotten to the end of the first half of the map, you're eager to turn it over to see what happens next."

The Masochists is Bertozzi's three-story graphic novel about an assortment of broken, sad characters. "Passing Out" delves into the horrors of adolescence, while the central character of "U.V. Katastrophe" is an older rock musician who has hit a creative wall, but who experiences a moment of transcendence when he sits in with his old band. "5/4" contains threads of obsession and self-mutilation and finds a young woman humiliated when she is exhibited, drunk and half-dressed, as part of an art show.

The woman, Donna, has a horrible family life that drives her. McElhatton wrote that "you can't help feeling sorry for her—doubly so after we see how she masks her mental pain with physical pain instead. It may be the hardest to find yourself having something in common with Donna, but I felt it was her story that I found the most heartrending of the three." McElhatton said of Bertozzi's artwork that "using a minimal amount of lines, his use of graytones works really well with the open expressions and backgrounds of his stories. People look real, something very important in three stories like those found in *The Masochists.*"

Peter Siegel reviewed *The Masochists* for *Artbomb. net,* saying that the book "is a very honest and compassionate look into their lives. . . . you'll be hard pressed to find a more oddly refreshing book with such an unflinching tone."

A *Publishers Weekly* contributor wrote that Bertozzi "infuses his stories with a deep melancholy and punctuates them with moments of genuine emotional discomfort that reveal his characters' most intimate and vulnerable sides."

Rubber Necker is Bertozzi's ongoing creation that includes stories such as *Drop Ceiling,* which features a young man whose place in the family business is at risk and who is looking for a special box left to him by his late father. Another story, *Belles Lettres,* is about a woman who develops and becomes obsessed with a new typeface.

Tim O'Shea interviewed Bertozzi for *Silver Bullet Comic Books* online and asked him how he felt after winning the Two Harvey awards for *Rubber Necker*. Bertozzi replied, "I'm really glad and astonished to have received the Harveys. The awards are kind of like nods from my friends and readers, telling me that I'm headed in the right direction with my comics."

Drop Ceiling examines why things are created. Bertozzi told O'Shea that he used Pawtucket, Rhode Island, as the model for the story's setting, where there is a distinct contrast between buildings constructed with care and those that have been merely thrown up. He said that "it's the contradiction of beauty and garishness that I find so appealing and a good subcurrent to the story." Bertozzi fits twenty panels per page, which he said is not hard, "since they consist of small shots. Most often, they're meant to give the reader the illusion of the main character's point of view. My perception of the world is pretty scattershot, so that's how I see the main character's vision: always floating around, eyes resting on different objects in a room. It's a manga trick."

Bertozzi posts updates of his online strip *The Salon* on the *Serializer* Web site. The story is set in 1907 Paris and revolves around the lives of artists like Picasso and writers such as Gertrude Stein. In preparing for the writing of this story, Bertozzi read the biographies of the main characters and histories of cubism in order to add factual information to his supernatural tale. The strip as he posts it is essentially the first draft of a project he intends to eventually publish.

BIOGRAPHICAL AND CRITICAL SOURCES:

PERIODICALS

Publishers Weekly, March 25, 2002, review of *The Masochists,* p. 48.

ONLINE

Alternative Comics, http://www.indyworld.com/ (December 9, 2003), Jesse Fuchs, interview with Bertozzi.

Artbomb.net, http://www.artbomb.net/ (December 9, 2003), Peter Siegel, review of *The Masochists.*

icomics, http://www.icomics.com/ (December 9, 2003), Greg McElhatton, reviews of *Boswash* and *The Masochists.*

Nick Bertozzi Home Page, http://www.nickbertozzi.com (December 9, 2003).

Serializer, http://www.serializer.net/ (December 9, 2003).

Silver Bullet Comic Books, http://www.silverbullet comicbooks/ (August 27, 2003), Tim O'Shea, interview with Bertozzi.*

*   *   *

BEY, Elihu

PERSONAL: Male.

ADDRESSES: Agent—Posro Media, LLC, P.O. Box 2197, Princeton, NJ 08543.

CAREER: Graphic artist, illustrator. Worked for Dow Jones, East Brunswick, NJ; Posro Komics (now Posro Media, LLC), illustrator, 1991—.

WRITINGS:

(Illustrator) Roland Owen Laird, Jr. and Taneshia Nash Laird, *Still I Rise: A Cartoon History of African Americans,* foreword by Charles Johnson, W.W. Norton (New York, NY), 1997.

Contributor of illustrations to the comic book series *MC Squared: A Man with a Serious Game Plan* and illustrator of the strip "The Griots."

SIDELIGHTS: Elihu Bey is a graphic artist and illustrator who first found work in that field when news that a position had opened reached him through his cartooning teacher. Bey jumped on it and was hired by Roland Laird, Willie Brown, and Taneshia Nash of Posro Komics, at the time one of just a few such black-owned companies in the country. The group created a comic series called *MC Squared: A Man with a Serious Game Plan,* about a Harlem barber and computer hacker, and "The Griots," a strip about a black newspaper family, which they self-syndicated to black newspapers. The Griots consist of parents Marcus and Monique and their children, Malika and Marvis. A *New York Times* contributor wrote that "the strip is full of witty lines, but also contains insights and black history and culture—a griot, in fact, is an African storyteller. . . . Mr. Bey, twenty-two, said black comic artists traditionally have drawn white characters or, at best, black superhero stereotypes. 'I want my drawings to convey emotion and spirituality,' he said. 'I want to portray black people as they really are.'"

The struggling young business suffered a major catastrophe when the home of Laird and Nash was destroyed in a gas explosion in 1993, four months after they married, resulting in the loss of all of their creative work and records. The next year, they were approached to do a graphic history of African Americans and had their book proposal ready soon after. They chose to publish with W.W. Norton, the second-highest bidder, because Norton agreed to do a hardcover version. Bey was recruited to illustrate the book, a job complicated by the fact that the writing and fact checking had to be completed before he could go to work. He managed to finish the project, including the penciling, inking, and lettering, in four months.

Still I Rise: A Cartoon History of African Americans portrays the struggles, dreams, and achievements of black Americans from 1618 to 1995. The title is taken from a poem by Maya Angelou. In *Library Journal* Stephen Weiner said the book "offers nuggets of little-known information on the impact of African Americans on American history."

Bey explains that the first African Americans to come to America were not slaves, but successful indentured servants and artisans who quickly bought out their contracts and those of others. This sparked resentment among the white population, servant and master alike. Contracts of blacks were illegally lengthened and buy-outs prohibited, causing some blacks to flee. When they were caught, their contracts were extended indefinitely, essentially marking the beginning of slavery. By 1677, slavery was official in all of the colonies. During the American Revolution the British offered slaves freedom for fighting and the Americans followed suit but slavery did not officially end with the war. When teh Dred Scott decision ruled that no slave could ever be free, escaped slaves and free blacks alike were kidnaped and returned to slavery.

Before its publication, the book was scrutinized for historical accuracy by Professors Nell Irvin Painter of Princeton University and Earl Lewis of the University of Michigan. Bey's volume includes black leaders and historical figures such as Harriet Tubman, Frederick Douglass, Ida B. Wells, Madame C.J. Walker, Malcolm X, and Martin Luther King. Also showcased are less well-known figures, including first female bank president Maggie Lena Walker, Benjamin Banneker, builder of the first striking clock made entirely with American-made parts, and Granville T. Woods, inventor of the third rail incorporated into subway systems.

A reviewer for *Rational Magic* online wrote that "touches of whimsy are plentiful, and Bey is very good at making even the background characters look like individuals. Although his people tend to be cartoony, he can draw them with great detail and accuracy when he desires." The reviewer said that "this is a fascinating book, jam-packed with information, yet presented in such a way that the story flows along smoothly, with little of the choppiness or 'episodicness' that often pervades such efforts."

Tori Still wrote for the alumni magazine of Brown University (Laird's alma mater) that "while *Still I Rise* is technically a comic book, it is less like *Superman* and more like Art Spiegelman's *Maus.*"

BIOGRAPHICAL AND CRITICAL SOURCES:

PERIODICALS

Brown Alumni, May, 1998, Torri Still, review of *Still I Rise: A Cartoon History of African Americans.*
Library Journal, February 1, 1998, Stephen Weiner, review of *Still I Rise,* p. 83.
New York Times, July 12, 1993, "At Posro Komics, hip hop heroes battle stereotypes."

ONLINE

Rational Magic, http://www.rationalmagic.com/ (June 24, 2006), review of *Still I Rise.**

*   *   *

BIERMAN, John 1929-2006
(John David Bierman)

OBITUARY NOTICE— See index for *CA* sketch: Born January 26, 1929, in London, England; died January 4, 2006. Journalist and author. Bierman achieved a remarkable career as an international correspondent for the BBC during conflicts in Africa, the Middle East, Asia, and Ireland. A child of divorced parents, he spent his early life being shuttled around by various relatives and attending almost a dozen different schools. Not old enough to fight during World War II, he did his military service shortly afterwards with the Royal Marine Commandos. After National Service, Bierman worked for a newspaper in Stoke-on-Trent and then moved to Canada to search for better journalism opportunities. With some experience under his belt, he returned to England and worked for such newspapers as the *Mirror* and *Daily Express* as a subeditor. This job would help him exercise his gift as a quick writer and expert reviser. In 1960, he was offered a new opportunity to be the editor of the *Nation* in Kenya. A few years later, he edited dailies in Trinidad before going back, once more, to England in 1967 to join the British Broadcasting Corporation. Here he worked as a television correspondent, covering such hot-spots as Israel during the 1967 Six-Day War, and in 1971 he reported on the war between India and Pakistan. Back in the United Kingdom in 1972, Bierman and his crew were covering what they thought would be an unspectacular demonstration in Londonderry when violence broke out between demonstrators and British soldiers. Now known as Bloody Sunday, the deadly incident was recorded on film only by Bierman and his colleagues because other crews lost their cameras to water cannons. Next, the journalist went to Iran, but was thrown out by the Shah after filming an unflattering documentary of the government there. In 1974, he found himself assigned to the conflict in Cyprus. Becoming enamored by the island, even in wartime, he would return to live there in 1991 after his retirement. Over the years, Bierman gained extensive knowledge of other peoples and countries that he would later draw upon for his acclaimed books. Among his publications are *Righteous Gentile: The Story of Raoul Wallenberg, Missing Hero of the Holocaust* (1981), *Dark Safari: The Life behind the Legend of Henry Morton Stanley* (1990), the co-written *Fire in the Night: Wingate of Burma, Ethiopia, and Zion* (1999), and *The Secret Life of Laszlo Almasy: The Real English Patient* (2005). At the time of his death, he was writing a novel.

OBITUARIES AND OTHER SOURCES:

PERIODICALS

Times (London, England), January 13, 2006, p. 72.

BIERMAN, John David
See BIERMAN, John

*   *   *

BIRDSALL, Jeanne 1952(?)-

PERSONAL: Born c. 1952; married Bill Diehl (a teacher), 1994; children: two stepchildren. *Education:* Attended Boston University, 1969, and California College of Arts and Crafts, 1972.

ADDRESSES: Home—Northampton, MA. *Agent*—Barbara S. Kouts Literary Agency, P.O. Box 560, Bellport, NY 11713.

CAREER: Photographer and children's book author. Also works as a technical writer. *Exhibitions:* Photographs exhibited at R. Michelson Galleries, Northampton, MA, and in permanent collections of Smithsonian Institution and Philadelphia Museum of Art.

AWARDS, HONORS: Booklist Top Ten First Novels for Youth inclusion, *School Library Journal* Best Books designation, and National Book Award for Young People's Literature, all 2005, all for *The Penderwicks.*

WRITINGS:

The Penderwicks: A Summer Tale of Four Sisters, Two Rabbits, and a Very Interesting Boy, Knopf (New York, NY), 2005.

ADAPTATIONS: The Penderwicks was adapted as an audiobook, Listening Library, 2006.

WORK IN PROGRESS: A sequel to *The Penderwicks.*

SIDELIGHTS: Inspired by the classic fantasy novels of Edward Eager and E. Nesbit, Jeanne Birdsall's 2005 book *The Penderwicks: A Summer Tale of Four Sisters, Two Rabbits, and a Very Interesting Boy* was described as "so retro, it's almost radical" by *School Library Journal* interviewer Rick Margolis. The novel surprised many—including its author—when it earned first-time writer Birdsall the National Book Award for Young People's Literature in 2005.

Growing up in Stratford, Pennsylvania, Birdsall had a childhood that was scarred by alcoholism, and reading quickly became a way for her to escape into another world. Her love of children's fantasy has stayed with her throughout her life, although in more recent years she has added Anthony Trollope, the Brontës, Leo Tolstoy, Dorothy Sayers, and other British writers to her list of favorites. Although in her primary career she has excelled at the visual arts and has become well known for her art photography, at age forty-two she decided to fulfill a childhood goal, and channel some creative energy into writing a book that carried on the legacy of Nesbit and Eager. *The Penderwicks* was the result.

Birdsall begins by introducing the Penderwick sisters: twelve-year-old Rosalind, eleven-year-old Skye, ten-year-old Jane, and four-year-old Batty. The widowed Mr. Penderwick—a loving but rather absentminded botany professor—take his daughters and the family dog to a cozy, rented cottage on a country estate called Arundel Hall. With few children living nearby, the girls soon befriend Jeffrey, the lonely son of the hall's upper-crusty owner, Mrs. Tifton. As the summer passes, the children encounter a series of adventures. Jeffrey's doom—to be sent to a dreaded military school—is something to be liberated from, while the usually dependable Rosalind suddenly finds herself doe-eyed over the hall's handsome young gardener. Feisty Skye fights the restrictions placed on the children by the snooty Mrs. Tifton, while Jane narrates the children's activities with a wry yet humorously melodramatic eye.

Praise for *The Penderwicks* was wide-ranging. Many critics acknowledged Birdsall's nod to other famous writers from Louisa May Alcott and Frances Hodgson Burnett to Elizabeth Enright and Lemony Snicket. "Nostalgic but never stale, this fresh, satisfying novel is like a cool breeze on a summer's day," concluded *Horn Book* contributor Carolyn Shute. She describes *The Penderwicks* as "suffused with affectionate humor." In her "timeless tale," Birdsall captures "spirited family dynamics and repartee," wrote a contributor to *Publishers Weekly,* adding that the Penderwick sisters exhibit "delightfully diverse personalities" that "propel the plot." Praising the author's "superb writing style," B. Allison Gray wrote in *School Library Journal* that Birdsall's "wonderful, humorous book . . . features characters whom readers will immediately love," characters who engage in what a *Kirkus Reviews* writer described as "the sorts of lively plots and pastoral pastimes we don't read much about these days."

As critics quickly perceived, her writing openly pays homage to the books she loved as a child: escapist fiction featuring a band of curious children, a daunting challenge, and an everyday world that is transformed by the imagination into a place rife with the possibility of adventure. When she first approached publishers, she was advised to add a strong dose of adolescent strife, and make her story reflect what publishers maintained is demanded by modern readers weaned on so-called "problem novels." Ultimately, her manuscript fell into the hands of a more open-minded editor at Knopf, and *The Penderwicks* was published with only relatively minor changes. As Birdsall explained to Rick Margolis in *School Library Journal,* "People are saying children who lead traumatic lives need books that validate the trauma, and I'm not saying they're wrong. But I also think because it worked so well for me, that there are children who lead difficult lives who need to understand that it doesn't have to be so bad. I also think that there are a lot of children out there who are still leading wonderful lives, and . . . they need to have something to read too."

Working on a sequel to her award-winning novel, Birdsall makes her home in Western Massachusetts, together with her husband and assorted cats, rabbits, a dog, and even a snail. As she remarked of writing in an interview on her home page: "Most authors do work very hard. I know that I do, partly because I write slowly, so I have to write almost every day to make any progress at all. But mostly I work hard because I'm happiest when I'm writing."

BIOGRAPHICAL AND CRITICAL SOURCES:

PERIODICALS

Bulletin of the Center for Children's Books, September, 2005, Timnah Card, review of *The Penderwicks: A Summer Tale of Four Sisters, Two Rabbits, and a Very Interesting Boy,* p. 9.

Horn Book, July-August, 2005, Carolyn Shute, review of *The Penderwicks,* p. 465.

Kirkus Reviews, June 1, 2005, review of *The Penderwicks,* p. 633.

Publishers Weekly, July 25, 2005, review of *The Penderwicks,* p. 77.

School Library Journal, July, 2005, B. Allison Gray, review of *The Penderwicks,* p. 95; January, 2006, Rick Margolis, "Seems Like Old Times" (interview), p. 60.

ONLINE

Boston Globe Online, http://www.boston.com/ (December 12, 2005), David Mehegan, "A Storybook Beginning."

Jeanne Birdsall Home Page, http://www.jeanne birdsall.com (April 26, 2006).

R. Michelson Galleries Web site, http://www. rmichelson.com/ (April 26, 2006), "Jeanne Birdsall."*

* * *

BISKUPIC, Joan 1956-

PERSONAL: Born 1956, in Chicago, IL, married; children: one daughter. *Education:* Marquette University, B.A., 1978; University of Oklahoma, M.A., 1986; Georgetown University, J.D., 1993.

ADDRESSES: Home—Washington, DC. *Office*—USA Today, 7950 Jones Branch Dr., McLean, VA 22108-0605. *E-mail*—jbiskupic@usatoday.com.

CAREER: Tulsa Tribune, Tulsa, OK, bureau chief and reporter, 1985-87; Washington correspondent for a Wisconsin newspaper, 1987-88; *Congressional Quarterly,* legal affairs reporter, 1989-92; *Washington Post,* Washington, DC, Supreme Court reporter, 1992-2000; *USA Today,* McLean, VA, 2000—.

WRITINGS:

The Supreme Court Yearbook: 1989-1990, Congressional Quarterly (Washington, DC), 1990.

The Supreme Court Yearbook: 1990-1991, Congressional Quarterly (Washington, DC), 1991.

(With Elder Witt) *Guide to the U.S. Supreme Court,* 3rd edition, two volumes, Congressional Quarterly (Washington, DC), 1997.

(With Elder Witt) *The Supreme Court and Individual Rights,* 3rd edition, Congressional Quarterly (Washington, DC), 1997.

(With Elder Witt) *The Supreme Court and the Powers of the American Government,* Congressional Quarterly (Washington, DC), 1997.

(With Elder Witt) *The Supreme Court at Work,* 2nd edition, Congressional Quarterly (Washington, DC), 1997.

Sandra Day O'Connor: How the First Woman on the Supreme Court Became Its Most Influential Justice (biography), Ecco (New York, NY), 2005.

SIDELIGHTS: A reporter with years of experience covering the U.S. Supreme Court, Joan Biskupic is the author of the biography *Sandra Day O'Connor: How the First Woman on the Supreme Court Became Its Most Influential Justice.* Published in 2005, the same year that O'Connor announced she would retire, the book has been called a timely work about the first woman to be appointed to the nation's highest court. In what *Booklist* contributor Vanessa Bush described as an "absorbing portrait," Biskupic conducted numerous interviews and researched court documents to describe how the conservative justice, who was selected by President Ronald Reagan in 1981, was influenced by her past and how she, in turn, influenced the Supreme Court. Generally viewed as a moderately conservative justice who resisted expressing her personal views about issues ranging from abortion to the death penalty, O'Connor proved to be a consensus builder between the more right-and left-leaning justices on the court. However, in Biskupic's view, this also made for a justice who became both praiseworthy for her lack of overt idealism and flawed for her general failure to be a bold leader on the bench. On the other hand, the biographer notes that O'Connor became a more confident and influential justice after surviving breast cancer in 1988.

Reviewers of *Sandra Day O'Connor* found that the book has many strong points. For example, Kathleen M. Sullivan, writing in the *Washington Post Book World,* wrote that the author "gives a fascinating account of O'Connor's political astuteness." In addition, Phillip Y. Blue, writing for *Library Journal,* was positive in his assessment, lauding Biskupic for revealing how O'Connor "moved the law—and society—in new directions" in "an insightful biography."

BIOGRAPHICAL AND CRITICAL SOURCES:

PERIODICALS

Booklist, September 1, 1999, Mary Ellen Quinn, review of *Guide to the U.S. Supreme Court,* p. 183; October 1, 2005, Vanessa Bush, review of *Sandra Day O'Connor: How the First Woman on the Supreme Court Became Its Most Influential Justice,* p. 4.

Library Journal, October 15, 2005, Philip Y. Blue, review of *Sandra Day O'Connor,* p. 63.

New York Times Book Review, February 6, 2006, review of *Sandra Day O'Connor,* p. 21.

Publishers Weekly, October 3, 2005, review of *Sandra Day O'Connor,* p. 66.

Washington Post Book World, December 25, 2005, Kathleen M. Sullivan, review of *Sandra Day O'Connor,* p. 3.

*   *   *

BITTLESTONE, Robert 1952-

PERSONAL: Born 1952; married; wife's name Jean; children: four. *Education:* Christ's College, Cambridge University, M.A. *Hobbies and other interests:* Skiing, wind-surfing.

ADDRESSES: Home—Kingston-upon-Thames, England. *Office*—Metapraxis Ltd., Hanover House, Coombe Road, Kingston-upon-Thames, Surrey KT2 7AH, England.

CAREER: Vickers, England, 1973-76; Roneo Vickers, England, head of financial analysis and group information, 1976-78; Metapraxis Ltd., Kingston-upon-Thames, England, founder, managing director, and chairman, 1979—.

MEMBER: Royal Society of Arts, Manufacturers and Commerce.

WRITINGS:

(With James Diggle and John Underhill) *Odysseus Unbound: The Search for Homer's Ithaca,* Cambridge University Press (New York, NY), 2005.

Author of the column *"The Soft Machine"* for *Chief Executive* magazine.

SIDELIGHTS: In *Odysseus Unbound: The Search for Homer's Ithaca,* amateur archeologist Robert Bittlestone and his coauthors, Cambridge University professor James Diggle and University of Edinburgh geographer John Underhill, claim they have discovered that the real Ithaca of Greek legend was not the island of Ithaki, but rather the peninsula of Paliki on the Greek island Cephalonia. Using satellite images to match the physical features of the island to the descriptions in Homer's *Odyssey,* Bittlestone worked with the Hellenic Ministry of Culture and the Institute of Geology and Mineral Exploration in Athens. Besides locating Ithaca, the researchers matched up twenty-five other locations mentioned in the *Odyssey* that are scattered around Paliki.

By profession, Bittlestone is a management consultant and the founder of Metapraxis Ltd.; he combined his business skills with his love of technology to examine various data that led him to new conclusions about the Trojan War. During trips to Greece, he used archeological data, 3-D imaging systems developed by NASA, and newly available geological data to make his discoveries. Bittlestone surmises that over the centuries, earthquakes have changed the landscape somewhat, making Homer's literary descriptions of the area unreliable.

Experts have long claimed that both Odysseus and Ithaca are far from historical fact, yet Bittlestone's discoveries have been enthusiastically received by Greek officials and history buffs alike. "Our purpose has been to demonstrate that there is something both very new and very old to be found at this new location and that we should now treat the existence of ancient Ithaca very seriously," Bittlestone told a reporter for the BBC News. He also declared that the discovery of Ithaca is as important as the 1870s discovery of ancient Troy in modern-day Turkey. Gilbert Taylor, writing in *Booklist,* was impressed by Bittlestone's investigation, which he called "enthralling," and the book's satellite photos, which he called "resplendent." T.L. Cooksey, writing in *Library Journal,* called *Odysseus Unbound* "a fascinating and compelling book." Michael Bywater, reviewing the book for the London *Telegraph,* was impressed with the authors' theories and evidence, yet retained a pragmatically critical eye regarding their conclusions. "The real Ithaca, if Ithaca ever was 'real'—emerges, recedes, relocates, proves impossible, proves magically possible, proves, finally, almost uncannily plausible, thanks to the Earth's own almost magical fluidity, its ability to rise, fall, shift and change shape."

BIOGRAPHICAL AND CRITICAL SOURCES:

PERIODICALS

Booklist, December 1, 2005, Gilbert Taylor, review of *Odysseus Unbound: The Search for Homer's Ithaca,* p. 13.
Charleston Post & Courier, January 8, 2006, Jeff Johnson, review of *Odysseus Unbound.*
Library Journal, October 15, 2005, T.L. Cooksey, review of *Odysseus Unbound,* p. 56.
Telegraph (London, England), October 10, 2005, Michael Bywater, review of *Odysseus Unbound.*

ONLINE

BBC News Web site, http://news.bbc.co.uk/ (February 24, 2006), "Search 'Locates' Homer's Ithaca."
MSNBC Web site, http://msmbc.msn.com/ (September 30, 2005), "Has *Odyssey* Hero's Land Been Found?"
Odysseus Unbound Web site, http://www.odysseus-unbound.org (February 24, 2006).*

*   *   *

BLAIR, Alison
    See LERANGIS, Peter

*   *   *

BLAIR, Steven N. 1939-
    (Steven Noel Blair)

PERSONAL: Born July 4, 1939, in Mankato, KS; son of Bernard (a farmer) and Wilma (a homemaker) Blair; married Jane Marie Pottberg (a psychologist),

April 10, 1965; children: Max Earl, Ann Marie Blair Kennedy. *Education:* Kansas Wesleyan University, B.A., 1962; Indiana University, M.S., 1965, P.E.D., 1968; Stanford University, postdoctoral studies in medicine, 1980. *Hobbies and other interests:* Gardening, jogging, theater.

ADDRESSES: Home—9316 Windycrest Dr., Dallas, TX 75243. *Office*—Cooper Institute for Aerobics Research, 12330 Preston Rd., Dallas, TX 75230; fax: 214-458-1675. *E-mail*—sblair@cooperinst.org.

CAREER: Kansas Wesleyan University, Salina, instructor in physical education and athletic coach, 1962-63; University of South Carolina, Columbia, from instructor to professor, 1966-84, founder and director of Human Performance Laboratory, 1966-78, adjunct professor of epidemiology and biostatistics, 1989—; Cooper Institute for Aerobics Research, Dallas, TX, director of epidemiology and clinical applications and director of research, 1980-2002, president and chief executive officer, 2002—. University of Texas Health Science Center, Houston, adjunct professor of epidemiology, 1989—; University of North Texas, Denton, adjunct professor at Academy for Research and Development, 1996—; University of Houston, TX, adjunct professor, 1998—.

Member of editorial board, *Exercise and Sport Sciences Reviews,* 1987-98, *Medicine and Science in Sports and Exercise,* 1988—, *Clinical Journal of Sports Medicine,* 1989—, *Current Issues in Exercise Science,* 1989—, *American Journal of Human Biology,* 1994—, *Biological and Pedagogical Problems of Physical Education and Sport,* 1995-98, *British Journal of Sports Medicine,* 1996-97, *Frontiers in Bioscience,* 1996-98, *American Journal of Medicine & Sports,* 2001—, and *Current Sports Medicine Reports,* 2002—; member of advisory board, *Medicine, Exercise, Nutrition, and Health,* 1991-97. University of Bristol, Bristol, England, Benjamin Meaker fellow, 2001. American College of Sports Medicine, member of board of trustees, 1981-84, vice president, 1990-92, president-elect, 1995-96, president, 1996-97. Member of council on nutrition, physical activity, and metabolism and of council on epidemiology, American Heart Association; member, American College of Epidemiology.

MEMBER: North American Association for the Study of Obesity, American Association for the Advancement of Science, American Public Health Association,

Society for Epidemiologic Research, American Epidemiological Society, Society for Behavioral Medicine, Human Biology Council, Society for Clinical Trials, American Academy of Kinesiology and Physical Education (president, 1994-95), American Alliance for Health, Physical Education, Recreation and Dance.

AWARDS, HONORS: South Carolina Scholar Award, American Alliance for Health, Physical Education, Recreation and Dance (AAHPERD), 1981; Health Educator of the Year Award, South Carolina Association for Health Education, 1982; Honor Award, AAHPERD, 1988; Distinguished Alumni Award, Wesleyan University, 1989; Scholar Award, AAHPERD (southern district), 1989-90; Honor Award, AAHPERD, 1991; W.W. Patty Distinguished Alumni Award, Indiana University, 1992; Scholar Award, AAHPERD, 1993-94; Wellner Distinguished Scholar, Frostburg State University, 1994; Citation Award, American College of Sports Medicine, 1994; R. Tait McKenzie Recognition Award, AAHPERD, 1995; distinguished scholar award, University of Memphis, 1995; named Healthy American Fitness Leader, 1995; Person of the Year, International Health, Racquet & Sportsclub Association (IHRSA), 1996; IDEA Lifetime Achievement Award, 1996; Gold Medal, International Council of Sports Science and Physical Education, 1996; Surgeon General's Medallion, 1996; Honor Award, Texas Regional Chapter, American College of Sports Medicine, 1997; Presidential Citation, AAHPERD, 1997; Award for Meritorious Achievement, American Heart Association, 1998; Lansdowne Scholar, University of Victoria (Canada), 1997; William G. Anderson Commemorative Award, 1998; named honorary member of the Order of the Horse Collar Knights of Kuopio University, 2001; Outstanding Service Award, Texas Health, IHRSA, 2001. D.H.C., Free University of Brussels, 1994; D.H.S., Lander University, 1996; D.Sc., Bristol University. Fellowships from American College of Epidemiology, American Epidemiological Society, American Heart Association, American College of Sports Medicine, American Academy of Kinesiology and Physical Education, Society of Behavioral Medicine, and North American Association for the Study of Obesity.

WRITINGS:

(Editor, with others) *Resource Manual for Guidelines for Exercise Testing and Prescription,* Lea & Febiger (Philadelphia, PA), 1988.

Living with Exercise, American Health (Dallas, TX), 1991.

(With others) *The LifeStyle Counselor's Guide for Weight Control,* edited by Brenda L. Wolfe, American Health (Dallas, TX), 1996.

(With Walter H. Ettinger, Jr., and Brenda S. Mitchell) *Fitness after 50: It's Never Too Late to Start!,* Beverly Cracom Publications (St. Louis, MO), 1996.

(With others) *Active Living Every Day: 20 Weeks to Lifelong Vitality,* Human Kinetics (Champaign, IL), 2001.

Contributor to numerous books and professional journals. Associate editor, *American Journal of Health Promotion,* 1986-99, and *American Journal of Epidemiology,* 1991-97.

SIDELIGHTS: An expert on diet and exercise, Steven N. Blair is a researcher and teacher who also has a background in epidemiology. One of the most significant epidemics that has become a vital issue in the United States in recent years is obesity. The sedentary lifestyle of most Americans, along with poor diet and stressful jobs, has made this a nation where the majority of people may be classified obese. For many years, obesity has been determined by the body mass index (BMI), a measurement that takes into account both weight and height. However, in his writings, Blair has asserted that simply plugging weight and height into a formula does not result in an accurate assessment of fitness. He weighs close to two hundred pounds and is only five feet, four inches tall; however, Blair runs four miles a day and has been deemed very fit by his physician. What is most important, insists Blair, is participating in a reasonable amount of activity daily, resulting in a sound heart rate and good blood circulation, among other benefits. Moreover, as he explains in such books as *Active Living Every Day: 20 Weeks to Lifelong Vitality,* a person need not endure intense weight training and aerobic exercise to achieve fitness. Instead, moderate exercise, including walking at a brisk pace for thirty minutes a day, is enough to add years to a person's life.

In research studies that Blair has conducted, he found "that about fifty percent of the obese people in his studies were fit," according to a *Jet* article. "There is a misdirected obsession with weight and weight loss," Blair stated in the article. "The focus is all wrong. It's fitness that is the key."

BIOGRAPHICAL AND CRITICAL SOURCES:

PERIODICALS

Dallas Morning News, August 30, 1999, Laura Beil, "Fatness vs. Fitness: Fatness, Fitness Can Co-exist," p. F1.

Internal Medicine News, October 1, 2004, Kate Johnson, "Emphasize Fitness over Weight Loss, Expert Says," interview with Steven N. Blair, p. 20.

Jet, November 26, 2001, "Heavy Can Mean Healthy If You're Active," p. 14.

Journal of the American Dietetic Association, April, 2003, review of *Active Living Every Day: 20 Weeks to Lifelong Vitality,* p. 526.

Library Journal, May 1, 2002, Susan B. Hagloch, review of *Active Living Every Day,* p. S4.

Nutrition Action Healthletter, December, 1993, David Schardt, "These Feet Were Made for Walking," interview with Steven N. Blair, p. 1.

People, December 2, 2002, "He Ain't Heavy: Fat but Fit? Researcher Steve Blair Says It's Possible, and He's Got the Data—and the Biceps—to Prove It," p. 199.

ONLINE

Cooper Institute Web site, http://www.cooperinst.org/ (January 16, 2006), biography of Steven N. Blair.*

*   *   *

BLAIR, Steven Noel
See BLAIR, Steven N.

*   *   *

BLANCHARD, Melinda

PERSONAL: Married Robert Blanchard (a restaurateur, businessman, and carpenter); children: Jesse.

ADDRESSES: *Office*—Blanchard's Restaurant, P.O. Box 898, Meads Bay, Anguilla, British West Indies; fax: 264-497-6161. *E-mail*—blanchards@lwyl.com.

CAREER: Restaurateur and businessperson. Owner, with husband, Robert Blanchard, of Blanchard's Restaurant, Anguilla, British West Indies. Host, with Robert Blanchard, of television shows for the Fine Living Network and Public Broadcasting Service.

AWARDS, HONORS: Blanchard's Restaurant received the Best in Caribbean Award.

WRITINGS:

WITH ROBERT BLANCHARD

A Trip to the Beach: Living on Island Time in the Caribbean (memoir), Clarkson Potter (New York, NY), 2000.

At Blanchard's Table: A Trip to the Beach Cookbook, photographs by Ben Fink, Clarkson Potter (New York, NY), 2003.

Cook What You Love: Simple Flavorful Recipes to Make Again and Again, photographs by Ellen Silverman, Clarkson Potter (New York, NY), 2005.

Live What You Love: Notes from an Unusual Life (memoir), Sterling Publishing (New York, NY), 2005.

ADAPTATIONS: Books adapted to audio include *A Trip to the Beach,* Brilliance Audio, 2000.

SIDELIGHTS: Melinda and Robert Blanchard met in college, and together they began their first business in Norwich, Vermont, where they developed a successful line of specialty foods and kitchen items under the name of Blanchard & Blanchard & Son. They followed their dream and opened a restaurant in Anguilla, British West Indies, which was destroyed in 1995 by Hurricane Luis, rebuilt and eventually became a four-star restaurant that is frequented by celebrities. It has been named the Best in the Caribbean and recognized by *Wine Spectator* for its extensive wine cellar.

The Blanchards wrote and sold their first book, *A Trip to the Beach: Living on Island Time in the Caribbean,* with the help of a literary agent who dined at their restaurant. It is a memoir of how they made the decision to open it, as well as the steps taken to begin, including locating suppliers and obtaining permits and dealing with red tape and bureaucracy. They had sold their specialty foods business, but what they had perceived as a stress-free island life soon became hectic as they imported building materials and equipment for the kitchen from the United States, created a menu, and trained staff. When after six years on the island they became homesick for Vermont, they taught their staff to run the restaurant during the off-season so that they could divide their time between their old home and their new one.

In an interview with *Yankee* contributor Amy Traverso, Melinda Blanchard said that "we missed just going to a movie or having Chinese food. We contemplated selling the business and moving on. Only we couldn't quite do it. Part of it is the people down there. They're not just employees. They've become central to our whole existence." In their memoir, the Blanchards include recipes, along with a description of life in Anguilla and the people who live there. *Library Journal* reviewer Alison Hopkins called the book "absorbing and well written."

In their cookbook *At Blanchard's Table: A Trip to the Beach Cookbook,* the Blanchards include such recipes as Vermont Cheddar Soup, Potato Salad with Lime and Sun-Dried Tomatoes, and Island Rice with Cumin and Coconut. Included are photographs of the island and the staff. A *Publishers Weekly* reviewer wrote that they "successfully blend New England practicality with the generosity and warmth of the islands."

The Blanchards wrote *Live What You Love: Notes from an Unusual Life,* in which they explain that "if we don't love it, we don't do it." They provide intimate details of their lives that will inspire readers who seek fulfillment and success. *Booklist* contributor Margaret Flanagan wrote that this book "will appeal to fans of inspirational literature."

BIOGRAPHICAL AND CRITICAL SOURCES:

BOOKS

Blanchard, Melinda, and Robert Blanchard, *A Trip to the Beach: Living on Island Time in the Caribbean,* Clarkson Potter (New York, NY), 2000.
Blanchard, Melinda, and Robert Blanchard, *Live What You Love: Notes from an Unusual Life,* Sterling Publishing (New York, NY), 2005.

PERIODICALS

Booklist, September 1, 2000, Brad Hooper, review of *A Trip to the Beach,* p. 58; November 1, 2005, Margaret Flanagan, review of *Live What You Love,* p. 15.
Entertainment Weekly, December 1, 2000, Daneet Steffens, review of *A Trip to the Beach,* p. 92.
Library Journal, September 1, 2000, Alison Hopkins, review of *A Trip to the Beach,* p. 238; February 15, 2003, Judith Sutton, review of *At Blanchard's Table: A Trip to the Beach Cookbook,* p. 164; September 1, 2005, Wendy Lee, review of *Live What You Love,* p. 163.
People, January 8, 2001, Kim Hubbard, review of *A Trip to the Beach,* p. 39.
Publishers Weekly, September 4, 2000, review of *A Trip to the Beach,* p. 94; January 6, 2003, review of *At Blanchard's Table,* p. 56.
Yankee, October, 2004, Amy Traverso, "From the Farm to the Islands" (interview) p. 95.

ONLINE

Blanchard's Restaurant Web site, http://www.blanchardsrestaurant.com (March 5, 2006).
Live What You Love Web site, http://www.livewhatyoulove.com (March 5, 2006).
Random House Web site, http://www.randomhouse.com/ (March 5, 2006), brief biography of authors.*

*   *   *

BLEVINS, Meredith

PERSONAL: Born in CA; married Win Blevins (a writer); children. *Education:* Attended several colleges in California. *Hobbies and other interests:* Recording music, tarot, spending time with family.

ADDRESSES: Home—UT. *Agent*—c/o Author Mail, Forge, 175 5th Ave., New York, NY, 10010. *E-mail*—meredith@meredithblevins.com.

CAREER: Writer and music therapist. Santa Rosa Junior College Community Services Department, Santa Rosa, CA, music therapist and founder of intergenerational program. Also held various jobs such as marketing for the food industry, writing financial columns, and lecturing on business to nonprofit farm organizations, food packing associations, and University of California extension programs.

MEMBER: American Association of Business Journalists.

WRITINGS:

ANNIE SZABO MYSTERIES

The Hummingbird Wizard, Forge (New York, NY), 2003.
The Vanished Priestess, Forge (New York, NY), 2004.
The Red Hot Empress, Forge (New York, NY), 2005.

SIDELIGHTS: When Meredith Blevins was growing up, all she wanted was to run off and become a Gypsy. Instead, she took the more common path of working, playing music, and raising a family. She never lost her fascination with the Gypsies, however, and incorporates that interest in her "Annie Szabo Mysteries." The first book in the series, *The Hummingbird Wizard,* introduces us to Annie Szabo, the widow of a Gypsy. When her oldest friend, a man who was married to Annie's sister-in-law, is murdered, she decides to investigate with the help of her colorful mother-in-law, Mina. Rex E. Klett, writing in a *Library Journal* review, applauded the story's "riveting characters, great plot, and insights into Gypsy culture." A *Publishers Weekly* contributor concurred, noting that the "fascinating gypsy lore, unforgettable characters and a wicked sense of humor distinguish Blevins's highly unusual mystery debut."

Blevins followed her successful first effort with *The Vanished Priestess.* This second novel in the series finds Annie's daughter and grandson coming to stay with her in an attempt to escape from Annie's abusive son-in-law, who comes looking for them shortly after their arrival. Meanwhile, a circus to support battered women opens in the yard next door, and when a murder occurs at the circus, Annie attempts to solve the crime. Klett, again writing in a *Library Journal* review, praised the book's "wild story, wonderful wit, and great characters." A *Publishers Weekly* contributor, however, was less satisfied, calling the book "uneven."

The third installment in the series, *The Red Hot Empress,* centers around Jimmy Qi, an Asian boy whose musical talent has healing powers. At the urging of Mina, Annie writes a newspaper feature about the boy, raising interest in Jimmy's music while simultaneously causing him trouble. Two suspicious-looking deaths cause Annie and Jimmy to hide from people who are only concerned with using Jimmy's abilities for their various causes. A *Publishers Weekly* reviewer praised the book, noting that it blends "humor, zany characters and the occult into an entertaining story with serious undertones." A contributor to *Kirkus Reviews* agreed, observing that while "at times the wackiness is forced," *The Red Hot Empress* "will have you howling, and everyone will want to adopt Jimmy."

BIOGRAPHICAL AND CRITICAL SOURCES:

PERIODICALS

Kirkus Reviews, August 15, 2003, review of *The Hummingbird Wizard,* p. 1046; July 1, 2005, review of *The Red Hot Empress,* p. 710.
Library Journal, August, 2003, Rex E. Klett, review of *The Hummingbird Wizard,* p. 138; October 1, 2004, Rex E. Klett, review of *The Vanished Priestess,* p. 62.
Publishers Weekly, August 4, 2003, review of *The Hummingbird Wizard,* p. 58; September 13, 2004, review of *The Vanished Priestess,* p. 62; July 25, 2005, review of *The Red Hot Empress,* p. 52.

ONLINE

Agony Column Book Reviews and Commentary, http://trashotron.com/ (March 17, 2006), review of *The Hummingbird Wizard.*
AllReaders.com, http://www.allreaders.com/ (March 17, 2006), reviews of the author's works.
Meredith Blevins Home Page, http://www.meredithblevins.com (March 19, 2006).
Reviewing the Evidence, http://www.reviewingtheevidence.com/ (March 17, 2006), review of *The Red Hot Empress.**

* * *

BO, Zhiyue 1958-

PERSONAL: Born May 11, 1958, in Taiyuan, Shanxi, China; immigrated to the United States, 1990; son of Tingxiang (a doctor of Chinese medicine) and Shaoqing (a doctor of Chinese medicine; maiden name,

Zhang) Bo; married Yan Dong (a computer programmer), 1987; children: Lin (son). *Ethnicity:* "Chinese." *Education:* Peking University, B.Law, 1985, M.Law, 1989; American University, doctoral study, 1990-91; University of Chicago, Ph.D., 1995.

ADDRESSES: Home—1006 W. Loyola, Apt. 2, Chicago, IL 60626. *Office*—Department of International Studies, St. John Fisher College, 3690 East Ave., Rochester, NY 14618; fax: 585-385-7311. *E-mail*—zbo@sjfc.edu.

CAREER: Beijing Nonferrous Metals Corp., Beijing, China, instructor in English, 1985-88; Peking University, Beijing, assistant professor, 1988-90; Roosevelt University, Chicago, IL, instructor, 1993-94, visiting assistant professor, 1995-96; Urban Innovation Analysis, Chicago, research director and postdoctoral fellow, 1996-98; St. John Fisher College, Rochester, NY, assistant professor of international studies and department chair, 1998-2003, associate professor and department chair of international studies, 2004—. Tarleton State University, Stephenville, TX, Joe and Teresa Long Endowed Chair in Social Science, 2005; Rochester Institute of Technology, research fellow at Center for International Business and Economic Growth, 2003; National University of Singapore, visiting research fellow at East Asian Institute, 2004; St. John Fisher College, trustees' distinguished scholar, 2004. American University, assistant professor and director of World Capitals Program in Beijing, China, 1997-98; University of Chicago, lecturer, 1997-98; guest speaker at other institutions, including Beijing Academy of Social Sciences, Harvard University, Columbia University, University of Chicago, and Tsinghua University; workshop presenter. International business consultant with International Orientation Resources, 1995—, Prudential Relocation Intercultural Services, 1995—, and Bennett and Associates, 1995-98.

MEMBER: American Political Science Association, Association for Asian Studies, Association of Chinese Political Studies (board member, 2002—), Midwest Political Science Association.

WRITINGS:

(Translator from the English) Morton A. Kaplan, *Guojizhengzhi de Xitong he Guocheng* (title means "System and Process in International Politics"), Zhongguo Renmin Gongandaxue Chubanshi (Beijing, China), 1989.

Chinese Provincial Leaders: Economic Performance and Political Mobility since 1949, M.E. Sharpe (Armonk, NY), 2002.
The History of Modern China, Mason Crest Publishers (Philadelphia, PA), 2004.

Contributor to books, including *The New Political Culture,* edited by Terry Nicholas Clark and Vincent Hoffmann-Martinot, Westview Press (Boulder, CO), 1998; *China's Leadership in the Twenty-first Century: The Rise of the Fourth Generation,* edited by David M. Finkelstein and Maryanne Kivlehan, M.E. Sharpe (Armonk, NY), 2003; and *Holding China Together,* edited by Barry Naughton and Dali Yang, Cambridge University Press (New York, NY), 2004. Contributor to periodicals, including *Provincial China, Chinese Social Sciences Review, Asian Profile,* and *Issues and Studies.* Guest editor and translator, *Chinese Law and Government,* 1999-2002, and *Journal of Contemporary China,* 2000; member of editorial advisory board, *Journal of Chinese Political Science,* 2003—.

WORK IN PROGRESS: Leaders and Institutions in Chinese Politics: From Mao Zedong to Hu Jintao; Who's Who in China: Provincial Leaders, 1949-2003.

SIDELIGHTS: Zhiyue Bo told *CA:* "Writing is essential for me because, through writing, I am telling people of different places and different times who I am. My favorite advice to my students in a writing class is: put the best of you into writing. I always remind them of eternal values of writing. In one hundred years, all of us will be gone, but our writings will remain if they are good enough to be published.

"My work has been influenced by leading scholars in the field of China studies such as William Parish, Joseph Fewsmith, Frederick C. Teiwes, David S.G. Goodman, Yasheng Huang, and Cheng Li.

"Writing is an ongoing process. It works 24/7. Starting a rough outline on scratch paper, I try to write as much as I can on a daily basis. Because I am thinking about my writing projects all the time, I often wake up with great ideas.

"I became interested in China studies when I was a doctoral student at the University of Chicago. Other scholars have studied provincial leaders in China, but none of them systematically dealt with the political mobility of China's provincial leaders. In order to fill this intellectual gap, I collected information on all provincial leaders in China since 1949 and applied the most sophisticated statistical models in my analysis. The book *Chinese Provincial Leaders: Economic Performance and Political Mobility since 1949* represents the most systematic, most comprehensive, and most sophisticated statistical analysis of these leaders. My research on China's provincial leaders has been widely cited by scholars of China studies from Australia, Hong Kong, South Korea, Singapore, France, Sweden, Germany, and the United States.

"I was born and grew up in Taiyuan, Shanxi province, China. In my early years, China had almost no contact with western countries. I learned Russian as my first foreign language at middle school. In order to take the college entrance examination, I taught myself English at the age of twenty-two and was subsequently admitted into the best university of the country: Beijing University. Upon graduation, I taught English to college students and corporate employees for three years. I began writing in English when I came to the United States in 1990."

BIOGRAPHICAL AND CRITICAL SOURCES:

PERIODICALS

Asian Studies Review, March, 2002, David S.G. Goodman, review of *Chinese Provincial Leaders: Economic Performance and Political Mobility since 1949,* pp. 99-100.
China Perspectives, March-April, 2004, Stephanie Balme, review of *Chinese Provincial Leaders,* pp. 166-168.
China Review, spring, 2003, Andrew Wedeman, review of *Chinese Provincial Leaders,* pp. 166-168.
China Review International, fall, 2002, Robert E. Gamer, review of *Chinese Provincial Leaders,* p. 366.

*   *   *

BOARDMAN, Alonzo
See WAGNER, Ralph D.

BOWEN, Mark
(Mark Stander Bowen)

PERSONAL: Male. *Education:* Massachusetts Institute of Technology, Ph.D. *Hobbies and other interests:* Mountain climbing.

ADDRESSES: Agent—Jessica Firger, Associate Publicist, Henry Holt and Company, 175 1st Ave., New York, NY 10010. *E-mail*—thinice@mark-bowen. com.

CAREER: Magazine journalist and photographer.

WRITINGS:

Thin Ice: Unlocking the Secrets of Climate in the World's Highest Mountains, Henry Holt (New York, NY), 2005.

Contributor to periodicals, including *Natural History* and *Climbing.*

SIDELIGHTS: After graduating from the Massachusetts Institute of Technology with a doctorate in physics, Mark Bowen became a magazine journalist and continued to pursue a love of mountaineering. Combining all three of his skills—writing, science, and climbing—he went on assignment to cover the story of Lonnie Thompson, an Ohio State University professor who was conducting research atop some of the world's tallest peaks. It is Thompson's contention that the strongest evidence for global warming can be found by taking samples from the snowy caps of mountains near the earth's equator. Bowen accompanied the scientist to expeditions above 18,000 feet on Mt. Kilimanjaro in Africa and Nevado Sajama in the Andes. He relates his experiences in his first book, *Thin Ice: Unlocking the Secrets of Climate in the World's Highest Mountains,* which also includes a history of climatology and information on the growing international debate on global warming. Mixed in with the more scientific details are Bowen's descriptions of the harrowing work involved in climbing mountains in a rarified atmosphere and bitter-cold conditions. Gloria Maxwell, writing in *Library Journal,* called *Thin Ice* "a gripping adventure tale," while *Mother Jones* contributor Elizabeth Gettelman maintained that the work "should correct the notion that climatologists are just number-crunching geeks." Not only is *Thin Ice* an exciting narrative, according to these critics, but a *Publishers Weekly* writer added that it "should be read by everyone concerned about the future of our planet" because of the convincing evidence it offers about what is happening to the earth's climate.

BIOGRAPHICAL AND CRITICAL SOURCES:

PERIODICALS

Booklist, September 1, 2005, George Cohen, review of *Thin Ice: Unlocking the Secrets of Climate in the World's Highest Mountains,* p. 33.
Kirkus Reviews, September 1, 2005, review of *Thin Ice,* p. 950.
Library Journal, October 1, 2005, Gloria Maxwell, review of *Thin Ice,* p. 104.
Mother Jones, November, 2005, Elizabeth Gettelman, review of *Thin Ice,* p. 86.
Publishers Weekly, August 8, 2005, review of *Thin Ice,* p. 220.
Science News, November 12, 2005, review of *Thin Ice,* p. 319.
Washington Post Book World, November 20, 2005, David Laskin, "The Great Meltdown," review of *Thin Ice,* p. 9.

ONLINE

Mark Bowen Home Page, http://www.mark-bowen.com (January 19, 2006).*

*   *   *

BOWEN, Mark Stander
   See BOWEN, Mark

*   *   *

BOZÓKI, András 1959-
   (Andras Bozoki)

PERSONAL: Born January 23, 1959, in Budapest, Hungary; son of Béla (an engineer) and Margit (an artist; maiden name, Baranyi) Bozóki; married Bernadette Czike (a psychologist), 1983; children: Bence,

Marcell, Raphaël. *Ethnicity:* "Hungarian." *Education:* Attended Eötvös University; Hungarian Academy of Sciences, Ph.D.

ADDRESSES: Office—1051 Budapest Nádor U.G., Hungary. *E-mail*—bozokia@ceu.hu.

CAREER: Eötvös University, Budapest, Hungary, assistant professor, 1983-93; Central European University, Budapest, associate professor, 1993—; Columbia University, New York, NY, visiting professor, 2004. Political advisor to the prime minister of Hungary, 2003-04; spokesperson for a democratic opposition party in Hungary, 1990. *Military service:* Served 1977-78.

MEMBER: International Political Science Association, Hungarian Political Science Association (chairman).

AWARDS, HONORS: Ferenc Erdei Prize, 1991; Hungarian Pulitzer Prize, 1993.

WRITINGS:

IN ENGLISH TRANSLATION

(Editor, with James Bak and Miklos Sukosd) *Liberty and Socialism,* Rowman & Littlefield (Lanham, MD), 1991.
(Editor, with Andras Korosenyi and George Schopflin, and contributor) *Post-Communist Transition: Emerging Pluralism in Hungary,* St. Martin's Press (New York, NY), 1992.
(Editor and contributor) *Democratic Legitimacy in Post-Communist Societies,* T-Twins Publishing House (Budapest, Hungary), 1994.
(Associate editor, with Bela K. Kiraly, and contributor) *Lawful Revolution in Hungary, 1989-1994,* Columbia University Press (New York, NY), 1994.
(Editor and contributor) *Intellectuals and Politics in Central Europe,* Central European University Press (Budapest, Hungary), 1999.
(Editor and contributor) *The Roundtable Talks of 1989: The Genesis of Hungarian Democracy,* Central European University Press (Budapest, Hungary), 2002.

(Editor, with John Ishiyama, and contributor) *The Communist Successor Parties of Central and Eastern Europe,* M.E. Sharpe (Armonk, NY), 2002.

(With Barbara Bősze) *Migrants, Minorities, Belonging, and Citizenship: The Case of Hungary,* Bric (Bergen, Norway), 2004.

(With Dario Castiglione, Philippe C. Schmitter, Alexandre Trechsel, and others) *The Future of Democracy in Europe: Trends Analyses, and Reforms,* Council of Europe Press (Strasbourg, France), 2004.

OTHER

(Editor) *A Szép Szó, 1936-39,* Kossuth-Magvetö (Budapest, Hungary), 1987.

(Editor, with Tamas Csapodt, Ervin Csizmadia, and Miklos Sukosd, and contributor) *Csendes? Forradalom? Volt?* (title means "Was It a Silent Revolution?"), T-Twins Publishing House (Budapest, Hungary), 1991.

(With Gabor Peli) *Társadalomismeret* (textbook; title means "Social Knowledge"), Tankönyvkiadó (Budapest, Hungary), 1991, 2nd edition, Nemzeti Tankönyvkiadó (Budapest, Hungary), 1995.

(Editor, with Miklos Sukosd, and contributor) *Anarchizmus* (title means "Anarchism"), Századvég (Budapest, Hungary), 1991.

(Editor, with Gabor Nagy) *Vannak-e emberi jogaik? A színesbörü diákok helyzete a fövárosban és a skinhead-jelenség* (title means "Do They Have Human Rights? The Situation of Black Students in Budapest and the Skinhead Phenomenon"), Budapest City Council (Budapest, Hungary), 1992.

(Editor) *Zsolt Béla: A végzetes toll* (title means "The Fatal Pen: From the Political Journalism of Béla Zsolt"), Századvég-Nyilvánosság Klub (Budapest, Hungary), 1992.

(Editor and contributor) *A Fidesz a magyar politikában 1988-1991* (title means "The Federation of Young Democrats in Hungarian Politics, 1988-1991"), Fidesz (Budapest, Hungary), 1992.

(With Agnes Heller and Ferenc Feher) *Polgárosodás, civil társadalom és demokrácia* (title means "'Embourgeoisement,' Civil Society, and Democracy"), MTA Politikai Tudományok Intézete (Budapest, Hungary), 1993.

(Editor, with Laszlo Seres and Miklos Sukosd, and contributor) *Anarchizmus ma* (title means "Contemporary Anarchist Thought"), T-Twins Publishing House (Budapest, Hungary), 1994.

(With Miklos Sukosd) *Az anarchizmus elmélete és magyarországi története* (title means "The Theory of Anarchism and Its History in Hungary"), Cserépfalvi (Budapest, Hungary), 1994.

Konfrontáció és konszenzus: a demokratizálás stratégiái (title means "Confrontation and Consensus: Strategies for Democratization"), Savaria University Press (Szombathely, Hungary), 1995.

Magyar panoptikum (title means "Hungarian Waxworks,"), KáVé (Budapest, Hungary), 1996.

(Editor and contributor) Paul Ignotus, *Vissza az értelemhez* (political essays; title means "Back to Reason"), Új Mandátum (Budapest, Hungary), 1997, 2nd edition, 1998.

(With Istvan Javorniczky and Istvan Stumpf) *Magyar politikusi arcképscarnok* (title means "Portraits of Hungarian Political Leaders"), Századvég (Budapest, Hungary), 1998.

(Editor, with Miklos Sukosd) *Magyar anarchizmus* (title means "Hungarian Anarchism,"), Balassi (Budapest, Hungary), 1998.

(Editor in chief) *A rendszerváltás forgatókönyve: kerekasztal-tárgyálasok 1989-ben* (title means "The Script of the Regime Change: The Minutes of the Hungarian Roundtable Negotiations in 1989"), Volumes 1-4, Magvetö (Budapest, Hungary), 1999, Volume 8 (with Marta Elbert) published as *Portrék és életrajzok: A rendszerváltás forgatókönyve* (title means "Portraits and Biographies: The Script of the Regime Change,"), Új Mandátum (Budapest, Hungary), 1999, Volumes 5-6 (with Marta Elbert and Zoltan Ripp), Új Mandátum (Budapest, Hungary), 2000, Volume 7 (editor and contributor) published as *Alkotmányos forraldalom: A rendszerváltás forgatókönyve* (title means "Constitutional Revolution: The Script of the Regime Change"), Új Mandátum (Budapest, Hungary), 2000.

Ignotus Pál, Új Mandátum (Budapest, Hungary), 2003.

Politikai pluralizmus Magyarországon, 1987-2002 (title means "Political Pluralism in Hungary, 1987-2002"), Századvég (Budapest, Hungary), 2003.

Contributor to periodicals. Founder and editor, *Hungarian Political Science Review;* founder, *Magyar Narancs* (weekly magazine).

SIDELIGHTS: András Bozóki told *CA:* "I already wanted a typewriter as a Christmas present from my parents at the age of nine. I enjoyed reading a lot of novels in my teenage years and started to write political essays and journalistic articles during my university years. At that time Hungary was not a free country, so I had no chance to be a publicist, so I decided to be a scholar in the social sciences. Politically I was influenced by the then emerging underground democratic opposition, and especially by the regime change and transition to democracy in 1989 and 1990. George Orwell, Arthur Koestler, Iván Szelényi, Miklós Szabó, Alexis de Tocqueville, and anarchist writers influenced me strongly.

"My interest in politics and society was shaped by history, and particularly certain historical events such as the Polish Solidarity Movement in 1980-81, the collapse of communism in central and eastern Europe in 1989-91, contemporary issues of war and peace, and the processes of democratization."

BIOGRAPHICAL AND CRITICAL SOURCES:

PERIODICALS

Sociology, May, 1994, Emanuela Todeva, review of *Post-Communist Transition: Emerging Pluralism in Hungary,* p. 622.

*   *   *

BOZOKI, Andras
    See BOZÓKI, András

*   *   *

BRISVILLE, Jean-Claude 1922-
    (Jean-Claude Gabriel Brisville)

PERSONAL: Born May 28, 1922, in Bois-Colombes/Hautes-de-Seine, France; son of Maurice and Geneviève (Gineste) Brisville; married second wife, Irène Kalaschnikowa, 1963; children: (first marriage) one son, one daughter. *Education:* Attended Lycée Jacques Decour, Paris, France.

ADDRESSES: Agent—c/o Author Mail, Éditions Stock, 31 rue de Fleurus, 75006 Paris, France.

CAREER: Reader for Hachette (publishing house), 1951-58; personal secretary to Albert Camus, 1957-58; Julliard (publishing house), Paris, France, deputy literary director, 1959-64, literary director, 1964-70; ORTF, head of drama video section, 1971-75; Livre de Poche (publishing house), literary director, 1976-81.

AWARDS, HONORS: Prix Sainte-Beuve, for *D'un amour;* Prix Ibsen and Prix de la Meilleure Création Dramatique, both for *Le Fauteuil à bascule;* Prix du Théâtre, Academie Française, for *Le souper;* Chevalier Légion d'Honneur; Chevalier des Arts et des Lettres; Prix du Théâtre de la Société des Auteurs et Compositeurs Dramatiques, SACD.

WRITINGS:

A la rencontre de Julien Green, La Sixaine (Brussels, Belgium), 1947.
Prologue (novel), Julliard (Paris, France), 1948.
La présence réelle, Gallimard (Paris, France), 1954.
D'un amour, Gallimard (Paris, France), 1954, reprinted, Stock (Paris, France), 1993.
Saint-Just (three-act play), Grasset (Paris, France), 1955.
Camus, Gallimard (Paris, France), 1959.
La fuite au Danemark (novel), R. Julliard (Paris, France), 1962.
Le rôdeur (three plays), Gallimard (Paris, France), 1970.
Un hiver dans la vie de Gros Ours (for children), illustrated by Danièle Bour, Grasset (Paris, France), 1973, new edition, 1983, translated by Anita Mondello as *Big Bear,* Prentice-Hall (Englewood Cliffs, NJ), 1973, translated by Peggy Blakeley as *The Dancer, the Bear and the Nobody Boy,* A. & C. Black (London, England), 1975.
Lançons le cerf-volant: deuxieme aventure, illustrated by Nicole Claveloux, Grasset (Paris, France), 1975.
La zone d'ombre, A. Michel (Paris, France), 1977.
Oleg, le leopard des neiges (for children), illustrated by Danièl Bour, Grasset (Paris, France), 1978, translated by Anthea Bell as *Oleg, the Snow Leopard,* Gollancz (London, England), 1978.
Oleg retrouve son royaume (for children), illustrated by Danièl Bour, Grasset/Fasquelle (Paris, France), 1981, translated as *King Oleg,* Gollancz (London, England), 1982.

La révélation d'une voix et d'un nom, P. Belfond (Paris, France), 1982.

Le fauteuil à bascule (produced at Petit-Odéon, 1982), L'Avant Scène (Paris, France), 1983.

Le bonheur à Romorantin (produced at Théâtre des Mathurins, 1983), Actes Sud (Arles, France), 1997.

L'entretien de M. Descartes avec M. Pascal le jeune (play; produced at Petit-Odéon, 1985; also see below), Papiers (Paris, France), 1986.

La villa bleue (produced at L'Espace Cardin, 1986), Papiers (Paris, France), 1986.

(Translator) Christopher Hampton, *Les liaisons dangereuses* (produced at Théâtre Édouard VII, 1988), Papiers (Paris, France), 1988.

Le souper (play; produced at Théâtre Montparnasse, 1989; also see below), Actes Sud (Arles, France), 1989.

(Translator) Férenc Molnàr, *L'officier de la garde* (play; produced at the Comédie des Champs-Élysées, 1990), Actes Sud (Arles, France), 1990.

L'antichambre (play; produced at l'Atelier, 1991; also see below), Actes Sud (Arles, France), 1991.

Contre-jour (play; produced at Studio des Champs-Élysées, 1993), Actes Sud (Arles, France), 1993.

La petite Marie (novel), Stock (Paris, France), 1993.

Le souper; suivi de L'entretien de M. Descartes avec M. Pascal le jeune et de L'antichambre, Actes Sud (Arles, France), 1994.

Le dernière salve (play; produced as Théâtre Montparnasse, 1995), Actes Sud (Arles, France), 1995.

(With Edouard Molinaro) *Beaumarchais, l'insolent* (screenplay), Gallimard (Paris, France), 1996, translated film produced as *Beaumarchais, the Scoundrel,* 1997.

De mémoire, Stock (Paris, France), 1998.

Vive Henri IV (novel), Fallois (Paris, France), 2001.

Quartiers d'hiver, Fallois (Paris, France), 2005.

Also author of preface to *Contes et romans,* by Voltaire, Éditions Rencontre, 1968.

SIDELIGHTS: French playwright, novelist, and children's author Jean-Claude Brisville is best known in the United States for his juvenile titles, since, with the exception of the 1997 film *Beaumarchais, the Scoundrel,* these are the only titles that have been translated into English. Brisville's *Oleg, the Snow Leopard* and *King Oleg* are animal tales about the adventures of a snow leopard named Oleg. In the former, Oleg flees his kingdom after being wounded by hunters, finding assistance from various animals such as a seal and a bear; in the sequel, Oleg has recovered and returns to his kingdom to find that his throne has been usurped by a cheetah. Reviewing *Oleg, the Snow Leopard,* a *Junior Bookshelf* critic called the tale "a pleasant, at times amusing, animal fantasy." *School Library Journal* reviewer Katharyn F. Crabbe praised the author for the way he "manages to give each animal a distinctive character."

Compared to his simple animal tales for children, Brisville's novels for adults are complex and challenging, according to critics. *La zone d'ombre,* for example, seems at first glance to be another story about a man who has lost his true love. Madeleine Rumeau-Smith, writing in *World Literature Today,* reported that the direction in which Brisville takes this basic premise proves to be "truly original." Unable to bring himself to commit suicide, the jilted protagonist instead tries to find solace in writing. This, too, however, fails as a form of therapy, and in a "skillful evocation of a double failure," Brisville concludes that both love and writing become mere illusions.

Brisville's *La révélation d'une voix et d'un nom* is about an attempt to uncover a lost revelation written in the time of Jesus Christ by Simon the Magician. Several characters in the novel go in search of the Gnostic text written by Simon—a real historical figure—and the narrator of the book eventually reveals its location accidentally to the others. The actual center of the book, however, is not the quest itself but rather the narrator's attempts to record it, thus creating a book about a book. *French Review* critic Robin Knee pointed out this play on reality versus fiction by the author, observing that the title of Brisville's novel is the same as that of Simon's mystical text: "Since Simon is a historical figure, the relationship between fiction and reality is brought to bear. The motif of the search for the original word/Word underscores writing as the central focus of the text."

BIOGRAPHICAL AND CRITICAL SOURCES:

PERIODICALS

French Review, December, 1984, Robin Knee, review of *La révélation d'une voix et d'un nom,* p. 305.
Junior Bookshelf, June, 1979, review of *Oleg, the Snow Leopard,* p. 153; August, 1982, review of *King Oleg,* p. 129.

National Review, December 8, 1997, John Simon, review of *Beaumarchais, l'insolent,* p. 56.

New York Times, October 24, 1997, Janet Maslin, "Film Review; Saga with Tight Corsets and a Loose Structure," review of *Beaumarchais, l'insolent.*

School Library Journal, September, 1977, Anne Hanst, review of *Big Bear,* p. 102; August, 1982, Katharyn F. Crabbe, review of *King Oleg,* p. 94.

Times Literary Supplement, April 2, 1976, Anne de la Presle, review of *Un hiver dans la vie de gros ours,* p. 374; March 26, 1982, Josephine Karavasil, "Matters of Rhythm and Register," review of *King Oleg,* p. 347.

World Literature Today, summer, 1978, Madeleine Rumeau-Smith, review of *La zone d'ombre,* p. 427; summer, 1983, J.L. Greenberg, review of *La révélation d'une voix et d'un nom,* p. 428.*

*   *   *

BRISVILLE, Jean-Claude Gabriel
See BRISVILLE, Jean-Claude

*   *   *

BROOKER, Alan M. 1934-

PERSONAL: Born September 20, 1934, in Lucknow, United Province (now Uttar Pradesh), India; immigrated to New Zealand, 1947; son of Richard Brooker (a teacher) and Iris (a teacher and clerical worker; maiden name, Hansford) Brooker; married Janice Gundersen, January 14, 1961 (divorced). *Ethnicity:* "European." *Education:* La Martinere College (India), teaching certificate. *Politics:* National. *Religion:* Anglican.

ADDRESSES: Home—23 Mako St., Taupo Bay, RD 1, Mangonui, Northland 0557, New Zealand. *E-mail*—ambrook@brookersworld.co.nz

CAREER: Otago Daily Times, Dunedin, Otago, New Zealand, reporter, 1954-56; Royal New Zealand Air Force, administrator, 1956-76; Zip Commercial Interiors, Wellington, New Zealand, administration manager, 1977-82; Kaipara Area Health Services, Dargaville, New Zealand, area manager; Ambro

Enterprises, Taupo Bay, New Zealand, founder, consultant, writer, 1995—. Northland Disabilitlies Resource Centre, trustee, 1995—; Whangaroa Health Services Trust, trustee, 2001—.

MEMBER: Wellington Badminton Association.

WRITINGS:

Dreams of Torment (fantasy), Xlibris (Princeton, NJ) 1998.

Dreams of Charni (fantasy; "Warrior of Earth Saga"), Amber Quill Press (Indian Hills, CO), 1998.

Bad Blood (science fiction), Xlibris (Princeton, NJ) 1998.

The Battle for Barnstable (horror), Amber Quill Press (Indian Hills, CO), 1998.

Journey of a Common Man (memoir) Xlibris (Princeton, NJ), 2000.

Tharne's Quest (horror), Amber Quill Press (Indian Hills, CO), 2000.

The Radicals, Amber Quill Press (Indian Hills, CO), 2001.

The Mean Green Machine, Amber Quill Press (Indian Hills, CO), 2002.

Killer Turtle (adventure), Amber Quill Press (Indian Hills, CO), 2004.

An Angel's Revenge (horror), Amber Quill Press (Indian Hills, CO), 2005.

The Ride to Revenge (fantasy; "Warrior of Earth Saga"), Amber Quill Press (Indian Hills, CO), 2005.

Author of *Food for Thought,* a cookbook on CD, a health and wellness column for the *The Whispers,* and an online newsletter for Northland Disabilities Resources.

SIDELIGHTS: Alan M. Brooker was a career officer with the Royal New Zealand Air Force, who held a number of positions before becoming a full-time writer and consultant. Many of Brooker's novels of fantasy and horror are in print and also available as electronic editions from Amber Quill Press and Xlibris.

In *Dreams of Charni,* the main character, Jason, has the same recurring dream. Each time he wakes remembering every detail, including the beautiful

Charni. After purchasing an old book of star charts and an amulet in a book store, he falls asleep to dream once again, but this time to awaken in the setting of the dream, the constellation Praesepe. Here he becomes a warrior who protects Charni from her evil brother and those who want to sacrifice her to the Evil Ones. *Road to Romance* reviewer Tina Burns wrote that "Brooker has taken the Sci-Fi genre, weaved in some romance, and created a fantastic melding of the two."

The protagonists of *Tharne's Quest* are Alison, Chad, a NASA scientist, and Tharne, an ancient entity that presents itself in a mist and which has come to earth to vanquish the Adept, a being that has been reincarnated in several bodies, including that of Hitler's deputy, Heinrich Himmler, and whose intention is to unite with Satan to destroy humanity. Susan DiPlacido stated in a review for *Blue Iris Journal* online that "Brooker's style is quick and captivating, and the chills are relentless."

The Radicals concerns a group of Maori who want to return to the old ways, including cannibalism. The group leaves the headless bodies of their victims in visible places. They also have connections to Mafia drug dealers. Al Brookes is the man put in charge of breaking up the drug ring. In a review for *All about Murder* online, Sumera Majid said that "to say this book is well-written, the characters well developed, the settings well drawn, the plot captivating, the action lively, is gross understatement. This is one of the most intense novels I've ever read."

A group of anarchistic New Zealanders will go to any lengths, including murder, to stop the degradation of their environment in *The Mean Green Machine*. Brookes is called in by police after six people are killed, and he is charged with breaking up the murderous group before they take control of the government.

Brooker once told *CA:* "My main drive is to get the stories circulating around my mind out into print to share them with others. I started writing many years ago as a form of stress release. It was fun to involve those giving me problems as characters I could do nasty things to without fear of reprisal—wonderful way to release pressure. I also get many of my ideas while I sleep, record the dreams and then incorporate them into my stories."

Brooker later told *CA:* "The sight of a police confrontation with a fleeing robber in India when I was around twelve years old first got me interested in writing. The chase ended just outside our front gate and was highly verbal as you can imagine in India. I wrote about it for the school magazine and have been writing ever since but not to the extent that I am now. This present burst started in the late 1980s as a 'stress relief' tool when I was the area manager of the Kaipara Health Services and was being forced to demolish a service I had helped build up. Many of the characters in my early books resemble some of the officials who wouldn't listen to reason—I could kill and mutilate them at night and then face them the next morning with much lower stress levels.

"My work is influenced by Dennis Wheatley and John Norman, with touches of Tolkien and Star Wars.

"My writing process is rip, shit and bust. Once I start I loose track of time and have been known to spend up to seven or eight hours on the computer without a break. Normally from skeleton to first draft takes three to four months. Working with the editors from Amber Quill it takes me around a week to ten days to turn around a manuscript sent for final edit.

"The most surprising thing I've learned as a writer is the strange gullibility of some readers. The world of Praesepe is my own creation. It is 545 light years away in the Crab nebulae (the Star does exist!) so nobody knows what it looks like because it's all mine and yet I have had an e-mail from a reader complaining because I got the geography wrong and had one of the rivers flowing the wrong way across the plains!

"Well, the Warrior of Earth Saga actually, all six volumes, is my favorite. It started life as a short story of 1,500 words for a competition but it sort of grew a wee bit and ended up over 450,000 words. I just let the characters drive the story and tell me where they wanted to go next. The skeleton for the series fitted within the covers of a six-by-four-inch school notebook."

BIOGRAPHICAL AND CRITICAL SOURCES:

BOOKS

Brooker, Alan M., *Journey of a Common Man*, Xlibris (Princeton, NJ), 2000.

ONLINE

Alan M. Brooker Home Page, http://www.igrin.co.nz/ ambro (September 13, 2005).

All about Murder, http://www16.brinkster.com/ allaboutmurder/ (November 9, 2003), Sumera Majid, review of *The Radicals.*

Amber Quill Press, http://www.amberquill.com/ (September 13, 2005).

Blue Iris Journal, http://blue_iris_journal.typepad. com/ (July, 2004), Susan DiPlacido, review of *Tharne's Quest.*

Road to Romance, http://www.roadtoromance.ca/ (February 5, 2004), Tina Burns, review of *Dreams of Charni.*

Roundtable Reviews, http://www.roundtablereviews. com/ (September 2, 2004), Pam Bless, review of *Dreams of Charni.*

*   *   *

BROUSSEAU, Francine 1951-

PERSONAL: Born September 6, 1951, in Amos, Quebec, Canada; daughter of Émilien (in sales) and Therese (an office clerk; maiden name, Baril) Brousseau; children: Christian Hudon, Nicolas Hudon. *Ethnicity:* "Canadian." *Education:* Laval University, B.A., 1974; National School of Public Administration (ENAP), M.P.A., 1994.

ADDRESSES: Office—Canadian Postal Museum, Canadian Museum of Civilization, 100 Laurier St., P.O. Box 3100, Station B, Gatineau, Quebec J8X 4H2, Canada. *E-mail*—francine_brousseau@sympatico.ca; francine.brousseau@civilization.ca.

CAREER: PLURAM, Inc., Quebec City, Quebec, Canada, project officer, 1975-81; Parks Canada, Quebec City, historian, 1977-78; National Assembly of Quebec, Quebec City, research officer, 1978-81, information officer, 1981; Société du Musée des Grandes-Rivières, Hull, Quebec, project director, 1981-83; National Postal Museum, Ottawa, Ontario, Canada, curator of works of art, 1984-88; National Postal Museum, Hull, curator of exhibitions, 1988-90; Canadian Museum of Civilization, Gatineau, Quebec, director of Canadian Postal Museum, 1990—, director

of exhibitions, 2000—. Centre psycho-pédagogique de Quebéc, Inc., teacher of French and geography, 1976-77; Parks Canada, architectural analyst, 1982; consultant in history and museology. Musée de la civilisation, Quebec City, board member, 1986-93; Commission des biens culturels du Québec, board member, 1994-98; Fondation des partenaires de la Biosphère de Montréal, board member, 1996—. *Exhibitions:* Curator of exhibitions for Canadian Museum of Civilization and Canadian Postal Museum, including "Jean Paul Lemieux: His Canada" and "Special Delivery: Canada's Postal Heritage."

MEMBER: International Association of Transport and Communication Museums (vice president and board member, 1998—), International Council of Museums, Canadian Museum Association (board member, 1998—; president, 2001-03;), American Association of Museums, Société des musées québécois (board member, 1993-96), Association régionale de natation de l'Outaouais (board member, 1986-90), Société du Musée des Grandes Rivières (board member, 1982-83), Club Aquatique de Gatineau (board member, 1985-90; board chair, 1998-90).

WRITINGS:

Jean Paul Lemieux: His Canada, Canadian Postal Museum (Gatineau, Quebec, Canada), 1998.

(Coeditor) *Special Delivery: Canada's Postal Heritage,* Goose Lane Editions (Fredericton, New Brunswick, Canada), 2001.

Also contributor to periodicals.

*   *   *

BRYANT, Sharon
(Sharon Haanes)

PERSONAL: Born in ME. *Education:* Vermont College, M.F.A.

ADDRESSES: Home—ME. *Agent*—c/o Author Mail, HarperCollins Publishers, 10 E. 53rd St., 7th Fl., New York, NY 10022.

CAREER: Writer.

WRITINGS:

The Earth Kitchen (novel; for young readers), Harper-Collins (New York, NY), 2002.

SIDELIGHTS: In her debut novel for young readers, The Earth Kitchen, Sharon Bryant chose the challenging topic of mental illness. The book is set in the 1960s and involves Gwen, a twelve-year-old girl who was orphaned at six. Since then, she has been under psychiatric care because she has been slipping in and out of mental illness. To cope with her parents' death in a car accident, Gwen, who imagines that their deaths were actually the result of an atomic bomb, creates a fantasy world called the Earth Kitchen that is inspired by her comforting memories of her beloved aunt. The environment at the hospital is not as emotionally supportive as she needs, though she enjoys the rare visits from Dr. Stone. The nurses are not as helpful as her psychiatrist, and the hospital's regular air-raid drills—it is the height of the Cold War and fear of a nuclear attack is always in the background—push Gwen deeper into her fantasy-land psychosis.

The story ends with Gwen eventually emerging from her illness, a development reviewers felt offered young audiences a positive message of hope. However, a number of critics believed that Bryant's complex narrative in which fantasy and reality are blended would confuse less sophisticated readers. "This is a complex book that may require too much of its audience," School Library Journal contributor Bruce Ann Shook stated. A Kirkus Reviews writer similarly commented that "confusion can arise" from the challenging use of a mentally ill person's point of view. However, the reviewer added that the novel is still a "suspenseful and thought-provoking piece." Several critics also complimented Bryant's writing skill, with Joanna Rudge Long asserting in the Horn Book Magazine that the tale is "vividly and concretely evoked"; a Publishers Weekly contributor concluded that the narrative is "sensually written."

BIOGRAPHICAL AND CRITICAL SOURCES:

PERIODICALS

Book World, May 12, 2002, review of The Earth Kitchen, p. 12; December 1, 2002, review of The Earth Kitchen, p. 6.

Horn Book Guide, fall, 2002, review of The Earth Kitchen, p. 368.
Horn Book Magazine, March-April, 2002, Joanna Rudge Long, review of The Earth Kitchen, p. 208.
Kirkus Reviews, March 15, 2002, review of The Earth Kitchen, p. 407.
Publishers Weekly, January 28, 2002, review of The Earth Kitchen, p. 292.
School Library Journal, March, 2002, Bruce Ann Shook, review of The Earth Kitchen, p. 225.
Voice of Youth Advocates, April, 2002, review of The Earth Kitchen, p. 38.*

*   *   *

BURDEN, Barry C. 1971-

PERSONAL: Born April 28, 1971, in Newark, OH; son of Robert A. and Karen S. (maiden name, Hirst; later surname, Selby) Burden; married Laura Read Hillman; children: Samantha, Davis. Ethnicity: "White." Education: Wittenberg University, B.A. (cum laude), 1993; Ohio State University, Ph.D., 1998. Religion: Unitarian-Universalist.

ADDRESSES: Home—21 Circle Dr., Framingham, MA 01702-5733. Office—Department of Government, Littauer Center 322 North Yard, Harvard University, Cambridge, MA 02138-3001; fax: 617-495-0438. E-mail—burden@fas.harvard.edu.

CAREER: Louisiana State University, Baton Rouge, assistant professor of political science, 1998-99; Harvard University, Cambridge, MA, assistant professor, 1999-2003, associate professor of government, 2003—, founder and coordinator of Political Psychology and Behavior Workshop, 2000—, faculty associate of Center for Basic Research in the Social Sciences, 2003—, member of executive committee of Center for American Political Studies, 2001-04. Active in congressional, state, and local political campaigns; guest on media programs.

MEMBER: Southern Political Science Association, Phi Beta Kappa.

AWARDS, HONORS: Outstanding Young Alumnus Award, Wittenberg University, 2002; grants from Joseph H. Clark Fund, Reischauer Institute for Japanese Studies, Dirksen Congressional Center, and Time-Sharing Experiments in the Social Sciences.

WRITINGS:

(With David C. Kimball) *Why Americans Split Their Tickets: Campaigns, Competition, and Divided Government,* University of Michigan Press (Ann Arbor, MI), 2002.
(Editor and contributor) *Uncertainty in American Politics,* Cambridge University Press (New York, NY), 2003.

Contributor to books, including *Democracy's Feast: Elections in America,* edited by Herbert F. Weisberg and Clyde Wilcox, Stanford University Press (Stanford, CA), 1995; *Great Theatre: The American Congress in the 1990s,* edited by Herbert F. Weisberg and Samuel C. Patterson, Cambridge University Press (New York, NY), 1998; *Congressional Primaries in the Politics of Representation,* edited by Peter F. Galderisi, Michael Lyons, and Marni Ezra, Rowman & Littlefield (Lanham, MD), 2001; *Models of Voting in Presidential Elections: The 2000 U.S. Election,* edited by Herbert F. Weisberg and Clyde Wilcox, Stanford University Press (Stanford, CA), 2003; and *CQ's Guide to Political Campaigns,* edited by Paul Herrnson, Congressional Quarterly Press (Washington, DC), in press. Contributor of articles and reviews to periodicals, including *Electoral Studies, British Journal of Political Science, Public Opinion Quarterly, Political Behavior, Political Analysis, American Journal of Political Science, Public Choice, Journal of Economic Literature, Foreview,* and *Legislative Studies Quarterly.*

WORK IN PROGRESS: The Limits of Representation.

BIOGRAPHICAL AND CRITICAL SOURCES:

PERIODICALS

Choice, December, 2003, review of *Why Americans Split Their Tickets.*
Legislative Studies Section Newsletter, July, 2003, review of *Why Americans Split Their Tickets.*
National Journal, March 6, 2003, review of *Why Americans Split Their Tickets.*
Party Politics, March, 2004, review of *Why Americans Split Their Tickets.*

Perspectives on Political Science, winter, 2004, Robert Heineman, review of *Uncertainty in American Politics,* p. 45.
Perspectives on Politics, December, 2003, review of *Why Americans Split Their Tickets.*
Public Choice, January, 2004, review of *Why Americans Split Their Tickets.*

ONLINE

Harvard University Web site, http://www.fas.harvard.edu/~burden (December 21, 2004) author profile.

*　　*　　*

BURKE, Morgan
　　See LERANGIS, Peter

*　　*　　*

BUXTON, Jayne

PERSONAL: Married; children: three.

ADDRESSES: Office—Flametree, Plumtree Court, London EC4A 4HT, England. *Agent*—Christy Fletcher, Fletcher & Parry, The Carriage House, 121 E. 17th St., New York, NY 10003.

CAREER: Flametree, London, England, cofounder and codirector; writer. Contributor to seminars, radio, and television discussions on the issues facing working parents. Consultant on work-life issues to private corporations.

MEMBER: National Work-Life Forum (United Kingdom).

WRITINGS:

Ending the Mother War: Starting the Workplace Revolution (nonfiction), Macmillan (London, England) 1998.

Lessons in Duck Hunting: A Novel, Ballantine Books, 2006, also published as *Lessons in Duck Shooting: A Novel,* Arrow, 2006.

SIDELIGHTS: Jayne Buxton is well known in the United Kingdom for her work as a consultant on work-life issues. After publishing *Ending the Mother War: Starting the Workplace Revolution* in 1998, Buxton became sought after as an expert on improving the balance between workplace demands and family life for all parents. With Rosemary Leith, Buxton founded Flametree, a partnership that works with corporations to implement policies that are more perceptive to the needs of working parents.

Buxton's professional concerns play a small part in her debut novel, *Lessons in Duck Hunting.* The romantic comedy centers on a divorced mother of two children, Ally, who has taken a dull job in order to spend more time at home. At the prodding of a friend who needs an undercover observer for a piece in a women's magazine, Ally signs up for a new dating service. A *Publishers Weekly* contributor described *Lessons in Duck Hunting* as "intelligent chick lit with a literary audience in mind." In addition, a *Kirkus Reviews* critic found the book "amiable—with some useful advice for meeting men."

BIOGRAPHICAL AND CRITICAL SOURCES:

PERIODICALS

Kirkus Reviews, October 15, 2005, review of *Lessons in Duck Hunting: A Novel,* p. 1097.
Publishers Weekly, October 31, 2005, review of *Lessons in Duck Hunting,* p. 31.

ONLINE

Flametree Web site, http://www.flametree.co.uk (December 9, 2005).*

*　　*　　*

BUZZELL, Colby

PERSONAL: Male.

ADDRESSES: Agent—c/o Author Mail, Penguin Group, G.P. Putnam's Sons Publicity, 375 Hudson St., New York, NY 10014. *E-mail*—mywarcbftw@gmail.com.

CAREER: Writer, soldier, and memoirist. Worked variously as a flower delivery person, valet, cashier, car washer, telemarketer, and retail clerk. *Military service:* U.S. Army, served in Iraq, became specialist.

WRITINGS:

My War: Killing Time in Iraq (memoir), Putnam (New York, NY), 2005.

SIDELIGHTS: While serving as a soldier in Iraq, Army specialist Colby Buzzell started a Web log, or blog, chronicling his experiences in the war-damaged, politically tumultuous, perpetually dangerous Iraqi city of Mosul. Posting under a pseudonym, Buzzell related the day-to-day events in his life, including stories of combat and firefights, daily routine and daily boredom, and the terrifying punctuation of those tense and frightening moments when injury and death were averted by luck, teamwork, and skill. In *My War: Killing Time in Iraq,* Buzzell tells his story as a soldier, as an unexpectedly influential blogger and critic of the Bush administration, and as a newly minted author. "In gutsy, sometimes profane prose, he takes you on a soldier's-eye view of the front lines of the war," noted Elise Soukup in *Newsweek.* Buzzell's military career started when, as a twenty-six-year-old slacker in a dead-end job who still lived at home with his parents, he was enticed to enlist by a recruiter's promises of sign-on bonuses and his choice of military specialty. Joining to overcome the interminable sameness of his civilian life, Buzzell soon enough found himself in Iraq, fighting against the insurgency as a gunner in a Stryker brigade, riding the quick-moving, rubber-tired vehicle into and out of harrowing combat situations.

Buzzell initially started his blog as a way to unwind from the intense pressures of combat duty, and as a means of recording his experiences for his own use and for readers in other areas of the world. Soon, however, his online combat diary attracted the attention of thousands of readers around the world, and Buzzell became well-known to those who followed his writings and had an interest in the day-to-day life of a modern combat soldier. Buzzell's online work also attracted the attention of his commanders, some of whom were not pleased with what he wrote. Because of security concerns, Buzzell's writings were eventually subjected to pre-publication screening. Despite interference by the brass, Buzzell's work remained available, and popular as ever. Much of the writing in *My War* originated on his blog, where his "incisive reportage and brutally honest take on the war" first appeared, noted a reviewer in *PR Newswire*. "Some of the sharpest writing comes from the author's blog," commented a *Kirkus Reviews* critic. *Booklist* reviewer Roland Green commented that even though it's too early to tell whether Buzzell has written the definitive account of the Iraq war, "he has written a book that stands quite tall in the literature of that conflict to date." In the end, "Buzzell's work never really wavers in its portrayal of American forces as the good guys in a dirty war," observed a *Publishers Weekly* reviewer.

Buzzell told *CA*: "An article in *Time* magazine called 'Meet Joe Blog' got me interested in writing. I was in Iraq when I read that article and after reading it I went and checked out some of the other blogs that were written by other people online and I was like, if they can do it I can do it too. So I went ahead and started a blog, where I just wrote about what I was experiencing over there in Iraq as an Infantry soldier, and one thing led to another and the next thing I knew I wrote a book and a couple things for *Esquire* magazine.

"When I write, I turn on the computer, open up Word, and then from there I just type away. I like to chain smoke and drink coffee when I write.

"The most surprising thing I've learned as a writer is that there are actually people out there who wanted to print and publish stuff that I've written. That still shocks me. I hope my book will make people want to publish and read more books by me."

BIOGRAPHICAL AND CRITICAL SOURCES:

BOOKS

Buzzell, Colby, *My War: Killing Time in Iraq,* Putnam (New York, NY), 2005.

PERIODICALS

Booklist, October 15, 2005, Roland Green, review of *My War,* p. 22.

Entertainment Weekly, October 14, 2005, Brian Raftery, "War Memoirs 101: Get a Piece of Iraq," review of *My War,* p. 157.
Kirkus Reviews, July 15, 2005, review of *My War,* p. 774.
Library Journal, September 1, 2005, John Riddick, "The Meaning of War: Afghanistan and Iraq in Six Titles," review of *My War,* p. 158.
Newsweek, October 10, 2005, Elise Soukup, "Memoirs: Gunning to Be in Print," review of *My War,* p. 10.
PR Newswire, January 31, 2005, "G.P. Putnam's Sons to Publish U.S. Army Soldier and Blogger Colby Buzzell's War Experiences on the Ground in Iraq."
Publishers Weekly, February 7, 2005, John F. Baker, "A Soldier-Blogger in Iraq," p. 12; August 1, 2005, review of *My War,* p. 59.
San Francisco Chronicle, September 13, 2005, C.W. Nevius, "*My War*—A Soldier's Wild Ride," review of *My War.*
Seattle Times, November 9, 2005, Alex Fryer, "Drifter, Soldier, Author: A Keen Eye on Iraq," review of *My War.*
Wall Street Journal, September 9, 2004, C.D.H. Cooper, Army Blogger's Tales Attract Censor's Eyes," p. B1.

ONLINE

1000 Words from Iraq Web Log, http://wordsfromiraq. blogspot.com/ (September 8, 2004), "Blogging in the News."
Chiasm, http://chiasm.blog-city.com/ (February 27, 2006), profile of Colby Buzzell.
My War Web log, http://cbftw.blogspot.com (February 27, 2006).

*   *   *

BYERS, Michael 1966-

PERSONAL: Born 1966. *Education:* University of Saskatchewan, B.A., 1988; McGill University, LL.B. and B.C.L., 1992; Queens' College, Cambridge University, Ph.D., 1996.

ADDRESSES: Office—Liu Institute for Global Issues, The University of British Columbia, 6476 N.W. Marine Dr., Vancouver BC V6T 1Z2, Canada. *E-mail*—Michael.byers@ubc.ca.

CAREER: Writer, educator, attorney, editor, and legal consultant. Jesus College, Oxford University, research fellow, 1996-99; Duke University School of Law, associate professor, 1999-2003, professor of law, 2003-04; University of British Columbia and Liu Institute for Global Studies, University of British Columbia, 2004—. Duke University, codirector, JD/LL.M program in International and Comparative Law and director, Center for Canadian Studies. Visiting Fellow, Max Planck Institute for Comparative Law and International Law, 1996-99; Peter North Visiting Fellow, Keble College & Centre for Socio-Legal Studies, Oxford University, 2001-02; Visiting scholar, Liu Institute for Global Issues, University of British Columbia, 2003; Commerzbank Visiting Professor, Bucerius Law School, Hamburg, Germany, 2003; visiting professor, Buchmann Faculty of Law, University of Tel Aviv, Israel, 2004; visiting professor, faculty of law, University of Cape Town, South Africa, 2005. Member of executive board, Center on Law, Ethics, and National Security. Frequent guest on television and radio programs on networks such as the BBC, Irish National Radio, CNN, CBC, Radio Australia, National Public Radio, PBS, and MSNBC.

WRITINGS:

Custom, Power, and the Power of Rules: International Relations and Customary International Law, Cambridge University Press (New York, NY), 1999.
(Editor) *The Role of Law in International Politics: Essays in International Relations and International Law,* Oxford University Press (New York, NY), 2000.
(Translator and revisor) Wilhelm G. Grewe, *The Epochs of International Law,* Walter de Gruyter (New York, NY), 2000.
(Editor, with Georg Nolte) *United States Hegemony and the Foundations of International Law,* Cambridge University Press (New York, NY), 2003.
War Law: Understanding International Law and Armed Conflict, Grove Press (New York, NY), 2006.

Contributor to books, including *Contemporary International Law Issues: New Forms, New Applications,* edited by Wybo Heere, T.M.C. Asser Institute (The Hague, Netherlands), 1998; *Liability of Multinational Corporations under International Law,* edited by Menno T. Kamminga and Saman Zia-Zarifi, Kluwer (The Hague, Netherlands), 2000; *Worlds in Collision,* edited by Ken Booth and Tim Dunne, Palgrave (Basingstoke, England), 2002; and *Humanitarian Intervention: Ethical, Legal, and Political Dilemmas,* edited by J.L. Holzgrefe and Robert Keohane, Cambridge University Press (Cambridge, England), 2003.

Contributor to periodicals, including *Ethics & International Affairs, Journal of Political Philosophy, European Journal of International Law, Guardian* (London, England), *McGill Law Journal, World Today, Independent on Sunday, European Human Rights Law Review, Duke Journal of Comparative and International Law, Nordic Journal of International Law, Michigan Journal of International Law, London Review of Books,* and *Times* (London, England).

SIDELIGHTS: Author, educator, and attorney Michael Byers is an expert in international law and related legal subjects. He is a frequent public speaker and presenter at seminars. A tenured professor of law at Duke University, Byers is a frequent contributor to journals and other periodicals, covering topics related to public policy, international law, and the application of law during wartime.

Byers is coeditor, with Georg Nolte, of *United States Hegemony and the Foundations of International Law.* The book contains eighteen essays by twelve scholars from around the world. The editors and contributors examine the more aggressive role in international affairs that the United States has taken since the September 11 terrorist attacks. More specifically, they carefully consider whether the expanded international presence and predominance of the United States is leading to fundamental changes in international law. The volume addresses how and why America is taking a larger role in the development of international law. Essayists cover topics related to areas such as sovereign equality, laws governing force, the law of treaties, and compliance with international law. A critic in *Contemporary Review* noted that the book's "range of topics is impressive and the collection will prove invaluable to students of international law and relations."

In *War Law: Understanding International Law and Armed Conflict,* Byers explores in depth the complex, often arcane area of international laws governing war and armed conflict. Byers delves into how that law applies to the United States and other countries, and how the U.S. tends to declare itself in compliance with relevant war law even when other countries believe America's actions are a violation. The author looks at the history and development of war law as it applies in five important categories: self defense, preemptive war, UN Security Council authorizations, humanitarian and pro-democratic intervention, and the protection of civilians and combatants during armed conflict. He explains the subtleties of arguments nations have used to justify their actions under international war law, and how such arguments and actions often coincide with a country's individual agenda rather than adherence to the letter of the law. Byers also looks at what seem to be contradictions in war law—for example, how Slobodan Milosevic can face an international tribunal to answer for war crimes, but how other leaders, such as Ariel Sharon or even Henry Kissinger, have not been tried for the same type of crime. In his final chapter, Byers looks at recent developments in American foreign policy and concludes that the United States consistently places its interests above international law. The book is "succinct, highly readable, and important," commented Brendan Driscoll in *Booklist.* A *Kirkus Reviews* contributor called *War Law* a "lucid primer" and "a thoughtful introduction to a complex, often baffling subject."

BIOGRAPHICAL AND CRITICAL SOURCES:

PERIODICALS

Booklist, November 15, 2005, Brendan Driscoll, review of *War Law: Understanding International Law and Armed Conflict,* p. 8.

Contemporary Review, November, 2003, review of *United States Hegemony and the Foundations of International Law,* p. 317.

Kirkus Reviews, November 1, 2005, review of *War Law,* p. 1168.

Publishers Weekly, October 17, 2005, review of *War Law,* p. 53.

ONLINE

Duke University School of Law Web site, http://www.law.duke.edu/ (February 27, 2006), biography of Michael Byers.

Liu Institute for Global Studies, University of British Columbia Web site, http://www.ligi.ubc.ca/ (February 27, 2006), biography of Michael Byers.*

C

CAMPBELL, Kellyna K. 1959-
(Kellyna Kaleolani Campbell)

PERSONAL: Born June 17, 1959, in Glendale, CA; daughter of Lewis (a business owner) and Jo (a homemaker; maiden name, Stoft) Falk; married Joseph Campbell (a healer), June 21, 2003. *Ethnicity:* "White." *Education:* University of California, Santa Cruz, B.S. *Hobbies and other interests:* Travel, hiking.

ADDRESSES: Agent—c/o Author Mail, Lehua Publishing, 708 Gravenstein Highway N., Ste. 40, Sebastopol, CA 95472.

CAREER: Lehua Center for Well-Being, Sebastopol, CA, cofounder, healer, and seminar leader. Creator of a line of natural healing products.

WRITINGS:

9 Inner Jewels, Lehua Publishing (Sebastopol, CA), 2004.

* * *

CAMPBELL, Kellyna Kaleolani
See CAMPBELL, Kellyna K.

* * *

CAREY, Charles W., Jr. 1951-

PERSONAL: Born June 16, 1951, in Norfolk, VA; son of Charles Sr. (an electronics engineer) and Jean Carey; married Deborah Lane (a registered nurse), June 15, 1974; children: Billy, Beth, Jeff, Diana. *Eth-* *nicity:* "Euro-American." *Education:* University of Virginia, B.A., 1973; Virginia Tech, M.A., 1995. *Politics:* Democrat. *Religion:* Roman Catholic. *Hobbies and other interests:* Canoeing, kayaking, miniature wargaming.

ADDRESSES: Home—1102 Biltmore Ave., Lynchburg VA 24502. *E-mail*—historian@centralva.net.

CAREER: Freelance writer, 1996—. Adjunct history instructor at colleges, including Central Virginia Community College, 1995-2004, Lynchburg College, 1997-2001, Virginia Tech, 2003—, Roanoke College, 2003—, and Radford University, 2004.

MEMBER: Virginia Social Science Association.

AWARDS, HONORS: Writing fellow, American Council of Learned Societies, 1996-98; Spur Award finalist for Best Western Juvenile Nonfiction, Western Writers of America, 2003, for *Mexican War.*

WRITINGS:

George Washington Carver, Child's World (Chanhassen, MN), 1999.
The Emancipation Proclamation, Child's World (Chanhassen, MN), 2000.
American Inventors, Entrepreneurs, and Business Visionaries, Facts on File (New York, NY), 2002.
The Mexican War: "Mr. Polk's War," Enslow Publishers (Berkeley Heights, NJ), 2002.

(Editor) *Life under Soviet Communism,* Greenhaven Press (San Diego, CA), 2003.

Eugene V. Debs: Outspoken Labor Leaders and Socialist, Enslow Publishers (Berkeley Heights, NJ), 2003.

(Editor) *Castro's Cuba,* Greenhaven Press (San Diego, CA), 2004.

(Editor) *The Kennedy Assassination,* Greenhaven Press (San Diego, CA), 2004.

African-American Political Leaders, Facts on File (New York, NY), 2004.

(Editor) *The American Revolution,* Greenhaven Press (San Diego, CA), 2004.

Living through the Korean War, Greenhaven Press (San Diego, CA), 2006.

American Scientists, Facts on File (New York, NY), 2006.

Contributor to books, including *Macmillan Encyclopedia of World Slavery,* Simon & Schuster, 1998; *American National Biography,* Oxford University Press, 1999; *New Encyclopedia of American Scandal,* Facts on File, 2001; *Encyclopedia of American Political History,* CQ Press, 2001; *Invisible Giants: Fifty Americans Who Shaped the Nation but Missed the History Books,* edited by Mark C. Carnes, Oxford University Press, 2002; and *Dictionary of Historical Documents,* Facts on File, 2003. Contributor to periodicals, including *Virginia Social Science Journal.*

WORK IN PROGRESS: African Americans in Science, for ABC-Clio.

SIDELIGHTS: Charles W. Carey Jr., once commented: "I knew I wanted to write for a living when I was ten years old, but I didn't actually start until I was in my forties. I always wanted to write the Great American Novel until I realized I wrote lousy fiction. But in graduate school I discovered that I could write pretty good history, and I've been doing it ever since."

BIOGRAPHICAL AND CRITICAL SOURCES:

PERIODICALS

Booklist, November 1, 2002, review of *American Inventors, Entrepreneurs, and Business Visionaries,* p. 522; July, 2004, review of *African-American Political Leaders,* p. 1860.

Choice, February, 2003, L. Kong, review of *American Inventors, Entrepreneurs, and Business Visionaries,* p. 965; July-August, 2004, N.M. Allen, review of *African-American Political Leaders,* p. 2024.

School Library Journal, January, 2003, review of *The Mexican War: "Mr. Polk's War,"* p. 150; October, 2003, Elizabeth Talbot, review of *Life under Soviet Communism,* p. 184; November, 2004, Doris Losey, review of *Castro's Cuba,* p. 160.

*   *   *

CARHEDEN, Göorel Kristina
See NÄASLUND, Göorel Kristina

*   *   *

CARNEY, John Otis 1922-2006

OBITUARY NOTICE— See index for *CA* sketch: Born February, 1922, in Chicago, IL; died of cancer, January 1, 2006, in AZ. Journalist and author. Carney was a former advertising writer and journalist who later became a successful novelist and scriptwriter for television. During World War II, he served with distinction as a Marine Corps pilot, earning five battle stars as well as a Presidential Unit Citation. After the war, he completed a B.A. at Princeton University in 1946, and the next year joined the advertising agency Louis de Rochemont Associates in New York City. From 1948 to 1949, he was a reporter for the *Minneapolis Star* before returning to advertising, this time with the J. Walter Thompson agency in Chicago. Having published his first novel, *Love at First Flight,* in 1943 with coauthor Charles Spalding, Carney was already a published author when he quit advertising completely in 1954. He found success writing for such television programs as *Zane Grey Theater* and *The Monroes,* while he continued to publish novels. Among these are *Yesterday's Hero* (1959), *The Paper Bullet* (1966), *Welcome Back Billy Rawls* (1977), and *Chihuahua, 1916* (1980).

OBITUARIES AND OTHER SOURCES:

PERIODICALS

Los Angeles Times, January 9, 2006, p. B9.

CARROLL, Linda 1944-

PERSONAL: Born 1944; adopted daughter of Jack and Louella Risi; biological daughter of Paula Fox (a writer); married; children: five.

ADDRESSES: Agent—c/o Author Mail, Doubleday, 1745 Broadway, New York, NY 10019. *E-mail*—lcbarr@aol.com.

CAREER: Writer, memoirist, and therapist.

WRITINGS:

Her Mother's Daughter: A Memoir of the Mother I Never Knew and of My Daughter, Courtney Love, Doubleday (New York, NY), 2005.

WORK IN PROGRESS: Return to Essence: Seven Stages of a Woman's Spiritual Journey, expected 2007.

SIDELIGHTS: Author, therapist, and memoirist Linda Carroll grew up as an adopted child in an affluent but emotionally difficult family setting. In *Her Mother's Daughter: A Memoir of the Mother I Never Knew and of My Daughter, Courtney Love,* Carroll tells the story of her own life, her search for her birth mother, and the tumultuous family connection between herself and her five children, one of whom is the controversial rock star Courtney Love. "At the core of her memoir is a mother-daughter legacy spanning three generations, rife with those elements that make such a story archetypal: conflict, love, loss and redemption," remarked Neva Chonin in the *San Francisco Chronicle.* Carroll describes her early life and how she was adopted by a wealthy couple, Louella and Jack Risi. Though they provided for her material comfort, she notes, they did not offer her emotional growth and stability. Her adoptive mother was emotionally distant, and her adopted father was sexually abusive. Following her rough and rebellious teenage years, she became friendly with a group of bohemian intellectuals in San Francisco, California. One of these individuals became Carroll's first husband and the father of her first child, who would later be known as Courtney Love. Carroll subsequently married twice more and gave birth to four more children. Her relationship with Courtney, however, was always tumultuous. In fact, the two became estranged and no longer spoke to one another. Years later, when Courtney was pregnant with her first child, Carroll began searching for her own birth mother, Paula Fox, a noted memoirist and children's author. Ultimately, as Carroll developed a relationship with her birth mother and watched helplessly as Courtney edged closer to self-destruction, she came to terms with her own dual role of mother and daughter and with the sometimes unpleasant but galvanizing past that forged her.

A *Kirkus Reviews* critic called the book "a surprisingly evocative account" and an "unassuming and reflective coming-of-age memoir." Similarly, *Booklist* reviewer Kristine Huntley called Carroll's book "a thoughtful memoir of one woman's coming-of-age in the turbulent 1960s and 1970s." A *Library Journal* reviewer, Amanda Glasbrenner, commented that the book is "a compelling read that delicately examines the nature of family, identity, and the links between them." A *Publishers Weekly* contributor noted that "Carroll's tender wit and poignant honesty . . . will keep readers soldiering through this often exhaustive history."

Carroll told *CA:* "In my memoir, *Her Mother's Daughter,* I worked very hard to show my adopted parents as the multidimensional people they were. My mother, Louella, although difficult and critical, was also tremendously loyal, gracious with her many friends, and genuinely wanted the best for me. My father, Jack, although he molested me as a young child, was also a man admired for his kindness, wit, and generosity. He remains one of the most generous people I have ever known. While I began life estranged from both of my mothers, I have been blessed with reconciliation with both.

"I resist this culture which tries to make people 'bad' and 'good,' when we are all woven of so many complexities and they all exist within us at once. As my birth mother, Paula, once remarked, 'Good things don't take away the bad, but bad things don't deny the good, either.'"

BIOGRAPHICAL AND CRITICAL SOURCES:

BOOKS

Carroll, Linda, *Her Mother's Daughter: A Memoir of the Mother I Never Knew and of My Daughter, Courtney Love,* Doubleday (New York, NY), 2005.

PERIODICALS

Booklist, December 1, 2005, Kristine Huntley, review of *Her Mother's Daughter,* p. 11.

Kirkus Reviews, November 1, 2005, review of *Her Mother's Daughter,* p. 1168.

Library Journal, November 1, 2005, Amanda Glasbrenner, review of *Her Mother's Daughter,* p. 84.

New York Observer, February 6, 2006, Tim Appelo, "The Sins of the Mother: Genetic Clues to Courtney Love," review of *Her Mother's Daughter,* p. 20.

Publishers Weekly, October 3, 2005, review of *Her Mother's Daughter,* p. 57.

San Francisco Chronicle, February 5, 2006, Neva Chonin, "Mothers & Daughters," review of *Her Mother's Daughter.*

*   *   *

CARTARESCU, Mircea 1956-

PERSONAL: Born June 1, 1956, in Bucharest, Romania. *Education:* University of Bucharest, Ph.D., 1980.

ADDRESSES: Office—Faculty of Letters, University of Bucharest, 68 Edgar Quinet St., Sector 1, Bucharest, Romania.

CAREER: School teacher in Bucharest, Romania, 1980-89; University of Bucharest, Bucharest, Romania, lecturer and chairman of Romanian literature history, 1991—. Writer in residence, Romanian Writers Union, 1991—. Visiting professor, University of Amsterdam, 1994-95. Participant in conferences, symposia, and seminars in America and Europe.

MEMBER: PEN (Romania), Romanian Writers Union, ASPRO.

AWARDS, HONORS: Romanian Writers Union prize, 1980, for *Faruri, vitrine, fotografii;* Romanian Academy prize, 1990, for *Visul;* Romanian Writers Union prize, 1990, for *Levantul;* "Flacara," "Ateneu," and "Cuvântul" prizes, 1990, 1996, and 1997; Union Latine prize (France), 1992; Romanian Writers Union prize, 1994, for *Travesti;* Romanian Writers Union, Republic of Moldova prize, 1994; ASPRO prize, 1994, for *Travesti,* and 1996, for *Orbitor.*

WRITINGS:

Faruri, vitrine, fotografii (title means "Headlights, Shop Windows, Photographs), Cartea Româneasca Publishing House (Bucharest, Romania), 1980.

(Contributor) *Aer cu diamante* (title means "Air and Diamonds"), Litera Publishing House (Bucharest, Romania) 1982.

Poeme de amor (title means "Love Poems"), 1983.

(Contributor) *Desant 83* (title means "Commando '83), Cartea Româneasca Publishing House (Bucharest, Romania), 1983.

Totul (title means "Everything"), 1985.

Visul, Cartea Româneasca Publishing House (Bucharest, Romania), 1989, translation by Andrei Codrescu published as *Nostalgia: A Novel,* New Directions (New York, NY), 2005.

Levantul (title means "Levant"), Cartea Româneasca Publishing House (Bucharest, Romania) 1990.

Visul chimeric (title means "The Chimerical Dream"), Litera Publishing House (Bucharest, Romania), 1992.

Travesti (title means "Travesty"), Humanitas Publishing House (Bucharest, Romania) 1994.

Dragostea (title means "Love"), Humanitas Publishing House (Bucharest, Romania) 1994.

(Contributor) *Antologia poeziei generaţiei '80* (title means "The Anthology of Generation '80 in Poetry"), Vlasie Publishing House (Piteşti, Romania), 1995.

Orbitor (title means "Dazzling"), Humanitas Publishing House (Bucharest, Romania) 1996.

Dublu CD: Antologie de poezie (title means "Double CD: Poetry Anthology") Humanitas Publishing House (Bucharest, Romania), 1998.

Postmodernismul romanesc (title means "The Romanian Post-Modernism"), Humanitas Publishing House (Bucharest, Romania) 1999.

(Contributor) *Generatia '80 în proza scurta,* (title means "Generation '80 in Short Stories"), Paralele 45 Publishing House (Piteşti, Romania), 1999.

Jurnal (title means "Journal"), Humanitas Publishing House (Bucharest, Romania) 2001.

Enciclopedia zmeilor, illustrated by Tudor Banus, Humanitas Publishing House (Bucharest, Romania) 2002.

Pururi tinar, infasurat in pixeli: din periodice, Humanitas Publishing House (Bucharest, Romania), 2003.

Plurivers, Humanitas Publishing House (Bucharest, Romania), 2003.

De ce iubim femeile, Humanitas Publishing House (Bucharest, Romania), 2004.

Contributor of poems and essays to periodicals. Work has been translated into French, Spanish, and German.

SIDELIGHTS: A reviewer for *Publishers Weekly* called Mircea Cartarescu "Romania's leading poet." Although not widely translated in English, Cartarescu is an important voice in Romanian letters, not only for his poetry, but also for his stories, novels, and essays. His novels in particular employ postmodern elements in the tradition of Franz Kafka, Jorge Luis Borges, and Gabriel Garcia Marquez. The same *Publishers Weekly* critic, considering Cartarescu's *Nostalgia: A Novel,* noted that the author's "prose shines." A *Kirkus Reviews* correspondent wrote that "a surrealist landscape stands revealed" in *Nostalgia,* concluding that Cartarescu's "phantasmagorical world is similar to Dali's dreamscapes."

BIOGRAPHICAL AND CRITICAL SOURCES:

PERIODICALS

Kirkus Reviews, October 1, 2005, review of *Nostalgia: A Novel,* p. 1043.

Publishers Weekly, October 3, 2005, review of *Nostalgia,* p. 49.

ONLINE

University of Bucharest Web Site, http://www.politice. snspa.ro/ (December 9, 2005), author's curriculum vitae.*

*   *   *

CASKIE, Kathryn

PERSONAL: Married; children.

ADDRESSES: Home—c/o Author Mail, Warner Books, 1271 Avenue of the Americas, New York, NY 10020. *E-mail*—kathryn@kathryncaskie.com.

CAREER: Writer. Has worked in marketing for America Online and worked variously as a magazine editor, television producer, and a copywriter for television, radio, commercials and the Internet.

AWARDS, HONORS: Golden Heart Award, Romance Writers of America, for *Rules of Engagement.*

WRITINGS:

"FEATHERTON" SERIES

Rules of Engagement, Warner Books (New York, NY), 2004.

Lady in Waiting, Warner Books (New York, NY), 2005.

A Lady's Guide to Rakes, Warner Forever (New York, NY), 2005.

Love Is in the Heir, Warner Forever (New York, NY), 2006.

SIDELIGHTS: Kathryn Caskie had a career in marketing and journalism, but when she moved into her 200-year-old home, she became inspired to write a historical novel. This inspiration ultimately resulted in a historical romance series featuring the Featherton sisters. The first book in the collection, *Rules of Engagement,* introduces the reader to Letitia and Viola Featherton, a pair of elderly sisters intent on finding a husband for their grandniece Eliza. To this end, they employ the advice of a military strategy book (aptly titled *Rules of Engagement*) that they mistake for a relationship guide. Critics welcomed the book with positive reviews. John Charles, writing in *Booklist,* found the debut "witty and wonderful," while *Romantic Times Book Club Online* contributor Kathe Robin observed that the book is "fresh, exciting and utterly charming." *Romance Readers Connection* reviewer Debora Hosey concurred, calling *Rules of Engagement* "absolutely fabulous," and designating it "one of the best debut books I've read in a long while."

Caskie next wrote *Lady in Waiting,* the story of Jenny, a lady's maid who dreams of someday becoming a lady herself. When she is mistaken for such by a handsome nobleman, the Featherton sisters—her employers—encourage her to keep up the pretense. At the same time, Jenny tries to prevent the Feathertons from finding out that she is the creator of a new, increasingly popular face cream. *Lady in Waiting* received mixed reviews. A *Publishers Weekly* contributor found it "far-fetched," yet *Booklist* reviewer Charles called *Lady in Waiting* "sweet, frothy and laughter-laced." Moreover, Robin, writing again in the *Romantic Times Book Club Online,* noted that "Caskie's unique wit sparkles."

Caskie's third book in the series is titled *A Lady's Guide to Rakes.* In this installment, the Featherton sisters once again play matchmaker, this time for their grandniece Meredith. In the meantime Meredith tries to prove that the womanizing Lord Lansing has not improved his behavior (as he claims he has) by attempting to seduce him. It turns out, however, that Lord Lansing truly has changed and that he sincerely wishes to marry her. Caskie's third book, like her second, was met with mixed reviews. A *Publishers Weekly* reviewer noted that the book has "little character depth," yet still felt that it "should satisfy most." *Booklist* contributor Charles, on the other hand, found only positives to speak of, calling this third novel "bright, breezy, and witty."

BIOGRAPHICAL AND CRITICAL SOURCES:

PERIODICALS

Booklist, May 15, 2004, John Charles, review of *Rules of Engagement,* p. 1603; December 1, 2004, John Charles, review of *Lady in Waiting,* p. 640; September 15, 2005, John Charles, review of *A Lady's Guide to Rakes,* p. 42.
Publishers Weekly, November 29, 2004, review of *Lady in Waiting,* p. 28; August 1, 2005, review of *A Lady's Guide to Rakes,* p. 50.

ONLINE

Kathryn Caskie Home Page, http://www.kathryn caskie.com (March 22, 2006).
Romance Junkies, http://www.romancejunkies.com/ (March 22, 2006), interview with author.

Romance Readers Connection, http://www.romance readersconnection.com/ (March 22, 2006), Debora Hosey, interview with author and review of *Rules of Engagement.*
Romantic Times Book Club Online, http://www. romantictimes.com/ (March 22, 2006), Kathe Robin, reviews of *Rules of Engagement* and *Lady in Waiting.*
Virginia Romance Writers Web site, http://www. virginiaromancewriters.com/ (March 22, 2006), brief biography of Kathryn Caskie.*

*   *   *

CASWAY, Jerrold
(Jerrold I. Casway)

PERSONAL: Male. *Education:* Temple University, B.A., M.A.; University of Maryland, Ph.D.

ADDRESSES: Office—Social Sciences/Education, Howard Community College, 10901 Little Patuxent Parkway, Columbia, MD 21044. *E-mail*—jcasway@ howardcc.edu.

CAREER: Professor, author. Howard Community College, Columbia, MD, professor of history, 1971—, division chair, director of Rouse Scholars.

WRITINGS:

NONFICTION

Owen Roe O'Neill and the Struggle for Catholic Ireland, University of Pennsylvania Press (Philadelphia, PA), 1984.
Ed Delahanty in the Emerald Age of Baseball, University of Notre Dame Press (Notre Dame, IN), 2004.

WORK IN PROGRESS: A nonfiction book examining the culture of nineteenth-century baseball.

SIDELIGHTS: A professor of history, Jerrold Casway has focused on Irish topics in works such as the 1984 title, *Owen Roe O'Neill and the Struggle for Catholic*

Ireland, and the 2004 book, *Ed Delahanty in the Emerald Age of Baseball.* The latter title focuses on Delahanty, an Irish baseball player who held the fourth highest batting average in the history of the sport. Delahanty's career was cut short, however, when his body was found at the foot of Niagara Falls in 1903. A flamboyant character, Delahanty was, according to Casway's account, fond of a life style that salary caps at the time thwarted.

Writing in *History: Review of New Books,* John E. Dreifort praised Casway for his "fascinating, carefully researched biography of a long-neglected baseball hero." Similarly, Laura Kopp, writing in Maryland's *Archivists' Bulldog,* found the book "a vivid portrait of how the sons of Irish famine immigrants revolution-ized the game of baseball in the late nineteenth century." For James Silas Rogers, reviewing the book in the *Irish Literary Supplement,* "Casway's account of the star's self-destructive end, which sifts through the competing accounts of his death, is particularly compelling."

BIOGRAPHICAL AND CRITICAL SOURCES:

PERIODICALS

American Historical Review, December, 1985, Colm Lennon, review of *Owen Roe O'Neill and the Struggle for Catholic Ireland,* p. 1205.
History: Review of New Books, fall, 2004, John E. Dreifort, review of *Ed Delahanty in the Emerald Age of Baseball,* p. 14.
Irish Literary Supplement, fall, 2004, James Silas Rogers, "Hitting for the Cycle," review of *Ed Delahanty in the Emerald Age of Baseball,* p. 10.

ONLINE

Archivists' Bulldog, http://www.mdarchives.state.md.us/ (August 15, 2005), Laura Kopp, review of *Ed Delahanty in the Emerald Age of Baseball.*
Howard Community College Web site, http://www.howardcc.edu/ (January 3, 2006), "Casway, Jerry."
Society for American Baseball Research Web site, http://www.sabr.org/ (July 7, 2004), "Women and Nineteenth Century Baseball/ Dr. Jerrold Casway."*

CASWAY, Jerrold I.
See CASWAY, Jerrold

*   *   *

CERF, Muriel 1951(?)-

PERSONAL: Born 1951 (one source says 1950), in Paris, France. *Education:* Studied Oriental art at École du Louvre.

ADDRESSES: Agent—c/o Author Mail, Editions du Rocher, 6 pl. St.-Sulpice, 75006 Paris, France. *E-mail*—mc.site@murielcerf.com.

CAREER: Writer.

AWARDS, HONORS: Valéry Larbaud Prize, 1975.

WRITINGS:

L'antivoyage, Mercure de France (Paris, France), 1974, reprinted, *Éditions J'ai lu,*1995.
Le diable vert (novel), Mercure de France (Paris, France), 1975, reprinted Actes Sud (Arles, France), 1997.
Les rois et les voleurs (novel), Mercure de France (Paris, France), 1975, translated by Dominic Di Bernardi as *Street Girl,* Dalkey Archive Press (Elmwood Park, IL), 1988.
Hiéroglyphes de nos fins dernières (novel), Mercure de France (Paris, France), 1977.
Le Lignage du serpent (novel), Mercure de France (Paris, France), 1978.
Les seigneurs du Ponant (novel), Mercure de France (Paris, France), 1979, reprinted, Éditions du Rocher (Monaco), 2001.
Amérindiennes (novel), Stock (Paris, France), 1979.
Une passion (novel), J.-C. Lattès (Paris, France), 1981.
Maria Tiefenthaler (novel), A. Muriel (Paris, France), 1982.
Une pâle beauté (novel), A. Michel (Paris, France), 1984.
Dramma per musica (novel), A. Michel (Paris, France), 1986.

Doux oiseaux de Galileé (novel), A. Michel (Paris, France), 1988.

La nativité à l'étoile (novel), A. Michel (Paris, France), 1989.

Primavera toscana: détail de la légende d'une florentine, Sand (Paris, France), 1989.

Julia M.; ou, Le premier regard (novel), R. Laffont (Paris, France), 1991.

Le verrou (novel), Actes Sud (Arles, France), 1997.

Ogres, et autres contes (short stories), Actes Sud (Arles, France), 1997.

Une vie sans secret, Éditions du Rocher (Monaco), 1998.

Servantes de l'oeil (novel), Actes Sud (Arles, France), 1999.

Ils ont tué Vénus Ladouceur, Éditions du Rocher (Monaco), 2000.

Triomphe de l'agneau, Éditions du Rocher (Monaco), 2000.

La lumière de l'île, Actes Sud (Arles, France), 2001.

La femme au chat (novel), Actes Sud (Arles, France), 2001.

Le bandit manchot (novel), Éditions du Rocher (Monaco), 2002.

L'homme du souterrain (novel), Éditions du Rocher (Monaco), 2003.

L'étoile de Carthage, Écriture (Paris, France), 2004.

La petite culotte, Maren Sell (Paris, France), 2005.

Bertrand Cantat; ou, le chant des automates, Écriture (Paris, France), 2006.

SIDELIGHTS: French novelist Muriel Cerf has been highly acclaimed for her intricate, challenging prose style that is rich in imagery and metaphor. In a review of the author's *Le Lignage du serpent,* for instance, *French Review* contributor Amy B. Millstone noted that the author's sentences are "often two pages long" and "undulate in serpentine fashion, embracing in their coils a rich series of mythological metaphors and sensual colors." Even those reviewers who have found flaws in her fiction have conceded that her stylistic skills are formidable. As *French Review* writer Michael G. Hydak wrote in his assessment of *Amérindiennes,* while the "narrative aspect of the book remains thin" the author still "redeems the book and asserts her skill as a writer" through her descriptions of settings and people. Critics similarly praised the writing in the more recent *Le verrou,* a novel in which "Cerf succeeds brilliantly in suffusing her pages with emotion and eroticism," according to Elisabeth Beyer in the *Times Literary Supplement.*

Most of Cerf's novels have yet to be translated into English, with the exception of *Street Girl,* the 1988 translation of the author's 1975 novel *Les rois et les voleurs.* The central character of *Street Girl* is Lydie Tristan, a spoiled French teenager living in 1960s France who indulges in sexual promiscuity and illegal activities in her attempt to experience life more intensely. "Cerf's prose will be too rich for some people's blood," predicted a *Kirkus Reviews* contributor: "This is as far from minimalism as we can get. But the rhetoric perfectly matches the adolescent sensibility." *Times Literary Supplement* critic Sara Rance described the style in the novel as "prose poetry." The reviewer added: "Cerf captures what it is like to be fifteen and female with a faultless touch; it is a major achievement to convey the benign contempt of the adolescent for authority and not compromise it with the hindsight of adulthood."

BIOGRAPHICAL AND CRITICAL SOURCES:

PERIODICALS

Bloomsbury Review, January, 1989, Barbara Loren, review of *Street Girl,* p. 17.

Economist, June 21, 1997, review of *Le verrou,* p. R14.

French Review, December, 1979, Amy B. Millstone, review of *Le Lignage du serpent,* p. 308; October, 1980, Michael G. Hydak, review of *Amérindiennes,* p. 189.

Kirkus Reviews, October 1, 1988, review of *Street Girl,* pp. 1421-1422.

Small Press, August, 1989, Thomas M. Reilly, review of *Street Girl,* p. 42.

Times Literary Supplement, October 13, 1989, Sara Rance, "Stormy Youth," review of *Street Girl,* p. 1130; October 10, 1997, Elisabeth Beyer, review of *Le verrou,* p. 25.

World Literature Today, autumn, 1979, Nicholas Catanoy, review of *Le Lignage du serpent,* p. 643.

ONLINE

Muriel Cerf Home Page, http://www.murielcerf.com (March 6, 2006).*

*   *   *

CHADWICK, Elizabeth
  (Susan E. Hicks)

PERSONAL: Born Susan E. Hicks.

ADDRESSES: Home—Nottingham, England. *Agent*—c/o Author Mail, St. Martin's Press, 175 5th Ave., New York, NY 10010. *E-mail*—Elizabeth.Chadwick@btinternet.com.

CAREER: Author.

AWARDS, HONORS: Betty Trask Award, England, for *The Wild Hunt;* shortlist, Parker Pen Award for Romantic Novel of the Year, Romantic Novelists Association, 1998, for *The Champion,* 2003, for *Winter Mantle,* and 2004, for *The Falcons of Montabard.*

WRITINGS:

NOVELS

The Wild Hunt, St. Martin's Press (New York, NY), 1991.

The Running Vixen, St. Martin's Press (New York, NY), 1992.

Children of Destiny, Michael Joseph (London, England), 1993.

The Leopard Unleashed, St. Martin's Press (New York, NY), 1993.

Shields of Pride, Ivy Books (New York, NY), 1994.

First Knight (novelization of the film), Boxwood (New York, NY), 1995.

Daughters of the Grail, Ivy Books (New York, NY), 1995.

The Conquest, St. Martin's Press (New York, NY), 1997.

The Champion, St. Martin's Press (New York, NY), 1998.

The Love Knot, St. Martin's Press (New York, NY), 1999.

The Marsh King's Daughter, St. Martin's Press (New York, NY), 2000.

Lords of the White Castle, St. Martin's Press (New York, NY), 2002.

The Winter Mantle, Little, Brown (London, England), 2002, St. Martin's Press (New York, NY), 2003.

The Falcons of Montabard, St. Martin's Press (New York, NY), 2004.

Shadows and Strongholds: A Novel, St. Martin's Press (New York, NY), 2005.

The Greatest Knight: The Story of William Marshall, Time/Warner (London, England), 2005.

Chadwick's books have been translated into Swedish, German, Czech, Russian, Spanish, Estonian, and Bulgarian.

ADAPTATIONS: The Champion was adapted for audiobook, Clipper Audio, 1997; *Lords of the White Castle* was adapted for audiobook, Clipper Audio, 2000; *The Winter Mantle* was adapted for audiobook, Soundings Audio, 2002; *Falcons of Montabard* was adapted for audiobook, Soundings Audio, 2003.

WORK IN PROGRESS: A sequel to *The Greatest Knight: The Story of William Marshall.*

SIDELIGHTS: British novelist Elizabeth Chadwick focuses on the Middle Ages for her popular historical romances. Inspired as a teenager by the movie *The War Lord,* starring Charlton Heston, Chadwick began to research the medieval world and write about it. Her first success came with the 1991 title, *The Wild Hunt,* and since then she has turned out about a book a year. In an interview for the Web site *All About Romance,* Chadwick noted, "My favourite period is the one I write about—1066-1250. My first novels were written in this period and it's the one I have researched in most depth."

Most of Chadwick's titles have been published in the United States. Reviewing her 2002 title, *Lords of the White Castle,* a *Publishers Weekly* contributor praised her medieval re-creation, noting that the author conveys a "vivid portrait of her native Britain in feudal times." For Harriet Klausner, writing on *AllReaders.com, Lords of the White Castle* "is biographical fiction at its most exciting best." Chadwick does not shy away from the rougher aspects of the medieval world. As Maureen Griffin noted in a *Kliatt* review of *The Marsh King's Daughter,* "Murder, sex, war, ransom are presented unflinchingly." Also reviewing *The Winter Mantle* for *Kliatt,* Griffin further observed that "there is considerable gore and explicit sex." Other reviewers have noted Chadwick's ability to combine thorough historical research with lively tales of love and war. Reviewing *The Winter Mantle* for *Booklist,* Margaret Flanagan called it, "a heartrending tale of love and loss." Writing on that same title for *AllReaders.com,* Klausner found the work "an exciting historical novel." *Booklist* contributor Kate Mediatore, reviewing *The Falcons of Montabard,* noted, "All characters, fictional and historical, are fully realized." Chadwick noted in her interview for *All About Romance,* "I enjoy writing historical fiction because it's a door to another world."

BIOGRAPHICAL AND CRITICAL SOURCES:

PERIODICALS

Booklist, April 15, 1992, Denise Perry Donavin, review of *The Running Vixen,* p. 1501; August, 1997, Margaret Flanagan, review of *The Conquest,* p. 1876; November 15, 1998, Patty Engelman, review of *The Champion,* p. 573; March 1, 2003, Margaret Flanagan, review of *The Winter Mantle,* p. 1145; May 15, 2004, Kate Mediatore, review of *The Falcons of Montabard,* p. 1607.

Kirkus Reviews, August 15, 1991, review of *The Wild Hunt,* p. 1026; April 1, 1992, review of *The Running Vixen,* p. 409; September 15, 2004, review of *Shadows and Strongholds: A Novel,* p. 991.

Kliatt, September, 2002, Maureen Griffin, review of *The Marsh King's Daughter* (audiobook), p. 54; January, 2004, Maureen Griffin, review of *The Winter Mantle* (audiobook), p. 51.

Library Journal, September 1, 1991, Mary Ann Parker, review of *The Wild Hunt,* p. 228; April 1, 1992, Mary Ann Parker, review of *The Running Vixen,* p. 145; July, 1997, Elizabeth Mary Mellett, review of *The Conquest,* p. 122; November 15, 1998, Elizabeth Mary Mellett, review of *The Champion,* p. 90; November 15, 1999, Kristin Ramsdell, review of *The Love Knot,* p. 54.

Publishers Weekly, August 16, 1991, review of *The Wild Hunt,* p. 47; March 29, 1993, review of *The Leopard Unleashed,* p. 38; July 3, 1995, review of *Daughters of the Grail,* p. 56; October 12, 1998, review of *The Champion,* p. 58; October 11, 1999, review of *The Love Knot,* p. 52; July 24, 2000, review of *The Marsh King's Daughter,* p. 71; February 18, 2002, review of *Lords of the White Castle,* p. 74;

School Library Journal, March, 1992, Sue Davis, review of *The Wild Hunt,* p. 266.

ONLINE

All About Romance, http://www.likesbooks.com/ (July 5, 2003), "Elizabeth Chadwick—The English One."

AllReaders.com, http://www.allreaders.com/ (January 4, 2006), Becky Lee, review of *First Knight, The Wild Hunt,* and *Running Vixen;* Harriet Klausner, review of *Lords of the White Castle, The Falcons of Montabard,* and *The Winter Mantle;* Annette Gisby, review of *The Love Knot.*

Elizabeth Chadwick Home Page, http://www.elizabethchadwick.com (January 4, 2006).

Historical Romance Writers, http://historicalromancewriters.com/ (January 4, 2006), "Meet Elizabeth Chadwick."

Suite101.com, http://www.suite101.com/ (January 4, 2006), Wendy J. Dunn, "Tudor England."*

*   *   *

CHANDLER, Glenn 1953-

PERSONAL: Born December 3, 1953, in Edinburgh, Scotland; son of Andrew (a professional musician) and Joan (Moy) Chandler. *Ethnicity:* "British." *Education:* Attended secondary school in Edinburgh, Scotland. *Politics:* "Anxious." *Hobbies and other interests:* Family history, hill walking, backpacking.

ADDRESSES: Agent—Diana Tyler, MBA Ltd., 62 Grafton Way, London W1T 5DW, England. *E-mail*—leavalleypress@yahoo.com.

CAREER: Writer. Creator of the television series *Taggart,* 1983.

WRITINGS:

Burning Poison (nonfiction), Lea Valley Press, 2000.

The Life and Crimes of William Palmer (television script), ITV Network (England), 2001.

A Is for Acid (television script), ITV Network (England), 2002.

The Brides in the Bath (television script), ITV Network (England), 2003.

Savage Tide (crime novel), Hodder & Stoughton (London, England), 2003.

Dead Sight (crime novel), Hodder & Stoughton (London, England), 2004.

Writer for the television series *Taggart,* c. 1983-99; also scriptwriter for episodes of other series, including *Crown Court,* Granada Television (England), and *In Suspicious Circumstances.* Also author of short stage plays.

WORK IN PROGRESS: Writing for television; research on death row in the United States.

SIDELIGHTS: Glenn Chandler told CA: "My primary motivation for writing is that I was hopeless at everything else at school except English! I made my first break in the theater circuit (London fringe) with a number of short plays. Harold Pinter was a great influence on me. Good, well-researched 'true crime' is also a great influence, for much of my fictional plotting sparks off from real-life events.;

"I start writing at 6:00 a.m. and finish at 2:00 in the afternoon—I have a life! Also, I feel fresher in the morning, and anything written by midnight oil will probably be in the wastepaper basket by morning.

"My inspiration for writing about crime came from an invitation by Granada Television to write for Crown Court in the seventies. I attended numerous famous murder trials and became hooked."

*   *   *

CHASE, Steven

PERSONAL: Male. Education: University of Washington, B.A.; Princeton Theological Seminary, M.Div.; Fordham University, Ph.D.

ADDRESSES: Office—Western Theological Seminary, 101 E. 13th St., Holland, MI 49423-3633. E-mail—steven.chase@westernsem.edu.

CAREER: Professor and writer. Jesuit School of Theology, Berkeley, CA, former adjunct professor; Graduate Theological Union, Berkeley, CA, former doctoral faculty member; Western Theological Seminary, Holland, MI, current associate professor of Christian spirituality. Center of Theological Inquiry, Princeton, NJ, two-time member-in-residence. Christian Spirituality Group, American Academy of Religion, founder and cochair; Society for the study of Christian Spirituality, member governing board; Institute of Spirituality at the Dominican Center, Grand Rapids, MI, former Director of Prayer Formation.

WRITINGS:

NONFICTION

Angelic Wisdom: The Cherubim and the Grace of Contemplation in Richard of St. Victor, University of Notre Dame Press (Notre Dame, IN), 1995.

(Editor) Doors of Understanding: Conversations in Global Spirituality in Honor of Ewert Cousins, Franciscan Press (Quincy, IL), 1997.
(Translator and author of introduction) Angelic Spirituality: Medieval Perspectives on the Ways of Angels, Paulist Press (New York, NY), 2002.
Contemplation and Compassion: The Victorine Tradition, Orbis Books (Maryknoll, NY), 2003.
The Tree of Life: Models of Christian Prayer, Baker Academic (Grand Rapids, MI), 2005.

SIDELIGHTS: Steven Chase is a professor of Christian spirituality who has authored several books on prayer, religious history, and on the role of angels in spirituality. In his 2003 title, Contemplation and Compassion: The Victorine Tradition, he examines aspects of the Order of St. Victor, founded in Paris, France, in 1110, which was influential in medieval thought. Joan M. Nuth, reviewing the title in Theological Studies, found it an "appealing account . . . [that] inspires in the reader the desire to learn more." In his 2005 book, The Tree of Life: Models of Christian Prayer, Chase presents, according to a reviewer for Library Journal, a "well argued" study. In the book, Chase surveys different categories of prayer, from transformational prayers to ones dealing with relationships, using the metaphor of a tree to represent the various types of prayer. Thus, prayer as conversation serves as the tree's roots, while the branches of the tree represent prayer as a form of journey. A reviewer for Publishers Weekly concluded of this book, "Chase sows seeds . . . [that] will spread deep roots and produce fragrant blossoms."

BIOGRAPHICAL AND CRITICAL SOURCES:

PERIODICALS

Library Journal, October 1, 2005, review of The Tree of Life: Models of Christian Prayer, p. 80.
Publishers Weekly, July 25, 2005, review of The Tree of Life, p. 69.
Theological Studies, June, 2005, Joan M. Nuth, review of Contemplation and Compassion: The Victorine Tradition, p. 491.

ONLINE

Western Theological Seminary Web site, http://www.westernsem.edu/ (January 4, 2006), "Steven Chase."*

CHÂTEAUREYNAUD, Georges-Olivier 1947-

PERSONAL: Born 1947.

ADDRESSES: Agent—c/o Author Mail, Zulma, 122, Bd. Haussmann, 75008 Paris, France.

CAREER: Writer.

AWARDS, HONORS: Grand Prix du Roman, 1974, for *Les messagers;* Prix Renaudot, 1982, for *La faculté des songes;* Goncourt Prize, for best short story.

WRITINGS:

Le fou dans la chaloupe, B. Grasset (Paris, France), 1973.

Les messagers (novel), B. Grasset (Paris, France), 1974, revised edition, La Table Ronde (Paris, France), 1990.

La belle charbonnière (short stories), B. Grasset (Paris, France), 1976.

Mathieu Chain (novel), B. Grasset (Paris, France), 1978.

Le Verger, Balland (Paris, France), 1978.

La faculté des songes (novel), B. Grasset (Paris, France), 1982.

Le congrès de fantomologie (novel), B. Grasset (Paris, France), 1985.

(With Danièle Thompson) *Le tiroir secret* (novel), B. Grasset (Paris, France), 1986.

La fortune: et autres textes, Castor Astral (Talence, France), 1987.

Le héros blessé au bras (short stories), B. Grasset (Paris, France), 1987.

Le jardin dans l'île (short stories), Presses de la Renaissance (Paris, France), 1989.

Le jardin d'Éden: la seule mortelle, illustrated by Georges Lemoine, Nompareille (Paris, France), 1992.

Nouvelles, 1972-1988 (short stories), Julliard (Paris, France), 1993.

Le kiosque et le tilleul (short stories), Julliard (Paris, France), 1993.

Le château de verre (novel), Julliard (Paris, France), 1994.

Monsieur d'Orsay, photographs by Philippe Bertin, Cercle d'Art (Paris, France), 1995.

Le Styx et autres nouvelles (short stories), Littéra (Arras, France), 1995.

Les ormeaux, Editions du Rocher (Monaco), 1996.

Le goût de l'ombre (short stories), Actes Sud (Arles, France), 1997.

Le démon à la crécelle (novel), B. Grasset (Paris, France), 1999.

Le conquête du Pérou: récit, Editions du Rocher (Monaco), 1999.

Les chevaliers sans nom (short stories), Nestiveqnen (Paris, France), 2001.

Civils de plomb, Editions du Rocher (Monaco), 2002.

Au fond du paradis (novel), B. Grasset (Paris, France), 2002.

(With Hubert Haddad and Frédérick Tristan) *Petite suite cherbourgeoise* (short stories), Editions du Rocher (Monaco), 2004.

Singe savant tabassé par deux clowns (short stories), B. Grasset (Paris, France), 2005.

SIDELIGHTS: Georges-Olivier Châteaureynaud is a French short story author and novelist whose partly surrealistic tales place him, according to critics like *Review of Contemporary Fiction* contributor John Taylor, into the "Romantic heritage" school of modern French storytellers. Taylor elaborated, "The fictional worlds he creates are reminiscent of but strangely apart from our own." In a review of Châteaureynaud's prize-winning novel *Les messagers,* Taylor noted in the *Times Literary Supplement* that Châteaureynaud's fiction is "an austere other-worldly mobile" that belongs with "the lineage of [Edgar Allan] Poe and [Franz] Kafka." The author's tales, which often feature ordinary, hapless main characters, are fairly realistic in nature but tinged with an element of fantasy.

Among the novels that fall into this somewhat other-worldly setting are Châteaureynaud's *La faculté des songes* and *Les messagers.* The first title, which earned the author the Prix Renaudot, features three lonely men who establish a sort of club in an abandoned house. There they find a measure of camaraderie, as well as a mother/lover figure in the form of Louise. Eventually, however, their oasis is lost and they must return to their real lives. Although Stephen Smith, writing in the *French Review,* found it difficult to suspend disbelief and become fully engaged in the story, the critic praised the "rich, precise vocabulary and the deft manipulation of literary French." *Les messagers,* which Taylor described in his *Times Literary Supplement* review as "a captivating exercise in intriguing symbolism," is about a young, aimless man who inherits the job of messenger from an acquaintance who has been traveling the world in an effort to deliver a message of unknown content.

A similar theme concerning the journey through life appears in the short story "La seule mortelle," published in *Le jardin d'Éden: la seule mortelle* and in the novel *Le château de verre*. In the short story, the narrator encounters a woman who was once mistaken for an immortal and allowed to live in a Tibetan Eden, but when she is found to actually be mortal, she is thrown out of paradise. After hearing the tale, the narrator similarly tells the woman to leave. He soon regrets the decision, however, and goes on a doomed quest to find her. In *Le château de verre*, two twelfth-century travelers, Job de Logonna and Marie de France, relate their life stories to each other while on their way to meet their loved ones. The story of Job from the Bible is clearly used as Châteaureynaud's inspiration for his character's tale, but he also draws on the epic romances of the Middle Ages. Thus, as Maryann De Julio commented in her *World Literature Today* review, *Le château de verre* "can be read as a literary history."

Many of Châteaureynaud's short stories bear similar qualities of surrealism and poetic use of language. In a review of *Le kiosque et le tilleul* for *World Literature Today*, critic Donald J. Dziekowicz indicated that the author's themes include "dream and reality, the effects of death upon a loved one, the ironies of fate, and the knowledge of one's mortality," all of which "are singularly presented in a quasi-surrealist mode." The reviewer complimented Châteaureynaud on the "versatility" in "his use of language" and concluded that the stories are "noteworthy for their originality as well as for the psychological territories they invite us to explore."

BIOGRAPHICAL AND CRITICAL SOURCES:

PERIODICALS

French Review, October, 1979, Paul A. Mankin, review of *Mathieu Chain,* p. 151; October, 1983, Stephen Smith, review of *La faculté des songes,* pp. 134-135.

Observer (London, England), January 2, 1983, John Weightman, "From the Crab Basket," review of *La faculté des songes,* p. 46.
Review of Contemporary Fiction, fall, 1989, John Taylor, review of *Le jardin dans l'île,* pp. 214-215.
Times Literary Supplement, September 7, 1990, John Taylor, "Deviations from the Real," review of *Les messagers,* p. 955; September 25, 1992, John Taylor, "Painless Progress," review of *Le jardin d'Éden: la seule mortelle,* pp. 13-14.
World Literature Today, autumn, 1994, Donald J. Dziekowicz, review of *Le kiosque et le tilleul,* p. 776; summer, 1995, Maryann De Julio, review of *Le château de verre,* p. 548.*

*   *   *

CHIHA, Kim
  See KIM, Chi-Ha

*   *   *

CHI-HA, Kim
  See KIM, Chi-Ha

*   *   *

CHURCH, Audrey P. 1957-
  (Audrey Puckett Church)

PERSONAL: Born December 12, 1957, in Richmond, VA; daughter of Aubrey Green (a farmer) and Faye (a nurse; maiden name, Fore) Puckett; married Michael Wayne Church (a banker), August 10, 1980; children: Samuel Michael, Chelsie Faye. *Ethnicity:* "Caucasian." *Education:* Bridgewater College, B.A.; Longwood College (now University), M.S. *Religion:* Methodist.

ADDRESSES: Office—School Library Media Program, Longwood University, 201 High St., Farmville, VA 23909. *E-mail*—churchap@longwood.edu.

CAREER: Library media specialist for public schools in Lunenburg County, VA, 1980-2000; Longwood University, Farmville, VA, coordinator of school library media program, 2000—.

MEMBER: American Library Association, American Association of School Librarians (member of Educators of Library Media Specialists Section, 2000—), Virginia Educational Media Association (president, 2001), Virginia Association for Supervision and Curriculum Development, Phi Delta Kappa, Delta Kappa Gamma.

AWARDS, HONORS: Certificate of commendation, American Association of School Librarians, 2003; Media Educator of the Year, Virginia Educational Media Association, 2004.

WRITINGS:

Leverage Your Library Program to Help Raise Test Scores: A Guide for Library Media Specialists, Principals, Teachers, and Parents, Linworth Publishing (Worthington, OH), 2003.

Contributor to journals, including *Today's School Media Specialist, Virginia Journal of Education, Multimedia and Internet at Schools,* and *Library Media Connection.*

WORK IN PROGRESS: Research on principal perceptions of school librarians, teacher perceptions of school librarians, and the history of school libraries in Virginia.

SIDELIGHTS: Audrey P. Church told *CA:* "Research studies have shown the tremendous impact that school library media programs and school library media specialists have on student academic achievement. I feel that this is one of the best-kept secrets in education. My primary motivation for writing is to share this information with others—parents, teachers, and administrators—so that libraries will be utilized to their fullest potential."

*　　*　　*

CHURCH, Audrey Puckett
　　See CHURCH, Audrey P.

*　　*　　*

CHWEDYK, Richard

PERSONAL: Born in Chicago, IL.

ADDRESSES: Home—7538 N. Bell Ave, Unit 3A, Chicago, IL 60645-1962. *E-mail*—rchwedyk@rcn.com.

CAREER: Oakton Community College, IL, part-time creative writing instructor.

AWARDS, HONORS: Nebula Award, 2002, Sturgeon Award, and Hugo Award nomination, all for "Bronte's Egg."

WRITINGS:

Bronte's Egg (novella), 2002.

Contributor of short stories, novellas, and poetry to magazines, including the *Magazine of Fantasy and Science Fiction, Amazing Stories, Stoney Lonesome, Science Fiction Chronicle,* and *Space and Time.* The novella "Bronte's Egg" was reprinted in *Nebula Awards Showcase 2004,* edited by Vonda M. McIntyre, Roc (New York, NY), 2004; the long short story "The Measure of All Things" was reprinted in *Year's Best SF 7,* edited by David Hartwell and Kathryn Cramer, Eos Books (New York, NY), 2002. Both "The Measure of All Things" and *Bronte's Egg* have been translated into Hebrew.

SIDELIGHTS: Richard Chwedyk is a poet and short story writer whose science fiction novella, *Bronte's Egg,* won a 2002 Nebula Award and a Sturgeon Award, as well as being nominated for a Hugo. The story deals with a refuge for dinosaurs that are intelligent and designed as toys. Called "saurs," these dinosaurs were genetically altered to be tiny and cute toys for little kids. Unexpectedly, the saurs also turned out to be very intelligent and to have life spans far longer than the tots who owned them; thus many end up in a shelter run by Tom Groverton after their owners have outgrown them. Chwedyk introduced his saurs in the 2001 short story "The Measure of All Things." Reviewing that title on the *Best SF* Web site, Mark Watson felt that Chwedyk "manages to keep the story from being too saccharin."

Chwedyk reprised his idea with the 2002 novella *Bronte's Egg,* in which one of the saurs at the refuge, young Axel, dreams of creating a robot. In the process, he saves the egg of another resident at the shelter, despite the efforts of the worried bioengineers who fear reproduction by their creations. For Watson, this second installment "veered toward a somewhat saccharin Disneyesque feel." Other reviewers, however, had much more positive assessments of this Nebula Award-winning story. David Soyka, writing for the *SF Site* thought the tale "quite silly and frothy, . . . but an apt breezy tonic." Higher praise came from *Greenman Review* contributor Matthew Winslow, who thought it was the "definitive winner for best story" in the issue of the *Magazine of Fantasy and Science Fiction* in which it appeared. Winslow went on to call the story "enjoyable," pointing out that "although Axel's antics are quite childish, . . . they still retain an adult sophistication." A reviewer for *Bluejack* likewise called *Bronte's Egg* "a fun romp."

Chwedyk told *CA:* "My interest in writing pre-dates my ability to read. I recall as a child filling notebooks with scrawled imitations of written text broken up by a few illustrations of lost islands and space capsules. In some way my hand started to work at writing before my brain did. If writing was not in my genes it was at least in my blood.

"My influences come from all over and would take much more time and space than I have here to describe. My writing process is chaotic. I haven't been able to settle down and write in one particular way, which has certainly affected my output but I hope not my quality. The best way I can answer this is to say that I usually start writing handwritten drafts and eventually move over to the computer. My goal is the old Joseph Conrad admonition: to make you see. I follow the story where it takes me. When I'm doing my best, the mantra is 'Trust the story! The story teaches you!' If it's any good, the exegeses can be worked out later.

"The most surprising thing I've learned should not have been a surprise: that an author is constantly writing from the self about the self, no matter the subject. This is not as insular as it sounds. In one respect an author is interpreting the 'lived in' world through the self, so the big picture is ultimately reflected in the author's work, but through the other end of the telescope.

"I can easily resort to the author's favorite answer, that I want my readers to enjoy themselves by living through my stories a bit and providing a good read, but I'd be ignoring the secret wish of most good writers—if I were to count myself among them, which I'm not sure I can—to say something more. I'm not sure if I can put that 'something more' into words—it's the part that readers have to provide for themselves—but I'll make an effort: I would like readers to get the feeling that there's more to us than we give ourselves credit for. We are remarkably complex, many-faceted and not easily duplicated. A mere reading of the newspaper demonstrates what we are at the lowest common denominator. What fiction writers and poets can do is demonstrate that the highest denominator is infinitely higher than the lowest, but not so far away as to be outside the reach of any one of us."

BIOGRAPHICAL AND CRITICAL SOURCES:

ONLINE

Best SF, http://www.bestsf.net/ (January 9, 2002), Mark Watson, review of *Bronte's Egg*; (August 3, 2002), Mark Watson, review of "The Measure of All Things."

Bluejack, http://www.bluejack.com/ (December 20, 2005), review of *Bronte's Egg*.

Greenman Review, http://www.greenmanreview.com/ (July 14, 2002), Matthew Winslow, review of *Bronte's Egg*.

SF Site, http://www.sfsite.com/ (December 20, 2005), David Soyka, review of *Bronte's Egg*.

*   *   *

CIABATTARI, Jane

PERSONAL: Born in Emporia, KS; married; husband's name Mark (a writer). *Education:* Stanford University, B.A.; San Francisco State University, M.A.

ADDRESSES: Home—Sag Harbor, NY; New York, NY; Windham, NY. *Agent*—Ellen Levine, Trident Media Group, LLC, 41 Madison Ave., 36th Fl., New York, NY 10010. *E-mail*—janeciab@aol.com.

CAREER: Journalist, editor, short story writer, teacher of writing. *Parade* magazine, former contributing editor; *California Living,* former managing editor; *Red-*

book, former managing editor; *Dial* magazine, former editor in chief; *McCall's,* senior consulting editor in fiction. Worked as a reporter and columnist for the *Montana Standard,* Butte, MT. Knox College, Galesburg, IL, Distinguished Writer in Residence/Visiting Professor of English, 2004; Columbia University's Graduate School of Journalism, New York, NY, writing instructor; New York University, New York, NY, writing instructor; Squaw Valley Community of Writers, writing instructor; Borderlands writing workshop, Tenants Harbor, ME, writing instructor; former fiction writer in residence, Chautauqua Institution's Writers' Center, 2003, 2005; associate faculty, Bennington College Low-Residency Writing Program, Bennington, VT. *Story* magazine, member of editorial board; Women's Media Group, past president; Overseas Press Club of America, former vice president; Women's Enews, member of the board and nominating chair; National Book Critics Circle, board member.

MEMBER: Authors Guild, PEN.

AWARDS, HONORS: Special Mention, Pushcart Prize, for "Payback Time"; Editors' Choice STUBBY Award, *Hampton Shorts,* 1996; fiction fellowships, New York Foundation for the Arts, the MacDowell Colony, and The Virginia Center for the Creative Arts.

WRITINGS:

Winning Moves: How to Come Out Ahead in a Corporate Shakeup, Penguin USA (New York, NY), 1989.
Stealing the Fire (short stories), Canio's Editions (Sagaponik, NY), 2002.

Contributor of short stories to the anthology *The Best Underground Fiction,* 2006, and to periodicals, including *Ms., North American Review, Denver Quarterly, Hampton Shorts, East Hampton Star, Blueline, Caprice,* and *Redbook.* Contributor of articles and reviews to *Los Angeles Times, Washington Post, San Francisco Chronicle, Chicago Tribune, Ms., Poets & Writers, East Hampton Star, Kirkus Reviews, Threepenny Review, Psychology Today,* and the *Columbia Journalism Review.*

SIDELIGHTS: A former contributing editor and columnist for *Parade* magazine, writer Jane Ciabattari has also authored book-length works, including the

nonfiction title, *Winning Moves: How to Come Out Ahead in a Corporate Shakeup,* and the highly praised 2002 collection of short stories, *Stealing the Fire.* Reviewing the latter title, a *Publishers Weekly* contributor noted that "dealing with loss" is the unifying theme in the "solid debut collection." Such loss is both very tangible, as in the death of a father in "Stealing the Fire," or the loss of innocence, as in "A Pilgrimage." A critic for *Kirkus Reviews* had further praise for the collection and Ciabattari, calling the author a "master of transformation." The same reviewer concluded that these stories were "written with heart." Similarly, Joyce Sparrow, writing in *Library Journal,* commended the stories that "explore how change affects our lives."

BIOGRAPHICAL AND CRITICAL SOURCES:

PERIODICALS

Kirkus Reviews, March 1, 2002, review of *Stealing the Fire,* p. 274.
Library Journal, April 15, 2002, Joyce Sparrow, review of *Stealing the Fire,* p. 127.
Publishers Weekly, April 8, 2002, review of *Stealing the Fire,* p. 205.
Southampton Press, August 8, 2002, review of *Stealing the Fire.*

ONLINE

Borderlands Magazine 2005, http://www.borderlands conference.com/ (January 5, 2006), "Jane Ciabattari."
Jane Ciabattari Home Page, http://www.janeciabattari. com (January 5, 2006).
Literary Mama, http://www.literarymama.com/ (January 5, 2006), Jane Ciabattari, "Hiding Out."

*   *   *

CLARKE, Brock 1968-

PERSONAL: Born November 15, 1968, in Springfield, MA; son of Peter Paslee (an English professor) and Elaine Giustina (a dental hygienist) Clarke; married Lane Ulrich, June 29, 1996; children: Quinn Alonzo. *Education:* Dickinson College, B.A., 1990; University of Rochester, Ph.D., 1998. *Religion:* "Lapsed Catholic."

ADDRESSES: *Home*—1712 Howland Pl., Cincinnati, OH 45223. *Office*—English Department, University of Cincinnati, P.O. Box 210069, Cincinnati, OH 45221. *E-mail*—clarkebl@excite.com.

CAREER: Cornell University, Ithaca, NY, lecturer in English, 1997-98; Clemson University, Clemson, SC, assistant professor of English, 1998-2001; University of Cincinnati, OH, assistant professor of English, 2001—.

MEMBER: Modern Language Association, Association of Writers and Writing Programs.

AWARDS, HONORS: Mary McCarthy Prize for short fiction, 2000, for *What We Won't Do;* Walter Dakin Fellowship, Sewanee Writers' Conference, 2002; Wesleyan Writers Conference fellow; Lightsey fellowship; Tennessee Williams scholarship; Bread Loaf Writers' Conference scholarship; New York State Writers' Institute award.

WRITINGS:

The Ordinary White Boy (novel), Harcourt (New York, NY), 2001.
What We Won't Do (short stories), Sarabande Books (Louisville, KY), 2002.
Carrying the Torch (short stories), University of Nebraska Press (Lincoln, NE), 2004.

Contributor to periodicals, including *New England Review, American Fiction, Brooklyn Review, South Carolina Review, Mississippi Review, Journal, Twentieth Century Literature, Southwestern American Literature,* and the *Chronicle of Higher Education.* Fiction editor, *Cincinnati Review.*

SIDELIGHTS: With his debut novel, *The Ordinary White Boy,* and two subsequent short story collections, Brock Clarke established a reputation as an author of fiction concerning average Americans learning to cope with failure or, at best, ordinariness in their lives. As Clarke admitted to *Collected Miscellany* interviewer Kevin Holtsberry, the idea behind his first novel was not exactly original, yet "I thought I had things to say about this man [Lamar.]" Set in Clarke's hometown of Little Falls, New York, the central story line in *The*

Ordinary White Boy is the disappearance of a black man in the town. Local boy Lamar, who has taken a reporter's job at his father's newspaper, sets out to investigate but finds himself repeatedly sidetracked by his indifference to the man's fate and the desire to find more entertaining things to do. In the end, Lamar discovers that the man was not the victim of racism after all and, in the process, confronts the unpleasant reality of who he, his friends, and his family truly are.

Booklist critic Gillian Engberg observed that although the novel's hero is not very sympathetic, "this messy honesty is the book's strength." Some reviewers considered the protagonist and story uninteresting, with one *Publishers Weekly* contributor describing it as a "rather dull tale" with a style "as flat as life in Little Falls." However, Joanna M. Burkhadt attested in *Library Journal* that the author offers "insightful philosophy about innocence and guilt, bravery and cowardice, substance and drama," and a contributor to the *Milwaukee Journal Sentinel* concluded that *The Ordinary White Boy* is "a subtle commentary on society."

Clarke's short story collections, *What We Won't Do* and *Carrying the Torch,* earned guarded praise from reviewers, who generally noted that Clarke continues to punch holes in the concept of the American dream. Reviewing *What We Won't Do,* a *Publishers Weekly* contributor commented that the author "probes the hearts and minds of the disaffected and the unfulfilled." The critic felt that Clarke sometimes falls short of conveying his premise effectively but added that the collection has "intriguing conceits . . . as well as flashes of talent." A *Kirkus Reviews* contributor faulted the author for being "too fond of novelty" in his stories, resulting in an "uneven debut." On the other hand, Tim Feeney noted in the *Review of Contemporary Fiction* that the stories "combine the comic and the deeply sad to create something at once bleak and radiant."

Carrying the Torch, according to a review in *Publishers Weekly,* is a compilation of nine stories that illustrate "the plight of . . . unfaithful husbands, dissatisfied wives and angry children in search of home and meaning." Reviewing the book for *Booklist,* Carol Haggas commented that the tales "are both subdued and effusive, simultaneously bitter with hard-won wisdom and giddy with dewy-eyed optimism."

BIOGRAPHICAL AND CRITICAL SOURCES:

PERIODICALS

Booklist, August, 2001, Gillian Engberg, review of *The Ordinary White Boy,* p. 2084; February 1, 2002, Bonnie Johnston, review of *What We Won't Do,* p. 921; September 1, 2005, Carol Haggas, review of *Carrying the Torch,* p. 62.

Kirkus Reviews, December 1, 2001, review of *What We Won't Do,* p. 1625.

Library Journal, August, 2001, Joanna M. Burkhadt, review of *The Ordinary White Boy,* p. 159.

Milwaukee Journal Sentinel, December 2, 2001, "Brock Clarke," review of *The Ordinary White Boy,* p. 9.

Publishers Weekly, August 6, 2001, Judith Rosen, review of *The Ordinary White Boy,* p. 47; August 13, 2001, review of *The Ordinary White Boy,* p. 283; December 24, 2001, review of *What We Won't Do,* p. 41; July 18, 2005, review of *Carrying the Torch,* p. 62.

Review of Contemporary Fiction, fall, 2002, Tim Feeney, review of *What We Won't Do,* p. 154.

ONLINE

Collected Miscellany, http://www.collectedmiscellany.com/ (September 29, 2003), Kevin Holtsberry, "Brock Clarke," interview with the author.*

*   *   *

CLARKE, Norma 1948-

PERSONAL: Born 1948. *Education:* Holds a doctorate.

ADDRESSES: Office—Kingston University, Penrhyn Rd., Kingston upon Thames, Surrey KT1 2EE, England. *E-mail*—N.Clarke@kingston.ac.uk.

CAREER: Kingston University, Surrey, England, senior lecturer.

WRITINGS:

Ambitious Heights: Writing, Friendship, Love: The Jewsbury Sisters, Felicia Hemans and Jane Welsh Carlyle (history and criticism), Routledge (London, England), 1990.

(With Helen Weinstein) *Spinning with the Brian: Women's Writing in Seventeenth Century England,* BBC (London, England), 1996.

Dr. Johnson's Women (biography), Hambledon & London (London, England), 2000.

The Rise and Fall of the Woman of Letters (history and criticism), Pimlico (London, England), 2004.

Contributor to works by others, including *Opening the Nursery Door: Reading, Writing and Childhood 1600-1900,* edited by Mary Hilton, Morag Styles, and Victor Watson, Routledge (London, England), 1997; and *Practical Visionaries: Women, Education and Social Progress 1790-1930,* edited by Pam Hirsch and Mary Hilton, Longman (Harlow, Englnad), 1998.

JUVENILE FICTION

Patrick in Person, illustrated by Vanessa Julian-Ottie, Faber & Faber (London, England), 1991.

Patrick and the Rotten Roman Rubbish, illustrated by Vanessa Julian-Ottie, Faber & Faber (London, England), 1993.

(With Peter Kavanagh) *Trouble on the Day,* A.&C. Black (London, England), 1995.

The Doctor's Daughter, illustrated by Michael Charlton, A.&C. Black (London, England), 1996.

Also author of the children's book *Theo's Time.*

SIDELIGHTS: Norma Clarke is a literary historian and an author of nonfiction for adults and fiction for children. She is perhaps best known for her nonfiction works. Her book *Ambitious Heights: Writing, Friendship, Love: The Jewsbury Sisters, Felicia Hemans and Jane Welsh Carlyle* is a study of four Victorian-era writers. Maria Jane Jewsbury was a literary journalist, while her sister, Geraldine, wrote novels and was a publisher's reader. Felicia Hemans was a very successful poet who wrote nearly one volume a year for two decades, from which she earned a handsome income. Clarke draws on the letters of these women and those of Jane Welsh Carlyle to study the state of women's professional lives, education, and marriages of the period. She particularly evaluates the level of acknowledgment, or lack thereof, of women's literary talent.

The biography *Dr. Johnson's Women* studies female writers in mid-eighteenth-century London by focusing on six who were acquaintances of Samuel Johnson.

They are Elizabeth Carter, Charlotte Lennox, Hester Thrale, Elizabeth Montagu, Hannah More, and Fanny Burney. Of these, only Thrale was connected romantically with Johnson, but Clarke uses Johnson only as a connecting figure to the women she considers independently as intellectuals and writers. Lance Wilcox wrote in the *Historian* that "Clarke does not so much argue a thesis as explore a social/professional world, which she peoples with an interesting and volatile cast." Wilcox concluded, "Her work is literate, graceful, and cagey; implicitly informed by theory without being bogged down by it; and possessing unusual narrative zest."

Clarke studies eighteenth-century women authors in *The Rise and Fall of the Woman of Letters,* including less well-known writers such as Aphra Behn, Elizabeth Singer, and Anne Seward. The book considers why many fine writers received little attention in comparison to those of similar abilities who received lavish praise. *Library Journal* critic Paolina Taglienti called the book "a scholastic achievement."

BIOGRAPHICAL AND CRITICAL SOURCES:

PERIODICALS

Biography, winter, 2003, Sarah R. Morrison, review of *Dr. Johnson's Women,* p. 160.

Historian, spring, 2003, Lance Wilcox, review of *Dr. Johnson's Women,* p. 751.

Library Journal, October 1, 2005, Paolina Taglienti, review of *The Rise and Fall of the Woman of Letters,* p. 74.

Modern Language Review, October, 2002, Judith Hawley, review of *Dr. Johnson's Women,* pp. 934-936.

Victorian Studies, spring, 1993, Deirdre David, review of *Ambitious Heights: Writing, Friendship, Love: The Jewsbury Sisters, Felicia Hemans and Jane Welsh Carlyle,* p. 399.

ONLINE

Kingston University Web site, http://fass.kingston.ac.uk/ (January 5, 2006), author profile.*

COBLE, Colleen 1952-
(Colleen Rhoads)

PERSONAL: Born January 19, 1952, in Wabash, IN; daughter of George (a guard) and Peggy (a homemaker; maiden name, Everroad) Rhoads; married David Coble (a buyer), October 30, 1971; children: David, Jr., Kara. *Ethnicity:* "White." *Education:* Attended Indiana Wesleyan University. *Politics:* Republican. *Religion:* Baptist. *Hobbies and other interests:* Reading, travel.

ADDRESSES: Agent—Karen Solem, Spencerhill Associates, 24 Park Row, P.O. Box 374, Chatham, NY 12037. *E-mail*—colleen@colleencoble.com.

CAREER: Romantic suspense novelist.

MEMBER: Romance Writers of America.

WRITINGS:

NOVELS

Where Leads the Heart, Barbour (Uhrichsville, OH), 1998.

Plains of Promise, Barbour (Uhrichsville, OH), 1999.

The Heart Answers, Barbour (Uhrichsville, OH), 1999.

To Love a Stranger, Barbour (Uhrichsville, OH), 2000.

From Russia with Love, Barbour (Uhrichsville, OH), 2000.

The Cattle Baron's Bride, Barbour (Uhrichsville, OH), 2001.

Love Ahoy, Barbour (Uhrichsville, OH), 2001.

Maggie's Mistake, Barbour (Uhrichsville, OH), 2002.

Red River Bride, Barbour (Uhrichsville, OH), 2002.

Without a Trace (romantic suspense), W. Publishing Group (Nashville, TN), 2003.

Beyond a Doubt (romantic suspense), WestBow Press (Nashville, TN), 2004.

Into the Deep (romantic suspense), WestBow Press (Nashville, TN), 2004.

Distant Echoes, WestBow Press (Nashville, TN), 2005.

(Under name Colleen Rhoads) *Great Lakes Legends,* Steeple Hill Books (Buffalo, NY), 2005.

Black Sands, WestBow Press (Nashville, TN), 2005.

Dangerous Depths, WestBow Press (Nashville, TN), in press.

Work represented in anthologies, including *Spring's Memory*, Barbour (Uhrichsville, OH), 1999; *Forever Friends*, Barbour (Uhrichsville, OH), 2000; *Reunions*, Barbour (Uhrichsville, OH), 2000; *Home for Christmas: Love Reunites Four Orphaned Siblings in Interwoven Novellas*, illustrated by Mari Goering, Barbour (Uhrichsville, OH), 2001; *Heirloom Brides*, Barbour (Uhrichsville, OH), 2001; *Aloha: Four Romances at a Hawaiian Hideaway*, Barbour (Uhrichsville, OH), 2002; *Blind Dates*, Barbour (Uhrichsville, OH), 2002; *Wyoming 4-in-1 Collection*, 2002; and *Gold Rush Christmas: Gold Fever Runs through Four Romantic Novellas*, Barbour (Uhrichsville, OH), 2003.

WORK IN PROGRESS: An "Aloha Reef" trilogy and a "Firejumper" series, both for WestBow Press (Nashville, TN).

SIDELIGHTS: Colleen Coble told *CA:* "Why did I decide to be a writer? I remember the night I finished a book and told the Lord how tired I was of reading books that assumed He didn't exist. I told God I'd do my best to write for him, but He would have to open the doors. I waited and nothing happened. I couldn't think of a thing worth saying.

"Then one night in August, 1990, everything changed. My brother Randy, the oldest of my three younger brothers, was killed by lightning. That tragedy showed me I didn't have time to wait to do what God was calling me to do. During a visit to Wyoming to see where Randy had lived for a time, the first idea for a book came to me, fully conceived. I was working full-time, so it took a year to write it, then seven years to sell it.

"What is my primary motivation for writing? I want to write great stories from a Christian worldview. Stories that are truly entertaining without an agenda like so many books have today.

"My work is influenced by Stephen King. I'm a huge fan of his work and have been since *Carrie* came out. No one can write characters like King. I want to get inside the character's head in the same way King does.

"What inspires me to write on the subjects I have chosen? I love to write suspense because it's all about justice. In my fiction, I can show how God walks with us even through the bad times and everything will be okay in the end."

BIOGRAPHICAL AND CRITICAL SOURCES:

PERIODICALS

Library Journal, April 1, 2004, Tamara Butler, review of *Beyond a Doubt*, p. 78.

ONLINE

Romantic Times, http://www.romantictimes.com/ (October, 2003), Jill Nelson, review of *Without a Trace;* (April, 2004), Jill Nelson, review of *Beyond a Doubt;* (October, 2004), Jill Nelson, review of *Into the Deep.*

*   *   *

COHEN, Edward Stone 1937-1999

PERSONAL: Born 1937, in MA; died, 1999; married; wife's name Fritzi.

CAREER: Environmental activist, hotelier. Owner of the Tabard Inn, Washington, DC, and Moby Dick, Nahcotta, WA.

WRITINGS:

Firewater: A Green Novel, Akashic Books (New York, NY), 2003.

SIDELIGHTS: Edward Stone Cohen's only book, *Firewater: A Green Novel*, was published posthumously and described by its publisher as "an environmental suspense novel." The story is set in Washington State, one of the locations where Cohen, during his lifetime, owned a hotel.

Along the shores of the coastal town, contaminated shellfish are dying, not far from a federally run genetics lab run by the Nazi-like Urbanchuk who sexually harasses Rhoda, one of the narrators. The main character is Chief Sheldrake, a proud Native American presidential candidate, with pronounced sexual appetites, running on environmental and human issues.

Sheldrake, who appears in the third person, is bombarded by the twin evils of government and big business with giant toxic clouds called tarbabies, superbacteria, and genetically mutated, automatic weapons-carrying dwarfs with oversized genitalia, all of which are constant distractions to his run for the White House.

Reviewing *Firewater* for the *Portland Mercury Online,* Erik Henriksen stated that there is no such genre as environmental suspense, and added that unlike the claim on the book's cover, the story "isn't 'brutally funny,' nor does it produce 'belly laughs.' It is brutal, but in a vicious, painful way, and it does produce something to do with my belly, that being a strong desire to eviscerate myself."

Justin Bauer wrote in a *Citypaper.net* review that "Cohen's sincerity as an environmentalist comes through" but "the values Cohen clearly sees as heroic come off flaky and mixed up, like month-old granola."

In a review for *Splendid* online, Jenn Sikes called Sheldrake "an Indian Bill Clinton" and noted that in this novel, Cohen "bares much anger toward the political state. He's gifted enough to make old metaphors do new tricks, and here, his constant prurient references reflect the Earth's condition. He sees it dying as swiftly as the salmonids tagged into futility by Rhoda. . . . It's in such bad shape it needs pills to pop out its shit. The book's thrust is to humorously comment upon the moral state informing our environmental choices. Cohen mixes in moral lessons, peeing a little wisdom by the trees or lakes his characters pass."

Sikes found Sheldrake to be a sympathetic character and an underdog to root for as he outwits the federals, but she wondered why Cohen gives his characters flaws unnecessary to the story, including his portrayal of Sheldrake as a heavy drinker, which she said "seems like a prop, intended to allow his Indians to talk about themselves in a way white people—his most likely readers—will immediately understand."

In *Library Journal* Jim Dwyer felt that inconsistencies in the text and the frequent references to bodily functions may "put off some readers, but others will be delighted by his wild romp."

BIOGRAPHICAL AND CRITICAL SOURCES:

PERIODICALS

Library Journal, April 1, 2003, Jim Dwyer, review of *Firewater: A Green Novel,* p. 128.

ONLINE

Citypaper.net (Philadelphia, PA), http://www.citypaper. net/ (June 26, 2003), Justin Bauer, review of *Firewater.*

Portland Mercury Online, http://portlandmercury.com/ (July 24, 2003), Erik Henriksen, review of *Firewater.*

Splendid, http://www.splendidezine.com/ (February 8, 2004), Jenn Sikes, review of *Firewater.**

*   *   *

COJOCARU, Steven

PERSONAL: Born in Montreal, Quebec, Canada.

ADDRESSES: Agent—c/o Author Mail, Random House, 1745 Broadway, New York, NY 10019.

CAREER: Journalist. *Flare,* Canada, correspondent, 1989-91; *People* (magazine), 1994—, began as a stringer, became West Coast style editor and columnist; *Today,* fashion correspondent; *Entertainment Tonight,* fashion correspondent. Contributor to and appearances on television shows, including VH1's *Behind the Music.*

WRITINGS:

Red Carpet Diaries: Confessions of a Glamour Boy, Ballantine Books (New York, NY), 2003.

Author of the columns "Hot Shots," and "Behind the Seams" (for *People*).

SIDELIGHTS: Steven Cojocaru has been a fashion correspondent since the 1980s when he covered parties for the Canadian fashion magazine *Flare.* He moved to Hollywood in the early 1990s, where he wrote a syndicated fashion column titled "Hot Shots," which ran in more than one hundred newspapers across the country. In 1994, Cojocaru joined *People* magazine as a stringer, and by 2000, he was their West Coast style editor and author of the column "Behind the Seams." Cojocaru has contributed to many television shows and specials, and he has written of his experiences in and rising to the limelight in his memoir, *Red Carpet Diaries: Confessions of a Glamour Boy.* A *Publishers Weekly* reviewer wrote that "from the inside scoop on Hollywood to enough zingers to placate the most starstruck reader, his book is dressed to thrill."

Cojocaru was born in Montreal to parents who emigrated from Romania. He credits his seamstress mother, in part, with his interest in fashion. He writes of fifth-grade taunts by classmates when he showed up for school in bell bottoms, disco shirts, and wooden clogs, and how, by the time he reached high school, he was accepted into the circle of the most popular girls because of his fashion sense.

The flamboyant Cojocaru describes his favorite outfits that consist of leather pants, white fur coats, "white, gauzy, balloon drawstring pants," and oversize sunglasses. *Bookreporter.com* reviewer Shannon Bloomstran wrote that "if you cannot recall ever seeing Steven, you should picture a cross between Aerosmith's lead singer, Steven Tyler, and Mick Jagger with Valerie Bertinelli's hair." Bloomstran noted that Cojocaru spends considerable time writing about his own hair.

An interviewer for *MSN Entertainment* said that Cojocaru "is obsessed with his hair—he calls a flat iron hairstyling tool one of his best friends—he says he didn't get an MTV VJ job because he showed up in a leather vest and no shirt."

As a fashion reporter for *People,* Cojocaru has worked both coasts and attended all the glamorous events, from the Academy Awards to the Golden Globes. *Maclean's* contributor Amy Cameron wrote that "every week, loyal stargazers and fashionistas flip to the back pages of the magazine [*People*] or tune into NBC's *Today* show to hear his latest diatribe on Melanie's large lips or J. Lo's unseemly panty line."

Library Journal's Rosellen Brewer commented that Cojocaru "dishes about the stars he's encountered." He names those he has found to be friendly, including Halle Berry and Meryl Streep, and those he has not, including Calista Flockhart and Helen Hunt. Berry shows up again in a tie with Nicole Kidman as Cojocaru's favorite red-carpet goddess.

Cojocaru recalls his meetings and gossip sessions with a number of stars, including the women of *Friends.* Amanda Cuda wrote in a review for *Curled Up with a Good Book* online that *Red Carpet Diaries* "is hardly an intellectual workout, but in times like this, a little well-written fluff is highly appreciated."

BIOGRAPHICAL AND CRITICAL SOURCES:

BOOKS

Cojocaru, Steven, *Red Carpet Diaries: Confessions of a Glamour Boy,* p. 86.

PERIODICALS

Library Journal, March 15, 2003, Rosellen Brewer, review of *Red Carpet Diaries: Confessions of a Glamour Boy,* p. 86.
Maclean's, April 14, 2003, Amy Cameron, review of *Red Carpet Diaries,* p. 55.
Publishers Weekly, February 10, 2003, review of *Red Carpet Diaries,* p. 173.
WWD, January 21, 2003, Merle Ginsberg, "Dishing with One of the Fashion World's Premier Funny Men, *People* Style Reporter Steven Cojocaru," p. 17.

ONLINE

Bookreporter.com, http://www.bookreporter.com/ (February 8, 2004), Shannon Bloomstran, review of *Red Carpet Diaries.*
Curled Up with a Good Book, http://www.curledup. com/ (February 8, 2004), Amanda Cuda, review of *Red Carpet Diaries.*
MSN Entertainment, http://entertainment.msn.com/ (March 19, 2003), interview with Cojocaru.*

*   *   *

CONRAD, Chris
See CONRAD, Christine

CONRAD, Christine 1946-
(Chris Conrad)

PERSONAL: Born 1946.

ADDRESSES: Office—Natural Woman Institute, 8539 Sunset Blvd., Los Angeles, CA 90069. *E-mail*—chriscoprd@aol.com.

CAREER: Writer, public speaker, administrator, and women's health activist. New York City film, television, and theater office, commissioner, 1970-74; Bantam Books and Warner Books, New York, NY, editor, 1974-82; screenwriter, 1982—. Natural Woman Institute (nonprofit women's health information organization), founder, 1997.

WRITINGS:

(With Kevin Wade) *Junior* (screenplay), Universal Pictures, 1994.
(With Marcus Laux) *Natural Woman, Natural Menopause,* HarperCollins Publishers (New York, NY), 1997.
A Woman's Guide to Natural Hormones, forewords by Leo Galland, Jesse Lynn Hanley, and Carolyn V. Shaak, Perigee Books (New York, NY), 2000.
Jerome Robbins: That Broadway Man, That Ballet Man (biography), Booth-Clibborn (London, England), 2000.
Mademoiselle Benoir (novel), Houghton Mifflin (Boston, MA), 2006.

SIDELIGHTS: Author Christine Conrad is a novelist, biographer, and women's health advocate. She is the founder of the Natural Women's Institute, a nonprofit organization that helps women find doctors in the United States and Canada who specialize in natural treatments for menopausal changes. Her *Natural Woman, Natural Menopause,* which was written with naturopathic doctor Marcus Laux, presents detailed information on what natural hormones are and how women who want to use them can find them. In addition to practical current advice, the authors offer a historical overview of the use of medicinal plants in alleviating menopausal symptoms, and a background of how the U.S. pharmaceutical industry has approached menopause treatment.

A Woman's Guide to Natural Hormones "provides the reader with the information needed to make an educated decision about hormone therapy," noted reviewer Janice Cuzzell in *Dermatology Nursing.* Conrad includes material for women experiencing typical symptoms such as insomnia, fatigue, decreased sex drive, and hot flashes. She explains how to choose over-the-counter natural hormone treatments and describes methods for focusing individual treatments on particular conditions or symptoms of menopause. Anthony L. Rosner, writing in *Alternative Therapies in Health and Medicine,* called Conrad's work a "clearly written, highly accessible, and engaging book," and concluded that "the material presented in Conrad's book is essential for women who plan to take a more activist role in restoring and maintaining their own health."

As a biographer, Conrad is the author of *Jerome Robbins: That Broadway Man, That Ballet Man.* Robbins was a brilliant choreographer and director with a reputation for being difficult to work with. Still, he was considered a genius by many of his peers and associates. Robbins was also well known—and vilified—for providing names of suspected Communists and associates in Hollywood to the notorious House Un-American Affairs Committee (HUAC) in 1953, which consequently harmed the careers of numerous performers. Still, his impact on the American theater was significant, and he worked on such high-profile, even iconic, productions as *The King and I, West Side Story,* and *Gypsy.*

Conrad was a friend of Robbins's for more than thirty years, and early in their relationship they even lived together for a time. The author's assessment of Robbins is therefore tempered by affection while enhanced by close familiarity. "Her view of her subject is not only kind, but sweet-natured," commented Doris Hearn in *Dance.* Through her own experiences with Robbins and considerable access to his papers by the Jerome Robbins Estate, Conrad "has come up with an enormously readable book, profusely illustrated with numerous photographs, many of which have never been seen previously," noted Jennie Schulman in *Back Stage.* Barbara Kudanis, writing in *Library Journal,* called Conrad's biography "a heartfelt tribute to a man she clearly loved who contributed much to his art."

In what a *Publishers Weekly* critic called "Conrad's pleasant first novel," *Mademoiselle Benoir* features an idealistic and romantic mathematics professor in his thirties. Tim Reinhart has moved to France, where he has bought a farm in the sparsely populated Midi region. While there, he works to renovate the house into proper living quarters including a studio for his fledgling interest in art. Told in the format of letters addressed to family and friends, the story unfolds as Reinhart tries to deal with unfamiliar laws and customs, accommodates his emotionally unpredictable girlfriend, Marcelline, and works on living what he calls "an authentic life." He makes the acquaintance of a prominent local family, the Benoirs, who welcome him hospitably. He becomes particularly great friends with Catherine Benoit, who is twenty years his senior, but as the novel progresses their friendship becomes deeper and eventually turns to love. When the two decide to marry, they face obstacles such as virulently disapproving family members, a stifling local bureaucracy, and the social pressure of longstanding French traditions. *Booklist* reviewer Laurie Sundborg called the novel "a thoroughly satisfying and thoughtful story of love triumphant." *Library Journal* contributor Christine DeZelar-Tiedman observed that "the characters are likable and engaging, and it's hard not to root for them."

BIOGRAPHICAL AND CRITICAL SOURCES:

PERIODICALS

Alternative Medicine Review, April, 1999, Kathleen Head, review of *Natural Woman, Natural Menopause,* p. 111.

Alternative Therapies in Health and Medicine, May-June, 2001, Anthony L. Rosner, review of *A Woman's Guide to Natural Hormones,* p. 150.

American Theatre, October, 2001, Mark Dundas Wood, "A Tyrant and His Whipping Boys," review of *Jerome Robbins: That Broadway Man, That Ballet Man,* p. 117.

Back Stage, May 4, 2001, Jennie Schulman, review of *Jerome Robbins,* p. 11.

Booklist, November 15, 2005, Laurie Sundborg, review of *Mademoiselle Benoir,* p. 18.

Dance, November, 2001, Doris Hearn, "Dancing around the Real Robbins," review of *Jerome Robbins,* p. 66.

Dermatology Nursing, August, 2000, Janice Cuzzell, review of *A Woman's Guide to Natural Hormones,* p. 272.

Health Naturally, December-January, 1998-1999, review of *Natural Woman, Natural Menopause,* p. 20.

Kirkus Reviews, October 1, 2005, review of *Mademoiselle Benoir,* p. 1044.

Library Journal, May 1, 1997, Kate Kelly, review of *Natural Woman, Natural Menopause,* p. 133; May 1, 2001, Barbara Kudanis, review of *Jerome Robbins,* p. 86; November 15, 2005, Christine DeZelar-Tiedman, review of *Mademoiselle Benoir,* p. 60.

Publishers Weekly, October 3, 2005, review of *Mademoiselle Benoir,* p. 47.

Total Health, May-June, 2000, review of *A Woman's Guide to Natural Hormones,* p. 14.

Variety, June 25, 2001, Wendy Smith, "Robbins' Twin Tomes," review of *Jerome Robbins,* p. 28.

ONLINE

Natural Woman Institute Web site, http://www.naturalwoman.org (January 15, 2006).

*   *   *

CONWAY, Rosaleen D.

PERSONAL: Born in Wellington, New Zealand; married; children: seven. *Ethnicity:* "New Zealand." *Religion:* Roman Catholic.

ADDRESSES: Home—14 Sunset Parade, Plimmerton, New Zealand. *E-mail*—rconway@paradise.net.nz.

CAREER: Writer. National Office of Catholic Communications, worked as journalist; *Marist Messenger,* work as proofreader for nearly twenty years; producer of a Catholic news program on local-access community radio network; freelance radio and print writer.

AWARDS, HONORS: Reader's Digest/New Zealand Society of Authors' Fellowship, Stout Research Centre, Victoria University of Wellington, New Zealand, 1997. Awards for stories from British Broadcasting Corporation and Commonwealth Broadcasting Association, 1997, 1999, and 2002.

WRITINGS:

Saints Alive (short stories), Marist Centre (Wellington, New Zealand), 1987.

Purely Business (novel), Col-Com Press (Orewa, New Zealand), 1995.

Feed My Revenge (contemporary novel), CA Publishing (Mana, NZ), 2003.

Other writings including a film script, *The Seeking Feet;* a short film, *The Birthday Party;* and writing for a children's television series. Contributor to periodicals and short story collections.

WORK IN PROGRESS: Research on Irish, Danish, and Maori backgrounds for a collection of short stories.

SIDELIGHTS: Rosaleen D. Conway told *CA:* "I spent four years researching and writing *Feed My Revenge,* studying documents and books I didn't expect ever to read. It's a contemporary novel about the Catholic church in the immediate future.

"My first published work was a report of my brother's christening when I was seven. I've never stopped writing. We have seven adult children, and during their growing-up years I found writing much better than dusting."

*   *   *

COOPER, M.E.
    See LERANGIS, Peter

*   *   *

COOPER, T.

PERSONAL: Born in Los Angeles, CA. *Education:* Graduated from Middlebury College; Columbia University, M.F.A.

ADDRESSES: Home—New York, NY. *Agent*—c/o Author Mail, Akashic Books, P.O. Box 1456, New York, NY 10009. *E-mail*—GoGetTCooper@hotmail. com.

CAREER: Taught high school English in New Orleans, LA; worked in the editorial departments of various New York publications; *Fish Tank* (zine), editor and publisher. Bronx Academy of Letters, writer-in-residence, 2004.

AWARDS, HONORS: Firecracker Alternative Book Award, 1999, for *Fish Tank;* MacDowell Colony fellow (twice); Lambda Literary Award finalist, and Barnes and Noble Discover Great New Writers pick, both for *Some of the Parts.*

WRITINGS:

Some of the Parts: A Novel, Akashic Books (New York, NY), 2002.

Lipshitz Six, or Two Angry Blondes (novel), Dutton Adult (New York, NY), 2006.

(Editor, with Adam Mansbach) *Fictional History of the United States with Huge Chunks Missing,* Akashic Books (New York, NY), 2006.

Contributor to anthologies and other volumes, including *The Future Dictionary of America* (includes CD), by Dave Eggers, Nicole Krauss, and others, edited by Jonathan Safran Foer, McSweeney's, 2004; and *The Insomniac Reader: Stories of the Night,* Manic D Press, 2005. Contributor to periodicals, including the *New York Times, Believer, Teen People, Out, Parenting,* and *Time for Kids.*

SIDELIGHTS: On her Web site, T. Cooper notes that while working for *Teen People* on stories about bands that included The Backstreet Boys, she decided to form an all-female band, which she named The Backdoor Boys. The four androgynous band members enhanced their boyish looks, and their performances were booked internationally, as far away as Malaysia.

Cooper's debut novel, *Some of the Parts: A Novel,* features four very diverse characters who include Isak, Taylor, Arlene, and Charlie. Taylor is Arlene's daughter, and Charlie is Arlene's brother. Arlene pops pills to forget the husband who left her and she owns a shop in Providence, Rhode Island. The androgynous and bisexual woman named Isak is a performance artist who lives in New York City. Isak lives with Charlie, who is HIV-positive, but she decides to leave him and move to Los Angeles. Taylor is also bisexual, and she meets Isak and begins a relationship with her in Los Angeles. These four characters are the "parts" of the title. In a review for the *San Francisco Chronicle Online,* Diane Anderson-Minshall described *Some of the Parts* as "a wry look at the intricacies of gender, sexuality and identity and how we use them as labels to make exiles of one another."

Lipshitz Six, or Two Angry Blondes is the story of a family of Russian Jews who immigrate to the United States in 1907. After arriving in New York, one of their young sons disappears from the immigration line. Five-year-old Reuven is blonde and, they tell authorities, doesn't look Jewish. He is never found, and the family settles in Texas. When Esther is told by a psychic that Reuven will become famous and then suffer a tragedy, she becomes convinced that Charles Lindbergh is her son and sends a constant stream of letters to the Lindberghs after their son is kidnapped in 1932. The story then moves to the year 2002, when a great-grandson, a blond rapper named T. Cooper (the author's name as well), loses his parents in a car crash and returns to Texas to make funeral arrangements. A *Publishers Weekly* critic wrote that Cooper adds to the themes of Jewish heritage and assimilation with "both postmodern parody and Chagallesque folk magic."

BIOGRAPHICAL AND CRITICAL SOURCES:

PERIODICALS

Advocate, January 21, 2003, review of *Some of the Parts: A Novel,* p. 89.
Booklist, November 1, 2005, John Green, review of *Lipshitz Six, or Two Angry Blondes,* p. 24.
Boston Phoenix, May 22, 2003, Amy Finch, review of *Some of the Parts.*
Kirkus Reviews, July 15, 2002, review of *Some of the Parts,* p. 974; October 15, 2005, review of *Lipshitz Six, or Two Angry Blondes,* p. 1099.
Lambda Book Report, April-July, 2003, Carol Rosenfeld, review of *Some of the Parts,* p. 19.
Publishers Weekly, September 2, 2002, review of *Some of the Parts,* p. 56; October 10, 2005, review of *Lipshitz Six, or Two Angry Blondes,* p. 32.

ONLINE

Brooklyn Rail Online, http://www.thebrooklynrail.org/ (December 20, 2005), Randolph Lewis, "T. Cooper: Portrait of a Young Novelist."

San Francisco Chronicle Online, http://sfgate.com/ (December 8, 2002), Diane Anderson-Minshall, review of *Some of the Parts.*
T. Cooper Home Page, http://www.t-cooper.com (January 5, 2006).*

* * *

**COPSEY, Jane
See FINNIS, Jane**

* * *

**COX, Ana Marie 1972-
(Ann O'Tate)**

PERSONAL: Born September 23, 1972, in Lincoln, NE; married Chris Lehmann (editor). *Education:* Graduated from the University of Chicago.

ADDRESSES: *Home*—Arlington, VA. *Agent*—c/o Riverhead Books Publicity, Penguin Group, 375 Hudson St., New York, NY 10014. *E-mail*—dogdaysgirl@gmail.com.

CAREER: Writer, editor, and journalist. *Mother Jones,* former features editor; *Suck.com,* former executive editor; *Wonkette.com,* Web log author, 2003-06, editor emeritus, 2006—. Affiliated with *National Geographic, Inside, Chronicle of Higher Education,* and *American Prospect.*

WRITINGS:

(Editor, with Joey Anuff) *Suck: Worst-Case Scenarios in Media, Culture, Advertising, and the Internet,* illustrated by Terry Colon, Wired (San Francisco, CA), 1997.
Dog Days (novel), Riverhead Books (New York, NY), 2006.

Contributor to periodicals, including *Feed, Spin,* and *Wired.* Contributor, as Ann O'Tate, to *Suck.com.*

WORK IN PROGRESS: "An anthropological study of the next generation of political leaders," for Riverhead Books.

SIDELIGHTS: Ana Marie Cox gained fame and some notoriety as the author of the satirical Web log *Wonkette.com.* The Web log features humorous commentary on national politics and current events. "I think what I have to be careful of is that I don't let an opportunity to make fun of anyone go by," Cox told Melissa P. McNamara in an interview posted on *Mediabistro.com.*

Cox retired her position as full-time author of the Web log in 2006 when her first novel, *Dog Days,* was published. Melanie Thorton, the story's protagonist, is a campaign staff member for the Democratic presidential candidate and is having an affair with a well-known, married journalist. At the same time, a group called the Citizens for Clear Heads is claiming that the Democratic candidate was brainwashed in college. In order to divert bad press away from herself and her boss, Melanie creates the fictional Web log of "Capitolette," a waitress whose many sexual partners include prominent politicians. Melanie hires a true, promiscuous waitress to play the role of Capitolette, but she does not expect the waitress to live up to her imagined reputation and rapid rise to fame.

The book mirrors the real-life scandal involving Jessica Cutler, a former Senate staff member who kept an online sex diary under the pseudonym "Washingtonienne." Cox helped reveal Cutler's identity by calling attention to the Washingtonienne's log on *Wonkette. com.* Cox's fictionalization of the event was met with mixed reviews. "Just call it Bridget Jones Goes to Washington or Sex and the Capital City," a *Kirkus Reviews* contributor observed. Although a *Publishers Weekly* reviewer wrote that the author's "powers of plot construction . . . don't match her political savvy: emotions are predictable, plot twists few," Christopher Buckley, writing in the *New York Times,* called the book a "brisk, smart, smutty, knowing and very well-written first novel." Buckley continued, "If this sparkly, witty—occasionally vicious—little novel is any indication of Wonkette's talent, then Cox ought to log out of cyberspace and start calling herself Novelette."

BIOGRAPHICAL AND CRITICAL SOURCES:

PERIODICALS

Booklist, December 1, 2005, Ilene Cooper, review of *Dog Days,* p. 4.

Kirkus Reviews, December 1, 2005, review of *Dog Days,* p. 1244.

New Yorker, January 23, 2006, review of *Dog Days,* p. 91.

New York Times, January 8, 2006, Christopher Buckley, "Web of Lies."

Publishers Weekly, December 12, 2005, review of *Dog Days,* p. 40.

Seattle Times, June 27, 2004, Susannah Rosenblatt, "Wonkette.com Author Ana Marie Cox Is Fearless Driver of Beltway Buzz."

U.S. News & World Report, January 16, 2006, Alex Kingsbury, "Tales of A Beltway Snarkster," p. 24.

Washington Post, January 4, 2006, Amy Argetsinger and Roxanne Roberts, "Wonkette's Sex Change," p. C1.

ONLINE

Ana Marie Cox Home Page, http://mtblog. anamariecox.com (March 16, 2006).

Mediabistro.com, http://mediabistro.com/ (March 30, 2004), Melissa P. McNamara, interview with author.

Rocky Mountain News Online, http://www. insidedenver.com/ (January 27, 2006), John Dicker, "Political Satire's All Bark, No Bite In *Dog Days.*"

St. Louis Post-Dispatch Online, http://www.stltoday. com/ (January 8, 2006), Harry Levins, review of *Dog Days.*

Antic Muse, http://www.theanticmuse.com (March 16, 2006), author's Web log.

Morning News, http://www.themorningnews.org/ (January 29, 2004), Rosecrans Baldwin, interview with author.

Village Voice Online, http://www.villagevoice.com/ (January 6, 2006), Izzy Grinspan, review of *Dog Days.**

*   *   *

CREEGAN, Nicola Hoggard
(Nicola Hoggard-Creegan)

PERSONAL: Female. *Education:* Victoria University, B.A. (with honors); Gordon Cornwell Theological Seminary, M.A.T.S.; Drew University, M.Phil, Ph.D.

ADDRESSES: Office—Bible College of New Zealand, 221 Lincoln Rd., PB 93104, Henderson, Waitakere City, New Zealand. *E-mail*—nicolahc@bcnz.ac.nz.

CAREER: Bible College of New Zealand, Auckland, lecturer, 2000—.

WRITINGS:

(With Christine D. Pohl) *Living on the Boundaries: Evangelical Women, Feminism, and the Theological Academy,* InterVarsity Press (Downers Grove, IL), 2005.

SIDELIGHTS: After finishing her studies at Drew University in New Jersey, Nicola Hoggard Creegan lectured at a Methodist university in North Carolina. Her research interests include the interface between science and theology, feminist theology, the theology of healing, human freedom, and issues in postmodernism and narrative theology. In keeping with her theological studies background, she wrote *Living on the Boundaries: Evangelical Women, Feminism, and the Theological Academy* with ethicist Christine D. Pohl. The focus of the book is the intersection of evangelical religion, feminism, and academic life. Commenting on the scarcity of publications with similar topics, Graham Christian, writing in *Library Journal,* called the book "groundbreaking and crucial." Reviewing *Living on the Boundaries* on the *Christians for Biblical Equality* Web site, Mary Stewart Van Leeuwen praised the book, describing it as "empirically and theoretically grounded . . . astute, timely, and compassionate."

BIOGRAPHICAL AND CRITICAL SOURCES:

PERIODICALS

Library Journal, October 1, 2005, Graham Christian, review of *Living on the Boundaries: Evangelical Women, Feminism, and the Theological Academy.*

ONLINE

Bible College of New Zealand Web site, http://www.bcnz.ac.nz/ (December 15, 2005), author profile.

Christians for Biblical Equality Web site, http://www.cbeinternational.org/ (December 15, 2005), Mary Stewart Van Leeuwen, review of *Living on the Boundaries.*

* * *

**CUNNINGHAM, Elin Hilderbrand
See HILDERBRAND, Elin**

* * *

**CUNQUEIRO, Álvaro 1911-1981
(Álvaro Cunqueiro Mora, Álvaro Labrado)**

PERSONAL: Born December 22, 1911, in Mondoñedo, Spain; died February 27, 1981, in Vigo, Spain; son of Joaquín (a pharmacist) and Josefa Mora de Cunqueiro. *Education:* Studied history at the University of Santiago de Compostela.

CAREER: Poet and author. Founder and editor of periodicals *Galiza,* 1920, and *Papel de Color,* 1932; *Pueblo Gallego* (daily newspaper), Vigo, Spain, staff writer, 1937-39; *Noche,* Madrid, Spain, staff writer, 1939-49; *A.B.C.,* Madrid, staff writer, 1939-49; *Faro de Vigo,* Vigo, editor; *Destino,* Madrid, associate editor.

AWARDS, HONORS: Nadal Prize, for *Un hombre que se parecía a Orestes.*

WRITINGS:

Balada de las damas del tiempo pasado, Alhambra (Madrid, Spain), 1930.
Mar ao norde, Nós (Santiago de Compostela, Spain), 1932.
Cantiga nova que se chama riveira, Resol (Santiago de Compostela, Spain), 1933.
Poemas do sí e non, Un (Lugo, Spain), 1933.
Poemas: Antología de inéditos, Descobrimento (Lisbon, Portugal), 1934.
Elegías y canciones, Apolo (Barcelona, Spain), 1940.
(Under pseudonym Álvaro Labrado) *San Gonzalo,* Nacional (Madrid, Spain), 1945.

Dona do corpo delgado, Soto (Pontevedra, Spain), 1950, new edition, 1957.

Crónica de la derrota de las naciones, Atlántida (Coruña, Spain), 1954.

Merlín e familia, i outras historias, Galaxia (Vigo, Spain), 1954, translated by Colin Smith as *Merlin and Company,* Charles E. Tuttle (Rutland, VT), 1996.

As crónicas do sochantre, Galaxia (Vigo, Spain), 1956, translation by the author published as *Las crónicas del sochantre,* AHR (Barcelona, Spain), 1959.

El caballero, La muerte y El diablo, y otras dos o tres historias, Grifón (Madrid, Spain), 1956.

(With José María Castroviejo Blanco Cicerón) *Teatro venatorio y coquinario gallego,* Monterrey (Vigo, Spain), 1958, published as *Viaje por los montes y chimeneas de Galicia: Caza y cocinas,* Espasa-Calpe (Madrid, Spain), 1962, revised and enlarged edition, 1978.

O incerto señor Don Hamlet, príncipe de Dinamarca, Galaxia (Vigo, Spain), 1958.

Escola de menciñeiros e Fabula de varia xente, Galaxia (Vigo, Spain), 1960.

Las mocedades de Ulises, Argos (Barcelona, Spain), 1960, 2nd edition, Destino (Barcelona, Spain), 1970.

Si o vello Sinbad volvese ás illas, Galaxia (Vigo, Spain), 1961, translated by the author as *Cuando el viejo Sinbad vuelva a las islas,* Argos (Barcelona, Spain), 1962.

Rutas de España: El camino de Santiago, Españolas (Madrid, Spain), 1962.

Itinerarios turístico-gastronómicos por la provincia de Pontevedra—Rias Bajas, Faro de Vigo (Vigo, Spain), 1964.

Tesouros novos e vellos, Galaxia (Vigo, Spain), 1964.

(With Gaspar Massó) *Pesca y conservas,* [Madrid, Spain], 1964.

El camino de Santiago, Faro de Vigo (Vigo, Spain), 1965, translated as *The Way of Saint James,* Faro de Vigo, 1965.

Rutas de España: Lugo, La Coruña, Pontevedra, Orense, Españolas (Madrid, Spain), 1967.

Lugo, Everest (León, Spain), 1968.

Flores del año mil y pico de ave, Taber (Barcelona, Spain), 1968.

El envés, Taber (Barcelona, Spain), 1969.

Un hombre que se parecía a Orestes, Destino (Barcelona, Spain), 1969.

La cocina cristiana de occidente, Taber (Barcelona, Spain), 1969.

Pontevedra—Rías Bajas, Taber (Barcelona, Spain), 1969.

Laberinto y cía, Taber (Barcelona, Spain), 1970.

El descanso del camellero, Taber (Barcelona, Spain), 1970.

Vigo y su ría, Everest (León, Spain), 1971.

Xente de aquí e de acolá, Galaxia (Vigo, Spain), 1971.

Vida y fugas de Fanto Fantini, Destino (Barcelona, Spain), 1972.

A cociña galega, Galaxia (Vigo, Spain), 1973, translated by the author as *Cocina gallega,* Everest (Madrid, Spain), 1981.

Don Hamlet e tres pezas mais, Galaxia (Vigo, Spain), 1974.

El año del cometa con la batalla de los cuatro reyes, Destino (Barcelona, Spain), 1974.

La otra gente, Destino (Barcelona, Spain), 1975.

Rías Bahas gallegas (in Spanish, French, and English), Everest (Madrid, Spain), 1975.

Tertulia de boticas prodigiosas y Escuela de curanderos, Destino (Barcelona, Spain), 1976.

Os outros feirantes, Galaxia (Vigo, Spain), 1979.

Obra en Galego completa (omnibus), Volume 1: *Poesía, teatro,* Volume 2: *Narrativa,* Volume 3: *Semblanzas,* Volume 4: *Ensaios,* Galaxia (Vigo, Spain), 1980–91.

(Editor and author of prologue) Alfonso X, King of Castile and Leon, *Cantigas de Santa Marí,* Galaxia (Vigo, Spain), 1980.

Vigo en su historia, Caja de Ahorros Municipal de Vigo (Vigo, Spain), 1980.

Las Historias gallegas, Banco de Crédito e Inversiones (Madrid, Spain), 1981.

Ver Galicia, photographs by Raimon Camprubi, Destino (Barcelona, Spain), 1981, Galician translation by the author published as *Ollar Galicia,* 1981.

Homenaxe a Alvaro Cunqueiro, University of Santiago de Compostela (Santiago de Compostela, Spain), 1982.

Rías Bajas Gallegas, photographs by Francisco Díez González and M. Luz Gutiérrez de Diez, Everest (Madrid, Spain), 1982.

Fábulas y leyendas de la mar, Tusquets (Barcelona, Spain), 1982.

Antología poética (in Galician and Castilian), translation by César A. Molina, Plaza & Janés (Barcelona, Spain), 1983.

Tesoros y otras magias, Tusquets (Barcelona, Spain), 1984.

Viajes imaginarios y reales, Tusquets (Barcelona, Spain), 1986.

Herba aquí ou acolá/Hierba aquí o allá (in Galician and Castilian), translation by César A. Molina, Visor (Madrid, Spain), 1988.

El pasajero en Galicia, selected and edited by César Antonio Molina, Tusquets (Barcelona, Spain), 1989.

Escritos recuperados, edited by Anxo Tarrió Varela, University of Santiago de Compostela (Santiago de Compostela, Spain), 1991.

Flor de diversos: escolma de poetas traducidos, edited by Xesús González Gómez, Galaxia (Vigo, Spain), 1991.

La bella del dragón: de amores, sabores y fornicos, selected by César Antonio Molina, Tusquets (Barcelona, Spain), 1991.

La historia del caballero Rafael, selected by Anxo Tarrio, Edhasa (Barcelona, Spain), 1991.

Alvaro Cunqueiro, edited by José Filgueira Valverde, Real Academia Galega (Coruna, Spain), 1991.

Alvaro Cunqueiro: (1911-1981), Xunta de Galicia (Santiago de Compostela, Spain), 1991.

Cunqueiro en la radio: Cada día tiene su historia y otras series, Fundación "Pedro Barrié de la Maza, Conde de Fenosa" (Coruna, Spain), 1991.

A máxia da palavra: Cunqueiro na rádio, Sotelo Blanco (Santiago de Compostela, Spain), 1991.

Cada dia tiene su historia y otras series: comentarios radiofónicos, Radio Nacional de España, Fundación "Pedro Barrié de la Maza, Conde de Fenosa" (Coruna, Spain), 1991.

Encuentros, caminos y noticias en el Reino de la Tierra, Compostela (Santiago de Compostela, Spain), 1991.

O reino da chuvia: artigos esquencidos (collection of articles), Servicio Publicaciones Diputación Provincial (Lugo, Spain), 1992.

Papeles que fueron vidas (collection of articles), edited by Xesús González, Tusquets (Barcelona, Spain), 1994.

Entrevistas a Cunqueiro (interviews), edited by Ramón Nicolás Rodriguez, 1994.

Narrativa curta: antoloxía, edited by María Xesús Nogueira, Asociación Socio-Pedagóxica Galega (Vigo, Spain), 1997.

Poesía en gallego completa, translated by Vicente Araguas and César Antonio Molina, Visor Libros (Madrid, Spain), 2003.

Contributor to periodicals, including *Escorial* and *Vértice.*

SIDELIGHTS: Described as the author of "the finest Galician poetry of the twentieth century" by *Dictionary of Literary Biography* contributor Xoan González-Millán, Álvaro Cunqueiro was a poet, essayist, and novelist known for his often fanciful works and love for his native Galician people, history, and landscape. A rising star prior to the Spanish Civil War, Cunqueiro initially wrote verses primarily in his native tongue. After Francisco Franco came to power, however, writers were persecuted for writing in anything but Castilian, and so Cunqueiro published works in this language for a time. However, he later managed to write in both Galician and Castilian, often translating his poetry and fiction into both tongues. His skill with language and ability to draw on archaic as well as modern terminology give his writings a unique and challenging character, while Cunqueiro's flights into fantasy, Roman and Celtic history, and mixture of literary traditions has also made him a distinctive voice in Spanish literature. As for his thematic concerns, the author sought his own path as well, focusing on his interest in Galician culture and history.

Influenced in his early works by the artistic trends of the time, including Cubism and Surrealism, Cunqueiro also wrote poems influenced by neotroubadorism, which was "based on the fin de siècle rediscovery of medieval Galician troubadours' verses," explained González-Millán. This is clearly seen in the poet's first successful collection, *Cantiga nova que se chama riveira.* Another early collection is his *Poemas do sí e non,* which contains free verse poems that show surrealistic influences, though to a decreasing degree. The poems that appear in Conqueiro's *Herba aquí ou acolá/Hierba aquí o allá* were written during the 1960s and 1970s, though the bilingual edition did not appear until 1988. Xoan González-Millán considered this work to be the poet's most extraordinary collection, with its "unrestrained musicality" and "existential uneasiness." The critic concluded: "Perhaps *Herba* will eventually be seen as a turning point in the development of Galician poetry in the twentieth century. With this work, Cunqueiro indicates the paths back to the poetry of the past, centered on the melancholy meditation on death, the nostalgia for a lost love, and the bitterness of old age."

With regard to his fiction, Cunqueiro has often been praised for his novels that take myths and legends from other literary traditions and place them into a Galician landscape and history. The author does this with the Greek stories of Orestes in *Un hombre que se parecía a Orestes* and Ulysses in *Las mocedades de Ulises,* and with the Arthurian character of Merlin the wizard in *Merlín e familia, i outras historias.* Unfortunately, the Galician world that Cunqueiro so loved had largely been overtaken by progress, even in the author's own time. Thus, his verse, fiction, and even essay collections repeatedly look to bygone days; "but then," commented Ricardo Landeira in *World Literature Today,* "sadly enough, that is all that remains recognizably Galician: history, literature, and superstition."

BIOGRAPHICAL AND CRITICAL SOURCES:

BOOKS

Dictionary of Literary Biography, Volume 134: *Twentieth-Century Spanish Poets,* Thomson Gale (Detroit, MI), 1993.

PERIODICALS

Hispania, March, 1970, John W. Kronik, review of *Un hombre que se parecía a Orestes,* p. 152; May, 1971, James A. Flightner, review of *Merlín e familia, i outras historias,* pp. 396-397; December, 1971, James A. Flightner, review of *Las mocedades de Ulises,* p. 971.
World Literature Today, winter, 1977, Olga Prjevalinskaya Ferrer, review of *Tertulia de boticas y Escuela de curanderos,* p. 70; winter, 1986, Ricardo Landeira, review of *Tesoros y otras magias,* p. 94; summer, 1987, David Ross Gerling, review of *Viajes imaginarios y reales,* p. 428; winter, 1993, Patricia Hart, review of *La bella del dragón: De amores, sabores y fornicos,* p. 171.*

* * *

**CUNQUEIRO MORA, Álvaro
See CUNQUEIRO, Álvaro**

D

DAISNE, Johan 1912-1978
[A pseudonym]
(Herman Thiery)

PERSONAL: Born September 2, 1912, in Ghent, Belgium; died from a heart attack, August 9, 1978, in Ghent, Belgium; married Polly van Dyck, 1944; married Marthe Kinaupenne, 1957. *Education:* University of Ghent, doctorate, 1936.

CAREER: Writer and librarian. Ghent Municipal Library, Ghent, Belgium, chief librarian, 1945-77; University of Ghent, professor of Germanic languages. Work-related activities include Royal Film Archive, administrative council; *Klaver(en)drie,* cofounder; *Nieuw Vlaams tijdschrift,* member of the editorial board.

MEMBER: PEN, Royal Flemish Academy of Language and Literature.

AWARDS, HONORS: Prize from the City of Ghent, 1944; Die Kogge International prize (Germany), 1967; Belgian State Prizes, 1944, 1960; Royal Flemish Academy prizes, 1957, 1958.

WRITINGS:

Maud Monaghan, Snoeck Ducaju (Ghent, Belgium), 1940.
De charade von advent (play; title means "The Advent Charade"), Manteau (Brussels, Belgium), 1942.

De trap van steen en wolken (novel; title means "The Staircase of Stone and Clouds"), Manteau (Brussels, Belgium), 1942, reprinted, 1969.
Zes domino's voor vrouwen, Manteau (Brussels, Belgium), 1944.
Hermine uit-de-storm, een cyclus verzen uit en voor het leven, Manteau (Brussels, Belgium), 1944.
Drie-hoog-voor, Manteau (Brussels, Belgium), 1945.
De liefde is een schepping van vergoding, Manteau (Brussels, Belgium), 1946.
In Memorium, Drukkerij A. Vandeweghe (Ghent, Belgium), 1946.
Het boek der zeven reizen . . . Verzamelde gedicthen, 1937-1944, De Sleutel (Antwerp, Belgium), 1946.
Schimmen om een schemerlamp, 1947, 3rd edition, Manteau (Brussels, Belgium), 1979.
De man die zijn haar kort liet knoppen, Manteau (Brussels, Belgium), 1947, reprinted, Paris-Manteau (Amsterdam), 1972, translated by S.J. Sackett as *The Man Who Had His Hair Cut Short,* Horizon (New York, NY), 1965.
Van nitsjevo tot chorosjo: Een geillustreerde en van bio-bibliografische aantekeningen voorziene anthologie der Russische literatuur (criticism), Electa (Brussels, Belgium), 1948.
Het eiland in de stille Zuidzee, Manteau (Brussels, Belgium), 1949.
De vrede van Wroclaw; of, Een proeve van spijkerschrift op het ijzeren gordijn, Uitgeverij Electa (Brussels, Belgium), 1949.
Met dertien aan tafel: of, Knalzilver met schelpgoud (short stories; title means "With Thirteen at Table"), Electa (Brussels, Belgium), 1950, selection published as *Dossier nr. 20.174: Een verhaal,* Manteau (Brussels, Belgium), 1966.

Het kruid aan-de-balk: Een bussel gedichten, Manteau (Brussels, Belgium), 1953.

Die vier heilsgeliefden, Ontwikkeling (Antwerp, Belgium), 1955.

Filmatiek; of, De film als levenskunst, Elsevier (Amsterdam, Netherlands), 1956.

't En is van U hiernederwaard, Manteau (Brussels, Belgium), 1956.

Lago Maggiore (novel), Manteau (Brussels, Belgium), 1957.

Lantarenmuziek, Nederlandsche Boekhandel (Antwerp, Belgium), 1957.

Letterkunde en Magie, S.M. Ontwikkeling (Antwerp, Belgium), 1958.

Grüsz Gott: Een idylle uit Carinthië, De Vlam (Ghent, Belgium), 1958.

Feest van de film: Het WT-festival Brussel '58, De Vlam (Ghent, Belgium), 1958.

De neusvleugel der muze (film novelization), Standaard-Boekhandel (Amsterdam, Netherlands), 1959.

Pierre Benoit; of de lof van de roman romanesque, Ontwikkeling (Antwerp, Belgium), 1960.

De nacht komt gauw genoeg, Desclée de Brouwer (Brugge, Belgium), 1961.

Met een inktvlek geboren; een ernstig-schalk zak-en zaakwoordenboekje, Heideland (Hasselt, Belgium), 1961.

Hoe schoon was mijn school (novel), Ontwikkeling (Antwerp, Belgium), 1961.

Baratzeartea: Een baskisch avontuur of de roman van een schrijver (novel), Manteau (Brussels, Belgium), 1963.

De bioscopiumschuiver: Een tweede pocket filmatiek (film reviews), Heideland (Hasselt, Belgium), 1963.

De trein der traagheid (film novelization), Manteau (Brussels, Belgium), 1963.

De wedloop der jeugd gevolgd door Het venster op het leven en de fan met aantekeningen door Jaak Frontier, Ontwikkeling (Antwerp, Belgium), 1964.

Als kantwerk aan de kim: Een roman van de stille week (novel), Manteau (Brussels, Belgium), 1964.

Charaban, Manteau (Brussels, Belgium), 1965.

De droom is een herinnering aan dat wat nimmer is gebeurd, Desclée de Brouwer (Brugge, Belgium), 1965.

Ganzeveer en kogelpen, of More or Less Brains. Een nieuwe "klapper gedachten," Heideland (Hasselt, Belgium), 1965.

Het geluk: Luisterspel [and] Wat is magisch-realisme (essays), Manteau (Brussels, Belgium), 1966.

Reveillon-reveillon. Een tweeluikroman, Manteau (Brussels, Belgium), 1966.

Ontnoeting in de zonne keer (novel), Manteau (Brussels, Belgium), 1967.

De Engelse groetenis (poetry), Manteau (Brussels, Belgium), 1967.

Twee schelpen en wat gruis, Manteau (Brussels, Belgium), 1967.

Ontmoeting in de zonnekeer (novel), Boekengilde de Clauwaert (Louvain, Belgium), 1967.

Fringilla: Een nieuwe [achtste] bundei filmatiek (film reviews), Heideland (Hasselt, Belgium), 1968.

Gojim, gevolgd door Zuster Sharon, Manteau (Brussels, Belgium), 1968.

Met zeven aan tafel, Manteau (Brussels, Belgium), 1969.

Filmografisch lexicon der werelditeratuur (title means "Filmographic Dictionary of World Literature"), Storyscientia (Gand, Belgium), Volume 1, 1971, Volume 2, 1977, Volume 3, 1978.

De Hollandse reis: Neder-Land richt zich op (poetry), Manteau (Paris, France), 1972.

De vier heilsgeliefden, Manteau (Paris, France), 1973.

Omnibus, Reinaert (Brussels, Belgium), 1974.

Trefwoorden: Een kleine verzameling (verhalende) aforismen, Orion (Brugge, Belgium), 1975.

Winterrozen voor een kwakzalver, Manteau (Brussels, Belgium), 1976.

Bloed op het witte doek (film reviews), Manteau (Brussels, Belgium), 1978.

Venezy, of, Het Eiland in de stille Zuidzee, Manteau (Brussels, Belgium), 1978.

Verzamelde gedichten, Gottmer (Nijmegen, Belgium), 1978.

Gepijnde honing, Elsevier (Amsterdam, Netherlands), 1979.

Over oude en nieuwe rolprenten: de dingen die niet voorbijgaan, Manteau (Antwerp, Belgium), 1980.

Zes liederen op gedichten van Johan Daisne (songs), music by Jean Baptiste Gyselynck, WLSK (Brussels, Belgium), 1984.

De beste verhalen van Johan Daisne, Manteau (Antwerp, Belgium), 1987.

Mijn huis van droom en werkelijkheid, Manteau (Antwerp, Belgium), 1998.

Work represented in anthologies; work translated into French and German.

SIDELIGHTS: Johan Daisne is the pen name of Herman Thiery, a prominent Belgian author who wrote poetry, fiction, and film criticism in Dutch. Prior to beginning his career as a librarian in the mid-1940s, Daisne began writing *De charade von advent,* a play, and *De trap van steen en wolken,* a novel. These two works, which appeared in 1942, marked Daisne as an artist with an interest in the fantastic and metaphysical. In his subsequent works, notably the novel *De man die zijn haar kort liet knoppen,* he continued to produce fiction that merged romance with both the realistic and the extraordinary. *De man die zijn haar kort liet knoppen,* which features a protagonist who is compelled to recall his past, has been ranked among the most significant achievements in modern Belgian fiction.

After publishing *De man die zijn haar kort liet knoppen,* which appeared in 1947, Daisne produced more than thirty additional works under the same pseudonym, including the poetry collection *Verzamelde gedichten,* which includes autobiographical verse, and the three-volume film dictionary *Filmografisch lexicon der wereldliteratuur,* which has been hailed as a major contribution to cinema studies due in part to its multi-language text. Appraising Daisne's body of work, an *Encyclopedia of World Literature in the Twentieth Century* contributor concluded that "the intellectual originality and richness of [his] major prose works put them in the first rank of modern European literature."

BIOGRAPHICAL AND CRITICAL SOURCES:

BOOKS

Apers, Michel, and others, *Johan Daisne: 10 films, 10 bioscopen* (exhibit catalogue), Internationaal Filmfestival van Wvlaanderen (Ghent, Belgium), 1994.
Encyclopedia of World Literature in the Twentieth Century, St. James Press (Detroit, MI), 1999.

PERIODICALS

American Book Review, annual, 1979, review of *Filmografisch lexicon der wereldliteratuur,* p. 508.
Choice, October, 1967, review of *The Man Who Had His Hair Cut Short,* p. 850; October 1976, review of *Dictionnaire Filmographique de la Litterature Mondiale,* p. 964.
De Vlaamse Gids, Volume 54, Number 6, 1970, "De man die zijn pen leeg laat lopen," pp. 17-18.

Dietsche Warande en Belfort, Volume 111, 1966, "Johan Daisne of het schrijven als een onderonsje," pp. 48-52; Volume 112, 1967, "Tweeluik van Daisne," pp. 385-388; Volume 124, 1979, Albert Westerlinck, "Oudere Dicters," pp. 42-43.
Nation, review of *The Man Who Had His Hair Cut Short,* December 13, 1965, p. 480.
New Leader, December 20, 1965, review of *The Man Who Had His Hair Cut Short,* p. 15.
New York Times Book Review, November 28, 1965, review of *The Man Who Had His Hair Cut Short,* p. 68.
Ons Erfdeel Volume 10, number 3, 1967, "Een Nederlands boek in het buitenland: The Reception of Johan Daisne in the United States," pp. 81-88; Volume 11, number 1, 1967, "Koggeliteratuurprijs voor Johan Daisne," p. 168.
Revue de Litterature Comparee, Volume 219, Number 3-4, 1981, Nathalie Sinaiski, "Echos de Dostevskij dans l'ouevre de Johan Daisne," pp. 401-418.
Saturday Review, December 18, 1965, review of *The Man Who Had His Hair Cut Short,* p. 35.
Spiegel der Letteren, Volume 15, 1974, pp. 241-262.
Tydskrif vir Letterkunde, Volume 8, number 2, 1970, "Spreken over en met Johan Daisne," pp. 54-58.
World Literature Today, autumn, 1965, review of *De droom is een herinnering aan dat wat nimmer is gebeurd,* p. 485.

ONLINE

International Movie Database, http://www.imdb.com/ (January 22, 2005).*

*   *   *

DALE, Anna 1971-

PERSONAL: Born 1971, in England. *Education:* Kent University, B.A., M.A. c. 2003. *Hobbies and other interests:* Walking with her dog.

ADDRESSES: Home—Southampton, England. *Agent*—c/o Author Mail, Bloomsbury Publishing, 38 Soho Sq., London W1D 3HB, England.

CAREER: Novelist. Works part time at a bookshop.

AWARDS, HONORS: Carnegie Medal longlist, 2004, for *Whispering to Witches.*

WRITINGS:

Whispering to Witches, Bloomsbury (New York, NY), 2004.
Dawn Undercover, Bloomsbury (New York, NY), 2005.

ADAPTATIONS: Dale's books have been adapted as audiobooks.

SIDELIGHTS: Anna Dale loved to tell stories as a child, and that hobby, along with her love of children's literature, has followed her into adulthood. When a temporary job at a book shop following college became something more permanent, Dale was inspired by her daily involvement with both children's books and their readers to do some writing of her own. Her first novel, *Whispering to Witches,* came out of her coursework toward a master's degree in creative writing and was actually written over a span of two months. While her more recent work has been less hurried, Dale has devised a useful strategy to combat writers' block. "If I'm struggling with a particularly troublesome sentence," she explained in an interview for the Bloomsbury Web site, "I find the consumption of chocolate an absolute necessity."

A fantasy involving a threat to British witchery, *Whispering to Witches* introduces Joe Binks, a twelve-year-old who becomes caught up with a coven of rather confused witches while taking the train from school to visit his mother and stepfather for Christmas break. He becomes friends with Twiggy, the youngest of the five members of the Deadnettle Coven, and through her becomes aware of a plot by the diabolical Logan Dritch to rid Earth of its spell-casting population through the use of a powerful hex. Dritch has acquired the hex by stealing page 513 from the powerful witches' reference, Mabel's Book, and the Deadnettles now hope to regain it, with Joe's help. Comparing *Whispering to Witches* to J.K. Rowling's "Harry Potter" books, a *Publishers Weekly* contributor wrote that the author "nimbly ties together the spidery threads of her story in a beguiling denouement," while in *Booklist* Kay Weisman praised Dale's story as "tightly plotted and with enough twists and turns to keep readers on

their toes." "Dale has fun creating the witch universe . . . and imbues it with some clever spells and tricks," according to *Rambles* online reviewer Celeste Miller, dubbing *Whispering to Witches* a "light and exciting tale."

From fantasy, Dale turns to the mystery genre in *Dawn Undercover.* In this middle-grade story, eleven-year-old Dawn Buckle longs for excitement, but because of her drab dress and unremarkable appearance she is often overlooked by everyone around her. Dawn's nondescript nature ultimately serves her well, however; while leaving school one day, she is recruited for a super-secret-spy organization, undergoes super-secret-spy training, and then embarks on her super-secret-spy mission: to travel to a small village and track down a fellow spy named Angela who has mysteriously vanished while on the trail of the evil Murdo Meek. While noting that Dale starts her story off slowly, a *Publishers Weekly* contributor cited the author's "ample humor" and quaint British references, concluding that the "complex" plotting of *Dawn Undercover* incorporates "false leads and tangles that will keep kids guessing." "Dawn's growth in self-esteem and confidence is believable," wrote Cindy Dobrez in a *Booklist* review of Dale's novel, adding that the book's "secondary characters are unique."

BIOGRAPHICAL AND CRITICAL SOURCES:

PERIODICALS

Booklist, November 15, 2004, Kay Weisman, review of *Whispering to Witches,* p. 601; March 1, 2005, Traci Todd, review of *Whispering to Witches* (audio version), p. 1218; October 15, 2005, Cindy Dobrez, review of *Dawn Undercover,* p. 50.
Kirkus Reviews, October 1, 2004, review of *Whispering to Witches,* p. 958; October 15, 2005, review of *Dawn Undercover,* p. 1135.
Kliatt, Carol Reich, review of *Whispering to Witches* (audio version), p. 58.
Publishers Weekly, October 4, 2004, review of *Whispering to Witches,* p. 88; December 20, 2004, "Flying Starts," p. 30; January 10, 2005, review of *Whispering to Witches,* p. 24; November 14, 2005, review of *Dawn Undercover,* p. 69.
School Library Journal, November, 2004, Elaine E. Knight, review of *Whispering to Witches,* p. 140; February, 2005, Cindy Lombardo, review of *Whispering to Witches* (audio version), p. 76.

ONLINE

Bloomsbury Web site, http://www.bloomsbury.com/childrens/ (May 1, 2006), "Anna Dale."
Rambles Online, http://www.rambles.net/ (February 5, 2005), Celeste Miller, review of *Whispering to Witches.**

*   *   *

DALEY, Michael J.

PERSONAL: Male. *Education:* Xavier University, B.A.; Villanova University, M.A.

ADDRESSES: Home—OH. *Agent*—c/o Author Mail, Holiday House, 425 Madison Ave., New York, NY 10017.

CAREER: Educator and writer. St. Xavier High School, Cincinnati, OH, teacher.

WRITINGS:

At Home with the Sun: Solar Energy for Young Scientists, Professor Solar Press, 1995.
Nuclear Power: Promise or Peril?, Lerner Publications (Minneapolis, MN), 1997.
Amazing Sun Fun Activities, illustrated by Buckley Smith, Learning Triangle Press (New York, NY), 1998.
Getting Around without Gasoline, Northeast Sustainable Energy Association, 2002.
(With William Madges) *Vatican II: Forty Personal Stories,* Twenty-third Publications, 2003.
(With Lee P. Yeazell) *In All Things: Everyday Prayers of Jesuit High-School Students,* Loyola Press, 2003.
Space Station Rat, Holiday House (New York, NY), 2005.

Contributor to periodicals, including *St. Anthony Messenger, Momentum, Youth Update, America,* and *Religion Teacher's Journal.*

SIDELIGHTS: Ohio author and educator Michael J. Daley has published several nonfiction titles for children and adults, many of which focus on science and nature. With *Space Station Rat,* Daley moves into fiction, spinning a futuristic story about a boy named Jeff who lives with his parents on a space observation station. The only young person on the station, Jeff is usually in the way or in trouble of one sort or another. Then adventure enters his life when he decides to help his robotic nanny find a space-station stowaway: a rodent who is chewing on and damaging the station's electrical wiring. Unknown to Jeff, the rat Nanny is hunting is not a normal rodent: an escaped lab rat, the creature is actually a smart, technologically proficient creature that has been trained to wiretap and retrieve confidential information. The Rat has also been taught to communicate on a computer keyboard, as Jeff learns when he begins receiving e-mails from the tiny typist. In Daley's novel, rat and boy learn to trust each other, thwart Nanny's efforts to destroy the rodent, and become friends despite their odd circumstances.

Chris Sherman, writing in *Booklist,* enjoyed *Space Station Rat,* writing that "short, snappy sentences, appealing characters, and tension between Nanny and Jeff combine with constant threats of ship malfunctions and Rat's struggle to survive to create a fast-paced story sure to please science fiction buffs." Elaine E. Knight, a reviewer for *School Library Journal,* called the book "a thoughtful and satisfying adventure for middle grade science-fiction fans," and a *Kirkus Reviews* critic predicted that "science geeks will enjoy the details of life on a space shuttle."

BIOGRAPHICAL AND CRITICAL SOURCES:

PERIODICALS

Booklist, November 1, 1997, Chris Sherman, review of *Nuclear Power: Promise or Peril?,* p. 459; August, 2005, Chris Sherman, review of *Space Station Rat,* p. 2026.
Kirkus Reviews, June 1, 2005, review of *Space Station Rat,* p. 635.
National Catholic Reporter, July 4, 2003, Dennis M. Doyle, "Reminiscences Bring Vatican II Era to Life," p. 16.
School Library Journal, January, 1998, Linda Wadleigh, review of *Nuclear Power,* p. 122; August, 2005, Elaine E. Knight, review of *Space Station Rat,* p. 126.*

DANCHEV, Alex

PERSONAL: Male. *Education:* Holds a P.G.C.E. and a Ph.D.

ADDRESSES: Office—The School of Politics and International Relations, University of Nottingham, University Park, Nottingham NG7 2RD, England. *E-mail*—alex.danchev@nottingham.ac.uk.

CAREER: Writer and educator. University of Nottingham, Nottingham, England, professor of international relations. Tate Museum, London, England, member of the Acquisition Committee of the Patrons of New Art.

AWARDS, HONORS: "Books of the Year" selection, *Observer,* 1993, for *Oliver Franks: Founding Father;* Whitbread Prize for Biography shortlist, for *Alchemist of War: The Life of Basil Liddell Hart.*

WRITINGS:

EDITOR

Establishing the Anglo-American Alliance: The Second World War Diaries of Brigadier Vivian Dykes, Brassey's Defence (London, England), 1990.

International Perspectives on the Falklands Conflict: A Matter of Life and Death, St. Martin's Press (New York, NY), 1992.

(With Dan Keohane) *International Perspectives on the Gulf Conflict, 1990-1991,* St. Martin's Press (New York, NY), 1994.

Fin de Siècle: The Meaning of the Twentieth Century, Tauris Academic Studies/St. Martin's Press (New York, NY), 1995.

(With Thomas Halverson) *International Perspectives on the Yugoslav Conflict,* Tauris Academic/St. Martin's Press (New York, NY), 1996.

(With Daniel Todman) Alan Brooke, *War Diaries, 1939-1945: Field Marshal Lord Alanbrooke,* University of California Press (Berkeley, CA), 2001.

(With John MacMillan) *The Iraq War and Democratic Politics,* Routledge (New York, NY), 2005.

NONFICTION

Very Special Relationship: Field-Marshall Sir John Dill and the Anglo-American Alliance, 1941-1944, Brassey's Defence (London, England), 1986.

The Franks Report: The Falkland Islands Review, 1992.

Oliver Franks: Founding Father, Clarendon Press (London, England), 1993.

On Specialness: Essays in Anglo-American Relations, St. Martin's Press (New York, NY), 1998.

Alchemist of War: The Life of Basil Liddell Hart, Weidenfeld & Nicolson (London, England), 2000.

Georges Braque: A Life, Arcade (New York, NY), 2005.

Contributor to periodicals, including the *Times Literary Supplement, Intelligence and National Security, Review of International Studies, Journal of Contemporary History,* and *International Affairs.* Contributor to books, including the *Oxford Dictionary of National Biography; The Oxford Companion to Military History,* 2001; *Telling Lives,* 2001; *September 2001: War, Terror & Judgement,* 2003; and *Closeness and Asymmetry: The Anglo-American and Mexican-American 'Special Relationships,'* 2005.

SIDELIGHTS: Alex Danchev is a prolific author and editor who specializes in biography and international conflict. A professor of international relations, Danchev is an expert in his field. His biographies, however (at least according to a profile posted on the *David Higham Associates* agency Web site), are a labor of love. And, of his many works, Danchev's biographies have been the most widely reviewed and praised.

Oliver Franks: Founding Father is the biography of the influential British political figure Oliver Franks. Franks worked his way through British bureaucratic positions during and after World War II. Danchev's biography notes that Franks was highly influential in shaping England's post-war policies. Franks was also the key figure who influenced America to join the North Atlantic Treaty Organization (NATO). Franks was a 'behind-the-scenes' political figure, noted *New Statesman* contributor John Campbell, and a "scholarly celebration of this paragon is therefore welcome." Campbell went on to note, however, that the book also "clearly demonstrate[s] why writing a biography of the boys in the backroom is so difficult." Dennis Kavanagh, writing in *Parliamentary Affairs,* was far more laudatory. He commented that Danchev's biography "provides a remarkable insight into policy making," and added that it is "an impressive piece of scholarship, written with style and sympathy."

Danchev also edited, with Daniel Todman, *War Diaries, 1939-1945: Field Marshal Lord Alanbrooke.* Lord Alanbrooke, also known simply as Alan Brooke, was a general in the British Army during World Wars I and II. Over the course of the latter, he came into constant conflict with the then prime minister, Winston Churchill. Many of these conflicts are recorded within Alanbrooke's diaries. Reviewers noted that Danchev's edition is the first unabridged and unadulterated version of the journals. Because of this, a *Biography* contributor called the volume "compelling." *Spectator* critic Michael Howard commented that "enough of the diaries remained unpublished to make this new, complete edition well worthwhile." Howard concluded that the book is a "reliable source for all historians of the second world war."

Georges Braque: A Life is Danchev's most acclaimed biography to date. Although overshadowed by his contemporaries, including artist Pablo Picasso, Georges Braque was one of the founders of the cubist movement. The two artists were friends, and while their friendship is explored in the book, so too are Braque's other personal relationships. This is of note because Braque was quite reclusive and secretive about his personal life. Thus, this particular aspect of the biography caused a *Publishers Weekly* reviewer to observe that the volume contains some "intriguing revelations." Although Braque's achievements are significant, a *Kirkus Reviews* contributor felt that Danchev may place too much significance upon them. "Scholars are unlikely to agree that Braque's reputation will come to rest as high as Danchev insists," noted the contributor. Regardless, most reviewers praised the biography. The *Publishers Weekly* reviewer called *Georges Braque* a "meticulous contribution to the study of cubism." *Booklist* critic Donna Seaman added: "Danchev is fluent in facts and penetrating in his analysis."

BIOGRAPHICAL AND CRITICAL SOURCES:

PERIODICALS

Biography, fall, 2001, review of *War Diaries, 1939-1945: Field Marshal Lord Alanbrooke,* p. 985.

Booklist, November 1, 2005, Donna Seaman, review of *Georges Braque: A Life,* p. 17.
English Historical Review, April, 1996, R.K. Middlemas, review of *Oliver Franks: Founding Father,* p. 541.
History: Review of New Books, spring, 1997, Julian Delgaudio, review of *Fin de Siècle: The Meaning of the Twentieth Century,* p. 139.
Kirkus Reviews, November 1, 2005, review of *Georges Braque,* p. 1169.
Middle Eastern Studies, October, 1997, Joseph Kostiner, review of *International Perspectives on the Gulf Conflict, 1990-1991,* p. 788.
New Statesman & Society, June 4, 1993, John Campbell, review of *Oliver Franks,* p. 32.
Observer (London, England), June 19, 2005, Peter Conrad, review of *Georges Braque.*
Parliamentary Affairs, January, 1994, Dennis Kavanagh, review of *Oliver Franks,* p. 146.
Publishers Weekly, November 21, 2005, review of *Georges Braque,* p. 44.
Spectator, June 2, 2001, Michael Howard, review of *War Diaries, 1939-1945,* p. 138; September 10, 2005, Richard Shone, review of *Georges Braque,* p. 44.
Sunday Times (London, England), June 19, 2005, Frank Whitford, review of *Georges Braque.*

ONLINE

David Higham Associates Web site, http://www.davidhigham.co.uk/ (March 16, 2005), author profile.
University of Nottingham Web site, http://www.nottingham.ac.uk/ (March 16, 2005), author profile.*

* * *

DAUMAL, René 1908-1944

PERSONAL: Born March 16, 1908, in Boulzicourt, France; died of tuberculosis, May 21, 1944, in Paris, France; married; wife's name Vera.

CAREER: Novelist, poet, essayist, dramatist, and short-story writer. Cofounder of literary journal *Le grand jeu,* 1928-c. 1930.

AWARDS, HONORS: Jacques Doucet Prize, 1936, for *Le Contre ciel.*

WRITINGS:

Le Contre ciel (poems), Université de Paris (Paris, France), 1936, published as *Le contre-ciel: suivi de les dernieres parole du poete,* Gallimard (Paris, France), 1970, translated by Kelton W. Knight as *Le contre-ciel,* Overlook Press (New York, NY), 2005.

Le grande beuverie (novel), Gallimard (Paris, France), 1938, translated by David Coward and E.A. Lovatt as *A Night of Serious Drinking,* Random House (New York, NY), 1979, reprinted, Overlook Press (Woodstock, NY), 2003.

La guerre sainte, Fontaine, 1940, translated by Peter Levi as *The Holy War,* illustrated by Alan Johnston, Morning Star Publications (Edinburgh, Scotland), 1995, translated by Louise Landes-Levi as *The Sacred War,* Coronamundi (Bangor, ME), 1997.

(Translator, with Jean Herbert and Camille Rao) Aurobindo Ghose, *La Kena upanishad,* A. Maisonneuve (Paris, France), 1943.

(Translator) Ernest Hemingway, *Mort dans l'aprè-midi = Death in the Afternoon,* Gallimard (Paris, France), 1949, published in *Nouvelles et récits,* Gallimard (Paris, France), 1963.

Le Mont Analogue (novel), Gallimard (Paris, France), 1952, translated by Roger Shattuck as *Mount Analogue: An Authentic Narrative,* Stuart (London, England), 1959, published as *Mount Analogue: A Novel of Symbolically Authentic Non-Euclidean Adventures in Mountain Climbing,* Pantheon (New York, NY), 1960, reprinted, Overlook Press (Woodstock, NY), 2004.

Essais et notes (essays), Gallimard (Paris, France), 1953, reprinted in two volumes, 1972.

Chaque fois que l'aube paraît, Gallimard (Paris, France), 1953.

Poésie noire, poésie blanche (poems), Gallimard (Paris, France), 1954.

(With Carlo Suarès and Joë Bousquet) *Critique de la raison impure: et les paralipomènes de la comedie psychologique,* 1955, reprinted, Stock (Brussels, Belgium), 1975.

René Daumal: letters à ses amis, Gallimard (Paris, France), 1958.

Le lyon rouge: suivi de la empete des cygnes, Collège de Pataphysique (Paris, France), 1963.

René Daumal, edited by Jean Biès, Seghers (Paris, France), 1967.

Tu t'es toujours trompé, Mercure de France (Paris, France), 1970, translated by Thomas Vosteen as *You've Always Been Wrong,* University of Nebraska Press (Lincoln, NE), 1995.

Bharata: l'origine du théâtre: la poésie et la musique en Inde, Gallimard (Paris, France), 1970.

L'évidence absurde (1926-1934), Gallimard (Paris, France), 1972.

Les pouvoirs de la parole (1935-1943), Gallimard (Paris, France), 1972.

Le grand jeu: collection complète (collection of articles), 1977.

Mugle (also see below), Éditions Fata Morgana (Montpellier, France), 1978, reprinted, 1995.

René Daumal; ou, Le retour à soi: textes inédits de René Daumal: études sur son oeuvre, L'Originel (Paris, France), 1981.

Rasa; or, Knowledge of the Self: Essays on Indian Aesthetics and Selected Sanskrit Studies, New Directions (New York, NY), 1982.

La Langue sanskrite: grammaire, poésie théâtre, L'Originel (Paris, France), c. 1985.

A Fundamental Experiment, translated by Roger Shattuck, Hanuman Books (New York, NY), 1987.

The Lie of the Truth: And Other Parables from The Way of Liberation, translated by Phil Powrie, Hanuman Books (New York, NY), 1989.

The Powers of the Word: Selected Essays and Notes, 1927-1943, translated by Mark Polizzotti, City Lights Books (San Francisco, CA), 1991.

Correspondence, three volumes, edited and with annotations by H.J. Maxwell, Gallimard (Paris, France), 1992–96.

Je ne parle jamais pour ne rien dire: lettres de René Daumal à Artür Harfaux, Éditions Le Nyctalope (Amiens, France), 1994.

Fragment inédits, 1932-99: Premiere etape vers la grand beuverie, Eolienne (Arcueil, France), 1996.

René Daumal's Mugle; and, The Silk, E. Mellen Press (Lewiston, NY), 1997.

Chroniques cinématographiques: 1934 (Aujourd'hui), Au Signe de la Licorne (Clermont-Ferrand, France), 2004.

SIDELIGHTS: René Daumal is known for his writings on spirituality and perception. He spent his youth in the company of several artists called Simplists, who delved into psychological exploration and used drugs. Daumal's own use of carbon tetrachloride, though nearly fatal, later inspired him to write *A Fundamental Experiment,* an essay in which he traces the expansion of his consciousness from simple awareness to drug-induced intuition to a renewed consciousness in which his perceptions were rationalized.

Daumal continued to concern himself with spiritual matters and altered states of consciousness in *Le Contre ciel* a collection of poems which earned him the Prix Jacques Doucet. By this time Daumal, under the tutelage of Gurdjieff disciple Alexandre de Salzmann, had taught himself Sanskrit and established himself as a Hindu scholar with translations of several sacred texts. But his greatest achievement from the 1930s is probably *Le grande beuverie* (later translated as *A Night of Serious Drinking*), a satire on French society in which the author poses the ascendance of a higher spiritual plane as an alternative to a superficial life. At his death, Daumal left unfinished *Le Mont Analogue* (translated as *Mount Analogue: A Novel of Symbolically Authentic Non-Euclidean Adventures in Mountain Climbing*), a novel in which he contends that transcendental knowledge is attained through an understanding of reality and communion with others.

A Night of Serious Drinking and *Mount Analogue* remain Daumal's most accomplished works, though since his death in 1944 many of his other writings have been published. While Michael Wood, writing in the *New York Review of Books,* pointed out that Daumal was not the equal of satirist Jonathan Swift, he added in his review of *Le grande beuverie* that there are "remarkable moments" in the book and some "fine touches of visionary realism." Reviewing the English translation of this book, *Listener* critic Malcolm Bowie asserted: "It is extraordinary that a work as intelligent as this, and one that enlists wit and satire in such a variety of unusual causes, should have had to wait so long before gaining, even in France, a more than minimal readership." Several critics of *Mount Analogue* have commented, too, that as a literary work it has some shortcomings. However, as Leon S. Roudiez stated in the *New York Times Book Review,* "the mature reader will be more intrigued by the mind of the author than impressed by his literary accomplishments." *New York Herald Tribune Book Review* writer Vernon Hall, Jr. praised the "wit and clarity of the prose, [which] reads as easily as a superior piece of Science Fiction."

BIOGRAPHICAL AND CRITICAL SOURCES:

BOOKS

Twentieth-Century Literary Criticism, Volume 14, Thomson Gale (Detroit, MI), 1984.

PERIODICALS

Choice, March, 1980, review of *A Night of Serious Drinking,* p. 79; January, 1996, F.C. St. Aubyn, review of *You've Always Been Wrong,* p. 798.
Listener, November 22, 1979, Malcolm Bowie, "Raising the Glass," review of *A Night of Serious Drinking,* pp. 712-713.
Modern Language Review, October, 1999, Jocelyn Dupont, review of *René Daumal's Mugle; and, The Silk,* p. 1111.
Nation, August 20, 1960, David L. Norton, "Return to the Heart's Longing," review of *Mount Analogue: An Authentic Narrative,* pp. 95-96.
New York Herald Tribune Book Review, August 14, 1960, Vernon Hall, Jr., review of *Mount Analogue,* p. 6.
New York Review of Books, April 17, 1980, Michael Wood, "The Great Game," review of *A Night of Serious Drinking,* pp. 41-43.
New York Times Book Review, July 10, 1960, Leon S. Roudiez, review of *Mount Analogue,* p. 26.
Publishers Weekly, August 27, 1979, review of *A Night of Serious Drinking,* p. 373.
Review of Contemporary Fiction, spring, 2005, Tim Feeney, review of *Mount Analogue,* p. 141.
Times Literary Supplement, October 25, 1996, Ian Pindar, "The Guru and the Gas," review of *You've Always Been Wrong,* p. 26; October 17, 1997, Ian Pindar, "The Last of Nath," review of *Correspondance,* p. 13.
Village Voice, February 11, 1980, Robert Richman, "Pwatt's Progress," review of *A Night of Serious Drinking,* pp. 40-41; October, 1989, Sally S. Eckhoff, "Little Bits," review of *A Fundamental Experiment,* p. 67.*

*   *   *

DAVIDSON, Craig 1976-
  (Patrick Lestewka)

PERSONAL: Born 1976. *Education:* Graduate of the University of New Brunswick.

ADDRESSES: Agent—c/o Author Mail, Penguin Group (Canada), 90 Eglinton Ave. E., Ste. 700, Toronto, Ontario M4P 2Y3, Canada.

WRITINGS:

Rust and Bone: Stories, W.W. Norton (New York, NY), 2005.

Contributor to periodicals, including *Prairie Fire, Fiddlehead, Event,* and *SubTerrain;* writes horror fiction under a pseudonym.

WORK IN PROGRESS: In the Pit (novel).

SIDELIGHTS: Craig Davidson has written stories for literary magazines, dark fantasy under the pseudonym, Patrick Lestewka, and now his first collection, *Rust and Bone: Stories.* Davidson follows a "Hemingway-esque tradition," noted a *Kirkus Reviews* contributor after reading *Rust and Bone.* The eight stories feature hard, damaged men, most of whom are addicted to alcohol, sex, gaming, or violence. They include a boxer, a dog fighter, a magician, a gambler, and a repo man. Davidson's characters have lost limbs, relationships, and the ability to change their lives.

The *Kirkus Reviews* writer concluded by noting that the stories are "thick with bleak characters and thin on redemption." *Booklist* reviewer Joanne Wilkinson described Davidson's prose as "ferociously detailed." A *Publishers Weekly* contributor called *Rust and Bone* an "accomplished, macabre first collection."

Prudence Peiffer commented in *Library Journal* that in addition to the hard-driving stories, "there are also quiet moments of grace." Peiffer found these moments in "On Sleepless Roads" and "An Apprentice's Guide to Modern Magic."

BIOGRAPHICAL AND CRITICAL SOURCES:

PERIODICALS

Booklist, September 1, 2005, Joanne Wilkinson, review of *Rust and Bone: Stories,* p. 56.
Kirkus Reviews, October 1, 2005, review of *Rust and Bone,* p. 1044.
Library Journal, October 15, 2005, Prudence Peiffer, review of *Rust and Bone,* p. 49.

Publishers Weekly, August 29, 2005, review of *Rust and Bone,* p. 29.

ONLINE

Banff-Calgary International Writers Festival Online, http://www.wordfest.com/ (January 5, 2006), profile of Davidson.
Craig Davidson Blog, http://www.penguinblogs.ca/ davidson (January 5, 2005).
Craig Davidson Web site http://www.craigdavidson.net (July 17, 2006).*

* * *

DAVIDSON, Larry 1960-

PERSONAL: Born December 31, 1960, in New York, NY; son of Bernard (an engineer) and Faye (a homemaker; maiden name, Bernstein) Davidson; married October 28, 1990; wife's name Maryanne (a nurse practitioner); children: Abigal, Alana, Alexa. *Ethnicity:* "Caucasian/Jewish." *Education:* Emory University, B.A. (psychology), B.A. (philosophy and religion), and M.A. (philosophy), all 1982; Duquesne University, M.A. (psychology), 1983, Ph.D., 1989; attended Yale University, between 1988 and 1992. *Politics:* "Democratic." *Religion:* Jewish. *Hobbies and other interests:* Cooking, family life.

ADDRESSES: Office—Department of Psychology, Yale University, 319 Peck St., Ste. 6W-1C, New Haven, CT 06513. *E-mail*—larry.davidson@yale.edu.

CAREER: Writer. Yale University, New Haven, CT, postdoctoral fellow in clinical and community psychology, 1990-92, instructor, 1992-93, assistant professor, 1993-99, associate professor of psychology, 1999—, fellow of Calhoun College and director of mental health education program, 1996—, director of program for recovery and community health, 2000—. Connecticut Mental Health Center, New Haven, assistant director for outpatient program development and research, 1994-96, coordinator of outpatient psychology training, 1995-96, associate director of outpatient division, 1996-97, director of psychosis program, 1996-2001, deputy director of clinical services, 1997-98, president of medical and professional staff, 1998-2000, director of clinical services, 1998-2000, director of behavioral health policy and research, 2000—. Mental Health Network of South Central Connecticut, chair of consumer involvement committee, 1991-94; Connecticut Department of Mental Health and Addiction Services, senior clinical officer and mental health policy director, 2000—. Guest lecturer at Trinity College, Burlington, VT, 1997, University of Toronto, 2000, and Nova Southeastern University, 2001; expert witness for legal proceedings; participant in conferences and symposia; consultant to John D. and Catherine T. MacArthur Foundation research network on mental health and the law.

MEMBER: American Psychological Association (president of Mutual Support Interest Group, 1998-2000; chair of systems reform and under-served populations committee, 2003—), American Psychiatric Association (member of Expert Panel on the Development of Practice Guidelines for the Psychosocial Treatment of Schizophrenia, 1998—), Society for Community Research and Action (fellow), Yale Society for Phenomenology and Psychiatry (member of organizing board, 1988-96), Phi Beta Kappa, Psi Chi, Phi Sigma Tau.

AWARDS, HONORS: Distinguished Young Investigator Award and Garmezy scholar, Society for Life History Research, 1990; Karl Jaspers Prize, Association for the Advancement of Philosophy and Psychiatry, 1991; Chairman's Award for outstanding clinical, teaching, and administrative contributions, Department of Psychiatry, School of Medicine, Yale University, 1998; Seton Elm and Ivy Award, Yale University and City of New Haven, 2002; grants from National Institute of Mental Health, State of Connecticut, National Institute on Drug Abuse, National Association of State Mental Health Program Directors, Substance Abuse and Mental Health Services Administration, National Alliance for Research on Schizophrenia and Depression, Eli Lilly Research Laboratories, and Donoghue Foundation.

WRITINGS:

Living outside Mental Illness: Qualitative Studies of Recovery in Schizophrenia, New York University Press (New York, NY), 2003.

Contributor to books, including *Psychological and Social Aspects of Psychiatric Disability,* edited by L. Spaniol, C. Gagne, and M. Koehler, Center for Psychiatric Rehabilitation, Boston University (Boston, MA), 1992; *The Humanistic Movement: Recovering the Person in Psychology,* edited by F.J. Wertz, Gardner Press (New York, NY), 1994; *Mental Disorder, Work Disability, and the Law,* edited by R. Bonnie and J. Monahan, University of Chicago Press (Chicago, IL), 1996; *Consumers As Providers in Psychiatric Rehabilitation,* edited by C.T. Mowbray, D.P. Moxley, and others, International Association for Psychosocial Rehabilitation Services (Columbia, MD), 1997; and *Psychological Treatments for Early Course Psychosis,* edited by J. Gleeson and P. McGorry, Whiley (London, England), 2004. Contributor of nearly 100 articles and reviews to medical and scientific journals, including *Journal of Phenomenological Psychology, Practice: Journal of Psychology and Political Economy, Hospital and Community Psychiatry, Journal of Mental Health Administration, Current Opinion in Psychiatry, American Journal of Psychiatry, Journal of Nervous and Mental Disease, Journal of Social Issues, Children's Services: Social Policy, Research, and Practice,* and *Humanistic Psychologist.* Member of editorial board, *Psychiatric Rehabilitation Journal,* 2004—.

*   *   *

DEAN, Bradley P. 1954-2006

OBITUARY NOTICE— See index for *CA* sketch: Born February 4, 1954, at Clark Air Force Base, the Philippines; died of a heart attack, January 14, 2006, in Bloomington, IN. Educator and author. Dean was best known for his research and editorial work on previously unpublished manuscripts by Henry David Thoreau. Born in the Philippines while his father served in the military, he joined the U.S. Navy himself as a construction mechanic in the mid-1970s. He then was an executive assistant manager for Thunderbird-Red Lion Motor Inns on the West Coast before going back to school and earning his A.A. from Spokane Community College. Dean then attended Eastern Washington University, where he finished a B.A. in 1982 and an M.A. in 1984. For his doctorate work, he attended the University of Connecticut, graduating in 1993. While attending graduate school, Dean began teaching English at Eastern Washington University and the University of Connecticut. From 1988 to 1998 he had joint occupations: the first was as the owner and consultant of Transpacific Communications in Ayden, North Carolina, and as international business communications coordinator for Sunstar, Inc.; the second was to continue his academic career. Briefly teaching at Rhode Island College and the University of Montana, he moved on to be an assistant and then adjunct professor at East Carolina University through much of the 1990s. A member of the Thoreau Society and the Thoreau Country Conservation Alliance, Dean was director of the media center at the Thoreau Institute in Lincoln, Massachusetts, from 1998 to 2005. Having edited the manuscript of Thoreau's *Faith in Seed: The Dispersion of Seeds and Other Late Natural History Writings* in 1993, he was most highly praised for editing the philosopher's *Wild Fruits: Thoreau's Rediscovered Last Manuscript* (2000). Dean next edited *Letters to a Spiritual Seeker* (2004), also by Thoreau. The scholarly community was very appreciative of Dean's work, which turned Thoreau's supremely difficult to read handwriting into valuable published documents that helped academics appreciate Thoreau's contributions to science. At the time of Dean's death, he was working on yet another such manuscript, *Indian Notebooks*.

OBITUARIES AND OTHER SOURCES:

PERIODICALS

Los Angeles Times, February 3, 2006, p. B9.
Washington Post, February 2, 2006, p. B6.

*   *   *

DEDINI, Eldon 1921-2006
   (Eldon Lawrence Dedini)

OBITUARY NOTICE— See index for *CA* sketch: Born June 29, 1921, in King City, CA; died of esophageal cancer, January 12, 2006, in Carmel Valley, CA. Cartoonist, artist, and author. Dedini was an award-winning cartoonist best known for his hundreds of contributions to the *New Yorker* and *Playboy* magazines. With a love for cartoons dating back to his childhood, Dedini began drawing when he was just five years old. Later, he went on to formally study art at Salinas Junior College (now Hartnell College), where he earned an A.A. in 1942. He also gained

experience by working as staff cartoonist for the *Salinas Index Journal and Salinas Morning Post*. He then moved to Los Angeles, working as a janitor to pay for his education at the Chouinard Art Institute, from which he graduated in 1944. Dedini was next hired by Walt Disney Studios to work in its storyboard department. Meanwhile, he strove to build his own freelancing career, but first he was hired by *Esquire* in Chicago to be its cartoonist from 1946 to 1950. Moving back to the Monterey Peninsula in California, near where he was born, Dedini started his freelance career in earnest. He found regular work contributing cartoons to the *New Yorker* and, beginning in 1959, to *Playboy* magazine as well. By this time, he had discovered the importance of writing good gags, concluding that even if a cartoonist had excellent artistic skills, it did not matter unless he or she could write a good joke as well. Dedini consequently became just as accomplished a writer as he was an artist. Because of his *Playboy* work, he became well known for drawing voluptuous cartoon women; but, beginning in 1985, he also found a kind of fame drawing broccoli. He was hired by Mann Packing Inc. in California to create advertising pieces promoting broccoli in a humorous way, doing so successfully for the next nine years. In addition to his cartooning, Dedini was also an accomplished painter, winning particular praise for the posters he created promoting the Monterey Jazz Festival and the Pebble Beach Concours d'Elegance classic car show. A four-time winner of the National Cartoonist Society's best magazine cartoonist award, Dedini collected many of his cartoons in the books *The Dedini Gallery* (1961) and *A Much, Much Better World* (1985).

OBITUARIES AND OTHER SOURCES:

PERIODICALS

Chicago Tribune, January 16, 2006, section 1, p. 13.
Los Angeles Times, January 20, 2006, p. B11.
New York Times, January 14, 2006, p. B14.
Washington Post, January 25, 2006, p. B6.

*   *   *

DEDINI, Eldon Lawrence
   See DEDINI, Eldon

DeFAZIO, Albert J. III

PERSONAL: Male. *Education:* University of Virginia, Ph.D., 1992.

ADDRESSES: Office—Department of English, George Mason University, Robinson A 487, 4400 University Dr., MSN 3E4, Fairfax, VA 22030. *E-mail*—adefazio@gmu.edu.

CAREER: George Mason University, Fairfax, VA, adjunct professor.

WRITINGS:

Literary Masterpieces: The Sun Also Rises ("Gale Study Guides to Great Literature" series), Thomson Gale (Detroit, MI), 2000.
(Editor) *Dear Papa, Dear Hotch: The Correspondence of Ernest Hemingway and A.E. Hotchner,* preface by A.E. Hotchner, University of Missouri Press (Columbia, MO), 2005.

Contributor to the *Hemingway Review, F. Scott Fitzgerald Society Newsletter, American Literary Scholarship: An Annual,* and the *Journal of Foreign Literature.*

SIDELIGHTS: Albert J. DeFazio III has taught introductory and advanced composition and literary surveys. He particularly focuses on the moderns, including Ernest Hemingway and F. Scott Fitzgerald. His *Literary Masterpieces: The Sun Also Rises* is a study guide for the Hemingway novel first published in 1926. The volume is divided into eight sections that contain a plot summary, profiles of the characters, themes, biographical information on Hemingway, and DeFazio's thirteen-page analysis. Ellen Andrews Knodt wrote in the *Hemingway Review* that the first section, titled "About *The Sun Also Rises,*" "is the most student-oriented of the sections with a chapter-by-chapter plot summary of the novel, sprinkled with quotations to anchor the key events in each chapter." The second section describes Hemingway's writing process and the revisions that were made before the manuscript was completed, as well as a discussion of the relationship between writer and editor. "In the third section on themes, DeFazio does a superb job of explaining Hemingway's use of irony and ambiguity to a readership who may not readily understand those ideas as expressed in literature," noted Knodt. The fourth section covers early criticism and reviews, with DeFazio providing a range of opinion. DeFazio includes sidebars that provide personal glimpses into Hemingway's life and thoughts, and includes quotes that include a line from a Nobel acceptance speech. Other sections deal with the novel in history, adaptations, resources and study questions, and an index.

DeFazio is also editor of *Dear Papa, Dear Hotch: The Correspondence of Ernest Hemingway and A.E. Hotchner,* a collection of letters between Hemingway and his good friend who sought out the writer while he was living in Cuba with his fourth wife, Mary. Hotchner originally contacted Hemingway to solicit writing for *Cosmopolitan,* then a general publication, and he became part of the author's entourage. The letters reveal Hemingway's ego. He felt he was the greatest of American writers and criticized the works of others. They note accidents and injuries he suffered while on fishing expeditions and safari and his crushes on young girls and women that Mary to become increasingly irritated. The man who had been held up as the model for the Lost Generation and decades of men became clinically depressed, and decided to take his own life. Mary, who was preparing to leave him, did not recognize the extent of his depression.

Carolyn See reviewed this volume for the *Washington Post,* writing: "What was it in 20th-century society that spawned Hemingway and his decision—all through life—to valorize death, melancholy, risk-taking and misery? Was it that emblematic injury in Italy when he felt his soul going out of his body like a handkerchief out of a pocket? His earliest stories insist on this nihilistic point of view. But the real question remains: Why did we buy it? Why did we enlist so easily in the vast army of the Lost Generation?" See called the collection "fascinating."

BIOGRAPHICAL AND CRITICAL SOURCES:

PERIODICALS

Hemingway Review, fall, 2002, Ellen Andrews Knodt, review of *Literary Masterpieces: The Sun Also Rises,* p. 128.
Library Journal, May 1, 2000, Paul D'Alessandro, review of *Literary Masterpieces,* p. 94.

Reference Reviews, 2000, William Baker, review of *Literary Masterpieces,* p. 35.

School Library Journal, August, 2000, Herman Sutter, review of *Literary Masterpieces,* p. 28.

Washington Post, January 13, 2006, Carolyn See, review of *Dear Papa, Dear Hotch: The Correspondence of Ernest Hamingway and A.E. Hotchner,* p. C4.

ONLINE

George Mason University, Department of English Web site, http://english.gmu.edu/ (March 30, 2006), brief biography of author.*

*   *   *

DELGADO, Ricardo

PERSONAL: Male.

ADDRESSES: Agent—c/o Author Mail, Dark Horse Comics, 10956 S.E. Main St., Milwaukie, OR 97222.

CAREER: Comic book artist, illustrator, storyboard artist/conceptual designer for films.

AWARDS, HONORS: Eisner award, for *Age of Reptiles.*

WRITINGS:

(Illustrator) Robert C. Welch, *Scary Stories for Sleep-Overs,* Price Stern Sloan (Los Angeles, CA), 1991.

Age of Reptiles: Tribal Warfare (collection), Dark Horse Comics (Milwaukie, OR), 1996.

Age of Reptiles: Carnivores #1 (limited edition lithographs), Dark Horse Comics (Milwaukie, OR), 1997.

Age of Reptiles: Carnivores #2 (limited edition lithographs), Dark Horse Comics (Milwaukie, OR), 1997.

Age of Reptiles: Carnivores #3 (limited edition lithographs), Dark Horse Comics (Milwaukie, OR), 1997.

Age of Reptiles: The Hunt (collection), Dark Horse Comics (Milwaukie, OR), 1997.

Age of Reptiles: Carnivores (collection), Dark Horse Comics (Milwaukie, OR), 1997.

Age of Reptiles: Carnivores #4 (limited edition lithographs), Dark Horse Comics (Milwaukie, OR), 1998.

Creator of comic book series, including *Age of Reptiles* and *Hieroglyph;* storyboard artist for films, including *Species, Star Trek: Deep Space Nine, Speed, Men in Black, Tomb Raider, Dinosaur, The Matrix Reloaded,* and *The Matrix Revolutions.*

SIDELIGHTS: Ricardo Delgado is an artist whose first comic book was his award-winning *Age of Reptiles,* a full-color series inspired by his own fascination with dinosaurs, and one that consisted entirely of art and is appropriate for all ages. Mike Richardson, the founder of Dark Horse Comics, offered Delgado the opportunity to draw a series after being impressed with the artist's work. Dark Horse published four limited editions of Delgado's dinosaur lithographs, signed and numbered by the artist, and *Age of Reptiles* has been collected in several volumes, including *Age of Reptiles: The Hunt,* in which a young Allosaur crosses Jurassic North America to escape the pack of Ceratosaurs that killed his mother.

In *Age of Reptiles: Tribal Warfare,* a Deinonychus band steals the eggs of a family of Tyrannosaurus rexes, who take revenge as the thieves concentrate on eating turtle eggs by the sea. The action picks up when an Ichthyosaur rises from the watery depths to join the fray.

Delgado's next series, *Hieroglyph,* features monsters and archeology. In an interview with Delgado, a *Dark Horse Comics Online* contributor said to him that in *Hieroglyph,* "you have a character who travels to another planet far on the other side of the solar system, and he encounters not only the contemporary lives that populate the planet, but he also learns a lot about the history of their ancestors. It's a neat setup for a science fiction comic." Delgado, who said he was influenced as a child by reading *National Geographic* and watching films like *The Seven Voyages of Sinbad,* replied, "there is a whole back story there that you can sort of vaguely figure out, which is all I want. I just want people to read this and say, 'You know there is a really unique history to this planet that might sort of resemble our own.' There are these ruins and fish mummies, and cool stuff, and there are mosaics that show people with cool robes and octopus heads."

The hero of the story is Francisco Chavez, an intellectual who has left his family to explore and chart the planet. Delgado notes that Chavez misses his family very much, "cries for them, and that is based on my love for my family. . . . I want my characters to be that well developed, so that you see their emotions and know them more deeply as a person and a character."

Delgado is also a storyboard artist for films, particularly action/adventure films like sequels to *The Matrix*. In an interview with Redpill for *Whatisthematrix* online, Delgado said that *Matrix* creators Larry and Andy Wachowski are comic book fans and have comics in their backgrounds, "so they try to get a comic book feel for their stories; that's why I'm here." The interview was conducted as Delgado was working on *The Matrix Revolutions*.

Redpill asked him to compare the art departments of the *Matrix* project and *Men in Black*, to which Delgado also contributed. He said that for *Men in Black*, he "was on very early in that film and did a lot of design work, leaving before the production actually started. So this is similar in the sense that we're working really early and developing ideas, even though we're supposedly making a movie in about six months or so, and I'll be leaving the show before the filming starts. That's sort of the role of the illustrator in film, you work on a film and a couple of years later . . . you see this thing on the screen, and that's always really interesting, sometimes to your enjoyment and sometimes not." Delgado said that this was the biggest film he had ever worked on, "a gargantuan story which needs to be designed and told."

Delgado told Redpill that he saw the first *Matrix* with his wife at her urging and didn't know anything about it except what he saw on the promotional poster. He said that "when you don't expect or know anything about a story, and you come in and it kind of floors you like that, watching the film for the first time . . . it was a real treat. And now, a couple of years later to be working on it is really cool. It doesn't get better than that."

BIOGRAPHICAL AND CRITICAL SOURCES:

ONLINE

Dark Horse Comics Online, http://www.darkhorse. com/ (August 31, 1999), interview with Delgado.
Whatisthematrix, http://whatisthematrix.warnerbros. com/ (November, 2000), Redpill, interview with Delgado.*

*   *   *

DELLASEGA, Cheryl 1953-

PERSONAL: Born December 12, 1953, in Patuxent River, MD; daughter of James Robert and Lillian Margaret (Diehl) Miller; married Paul Dellasega, August, 1984; children: Matthew, Ellen, Joe. *Education:* Lancaster General Hospital, Lancaster, PA, R.N. diploma, 1974; Millersville University, B.S., 1981; University of Delaware, M.S., G.N.P., 1982; Temple University, Ph.D., 1988.

ADDRESSES: Home—8 Boxwood Dr., Hershey, PA 17033. *Office*—H134 Humanities, Hershey Medical Center, Hershey, PA 17033. *E-mail*—opheliasmother@ aol.com; cdellasega@aol.com; cxd6@psu.edu.

CAREER: Nurse and author. Hospital of the University of Pennsylvania, Philadelphia, PA, staff nurse, 1974-75; Medox Nursing Pool, Philadelphia, PA, staff nurse, 1975-76; Lancaster General Hospital, Lancaster, PA, CCU staff nurse, 1976; Muhlenburg Hospital, South Plainfield, NJ, CCU staff nurse, 1977; Centre Community Home Health Agency, Bellefonte, PA, visiting nurse and team coordinator, 1977-78; St. Joseph's Hospital and Health Care Center, Lancaster, infirmary charge nurse, 1978-80; Lancaster General Hospital, recovery room staff nurse, 1980-81; Susquehanna Nursing Services, Harrisburg, PA, nurse practitioner, 1985; Rehab Hospital for Special Services, Bellefonte, PA, nurse practitioner, 1987; South Huntingdon County Family Health Center, Orbisonia, PA, nurse practitioner in rural primary care, 1988; geriatric nurse practitioner for Dr. Betsy Eggler, Reedsville, PA, 1989; geriatric nurse practitioner for Dr. Jon Evans, State College, PA, 1992-93; Geisinger Medical Group, State College, geriatric nurse practitioner, 1994-96. Lancaster General Hospital, clinical instructor, school of nursing, 1982; Millersville University, Millersville, PA, instructor, 1982-84; Messiah College, Grantham, PA, instructor, 1984-85; Pennsylvania State University School of Nursing, instructor, 1986-88, assistant professor, 1988-95, associate professor of humanities, 1998—. Visiting scholar, John Hartford Institute for Geriatric Nursing, New York University, 1997; visiting professor, Halshogskolan, Jonkoping, Sweden, 1992, 1997.

MEMBER: American Nursing Association, American Public Health Association, National League of Nursing, American Society on Aging, American Association of University Women, Gerontological Society of America, Pennsylvania Nurses Association, Pennsylvania Long Term Care Council, Sigma Theta Tau, Phi Delta Kappa.

AWARDS, HONORS: Faculty Fellowship, Institute of Aging, Temple University, 1987; Outstanding Alumni Award, Millersville University, 1992; Penn State University Outreach Award, 2004, for work with women and girls; GSA postdoctoral fellowship.

WRITINGS:

Surviving Ophelia: Mothers Share Their Wisdom in Navigating the Tumultuous Teenage Years, Perseus (Cambridge, MA), 2001.
(With Charisse Nixon) *Girl Wars: 12 Strategies That Will End Female Bullying,* Simon & Schuster (New York, NY), 2003.
Mean Girls Grown Up: Adult Women Who Are Still Queen Bees, Middle Bees, and Afraid-to-Bees, John Wiley (Hoboken, NJ), 2005.
The Starving Family: Caregiving Mothers and Fathers Share Their Eating Disorder Wisdom, Champion Press (Fredonia, WI), 2005.
Artolescence: Ten Art-based Activities for Adolescent Girls to Overcome Relational Aggression, Champion Press (Belgium, WI), 2005.
The Girl's Friendship Journal, Champion Press (Belgium, WI), 2006.

Contributor of articles to professional journals and periodicals.

SIDELIGHTS: Cheryl Dellasega is a nurse and counselor who specializes in issues that confront women and girls, mothers and daughters, and the fam-

ily members who support and care for them. Among the topics she covers in her books are relational aggression, or female bullying; eating disorders and body image disorders; the Ophelia Syndrome and adolescent emotional disturbances; and depression and other problems in women and teens. She operates Club Ophelia and Camp Ophelia, a Web site and after-school program respectively, for girls and young women who are experiencing interpersonal conflict, peer pressure, bullying, and other social difficulties. These programs "have helped hundreds of teens learn healthy relationship skills through an arts-based curriculum and mentoring," Dellasega stated on her home page. She is also concerned with making sure that girls who find themselves playing the role of bully or victim in their childhood and teen years do not carry those destructive roles forward into their adult lives.

Surviving Ophelia: Mothers Share Their Wisdom in Navigating the Tumultuous Teenage Years contains the stories of several mothers of troubled teenage girls who helped their daughters overcome, or at least cope with, a variety of emotional and social problems. Included are stories of mothers and daughters facing depression, criminal activity, sexual promiscuity, eating disorders, and other troubles. The participants offer practical suggestions and techniques for confronting and overcoming these difficulties, as well as advice on how families can live with them when their best efforts fail to solve the problem. A reviewer for *Daughters* called *Surviving Ophelia* an "honest book," while a *Publishers Weekly* contributor noted that "there are lessons here that will help every mother dealing with an adolescent daughter."

Girl Wars: 12 Strategies That Will End Female Bullying offers twelve tested strategies and techniques for facing and overcoming relational aggression, or female bullying. Dellasega includes a number of true stories of the effects of bullying, which are "heart-wrenching and call for intervention," observed a *Psychology Today* reviewer. Among Dellasega's suggestions are acquiring preventive skills, developing coping mechanisms, involving fathers in issues of bullying, seeking the support of community organizations in confronting bullying and bullies, and promoting anti-bullying behavior. With a goal of strengthening the personalities and resolve of young women facing bullying, Dellasega strives to also create a level of social change that discourages bullying and instead calls for "confident kindness."

Recognizing that bullying and abusive behavior among girls is not always effectively controlled, Dellasega acknowledges that it also does not always go away when bullies and bullying victims reach adulthood. In *Mean Girls Grown Up: Adult Women Who Are Still Queen Bees, Middle Bees, and Afraid-to-Bees* Dellasega breaks the participants into three categories: queen bees, or the aggressors; middle bees, or those who enable the aggressors; and afraid-to-bees, those who experience the bullying. She addresses how aggressive and bullying behavior might manifest itself in adults in the workplace, church, school, the family, and organizations. She includes a number of anecdotes that illustrate the very real damage that such unchecked behavior can cause, including sabotage by colleagues, professional damage inflicted by aggressive supervisors, and relationship damage caused by overly critical mothers-in-law. Among her suggestions for dealing with the problem are the cultivation of self-awareness, positive and nonthreatening confrontation, and establishing more satisfying relationships with other women in other contexts.

Dellasega once again collects the wisdom of those who have faced their children's troubles head-on in *The Starving Family: Caregiving Mothers and Fathers Share Their Eating Disorder Wisdom.* She presents observations, suggestions, and strategies from the parents of young women suffering from anorexia, bulimia, and a variety of other eating disorders. Dellasega also offers material on boys and eating disorders, "which alone is worth the investment in this important and innovative contribution to the field," commented Dale Ferris in *Library Journal.* Based on a number of anonymous case studies, the stories present information on topics such as discovering the disorder, the effects of the disorder on siblings and parents, finding professional help, dealing with insurance companies, and the expected results after treatment. "What sets the work apart, though, is its emphasizing the need to integrate parents into the treatment process," Ferris concluded.

BIOGRAPHICAL AND CRITICAL SOURCES:

PERIODICALS

Daughters, May-June, 2002, "When Girls Get in Trouble," review of *Surviving Ophelia: Mothers Share Their Wisdom in Navigating the Tumultuous Teenage Years,* p. 3.

Education Week, October 15, 2003, review of *Girl Wars: 12 Strategies That Will End Female Bullying,* p. 38.

Entrepreneur, August, 2004, Aliza Pilar Sherman, "Under Attack? Think Another Woman Is Out to Get You? Here's How to Watch Your Back," p. 36.

Library Journal, August, 2003, Antoinette Brinkman, review of *Girl Wars,* p. 120; February 1, 2005, Dale Farris, review of *The Starving Family: Caregiving Mothers and Fathers Share Their Eating Disorder Wisdom,* p. 103; October 1, 2005, Kay Brodie, review of *Mean Girls Grown Up: Adult Women Who Are Still Queen Bees, Middle Bees, and Afraid-to-Bees,* p. 96.

Psychology Today, September-October, 2003, review of *Girl Wars,* p. 82.

Publishers Weekly, September 10, 2001, review of *Surviving Ophelia,* p. 77; July 18, 2005, review of *Mean Girls Grown Up,* p. 197.

Reference & Research Book News, May, 2003, review of *Surviving Ophelia,* p. 136.

Tribune Books (Chicago, IL), December 15, 2002, review of *Surviving Ophelia,* p. 6.

Voice of Youth Advocates, December, 2004, Charisse Nixon, review of *Girl Wars,* p. 425.

ONLINE

Cheryl Dellasega Home Page, http://www.cheryl dellasega.com (January 15, 2006).

Club Ophelia Web site, http://www.clubophelia.com (January 15, 2006).

Penn State Outreach Magazine Web site, http://www. outreach.psu.edu/ (February 8, 2006), Melissa W. Kaye, "Academia Meets Artistic Ability," profile of Cheryl Dellasega.

Relational Aggression Web site, http://www.relational aggression.net (January 15, 2006).*

*   *   *

de los SANTOS, Marisa 1966-

PERSONAL: Born 1966; married David Teague; children: Charles, Annabel. *Education:* University of Virginia, B.A.; Sarah Lawrence College, M.F.A.; University of Houston, Ph.D.

ADDRESSES: *Home*—Wilmington, DE. *Agent*—Jennifer Carlson, Dunow, Carlson & Lerner Literary Agency, 27 W. 20th St., Ste. 1003, New York, NY 10011. *E-mail*—Marisa@LoveWalkedIn.com.

CAREER: University of Delaware, Newark, DE, former English instructor.

AWARDS, HONORS: Delaware Arts Council grant; Rona Jaffe Writers Award.

WRITINGS:

From the Bones Out: Poems, University of South Carolina Press (Columbia, SC), 2000.
Love Walked In: A Novel, Dutton (New York, NY), 2006.

Contributor of poetry to journals, including the *Antioch Review, Poetry, Prairie Schooner, Western Humanities Review, Chelsea,* and *Virginia Quarterly Review.*

ADAPTATIONS: A film version of *Love Walked In* is planned, starring Sarah Jessica Parker, who will co-produce with Michael London Productions.

WORK IN PROGRESS: A novel.

SIDELIGHTS: Marisa de los Santos is a contributor of poetry to literary journals. Her first published collection, *From the Bones Out: Poems,* was called "crisp and uncanny" by *Poetry* reviewer Bill Christophersen, who also wrote that "the excellence of this collection begins with its fresh renderings and extends to the way many of the poems segue to form a whole." Christophersen noted four consecutive poems that he felt "trace a cycle of loss, recovery, bitterness, and loss revisited that informs the book." They are "For a Stillborn," "Monologue of One Returned," "Bible Stories," and "Luray Caverns: The Discovery." A *Publishers Weekly* contributor concluded that the book "offers a formula of hope and clarity when confronting life's trials and tribulations."

Love Walked In: A Novel is de los Santos's contemporary story about a woman who loves film classics. Cornelia Brown manages a café while dreaming of the day that her leading man might enter her life. When Martin Grace comes to the café, she's sure she's found him. In addition to adoring Martin, Cornelia becomes an anchor for Clare, a fifth-grader whose beautiful mother has no time for her daughter. Sarah Lomas, who reviewed the book for *MyShelf.com,* wrote, "I have not read a book this real and rich in a long time." She also noted that the characters' "ideas, dreams, and fears are eloquently and realistically revealed." A film based on the book will star Sarah Jessica Parker, who will also coproduce with Michael London.

BIOGRAPHICAL AND CRITICAL SOURCES:

PERIODICALS

Library Journal, September 15, 2005, Beth Gibbs, review of *Love Walked In: A Novel,* p. 55.
Poetry, January, 2002, Bill Christophersen, review of *From the Bones Out: Poems,* p. 217.
Publishers Weekly, March 27, 2000, review of *From the Bones Out,* p. 74; September 12, 2005, review of *Love Walked In,* p. 37.

ONLINE

Marisa de los Santos Home Page, http://www.lovewalkedin.com (January 6, 2006).
MyShelf.com, http://www.myshelf.com/ (January 6, 2006), Sarah Lomas, review of *Love Walked In.*

* * *

DEMERS, Patricia 1946-
(Patricia A. Demers)

PERSONAL: Born 1946; daughter of a teacher (mother). *Education:* McMaster University, B.A., M.A.; University of Ottawa, Ph.D.

ADDRESSES: *Office*—Department of English, University of Alberta, 3-5 Humanities Centre, Edmonton, Alberta T6G 2E5, Canada. *E-mail*—patricia.demers@ualberta.ca.

CAREER: Writer, researcher, and educator. Social Sciences and Humanities Research Council of Canada, vice president, 1998-2002; University of Alberta, Alberta, Canada, department chair 1995-98, professor of English and film studies. Also worked as a high school English and French teacher.

MEMBER: The Royal Society of Canada (president, 2005-07).

AWARDS, HONORS: Rutherford Award for Excellence in Undergraduate Teaching, University of Alberta; Arts Faculty Teaching Award, University of Alberta; McCalla Research Professorship Award, University of Alberta; University Cup, University of Alberta, 2005.

WRITINGS:

EDITOR

(With Gordon Moyles) *From Instruction to Delight: An Anthology of Children's Literature to 1850,* Oxford University Press (Toronto, Ontario, Canada), 1982.

A Garland from the Golden Age: An Anthology of Children's Literature from 1850 to 1900, Oxford University Press (Toronto, Ontario, Canada), 1983.

(And author of introduction) *The Creating Word: Papers from an International Conference on the Learning and Teaching of English in the 1980s,* University of Alberta Press (Edmonton, Alberta, Canada), 1986.

Scholarly Publishing in Canada: Evolving Present, Uncertain Future/L'Edition savante au Canada: tendances actuelles et perspectives d'avenir (bilingual edition), Aid to Scholarly PublicationsProgramme/University of Ottawa Press (Ottawa, Ontario, Canada), 1988.

Science and Ethics: Proceedings of a Symposium Held in November 2000 under the Auspices of the Royal Society of Canada/La science et lethique: actes d'un colloque tenu en Novembre 2000 sous les auspices de la Société royale du Canada (bilingual edition), University of Toronto Press (Toronto, Ontario, Canada), 2001.

NONFICTION

P.L. Travers (biography; "Twayne's English Authors" series), Twayne (Boston, MA), 1991.

Women As Interpreters of the Bible, Paulist Press (New York, NY), 1992.

Heaven upon Earth: The Form of Moral and Religious Children's Literature to 1850, University of Tennessee Press (Knoxville, TN), 1993.

The World of Hannah More (biography), University Press of Kentucky (Lexington, KY), 1996.

Women's Writing in English: Early Modern England, University of Toronto Press (Toronto, Ontario, Canada), 2005.

WORK IN PROGRESS: Developing the online magazine *WWR* (Women Writing and Reading).

SIDELIGHTS: A professor of English and film studies, Patricia Demers has written and edited several nonfiction books on the topics of children's literature, scholarly publishing, and the Bible. Demers attributes her love of learning to her school-teacher mother. "The breakfast table would be filled with exams or essays she was marking and there would be science experiments of some sort on the kitchen stove," she told Bev Betkowski in an article for the *University of Alberta ExpressNews.*

Demers's treatise *Women As Interpreters of the Bible,* is a prime example of the author's varied interests. The book discusses the many interpretations of the Bible made by Western European and North American women from the tenth century to the twenty-first. Demers divides the book into five chapters that explore the various intellectual schools of thought used to approach the Bible. The discussions of "renaissance exegetes" and "governesses and matriarchs" are, according to *Theological Studies* contributor Patricia M. McDonald, "the most interesting chapters" because they lie at the heart of the author's scholarly expertise. Avril M. Makhlouf, writing in *Interpretation,* explained that "Demers has covered an enormous amount of material in a succinct manner," and went on to comment that "one has confidence in her scholarship and admires the honesty that leads her to admit her preference for the transcendent, rather than the immanent, God." Because of the scope of the book, McDonald concluded that Demers, "by demonstrating (and documenting) well the variety of ways in which women have used the Bible . . . has opened a potentially rich vein that could be mined" by scholars in several disciplines.

The World of Hannah More is a biography and literary critique that "sets out to rescue Hannah More from the hostility of her recent feminist critics," observed Robert Markley in *Studies in English Literature, 1500-1900.* Hannah More was a nineteenth-century Evangelical writer of tracts, plays, essays, and novels who believed in social hierarchy (i.e., that the poor should be poor and the rich should be rich). More's writings and her many charitable works were influenced, if not motivated by, this belief and have thus been criticized on that account. Demers's biography attempts to "vindicate what now seems a paternalistic" worldview, Markley stated. Critics noted the volume's unorthodox format but ultimately concluded that *The World of Hannah More* is a worthwhile effort. *ANQ* reviewer Eleanor Ty observed that the book "contains a number of unexpected, unconventional moments—the free use of personal anecdotes, the interweaving of the past with the present, playful puns, and colloquial language." While Ty felt that this results in a "very full and thorough, though at times somewhat plodding, narrative," she also stated that the author's "excellent observations" are "a valuable contribution to Hannah More scholarship."

BIOGRAPHICAL AND CRITICAL SOURCES:

PERIODICALS

ANQ, summer, 1999, Eleanor Ty, review of *The World of Hannah More,* p. 57.

Interpretation, July, 1993, Avril M. Makhlouf, review of *Women As Interpreters of the Bible,* p. 322.

Studies in English Literature, 1500-1900, summer, 1997, Robert Markley, review of *The World of Hannah More,* p. 637.

Theological Studies, March, 1993, Patricia M. McDonald, review of *Women As Interpreters of the Bible,* p. 194.

University of Alberta ExpressNews, September 9, 2005, Bev Betkowski, "Demers Awarded University Cup."

ONLINE

University of Alberta Web site, http://www.humanities.ualberta.ca/ (March 17, 2006), author profile.*

DEMERS, Patricia A.
   See DEMERS, Patricia

*   *   *

DIXON, Franklin W.
   See LERANGIS, Peter

*   *   *

DONOVAN 1946-
   (Donovan P. Leitch)

PERSONAL: Born May 10, 1946, in Glasgow, Scotland; son of Donald and Winifred Leitch; married Linda Lawrence, October, 1970; children: (with Enid Stulberger) Donovan Leitch, Jr., Ione Skye; (with Linda Lawrence) Astrelia Celeste, Oriole Nebula, Julian (stepson). *Education:* Attended Welwyn Garden City College.

ADDRESSES: Home—Ireland. *Agent*—c/o Author Mail, St. Martin's Press, 175 5th Ave., New York, NY 10010.

CAREER: Singer, songwriter, and recording artist. Worked at odd jobs and performed in clubs and bars throughout England, c. 1963-65; performed on British television program *Ready Steady Go,* 1965. Actor in films, including *If It's Tuesday, This Must Be Belgium* and *The Pied Piper.*

WRITINGS:

SOUND RECORDINGS

Catch the Wind, Hickory, 1965.
Sunshine Superman, Epic (New York, NY), 1966.
Mellow Yellow, Epic (New York, NY), 1967.
In Concert, Epic (New York, NY), 1968.
Hurdy Gurdy Man, Epic (New York, NY), 1968.
A Gift from a Flower to a Garden, 1968.
(With Jeff Beck) *Barabajagal,* 1968.
For Little Ones, Epic (New York, NY), 1968.
Greatest Hits, Epic (New York, NY), 1969.

Open Road, Epic (New York, NY), 1970.
Colours, Hallmark, 1972.
Cosmic Wheels, Epic (New York, NY), 1973.
7-Tease, Epic (New York, NY), 1974.
Slow Down World, Epic (New York, NY), 1976.
Donovan, Rak, 1977.
The Donovan File, Pye, 1977.
Greatest Hits, Embassy, 1979.
Donovan: The Classics Live, Great Northern Arts, 1991.
Sunshine on the Mountain, Sony, 1991.
Troubadour: The Definitive Collection, 1964-76, Epic/Legacy, 1992.
Desert Island Disc: Donovan, Armed Forces Radio and Television Service (Los Angeles, CA), 1993.
Sutras, American Recordings (Burbank, CA), 1996.
Summer Day Reflection Songs, Castle Records (New York, NY), 2001.
Pied Piper, Music for Little People (Redway, CA), 2002.
Fairytale, Sanctuary (New York, NY), 2002.
The Very Best of Donovan, Castle Music (New York, NY), 2002.
The Essential Donovan, Epic/Legacy (New York, NY), 2004.
Beat Café, Appleseed Records, 2004.

Also released albums *The Real Donovan, H.M.S. Donovan, Love Is Only Feeling, Lady of the Stars,* and *Neutronica.* Composer of film scores.

BOOKS

Dry Songs and Scribbles, Doubleday (Garden City, NY), 1971.
(As Donavan Leitch) *The Autobiography of Donovan: The Hurdy Gurdy Man,* St. Martin's Press (New York, NY), 2005.

SIDELIGHTS: Donovan attained fame during the 1960s and 1970s. The singer-songwriter's style and music combines folk stylings, psychedelic influences, and a cheerful naivete. Donovan's hits, such as "Sunshine Superstar" and "Mellow Yellow," became classics of the flower-power era. Donovan began writing poetry and music lyrics as a child, and by the time he was in his teens he was performing in coffeehouses, singing protest music with a folk feel,

much as the American singer Bob Dylan did early in his career. Donovan's image gradually changed from activist to peace-loving hippie, and he incorporated diverse influences into his work. He traveled to India with the Beatles to visit the Maharishi Mahesh Yogi and studied meditation. His popularity continued throughout the late 1960s, but he faded from the limelight as the 1970s progressed. During this period he wrote scores for films and worked on conceptual works such as *7-Tease,* an album connected to a theatrical show featuring Donovan and a company of dancers. During the 1980s he devoted much of his energy to working for the peace movement in Europe, while in the 1990s he enjoyed some revival of his popularity, as contemporary bands released cover versions of his songs. "Although his heyday was relatively short-lived, Donovan's impact on popular music has been significant," stated a writer for *Contemporary Musicians.* "Many of his songs have stood the test of time, sounding fresh decades later—testimony to their irresistible hooks, unusual orchestration, and lyrical creativity."

Donovan tells his life story in *The Autobiography of Donovan: The Hurdy Gurdy Man,* published in 2005. *Booklist* reviewer June Sawyers described the musician's memoir as "a warm, gentle recollection of a turbulent time." A *Publishers Weekly* reviewer concurred that the book is an enjoyable read, stating, "Donovan writes his bohemian manifesto personably and earnestly."

BIOGRAPHICAL AND CRITICAL SOURCES:

BOOKS

Contemporary Musicians, Volume 9, Thomson Gale (Detroit, MI), 1993.
Leitch, Donovan, *The Autobiography of Donovan: The Hurdy Gurdy Man,* St. Martin's Press (New York, NY), 2005.
St. James Encyclopedia of Popular Culture, Thomson Gale (Detroit, MI), 2000.

PERIODICALS

Booklist, November 15, 2005, June Sawyers, review of *The Autobiography of Donovan,* p. 12.

Bookseller, September 23, 2005, review of *The Autobiography of Donovan,* p. 10.

Entertainment Weekly, December 9, 2005, David Browne, review of *The Autobiography of Donovan,* p. 94.

Kirkus Reviews, October 15, 2005, review of *The Autobiography of Donovan,* p. 1124.

Publishers Weekly, October 3, 2005, review of *The Autobiography of Donovan,* p. 61.

ONLINE

Donovan Home Page, http://www.donovan.ie (January 20, 2006).*

*   *   *

D'ORMESSON, Jean Bruno Waldemar François-de-Paule Lefevre
     See D'ORMESSON, Jean

*   *   *

d'ORMESSON, Jean 1925-
     (Bruno Waldemar Francois-de-Paule Lefevre d' Ormesson, Jean Bruno Waldemar François-de-Paule Lefevre d'Ormesson)

PERSONAL: Born June 15, 1925, in France; son of the Marquis d'Ormesson; married Françoise Béghin, 1962; children: one.

ADDRESSES: Home—10 avenue du Parc-Saint-James, 92200 Neuilly-sur-Seine, France. *Office*—Le Figaro, 37 rue du Louvre, Paris, France.

CAREER: Journalist and writer. International Council for Philosophy and Humanistic Studies, UNESCO, deputy secretary-general, 1950-71, secretary-general, 1971; member of staff for various French government ministries, 1958-66; *Diogèenes* (journal), deputy editor, 1952-72, member of magazine committee, 1972; *Le Figaro* (journal), Paris, France, columnist and editor in chief, 1972-77, director general, beginning 1976, lead writer, beginning 1977. Member, ORTF, 1960-62.

AWARDS, HONORS: Grand Prix du Roman, 1971, for *The Glory of the Empire;* named Officier Légio d'honneur, Officier Ordre Nationale du Mérite, and Chevalier des Palmes académiques.

WRITINGS:

La gloire de l'Empire (novel), J. Tallandier, 1972, translated by Barbara Bray as *The Glory of the Empire: A Novel, a History,* Knopf (New York, NY), 1974.

Au plaisir de Dieu, Gallimard (Paris, France), 1974, translated by Barbara Bray as *At God's Pleasure,* Knopf (New York, NY), 1977.

Au revoir et merci, Gallimard (Paris, France), 1976.

Du côte de chez Jean, Gallimard (Paris, France), 1978.

L'enfant qui attendait le train, Editions G.P., 1979.

Dieu: sa vie son oeuvre, Gallimard (Paris, France), 1980.

Mon dernier rêve sera pour vous: une biographie sentimentale de Chateaubriand, J.C. Lattés (Paris, France), 1982.

Jean qui grogne et Jean quit rit, J.C. Lattés (Paris, France), 1984.

Le vagabond qui passe sous une ombrelle troué, Gallimard (Paris, France), 1985.

Le vent du soir (novel), J.C. Lattés (Paris, France), 1985.

Tout les hommes en sont fous (novel), J.C. Lattés (Paris, France), 1986.

Discours de réception de Michel Mohrt à l'Académie française et réponse de Jean d'Ormesson, Gallimard (Paris, France), 1987.

Le bonheur à San Miniato (novel), J.C. Lattés (Paris, France), 1987.

Album Chateaubriand, Gallimard (Paris, France), 1988.

Garçon de quoi écrire, Gallimard (Paris, France), 1989.

(With Emmanuel Berl) *Tant que vous penserez à moi,* Grasset (Paris, France), 1992.

La douane de mer (novel), Gallimard (Paris, France), 1993.

Presque rien sur presque tout (novel), Gallimard (Paris, France), 1996.

Aragon parmi nous, Éditions Cercle d'Art, 1997.

Casimir mene la grande vie, Gallimard (Paris, France), 1997.

Une autre histoire de la litterature française, Nil Éditions, 1997–1998.

Le rapport Gabriel (novel), Gallimard (Paris, France), 1999.

Voyez comme on danse (novel), Laffont (Paris, France), 2001.

Et toi mon coeur pourquoi bats-tu, R. Laffont (Paris, France), 2003.

C'était bien, Gallimard (Paris, France), 2003.

Une fête en larmes (novel), Laffont (Paris, France), 2005.

Member of editorial committee, Gallimard.

SIDELIGHTS: Long associated with the French journal *Le Figaro,* where he has been an editor in chief and director general, Jean d'Ormesson burst onto the literary scene in 1972 with his first novel, *La gloire de l'Empire* which was published in English two years later as *The Glory of the Empire: A Novel, a History.* What makes the epic book about the rise and fall of an immense chimerical empire so unique, commented reviewers, is how d'Ormesson worked so assiduously to make it appear as if it were an actual history. The author includes extensive footnotes, for example, often citing real-life scholars but crediting their names to fictional publications. He writes about such characters in his books as the barbarian Arsaphes and Emperor Alexis as if they were real historical figures, and traces the thousand-year history of his empire in loving detail. "This has to be one of the most engrossing histories every written," wrote William Beauchamp in the *New York Times Book Review,* "yet not a word of it is true."

According to several critics, though, one problem with the author's approach is that it prevents him from making his characters living, breathing people. Instead, the author "must view his characters from a distance," noted Ronald A. Carter in the *Library Journal,* adding that the "pendantic style . . . makes for ponderous reading." While a *Publishers Weekly* reviewer similarly noted that the author's conceit might be carried too far, the critic added that he "is never less than clever and is strikingly so in his pseudo-historical citations."

D'Ormesson took a somewhat similar approach to fiction with some of his other ambitious novels, including *Dieu: sa vie son oeuvre* ("God: His Life, His Works"). In the latter title, d'Ormesson embarks on a kind of biography of the Supreme Being in which the creativity of God, and not the Christian message of the redemption of mankind through His son, is emphasized. As Peter G. Christensen pointed out in a *Literature and Philosophy* essay, "D'Ormesson's preference for the idea of a suffering God rather than a suffering Christ as a response to death-of-God pessimism leads him to express greater concern for the creative sphere of life than for the moral. More important to d'Ormesson than attributing to God a moral code to be obeyed is an acceptance of what an idea of God offers for him personally as a dreamer and writer." The author, related Christensen, concludes that "God is real even if he is only imagined."

In addition to tackling history and philosophy, the author created an ambitious fictional family saga with *Au plaisir de Dieu* (translated as *At God's Pleasure*). The multigenerational tale concerns a wealthy family's vain struggle to maintain its status and possessions in a changing world. While a *Publishers Weekly* contributor admitted that the story possesses a "beguiling charm," the reviewer commented: "The reader may wish there were sharper characterization and more story." A *Kirkus Reviews* writer had a similar complaint, while admitting that at its "high point" the novel provides "sentiment given a rare legitimization."

BIOGRAPHICAL AND CRITICAL SOURCES:

PERIODICALS

Booklist, March 15, 1975, review of *The Glory of the Empire: A Novel, a History,* p. 724.

Kirkus Reviews, September 15, 1977, review of *At God's Pleasure,* p. 1004.

Library Journal, March 15, 1975, Ronald A. Carter, review of *The Glory of the Empire,* p. 602.

Literature and Philosophy, December, 1994, Peter G. Christensen, "*Dieu, Sa Vie, Son Oeuvre:* Jean D'Ormesson's Attack on 'Apatheia' as a Quality of God," pp. 405-420.

New York Times Book Review, January 19, 1975, William Beauchamp, review of *The Glory of the Empire,* pp. 34-35.

Publishers Weekly, October 28, 1974, review of *The Glory of the Empire,* p. 42; September 19, 1977, review of *At God's Pleasure,* p. 140.

Times Literary Supplement, November 5, 1982, Patrick Lindsay Bowles, "The Play of Desire," review of *Mon dernier rêve sera pour vous: une biographie sentimentale de Chateaubriand,* p. 1222.*

*   *   *

DOVAL, Alexis J. 1953-

PERSONAL: Born November 25, 1953, in Sacramento, CA; son of John H. (a physician) and Patricia Doval; married Felicidad Oberholzer (a professor of theology). *Ethnicity:* "White." *Education:* Saint Mary's College of California, B.A., 1976; Oxford University, B.A. and M.A., 1984, D.Phil., 1993.

ADDRESSES: Home—42 Alta Vista, Orinda, CA 94563. *Office*—Saint Mary's College, Moraga, CA 94575. *E-mail*—adoval@stmarys-ca.edu.

CAREER: Writer. Saint Mary's College of California, Moraga, professor of theology.

MEMBER: North American Patristics Society, College Theology Society, Catholic Theological Association of America.

WRITINGS:

Cyril of Jerusalem, Mystagogue: The Authorship of the Mystagogic Catecheses, Catholic University of America Press (Washington, DC), 2001.

BIOGRAPHICAL AND CRITICAL SOURCES:

PERIODICALS

Journal of Ecclesiastical History, October, 2003, Bryan D. Spinks, review of *Cyril of Jerusalem, Mystagogue: The Authorship of the Mystagogic Catecheses,* p. 739.
Journal of Religion, July, 2004, Paul M. Blowers, review of *Cyril of Jerusalem, Mystagogue,* p. 471.

DUBROW, Gail Lee

PERSONAL: Female. *Education:* University of Oregon, B.Arch., 1980; University of California, Los Angeles, Ph.D., 1991.

ADDRESSES: Office—University of Washington, College of Architecture & Urban Planning, 410 Gould Hall, Box 35570, Seattle, WA 98195-5720. *E-mail*—dubrow@u.washington.edu.

CAREER: Writer and educator. University of Washington, Seattle, professor of architecture, urban design, and planning, associate dean for research and computing, adjunct professor of history and women's studies, director of preservation planning and design certificate program. Member of Seattle Design Commission, 1996-2000; member of board of directors, Vernacular Architecture Forum, 2001-04.

MEMBER: Association of Collegiate Schools of Architecture (western regional director, 2001-04).

AWARDS, HONORS: Recipient of grants and fellowships from the American Institute of Architects/American Architectural Foundation, the American Association of University Women, National Endowment for the Humanities, and the U.S. National Park Service.

WRITINGS:

(Designer, with Judy Anderson and John Koval) *The Library Book: A Good Book for a Rainy Day,* Seattle Arts Commission (Seattle, WA), 1991.
(With Donna Graves) *Sento at Sixth and Main: Preserving Landmarks of Japanese American Heritage,* Seattle Arts Commission (Seattle, WA), 2002.
(Editor, with Jennifer B. Goodman) *Restoring Women's History through Historic Preservation,* Johns Hopkins University Press (Baltimore, MD), 2003.

Contributor to books, including *Architecture: A Place for Women,* edited by Ellen Perry Berkeley, Smithsonian Institution Press (Washington, DC), 1989; *Re-*

claiming the Past, edited by Page Putnam Miller, Indiana University Press (Bloomington, IN), 1992; *Making the Invisible Visible,* edited by Leonie Sandercock, University of California Press (Berkeley, CA), 1998; and *Preserving Cultural Landscapes in America,* edited by Arnold R. Alanen and Robert Z. Melnick, Johns Hopkins University Press (Baltimore, MD), 2000.

Contributor to periodicals, including *CRM* and *Planning Theory.* Member of editorial board, *Journal of Architectural Education,* 2000-03.

SIDELIGHTS: Author Gail Lee Dubrow is a professor of architecture, urban design, and planning at the University of Washington. She frequently teaches on topics related to American urban history and on architectural preservation. Her research interests include topics such as historic preservation, history of the built environment, and women's studies.

Her coauthored book *Sento at Sixth and Main: Preserving Landmarks of Japanese American Heritage* offers consideration and analysis of the experiences of Japanese Americans, both *issei* (first-generation immigrants) and *Nisei* (second-generation Japanese Americans). Dubrow and coauthor Donna Graves look at ten landmarks in Washington and California that are important to Japanese-American heritage, and discuss in depth how these landmarks were and are important to Japanese Americans. "With the aid of oral histories, Dubrow and Graves skillfully let material objects and photographic images tell nuanced stories of work, recreation, community, and family among Japanese Americans," noted reviewer Eiichiro Azumo in the *Oregon Historical Quarterly.*

Restoring Women's History through Historic Preservation, which Dubrow coedited, includes twenty-one essays that examine the role of women in historic preservation as well as the activities of women who inhabited historic sites. The book is divided into five sections that cover the history of women in the preservation movement; women's lives at historic houses and museums; claiming new space for women in the built environment and cultural landscape; exemplary projects; and developing an inclusive future agenda for preservation policy. Most of the essays in the book are "concerned with rethinking the interpretation at historic sites and museums so that women's roles become central to the story," observed Martha Norkunas in the *Women's Review of Books.* Daphne Spain, writing in the *Journal of the American Planning Association,* called the book "a solid addition to the literature on women and preservation."

BIOGRAPHICAL AND CRITICAL SOURCES:

PERIODICALS

Choice, December, 2003, J.M. Lewis, review of *Restoring Women's History through Historic Preservation,* p. 774.
Journal of the American Planning Association, spring, 2004, Daphne Spain, review of *Restoring Women's History through Historic Preservation,* p. 243.
Oregon Historical Quarterly, summer, 2003, Eiichiro Azumo, review of *Sento at Sixth and Main: Preserving Landmarks of Japanese American Heritage,* p. 273.
Public Historian, winter, 2003, Nadine Ishitani Hata, review of *Sento at Sixth and Main,* p. 106; fall, 2004, Anne M. Valk, review of *Restoring Women's History through Historic Preservation,* p. 119.
Women's Review of Books, September, 2004, Martha Norkunas, "Shaping the Past," review of *Restoring Women's History through Historic Preservation,* p. 23.

ONLINE

H-Net: Humanities and Social Sciences Online, http://www.h-net.org/ (January 15, 2006), review of *Sento at Sixth and Main;* Elizabeth Wiatr, review of *Sento at Sixth and Main.*
University of Washington College of Architecture Web site, http://depts.washington.edu/archdept/ (January 15, 2006), biography of Gail Lee Dubrow.*

*   *   *

DUNLOP, Nic 1969-

PERSONAL: Born 1969.

ADDRESSES: *Home*—Bangkok, Thailand. *Agent*—Robert Kirby, PFD, Drury House, 34-43 Russell Street, London WC2B 5HA, England. *E-mail*—nicphoto@ksc.th.com.

CAREER: Writer and photojournalist.

AWARDS, HONORS: Award for Excellence in International Journalism, from Johns Hopkins University, for his work in finding and exposing Comrade Duch of the Khmer Rouge, 1999.

WRITINGS:

(Photographer) Paul Davies, *War of the Mines: Cambodia, Landmines, and the Impoverishment of a Nation,* Pluto Press (Boulder, CO), 1994.

The Lost Executioner: A Journey to the Heart of the Killing Fields, Bloomsbury (London, England), 2005, Walker (New York, NY), 2006.

Contributor of photographs to such periodicals as the *Guardian, Independent, New York Times,* and *Sydney Morning Herald,* and of articles to *Prospect, HQ,* and the *South China Morning Post.*

SIDELIGHTS: Photographer and journalist Nic Dunlop has worked around the world as a freelancer, with a particular focus on southern Asia. Based in Bangkok, he has taken photographs and written articles for numerous publications, such as the *Guardian, Independent, New York Times,* and *South China Morning Post.* In 1994 he provided the photographs for Paul Davies's *War of the Mines: Cambodia, Landmines, and the Impoverishment of a Nation,* which illustrated in detail the effects of landmines on the poverty-stricken, rural areas of Cambodia. In *The Lost Executioner: A Journey to the Heart of the Killing Fields,* Dunlop recounts his experiences while investigating the aftermath of the Khmer Rouge communist regime in Cambodia, a trip that included a successful search for Comrade Duch, who had been Pol Pot's chief executioner during the war. Part travelogue and part political history, the book describes Dunlop's encounter with Duch, who had changed his name and

started a new life as a Baptist lay pastor. Dunlop was awarded the Johns Hopkins Award for Excellence in International Journalism in 1999 for the investigative work that provided the foundation for *The Lost Executioner.* Allison Block, in a review for *Booklist,* remarked that "Dunlop's interviews with former Khmer Rouge members are both wrenching and revelatory." A contributor for *Spike Online* noted, "Perhaps because Dunlop's profession is as a photographer, there is never a sense of getting lost within his narrative. His prose has a real composure to it—it's extremely simple without being simplistic, and there is not one verbose word or overwrought sentence here. The understated tone of Dunlop's journalism allows the appalling facts of his narrative to speak for themselves."

BIOGRAPHICAL AND CRITICAL SOURCES:

BOOKS

Dunlop, Nic *The Lost Executioner: A Journey to the Heart of the Killing Fields,* Walker (New York, NY), 2006.

PERIODICALS

Biography, fall, 2005, Ron Gluckman, review of *The Lost Executioner,* p. 709.
Booklist, December 1, 2005, Allison Block, review of *The Lost Executioner,* p. 16.
Kirkus Reviews, November 1, 2005, review of *The Lost Executioner,* p. 1170.
Publishers Weekly, October 24, 2005, review of *The Lost Executioner,* p. 47.

ONLINE

Asia Times Online, http://www.atimes.com/ (March 20, 2006), Julian Gearing, "The Executioner's Tale," review of *The Lost Executioner.*
British Press Photographers Web site, http://www.thebbpa.com/ (March 20, 2006), information about author.

PFD Talent Agency Web site, http://www.pfd.co.uk/ (March 20, 2006), author profile.

Spike Online, http://www.spikemagazine.com/ (March 20, 2006), review of *The Lost Executioner.*

Telegraph Online, http://www.telegraph.co.uk/ (March 20, 2006), Lewis Jones, "While Getting Lashed You Must Not Cry," review of *The Lost Executioner.**

* * *

DURCAN, Liam

PERSONAL: Born in Winnipeg, Ontario, Canada; married; wife's name Florence (a veterinarian); children: two. *Education:* Attended medical school at the University of Manitoba.

ADDRESSES: Home—Montreal, Quebec, Canada. *Office*—Montreal Neurological Hospital and Institute, 3801 University Ave., Montreal, Quebec H3A 2B4, Canada. *Agent*—c/o Author Mail, Véhicule Press, P.O. Box 125, Place du Parc Station, Montreal, Quebec H2X 4A3, Canada. *E-mail*—ldurcan@sympatico.ca; liam.durcan@mcgill.com.

CAREER: Writer, educator, and neurologist. Montreal Neurological Hospital and Institute, neurologist; McGill University, assistant professor.

AWARDS, HONORS: Quebec Writers' Federation/ CBC Quebec short story competition winner, 2004, for "Kick."

WRITINGS:

A Short Journey by Car (short stories), Véhicule Press (Montreal, Quebec, Canada), 2004.

Contributor to periodicals, including *Antigonish Review, Fiddlehead, Zoetrope* and the *Paumanok Review.*

SIDELIGHTS: Canadian Liam Durcan is a practicing neurologist and professor who writes fiction on the side. He started writing before going to medical school, but during his medical training and residency he had to put writing aside. After establishing a neurological practice, the urge to write returned, nurtured by a 2001 workshop presented by the Quebec Writer's Federation. After learning to edit and revise his work, Durcan successfully submitted numerous short stories to literary journals.

In his debut short story collection, *A Short Journey by Car,* "Durcan operates successfully on both the brain and the heart," remarked *Library Journal* reviewer Jim Dwyer. The sixteen stories in the collection tell of "ordinary people thrust into extraordinary situations," noted Martin Levin and H.J. Kirchhoff in the *Globe and Mail.* In the title story, Moscow dentist Yevgeny Mikailovich is whisked away in the night by the secret police. Arriving at his dental office, he is surprised to see Stalin himself wracked with pain from a toothache and requesting that the dentist use a new type of anesthetic. Yevgeny becomes Stalin's de facto personal dentist, though he is terrified that a mistake will lead to a sentence to the Gulag or worse. Yevgeny begins to believe that the now-friendly Stalin will help his academic career, but his newfound success is short-lived.

Gerald, the protagonist of "Control," volunteers for an experimental drug trial, hoping it will pull him out of the doldrums at his insurance company job. The pills he is given evoke a blissful state of near-Nirvana so delightful that Gerald is hesitant to even record his experiences in his treatment journal. Beyond the drug-induced euphoria, however, the hard-edged world of reality waits to reclaim Gerald. In "Nightflight," a contentious cab driver and his passenger get lost in the dark in rural Vermont; they abandon their antagonism toward each other in order to find their way out of an unfamiliar and menacing rural countryside. "Lumier" chronicles the amazement of the Parisian crowd that witnessed the technological marvel of the century: the debut of the first motion picture. In "American Standard" a trucker trying to cross the U.S./Canada border stakes his financial solvency on the illegal U.S. sale of two hundred toilets that use more water than allowed by federal standards. "For a tale turning on litres per flush, it's strangely solemn," observed reviewer Jim Bartley in the *Globe and Mail.* "Durcan's greatest gift is for imagining his way into worlds he can't possibly have known," commented Bartley. "Where he soars, in full flight with his muse, is in stories that vault us out of the contemporary."

BIOGRAPHICAL AND CRITICAL SOURCES:

PERIODICALS

Globe and Mail (Toronto, Ontario, Canada), October 23, 2004, Jim Bartley, "No First-Book Nerves Here," review of *A Short Journey by Car*, p. D23; November 27, 2004, Martin Levin and H.J. Kirchhoff, "The Globe 100: Of All the Year's Writings, Few Meet the Test," review of *A Short Journey by Car*, p. D3.

JAMA, The Journal of the American Medical Association, May 18, 2005, Peter W. Graham, review of *A Short Journey by Car*, p. 2414.
Library Journal, June 15, 2005, Jim Dwyer, review of *A Short Journey by Car*, p. 62.
Medical Post (Toronto, Ontario, Canada), February 8, 2005, Kylie Taggart, "Not the Stories of His Life," review of *A Short Journey by Car*, p. 21.

ONLINE

Absinthe Literary Review, http://www.absinthe-literary-review.com/ (January 15, 2006), biography of Liam Durcan.
Bukowski Agency Web site, http://www.thebukowski agency.com/ (January 15, 2005), biography of Liam Durcan.*

E

EAVES, Will 1967-

PERSONAL: Born 1967, in England. *Education:* Attended King's College, Cambridge University, Cambridge, England.

ADDRESSES: Home—London, England. *Agent*—David Miller, Rogers, Coleridge, and White, 20 Powis Mews, London W11 1JN, England.

CAREER: Times Literary Supplement, London, England, arts editor.

WRITINGS:

The Oversight, Picador (London, England), 2001.
Nothing to Be Afraid Of, Picador (London, England), 2005.

SIDELIGHTS: British writer Will Eaves began his career with high honors when his first novel, *The Oversight,* was short-listed for the Whitbread Award for first novels. The coming-of-age story follows Dan Rathbone as he tries to reconstruct his past through a series of letters and photographs he finds in an heirloom writing box that his father leaves to him. The memorabilia are at odds with Dan's own memories, forcing him to delve into family secrets. Readers are given glimpses not only of Dan's own childhood and teen years as he struggles to come to grips with his homosexuality, but back one generation to Dan's parents and their courtship, offering a contrast between both time periods and sexual preferences. James Hopkin, in a review for the *New Statesman,* found the technique distracting, remarking that "suddenly, there are too many characters, all of the same age, all looking for sex and stability, and Dan's parents are lost in the rush." Hopkin concluded, however, "This fine novel improves, as slowly more and more family secrets are leaked or conceded." A contributor for the *Economist* stated, "Eaves has a very sharp eye for images, and his prose is carefully wrought without ever being baroque."

In *Nothing to Be Afraid Of,* Eaves sets his story against the backdrop of the theater world, but his focus is really on the daily lives of the players themselves. The story revolves around two sisters, Alice and Martha, both of whom are actors, and their experiences with Shakespeare and a host of other theatrical productions. Eaves concentrates on the plainer, financially challenged end of the theater world, ignoring more glamorous aspects of the industry. David Jays, reviewing for the *Observer Online,* called the book "a fantastic pageant of layered identities."

BIOGRAPHICAL AND CRITICAL SOURCES:

PERIODICALS

Economist, March 31, 2001, "Winding Up," review of *The Oversight,* p. 5.
New Statesman, April 2, 2001, James Hopkin, "Novel of the Week," review of *The Oversight,* p. 55.

ONLINE

Guardian Online, http://books.guardian.co.uk/ (March 20, 2006), Alfred Hickling, review of *Nothing to Be Afraid Of.*

Observer Online, http://books.guardian.co.uk/ (March 20, 2006), David Jays, review of *Nothing to Be Afraid Of.*

Scotland on Sunday Online, http://www.scotsman. com/ (March 20, 2006), Andrew Biswell, "Bed Hopping and Time Leaping," review of *Nothing to Be Afraid Of.*

Telegraph Online, http://www.telegraph.co.uk/ (March 20, 2006), Robert Douglas-Fairhurst, "Seismic Tremors, Human Aftershocks," review of *Nothing to Be Afraid Of.*

Times Online (London, England), http://www. timesonline.co.uk/ (March 20, 2006), Hugo Barnacle, review of *Nothing to Be Afraid Of;* Tom Gatti, review of *Nothing to Be Afraid Of.*

*   *   *

EDWARDS, Johanna 1978-

PERSONAL: Born 1978, in Memphis, TN. *Education:* University of Memphis, B.A. (with honors), 2001. *Hobbies and other interests:* Travel, movies, television, reading.

ADDRESSES: Agent—Jenny Bent, Trident Media Group, LLC, 41 Madison Ave., 36th Fl., New York, NY 10010. *E-mail*—johanna@johannaedwards.com; edwardsj@memphis.lib.tn.us.

CAREER: Radio and television producer, journalist, and freelance writer. *Daily Helmsman,* Memphis, TN, arts and entertainment editor, c. 1999-2001; Blockbuster Video, staff member in London, England, 2002; WYPL, Memphis, producer of radio program *Book Talk,* 2003—.

AWARDS, HONORS: Hearst Award, for story published in the *Daily Helmsman.*

WRITINGS:

The Next Big Thing (novel), Berkley Books (New York, NY), 2005.
Your Big Break (novel), Berkley Books (New York, NY), 2006.

WORK IN PROGRESS: Love Undercover, for Simon Pulse, expected 2007.

SIDELIGHTS: Describing herself as a "chick lit" writer, Johanna Edwards burst onto the scene in 2005 with her debut novel, *The Next Big Thing.* Edwards, a Memphis radio show producer, wrote her first novel quickly and, after shopping it around to about two dozen agents, sold the manuscript in 2003 for a reported six-figure royalty advance. *The Next Big Thing* draws on the author's knowledge of the media to spoof the reality television show craze, while Edwards also created what critics considered to be a very realistic and enjoyable heroine. Kat Larson is a twenty-seven-year-old woman who works at a public relations firm. She hates her boss, but this is balanced by her good relationship with loving parents and her best friend. She is unhappy with her weight and has been telling her online boyfriend, whom she has yet to meet, that she is actually a size four. Believing that she can only gain true happiness by shedding pounds, Kat agrees to go on the television show *From Fat to Fabulous,* where she is forced to perform embarrassing acts that will supposedly make her lose weight as she entertains the audience. One of the stunts she goes through is a blind date who turns out to be her online boyfriend; he shows his true colors by breaking up with her when he sees that she weighs over two hundred pounds.

Describing the novel as "better-than-average chick lit," Diane White went on to write in her review for *Boston.com* that "Edwards is good where it counts. She's written a pointed comedy about a woman learning to accept herself, flaws and all." Many reviewers were even more positive in their assessments. *USA Today* critic Deirdre Donahue asserted that *The Next Big Thing* is "a light-hearted, well-plotted debut with a surprise romantic ending and over-the-top charm." "Edwards," concluded Aleksandra Kostovski in *Booklist,* "addresses image issues with wit and candor."

In her follow-up novel, *Your Big Break,* Edwards tells the story of a woman who works for an agency that specializes in helping women break up with their boyfriends. During one assignment, however, she finds herself falling in love with the man her client is breaking up with. Consequently, her entire perspective shifts and she ends up working for a match-making company in what reviewer Jason Anthony described in *Publishers Weekly* as a "down-the-middle romantic comedy."

Edwards plans to continue writing novels in the "chick lit" genre. "What I love most about chick lit is that it's so REAL," the author told an interviewer for *Chick Lit Books* online. "Finally, we have lead characters who we can relate to! It's great to read these books and realize that you're not the only one who has lousy dates, or bad break-ups, or self-confidence issues. Plus, the genre is really evolving and growing, which is great!"

BIOGRAPHICAL AND CRITICAL SOURCES:

PERIODICALS

Booklist, March 1, 2005, Aleksandra Kostovski, review of *The Next Big Thing,* p. 1136.

Publishers Weekly, June 27, 2005, Jason Anthony, "Boy Meets Girl," review of *Your Big Break,* p. 10.

School Library Journal, November, 2005, Mary R. Hoffman, review of *The Next Big Thing,* p. 59.

USA Today, June 1, 2005, Deirdre Donahue, "Female Writers Bare Their Souls about Being Fat," review of *The Next Big Thing,* p. D11.

Us Weekly, March 21, 2005, Eugena Pilek, "Hot Book Picks: Showbiz Satires!," review of *The Next Big Thing,* p. 89.

ONLINE

Best Reviews, http://thebestreviews.com/ (March 5, 2005), Harriet Klausner, review of *The Next Big Thing.*

Boston.com, http://www.boston.com/ (March 13, 2005), Diane White, "Shedding Ties, and Those Pesky Extra 100 lbs.," review of *The Next Big Thing.*

Chick Lit Books, http://www.chicklitbooks.com/ (January 23, 2006), interview with Johanna Edwards.

Johanna Edwards Home Page, http://www.johannaedwards.com (January 22, 2006).

Memphis Magazine, http://www.memphis.edu/magazine/ (January 23, 2006), Jamie Peters, "Novel Ambitions."*

*   *   *

EDWARDS, Michael B.

PERSONAL: Married; wife's name Sylvia; children: three.

ADDRESSES: Agent—c/o Author Mail, Academy Chicago Publishers, 363 W. Erie St., #7E, Chicago, IL 60610.

CAREER: Writer, advocate, and soldier. U.S. Army, career officer, retired as lieutenant colonel; currently works as a veterans' advocate.

WRITINGS:

Murder at the Panionic Games (mystery novel), Academy Chicago Publishers (Chicago, IL), 2002.

WORK IN PROGRESS: Murder at the Festival of Apaturia, a second Bias of Priene historical mystery novel, for Academy Chicago Publishers.

SIDELIGHTS: Novelist Michael B. Edwards is a retired U.S. Army lieutenant colonel who currently works as a veterans' advocate. He developed an interest in ancient Greece and the Ionic League while stationed in Izmir, Turkey, in the 1980s. Since then, he has visited every Ionic League site, and this inspired him to write his first mystery novel, *Murder at the Panionic Games.* It is Edwards's deep knowledge of the historical setting he writes about that "makes all the difference between a costume drama that uses the trappings of the period and one like this that really manages to get under the ancient Greek skin," observed a reviewer on *MyShelf.com.*

In 650 B.C.E. Greece, the twelve nation-states of the Ionic Greek league bought together their athletic champions for a series of games and competitions in Pirene. The games' opening ceremonies were held in the temple where sacrifices were made to Poseidon and where Bias, the novel's narrator, serves as a subpriest. When the local star athlete Tyrestes is poisoned following the initial sacrifice, he collapses and is caught by Bias and another athlete, Endemion. Because of his proximity to the dead man, Bias is assumed to be living under a "miasma," a taint or pollution caused by any murder on sacred ground. This miasma is thought to have a negative effect on the games as well as on the state of Pirene, and the local officials suggest that Bias should assume a great interest in solving the murder in order to lift the dead man's taint from the games and from the state. Bias works his way through a selection of likely suspects, including Endemion; magistrate Nolarion, Endemion's father and a former athletic champion; a group of beautiful girls; and two other magistrates. During his investigations, a prominent athlete from the state of Miletus is killed, raising the stakes from athletic competition to full-scale conflict between states. The meek and timid Bias must redouble his efforts to solve the crimes, not only to bring the murderers to justice but to prevent the outbreak of war.

A *Kirkus Reviews* critic remarked that "Bias spends too much time mulling over motive and alibi, but his wry perspective makes an otherwise conventional debut appealing." A *Publishers Weekly* contributor called the book a "cleanly plotted tale," but noted that the story is "so simply told it might almost be aimed at the young adult market." Other critics were more pleased overall with the tale. "The period detail is fascinating . . . the plot clever, and the humor surprisingly contemporary but never anachronistic," commented Wes Lukowsky in *Booklist*.

BIOGRAPHICAL AND CRITICAL SOURCES:

PERIODICALS

Aethlon: The Journal of Sport Literature, spring, 2003, review of *Murder at the Panionic Games*, p. 185; spring, 2003, review of *Murder at the Panionic Games*, p. 197.
Booklist, May 1, 2002, Wes Lukowsky, review of *Murder at the Panionic Games*, p. 1474.
Kirkus Reviews, March 1, 2002, review of *Murder at the Panionic Games*, p. 291.
New York Times Book Review, May 5, 2002, Marilyn Stasio, review of *Murder at the Panionic Games*, p. 24.
Publishers Weekly, April 8, 2002, review of *Murder at the Panionic Games*, p. 209.

ONLINE

Michael B. Edwards Home Page, http://www.michaelbedwards.com (January 15, 2006).
MyShelf.com, http://www.myshelf.com/ (January 15, 2006), review of *Murder at the Panionic Games*.*

ENGLISH, Camper

PERSONAL: Male. *Education:* Attended college in Boston, MA.

ADDRESSES: Home—San Francisco, CA. *Agent*—c/o Author Mail, Alyson Publications, 6922 Hollywood Blvd., 10th Fl., Los Angeles, CA 90028. *E-mail*—camper@cramper.com.

CAREER: Freelance writer. Worked briefly as a computer programmer.

WRITINGS:

Party Like a Rockstar (Even When You're Poor As Dirt), Alyson Books (Los Angeles, CA), 2005.

Contributor to numerous print and online publications including *Instinct, San Francisco, San Francisco Bay Guardian, San Francisco Chronicle, Lonely Planet Guides, CitySearch.com, DigitalCity.com,* and *SFGate.com.*

SIDELIGHTS: Writer Camper English worked briefly as a computer programmer before being laid off at the end of the dot-com craze. He turned to a career as a freelance writer, focusing particularly on the world he knew best from his own experiences: the club scene. He has written extensively about nightlife and culture, his articles and reviews appearing in such publications as *Instinct, San Francisco, San Francisco Bay Guardian, San Francisco Chronicle,* and the *Lonely Planet Guides.* He has also written for a number of online resources, including *CitySearch.com, DigitalCity.com,* and *SFGate.com.* English's first book, *Party Like a Rockstar (Even When You're Poor As Dirt),* takes an irreverent look at nightlife and club hopping, with instructions on how to live a swinging social life on a very low budget. Basing much of his advice on his own struggles to manage on a freelancer's inconsistent income, English offers tips on how to get things for free as well as on how to make a dollar stretch. Deborah Bigelow, in a review for *Library Journal,* remarked that the book is "destined to be read by many twentysomethings." Writing for *SFWeekly.com,* Brock Keeling remarked, "Smart and funny, the book makes for an easy and enlightening read."

BIOGRAPHICAL AND CRITICAL SOURCES:

PERIODICALS

Advocate, June 21, 2005, Anne Stockwell, "Party Miser," p. 188.
Library Journal, July 1, 2005, Deborah Bigelow, review of *Party Like a Rockstar (Even When You're Poor As Dirt),* p. 104.

ONLINE

Camper English Home page, http://www.cramper.com (March 20, 2006).
Gay.com, http://www.gay.com/ (March 20, 2006), Julie Ross, "Fabulous and Frugal: An Interview with Party Boy Camper English."
Guardian Online, http://www.guardian.co.uk/ (March 20, 2006), Phelim O'Neill, review of *Party Like a Rockstar (Even When You're Poor As Dirt).*
PostHoc Online, http://www.posthoc.com/ (March 20, 2006), information about author.
SFGate.com, http://www.sfgate.com/ (March 20, 2006), Joe Brown, "Camper Saves," author profile.
SF Weekly.com, http://www.sfweekly.com/ (March 20, 2006), Brock Keeling, "Poverty Stricken? This Handy Guide Will Teach You How to Live Richly."*

*   *   *

ENRIGHT, Michael 1958-

PERSONAL: Born 1958, in Chicago, IL. *Religion:* Roman Catholic.

ADDRESSES: Home—Chicago, IL. *Agent*—c/o Author Mail, Tor Books, 175 5th Ave., New York, NY 10010.

CAREER: Roman Catholic priest.

WRITINGS:

Daisies in the Junkyard (novel), Tor Books (New York, NY), 2002.

SIDELIGHTS: In his first novel, *Daisies in the Junkyard,* Catholic priest Michael Enright discusses the issues and challenges that face families growing up in the barrios of modern Chicago. The novel centers on the adventures of Tony and Carlos, two young Latin American men about to graduate from high school. Through no fault of their own, the two are drawn into the circle of violence that continues to plague their South Chicago neighborhood. Although they have constantly struggled to avoid being sucked into gangs themselves, the fighting seems to seek them out. Tony is caught in the crossfire between gangs, taking a bullet to the hand, and Carlos's younger brother is murdered. Eventually, the violence costs both young men their jobs with UPS, and they are reduced to working in a junkyard that doubles as a site for fencing stolen cars.

Enright emphasizes two points in his novel: The situation in which Tony and Carlos find themselves is not their fault, and that there are no easy answers to their problems. Critics respected the author's forthright approach. Although the Church does figure prominently in the novel as a temporary refuge for the boys, neither parents nor authority figures, including the local priest, seem to have any answers. "Enright," stated a reviewer for *Publishers Weekly,* "ably captures the experiences of the boys." "Though Enright falls at times into bathos," a *Kirkus Reviews* contributor concluded, "for the most part he shaves things close to the bone."

BIOGRAPHICAL AND CRITICAL SOURCES:

PERIODICALS

Kirkus Reviews, May 1, 2002, review of *Daisies in the Junkyard,* p. 595.
Publishers Weekly, May 6, 2002, "May Publications," review of *Daisies in the Junkyard,* p. 38.*

*   *   *

ERMATINGER, James W. 1959-

PERSONAL: Born 1959. *Education:* San Diego State University, B.S., 1980, M.A., 1982; Indiana University, Ph.D., 1988.

ADDRESSES: Office—Department of History, Southeast Missouri State University, One University Plaza, MS 2960, Cape Girardeau, MO 63701. *E-mail*—jermatinger@semo.edu.

CAREER: Educator and writer. Earlham College, Richmond, IN, instructor in history, 1988; Wright State University, Dayton, OH, instructor in history, 1989; Kearney State College, Kearney, NE, instructor in history, 1989-91; University of Nebraska at Kearney, assistant professor then professor of history, 1991-95; Lourdes College, Sylvania, OH, professor of history, 1995-01; Southeast Missouri State University, Cape Girardeau, MO, professor of history and chair of department, 2001—.

MEMBER: Association of Ancient Historians, American Numismatic Society, American Historical Association, American Society of Papyrologists, American Philological Association.

AWARDS, HONORS: University of Nebraska at Kearney research services council grant, 1990-93, 1994-95, and summer research fellowship, 1993; Distinguished Faculty Award, Honors Program, University of Nebraska at Kearney, 1995; Lourdes College summer grant, 1999; National Endowment for the Humanities.

WRITINGS:

The Economic Reforms of Diocletian, Scripta Mercaturae (St. Katharinen, Germany), 1996.
The Decline and Fall of the Roman Empire ("Greenwood Guides to Historic Events of the Ancient World" series), Greenwood Press (Westport, CT), 2004.

Contributor to numerous publications, including *American Journal of Numismatic* and *Historia.*

BIOGRAPHICAL AND CRITICAL SOURCES:

PERIODICALS

Choice, October, 2005, review of *The Decline and Fall of the Roman Empire.*

Reference & Research Book News, February, 2005, review of *The Decline and Fall of the Roman Empire,* p. 43.
School Library Journal, August, 2005, Joanne K. Cecere, review of *The Decline and Fall of the Roman Empire,* p. 142.

ONLINE

Southeast Missouri State University Web site, http://www4.semo.edu/ (April 11, 2006), "James W. Ermatinger."
Greenwood Press Web site, http://www.greenwood.com/ (April 11, 2006).*

*   *   *

ESHUN, Ekow 1968-

PERSONAL: Born May 27, 1968, in London, England. *Education:* London School of Economics, B.Sc. *Hobbies and other interests:* Contemporary art, fashion design.

ADDRESSES: Home—London, England. *Office*—Institute of Contemporary Arts, The Mall, London SW1Y 5AH, England.

CAREER: Kiss FM radio, London, England, broadcaster, 1987-88; freelance journalist, 1990-93; assistant editor for *The Face,* 1993-96; *Arena* (magazine), former editor, beginning c. 1996; Institute of Contemporary Arts, London, England, council member, 1999-2003, artistic director, 2005—; Bug Cultural Consultancy, London, England, director, 2000-04; has also worked as editorial director of *Tank* magazine, and as editor of *Mined* and *Hot Air.* Board member of London Arts Board, 1999—, and Tate Members, London, 2003—; governor of University of Arts, London, 2001—.

AWARDS, HONORS: Christian Aid Lifestyle Award (with Jon Snow), One World Media Awards, 2000, for work on documentary *Living on the Line.*

WRITINGS:

Black Gold of the Sun: Searching for Home in England and Africa, illustrated by Chris Ofili, Hamish Hamilton (New York, NY), 2005.

Contributor to periodicals, including the London *Observer, Guardian, Sunday Times, New Statesman,* and *Sleaze,* as well as to *BBC Radio.*

SIDELIGHTS: In 2002 London-born journalist Ekow Eshun traveled to his family's home in Ghana in an attempt to trace his roots and to study the issues of race and identity in both that country and his own. The resulting memoir, *Black Gold of the Sun: Searching for Home in England and Africa,* traces his journey from Accra to Cape Coast, and from the Ashanti region to northern Ghana. Eshun compares his own route to those taken by other notable Africans, as well as his own parents and grandparents and, going back even farther, to the journeys of slaves. Not only does the author examine a wide range of history and culture, but he also weaves his findings with his own personal history and experiences and his reactions to what he learned on his trip. His discoveries were not all pleasant, or even anticipated. At one point, Eshun learned one of his ancestors was a slave trader. In an article for *Time International,* he told Daneet Steffens: "I haven't really come to terms with it. It's a very salient daily reminder of the fact that there's no such thing as black and white, that everything we do is a kind of mixing up. Everything we do is about contradictions, really." Margaret Busby, in a review for the *New Statesman,* observed that "whorls of memories of family life—particularly his interaction with his older brother Kodwo—are imaginatively layered with vivid observation, convincing speculation, recherche nuggets of information."

BIOGRAPHICAL AND CRITICAL SOURCES:

BOOKS

Eshun, Ekow, *Black Gold of the Sun: Searching for Home in England and Africa,* Hamish Hamilton (New York, NY), 2005.

PERIODICALS

African Business, October, 2005, review of *Black Gold of the Sun,* p. 64.

Art in America, June-July, 2005, "Institute of Contemporary Arts," p. 206.

Design Week, March 17, 2005, "ICA Seeks to Appoint MD," p. 3.

Marketing Week, March 29, 2001, "Ekow Eshun," p. 13.

New Statesman, January 1, 2005, "No Place Like Home: When Ekow Eshun Visited Ghana in Search of His Roots, He Was Troubled by What He Dug Up," p. 80; May 30, 2005, Margaret Busby, "Homing Instinct," review of *Black Gold of the Sun,* p. 55.

Time International, June 27, 2005, Daneet Steffens, "A Secret History: In a Moving Memoir, British Journalist Ekow Eshun Returns to Ghana and Discovers Some Painful Truths," p. 74.

ONLINE

BBC News Web site, http://news.bbc.co.uk/ (March 4, 2006), brief author biography.

Black in Britain, http://www.blackinbritain.co.uk/ (March 4, 2006), brief author biography.

Contemporary African Database, http://people.africadatabase.org/ (March 4, 2006), information about author.

ICA.org, http://www.ica.org.uk/ (March 4, 2006), article about author.*

*   *   *

EVANS, Elodia
See TATE, Elodia

F

FALK, Barbara J. 1962-

PERSONAL: Born August 25, 1962, in Calgary, Alberta, Canada; daughter of Mearl Elmer (a machinist) and Faith Irene (a bookkeeper; maiden name, Vetter) Falk; married Jules Barry Bloch (a lawyer and arbitrator), June 30, 1991; children: Alannah Ada. *Ethnicity:* "Canadian." *Education:* Attended Carleton University, 1980-81; University of Victoria, B.A. (with distinction), 1983; York University, M.A. (with distinction), 1986, Ph.D., 1999; also attended George Brown College and Goethe Institute. *Religion:* Christian.

ADDRESSES: Office—Department of Political Science, University of Toronto, Toronto, Ontario M5S 1A1, Canada. *E-mail*—falkb@sympatico.com.

CAREER: Writer. Ontario Women's Directorate, policy analyst for pay equity project, 1985-87, executive assistant to the assistant deputy minister, 1987-88; Pay Equity Commission of Ontario, senior policy advisor to policy and research branch, 1988-89; Sony Music Entertainment (Canada), Inc., director of human resources, 1989-91; Government of Ontario, director of compensation policy branch, 1991-95; York University, Downsview, Ontario, Canada, teacher of political science, 1998-2000; University of Toronto, Toronto, Ontario, fellow at the Centre for Russian and East European Studies, 2000—, lecturer in political science, 2003—. Seneca College, instructor in human resources management, 1989-91; George Brown College, instructor, 1989-91; University of Victoria, course director, summers, 2000-01; Humber College, professor, 2000-03. Network for East-West Women, member, 1995—; Skilling Seminar on Czech and Central European Studies, founder, 1996, member, 1996—; guest speaker in Canada, the United States, and Central Europe. Charles Hastings Housing Cooperative, president and member of board of directors, 1986-88; East End Literacy, volunteer adult literacy tutor, 1987-89; Co-operative Housing Federation of Toronto, member of board of directors, 1988-89, president, 1989; Inner City Non-Profit Dwellings, Inc., member of board of directors, 1988-89; mediator and arbitrator in employment disputes, 1991—; volunteer for schools, youth organizations, and religious groups.

MEMBER: Canadian Political Science Association, Association for the Study of Nationalities, American Association for the Advancement of Slavic Studies.

AWARDS, HONORS: Alice Wilson Award, Canadian Federation of University Women, 1993; grants from Social Science and Humanities Research Council of Canada, 2002, 2003, Canada Council, 2004, and Canada Council for the Arts, 2004.

WRITINGS:

The Dilemmas of Dissidence in East-Central Europe, Central European University Press (New York, NY), 2002.

Contributor of articles and reviews to periodicals, including *Canadian Slavonic Papers, Core Issues,* and *Canadian Journal of Political Science.*

WORK IN PROGRESS: Comparative research on Cold War political trials, completion expected in 2007.

* * *

FÉLIX, Moacyr 1926-2005

PERSONAL: Born March 11, 1926, in Rio de Janeiro, Brazil; died October 25, 2005; married Birgitta Lagerblad, 1953 (died, 2003). *Education:* Attended Universidade Católica do Rio; attended the Sorbonne, 1950-53, and College de France, 1953.

CAREER: Company Auxiliary of Electric Companies, lawyer in legal department, 1946-49; member of Brazilian Institute of Economy, Sociology, and Politics, 1954-55; editor and broadcaster for weekly television program on literature in Brazil, 1955-56; *Para Todos* (periodical), writer and editor of poetry section, 1956-58; freelance writer, 1955-60; *Jornal de Letras,* editor in chief, 1955-62; Brazilian Civilization (publishing company), managing editor of *Poesia Hoje,* 1963-71, and *Perpectivas do Homem,* 1966-92; *Encontros com a Civilização* (magazine), publisher, 1978-82; editorial manager for Rio-Arte Foundation, Municipal Institute Rio-Arte, 1987-88.

MEMBER: Comando de Trabalhadores Intelectuals (cofounder).

WRITINGS:

Singular plural: história e poesia em Moacyr Félix, 1944, 2nd edition, Editora Record (Rio de Janeiro, Brazil), 1998.
Canção do exílio aqui, Civilização Brasileira (Rio de Janeiro, Brazil), 1977.
Neste lençol, Civilização Brasileira (Rio de Janeiro, Brazil), 1977, 2nd edition, 1992.
Invenção de crença e descrença, Civilização Brasileira (Rio de Janeiro, Brazil), 1978.
Em nome da vida, Civilização Brasileira (Rio de Janeiro, Brazil), 1981.
Antologia poética, República Federativa do Brasil (Rio de Janeiro, Brazil), 1993.
Introdução a escombros, Ministry of Culture (Rio de Janeiro, Brazil), 1998.

(Compiler, with Adriano Espínola) *41 poetas do Rio,* Ministry of Culture (Rio de Janeiro, Brazil), 1998.
(Compiler and selector) Enio Silveira, *Enio Silvaira: arquiteto de liberdades,* Bertrand Brasil (Rio de Janeiro, Brazil), 1998.
O pensar e o sentir na obra de Moacyr Félix, Ministry of Culture (Rio de Janeiro, Brazil), 2001.

Author of additional poetry collections and other books. Managing editor of series *Violão de Rua,* 1962-63; managing editor of magazine *Revista da Civilização,* 1966-72, and *Alguma Poesia,* 1983-85; director of *Paz e Terra,* beginning 1969; editorial advisory board member, *Novos Rumos,* 1990-91. Contributor to periodicals, including *Teologia da Libertação.*

SIDELIGHTS: Moacyr Félix was a Brazilian poet who, as an editor of numerous journals and magazines over the years, was also an influential voice within his country's literary circles. As an outspoken champion of the poor, he was known in Brazil for his criticism of the rich and powerful and for championing a socialist system of government. His poetry had not been translated into English at the time of his death in 2005, but some reviews of his Portuguese verses were written in such periodicals as *World Literature Today.* In one issue, Wilson Martins reviewed *Canção do exílio aqui,* pondering its apparent contradictions. According to Martins, Félix "seems intellectually leftist but finds himself 'exiled' in a number of leftist positions." Yet the poet also rejects the ideology of the right. Thus, while Martins found some of the poems "beautiful and melancholy," he complained that the poet's attempts at political messages strike a discordant chord. Gerald M. Moser, reviewing *Neste lençol* in another *World Literature Today* issue, noted the themes of this collection, which predominantly contains poems about physical sex tinged with feelings of despair and sadness. The critic asserted that Félix was capable of writing in "a powerful poetic vein."

BIOGRAPHICAL AND CRITICAL SOURCES:

PERIODICALS

World Literature Today, summer, 1978, Wilson Martins, review of *Canção do exílio aqui,* p. 449; autumn, 1978, Gerald M. Moser, review of *Neste lençol,* p. 612.*

FENTON, Peter 1949-

PERSONAL: Born 1949.

ADDRESSES: Home—Eugene, OR. *Agent*—c/o Author Mail, Simon & Schuster, 1230 Avenue of the Americans, New York, NY 10020.

CAREER: Writer. Worked as a tabloid reporter for the *National Enquirer* for fifteen years, then as editor of the *Secrets Exchange.*

WRITINGS:

I Forgot to Wear Underwear on a Glass-Bottom Boat: Real People, True Secrets, St. Martin's Press (New York, NY), 1997.

Truth or Tabloid? (novelty), Three Rivers Press (New York, NY), 2003.

Eyeing the Flash: The Education of a Carnival Con Artist (memoir), Simon & Schuster (New York, NY), 2005.

SIDELIGHTS: Peter Fenton is a former tabloid reporter and author of the memoir *Eyeing the Flash: The Education of a Carnival Con Artist.* During his junior year of high school, Fenton became friends with Jackie Barron, whose family operated traveling carnivals, and it was Barron who taught Fenton how to apply his skills in math to less than scrupulous pursuits, starting with setting up a casino for their fellow students in his basement. Fenton learned the art of counting cards and maintaining a balance between winning and losing so that the house would stay ahead. Fenton later joined Barron in running a carnival. Their adventures serve as the basis for Fenton's humorous memoir. Reviews of the book were predominantly positive. Barry X. Miller, writing for *Library Journal,* called Fenton's book "a contemporary carnival classic." In addition, a contributor for *Publishers Weekly* found it "instantly engrossing" and "at once entertaining and informative."

BIOGRAPHICAL AND CRITICAL SOURCES:

BOOKS

Fenton, Peter, *Eyeing the Flash: The Education of a Carnival Con Artist,* Simon & Schuster (New York, NY), 2005.

PERIODICALS

Kirkus Reviews, October 15, 2004, review of *Eyeing the Flash: The Education of a Carnival Con Artist,* p. 993.

Library Journal, December 1, 2004, Barry X. Miller, review of *Eyeing the Flash,* p. 130.

Psychology Today, January-February, 2005, review of *Eyeing the Flash,* p. 36.

Publishers Weekly, April 14, 1997, review of *I Forgot to Wear Underwear on a Glass-Bottom Boat: Real People, True Secrets,* p. 68; November 8, 2004, review of *Eyeing the Flash,* p. 43.

School Library Journal, March, 2005, Matthew L. Moffett, review of *Eyeing the Flash,* p. 244.

ONLINE

San Francisco Gate Online, http://www.sfgate.com/ (January 16, 2005), Elizabeth Corcoran, "Memoir of a Scam Artist Reads Like Another Trick."

*   *   *

FERRIÈRES, Madeleine

PERSONAL: Female.

ADDRESSES: Home—Avignon, France. *Office*—Université d'Avignon, 74 rue Louis Pasteur, 84029 Avignon Cedex 1, France. *Agent*—c/o Author Mail, Columbia University Press, 61 W. 62nd St., New York, NY 10023.

CAREER: University of Avignon, Avignon, France, professor of social history.

WRITINGS:

Histoire des Peurs Alimentaires: du Moyen Âge à l'aube du XXe Siècle, Editions du Seuil (Paris, France), 2002, translation by Jody Gladding published as *Sacred Cow, Mad Cow: A History of Food Fears,* Columbia University Press (New York, NY), 2005.

Le Bien des Pauvres: La Consommation Populaire en Avignon, 1600-1800, Champ Vallon (Seyssel, France), 2004.

SIDELIGHTS: French writer Madeleine Ferrières is a professor of social history. In her book *Sacred Cow, Mad Cow: A History of Food Fears,* she traces the history of people's anxieties regarding food. Her investigation relies upon medical and veterinary journals, public health records, cook books, and agricultural statistics. Ferrières regards food fears from two distinct angles (worry over the quantity of food and concerns over the quality of food), and includes numerous intriguing anecdotes, such as the story of a seventeenth-century lawsuit based upon the supposition that yeast made bakery bread unhealthy. The book concentrates primarily on food culture in Europe, with the occasional reference to the United States, including a discussion of Upton Sinclair's work *The Jungle,* and the enactment of the Pure Food and Drug Act. Mark Knoblauch, in a review for *Booklist,* found Ferrières's effort to be "highly scholarly," and "a historical foundation for anyone interested in development of public policy regarding what we eat." A contributor for *Kirkus Reviews* was also impressed, remarking that the book was "filled with choice nuggets of food lore, culinary information and social history."

Ferrières told *CA:* "The starting point for my work is the strong conviction that food-related behaviour, both presently and in former times, is determined by cultural representation. While observing the behaviour of consumers faced with Mad Cow disease, or bird flu, I have become thoroughly convinced of this opinion. Therefore I have studied the cultural representations throughout an extensive period (1300-1900), to be able to locate constancies and divisions, and across a wide area, on both sides of the Atlantic.

"From our past eating habits, I think that I have revealed several keys in order to understand the present; for example, by studying the first measures of systematic culling of cows during the bovine plague epidemic in Europe between 1711-1714, on the advice of Lancisi, the Pope's chief doctor. Or, for example, by observing that all the pigeons in Paris were killed at the time of Louis XIV, for fear of the transmission of a disease from birds to man. My standpoint is at the same time that of an historian of the countryside specialised in agriculture, and an historian of representa-

tions; I am also able to piece together all the food related processes, from production to consumption. My present work also concerns everyday foodstuffs, and ingredients which are the base of traditional French cuisine."

BIOGRAPHICAL AND CRITICAL SOURCES:

PERIODICALS

Actualité, March 1, 2003, review of *Histoire des Peurs Alimentaires: du Moyen Âge à l'aube du XXe Siècle,* pp. 75-76.
Booklist, October 15, 2005, Mark Knoblauch, review of *Sacred Cow, Mad Cow: A History of Food Fears,* p. 16.
Kirkus Reviews, October 15, 2005, review of *Sacred Cow, Mad Cow,* p. 1122.

ONLINE

Columbia University Web site, http://www.columbia.edu/ (January 15, 2005), "Madeleine Ferrières."

*   *   *

FINNIS, Jane (Jane Copsey)

PERSONAL: Born in Yorkshire, England; married Richard Copsey. *Education:* Attended London University. *Hobbies and other interests:* Traveling, gardening, playing guitar.

ADDRESSES: *Home*—North Yorkshire, England. *Home and office*—98 Bridlington St., Hunmanby, Filey, North Yorkshire YO14 0LP, England. *E-mail*—janefinnis@ukf.net.

CAREER: Writer. Worked variously as a freelance broadcaster for BBC Radio, a computer programmer, and a shopkeeper.

WRITINGS:

MYSTERY NOVELS

Get Out or Die, Poisoned Pen Press (Scottsdale, AZ), 2004.

A Bitter Chill, Poisoned Pen Press (Scottsdale, AZ), 2005.

Also contributor of short stories to anthologies, including *The Mammoth Book of Roman Whodunnits,* edited by Mike Ashley, Carroll & Graf (New York, NY), 2003.

SIDELIGHTS: Mystery writer Jane Finnis became fascinated with history as a child growing up in East Yorkshire, England, surrounded by the old city walls and the roads originally marked out by the Romans. Her interest was further sparked through reading the works of Robert Graves, and she went on to study history at London University. Finnis worked in various fields after graduation, but her love of history endured. When she attempted to write her first mystery novel, *Get Out or Die,* it was a natural choice to set the book during the Roman era. The story takes place in northern Britain in 91 C.E., and introduces heroine Aurelia Marcella and her sister, keepers of an elite inn. Aurelia finds herself in the middle of a plot to rid the area of Roman occupiers, and she is forced to turn detective in order to find the traitor responsible for a series of local murders. A reviewer for *Publishers Weekly* called the novel a "lively debut" and remarked that "the plot is timely as conquerors seek to impose civilization on a barbarian culture."

Finnis finds researching the time period just as enjoyable as plotting out and writing the mysteries themselves. She has continued her series with another mystery for Aurelia Marcella to solve in *A Bitter Chill.* Margaret Flanagan, reviewing the novel for *Booklist,* called Finnis's mystery "a suspenseful and authentically detailed historical whodunit."

Finnis told *CA:* "I've always enjoyed writing, and when I worked for BBC Radio I was given the chance to write scripts and documentaries on every topic under the sun, but of course they were fact, not fiction. When I retired from full-time work, trying my hand at a novel was at the top of my "To Do" list.

"I try hard not to be influenced by other fiction writers; I never read any fiction set in Roman times while I'm working on a book. Though I'd never dream of plagiarising, you can't be sure how ideas cross-fertilise each other. I enjoy reading the factual history of the Roman Empire, and I try to choose topics and events for my stories that fit well into what we know of first-century Roman Britain. Looking back at life in the ancient past is like standing in the dark outside a large house, (a villa perhaps?) and trying to peer in through the windows to examine the many rooms inside. Some rooms are brightly lighted, some tantalisingly dim, and others pitch black. So parts of the house are plainly visible in great detail, but not all, and the lighted rooms are scattered, not adjacent. Similarly, we know only certain aspects of the history of Britannia in real depth. Our knowledge is growing all the time, but can never be complete. This is a pain or a challenge, depending on your standpoint. To me, a writer who cares about historical truth, it is both.

"I like to start a novel knowing the beginning, the end, and whodunnit. I then try to plot the action in detail, but am not very good at sticking to my carefully prepared synopsis. Only when I'm sitting at my word processor can I be sure if something works, and even then I don't always get it right first time. Thank goodness for computers, I say; it's much easier to re-jig, re-order, cut, paste, delete, whatever, with an electronic manuscript than it must have been with a real one. Before I started writing, I used to be sceptical of authors who said that their characters often dictated their plots. But now I've found it can be true. If you've created characters in enough detail that you feel you actually know them, then you'll realise there are certain actions they wouldn't take, certain things they wouldn't say, and if you force them to, your plot won't flow.

"The most surprising thing I've learned as a writer is that, thanks to e-mail and the Internet, being a writer doesn't have to mean you are lonely and isolated in the way that many authors felt themselves to be in years gone by. The process of getting my words down is solitary, but I can be in touch with other writers and readers all around the world. I can share thoughts and feelings, compare experiences, and seek practical information. People are extremely generous about sharing their expertise on subjects as varied as how long a dead body would remain recognisable when it's been in the sea, to the most effective sort of press release to send out before a book-signing tour.

"I can't give a sensible answer to which of my books is my favorite; it's like asking a mother which of her children she loves best. If I'm honest, I think I'll always have a special soft spot for *Get Out or Die,* just because it was my first. I still remember the thrill of seeing that first copy, a real book, with my name on it.

"First and foremost, I want people to enjoy my books, and feel, when they get to the end, that they've had a satisfying read. I hope that readers with some knowledge of Roman Britain will feel I've caught the spirit of that far-off place and time, and also that those who are new to ancient history will find their interest kindled, and maybe go on to read more books on the subject—mine and other people's."

BIOGRAPHICAL AND CRITICAL SOURCES:

PERIODICALS

Booklist, September 1, 2005, Margaret Flanagan, review of *A Bitter Chill,* p. 68.
Chicago Tribune, January 25, 2004, Dick Adler, review of *Get Out or Die,* p. 4; September 18, 2005, Dick Adler, review of *A Bitter Chill,* p. 2.
Publishers Weekly, December 1, 2003, review of *Get Out or Die,* p. 44; July 25, 2005, review of *A Bitter Chill,* p. 52.

ONLINE

AllReaders.com, http://www.allreaders.com/ (March 6, 2006), Harriet Klausner, review of *Get Out or Die;* Alan J. Bishop, review of *A Bitter Chill.*
Jane Finnis Home Page, http://www.janefinnis.com (March 6, 2006).
MyShelf.com, http://www.myshelf.com/ (May 31, 2006), Rachel A. Hyde, review of *Get Out or Die;* Kim Malo, review of *A Bitter Chill.*

*   *   *

FISHER, Julieta Dias 1947-

PERSONAL: Born January 1, 1947, in Mombasa, Kenya; naturalized U.S. citizen, 1976; daughter of Roque Felix (a Portuguese diplomat) and Silvia Asucena (de Menezes) Dias; married, 1971; children: Joscelyn Elizabeth, Ian Benjamin. *Education:* At-

tended Royal Irish Academy of Music, 1959-63; Immaculata College, Washington, DC, A.A., 1966; attended University of Lisbon, 1967, 1968; American University, B.A., 1968; Glassboro State College, M.A., 1975; also attended University of the Arts, Philadelphia, PA, and Rowan University, 1996. *Hobbies and other interests:* Cooking, reading, travel, music, dancing.

ADDRESSES: Office—Washington Township High School, 519 Hurffville-Crosskeys Rd., Sewell, NJ 08080. *E-mail*—jfisher@wtps.org.

CAREER: Writer and librarian. American Security and Trust Co., Washington, DC, bank teller, 1968-69; International Bank for Reconstruction and Development (now World Bank), Washington, DC, records assistant and classifier, 1969-71; Southwest Citizens' Organization for Poverty Elimination, Glassboro, NJ, director of Glassboro area center, 1973-74; McCowan Memorial Library, Pitman, NJ, senior library clerk, 1977-83, assistant director, 1983-87; Washington Township School District, Sewell, NJ, school librarian and media specialist at Wedgewood Elementary School, 1987-89, Orchard Valley Middle School, 1989-97, and Washington Township High School, 1997—. Rowan University, librarian at Schaub Curriculum Lab, 1987; Camden County College, reference librarian, 2000-03; workshop presenter. Member of Washington Township District Multicultural Committee, member, 1991—, Washington Township Technology Committee, 1998—, Washington Township Acceptable Use Committee, 1998—, and Cultural and Heritage Commission of Gloucester County, NY, 2001-03; volunteer for Pitman Manor and Literacy Volunteers of America.

MEMBER: American Library Association, National Education Association, Educational Association of New Jersey, Tri-County Educational Media Association, Camden County Educational Media Association (member of executive board, 1997-99).

AWARDS, HONORS: Progressive Media Award, New Jersey Educational Media Association, 1999.

WRITINGS:

(With Ann M. Hill) *Tooting Your Own Horn: Web-Based Public Relations for the Twenty-first Century Librarian,* Linworth Publications (Worthington, OH), 2002.

(Editor and contributor) *Ready to Present,* Linworth Publications (Worthington, OH), 2004.

Contributor to periodicals, including *Library Media Connection, New Jersey Library Association Newsletter,* and *Library Talk.*

SIDELIGHTS: Julieta Dias Fisher told *CA:* "I was an avid reader from the time I was a little girl. I devoured books with the same frequency as I did the plentiful bananas in Kenya! At the age of eleven I went to an Irish boarding school in Dublin, where I completed my secondary education. In Ireland, books were my sole companions and my solace against homesickness for my family in Mombasa. Books of all kinds have been my drug of choice throughout my life. Because of the different locales where I have lived, from equatorial to temperate, my readings and writings reflect the flavor of multicultural and cross-cultural similarities as well as differences. I am in the process of writing about these at the moment.

"Aside from reading, I love cooking various types of meals, traveling, music (piano), and dancing. I have traveled extensively to such places as Austria, Bermuda, Brazil, Canada, the Caribbean, England, France, Germany, Greece, Goa, India, Iceland, Ireland, Italy, Kenya, Mexico, Portugal, Spain, Sweden, Tanzania, and Turkey. I am fluent in English, Portuguese, and Spanish, and proficient in French and Italian.

"As a librarian, I was fortunate to work with a colleague, Ann M. Hill, whose expertise as a teacher complemented my lack of it. Together we were responsible for creating a twenty-first-century library. In the process of incorporating the latest technology, we wanted to share our exciting experiences with colleagues. We conducted various workshops for our school district, librarian associations, and the New Jersey Department of Education. From these experiences came our articles and our book on using technology to publicize libraries and all they accomplish."

BIOGRAPHICAL AND CRITICAL SOURCES:

PERIODICALS

Multimedia Schools, October, 2003, Jean Reese, review of *Tooting Your Own Horn: Web-Based Public Relations for the Twenty-first Century Librarian,* p. 46.

School Library Journal, December, 2003, Jessica Foster, review of *Tooting Your Own Horn,* p. 180.

* * *

FLANAGAN, Erin 1971-

PERSONAL: Born 1971. *Education:* University of Nebraska—Lincoln, B.A., 1994, M.A., 2000, Ph.D., 2004.

ADDRESSES: *Home*—Dayton, OH. *Office*—Wright State University, Department of English, 463 Millett Hall, Dayton, OH 45435. *E-mail*—erin.flanagan@wright.edu.

CAREER: Wright State University, Department of English, Dayton, OH, assistant professor.

WRITINGS:

The Usual Mistakes (short stories), University of Nebraska Press (Lincoln, NE), 2005.

Contributor of short fiction to periodicals, including the *Colorado Review* and the *Baltimore Review,* as well as to the anthology *Best New American Voices,* edited by Charles Baxter.

SIDELIGHTS: Erin Flanagan is a university faculty member who has focused on creative writing and women's studies. Her own writing interests have led to a series of short stories and contributions to literary journals. Her first collection of stories, *The Usual Mistakes,* includes twelve pieces, all of which center around Midwestern characters who are dealing with the consequences of their choices. In one story, a man tries to start his life over after killing a girl while driving drunk; another story depicts a man now living in a truck following a bout of infidelity. The lead story tells of Eleanor, a former motel receptionist who now works as a medical assistant thanks to fake credentials; yet she still needs to take on a boarder in order to make her mortgage payment. A reviewer for *Publishers Weekly* remarked that "the homogeneity of Flanagan's characters . . . threatens to spoil the whole, but the inventiveness of her . . . plots keep[s] common themes fresh." Annie Tully, writing for *Booklist,* stated that the works "lack the undercurrent of humor and pain that Flanagan seems to intend," but concluded they are "well told."

BIOGRAPHICAL AND CRITICAL SOURCES:

PERIODICALS

Booklist, September 1, 2005, Annie Tully, review of *The Usual Mistakes,* p. 63.
Publishers Weekly, August 1, 2005, review of *The Usual Mistakes,* p. 44.

ONLINE

Wright State University Web site, http://www.wright. edu/ (March 6, 2006), "Erin Flanagan."

*   *   *

FLUTSZTEJN-GRUDA, Ilona 1930-

PERSONAL: Born 1930, in Varsovie, Poland; immigrated to Canada, 1968; children: three. *Education:* Earned college degree, 1966.

ADDRESSES: Home—Quebec, Canada. *Agent*—c/o Author Mail, Sumach Press, 1415 Bathurst St., Ste. 202, Toronto, Ontario M5R 3H8, Canada. *E-mail*—gruda@videotron.ca.

CAREER: University of Quebec, Trois-Rivières, Quebec, Canada, professor of chemistry, 1968-91; writer. Affiliated with Polish Jewish Heritage Foundation.

WRITINGS:

L'aïeule (novel), translated from the Polish by Joanna Gruda, Éditions David (Ottawa, Ontario, Canada), 2004.
When Grownups Play at War: A Child's Memoir, translated from the Polish by Sarah Cummins, Sumach Press (Toronto, Ontario, Canada), 2005.

SIDELIGHTS: *When Grownups Play at War: A Child's Memoir* is Ilona Flutsztejn-Gruda's account of her experiences living in eastern Europe during World War II. At age nine, Flutsztejn-Gruda and her family fled from their home in Warsaw, Poland, in the wake of the Nazi invasion. After a grueling six-year journey, they finally settled on a collective farm in Uzbekistan where they learned to adapt to a rural lifestyle. The author recounts the hardships of this forced relocation as well as the anti-Semitism that was so prevalent during the war years. She also shares the emotional toll on her family; her mother, for example, carried a terrible guilt over the fact that her own sister had to be left behind in Poland due to illness. When the Flutsztejn family returned to Poland, all 0their relatives had vanished and no record of them remained.

Noting that Flutsztejn-Gruda's account of her family's "leave-taking . . . is most memorable," Hazel Rochman wrote in a *Booklist* review that *When Grownups Play at War* "speaks with immediacy about a refugee child's trauma and survival." Andrea Belcham, writing in the *Montreal Review of Books,* commented that "Flutsztejn-Gruda advances her narrative at a rapid pace, with only the sparest of passages devoted to self-reflection, though her attention to the physical details of the foreign lands and situations that she and her family encounter are astute."

After completing her college degree, Flutsztejn-Gruda immigrated to eastern Canada, and taught chemistry at the University of Quebec for over two decades. She wrote her memoir in Polish, shortly after retiring from her university post, and has also gone on to pen a novel, published in French. "I always told my story of wartime survival to my family—first to my children and then to my grandchildren," she commented to Stuart Nulman for the Canadian *Jewish Tribune.* In addition to publishing her own story of survival, Flutsztejn-Gruda has also been an active participant in the Polish Jewish Heritage Foundation, helping other Holocaust survivors record their stories. "It is very important to get as many remaining Holocaust survivors as possible to write about their experiences and to give witness to this tragic period in history," she told Nulman.

BIOGRAPHICAL AND CRITICAL SOURCES:

BOOKS

Flutsztejn-Gruda, Ilona, *When Grownups Play at War: A Child's Memoir,* translated by Sarah Cummins, Sumach Press (Toronto, Ontario, Canada), 2005.

PERIODICALS

Booklist, October 1, 2005, Hazel Rochman, review of *When Grownups Play at War,* p. 46.
Montreal Review of Books, winter, 2006, Andrea Belcham, "The Will to Live."

ONLINE

Canadian Review of Materials, http://www.umanitoba.ca/ (April 11, 2006).
Jewish Tribune Online, http://www.jewishtribune.ca/ (April 11, 2006), Stuart Nulman, "From Poland to Uzbekistan."
Sumach Press Web site, http://www.sumachpress.com/ (April 11, 2006).*

* * *

FORBES, Elliot 1917-2006

OBITUARY NOTICE— See index for *CA* sketch: Born August 30, 1917, in Cambridge, MA; died January 10, 2006, in Cambridge, MA. Educator and author. Particularly noted as a scholar of Ludwig von Beethoven, Forbes was Fanny Peabody Professor of Music emeritus at Harvard University. After studying music at the Milton Academy for four years, he attended Harvard, completing a B.A. in 1941 and an M.A. in 1947. Between degrees, he taught music at schools in California and Massachusetts. From 1947 to 1958, Forbes was on the faculty at Princeton University, where he rose to the post of associate professor of music. He then returned to Harvard to become a professor of music and, in 1961, Fanny Peabody Professor of Music. In addition to teaching, during the 1960s he was the conductor for the Harvard Glee Club and the Radcliffe Choral Society, a noteworthy accomplishment given that he was physically hampered as the result of suffering from polio. Though he loved many forms of music, including blues and jazz, Forbes became most noted for his Beethoven scholarship, particularly after revising, editing, and updating the nineteenth-century biography of Beethoven written by Alexander Wheelock Thayer. The result, *Life of Beethoven* (1964; revised edition, 1967) is a two-volume work of scholarship that has been widely praised by academics. Forbes also wrote or edited a number of other music books, including *The Choral Music of Beethoven* (1969) and *A History of Music at Harvard to 1972* (1972; reprinted, 1988). Retiring in 1984, Forbes continued his association with Harvard for many years as a professor emeritus, including as editor of *A Report of Music at Harvard* until 1990.

OBITUARIES AND OTHER SOURCES:

PERIODICALS

New York Times, January 14, 2006, p. B14.

* * *

FORDE, Catherine 1961-

PERSONAL: Born 1961; children: two sons. *Hobbies and other interests:* Reading, swimming, jogging, walking, skiing, music.

ADDRESSES: Home—Glasgow, Scotland. *Agent*—c/o Author Mail, Egmont Books, 239 Kensington High St., London W8 6SA, England. *E-mail*—info@catherineforde.co.uk.

CAREER: Educator and writer. Collins (publisher), former lexicographer; secondary school teacher in Scotland.

AWARDS, HONORS: Blue Peter "Book I Couldn't Put Down" designation shortlist, and Booktrust Teenage Book Award shortlist, both 2004, and Grampian Book Award, 2005, all for *Fat Boy Swim;* North Lanarkshire Book Award shortlist, Calderdale Teenage Book Award shortlist, Renfewshire Teenage Book Award shortlist, Angus Award shortlist, and Scottish Arts Council award, all 2005, all for *Skarrs.*

WRITINGS:

Think Me Back, House of Lochar (Colonsay, Scotland), 2001.
The Finding, House of Lochar (Conosay, Scotland), 2002.

Fat Boy Swim, Egmont Books (London, England), 2003, Delacorte Press (New York, NY), 2004.

Skarrs, Egmont Books (London, England), 2004.

I See You Baby . . . , Barrington Stoke (Edinburgh, Scotland), 2005.

The Drowning Pond, Egmont Books (London, England), 2005.

Firestarter, Egmont Books (London, England), 2006.

WORK IN PROGRESS: The novel *Tug of War.*

SIDELIGHTS: Scottish writer Catherine Forde worked as a secondary-school English teacher until making the transition to children's book author. Publishing her first book in 2001, Forde earned particular praise two years later, when her young-adult novel *Fat Boy Swim* was released. Also released in the United States, the novel introduces fourteen-year-old Jimmy, a Scottish boy who is sorely overweight and known around school as "Fat Boy Fat." Asthmatic and chronically bullied by classmates, Jimmy has little to feel upbeat about, and his down-in-the-dumps attitude worries his overly protective mother as posing a direct threat to the teen's health. Fortunately, his upbeat Aunt Pol is a proactive force in Jimmy's life and helps him sustain a sense of humor, so when Jimmy meets a local priest nicknamed GI Joe, he takes to heart the man's encouragement that he take up swimming and cooking. In the water, Jimmy discovers a natural talent and learns that he is capable of changing his life. Meanwhile, a love interest bubbles to the surface in his cooking class.

Fat Boy Swim was praised by several critics for its realistic portrayal of a troubled teen. While noting that Forde is "a bit heavy-handed" in defending her young protagonist, *Booklist* Gillian Engberg added that her novel's "messy ending is satisfyingly realistic; despite his newfound swimming talent . . . Jim still has complicated, unresolved questions about who he wants to be." A *Kirkus Reviews* critic called the novel "warm and full of vivid imagery," while Francisca Goldsmith stated in *School Library Journal* that "each character is developed and interesting."

Forde has continued her writing career with the Y-A novels *The Drowning Pond* and *Firestarter,* the former a mix of supernatural and frustrated adolescence that a *Bookseller* contributor dubbed "bleakly uncompromising" and full of "historical parallels." She discussed her craft in an interview posted on the Egmont Books Web site, noting: "I always promised myself I'd write a book some day, but didn't actually start writing properly until my younger son started school. . . . Sick of doing more housework to keep myself busy, I sat down at the computer and I haven't stopped writing since." "I enjoy putting characters in difficult situations or involving them in conflict to see how they will develop," Forde added. "Things that have happened in my own life can creep into my writing demanding to be relived or explored, and people who are important to me often become characters in my story."

BIOGRAPHICAL AND CRITICAL SOURCES:

PERIODICALS

Booklist, September 1, 2004, Gillian Engberg, review of *Fat Boy Swim,* p. 110; Feburary 1, 2005, Anna Rich, review of *Fat Boy Swim,* p. 988.

Kirkus Reviews, September 1, 2004, review of *Fat Boy Swim,* p. 864.

School Library Journal, September, 2004, Joel Shoemaker, review of *Fat Boy Swim,* p. 204; February, 2005, Francisca Goldsmith, review of *Fat Boy Swim,* p. 76.

ONLINE

Catherine Forde Home Page, http://www.catherine forde.co.uk (April 11, 2006).

Egmont Books Web site, http://www.egmont.co.uk/ (April 11, 2006), "Catherine Forde."*

*   *   *

FRASCELLA, Lawrence

PERSONAL: Born in New York, NY.

ADDRESSES: *Home*—New York, NY *Agent*—c/o Author Mail, Simon & Schuster, 1230 Avenue of the Americans, New York, NY 10020. *E-mail*—rebels@ livefastdieyoungbook.com.

CAREER: Writer. Has worked variously as an editor for periodicals, including *Aperture, Camera Arts,* and *Photo/Design,* and as a book editor for Aperture Publishing.

WRITINGS:

The American Cowboy: Tribute to a Vanishing Breed, photographs by Michael Rutherford, foreword by Charlie Daniels, Moore & Moore Publishing (New York, NY), 1990.

(With Al Weisel) *Live Fast, Die Young: The Wild Ride of Making "Rebel without a Cause,"* Simon & Schuster (New York, NY), 2005.

Contributor to periodicals, including *Harper's Bazaar, Rolling Stone, Advocate, Sunday Times Magazine,* and *Entertainment Weekly,* and to Web sites, including *CD-Now* and AOL's *Critics Choice.* Former movie critic for *Us* magazine; former theater critic for *Entertainment Weekly.*

SIDELIGHTS: Lawrence Frascella began his career as a freelance journalist, writing primarily about pop culture and the entertainment industry. He served as the movie critic for *Us* and covered theater for *Entertainment Weekly.* He has written profiles of the likes of Martin Scorsese, Tina Turner, Brian Wilson, Sarah Jessica Parker, and Kevin Kline. In addition, he has edited a number of visual arts periodicals and books. Frascella's book *Live Fast, Die Young: The Wild Ride of Making "Rebel without a Cause,"* written with Al Weisel, was released to commemorate the fiftieth anniversary of James Dean's death. The volume offers an insider's view of the making of the landmark film in which Dean starred, including interviews with the surviving cast members and numerous facts and anecdotes taken from previously inaccessible studio archives. A contributor for *Kirkus Reviews* called the book "a passionate depiction of how art can create, inspire and destroy—all at the same time." Chris Barsanti remarked in the *Hollywood Reporter* that "there's no end to the drama inherent in this overstuffed narrative." *Library Journal* critic Rosellen Brewer concluded that Franscella's effort is a "well-researched study of a groundbreaking film."

BIOGRAPHICAL AND CRITICAL SOURCES:

PERIODICALS

Advocate, November 8, 2005, David Ehrenstein, "Crazy for Dean," review of *Live Fast, Die Young: The Wild Ride of Making "Rebel without a Cause,"* p. 64.

Booklist, September 15, 2005, Gordon Flagg, review of *Live Fast, Die Young,* p. 17.

Boston Globe, October 30, 2005, Chris Fujiwara, "The Rebel."

Hollywood Reporter, October 10, 2005, Chris Barsanti, "Tomorrow Is Another Day for Quartet of Literary Thrill Rides," review of *Live Fast, Die Young,* p. 10.

Kirkus Reviews, September 1, 2005, review of *Live Fast, Die Young,* p. 954.

Library Journal, October 1, 2005, Rosellen Brewer, review of *Live Fast, Die Young,* p. 77.

Publishers Weekly, August 29, 2005, review of *Live Fast, Die Young,* p. 46.

ONLINE

Boston Phoenix Online, http://www.bostonphoenix.com/ (October 14, 2005), Gerald Peary, "Worthy Cause," review of *Live Fast, Die Young.*

Hollywood Reporter Online, http://www.hollywoodreporter.com/ (November 28, 2005), Gregory McNamee, review of *Live Fast, Die Young.**

*   *   *

FRÉNAUD, André 1907-1993

PERSONAL: Born July 26, 1907, in Montceau-les-Mines, Saô-et-Loire, France; died, 1993; married second wife, Monique Mathieu, 1971. *Education:* Attended University of Dijon; Sorbonne, received law degree.

CAREER: University of Lvov, lecturer, 1930; Ministry of Public Works, Paris, France, civil administrator, 1937-40, 1945-63; Communauté Européenne des Écrivains, member of executive committee, 1963-68. *Military service:* French Army; served during World War II; prisoner of war, 1940-42; served in French Resistance movement.

AWARDS, HONORS: Etna-Taormina Prize, 1973; grand prize for poetry, Académie Française, 1973; poetry prize, Ministry of Culture and Communication, 1988; grand prize, Société des Gens de Lettres, 1989.

WRITINGS:

POETRY

Les rois mages, Seghers (Paris, France), 1943, revised edition, Gallimard (Paris, France), 1977.

Les mystères de Paris, Seuil (Paris, France), 1943.

La noce noire (also see below), Seghers (Paris, France), 1946.

Soleil irréductible, Ides et Calendes (Paris and Neuchâtel, France), 1946.

La femme de ma vie, Blaizot, 1947.

Poèmes de Brandebourg, Gallimard (Paris, France), 1947.

Poèmes de dessous le plancher; La noce noire, Gallimard (Paris, France), 1949.

L'Énorme figure de la Déesse Raison, illustrated by Raoul Ubac, privately printed, 1950.

Les Paysans, Jean Aubier, [Paris, France],1951.

Source entière, Seghers (Paris, France), 1953.

André Frénaud, edited by G.E. Clancier, Seghers (Paris, France), 1953.

Dans l'arbre ténébreux, Benoit (Alès, France), 1956.

La nuit des prestiges, Benoit (Alès, France), 1956.

Chemins du vain espoir, De Romilly, 1956.

Passage de la visitation, GLM (Paris, France), 1956.

Coeur mal fléché, Benoit (Alès, France), 1957.

Pays retrouvé, Benoit (Alès, France), 1957.

Excrétion, misère et facéties, Sciascia (Rome and Caltanissetta, Italy), 1958.

Noël au chemin de fer, Benoit (Alès, France), 1959.

L'Agonie du Général Krivitski, illustrated by André Masson, Oswald (Paris, France), 1960.

L'Amitié d'Italie, Strenna per Gli Amici (Milan, Italy), 1961.

Pour l'office des morts, Benoit (Alès, France), 1961.

Il n'y a pas de paradis, Gallimard (Paris, France), 1962.

L'Étape dans la clairièrer; Pour une plus haute flamme par le défi, Gallimard (Paris, France), 1966.

Vieux pays; Campagne, Maeght (Paris, France), 1967.

La Sainte Face, Gallimard (Paris, France), 1968, revised edition, 1985.

Depuis toufours déjà: poèmes, 1953-1968, Gallimard (Paris, France), 1970.

Le miroir de l'homme par les bêtes, Maeght (Paris, France), 1972.

Qui possède quoi? (in French and English), translations by Serge Gavronsky, Greenwood Press (San Francisco, CA), 1972.

La sorcière de Rome, Gallimard (Paris, France), 1973, translated by Keith Bosley as *Rome, the Sorceress,* Bloodaxe (Newcastle-upon-Tyne, England), 1996.

Mines de rien, petits délires, Puel (Veilhes, France), 1974.

A Round O, translation by Keith Bosley, Interim Press (Egham, Surrey, England), 1977.

November, translation by John Montague and Evelyn Robson, Golden Stone Press (Cork, Ireland), 1977.

La vie comme elle tourne et par exemple, Maeght (Paris, France), 1979.

Alentour de la montagne, Galanis (Paris, France), 1980.

Haeres: poèmes, 1968-1981, Gallimard (Paris, France), 1982.

Nul ne s'égare; La vie comme elle tourne et par exemple; Comme un serpent remonte les rivières (omnibus), Gallimard (Paris, France), 1986.

André Frénaud ontologique: 11 poèmes, Bedou (Gourdon, France), 1986.

Also author of poetry collection *Le tombeau de mon père,* Galanis (Paris, France).

OTHER

(With Jean Lescure and Jean Tardieu) *Bazaine, Estè, Lapicque,* Carré (Paris, France), 1945.

(With Maurice Estève) *C'est à valoir,* Benoit (Alès, France), 1955.

A. Beaudin, peinture, 1927-1957 (exhibition catalog), Galerie Leiris (Paris, France), 1957.

Le château et la quête du poète, Benoit (Alès, France), 1957.

Chant de Marc Chagall, Maeght (Paris, France), 1969.

(With Bernard Pingaud) *Notre inhabileté fatale* (interview), Gallimard (Paris, France), 1979.

Miró, comme un enchanteur, Maeght (Paris, France), 1983.

Ubac et les fondements de son art, Maeght (Paris, France), 1985.

A collection of Frénaud's manuscripts is maintained at Harvard University.

SIDELIGHTS: Originally content in his work as a civil servant in France, it was his bleak experiences during World War II, including two years as a prisoner of war, that inspired André Frénaud to turn to writing poetry. His verses are characterized by their sense of futility, pessimism, and stoicism. While Peter Broome pointed out in his *Contemporary World Writers* essay that titles such as *Les rois mages* ("The Magi") and *Il n'y a pas de paradis* ("There Is No Paradise") "suggest a religious preoccupation . . . [there is actually] an impetus which negates itself, sees no afterlife, end, or redemption." Frénaud also often wrote about war, such as World War II in *Poèmes de Brandebourg* and the Spanish Civil War in *La Sainte Face,* while his love poems "rarely . . . transcend solitude or exorcize the haunting and tormented images of a restless subconscious."

Among Frénaud's most often praised collections is *La sorcière de Rome,* which was translated and published as *Rome, the Sorceress.* In this complex work, the poet offers an extended contemplation of the title city, ruminating on its pagan past and religious-center present alike, "often in relation to religious and mythological themes," according to Gary Cookson in the *Modern Language Review.* Divided into fifteen movements, the verses "explore in a sort of pulsating rhythm the human search for response from a supporting, expansive divinity," explained Elizabeth R. Jackson in the *French Review.* However, the poet concludes that those who promise help and salvation through God are "cheats" whose "promises make way for cold reality," according to a *Times Literary Supplement* reviewer, who concluded that *La sorcière de Rome* is Frénaud's "finest creation in this genre."

Frénaud received the same kind of praise nearly ten years later for his *Haeres: poèmes, 1968-1981,* which critics felt bore further evidence that the poet was still going strong four decades after his early work earned him acclaim. The writer's thematic concerns and position remain remarkably consistent, while his willingness to experiment with style and content also continues here. "*Haeres,*" reported Moira McCluney in the *French Review,* "is the poet's questioning dialogue with himself, written in sober, meditative, 'versets,' followed by elaborations approaching the explanatory essay form." Michael Bishop, writing in *World Literature Today,* described *Haeres* as a "lucidly benign mediation of the light and darkness traversed, briefly, by a great poet."

Reviewers of one of Frénaud's last verse collections, *Nul ne s'égare; La vie comme elle tourne et par exemple; Comme un serpent remonte les rivières,* took the opportunity to assert their high opinion of the poet. Here, the poems still convey a perturbed sense of fate and disintegration, while the author maintains a sense of "something quite 'imperceptible' occurring, displaying itself parabolically, in symbols no doubt only decipherable by the heart and the soul," according to Bishop in another *World Literature Today* review. Bishop concluded that *Nul ne s'égare* offers more evidence that Frénaud "is one of France's greatest . . . poets."

BIOGRAPHICAL AND CRITICAL SOURCES:

BOOKS

Contemporary World Writers, St. James Press (Detroit, MI), 1993.

PERIODICALS

French Review, May, 1975, Elizabeth R. Jackson, review of *La sorcière de Rome,* pp. 1063-1064; December, 1984, Moira McCluney, review of *Haeres: poèmes, 1968-1981,* pp. 313-314.
Modern Language Review, April, 1985, Gary Cookson, review of *La sorcière de Rome,* pp. 477-478; January, 1998, Andrew Rothwell, review of *Rome, the Sorceress,* pp. 232-233.
Times Literary Supplement, October 12, 1973, "Subterranean Truths," review of *La sorcière de Rome,* p. 1244; April 22, 1988, Mark Hutchinson, "A Basis for Beneficence," review of *André Frénaud,* p. 456.
World Literature Today, spring, 1980, Michael Bishop, "Interviews," review of *Notre inhabileté fatale,* p. 253; summer, 1983, Michael Bishop, review of *Haeres,* pp. 423-424; winter, 1988, Michael Bishop, review of *Nul ne s'égare; La vie comme elle tourne et par exemple; Comme un serpent remonte les rivières,* p. 89.*

*   *   *

FUGARD, Lisa 1961-

PERSONAL: Born 1961, in Port Elizabeth, South Africa; immigrated to the United States, 1980; daughter of Athol (a playwright) and Sheila (a writer) Fugard; children: one son. *Education:* Attended Rhodes University; studied acting in New York, NY.

ADDRESSES: Home—CA. *Agent*—c/o Author Mail, Scribner Publicity Department, Simon & Schuster, Inc., 1230 Avenue of the Americas, New York, NY 10020.

AWARDS, HONORS: Robie Macauley fellowship for short fiction, 1997.

WRITINGS:

Skinner's Drift: A Novel, Scribner (New York, NY), 2006.

Contributor to periodicals, including the *New York Times;* work represented in anthologies, including *Getting Here from There: Selected Shorts, a Celebration of the Short Story.*

SIDELIGHTS: Lisa Fugard is the daughter of two writers, Sheila and playwright Athol Fugard. Born in South Africa, she moved to New York with her parents in 1980 after completing one year at Rhodes University. She studied acting and performed on stage, including in her father's plays, before turning to writing.

Fugard has written nature and travel articles, and she is the author of *Skinner's Drift: A Novel,* inspired by an actual event. Eva von Rensburg left South Africa ten years earlier in 1987, after the death of her mother, Lorraine, and she now returns to care for her dying father, Martin. The story includes flashbacks that reflect the atmosphere of apartheid, her father's forays into the night, and the young Eva's relationships with the black workers on their farm in the Limpopo Valley, all of which come back to her when Eva discovers her mother's diaries.

A *Kirkus Reviews* contributor noted Fugard's "ability to effectively explore broad themes through a family story." Rachel Hore noted in a review for the *Guardian Online* that Fugard not only provides a glimpse into South African history, but also of "the breathtaking beauty of landscape, flora and fauna."

BIOGRAPHICAL AND CRITICAL SOURCES:

PERIODICALS

Booklist, October 1, 2005, Hazel Rochman, review of *Skinner's Drift: A Novel,* p. 33.
Kirkus Reviews, September 15, 2005, review of *Skinner's Drift,* p. 993.
Library Journal, November 1, 2005, Kellie Gillespie, review of *Skinner's Drift,* p. 64.
Publishers Weekly, October 3, 2005, review of *Skinner's Drift,* p. 45.

ONLINE

Exclusive Books.com, http://www.exclusivebooks.com/ (April 22, 2005), interview with Fugard.
Guardian Online, http://books.guardian.co.uk/ (April 16, 2005), Rachel Hore, review of *Skinner's Drift.*
LitNet, http://www.litnet.co.za/ (January 3, 2006), profile of Fugard.
Penguin UK Online, http://www.penguin.co.uk/ (January 3, 2006), profile of Fugard.

G

GABRIELE, Lisa

PERSONAL: Born in Windsor, Ontario, Canada. *Education:* Graduate of the Ryerson School of Journalism.

ADDRESSES: Home—New York, NY. *Agent*—c/o Author Mail, Random House of Canada Limited, One Toronto St., Unit 300, Toronto, Ontario M5C 2V6, Canada.

CAREER: Worked variously as a cab driver, barmaid, waitress, and salesperson; Canadian Broadcasting Corporation, producer, writer, reporter, and researcher; LifeSize Television (television production company), Toronto, Ontario, Canada, executive producer. Producer for the History Channel and Life Network.

WRITINGS:

Tempting Faith DiNapoli (novel), Simon & Schuster (New York, NY), 2002.

Columnist for *Vice;* contributor to periodicals, including *Nerve, National Post,* and *Washington Post.*

WORK IN PROGRESS: A novel.

SIDELIGHTS: Lisa Gabriele is a writer who has also worked as a producer and cinematographer, first for the Canadian Broadcasting Corporation and others, then for her own documentary-production company,

LifeSize Television, in Toronto. With the publication of her debut novel, *Tempting Faith DiNapoli,* she moved to New York City to begin work on another book.

The protagonist of *Tempting Faith DiNapoli,* Faith, is one of four children of Joe, an Italian immigrant, and Nancy, who discards Catholicism on the day of Faith's First Communion. Soon Nancy becomes a rebellious chain-smoking and drinking mother who, although she smacks them around, deeply loves her children. When her father finds work in Calgary, Faith's parents, whose marriage was not strong to begin with, separate. Faith, who had tried to keep the family's religion alive, becomes distracted by boys, sex, and the temptations of shoplifting, and she is eventually sent to a Church retreat for troubled children. When she reads her mother's diaries, Faith discovers that her mother had lived fast and loose at her age and that she has a dark secret that helps to explain the family history.

Booklist reviewer Joanne Wilkinson commented that "Faith may be more sinner than saint," but she also serves as an "inspiration to good Catholic girls everywhere." Amy Brozio-Andrews wrote in *Library Journal* that Gabriele's debut "is emotionally intense and ultimately satisfying."

BIOGRAPHICAL AND CRITICAL SOURCES:

PERIODICALS

Booklist, June 1, 2002, Joanne Wilkinson, review of *Tempting Faith DiNapoli,* p. 1681.

Chatelaine, August, 2002, Bonnie Schiedel, review of *Tempting Faith DiNapoli,* p. 16.

Kirkus Reviews, April 15, 2002, review of *Tempting Faith DiNapoli,* p. 513.

Library Journal, June 1, 2002, Amy Brozio-Andrews, review of *Tempting Faith DiNapoli,* p. 194.

ONLINE

Bookreporter.com, http://www.bookreporter.com/ (January 3, 2006), Melissa Morgan, review of *Tempting Faith DiNapoli.*

Homemakers.com, http://www.homemakers.com/ (January 3, 2006), Kathy English, interview with Gabriele.

January Magazine, http://www.januarymagazine.com/ (January 31, 2006), Margaret Gunning, review of *Tempting Faith DiNapoli.*

Virago Online, http://www.virago.co.uk/ (January 3, 2006), interview with Gabriele.*

*   *   *

GALLIGAN, John

PERSONAL: Born in Spokane, WA; married; wife's name Jinko; children: Sam, Joe. *Education:* University of Wisconsin, Madison, B.S., M.A.

ADDRESSES: Home—Madison, WI. *Office*—Madison Area Technical College, 3550 Anderson St., Madison, WI 53704.

CAREER: Worked variously as a newspaper journalist, screenwriter, house painter, au pair, ESL teacher, cab driver, and in a salmon cannery. Teacher in Japan. Madison Area Technical College, Madison, WI, writing teacher.

AWARDS, HONORS: Epiphany Best Story award; Crime Fiction Book of the Year, *Crimespree* magazine, 2005, for *The Blood Knot.*

WRITINGS:

Red Sky, Red Dragonfly (novel), paperback edition, Bleak House Books (Madison, WI), 2001, hardcover edition, 2003.

The Nail Knot ("Fly Fishing Mystery" series), Bleak House Books (Madison, WI), 2003.

Oh Brother! Said the Mother of Tony Pepperoni (juvenile), Bleak House Books (Madison, WI), 2003.

The Blood Knot ("Fly Fishing Mystery" series), Bleak House Books (Madison, WI), 2005.

Author of short stories and screenplays.

WORK IN PROGRESS: Books in the "Fly Fishing Mystery" series.

SIDELIGHTS: John Galligan's first novel, *Red Sky, Red Dragonfly,* is a mystery inspired by the time he spent living and teaching in Japan. It is the story of the divide between the two Japans, one old and one contemporary. The protagonist, Tommy Morrison, like Galligan, is an English teacher who takes a position in the small town of Kitayama. Upon arriving, he learns that the previous teacher has disappeared. Characters include the school manager, Noriko Yamaguchi, who dislikes life in the small town and longs to be with her mother and brother in the city; and Miwa Sato, a teen who is in love but hides it from her traditional grandfather.

Galligan began his series featuring Ned "Dog" Oglivie with *The Nail Knot.* Dog is a former security consultant who spends his time traveling around the country trout fishing after experiencing a personal tragedy. While in the town of Black Earth, he discovers the body of fisherman Jake Jacobs, whose ponytail has been cut off and stuffed into his mouth. At the urging of local Melvina O'Malley, he stays in town and becomes involved in the investigation of the crime.

The Blood Knot finds Dog camping in Avalanche, Wisconsin, home to a number of Amish families and the Kussmauls, a clan that includes Eve, who was banned by the Amish and whose young son, Deuce, claims to have killed local artist Annie Adams. Eve, who treats Dog's beaver bite, asks him to help prove the boy's innocence, even though Dog saw him fire his .22 into the woman's body.

A *Kirkus Reviews* contributor described *The Blood Knot* as being "the tetchy xenophobia of *Witness* combined with the unbridled energy of *Deliverance* and a touch of *The Compleat Angler:* one helluva story."

BIOGRAPHICAL AND CRITICAL SOURCES:

PERIODICALS

Children's Bookwatch, February, 2003, review of *Oh Brother! Said the Mother of Tony Pepperoni,* p. 3.

Kirkus Reviews, August 15, 2005, review of *The Blood Knot,* p. 884.

Library Journal, December, 2003, Rex E. Klett, review of *The Nail Knot,* p. 171; June 1, 2005, Ann Kim, review of *The Blood Knot,* p. 106.

Publishers Weekly, September 12, 2005, review of *The Blood Knot,* p. 46.

School Library Journal, August, 2003, review of *Oh Brother! Said the Mother of Tony Pepperoni,* p. 140.

ONLINE

Badger Herald Online (University of Wisconsin), http://badgerherald.com/ (March 5, 2002), review of *Red Sky, Red Dragonfly.*

Dispatch (Eatonville, WA), http://www.dispatchnews. com/ (November 15, 2005), Terri Schlichenmeyer, review of *The Blood Knot.*

John Galligan Home Page, http://www.johngalligan. com (January 3, 2006).

Madison.com, http://www.madison.com/ (May 28, 2004), Rob Thomas, review of *The Nail Knot.*

* * *

GELB, Jeff

PERSONAL: Male.

ADDRESSES: Agent—c/o Author Mail, Mysterious Press, Warner Books, 1271 Avenue of the Americas, New York, NY 10020.

CAREER: Writer, editor, teacher. Worked as a disc jockey and music columnist; producer of fanzine *Men of Mystery.*

WRITINGS:

EDITOR; "HOT BLOOD" ANTHOLOGY SERIES

(With Lonn Friend) *Hot Blood: Tales of Erotic Horror,* Pocket Books (New York, NY), 1989.

(With Michael Garrett) *Hotter Blood: More Tales of Erotic Horror,* Pocket Books (New York, NY), 1991.

(With Michael Garrett) *Hottest Blood,* Pocket Books (New York, NY), 1993.

(With Michael Garrett) *Deadly after Dark,* Pocket Books (New York, NY), 1994.

(With Michael Garrett) *Seeds of Fear,* Pocket Books (New York, NY), 1995.

(With Michael Garrett) *Stranger by Night,* Pocket Books (New York, NY), 1995.

(With Michael Garrett) *Fear the Fever,* Pocket Books (New York, NY), 1996.

(With Michael Garrett) *Kiss and Kill,* Pocket Books (New York, NY), 1997.

(With Michael Garrett) *Hot Blood: Crimes of Passion,* Pocket Books (New York, NY), 1997.

(With Michael Garrett) *Hot Blood X,* Pocket Books (New York, NY), 1998.

(With Michael Garrett) *Hot Blood XI: Fatal Attractions,* Kensington (New York, NY), 2003.

EDITOR; "FLESH AND BLOOD" ANTHOLOGY SERIES

(With Max Allan Collins) *Flesh and Blood: Erotic Tales of Crime and Passion,* Mysterious Press (New York, NY), 2001.

(With Max Allan Collins) *Flesh and Blood: Dark Desires: Tales of Crime and Passion,* Mysterious Press (New York, NY), 2002.

(With Max Allan Collins) *Flesh and Blood: Guilty As Sin: Erotic Tales of Crime and Passion,* Mysterious Press (New York, NY), 2003.

OTHER

Specters (novel), Bart Books, 1988.

(Editor) *Shock Rock* (anthology), foreword by Alice Cooper, Pocket Books (New York, NY), 1992.

(Editor) *Shock Rock II* (anthology), foreword by Lonn Friend, Pocket Books (New York, NY), 1994.

(Editor) *Fear Itself* (anthology), Warner Aspect (New York, NY), 1995.

Also author of short stories.

SIDELIGHTS: Jeff Gelb is a writer who is best known for cocreating and editing the "Hot Blood" anthology series and his newer "Flesh and Blood" series, as well as for *Shock Rock* and its sequel. One of Gelb's own novels, *Specters,* finds thirteen-year-old Paul communicating with souls that enable him to see the perpetrators of various murders. *Science Fiction Chronicle* reviewer Don D'Ammassa saw similarities between this novel and Stephen King's *The Dead Zone.* A contributor to *West Coast Review of Books* called the pacing "slick and fast. The book speeds by so quickly, the reader has little time to question what's happening." Gelb frequently contributes to the anthologies he edits.

Gelb and coeditor Michael Garrett were interviewed in 2003 by a writer for *Bookreporter.com,* who talked with them about their latest, *Hot Blood XI,* and the beginnings of the series. The interviewer noted that Garrett was the first to publish King. The two shared a love of comic books, and Garrett and a friend published a fanzine in which King's first story, "I Was a Teenage Grave Digger," appeared. Gelb and Garrett were already friends at the time.

The interviewer asked them how the "Hot Blood" series got started, and Gelb said that he and Garrett "grew up reading horror fiction and *Playboy* in the sixties, and one day a light bulb went off in our heads that it would be fun to write stories that combined the best of both worlds." They wrote and sold several to men's magazines, then decided to create their own market. This was an opportune time, since horror as a genre was gaining popularity, generated in large part by the work of King and Dean Koontz. When they put out a call for submissions, Gelb and Garrett were flooded. Gelb said, "We had obviously tapped into a very rich vein, as it remains to this day."

Gelb noted that when they began, the series was written for a male audience, but that the writers in *Hot Blood XI* are about evenly split between male and female. He said that he and Garrett have talked about doing an all-female issue. In *Publishers Weekly* Penny Kaganoff reviewed the first issue, which Gelb coedited with Lonn Friend, in 1989, commenting on the fact that of the twenty-five contributors, there is only one female. She also said that there is a "redundancy here of female vampires and other monsters, variously seductive and castrating."

Robert Morrish, a contributor to *Voice of Youth Advocates,* called the first anthology "an excellent collection," adding that it "unabashedly flaunts sex and hor-

ror, its various authors gleefully airing the darkest skeletons from their closets, its editors seemingly reveling in the titillating fare—this one is sure to make the Moral Majority blush, if not more." Morrish felt the best story to be Ray Garton's "Punishments," a critique of organized religion, in this case the Seventh-Day Adventist Church, and which reveals the consequences of taking guilt to the extreme.

Edward Bryant reviewed a number of the "Hot Blood" titles for *Locus,* beginning with the first. He also felt that "some diverse viewpoints would have been welcome. After all, sex and eroticism are hardly exclusive male preserves." Of *Hotter Blood: More Tales of Erotic Horror,* which began Gelb's collaboration with Garrett on the series, Bryant wrote that it is "a more successful collection. . . . Both the levels of ambition and of execution are generally higher. . . . *Hotter Blood* is acutely readable, occasionally punctuated with moments of genuine stimulation."

The next book is titled *Hottest Blood,* and Bryant joked that "many of us were wondering what comparative would come next." But the fourth book in the series is titled *Deadly after Dark.* Bryant continued his questioning of the word erotic in the description of the stories of the series, emphasizing that erotic indicates sexual titillation, which he feels is not a component. "Now 'sexual horror' I'd have no problem with," said Bryant, who added that "erotic or sexual, sexy or cautionary, here are fourteen new stories that should arouse a variety of responses, ranging from 'Oooh, wow' to 'Yuck.' As with every preceding volume of this series, there's some extremely effective material."

New volumes of the series were published regularly until 1998, but there was a gap of several years before *Hot Blood XI* was published. Gelb said that he is proud "that we use so many new names in each volume. It's great to have our 'usual cast' of phenomenal writers, but we also love finding raw talent and working with them to give us fresh takes on 'Hot Blood' themes."

Bookreporter.com contributor Joe Hartlaub reviewed the most recent volume, noting that *Hot Blood XI* "contains graphic descriptions of sexual encounters, some of them quite, ah, innovative, to say the least. None of them are gratuitous, though. The erotica, however, is not the common thread that ultimately unites all of the stories in *Hot Blood XI* into a common tapestry. No, there is an almost biblical morality infused into each of these tales or, if you will, a graphic illustration of the ancient caveat that 'one must be careful with what one wishes for.'" Hartlaub praised the editors' contributions, Gelb's "Night of the Giving Head" and Garrett's "One to Die For," and called this volume "by far the best of a heretofore terrific series."

Shock Rock and *Shock Rock II* contain dark tales with a rock 'n' roll theme, and the former includes one by King about a husband and wife who take the wrong road and find themselves in the haunted town of Rock and Roll Heaven, Oregon, presided over by Mayor Elvis Presley.

Gelb edits the "Flesh and Blood" anthologies with Max Allan Collins. *Dark Desire,* the second volume of the sex-and-violence series, was called "much better than its predecessor" by a *Kirkus Reviews* contributor who singled out as outstanding "O'Neil De Noux's titillating comeuppance for a mob holdout, Jon L. Breen's audition for a role in a nonexistent sex film, and Paul Bishop's TV-drama-triangle . . . models of their kind."

The third entry in the series, *Guilty As Sin,* includes contributors who write as couples, including Annette and Martin Meyers and Michael Collins, a.k.a. Dennis Lynds, and Gayle Lynds. Barbara Collins offers up "Dalliance at Sunnydale," about sex, life, and death in an assisted-living facility, and her husband, Max, wrote "Lie beside Me," about a retired spy, with Matthew V. Clemens. A *Publishers Weekly* critic wrote that "Low Tide," the opening story by Dick Lochte, "is a solid hit about a bank robbery with some unusual aftereffects."

BIOGRAPHICAL AND CRITICAL SOURCES:

PERIODICALS

Booklist, January 15, 1992, Gordon Flagg, review of *Shock Rock,* p. 909.
Kirkus Reviews, February 1, 2001, review of *Flesh and Blood: Erotic Tales of Crime and Passion,* p. 146; March 15, 2002, review of *Flesh and Blood: Dark Desires: Tales of Crime and Passion,* p. 370; February 15, 2003, review of *Flesh and Blood: Guilty As Sin: Erotic Tales of Crime and Passion,* p. 272.

Locus, July, 1989, review of *Hot Blood: Tales of Erotic Horror,* pp. 23, 25; February, 1991, Edward Bryant, review of *Hotter Blood: More Tales of Erotic Horror,* pp. 23, 25; February, 1992, Edward Bryant, review of *Shock Rock,* pp. 19, 21, 58; February, 1995, Edward Bryant, review of *Deadly after Dark,* pp. 25, 27, 61.
Publishers Weekly, April, 1989, Penny Kaganoff, review of *Hot Blood,* p. 63; March 19, 2001, review of *Flesh and Blood: Erotic Tales of Crime and Passion,* p. 79; April 1, 2002, review of *Flesh and Blood: Dark Desires,* p. 56; March 17, 2003, review of *Flesh and Blood: Guilty As Sin,* p. 58.
Science Fiction Chronicle, November, 1988, Don D'Ammassa, review of *Specters,* p. 43.
Voice of Youth Advocates, August, 1989, Robert Morrish, review of *Hot Blood,* pp. 165-166; April, 1995, Mary Lee Tiernan, review of *Fear Itself,* p. 33.
West Coast Review of Books, Volume 14, issue 1, review of *Specters,* p. 34.

ONLINE

Bookreporter.com, http://www.bookreporter.com/ (February 14, 2003), interview with Gelb and Garrett; (December 24, 2003), Joe Hartlaub, review of *Hot Blood XI: Fatal Attractions.**

*   *   *

GERSON, Lloyd P.
(L.P. Gerson)

PERSONAL: Male. *Education:* Grinnell College, B.A.; University of Toronto, M.A., Ph.D.

ADDRESSES: Office—Department of Philosophy, University of Toronto, 81 Saint Mary St., Toronto, Ontario M5S 1J4, Canada; fax: 416-926-2070. *E-mail*—lloyd.gerson@utoronto.ca.

CAREER: Writer, philosopher, and educator. University of Toronto, Toronto, Ontario, Canada, professor of philosophy.

WRITINGS:

NONFICTION

(As L.P. Gerson) *God and Greek Philosophy: Studies in the Early History of Natural Theology,* Routledge (New York, NY), 1990.

Plotinus ("*Arguments of the Philosophers*" series), Routledge (New York, NY), 1994.

(Author of foreword) R.T. Wallis, *Neoplatonism,* 2nd edition, Hackett (Indianapolis, IN), 1995.

Knowing Persons: A Study in Plato, Oxford University Press (New York, NY), 2003.

Aristotle and Other Platonists, Cornell University Press (Ithaca, NY), 2005.

TRANSLATOR

(And editor, with Hippocrates G. Apostle) Aristotle, *Selected Works,* Peripatetic Press (Grinnell, IA), 1982, 3rd edition, 1991.

(And author of commentaries, with Hippocrates G. Apostle) *Aristotle's Politics,* Peripatetic Press (Grinnell, IA), 1986.

(And author of introduction and notes, with Brad Inwood; as L.P. Gerson) *Hellenistic Philosophy: Introductory Readings,* Hackett (Indianapolis, IN), 1988, 2nd edition 1997.

(And editor and author of notes, with Brad Inwood; as L.P. Gerson) *The Epicurus Reader: Selected Writings and Testimonia,* Hackett (Indianapolis, IN), 1994.

EDITOR

Graceful Reason: Essays in Ancient and Medieval Philosophy Presented to Joseph Owens, on the Occasion of his Seventy-fifth Birthday and the Fiftieth Anniversary of his Ordination, Pontifical Institute of Mediaeval Studies (Toronto, Ontario, Canada), 1983.

(With others) *Hamartia,* Edwin Mellen Press (Lewiston, NY), 1983.

The Cambridge Companion to Plotinus, Cambridge University Press (New York, NY), 1996.

Aristotle: Critical Assessments, four volumes, Routledge (New York, NY), 1999.

(With John Dillon) *Neoplatonic Philosophy: Introductory Readings,* Hackett (Indianapolis, IN), 2004.

(And author of preface) Joseph Owens, *Aristotle's Gradations of Being in Metaphysics E-Z,* St. Augustine's Press (South Bend, IN), 2005.

Contributor to many books, including *Proceedings of the Boston Area Colloquium in Ancient Philosophy,* edited by J. Cleary, University Press of America (Washington, DC), 1988; *Encyclopedia of Classical Philosophy,* edited by Donald J. Zeyl, Greenwood (Westport, CT), 1997; *Who Speaks for Plato?,* edited by Gerald Press, Rowman & Littlefield (Lanham, MD), 2000; *Plato's Forms: Varieties of Interpretation,* edited by William Welton, Lexington Books (Lanham, MD), 2003; *Plato Ethicus,* edited by Maurizio Migliori, Academica Verlag (Sankt Augustin, Germany), 2004.

Contributor to scholarly journals, including the *Bryn Mawr Classical Review, Journal of the International Society for the Study of European Ideas, Ancient Philosophy, Journal of the History of Philosophy, Religious Studies, Canadian Philosophical Reviews,* and *Philosophical Quarterly.*

WORK IN PROGRESS: The Morality of Nations: An Aristotelian Approach; editing, with N.D. Smith, *Blackwell's Readings in Ancient Philosophy.*

SIDELIGHTS: Lloyd P. Gerson is a professor of philosophy who has written, translated, and edited many books on philosophical topics. He has analyzed the works of great philosophers such as Plotinus, Plato, and Aristotle. One such work, published in 1994, is *Plotinus,* the first book in the Routledge "Arguments of the Philosophers" series. In the book Gerson writes about and analyzes a variety of Plotinus's arguments while emphasizing their importance in relation to Aristotle. This approach is "the most original and valuable aspect of the book," according to Eric D. Perl in the *Review of Metaphysics.* Perl further commented: "The book is thus of value principally to those who have sufficient familiarity with Plotinus' thought to be able to read it critically, making the most of Gerson's insightful explanations of many individual issues."

In 1996 Gerson edited *The Cambridge Companion to Plotinus,* which M.G.J. Beets, writing in the *Review of Metaphysics,* called an "attractive, well-produced book." The volume is a collection of scholarly contributions which serves as a research guide to Plotinus's philosophy. Beets also acknowledged that "the reader is provided with all the information he needs to proceed by himself, making it an efficient companion." In addition, Beets noted, "there is no treatise and no facet of Plotinus' philosophy that is not given adequate and expert attention."

Gerson later authored *Aristotle and Other Platonists.* The book introduces the unconventional idea that the central philosophies of Aristotle and Plato complement each other rather than conflict with one another. Leon H. Brody, writing in *Library Journal,* felt that the text is "a scholarly, highly technical treatise." Other critics were equally impressed; Michael Ewbank, writing in the *Review of Metaphysics,* called *Aristotle and Other Platonists* "remarkable" and thought that "Gerson's thorough reflections . . . clarify enduring philosophical problems" and "encourage more exacting comprehension of subsequent renown speculators."

BIOGRAPHICAL AND CRITICAL SOURCES:

PERIODICALS

Library Journal, December 1, 2004, Leon H. Brody, review of *Aristotle and Other Platonists,* p. 121.
Review of Metaphysics, December, 1996, Eric D. Perl, review of *Plotinus,* p. 399; March, 1998, M.G.J. Beets, review of *The Cambridge Companion to Plotinus,* p. 685; September, 2005, Michael Ewbank, review of *Aristotle and Other Platonists,* p. 175.

ONLINE

University of Toronto Web site, http://www.utoronto.ca/ (March 20, 2006), author's curriculum vitae.*

*   *   *

GERSON, L.P.
   See GERSON, Lloyd P.

*   *   *

GIESBERT, Franz-Olivier 1949-

PERSONAL: Born January 18, 1949, in Wilmington, DE; immigrated to France, c. 1952; son of Frederick (an artist) and Marie (a nurse; maiden name, Allain) Giesbert; children: Aurélien, Claire, Alexandre, Julien. *Education:* Studied law; graduate of the Centre de Formation des Journalistes (journalism school; Paris, France).

ADDRESSES: Home—Paris, France. *Agent*—c/o Author Mail, Éditions Gallimard, 5 rue Sébastien-Bottin, 75328 Paris Cedex 07, France.

CAREER: Le Nouvel Observateur, Paris, France, journalist, 1971-85, editor-in-chief, 1985-88; *Le Figaro,* Paris, editor-in-chief, 1988-2000, publisher, 1999-2000; *Le Point,* Paris, publisher, 2000—.

WRITINGS:

(Editor, with Lucien Rioux) Pierre Mauroy, *Heritiers de l'avenir,* Stock (Paris, France), 1977.
Francois Mitterrand: ou, la tentation de l'histoire (biography), Seuil (Paris, France), 1977.
Monsieur Adrien (novel), Seuil (Paris, France), 1982.
Jacques Chirac (biography), Seuil (Paris, France), 1987.
Le President (biography of Charles de Gaulle), Seuil (Paris, France), 1990.
L'affreux (novel), Bernard Grasset (Paris, France), 1992.
La fin d'une epoque, Seuil (Paris, France), 1993.
La souille (novel), Bernard Grasset (Paris, France), 1995.
Francois Mitterrand: une vie (biography), Seuil (Paris, France), 1996.
Le sieur Dieu (novel), Bernard Grasset (Paris, France), 1998.
Dying without God: Francois Mitterand's Meditations on Living and Dying (biography; originally published in French as *Vieil homme et la mort*), translated by Richard Seaver, introduction by William Styron, Arcade (New York, NY), 1998.
Mort d'un berger (novel), Gallimard (Paris, France), 2002.
L'abatteur (novel), Gallimard (Paris, France), 2003.
L'Americain (memoir), Gallimard (Paris, France), 2004, translation by Barbara Johnson published as *The American,* Pantheon Books (New York, NY), 2005.

SIDELIGHTS: Franz-Olivier Giesbert was born in the United States to an American father and a French mother, and the family moved to France when he was a small child. His father and grandfather were both artists, his grandfather also being on the faculty of the Art Institute of Chicago. Giesbert is a career journalist and the author of novels, biographies, and other nonfiction works, several of which have been translated into English.

Among these is *Dying without God: Francois Mitterand's Meditations on Living and Dying,* a biography of the French president who served his country in that capacity for fourteen years and who died in 1996 of the prostate cancer that had plagued him for years. Giesbert spent a considerable amount of time with Mitterand toward the end of his life, during which they discussed history, politics, and religion. At the time that Mitterand asked for their meetings, Giesbert was editor-in-chief of *Le Figaro.* As Bonnie Smothers noted in *Booklist,* the book reflects Giesbert's "love/hate relationship over the years with Mitterand." Mitterand read the bible but rejected Catholicism for atheism, and his lack of belief is reflected in his observations about his coming death.

The American is Giesbert's memoir, which delves into his relationship with his father, whose experiences during World War II negatively impacted his and his family's lives. Frederick Giesbert was an American soldier who landed on Omaha Beach in Normandy during the D-Day invasion and who stayed and married Giesbert's mother, a nurse. The couple moved to the United States, where the author was born, before returning to Normandy when he was several years old to live on a farm. Although the elder Giesbert had the benefit of a privileged childhood, he came to despise American music, culture, and materialism. Giesbert tells of the beatings he, his siblings, and particularly his mother, received at the hands of his tormented father, and how his hatred of his father dominated his life. He writes of his plans to kill his father, although he never came close to carrying them out.

A *Publishers Weekly* contributor wrote that "the palpable taste of hatred lingers even as an odor of regret pervades this work." Jonathan Yardley wrote in the *Washington Post* that "our parents shape us whether we love them or loathe them, which is one lesson the reader can take away from Giesbert's painfully honest book."

BIOGRAPHICAL AND CRITICAL SOURCES:

BOOKS

Giesbert, Franz-Olivier, *L'Americain* (memoir), Gallimard (Paris, France), 2004, translation by Barbara

Johnson published as *The American,* Pantheon Books (New York, NY), 2005.

PERIODICALS

Booklist, March 15, 1998, Bonnie Smothers, review of *Dying without God: Francois Mitterand's Meditations on Living and Dying,* p. 1197.
Economist, June 30, 1990, review of *Le President,* p. 83; June 5, 2004, review of *L'Americain,* p. 79.
Kirkus Reviews, October 15, 2005, review of *The American,* p. 1123.
Library Journal, April 1, 1998, Augustine J. Curley, review of *Dying without God,* p. 94; November 15, 2005, Susan McClellan, review of *The American,* p. 74.
Publishers Weekly, February 9, 1998, review of *Dying without God,* p. 87; September 5, 2005, review of *The American,* p. 42.
Washington Post, December 6, 2005, Jonathan Yardley, review of *The American,* p. C8.

ONLINE

Arcade Publishing Web site, http://www.arcadepub. com/ (January 4, 2006), profile of Giesbert.*

*   *   *

GLASER, Michael S. 1943-
(Michael Schmidt Glaser)

PERSONAL: Born March 20, 1943, in Chicago, IL; son of Milton A. (a chemist) and Rona (a philosopher; maiden name, Schmidt) Glaser; married Kathleen W. (an educator), May 8, 1976; children: Brian, Joshua, Daniel, Amira, Eva. *Ethnicity:* "Russian/Polish/German." *Education:* Denison University, B.A., 1965; Kent State University, M.A., 1967, Ph.D., 1971; postdoctoral studies at University of California at San Diego, 1974-75. *Politics:* "Kindness." *Religion:* Jewish. *Hobbies and other interests:* Gardening, hiking, travel.

ADDRESSES: Home—P.O. Box 1, St. Mary's City, MD 20686. *Office*—St. Mary's College of Maryland, E. Fisher Rd., St. Mary's City, MD 20686-3001. *E-mail*—msglaser@smcm.edu.

CAREER: Kent State University, Kent, OH, teaching fellow, 1966-70; St. Mary's College of Maryland, St. Mary's City, MD, assistant professor, 1970-74, associate professor, 1974-82, professor, 1982—, chair of arts and letters division, 1979-81, 2001-04, chair of English department, 1996—. Poet laureate of Maryland, 2004—. Chair, Institute of Humanistic Education, 1974-85; has also chaired the St. Mary's County Council of PTAs; served as director of the St. Mary's College of Maryland Oxford Program and Festival of Poets and Poetry/Literary Festival at St. Mary's, 1980—. Has also served on the board for the poetry committee of the Greater Washington, DC, Area, the St. Mary's County Housing Authority, and the St. Mary's Women's Center. Participates in Poet-in-the-Schools project, Maryland State Arts Council, Baltimore, 1985—.

MEMBER: Academy of American Poets, Poetry Society of America, Writer's Center.

AWARDS, HONORS: Faculty student life award, St. Mary's College of Maryland, 1992; Columbia Award, PCGWA, 1995, for service to poetry; Painted Bride Chapbook Award, Painted Bride Quarterly, 1996; Individual Artist Award for poetry, Maryland State Arts Council, 1997; Homer Dodge Endowed Award for Excellence in Teaching, St. Mary's College of Maryland, 2003; Named Poet Laureate for the State of Maryland, 2004.

WRITINGS:

(Editor) *The Cooke Book: A Seasoning of Poets* (poetry anthology), SCOP Publications (College Park, MD), 1987.
The Poet and the Poem (sound recording), first broadcast on WPFW Radio, Washington, DC, 1987.
A Lover's Eye (poetry), Bunny & Crocodile Press (Washington, DC), 1989, 2nd edition, 1991.
In the Men's Room and Other Poems (poetry chapbook), Painted Bride Quarterly, 1996.
The Poet and the Poem from the Library of Congress (sound recording), Library of Congress (Washington, DC), 1998.
Weavings 2000: The Maryland Millennial Anthology, Forest Woods Media Productions (MD), 2000.
Greatest Hits (poetry), Pudding House Publications (Columbus, OH), 2001.

Being a Father (poetry), Bunny & Crocodile Press (Washington, DC), 2004.

Contributor of poems to anthologies, including *Anthology of Magazine Verse and Yearbook of American Poetry, Unsettling America: Race & Ethnicity in America, Welcome to Your Life, Identity Lessons: Learning American Style, Outsiders,* and *Light-Gathering Poems.* Contributor to periodicals, including the *Progressive, Nimrod, First Things, Plum Review, Christian Science Monitor, American Studies, Midstream, Poet Lore, Friends Journal, America, Prairie Schooner, Antioch Review, The American Scholar, The Sun, New Letters, Sacred Journey,* and the *Paterson Literary Review.*

SIDELIGHTS: Named the Poet Laureate for the State of Maryland in 2004, Michael S. Glaser is respected for writing deceptively simple prose poems that are typically based on his own ordinary life experiences. His view of poetry is that it should serve as a medium for sharing experiences between people; verse, he has maintained, should not be an intimidating form of literature, but rather a way to learn about life. As the author put it in an interview for the *Washington Post,* "I'm less interested in poetry as an academician than I am as a person. I read literature because it helps me understand and make sense of my life, not because it's an academic discipline." Also wishing to share the world of poetry with others, Glaser not only composes verse himself, but is well known in Maryland as a teacher of writing and as the director of the Festival of Poets and Poetry/Literary Festival at St. Mary's as well as the annual Voices Reading series at St. Mary's College of Maryland.

Critics of Glaser's works have found his compositions to be intimate works that aim for the heart. In one of his more recent collections, *Being a Father,* for instance, James R. Sims wrote in the *Montserrat Review,* "*Being a Father* disarms me, touches my heart, and deepens my understanding of parenthood through the freshness of the poetic experience."

After accepting the unpaid post of Maryland's poet laureate, Glaser planned to work with teachers around the state to include more poetry in the classroom. "I'm looking forward . . . to sharing more broadly something that I truly love," he told Karen Buckelew in the *Jewish Times.*

Glaser told *CA:* "For influencing my work, I am especially grateful to William Wordsworth for his belief in the everyday language of the common man; Galway Kinnell for his elegance; Sharon Olds for her bravery; Lucille Clifton for her wisdom; Mary Oliver for her perspective; William Stafford for his compassion and Grace Cavalieri for her joyous idiosyncrasies."

BIOGRAPHICAL AND CRITICAL SOURCES:

PERIODICALS

Jewish Times (Baltimore, MD), August 13, 2004, Karen Buckelew, "Maryland State Poet's Jewish Angle."

Small Press Bookwatch, November, 2004, review of *Being a Father.*

Washington Post, August 8, 2004, "Questions and Answers With . . . ," interview with Glaser, p. C4.

ONLINE

Maryland State Arts Council Web site, http://www.marylandstateartscouncil.org/ (August 2, 2004), "Michael S. Glaser Named Maryland's New Poet Laureate."

Montserrat Review, http://www.themontserratreview.com/ (November 14, 2005), James R. Sims, review of *Being a Father.*

St. Mary's College of Maryland Web site, http://www.smcm.edu/ (October 17, 2005), "Michael S. Glaser: Poet Laureate of Maryland."

*   *   *

GLASER, Michael Schmidt
See GLASER, Michael S.

*   *   *

GLUCKSMANN, André 1937-

PERSONAL: Born 1937, in Boulogne, France.

ADDRESSES: Agent—c/o Author Mail, Plon-Perrin, 76, rue Bonaparte, 75006 Paris, France.

CAREER: Philosopher and writer.

WRITINGS:

Le discours de la guerre (title means "The Discourse of War"), l'Herne (Paris, France), 1967, published as *Le discours de la guerre, précédé de, Europe 2004,* B. Grassett (Paris, France), 1979.

Stratégie de la révolution, introduction, C. Bourgois (Paris, France), 1968.

(With Jean Ipoustéguy) *Ipoustéguy, marbres* (exhibition text), Galerie Claude Bernard (Paris, France), 1968.

Violence on the Screen: A Report on Research into the Effects on Young People of Scenes of Violence in Films and Television, translated by Susan Bennett, foreword by Paddy Whannel, afterword by Dennis Howitt, British Film Institute (London, England), 1971.

La cuisinière et le mangeur d'hommes; essai sur les rapports entre l'État, le marxisme et les camps de concentration (title means "The Cook and the Devourer of Men: An Essay on the Relationships between the State, Marxism, and the Concentration Camps"), Éditions du Seuil (Paris, France), 1975.

Les Maîtres penseurs, B. Grasset (Paris, France), 1977, translation by Brian Pearce published as *The Master Thinkers,* Harper & Row (New York, NY), 1980.

Cynisme et passion (title means "Cynicism and Passion"), B. Grasset (Paris, France), 1981.

La force du vertige (title means "The Force of Vertigo"), B. Grassett (Paris, France), 1983.

Le Bétise, B. Grassett (Paris, France), 1985.

(With Thierry Wolton) *Silence, on tue* (title means "Quiet, One Is Killing"), B. Grassett (Paris, France), 1986.

Descartes, c'est la France (title means "Descartes, That's France"), Flammarion (Paris, France), 1987.

Le XIe commandement (title means "The Eleventh Commandment"), Flammarion (Paris, France), 1992.

La fêlure du monde: éthique et SIDA (title means "The Wound of the World: Ethics and AIDS"), Flammarion (Paris, France), 1994.

De Gaulle òu es-tu? (title means "De Gaulle, Where Are You?"), J.C. Lattès (Paris, France), 1995.

Le bien et le mal: letters immorales d'Allemagne et de France (title means "Good and Evil: Immoral Letters from Germany and France"), R. Laffont (Paris, France), 1997.

La troisième mort de Dieu (title means "The Third Death of God"), Nil (Paris, France), 2000.

Doestoïevski à Manhattan (title means "Dostoevsky in Manhattan"), Laffon (Paris, France), 2002.

L'Ouest contre ouest (title means "The West versus the West"), Plon (Paris, France), 2003.

Le discours de la haine, Plon (Paris, France), 2004.

Also author of *Tché, le déshonneur russe,* 2004. Contributor to books, including *Debakel einer Utoopie,* Union Verlag (Berlin, German), 1990; *Tchétchénie: la guerre jusqu'au dernier,* under the direction of de Frédérique Longuet Marx, Mille et une nuits (Paris, France), 2003; and *Open Wound: Chechnya, 1994 to 2003,* by Stanley Greene, Trolley (London, England), 2003.

SIDELIGHTS: André Glucksmann is a French writer who specializes in philosophical and political topics. He is a member of a group of French writers called *les nouveaux philosophes* ("the new philosophers"), a term that denotes these writers' rejection of the Communist fealties of their youth and pays homage to Enlightenment philosophers such as Voltaire. Born to German refugee parents in Boulogne, France, Glucksmann helped found the newspaper *J'accuse,* which became a forerunner of the left-wing paper *Libération.* His writings, many of which concern different manifestation of violence, include *Le discours de la guerre; Stratégie de la révolution, introduction; Les Maîtres penseurs;* and *La force du vertige.*

Glucksmann's first book, *Le discours de la guerre,* deals with theories associated with war and the use of military force, and also includes a study of the military aspects of Mao Zedung's philosophy. *Stratégie de la révolution, introduction* offers a political analysis of the student and worker uprisings in the spring of 1968 that stopped just short of revolution. The book draws on Marx's writings on France, particularly his criticism of French statism. Glucksmann rejects the idea that the consumer culture was the enemy. Instead, he bemoans the domination of French society by the state, and suggests a highly decentralized approach to revolution. "In a society ripe for socialism," he wrote in *Stratégie de la révolution, introduction,* "counterpower is created by the multiplication of centres first of contestation and then of decision which paralyze the central State power." In an essay for the *New York Review of Books,* George Lichtheim praised Glucksmann's analysis as "original . . . though a trifle perverse."

By the early 1970s, Glucksmann was associated with a Maoist group called La Gauche Prolétarienne, which supported resistance against the state. Eschewing a politics of class, the group trained its focus on individual resistors, including farmers, immigrant workers, slum dwellers, and prisoners, and saw some of its members imprisoned. Over time, Glucksmann was also influenced by French philosopher and social critic Michel Foucault, who focused on the diffusion of power throughout society.

Glucksmann's evolving politics were also deeply affected by the works of preeminent Russian critic Aleksandr Solzhenitsyn, who was a survivor of the Soviet prison camps that he described in *The Gulag Archipelago.* In 1975, in *La cuisinière et le mangeur d'hommes; essai sur les rapports entre l'État, le marxisme et les camps de concentration,* Glucksmann attacked the Soviet state and Lenin himself, exploring their links to the Gulag. Two years later, *Les Maîtres penseurs,* a widely reviewed work that was translated into English as *The Master Thinkers,* marked Glucksmann's final break with Marxism. It was published in France the same year as Bernard-Henri Levy's *Barbarism with a Human Face,* which expresses similar concerns. *Les Maîtres penseurs* is a dissection and critique of such philosophers as Johann Gottlieb Fichte, Georg Wilhelm Friedrich Hegel, Marx, and Friedrich Nietzsche, all condemned by Glucksmann for their universalistic thinking. Reviewing the English translation for the *New York Times Book Review,* Werner J. Dannhauser wrote: "At his best Mr. Glucksmann forces us to reconsider the most cherished foundations of modernity—such as the collapse of the traditional distinction between theory and practice—and questions them in a sober, sobering spirit." In the *National Review,* Arnold Beichman took Glucksmann to task for seeming to blame German idealism for the great crimes of the twentieth century; for neglecting the influence of other major thinkers, including Sigmund Freud and Max Weber, on French intellectuals; and for being guilty of "too little too late" in his renunciation of Marxism.

In *La force du vertige,* Glucksmann takes up the subject of the arms race and the European peace movement, which he criticizes as a form of moral abdication and zealotry. The work marks a further distancing from his past positions. It treats the Soviet Union and its nuclear weapons as an imminent threat to the West, worth fighting against at the risk of death. *Times Literary Supplement* reviewer Michael Ignatieff credited the book with making "useful points" about Europe's vulnerability to nuclear attack.

Silence, on tue, which Glucksmann wrote with Thierry Wolton, demonstrates how political expediency, and in particular the tactics of Colonel Mengitsu Haile Mariam, had worsened the mass famine in Ethiopia. The coauthors describe how similar tactics had been used by past regimes to turn the natural disaster of famine into an even greater man-made one. In his *Encounter* review, Jean-François Revel called the book "unassailable in its documentation, irrefutable in its arguments, and implacable in its tone." He also credited the authors with having the "moral courage" to ask: "Why does a crime against humanity cease to be a crime against humanity when it is Blacks who are killing other Blacks?"

In other works, Glucksmann has tackled the subject of AIDS (*La fêlure du monde: éthique et SIDA*); good and evil (*Le bien et le mal: letters immorales d'Allemagne et de France*); and such figures as René Descartes, Fedor Mikhailovich Dostoevsky, Charles De Gaulle, and even God. Since the 1980s, his writings have reflected a preoccupation with questions of morality.

In *L'Ouest contre ouest,* which means "The West versus the West," Glucksmann addresses the issue of European criticism following the American invasion of Iraq in 2003. For the most part, the author stands up for President George W. Bush and the United States and writes about the failure of many groups to realize just how evil the terrorist attacks of September 11, 2001 were. The author also notes that the United States, more than any other country, represents the whole of mankind. "In equating America with civilization, Glucksmann says the term has a double sense: the state of being civilized and the act of civilising," noted David Lawday in the *New Statesman,* adding that the author notes that the duty of civilizations sometimes lies in waging war.

BIOGRAPHICAL AND CRITICAL SOURCES:

BOOKS

Glucksmann, André, *Stratégie de la révolution,* introduction, C. Bourgois (Paris, France), 1968.

PERIODICALS

Booklist, December 15, 1994, review of *La fêlure du monde: éthique et SIDA,* p. 741.

Commonweal, June 6, 1969, Staughton Lynd, "Almost Making It: One View on the Meaning of France's Revolution," pp. 345-347.

Critic, September 1, 1980, review of *The Master Thinkers,* p. 2.

Encounter, July, 1971, Roger Manvell, "The Explosion of Film Studies," pp. 67-74; April, 1987, Jean-François Revel, "Famine, and the School for Dictators," pp. 39-40.

Human Events, March 1, 1980, review of *The Master Thinkers,* p. 7.

Journal of Politics, August, 1981, review of *The Master Thinkers,* p. 923.

Kirkus Reviews, February 1, 1980, review of *The Master Thinkers,* p. 181.

L'Express International, April 21, 1994, Luc Ferry, review of *La fêlure du monde,* pp. 58-59; March 23, 1995, Michel-Antoine Burnier, review of *De-Gaulle òu es-tu?,* p. 63.

Library Journal, May 1, 1980, review of *The Master Thinkers,* p. 1086.

Nation, January 12, 2004, Stephen Sartarelli, "Where Did Our Love Go?," review of *Doestoïevski à Manhattan* p. 29.

National Review, August 8, 1980, Arnold Beichman, "Jacquerie," pp. 970-972.

New Statesman, September 22, 2003, David Lawday, "Now French Intellectuals Love America," p. 32.

New York Review of Books, January 30, 1969, George Lichtheim, "A New Twist in the Dialectic," pp. 33-38.

New York Times, December 26, 1984, John Vinocur, "With Socialist Theory Discredited, French Left Looks for a 'New Frontier,'" p. 6.

New York Times Book Review, September 28, 1980, Werner J. Dannhauser, "A Frenchman Says No to Marx," pp. 12, 40.

New York Times Magazine, April 29, 1984, John Vinocur, "Europe's Intellectuals and American Power," pp. 60-69.

Publishers Weekly, January 25, 1980, review of *The Master Thinkers,* p. 334.

Reflections, spring, 1984, review of *La force du vertige,* p. 18.

Times Literary Supplement, June 1, 1984, Michael Ignatieff, "The Threat of Destruction," pp. 603-604.

Virginia Quarterly Review, autumn, 1980, review of *The Master Thinkers,* p. 148.

ONLINE

Dropping Knowledge, http://www.droppingknowledge. org/ (March 3, 2006), profile of author.

Independent Media Center, http://www.indymedia.org/ (May 7, 2002), Hichem Karoui, "14 Days That Changed France," includes brief discussion of author.

Signandsight, http://www.signandsight.com/ (November 15, 2005), "Integration through Negation," interview with author.*

*   *   *

GOLDSMITH, Andrea 1950-

PERSONAL: Born 1950, in Melbourne, Victoria, Australia.

ADDRESSES: Agent—Barbara Mobbs, P.O. Box 126, Edgecliff, New South Wales 2027, Australia.

CAREER: Worked as a speech pathologist until 1987; creative writing teacher.

AWARDS, HONORS: Australia Council grants; Arts Victoria Award.

WRITINGS:

NOVELS

Gracious Living, Penguin Books (Ringwood, Victoria, Australia), 1990.

Modern Interiors, Penguin Books (Ringwood, Victoria, Australia), 1991.

Facing the Music, Penguin Books (Ringwood, Victoria, Australia), 1994.

Under the Knife, Allen & Unwin (Sydney, New South Wales, Australia), 1998.

The Prosperous Thief, Allen & Unwin (Sydney, New South Wales, Australia), 2002.

Contributor of essays to books, including *Best Australian Essays,* 2004. Also contributor of essays to periodicals, including *Australian Book Review;* contributor of articles to newspapers.

SIDELIGHTS: Before beginning her writing career in the 1980s, Australian novelist Andrea Goldsmith was a speech pathologist who worked with children with communication disabilities. Goldsmith's fourth novel, *Under the Knife,* is a modern tragedy. In the story, Alexander Otto is an eminent gastroenterologist who becomes obsessed with his biographer, Edwina Frye. The official biography is straightforward, but Edwina also writes a parallel fiction biography, which reveals the faults of Alexander's seemingly perfect life. When Alexander believes his long-buried transgressions have been discovered, his life unravels in a murky exploration of failure and regret. Reviewers praised the novel. Indeed, Wendy Cavenett, in a review posted on the *i Magazine* Web site, wrote, "*Under the Knife* is a riveting experience. . . . Goldsmith mainlines discomfort as naturally as breathing and what she creates is truly unforgettable."

A *Publishers Weekly* contributor wrote that Goldsmith's next book, *The Prosperous Thief,* "has undeniable power." The novel opens in the mean streets of 1910 Berlin with the birth of Heinrik Heck. Heinrik's impoverished circumstances and dismal future are in sharp contrast with those of the Lewins, a secular Jewish family living near Düsseldorf. However, everything changes once Hitler comes to power. Outside the Belsen concentration camp at the end of the war, the fates of both families are cemented together in an act with far-reaching repercussions. Later, the descendents of both families, each of which has dealt with their legacy from the past in different ways, confront each other. A *Kirkus Reviews* critic described *The Prosperous Thief* as "compulsively readable, almost hypnotic in its ability to draw the reader in."

BIOGRAPHICAL AND CRITICAL SOURCES:

PERIODICALS

Kirkus Reviews, September 15, 2005, review of *The Prosperous Thief,* p. 994.
People, November 28, 2005, Natalie Danford, review of *The Prosperous Thief,* p. 67.
Publishers Weekly, September 26, 2005, review of *The Prosperous Thief,* p. 63.

ONLINE

Allen & Unwin Web site, http://www.allenandunwin. com/ (January 4, 2006), interview with Andrea Goldsmith.
Compulsive Reader, http://www.compulsivereader. com/ (January 4, 2006), Magdalena Ball, review of *The Prosperous Thief,* and "Interview with Andrea Goldsmith."
i Magazine, http://www.thei.aust.com/ (April 17, 2006), Wendy Cavenett, review of *Under the Knife.*

*   *   *

GOODMAN, Amy

PERSONAL: Female.

ADDRESSES: Agent—c/o Author Mail, Hyperion Editorial Department, 77 W. 66th St., 11th Fl., New York, NY 10023.

CAREER: Journalist. WBAI (radio station), New York, NY, staff member, 1985—; founder and executive producer of syndicated radio program *Democracy Now!,* 1996—.

AWARDS, HONORS: With Allan Nairn, Robert F. Kennedy Prize for international reporting, Alfred I. DuPont-Columbia Award, Armstrong Award, Radio/ Television News Directors Award, and awards from the Associated Press, United Press International, and the Corporation for Public Broadcasting, all for the

documentary *Massacre: The Story of East Timor;* with Jeremy Scahill, George Polk Award, Golden Reel for best national documentary, and Project Censored Award, all for the documentary *Drilling and Killing: Chevron and Nigeria's Oil Dictatorship.*

WRITINGS:

(With Noam Chomsky and Paul Farmer) *Getting Haiti Right This Time: The U.S. and the Coup,* Common Courage Press (Monroe, ME), 2004.
(With brother, David Goodman) *The Exception to the Rulers: Exposing Oily Politicians, War Profiteers, and the Media That Love Them,* Hyperion (New York, NY), 2004.

Writer and producer of documentaries, including, with Allan Nairn, *Massacre: The Story of East Timor,* and, with Jeremy Scahill, *Drilling and Killing: Chevron and Nigeria's Oil Dictatorship.*

SIDELIGHTS: Progressive journalist Amy Goodman began reporting the news for Pacifica Radio in 1985, and went on to cover U.S. foreign policy from Mexico, Haiti, and Indonesia. In 1990 and 1991, she and colleague Allan Nairn were beaten after witnessing the execution of 270 East Timorese by Indonesian occupation forces bearing U.S.-made M-16s. Allan suffered a cracked skull, and both stood in a firing line before their captors changed their mind. Their documentary, *Massacre: The Story of East Timor,* based on this experience, received numerous awards.

Goodman is a founder of Democracy Now!, a radio program for activists and others that airs through regular channels, as well as online, on public access television, and on Free Speech TV. The show ran Goodman's documentary *Drilling and Killing: Chevron and Nigeria's Oil Dictatorship,* produced with Jeremy Scahill. The documentary exposed Exxon's part in the killing of two Nigerian villagers who protested an oil spill in their community. In 1999 Goodman interviewed political prisoner Lori Berenson in Peru, and she covered the return of exiled Haitian President Jean-Bertrand Aristide.

In an interview for the *Women's Review of Books,* Harriet Malinowitz asked Goodman about her influences. Goodman replied that her father had been an activist for integration and her mother taught working-class people at a community college so that they could get ahead. She said that she become involved in independent media after writing her college thesis in medical anthropology on the cancer-causing contraceptive Depo Provera. She noted that the corporate media has control of the news and said that her book, *The Exception to the Rulers: Exposing Oily Politicians, War Profiteers, and the Media That Love Them,* written with her brother, David Goodman, "may introduce people to independent media who haven't experienced it, and let them know where it is. I also want to encourage people to challenge the corporate media, because they're using our national treasure—the public airwaves." Speaking of *The Exception to the Rulers, Booklist* reviewer Brendan Driscoll wrote that "Goodman's vision for media's role in society is as vigorous as her confidence in the power of motivated communities."

BIOGRAPHICAL AND CRITICAL SOURCES:

PERIODICALS

Booklist, April 15, 2004, Brendan Driscoll, review of *The Exception to the Rulers: Exposing Oily Politicians, War Profiteers, and the Media That Love Them,* p. 1419.
Kliatt, September, 2005, Nola Theiss, review of *The Exception to the Rulers,* p. 37.
Publishers Weekly, March 15, 2004, review of *The Exception to the Rulers,* p. 64.
Women's Review of Books, September, 2004, Harriet Malinowitz, "The Sword and the Shield: A Conversation with Independent Journalist Amy Goodman" (interview), p. 20.

ONLINE

Democracy Now Web site, http://www.democracynow. org (March 6, 2006), author biography.*

*　　*　　*

GORRELL, Gena K. 1946-
(Gena Kinton Gorrell)

PERSONAL: Born July 14, 1946, in Toronto, Ontario, Canada; daughter of John Stobie (an art director) and Laura (a musician) Muir; married W. Peter Gorrell (a manager), May 21, 1966. *Education:* Attended University of Toronto.

ADDRESSES: Agent—c/o Author Mail, Tundra Books, 481 University Ave, Ste. 900, Toronto, Ontario M5G 2E9, Canada. *E-mail*—gorrell@netrover.com.

CAREER: Lester & Orpen Dennys (publisher), Toronto, Ontario, Canada, editor, 1978-91; freelance editor and writer. Toronto Police, volunteer constable in marine unit, 1991-2005; volunteer first-aid instructor for St. John Ambulance, 1991-2003.

AWARDS, HONORS: Parents' Choice Award, 1997, for *North Star to Freedom;* Norma Fleck Award for Outstanding Nonfiction for Children shortlist, 1999, and New York Public Library Books for the Teen Age selection, and Canadian Children's Book Centre Choice, both 2000, all for *Catching Fire;* New York Public Library Books for the Teen Age selection, and Norma Fleck Award, both 2001, and Hackmatack Children's Choice Book Award, shortlist, 2002, all for *Heart and Soul;* American Society for the Prevention of Cruelty to Animals Henry Bergh Children's Book Award, 2004, for *Working Like a Dog.*

WRITINGS:

Stories of the Witch Queen, illustrations by N.R. Jackson, Peppermint Press (Cavan, Ontario, Canada), 1985.
North Star to Freedom: The Story of the Underground Railroad, foreword by Rosemary Brown, Stoddart (Toronto, Ontario, Canada), 1996, Delacorte Press (New York, NY), 1997.
Catching Fire: The Story of Firefighting, Tundra Books (Plattsburgh, NY), 1999.
Heart and Soul: The Story of Florence Nightingale, Tundra Books (Toronto, Ontario, Canada), 2000.
Working Like a Dog: The Story of Working Dogs through History, Tundra Books (Plattsburgh, NY), 2003.

SIDELIGHTS: Canadian writer Gena K. Gorrell moved into writing after working for several years as a book editor and researcher. Drawing on her curiosity and her personal interests, she has produced a number of highly praised nonfiction titles that range from biographies and social history to *Catching Fire: The Story of Firefighting.* Inspired by Gorrell's experiences in emergency services as a volunteer police officer and first-aid instructor, *Catching Fire* reveals the history of major fires, the job of fire investigators, the scientific background necessary to battle fires and discusses the many different dangers modern firefighters must confront during the course of their dangerous but necessary job.

Man's best friend earns his reputation for a good reason, as Gorrell shows in *Working Like a Dog: The Story of Working Dogs through History.* Evolved from wolves, canines have skills that have aided mankind throughout history, such as their ability to scent out danger, retrieve game during a hunt, herd livestock, guard against predators, and pull sleds. Beginning with an outline of dog history and evolution, Gorrell introduces readers to modern canine heroes, including a yellow lab who works as a guide dog for the blind, the search-and-rescue dogs that aided firefighters and police during the 9/11 tragedy, and dogs who are trained to nose out everything from illegal drugs to dangerous snakes to hidden caches of fish. Winner of the American Society for the Prevention of Cruelty to Animals' Henry Bergh Children's Book Award, *Working Like a Dog* was praised by Anne Chapman Callaghan in *School Library Journal* as "a thoroughly researched and captivating offering," while *Resource Links* contributor Carol-Ann Hoyte dubbed it "fascinating and comprehensive." In *Quill & Quire,* John Wilson wrote that in Gorrell's "splendid, in-depth book . . . even the most fanatical dog lover will discover something new."

North Star to Freedom: The Story of the Underground Railroad and *Heart and Soul: The Story of Florence Nightingale* focus on America's past. *North Star to Freedom* profiles the men and women who, in order to escape slavery in the American south, risked their lives on the dangerous trek north to freedom. Harriet Tubman and Henry "Box" Brown are among the people covered in Gorrell's inspirational book. The English nurse who became known as the "Lady of the Lamp" due to her work reforming hospital care is the subject of the award-winning *Heart and Soul,* a work described by a *Resource Links* contributor as a "compelling biography" that presents "both Florence's passion to

help others who were less fortunate and her own 'inner struggles.'" Now considered the founder of modern nursing, Nightingale rejected the prospects of making a good marriage match in favor of contributing to society's betterment by studying nursing. In charge of hospital nursing care during the Crimean War, she witnessed the appalling conditions of battlefield medicine and spent the rest of her life battling to improve standards of care. Considered difficult and uncompromising in person, Nightingale nonetheless achieved her goal, as Gorrell shows in a work that "succeeds in separating myth from reality, smoothly crafting a picture of a gifted individual who was also wholly human," according to *School Library Journal* reviewer Cindy Darling Codell.

Gorrell once commented: "How are kids today supposed to learn about their world? The past gets longer and longer—not just literally, but also because we're expected to know more about it than our grandparents were—while much of our emerging knowledge is beyond a lay person's comprehension. I'm concerned that some kids may feel overwhelmed, and may give up trying to understand where we've come from and where we're going, leading to a sense of apathy, futility, and inadequacy.

"My goal in each book is to explain a small corner of the world, focusing on what's interesting and memorable (not all that stuff you forget as soon as you turn the page). I try to put the topic in context, tying it to other times and places. I hope to give kids some of those 'aha!' moments when a piece of the jigsaw suddenly fits into place, and the puzzle of our world seems a little less impenetrable."

BIOGRAPHICAL AND CRITICAL SOURCES:

PERIODICALS

Booklist, February 15, 1997, Hazel Rochman, review of *North Star to Freedom: The Story of the Underground Railroad,* p. 1012; January 1, 2001, Carolyn Phelan, review of *Heart and Soul: The Story of Florence Nightingale,* p. 944; November 1, 2003, Lauren Peterson, review of *Working Like a Dog: The Story of Working Dogs through History,* p. 494.

Bulletin of the Center for Children's Books, February, 1997, review of *North Star to Freedom,* p. 205; May, 1999, review of *Catching Fire: The Story of Firefighting,* p. 314.

Canadian Book Review Annual, 2000, review of *Heart and Soul,* p. 532.

Horn Book, January, 2001, Anita L. Burkam, review of *Heart and Soul,* p. 110.

Publishers Weekly, December 16, 1996, review of *North Star to Freedom,* p. 61.

Quill & Quire, April, 1996, review of *North Star to Freedom,* p. 41; April, 1999, review of *Catching Fire,* p. 35; January, 2001, review of *Heart and Soul,* p. 36; October, 2003, John Wilson, review of *Working Like a Dog.*

Resource Links, June, 1997, John Fielding, review of *North Star to Freedom,* p. 229; October, 1999, review of *Catching Fire,* p. 17; February, 2001, review of *Heart and Soul,* p. 22; October, 2003, Carol-Ann Hoyte, review of *Working Like a Dog,* p. 22.

School Library Journal, January, 1997, Shirley Wilton, review of *North Star to Freedom,* p. 125; June, 1999, William C. Schadt, review of *Catching Fire,* p. 146; December, 2000, Cindy Darling Codell, review of *Heart and Soul,* p. 161; December, 2003, Anne Chapman Callaghan, review of *Working Like a Dog,* p. 167.

Voice of Youth Advocates, February, 1998, review of *North Star to Freedom,* p. 364; February, 2001, review of *Heart and Soul,* p. 441; February, 2004, Michele Winship, review of *Working Like a Dog,* p. 510.

ONLINE

Gena K. Gorrell Home Page, http://www.netrover.com/~gorrell (May 18, 2005).

Canadian Review of Materials Online, http://www.umanitoba.edu/cm/ (September 5, 2003), review of *Working Like a Dog.*

* * *

GORRELL, Gena Kinton
  See GORRELL, Gena K.

GORRINGE, Tim J.
  See GORRINGE, Timothy

* * *

GORRINGE, Timothy
  (T.J. Gorringe, Tim J. Gorringe, Timothy J. Gorringe)

PERSONAL: Male. *Hobbies and other interests:* Bee keeping, poultry keeping, going to the theater, wine making, political activism.

ADDRESSES: Office—Department of Theology, University of Exeter, Queen's Building, The Queen's Drive, Exeter EX4 4QH, England. *E-mail*—t.j.gorringe@exeter.ac.uk.

CAREER: Theologist, writer, and educator. Worked in parishes for six years; Tamil Nadu Theological Seminary, India, teacher of theology for seven years; St John's College, Oxford, England, chaplain, fellow, and tutor in theology for nine years; University of St. Andrews, Fife, Scotland, reader in contextual theology, 1995-98; University of Exeter, Exeter, England, St Luke's Professor of Theological Studies, 1998—.

WRITINGS:

THEOLOGICAL NONFICTION

Redeeming Time: Atonement through Education, foreword by Lesslie Newbigin, Darton, Longman & Todd (London, England), 1986.

(As T.J. Gorringe) *Discerning Spirit: A Theology of Revelation,* Trinity Press International (Philadelphia, PA), 1990.

(As Timothy J. Gorringe) *Capital and the Kingdom: Theological Ethics and Economic Order,* Orbis Books (Maryknoll, NY), 1994.

God's Just Vengeance: Crime, Violence, and the Rhetoric of Salvation, Cambridge University Press (New York, NY), 1996.

Fair Shares: Ethics and the Global Economy, Thames & Hudson (New York, NY), 1999.

Karl Barth: Against Hegemony, Oxford University Press (New York, NY), 1999.

(As T.J. Gorringe) *The Education of Desire: Towards a Theology of the Senses,* Trinity Press International (Harrisburg, PA), 2002.

(As T.J. Gorringe) *A Theology of the Built Environment: Justice, Empowerment, Redemption,* Cambridge University Press (New York, NY), 2002.

(As T.J. Gorringe) *Furthering Humanity: A Theology of Culture,* Ashgate (Burlington, VT), 2004.

Also author of *God's Theatre: A Theology of Providence,* SCM, 1991; *Alan Ecclestone: Priest As Revolutionary,* Cairns, 1994; and *Crime,* SCM, 2004.

SIDELIGHTS: Timothy Gorringe is a theologian with a strong background in teaching. Nearly all of the books he has written attempt to place everyday items and/or issues within a theological context. For instance, in *God's Just Vengeance: Crime, Violence, and the Rhetoric of Salvation,* Gorringe provides an exploration of the theological origins of the idea of atonement and how that idea has influenced penal codes and systems (and vice versa). The book is large in its scope, and it traces the theory of atonement and its development from the eleventh century to the present. Gorringe uses this historical approach to show how societal views of crime and punishment have changed over the centuries and how the concept of atonement has factored into these changes. According to Gorringe, once atonement became equated with retribution, penal codes began to reflect this by seeking to punish the perpetrator/s rather than to promote restoration to the damaged party or community. Part of Gorringe's thesis also claims that it is this shift in attitude that moved the Crucifixion to the center of Western theology. Thus, the teachings of Jesus Christ became less central than the fact that Christ 'paid' for the sins of others with his death.

Reviewers were intrigued by *God's Just Vengeance;* they noted the book's complexity and concluded that it is a valuable tome. Keith Clements, writing in the *Journal of Ecclesiastical History,* stated that the book "provides an impressively thorough and at times provocative survey." And, although *Theological Studies* contributor James J. Megivern felt that the the book's thesis was not always "adequately established," he nevertheless concluded that Gorringe "has done a fine piece of detective work." Pointing out the breadth of Gorringe's undertaking, *British Journal of Criminology* critic Jan A. Nijboer noted that the author's "point of view is not only theological, but also sociological and sometimes psychological." Nijboer ultimately concluded: "Gorringe has written a many layered and well documented, but also complicated book."

In a departure from his usual topic matter, Gorringe published *Karl Barth: Against Hegemony.* The book is an exploration of the work of theologian Karl Barth (1886-1968), and an attempt to explain Barth's often controversial work in light of the political climate of his time. Stating that this approach was too narrow, *Interpretation* contributor William W. Young III felt that the book calls for "greater focus on specific cases and a closer analysis of the ideological context" (aside from the political context) of Barth's ideas. Young conceded, however, that the book "enriches understanding of Barth's work as a response to issues and movements of his time." Gorringe's explication "successfully argues that Barth's theology is written to and for a world in crisis," Young added. Other critics also proffered praise for the book and once again remarked upon Gorringe's dense and intricate prose. Writing in the *Journal of Religion,* Kathryn Tanner concluded that "the virtues of Gorringe's approach come through, indeed, in the nuanced complexity of his analysis of particulars."

BIOGRAPHICAL AND CRITICAL SOURCES:

PERIODICALS

British Journal of Criminology, summer, 1997, Jan A. Nijboer, review of *God's Just Vengeance: Crime, Violence, and the Rhetoric of Salvation,* p. 461.

First Things: A Monthly Journal of Religion and Public Life, April, 2000, review of *Karl Barth: Against Hegemony,* p. 77.

Interpretation, July, 1996, Michael Novak, review of *Capital and the Kingdom: Theological Ethics and Economic Order,* p. 326; April, 2001, William W. Young III, review of *Karl Barth,* p. 212.

Journal of Ecclesiastical History, July, 1998, Keith Clements, review of *God's Just Vengeance,* p. 573.

Journal of Religion, April, 2003, Kathryn Tanner, review of *Karl Barth,* p. 298; October, 2003, Cabell King, review of *A Theology of the Built Environment: Justice, Empowerment, Redemption,* p. 642.

Theological Studies, June, 1998, James J. Megivern, review of *God's Just Vengeance,* p. 357.

ONLINE

Exeter University Web site, http://www.huss.ex.ac.uk/ (March 20, 2006), author profile.*

GORRINGE, Timothy J.
See GORRINGE, Timothy

*   *   *

GORRINGE, T.J.
See GORRINGE, Timothy

*   *   *

GRABENSTEIN, Chris

PERSONAL: Born in Buffalo, NY; married; wife's name Jennifer. *Education:* University of Tennessee, earned degree.

ADDRESSES: Home—New York, NY. *Agent*—Spieler Agency, 154 W. 57th St., Rm. 135, New York, NY 10019. *E-mail*—author@chrisgrabenstein.com.

CAREER: Worked at a bank in New York, NY; comedian in New York clubs; J. Walter Thompson (advertising agency), New York, copywriter; Young & Rubicam (advertising agency), New York, group creative director; Bart and Chris (radio creative services), New York and Seattle, WA, cofounder.

MEMBER: Mystery Writers of America.

WRITINGS:

Tilt-a-Whirl (crime novel; "Jersey Shore" series), Carroll & Graf (New York, NY), 2005.
Mad Mouse (crime novel; "Jersey Shore" series), Carroll & Graf (New York, NY), 2006.

Also author of movie and television scripts.

WORK IN PROGRESS: Whack-a-Mole, the third book in the "Jersey Shore" series, expected 2007; *Slay Ride,* the first book in a new series.

SIDELIGHTS: Chris Grabenstein graduated from the University of Tennessee at Knoxville, where he spent his available time acting at the university's Clarence Brown Theatre. He then left Knoxville for New York City, working evenings during the early 1980s as an improvisational comedian in a troupe that included Bruce Willis and now-television star Kathy Kinney; he supported himself by day with a clerical job in a bank. Grabenstein's first writing job was for the advertising agency J. Walter Thompson. For nearly two decades, he wrote commercials there, as well as for Young & Rubicam. In 2001 he made the break to novelist by penning his crime story *Tilt-a-Whirl,* which became the first in his "Jersey Shore" series.

The novel features policeman John Ceepak, a veteran of the Iraq conflict who lives his life by a strict moral code. His partner for the tourist season is the more lighthearted Danny Boyle, who shares Ceepak's love for Bruce Springsteen music. The title refers to the amusement park ride at the resort town of Sea Haven, New Jersey, where the pair investigate the disappearance of Ashley. She is the daughter and heir of real estate magnate Reginald Hart, who is shot while father and daughter are riding on the Tilt-a-Whirl. Nicole A. Cooke noted in a *Library Journal* review that "though a bit surreal, the ending is unexpected and satisfying and wraps up a good pace." *Booklist* contributor Jenny McLarin, who considered this debut to be "refreshingly different," concluded that it is Grabenstein's "development of the Ceepak-Boyle relationship that makes this an absolute triumph."

BIOGRAPHICAL AND CRITICAL SOURCES:

PERIODICALS

Booklist, September 1, 2005, Jenny McLarin, review of *Tilt-a-Whirl,* p. 69.
Detroit Free Press, October 19, 2005, Ron Bernas, review of *Tilt-a-Whirl.*
Kirkus Reviews, August 1, 2005, review of *Tilt-a-Whirl,* p. 818.
Library Journal, September 15, 2005, Nicole A. Cooke, review of *Tilt-a-Whirl,* p. 60.
Publishers Weekly, August 8, 2005, review of *Tilt-a-Whirl,* p. 216.
South Florida Sun-Sentinel, January 4, 2006, Oline H. Cogdill, review of *Tilt-a-Whirl.*

ONLINE

Beatrice, http://www.beatrice.com/ (September 29, 2005), Ron Hogan, "Guest Author: Chris Grabenstein."

BookReporter.com, http://www.bookreporter.com/ (February 23, 2006), Joe Hartlaub, review of *Tilt-a-Whirl.*

Boston Globe Online, http://www.boston.com/ (October 30, 2005), Hallie Ephron, review of *Tilt-a-Whirl.*

Mystery Reader, http://www.themysteryreader.com/ (February 23, 2006), review of *Tilt-a-Whirl;* Kathy Sova, "New Faces 41—Chris Grabenstein."

*   *   *

GRAHAM, Laurie 1947-

PERSONAL: Born 1947, in England; married to second husband; children: (first marriage) four.

ADDRESSES: Home—Venice, Italy. *Agent*—Mic Cheetham Literary Agency, 11 Dover St., London W1S 4LJ, England.

CAREER: Writer.

WRITINGS:

The Man for the Job, Penguin (London, England), 1988.

A Marriage Survival Guide, cartoons by Gray Jolliffe, Chatto & Windus (London, England), 1988.

Getting It Right: A Survival Guide to Modern Manners, cartoons by Gray Jolliffe, Chatto & Windus (London, England), 1989.

The British Abroad: A Survival Guide, Chatto & Windus (London, England), 1991.

The Ten o'Clock Horses (stories), Black Swan (London, England), 1996.

Perfect Meringues (stories), Black Swan (London, England), 1997.

The Dress Circle (novel), Black Swan (London, England), 1998.

Dog Days, Glen Miller Nights (stories), Black Swan (London, England), 2000.

The Future Homemakers of America (novel), Fourth Estate (London, England), 2001, Warner Books (New York, NY), 2002.

The Unfortunates (novel), Fourth Estate (London, England), 2002.

The Great Husband Hunt (novel), Warner Books (New York, NY), 2003.

Gone with the Windsors (novel), Fourth Estate (London, England), 2005, HarperCollins (New York, NY), 2006.

Mr. Starlight (novel), HarperCollins (London, England), 2005.

Also author of radio plays for the British Broadcasting Corporation (BBC); contributing editor to *Cosmopolitan UK;* former columnist for the *Daily Telegram.*

ADAPTATIONS: Works that have been adapted for audio include *Gone with the Windsors* (unabridged; fourteen CDs), Audio Books, 2005.

WORK IN PROGRESS: A screenplay adaptation of *The Dress Circle.*

SIDELIGHTS: Laurie Graham was born in post-World War II England, and noted on the *Warner Books* Web site that she "was five years old before I tasted candy, nearer ten years old before I rode in a car." Graham attended college, married, and had four children in four years. She had never before pursued a career, and so when her marriage deteriorated she decided to try her hand at writing out of "sheer desperation." Five years passed before her articles were published, the first in the British edition of *Cosmopolitan.* This success eventually led to stories and books. With her children now gone, Graham has settled in Venice, Italy, where she lives with her second husband and continues to work as a writer.

Among Graham's novels is *The Future Homemakers of America,* the story of five American women who become friends after meeting on the U.S. Air Force base where their husbands are stationed in England. The narrator is Texan Peggy Dewey, and the others are Audrey, Gayle, Lois, and Betty. A sixth woman, British Kath, joins the group after they meet her at the funeral procession of King George. The lives of these friends are followed through four decades, during which time they experience the joy and pain of births, raising children, marriages, infidelities, divorces, and deaths. *Booklist* reviewer Carol Haggas noted that in Britain, Graham is compared to Helen Fielding and Nick Hornsby, but that American readers will more likely be reminded of Fannie Flagg and Rebecca Wells.

Haggas called *The Future Homemakers of America* a "fast-paced and funny, timely and tender tribute to the mysteries and magic of true friendship."

Claire Zulkey reviewed the novel for *PopMatters* on-line, observing that Graham's "storytelling style is linear and straightforward, real-seeming and lacking many of the contrivances used in such stories. . . . As in real life, some characters go away and don't come back. Some friends lose touch and, believe it or not, do not all reunite for a grand conclusion. Some children are horrible, hopeless messes and there is no teary reconciliation. Some people make bad, bad mistakes and nothing can be done to fix them." Shelley Mosley commented in *Library Journal* that readers who have enjoyed such novels as *Circle of Friends* by Maeve Binchey, *Divine Secrets of the Ya-Ya Sisterhood* by Rebecca Wells, and Terry McMillan's *Waiting to Exhale* "will relish the humor and pathos, as well as the well-defined characters" in Graham's fiction.

The Great Husband Hunt is a fictional memoir narrated by Poppy Minkel, who inherits her father's fortune after the founder of Minkel's Mighty Fine Mustard dies in the Titanic disaster. Vin Patel reviewed this novel for *Bookreporter.com*, saying that he found Graham's "writing and storytelling to be a joy. I became so involved with her characters that I did not want the story to end." Poppy recounts her life from her father's death until the late 1970s, when she is an old woman. Her first marriage ends in divorce, and her second is to a man distantly related to the British Royals. When he dies, she goes to Paris, just as the Germans are advancing on the city. When she returns to New York, she opens an avant garde art gallery. As she goes through life, wealthy even during the Great Depression, Poppy exhibits independence in her choices regarding work, sex, child rearing, and her religion, Judaism, which does not play an important role for her. She considers herself "Jewish, to just the right degree." A *Publishers Weekly* critic noted that "Graham's protagonist is much less conventional than the book's title leads readers to expect; those looking for ordinary historical romance will get more than they bargained for."

Gone with the Windsors is a fictional recounting of the love of King Edward VIII and twice-divorced American Wallis Simpson, for whom he gave up the crown. The story is told through the diary of Maybell Brumby, a fictional friend of Simpson's from their school days

in Baltimore. They are reunited in 1932, when the wealthy Brumby and well-connected Wallis pursue their dreams in London society. The diary follows the romance of Wallis and Edward as they cavort on the Mediterranean and in the English countryside, as well as his abdication and exile, and provides a history of 1930s London as war approaches.

BIOGRAPHICAL AND CRITICAL SOURCES:

PERIODICALS

Booklist, August, 2002, Carol Haggas, review of *The Future Homemakers of America*, p. 1919; September 1, 2003, Carol Haggas, review of *The Great Husband Hunt*, p. 56.

Kirkus Reviews, August 1, 2002, review of *The Future Homemakers of America*, p. 1060; July 15, 2003, review of *The Great Husband Hunt*, p. 926.

Library Journal, September 15, 2002, Shelley Mosley, review of *The Future Homemakers of America*, p. 90.

Publishers Weekly, September 2, 2002, review of *The Future Homemakers of America*, p. 52; August 25, 2003, review of *The Great Husband Hunt*, p. 37.

ONLINE

AllReaders.com, http://www.allreaders.com/ (February 25, 2006), Harriet Klausner, reviews of *The Future Homemakers of America* and *The Great Husband Hunt.*

BookReporter.com, http://www.bookreporter.com/ (February 25, 2006), Vin Patel, review of *The Future Homemakers of America.*.

GirlPosse.com, http://www.girlposse.com/ (February 25, 2006), reviews of *The Future Homemakers of America* and *The Great Husband Hunt.*

Laurie Graham Home Page, http://www.lauriegraham.com (February 25, 2006).

PopMatters, http://www.popmatters.com/ (December 4, 2002), Claire Zulkey, review of *The Future Homemakers of America.*.

Warner Books Web site, http://www.twbookmark.com/ (February 25, 2006), Laurie Graham, brief autobiography.*

*   *   *

GREGOR, Joseph 1888-1960

PERSONAL: Born October 26, 1888, in Czernowitz (now Chernovtsy), Ukraine; died October 12, 1960, in Vienna, Austria.

CAREER: University professor, librarian, poet, writer, and dramatist; founder of the theater collection of the Austrian National Library (later renamed the Austrian Theatre Museum), 1923, head of library, 1923-54.

WRITINGS:

Das Theater in der Wiener Josefstadt, Wiener Drucke (Vienna, Austria), 1924.

Das amerikanische Theater und kino, zwei kulturge-schichtliche Abhandlungen, Amaltheaverlag (Zurich, Switzerland), 1931.

Weltgeschichte des Theaters (history), Phaidon (Zurich, Switzerland), 1933.

Shakespeare: Der Aufbau eines Zeitalters: mit 136 Kupfertiefdruckbildern, Phaidon (Vienna, Austria), 1935.

Die Masken der Erde: mit 255 Bildern, darunter 15 farbigen, R. Piper (Munich, Germany), 1936, translated as *Masks of the World: An Historical and Pictorial Survey of Many Types and Times,* B.T. Bates (London, England), 1937, published as *Masks of the World: With 255 Photographs,* Dover (Mineola, NY), 2001.

Das spanische Welttheater: Weltanschauung, Politik und Kunst im Zeitalter der Habsburger, H. Reichner (Vienna, Austria), 1937.

Stefan Zweig, Joseph Gregor: Correspondence, 1921-1938, edited by Kenneth Birkin, University of Otago (Dunedin, New Zealand), 1938.

(Author of libretto) Richard Strauss, *Friedenstag* (opera), first produced in Munich, Germany, 1938.

Alexander der Grosse: die Weltherrschaft einer Idee, R. Piper (Munich, Germany), 1940.

Das Theater des Volkes in der Ostmark, mit 50 Abbildungen, Deutscher (Vienna, Austria), 1943.

Kulturgeschichte des Balletts, seine Gestaltung und Wirksamkeit in der Geschichte und unter den Kunsten, Gallus (Vienna, Austria), 1946.

(Selector and author of introduction) Hermann Bahr, *Meister und Meisterbriefe um Hermann Bahr; aus seinen Entwürfen, Tagebüchern und seinem Briefwechsel mit Richard Strauss,* H. Bauer (Vienna, Austria), 1947.

Geschichte des osterreichischen Theaters von seinen Ursprungen bis zum Ende der ersten Republik (history), Donau (Vienna, Austria), 1948.

Kulturgeschichte der Oper: Ihre Verbindung mit dem Leben, den Werken des Geistes und der Politik, 2nd revised edition, Gallus (Vienna, Austria) 1950.

Gerhart Hauptmann, das Werk und unsere Zeit, Diana (Vienna, Austria), 1951.

(Author of libretto) Richard Strauss, *Die Liebe der Danae* (opera; first performed as a radio broadcast in Salzburg, Austria, 1952), J. Örtel (Berlin-Grunewald, Germany), 1944.

Der Schauspielfuhrer, Hiersemann (Stuttgart, Germany), 1953.

Clemens Krauss, seine musikalische Sendung, W. Krieg (Bad Bocklet, Germany), 1953.

Clemens Holzmeister: Das architektonische Werk, Osterreichischen (Vienna, Austria), 1953.

Richard Strauss und Joseph Gregor Briefwechsel, 1934-1949 (correspondence), O. Muller (Salzburg, Austria), 1955.

Europa: Hauptdenkmaler der west-ostlichen geistigen und kunstlerischen Bewegung, Kremayr & Scheriau (Vienna, Austria), 1957.

Die Theaterregie in der Welt unseres Jahrhunderts: Grosse Regisseure der modernen Buhne, UNESCO (Vienna, Austria), 1958.

(With Rene Fulop-Miller) *The Russian Theatre: Its Character and History with Especial Reference to the Revolutionary Period,* translated by Paul England, B. Blom (New York, NY), 1968.

Also author of libretto for opera *Daphne,* by Richard Strauss. Author of introduction, *Der Nachlass Josef Kainz: Katalogaufnahme nach den Beständen der Nationalbibliothek,* by Bertha Niederle, O. Harrassowitz (Leipzig, Germany), 1942.

SIDELIGHTS: Joseph Gregor was a student of literary and theatrical sciences, a professor, and a poet, writer, and author of librettos, particularly for the musical compositions of Richard Strauss. Two of these are *Friedenstag* and *Die Liebe der Danae.* The former features male singers, with one female lead, Marie, who is the wife of a commandant during the Thirty Years War. This twelfth Strauss opera is unique in that the composer had, until that time, favored soprano voices, including that of his wife, for whom he often wrote. Gregor completed the libretto in June 1936, following the German remilitarization of the Rhineland, and the opera premiered two years later following the annexation of Austria and German preparedness for war. Intended for German-speaking audiences it became popular despite of its antiwar theme, but once World War II erupted it was seldom performed again.

Die Liebe der Danae was first scheduled to premiere during the 1944 Salzburg Festival, but it never went beyond the dress rehearsal when Joseph Goebbels, Hitler's minister of propaganda, declared "total war." It would finally premier as a radio broadcast in 1952, and until 2001 this would be the only recording of its performance. Gregor's libretto describes the pursuit of Danae by both Jupiter and Midas. *Opera News* critic Paul Thomason reviewed the recording performed by the American Symphony Orchestra, writing that "if this extraordinary recording of Strauss's undervalued *Die Liebe der Danae* does not jolt opera companies into staging the work, the world will be a poorer place."

BIOGRAPHICAL AND CRITICAL SOURCES:

BOOKS

Birkin, Kenneth, *Stefan Zweig, Joseph Gregor: Correspondence, 1921-1938,* University of Otago (Dunedin, New Zealand), 1938.
Richard Strauss und Joseph Gregor Briefwechsel, 1934-1949, O. Muller (Salzburg, Austria), 1955.

PERIODICALS

Opera News, November, 1999, Bryan Gilliam, review of *Friedenstag,* p. 64; June, 2001, Paul Thomason, review of *Die Liebe der Danae,* p. 54; June, 2002, Paul Thomason, review of *Friedenstag,* p. 57.*

*   *   *

GREMILLION, Helen 1965-
(Helen C. Gremillion)

PERSONAL: Born March 20, 1965, in Corona, CA; daughter of Michael (an aeronautical engineer) and Virginia (a hospital patient-relations director; maiden name, Dubroc) Gremillion; married Nigel Pizzini (an academic advisor), May 24, 2003. *Ethnicity:* "Caucasian." *Education:* Boston University, B.A. (summa cum laude), 1988; University of Chicago, M.A., 1991; Stanford University, Ph.D., 1996. *Hobbies and other interests:* Singing with Bloomington Chamber Singers.

ADDRESSES: Office—Department of Gender Studies, Indiana University—Bloomington, Bloomington, IN 47405-2201.

CAREER: Stanford University, Stanford, CA, fellow, 1994-95, lecturer in anthropology, 1996-98; Indiana University—Bloomington, assistant professor, 1998-2004, associate professor of gender studies, 2004—, holder of Peg Zeglin Brand chair, 1998—, adjunct professor of anthropology, 1998, cultural studies, 2000, and American studies, 2003, fellow of Research and University Graduate School, 2001, and Freshman Learning Project, 2004. Guest lecturer at University of Washington, Seattle, 1994, and UNITEC University and University of Waikato, 2000; workshop presenter; guest on local media programs. Progressive Faculty Coalition, member, 2001—; Friends of Kinsey, board member.

MEMBER: American Anthropological Association, Association for Medical Anthropology, Association for Feminist Anthropology, National Women's Studies Association, Phi Beta Kappa.

AWARDS, HONORS: Research grant, National Science Foundation, 1993-94; American Fellowship, American Association of University Women, 1995-96; travel grants for Australia, Indiana University—Bloomington, 2000.

WRITINGS:

Feeding Anorexia: Gender and Power at a Treatment Center, Duke University Press (Durham, NC), 2003.

Contributor of articles and reviews to academic journals, including *Journal of Constructivist Psychology, Signs: Journal of Women in Culture and Society,* and *Social Science and Medicine.*

WORK IN PROGRESS: Ethnographic Therapies: Lessons for an Engaged Anthropology (tentative title).

SIDELIGHTS: Helen Gremillion told *CA:* "My writing is inspired by a desire to produce interdisciplinary scholarship that can contribute to new knowledge and to social change. For example, my book, *Feeding An-*

orexia: Gender and Power at a Treatment Center, is a cultural analysis of psychiatric treatments that challenges both the disciplinary boundaries of biomedicine and the lack of attention to the material body in some cultural studies literature, and it aims to help improve treatments for 'eating disorders.' My current work examines intersections among talk therapies, cultural studies, literary theory, and poststructuralist theories and aims to help shift dominant psychotherapeutic paradigms. My writing process is collaborative (without strict divisions between 'studier' and 'studied'), in keeping with the goals of my work."

BIOGRAPHICAL AND CRITICAL SOURCES:

BOOKS

Working with the Stories of Women's Lives, Dulwich Centre Publications (Adelaide, Australia), 2001.

PERIODICALS

Canadian Review of Sociology and Anthropology, February, 2004, Richard O'Connor, review of *Feeding Anorexia: Gender and Power at a Treatment Center,* p. 90.

*   *   *

GREMILLION, Helen C.
    See GREMILLION, Helen

*   *   *

GRIERSON, Philip 1910-2006

OBITUARY NOTICE— See index for *CA* sketch: Born November 15, 1910, in Dublin, Ireland; died January 15, 2006. Historian, numismatist, educator, and author. A professor emeritus and former president of Gonville and Caius College, Grierson was a medieval historian who was most often recognized as an authority on medieval European and Byzantine coins. A 1936 graduate of Gonville and Caius, Cambridge, where he earned his M.A., he joined the staff there as a fellow in 1935. Over the years, he would serve in various

positions at the college, including as librarian from 1944 to 1969, lecturer, reader, professor of numismatics from 1971 to 1978, president from 1966 to 1976, and honorary keeper of coins at the Fitzwilliam Museum. His interest in ancient coinage was inspired in 1945, when he was going through some of his father's collection and discovered a coin he did not recognize. Researching it, he learned that it came from the early seventh-century Roman Emperor Phocas. At the time, there were no relevant reference books about such coins, so Grierson set out to rectify the problem. He began collecting ancient coins himself, creating one of the best collections in the world of Byzantine, and later medieval European coins. He also began publishing works on the subject, including *Numismatics and History* (1951), *Coins and Medals: A Select Bibliography* (1954), and the five-volume *Catalogue of the Byzantine Coins in the Dumbarton Oaks Collection and in the Whittemore Collection* (1966-99). After accepting a post as advisor to the Byzantine Institute at Dumbarton Oaks at Harvard University, Grierson felt that keeping his own collection of Byzantine coins represented a conflict of interest. He therefore donated these to Dumbarton Oaks and focused on his medieval Europe collection, which were later also donated to the Fitzwilliam Museum at Cambridge. Meanwhile, Grierson was widely appreciated for his work on numismatics. He was named a member of the British Academy, which named him the Sylloge of Coins of the British Isles, received honorary doctorates, and was presented with the Medal of the Royal Numismatic Society in 1958. His more recent work includes such publications as *Byzantine Coins* (1982) and *The Coins of Medieval Europe* (1990). At the time of his death, he was orchestrating a multi-scholar effort to publish a seventeen-volume work on medieval coins. Anticipated by his three-hundred-page book *Monnaies du Moyen Age* (1976), the project began in 1982, with work continuing after his death. A multilingual scholar who lectured around the world, Grierson was also a former president of the Royal Numismatic Society and former literary director of the Royal Historical Society.

OBITUARIES AND OTHER SOURCES:

PERIODICALS

Times (London, England), January 20, 2006, p. 68.

GROSS, Andrew

PERSONAL: Married; wife's name Lynn; children: three.

ADDRESSES: Home—Westchester County, NY. Agent—c/o Author Mail, Little, Brown and Company, 1271 Avenue of the Americas, New York, NY 10020.

CAREER: Writer.

WRITINGS:

NOVELS

(With James Patterson) *2nd Chance* ("Women's Murder Club" series), Little, Brown (Boston, MA), 2002.
(With James Patterson) *The Jester,* Little, Brown (Boston, MA), 2003.
(With James Patterson) *3rd Degree* ("Women's Murder Club" series), Little Brown (New York, NY), 2004.
(With James Patterson) *Lifeguard,* Little, Brown (New York, NY), 2005.

ADAPTATIONS: Books adapted for audio include *2nd Chance* (unabridged; seven CDs), Time Warner; *The Jester* (unabridged; eleven CDs), Time Warner, 2003; *3rd Degree* (unabridged; six CDs), Time Warner, 2004; and *Lifeguard* (unabridged; seven CDs), Time Warner, 2005.

SIDELIGHTS: Andrew Gross has written several novels with James Patterson, the first being *2nd Chance* for the "Women's Murder Club" series, which Patterson launched with a previous book, *1st to Die.* The four females who make up the club are newspaper reporter Cindy Thomas, district attorney Jill Bernhardt, medical examiner Claire Washburn, and San Francisco homicide detective Lindsay Boxer. In *2nd Chance* Lindsay is recovering from the death of her lover and conflicted about meeting her father, who abandoned the family when she was a child. She investigates the shooting of a black girl on the steps of a church, and Cindy makes the connection between this murder and another that was racially motivated. However, when two police officers are also killed they realize that these are more than just hate crimes. *Booklist* contributor Kristine Huntley wrote that "this novel solidifies the new series," while *People* reviewer Samantha Miller called *2nd Chance* "a solidly engineered whodunit."

In the next book in the series, *3rd Degree,* Lindsay comes up against a group of terrorists called the August Spies, who are committing crimes against the privileged and the wealthy. Lindsay and Jill are jogging when they witness such a crime, and Lindsay enters a burning townhouse and saves a child. Terrorism is one timely topic addressed in this story; the other is abuse. Lindsay notices bruising on Jill's shoulder and discovers that there is trouble at home. Meanwhile, Department of Homeland Security agent Joe Molinari becomes the new man in Lindsay's life.

The Jester is a very different novel set in the Middle Ages. The book begins in the year 1096 and was described as a "bodice-ripper-for-guys" by Sean Daly in *People.* Hugh De Luc is an innkeeper whose wife, Sophie, is kidnapped and whose son is killed by Lord Baldwin while he is off fighting in the Crusades. Seeking revenge, Hugh poses as a jester and gains entrance to Baldwin's castle, where he loses one love and finds another, but his life remains in danger because Baldwin seeks a relic he believes Hugh brought back from the Crusades. A *Publishers Weekly* reviewer wrote that "from start to finish, this is supersmart popular fiction, slick yet stirring, packed with colorful details of medieval life, bursting with unforgettable characters and clever tropes and themes."

Returning to contemporary times, *Lifeguard* is about a robbery gone bad. Nick Kelly and four of his friends have moved from Brockton, Massachusetts, to West Palm Beach, Florida, where Ned has a job as a resort lifeguard. There he meets the beautiful and wealthy Tess McAuliffe and falls in love. He also becomes involved with his friends in a plan to steal artworks from a wealthy collector, a job they hope will pay five million dollars. Ned's role is to set off alarms in other homes to confuse the police. When the four friends break into the house, however, they find that the paintings are not there. Both they and Tess are killed, and Ned's name goes to the top of the FBI's most wanted list. Ned returns to Boston but is captured by FBI agent Ellie Shurtleff, and after he convinces her that he has been set up as a serial killer, they try to find the actual murderers and thieves. *Library Journal* contributor

Ken Bolton declared *Lifeguard* to be "the quintessential summer read."

BIOGRAPHICAL AND CRITICAL SOURCES:

PERIODICALS

Booklist, January 1, 2002, Kristine Huntley, review of *2nd Chance,* p. 777; February 1, 2003, Kristine Huntley, review of *The Jester,* p. 956.

Library Journal, July 1, 2005, Ken Bolton, review of *Lifeguard,* p. 70.

People, March 18, 2002, Samantha Miller, review of *2nd Chance,* p. 43; March 10, 2003, Sean Daly, review of *The Jester,* p. 45.

Publishers Weekly, February 3, 2003, review of *The Jester,* p. 55; February 23, 2004, review of *3rd Degree,* p. 49; May 16, 2005, review of *Lifeguard,* p. 35.

Reviewer's Bookwatch, October, 2004, Marty Duncan, review of *The Jester;* March, 2005, Gary Roen, review of *3rd Degree.*

ONLINE

BookReporter.com, http://www.bookreporter.com/ (January 7, 2006), Joe Hartlaub, review of *The Jester.*

Books 'n' Bytes, http://www.booksnbytes.com/ (January 7, 2006), Pat Reid, reviews of *2nd Chance* and *3rd Degree;* Harriet Klausner, reviews of *2nd Chance* and *3rd Degree;* Fiona Walker, review of *The Jester;* and Luke Croll, review of *3rd Degree.*

MostlyFiction.com, http://mostlyfiction.com/ (October 30, 2005), Kam Aures, review of *Lifeguard.*

Seattle Post-Intelligencer Online, http://seattlepi. nwsource.com/ (March 7, 2003), Jill Barton, review of *The Jester.**

*   *   *

GUSHEE, David P. 1962-
(David Paul Gushee)

PERSONAL: Born June 17, 1962, in Frankfurt, Germany; married; wife's name Jeanie (a nurse, poet, and homemaker), 1984; children: Holly, David, Marie, Madeleine. *Education:* College of William and Mary,

B.A., 1984; Southern Baptist Theological Seminary, M.Div., 1987; Union Theological Seminary, M.Phil., 1990, Ph.D., 1993. *Religion:* Christian.

ADDRESSES: Home—Jackson, TN. *Office*—Union University, 1050 Union University Dr., Jackson, TN 38305. *E-mail*—dgushee@uu.edu.

CAREER: Walnut Hills Baptist Church, Williamsburg, VA, youth minister, 1983-84; St. Matthews Baptist Church, youth minister, 1984-86; ordained to the Christian ministry, Walnut Hills Baptist Church, 1987; Evangelicals for Social Action, staff, 1990-93; Southern Baptist Theological Seminary, Louisville, KY, assistant professor of Christian ethics,1993-96, acting associate dean of school of theology and acting director of professional studies, 1995-96; Union University, Jackson, TN, associate professor of Christian studies, 1996-99, Graves Associate Professor of Moral Philosophy, 1999-2003, Graves Professor of Moral Philosophy, 2003—; Carl F.H. Henry Center for Christian Leadership, senior fellow, 2000—. Northbrook Church, Jackson, member of the Pastoral Leadership Team, 1997-2004; First Presbyterian Church, Humboldt, TN, interim pastor, 2004-05. Affiliated with the Wilberforce Forum, Center for Public Justice, and Empowering the Poor; lecturer and guest professor at colleges and universities in the United States and abroad.

MEMBER: Baptist World Alliance, Society of Christian Ethics, American Academy of Religion, National Association of Evangelicals, Baptist Association of Philosophy Teachers, Society of Christian Ethics, Phi Eta Sigma, Phi Beta Kappa.

AWARDS, HONORS: Francisco Preaching Scholarship, Southern Baptist Theological Seminary, 1985; journalism awards, Evangelical Press Association, 1991, 1992, 1997; named one of fifty "Up and Coming" evangelical leaders under forty by *Christianity Today,* 1996; named one of the Outstanding Young Men of America, 1996; Pew research grants, 1997, 2005; Outstanding Young Religious Leader award from the Jaycees, Jackson, TN, 1998; Faculty of the Year Award, Union University, 2000; *Kingdom Ethics: Following Jesus in Contemporary Context* was named the Theology/Ethics Book of the Year by *Christianity Today,* 2004.

WRITINGS:

The Righteous Gentiles of the Holocaust: A Christian Interpretation, Fortress Press (Minneapolis, MN),

1994, revised and reprinted as *Righteous Gentiles of the Holocaust: Genocide and Moral Obligation,* Paragon House (St. Paul, MN), 2003.

(Editor, with Walter C. Jackson) *Preparing for Christian Ministry: An Evangelical Approach,* Victor Books (Wheaton, IL), 1996.

(With Robert H. Long) *A Bolder Pulpit: Reclaiming the Moral Dimension of Preaching,* Judson Press (Valley Forge, PA), 1998.

(Editor, with David S. Dockery) *The Future of Christian Higher Education,* Broadman & Holman Publishers (Nashville, TN), 1999.

(Editor) *Toward a Just and Caring Society: Christian Responses to Poverty in America,* Baker Books (Grand Rapids, MI), 1999.

(Editor) *Christians and Politics beyond the Culture Wars: An Agenda for Engagement,* Baker Books (Grand Rapids, MI), 2000.

(With Glen H. Stassen) *Kingdom Ethics: Following Jesus in Contemporary Context,* InterVarsity Press (Downers Grove, IL), 2003.

Getting Marriage Right: Realistic Counsel for Saving and Strengthening Relationships, Baker Books (Grand Rapids, MI), 2004.

Only Human: Christian Reflections on the Journey toward Wholeness ("Enduring Questions in Christian Life" series), foreword by Stanley Hauerwas, Jossey-Bass (San Francisco, CA), 2005.

Contributor to books by others, including *Toward an Evangelical Public Policy: Political Strategies for the Health of the Nation,* edited by Ronald J. Sider and Diane Knippers, Baker Books (Grand Rapids, MI), 2005, and *Doing Right and Doing Good: Classical and Contemporary Readings in Christian Ethics,* edited by David Ahearn and Peter Gathje, Liturgical Press (Collegeville, MN), 2005. Contributor to periodicals, including *Christianity Today, Christian Century, Perspectives in Religious Culture, Books and Culture, Sojourners, Journal of Church and State, Catholic Digest, Annals of the American Academy of Political and Social Science, Journal of Family Ministry, Holocaust and Genocide Studies, Theology Today,* and *Annals of the Society of Christian Ethics.* Also author of columns for the *Jackson Sun,* Religion News Service, and *Beliefnet;* serves on the editorial boards of periodicals, including *Prism* and *Faithworks;* editor of the "Enduring Questions in Christian Life" series, Jossey-Bass.

WORK IN PROGRESS: The Sanctity of Life: A Christian Exploration; Moral Philosophy: Tracing the Traditions, for Chalice Press.

SIDELIGHTS: David P. Gushee, whose field of interest is Christian ethics, is the author of nonfiction books that instruct and guide, as well as those that examine history and culture as they relate to Christian life. His first book, *The Righteous Gentiles of the Holocaust: A Christian Interpretation,* later revised as *Righteous Gentiles of the Holocaust: Genocide and Moral Obligation,* examines the part played by Gentiles in rescuing Jews from the Nazis during the Holocaust and then analyzes how these acts of valor should be viewed in the present time. Gushee estimates the number of rescuers to be between 100,000 and 250,000 and considers what it was about these people that they would take such risks to help the Jews. John K. Roth, who reviewed the original edition in *Christianity Today,* wrote that "Gushee locates that 'something' in qualities of character—for example, self-esteem, independence, willingness to stand up for beliefs—and in communal support that encourage those traits. That support nurtured a sense of responsibility rooted both in moral commitment to love, justice, and mercy and in an inclusive, democratic, life-and-justice-affirming patriotism and political orientation." *America* contributor Michael B. McGarry concluded that "Gushee has done a great service by marshaling the history, data and thoughts of the Christian rescuers into a well-written, cogent volume."

In *Kingdom Ethics: Following Jesus in Contemporary Context,* Gushee and collaborator Glen H. Stassen state that their intent is "to reclaim Jesus Christ for Christian ethics and for the moral life of the churches." The book approaches ethics in relation to the Sermon on the Mount, which the authors note is little studied, and applies the principles drawn from it to such social issues as abortion, cloning, stem cell research, genetic engineering, and homosexuality. Reviewing the volume in the *Journal of Church and State,* L. Manning Garrett III wrote that "in that vein, it clearly attempts to illuminate the interfacing of church and state." In later chapters Gushee and Stassen study ethics with regard to such issues as politics, the environment, and capital punishment. "Resisting postmodernism, Stassen and Gushee insist that Jesus taught rules—concrete directions for action applying to many situations—and the general principles underlying them," commented Thomas Finger in the *Christian Century.* "More like postmodernists, however, they consider few principles absolute. . . . The book should appeal to the large, somewhat amorphous but increasingly visible audience that is neither traditionally ecumenical nor evangelical."

The state of contemporary marriage is the topic of *Getting Marriage Right: Realistic Counsel for Saving and Strengthening Relationships,* in which Gushee includes advice for churches as to how they can help prevent divorce and strengthen marriage. Although he asserts that the bond of marriage should not be easily broken, he acknowledges that in marriages where there is violence, desertion, and infidelity, divorce, according to the Bible, may be justified. He also considers how stronger marriage and divorce laws might prevent broken homes, and in particular the negative impact on the lives of children.

Gushee is also the editor of such books as *Toward a Just and Caring Society: Christian Responses to Poverty in America* and *Christians and Politics beyond the Culture Wars: An Agenda for Engagement.* The former is a collection of essays by Christian scholars that deal with economic justice and suggest that the church and the state must work together in addressing poverty and the social ills that result, naming them as problems that must be shared equally by the public and private sectors. The latter book includes essays that were part of the proceedings of a conference at Union University. Subjects include education, welfare reform, divorce, abortion, refugees, and Third World relationships. Richard J. Mouw noted in *Theology Today* that although the contributors to *Christians and Politics beyond the Culture Wars* do not always agree, "taken together, [they] exemplify a position that does not fit nicely into current 'left' or 'right' categories."

The editor of the "Enduring Questions in Christian Life" series, Gushee wrote its first volume, *Only Human: Christian Reflections on the Journey toward Wholeness.* Here he explores what it means to be human, the concept of human nature, and how there can be such differences in the behavior of humans. He studies humans as a composite of body, soul, and spirit who are tempted by sin on the way to finding wholeness. Steve Young wrote in *Library Journal* that Gushee's discussion of how virtue can grow, as well the biographies he presents that demonstrate how moral people have improved our world, are "his most illuminating contribution."

Gushee told *CA:* "All doctoral students write dissertations, and most of them are arduous and unmemorable, but I found that I really enjoyed writing mine. It became my first book, *The Righteous Gentiles of the Holocaust,* and launched me on a book-writing career that hasn't slowed down since then. Another major factor in developing my writing was three years of service as an editor for the publications of Evangelicals for Social Action. This gave me numerous opportunities to write shorter articles and also to sharpen my craft through constant editing of the work of others. Together, book writing and essay writing/editing have continued to be central to my work since that time.

"I have been surprised by the hunger that so many people show for good writing. Even in this supposedly post-literary era, I find that people of all types respond passionately to my writing when I am at my best. And one of the benefits of the Internet is that my writing finds audiences I could never have planned, anticipated, or controlled. Once the words leave my 'pen,' they belong to the audience, for better or for worse.

"My personal mission statement is to contribute to the moral and spiritual renewal of the church and American society through scholarship in Christian ethics and its public articulation. So the main thing I hope that my books will do is to somehow serve this overall mission. I want to help people, especially Christians, think rightly, and live rightly, as this is understood from within the frameowrk of the Christian faith. Secondarily, it is important to me to offer a peaceable, reconciling voice that can build bridges in our deeply divided society."

BIOGRAPHICAL AND CRITICAL SOURCES:

PERIODICALS

America, October 14, 1995, Michael B. McGarry, review of *The Righteous Gentiles of the Holocaust: A Christian Interpretation,* p. 27.

Booklist, September 1, 2005, Donna Chavez, review of *Only Human: Christian Reflections on the Journey toward Wholeness,* p. 25.

Christian Century, May 17, 1995, Wynn M. Goering, review of *The Righteous Gentiles of the Holocaust,* p. 547; September 7, 2004, Thomas Finger, review of *Kingdom Ethics: Following Jesus in Contemporary Context,* p. 51.

Christianity Today, March 6, 1995, John K. Roth, review of *The Righteous Gentiles of the Holocaust,* p. 36; July, 2004, Andy Crosby, review of *Getting Marriage Right: Realistic Counsel for Saving and Strengthening Relationships,* p. 66.

International Bulletin of Missionary Research, October, 2005, Joon-Sik Park, review of *Kingdom Ethics,* p. 211.

Journal of Church and State, spring, 2002, Paul Mastin, review of *Toward a Just and Caring Society: Christian Responses to Poverty in America,* p. 370; winter, 2005, L. Manning Garrett III, review of *Kingdom Ethics,* p. 158.

Library Journal, October 1, 2005, Steve Young, review of *Only Human,* p. 84.

Theology Today, January, 2002, Richard J. Mouw, review of *Christians and Politics Beyond the Culture Wars: An Agenda for Engagement,* p. 651.

ONLINE

David P. Gushee Home Page, http://www.davidgushee.com (February 23, 2006).

Union University Web site, http://www.uu.edu/ (January 8, 2006), author profile.

*   *   *

GUSHEE, David Paul
    See GUSHEE, David P.

H

HAANES, Sharon
See BRYANT, Sharon

*   *   *

HAMBLYN, Richard 1965-

PERSONAL: Born 1965.

ADDRESSES: Agent—c/o Author Mail, Farrar, Straus and Giroux, 19 Union Square W., New York, NY 10003.

CAREER: Geologist. Nottingham University, Nottingham, England, postdoctoral research fellow.

WRITINGS:

The Invention of Clouds: How an Amateur Meteorologist Forged the Language of the Skies, Farrar, Straus (New York, NY), 2001.
(Editor) *Earthly Powers* (Volume 3 of "Literature and Science, 1660-1834" series), Pickering & Chatto (London, England), 2003.
(Editor and author of introduction and notes) Daniel Defoe, *The Storm,* Penguin (New York, NY), 2005.

Also reviewer for the *London Review of Books.*

WORK IN PROGRESS: Terra: Tales of the Earth.

SIDELIGHTS: Geologist Richard Hamblyn's research and writings focus on the natural world. His first book, *The Invention of Clouds: How an Amateur Meteorologist Forged the Language of the Skies,* was published on the two-hundredth anniversary of Luke Howard's presentation to the Askesian Society of his list of cloud names. Howard, an amateur British scientist, first named the clouds we continue to identify as cirrus, cumulus, stratus, as well as nimbus, a cloud that he considered a combination of the primary three. Hamblyn offers both an overview of Howard's life and the science of clouds, and as a writer who compares science and art, he includes anecdotes and poetry that demonstrate those relationships. Howard was a Quaker and an apprentice chemist (druggist) when he began to study clouds. His paper was titled *On the Modifications of Clouds,* and after it was published in a journal, like-minded naturalists praised his work, including Johann Wolfgang von Goethe, who wrote a series of poems in honor of Howard.

Alfred Corn noted in the *New York Times Book Review* that "the Romantics, turning inward to private consciousness, found a fluidity for which clouds are an especially apt metaphor." As Hamblyn notes in his tribute, "by naming the clouds, by giving language and a greater visibility to things that had hitherto been nameless and unknowable, he completely transformed the relationship between the world and its overarching sky." *Weatherwise* reviewer Stanley David Gedzelman wrote that "from the first page, I felt transported back to a time when the face of the modern world was taking shape and when a humble man put an indelible stamp on the clouds, forever changing their place in our minds and in our imaginations."

Hamblyn also edited *Earthly Powers,* the third volume in the "Literature and Science, 1660-1834" series published by Pickering & Chatto. The book studies the perception of natural events, including volcanic eruptions, earthquakes, energy storms, and less violent "powers," such as tides and clouds, by eighteenth-and nineteenth-century writers and philosophers. Hamblyn is also editor of the reprint of Daniel Defoe's *The Storm,* an account of the devastation caused by the hurricane that traveled from the Caribbean to strike England on November 26, 1703, causing the loss of eight thousand lives.

BIOGRAPHICAL AND CRITICAL SOURCES:

PERIODICALS

Book, July, 2001, review of *The Invention of Clouds: How an Amateur Meteorologist Forged the Language of the Skies,* p. 13.

Booklist, June 1, 2001, Gilbert Taylor, review of *The Invention of Clouds,* p. 1809.

Bulletin of the American Meteorological Society, May, 2002, Walt Lyons, review of *The Invention of Clouds,* p. 742.

Entertainment Weekly, August 3, 2001, Suzanne Ruta, review of *The Invention of Clouds,* p. 62.

Forbes, August 6, 2001, Susan Adams, review of *The Invention of Clouds,* p. 114.

Harper's, January, 2002, Guy Davenport, review of *The Invention of Clouds,* p. 64.

M2 Best Books, December 9, 2002, Jamie Ayres, review of *The Invention of Clouds.*

New York Times Book Review, July 29, 2001, Alfred Corn, review of *The Invention of Clouds,* p. 22.

Publishers Weekly, June 11, 2001, review of *The Invention of Clouds,* p. 74.

School Library Journal, December, 2001, Barbara A. Genco, review of *The Invention of Clouds,* p. 58.

Science, March 5, 2004, review of *The Storm,* p. 1471.

Scientific American, January, 2002, review of *The Invention of Clouds,* p. 95.

Weatherwise, January-February, 2002, Stanley David Gedzelman, review of *The Invention of Clouds,* p. 42.

Wordsworth Circle, fall, 2003, Ashton Nichols, review of *Earthly Powers,* p. 234.*

HAN, Béatrice 1963-

PERSONAL: Born May 16, 1963, in Paris, France; daughter of René (a writer) and Danièle (a pharmacist; maiden name, Dupont) Han; married Edward Pile (an artist), May 19, 2001. *Ethnicity:* "Half French, half Chinese." *Education:* École Normale Supérieure, Paris, graduated, 1983; University of Paris XII, doctorate, 1995.

ADDRESSES: Home—Elm Cottage, 9 Park Rd., Wivenhoe, Colchester CO7 9NG, England. *Office*—Department of Philosophy, University of Essex, Wivenhoe Park, Colchester CO4 3SQ, England; fax: 01-206-873377. *E-mail*—beatrice@essex.ac.uk.

CAREER: University of Paris IV, Sorbonne, Paris, France, assistant, 1987-91; University of Reims, Reims, France, assistant, 1992-95; University of Amiens, Amiens, France, assistant, 1996-97; University of Essex, Colchester, England, reader, 1997—.

AWARDS, HONORS: Award from Arts and Humanities Research Board, 2003.

WRITINGS:

L'ontologie manquée de Michel Foucault, Editions Jérôme Millon (Grenoble, France), 1998.

Foucault's Critical Project: Between the Transcendental and the Historical, Stanford University Press (Stanford, CA), 2002.

Transcendence without Religion, Routledge (New York, NY), 2005.

Contributor to books, including *Heidegger, Authenticity, and Modernity: Essays in Honor of Hubert L. Dreyfus,* Volume 1, edited by M. Wrathall, MIT Press (Cambridge, MA), 1999; *Nietzsche and the Divine,* edited by J. Lippitt and J. Urpeth, Clinamen Press (London, England), 2000; *Religion,* edited by J. Faulconer, Indiana University Press (Bloomington, IN), 2003; *Companion to Modern French Thought,* Fitzroy (London, England), 2004; *The Blackwell Companion to Existentialist Philosophy,* Blackwell, 2004; *The Blackwell Companion to Heidegger,* Blackwell, 2005; and *The Cambridge Companion to Foucault,* Cambridge, 2005. Contributor to academic journals, including *Epoche, Journal of the Institute of Romance Studies, La Recherche Photographique,* and *Kairos.*

SIDELIGHTS: Béatrice Han told *CA:* "My writing process includes a long research time, during which I gather material and think about it. Then comes a very intensive writing period, with a first draft that will need modification. I researched *Foucault's Critical Project: Between the Transcendental and the Historical* for a few years and wrote the book in exactly nine months, writing every day without interruption. I am driven by a desire to understand some aspects of the world and times I live in and to communicate this understanding to others."

*   *   *

HANHIMÄKI, Jussi M. 1965-
(Jussi Markus Hanhimäki)

PERSONAL: Born February 3, 1965, in Espoo, Finland; son of Jussi Kalervo and Hilkka Doris (Uuskallio) Hanhimäki; married Holli Tina Schauber, June 17, 1990. *Education:* Tampere University (Tampere, Finland), B.A., 1987; Boston University, M.A., 1988, Ph.D., 1993. *Hobbies and other interests:* Tennis, jogging.

ADDRESSES: Office—Graduate Institute of International Studies, rue de Lausanne 132, Case postale 36, CH-1211 Geneva 21, Switzerland. *E-mail*—hanhimak@hei.unige.ch.

CAREER: Researcher, historian, writer, and educator. Massachusetts Institute of Technology, Cambridge, lecturer, 1990-91; United States Institute of Peace, Washington, DC, researcher, 1991-92; Bishop's University, Lennoxville, Quebec, Canada, assistant professor, 1992-93; Harvard University, Cambridge, MA, research fellow, 1993-94; Ohio University, Athens, research fellow, 1994-95; London School of Economics, London, England, lecturer, 1995-2000; Institute of International Studies, Geneva, Switzerland, professor, 2000—. Nobel Institute, fellow, 1997.

MEMBER: Finnish Historical Society, American Historical Association, Society for Historians of American Foreign Relations.

WRITINGS:

NONFICTION

Rinnakkaiseloa patoamassa: Yhdysvallat ja Paasikivien linja 1948-1956, Suomen Historiallinen Seura (Helsinki, Finland), 1996.
Containing Coexistence: America, Russia, and the "Finnish Solution," Kent State University Press (Kent, OH), 1997.
Scandinavia and the United States: An Insecure Friendship, Twayne (New York, NY), 1997.
(Editor, with Odd Arne Westad) *The Cold War: A History in Documents and Eyewitness Accounts,* Oxford University Press (New York, NY), 2003.
The Flawed Architect: Henry Kissinger and American Foreign Policy, Oxford University Press (New York, NY), 2004.

Coeditor of the journal *Cold War History.*

WORK IN PROGRESS: Researching Henry Kissinger and triangular diplomacy, and European perceptions of McCarthyism.

SIDELIGHTS: Finnish professor Jussi M. Hanhimäki is a historian who specializes in foreign relations and Cold War history. Both topics come to the fore in *Containing Coexistence: America, Russia, and the "Finnish Solution."* The book examines American policy and attitude towards Finnish-Soviet relations, especially after the 1948 signing of the Soviet-Finnish Treaty of Friendship, Cooperation, and Mutual Assistance (FCMA). While the treaty allowed Finland to coexist independently of and peacefully with Russia, American leaders were wary of the agreement (they viewed it as a strategical move indicating Russia's intent to absorb or takeover Finland). The book's "source base is broad and up to date and includes the pertinent records in American, Finnish, and British archives," noted H. Peter Krosby in *Scandinavian Studies.* However, Gordon L. Shull, writing in *Perspectives on Political Science,* remarked upon the noticeable absence of Soviet sources. Still, both reviewers found much of the book to be of value. While Shull felt that the window of time covered in the book was too narrow, and that this led to the omission of later events that are pertinent to the topic, he did comment that "the author's close attention to U.S.

perceptions and policies . . . are its distinguishing features." Krosby was far more enthusiastic in his summation, stating that "Hanhimäki's very well-written book is a fine addition to the history of the early Cold War."

Among Hanhimäki's other reviewed books are *Scandinavia and the United States: An Insecure Friendship* and *The Cold War: A History in Documents and Eyewitness Accounts.* The former volume picks up largely where *Containing Coexistence* ends; it focuses not only on America's Cold War concerns regarding Finland, but on America's concerns with the whole of Scandinavia as well. Indeed, Hanhimäki "is the first to survey this broad subject in its entirety," noted *Scandinavian Studies* contributor John Pederson. Likewise, a *Contemporary Review* critic noted that *The Cold War,* which Hanhimäki coedited, is also a unique volume. The critic stated that it is an "original collection [that] reflects the changing nature of Cold War studies based, in large part, on historians' new access to Communist material."

The Flawed Architect: Henry Kissinger and American Foreign Policy also relies on previously unavailable material, and it is perhaps Hanhimäki's most widely-reviewed work to date. The book is an in-depth look at Henry Kissinger, the highly controversial American diplomat who was instrumental in directing American policies in regard to the Vietnam War. Hanhimäki chronicles Kissinger's career and provides an analysis of his policies and their results. This aspect of the book is particularly relevant because of Hanhimäki's access to declassified government documents that were previously unavailable to the public. The result is "a useful if at times dense analysis of the available material," commented *Foreign Affairs* writer Lawrence D. Freedman. Several critics also noted Hanhimäki's neutral discussion of Kissinger's legacy. The author gives "due credit for his [Kissinger's] very real accomplishments while not concealing unpleasant facts," *Library Journal* reviewer Marcia L. Sprules observed. *Contemporary Review* contributor Ian Jackson also felt that Hanhimäki "provides a balanced and lucid analysis."

BIOGRAPHICAL AND CRITICAL SOURCES:

PERIODICALS

Biography, fall, 2005, James M. Murphy, review of *The Flawed Architect: Henry Kissinger and American Foreign Policy,* p. 714.

Contemporary Review, March, 2004, review of *The Cold War: A History in Documents and Eyewitness Accounts,* p. 191; July, 2005, Ian Jackson, review of *The Flawed Architect,* p. 47.
Foreign Affairs, March-April, 2005, Lawrence D. Freedman, review of *The Flawed Architect,* p. 156.
Library Journal, August, 2004, Marcia L. Sprules, review of *The Flawed Architect,* p. 99.
Perspectives on Political Science, spring, 1998, Gordon L. Shull, review of *Containing Coexistence: America, Russia, and the "Finnish Solution,"* p. 106.
Publishers Weekly, August 9, 2004, review of *The Flawed Architect,* p. 241.
Scandinavian Studies, spring, 1998, H. Peter Krosby, review of *Containing Coexistence,* p. 143; winter, 1998, John Pederson, review of *Scandinavia and the United States: An Insecure Friendship,* p. 533.

ONLINE

Graduate Institute of International Studies Web site, http://hei.unige.ch/ens/ (March 20, 2006), author profile.*

*   *   *

HANHIMÄKI, Jussi Markus
   See HANHIMÄKI, Jussi M.

*   *   *

HANNIGAN, Katherine

PERSONAL: Born in western NY. *Education:* State University of New York, B.S., 1987, B.F.A., 1997; Rochester Institute of Technology, M.F.A., 1991.

ADDRESSES: Home—IA. *Agent*—c/o Author Mail, Greenwillow Press/HarperCollins Children's Books, 1350 Avenue of the Americas, New York, NY 10019.

CAREER: Educator and writer. Head Start, former education coordinator; instructor at Rochester Institute of Technology, Rochester, NY, Buffalo State College, Buffalo, NY, and Niagara County Community College,

Sanborn, NY; Iowa State University, Ames, instructor in drawing, then assistant professor of art and design, 2001-c. 04; full-time writer.

AWARDS, HONORS: Book Sense Book of the Year Honor Book designation, Best Book of the Year designations from School Library Journal, Publishers Weekly, and Child magazine, and Gold Award, Parents' Choice, all 2005, all for Ida B . . . and Her Plans to Maximize Fun, Avoid Disaster, and (Possibly) Save the World.

WRITINGS:

Ida B . . . and Her Plans to Maximize Fun, Avoid Disaster, and (Possibly) Save the World, Greenwillow Press (New York, NY), 2004.

ADAPTATIONS: Ida B . . . and Her Plans to Maximize Fun, Avoid Disaster, and (Possibly) Save the World was adapted as an audiobook read by Lili Taylor, Books on Tape, 2004.

WORK IN PROGRESS: Two stories for middle-grade children.

SIDELIGHTS: Growing up in western New York, Katherine Hannigan was constantly surrounded by books, rodents adopted as family pets, and stray cats and dogs. With a vivid imagination, she developed a knack for creating stories involving playthings, such as a pair of clay figures which she manipulated from behind her second-grade pop-up desk; paper characters cut from her Valentine's Day cards; and the dolls populating her closet and who starred in Hannigan's early theatrical performances. Continuing to draw on that imagination as an adult, Hannigan is the author of the entertaining middle-school novel Ida B . . . and Her Plans to Maximize Fun, Avoid Disaster, and (Possibly) Save the World.

Before beginning her writing career, Hannigan studied art in New York and obtained bachelor's and master's degrees in painting. After teaching in upstate New York for several years, she moved west, teaching art and design at Iowa State University. While in Iowa, Hannigan once again found inspiration in her surroundings, and she began to develop the title character for her first children's book. Ida B . . . and Her Plans to Maximize Fun, Avoid Disaster, and (Possibly) Save the World was still in its draft stage when Hannigan decided to take a writing workshop conducted by children's author Kate DiCamillo in 2002. After Hannigan submitted a chapter from her unpublished work and won the praise of DiCamillo, DiCamillo passed along the manuscript to a literary agent and the novel was published by Greenwillow Books in 2004. Ida B . . . and Her Plans to Maximize Fun, Avoid Disaster, and (Possibly) Save the World became a New York Times best-seller and won numerous accolades from critics.

In an interview with an online BookBrowse contributor, Hannigan noted that her title character, Ida B, was developed from "a love of laughter," and "a fondness for people with a good dose of punkishness in them." Ida B is, indeed, a distinctive and "unforgettable heroine" as School Library Journal contributor Faith Brautigam declared. A Publishers Weekly critic also remarked that heroine Ida B is a "firecracker of a character." In the book nine-year-old Ida B speaks to the trees and the brooks that surround her family farm and spends the majority of her free time making arts and crafts. Ida B has been home-schooled throughout her life and enjoys the freedom and tranquility of being taught at home. Things drastically change for the girl, however, when her mother develops cancer and her parents decide to sell a portion of the apple grove—which also happens to be Ida B's playground—to help pay medical bills. Matters are exacerbated when Ida B is sent to public school, but it is at this point that the girl decides to deal directly with the changes that are taking place around her. As pressures mount, she becomes an embittered nine-year-old and feels as if every thing in her life has betrayed her.

Reviewing Ida B . . . and Her Plans to Maximize Fun, Avoid Disaster, and (Possibly) Save the World, critics hailed Hannigan for her ability to realistically portray the mind-set of a nine-year-old. Faith Brautigam, writing in School Library Journal, noted that "Ida B is a true character in every sense of the word." Likewise, Booklist contributor Ilene Cooper commented on Hannigan's ability to fully capture "the fury [that] children can experience" and "the tenacity with which they can hold on to their anger." Another tactic Hannigan employs can be seen in the resolution of the author's story, as Ida B begins to appreciate the changes in her life. Susan Dove Lempke stated that

Hannigan "skillfully depicts the slow climb back . . . where Ida B can allow herself to express happiness again."

With her adept skills in characterization, plot, storyline, and writing style, Hannigan impressed many critics. Ilene Cooper, writing in *Booklist,* noted that "Hannigan gets it down brilliantly," while a *Publishers Weekly* reviewer regarded *Ida B . . . and Her Plans to Maximize Fun, Avoid Disaster, and (Possibly) Save the World* as an "insightful, seemingly intuitive first novel." In a similar fashion, a *Kirkus Reviews* critic noted that the book is a "funny debut from a promising new author," while *Horn Book* contributor Susan Dove Lempke, described Hannigan as "clearly an author to watch."

BIOGRAPHICAL AND CRITICAL SOURCES:

PERIODICALS

Booklist, September, 2004, Ilene Cooper, review of *Ida B . . . and Her Plans to Maximize Fun, Avoid Disaster, and (Possibly) Save the World,* p. 1924; January 1, 2004, Jennifer Mattson, interview with Hannigan, p. 843.
Horn Book, November-December, 2004, Susan Dove Lempke, review of *Ida B . . . and Her Plans to Maximize Fun, Avoid Disaster, and (Possibly) Save the World,* p. 709.
Kirkus Reviews, July 15, 2004, review of *Ida B . . . and Her Plans to Maximize Fun, Avoid Disaster, and (Possibly) Save the World,* p. 686.
Publishers Weekly, July 26, 2004, review of *Ida B . . . and Her Plans to Maximize Fun, Avoid Disaster, and (Possibly) Save the World,* p. 55; September 13, 2004, review of audio cassette *Ida B . . . and Her Plans to Maximize Fun, Avoid Disaster, and (Possibly) Save the World,* p. 36; December 12, 2004, Jennifer M. Brown, "Katherine Hannigan," pp. 30-34.
School Library Journal, August, 2004, Faith Brautigam, review of *Ida B . . . and Her Plans to Maximize Fun, Avoid Disaster, and (Possibly) Save the World,* p. 122.

ONLINE

BookBrowse, http://www.bookbrowse.com/ (April 10, 2006), interview with Hannigan.

HarperCollins Children's Books, http://www.harperchildrens.com/ (April 10, 2006), author profile.

*   *   *

HANSEN, Suzanne

PERSONAL: Married; children: two. *Education:* Attended Northwest Nannies Institute, Portland, OR; Linfield College, B.S.

ADDRESSES: Home—Portland, OR. *Agent*—c/o Sarah Chance, Crown Publishing/Random House, Inc., 1745 Broadway, 13th Fl., New York, NY 10019.

CAREER: Worked as a nanny, labor and delivery nurse, lactation specialist, and childbirth educator.

WRITINGS:

You'll Never Nanny in This Town Again! The Adventures and Misadventures of a Hollywood Nanny (memoir), Ruby Sky Publishing (Beaverton, OR), 2003, reprinted as *You'll Never Nanny in This Town Again: The True Adventures of a Hollywood Nanny,* Crown Publishers (New York, NY), 2005

SIDELIGHTS: Suzanne Hansen attended Northwest Nannies Institute in her home state of Oregon before moving to Los Angeles to work as a live-in nanny. She later went on to earn a nursing degree and work in that profession, marry, and have children of her own. In *You'll Never Nanny in This Town Again! The True Adventures of a Hollywood Nanny,* she recalls that earlier experience, including the years she worked for celebrities that included Michael Ovitz, Debra Winger, and Rhea Perlman and Danny DeVito. She depicts the life of the nanny to the stars as one of low pay, overwork, and dealing not only with the children but also with the parents themselves. Hansen provides details of the perks, as well, including parties and trips and the opportunities to meet celebrities and visit production sets. "Hardly backstabbing, this entertaining book possesses a sincerity other nannying tomes lack," concluded a *Publishers Weekly* reviewer. A

Kirkus Reviews contributor wrote that Hansen offers "sympathetic and nuanced analyses of the wealthy, and insights into parenthood and childrearing."

On her Web site, Hansen provides her views about "children who are raised materially instead of maternally," saying that "all children want (and need) their parents' time and attention. Even though these children have flown around the world, been on exotic vacations, and are waited on by a staff, what they really desire is individual attention from their parents. I have never seen an expensive toy or extravagant birthday party ever replace a child's daily longing for parental involvement."

BIOGRAPHICAL AND CRITICAL SOURCES:

BOOKS

Hansen, Suzanne, *You'll Never Nanny in This Town Again! The True Adventures of a Hollywood Nanny,* Crown Publishers (New York, NY), 2005.

PERIODICALS

Kirkus Reviews, September 15, 2005, review of *You'll Never Nanny in This Town Again,* p. 1012.
Publishers Weekly, September 19, 2005, review of *You'll Never Nanny in This Town Again,* p. 51.

ONLINE

Suzanne Hansen Home Page, http://www.hollywood nanny.com (January 8, 2006).*

*   *   *

HANSON, David D. 1968-

PERSONAL: Born January 4, 1968, in Hastings, NE; son of W. Dean (a farmer) and Mary (a counselor; maiden name, Beekman) Hanson; married Deborah Pavelka (an actress), December 28, 1991; children: D. Henry, De Annajoyce. *Ethnicity:* "Caucasian." *Education:* Trinity University, B.A., 1990; University of Southern California, M.P.W., 1991; Emporia State University, M.L.S. 2005. *Politics:* Independent. *Religion:* Christian. *Hobbies and other interests:* Raising cattle.

ADDRESSES: Home—7230 Gleason, Shawnee, KS 66227. *E-mail*—dhanson193@aol.com.

CAREER: New York Public Library, New York, NY, information associate, 1992-95; Dreyfus Corp., New York, NY, senior research specialist, 1995-97; Kansas City Public Library, Kansas City, KS, fiction specialist, 1998; writer, 1998—.

WRITINGS:

Clearance Sale at the Five and Dime (play), 1995.
101 Reasons to Hate Dennis Rodman (humor), Avon Publishing (New York, NY), 1996.
The Spring Habit (novel), Ad Lib Books (Raymore, MO), 2004.

Assistant editor, *Southern California Anthology,* 1990.

SIDELIGHTS: David D. Hanson told *CA:* "I have always been drawn to the characters and stories of the American Heartland: the quiet and strong characters who face life beyond the city limits."

*   *   *

HARRER, Heinrich 1912-2006

OBITUARY NOTICE— See index for *CA* sketch: Born July 6, 1912, in Knappenberg, Carinthia, Austria; died January 7, 2006, in Friesach, Austria. Adventurer, filmmaker, and author. Harrer was a mountaineer and explorer best known for his memoir *Seven Years in Tibet,* which was later adapted to film. Graduating from the University of Graz in 1938 with a degree in geography, Harrer quickly began making a name for himself when he climbed the 13,025-foot Eiger peak in the Alps. Already a 1936 Olympic athlete for the German ski team, Harrer was made a hero by Hitler and the Nazis for his feat, and Harrer, who had joined the Nazi storm troopers in 1933 and the SS in 1938, was congratulated by the Fuhrer himself. Much later, in 1997, the fact that Harrer had been a Nazi was publicized by the German magazine *Stern.* Harrer, however, explained that he had joined the Nazis only so he could gain membership to a teacher's organization that made it possible for him to pursue his expeditions. In 1939, Harrer set out to climb Nanga Parbat in northern India. Before he had a chance to attempt the ascent, however, World War II broke out and the British, who controlled India, captured and imprisoned Harrer and his party. After making two unsuccessful escape attempts, Harrer managed to flee his prison in 1944. He headed for Tibet, eventually reaching the capital of Lhasa. Working as a gardener, he used his language skills and good will to befriend the Tibetans. He gained their trust to such an extent that he was introduced to the young Dalai Lama, whom he would befriend and to whom he served as a teacher. Harrer fell in love with Tibet and wanted to remain there, but when the Chinese invaded in 1950 he had to leave the country the next year. For many decades thereafter, he traveled the world, climbing peaks and exploring remote landscapes. He led expeditions in the Andes, Alaska, Africa, West New Guinea, Nepal, Surinam, Sudan, North Borneo, Alaknanda, the Andaman Islands, Brazil, and Zangkar-Ladakh. Throughout his travels, though, Harrer would say he always longed to return to his time in Tibet, which he described as having been the happiest time of his life. His book about that experience, originally published in German as *Sieben Jahre in Tibet* in 1952 and translated into English two years later, would sell over three million copies and was his best-known work. He would go on to publish many more books, however, including the translated titles *I Come from the Stone Age* (1964), *Ladakh: Gods and Mortals behind the Himalayas* (1981), *Return to Tibet* (1984), and *Lost Lhasa: Heinrich Harrer's Tibet* (1992). In addition to his publications, Harrer made numerous documentary films about his travels. The controversy that made the news in 1997 when the Brad Pitt film *Seven Years in Tibet* was released was resolved when Nazi hunter Simon Wiesenthal himself declared that Harrer was guiltless of any war crimes. Harrer, who embraced the peaceful philosophy of his adopted Tibet, would denounce those years in Germany as a big mistake.

OBITUARIES AND OTHER SOURCES:

PERIODICALS

Chicago Tribune, January 10, 2006, section 2, p. 9.
Los Angeles Times, January 10, 2006, p. B10.

New York Times, January 10, 2006, p. A25.
Times (London, England), January 9, 2006, p. 46.
Washington Post, January 9, 2006, p. B6.

* * *

HARRISON, Kathy A. 1952-

PERSONAL: Born July 29, 1952, in Pittsfield, MA; daughter of a police officer and a schoolteacher; married Bruce Harrison, 1973; children: Bruce, Jr., Nathan, Ben; adopted children: Neddy, Angie, Karen. *Ethnicity:* "Caucasian."

ADDRESSES: Agent—Curtis Brown Ltd., 10 Astor Pl., New York, NY 10003.

CAREER: Writer and professional foster parent. Formerly worked as preschool teacher.

WRITINGS:

Another Place at the Table: A Story of Shattered Childhoods Redeemed by Love (memoir), Jerome P. Tarcher (New York, NY), 2003.

SIDELIGHTS: Kathy A. Harrison told *CA:* "Writing helps me process my children's histories. It also defines me and what I do. As a writer, I have been most influenced by Marion Wright Edelman and Tory Hayden. I wish I had a writing process. I keep notes on bits of paper, tucked here and there. When deadlines loom, I put in four to five hours a day to finish. I rewrite five to six times. My first book will always be my baby, but my favorite is always the book I want to write next.

"The most surprising thing I've learned as a writer is that people feel free to contact me and tell me incredibly personal and painful things."

BIOGRAPHICAL AND CRITICAL SOURCES:

BOOKS

Harrison, Kathy A., *Another Place at the Table: A Story of Shattered Childhoods Redeemed by Love,* Jeremy P. Tarcher (New York, NY), 2003.

PERIODICALS

Booklist, April 15, 2003, Vanessa Bush, review of *Another Place at the Table,* p. 1431.

Kirkus Reviews, January 1, 2003, review of *Another Place at the Table,* p. 38.

People, June 9, 2003, Thomas Fields-Meyer, "100 Kids and Counting: When It Comes to Helping Children, Foster Mom Kathy Harrison Can't Say No," p. 131.

Redbook, May, 2003, "The Bravest Mom We've Ever Met: If They Gave Medals to Parents for Hard Work (and They Should!), Kathy Harrison Would Take the Gold Every Time," p. 158.

Publishers Weekly, January 27, 2003, review of *Another Place at the Table,* p. 244.

Women's Review of Books, April, 2003, Edith Milton, review of *Another Place at the Table,* p. 13.

*   *   *

HART, Lorenz 1895-1943
(Lorenz Milton Hart)

PERSONAL: Born May 2, 1895, in New York, NY; died of pneumonia, November 22, 1943, in New York, NY; son of Max M. and Frieda (Isenberg) Hart. *Education:* Attended the Columbia School of Journalism. *Religion:* Jewish.

CAREER: Lyricist, songwriter, and composer. Producer of Broadway musicals.

AWARDS, HONORS: Commemorated on a U.S. postage stamp, 1999.

WRITINGS:

LYRICIST FOR MUSICALS

Fly with Me, 1920.
The Garrick Gaieties, Garrick Theater, 1925.
Dearest Enemy, 1925.
Betsy, 1926.
The Fifth Avenue Follies, 1926.
The Girlfriend, 1926.
Lido Lady, 1926.

Peggy-Ann, 1926.
One Dam Thing after Another, 1927.
A Connecticut Yankee, 1927, revised 1943.
Present Arms (also see below), 1928.
She's My Baby, 1928.
Chee-Chee, Mansfield Theater, 1928.
Heads Up! (also see below), 1929.
Evergreen, 1930.
Simple Simon, 1930.
America's Sweetheart, 1931.
Jumbo (also see below), 1935.
Babes in Arms (also see below), 1936.
The Show Is On, 1936.
I'd Rather Be Right, 1937.
I Married An Angel (also see below), 1938.
The Boys from Syracuse (also see below), 1938.
Too Many Girls (also see below), 1939.
Higher and Higher (also see below), 1940.
Pal Joey (also see below), 1940.
By Jupiter, 1942.

Contributor, with Richard Rodgers, to *A Lonely Romeo,* 1919; and *Poor Little Ritz Girl,* 1920. Also translated operettas and plays from German to English.

LYRICIST FOR FILMS

Present Arms, 1930.
Spring Is Here, 1930.
Heads Up!, 1931.
The Hot Heiress, 1931.
Love Me Tonight, 1932.
The Phantom President, 1932.
Dancing Lady, 1933.
Hallelujah, I'm a Bum, 1933.
Hollywood Party, 1934.
The Merry Widow, 1934.
Nana, 1934.
Manhattan Melodrama, 1934.
Mississippi, 1935.
The Dancing Pirate, 1936.
Fools for Scandal, 1938.
Babes in Arms, 1939.
On Your Toes, 1939.
Too Many Girls, 1940.
The Boys from Syracuse, 1940.
They Met in Argentina, 1941.
I Married an Angel, 1942.
Higher and Higher, 1943.

Pal Joey, 1957.
Jumbo, 1962.

SIDELIGHTS: Lorenz Hart was an extremely success-ful lyricist of Broadway musicals produced from 1920 to 1942 (Hart died in 1943). Hart was writing songs and lyrics over a period of time known today as the golden age of American songwriting, and several of Hart's musicals have since been revived and produced (many nearly sixty years after his death). Numerous individual songs from Hart's many musicals are considered American standards. Perhaps his most famous singles are "The Lady Is a Tramp," "Blue Moon," and "My Funny Valentine." It is important to note that throughout his career, Hart worked with composer Richard Rodgers. For the most part, Rodg-ers would first compose the score, and Hart would next write the lyrics. Hart, then, is perhaps best recognized as the latter half of 'Rodgers & Hart,' as the duo and their work was, and is, known by audiences.

Hart also adapted several of his musicals for film, and he composed the lyrics for several original films as well. Perhaps the most popular original film that Hart worked on is *Love Me Tonight.* Released in 1932, the film became a success at the height of Hart's career.

According to a *Dictionary of American Biography* writer, Hart "contributed to musical comedies sharp, tasteful lyrics finely coordinated with rhythm and melody and with the plot, mood, and action of the play." These qualities can be seen in Hart's earliest musicals, such as the 1925 production of *The Garrick Gaieties* a humorous review akin to the famous Zieg-feld follies. The same irreverent wit can be seen in later musicals as well, including *The Boys from Syra-cuse,* which premiered in 1938. The musical was adapted as a film a few years later, but it has remained relevant and popular in its original form, and was last revived on Broadway in 2002.

Slowly, Hart began to move away from his more comedic, stylized musicals in an attempt to create a more naturalistic theater experience. Hart's last musicals, *Pal Joey* (1940) and *By Jupiter* (1942), reflect this. A contributor to the *St. James Encyclopedia of Popular Culture* noted that, with *Pal Joey,* Hart "departed from conventional musical theater practice and built the production around a much darker subject

than Broadway was accustomed to contemplating." The musical is about a nightclub worker who leaves his girlfriend for a wealthier woman. Even though the wealthy woman builds her new lover a nightclub, she eventually leaves him also. Although the musical was not a hit, the movie, starring Frank Sinatra, has assured its longevity and prominence.

Despite his numerous successes, Hart was an alcoholic, perhaps due to the fact that he was a homosexual liv-ing in a time historically unkind to those with alterna-tive sexual orientations. Although Hart died at the early age of forty-eight from pneumonia, it is likely that the initial deterioration that caused the illness was a result of his alcoholism. Hart's death, however, has had little effect on his legacy. In 1995 New York City celebrated the centennial of Hart's birth, and in 1999 Hart was honored with a commemorative U.S. postage stamp. Review performances of Hart's songs also continue to be produced.

BIOGRAPHICAL AND CRITICAL SOURCES:

BOOKS

Dictionary of American Biography, Supplement 3: *1941-1945,* American Council of Learned Societ-ies (New York, NY), 1973.
St. James Encyclopedia of Popular Culture, St. James Press (Detroit, MI), 2000.

PERIODICALS

Back Stage, May 9, 1997, David A. Rosenberg, review of *The Boys from Syracuse,* p. 52; February 26, 1999, David A. Rosenberg, review of *Babes in Arms,* p. 59.
Commentary, April, 2002, Terry Teachout, review of "Glad to be Unhappy," p. 57.
Daily Variety, August 19, 2002, review of *The Boys from Syracuse,* p. 2.
New Statesman, February 12, 1999, Richard Cook, review of "Funny Valentine," p. 45.
Newsweek, May 15, 1995, Jack Kroll, review of *Pal Joey,* p. 45.
Opera News, August, 1998, review of *The Boys from Syracuse,* p. 38.
Variety, September 2, 2002, Markland Taylor, review of *Babes in Arms,* p. 33.

ONLINE

Guide to Musical Theater, http://www.nodanw.com/ (March 21, 2006), author profile.
Lorenz Hart, http://www.lorenzhart.org (March 21, 2006), author profile and bibliography.
Songwriters Hall of Fame Web site, http://www. songwritershalloffame.org/ (March 21, 2006), author profile.*

* * *

HART, Lorenz Milton
   See HART, Lorenz

* * *

HARVEY, Kenneth J. 1962-

PERSONAL: Born 1962.

ADDRESSES: Home—Burnt Head, Newfoundland, Canada. *Agent*—c/o Publicity Department, St. Martin's Press, 175 5th Ave., New York, NY 10010. *E-mail*—kennethjharvey@hotmail.com; sculpin@KennethJHarvey.com.

CAREER: Poet, short story writer, essayist, and novelist. Founder of ReLit Awards, 2000; University of New Brunswick, New Brunswick, Canada, former writer-in-residence; Memorial University, Newfoundland, Canada, former writer-in-residence; has also worked as an assistant film editor, graphic designer, magazine editor, short-order cook, trade show promoter, and amusement park manager.

MEMBER: PEN, Writers' Union of Canada.

AWARDS, HONORS: Newfoundland Arts & Letters Award, several awards for poetry, short fiction, drama, and photography.

WRITINGS:

No Lies: And Other Stories, Robinson-Blackmore (St. John's, Newfoundland, Canada), 1985.

Directions for an Opened Body (stories), Mercury Press (Toronto, Ontario, Canada), 1990.
Brud: A Parable, Little, Brown (Toronto, Ontario, Canada), 1992.
The Hole That Must Be Filled (stories), Little, Brown (Toronto, Ontario, Canada), 1994.
Stalkers, Stoddart (Toronto, Ontario, Canada), 1994.
Kill the Poets: Anti-verse, Exile Editions (Toronto, Ontario, Canada), 1995.
The Great Misogynist, Exile Editions (Toronto, Ontario, Canada), 1996.
Heart to Heart, Plowman (Whitby, Ontario, Canada), 1996.
Nine-tenths Unseen: A Psychological Mystery, Somerville House Publishing (Toronto, Ontario, Canada), 1996.
Lift Up Your Eyes (poems), Plowman (Whitby, Ontario, Canada), 1997.
We Must Let Him Know, Plowman (Whitby, Ontario, Canada), 1997.
The Flesh So Close: Stories, Mercury Press (Toronto, Ontario, Canada), 1998.
The Woman in the Closet (mystery novel), Mercury Press (Toronto, Ontario, Canada), 1998.
As Time Winds Down, Plowman (Whitby, Ontario, Canada), 1998.
Everyone Hates a Beauty Queen: Provocative Opinions and Irrelevant Humor, Exile Editions (Toronto, Ontario, Canada), 1998.
Skin Hound (There Are No Words): A Transcomposite Novel, Mercury Press (Toronto, Ontario, Canada), 2000.
Sense the Need, Plowman (Whitby, Ontario, Canada), 2000.
(With Eve Mills Nash) *Little White Squaw: A White Woman's Story of Abuse, Addiction, and Reconciliation,* Beach Holme (Vancouver, British Columbia, Canada), 2002.
Artists United, Plowman (Whitby, Ontario, Canada), 2003.
The Town That Forgot How to Breathe (novel), Raincoast Books (Vancouver, British Columbia, Canada), 2003, St. Martin's Press (New York, NY), 2005.
Heaven Only, Plowman (Whitby, Ontario, Canada), 2004.
Shack: The Cutland Junction Stories, Mercury Press (Toronto, Ontario, Canada), 2004.
The Path of Life, Plowman (Whitby, Ontario, Canada), 2005.
Inside, Random House Canada (Toronto, Ontario, Canada), 2006.

Contributor to periodicals, including *Globe & Mail, National Post, Ottawa Citizen, Vancouver Province, Halifax Daily News, Toronto Star,* and the Newfoundland *Sunday Independent.*

SIDELIGHTS: Kenneth J. Harvey is a Newfoundland-based writer who has published poetry, short stories, essays, editorials, and novels. In 2000 he also founded the ReLit Awards, which take place annually in British Columbia and Newfoundland, Canada. Short for Regarding Literature, Reinventing Literature, Relighting Literature, etc., the ReLit Awards recognize new writing published by independent Canadian presses.

Harvey's novel *The Town That Forgot How to Breathe* marked his debut in the United States. Set in a depressed fishing village in Newfoundland, the story has elements of romance, horror, mystery, and regionalism. Many of the town's inhabitants are suffering from a strange respiratory illness, long-lost bodies are washing up from the sea with no signs of decomposition, and mythical sea creatures are brought in by the fishermen's nets. With the number of characters and sub-storylines, a reviewer for *Kirkus Reviews* felt this was a "messy disaster novel" with a "lack of focus." A contributor to *Publishers Weekly* however, commended Harvey's "literary flair," while a reviewer for the *Detroit Free Press* noted that the "characters and their world . . . are meticulously created." Ann H. Fisher wrote in *Library Journal* that *The Town That Forgot How to Breathe* is "mystical, complicated, and always compelling."

BIOGRAPHICAL AND CRITICAL SOURCES:

PERIODICALS

Detroit Free Press, November 2, 2005, review of *The Town That Forgot How to Breathe.*
Kirkus Reviews, August 15, 2005, review of *The Town That Forgot How to Breathe,* p. 872.
Library Journal, October 15, 2005, Ann H. Fisher, review of *The Town That Forgot How to Breathe,* p. 45.
Publishers Weekly, August 8, 2005, review of *The Town That Forgot How to Breathe,* p. 208.

ONLINE

Danforth Review, http://www.danforthreview.com/ (March 21, 2006), interview with Kenneth J. Harvey.

Kenneth J. Harvey Home Page, http://www.kennethjharvey.com (February 28, 2006).
Kenneth J. Harvey Web log, http://www.blogger.com/profile/9404652 (February 28, 2006).
Writers in Electronic Residence Web site, http://www.wier.ca/ (February 28, 2006), biography of Kenneth J. Harvey.
Writers' Union of Canada Web site, http://www.writersunion.ca/ (February 28, 2006), biography of Kenneth J. Harvey.*

*   *   *

HAYTER, Alethea 1911-2006
(Alethea Catharine Hayter)

OBITUARY NOTICE— See index for *CA* sketch: Born November 7, 1911, in Cairo, Egypt; died January 10, 2006. Civil servant and author. Hayter was widely recognized for inventing a new subgenre of biography in which she focused on a very brief time period of a few weeks, describing events in great detail. The daughter of a British legal advisor to the Egyptian government, she spent her first eleven years very happily in Cairo. After her father died, she and her family moved to England, where she attended Lady Margaret Hall, Oxford, and earned a bachelor's degree in 1932. She then worked on the editorial staff of *Country Life* magazine before the onset of World War II. During the war, she functioned as what she would describe as a very tangential sort of spy for the Postal Censorship department, conducting minor operations in Gibraltar, Bermuda, Trinidad, and London. From 1945 to 1967, she worked for the British Council in such locations as London, Athens, and Paris. Finally, from 1967 to 1971, Hayter was a cultural attaché for the British Embassy in Belgium and then Luxembourg. Retiring in 1971, she remained active as governor of the Old Vic Theatre and the Sadler's Wells Theatre. As an author, Hayter was interested in biography, with her first publication being *Mrs. Browning: A Poet's Work and Its Setting* (1962). She then had the sudden inspiration to focus her writing on a very specific point in time, describing for readers settings, dress, food, and even the weather occurring during an event in meticulous detail. She assembled such information based on letters, diaries, and other primary research sources. The first book in her newly created subgenre is *A Sultry Month: Scenes of London Literary Life in 1846* (1965). Others in this vein include *A Voyage in*

Vain: Coleridge's Journey to Malta in 1804 (1973) and her last book, *The Wreck of the Abergavenny* (2002). Despite the critical success of such works, however, Hayter received the most attention for her *Opium and the Romantic Imagination* (1968), later published as *Opium and the Romantic Imagination: Addiction and Creativity in De Quincey, Coleridge, Baudelaire, and Others* (1988). Hayter, who also edited De Quincey's *Confessions of an English Opium Eater* (1971), was particularly praised for her ability to described in horrifying psychological detail the terrible effects of opium addiction. Hayter, who was appointed to the Order of the British Empire in 1970, was also the author of many other books, including *Elizabeth Barrett Browning* (1965), the fiction work *Horatio's Version* (1972), and *A Wise Woman: A Memoir of Lavinia Mynors from Her Diaries and Letters* (1996).

OBITUARIES AND OTHER SOURCES:

PERIODICALS

Times (London, England), January 12, 2006, p. 66.

*　　*　　*

HAYTER, Alethea Catharine
　　See HAYTER, Alethea

*　　*　　*

HEADLEY, Maria Dahvana 1977-

PERSONAL: Born 1977, in ID; married Robert Schenkkan (a playwright and screenwriter), 2003; stepchildren: two. *Education:* Attended New York University.

ADDRESSES: *Home*—Seattle, WA. *Agent*—William Morris Agency, 1325 Avenue of the Americas, New York, NY 10019. *E-mail*—theyearofyes@hotmail.com.

CAREER: Writer.

MEMBER: The Memoirist's Collective.

AWARDS, HONORS: TenTen Award for Fiction, *Word Smitten,* Web site, 2003; MacDowell Colony fellow, 2006.

WRITINGS:

The Year of Yes (memoir), Hyperion (New York, NY), 2006.

Also author of plays and short works of fiction.

ADAPTATIONS: Paramount Pictures has aquired the movie rights for *The Year of Yes,* which will be produced by Dan Jinks and Bruce Cohen.

SIDELIGHTS: Maria Dahvana Headley is a fiction and nonfiction writer who studied dramatic writing at New York University's Tisch School of the Arts in the 1990s. Having grown up in Idaho feeling as if she did not fit in, the move to New York City offered her many new opportunities. However, after dating a number of men she thought she would like but ultimately did not, Headley decided to agree to any man or woman who asked her out on a date. Making only a few exceptions, such as not agreeing to meet up with someone who is drunk or high, she realized that dating among a larger pool of people would increase her chances of finding someone she liked. For one year, she followed her plan and ultimately married someone she met during that period.

It wasn't until a decade later that she published her memoir based on that year of dating adventures, *The Year of Yes.* In a *Newsweek* article, she said of her year of dating: "It's something I never would have picked, but it's turned out to be this kind of amazing experience." Reviews for *The Year of Yes* were mostly positive. A reviewer in *Publishers Weekly* labeled it "sheer chick fluff" but admitted it was "amusing." Leah Greenblatt praised the memoir in *Entertainment Weekly* saying it was "charming, hyperliterate," and "laugh-out-loud funny." Elizabeth Morris's review in *Library Journal* was not as complimentary. Calling it "hollow and tragic," Morris wrote that "the story has a rambling, breathless quality." Kristine Huntley, writing in *Booklist,* however, had a positive perception of the book: "Snappy and readable, Headley's fun memoir will be sought out by singletons everywhere."

Headley told *CA:* "I got interested in writing because I'm a reader. In *The Year of Yes,* I talk about how I started in the A section of the library and worked my way through to N, as a kid. I come from a small town. There's not a lot to do. The library is where town freaks often hang out, and I'm no exception. Fairly quickly, I realized that a lot of town freaks turn into writers, and I thought I might be able to find my comrades in the writing world. . . which, alas, is a pretty solitary place. My work is influenced by everything I've ever read—if something is really great, I try to figure out how the writer accomplished it—as well as by everything I've ever heard. I listen to music as I write, and the mood of whatever song I'm hearing often dictates the mood of the writing. I'm a huge Tom Waits fan. Bob Dylan too. Anyone who loves words and has a story to tell, basically, can win me over. My writing process is similar to dumping a 1,000 piece puzzle on the floor and trying to put it together without any idea of what the whole thing ought to look like. I usually find myself sitting amid a heap of disparate bits, with no idea what will string them together. Finally, though, I find a piece that fits, and then another, and soon it's all linked. Or, at least, in a best case scenario, that's what happens. Sometimes I find myself with a picture of something that still doesn't make sense. That's when I get out the scissors and start illegally snipping puzzle pieces. Like all writers I know, I have a drawer full of things that just didn't quite get there. That drawer is great for procrastination.

"*The Year of Yes* has been a lesson in the diversity of this country. Everyone, and I mean everyone, has a different favorite part. . . people also have all kinds of different most-hated parts, though the people that hated me most tend not to have actually read the book. A lot of people got really up in arms after reading an article about me, or seeing me on TV. This was odd. Their response had very little to do with the book, and a lot to do with the fact that by saying 'yes' to dates with everyone who asked, I'd broken some deep social rules—largest among them, 'don't talk to strangers.' While promoting this book, I got everything from love letters, to preachers preaching against me. I was amazed, and kind of thrilled, by how much my subject matter seemed to galvanize people. Plenty of people have embarked on their own 'year of yes' as a result of reading the book, and that is pretty great.

"As for favorite books—I only have one out, so far. When my next one comes out, though, I'll change allegiances. Every writer's favorite book is the one they're working on—or at least, that's the case with the writers I know. The ideal situation is to feel as though you're becoming a better writer the more you write.

"I hope *The Year of Yes* first and foremost makes people laugh. As well, I hope it inspires people to be less judgmental in their own lives. I think that'd be a pretty great effect to have on your readers. The thing I love best when I'm reading, is the sense that I'm being taken away for a while, swept up into a story, and emotionally effected by it. That's what I hope happens with my work."

BIOGRAPHICAL AND CRITICAL SOURCES:

BOOKS

Headley, Maria Dahvana, *The Year of Yes,* Hyperion (New York, NY), 2006.

PERIODICALS

Booklist, January 1, 2006, Kristine Huntley, review of *The Year of Yes,* p. 34.
Entertainment Weekly, January 13, 2006, Leah Greenblatt, review of *The Year of Yes,* p. 83.
Library Journal, January 1, 2006, Elizabeth Morris, review of *The Year of Yes,* p. 130.
Newsweek, January 16, 2006, Daniel McGinn, "Dating: Positive Thinking."
People, February 13, 2006, Judith Newman, review of *The Year of Yes,* p. 51.
Publishers Weekly, November 7, 2005, review of *The Year of Yes,* p. 66.
Time, February 10, 2006, Andrea Sachs, "A Year in the Underbelly of Sex in the City."

ONLINE

Maria Dahvana Headley Web log, http://www.myspace.com/mariadahvanaheadley (April 12, 2006).
Mumpsimus Web log, http://mumpsimus.blogspot.com/ (December 27, 2005), author interview.

My Space, The Memoirist's Collective, http://www.my space.com/thememoiristscollective (June 1, 2006).

Year of Yes Web site, http://www.theyearofyes.com (April 12, 2006).

Washington Post Online, http://www.washingtonpost. com/ (February 7, 2006), online author chat.

Word Smitten, http://www.wordsmitten.com/ (April 12, 2006), author award information.

*   *   *

HENDERSON, Kristin

PERSONAL: Born in New York, NY; married a Marine chaplain. *Education:* Attended the University of Florida. *Religion:* Quaker. *Hobbies and other interests:* Amateur autocross racing.

ADDRESSES: Home—Washington, DC. *Agent*—c/o Author Mail, Houghton Mifflin Company, Trade Division, Adult Editorial, 8th Fl., 222 Berkeley St., Boston, MA 02116-3764. *E-mail*—kh@kristin henderson.com.

CAREER: Writer. Volunteer for Marine Corps' family support program and Compass, the Navy's spouse mentoring program.

MEMBER: National Military Family Association, National Writers Union, Military Reporters and Editors, Orlando Place Writers Group, Resolve, Religious Society of Friends.

WRITINGS:

Driving by Moonlight: A Journey through Love, War, and Infertility (memoir), Seal Press (New York, NY), 2003.

While They're at War: The True Story of American Families on the Homefront, Houghton Mifflin (Boston, MA), 2006.

Contributor to the *Washington Post* magazine. Also contributor of short stories to various literary journals.

WORK IN PROGRESS: Sisterhood of War, for Houghton Mifflin.

SIDELIGHTS: After Kristin Henderson's Marine chaplain husband was sent to Afghanistan following the September 11, 2001, terrorist attacks, she decided to drive across the country in her Corvette with her German shepherd. The trip resulted in her memoir, titled *Driving by Moonlight: A Journey through Love, War, and Infertility.* In the book, Henderson examines her contradicting beliefs about religion and politics and recounts both her physical and emotional journeys. She also reflects on the painful fertility treatments she endured during an unsuccessful attempt to conceive a child. Many critics praised the work; Nancy R. Ives, writing in the *Library Journal,* called it "an evocative story." A *Publishers Weekly* contributor acknowledged that Henderson is "a sophisticated and humorous writer," and Patricia Monaghan, writing for *Booklist,* maintained that "Henderson's complex, compelling, timely story will haunt her readers."

Henderson's second book, *While They're at War: The True Story of American Families on the Homefront,* is a collection gathered from over one hundred interviews with military families. Henderson focuses on the lives of two women, Beth Pratt and Marissa Bootes, as they try to cope with their husbands' deployment and their own adjustment to the military base in Fort Bragg, North Carolina. "I chose Beth and Marissa because they were very different in many ways, with different experiences. Together they give you a hint of the many different facets of the military spouse experience," Henderson explained during a question-and-answer session posted on *Washington Post Online.* According to reviewers, the approach was effective. "This powerful, revealing, and sometimes painful book offers a look behind the scenes of military families," Vanessa Bush remarked in *Booklist.* A contributor to *Publishers Weekly* had a similar opinion: "This is an emotional book that effectively plies the complexities of military life."

BIOGRAPHICAL AND CRITICAL SOURCES:

BOOKS

Henderson, Kristin, *Driving by Moonlight: A Journey through Love, War, and Infertility,* Seal Press (New York, NY), 2003.

PERIODICALS

Booklist, October 15, 2003, Patricia Monaghan, review of *Driving by Moonlight,* p. 381; November 1, 2005, Vanessa Bush, review of *While They're at War: The True Story of American Families on the Homefront,* p. 16.

Kirkus Reviews, November 1, 2005, review of *While They're at War,* p. 1172.

Library Journal, December, 2003, Nancy R. Ives, review of *Driving by Moonlight,* p. 132.

Publishers Weekly, August 25, 2003, review of *Driving by Moonlight,* p. 50; December 12, 2005, review of *While They're at War,* p. 48.

ONLINE

Kristin Henderson Home Page, http://www.kristinhenderson.com (March 20, 2006).

Mother Jones Online, http://www.motherjones.com/ (March 20, 2006), author profile.

Washington Post Online, http://www.washingtonpost.com/ (October 12, 2004), question-and-answer session with author.*

*　　　*　　　*

HICKS, Susan E.
　　See CHADWICK, Elizabeth

*　　　*　　　*

HIETALA, Thomas R. 1952-

PERSONAL: Born February 1, 1952, in Biwabik, MN; son of Lloyd C. (a truck driver) and Angeline O. (a homemaker; maiden name, Miletich) Hietala; married Heather T. Kenvin, July 1, 1989; children: Kyle A. *Ethnicity:* "Finnish, Croatian, Slovenian." *Education:* Gustavus Adolphus College, graduated (summa cum laude), 1974; Yale University, M.A., 1975, Ph.D., 1979. *Politics:* Democrat/Progressive. *Religion:* Catholic.

ADDRESSES: *Home*—26 Fore Seasons Dr., Grinnell, IA 50112-3006. *Office*—215 Mears Cottage, 1213 6th Ave., Grinnell, IA 50112-1690.

CAREER: Yale University, New Haven, CT, lecturer in history, 1979-80; Dartmouth College, Hanover, NH, visiting assistant professor of history, 1980-85; Grinnell College, Grinnell, IA, assistant professor, 1985-89, associate professor, 1989-99, professor of history, 1999—.

AWARDS, HONORS: Danforth fellow, 1974-78; Distinguished Teaching Award, Yale University, 1979; cited for "outstanding academic title," *Choice,* 2003, for *The Fight of the Century: Jack Johnson, Joe Louis, and the Struggle for Racial Equality.*

WRITINGS:

Manifest Design: Anxiety and Aggrandizement, Cornell University Press (Ithaca, NY), 1985, revised edition published as *Manifest Design: American Exceptionalism and Empire,* 2003.

The Fight of the Century: Jack Johnson, Joe Louis, and the Struggle for Racial Equality, M.E. Sharpe (Armonk, NY), 2002.

WORK IN PROGRESS: A book "that will revisit and reassess boxer Muhammad Ali and his career and historical context, particularly in the 1960s and 1970s."

SIDELIGHTS: Thomas R. Hietala told *CA:* "As a scholar and writer, I strive to produce well-researched, informative, lively, and persuasive texts that examine and reinterpret past events, issues, and people of significance. History can instruct and humanize in many ways, but only if historians define topics and compose works that attract and engage a wide audience. Historical literacy promotes understanding of cultures and institutions and thereby fosters civic awareness and a capacity to transcend today's parochialism and partisanship. Good history teaches vital lessons about the primacy of evidence, the value of extensive research, the importance of questioning assumptions, and proper methods for analyzing and interpreting data. History is a way of learning and knowing that is applicable to virtually all disciplines and professions.

"My writing is a complement to my teaching, and my teaching informs my writing. My recent book, *The Fight of the Century: Jack Johnson, Joe Louis, and the Struggle for Racial Equality,* places boxing champions Jack Johnson and Joe Louis in a rich and revealing historical context and traces the deep and stubborn roots of American racist notions, habits, and policies. *Manifest Design: Anxiety and Aggrandizement,* my first book, challenged the popular slogan 'manifest destiny' as an explanation for American westward expansion. Americans often live blithely behind a veil of comforting assumptions and illusions about themselves and their heritage. My scholarship seeks to uncover and expose a more contradictory and troubling past, a legacy of splendid achievements and tragic failures that link past to present.

"I view writing as both process and product. The author sculpts multiple drafts until the final version attains the right economy of language, vivid imagery, and clarity of meaning. To that end, good writing shares stellar qualities whether labeled prose or poetry, fiction or nonfiction. Among my favorite authors are Charles Dickens, Mark Twain, Langston Hughes, George Orwell, and William Faulkner. In different ways, these writers instruct and entertain as they invite readers to see life through different lenses. Society would do well to encourage more reading, writing, and thinking, and less talking. The well-written text remains an indispensable antidote to the toxins of the sound-bite and one-liner."

BIOGRAPHICAL AND CRITICAL SOURCES:

PERIODICALS

Booklist, September 15, 2002, John Green, review of *The Fight of the Century: Jack Johnson, Joe Louis, and the Struggle for Racial Equality,* p. 193.
History: Review of New Books, winter, 2003, Phillip H. Vaughan, review of *The Fight of the Century,* p. 56.
Publishers Weekly, August 26, 2002, review of *The Fight of the Century,* p. 61.

*   *   *

HIGHTMAN, Jason 1971(?)-

PERSONAL: Born c. 1971; married; children: one daughter. *Education:* University of Southern California, B.A., 1993.

ADDRESSES: Home—CA. *Agent*—c/o Author Mail, HarperCollins Publishers, 10 E. 53rd St., 7th Fl., New York, NY 10022. *E-mail*—jason@jasonhightman.com.

CAREER: Film writer, director, and producer. Screenwriter for film studios, including Touchstone, Warner Films, and Columbia Pictures.

MEMBER: Writers Guild of America.

AWARDS, HONORS: New York Independent Film and Video Festival awards for best writing, direction, and best of show, all 2003, all for *Delusion;* also winner of several student filmmaking awards.

WRITINGS:

(And director) *Delusion* (short film), 2003.
The Saint of Dragons (fantasy novel), Eos (New York, NY), 2004.

Also author of screenplay *World War III,* Columbia Pictures.

ADAPTATIONS: Film rights to *The Saint of Dragons* have been purchased by Universal Pictures.

WORK IN PROGRESS: Writing the screenplay adaptation of *The Saint of Dragons.*

SIDELIGHTS: Jason Hightman is a screenwriter and award-winning director. Since he was about seventeen, however, Hightman had been mulling over a story idea involving the descendants of St. George the dragon slayer. Then, as the author revealed in an interview on the HarperCollins Children's Books Web site, "the idea of dragons reoccurred to me with special strength after the September 11 tragedy." The existence of evil in the world—made so apparent by the terrorist attacks on New York City and Washington, DC, led Hightman to decide to tackle the issue metaphorically through a fantasy novel. The result became *The Saint of Dragons,* his first novel.

Set in contemporary times, the premise of the book is that dragons, who are evil creatures and the source of all of humanity's misery, still exist and hide among people disguised as human beings. Simon St. George, the thirteen-year-old protagonist, learns from his long-absent father, Aldric, that he is a descendant of the dragon slayers. Because the dragons know of Simon's existence, he is in danger, and Aldric takes him out of school to train him in the family trade. Together, and with the additional assistance of the wizard Alaythia, they must seek out the dragons and slay them before their nefarious plot to destroy the world comes to fruition.

Critics of *The Saint of Dragons* considered it a rollicking, if rather shallow, adventure that should appeal to many teenage readers. For example, a *Kirkus Reviews* contributor commented that there is a lot of the book's action that will "distract readers from the clunky prose, wooden characters, and nonsensical, cliché-ridden plot." Susan L. Rogers, writing in the *School Library Journal,* described the novel as "a long series of sword-and-sorcery adventures heavy on action and light on plot." *Booklist* critic Sally Estes similarly attested that "the humor-laced story is preposterous to be sure," but added that audiences "will enjoy going along on the adventure."

BIOGRAPHICAL AND CRITICAL SOURCES:

PERIODICALS

Booklist, August, 2004, Sally Estes, review of *The Saint of Dragons,* p. 1920.

Bulletin of the Center for Children's Books, October, 2004, Timnah Card, review of *The Saint of Dragons,* p. 77.

Kirkus Reviews, September 1, 2004, review of *The Saint of Dragons,* p. 866.

Kliatt, July, 2004, Claire Rosser, review of *The Saint of Dragons,* p. 8; September, 2005, Claire Rosser, review of *The Saint of Dragons,* p. 28.

Publishers Weekly, December 6, 2004, review of *The Saint of Dragons,* p. 60.

School Librarian, winter, 2004, Dorothy Atkinson, review of *The Saint of Dragons,* p. 214.

School Library Journal, September, 2004, Susan L. Rogers, review of *The Saint of Dragons,* p. 208.

Voice of Youth Advocates, December, 2004, review of *The Saint of Dragons,* p. 406.

ONLINE

HarperCollins Children's Books, http://www.harperchildrens.com/ (January 20, 2006), interview with Jason Hightman.

Jason Hightman Home Page, http://www.jasonhightman.com (January 20, 2006).*

*   *   *

HILDERBRAND, Elin
(Elin Hilderbrand Cunningham)

PERSONAL: Married Chip Cunningham; children: Max, Dawson. *Education:* Graduate of Johns Hopkins University and the University of Iowa.

ADDRESSES: Home—Nantucket, MA. *Office*—Nantucket Preservation Trust, 2 Union St., Nantucket Island, MA 02554.

CAREER: Worked as a paralegal for attorney Richard Loftin, Nantucket, MA; Nantucket Preservation Trust, Nantucket, director.

WRITINGS:

The Beach Club (novel), St. Martin's Press (New York, NY), 2000.

Nantucket Nights (novel), St. Martin's Press (New York, NY), 2002.

Summer People (novel), St. Martin's Press (New York, NY), 2003.

The Blue Bistro (novel), St. Martin's Press (New York, NY), 2005.

Contributor to journals, including *Massachusetts Review* and *Colorado Review.*

SIDELIGHTS: Elin Hilderbrand is the author of a number of novels that are all set on the historic island of Nantucket, which is also her home. Her first novel, *The Beach Club,* features Mack Peterson, a man originally from Iowa who has been managing the Nantucket Beach Club and Hotel for eleven years. As the new season begins, he considers whether he would like to buy the hotel from owners Bill and Therese Elliot, the parents of rebellious eighteen-year-old Cecily. Mack has a beautiful girlfriend, Maribel Cox, who is hinting about a wedding, an elderly friend named Lacey Gardner, and an enemy, Vance Robbins, who once vied with Mack for his job but who is now a bellboy. Other characters include a new receptionist who has a special reason for finding a man, and another man who gives Mack competition for Maribel. The relationships between the characters are complicated when a hurricane threatens the resort. A *Publishers Weekly* reviewer wrote that "though somewhat predictable, these summer escapades have a strong emotional pull, and readers will remain absorbed until the surprising denouement." *Booklist* contributor Deborah Rysso considered *The Beach Club* to be a "delectably dramatic debut novel."

In *Nantucket Nights* the main characters are Kayla, Antoinette, and Valerie, three women who have known each other for two decades. The novel is about their relationships as they continue their tradition of celebrating over the Labor Day weekend with lobster, champagne, skinny dipping, and soul-baring. This story was followed by *Summer People,* which also features a woman character and a vacation tradition on Nantucket. Beth Newton and her teenage twins, Garrett and Winnie, are beginning their annual Nantucket vacation without their father, Arch, as the book opens. Arch is not there with them because he perished in a plane crash. However, before he died, he invited Marcus, the son of a black woman he was defending in a murder trial. Added to this mix during an unusual vacation for the family is David, an old love of Beth's who is showing new interest in her. The story was characterized as "more entertaining beach reading" by *Booklist* contributor Beth Leistensnider.

The eatery in *The Blue Bistro* is an exclusive oceanside restaurant owned by Thatcher Smith, who plans to close it after the season ends. His talented chef is the reclusive Fiona Kemp, with whom he eats dinner every night after the restaurant closes. Into their lives comes Adrienne Dealey, a seasonal worker newly arrived from Aspen who is looking for employment. Although she has no restaurant experience, Thatcher hires her anyway, and she proves to be a quick learner. She soon finds herself falling in love with Thatcher, but she is confused as to why Fiona is so abrupt with her. The other question in this novel is why such a fabulous, popular restaurant is closing. Other characters include a handsome bartender and an ambitious pastry chef. As with her previous novels, Hilderbrand provides more than a story as she describes the beautiful island of Nantucket and all that it has to offer. Joanne Wilkinson, writing in *Booklist,* called the novel "fun, stylish, and absorbing vacation reading."

BIOGRAPHICAL AND CRITICAL SOURCES:

PERIODICALS

Booklist, May 15, 2000, Deborah Rysso, review of *The Beach Club,* p. 1730; March 15, 2002, Beth Warrell, review of *Nantucket Nights,* p. 1211; June 1, 2003, Beth Leistensnider, review of *Summer People,* p. 1743; May 15, 2005, Joanne Wilkinson, review of *The Blue Bistro,* p. 1636.

Kirkus Reviews, March 1, 2002, review of *Nantucket Nights,* p. 278; April 1, 2005, review of *The Blue Bistro,* p. 374.

Publishers Weekly, May 29, 2000, review of *The Beach Club,* p. 51; May 27, 2002, review of *Nantucket Nights,* p. 39; May 30, 2005, review of *The Blue Bistro,* p. 40.

ONLINE

AllReaders.com, http://www.allreaders.com/ (January 10, 2006), Sandra Calhoune, review of *The Blue Bistro.**

*   *   *

HILL, Laban Carrick

PERSONAL: Male. *Education:* Earned Ph.D.

ADDRESSES: Home—VT. *Agent*—c/o Author Mail, Watson-Guptill Publications, 770 Broadway, New York, NY 10003. *E-mail*—labanhill@yahoo.com.

CAREER: Poet, children's writer, lecturer, and educator. Previously taught writing at Columbia University, New York, NY; Baruch College, City University of New York; and St. Michael's College, VT. Lecturer to U.S. Embassy in Egypt, 2006.

MEMBER: Authors Guild, Author's League of America.

AWARDS, HONORS: National Book Award finalist, 2004, for *Harlem Stomp!*

WRITINGS:

Bugged Out!, illustrated by Bill Schmidt, Gareth Stevens (Milwaukee, WI), 1997.

Watch Out for Room 13, illustrated by Bill Schmidt, Gareth Stevens (Milwaukee, WI), 1997.

The Evil Pen Pal, illustrated by Bill Schmidt, Gareth Stevens (Milwaukee, WI), 1998.

The Toy Shop of Terror, illustrated by Bill Schmidt, Gareth Stevens (Milwaukee, WI), 1998.

Welcome to Horror Hospital, illustrated by Bill Schmidt, Gareth Stevens (Milwaukee, WI), 1998.

Jonathan Franzen's "The Corrections" ("Spark Notes"), Spark Publishers (New York, NY), 2003.

Harlem Stomp!: A Cultural History of the Harlem Renaissance, Little, Brown (New York, NY), 2003.

The Spy's Survival Handbook, Scholastic (New York, NY), 2004.

Casa Azul: An Encounter with Frida Kahlo (young-adult novel), Watson-Guptill (New York, NY), 2005.

Contributor of poetry to anthology *Contemporary Poetry of New England* and to periodicals, including *Tar River Review, Denver Quarterly,* and *American Letters & Commentary.* Contributor of articles to Scribner's "American Writers" and "British Writers" series.

"X-TREME MYSTERIES" NOVEL SERIES

Deep Powder, Deep Trouble, Hyperion (New York, NY), 1998.

Crossed Tracks, Hyperion (New York, NY), 1998.

Rocked Out: A Summer X-Games Special, Hyperion (New York, NY), 1998.

Half Pipe Rip-off, Hyperion (New York, NY), 1998.

Lost Wake, Hyperion (New York, NY), 1998.

Out of Line, Hyperion (New York, NY), 1998.

Spiked Snow, Hyperion (New York, NY), 1998.

Total White Out, Hyperion (New York, NY), 1998.

SIDELIGHTS: Laban Carrick Hill is the author of several titles for young readers and young adults, including illustrated chapter books for early readers, nonfiction and historical fiction for older readers, and novels in the "X-treme Mysteries" series. His highly praised nonfiction title *Harlem Stomp!: A Cultural*

History of the Harlem Renaissance was a finalist for the National Book Award for young people's literature. In addition to books, Hill is a published poet and has contributed biographical essays to Scribner's "American Writers" and "British Writers" series, and his synopsis and analyses of *The Corrections* by Jonathan Franzen was published as *Jonathan Franzen's "The Corrections"* for the "Spark Notes" series.

Harlem Stomp! delves into the Harlem Renaissance, the period from 1900 to 1924 when music, literature, and art surged from the African-American community in Harlem, New York. Covering such noteworthy figures as Booker T. Washington, W.E.B. DuBois, Sgt. Henry Johnson, and Charles Spurgeon Johnson, Hill includes short biographies, analyses of opposing viewpoints of the time, and background information on the factors leading up to this cultural awakening. "This compelling history will leave readers familiar or unfamiliar with this high-flying period eager to discover more," wrote a contributor to *Publishers Weekly.* A *Kirkus Reviews* critic considered the book "clearly a labor of love," and Joanne K. Cecere wrote in *School Library Journal* that "the words and images bring this extraordinary period to life." Noting that Hill includes excerpts of "great selections from literature and journalism of the period" in his book, Hazel Rochman commented in her *Booklist* review that, while the biographies occasionally lag, "far livelier are discussions of their works, which show how the writers changed the view of blacks." To help teachers introduce *Harlem Stomp!* to students, the publisher has also provided a downloadable teacher's guide.

Hill's historical fiction title, *Casa Azul: An Encounter with Frida Kahlo,* is part of the "Art Encounters" series of historical novels that introduces young-adult readers to famous artists. Drawing on Kahlo's painting "Self Portrait (with Monkey and Hummingbird)" for inspiration, Hill's story centers around two young people—fourteen-year-old Maria Ortiz, and Victor, Maria's younger brother—who are invited to stay in Kahlo's mysterious house, where what is real and what is fantastic are often the very same thing. Other residents of Kahlo's home are Fuland the monkey and Chica the cat, both of whom are able to speak. "In the spirit of Kahlo's life and art, the magical realism is both playful and dark," noted Rochman in a *Booklist* review. Steev Baker, writing in *School Library Journal,* commented that "Hill's short art-history novel accomplishes with style what it is meant to do," while

Magazine of Fantasy and Science Fiction contributor Charles de Lint deemed the novel "a terrific introduction to magical fantasy and the creative impulse." A *Kirkus Reviews* critic also noted the similarities between the novel and Kahlo's creative work, writing that "Hill's blend of realism, fantasy, and Aztec myth nicely mirrors Kahlo's surreal juxtaposition of real and unreal."

Along with his historical and historical fiction titles, Hill has published several titles for young mystery lovers. The "X-treme Mysteries" center around young sleuths who enjoy such extreme sports as rock climbing, snowboarding, and skate boarding. When their respective sports are endangered by nefarious activities, the kids rise to the challenge to solve the mystery. In *The Spy's Survival Handbook* Hill explores codes and gives helpful hints on how to successfully shake someone following you or create an effective disguise. "Young secret agents can hone their skills," a *Publishers Weekly* critic commented in a review of the title.

BIOGRAPHICAL AND CRITICAL SOURCES:

PERIODICALS

Booklist, February 15, 2004, Hazel Rochman, review of *Harlem Stomp!: A Cultural History of the Harlem Renaissance,* p. 1065; October 1, 2005, Hazel Rochman, review of *Casa Azul: An Encounter with Frida Kahlo,* p. 48.
Bulletin of the Center for Children's Books, April, 2004, Elizabeth Bush, review of *Harlem Stomp!,* p. 330.
Kirkus Reviews, November 15, 2003, review of *Harlem Stomp!,* p. 1360; June 15, 2005, review of *Casa Azul,* p. 683.
Kliatt, May, 2005, Janis Flint-Ferguson, review of *Casa Azul,* p. 13.
Magazine of Fantasy and Science Fiction, August, 2005, Charles de Lint, review of *Casa Azul,* p. 27.
Publishers Weekly, December 22, 2003, review of *Harlem Stomp!,* p. 63; June 7, 2004, "Spy vs. Spy," p. 53.
School Library Journal, January, 2004, Joanne K. Cecere, review of *Harlem Stomp!,* p. 148; October, 2004, review of *Harlem Stomp!,* p. S66; September, 2005, Steev Baker, review of *Casa Azul,* p. 204.

Voice of Youth Advocates, February, 2004, Valerie Ott, review of *Harlem Stomp!,* p. 511; April, 2004, "Pure Poetry," p. 16.

ONLINE

Laban Carrick Hill Home Page, http://www.labanhill.com (April 4, 2006).
National Book Foundation Web site, http://www.nationalbook.org/ (April 8, 2006), "Laban Carrick Hill."*

*   *   *

HILL, Lynn 1961(?)-

PERSONAL: Born c. 1961, in Los Angeles, CA; married Russ Raffa (a salesperson), 1988 (marriage ended); children: Owen. *Education:* College at New Paltz, B.S., c. 1983.

ADDRESSES: Office—P.O. Box 383, Eldorado Springs, CO 80025. *E-mail*—lynn@lynnhillblogs.com.

CAREER: Professional rock climber. Lynn Hill Climbing Camps, Eldorado Springs, CO, owner. Member, Access Fund.

AWARDS, HONORS: First woman to complete a grade 5.14 climb, 1990, in Cimai, France; first woman to scale a grade 5.14 climb, 1991, Mass Critique in Cimai, France; has won more than thirty international climbing competitions.

WRITINGS:

(With Greg Child) *Climbing Free: My Life in the Vertical World* (autobiography), foreword by John Long, W.W. Norton (New York, NY), 2002.

SIDELIGHTS: Lynn Hill started rock climbing when she was just fourteen years old, and since then she has become one of the world's leading sport climbers. As distinguished from mountain climbing, sport climbing is the difficult and dangerous competition of ascending mountains and cliff faces without the benefit of any equipment whatsoever. A woman in a field dominated by men, especially in the sport's earlier years, Hill has set numerous records, including being the first and only person to climb the three-thousand-foot face of El Capitan in Yosemite without mountaineering equipment. Her autobiography, *Climbing Free: My Life in the Vertical World*, is a reminiscence of her years in the sport, as well as a reflection on her personal and professional life. Hill talks about the challenges of competition, the famous climbers she has met and befriended—some of whom would later die in climbing accidents—and her marriage and decision to become a mother. She also offers rock climbing tips.

Reviewers of the book enjoyed *Climbing Free* as both an entertaining and informative work. A *Publishers Weekly* contributor, for example, called it "remarkably entertaining." David Pitt, writing in *Booklist*, appreciated how the author avoids "ego or pretension," despite her amazing success in the sport, calling the autobiography a "quietly inspiring" work that "is a must-read for fans of sport climbing." *Climbing* writer Susan Fox Rogers concluded that *Climbing Free* "is a wonderfully universal story, as perfectly balanced and strong as Hill is on the rock."

BIOGRAPHICAL AND CRITICAL SOURCES:

BOOKS

Great Women in Sports, Visible Ink Press (Detroit, MI), 1996.
Hill, Lynn, and Greg Child, *Climbing Free: My Life in the Vertical World,* W.W. Norton (New York, NY), 2002.
Newsmakers 1991, Thomson Gale (Detroit, MI), 1991.
Notable Sports Figures, Thomson Gale (Detroit, MI), 2004.

PERIODICALS

Booklist, March 15, 2002, David Pitt, review of *Climbing Free,* p. 1203.
Book World, May 5, 2002, review of *Climbing Free,* p. 4.
Books Magazine, summer, 2002, review of *Climbing Free,* p. 20.

Climbing, September 15, 2002, Susan Fox Rogers, review of *Climbing Free,* p. 120.
Kirkus Reviews, March 1, 2002, review of *Climbing Free,* p. 309.
Life, August, 1989, "Upward Mobility: The Best Woman Climber in the World Gets Paid for Going Higher," p. 104.
Los Angeles Times, May 19, 2002, review of *Climbing Free,* p. 15.
O, the Oprah Magazine, July, 2002, James B. Meigs, "Extreme Living: Adventure Isn't about Risk or Thrill Seeking or Proving Your Mettle. It's about Going for Something with All Your Heart," p. 35.
Publishers Weekly, December 13, 1999, John F. Baker, "Three on the Rope," p. 16; April 29, 2002, review of *Climbing Free,* p. 54.

ONLINE

Altrec.com Outdoors, http://www.altrec.com/ (January 24, 2006), Peter Potterfield, "Lynn Hill: One of the Great Rock Climbers of the Era Takes on Writing and Motherhood."
Lynn Hill Climbing Camps, http://www.lynnhillclimbs.com (January 24, 2006).*

*   *   *

HIMMELFARB, Milton 1918-2006

OBITUARY NOTICE— See index for *CA* sketch: Born October 21, 1918, in New York, NY; died of complications from skin cancer, January 4, 2006, in New York, NY. Editor, researcher, educator, and author. Himmelfarb was best remembered as a commentator on Jewish issues, especially as an essayist for *Commentary* magazine. A graduate of the City College (now of the City University of New York), he completed his master's degree there in 1939. That same year, he also received a degree in Hebrew literature from the Jewish Theological Seminary of America and a diploma from the University of Paris. After taking post-graduate courses at Columbia University through 1947, his first important job was with the American Jewish Committee in New York City, where he became director of information and research in 1955. Himmelfarb would remain associated with the committee for the next thirty years, becoming the editor of *The American Jewish Yearbook* in 1959 and a contributing editor to *Commentary*. His essays for the latter made him famous for his wry observations about the Jewish people. A conservative writer, he expressed his opposition to historians who held that the Holocaust was a result of historical trends and not just Adolf Hitler's doing; Himmelfarb, to the contrary, asserted that blame for the Holocaust could be laid entirely at Hitler's feet. He also warned that birth control and intermarriage practices were diluting the purity of the Jewish race. Himmelfarb, who also occasionally taught as a visiting professor at such institutions as the Jewish Theological Seminary and the Reconstructionist Rabbinical College, retired from the committee and as contributing editor to *Commentary* in 1986. His publications include *The Jews in Modernity* (1973) and the coedited *Zero Population Growth—for Whom? Differential Fertility and Minority Group Survival* (1978).

OBITUARIES AND OTHER SOURCES:

PERIODICALS

Los Angeles Times, January 18, 2006, p. B10.
New York Times, January 15, 2006, p. A23.

*   *   *

HINTON, J. Lynne
    See HINTON, Lynne

*   *   *

HINTON, Lynne
    (J. Lynne Hinton, Jackie Lynn)

PERSONAL: Born in Durham, NC; daughter of Jack (a reverend) and Shirley Hinton; married Bob Branard. *Education:* University of North Carolina at Greensboro, undergraduate degree; Pacific School of Religion, M.Div.; also studied at Wake Forest University and North Carolina School of the Arts, 1997.

ADDRESSES: Home—Denton, NC. *Agent*—c/o Author Mail, Publicity Department, St. Martin's Press, 175 5th Ave., New York, NY 10010.

CAREER: Pastor and writer. Ordained Baptist minister, 1990; Hospice of Rockingham County, chaplain, beginning 1990; Hospice of Alamance-Caswell, chaplain; Mount Hope United Church of Christ, Guilford County, NC, pastor, 1992; First Congregational United Church of Christ, Asheboro, NC, pastor, 1998; *Charlotte Observer,* Charlotte, NC, columnist.

WRITINGS:

(As J. Lynne Hinton) *Meditations for Walking* (nonfiction), Smyth & Helwys Publishers (Macon, GA), 1999.
Friendship Cake (novel), HarperSanFrancisco (San Francisco, CA), 2000.
The Things I Know Best (novel), HarperSanFrancisco (San Francisco, CA), 2001.
Garden of Faith (novel), HarperSanFrancisco (San Francisco, CA), 2002.
Forever Friends (novel), HarperSanFrancisco (San Francisco, CA), 2003.
The Last Odd Day (novel), HarperSanFrancisco (San Francisco, CA), 2004.
The Arms of God (novel), St. Martin's Press (New York, NY), 2005.

WORK IN PROGRESS: "Shady Grove" mystery series for St. Martin's Press, under the pseudonym Jackie Lynn.

SIDELIGHTS: Having grown up in and around the church, it was not surprising that Lynne Hinton would become an ordained Baptist minister in 1990. The religious upbringing she received also pervades many of her books. *Friendship Cake,* for example, tells the story of five women from the same church group who strengthen their friendship and faith by collaborating on a cookbook. A reviewer for *Publishers Weekly* described the novel as "sincere but frothy." In the sequel, *Garden of Faith,* many of the characters are losing control of their lives, ranging from Pastor Charlotte's faith-trying experiences to Jessie's newfound health problems. While noting some flaws in the work, *Booklist* critic Melanie Duncan believed that "fans of the first book will want to read the second."

The Things I Know Best mixes the sacred with the profane as members of a small-town family deal with and apply their abilities to tell the future. Danise

Hoover, writing in *Booklist,* praised Hinton's "deep understanding of the psyche of the women she writes about." In *The Arms of God* Olivia meets the mother who abandoned her as a child. When her mother dies, Olivia is left alone in the task of putting the pieces of the past back together. A contributor to *Kirkus Reviews* reasoned that despite some "uneven lyricism," Hinton creates "some fine characterizations."

BIOGRAPHICAL AND CRITICAL SOURCES:

PERIODICALS

Booklist, May 15, 2001, Danise Hoover, review of *The Things I Know Best,* p. 1731; May 1, 2002, Melanie Duncan, review of *Garden of Faith,* p. 1507.

Charlotte Observer, November 19, 2005, "Five Questions for Lynne Hinton."

Kirkus Reviews, March 15, 2004, review of *The Last Odd Day,* p. 242; September 1, 2005, review of *The Arms of God,* p. 935.

Library Journal, June 1, 2000, Melanie C. Duncan, review of *Friendship Cake,* p. 106.

Publishers Weekly, March 22, 1999, review of *Meditations for Walking,* p. 88; April 10, 2000, review of *Friendship Cake,* p. 74; August 7, 2000, Barbara Roether, review of *Friendship Cake,* p. 24; April 23, 2001, review of *The Things I Know Best,* p. 50; February 11, 2002, review of *Garden of Faith,* p. 159; May 24, 2004, review of *The Last Odd Day,* p. 45; September 5, 2005, review of *The Arms of God,* p. 32.

Tribune Books (Chicago, IL), December 28, 2003, review of *The Things I Know Best,* p. 6.

ONLINE

BookReporter.com, http://www.bookreporter.com/ (January 17, 2006), brief biography of J. Lynne Hinton.

Lynne Hinton Home Page, http://www.lynnehinton.com (January 17, 2006).

Southern Scribe, http://www.southernscribe.com/ (January 17, 2006), Joyce Dixon, interview with J. Lynne Hinton.

TeenReads.com, http://www.teenreads.com/ (January 17, 2006), Jana Siciliano, review of *The Things I Know Best.*

Writer's E-Zine, http://www.thewritersezine.com/ (January 17, 2006), Janet Smith, interview with J. Lynne Hinton.*

* * *

HOBAN, Tana 1917(?)-2006

OBITUARY NOTICE— See index for *CA* sketch: Born c. 1917, in Philadelphia, PA; died January 27, 2006, in Louveciennes, France. Photographer and author. Hoban was an award-winning photographer and prolific author of children's nonfiction books whose emphasis on presenting ordinary objects in new ways was considered revolutionary. After graduating from what is now the Moore College of Art and Design in 1938, she studied painting in the Netherlands and England. Returning to America, she worked as an illustrator and graphic artist before becoming an editorial and advertising photographer for such magazines as *Life* and *McCall's.* Opening a studio in Philadelphia in 1946, she began to focus her work more and more on children, using them as her subjects in photographs that were exhibited at the Museum of Modern Art in 1949 and again in 1955. Four years later, she was named one of the ten top women photographers in the country. Beginning in 1970, Hoban started using her photographs to illustrate her own children's books. Her main focus was to take photos of everyday objects and present them in new and interesting ways; then, she would use these pictures to illustrate basic principles such as counting, the alphabet, shapes, and other fundamental concepts. She produced dozens of children's books over the next three decades, with her last being 2000's *Cubes, Cones, Cylinders and Spheres.* Many of these works won awards, such as the Golden Eagle Award for *Look Again!* (1971), the Washington Children's Book Guild Nonfiction Award for *More Than One* (1981), the George C. Stone Recognition of Merit Award in 1986 for her body of work, and the lifetime achievement award from the American Society of Media Photographers in 1998, not to mention many notable book citations from the American Library Association and other honors. Hoban moved to France permanently in 1983, where she also occupied her time forming the Americans for Peace group that staged protests at the U.S. Embassy. In later life, a series of strokes limited her ability to continue working.

OBITUARIES AND OTHER SOURCES:

PERIODICALS

Los Angeles Times, February 20, 2006, p. B13.
New York Times, February 4, 2006, p. A11.
Washington Post, February 10, 2006, p. B6.

* * *

HOGGARD-CREEGAN, Nicola
    See CREEGAN, Nicola Hoggard

* * *

HOLLAND, David

PERSONAL: Male. *Education:* Purdue University, M.A.

ADDRESSES: Office—84WHAS Radio, 4000 Radio Dr., Louisville, KY 40218.

CAREER: WHAS Radio, Louisville, KY, creative director. Has also worked as freelance journalist, college teacher, and advertising copywriter.

WRITINGS:

NOVELS

Murcheston: The Wolf's Tale, Forge (New York, NY), 2000.
Devil in Bellminster: An Unlikely Mystery, Thomas Dunne Books (New York, NY), 2002.
Devil's Acre: An Unlikely Mystery, Thomas Dunne Books (New York, NY), 2003.
Devil's Game: An Unlikely Mystery, Thomas Dunne Books (New York, NY), 2005.

SIDELIGHTS: David Holland's educational background in Victorian-era literature imbues the themes and settings of his first four novels. His debut, *Murcheston: The Wolf's Tale,* is told in a Victorian style that, according to several reviewers, is similar to the works of Charles Dickens and Bram Stoker. His next three novels, the "Unlikely Mysteries," introduce the character of Reverend Tuckworth, a vicar who finds himself investigating mysterious circumstances in Victorian England.

Murcheston relates the story of a nobleman who turns into a werewolf after having been clawed by one near his estate. Although not a fan of werewolf novels, Don D'Ammassa, writing in the *Science Fiction Chronicle,* praised the "extremely witty" story, saying it "stands far ahead of the pack." Writing for the *Books 'n' Bytes* Web site, Harriet Klausner similarly commented that *Murcheston* "will set the standard for future such books to be measured against."

Devil in Bellminster: An Unlikely Mystery introduces Tuckworth's sleuthing abilities as he investigates two homicides in tiny Bellminster, England. A reviewer for *Publishers Weekly* thought Holland used "old-fashioned language inconsistently, breaking the period spell." Writing again for *Books 'n' Bytes,* Harriet Klausner, however, felt the "story line is cleverly developed." *Devil's Acre: An Unlikely Mystery* follows Tuckworth to London in his attempt to secure money for his cathedral while investigating a murder. While Klausner believed that the story is "rich in the era so much so that nineteenth-century readers will appreciate the depth," Sue O'Brien commented in *Booklist* that "Holland ladles on the atmosphere with a bit of a heavy hand." In *Devil's Game: An Unlikely Mystery,* Tuckworth investigates the mysterious events surrounding the murder of Bellminster's member of Parliament and the subsequent rush to replace his seat. A reviewer for *Publishers Weekly* noted that Holland "does an excellent job at evoking the desperate claustrophobia of the town." Margaret Flanagan concluded in *Booklist* that Holland "manages to evoke the Victorian temperament and psyche."

BIOGRAPHICAL AND CRITICAL SOURCES:

PERIODICALS

Booklist, November 1, 2003, Sue O'Brien, review of *Devil's Acre: An Unlikely Mystery,* p. 482; November 1, 2005, Margaret Flanagan, review of *Devil's Game: An Unlikely Mystery,* p. 28.
Boston Book Review, May, 2005, review of *Murcheston: The Wolf's Tale,* p. 39.

Drood Review of Mystery, May, 2002, review of *Devil in Bellminster: An Unlikely Mystery,* p. 10.

Kirkus Reviews, December 15, 2001, review of *Devil in Bellminster,* p. 1725; September 15, 2003, review of *Devil's Acre,* p. 1157; September 15, 2005, review of *Devil's Game,* p. 1002.

Library Journal, February 15, 2000, Jackie Cassada, review of *Murcheston,* p. 202; February 1, 2002, Rex E. Klett, review of *Devil in Bellminster,* p. 136; November 1, 2003, Rex E. Klett, review of *Devil's Acre,* p. 128.

Publishers Weekly, January 3, 2000, review of *Murcheston,* p. 61; February 11, 2002, review of *Devil in Bellminster,* p. 165; September 29, 2003, review of *Devil's Acre,* p. 46; September 26, 2005, review of *Devil's Game,* p. 65.

Science Fiction Chronicle, June, 2001, Don D'Ammassa, review of *Murcheston,* p. 40.

ONLINE

Books 'n' Bytes, http://www.booksnbytes.com/ (December 15, 2005), Harriet Klausner, review of *Devil in Bellminster, Devil's Acre,* and *Murcheston.*

Rambles, http://www.rambles.net/ (December 15, 2005), Laurie Thayer, review of *Murcheston.*

Reviewing the Evidence, http://reviewingtheevidence. com/ (February 7, 2006), Sarah Dudley, review of *Devil's Acre.**

* * *

HOLLAND, Endesha Ida Mae 1944-2006

OBITUARY NOTICE— See index for *CA* sketch: Born August 29, 1944, in Greenwood, MS; died of complications from ataxia, January 25, 2006, in Los Angeles, CA. Educator, activist, and author. A Pulitzer Prize-nominated playwright, Holland was an emeritus professor at the University of Southern California best known for her play *From the Mississippi Delta.* The daughter of a desperately poor Mississippi family, she knew a life of extreme hardship as a child. Raped by a white man when she was just eleven years old, she would later see prostitution as her only means of income. That changed, however, when she discovered the Student Nonviolent Coordinating Committee and became involved in the Civil Rights movement. This involvement, however, also turned to tragedy when her family became a target of white violence. Her house was burned down, killing her wheelchair-bound mother inside. Holland soon left the South after that. Moving north, she continued her activism by becoming the founding director of Women Helping Offenders, Inc., in Minneapolis from 1971 to 1975, serving as chair from 1975 to 1977. Deciding the best way to try to wash away her feelings of guilt about her past was to become well educated, she attended the University of Minnesota, earning a doctorate in 1986. Holland also found solace in writing, producing the plays *Second Doctor Lady* (1981), which won the National Lorraine Hansberry award, *The Reconstruction of Dossie Ree Hemphill* (1981), *Miss Ida B. Wells* (1982), and *Parader without a Permit* (1985). *Second Doctor Lady,* first produced at London's Young Vic Theatre in 1979, would be revised as the Pulitzer-nominated *From the Mississippi Delta* (1988), which would be produced Off-Broadway with financial backing from talk-show host Oprah Winfrey. Holland also had a productive teaching career. She was an instructor in the women's study program, which she helped create, at the University of Minnesota from 1982 to 1985. Moving on to the State University of New York at Buffalo, she was a professor there from 1985 to 1993. Her last position was at the University of Southern California, where she taught until 2003, leaving the school when her ataxia began to hamper her ability to speak. In 1997, she related her life's story in *From the Mississippi Delta: A Memoir.*

OBITUARIES AND OTHER SOURCES:

BOOKS

Holland, Endesha Ida Mae, *From the Mississippi Delta: A Memoir,* Simon & Schuster (New York, NY), 1997.

PERIODICALS

Los Angeles Times, January 30, 2006, p. B9.
New York Times, February 1, 2006, p. A23.
Washington Post, February 4, 2006, p. B6.

* * *

HORN, James
(James P.P. Horn)

PERSONAL: Married; wife's name Sally; children: Ben, Lizzie. *Education:* University of Sussex, D.Phil., 1982.

ADDRESSES: Office—John D. Rockefeller, Jr. Library, 313 1st St., Williamsburg, VA 23187. *E-mail*—jhorn@cwf.org.

CAREER: University of Brighton, England, head of the School of Historical and Critical Studies; Omohundro Institute of Early American History and Culture, Williamsburg, VA, visiting editor of publications; Thomas Jefferson Foundation, International Center for Jefferson Studies, Charlottesville, VA, Saunders Director; Colonial Williamsburg Foundation, Williamsburg, VA, began as deputy research division administrator and director of John D. Rockefeller, Jr. Library, became director of research and O'Neill Director of the John D. Rockefeller, Jr. Library.

AWARDS, HONORS: Fulbright scholar; research fellow, Omohundro Institute, American Council of Learned Societies, Charles Warren Center at Harvard University, and the Royal Historical Society.

WRITINGS:

(Editor, with Ida Altman) *"To Make America": European Emigration in the Early Modern Period,* University of California Press (Berkeley, CA), 1991.

Adapting to a New World: English Society in the Seventeenth-Century Chesapeake, University of North Carolina Press (Chapel Hill, NC), for the Omohundro Institute of Early American History and Culture, 1994.

(Editor, with Jan Ellen Lewis and Peter S. Onuf) *The Revolution of 1800: Democracy, Race, and the New Republic* ("Jeffersonian America" series), University of Virginia Press (Charlottesville, VA), 2002.

A Land As God Made It: Jamestown and the Birth of America, Basic Books (New York, NY), 2005.

SIDELIGHTS: James Horn, a scholar of Colonial America, has written or edited a number of books about early American history; he is the author of *A Land As God Made It: Jamestown and the Birth of America.* The history covers the period from the Jamestown colony's beginnings in 1607 to 1622, the year after it was attacked by the Pamunkey Native American tribe. Although Horn touches on the foundations of the colony, he concentrates more on day-to-

day events and the settlers' methods of surviving, especially their dependence on the Powhatan Native Americans who supplied them with food.

Critics reacted to the book with enthusiasm. *Booklist* reviewer Gilbert Taylor called the history "a solid rendition of the [Jamestown] saga." Jonathan Yardley wrote in the *Washington Post* that *A Land As God Made It* is "an exemplary account of the settlement and development of Jamestown" and commented that Horn's "treatment of the Indian tribes and their leaders is extensive and fair but never sentimental. . . . All in all, an absolutely terrific book."

BIOGRAPHICAL AND CRITICAL SOURCES:

PERIODICALS

Booklist, October 1, 2005, Gilbert Taylor, review of *A Land As God Made It: Jamestown and the Birth of America,* p. 20.
Publishers Weekly, August 22, 2005, review of *A Land As God Made It,* p. 55.
Washington Post, October 25, 2005, Jonathan Yardley, review of *A Land As God Made It,* p. C8.

*   *   *

HORN, James P.P.
See HORN, James

*   *   *

HUNDLEY, Jessica

PERSONAL: Female. *Education:* Degree in creative writing.

ADDRESSES: Agent—c/o Author Mail, Thunder's Mouth Press, 245 W. 17th St., 11th Fl., New York, NY 10011-5300.

CAREER: Journalist and filmmaker. Boston Phoenix, Boston, MA, arts contributor, 1992; *Mommy and I Are One* (magazine), founder and editor, 1992-2000.

WRITINGS:

(Editor, with Jon Alain Guzik) *Horny? Los Angeles: A Sexy, Steamy, Downright Sleazy Handbook to the City,* Really Great Books (Los Angeles, CA), 2001.
(With Polly Parsons) *Grievous Angel: An Intimate Biography of Gram Parsons,* Thunder's Mouth Press (New York, NY), 2005.

Also contributor to periodicals and Web sites, including *Los Angeles Times, Blender, Mojo, Black Book, Dazed and Confused, Flaunt, New York Press, Paper, Salon.com, Hustler, Playboy, Nerve.com,* and *Soma.*

WORK IN PROGRESS: Editing a feature film, writing a screenplay, and working on several shorts.

SIDELIGHTS: Jessica Hundley is a freelance author and journalist who has written for a number of publications. After completing her creative writing degree, Hundley came up with the idea to start her own magazine while on a cross-country trip. With assistance from Andy Hunter, the first issue of *Mommy and I Are One* was published two years later. The magazine covered alternative music, art, and independent film, subjects addressed throughout most of her writings.

In *Grievous Angel: An Intimate Biography of Gram Parsons,* Hundley collaborated with Polly Parsons, daughter of the book's subject, to illustrate the short life of one of the first musicians to successfully mix country and rock music. A reviewer for *Publishers Weekly* wrote that *Grievous Angel* is a "fluffy, interview-packed biography" that does not "provide more than a superficial portrait." Writing in *Library Journal,* however, James E. Perone believed that Hundley discusses her subject "with sensitivity and attention to detail." Overall, he praised the authors for telling "Parsons's tragic story . . . very well."

BIOGRAPHICAL AND CRITICAL SOURCES:

PERIODICALS

Library Journal, October 1, 2005, James E. Perone, review of *Grievous Angel: An Intimate Biography of Gram Parsons,* p. 78.

Publishers Weekly, September 5, 2005, review of *Grievous Angel,* p. 47.

ONLINE

Book of Zines, http://www.zinebook.com/ (January 3, 2006), interview with Jessica Hundley.
Club Free Time, http://www.clubfreetime.com/ (January 3, 2006), brief biography of Jessica Hundley.*

*   *   *

HUNTER, Robin
  See NEILLANDS, Robin

*   *   *

HUTTON, Deborah 1955-2005
  (Deborah Helen Hutton)

PERSONAL: Born September 7, 1955, in England; died of lung cancer, July 15, 2005; father a farmer; married Charlie Stebbings (a photographer and film director), 1984; children: Archie, Romilly, Clemmie, Freddie. *Education:* York University, B.A. (with first-class honors)

CAREER: Worked for the British Council after college; *Vogue* (magazine), New York, NY, former staff writer; became freelance writer in late 1990s.

AWARDS, HONORS: Won *Vogue* magazine talent contest.

WRITINGS:

Vogue Complete Beauty, Harmony Books (New York, NY), 1982, published as *Vogue Beauty,* 1984.
(General editor) *Vogue Complete Diet and Exercise,* Harmony Books (New York, NY), 1985.
(With Ivan Sokolov) *The Parents Book: Getting On Well with Our Children,* Thorsons Publishing Group (Wellingborough, England), 1988.
Vogue Beauty for Life: Health, Fitness, Looks, and Style for Women in their 30s, 40s, 50s—, Crown (New York, NY), 1994.

"Vogue" Futures: Beauty for Life, Ebury Press (London, England), 1994.

What Can I Do to Help? 75 Practical Ideas for Family and Friends from Cancer's Frontline, Short Books (London, England), 2005.

SIDELIGHTS: When health writer Deborah Hutton was diagnosed with stage-four adenocarcinoma—advanced lung cancer—in November 2004, it came as a complete shock. Although Hutton had been a smoker in her twenties, she had quit long ago and had for many years followed a healthy lifestyle of careful diet and regular exercise. A winner of the *Vogue* writing contest in the 1980s, she had also become a health columnist for the magazine, and later, a freelancer who had published several books on food and exercise, including the popular *Vogue Complete Beauty.* Lung cancer has a high mortality rate, and Hutton knew her prospects were not good. She spent her remaining time campaigning in her native England for better funding for a disease that, though it causes twenty percent of all cancer deaths, only receives three percent of government cancer research funding. She also managed to publish a final book, *What Can I Do to Help? 75 Practical Ideas for Family and Friends from Cancer's Frontline.*

What Can I Do to Help? is a frank and honest guide aimed at the family and friends of those who are suffering from cancer. "The great strength of this anthology," reported Hugh Massingberd for the *Spectator,* "is that it gives clear and supremely practical guidance to the family and friends . . . who long to do something to help but don't know how to go about it." Hutton's advice includes telling readers that they should do all they can to maintain a sense of normalcy in the cancer patient's life, listen to what they have to say—even when it is a complaint that has been stated repeatedly—without offering judgment, refraining from asking "How are you?" all the time, and advis-

ing the person on how to treat his or her illness. One of Hutton's last acts was to designate that all royalties from her book should be donated to the Macmillan Cancer Relief fund.

BIOGRAPHICAL AND CRITICAL SOURCES:

PERIODICALS

Booklist, January 1, 1983, review of *Vogue Complete Beauty,* p. 592; April 15, 1985, review of *Vogue Complete Diet and Exercise,* p. 1147.
Kliatt, winter, 1985, review of *Vogue Beauty,* p. 42.
Library Journal, February 1, 1983, review of *Vogue Complete Beauty,* p. 206.
New Scientist, April 16, 1994, Gail Vines, review of *"Vogue" Futures: Beauty for Life,* p. 43.
Observer (London, England), November 14, 1982, review of *Vogue Complete Beauty,* p. 27.
Spectator, July 30, 2005, Hugh Massingberd, "Bring on the Colander Girls," review of *What Can I Do to Help? 75 Practical Ideas for Family and Friends from Cancer's Frontline,* p. 35.
Times Educational Supplement, December 23, 1988, Sarah Jane Evans, review of *The Parents Book: Getting On Well with Our Children,* p. 21.

OBITUARIES

PERIODICALS

Daily Telegraph (London, England), July 16, 2005.
Guardian (London, England), July 17, 2005.
Times (London, England), July 21, 2005, p. 61.*

* * *

HUTTON, Deborah Helen
  See HUTTON, Deborah

I-J

INDRIDASON, Arnaldur
See INDRIÐASON, Arnaldur

* * *

INDRIÐASON, Arnaldur 1961-
(Arnaldur Indridason)

PERSONAL: Born January 8, 1961, in Iceland; married; children: three. *Education:* University of Iceland, B.A., 1996.

ADDRESSES: Home—Reykjavik, Iceland. *Agent*—c/o Author Mail, St. Martin's Minotaur, Publicity Department, 175 5th Ave., New York, NY 10010.

CAREER: Journalist and writer. *Morgunblaðið,* Reykjavik, Iceland, journalist, 1981-82, film critic, 1986-2001.

AWARDS, HONORS: Glass Key Prize, Crime Writers of Scandinavia, 2002, for *Jar City,* and 2003, for *Silence of the Grave;* Golden Dagger, Crime Writers Association of Great Britain, 2005, for *Silence of the Grave.*

WRITINGS:

CRIME FICTION

Mýrin, Vaka-Helgafell (Reykjavik, Iceland), 2000, translated as *Jar City,* by Bernard Scudder, Harvill Press (London, England), 2004.

Grafarthogn, Vaka-Helgafell (Reykjavik, Iceland), 2001, translated as *Lady in Green,* St. Martin's Press (New York, NY), 2006.
Kleifarvatn (title means "The Lake"), Vaka-Helgafell (Reykjavik, Iceland), 2004.
Voices, Harvill Press (London, England), 2006.
Silence of the Grave, St. Martin's Minotaur (New York, NY), 2006.

Also author of other novels, including *Synir Duftsins* (title means "Sons of Earth"), 1997; *Daudarosir* (title means "Silent Kill"), 1998; *Napoléonskjölin* (title means "Operation Napoleon"), 1999; *Betty,* 2004; and *Vetrarborgin* (title means "Arctic Chill"), 2005.

SIDELIGHTS: Arnaldur Indriðason is one of Iceland's most successful crime fiction novelists. Shortly after finishing secondary school, he began working for *Morgunblaðið* newspaper in Reykjavik as a journalist and later as a film critic. He began writing full time shortly before the publication of his first internationally successful book, *Mýrin,* translated as *Jar City. Jar City* has been nominated for numerous international awards and won Britain's Golden Dagger award from the Crime Writers Association. *Jar City* takes place in Reykjavik and follows detective Erlendur Sveinnson's investigation of an elderly man's murder. While most murders in Iceland are purportedly easily solved, this particular case draws connections across the entire community, where most people are associated to each other in some manner.

Many reviews of *Jar City* were favorable. *Booklist* reviewer Bill Ott called it a "powerful, psychologically acute procedural drama," while a critic in *Kirkus*

Reviews felt it was "a model puzzle presented with clarity and crisp economy." Rex E. Klett, reviewing the book for *Library Journal,* stated that the book "captures the reader's attention with its direct prose and depiction of a distinctive culture." This distinct culture also received mention in Kara Kellar Bell's review on the *Laura Hird* Web site. "This is a culture which is both familiar and a little different, and that ought to appeal to the less adventurous readers of police procedurals who might otherwise be reluctant to read foreign language translation out of a fear of massive culture shock." Bell concluded: "*Jar City* is an entertaining book that moves along very fast . . . [that] favours dialogue and pace over description or long introverted passages."

BIOGRAPHICAL AND CRITICAL SOURCES:

PERIODICALS

Booklist, October 15, 2005, Bill Ott, review of *Jar City,* p. 32.
Guardian (Manchester, England), November 10, 2005, John Ezard, review of "Icelandic Author Wins Crime Writing Prize."
Kirkus Reviews, August 15, 2005, review of *Jar City,* p. 885.
Library Journal, October 1, 2005, Rex E. Klett, review of *Jar City,* p. 62.
M2 Best Books, November 10, 2005, "Winner of the Golden Dagger Award Announced."
Publishers Weekly, September 5, 2005, review of *Jar City,* p. 35.
Shots, May, 2005, L.J. Hurst, review of *Silence of the Grave.*

ONLINE

Bokmenntir, http://www.bokmenntir.is/ (April 14, 2006), author profile.
Fantastic Fiction, http://www.fantasticfiction.co.uk/ (April 14, 2006), author profile.
Laura Hird Web site, http://www.laurahird.com/ (April 14, 2006), Kara Kellar Bell, review of *Jar City.**

*   *   *

JACOBS, Joanne 1952-

PERSONAL: Born March 31, 1952, in Chicago, IL; daughter of Alan Joseph and Phyllis (Leaf) Jacobs; married Colin Bowman Hunter, June 18, 1977 (divorced, 1985); children: Allison Sarah. *Education:*

Stanford University, B.A., 1974. *Hobbies and other interests:* Charter school volunteer.

ADDRESSES: Agent—c/o Author Mail, Palgrave Macmillan, 175 5th Ave., New York, NY 10010. *E-mail*—Joanne@joannejacobs.com; joanne@readjacobs.com.

CAREER: Journalist and freelance writer. Suburban Newspapers, Cupertino, CA, copy editor and reporter, 1974-76; Super 8 Filmmaker, San Francisco, CA, associate editor, 1976-78; *San Jose Mercury News,* San Jose, CA, copywriter, 1978-80, editorial writer, 1980-84, columnist and editorial writer, 1984-2001. Also has been a Michigan Journalism Fellow, 1991-92; Casey Fellow, 1994; and a media fellow at the Hoover Institution at Stanford University and at the Pacific Research Institute for Public Policy, San Francisco. Member of board of directors, Women's Freedom Network, Washington, DC, 1993.

AWARDS, HONORS: Casey Medal, for column "Making Welfare Work," 1999.

WRITINGS:

Our School: The Inspiring Story of Two Teachers, One Big Idea, and the School That Beat the Odds, Palgrave Macmillan (New York, NY), 2005.

SIDELIGHTS: Joanne Jacobs wrote for the *San Jose Mercury News* for over fifteen years, primarily covering education topics, before leaving to pursue a freelance career. In 2001 she began volunteering at Downtown College Prep, a charter school of 102 ninth-grade students in San Jose, California, to get first-hand experience on the workings and culture of charter schools. Made up primarily of low-income Mexican-American students, the school's purpose is to prepare these students for college despite the prevailing influence of local gangs.

Many reviewers of *Our School: The Inspiring Story of Two Teachers, One Big Idea, and the School That Beat the Odds* commented that the concept of the book provides interesting insight into this alternative education system. A reviewer for *Kirkus Reviews,* for one, called the reporting "balanced" and "persuasive." Curt Schleier, writing in the *Journal Sentinel,* similarly stated that the writing is balanced, but he added that the book is "written and researched too early," leaving several questions "unanswered" and "unasked." With "some useful data," commented a reviewer for *Publishers Weekly, Our School* is a "fascinating case study." Overall, *Booklist* contributor Deborah Donovan lauded how "Jacobs vividly portrays everyday life at the school . . . [in this] remarkable story."

BIOGRAPHICAL AND CRITICAL SOURCES:

PERIODICALS

Booklist, December 1, 2005, Deborah Donovan, review of *Our School: The Inspiring Story of Two Teachers, One Big Idea, and the School That Beat the Odds,* p. 10.

Journal Sentinel, December 10, 2005, Curt Schleier, review of *Our School.*

Kirkus Reviews, October 1, 2005, review of *Our School,* p. 1063.

Publishers Weekly, October 3, 2005, review of *Our School,* p. 61.

ONLINE

Joanne Jacobs Home Page, http://www.joannejacobs. com (December 15, 2005).

TCS Daily Online, http://www.techcentralstation.com/ (December 15, 2005), brief biography of Joanne Jacobs.*

*   *   *

JACOBS, Laura

PERSONAL: Married James Wolcott (a journalist and editor).

ADDRESSES: Home—Manhattan, NY. *Agent*—c/o Author Mail, Viking Publicity, 375 Hudson St., New York, NY 10014.

CAREER: Journalist and author. Dance critic for *New Criterion;* contributing editor, *Vanity Fair.*

WRITINGS:

Barbie: What a Doll!, Artabras (New York, NY), 1994, 2nd edition, 1999.

Barbie: In Fashion, 2nd edition, Abbeville Press (New York, NY), 1994, revised edition published as *Barbie: Four Decades in Fashion,* 1998.

(Author of text) Victor Skrebneski, *The Art of Haute Couture,* Abbeville Press (New York, NY), 1995.

Beauty and the Beene: A Modern Legend, illustrated by Sirichai, Abrams (New York, NY), 1999.

Women about Town (novel), Viking (New York, NY), 2002.

(With Geoffrey Beene, Marylou Luther, and Pamela A. Parmal) *Beene by Beene,* introduction by James Wolcott, Vendome Press (New York, NY), 2005.

Contributor to periodicals, including the *Atlantic Monthly, New Republic, Chicago Reader, Village Voice,* and *Boston Phoenix.*

WORK IN PROGRESS: A novel featuring one of the characters from *Women about Town.*

SIDELIGHTS: A contributing editor to *Vanity Fair* who also writes dance criticism for the *New Criterion,* Laura Jacobs is knowledgeable about the art and fashion world of New York City. She drew on this background to write her first novel, *Women about Town,* which tells of two career women trying to balance their work and social lives in the Big Apple. Forty-year-old Iris Biddle is a divorced designer of high-end lampshades that sell for thousands of dollars, while Lana Burton is thirty-four and writes about dance for a magazine. Jacobs parallels their stories in alternating chapters and has the two characters come together only near the end of her novel. What could have degenerated into a gossipy, shallow tale of glamorous socialites, however, turns into what Beth Warrell called in *Booklist* an "insightful look at the lives of today's career woman." While a *Kirkus Reviews* critic did label the novel "superficial," many other reviewers had much higher praise for Jacobs's debut. A *Publishers Weekly* writer insisted that the author "effectively avoids cliché by treating Iris and Lana with gravity and respect," and *People* critic Joyce Cohen wrote that Jacobs "writes with intelligence, grace and an utterly female sensibility."

BIOGRAPHICAL AND CRITICAL SOURCES:

PERIODICALS

Booklist, April 15, 2002, Beth Warrell, review of *Women about Town,* p. 1382.

Book World, May 19, 2002, review of *Women about Town,* p. 4.

Kirkus Reviews, March 15, 2002, review of *Women about Town,* p. 359.

People, July 8, 2002, Joyce Cohen, "Pages," review of *Women about Town,* p. 35.

Publishers Weekly, April 22, 2002, review of *Women about Town,* p. 47; October 10, 2005, review of *Beene by Beene,* p. 52.

Tribune Books (Chicago, IL), May 18, 2003, review of *Women about Town,* p. 7.*

*　　*　　*

JEFFERSON, Margo 1947-

PERSONAL: Born October 17, 1947, in Chicago, IL; daughter of Ron (a doctor) and Irma (a teacher and social worker) Jefferson. *Education:* Brandeis University, B.A., 1968; Columbia University, M.S.

ADDRESSES: Agent—c/o Author Mail, Pantheon Books, 1745 Broadway, New York, NY 10019.

CAREER: Journalist. *Newsweek,* New York, NY, associate editor, 1973-78; New York University, New York, NY, assistant professor, 1979-83, 1989-91; *Vogue,* New York, NY, contributing editor, 1984-89; *7 Days,* contributing editor, 1988-89; Columbia University, New York, NY, lecturer, then assistant professor, 1991; *New York Times,* New York, NY, critic, 1993—. Also visiting lecturer at New School for Social Research, New York, NY.

AWARDS, HONORS: Pulitzer Prize, 1995; Alumni Achievement Award, Brandeis University, 1995.

WRITINGS:

On Michael Jackson, Pantheon Books (New York, NY), 2006.

Contributor to periodicals, including *Nation, Vogue, Grand Street, Village Voice, American Theatre, Dance Ink, Ms., New York Times Book Review, Soho Weekly News, Lear's, Alt, Denmark, NRC Handelsblad* and *Harper's Magazine.*

SIDELIGHTS: Margo Jefferson is a Pulitzer Prize-winning critic for the *New York Times.* Gaining experience with various periodicals and lecturing positions at Columbia University and New York University, Jefferson began working on staff with the *New York Times* in 1993 as a culture critic and later as a theater critic. After winning her Pulitzer, she became critic-at-large for the paper while contributing to a number of other publications, including the *Nation* and *Village Voice.* With her wide-ranging experience, it was only natural for Jefferson to cover Michael Jackson and the highly publicized events surrounding his life. In 2006, she published *On Michael Jackson,* with topics ranging from the psychology of his celebrity upbringing to his fascination with P.T. Barnum's circus and through his child molestation court case.

Critics who reviewed *On Michael Jackson* had mostly positive comments about the book. A reviewer for *Essence* called the "evenhanded portrait . . . piercingly honest" and "flawlessly written." Despite the familiarity the average television viewer has with the life and scandals of Michael Jackson, several critics noted that Jefferson does not simply summarize what has already been reported and published. Robert Morast, writing in the *Library Journal,* commented that Jefferson's "book manages to be almost as fresh as it is entertaining." Francine Prose had a similar viewpoint in her review of *On Michael Jackson* in *O, the Oprah Magazine.* She went even further in her praise by adding that "watching Margo Jefferson's mind at work is as pleasurable and thrilling as seeing Michael Jackson dance."

BIOGRAPHICAL AND CRITICAL SOURCES:

BOOKS

Notable Black American Women, Thomson Gale (Detroit, MI), 2002.

PERIODICALS

Booklist, November 15, 2005, Ray Olson, review of *On Michael Jackson,* p. 4.

Detroit Free Press, January 23, 2006, Marta Salij, "Never Can Say Goodbye"; January 25, 2006, "Margo Jefferson Bio."

Ebony, January, 2006, review of *On Michael Jackson,* p. 28.

Essence, February, 2006, review of *On Michael Jackson,* p. 95.

Hollywood Reporter, January 17, 2006, Gregory Mc-Namee, review of *On Michael Jackson,* p. 23.

Houston Chronicle, March 3, 2006, Roger Catlin, "Michael Jackson after the Hits."

Kirkus Reviews, November 15, 2005, review of *On Michael Jackson,* p. 1222.

Library Journal, December 1, 2005, Robert Morast, review of *On Michael Jackson,* p. 132.

O, the Oprah Magazine, January, 2006, Francine Prose, review of *On Michael Jackson,* p. 87.

Playbill, July 29, 2004, Robert Simonson, "Margo Jefferson Out."

Publishers Weekly, November 28, 2005, review of *On Michael Jackson,* p. 41.

ONLINE

New School for Social Research Web site, http://www.newschool.edu/ (April 15, 2006), profile of Jefferson.

New York Writer's Institute Web site, http://www.albany.edu/writers-inst/ (April 15, 2006), profile of Jefferson.

Public Broadcast Service, http://www.pbs.org/ (April 15, 2006), profile of Jefferson.*

* * *

JEUNET, Jean-Pierre 1955-

PERSONAL: Born September 3, 1955, in Roanne, Loire, France; married Liza Sullivan. *Education:* Studied animation at Cinémation Studios.

ADDRESSES: Agent—Bertrand de Labey, Artmédia, 20, avenue Rapp, 75007 Paris, France.

CAREER: Film writer and director. Codirector of numerous films with Marc Caro, including the animated shorts *L'Évasion,* 1978, and *Le Manège,* 1980; director of feature film *Alien: Resurrection,* 1997. Also director of various television commercials, for products such as Lactel and Malabar, and music videos, including Etienne Daho's *Tombe pour la France.* Cannes Film Festival, "Courts-métrages" (shorts) jury member and Grand Jury member, 1998; Cinéfondation (provides funds for young directors), head.

AWARDS, HONORS: Best Director and Prize of the Catalan Screenwriter's Critic and Writer's Association, Catalonian International Film Festival, 1991, Best Film not in the English Language nomination, Film Awards, British Academy of Film and Television Arts (BAFTA), 1993, all for *Delicatessen;* Golden Palm nomination, Cannes Film Festival, 1995, for *La Cité des enfants perdus;* Audience Award, Canberra International Film Festival, People's Choice award, Toronto International Film Festival, and Berlin European Film Award, all 2001, all for *Le Fabuleux destin d'Amélie Poulain;* César Award for best picture and best director, Académie des Arts et Techniques du Cinema, Best Screenplay—Original, Film Awards, BAFTA, Best Foreign Feature Film, Amanda Awards (Norway), Academy Award nomination for best original screenplay, Academy of Motion Picture Arts and Sciences, Discover Screenwriting award nomination, American Screenwriters Association, Best Film not in the English Language nomination, Film Awards, BAFTA, and David Lean Award for Direction nomination, BAFTA, all 2002, all for *Le fabuleux destin d'Amélie Poulain;* International Achievement in Filmmaking Award, ShoWest, 2002; Best Film not in the English Language nomination, Film Awards, BAFTA, César Award nominations for best picture, best screenplay and best director, Académie des Arts et Techniques du Cinema, all 2005, for *Un long dimanche de fiançailles;* named member of the Legion d'Honneur, France, 2006.

WRITINGS:

SCREENPLAYS

(With Gilles Adrien and Marc Caro; also actor and co-director, editor, cinematographer, set decorator and costume designer, all with Marc Caro) *Le bunker de la dernière rafale* (released in America as *The Bunker of the Last Gunshots*), Zootrope, 1981.

(And director) *Pas de repos pour Billy Brakko* (animated short film), 1984.

(With Bruno Delbonnel; also director and editor) *Foutaises* (short film; released in United Kingdom as *Things I Like, Things I Don't Like*), Zootrope, 1989.

(With Guillaume Laurant; and director) *Le Fabuleux destin d'Amélie Poulain* (released in America as *Amélie*), Victoires Productions, 2001.

(With Guillaume Laurant; and director) *Un long dimanche de fiançailles* (released in America as *A Very Long Engagement*), Warner Brothers, 2004.

SCREENPLAYS; WITH MARC CARO AND GILLES ADRIEN

(And director, with Marc Caro) *Delicatessen,* Victoires Productions, 1991; Miramax, 1992.

(And director, with Marc Caro) *La Cité des enfants perdus* (released in America as *The City of Lost Children*), Victoires Productions, 1995.

Contributor to *Fluide Glacial.*

WORK IN PROGRESS: A film adaptation of Yann Martel's *Life of Pi,* for Fox 2000 Pictures, expected 2007.

SIDELIGHTS: Jean-Pierre Jeunet is one of those rare screenwriters who also directs all of his own works to ensure his original vision is not tampered with. Beginning his film-making career by collaborating with Marc Caro on short films, both animated and live action, Jeunet ventured into feature film with 1991's *Delicatessen.* Written with Caro and Gilles Adrien, *Delicatessen* is a black comedy set in a post-apocalyptic world where hunger is the norm. In a run-down apartment building perched atop the remains of a deli, a myriad of strange characters—including a woman constantly dreaming up new, unsuccessful ways to kill herself and a man cohabiting with assorted amphibians—lead dreary lives. Perhaps the strangest of these tenants is the deli's butcher, who feels that it is his job to keep his neighbors as well-fed as possible. To this end, he finds a new source of meat—newcomers to the building are ultimately killed and served to the longtime residents. This seems to work out well for all except the victims, until a good-hearted clown moves in and attempts to win the heart of the butcher's daughter. *People* contributor Joanne Kaufman found the movie "hilarious," and noted "an undeniable sweetness," despite the fact that the film "occasionally gets mired in metaphor and symbolism." Georgia Harbison, writing in *Time,* was far more laudatory. The film "can be lots of fun," she

commented. Harbison concluded: "Part circus, part zoo, the film's milieu is a nice metaphor for the rudderless morals of post-Everything Europe."

The 1995 release of another Jeunet-Caro joint effort, *La Cité des enfants perdus,* was also released in the United States as *The City of Lost Children.* The film is purportedly a children's movie, despite the "R" rating it was given in America. The action moves between a dystopian city and an oil rig long unused for its original purpose. Though there are subplots involving bizarre characters, such as a set of twins so close they finish each other's actions, and a former circus owner whose trained fleas assist him in controlling the minds of others, the main focus of the story involves a madman, Krank, created by a scientist and living on the oil rig with six clones of that scientist, as well as a midget and a talking brain in a jar. Krank was created without the ability to dream, and he sends out minions to kidnap small children so he can transfer their dreams to himself, through the use of a sinister-looking machine. When the little brother of a carnival strongman named One is taken by Krank's thugs, One goes on a search-and-rescue mission, enlisting the aid of street urchin Miette along the way. Stephen Holden, in a *New York Times* review of the film, observed that the movie "carries little allegorical resonance. While its story seems to warn about the loss of imagination in an overly technologized world, it is too disjointed to carry much weight." *Los Angeles Times* writer Kevin Thomas disagreed, noting that "*The City of Lost Children* is a stunningly surreal fantasy, a fable of longing and danger, of heroic deeds and bravery, set in a brilliantly realized world of its own." Thomas stated: "It is one of the most audacious, original films of the year."

After taking a break from writing to direct *Alien: Resurrection* in America, Jeunet returned to France to resume making his own movies, this time with cowriter Guillaume Laurant. *Le Fabuleux destin d'Amélie Poulain,* released as simply *Amélie* in the United States, is Jeunet's most acclaimed effort to date, earning the adulation of critics and the viewing public alike. The story, which *French Politics, Culture and Society* contributor Sylvie Waskiewicz considered "a poetic love story with comic touches" and a "hip antidote to the recent trend towards gritty realism," centers around Amélie Poulain, an unusual young woman whose life story, along with her strange list of likes and dislikes, is shared with the viewer as the film opens. The discovery of a small, long-forgotten box hidden inside her apartment's walls sends Amélie on a journey to find the owner of the box and, subsequently, attempt to improve the lives of others with small, anonymous gestures. Along the way she discovers joy—and ultimately love—for herself. *Variety* contributor Lisa Nesselson found *Amélie* "fresh, funny, [and] exquisitely bittersweet," noting that "the beauty of the film's mechanism . . . is that every poignant or silly little detail contributes to the story." Rex Roberts, in an *Insight on the News* review, called the movie "a thoroughly amusing entertainment that transcends its genre," and stated that "the wit with which the writers have woven together the subplots, all illustrating the timeless truths of hope, faith and charity, is rare in cinema."

Jeunet and Laurant once again collaborated to write 2004's *Un long dimanche de fiançailles*, released in the United States as *A Very Long Engagement*. The film was embroiled in controversy over its funding. Because the film was produced in part by a French subsidiary of Warner Brothers, many decried the additional use of grant money meant strictly for French film-making. *Variety* writer Nesselson, however, commented that "financing is—or should be—beside the point, for the result is French to the tips of its widescreen celluloid toes." *A Very Long Engagement* follows the tale of Mathilde and Manech, young lovers separated when Manech leaves to fight in World War I. Manech attempts self-mutilation to get excused from duty, leading to a court martial and sentence of death. He is led to the 'no man's land' between the French and German lines and left for dead. Mathilde, however, believes that if he had truly died, she would know. When the war ends, she hires a detective to find out exactly what happened to Manech, also doing some investigating on her own. While Bruce Handy, writing in a *Vanity Fair* review, noted that the film "is less concerned with combat than it is with the perseverance of true love against awful odds," Nesselson disagreed, observing that it is a "love story with haunting digressions into misfortune, but in its portrait of the trenches and the consequences of soul-searing combat, [the] result is as antiwar as Kubrick's *Paths of Glory*."

BIOGRAPHICAL AND CRITICAL SOURCES:

PERIODICALS

Entertainment Weekly, June 5, 1992, Owen Gleiberman, review of *Delicatessen*, p. 39; July 26, 1996,

Nisid Hajari, review of *The City of Lost Children*, p. 62; November 9, 2001, Lisa Schwarzbaum, "The It Fille: A French Beauty Brings Joy to Those around Her in *Amélie*," p. 83.

Film Journal International, November, 2001, Harry Haun, "Fantasy in Paris: Jean-Pierre Jeunet Delights Audiences with Tale of Amélie," p. 14.

French Politics, Culture and Society, spring, 2002, Sylvie Waskiewicz, review of *Le Fabuleux destin d'Amélie Poulain*, p. 152.

Guardian (London, England), May 18, 1995, Derek Malcolm, review of *The City of Lost Children*, p. 2.

Insight on the News, November 19, 2001, Rex Roberts, review of *Amélie*, p. 29.

Los Angeles Times, December 22, 1995, Kevin Thomas, review of *The City of Lost Children*, p. 8.

Nation, November 12, 2001, B. Ruby Rich, review of *Amélie*, p. 44.

New Statesman, October 1, 2001, Philip Kerr, review of *Amélie*, p. 66.

New York Times, December 15, 1995, Stephen Holden, review of *The City of Lost Children*, p. C34.

People, June 22, 1992, Joanne Kaufman, review of *Delicatessen*, p. 21; December 13, 2004, review of *A Very Long Engagement*, p. 31.

Time, March 20, 1992, Georgia Harbison, review of *Delicatessen*, p. 14; November 12, 2001, review of *Amélie*, p. 93; November 29, 2004, Richard Corliss, review of *A Very Long Engagement*, p. 148.

Time International, May 21, 2001, Bruce Crumley, review of *Le Fabuleux destin d'Amélie Poulain*, p. 71.

Vanity Fair, December, 2004, Bruce Handy, review of *A Very Long Engagement*, p. 150.

Variety, April 30, 2001, Lisa Nesselson, review of *Le Fabuleux destin d'Amélie Poulain*, p. 26; November 1, 2004, Lisa Nesselson, review of *A Very Long Engagement*, p. 27.

ONLINE

International Movie Database, http://www.imdb.com/ (February 28, 2006), biography of Jean-Pierre Jeunet.

Jean-Pierre Jeunet Home Page, http://jpjeunetlesite.online.fr (February 28, 2006).*

JOHANSSON, M. Jane 1963-

PERSONAL: Born January 19, 1963, in Shawnee, OK; daughter of Lloyd Jack (a pharmacist) and Belle (a pharmacist; maiden name, Standifer) Harris; married David H. Johansson (a public library director), June 3, 1989. *Ethnicity:* "Caucasian." *Education:* Oklahoma Baptist University, B.A., 1985; University of North Texas, M.S., 1987, Ph.D., 1993. *Politics:* Democrat. *Religion:* United Methodist. *Hobbies and other interests:* Music, travel, astronomy.

ADDRESSES: Office—Department of Social and Behavioral Sciences, Rogers State University, 421 South Elliott, Pryor, OK 74361. *E-mail*—jjohansson@ rsu.edu.

CAREER: Tarrant County Junior College, Fort Worth, TX, adjunct instructor in history, 1993-94; Rogers State University, Pryor, OK, adjunct instructor in history, 1994-97; Northeastern State University, Tahlequah, OK, adjunct instructor in history, 1997-2000; Rogers State University, adjunct instructor, 2000-01, assistant professor of history, 2001—. Pryor Area Arts and Humanities Council, humanities project director, 1995-2001; Friends of the Pryor Public Library, secretary, 1996-99, 2001-2005.

MEMBER: Organization of American Historians, Southern Historical Association, Oklahoma Historical Society, Texas State Historical Association, P.E.O. (GL chapter; president, 2000-02)

AWARDS, HONORS: Ottis Lock Endowment Award, best book of the year on East Texas, East Texas Historical Association, 1999, for *Peculiar Honor: A History of the 28th Texas Cavalry, 1862-1865.*

WRITINGS:

Peculiar Honor: A History of the 28th Texas Cavalry, 1862-1865, University of Arkansas Press (Fayetteville, AR), 1998.

(Editor) *Widows by the Thousand: The Civil War Letters of Theophilus and Harriet Perry, 1862-1864,* University of Arkansas Press (Fayetteville, AR), 2000.

Contributor to periodicals, including *Military History of the West, Civil War Regiments, Civil War History, Military History of the West,* and *Southwestern Historical Quarterly.*

WORK IN PROGRESS: Coeditor of *The Papers of Will Rogers,* Volumes 4-5, for University of Oklahoma Press (Norman, OK); research on the Adams-Gibson Louisiana brigade during the American Civil War.

SIDELIGHTS: M. Jane Johansson told *CA:* "Since I was about ten years old, the American Civil War has fascinated me. The fact that several of my ancestors served in the Civil War enthralled me, and beginning at a young age I read many books about the war.

"The books that interested me the most were volumes about specific units during the war and books by or about common soldiers. Bruce Catton's gracefully written trilogy about the Army of the Potomac (*Mr. Lincoln's Army, Glory Road,* and *A Stillness at Appomattox*) and John J. Pullen's *The 20th Maine* influenced me considerably. Reading about unit 'personalities' and unit actions during the war were of utmost interest. In addition, books about the common soldiers of the war were instructive, particularly Bell Irvin Wiley's *The Life of Billy Yank* and *The Life of Johnny Reb.* Although I enjoy many different kinds of Civil War books, I am most attracted to those that deal with units or individuals because one can then understand the impact of the war on a personal level. In my writing about the war, I like to work on topics that deal with a smaller and more personal world.

"With the guidance of my major advisor, Dr. Richard Lowe at the University of North Texas, I selected my dissertation topic (a history of the 28th Texas Cavalry). This topic combined two major interests: an interest in unit histories and a growing interest in the history of Confederate soldiers in the Trans-Mississippi Confederacy. Although older unit histories influenced me in regard to organization and major topics, a newer wave of unit histories greatly influenced me. Contemporary historians have mined census records, tax records, and service records to find out more about the kinds of men who went to war. In my case, Douglas Hale's *The 3rd Texas Cavalry in the Civil War* not only provided data for comparison purposes, but also provided guidance on research ideas.

"In the late 1990s, I began working on a spin-off project. In writing *Peculiar Honor: A History of the 28th Texas Cavalry, 1862-1865,* I utilized an important source, the correspondence of Captain Theophilus Perry and his wife, Harriet. Captain Perry served in the 28th Texas Cavalry and was mortally wounded at the battle of Pleasant Hill in Louisiana in April, 1864. The Perrys suffered many tragedies during the war, and their letters show the impact of the war on one southern family. As I deciphered and transcribed their letters, for the first time I became interested in the topic of women during the war. Two books that were of particular use in regard to background material were Drew Gilpin Faust's *Mothers of Invention: Women of the Slaveholding South in the American Civil War* and Sally G. McMillan's *Motherhood in the Old South: Pregnancy, Childbirth, and Infant Rearing.* The process of adding identifications of people, places, and events was a time-consuming but rewarding project."

BIOGRAPHICAL AND CRITICAL SOURCES:

PERIODICALS

Civil War History, March, 2003, Frances S. Pollard, review of *Widows by the Thousand: The Civil War Letters of Theophilus and Harriet Perry, 1862-1864,* p. 87.
Journal of Southern History, August, 2002, Betsy Glade, review of *Widows by the Thousand,* p. 706.

* * *

JOHNSON, Adam 1967-

PERSONAL: Born July 12, 1967, in SD; married Stephanie Harrell, 2000; children: James Geronimo, Jupiter. *Education:* Arizona State University, B.A., 1992; McNeese State University, M.A., M.F.A., 1996; Florida State University, Ph.D., 2001.

ADDRESSES: Home—San Francisco, CA. *Office*—English Department, Stanford University, Stanford, CA 94305. *E-mail*—adamjohn@stanford.edu.

CAREER: Educator and author. Stanford University, Stanford, CA, Jones Lecturer in creative writing and fiction, 2001—.

AWARDS, HONORS: Wallace Stegner Fellowship, Stanford University, 2001; California Book Award, 2003, for *Parasites Like Us.*

WRITINGS:

Emporium (short stories), Viking (New York, NY), 2002.
Parasites Like Us (novel), Viking (New York, NY), 2003.

Also contributor of short stories to numerous publications, including *Paris Review, Esquire,* and *Harper's.*

WORK IN PROGRESS: A novel set in contemporary Los Angeles.

SIDELIGHTS: In an interview for *Barnes & Noble. com,* author Adam Johnson admitted that he began writing creatively "by mistake." While attempting to sign up for a poetry course during college, he accidentally enrolled in a fiction class. "Immediately I knew writing was for me—suddenly my penchant for daydreaming, exaggerating, and lying all became useful and constructive, and I never looked back." Since then, Johnson has earned his Ph.D. from Florida State University, landed a lectureship in creative writing and fiction at Stanford University, and has begun publishing his fiction.

Among the stories in Johnson's first effort, *Emporium,* are "Trauma Plate," featuring the owners of a mom-and-pop bullet-proof vest rental shop; "Your Own Backyard," a story about a police officer turned zoo security guard who begins to notice his son's disturbing obsession with guns and desensitization to violence; and "Teen Sniper," which focuses on a fifteen-year-old sniper whose job is to shoot and kill disgruntled corporate employees. A reviewer for the *New Yorker* noted that the stories in *Emporium* capture "the loneliness of youth, the failure of parents, and the yearning for connection." A *Publishers Weekly* contributor commented, "Each of these unusual, skillful stories exhibits a fierce talent, showcasing Johnson's quirky humor and slicing insight." *Booklist* reviewer James O'Laughlin determined that "Johnson's is a distinctive new fictional sensibility," and a *Kirkus Reviews* critic observed that "Johnson's unique premises, hybrids of realism and allegory, blends of pedestrian, pop, and the bizarre, create unnerving moods."

Johnson followed *Emporium* with his first novel, *Parasites Like Us,* in which, according to a *Publishers Weekly* reviewer, "an archeological find sets off an apocalyptic epidemic." The book features archeology professor Hank Hannah and his two graduate students, Trudy and Eggers, who discover an ancient burial site of the prehistoric Clovis people and unwittingly release a deadly plague on the world. Writing for the *Magazine of Fantasy and Science Fiction,* Elizabeth Hand termed Johnson's work "the novelistic equivalent of a long drunken whacked-out binge with your closest, smartest, craziest friend." Michele Leber, writing in *Booklist,* depicted *Parasites Like Us* as a "weird but masterfully written debut novel" full of "inventiveness, black humor, and penetrating insight."

In his interview with *Barnes & Noble.com,* Johnson offered this advice to aspiring writers: "Find a mentor. . . . They have a lot to teach and share if you're willing to seek them out. Be humble, think of writing as a lifelong process of learning, and your audience will come."

BIOGRAPHICAL AND CRITICAL SOURCES:

PERIODICALS

Book, May-June, 2002, Kevin Greenberg, review of *Emporium,* p. 84; September-October, 2003, Kevin Greenberg, review of *Parasites Like Us,* p. 91.

Booklist, March 15, 2002, James O'Laughlin, review of *Emporium,* p. 1212; August, 2003, Michele Leber, review of *Parasites Like Us,* p. 1953.

Esquire, September, 2003, "Two More Books for Your Shelf," review of *Parasites Like Us,* p. 66.

Kirkus Reviews, February 1, 2002, review of *Emporium,* p. 127; June 15, 2003, review of *Parasites Like Us,* p. 826.

Magazine of Fantasy and Science Fiction, March, 2004, Elizabeth Hand, review of *Parasites Like Us,* p. 34.

New Yorker, April 22, 2002, "Briefly Noted," review of *Emporium,* p. 201.

Publishers Weekly, February 11, 2002, review of *Emporium,* p. 158; June 23, 2003, review of *Parasites Like Us,* p. 44.

ONLINE

Barnes & Noble.com, http://www.barnesandnoble. com/ (January 10, 2006), "Meet the Writers: Adam Johnson."

KQED Web site, http://www.kqed.org/ (January 10, 2006), "The Writers' Block: Adam Johnson."

Stanford Daily/Intermission, http://daily.stanford.edu/ (November 14, 2003), Anthony Ha, "*Intermission* Interviews Adam Johnson: Johnson Discusses His First Novel *Parasites Like Us.*"

Stanford University Web site, http://www.stanford.edu/ (January 10, 2006), "English Department Faculty."*

*   *   *

JOHNSON, Stephen P. 1952-

PERSONAL: Born 1952. *Education:* University of Houston, B.A., 1976.

ADDRESSES: Agent—c/o Author Mail, Wiley Books, 111 River St., Hoboken, NJ 07030-5774.

CAREER: Journalist. *Houston Chronicle,* Houston, TX, staff member, 1979—.

WRITINGS:

The Complete Idiot's Guide to Sunken Ships and Treasures, Alpha Books (New York, NY), 2000.

(With Roberto T. Leon) *Encyclopedia of Bridges and Tunnels,* Checkmark Books (New York, NY), 2002.

Silent Steel: The Mysterious Death of the Nuclear Attack Sub USS Scorpion, Wiley Books (Hoboken, NJ), 2006.

SIDELIGHTS: Stephen P. Johnson is a longtime journalist with the *Houston Chronicle* who has written several books about highly technical subjects.

Johnson's 2002 publication, *Encyclopedia of Bridges and Tunnels,* was written with Dr. Roberto T. Leon. This work covers the vast array of technologies, circumstances, and people involved in the creation and design of bridges and tunnels around the world. A *Booklist* contributor praised the accessibility of the work as the "reading level is not too technical and is appropriate for general readers." Dorothy F. Byers, writing in the *Reference and User Services Quarterly,* found that "it occupies the niche between elementary and highly technical readers" with its "jargon-free entries."

A series of articles Johnson wrote about the disappearance of the American nuclear submarine, the *USS Scorpion,* resulted in his 2006 publication, *Silent Steel: The Mysterious Death of the Nuclear Attack Sub USS Scorpion.* The *USS Scorpion* was lost mysteriously in the Atlantic in 1968. In his book, Johnson analyzes many possibilities in trying to uncover the ship's fate, including poor maintenance, torpedo malfunction, and a potential Soviet attack. Frieda Murray, writing in *Booklist,* called this account "very readable." A reviewer on the *Science a GoGo* Web site dubbed Johnson as the "expert on the disappearance of the *Scorpion*" and went on to call the book an "utterly riveting mystery choc-a-block full of well-researched technical specs and details." A critic for *Kirkus Reviews* called it an "engrossing documentation of haunting, grisly what-ifs."

BIOGRAPHICAL AND CRITICAL SOURCES:

PERIODICALS

Booklist, December 1, 2002, review of *Encyclopedia of Bridges and Tunnels,* p. 698; January 1, 2006, Frieda Murray, review of *Silent Steel: The Mysterious Death of the Nuclear Attack Sub USS Scorpion,* p. 34.

Kirkus Reviews, November 1, 2005, review of *Silent Steel,* p. 1172.

Publishers Weekly, October 31, 2005, review of *Silent Steel,* p. 45.

Reference and User Services Quarterly, spring, 2003, Dorothy F. Byers, review of *Encyclopedia of Bridges and Tunnels,* p. 264.

ONLINE

Science a GoGo Web site, http://www.scienceagogo. com/ (February 22, 2006), review of *Silent Steel.**

K

KAGANA, Ella Iurievena
See TRIOLET, Elsa

*   *   *

KANE, Larry 1942-
   (Lawrence Kanowitz)

PERSONAL: Born Lawrence Kanowitz, October 21, 1942, in Brooklyn, NY; married, May 24, 1970; wife's name Donna (business owner and executive); children: Alexandra, Michael.

ADDRESSES: Home—PA. *Agent*—c/o Author Mail, Running Press, 125 S. 22nd St., Philadelphia, PA 19103-4399. *E-mail*—info@larrykane.com.

CAREER: Broadcast journalist and writer. WQAM, broadcast journalist; WAME and WFUN, broadcast journalist; WFIL Radio, Philadelphia, PA, anchor, 1966; WFIL Radio sister television station (now WPVI), Philadelphia, general assignment reporter, 1966; WPVI, Philadelphia, *Action News* anchor, 1970; WABC-TV, New York, NY, *Eyewitness News* anchor, 1977-78; WCAU, Philadelphia, primary anchor; KYW-TV, Philadelphia, anchor, 1993-2002.

Dynamic Images Incorporated (mentoring service for reporters and anchors), co-owner (with wife, Donna); consultant to corporations and media companies, Larry Kane Consulting (part of Dynamic Images Incorporated); hosted *The Bulletin with Larry Kane,* KYW-TV; contributor of commentary to KYW News Radio 1060; host of *Larry Kane: Voice of Reason,* Comcast's CN8 channel, 2006; campaign chairman of the Delaware Valley Multiple Sclerosis Society.

AWARDS, HONORS: Emmy Award, Academy of Television Arts and Sciences; Governor's Award for Lifetime Achievement, Mid-Atlantic Emmy Organization; Alfred I. duPont-Columbia University Award, 1985, for news coverage of the confrontation between the extremist group MOVE and the Philadelphia Police force; Broadcast Pioneers of Philadelphia Hall of Fame induction, 1994; Diamond in the Rough Leadership Award, Temple University Young Alumni Association Award, 2000; Person of the Year award, Broadcast Pioneers of Philadelphia, 2002.

WRITINGS:

NONFICTION

Larry Kane's Philadelphia, foreword by Dan Rather, Temple University Press (Philadelphia, PA), 2000.
Ticket to Ride: Inside the Beatles' 1964 & 1965 Tours That Changed the World (with compact disc), Running Press (Philadelphia, PA), 2003.
Lennon Revealed (with digital video disc), Running Press (Philadelphia, PA), 2005.

SIDELIGHTS: Broadcast journalist Larry Kane is an Emmy-award winner with over four decades of experience in his field. Most of Kane's anchorage was based in Philadelphia, Pennsylvania, which is why he has been called "the dean of Philadelphia television news anchors." As an anchorman, he covered local news and interviewed several important figures. Kane's experiences to this effect are disclosed in his first book, *Larry Kane's Philadelphia.*

Kane is perhaps best known, however, as the only journalist to accompany the British band the Beatles for the entirety of their first North American tours in the mid-1960s. Thus his second book, *Ticket to Ride: Inside the Beatles' 1964 & 1965 Tours That Changed the World,* is a story that only Kane can tell. The book is also accompanied by a compact disc containing some of the interviews that Kane recorded with the band members during the tours. In his book, Kane, who was only twenty-one years old when he joined the Beatles tour, relates how fans attacked the band members in unprecedented frenzies and describes the band's interactions with celebrities and groupies alike. It is interesting to note that Kane's experiences on the tour led him to view the Beatles mostly as four regular boys. Although a *Kirkus Reviews* critic called the account "heartfelt," the critic also commented that it is "threadbare of fresh material." Based on the singular nature of Kane's perspective, however, most reviewers disagreed with this view. A *Publishers Weekly* contributor stated that *Ticket to Ride* is "one of the few books on the band written in the past decade that can be considered indispensable." The same reviewer also commented on the in-depth interviews that "Kane skillfully uses throughout" the book to portray the Beatles' views. Gordon Flagg, writing in *Booklist,* concluded that Kane provides "terrific fly-on-the-wall stuff about a unique pop-cultural event."

After publishing *Ticket to Ride* Kane continued to explore the Beatles by writing *Lennon Revealed,* which was released around the twenty-fifth anniversary of Beatles bandleader John Lennon's death. The book calls on Kane's recollections of the early tours as well as later interviews with Lennon's friends and family. Unfortunately, *Lennon Revealed* was not as critically successful as its predecessor. Flagg, writing again in *Booklist,* called the book an "affectionate but dear-eyed look at the musician's life." While *Library Journal* reviewer James E. Perone felt that Kane "does not necessarily 'reveal' anything" about Lennon that fans don't already know, he did state, on the other hand, that Kane "does strike a nice balance" between biographers who are overly positive or overly negative. Additionally, a *Publishers Weekly* reviewer

concluded that, while "there are certainly better books on Lennon, . . . readers should enjoy Kane's personal, honest recollections."

BIOGRAPHICAL AND CRITICAL SOURCES:

BOOKS

Kane, Larry, *Larry Kane's Philadelphia,* Temple University Press (Philadelphia, PA), 2000.
Kane, Larry, *Ticket to Ride: Inside the Beatles' 1964 & 1965 Tours That Changed the World,* Running Press (Philadelphia, PA), 2003.

PERIODICALS

America's Intelligence Wire, September 18, 2003, Miles O'Brien and Kyra Phillips, "Interview with Larry Kane."
Booklist, August, 2003, Gordon Flagg, review of *Ticket to Ride,* p. 1941; October 15, 2005, Gordon Flagg, review of *Lennon Revealed,* p. 19.
Kirkus Reviews, June 15, 2003, review of *Ticket to Ride,* p. 846.
Library Journal, September 15, 2005, James E. Perone, review of *Lennon Revealed,* p. 66.
Publishers Weekly, May 26, 2003, review of *Ticket to Ride,* p. 58; August 29, 2005, review of *Lennon Revealed,* p. 46.

ONLINE

Broadcast Pioneers of Philadelphia Web site, http://www.geocities.com/broadcastpioneers/ (March 21, 2006), author profile.
Greenman Review, http://www.greenmanreview.com/ (March 21, 2006), Gary Whitehouse, review of *Ticket to Ride.*
Larry Kane Consulting Web site, http://www.larrykane.com (March 21, 2006).
Lennon Revealed Web site, http://www.lennonrevealed.com (March 21, 2006).
PopMatters, http://www.popmatters.com/ (March 21, 2006), John Bergstrom, review of *Lennon Revealed.**

*   *   *

KANOWITZ, Lawrence
  See KANE, Larry

KAPLAN-MAXFIELD, Thomas 1952-

PERSONAL: Born October 17, 1952, in Chicopee, MA; son of Gerald and Julie (Rodoreda) Maxfield; married June 5, 1976; wife's name Ellen Kaplan (a web-designer). *Education:* Boston College, Ph.D. *Politics:* "Progressive"

ADDRESSES: Office—Boston College, Carney Hall 331, 140 Commonwealth Ave., Chestnut Hill, MA 02467. *Agent*—c/o Author Mail, Kepler Press, P.O. Box 400326, Cambridge, MA 02140. *E-mail*—thomas.kaplan-maxfield.1@bc.edu.

CAREER: Writer. Tufts University, Boston, MA, instructor; Boston College, Chestnut Hill, MA, instructor.

WRITINGS:

Memoirs of a Shape-Shifter (novel), Kepler Press (Cambridge, MA), 2005.

Contributor to periodicals, including *Poets and Writers.*

SIDELIGHTS: Thomas Kaplan-Maxfield published *Memoirs of a Shape-Shifter* in 2005. The contemporary gothic novel tells the story of Nikki Helmik, a forty-year-old woman who quits her law career and returns to her hometown of Gloucester, Massachusetts. In Gloucester she falls in love with the son of her childhood mentor, the cruel Rose Eveless, who is obsessed with the idea of eternal youth. Rose doesn't approve of the relationship but will allow it if Nikki promises to find the lost journal of Anne Cleves, a Druid magician who lived in colonial New England and was an ancestor of Nikki's. The novel alternates between Nikki's present-day narration and her ancestor's journal, which reveals just as much about Nikki as it does about its writer.

On the Web site *Curled Up with a Good Book,* Mayra Calvani noted that the dialogue in this study of the female psyche "flows naturally and sparkles with genuineness, and the author does an excellent job putting himself in the mind of the female protagonist." In addition, a contributor to the *Small Press Bookwatch* described the book as "entangled," and added that the story "does not let go until the final page."

On his home page, Kaplan-Maxfield credits writing with keeping him alive. In a welcoming message on the Web site, the writer tells a story of his fictional heart transplant, which included complications and a dream in which the donor told him he needed to write in order to stay alive. His stories, he reflected, are "all fundamentally about love; from the heart."

Kaplan-Maxfield told *CA:* "I became a writer in fifth grade, when I simultaneously discovered, via watching a movie called *The Cardinal,* that I did not want to become a priest, that I could enter the fictional world via writing, that that world felt like home to me, and when I kissed my first girl. Since then writing, 'truth' in some sense, and women have been entangled in my imagination.

"I was a friend of Lawrence Durrell for many years, and published an article about that friendship in *Poets and Writers* in 1993, after Mr. Durrell's death. He has been a major influence on my writing.

"What I've learned as a writer is perhaps not so much surprising as crucial: it's to ignore the voice that says 'this is awful' as well as 'this is great.' I consider both voices the same, essentially, and equally to be ignored. It is not the artist's job to judge the work, but rather to perform his job as well as he can. Having a favorite book seems like having a favorite child; in some way it would feel like a betrayal of the others. *Memoirs of a Shape-Shifter* is the book that's out there in the world right now and just getting going, and so it is taking my attention.

"I consider myself growing on the same tree as Thoreau, Henry Miller, Kerouac, Durrell and others who assumed a connection between life and art, between belief and action, fantasy and behavior. Thus I would like my work to immerse the reader in that sense— that always and everywhere art is life and life art. Because love is the activity where we most feel and see the connection between our feelings and our behaviors, I have had many 'heart transplants.' As I say in my readings for *Memoirs of a Shape-Shifter,* which is about the ancient art of shape-shifting, when one falls in love, one's shape is shifted by the other. One gives one's heart away and in a sense takes on another one. This is the way in which I intended the story of the heart transplant on my Web site, for it delineates most precisely my approach to life."

BIOGRAPHICAL AND CRITICAL SOURCES:

PERIODICALS

Small Press Bookwatch, September, 2005, review of *Memoirs of a Shape-Shifter.*

ONLINE

Curled Up with a Good Book, http://www.curledup.com/ (January 11, 2006), Mayra Calvani, review of *Memoirs of a Shape-Shifter.*

Kepler Press Web site, http://www.keplerpress.com/ (January 11, 2006), biography of Thomas Kaplan-Maxfield.

Thomas Kaplan-Maxfield Home Page, http://www.tkaplanmaxfield.com (January 11, 2006).

*   *   *

KAVENNA, Joanna

PERSONAL: Female. *Education:* Studied at Oxford University, University of Oslo, and Munich University.

ADDRESSES: Home—Duddon Valley, Cumbria, England. *Agent*—Anna Webber, PFD, Drury House, 34-43 Russell St., London WC2B 5HA, England. *E-mail*—jk@joannakavenna.com.

CAREER: Writer. Held writing fellowships at St. Antony's College, Oxford, England, and St. John's College, Cambridge, England.

WRITINGS:

The Ice Museum: In Search of the Lost Land of Thule, Viking (London, England), 2005.

Contributor to *London Review of Books, Guardian, Observer, Times Literary Supplement, Spectator, Telegraph,* and the *International Herald Tribune.*

WORK IN PROGRESS: Inglorious, "a novel about the slow disintegration of a perfectly functioning mind, set against the backdrop of a disconcerting London," for Faber & Faber.

SIDELIGHTS: Author Joanna Kavenna was intrigued by the story of a mythical northern land called Thule, first sighted by the Greek explorer Pytheas in the fourth century before the common era. This land, described as being a six-day sail away from Scotland, continues to elude exact identification. *The Ice Museum: In Search of the Lost Land of Thule* describes Kavenna's journey to find Thule based on historical reports, old Nazi propaganda, linguistic connections, and other sources.

Many critics found much to enjoy in *The Ice Museum.* Writing in the London *Observer,* Kelly Grovier lauded Kavenna's "elegant debut" saying that she "has created an enchanting work that transcends conventional genres, full of poise and passion." Paul Watkins, writing for the London *Times,* similarly called it "compelling" and praised this "beautifully recorded . . . exceptionally readable narrative."Labeling Kavenna a "natural writer," Nick Smith concluded in *Geographical* that *The Ice Museum* "is a dazzling mix of polar history, personal anecdote, and literary erudition."

BIOGRAPHICAL AND CRITICAL SOURCES:

PERIODICALS

Geographical, April, 2005, Nick Smith, review of *The Ice Museum: In Search of the Lost Land of Thule,* p. 68.

Kirkus Reviews, January 1, 2006, review of *The Ice Museum,* p. 29.

Observer (London, England), February 27, 2005, Kelly Grovier, review of *The Ice Museum.*

Publishers Weekly, January 2, 2006, review of *The Ice Museum,* p. 50.

Spectator, March 12, 2005, Paul Binding, review of *The Ice Museum,* p. 48.

Times (London, England), February 26, 2005, Paul Watkins, review of *The Ice Museum.*

ONLINE

Joanna Kavenna Home Page, http://www. joannakavenna.com (March 1, 2006).
Peters, Fraser, and Dunlop (PFD) Web site, http:// www.pfd.co.uk/ (March 1, 2006), profile of Joanna Kavenna.

*   *   *

KEENE, Carolyn
See LERANGIS, Peter

*   *   *

KENYON, Nate
(Nathaniel Kenyon)

PERSONAL: Married Nicole Malec (a Web site and multimedia designer); children: Emily, Harrison, Abbey. *Education:* Trinity College, B.A., 1993.

ADDRESSES: Home—Boston, MA. *Office*—Boston College Law School, Stuart House M305, 885 Centre St., Newton, MA 02459. *E-mail*—nate@natekenyon. com; nathaniel.kenyon.1@bc.edu.

CAREER: Brookline Public Library, Brookline, MA, former staff member; Boston College Law School, Newton, MA, director of marketing and communications.

MEMBER: International Thriller Writers, Horror Writers Association.

WRITINGS:

Bloodstone (novel), Five Star Press (Waterville, ME), 2006.

Also contributor to *Terminal Frights, Volume One* (horror anthology), edited by Ken Abner, Terminal Frights Press (Black River, NY), 1997. Contributor of online book reviews to *Horror World Book Reviews;* contributor of stories to various magazines.

SIDELIGHTS: Nate Kenyon's debut horror novel, *Bloodstone,* is set in a small town in Maine that is much like the one where the author spent his childhood. The story tells the tale of Billy Smith, an ex-convict who is released from jail after serving ten years for taking the lives of a mother and her two children while driving drunk. Shortly after his release, Billy begins to have dark, disturbing dreams and visions of a beautiful young woman. Menacing, unsettling voices fill his head, persuading him to perform evil actions. When Billy sees the woman from his dreams on a beach, he is compelled to kidnap her and take her to the small town of White Falls, Maine. As it turns out, the woman, a prostitute and junkie named Angel, is afflicted by similar sinister dreams. She relents to being kidnapped and joins Billy in an attempt to discover why they have been brought together. When a local boy falls under the spell of an old amulet, it becomes apparent that an event in White Falls history has drawn them to the town and that evil forces at large will not rest until they have engulfed everyone in the town.

Many critics compared Kenyon to well-known writers who helped to established horror as a mainstream genre. One *Publishers Weekly* contributor found that "Stephen King's influence is apparent in Kenyon's debut spooker," further commenting on the story's "impressive panoramic sweep." In a review for the *Horror World Book Reviews* Web site, contributor Mark Justice suggested that *Bloodstone* is a "dark thrill ride" and reported that the story "will live on in your nightmares long after you've finished it." Justice also wrote that Kenyon's characters are "so three-dimensional that they threaten to step off the page." Offering similar praise, reviewer Harriet Klausner wrote on her Web site that the characters "come across as believable."Klausner termed the book "horrifying," "chilling," and "original and frightening." Finally, she observed that *Bloodstone* "will make readers want to sleep with all the lights in the neighborhood shining brightly."

In an interview on his Web site, Kenyon revealed, "I never set out to write horror; in fact, most of my writing would be considered more dark suspense, with an emphasis on dark. Whatever I write does tend to get scary in some way, even if there aren't monsters, ghouls, or ghosts wandering around."

BIOGRAPHICAL AND CRITICAL SOURCES:

PERIODICALS

Kirkus Reviews, October 15, 2005, review of Bloodstone, p. 1110.
Publishers Weekly, November 7, 2005, review of Bloodstone, p. 58.

ONLINE

Harriet Klausner's Review Archive, http://harrietklausner.wwwi.com/ (January 11, 2006), Harriet Klausner, review of Bloodstone.
Horror World Book Reviews, http://www.horrorworld.org/ (January 11, 2006), Mark Justice, review of Bloodstone.
Nate Kenyon Home Page, http://www.natekenyon.com (January 11, 2006).
WritersNet, http://www.writersnet.com/ (January 11, 2006), profile of Nate Kenyon.*

*   *   *

KENYON, Nathaniel
    See KENYON, Nate

*   *   *

KERT, Bernice 1923-2005
    (Bernice Galansky Kert)

PERSONAL: Born October 4, 1923, in St. Louis, MO; died of respiratory failure, July 23, 2005, in Los Angeles, CA; daughter of Gus D. (a wholesale grocer) and Mary (Katanik) Galansky; married Morley J. Kert (a physician), January 14, 1945 (died May, 1990); children: Elizabeth, Kathryn Green, Charles. Education: University of Michigan, B.A., 1944. Politics: Democrat.

CAREER: Writer. University of Michigan, Ann Arbor, teaching fellow in English, 1946-47. Scholar in residence, Bellagio Study Center (Italy), 1991.

MEMBER: Hemingway Society, Authors Guild, Authors League of America, J.B. Berland Foundation, Hillcrest Country Club.

AWARDS, HONORS: Avery Hopwood Award, University of Michigan, c. 1944; Guggenheim fellowship, 1988.

WRITINGS:

The Hemingway Women, W.W. Norton (New York, NY), 1983.
Abby Aldrich Rockefeller: The Woman in the Family, Random House (New York, NY), 1993.

Member of editorial board, Hemingway Review, 1992-2005.

SIDELIGHTS: Bernice Kert's prospects for becoming a successful writer began well when she won the prestigious Avery Hopwood Award at the University of Michigan. She began writing short stories after graduating from college and sold her first, "Look at Me, Lorrie," to Seventeen magazine in 1946. However, her marriage to a busy doctor and raising three children soon occupied much of her time, and she did not return to writing seriously until the late 1980s. In addition to completing three unpublished novels and a variety of short stories, she managed to produce two well-received books later in her life: The Hemingway Women and Abby Aldrich Rockefeller: The Woman in the Family.

After learning that little had been written about author Ernest Hemingway's mother, four wives, and mistresses, Kert decided to rectify this oversight. She managed to interview three of Hemingway's former wives (one, Pauline Pfeiffer, had died in 1951), as well as mistresses, such as Jane Mason. The result is a unique portrait of the famous author as seen through the eyes of the women in his life, many of whom inspired the fictional female characters of his novels. What emerges is a rather unflattering portrait of a misogynist who had serious emotional issues about his mother that carried into his adult life, during which he severely mistreated other women. Hemingway, Kert shows, expected his wives and other women to be subordinate to him; however, ironically, if they did bow to his will he lost all respect for them and soon ended the relationship. *National Review* contributor Jeffrey Meyers noted that Kert offers a sympathetic portrayal of Hemingway's mother, Grace, and reveals new facts about her subjects, such as the lesbianism of his sister-in-law, Jinny Pfeiffer. While Meyers felt the book suffers somewhat from Kert's lack of a thorough knowledge of Hemingway's writings, he asserted that *The Hemingway Women* is "an original and useful book." Although this portrait "doesn't hurt [Hemingway's] reputation as a writer," concluded a *People* critic, "it won't do much to help his image as a human being."

Kert later completed *Abby Aldrich Rockefeller,* a biography of the wife of wealthy industrialist John D. Rockefeller that gives her credit as "the driving force behind the founding of" the Museum of Modern Art in Manhattan, as a *Publishers Weekly* critic related. It also reveals how she influenced the Rockefeller clan to become more liberal and charitable philanthropists. Abby Rockefeller, Kert further points out, was an important backer of the restoration of colonial Williamsburg. Thanks to Kert, stated the *Publishers Weekly* writer, "Abby Rockefeller emerges as a loveable and intelligent woman."

BIOGRAPHICAL AND CRITICAL SOURCES:

PERIODICALS

Booklist, June 15, 1983, review of *The Hemingway Women,* p. 1320; September 15, 1993, Donna Seaman, review of *Abby Aldrich Rockefeller: The Woman in the Family,* p. 116.
Historian, summer, 1994, Lynn Y. Weiner, review of *Abby Aldrich Rockefeller,* p. 753.
Journal of American History, March, 1995, Marsha Shapiro Rose, review of *Abby Aldrich Rockefeller,* p. 1777.
Kirkus Reviews, August 1, 1993, review of *Abby Aldrich Rockefeller,* p. 982.
Library Journal, May 15, 1983, review of *The Hemingway Women,* p. 1004; October 1, 1993, Caroline Mitchell, review of *Abby Aldrich Rockefeller,* p. 102.
Los Angeles Times, July 3, 1983, Carol Ames, review of *The Hemingway Women,* p. B2; July 10, 1994, review of *Abby Aldrich Rockefeller,* p. 10.
National Review, August 19, 1983, Jeffrey Meyers, review of *The Hemingway Women,* p. 1027.

New York Times Book Review, July 17, 1983, Aaron Latham, review of *The Hemingway Women,* p. 8; February 9, 1986, Patricia T. O'Conner, review of *The Hemingway Women,* p. 38; March 21, 1999, review of *Abby Aldrich Rockefeller,* p. 32.
People, August 8, 1983, review of *The Hemingway Women,* p. 10.
Publishers Weekly, August 9, 1993, review of *Abby Aldrich Rockefeller,* p. 426.
Times Literary Supplement, May 10, 1985, review of *The Hemingway Women,* p. 524.
Tribune Books (Chicago, IL), review of *Abby Aldrich Rockefeller,* p. 2.

OBITUARIES

PERIODICALS

Los Angeles Times, July 26, 2005, p. B10.*

*   *   *

**KERT, Bernice Galansky
See KERT, Bernice**

*   *   *

**KIM, Chi-Ha 1941-
(Kim Chi Ha, Kim Chi-Ha, Kim Chiha)**

PERSONAL: Born February 4, 1941, in Mokpo, South Chôlla Province, South Korea. *Education:* Seoul National University, graduated from Liberal Arts College. *Religion:* Catholic.

ADDRESSES: Agent—c/o Author Mail, White Pine Press, P.O. Box 236, Buffalo, NY 14201.

CAREER: Poet, writer, and activist.

AWARDS, HONORS: Lotus Special Award, Asian and African Writers' Council, 1975; Nobel Peace Prize nominations in Peace and Literature, 1975; Great Poet Award, Poetry International, 1981; Bruno Chriski Human Rights Award, Chriski Human Rights Award

Committee of Austria, 1981; Isan Literature Prize, 1993; honorary doctorate in literature, Sogang University, 1993.

WRITINGS:

ENGLISH TRANSLATIONS

Cry of the People and Other Poems, Autumn Press (Hayama, Japan), 1974.

The Gold-Crowned Jesus and Other Writings, Orbis Books (Maryknoll, NY), 1978.

The Middle Hour: Selected Poems of Kim Chi Ha, translated by David R. McCann, preface by Denise Levertov, Human Rights Publishing Group (Stanfordville, NY), 1980.

Heart's Agony: Selected Poems, translated by Won-Chung Kim and James Han, White Pine Press (Fredonia, NY), 1998.

Also author of the collection *Yellow Earth Road,* 1970.

IN KOREAN

Kim Chi-ha chakpum sonjip: Nam Choson aeguk siin (selections), Yonyong Inmin Chulpansa Yonyongsong Sinhwa Sojom parhaeng, (Sinhwa, South Korea), 1982.

Minjok ui norae minjung ui norae, Tonggwang Chulpansa (Seoul, South Korea), 1984.

Aerin Silchon Munhaksa (Seoul, South Korea), 1986.

Ojok, Tonggwang Chulpansa (Seoul, South Korea), 1987.

Sallim, Tonggwang Chulpansa (Seoul, South Korea), 1987.

Naui omoni, Chayu Munhaksa (Seoul, South Korea), 1988.

I kamun nal e pi kurum, Yeni, 1988.

Pyol pat ul urorumyo, Tonggwang Chulpansa (Seoul, South Korea), 1989.

Tanun mongmarum eso saengmyong ui pada ro, Tonggwang Chulpansa (Seoul, South Korea), 1991.

Ttongttakki ttongttak, Tonggwang Chulpansa (Seoul, South Korea), 1991.

Han sarang i taeonamuro, Tonggwang Chulpansa (Seoul, South Korea), 1991.

Igot kurigo chogot, Tonggwang Chulpansa (Seoul, South Korea), 1991.

Kim Chi-ha chonjip (works), Tonggwang Chulpansa (Seoul, South Korea), 1991.

Malttugi ippal un palman-sachon-kae, (works), Tonggwang Chulpansa (Seoul, South Korea), 1991.

Mungchimyon chukko hechimyon sanda, (works), Tonggwang Chulpansa (Seoul, South Korea), 1991.

Saengmyong, i challanhan chongche (works), Tonggwang Chulpansa (Seoul, South Korea), 1991.

Moro nuun tol pucho, Nanm (Seoul, South Korea), 1992.

Saengmyong, Sol (Seoul, South Korea), 1992.

Kyolchongbon Kim Chi-ha si chonjip, Sol (Seoul, South Korea), 1993.

Ongchi kyok, Sol (Seoul, South Korea), 1993.

Pam nara, Sol (Seoul, South Korea), 1993.

Chungsim ui koeroum, Sol (Seoul, South Korea), 1994.

Tonghak iyagi, Sol (Seoul, South Korea), 1994.

Nim: yojum sesang e taehayo, Sol (Seoul, South Korea), 1995.

Pin san: Kim Chi-ha sijip, Sol (Seoul, South Korea), 1996.

Sasang kihaeng, Silchon Munhaksa (Seoul, South Korea), 1999.

Mi ui yojong, Kim Chi-ha ui mungnan, Hakkojae (Seoul, South Korea), 2001.

Hwagae, Silchon Munhaksa (Seoul, South Korea), 2002.

Kim Chi-ha chonjip, Silchon Munhaksa (Seoul, South Korea), 2002.

Chol, ku onjori: Kim Chi-ha sumuk sihwachop, Changjak kwa Pipyongsa (Seoul, South Korea), 2003.

Kim Chi-ha ui hwadu: pulgun angma wa chotpul, Hwanam (Seoul, South Korea), 2003.

Talchum ui minjok mihak, Silchon Munhaksa (Seoul, South Korea), 2004.

Also author of *Hwangto,* 1970; *Nagai kurayami no kanata ni,* 1971; *Kin Shika shishu,* 1974; *Minshuno koe,* 1974; *Ryoshin sengen,* 1975; *Fuki,* 1975; *Kim Chi-ha cho njip,* 1975; *Kim Chi-ha tamsijip,* 1975; *Kin Shika sakuhin shu,* 1976; *Gokuchu kara,* 1977; *Kugyo,* 1978; *Tanun mongmarum uro: Kim Chi-ha sisonjip,* 1982; *Tongyang chongsin kwa ijil munhwa kan ui taehwa,* 1984; *Pap: Kim Chi-ha iyagi moum,* 1984; *Pap,* 1984; *Susan,* 1984; *Taesol nam,* 1984; *Komun san hayan pang,* 1986; and *Yumok kwa undun: Kim Chi-ha sijip,* 2005.

Contributor to numerous books, including *Chejari rul channun si*, 1985; *Sam inya chugum inya*, 1985; *Nam-nyok ttang paennorae*, 1985; *Nunmul ul samkimyo*, 1988; *Chinae hanun kungmin yorobun!: chongchi pungja sijip*, 1989; *Han-guk munhak pirhwa chak-pumjip*, 1989; *70, 80-yondae kongyon kumji huigok sonjip*, 1990; and *Cracking the Shell: Three Korean Ecopoets: Seungho Choi, Chiha Kim, Hyonjong Chong*, edited and translated by Won-Chung Kim, Homa & Sekey Books (Paramus, NJ), 2006.

Contributor of poetry, essays, and other writings to periodicals, including *Shiin* and *Sasanggye;* made sound recording *Shin ya*, 1976.

SIDELIGHTS: Kim Chi-Ha was sentenced to death in 1974 for his poetry provoking South Korean President Chunghee Park. His sentence was eventually commuted in 1980 due to a worldwide effort to save him. Much of Kim's poetry has been published in English, including the collection of poems that got him arrested, *Cry of the People and Other Poems*. Writing in *Book World*, Don Oberdorfer noted that the volume was "a polemical call to arms written for the antigovernment student demonstrations." Oberdorfer also wrote that, despite the difficulties that translations can make in poetry, the poet's "anger, earthiness and sense of irony somehow manage to shine throughout." Julia Morrison, writing in the *Library Journal*, remarked that Kim's "powerful reactions to his environment have an impact on the reader." Writing in the *Catholic Library World*, Harry James Cargas noted that the collection "makes very powerful reading."

The Gold-Crowned Jesus and Other Writings presents various writings by the author, including poems, a play, and essays. For example, in "Declaration of Conscience," which the poet wrote while on trial, Kim tells about his interrogation in court. Another essay, "Torture Road," also looks askance at government efforts at repression. The title of the book is a play that features Jesus relinquishing His gold crown to be with the downtrodden. Writing about the play in the *Christian Century*, Deane William Ferm noted that the play "portrays Christ as an inert figure of gold imprisoned in concrete by his political and religious oppressors. A leper, the advocate of the oppressed, tries to liberate Jesus by removing the gold crown from his head, and Jesus encourages the leper." Cargas commented that the play "is powerful not highly polished theatre."

Thomas C. Hunt, writing in the *Library Journal*, commented that the entire volume "portrays the agony and frustration of revolutionary-minded Catholics under" the regime of Korea at the time. *World Literature Today* contributor Peter H. Lee noted the author's use in his poems of "the rhetorical device of *place* (sporadic word repetition), the recurrence of certain sounds, and association of words."

Another collection of poems, *The Middle Hour: Selected Poems of Kim Chi Ha*, includes a wide selection of the author's works. Writing in the *Library Journal*, Robert Hudzik called the poems "angry, sad, and, remarkably, touched with humor." In a review of another collection of poems titled *Heart's Agony: Selected Poems*, *World Literature Today* contributor Edgar C. Knowlton, Jr. noted that the volume "fills a desirable function, giving samples from both the earlier and later styles of this gifted poet, together with a sophisticated analysis thereof." Knowlton went on to note that the poet "is a virtuoso, entertaining as well as brilliant."

BIOGRAPHICAL AND CRITICAL SOURCES:

PERIODICALS

Book World, April 6, 1975, Don Oberdorfer, review of *Cry of the People and Other Poems*, p. 3.

Catholic Library World, October, 1982, Harry James Cargas, "Korea's Catholic Martyr," discusses author's life and works, pp. 129-130.

Choice, June, 1985, Deane William Ferm, review of *The Gold-Crowned Jesus and Other Writings*, p. 1454.

Christian Century, January 25, 1984, Deane William Ferm, "Outlining Rice-Roots Theology," discusses author and work, pp. 78-80.

Library Journal, March 15, 1978, Thomas C. Hunt, review of *The Gold-Crowned Jesus and Other Writings*, p. 673; June 1, 1975, Julia Morrison, review of *Cry of the People and Other Poems*, p. 1134; August, 1980, Robert Hudzik, review of *The Middle Hour: Selected Poems of Kim Chi Ha*, p. 1640.

World Literature Today, winter, 1980, Peter H. Lee, review of *The Gold-Crowned Jesus and Other Writings*, p. 173; summer, 1999, Edgar C. Knowlton, Jr., review of *Heart's Agony: Selected Poems*, pp. 602-603; spring, 2002, Oe Kenzaburo, "Can Literature Bridge the Gap among the Countries of Asia?," p. 24.

                              *   *   *

KIMMEL, Elizabeth Cody

PERSONAL: Born New York, NY; married; children: Emma. *Education:* Attended Kenyon College. *Hobbies and other interests:* Reading, hiking, singing, rock climbing.

ADDRESSES: Home—Cold Spring, NY. *Agent*—c/o Author Mail, HarperCollins, 10 E. 53rd St., 7th Fl., New York, NY 10022. *E-mail*—codykimmel@ earthlink.net.

CAREER: Children's book writer.

WRITINGS:

FICTION

In the Stone Circle, Scholastic (New York, NY), 1998.

Balto and the Great Race, illustrated by Nora Koerber, Random House (New York, NY), 1999.

Visiting Miss Caples, Dial (New York, NY), 2000.

To the Frontier ("Adventures of Young Buffalo Bill" series), HarperCollins (New York, NY), 2001.

One Sky above Us ("Adventures of Young Buffalo Bill" series), illustrated by Scott Snow, Harper-Collins (New York, NY), 2002.

My Wagon Will Take Me Anywhere, illustrated by Tom Newsom, Dutton (New York, NY), 2002.

In the Eye of the Storm ("Adventures of Young Buffalo Bill" series), HarperCollins (New York, NY), 2003.

West on the Wagon Train ("Adventures of Young Buffalo Bill" series), illustrated by Scott Snow, HarperCollins (New York, NY), 2003.

Lily B. on the Brink of Cool, HarperCollins (New York, NY), 2003.

What Do You Dream?, Candlewick (Cambridge, MA), 2003.

My Penguin Osbert, illustrated by H.B. Lewis, Candlewick (Cambridge, MA), 2004.

Lily B. on the Brink of Love, HarperCollins (New York, NY), 2005.

Lily B. on the Brink of Paris, HarperCollins (New York, NY), 2006.

Kimmel's "Lily B." books have been translated into several languages.

NONFICTION

Ice Story: Shackleton's Lost Expedition, Clarion (New York, NY), 1999.

Before Columbus: The Leif Eriksson Expedition, Random House (New York, NY), 2003.

As Far As the Eye Can Reach: Lewis and Clark's Westward Quest, Random House (New York, NY), 2003.

The Look-It-Up Book of Explorers, Random House (New York, NY), 2004.

Ladies First: Forty Daring American Women Who Were Second to None, National Geographic (Washington, DC), 2005.

WORK IN PROGRESS: Osbert in Love, for Candlewick Press; a book for the "Little House" series published by HarperCollins.

SIDELIGHTS: Elizabeth Cody Kimmel grew up in both New York and Brussels, Belgium. As a writer of fiction and nonfiction for children and young adults, she has worked to weave subjects she finds interesting—from Antarctica to ghost stories and medieval history—into her books. Many of her nonfiction titles, such as *Ice Story: Shackleton's Lost Expedition* and *As Far As the Eye Can Reach: Lewis and Clark's Westward Quest* tell the stories of explorers, while her teen novels deal with such themes as multi-generational friendships and being yourself.

The Lewis and Clark Expedition is the subject of *As Far As the Eye Can Reach,* which follows their efforts to locate a northern route to the Pacific Ocean. The book was considered "a well written, lively account for young readers" by a contributor to *Kirkus Reviews.* As *Booklist* critic Carolyn Phelan commented, "This clearly written summary provides a useful overview for students." Renee Steinberg, writing for *School Library Journal,* commented that "a book such as this can excite young readers to delve further into U.S. history." Another of Kimmel's nonfiction titles, *Before Columbus: The Leif Eriksson Expedition,* introduces readers to the Viking exploration of the Americas. The book is a "small, readable volume," according to *Booklist* contributor Roger Leslie, while a *Kirkus Reviews* contributor deemed it "more a quick once-over than a systematic study" and "well designed to stimulate an early interest" in its subject. Ginny Gustin, writing in *School Library Journal,* noted that the nonfiction title reads more like an historical novel, and acknowledged that "Kimmel's book will captivate and entertain young readers." The author's reference resource, *The Look-It-Up Book of Explorers,* covers the expeditions of explorers through the ages. Carol Wichman, writing in *School Library Journal,* considered the work "a concise and useful guide to virtually all of the explorers usually studied in public schools."

Kimmel's first teen novel, *Visiting Miss Caples,* is the story of thirteen-year-old Jenna, whose father abandons her family. To make things worse, her best friend no longer speaks to her. Jenna assumes that a class project to visit an elderly shut-in will be another bad thing in her year, but she learns that Miss Caples, despite her difference in age, understands a lot of what Jenna is going through. "Kimmel ably articulates a young person's experience," wrote Gillian Engberg in *Booklist.*

Kimmel has written three books in the "Lily B." series, all of them featuring teen heroine Lily B. and her misadventures. In *Lily B. on the Brink of Cool,* Lily is convinced that her family is anything but cool. When she meets distant cousin Karma and Karma's family, Lily is determined to fit in, becoming more sophisticated by proximity. However, it soon appears that Karma's family has more in mind than befriending Lily, and the teen ultimately learns that sometimes first impressions are deceiving. "Lily is a likable teen who wants more than she has, only to discover that what she has is pretty darn good," wrote Linda Binder in *School Library Journal.* A *Kirkus Reviews* contributor found Lily to be "a delightful heroine, sweeter than [other teen heroines] and hilarious," while Louise Brueggemann noted in her *Booklist* review that the book is a "funny, fast-moving, if somewhat self-conscious, novel." A *Publishers Weekly* critic considered Lily "by turns chirpy, sardonic, glib, and melodramatic—and always likable." Lily's adventures continue in *Lily B. on the Brink of Love* when, as her middle-school paper's advice columnist, she discovers

that love in her own life is more difficult than answering readers' love questions. "Lily's journal entries and advice columns . . . deliver laughs and substance," wrote Wendi Hoffenberg in *School Library Journal.* A *Kirkus Reviews* contributor found the book to be "heartwarming and funny," and Heidi Hauser Green in *Kliatt* felt that "Lily's over-the-top narrative voice will likely appeal to many middle school readers."

Along with nonfiction and novels, Kimmel has also crafted picture books, including *My Penguin Osbert.* The book tells the story of a Christmas wish gone wrong; Joe wanted a live penguin, but when Osbert is delivered by Santa, the boy realizes that having a pet penguin is not quite what he imagined. When Joe finally brings Osbert to a new home in the zoo, both boy and penguin end up happy. "Kimmel sneaks some sly humor into the well-told, nicely paced tale," wrote Ilene Cooper in *Booklist.* A *Kirkus Reviews* contributor found the tale to be "salutary reading for all children campaigning for a pet," and *Horn Book* critic Lauren E. Raece likewise found the story to be a "satisfying tale." Readers should "find much to enjoy in this lighthearted fantasy with realistic holiday roots," according to a *Publishers Weekly* contributor.

On her home page, Kimmel explained where she came up with the idea for *My Penguin Osbert.* "I love the idea of all that ice and snow and wind," she wrote, referring to the weather in Antarctica, "and I can imagine myself bundling up to hike through the winter wonderland. But when reality sets in, I can't stand the cold, and I think that is how Osbert was born." Kimmel expects to write additional books about Osbert, and has begun working on *Osbert in Love.*

BIOGRAPHICAL AND CRITICAL SOURCES:

PERIODICALS

Booklist, May 15, 2000, Gillian Engberg, review of *Visiting Miss Caples,* p. 1739; January 1, 2003, Carolyn Phelan, "Lewis & Clark on the Road Again," p. 885; July, 2003, Roger Leslie, review of *Before Columbus: The Leif Eriksson Expedition* p. 1882; October 1, 2003, Lauren Peterson, review of *What Do You Dream?,* p. 328; December 1, 2003, Louise Brueggemann, review of *Lily B. on the Brink of Cool,* p. 666; December 1, 2004, Ilene Cooper, review of *My Penguin Osbert,* p. 659; October 1, 2005, Anne O'Malley, review of *Lily B. on the Brink of Love,* p. 58.

Bulletin of the Center for Children's Books, April, 2000, review of *Visiting Miss Caples,* p. 285; February, 2004, review of *Lily B. on the Brink of Cool,* p. 237.

Horn Book, November-December, 2004, Lauren E. Raece, review of *My Penguin Osbert,* p. 662.

Kirkus Reviews, December 15, 2002, review of *As Far As the Eye Can Reach,* p. 1851; July 15, 2003, review of *Before Columbus,* p. 965; October 15, 2003, review of *Lily B. on the Brink of Cool,* p. 1272; November 1, 2004, review of *My Penguin Osbert,* p. 1051; August 1, 2005, review of *Lily B. on the Brink of Love,* p. 851.

Kliatt, July, 2004, Sherri Ginsberg, review of *Lily B. on the Brink of Cool,* p. 53; September, 2005, Heidi Hauser Green, review of *Lily B. on the Brink of Cool,* p. 20.

Publishers Weekly, December 10, 2001, review of *Visiting Miss Caples,* p. 73; June 9, 2003, review of "Adventures of Young Buffalo Bill" series, p. 54; December 8, 2003, review of *Lily B. on the Brink of Cool,* p. 62; June 14, 2004, audiobook review of *Lily B. on the Brink of Cool,* p. 38; November 22, 2004, review of *My Penguin Osbert,* p. 60.

School Librarian, autumn, 2004, Chris Brown, review of *Lily B. on the Brink of Cool,* p. 156.

School Library Journal, July, 2002, Anne Knickerbocker, review of *My Wagon Will Take Me Anywhere,* p. 94; March, 2003, Renee Steinberg, review of *As Far As the Eye Can Reach,* pp. 172, 253; October, 2003, Ginny Gustin, review of *Before Columbus,* p. 152, and Linda Binder, review of *Lily B. on the Brink of Cool,* p. 169; February 2004, Sanda Kitain, review of *What Do You Dream?,* p. 116; January, 2005, Wendi Hoffenberg, review of *Lily B. on the Brink of Love,* p. 104, and Carol Wichman, review of *The Look-It-Up Book of Explorers,* p. 149; October, 2005, review of *The Look-It-Up Book of Explorers,* p. S48.

Voice of Youth Advocates, August, 2000, review of *Ice Story,* p. 165; October, 2003, review of *Lily B. on the Brink of Cool,* p. 312.

ONLINE

Elizabeth Cody Kimmel Home Page, http://www.codykimmel.com (April 27, 2006).

Kids Reads Web site, http://www.kidsreads.com/ (April 27, 2006), profile of Kimmel.*

* * *

KING, Coretta Scott 1927-2006

OBITUARY NOTICE— See index for *CA* sketch: Born April 27, 1927, in Marion, AL; died of heart and respiratory arrest, January 31, 2006, in Rosarito Beach, Mexico. Activist and author. The widow of civil rights leader Rev. Dr. Martin Luther King, Jr., King herself was a dominant leader in equal rights for minorities and women, as well as a champion of political causes. Although her childhood in Alabama was marked by poverty, her parents were hard workers and, overall, they were more financially secure than many blacks in the South at the time. They believed in a good education, and King was able to attend a private missionary school before continuing her education at Antioch College. There she earned her B.A., then she studied at the New England Conservatory of Music, where she completed a Mus.B. in 1954; later, in 1971, she also received a doctorate from that institution. It was here that she first met her future husband, who was immediately entranced by her intelligence and beauty. King herself was less impressed with his effusive initial declarations of love, but was eventually won over by the young philosophy student from a prominent family of ministers. They married in 1953, and King followed her husband to Atlanta and then Montgomery. She never anticipated what was to come in 1955, when Reverend King was thrust into a prominent role during the Montgomery Bus Boycott. While her husband became more and more famous, King resolved not to be merely a supportive wife but also a participant in the civil rights movement. Her husband resisted at first, but later admitted that she was a strong woman who deserved to be in the forefront of the fight for equal rights. King became particularly active in organizing dozens of Freedom Concerts to promote their cause and raise money. After her husband's 1968 assassination, she resolved to take up his banner and continue to work for his cause. Gradually finding her own voice, King was active in the Southern Christian Leadership Conference (SCLC) and expanded her husband's initial goals to include not only minority, but also women's rights. She joined the National Organization for Women and would later take up such international causes as the struggle against apartheid in South Africa. Keeping her husband's memory alive was of huge importance to the widow, as well, and she successfully lobbied the federal government to establish Martin Luther King, Jr. day, which was first celebrated in 1986. She also founded the Martin Luther King, Jr. Center for Non-Violent Social Change in Atlanta. Unfortunately, sometimes such activities were criticized. For example, some complained that her focus on the center took much-needed funds away from the SCLC. Others were puzzled, too, when King declared that she believed her husband's accused killer, James Earl Ray, was innocent; Ray died in 1998 before a new trial was ever set. Despite such occasional controversies, however, King remained a beloved leading figure for equal rights throughout her life. A heart attack and stroke in 2005 slowed her down, though, and she also suffered from ovarian cancer and cerebral vascular disease, which would eventually contribute to her death. The recipient of numerous awards and prizes for her commitment to human rights, King was the author of *The Martin Luther King, Jr. Companion: Quotations from the Speeches, Essays, and Books of Martin Luther King, Jr.* (1999) and the autobiography *My Life with Martin Luther King, Jr.* (1969).

OBITUARIES AND OTHER SOURCES:

BOOKS

King, Coretta Scott, *My Life with Martin Luther King, Jr.,* Holt (New York, NY), 1969.

PERIODICALS

Chicago Tribune, February 1, 2006, section 1, pp. 1, 14.
Los Angeles Times, February 1, 2006, pp. A1, A10-11.
New York Times, February 1, 2006, pp. A1, A22.
Times (London, England), February 1, 2006, p. 60.
Washington Post, February 1, 2006, pp. A1, A6.

*   *   *

KIRBY, Susan E. 1949-
(Suzanne Stephens, Suzanne Wade)

PERSONAL: Born August 10, 1949, in Bloomington, IL; daughter of Stephen F. (a farmer) and Glaida (a homemaker; maiden name, Wade) Funk; married John R. Kirby (a mechanic), June 27, 1969; children: John R. II, A. Levi. *Education:* Attended Illinois State University, 1967-68. *Religion:* "Protestant-Christian."

ADDRESSES: Agent—c/o Author Mail, Aladdin Publicity Department, Simon & Schuster, Inc., 1230 Avenue of the Americas, New York, NY 10020.

CAREER: Writer. Has also worked as a school cook and postal worker.

WRITINGS:

FOR CHILDREN

Ike and Porker, Houghton Mifflin (Boston, MA), 1983.
Culligan Man Can, illustrated by Jim Spence, Abingdon (Nashville, TN), 1988.
Shadow Boy, Orchard Books (New York, NY), 1991.
Tear Jerkers: Once in a Blue Moon, Pan Macmillan (New York, NY), 1996.

"AMERICAN QUILT" SERIES; FOR CHILDREN

Ellen's Story, Aladdin (New York, NY), 2000.
Hattie's Story, Aladdin (New York, NY), 2000.
Daniel's Story, Aladdin (New York, NY), 2000.
Ida Lou's Story, Aladdin (New York, NY), 2001.

"MAIN STREET" SERIES; FOR CHILDREN

Home for Christmas, Harper Trophy (New York, NY), 1994.
Lemonade Days, Avon Books (New York, NY), 1994.
Home Front Hero, Avon Books (New York, NY), 1994.
Goodbye, Desert Rose, Camelot (New York, NY), 1995.

ROMANCE NOVELS

The Maple Princess, Bouregy (New York, NY), 1982.
Lessons for the Heart, Bouregy (New York, NY), 1982.
Blizzard of the Heart, Bouregy (New York, NY), 1982.
Chasing a Dream, Bouregy (New York, NY), 1982.
Love's Welcome Home, Bouregy (New York, NY), 1983.

Reach for Heaven, Bouregy (New York, NY), 1983.

One Whispering Voice, Silhouette (Buffalo, NY), 1984.

Love's Secret Game, Bouregy (New York, NY), 1985.

(Under pseudonym Suzanne Stephens) *The Proud Heart,* Bouregy (New York, NY), 1986.

Heart Aflame, Zondervan (Grand Rapids, MI), 1986.

Butterscotch Moon, Thomas Nelson (Nashville, TN), 1986.

Cries the Wilderness Wind, Zondervan (Grand Rapids, MI), 1987.

Love, Special Delivery, Butterfield (Lindsborg, KS), 1987.

In Perfect Harmony, Butterfield (Lindsborg, KS), 1988.

Leah's Love Song, Bouregy (New York, NY), 1990.

Too Good to Be True, Bantam (New York, NY), 1991.

(As Suzanne Wade) *Candy Kisses,* Bouregy (New York, NY), 1991.

My Secret Heart, Bantam (New York, NY), 1993.

Partners in Love, Bantam (New York, NY), 1993.

Picture Perfect, Heartsong Presents (Uhrichsville, OH), 1993.

The Field, Kensington Publishing (New York, NY), 1995.

Prairie Rose, Avon Books (New York, NY), 1997.

Blue Moon, Berkeley Publishing Group (New York, NY), 1997.

When the Lilacs Bloom, Avon Books (New York, NY), 1997.

As the Lily Grows, Avon Books (New York, NY), 1997.

Your Dream and Mine, Steeple Hill Books (Buffalo, NY), 1999.

Love Sign, Steeple Hill Books (Buffalo, NY), 2001.

Love Knot, Steeple Hill Books (Buffalo, NY), 2004.

Contributor of over two hundred short stories to periodicals, including *Scholastic Scope;* contributor of short stories to anthologies.

SIDELIGHTS: Susan E. Kirby is an award-winning author who primarily writes Christian romance, historical fiction, and children's books. Kirby's young adult "Main Street" series spans four decades and three generations of an American family with a connection to America's main street, Route 66. The remnants of the highway which skirts Kirby's childhood home in Illinois inspired her to embellish Route 66 experiences drawn from family and friends into chapter books, each reflecting a different mood of the highway.

Kirby is also the author of the "American Quilt" series for children. The second book in this series is titled *Hattie's Story,* a tale about a girl coping with her parents' involvement in the Illinois Underground Railroad and her friend's family's actions to stop it. Angela J. Reynolds, writing in the *School Library Journal,* noted that the "suspense carries much of the plot" in this story. Another regional book by Kirby is *When the Lilacs Bloom,* which is set in the early twentieth century. Kristin Ramsdell, reviewing the work in *Library Journal,* complimented the author's use of descriptive details and noted that the "characters are nicely rendered" as well.

Kirby told *CA:* "My interest in writing was a natural outgrowth of my love of reading. I did not plan or prepare for a career in writing. When the urge to express myself in short stories became too strong to ignore, I was the mother of two young, active boys with little spare time. I failed at balancing motherhood and all its constant yet satisfying demands, so though I'd managed to sell a few short stories, I postponed my writing ambitions until my youngest started school. The time was right! God blessed my efforts. I began to sell short stories regularly. My first children's novel knocked around a bit before it found a home with Houghton Mifflin. It was a delight to do this story of a sensitive pioneer boy who, like my own boys, was a bit timid of the dark, yet full of bright bold ideas and ambitions.

"My children's book *Culligan Man Can* is a story of perseverance, and leaves readers cheering for the creative young hero who struggles with a learning disability. Also of importance to me is [*Shadow Boy.*] Of a more serious tone, this novel is the story of a teenage girl's gradual acceptance of the changes in her life brought about by an accident which left her younger brother brain-injured. It is a story of strained loyalties, old and new friendships, and love tested to the limits.

"Writing is and will always be a joy to me. Yet it is also a driving force that continually looks ahead to the next challenge."

Kirby further commented: "As a child, my father's stories of my pioneering ancestors brought history to life for me. I try to do the same for my readers in the 'American Quilt' series. The books blend some my favorite things—people, history, stories and quilts. My favorite book in the series is *Hattie's Story*, an Underground Railroad story that has proved popular with readers and teachers alike.

"Often, I'm invited to speak for schools, libraries, civic and church groups, and quilt venues, which I enjoy. I also like to play the organ for worship services at my home church. I'm very grateful for the gift of imagination which lends itself so well to the things I enjoy most—not the least of which is my grandchildren.

"My interest in writing is a gift from God. I was blessed with a fertile imagination and am a day-dreamer. Writing fiction is daydreaming on paper.

"A love for people heavily influences my work. As does an appreciation for nature. I've come to think of the world as a really big garden, beautifully landscaped by our Creator with startling surprises around every bend.

"My writing process, like music, is all about tension and resolution.

"The two most surprising things I've learned as a writer are, one—that a neat, orderly book emerges from the chaos of the writing process is a constant surprise and delight to me! Two—that my happiness is not bound up in my writing. I can walk away from it. Learning that has liberated me from the guilt of 'not writing' when 'abundant living' leaves little time for daydreaming on paper."

BIOGRAPHICAL AND CRITICAL SOURCES:

PERIODICALS

Book Report, September-October, 1991, Donna Dalton, review of *Shadow Boy,* p. 50.
Booklist, June 1, 1991, review of *Shadow Boy,* p. 1868.
Bulletin of the Center for Children's Books, February, 1984, review of *Ike and Porker,* p. 109; February, 1991, review of *Shadow Boy,* p. 144.
Children's Book Review Service, April, 1991, review of *Shadow Boy,* p. 106.
Horn Book Magazine, December, 1983, Nancy C. Hammond, review of *Ike and Porker,* p. 710; fall, 1991, review of *Shadow Boy,* p. 276.
Kirkus Reviews, April 1, 1991, review of *Shadow Boy,* p. 473.
Kliatt, March, 1997, review of *Prairie Rose,* p. 10.
Library Journal, November 15, 1997, Kristin Ramsdell, review of *When the Lilacs Bloom,* p. 48.
Library Media Connection, September, 1991, review of *Shadow Boy,* p. 50.
School Library Journal, February, 1984, review of *Ike and Porker,* p. 74; October, 1988, Susannah Price, review of *Culligan Man Can,* p. 146; March, 1991, Libby K. White, review of *Shadow Boy,* p. 212; January, 1998, Alison Follos, review of *Blue Moon,* p. 114; March, 2001, Angela J. Reynolds, review of *Hattie's Story,* p. 252; December, 2001, Kristen Oravec, review of *Ida Lou's Story,* p. 138.
Voice of Youth Advocates, April, 1991, review of *Shadow Boy,* p. 32.

ONLINE

All Readers, http://www.allreaders.com/ (March 6, 2006), review of *Shadow Boy.*
University of Illinois at Urbana-Champaign Web site, http://www.uiuc.edu/ (March 6, 2006), profile of Susan E. Kirby.

*   *   *

KIRSCHNER, Marc
See KIRSCHNER, Marc W.

*   *   *

KIRSCHNER, Marc W. 1945-
(Marc Kirschner, Marc Wallace Kirschner)

PERSONAL: Born February, 28, 1945, in Chicago, IL. *Education:* Northwestern University, B.A., 1966; University of California, Berkeley, Ph.D., 1971.

ADDRESSES: Office—Harvard Medical School, Alpert 536, Systems Biology, 200 Longwood Ave., Boston, MA 02115. *E-mail*—marc@hms.harvard.edu.

CAREER: Biochemist, educator, and author. Princeton University, Princeton, NJ, assistant professor of biochemistry, 1972-78; University of California, San Francisco, professor of biochemistry, 1978-93; Harvard University, Boston, MA, professor and chair of cell biology, 1993-2003, professor of systems biology and chair of department, 2003—.

MEMBER: American Society of Biological Chemisry, American Society for Cell Biology, American Academy of Arts and Sciences, National Academy of Sciences, Royal Society of London.

AWARDS, HONORS: National Science Foundation fellowship, University of California, 1971-72; Research Career Development Award, National Institutes of Health, 1975-80; Richard Lounsberg Award, National Academy of Sciences, 1991; William C. Rose Award, American Society for Biochemistry and Molecular Biology, 2001; International Award, Gairdner Foundation of Toronto, 2001; Rabbi Shai Shacknai Lectureship Prize, Lautenberg Center for General and Tumor Immunology, 2003; Dickson Prize, Carnegie Mellon University, 2004, for making the greatest strides in a scientific field in the past year.

WRITINGS:

(As Marc Kirschner; with John C. Gerhart) *Cells, Embryos, and Evolution: Toward a Cellular and Developmental Understanding of Phenotypic Variation and Evolutionary Adaptability,* illustrated by Eileen Starr Moderbacher, Blackwell Science (Malden, MA), 1997.
(With John C. Gerhart) *The Plausibility of Life: Resolving Darwin's Dilemma,* Yale University Press (New Haven, CT), 2005.

Also contributor to periodicals, including *Cell, Nature, Science, Current Biology,* and *Public Library of Science.*

SIDELIGHTS: In 1997 biology professors Marc W. Kirschner and John C. Gerhart published *Cells, Embryos, and Evolution: Toward a Cellular and Developmental Understanding of Phenotypic Variation and Evolutionary Adaptability.* The book examines how cellular processes have influenced the course of physical evolution. The authors explain that the same core cellular processes that create eyes also create elbows, and that those core processes also explore possible evolutionary changes.

According to Kirschner and Gerhart, the core cellular processes that make up our basic physical features are exploratory, meaning they attempt different outcomes to address new environmental circumstances. These processes also regulate themselves. When exploratory procedures are unsuccessful, the processes adjust so that the organism is not adversely affected by mutations. Cells adapt to disturbances created by the processes so that they do not affect basic cellular processes in the organism. The writers call this "robust flexibility," meaning that a few core cellular processes can direct many more diverse processes, even those that cause the evolution of many differing phenotypes. The book revolves around the hypothetical idea that the body has a built-in capacity for evolution, which the authors call "evolvability." Darwin suggested that animals that evolve are naturally selected; however, Kirschner and Gerhart assert that animals are naturally selected because of their ability to evolve.

In 2005 Kirschner and Gerhart published *The Plausibility of Life: Resolving Darwin's Dilemma,* which addresses the same ideas explored in *Cells, Embryos, and Evolution,* but it presents further research on the topic. This book examines the origins of new adaptations. Darwin asserted that random and gradual change in organisms is responsible for species variation, but Kirschner and Gerhart suggest a theory of "facilitated variation," in which core processes are responsible for the range of possible physiological responses that allow an organism to adapt to environmental conditions. Many adaptations, the scientists explain, are "exploratory" in response to circumstances; biological differences occur when plants and animals need them most, not just as a matter of chance. In *The Plausibility of Life* the writers anticipate and address counter-theories and suggest areas for further research. *Library Journal* contributor Gregg Sapp found that the authors "skillfully lay out their arguments so that, while drawing on current research, their work is remarkably comprehensible to general readers."

Kirschner told *CA:* "As a scientist, writing is an essential and common task, but writing books for lay people and/or for scientists are very different tasks. I very much enjoyed writing two books on evolution with my close scientific colleague, John Gerhart. Amazingly, though we live on opposite coasts, we managed to write both books entirely in each other's presence. Having written the two books, one very scientific, and the other for an educated but lay audience and scientists as well, I feel it difficult to choose my favorite. I could not imagine ever again amassing the material of the first book, *Cells, Embryos, and Evolution*—it took ten years. The second book was much more polished as a literary product.

"I hope my books will inspire people to appreciate what the organism brings to evolution. This was largely missing from Darwin and was impossible to comprehend until very recently. It makes life and evolution seem more plausible, and more interesting."

BIOGRAPHICAL AND CRITICAL SOURCES:

PERIODICALS

Booklist, September 15, 2005, Bryce Christensen, review of *The Plausibility of Life: Resolving Darwin's Dilemma,* p. 16.

Cell, August 22, 1997, Kathryn V. Anderson, review of *Cells, Embryos, and Evolution: Toward a Cellular and Developmental Understanding of Phenotypic Variation and Evolutionary Adaptability,* p. 593.

Evolution, February, 1998, Gregory A. Wray, review of *Cells, Embryos, and Evolution,* p. 291.

Library Journal, September 15, 2005, Gregg Sapp, review of *The Plausibility of Life,* p. 87.

Nature, June 26, 1997, J.M.W. Slack, review of *Cells, Embryos, and Evolution,* p. 866.

Publishers Weekly, September 5, 2005, review of *The Plausibility of Life,* p. 52.

Science, August 8, 1997, Anthony P. Mahowald, review of *Cells, Embryos, and Evolution,* p. 772.

Times Higher Education Supplement, February 20, 1998, Mark Pagel, review of *Cells, Embryos, and Evolution,* p. 36.

Trends in Biochemical Sciences, December, 1997, Gilean T. McVean, review of *Cells, Embryos, and Evolution,* p. 495.

ONLINE

Cytokinetics, http://www.cytokinetics.com/ (January 13, 2006), biography of Marc W. Kirschner.

Harvard Medical School Web site, http://www.med.harvard.edu/ (January 13, 2006), biography of Marc W. Kirschner.

Marine Biological Laboratory Home Page, http://www.mbl.edu/ (January 13, 2006), biography of Marc W. Kirschner.

Mellon College of Sciences News Page, http://www.cmu.edu/mcs/ (January 13, 2006), "Carnegie Mellon to Award Dickson Prize to Top Cell Biologist."

* * *

KIRSCHNER, Marc Wallace
 See KIRSCHNER, Marc W.

* * *

KLAHR, David

PERSONAL: Male. *Education:* Massachusetts Institute of Technology, S.B., 1960; Carnegie-Mellon University, M.S., 1965, Ph.D., 1968.

ADDRESSES: Home—1212 Heberton St., Pittsburgh, PA 15206. *Office*—Department of Psychology, Carnegie-Mellon University, Pittsburgh, PA 15213; fax: 412-268-2798. *E-mail*—klahr@cmu.edu.

CAREER: Wolf Research and Development Corp., Bedford, MA, designer, 1960-61; North American Air Defense Command Headquarters, Colorado Springs, CO, developer of systems programs, 1961-62; Federal Aviation Agency, National Aviation Facilities Experimental Center, Northfield, NJ, statistical analyst and programmer, 1963; Westinghouse Electric Corp., Pittsburgh, PA, researcher, 1964; Carnegie Institute of Technology (now Carnegie-Mellon University), Pittsburgh, instructor in mathematics, 1964-66; University of Chicago, Chicago, IL, instructor in business, 1966-67, assistant professor of behavioral and information sciences, 1967-69; Carnegie-Mellon University, Pittsburgh, associate professor, 1969-76, professor of psychology, 1976—, department head, 1983-93, director of Literacy in Science Center, 1988-96. University of Stirling, visiting research fellow in education, 1968; University of London, London Graduate School of Business Studies, visiting Fulbright lecturer, 1969; guest lecturer or scholar at other institutions in the United State and abroad, including University of Colorado, University of Chicago, University of California, Berkeley, Dartmouth College, University of Virginia, University of Iowa, Stanford University, Deakin University, Bowling Green State University, University of Chicago, Naval War College, and Trinity College, Dublin; organizer of symposia. Tel Aviv University, member of international advisory board for human development unit, 1987—.

MEMBER: American Psychological Association (fellow), American Psychological Society (founding fellow), Cognitive Science Society, Cognitive Development Society (member of board of governors), Psychonomic Society, Society for Research in Child Development, Council of Graduate Departments of Psychology (member of executive board, 1986-89), Sigma Xi.

AWARDS, HONORS: Ford Foundation fellow, 1964-66; Social Science Research Council fellow in Scotland, 1968; J.M. Cattell sabbatical award, 2001-02; grants from Spencer Foundation, National Science Foundation, National Institute of Education, A.W. Mellon Foundation, National Institute of Child Health and Human Development, McDonnell Foundation, and Institute for Education Science.

WRITINGS:

Cognition and Instruction, Lawrence Erlbaum Associates (Hillsdale, NJ), 1976.
(With J.G. Wallace) *Cognitive Development: An Information Processing View,* Lawrence Erlbaum Associates (Hillsdale, NJ), 1976.
(Editor, with P. Langley and R. Neches) *Production System Models of Learning and Development,* MIT Press (Cambridge, MA), 1987.
(Editor, with K. Kotovsky) *Complex Information Processing: The Impact of Herbert A. Simon,* Lawrence Erlbaum Associates (Hillsdale, NJ), 1989.
Exploring Science: The Cognition and Development of Discovery Processes, MIT Press (Cambridge, MA), 2000.
(Editor, with S.M. Carver, and contributor) *Cognition and Instruction: 25 Years of Progress,* Erlbaum (Mahwah, NJ), 2001.

Series editor, "Carnegie Mellon Symposia on Cognition." Contributor to books, including *Concept Formation: Knowledge and Experience in Unsupervised Learning,* edited by D. Fisher and M. Pazzani, Morgan Kauffman (San Mateo, CA), 1991; *Developing Cognitive Competence: New Approaches to Process Modeling,* edited by T. Simon and G. Halford, Lawrence Erlbaum Associates (Hillsdale, NJ), 1995; *Conceptual Development: Piaget's Legacy,* edited by E.K. Scholnick and others, Lawrence Erlbaum Associates (Hillsdale, NJ), 1999; *Designing for Science: Implications from Professional, Instructional, and Everyday Science,* edited by K. Crowley, C.D. Schunn, and T. Okada, Erlbaum (Mahwah, NJ), 2001; and *Models of a Man: Essays in Memory of Herbert A. Simon,* edited by M. Augier and J.G. March, MIT Press (Cambridge, MA), in press. Contributor to periodicals, including *Child Development, Developmental Science, Journal of Cognition and Development, Machine Learning, Cognition and Instruction, Science, Memory and Cognition, Contemporary Psychology, Journal of Experimental Psychology: Learning, Memory, and Cognition,* and *Psychological Science.* Served on editorial boards of cognitive science journals.

Some of Klahr's writings have been translated into German, Japanese, and Spanish.

WORK IN PROGRESS: Research on cognitive psychology, especially information-processing analysis of cognitive development, problem-solving instruction, scientific discovery in children and adults, and instructional interventions in science.

BIOGRAPHICAL AND CRITICAL SOURCES:

ONLINE

Carnegie-Mellon University Web Site: David Klahr Home Page, http://www.psy.cmu.edu/psy/faculty/dklahr.html (December 27, 2004).

*   *   *

KLINE, David 1950-

PERSONAL: Born 1950.

ADDRESSES: Agent—c/o Author Mail, CDS Books, 425 Madison Ave., New York, NY 10017. *E-mail*—david@blogrevolt.com; dkline@well.com.

CAREER: Journalist, writer, business consultant. Former columnist for *Wired* and *Upside* magazines; reporter for *New York Times, Christian Science Monitor, Atlantic, NBC News, CBS News,* and *Rolling Stone;* consultant to Microsoft, Sun Microsystems, Hewlett-Packard, Accenture, Discovery Channel, Network Associates, Cordant Technologies, and InteCap. Has also worked as a radio commentator and business speaker.

AWARDS, HONORS: Pulitzer Prize nomination for international reporting.

WRITINGS:

NONFICTION

(With Daniel Burstein) *Road Warriors: Dreams and Nightmares along the Information Highway,* Dutton (New York, NY), 1995.
(With Kevin G. Rivette) *Rembrandts in the Attic: Unlocking the Hidden Value of Patents,* Harvard Business School Press (Boston, MA), 2000.
(With Daniel Burstein) *Blog! How the Newest Media Revolution Is Changing Politics, Business, and Culture,* edited by Arne J. De Keijzer and Paul Berger, CDS Books (New York, NY), 2005.

Contributor to business periodicals, including *Harvard Business Review, Chief Executive, Business 2.0,* and *Sloan Management Review.*

WORK IN PROGRESS: A book about business Web logging.

SIDELIGHTS: As a successful journalist, David Kline has covered stories for a wide range of media. He has reported in several countries, including Bolivia, Ethiopia, and Afghanistan. Kline was nominated for the Pulitzer Prize in international reporting for his 1979 work in Afghanistan. In addition to his work as a journalist, he also serves as a business consultant to large corporations and is the author of several books.

Kline's first nonfiction work, written with Daniel Burstein, is *Road Warriors: Dreams and Nightmares along the Information Highway.* In it, the authors provide an analysis of significant advancements made in information technology during the twentieth century by examining events that led up to each innovation and by discussing the specific consequences that followed them. The book also contains interviews with key figures in technology companies who give various points of view on the 'digital revolution.'

Reviewers' reactions to the book varied. Rick Tetzeli, writing in *Fortune,* found that "reading *Road Warriors* is like catching up on three years' worth of technological trends without having to sift through the boring stuff." Tetzeli went on to note, however, that the book "covers so many topics that reading it straight through is dissatisfying." Alternately, Mary Paulson, a reviewer for *PC* magazine, thought that "further discussions about privacy issues, the debate over government intervention, and the ever-increasing split between the haves and the have-nots give the book an added human dimension." Paulson also pointed out that the book "is an intelligently written, enjoyable read."

Kline's next nonfiction work, *Rembrandts in the Attic: Unlocking the Hidden Value of Patents,* was published in 2000. The book, which Kline wrote with patent attorney Kevin G. Rivette, stresses the value of intellectual property and claims that companies that capitalize on patents and copyrights will gain an advantage over those that do not. "This book makes it utterly clear that executives should be sure they are patenting, or at least assessing, every idea their companies have," observed a reviewer for *Whole Earth.*

Rembrandts in the Attic was followed in 2005 by *Blog! How the Newest Media Revolution Is Changing Politics, Business, and Culture.* The book, which Kline wrote with Burstein, is a combination of interviews and essays concerning online Web logs, or 'blogs.' The authors argue that blogs are revolutionary and they analyze the effects of blogs on business, politics, and culture. Carlin Romano, reviewing the book for the *Philadelphia Inquirer,* stated that *Blog!* "provides a sophisticated intro to a new container of writing that resembles its predecessors, but also counts as an advance." Other reviewers similarly praised the work. Keir Graff, writing in *Booklist,* noted that the book "focuses on the larger issues . . . while steering clear of details that will date quickly." Graff thus concluded that the book is "well worthwhile."

BIOGRAPHICAL AND CRITICAL SOURCES:

PERIODICALS

Booklist, November 1, 2005, Keir Graff, review of *Blog! How the Newest Media Revolution Is Changing Politics, Business, and Culture,* p. 6.

Fortune, November 13, 1995, Rick Tetzeli, review of *Road Warriors: Dreams and Nightmares along the Information Highway,* p. 237.

PC, November 21, 1995, Mary Paulson, review of *Road Warriors,* p. 69.

Philadelphia Inquirer, November 16, 2005, Carlin Romano, review of *Blog!*

Sloan Management Review, winter, 2000, Judith Maas, review of *Rembrandts in the Attic: Unlocking the Hidden Value of Patents,* p. 99.

Whole Earth, winter, 2000, review of *Rembrandts in the Attic,* p. 44.

ONLINE

David Kline Web log, http://www.blogrevolt.com (March 22, 2006).

Jane Genova Web log, http://speechwriting-ghost writing.typepad.com/ (October 27, 2005), interview with author.*

*   *   *

KNELL, Hermann 1926-

PERSONAL: Born November 1, 1926, in Würzburg, Germany; naturalized Canadian citizen; son of Hermann (a merchant) and Therese (Gross) Knell; married Maia Liiv (a chemical engineer), July 14, 1954 (deceased); children: Eva. *Ethnicity:* "German." *Education:* Earned a diploma in mechanical engineering from a technical university, 1952. *Politics:* "None."

ADDRESSES: Agent—c/o Author Mail, Da Capo Press, 11 Cambridge Center, Cambridge, MA 02142. *E-mail*—knellh@shaw.ca.

CAREER: Paper research engineer in Sweden, 1952-53; paper mill design engineer in Canada, 1953-60; paper mill consultant and project manager in Canada, the United States, Asia, South America, Africa, and Europe, between 1961 and 1992; retired, 1992.

MEMBER: Professional Engineers of British Columbia.

WRITINGS:

To Destroy a City: Strategic Bombing and Its Human Consequences in World War II, Da Capo Press (Cambridge, MA), 2003.

BIOGRAPHICAL AND CRITICAL SOURCES:

BOOKS

Knell, Hermann, *To Destroy a City: Strategic Bombing and Its Human Consequences in World War II,* Da Capo Press (Cambridge, MA), 2003.

PERIODICALS

History: Review of New Books, fall, 2003, Ronald D. Cassell, review of *To Destroy a City,* p. 18.

Parameters, spring, 2004, Jeffrey Record, review of *To Destroy a City,* p. 137.

*   *   *

KNIGHT, R.J.B.
    See KNIGHT, Roger

*   *   *

KNIGHT, Roger
    (R.J.B. Knight)

PERSONAL: Married. *Education:* University of Dublin, M.A.; University of Sussex, P.G.C.E.; University of London, Ph.D.

ADDRESSES: Office—Greenwich Maritime Institute, University of Greenwich, Old Royal Naval College, Park Row, Greenwich, London SE10 9LS, England.

CAREER: Maritime scholar. Greenwich Maritime Institute, Greenwich, England, visiting professor; National Maritime Museum, Greenwich, England, former deputy director. Member, British Commission for Maritime History.

MEMBER: Society for Nautical Research (former vice president), Royal Historical Society (fellow), Navy Records Society (former vice president).

WRITINGS:

Valuing English: Reflections on the National Curriculum, David Fulton Publishers (London, England), 1996.
The Pursuit of Victory: The Life and Achievement of Horatio Nelson, Basic Books (New York, NY), 2005.

Also author of scholarly maritime history books under name R.J.B. Knight; member of editorial board for journals, including *Mariner's Mirror* and *Journal for Maritime Research;* consulting editor for the *Oxford Encyclopedia of Maritime History.*

SIDELIGHTS: Roger Knight has devoted a large part of his life to maritime history and archival research. His experience ranges from a number of British and international maritime organizations, museums, and universities. His 2005 publication, *The Pursuit of Victory: The Life and Achievement of Horatio Nelson,* is a biography of British Admiral Horatio Nelson, who first achieved notoriety by defeating Napoleon's fleet during the Battle of the Nile in 1798 and the battle of Trafalgar in 1805, when Nelson was killed.

Comparing the book to other biographies on Nelson, a reviewer in *Publishers Weekly* stated that "Knight's book may be the best." The same reviewer went on to note that the author "paints a vivid picture," making all the details clear in this "highly readable, authoritative, and deeply satisfying biography." A reviewer for the *Economist* similarly felt that "there is every reason to think that this superb work will become the definitive Nelson biography."

BIOGRAPHICAL AND CRITICAL SOURCES:

PERIODICALS

Booklist, December 1, 2005, Gilbert Taylor, review of *The Pursuit of Victory: The Life and Achievement of Horatio Nelson,* p. 17.

Bookseller, June 17, 2005, review of *The Pursuit of Victory,* p. 38.
Economist, June 25, 2005, review of *The Pursuit of Victory,* p. 83.
Kirkus Reviews, October 15, 2005, review of *The Pursuit of Victory,* p. 1123.
Publishers Weekly, October 31, 2005, review of *The Pursuit of Victory,* p. 46.
Times Literary Supplement, September 23, 2005, N.A.M. Rodger, review of *The Pursuit of Victory.*
Weekly Standard, October 24, 2005, Henrik Bering, review of *The Pursuit of Victory,* p. 35.

ONLINE

Greenwich Maritime Institute Web site, http://www.gre.ac.uk/ (March 2, 2006), profile of Roger Knight.

* * *

KOPPEL, Tom

PERSONAL: Married. *Education:* University of Pennsylvania, B.A., 1966; University of Wisconsin, Ph.D., 1972.

ADDRESSES: Home—193 Richard Flack Rd., Salt Spring Island, British Columbia V8K 1N4, Canada. *E-mail*—koppel@saltspring.com.

CAREER: Journalist, beginning c. 1985; *Rabochaya Gazeta,* Kiev, Ukraine, visiting staff, 1989-90.

MEMBER: Periodical Writers Association of Canada (Victoria Chapter).

AWARDS, HONORS: Public Writing Award, Canadian Archaeological Association, 1992, for *Canadian Geographic* article "The Peopling of North America"; Public Communications Award, Canadian Archaeological Association, 1996, for *Canadian Geographic* feature "The Spirit of Haida Gwaii"; British Columbia Arts Council grant, 1998, for research and writing of a book on the Ballard fuel cell; also earned awards from the Canadian Science Writers' Association for his investigative research.

WRITINGS:

Kanaka: The Untold Story of Hawaiian Pioneers in British Columbia and the Pacific Northwest, Whitecap Books (Vancouver, British Columbia, Canada), 1995.

Powering the Future: The Ballard Fuel Cell and the Race to Change the World, Wiley (New York, NY), 1999.

Lost World: Rewriting Prehistory; How New Science Is Tracing America's Ice Age Mariners, Atria Books (New York, NY), 2003.

Also author of several features for the British Columbia Ministry of the Secretary of State, the British Columbia Ministry of Education, and the British Columbia Ministry of Municipal Affairs, Recreation and Culture. Contributor of articles to periodicals, including the *Seattle Post-Intelligencer,* the *Vancouver Sun, Porthole Magazine, Quill & Quire, Canadian Geographic, Canadian Living,* and *Reader's Digest.*

SIDELIGHTS: Canadian journalist Tom Koppel has written everything from feature articles and profiles to technical reports and books. His subjects are drawn from many different fields, including geography, archeology, history, science, and travel. His first book, *Kanaka: The Untold Story of Hawaiian Pioneers in British Columbia and the Pacific Northwest,* chronicles the lives of the Kanakas, a group of Hawaiian people who settled in the Salt Spring Island region of British Columbia, where Koppel himself resides.

In 1999 Koppel published *Powering the Future: The Ballard Fuel Cell and the Race to Change the World.* "This book tells the fascinating story of the development of the Ballard fuel cell and how a small Canadian company grew to world-class stature and went on to form partnerships with some of the largest companies in the world," stated Timothy E. Lipman in the *American Scientist.* The purpose of fuel cell technology is to create an environment-friendly alternative to the internal combustion engine. Fuel cells use hydrogen and oxygen, rather than gasoline or other polluting fuels, to generate electricity. Koppel's book traces the history of Ballard Power Systems, the small Canadian research company that fine-tuned fuel cell design and went on to achieve amazing success. The book includes many quotations from the cofounders of Bal-

lard Power Systems, including Geoffrey Ballard, Paul Howard, and Keith Prater, as well as Firoz Rasul, who took over as president and chief executive officer when the company began to transform into a manufacturing facility.

Writing for *Library Journal,* Eric C. Shoaf felt that *Powering the Future* relies too heavily on technical jargon, but the critic believed that "the technically advanced may find this book compelling." Lipman expressed an opposing sentiment, regarding the book as "entertaining and generally nontechnical" and recommending it "for those in or out of the energy and transportation fields." In a review for *Environment,* Robert M. Margolis acknowledged that "*Powering the Future* is an interesting and timely account" of Ballard's success.

Koppel's next book, *Lost World: Rewriting Prehistory; How New Science Is Tracing America's Ice Age Mariners,* follows a team of scientists as they try to determine how the first people arrived in North America. A long-standing and widely accepted theory is that the first people to arrive in America were big-game hunters from Asia who crossed a land bridge over the Bering Strait. Koppel, and the scientists whom he follows, believe that the first people in America did not come by land, but rather came via coastal migration, arriving along the coast by water. Koppel takes readers along as scientists crawl through caves, dive beneath the sea, camp in the woods, gather scientific data, and celebrate new discoveries.

In a *Kirkus Reviews* critique, one contributor noted that "despite the author's overt cheerleading for the coastal theory," *Lost World* is "a good overview of a fascinating slice of prehistory." *Library Journal* contributor Ann Forister observed that the author slowly breaks down the big-game hunter theory and "begins building a new one of how and when the earliest humans arrived" in North America. One "highlight" of this book, according to Thomas Dillehay in *American Antiquity,* is "a review of a wide variety of underwater and other exploratory techniques and of key happenings in archeology, geology, and paleontology." Dillehay went on to say that "the story and some ideas are interesting, stimulating even."

BIOGRAPHICAL AND CRITICAL SOURCES:

PERIODICALS

American Antiquity, January, 2005, Thomas Dillehay, review of *Lost World: Rewriting Prehistory; How*

New Science Is Tracing America's Ice Age Mariners, p. 202.

American Scientist, September, 2000, Timothy E. Lipman, "Fuel Cell Start-Up," review of *Powering the Future: The Ballard Fuel Cell and the Race to Change the World,* p. 468.

Environment, July, 2000, Robert M. Margolis, review of *Powering the Future,* p. 43.

Kirkus Reviews, April 15, 2003, review of *Lost World,* p. 588.

Library Journal, November 1, 1999, Eric C. Shoaf, review of *Powering the Future,* p. 121; June 15, 2003, Ann Forister, review of *Lost World,* p. 96.

Mechanical Engineering-CIME, June, 2000, review of *Powering the Future,* p. 96.

Natural Life, January-February, 2000, review of *Powering the Future,* p. 29.

ONLINE

Periodical Writers Association of Canada, Victoria Chapter Web site, http://www.islandnet.com/pwacvic/ (January 19, 2006), "Author Profiles: Tom Koppel."

Simon & Schuster Web site, http://www.simonsays.com/ (January 19, 2006), description of *Lost World* and biography of Tom Koppel.*

*   *   *

KOUMANDAREAS, Menis 1931-
(Menes Koumantareas)

PERSONAL: Born 1931, in Athens, Greece.

ADDRESSES: Agent—c/o Author Mail, Dalkey Archive Press, ISU Campus 8905, Normal, IL 61790-8905.

CAREER: Writer. Has worked for insurance and shipping companies.

AWARDS, HONORS: Ford Foundation grant, for completion of *Glass Factory;* German Academic Exchange Service (DAAD) scholarship, 1972; Greek State Prize, 1976, for *Glass Factory;* Blue Book Award, International Book Festival (Frankfurt, Germany), 2001, for *The Handsome Lieutenant.*

WRITINGS:

To armenisma, 1966.

Ta kaemena, Kedros (Athens, Greece), 1972.

Viotechnia hyalikon (title means "Glass Factory"), 1975, reprinted, Kedros (Athens, Greece), 1982.

He kyria Koula, Kedros (Athens, Greece), 1978, published as *Koula,* Kedros (Athens, Greece), 1991, English translation by Kay Cicellis published as *Koula,* Dalkey Archive Press (Normal, IL), 2005.

Serapheim kai Cherouveim (title means "Seraphim and Cherubim"), Kedros (Athens, Greece), 1981.

Ho horaios lochagos (title means "The Handsome Lieutenant"), Kedros (Athens, Greece), 1983.

Planodios salpinktes: dekatessera keimena, Kedros (Athens, Greece), 1989.

He symmoria tes arpas (title means "Harp's Gang"), Kedros (Athens, Greece), 1993.

He myrodhia tous me kani na kleo (short stories; title means "Their Smell Makes Me Want to Cry"), c. 1997.

I mera gia ta grapta kai I nihta gia to soma (essays; title means "Daytime Is for Writing and Nighttime for the Body"), Kedros (Athens, Greece), 1999.

(Author of text) Costas Ordolis, *Athenaioi* (title means "Athenians"), Ekdoseis Kastaniote (Athens, Greece), 2000.

Dyo phores Hellenas (title means "Two Times Greek"), Kedros (Athens, Greece), 2001.

Noe (novel; title means "Noah"), Kedros (Athens, Greece), 2003.

Also author of short story collection whose Greek title means "Pin-Ball Machines" (short stories), 1962, and of *Vest No. 9.* Translator of works by Edgar Allan Poe, Herman Melville, Ernest Hemingway, Carson McCullers, William Faulkner, and F. Scott Fitzgerald.

ADAPTATIONS: Vest No. 9 was adapted for film by Greek filmmaker Pandelis Voulgaris; *Koula* was filmed for Greek Television. Many of Koumandareas's works have been translated into other languages.

SIDELIGHTS: The Foundation for Hellenic Culture in New York has called Menis Koumandareas "the foremost representative of the school of social realism in contemporary Greek literature," according to the Art News Channel Web site. Known for his detailed depictions of contemporary urban life in Greece, Koumandareas has authored a number of award-winning works, among them *Glass Factory* and *The Handsome Lieutenant*. His *Koula*, first published in Athens in 1978, was translated by Kay Cicellis and released in the United States in 2005.

The story in *Koula* is familiar: two strangers (Koula, the bored, frustrated, married mother of two, and Dmitri, a charming, handsome young college student) meet on a train, fall in love, embark on a steamy affair, and eventually go their separate ways. Though the storyline might seem less than original to avid readers, several reviewers felt that in Koumandareas's hands it is anything but clichéd. Brad Hooper acknowledged in *Booklist* the author's "spare, immaculate prose," and concluded that *Koula* is "a short novel as perfectly structured and luminescent as a gemstone." Sharing a similar sentiment, a contributor to *Publishers Weekly* observed that Koumandareas "pack[s] a full novel's worth of drama, passion and sex into a novella."

In his 1993 novel, *He symmoria tes arpas* ("Harp's Gang"), Koumandareas details the life of an aged, reclusive, failed composer whose only link to the world is through his fourteen-year-old bride and her relationships with the other two male characters in the story. In a review of the novel for *World Literature Today*, Theodore Sampson noted, "Koumandareas fleshes out his narrative skillfully through his expert handling of dialogue and psychological nuance." Sampson continued, "This is far more than the average, run-of-the-mill novel can give to a sophisticated reader of fiction."

Like his longer works, Koumandareas's short stories have also received positive critical attention. In the collection *He myrodhia tous me kani na kleo* ("Their Smell Makes Me Want to Cry,") a barber named Euripides listens as a steady stream of clients take a seat in his old barbershop chair and relate their depressing stories. As Sampson pointed out in another *World Literature Today* review, when the stories finally end "we realize that what they have given us is a revealing and disturbing glimpse of a society in crisis." He went on to note that Koumandareas has been classified "as one of the major writers of his generation, a reputation fully reconfirmed by the present volume."

BIOGRAPHICAL AND CRITICAL SOURCES:

PERIODICALS

Booklist, October 15, 2005, Brad Hooper, review of *Koula,* p. 30.

Kirkus Reviews, September 15, 2005, review of *Koula,* p. 996.
Publishers Weekly, September 26, 2005, review of *Koula,* p. 62.
World Literature Today, summer, 1994, Theodore Sampson, review of *He simmoria tes arpas,* p. 610; spring, 1997, Theodore Sampson, review of *He myrodhia tous me kani na kleo,* p. 427.

ONLINE

Art News Channel, http://www.artnewschannel.net/ (January 20, 2006), "A Literary Evening Honoring Menis Koumandareas," press release of the Foundation for Hellenic Culture.
Center for Book Culture Web site, http://www.centerforbookculture.org/ (January 20, 2006), Ana Lucic, "Dalkey Archive, Author Interviews: Menis Koumandareas."
Internationales Literaturfestival Berlin Web site, http://www.literaturfestival.com/ (January 20, 2006), "Authors: Menis Koumandareas."

*   *   *

KOUMANTAREAS, Menes
See KOUMANDAREAS, Menis

*   *   *

KRYSTAL, Arthur

PERSONAL: Male.

ADDRESSES: Agent—c/o Author Mail, Yale University Press, P.O. Box 209040, New Haven, CT 06520-9040.

CAREER: Literary critic, writer, editor.

WRITINGS:

(Editor) Jacques Barzun, *The Culture We Deserve,* Wesleyan University Pres (Middletown, CT), 1989.

(Editor and author of introduction) *A Company of Readers: Uncollected Writings of W.H. Auden, Jacques Barzun, and Lionel Trilling from the Readers' Subscription and Mid-Century Book Clubs,* Free Press (New York, NY), 2001.

Agitations: Essays on Life and Literature, Yale University Press (New Haven, CT), 2002.

Contributor to periodicals, including the *Times Literary Supplement, New York Times Book Review, Harper's, New Yorker, Wall Street Journal, American Scholar,* and *Art and Antiques.*

SIDELIGHTS: Arthur Krystal is a writer and literary critic, and also an editor, including of Jacques Barzun's *The Culture We Deserve,* twelve essays by the scholar. Barzun was born in France but spent nearly his entire life at Columbia University from the time he entered as a student at the age of fifteen. In this volume, he emphasizes the decline of culture in all areas, including education, politics, and the arts. Barbara Fisher Williamson, who reviewed the book for the *New York Times Book Review,* felt that the most informative entries focus on the writing of history.

Krystal is also editor of *A Company of Readers: Uncollected Writings of W.H. Auden, Jacques Barzun, and Lionel Trilling from the Readers' Subscription and Mid-Century Book Clubs.* The Readers' Book Club was in existence from 1951 to 1963. It was published by Gilman Kraft, brother of columnist Joseph Kraft, with its first editor, Lionel Trilling, who had been Gilman's teacher. Trilling went to Jacques Barzun, who had taught Joseph Kraft, and invited him to become part of the venture. Barzun agreed and solicited W.H. Auden, who became the third editor.

The club, which its founders considered to be a step up from the everyman's Book of the Month Club, underwent only one change of name, to the Mid-Century Book Club, and publisher. A book was offered to members every four weeks. Some were new titles, while others were reprints. Each book was introduced in the club's newsletter with an essay by one of the editors, and a total of 173 essays were eventually published. Krystal collected forty-five of them for this volume, and all but one have never before been reprinted.

Louis Menand noted in the *New Yorker* that Krystal writes that these essays "constitute 'some of the last examples of literary criticism aimed at a general audi-

ence by professional critics.' But the pieces are not criticism; they are blurbs, blurbs of rare discernment, perhaps, but blurbs. Their purpose, after all, was to persuade subscribers to buy the selections—and to keep on subscribing." Menand felt that it was not just the books the editors were promoting, "it was a sense of intellectual ease and familiarity that readers might, through a steady consumption of such books, hope to acquire themselves. 'Read this,' the editors seem to say, 'and sound like us.'"

Menand assessed the contributions of the editors, writing that "as it turned out, the only one with a knack for the style of relaxed erudition that the circumstances called for—the only one you can imagine anybody wanting to sound like, even in 1951—was Barzun. This is a little unexpected, for Barzun's take on modern life is fairly severe. He was born in Paris in 1907, and was raised in the world of the French prewar avant-garde. . . . The war ended all that . . . and Barzun never developed a taste for the art and literature that came afterward. . . . Most art and literature after 1914 seemed to him stylistically incoherent and filled with nihilism and disgust." Menand felt that the reason for Barzun's responsiveness and open-mindedness is that they "were features of the Romantic and early avant-garde culture he admired. But part of the reason is that he had a trick that seems to have escaped the other two: he picked his occasions. He wrote on subjects he knew something about, and therefore had points to make."

Menand wrote that Trilling "labored under a ponderous theoretical apparatus, whose elements he took from Hegel, Nietzsche, and Freud. There was nothing ad hoc or belletristic about his criticism; it was theoretical to the last degree. . . . Trilling was also a kind of cultural neurasthenic. His reaction to art that he suspected of lacking the proper gravitas was to avoid it."

Washington Post Book World's George Scialabba called the tone of the reviews "authoritative yet informed, earnest yet relaxed, frequently personal, regularly wry, and once—Trilling on Eliot's recording of *Old Possum's Book of Practical Cats*—memorably whimsical. Auden's is perhaps the most distinctive style, varying the general urbanity now and then with puckishness or crotchet."

In a *Wall Street Journal* review, Terry Teachout called *A Company of Readers* "one of those brilliant book ideas so 'obvious' that nobody ever thinks to carry them out. . . . The Readers' Subscription may have been, in reality, more highbrow than its competitors, but never self-consciously so. All three judges wrote of books in the clear, elegant language of learned men who devoutly believed that culture is accessible to the nonspecialist, whatever his background or condition of life. In a larger sense, one might well define culture as the tribute the uneducated pay to education: They take it on faith that learning is a virtue, and some of them actually do something about it."

Agitations: Essays on Life and Literature is a collection of Krystal's own writings, essays, and reviews that span two decades, and most come from the *New York Times Book Review, American Scholar,* and *Harper's.* His subjects are reading and writing, the relationship between life and literature, the nature of God and death, and his dissatisfaction with the literary scene. "Krystal celebrates the author compelled to write by a sense of mortality and the critic qualified to judge literature by traits of temperament and taste," commented Elizabeth Mary Sheehan in the *New York Times Book Review.*

Library Journal's Mary Paumier Jones noted that the best-known of the essays, "Closing the Books: A Once-Devoted Reader Arrives at the End of the Story," "attempts to come to terms with his own loss of interest in reading. Is it his age, he wonders, or the age."

A *Kirkus Reviews* critic stated that "for someone who has gained a modest reputation as a bumptious crank, critic Krystal . . . comes across here as sensible, personable, and unafraid of his own ideas. . . . This poke in the eye of literary opinion and knowledge feels oddly good."

BIOGRAPHICAL AND CRITICAL SOURCES:

PERIODICALS

American Spectator, October, 1989, John Simon, review of *The Culture We Deserve,* pp. 41-44.

Kirkus Reviews, July 15, 2002, review of *Agitations: Essays on Life and Literature,* p. 1012.

Library Journal, June 15, 2001, Ali Houissa, review of *A Company of Readers: Uncollected Writings of W.H. Auden, Jacques Barzun, and Lionel Trilling from the Readers' Subscription and Mid-Century Book Clubs,* p. 72; September 1, 2002, Mary Paumier Jones, review of *Agitations,* p. 176.

National Review, August 4, 1989, Stephen J. Tonsor, review of *The Culture We Deserve,* p. 41.

Newsweek, August 13, 2001, David Gates, review of *A Company of Readers,* p. 59.

New Yorker, October 15, 2001, Louis Menand, review of *A Company of Readers,* p. 202.

New York Times Book Review, September 17, 1989, Barbara Fisher Williamson, review of *The Culture We Deserve,* p. 25; February 2, 2003, Elizabeth Mary Sheehan, review of *Agitations,* p. 20.

Wall Street Journal, August 6, 2001, Terry Teachout, review of *A Company of Readers,* p. A11.

Washington Post Book World, September 30, 2001, George Scialabba, review of *A Company of Readers,* p. T10.

Wilson Quarterly, autumn, 2001, Michael Dirda, review of *A Company of Readers,* pp. 144-145.*

L

LABRADO, Álvaro
See CUNQUEIRO, Álvaro

* * *

LAIRD, Nick 1975-

PERSONAL: Born 1975, in Northern Ireland; married Zadie Smith (a writer). *Education:* Attended Cambridge University.

ADDRESSES: Agent—c/o Author Mail, HarperCollins Publishers, 10 E. 53rd St., New York, NY 10022.

CAREER: Writer. Visiting fellow, Harvard University.

AWARDS, HONORS: Rooney Prize for Irish Literature, 2005.

WRITINGS:

To a Fault (poetry), Faber & Faber (London, England), 2005.
Utterly Monkey (novel), Fourth Estate (New York, NY), 2005.

WORK IN PROGRESS: A novel, for Fourth Estate.

SIDELIGHTS: Nick Laird's debut novel *Utterly Monkey* relates the story of Danny Williams, a young Irishman who leaves Belfast for a position at a London law firm. His urbane new life takes its toll on Danny's spirit, and he is thoroughly disrupted when Geordie, a friend from high school who has become entangled with the Irish Republican Army (IRA), shows up at Danny's home one night. Danny eventually learns that Geordie has made off with a large amount of money the IRA had earmarked for their use. When Danny's employers send him to Northern Ireland to oversee a corporate takeover, the two men join forces. Six days of their lives are recorded in the novel, including their sexual misadventures and emotional revelations. A *Kirkus Reviews* writer noted that Laird seems unconcerned with creating a plausible plot, but noted that the author's "empathy" for his characters "give[s] the writing a richness beyond the chance encounters and coincidences on which the novel relies."

Utterly Monkey was well received by critics. The book is "a strange combination of thriller and office drama," noted *New Statesman* reviewer Alastair Sooke. Although the action is sometimes "cartoonish," the book is more than merely a humorous offering; it is "a raging, often darkly hilarious meditation on the modern workplace" and a "deft, highly enjoyable book," according to Sooke.

BIOGRAPHICAL AND CRITICAL SOURCES:

PERIODICALS

Booklist, November 15, 2005, Allison Block, review of *Utterly Monkey,* p. 22.

Bookseller, February 4, 2005, review of *Utterly Monkey,* p. 33.

Kirkus Reviews, October 15, 2005, review of *Utterly Monkey,* p. 1102.

New Statesman, May 23, 2005, Alastair Sooke, review of *Utterly Monkey,* p. 53.

Publishers Weekly, November 14, 2005, review of *Utterly Monkey,* p. 43.*

*   *   *

LAMBERT, Lee
See MINGAY, G.E.

*   *   *

LANE, John 1954-
(John Edward Lane)

PERSONAL: Born John Edward Lane, October 29, 1954, in Southern Pines, NC; son of John and Mary Brown (a housewife) Lane; married Margaret Groos (divorced); married Betsy Wakefield Teter. *Education:* Wofford College, B.A., 1977; Bennington College, M.F.A., 1995. *Politics:* "Liberal Democrat." *Hobbies and other interests:* Whitewater kayaking, hiking, contemporary architecture.

ADDRESSES: Office—Wofford College, 326-A Main Building, 429 North Church St., Spartanburg, SC 29303. *E-mail*—Laneje@Wofford.edu.

CAREER: Poet, writer, editor, and educator. Wofford College, Spartanburg, SC, associate professor of English and writing, 1988—; Hub City Writers Project, Spartanburg, project director; Holocene Publications, editor.

Served on the boards of directors of Upstate Forever and Hub City Writers Project and on the advisory board of the South Carolina Writers Workshop.

MEMBER: Association for Study of Literature and the Environment (ASLE), Associated Writing Programs (AWP).

AWARDS, HONORS: Hoyns Fellowship in poetry, University of Virginia, 1980; South Carolina Fellowship in poetry, South Carolina Arts Commission, 1984;

Louisville Review Prize in Poetry, *Louisville Review,* 1991; Phillip K. Reed Memorial Award for outstanding writing on the Southern environment, Southern Environmental Law Center, 2001.

WRITINGS:

Quarries, Briarpatch Press (Davidson, NC), 1984.

As the World around Us Sleeps (poetry), Briarpatch Press (Charlotte, NC), 1992.

Weed Time: Essays from the Edge of a Country Yard, Briarpatch Press (Charlotte, NC), 1993.

Against Information and Other Poems, New Native Press (Cullowhee, NC), 1995.

The Pheasant Cage (one-act play; performed at Presbyterian College and Ohio University, 1995), Palmetto Play Services Acting Editions (Seneca, SC), 1997.

The Empty Pot (CD-ROM; adaptation of Chinese folk tale), Little Planet Publishing (Nashville, TN), 1996.

The Dead Father Poems, Horse & Buggy Press (Raleigh, NC), 2000.

Waist Deep in Black Water (essays), University of Georgia Press (Athens, GA), 2002.

Chattooga: Descending into the Myth of Deliverance River (personal narrative), University of Georgia Press (Athens, GA), 2004.

EDITOR AND CONTRIBUTOR

Usumacinta Journey—a Collaborative Journal from Mexico, Holocene (Spartanburg, SC), 1992.

(With Betsy Wakefield Teter) *Hub City Anthology: Spartanburg Writers & Artists* (essays), Hub City Writers Project/Holocene (Spartanburg, SC), 1996.

(With Betsy Wakefield Teter) *Hub City Christmas: 32 Spartanburg Writers Trim the Literary Tree* (essays), Hub City Writers Project/Holocene (Spartanburg, SC), 1998.

(With Gerald Thurmond) *The Woods Stretched for Miles: New Nature Writing from the South* (essays), University of Georgia Press (Athens, GA), 1999.

(With Jeremy Jones) *The Once-Again Wilderness: Following Wendell Berry into Kentucky's Red River Gorge,* Holocene (Spartanburg, SC), 2000.

Also author of *Thin Creek,* Copper Canyon Press (Port Townsend, WA), 1978; *Quartz Mountain Daybook,* OSAI (Oklahoma city, OK), 1987; *Body Poems,* New

Native Press (Cullowhee, NC), 1991; and *Something Rare As a Dwarf-Flowered Heartleaf (Save the Mary Elizabeth Woods)*, 1999.

Contributor of poetry, fiction, and articles to magazines and periodicals, including *Voice Literary Supplement, Southern Review, State Paper, Upstate Advocate, Fourth Genre, Tar River Poetry, Poetry Motel, New Review, Quarter after Eight, Isle, Chattahoochee Review, W.P. Journal, Alkali Flats, Interim, Poetry Northwest, Tar River Poetry, Wofford Journal, Virginia Quarterly Review, Point, Hampden-Sydney Poetry Review, Higgensville Reader, Patagonia Winds, Asheville Poetry Review, New Review, Nexus, Mount Olive Review, Charleston News & Courier, South Florida Poetry Review, St. Andrews Review, Loblolly,* and *Ploughshares.*

Contributor to numerous anthologies, including *45/96: An Anthology of South Carolina Poets,* edited by William Aarns, Ninety-Six Press (Greenville, SC), 1995; *You Year: New Poems by Point Poets,* edited by Thomas Johnson, Harbinger (Columbia, SC), 1996; *Coffee House Poetry Anthology,* edited by June King and Larry Smith, Bottom Dog Press (Huron, OH), 1996; *In Short: An Anthology of Short Creative Nonfiction,* edited by Judith Kitchen and Mary Paumier Jones, Norton (New York, NY), 1996; *The Heart of America: Celebrating the American Landscape,* National Geographic Books, 2000; *A Year in Place,* edited by Bret Lott, The University of Utah Press, 2000; *Heart of a Nation: Writers and Photographers Inspired by the American Landscape,* National Geographic Press (Washington, DC), 2000; *Adventure America,* National Geographic Press (Washington, DC), 2000 and 2002; *Elemental South,* edited by Dorinda Dalmeyer, University of Georgia Press (Athens, GA), 2004.

SIDELIGHTS: John Lane writes poetry, essays, fiction, and screenplays, much of which features place and wilderness as critical themes. His focus on these themes comes from his love of the outdoors and his outdoor experiences, which include living off of the coast of Georgia on a wilderness island and travels to such exotic places as Central America, the remote rain forest of Surinam, and even wilderness gems located in the United States. For example, in his collection of eighteen essays titled *Waist Deep in Black Water,* Lane writes about a variety of places throughout America, from his home turf of South Carolina to a gorge in Kentucky to the wild's of South America. His essays touch upon topics such as a medicine wheel in Wyoming, the Mayan sense of time, and saving a Girl Scout camp called the Mary Elizabeth Woods that harbors the endangered dwarf-flowered heartleaf. A *Kirkus Reviews* contributor noted that the author "tries to get into a place intuitively" and also commented, "Lane has a fluid eye . . . and it's energizing to see through that eye, open as it is to both light and darkness." Eric Chaney, writing in *Southern Living,* commented that the collection "features exquisite descriptions."

Chattooga: Descending into the Myth of Deliverance River is the author's personal narrative of his journey on the Chattooga River, made somewhat infamous as the setting for the novel *Deliverance* by James Dickey, which was also made into a movie. Lane describes both his experiences on the trip and also looks at the river in relation to Dickey's book. The author describes many of the people who live by the river and recounts how they feel about Dickey's portrayal of some of them as dangerous backwoods inhabitants. A *Publishers Weekly* contributor noted that the author "artfully applies his poetic sensibility to the river."

Lane has also edited or coedited numerous books, including the collection of essays *The Woods Stretched for Miles: New Nature Writing from the South,* which he edited with Gerald Thurmond. The volume features eighteen essays and such noted nature writers as Wendell Berry and Barry Lopez, as well as lesser-known authors, including six women writers. Writing in the *Mississippi Quarterly,* F. Waage noted, "These personal narratives . . . are mainly in the storytelling, feature-journalistic mode, journey-based, and often laced with dialogue between the tellers and other picturesque Southerners." A *Publishers Weekly* contributor wrote that the collection "is full of indelible forays deep into nature." The reviewer went on to note, "These vibrant essays . . . scour nature . . . for keys to earth's renewal and untapped potential." Commenting on the individual essays in a review in the *Library Journal,* Sue Samson wrote, "All are well crafted."

BIOGRAPHICAL AND CRITICAL SOURCES:

PERIODICALS

Kirkus Reviews, September 1, 2002, review of *Waist Deep in Black Water* p. 1283.

Library Journal, April 15, 1999, Sue Samson, review of *The Woods Stretched for Miles: New Nature Writing from the South,* p. 141.

Mississippi Quarterly, winter, 1999, F. Waage, review of review of *The Woods Stretched for Miles,* p. 143.

Publishers Weekly, March 29, 1999, review of *The Woods Stretched for Miles,* p. 85; February 16, 2004, review of *Chattooga: Descending into the Myth of Deliverance River,* p. 162.

Southern Living, April, 2003, Eric Chaney, review of *Waist Deep in Black Water,* p. 54.

ONLINE

Wofford College Web site, http://www.wofford.edu/ (January 28, 2006), faculty profile of author.

*   *   *

LANE, John Edward
See LANE, John

*   *   *

LAURENT, Daniel
See TRIOLET, Elsa

*   *   *

LAYTON, Irving 1912-2006
(Irving Peter Layton)

OBITUARY NOTICE— See index for *CA* sketch: Born March 12, 1912, in Neamtz, Romania; died of Alzheimer's disease, January 4, 2006, in Montréal, Quebec, Canada. Educator and author. Layton was one of Canada's most prominent poets and authors and was known for his often passionate, angry, and sometimes erotic verses. Born Israel Lazarovitch to a Jewish family living in Romania, he was brought to Canada with his parents in 1913. They settled in Montréal, and Layton, who later changed his name legally, completed a bachelor's degree in agriculture from McDonald College in 1939. When Canada entered World War II, he joined the Canadian Army as a lieutenant.

After the war, he returned to school and finished a master's in economics and political science at McGill University in 1946. Over the next decades, Layton pursued dual careers as an educator and poet. He was a lecturer at the Jewish Public Library in Montréal from 1943 to 1958, and a high school teacher in Montréal from 1945 to 1960. He also lectured at Sir George Williams University until 1965, and was a poet in residence there through the late 1960s. From 1970 through 1978, Layton was a professor of English literature at York University in Toronto. He also held various poet-and writer-in-residence positions at various universities, including the University of Ottawa and Concordia University. Layton began publishing collections of his verses in 1945, with the release of *Here and Now.* Over the next few years he became known for what were then considered bawdy and gritty verses. His purpose, the poet would declare, was to shock Canadians out of their complacency with life. Layton's ego about his writing accomplishments sometimes overshadowed his work, and he declared himself on several occasions to be just as accomplished a writer as Wordsworth or Shakespeare. Though few literary critics would place him in that high a category, many would come to agree that Layton was one of Canada's best poets, with some even declaring him a great artist. An incredibly prolific writer, he would produce over fifty verse collections over the years, as well as several nonfiction books and a number of edited works. He earned Canada's Governor-General's Award in 1959 for *A Red Carpet for the Sun,* a Prix Litteraire de Quebec in 1963 for *Balls for a One-Armed Juggler,* and a Life Achievement Award from the *Encyclopedia Britannica* in 1978. Also nominated for a Nobel Prize in 1982, Layton's highest honor came when he was appointed to the Order of Canada in 1976.

OBITUARIES AND OTHER SOURCES:

BOOKS

Contemporary Poets, 7th edition, St. James Press (Detroit, MI), 2001.

PERIODICALS

Los Angeles Times, January 14, 2006, p. B15.
New York Times, January 13, 2006, p. A21.

Times (London, England), February 16, 2006, p. 67.
Washington Post, January 9, 2006, p. B5.

* * *

LAYTON, Irving Peter
　　See LAYTON, Irving

* * *

LAZENBY, Roland

PERSONAL: Male. *Education:* Virginia Military Institute, B.A., 1975; Hollins University, M.A., 1985.

ADDRESSES: Home—Roanoke, VA. *Office*—Virginia Polytechnic Institute and State University, Department of Communication, 106 Shanks Hall, Mail Code 0311, Blacksburg, VA 24061. *E-mail*—rllazenby@aol.com.

CAREER: Writer, journalist, educator, and coach. Virginia Polytechnic Institute and State University, Blacksburg, faculty member.

WRITINGS:

NONFICTION SPORTS BOOKS

(With Billy Packer) *Hoops! Confessions of a College Basketball Analyst,* Contemporary Books (Chicago, IL), 1985.
(With Ed Green and David Meador) *Championship Basketball: Top College Coaches Present Their Winning Strategies, Tips, and Techniques for Players and Coaches,* Contemporary Books (Chicago, IL), 1987.
(With Billy Packer) *Fifty Years of the Final Four: Golden Moments of the NCAA Basketball Tournament,* Taylor (Dallas, TX), 1987, revised edition published as *Golden Moments of the Final Four: A Retrospective of the NCAA Basketball Tournament,* Jefferson Street Press (Dallas, TX), 1989.
100 Greatest Quarterbacks, Crescent Books (New York, NY), 1988.
(With Billy Packer) *College Basketball's 25 Greatest Teams,* Sporting News (St. Louis, MO), 1989.

The NBA Finals: The Official Illustrated History, foreword by Joe Dumars, introduction by Bob Ryan, Taylor (Dallas, TX), 1990.
(With Jeffrey Denberg and Tom Stinson) *From Sweet Lou to 'Nique,* edited by Arthur Triche, Longstreet Press (Atlanta, GA), 1992.
The Lakers: A Basketball Journey, St. Martin's Press (New York, NY), 1993, 50th anniversary edition, Masters Press (Indianapolis, IN), 1995.
(With Doug Doughty) *'Hoos 'n' Hokies: The Rivalry: 100 Years of Virginia/Virginia Tech Football,* Taylor (Dallas, TX), 1995.
And Now, Your Chicago Bulls! A Thirty-Year Celebration!, Taylor (Dallas, TX), 1995.
Airballs! Notes from the NBA's Far Side, Masters Press (Indianapolis, IN), 1996.
Bull Run! The Story of the 1995-96 Chicago Bulls: The Greatest Team in Basketball History, foreword by Phil Jackson, photography by Bill Smith, Addax (Lenexa, KS), 1996.
The NBA Finals: A Fifty-Year Celebration, introduction by Bob Ryan, Masters Press (Indianapolis, IN), 1996.
Chicago Bulls: The Authorized Pictorial, photography by Bill Smith, Summit (Arlington, TX), 1997.
Smashmouth: Attitude between the Lines, Addax (Lenexa, KS), 1997.
Yo, Baby, It's Attitude! The New Bad Boyz of the NBA Take the Jordan Test, Addax (Lenexa, KS), 1997.
Blood on the Horns: The Long Strange Ride of Michael Jordan's Chicago Bulls, Addax (Lenexa, KS), 1998.
The Unofficial Chicago Bulls Pocket Primer, Addax (Lenexa, KS), 1998.
Stockton to Malone: The Rise of the Utah Jazz, Addax (Lenexa, KS), 1998.
Bird: Portrait of a Competitor, photography by Steve Lipofsky, Addax (Lenexa, KS), 1998.
(With Billy Packer) *Why We Win: Great American Coaches Offer Their Strategies for Success in Sports and Life,* Masters Press (Lincolnwood, IL), 1999.
Love at First Light: Michael Jordan and the Romance of Golf, Sports (Champaign, IL), 1999.
Mad Game: The NBA Education of Kobe Bryant, Masters Press (Lincolnwood, IL), 2000, revised edition, Contemporary Books (Chicago, IL), 2002.
(Editor) *Chicago Sports Century,* Sports (Champaign, IL), 2000.
Mindgames: Phil Jackson's Long, Strange Journey, Contemporary Books (Lincolnwood, IL), 2001.

The Pictorial History of Football, Thunder Bay Press (San Diego, CA), 2002.
Johnny Unitas: The Best There Ever Was, Triumph Books (Chicago, IL), 2002.
Ichiro: The Making of an American Hero, Triumph Books (Chicago, IL), 2002.
(With Bob Schron) *Tom Brady: Sudden Glory,* Triumph Books (Chicago, IL), 2002.
(With Mike Ashley) *Emmitt Smith: Record-Breaking Rush to Glory,* Triumph Books (Chicago, IL), 2002.
The Show: The Inside Story of the Spectacular Los Angeles Lakers in the Words of Those Who Lived It, McGraw-Hill (New York, NY), 2005.

Also author of annual publications *Official Boston Celtics Greenbook* and *Official Detroit Pistons Yearbook.* Contributor to books, including *Michael Jordan Scrapbook,* Publications International (Lincolnwood, IL), 1998.

Contributor to periodicals, including *Sporting News, Chicago Sun-Times,* and *Dunkshoot.*

SIDELIGHTS: Since the mid-1980s, prolific sports writer Roland Lazenby has authored over two dozen books on various sports topics. Some of his titles include, *Airballs! Notes from the NBA's Far Side, Smashmouth: Attitude between the Lines, Mad Game: The NBA Education of Kobe Bryant,* and *Mindgames: Phil Jackson's Long, Strange Journey.*

In 1993 Lazenby published *The Lakers: A Basketball Journey.* The book gives a history of the famous Los Angeles professional basketball team dating back to their formation in Minneapolis, Minnesota, in 1946. Lazenby also addresses such high-profile events as when team-member Magic Johnson was diagnosed with the Human Immunodeficiency Virus (HIV). The author also provides behind-the-scenes insights into legendary Lakers, including George Mikan, Elgin Baylor, Kareem Abdul-Jabbar, and coach Pat Riley. Overall, critics praised the work. A *Publishers Weekly* reviewer noted that "the author is clearly well informed." Additionally, William Ladson, writing in *Sport,* acknowledged that "if you want to reminisce about the glory days, this is the book to read."

The Los Angeles Lakers are also the topic of Lazenby's 2005 book, *The Show: The Inside Story of the Spectacular Los Angeles Lakers in the Words of Those*

Who Lived It. In this comprehensive oral history of the basketball franchise, Lazenby "pulls the reader into the tale with humorous quotes and innumerable first-person accounts," according to *Library Journal* contributor Todd Spires. The book is a compilation of interviews with prominent players such as Kobe Bryant and Shaquille O'Neal, and head coach Phil Jackson. Lazenby examines the off-court activities of the Lakers that made them one of the best-known teams in history. The book, ultimately, received mixed reviews. A *Kirkus Reviews* contributor called it "informative, but stylistically uneven," while Wes Lukowsky, writing in *Booklist,* felt that *The Show* "is must reading for NBA fans both young and old."

BIOGRAPHICAL AND CRITICAL SOURCES:

PERIODICALS

Booklist, November 15, 2005, Wes Lukowsky, review of *The Show: The Inside Story of the Spectacular Los Angeles Lakers in the Words of Those Who Lived It,* p. 13.
Kirkus Reviews, November 1, 2005, review of *The Show,* p. 1174.
Library Journal, November 15, 2005, Todd Spires, review of *The Show,* p. 73.
Publishers Weekly, October 18, 1993, review of *The Lakers: A Basketball Journey,* p. 59; October 31, 2005, review of *The Show,* p. 44.
Sport, July, 1994, William Ladson, review of *The Lakers,* p. 16.

ONLINE

Los Angeles Lakers Web log, http://lakersblog.latimes.com/ (March 23, 2006), interview with author.
True Hoop, http://www.truehoop.com/ (January 19, 2006), Henry Abbott, interview with author.
Virginia Polytechnic Institute and State University, Department of Communication Web site, http://www.comm.vt.edu/ (March 23, 2006), author profile.*

*   *   *

LEHMANN, Debra Lynn
See VANASSE, Deb

LEITCH, Donovan P.
   See DONOVAN

*　　*　　*

LERANGIS, Peter 1955-
   (Alison Blair, Morgan Burke, M.E. Cooper, Franklin W. Dixon, a house pseudonym, Carolyn Keene, a house pseudonym, A.L. Singer, George Spelvin, Artie Sprengle, Dr. R.E. Volting)

PERSONAL: Born August 19, 1955, in New York, NY; son of Nicholas P. (a telephone company employee) and Mary (a school secretary; maiden name, Condos) Lerangis; married Cristina L. DeVaron (a singer, pianist, and songwriter), September 4, 1983; children: Nicholas James, Joseph Alexander. *Education:* Harvard College, A.B., 1977. *Hobbies and other interests:* Photography, jogging, singing, piano.

ADDRESSES: Home—7 W. 96th St., New York, NY 10025. *Agent*—George Nicholson, Sterling Lord Literistic, 65 Bleecker St., New York, NY 10012-2420.

CAREER: Actor and singer in New York, NY, 1978-89; freelance copyeditor, 1979-85; freelance writer, 1986—. Has also taught at the City University of New York Graduate Center, 1985-86.

MEMBER: Society of Children's Book Writers and Illustrators, PEN, Actors Equity Association, Screen Actors Guild, American Federation of Television and Radio Artists, Harvard Krokodiloes Board.

AWARDS, HONORS: Children's Choice Award, International Reading Association, 2000, for *War;* Bank Street Best Children's Book, 2006, for *Smiler's Bones.*

WRITINGS:

YOUNG ADULT FICTION

Foul Play ("Three Investigators Crimebusters" series), Knopf (New York, NY), 1990.
The Yearbook, Scholastic (New York, NY), 1994.

Driver's Dead, Scholastic (New York, NY), 1994.
Spring Fever, Scholastic (New York, NY), 1996.
Spring Break, Scholastic (New York, NY), 1996.
It Came from the Cafeteria, Scholastic (New York, NY), 1996.
Attack of the Killer Potatoes, Scholastic (New York, NY), 1997.
Antarctica #1: Journey to the Pole, Scholastic (New York, NY), 2000.
Antarctica #2: Escape from Disaster, Scholastic (New York, NY), 2000.
Smiler's Bones, Scholastic (New York, NY), 2005.
WTF, Simon Pulse (New York, NY), 2007.

"WATCHERS" SERIES

Last Stop, Scholastic (New York, NY), 1998.
Rewind, Scholastic (New York, NY), 1998.
I.D., Scholastic (New York, NY), 1999.
War, Scholastic (New York, NY), 1999.
Lab 6, Scholastic (New York, NY), 1999.

"ABRACADABRA!" SERIES

Poof! Rabbits Everywhere!, Scholastic (New York, NY), 2001.
Boo! Ghosts in the School!, Scholastic (New York, NY), 2001.
Presto! Magic Treasure!, Scholastic (New York, NY), 2002.
Yeeps! Secret in the Statue!, Scholastic (New York, NY), 2002.
Zap! Science Fair Surprise!, Scholastic (New York, NY), 2002.
Whoa! Amusement Park Gone Wild!, Scholastic (New York, NY), 2003.
Wow! Blast from the Past!, Scholastic (New York, NY), 2003.

"X ISLE" SERIES

X Isle, Scholastic UK (London, England), 2003.
Return to X Isle, Scholastic UK (London, England), 2003.

"SPY X" SERIES

The Code, Scholastic (New York, NY), 2004.
Hide and Seek, Scholastic (New York, NY), 2004.

Proof Positive, Scholastic (New York, NY), 2005.
Tunnel Vision, Scholastic (New York, NY), 2005.

PUZZLE BOOKS

Puzzles and Games, Macmillan Educational (New York, NY), 1984.
Mickey's Drill-a-Days: Letters and Words, Simon & Schuster (New York, NY), 1985.
Star Trek Activity Book, Simon & Schuster (New York, NY), 1986.
Star Trek Puzzle Book, Simon & Schuster (New York, NY), 1986.
Super Puzzle #1: Going Batty, Troll, 1988.
Super Puzzle #3: Camp Craziness, Troll, 1988.

SCREENPLAY NOVELIZATIONS

Young Sherlock Holmes (based on the screenplay by Chris Columbus), Simon & Schuster (New York, NY), 1985.
Star Trek IV: The Voyage Home (based on the screenplay by Steve Meerson), Simon & Schuster (New York, NY), 1986.
(Under pseudonym A.L. Singer) *License to Drive* (based on the screenplay by Neil Tolkin), Scholastic (New York, NY), 1988.
(Under pseudonym A.L. Singer) *Little Monsters* (based on the screenplay by Terry Rossio and Ted Elliott), Scholastic (New York, NY), 1989.
(Under pseudonym A.L. Singer) *Sing* (based on the screenplay by Dean Pitchford), Scholastic (New York, NY), 1989.
(Under pseudonym A.L. Singer) *Rescuers Down Under* (based on the Disney film of the same title), Scholastic (New York, NY), 1990.
(Under pseudonym A.L. Singer) *Dick Tracy* (based on the screenplay by Jim Cash and Jack Epps, Jr.), Western Publishing (Racine, WI), 1990.
(Under pseudonym A.L. Singer) *Disney's Beauty and the Beast* (based on the screenplay by Linda Woolverton), illustrated by Ron Dias and Ric Gonzalez, Disney Press (New York, NY), 1991.
(Under pseudonym A.L. Singer) *Davy Crockett and the Pirates at Cave-In Rock* (based on the Disney television series), Disney Press (New York, NY), 1991.
(Under pseudonym A.L. Singer) *Bingo* (based on the screenplay by Jim Strain), Scholastic (New York, NY), 1991.

(Under pseudonym A.L. Singer) *Aladdin,* Disney Press (New York, NY), 1992.
(Under pseudonym A.L. Singer) *Home Alone II: Lost in New York,* Scholastic (New York, NY), 1992.
(Under pseudonym A.L. Singer) *Robin Hood,* Disney Press (New York, NY), 1992.
(Under pseudonym A.L. Singer) *Young Indiana Jones Chronicles: Safari Sleuth* (based on the screenplay by Matthew Jacobs), Random House (New York, NY), 1992.
(Under pseudonym A.L. Singer) *Little Mermaid,* Disney Press (New York, NY), 1993.
(Under pseudonym A.L. Singer) *Sleeping Beauty,* Disney Press (New York, NY), 1993.
(Under pseudonym A.L. Singer) *Surf Warriors* (based on the screenplay by Dan Gordon), Dell (New York, NY), 1993.
(Under pseudonym A.L. Singer) *The Swan Princess,* Scholastic (New York, NY), 1994.
(Under pseudonym A.L. Singer) *Miracle on Thirty-fourth Street,* Scholastic (New York, NY), 1994.
(Under pseudonym A.L. Singer) *Mufasa's Little Instruction Book,* Disney Press (New York, NY), 1994.
(Under pseudonym A.L. Singer) *Jumanji* (picture book), Scholastic (New York, NY), 1995.
(Under pseudonym George Spelvin) *Jumanji* (young adult), Scholastic (New York, NY), 1995.
(Under pseudonym A.L. Singer) *The Amazing Panda Adventure,* Scholastic (New York, NY), 1995.
(Under pseudonym A.L. Singer) *Baby-Sitters Club,* Scholastic (New York, NY), 1995.
(Under pseudonym A.L. Singer) *Anastasia,* HyperActive (New York, NY), 1997.
Sleepy Hollow: A Novelization, Simon & Schuster (New York, NY), 1999.
The Road to El Dorado, Penguin Putnam (New York, NY), 2000.
M. Night Shyamalan's The Sixth Sense, Scholastic (New York, NY), 2000.
Batman Begins, Scholastic (New York, NY), 2005.

OTHER MOVIE TIE-IN BOOKS

(Under pseudonym A.L. Singer) *Star Wars—Episode One Adventure and Game Books,* Scholastic (New York, NY), 2000.
(Under pseudonym Dr. R.E. Volting) *Shrek Gag Book,* Penguin Putnam (New York, NY), 2001.

(Under pseudonym Artie Sprengle) *Madagascar Joke Book,* Scholastic (New York, NY), 2005.

INTERACTIVE

The Amazing Ben Franklin, Bantam (New York, NY), 1987.

In Search of a Shark, Scholastic (New York, NY), 1987.

The Last of the Dinosaurs, Bantam (New York, NY), 1988.

World War II Codebreakers, Bantam (New York, NY), 1989.

NONFICTION

A Kid's Guide to New York City, illustrated by Richard E. Brown, Harcourt Brace Jovanovich (San Diego, CA), 1988.

Teacher Guide to Square One TV Show, Children's Television Workshop, 1989.

(With Peter Dodson) *Dinosaur Bookshelf: Giant Dinosaurs,* illustrated by Alex Nino, Scholastic (New York, NY), 1990.

(With Peter Dodson) *Dinosaur Bookshelf: Baby Dinosaurs,* illustrated by Alex Nino, Scholastic (New York, NY), 1990.

UNDER PSEUDONYM FRANKLIN W. DIXON

The Genius Thieves, Archway (New York, NY), 1987.

The Borgia Dagger, Archway (New York, NY), 1988.

A Killing in the Market, Archway (New York, NY), 1988.

Danger Zone, Archway (New York, NY), 1990.

UNDER PSEUDONYM CAROLYN KEENE

A Crime for Christmas, Archway (New York, NY), 1988.

Shock Waves, Archway (New York, NY), 1989.

Buried in Time, Archway (New York, NY), 1990.

UNDER PSEUDONYM A.L. SINGER

The Sultan's Secret, Ballantine (New York, NY), 1988.

Blaster Master, Scholastic (New York, NY), 1990.

Ninja Gaiden, Scholastic (New York, NY), 1990.

Dick Tracy Catch-a-Crook Adventure, Western Publishing (Racine, WI), 1990.

Infiltrator, Scholastic (New York, NY), 1991.

Bases Loaded 2, Scholastic (New York, NY), 1991.

UNDER PSEUDONYM MORGAN BURKE

The Party Room #1: Get It Started, Simon Pulse (New York, NY), 2005.

The Party Room #3: Last Call, Simon Pulse (New York, NY), 2005.

OTHER

(Under pseudonym Alison Blair) *Campus Fever,* Ballantine (New York, NY), 1988.

(Under pseudonym M.E. Cooper) *Falling for You,* Scholastic (New York, NY), 1988.

Also author of books in the "Baby-Sitters Club," "California Diaries," "Sweet Valley High," and "Sweet Valley Twins" series; contributor of short stories to anthologies, including *Unexpected: 11 Mysterious Stories,* edited by Laura E. Williams, Scholastic (New York, NY), 2005.

WORK IN PROGRESS: Four books in the "Drama Club" series, for Penguin Putnam, expected 2007.

SIDELIGHTS: Peter Lerangis is a prolific author of children's books written under his own name and various pseudonyms. The author won praise from numerous critics for his novel *Smiler's Bones,* which is intended for an audience of middle-schoolers and older. The book is based on a real incident that took place in 1897, in which the Arctic explorer Robert Peary brought six Inuit people from their northern homes to New York City. They were treated like curiosities and displayed at the American Museum of Natural History as part of a living exhibit. The youngest member of the group, and the focus of the story, is an eight-year-old Inuit boy named Minik. Coming from a frozen land where he has never even seen a tree, the trusting child is happy enough to experience the pleasures of candy, circuses, and other amusements never dreamed of in his homeland. His perception of this new world is portrayed in a way that is "brilliant," according to a *Kirkus Reviews* writer. Minik's father, who is known as Qisuk or "Smiler," is also part of the exhibit, but when he and three other adult members of the party die of disease, and the other heads back to the Arctic, Minik comes under the care of a museum curator he knows as "Uncle Will."

The chapters of the book alternate between the innocent viewpoint of young Minik and that of the confused, cynical, and isolated teenager he becomes with the passing of years. Minik's inner life is convincingly drawn, according to numerous reviewers. Although his dream life provides a link between him and his distant family, Minik also comes to realize how terribly alone he is. Eventually, he even learns that Uncle Will, whom he trusted, has horribly betrayed him and his culture by allowing the bones of Qisuk to be stored in a drawer as a museum artifact rather than properly burying the body, though he and other museum officials had staged a fake burial to fool Minik into believing that his father was buried according to Inuit custom. By 1909, Minik is living in Quebec City and is suicidal. The author's notes inform readers that although Minik did eventually return to his birthplace in Greenland, he was not able to reintegrate successfully into his old culture; he ended up traveling to New Hampshire and working in a logging camp there until his death from influenza in 1918. According to *Kliatt* reviewer Paula Rohrlick, Lerangis does a fine job making Minik and his story vivid, showing "how he was exploited and illuminating a dark corner of history . . . . Thoughtful readers will appreciate its message about respecting other cultures and how it feels to belong nowhere." According to Vicki Reutter in *School Library Journal,* Minik is a memorable character, and "issues of racism and scientific arrogance will not be lost on readers." The use of many flashbacks may be "disorienting" to some readers, cautioned *Booklist* reviewer Jennifer Mattson, but she concluded that "the incisive emotions are unforgettable." Noting the tragic elements of the story, Deborah Stevenson nevertheless commented in her review for the *Bulletin of the Center for Children's Books* that Lerangis somehow manages to present Minik's history as "a tale of hard-won resilience and hope rather than annihilation, and the darkness is counterbalanced with human goodness and touches of quiet humor."

Lerangis once told *CA:* "When I was in fourth grade, I used to hide spiral notebooks in my math textbook. My teacher, Ms. Scuderi, thought I was deeply involved in my multiplication tables. I wasn't. I was busy writing stories. (I thought they would be books, but I never seemed to be able to finish them.) My main interest back then was science fiction, and my stories were usually about kids stowing away on rockets to other planets.

"To me, the best thing about writing was this: I could completely escape my house, my town, my family, my body, *everything.* I could fly, burrow, travel in time; I could create people and creatures, tell them what to say, give them powers, kill them off, make them grow old—and when I was done, there'd still be dinner on the table and a nice cozy bed to sleep in. Why did I want to escape? I had a pretty happy, normal life on the outside. *Inside,* though, things weren't so great.

"I grew up in Freeport, New York, a suburb. Until high school I was a pretty fat kid (87 pounds in second grade). I was horrible in gym class. When it came time to pick teams, I tried to be invisible. It never worked. Inevitably someone would say, 'You got *Lerangis,*' as if 'Lerangis' was some kind of annoying condition, like the flu. One time, as I was ducking a fly ball that dropped for a hit, a classmate screamed out, 'Lerangis, you're the worst athleek I ever saw." I took comfort in the fact that I knew how to say *athlete.* Even spell it.

"The other problem was clothes. My mom used to choose and buy them for me. I thought she did an okay job, but by eighth grade I thought I should take matters into my own hands. I had my eye on a Nehru jacket on sale at Macy's and begged Mom to let me buy it. (Nehru jackets were very hip in 1969. They were tight-fitting, with many buttons up the middle and a priest-like collar.) This one was made of stiff marbled vinyl, like the fabric on a TV-room lounge chair. But it was the one thing I wanted in life. It was going to change my image in school. With a look of compassion and pity, Mom agreed to buy it for me. I was elated. The next day I proudly wore it to John W. Dodd Junior High.

"It did change my image, all right. The hoots of laughter on the playground were heard in the next town. I felt humiliated. That evening I took it off and hung it in the attic. My mom was wise enough not to ask too much about it. (I wore it only once again, when I played the Fairy Godmother in a comedy version of *Cinderella*).

"When I was reading or writing, I didn't have to worry about other kids' opinions. Not that my life was so awful. I did have fun as a kid. I could make people laugh. I did good imitations, which sometimes grew into shows (and sometimes got me into big trouble). Between eighth and ninth grade, things changed a lot. I grew about five inches and didn't look so fat anymore. I started getting bad grades on purpose to be cooler (not a great idea, in retrospect). I began playing sports a little and got more involved in drama and music—and girls. My first girlfriend was the sports editor of the high-school newspaper. When she read a poem I'd written (a spoof on 'Casey at Bat,' about a basketball player who stuffs his own team's hoop), she got me a spot on the newspaper right away.

"Newspaper writing taught me a lot about organizing my thoughts concisely. But even though fiction writing was my real love, I was hardly doing it at all. I somehow managed to finish first in my high-school class, and a lot of colleges accepted me, so I felt major pressure to do something noble, upstanding, and respectable. Writing was not one of those things. Acting? Forget it. The immigrant ethic was strong in my family. My grandparents had come from Greece with no education or money (my grandfather's last name was Lirantzis, which means 'lyre player'; the name became 'Lerangis' at Ellis Island). My parents grew up poor and worked hard to rise into the American middle class. Me? I was the first-born in my generation, which was expected to be chock-full of doctors, lawyers, and tycoons.

"Well, I didn't want to be any of those things. But everyone insisted that a life of writing, theater, or music would be full of despair and wasted effort. I went to Harvard College and majored in biochemistry. I guess I thought if I forced the issue, I might magically become interested in medicine after all. Guess what became of that idea?

"In college I did practically no creative writing. (I tried to get into a creative-writing program, but I was rejected.) My main extra activity was singing. I joined a twelve-member a cappella group and became its director. I acted in a play or two. And I didn't do very well in biochemistry.

"After college lots of my friends were going to law school, so I thought I might try that. I applied, got in, sent a deposit, even got a job as a paralegal for a few months. I became pretty miserable and left to be a singing waiter in Nantucket for a summer. That fall I chucked law school and went to New York to try to be an actor. I did *that* for eight years, performing in musical theater. I was even in a Broadway show. In between acting jobs, I waited on tables, but I kept getting fired. In desperation, I tried freelance copyediting, which means checking authors' manuscripts for grammar, spelling, accuracy. It was flexible work and I could go to auditions and classes. I ended up reading an awful lot of books—some of them *quite* awful! I figured, 'I can do better than that!' So I tried my hand at writing again.

"It had been over ten years since I'd done any creative writing at all, and I was nearly thirty. By 1986 I was writing full-time. I found out that (1) It's never too late to start doing something you love, and (2) *everything* you've done in your life makes your writing rich and unique. My acting experience gave me a good ear for dialogue and an ability to slip in and out of my characters' personalities. My introverted years gave me the patience to sit alone for hours and think and write. Being the oldest in my family, watching sixteen siblings and cousins grow up, gave me insights into kids' ways of thinking. As for the rest—the stories that have nothing to do with life experiences—that's what imagination is for! In writing, the possibilities are endless. If you have a little talent and a lot of passion for it, then the only remaining necessary ingredient is discipline. And *that* is something anyone can learn (even a horrendous procrastinator like me).

"I live in an apartment in New York City, near Central Park. My wife is a singer and pianist and songwriter. I've written over one hundred forty books. In the early days, I used a lot of pen names, but now almost all of my books are under my own name. I do lots of different kinds of writing. *Smiler's Bones* is a historical novel about a true character named Minik, a Polar Eskimo boy who was orphaned in New York City in 1897. The 'Spy X' series is about 11-year-old twins who must try to find their missing mother by solving mysterious codes and using odd equipment that they receive anonymously. The 'Antarctica' series is about a fictional 'lost' voyage to the South Pole by an American explorer and a crew that includes his two teenage sons. Translated into many languages, the 'Watchers' books are mysteries with wild unexpected twists in a 'Twilight Zone' vein, which explore topics like cloning, alternate realities, time travel, and artificial humans. For younger (chapter book) readers, the 'Abracadabra' series follows a fourth-grade magic club who use their knowledge of magic tricks to solve mysteries in their school and town. Some of my earlier books were horror-related (and some horror spoofs), but all of those are out of print. And I still write occasional movie novelizations, because, well, I LOVE movies!"

BIOGRAPHICAL AND CRITICAL SOURCES:

PERIODICALS

Booklist, April 1, 2005, Jennifer Mattson, review of *Smiler's Bones,* p. 1354.

Bulletin of the Center for Children's Books, June, 2005, Deborah Stevenson, review of *Smiler's Bones,* p. 446.

Kirkus Reviews, March 15, 2005, review of *Smiler's Bones,* p. 354.

Kliatt, May, 2005, Paula Rohrlick, review of *Smiler's Bones,* p. 15.

Publishers Weekly, November 23, 1998, review of *Last Stop,* p. 67.

School Library Journal, October, 1987, Elaine E. Knight, review of *The Amazing Ben Franklin,* p. 151; April, 1988, Elaine E. Knight, review of *In Search of a Shark,* p. 120; January, 1990, Elaine E. Knight, review of *World War II Codebreaker,* p. 104; June, 2005, Vicki Reutter, review of *Smiler's Bones,* p. 161.

*　　*　　*

LESTEWKA, Patrick
See DAVIDSON, Craig

*　　*　　*

LEVY, Thomas 1950-
　　(Thomas Edward Levy)

PERSONAL: Born November 30, 1950, in Biloxi, MS; son of Isaac (an electrician) and Catherine (a homemaker; maiden name, Kurtz) Levy. *Ethnicity:* "Caucasian." *Education:* Johns Hopkins University, B.A., 1972; Tulane University School of Medicine, M.D., 1976; University of Denver, J.D., 1998. *Politics:* Republican. *Hobbies and other interests:* Golf.

ADDRESSES: Home—1585 Mesa Rd., Colorado Springs, CO 80904. *E-mail*—televymd@yahoo.com.

CAREER: Tulane University Medical School, New Orleans, LA, assistant professor of medicine, 1981-83, instructor in radiology, 1983-84, clinical assistant professor of medicine, 1983-86; Iberia General Hospital, New Iberia, LA, staff member, 1984-91; Memorial Hospital, Colorado Springs, CO, staff member, beginning 1991; Denver General Hospital, Denver, CO, staff member, 1995-96; Capital University of Integrative Medicine, Washington, DC, associate professor, 1999—. Admitted to the Bar of Colorado, 1998; admitted to the Bar of the District of Columbia, 1999.

MEMBER: American College of Cardiology (fellow), American Inn of Court (associate barrister), Colorado Bar Association.

WRITINGS:

(With Hal A. Huggins) *Uninformed Consent: The Hidden Dangers in Dental Care,* Hampton Roads Publishing (Charlottesville, VA), 1999.

Optimal Nutrition for Optimal Health, foreword by Robert C. Atkins, Keats (Chicago, IL), 2001.

(With Robert Kulacz) *The Roots of Disease: Connecting Dentistry and Medicine,* foreword by James Earl Jones, Xlibris (Philadelphia, PA), 2002.

Vitamin C, Infectious Diseases, and Toxins: Curing the Incurable, Xlibris (Philadelphia, PA), 2002.

Contributor to medical journals, including *Anesthesiology, Annals of Emergency Medicine, Journal of Advancement in Medicine,* and *Alternative Medicine Review.*

SIDELIGHTS: Thomas Levy is a physician who explores alternative ways of dealing with illness and disease. Levy addressed the dangers of toxic dental treatments with coauthor Hal A. Huggins in *Uninformed Consent: The Hidden Dangers in Dental*

Care. The authors detail the illnesses suspected to be caused by toxic dental materials and offer ways of dealing with that toxicity. *Library Journal* contributor Kristine Benishek felt that it is "an authoritative book that accomplishes their stated purpose."

In *Vitamin C, Infectious Diseases, and Toxins: Curing the Incurable,* Levy details the use of vitamin C (ascorbic acid) in treating a variety of ailments. Levy cites more than 1,200 articles from medical and scientific journals, including the *New England Journal of Medicine, Lancet,* and the *Journal of the American Medical Association,* that show that viral diseases such as hepatitis, encephalitis, and polio, have been cured by intravenous injections of vitamin C. Among the research cited is the work of vitamin C researchers Frederick Klenner and Robert Cathcart, doctors who have documented the positive use of the vitamin in treating their patients with AIDS. The book includes a chapter that offers evidence that vitamin C has been shown to neutralize toxins for which there is no other treatment, and that snakebite and spider venom, tetanus toxin, and heavy leads can be neutralized in this manner. Levy recommends an adult dose of vitamin C of between 6,000 and 12,000 mg. or six to twelve grams daily, adding that most adults need the higher dose. He covers the more widely discussed uses of vitamin C as a deterrent against aging, colds, heart disease, and cancer, but goes further in claiming that it is a natural and safe weapon against a wide range of bacterial and viral diseases. Owen Fonorow wrote in the *Townsend Letter for Doctors and Patients* that "Levy's book is unmatched in the medical literature." A reviewer for the *International Council for Health Freedom* online said that Levy "joins the ranks of the major researchers/proponents of vitamin C, and this recently released work stands shoulder-to-shoulder with the already existing studies of the best-studied controversial nutrient of them all." Sandra Goodman of *Positive Health* online felt that Levy "has rendered an invaluable service to us with this superb book which should be mandatory not only for physicians and health practitioners, but for all health-conscious individuals."

Levy once told *CA:* "My primary motivation for my writings has been the incredible privilege to observe so many 'impossible' clinical responses of many critically and chronically ill patients to treatments largely ignored and even scorned by the mainstream. I feel a strong obligation and passion to disseminate as much of this information as possible whenever and wherever

I can. Although life is certainly not always pleasant when you are perceived and treated as a renegade and an outsider by many of your professional peers, I have always been compelled to ignore this treatment. I will continue to remain dedicated to illuminating what I consider to be critical and grossly neglected medical and scientific truths."

BIOGRAPHICAL AND CRITICAL SOURCES:

PERIODICALS

Library Journal, December, 1998, Kristine Benishek, review of *Uninformed Consent: The Hidden Dangers in Dental Care,* p. 144.
Townsend Letter for Doctors and Patients, May, 2003, Owen Fonorow, review of *Vitamin C, Infectious Diseases, and Toxins: Curing the Incurable,* p. 125.

ONLINE

DoctorYourself.com, http://www.doctoryourself.com/ (September 18, 2005), Andrew Saul, review of *Vitamin C, Infectious Diseases, and Toxins.*
International Council for Health Freedom Web site, http://ichf.info/ (September 18, 2005), review of *Vitamin C, Infectious Diseases and Toxins.*
Positive Health, http://www.positivehealth.com/ (September 18, 2005), Sandra Goodman, review of *Vitamin C, Infectious Diseases and Toxins.*
Tom Levy Home Page, http://www.tomlevymd.com (September 18, 2005).

*   *   *

LEVY, Thomas Edward
    See LEVY, Thomas

*   *   *

LIEBOVICH, Louis W.

PERSONAL: Born in Rockford, IL; son of Albert (a steel company owner) and Dorothy (a homemaker; maiden name, Pollard) Liebovich; married Shirley Townsend (a homemaker), June 13, 1971; children: Cynthia, Andrew, Rebecca. *Education:* University of Illinois at Urbana-Champaign, B.A. (with distinction), 1971, M.S., 1972; University of Wisconsin—Madison, Ph.D., 1986.

ADDRESSES: *Office*—Department of Journalism, University of Illinois at Urbana-Champaign, Urbana, IL 61801. *E-mail*—liebovic@uiuc.edu.

CAREER: Writer. *Champaign-Urbana Courier,* reporter, 1971-72; *Rockford Register-Republic,* Rockford, IL, reporter and acting city editor, 1972-76; *Milwaukee Sentinel,* reporter and assistant city editor, 1976-80; University of Wisconsin—Milwaukee, instructor in journalism, 1978-81; University of Wisconsin—Whitewater, instructor in journalism, 1982-85; University of Illinois at Urbana-Champaign, Urbana, assistant professor, 1985-91, associate professor, 1991-97, professor of journalism and research professor at Institute of Communications Research, 1997—, director of graduate studies in journalism, 1997-2004. Seminar presenter; speaker at academic conferences and conventions; public speaker; guest on media programs.

MEMBER: Asssociation for Education in Journalism and Mass Communications.

AWARDS, HONORS: Journalism awards include three Pulitzer Prize nominations; first-place awards for investigative reporting, Illinois Associated Press, 1974, and Wisconsin Newspaper Association, 1977, 1978; citation for outstanding academic book of 1998, *Choice,* for *The Press and the Modern Presidency: Myths and Mindsets from Kennedy to Clinton.*

WRITINGS:

The Press and the Origins of the Cold War, Praeger Publishers (Westport, CT), 1988.
(With Shraga Feivel Bielawski) *The Last Jew from Wegrow,* Praeger Publishers (Westport, CT), 1991.
Bylines in Despair: Herbert Hoover, the Great Depression, and the U.S. News Media, Praeger Publishers (Westport, CT), 1994.
The Press and the Modern Presidency: Myths and Mindsets from Kennedy to Clinton, Praeger Publishers (Westport, CT), 1998, 2nd edition, 2001.
Richard Nixon, Watergate, and the Press: A Historical Retrospective, Praeger Publishers (Westport, CT), 2003.
Abraham's Rhyme: The Story of an American Family, in press.

Contributor to books, including *Last Rights,* University of Illinois Press (Champaign, IL), 1995. Contributor of articles and reviews to periodicals, including *Journalism Educator, Presidential Studies Quarterly,* and *Journalism Monographs.* Corresponding editor, *Journalism History,* 1990-98; member of editorial board, *Journalism Quarterly,* 1995—.

BIOGRAPHICAL AND CRITICAL SOURCES:

PERIODICALS

Library Journal, June 1, 2003, Karl Helicher, review of *Richard Nixon, Watergate, and the Press: A Historical Retrospective,* p. 141.
Presidential Studies Quarterly, June, 2004, Michael A. Genovese, review of *Richard Nixon, Watergate, and the Press,* p. 455.

*   *   *

LILIENFELD, Scott O. 1960-

PERSONAL: Born December 23, 1960, in New York, NY; son of Ralph M. (a physician) and Thelma (Farber) Lilienfeld; married Lori A. Marino (divorced, 2004). *Education:* Cornell University, A.B., 1982; University of Minnesota, Ph.D., 1990.

ADDRESSES: *Home*—250 10th St., Apt. 3403, Atlanta, GA 30309. *Office*—Department of Psychology, Room 206, Emory University, Atlanta, GA 30322. *E-mail*—slilien@emory.edu.

CAREER: Emory University, Atlanta, GA, associate professor of psychology, 1994—.

WRITINGS:

Seeing Both Sides: Classic Controversies in Abnormal Psychology, Brooks/Cole (Pacific Grove, CA), 1995.
(With James M. Wood, M. Teresa Nezworski, and Howard N. Garb) *What's Wrong with the Rorschach?,* Jossey-Bass (San Francisco), CA, 2003.

(Editor, with Steven Jay Lynn and Jeffrey M. Lohr, and contributor) *Science and Pseudoscience in Clinical Psychology,* Guilford Press (New York, NY), 2003.

Contributor to periodicals, including *Skeptical Inquirer.*

WORK IN PROGRESS: The Fifty Great Myths of Popular Psychology, completion expected in 2006; *Introductory Psychology: A Critical Thinking Approach,* 2007; research on the assessment and causes of psychopathic personality.

BIOGRAPHICAL AND CRITICAL SOURCES:

PERIODICALS

Journal of Social Work Education, spring-summer, 2003, Susan Sarnoff, review of *Science and Pseudoscience in Clinical Psychology,* p. 349.
Skeptical Inquirer, July-August, 2003, Brandon A. Gaudiano, review of *Science and Pseudoscience in Clinical Psychology,* p. 48; September-October, 2003, Terence Hines, review of *What's Wrong with the Rorschach?,* p. 53.

*   *   *

LINTON, Simi 1947-

PERSONAL: Born 1947; married. *Education:* Columbia University, B.S.; New York University, Ph.D., 1985.

ADDRESSES: Agent—Lescher and Lescher, Ltd., 47 E. 19th St., New York, NY 10003. *E-mail*—disabilityarts@yahoo.com.

CAREER: Hunter College of the City University of New York, New York, NY, associate professor of psychology, c. 1984-98, and codirector of Disabilities Studies Project. Disability rights activist; president, Disability/Arts. Consultant to theatre companies, arts organizations, museums, and film and television producers.

AWARDS, HONORS: Switzer Distinguished Fellowship, National Institute on Disability and Rehabilitation Research.

WRITINGS:

Claiming Disability: Knowledge and Identity (nonfiction), New York University Press (New York, NY), 1998.
My Body Politic: A Memoir, University of Michigan Press (Ann Arbor, MI), 2006.

SIDELIGHTS: Simi Linton was on her way to protest the Vietnam War in 1971 when she was involved in a car accident that took the lives of her husband and best friend and left her unable to walk. She spent nearly a year in hospitals and rehabilitation facilities. Living in Manhattan in the days before there were laws governing disability access, she struggled to conduct her life as normally as possible. After a move to the West Coast, she discovered the emerging disability-rights movement and began to work for political solutions to the difficulties faced by disabled people. In *Claiming Disability: Knowledge and Identity* Linton puts forth the argument that there should be more disability studies in all areas of curriculum. She criticizes the concept of "special education," in which disabled children are segregated, and contemporary practices of "mainstreaming," in which only some disabled children are assimilated into standard classrooms. Commenting on the book in *Signs,* Rachel Adams noted, "The anger evident in Linton's criticism of current disciplinary and social formations is balanced by her pragmatic account of how and why it is crucial to incorporate disability studies more effectively into the university."

Linton told her own story in *My Body Politic: A Memoir.* It serves as "a passionate guide to a world many outsiders, and even insiders, find difficult to navigate: the world of the differently-abled," according to a *Publishers Weekly* reviewer. A *Kirkus Reviews* contributor described the book as a "wholly enjoyable" work that reveals the author's "crackle, irreverence and intelligence."

BIOGRAPHICAL AND CRITICAL SOURCES:

BOOKS

Linton, Simi, *My Body Politic: A Memoir,* University of Michigan Press (Ann Arbor, MI), 2006.

PERIODICALS

Kirkus Reviews, October 1, 2005, review of *My Body Politic,* p. 1064.
Publishers Weekly, August 8, 2005, review of *My Body Politic,* p. 220.
Signs, autumn, 2000, Rachel Adams, review of *Claiming Disability: Knowledge and Identity,* p. 295.

*   *   *

LLOYD, Christopher 1921-2006

OBITUARY NOTICE— See index for *CA* sketch: Born March 2, 1921, in Northiam, England; died of complications following a stroke after a knee operation, January 27, 2006, in Hastings, England. Horticulturist and author. A renowned English gardener, Lloyd was a columnist and author whose gardens at his Great Dixter home are considered a national treasure. The son of a landscape architect father and a mother who also enjoyed gardening, Lloyd was enamored of horticulture from childhood. However, upon enrolling at King's College, Cambridge, he studied modern languages. World War II interrupted his studies, but he returned to complete a master's degree in 1947. Lloyd then studied horticulture at Wye College at the University of London, where he earned a B.Sc. in decorative horticulture in 1950. He lectured there for the next four years before devoting his full attention to the family estate at Great Dixter. Earning an income as a book writer, lecturer, and popular columnist for *Country Life* magazine, he created spectacular gardens surrounding his home that were especially noted for Lloyd's trademark love of brilliant colors. He encouraged other gardeners to be daring in their plantings and to express their own personalities through gardening. Opened to the public, tens of thousands of people visit the grounds around Great Dixter each year. Toward the end of his life, Lloyd created the Great Dixter Charitable Trust to ensure that his gardens would be managed properly long after his death. He was recognized for his contributions with an honorary doctorate from Open University in 1996 and an appointment to the Order of the British Empire in 2000. Among his many books are *The Well-Tempered Garden* (1970; revised edition, 1985), *The Adventurous Gardener* (1983), *In My Garden* (1993), *Colour for Adventurous Gardeners* (2001), *Meadows* (2004), and *Succession Planting for Adventurous Gardeners* (2005).

OBITUARIES AND OTHER SOURCES:

PERIODICALS

Los Angeles Times, February 4, 2006, p. B15.
New York Times, January 31, 2006, p. A20.
Times (London, England), January 30, 2006, p. 52.

*   *   *

LÓPEZ, Lorraine 1956-

PERSONAL: Born 1956. *Education:* California State University at Northridge, B.A.; University of Georgia, M.A., Ph.D., 2000.

ADDRESSES: Office—Department of English, Vanderbilt University, Box 1654, Station B, 331 Benson Hall, Nashville, TN 37235. *E-mail*—lorraine.lopez@vanderbilt.edu.

CAREER: Educator and author. Has taught at middle schools, high schools, and universities. Brenau University, Gainesville, GA, former faculty member; Vanderbilt University, Nashville, TN, professor of English, 2002—. Institute for Violence Prevention, Athens, GA, cofounder and director of education programs.

AWARDS, HONORS: Miguel Marmól Prize for fiction from Curbstone Press, Independent Publishers Book Award for multicultural fiction, and Latino Book Award for short stories from the Latino Literary Hall of Fame, all for *Soy la Avon Lady and Other Stories.*

WRITINGS:

Soy la Avon Lady and Other Stories, Curbstone Press (Willimantic, CT), 2002.
Call Me Henri (novel), Curbstone Press (Willimantic, CT), 2006.

Contributor to books, including *The Mammoth Anthology of Short Fiction,* and of poetry and prose pieces to periodicals, including *Prairie Schooner, U.S. Latino Review, Flagpole Magazine, Northridge Review, Crab Orchard Review,* and *New Letters.*

SIDELIGHTS: Lorraine López is an English professor whose first work of fiction, the short story collection *Soy la Avon Lady and Other Stories,* was warmly received by critics and won several awards. The eleven stories contained here explore issues of identity and present characters trying to fit into society or establish good relationships with their family and peers. Sometimes the characters struggle with cultural differences; sometimes they struggle with self-image or with alcoholism and other addictions. Reviewers of the collection praised both López's characterizations and her skillful narrative technique. Discussing the latter, reviewer Ranjana Varghese commented in the *Gulf Coast Magazine Online* that López "is a master of illusion" who is able to lull her readers into complacency just before surprising them with revelations; she is also able to reveal "the exotic, the novel, or the purely strange" in ordinary people. *Booklist* contributor Carlos Orellana called *Soy la Avon Lady and Other Stories* "a vibrant and memorable collection," Mary Margaret Benson declared it to be a "superb collection" in her *Library Journal* review, and a *Kirkus Reviews* writer concluded that "López is an original, and this is a fine collection." Noting the trend in literature by minority writers to point out the positive aspects of minority communities in America and to enlighten readers about them, Varghese asserted that "an attempt to fit López's fiction into any of these categories would be disastrous at worst, unfair at best. López's story collection exceeds these boundaries."

When asked by interviewer Jantje Tielken of the *Curbstone Press* Web site about the role of Chicano literature in today's society, López replied: "The role of literature is the same as the role of art which is to expand upon a person's store of knowledge and experience in such a way that the person perceives the world differently, more comprehensively. Obviously, the role of Chicano literature is the same for me."

BIOGRAPHICAL AND CRITICAL SOURCES:

PERIODICALS

Booklist, August, 2002, Carlos Orellana, review of *Soy la Avon Lady and Other Stories,* p. 1922.
Choice, January, 2003, R.B. Shuman, review of *Soy la Avon Lady and Other Stories,* p. 826.
Kirkus Reviews, May 1, 2002, review of *Soy la Avon Lady and Other Stories,* p. 613.

Library Journal, June 1, 2002, Mary Margaret Benson, review of *Soy la Avon Lady and Other Stories,* p. 1999.

ONLINE

Curbstone Press Web site, http://www.curbstone.org/ (January 24, 2006), Jantje Tielken, interview with Lorraine López.
Gulf Coast Magazine Online, http://www. gulfcoastmag.org/ (January 24, 2006), Ranjana Varghese, review of *Soy la Avon Lady and Other Stories.*
NewPages.com, http://www.newpages.com/ (January 24, 2006), Denise Bazzett, review of *Soy la Avon Lady and Other Stories.* *

*   *   *

LOUNDAGIN, Choeleen N. 1967-

PERSONAL: Born August 4, 1967, in Santa Rosa, CA; daughter of W.H. "Itchy" (an owner of a garage and towing service) and Leellen (a grocery store clerk; maiden name, Fleming; later surname, Trayler) Loundagin. *Ethnicity:* "Caucasian." *Education:* Santa Rosa Junior College, A.A., 1986; San Diego State University, B.A., 1988; John F. Kennedy University, M.A., 1992. *Hobbies and other interests:* Hiking, gardening, baking, roller-blading.

ADDRESSES: Office—InnerChamp Books, P.O. Box 11362, Santa Rosa, CA 95406. *E-mail*—choeleen@ innerchamp.com.

CAREER: Ice skating coach and performance enhancement consultant in Santa Rosa, CA, 1992—. InnerChamp Books, affiliate; seminar presenter. Professional Skaters Association, master rated for coaching figure skating, 2000; Santa Rosa Figure Skating Club, coach liaison.

MEMBER: U.S. Figure Skating Sport Science Society, United States Figure Skating Association, Professional Skaters Association, Association for the Advancement of Applied Sport Psychology.

AWARDS, HONORS: Gold medals for figure skating, United States Figure Skating Association, 1983, 1995.

WRITINGS:

The Inner Champion: A Mental Toughness Training Manual for Figure Skaters, InnerChamp Books (Santa Rosa, CA), 1997, revised edition, 2004.
(With Tom Mitchell) *Sport and Soul: Skate for the Love* (audio recording), Sport and Soul Publishing (Windsor, CA), 1999.

Contributor to periodicals, including *Skating, Professional Skater,* and *Recreational Ice Skater.*

SIDELIGHTS: Choeleen N. Loundagin told *CA:* "The quest for athletic excellence has been a passion throughout my life. I was inspired to choose a career in the field of sport psychology after experiencing the positive effects of mental toughness training as a teenage competitive figure skater. Now I enjoy helping athletes throughout the world bring more enjoyment to their sport experience and achieve their personal best. My master's degree in sport psychology and my figure skating background as a competitor, gold medalist, master-rated coach, and international performer lend me special insight into the particular needs of skaters."

*   *   *

LOVRIC, Michelle 1959-

PERSONAL: Born 1959, in Sydney, New South Wales, Australia.

ADDRESSES: Agent—c/o Author Mail, A.M. Heath, 6 Warwick Ct., London, WC1R 5DJ, England. *E-mail*—michelle@lovric.demon.co.uk.

CAREER: Writer and anthologist.

AWARDS, HONORS: London Arts Writer's Award.

WRITINGS:

(Compiler) *Birds: An Illustrated Treasury,* Courage Books (Philadelphia, PA), 1992.

(Compiler) *Cats: An Illustrated Treasury,* Courage Books (Philadelphia, PA), 1992.
(Compiler) *Love: An Illustrated Treasury,* Courage Books (Philadelphia, PA), 1992.
(Compiler) *Women: An Illustrated Treasury,* Courage Books (Philadelphia, PA), 1993.
(Compiler) *Seasons: An Illustrated Treasury,* Courage Books (Philadelphia, PA), 1993.
(Compiler) *Mothers: An Illustrated Treasury of Motherhood,* Courage Books (Philadelphia, PA), 1993.
(Compiler) *Friends: An Illustrated Treasury of Friendship,* Courage Books (Philadelphia, PA), 1993.
(Compiler) *Christmas: An Illustrated Treasury,* Courage Books (Philadelphia, PA), 1994.
(Compiler) *Horses: An Illustrated Treasury,* Courage Books (Philadelphia, PA), 1994.
(Compiler) *Kittens: An Illustrated Treasury,* Courage Books (Philadelphia, PA), 1994.
(Compiler) *Love Letters: An Illustrated Treasury,* Courage Books (Philadelphia, PA), 1994.
(Adaptor) James Beresford, *The Miseries of Human Life,* St. Martin's Press (New York, NY), 1995.
(Compiler) *Roses: An Illustrated Treasury,* Courage Books (Philadelphia, PA), 1995.
(Creator of original scrapbook) Maggie Philo, *Victorian Christmas: Sourcebook with 10 Projects,* photography by Debbie Patterson, Welcome Rain Books (New York, NY), 1995.
(Compiler) *The Countryside: An Illustrated Treasury,* Courage Books (Philadelphia, PA), 1995.
Love Letters: An Anthology of Passion, Shooting Star Press (New York, NY), 1995.
(With Nikiforos Doxiadis Mardas) *The Sweetness of Honey and the Sting of Bees: A Book of Love from the Ancient Mediterranean,* Stewart, Tabori & Chang (New York, NY), 1997.
(Compiler) *Deadlier Than the Male: Dangerously Witty Quotations by Women about Men,* St. Martin's Press (New York, NY), 1997.
(Compiler) *Woman to Woman: Letters to Mothers, Sisters, Daughters, Friends,* Andrews McMeel (Kansas City, MO), 1998.
(With Nikiforos Doxiadis Mardas) *How to Insult, Abuse, & Insinuate in Classical Latin,* Barnes & Noble (New York, NY), 1998.
(Editor) *Bleeding Hearts: Love Poems for the Nervous & Highly Strung,* St. Martin's Press (New York, NY), 1998.
(With Lea Chambers) *Latin Stuff & Nonsense,* Barnes & Noble (New York, NY), 1999.

Carpaccio's Cat, illustrated by Geoffrey Appleton, Artisan (New York, NY), 1999.

(With Mimma Balia) *Ruskin's Rose: A Venetian Love Story,* collages by Ann Field, Artisan (New York, NY), 2000.

(Compiler) *Cats Behaving Badly: An Anthology of Feline Misdemeanors,* illustrated by Lynne Curran, Barnes & Noble (New York, NY), 2000.

(Editor) *Weird Wills & Eccentric Last Wishes,* Barnes & Noble (New York, NY), 2000.

(Editor) *Eccentric Epitaphs: Gaffes from beyond the Grave,* Barnes & Noble (New York, NY), 2000.

Carnevale (novel), Virago (London, England), 2001.

Cleopatra's Face: Fatal Beauty, Field Museum (Chicago, IL), 2001.

Women's Wicked Wit: From Jane Austen to Roseanne Barr, Chicago Review Press (Chicago, IL), 2002.

(Selector and author of introduction) *The Virago Book of Christmas,* Virago (London, England), 2002.

Love.Bytes: 10,000 Romantic Email Postcards for Him and Her, Duncan Baird (London, England), 2002.

Insult and Curse Book, Prion Books (London, England), 2002.

The Floating Book (novel), Regan Books (New York, NY), 2003.

(Compiler, with assistance from Irving Y. Lo) *Oriental Love Poems,* Andrews McMeel (Kansas City, MO), 2003.

Venice: Tales of the City, Little, Brown (New York, NY), 2003.

(With Jenny Quickfall) *How to Seduce, Pleasure, & Titillate in Classical Latin,* Barnes & Noble (New York, NY), 2004.

How to Write Love Letters, Chicago Review Press (Chicago, IL), 2004.

(Compiler and Editor) *The World's Greatest Letters: From Ancient Greece to the Twentieth Century,* Chicago Review Press (Chicago, IL), 2004.

Women's Wicked Wisdom, Chicago Review Press (Chicago, IL), 2004.

More Women's Wicked Wit, Carlton Books (London, England), 2005.

The Remedy: A Novel of London and Venice, Regan Books (New York, NY), 2005.

(Compiler) *Cats and Their Slaves: An Anthology of Worship,* Chicago Review Press (Chicago, IL), 2006.

Also editor of over 100 anthologies and gift books.

SIDELIGHTS: Michelle Lovric shuttles between her homes in London and Venice, a city that receives a great deal of attention in several of her books. Lovric commented in an interview on the *Virago Publishers* Web site that since reading her first book, she knew she wanted to be a writer. Having published several novels and edited or compiled numerous anthologies, Lovric has done just that.

Among the books she has compiled is *Victorian Christmas: Sourcebook with 10 Projects.* Lovric created the original Victorian scrapbook used in the various projects the book presents. A reviewer in *Publishers Weekly* said Lovric's portfolio was "appealingly designed." Lovric both edited and compiled *The World's Greatest Letters: From Ancient Greece to the Twentieth Century.* This collection includes everything from Virginia Woolfe's suicide letter to her husband to an account of the eruption of Mt. Vesuvius as recorded by Pliny. Jan Brue Enright reviewed this book in *Library Journal* and took notice of "the importance of letter writing in telling the story of individuals in history."

In 2001, Lovric penned her first novel, *Carnevale.* Cecilia, the protagonist, is the artistic daughter of an eighteenth-century Venetian merchant. She leads a passionate life full of food, drink, and lovers, who include the infamous Casanova and Lord Byron. "In Lovric's collation of narrative, recipes, letters, and inventories, [Venice] overflows with pungent smells, strange noises and the fading decadence of a magical city," noted Melissa Katsoulis in the London *Times.* Other reviewers also praised the novel. Janet Mary Tomson, writing in the *Historical Novels Review,* pointed out that Lovric "has a gift for the poetic that captures the heightened state of Cecilia's emotions," concluding that the book is "very readable" and "enjoyable."

Lovric's second novel, *The Floating Book,* was published in 2003. The story takes place in fifteenth-century Venice and concerns that city's early printing press business. A number of the characters are actual historical figures, ranging from witchcraft-practicing nuns to debauched scribes. Kristine Huntley, writing in *Booklist,* praised the "vibrant cast of characters" in this "big, lush novel." A reviewer in *Publishers Weekly* complimented Lovric's "eye for sensual detail, conveying the sights and smells of the city's markets and palazzi." A contributor to *Kirkus Reviews* summed up *The Floating Book* by commenting that it was "maddeningly over the top and self-important, but as seductive as Venice."

The Remedy: A Novel of London and Venice is set in eighteenth-century Venice and London and centers around the relations between a Venetian noblewoman and the leader of London's medical underworld. A contributor to *Kirkus Reviews* commented that "despite the merciless plot twists, Lovric's real fascination is with the cities she describes in loving if endless detail." Leah Greenblatt, writing in *Entertainment Weekly,* also took note of the amount of detail and overall density of the book, stating that some readers might develop a "serious case of literary indigestion." However, Kristine Huntley in *Booklist* lauded Lovric as a "gifted novelist," and concluded that *The Remedy* is "historical fiction at its finest."

BIOGRAPHICAL AND CRITICAL SOURCES:

PERIODICALS

Booklist, November 15, 2003, Kristine Huntley, review of *The Floating Book,* p. 580; November 15, 2005, Kristine Huntley, review of *The Remedy: A Novel of London and Venice,* p. 27.

Bookwatch, September, 2005, review of *Venice: Tales of the City.*

Entertainment Weekly, November 25, 2005, Leah Greenblatt, review of *The Remedy,* p. 108.

Historical Novels Review, December, 2001, Janet Mary Tomson, review of *Carnevale.*

Kirkus Reviews, October 15, 2003, review of *The Floating Book,* p. 1247; November 15, 2005, review of *The Remedy,* p. 1207.

Library Journal, November 1, 2003, Kim Uden Rutter, review of *The Floating Book,* p. 124; September 1, 2004, Jan Brue Enright, review of *The World's Greatest Letters: From Ancient Greece to the Twentieth Century,* p. 151; January 1, 2006, Mary Kay Bird, review of *The Remedy,* p. 99.

New York Times, February 8, 1995, Mary B.W. Tabor, review of *Love Letters: An Anthology of Passion.*

Publishers Weekly, September 11, 1995, review of *Victorian Christmas: Sourcebook with 10 Projects,* p. 82; October 20, 2003, review of *The Floating Book,* p. 32; November 7, 2005, review of *The Remedy,* p. 55.

Times (London, England), July 3, 2002, Melissa Katsoulis, review of *Carnevale.*

Victoria Magazine, February, 1995, "Oh, What It Is to Love Like This!," review of *Love Letters*

Washington Post, January, 2004, Edward Docx, review of *The Floating Book.*

ONLINE

Michelle Lovric Home Page, http://www.michelle lovric.com (April 18, 2006).

Virago Publishers Web site, http://www.virago.co.uk/ (February 22, 2006), author interview.

* * *

LUNA, Félix 1925-

PERSONAL: Born September 30, 1925, in Buenos Aires, Argentina. *Education:* National University of Buenos Aires, 1951.

ADDRESSES: Agent—c/o Author Mail, Editoral Sudamericana SA, Division of Random House-Mondadori, Humbert 1 555, C1103ACK Buenos Aires, Argentina.

CAREER: Writer, journalist, historian. *Todo es Historia* magazine, founder and director; Municipality of the City of Buenos Aires, secretary of culture, 1986-89; University of Buenos Aires, professor.

MEMBER: National Academy of History.

AWARDS, HONORS: Commander of the Order of Merit, France, 1988; Commander of the Order of the Sun, Peru, 1990; Prize Konex de Platino, 1994; Prize National Consecration, Secretariat of Culture of the Nation.

WRITINGS:

La Rioja despeés de la Batalla de Vargas, [Tucumán, Argentina], 1950.

Rosás: balance y memoria, Museo Cultura Riojano (La Rioja, Argentina), 1952.

Yrigoyen, el templario de la libertad, Editorial Raigal (Buenos Aires, Argentina), 1954, reprinted, Editorial Sudamericana (Buenos Aires, Argentina) 1988.

La última montonera: cuentos bárbaros, Ediciones Doble (Buenos Aires, Argentina), 1955, reprinted, Beas Edicionies (Buenos Aires, Argetina), 1992.

Guía elemental para una reforma de la constitución, Editorial Perrot (Buenos Aires, Argentina), 1957.

Alvear, Libros Argentinos (Buenos Aires, Argentina), 1958, reprinted, Editorial Sudamericana (Buenos Aires, Argentina), 1988.

(With Arturo Frondizi) *Diálogos con Frondizi,* 2nd edition, Editorial Desarrollo (Buenos Aires, Argentina), 1963, reprinted, Planeta (Buenos Aires, Argentina), 1998.

La noche de la alianza; [cuentos], Editorial Desarrollo (Buenos Aires, Argentina), 1964.

La historia argentina en funció de los objectivos nacionales, Editorial Cen (Buenos Aires, Argentina), 1965.

Los caudillos, Editorial J. Alvarez (Buenos Aires, Argentina), 1966, reprinted, Planeta (Buenos Aires, Argentina), 1993.

La útima Motonero, Editorial J. Alvarez (Buenos Aires, Argentina), 1969.

El 45, Editorial J. Alvarez (Buenos Aires, Argentina), 1969, reprinted, Hyspamerica (Buenos Aires, Argentina), 1984.

Historia para un país maduro, Centro de Documentación e Información Educativas de la Escuela Normal Victor Mercante (Villa Maria, Argentina), 1969.

(Author of lyrics) *Mujeres argentines* (music and lyrics), music by Ariel Ramirez, Editoral Lagos (Buenos Aires, Argentina), 1971.

Argentina de Péron a Lanusse, 1943-1973, Planeta (Barcelona, Spain), 1972, reprinted, Planeta, 1993.

Qué Argentina queremos los argentinos?, Ediciones La Bastilla (Buenos Aires, Argentina), 1973.

(With Atahualpa Yupanqui) *Atahualpa Yupanqui,* Ediciones Júcar (Madrid, Spain), 1974.

Las crisis en la Argentina, Schapire Editor (Buenos Aires, Argentina), 1976.

De comicios y entreveros, Schapire Editor (Buenos Aires, Argentina), 1976.

Conversaciones con José Luis Romero, sobre una Argentina, con historia, política y democracia, Timerman Editores (Buenos Aires, Argentina), 1976.

(With Susana B. Sigwal Carioli) *Inmigrantes y colonos,* Todo es Historia S.R.L. (Argentina), 1976.

Ortiz: Reportaje a la Argentina opulenta, Editorial Sudamericana (Buenos Aires, Argentina), 1978.

Conflictos y armonías en la historia argentina, Editorial de Belgrano (Buenos Aires, Argentina), 1980.

Buenos Aires y el país, Editorial Sudamericana (Buenos Aires, Argentina), 1982, reprinted, 2000.

Golpes militares y salida electorales, Editorial Sudamericana (Buenos Aires, Argentina), 1983.

Peró y su tiempo, Editorial Sudamericana (Buenos Aires, Argentina), 1984.

(With Enrique Mario Mayochi and Ulises Petit de Murat) *Tres intendentes de Buenos Aires,* Municipalidad de la Ciudad de Buenos Aires, Secretaria de Cultura, Instituto Histórico de la Ciudad de Buenos Aires (Buenos Aires, Argentina), 1985.

La noche de la alianza, Hyperamerica (Madrid, Spain), 1985.

Fuerzas hegemónicas y partidos políticos, Editorial Sudamericana (Buenos Aires, Argentina), 1988.

Desde Campora hasta Alfonsíin, Editorial Abril (Buenos Aires, Argentina), 1988.

La Inestablilidad constitucional, Editorial Abril (Buenos Aires, Argentina), 1988.

El Desarrollo de la Patagonia, Editorial Abril (Buenos Aires, Argentina), 1988.

La Déada infame, Editorial Abril (Buenos Aires, Argentina), 1988.

El Radicalismo, Editorial Abril (Buenos Aires, Argentina), 1988.

Las Grandes huelgas, Editorial Abril (Buenos Aires, Argentina), 1988.

Fundación de ciudades, Editorial Abril (Buenos Aires, Argentina), 1988.

Orígenes de los partidos políticos, Editorial Abril (Buenos Aires, Argentina), 1988.

500 años historia argentina: Las misiones jesuíticas, Editorial Abril (Buenos Aires, Argentina), 1988.

La Crisis del 90 y los albores del siglo XX, Editorial Abril (Buenos Aires, Argentina), 1988.

San Martín, Editorial Abril (Buenos Aires, Argentina), 1988.

La organización nacional, Editorial Abril (Buenos Aires, Argentina), 1988.

El Peronismo, Editorial Abril (Buenos Aires, Argentina), 1988.

Rosas y la sociedad federal, Editorial Abril (Buenos Aires, Argentina), 1988.

La Aventura del Rio de la Plata, Editorial Abril (Buenos Aires, Argentina), 1988.

El Decubrimiento de América, Editorial Abril (Buenos Aires, Argentina), 1988.

Las Mujeres y sus luchas, Editorial Abril (Buenos Aires, Argentina), 1988.

Colonos, indios y gauchos, Editorial Abril (Buenos Aires, Argentina), 1988.

La Civilización cosmopolita, Editorial Abril (Buenos Aires, Argentina), 1988.

500 años historia argentina: la inmigración, Editorial Abril (Buenos Aires, Argentina), 1988.

El roquismo y los notables, Editorial Abril (Buenos Aires, Argentina), 1988.

Primeros gobiernos revolucionarios, Editorial Abril (Buenos Aires, Argentina), 1988.

Soy Roca, Editorial Sudamericana (Buenos Aires, Argentina), 1989.

Confluencias, Editorial Sudamericana (Buenos Aires, Argentina), 1991.

Fracturas y continuidades en la historia argentina, Editorial Sudamericana (Buenos Aires, Argentina), 1992.

(With Rafael Segura) *Matías cruza los Andes* (juvenile), Atlántida (Buenos Aires, Argentina), 1992.

Breve historia de los argentinos, Planeta (Buenos Aires, Argentina), 1993, translation published as *A Short History of Argentina,* Planeta (Buenos Aires, Argentina), 2000.

Historia integral de la Argentina (title means "A Brief History of Argentina"), Planeta (Buenos Aires, Argentina), 1994.

Diálogos con la historia y la política, Editorial Sudamericana (Buenos Aires, Argentina), 1995.

Encuentros, Editorial Sudamericana (Buenos Aires, Argentina), 1996.

Sarmiento y sus fantasmas: encuentros imaginarios, Editorial Atlantida (Buenos Aires, Argentina), 1997.

La emancipación argentina y americana (title means "The Emancipation of Argentina and America"), Planeta (Buenos Aires, Argentina), 1998.

La cultura en tiempos de la colonia, Planeta (Buenos Aires, Argentina), 1998.

La santa federacyón, Planeta (Buenos Aires, Argentina), 1998.

Así se hizo la patira: desde el Virreinato a la actualidad, Billiken (Buenos Aires, Argentina), 1998.

La época de Roca, Planeta (Buenos Aires, Argentina), 1998.

La cultura desde la independencia hasta el centenario, Planeta (Buenos Aires, Argentina), 1998.

(With Prilidiano Pueyrredón and Roberto Amigo Cerisola) *Prilidiano Pueyrredón: Proyecto Cultural Artistas del Mercosur,* Banco Velox (Argentina), 1999.

Segunda fila: personajes olvidados que también hicieron historia, Planeta (Buenos Aires, Argentina), 1999.

Puerto Madero, Ediciones Larivière (Buenos Aires, Argentina), 1999.

Grandes protagonistas de la historia argentina (title means "Great Protagonists in the History of Argentina"), Planeta (Buenos Aires, Argentina), 1999.

Palabra de historiador: en busca de la memoria argentina, Editorial Sudamericana (Buenos Aires, Argentina), 1999.

Los hechos y sus consecuencias, TIYM (McLean, VA), 1999.

Juana Azurduy, Editorial Planeta Argentina (Buenos Aires, Argentina), 1999.

Buenos Aires 1910: patrimonio, productividad, porvenir = patrimony, productivity, future, Exxel Group (Buenos Aires, Argentina), 1999.

Conflictos en la Argentina próspera: de la Revolución del Parque a la restauración conservadora, Planeta (Buenos Aires, Argentina), 2000.

Martín Aldama: un soldado de la Independencia, Planeta (Buenos Aires, Argentina), 2001.

Golpes militares: de la dictadura de Uriburu al terrorismo de Estado, Planeta (Buenos Aires, Argentina), 2001.

Lo mejor de Todo es historia, Taurus (Buenos Aires, Argentina), 2002.

El despertar de una Nación: fotografía argentina del siglo XIX, EDODAL (Buenos Aires, Argentina), 2004.

Temas de historia colonial de La Rioja, Nexo Communicación (La Rioja, Argentina), 2004.

1925: historias de un año sin historia, Sudamericana (Buenos Aires, Argentina), 2005.

Author of introduction to *Archivo del Brigadier General Juan Facundo Quiroga. Tomo III (1824-1825),* Universidad de Buenos Aires (Buenos Aires, Argentina), 1986.

Also writer of lyrics for songs and recordings, including *Misa Criolla: para solistas, coro y orquesta,* Phillips, c. 1969; *Mujere argentines,* Phillips, 1970; *Cantata sudamericana,* Phillips, 1973.

SIDELIGHTS: Argentine writer Félix Luna is recognized widely in his own country as having made the history of Argentina accessible to the broad general public. In *Ortiz: Reportaje a la Argentina opulenta,* the author delves into the history of Argentina via a biography of its one-time president Robert M. Ortiz, who was known for his adherence to democratic principles even as he dealt with the corruption of politics. Writing in the *Hispanic American Historical Review,* Ronald C. Newton noted that Ortiz may have been "the last Argentine of stature potentially capable of restoring and modernizing the country's representative system." Luna looks both at the public persona and the personal side of Oritz, who suffered from diabetes and oncoming blindness. Newton commented that readers will "learn about the progress of Ortiz's disease and also about his household economy, as both his doctors and his servants have unburdened themselves."

Soy Roca is written as though it is a first-person memoir, telling the history of Argentina in the 1880s through the personage of Argentinean political figure Julio A. Roca. "Luna is a superb writer, imaginative and knowledgeable, and his able prose produces a compelling narrative," wrote Douglas W. Richmond in the *Hispanic American Historical Review.* Richmond went on note that the author "has produced an interesting book." Luna is also the author of the introduction to *Archivo del Brigadier General Juan Facundo Quiroga. Tomo III (1824-1825),* which *Hispanic American Historical Review* contributor David Bushnell called "an exceptionally valuable source collection." The volume contains a wide range of materials, including correspondence and other documents from the early nineteenth century.

BIOGRAPHICAL AND CRITICAL SOURCES:

PERIODICALS

Hispanic American Historical Review, August, 1980, Ronald C. Newton, review of *Ortiz: Reportaje a la Argentina opulenta,* pp. 523-525; May, 1987, David Bushnell, review of *Archivo del Brigadier General Juan Facundo Quiroga. Tomo III (1824-1825),* pp. 355-357; August, 1991, Douglas W. Richmond, review of *Soy Roca,* p. 643.

ONLINE

Collegio Cardinal Newman Web site, http://www. cardenal-newman.edu/ (March 4, 2006), "Experts' Opinons: Felix Luna's Interview Report."

Konex Foundation Web site, http://www. fundacionkonex.com.ar/ (March 4, 2006), information on author.

*   *   *

LYNN, David
    See LYNN, David H.

*   *   *

LYNN, David H.
    (David Lynn)

PERSONAL: Married Wendy Singer (a college professor); children: Aaron, Elizabeth. *Education:* Kenyon College, B.A.; University of Virginia, M.A., Ph.D.

ADDRESSES: Home—Gambier, OH. *Office*—Kenyon Review, Walton House, Kenyon College, Gambier, OH 43022-9623. *E-mail*—lynnd@kenyon.edu.

CAREER: Kenyon College, Gambier, OH, professor of English and editor of the *Kenyon Review,* 1994—. Member of board of directors, Council of Literary Magazines and Presses.

AWARDS, HONORS: Fulbright scholarship, 1995-96.

WRITINGS:

The Hero's Tale: Narrators in the Early Modern Novel, St. Martin's Press (New York, NY), 1989.
Fortune Telling (short stories), Carnegie-Mellon University Press (Pittsburgh, PA), 1998.
Wrestling with Gabriel (novel), Carnegie-Mellon University Press (Pittsburgh, PA), 2002.
(Editor) *The Best of the Kenyon Review,* introduction by Joyce Carol Oates, Sourcebooks (Naperville, IL),2003.
Year of Fire (short stories), Harcourt (Orlando, FL), 2005.

Also contributor to periodicals.

SIDELIGHTS: An English professor who has served as editor of the *Kenyon Review* for many years, David H. Lynn has also published several well-received short-story collections. The author's stories are typically set in modern times and are character-driven tales covering a wide range of themes. *Fortune Telling,* his first short-story collection, includes tales about school bullying, arranged marriages, and Jewish characters trying to adjust to mainstream America. Praising both the dialogue and prose of the collection, *Library Journal* critic Doris Lynch declared *Fortune Telling* to be a "fine, first collection." A *Publishers Weekly* contributor praised the collection's "dry, credible sketches."

Lynn's second story collection, *Year of Fire,* contains nineteen tales on such topics as loneliness, aging, racism, and "human foibles and failings," according to a *Kirkus Reviews* writer. The reviewer felt that "Lynn's skill is at times considerable." In *Booklist,* Ellen Loughran indicated that *Year of Fire* shows that Lynn is "a master of the ambivalent resolution" whose work contains "some really brilliant writing."

BIOGRAPHICAL AND CRITICAL SOURCES:

PERIODICALS

Booklist, October 15, 2003, John Green, review of *The Best of the Kenyon Review,* p. 379; November 1, 2005, Ellen Loughran, review of *Year of Fire,* p. 24.
Bookwatch, June, 1998, review of *Fortune Telling,* p. 8.

Choice, June, 1989, review of *The Hero's Tale: Narrators in the Early Modern Novel,* p. 1683.
Kirkus Reviews, October 15, 2005, review of *Year of Fire,* p. 1103.
Library Journal, May 1, 1991, Bill Katz, review of *The Best of the Kenyon Review,* p. 114; June 15, 1998, Doris Lynch, review of *Fortune Telling,* p. 109; November 1, 2003, Kathryn R. Bartelt, review of *The Best of the Kenyon Review,* p. 81; May 1, 2005, Susan Lense, "The Kenyon Review: Incubator for Good Fiction," p. 130.
Modern Fiction Studies, winter, 1989, Marvin Magalaner, review of *The Hero's Tale,* p. 849.
Publishers Weekly, June 1, 1998, review of *Fortune Telling,* p. 48; September 26, 2005, review of *Year of Fire,* p. 61.
Virginia Quarterly Review, spring, 1990, review of *The Hero's Tale,* p. 48.

ONLINE

Kenyon College Web site, http://www.kenyon.edu/ (January 23, 2006), brief biography of David H. Lynn.
Kenyon Review Online, http://www.kenyonreview.org/ (January 23, 2006), brief biography of David H. Lynn.

*   *   *

LYNN, Jackie
See HINTON, Lynne

M

MADDIGAN, Beth 1967-

PERSONAL: Born February 1, 1967, in St. John's, Newfoundland, Canada; daughter of Philip (an airport manager) and Christine (a bank teller; maiden name, Crummey) Maddigan; married Robert Pound (a courier), April 4, 1998. *Education:* Memorial University of Newfoundland, B.A., 1990; University of Western Ontario, M.L.I.S., 1996.

ADDRESSES: Home—10 Ivy Cres., Paris, Ontario N3L 4A9, Canada. *Office*—Cambridge Libraries and Galleries, 1 North Sq., Cambridge, Ontario N1S 2K6, Canada. *E-mail*—bmaddigan@library.cambridge.on.ca.

CAREER: A.C. Hunter Children's Library, St. John's Newfoundland, Canada, library assistant, 1990-94, branch head, 1994-96; Cambridge Libraries and Galleries, Cambridge, Ontario, Canada, children's services librarian, 1997-99, children's services coordinator, 1999—. Memorial University of Newfoundland, instructor, 1997-2003; University of Western Ontario, sessional instructor; presenter of workshops for librarians.

MEMBER: Ontario Library Association (member of Child and Youth Services Task Force, 2003—).

WRITINGS:

(With Stefanie Drennan) *The Big Book of Stories, Songs, and Sing-Alongs: Programs for Babies, Toddlers, and Families,* illustrated by Roberta Thompson, Libraries Unlimited (Westport, CT), 2003.

(With Stefanie Drennan) *The Big Book of Reading Fun,* illustrated by Roberta Thompson, Libraries Unlimited (Westport, CT), in press.

BIOGRAPHICAL AND CRITICAL SOURCES:

PERIODICALS

Canadian Materials, September 19, 2003, Lorraine Douglas, review of *The Big Book of Stories, Songs, and Sing-Alongs: Programs for Babies, Toddlers, and Families.*
Children and Libraries, summer-fall, 2004, Junko Yokota, review of *The Big Book of Stories, Songs, and Sing-Alongs,* p. 58.
School Library Journal, January, 2004, Leslie Barban, review of *The Big Book of Stories, Songs, and Sing-Alongs,* p. 167.

*   *   *

MARANGONI, Alejandro G. 1965-

PERSONAL: Born January 17, 1965, in Guayaquil, Ecuador; son of Paolo (a physician) and Rosita (Bertini) Marangoni; married Dianne Del Zotto (a food specialist), August 17, 1990; children: Isaac Paul, Joshua Paul. *Ethnicity:* "Caucasian." *Education:* McGill University, B.Sc., 1987; University of Guelph, Ph.D., 1990. *Politics:* Liberal. *Religion:* Roman Catholic. *Hobbies and other interests:* Whitewater kayaking and canoeing, canoe tripping, technical rock climbing, mountaineering, mountain biking.

ADDRESSES: Office—Department of Food Science, University of Guelph, Guelph, Ontario N1G 2W1, Canada; fax: 519-824-6631. *E-mail*—amarango@uoguelph.ca.

CAREER: University of Guelph, Guelph, Ontario, Canada, professor of food science, 1991—, Canada Research Chair in food and soft materials science, 2000—.

MEMBER: American Chemical Society, American Physical Society, American Oil Chemists' Society, Sigma Xi.

AWARDS, HONORS: Premier's Research Excellence Award, Ontario Ministry of Energy, Science, and Technology, 1999; American Oil Chemists' Society, Young Scientist Research Award, 2000, T.L. Mounts Award, 2004; Natural Sciences and Engineering Research Council of Canada, Canada research chair, 2001, E.W.R. Steacie memorial fellowship, 2002; grants from Canada Foundation for Innovation, Ontario Innovation Trust, Ontario Ministry of Agriculture and Food, and Agriculture and Agrifood Canada.

WRITINGS:

(Editor, with Suresh S. Narine) *Physical Properties of Lipids,* Marcel Dekker (New York, NY), 2002.

Enzyme Kinetics: A Modern Approach, John Wiley (New York, NY), 2002.

(Editor, with John R. Dutcher) *Soft Materials: Structure and Dynamics,* Marcel Dekker (New York, NY), 2004.

Fat Crystal Networks, Marcel Dekker (New York, NY), 2004.

Editor in chief, *Food Research International,* 1998—.

WORK IN PROGRESS: Food Chemistry Essentials, for John Wiley.

SIDELIGHTS: Alejandro G. Marangoni told *CA:* "I enjoy the writing process and putting together a body of knowledge in a logical, readable fashion. I try to write in a very concise fashion, while remaining as thorough as possible. I like to write about things I know, and I try explain them in a clear and concise fashion."

BIOGRAPHICAL AND CRITICAL SOURCES:

ONLINE

University of Guelph Web site: Alejandro G. Marangoni Home Page, http://www.uoguelph.ca/~amarango (December 29, 2004).

*   *   *

MARCHANT, Anyda 1911-2006
(Sarah Aldridge)

OBITUARY NOTICE— See index for *CA* sketch: Born January 27, 1911, in Rio de Janeiro, Brazil; died of congestive heart failure, January 11, 2006, in Rehoboth Beach, DE. Lawyer, publisher, and author. Marchant was the cofounder of the publishing houses Naiad Press and A&M Books, which released feminist and lesbian books, including Marchant's own novels. Marchant had been interested in writing since her childhood, but she pursued a law degree in school instead of literature. She graduated from what is now George Washington University with a B.A. in 1931, an M.A. in 1933, and an LL.B. in 1936. While still a student, she was inspired by women's rights leader Alice Paul, whom she assisted during Paul's research for the Equal Rights Amendment proposal. Women' rights and feminism would become of central importance to Marchant for the rest of her life. One of the few women lawyers in the country at the time, during World War II Marchant worked in the Law Library for the Library of Congress. However, she quit the job when she was told to take a lower-paying position after a male colleague returned from the war. Refusing to compromise, she moved to Brazil for a time and worked as an interpreter. She came back to the United States, however, and worked for the law firm Covington & Burling in Washington, DC. From 1951 to 1953 she was on the staff of the Bureau of Foreign and Domestic Commerce in Washington, and she spent the next twenty years as an attorney for the World Bank. After retiring in 1972, Marchant founded Naiad Press with her partner, Muriel Crawford. The first book the publishing house released was Marchant's debut novel, *The Latecomer* (1974), which was printed under the pen name Sarah Aldridge. Marchant would go on to write a dozen more novels under the Aldridge name, including *All True Lovers* (1978),

Misfortune's Friend (1985), and *Nina in the Wilderness* (1997). A publishing dispute caused Marchant and Crawford to split from their other shareholders in 1995, and together they created a new publishing company, A&M Books.

OBITUARIES AND OTHER SOURCES:

PERIODICALS

Washington Post, February 7, 2006, p. B6.

*   *   *

MARK, Jan 1943-2006
(Janet Marjorie Mark)

OBITUARY NOTICE— See index for *CA* sketch: Born June 22, 1943, in Welwyn, Hertfordshire, England; died January 16, 2006. Author. Mark was a two-time Carnegie Medal-winning author of stories for children who wrote for all ages, including novels for adults. She was interested in writing from a young age, and when she was just fifteen years old she entered a writing competition for the *Daily Mirror* and won second place. She earned a degree from the Canterbury College of Art in 1965 and then embarked on a teaching career. Teaching English and art at Southfields School in Kent until 1971, she left that occupation to focus on her family. When the publisher Kestrel Books established the *Guardian* Award for best children's book by a new talent, however, Mark could not resist submitting an entry. Her *Thunder and Lightnings* (1976) won the competition handily, as well as the Carnegie, and thus began what would be a prolific career. Mark found that she could write everything from picture books for young children to young adult titles and from short stories to adult novels with great success. She also wrote science fiction, including the trilogy comprised of *The Ennead* (1978), *Divide and Rule* (1979), and *Aquarius* (1982). In addition, Mark was versatile in the type of stories she wrote, with critics labeling some of her books as having very bleak moods, while others have been more lighthearted and witty; furthermore, she received praise for her strong characterizations and depictions of human relationships. Among her more recent titles, too, are the adult novels *The Eclipse of the Century*

(1999) and *Useful Idiots* (2004). Also earning a Carnegie Medal for *Handles* (1983), Mark won many other honors over the years. Concerned about the state of children's literature and its seeming continued lack of respect from critics, she also earned praise for editing *The Oxford Book of Children's Stories* (1993).

OBITUARIES AND OTHER SOURCES:

PERIODICALS

Times (London, England), January 23, 2006, p. 53.

*   *   *

MARK, Janet Marjorie
See MARK, Jan

*   *   *

MARQUARDT, Elizabeth

PERSONAL: Married; husband's name Jim (a college professor); children: two. *Education:* Wake Forest University, B.A.; University of Chicago, M.A., M.Div.

ADDRESSES: Home—Chicago, IL. *Office*—Institute for American Values, 1841 Broadway, Ste. 211, New York, NY 10023; fax: 212-541-6665. *E-mail*—elizabeth@familyscholars.org.

CAREER: Institute for American Values, New York, NY, director of the Center for Marriage and Families. Guest on radio and television programs, including *All Things Considered, O'Reilly Factor,* and *Today.* Public speaker.

WRITINGS:

Between Two Worlds: The Inner Lives of Children of Divorce (nonfiction), Crown Publishers (New York, NY), 2005.

Coauthor of study, *"Hooking Up, Hanging Out, and Hoping for Mr. Right: College Women on Dating and Mating Today."* Contributor to periodicals, including

Christian Science Monitor, Chicago Tribune Magazine, Philadelphia Inquirer, New York Times, Washington Post, Los Angeles Times, and *Christian Century.*

SIDELIGHTS: Elizabeth Marquardt paints a stark picture of the effect of divorce on children in her book *Between Two Worlds: The Inner Lives of Children of Divorce.* Marquardt challenges the common wisdom that an amicable divorce is better for children than parents who remain married despite problems. Her studies show that while divorce may be less destructive to children's psyches than living in a home that is actually dangerous due to violence or extreme tension in the marriage, most divorces today do not fall into that category, and children whose parents divorce even though their problems create a low amount of stress in the family may fare far worse than others. Marquardt believes that children of divorce frequently become caretakers of their parents rather than vice versa, and are burdened with the perplexing problem of reconciling their parents' differing values and beliefs. She also finds that children of divorce are often inappropriately entrusted with their parents' secrets. Remarriage does little to heal the sense of brokenness that often overcomes a child of divorce, and such individuals frequently seem to be at increased risk for substance abuse, pedophilic attacks, and other social ills.

The author's contention that strong marriages are better for children than divorce is largely uncontested, but some reviewers fault her for focusing so much on what Kay Brodie called in *Library Journal* "a largely unattainable ideal for society." Marquardt states that her work stems from her own experiences as a child of divorce as well as a survey of 1,500 young adults. *National Review* contributor Allan Carlson found that the author's inclusion of her personal story "saves her book" from becoming maudlin, "and turns it instead into a fresh, cogent, and compelling testimony."

BIOGRAPHICAL AND CRITICAL SOURCES:

PERIODICALS

First Things, November, 2005, review of *Between Two Worlds: The Inner Lives of Children of Divorce,* p. 60.
Library Journal, July 1, 2005, Kay Brodie, review of *Between Two Worlds,* p. 100.

National Review, November 7, 2005, Allan Carlson, review of *Between Two Worlds,* p. 54.
Newsweek, October 24, 2005, Peg Tyre, interview with Elizabeth Marquardt, p. 14.
Publishers Weekly, June 13, 2005, review of *Between Two Worlds,* p. 42.

ONLINE

Between Two Worlds Web site, http://www.betweentwoworlds.org (April 18, 2006).
CNN Online, http://transcripts.cnn.com/ (March 8, 2006), transcript of Anderson Cooper interview with Elizabeth Marquardt.
Dallas Morning News Online, http://www.dallasnews.com/ (January 20, 2006), transcript of chat session with Elizabeth Marquardt.
Institute for American Values Web site, http://www.americanvalues.org/ (March 8, 2006), biographical information about Elizabeth Marquardt.
uExpress, http://www.uexpress.com/ (November 25, 2003), "Massachusetts Decision Ignores Fate of Children."
Washington Post Online, http://www.washingtonpost.com/ (November 7, 2005), transcript of chat session with Elizabeth Marquardt.

*   *   *

MARTÍNEZ, Guillermo 1962-

PERSONAL: Born July 29, 1962, in Bahía Blanca, Argentina. *Education:* Holds a Ph.D.

ADDRESSES: *Agent*—Carmen Balcells Agency, Diagonal 580 (08021), Barcelona, Spain. *E-mail*—infogmartinez@yahoo.com.ar.

CAREER: Writer and mathematician.

AWARDS, HONORS: Premio del Fondo de las Artes, 1988, for *Infierno Grande;* Fundación Antorchas scholarship, 1999; MacDowell scholarships, 2000, 2001; Premio Planeta, 2003, for *Crímenes imperceptibles;* Civitella Ranieri Foundation scholarship, 2004.

WRITINGS:

FICTION

Infierno grande (short stories), Editorial Legasa (Buenos Aires, Argentina), 1989, new edition, Planeta (Buenos Aires, Argentina) 2006.

Acerca de Roderer (novel), Planeta (Buenos Aires, Argentina), 1992, translated by Laura Dail as *Regarding Roderer,* St. Martin's Press (New York, NY), 1994.

La mujer del maestro (novel), Planeta (Buenos Aires, Argentina), 1998.

Crímenes imperceptibles (novel), Planeta (Buenos Aires, Argentina), 2003, translated by Sonia Soto as *The Oxford Murders,* MacAdam/Cage (New York, NY), 2005.

NONFICTION

Borges y la matemática, Editorial Universitaria de Buenos Aires (Buenos Aires, Argentina), 2003.

La fórmula de la inmortalidad, Seix Barral (Buenos Aires, Argentina), 2005.

Contributor of short stories to anthologies; also contributor of reviews to periodicals, including *La Nación.* Author's writings have been translated into several languages.

ADAPTATIONS: Crímenes imperceptibles has been adapted for film, directed by Alex de la Iglesia.

SIDELIGHTS: Argentinian author Guillermo Martínez has written several novels and short stories, earning him some of his country's top literary prizes. Martínez is the author of six books, two of which have been translated into English. The first translation, *Regarding Roderer,* was published in 1994. The novel's protagonist is a schoolboy—the unnamed first-person narrator—and his position as the smartest boy in class is threatened by the arrival of new student Gustavo Roderer. The boys begin a fragile friendship; ultimately, the narrator's sister falls in love with Gustavo, but Gustavo is more interested in thinking than he is in being in love. Indeed, Gustavo lives only to come up with a philosophical thought that has not been thought of before. As both boys grow older, the narrator, who is much more of a pragmatist than his companion, enters college and then goes, briefly, to fight in the Malvinas/Falklands war. Gustavo, on the other hand, continues his abstract intellectual pursuits, falls sick, and dies alone.

The novel, which was described by critics as brief and ascetic, received high appraisal in Argentina and mixed reviews in the United States. A *Publishers Weekly* reviewer stated that the story rests upon Gustavo's decline, yet "the narrator's voice, which seems sometimes selfishly recalcitrant, does little to generate interest" in Gustavo. Nonetheless, the reviewer did find the book to be "provocative." Moreover, Brad Hooper, writing in *Booklist,* found much to praise in the novel. After calling the novel "austere," Hooper stated that the story "transcends any cultural attachments to reveal universal truths."

Martínez's second book in English translation, *The Oxford Murders,* was published eleven years after the release of *Regarding Roderer.* The book draws on Martínez's background as a mathematician, a subject in which the author holds a doctorate. Set in Oxford, England, the story portrays a young Argentinian student of mathematics and his mentor, a logician named Arthur Seldom. The student, who is also the narrator, again remains nameless. When the narrator's landlady, a retired mathematician herself, is killed, a note from the killer, complete with mathematical clues is sent to Arthur. As the student and Arthur attempt to solve the crime, more murders are committed, and new notes with clues begin to appear.

Most critics reacted positively to the use of math as a plot device; they argued that it added an intriguing intellectual aspect to the murder-mystery story. *Booklist* contributor Connie Fletcher felt that the "fascinating applications of logical sequences" are an "extreme" version of the work of famous mystery-novelist Agatha Christie. London *Independent* reviewer Emma Hagestadt stated: "Read it, and be temporarily convinced that applied mathematics is suddenly within your grasp." Critics additionally praised Martínez's writing style; while a *Kirkus Reviews* writer called the book "soft-spoken, smart and satisfying," a *Publishers Weekly* reviewer noted that Martínez "writes with a restrained, elegant style."

BIOGRAPHICAL AND CRITICAL SOURCES:

PERIODICALS

Booklist, November 1, 1994, Brad Hooper, review of *Regarding Roderer,* p. 475; September 1, 2005, Connie Fletcher, review of *The Oxford Murders,* p. 70.

Independent (London, England), January 27, 2006, Emma Hagestadt, review of *The Oxford Murders.*

Guardian (London, England), February 5, 2005, Marcus du Sautoy, review of *The Oxford Murders.*

Kirkus Reviews, August 1, 2005, review of *The Oxford Murders,* p. 809.

Publishers Weekly, September 19, 1994, review of *Regarding Roderer,* p. 50; August 1, 2005, review of *The Oxford Murders,* p. 41.

San Francisco Chronicle, October 2, 2005, David Lazarus, review of *The Oxford Murders.*

Times (London, England), March 12, 2005, Marcel Berlins, review of *The Oxford Murders.*

ONLINE

Guillermo Martinez Home Page (Spanish language), http://www.guillermomartinez.8m.net (March 23, 2006).

* * *

MARZLUFF, John
   See MARZLUFF, John M.

* * *

MARZLUFF, John M.
   (John Marzluff)

PERSONAL: Male. *Education:* Degree in wildlife biology, 1980; attended Northern Arizona University and University of Vermont.

ADDRESSES: Office—College of Forest Resources, University of Washington, Box 352100, Seattle, WA 98195-2100. *E-mail*—corvid@u.washington.edu.

CAREER: University of Washington, Seattle, began as associate professor of ecosystem sciences, became Denman Professor of Sustainable Resource Science and professor of wildlife science. Leader of U.S. Fish and Wildlife Service's Recovery Team for the Mariana Crow; Cooper Ornithological Society, board member.

MEMBER: American Ornithologist's Union (councilor).

AWARDS, HONORS: H.R. Painton Award, 1989, for outstanding paper published in *The Condor.*

WRITINGS:

NONFICTION

(With Russell P. Balda) *The Pinyon Jay: Behavioral Ecology of a Colonial Cooperative Corvid,* illustrated by Tony Angell and Caroline Bauder, Poyser (London, England), 1992.

(Editor, with Rex Sallabanks) *Avian Conservation: Research and Management,* Island Press (Washington, DC), 1998.

(Editor, with Reed Bowman and Roarke Donnelly) *Avian Ecology and Conservation in an Urbanizing World,* Kluwer Academic Publishers (Boston, MA), 2001.

(Editor) *Radiotelemetry and Animal Populations,* Academic Press (Burlington, MA), 2001.

(With Tony Angell) *In the Company of Crows and Ravens,* illustrated by Tony Angell, Yale University Press (New Haven, CT), 2005.

Also author of numerous scientific papers on bird behavior and wildlife management. Member of editorial boards, *Bird Behavior, Acta Ornithologica, Ecological Applications.*

SIDELIGHTS: John M. Marzluff is an ornithologist who has published several books about bird life and wildlife conservation. Along with Rex Sallabanks, he edited *Avian Conservation: Research and Management,* a collection of papers that cover past and present philosophies of conservation, techniques used in conservation research, and conservation methods suitable to working with endangered species, forested and non-forested landscapes, and even urban landscapes. According to Robert W. Butler in the *Wilson Bulletin,* "Marzluff and Sallabanks should be commended for assembling concise reviews of many important topics for conservationists and applications for land managers. . . . This book contains a wealth of information and is an excellent review of the topic."

In the Company of Crows and Ravens, written with and illustrated by Tony Angell, is of more interest to general readers. The authors point out that crows share many traits with humans, including large brains, complex social orders, and extensive vocabularies. They go on to document the ways in which humans and crows have interacted over the years. Human reaction to crows has ranged from respect to hatred, and even attempts at extermination. The authors analyze the current trends in crow population and ways to control crows. Nancy Bent, a reviewer for *Booklist,* wrote that the text's coverage of science, folklore, and literature, along with the "lively" illustrations, "recommends this book highly."

Marzluff told *CA:* "I got interested in writing as a way to share my fascination with the natural world with others. I studied with Bernd Heinrich, whose writing has influenced my scientific and literary approach to nature. I am most surprised by strange encounters other people have had with the animals I write about. By stimulating others to consider my interests, I learn secondhand much more than I could directly experience. In this way, I learn from readers about strange and intriguing bird behavior (like the crow that landed on a sunbather and left her a wooden bead) that will fuel my scientific curiosity for decades. My book with Tony Angell on the mutual interactions between people and crows (*In the Company of Crows and Ravens,*) is my favorite because it summarizes my (and my students') long-term scientific investigations of these amazing birds in a way that I have tried to make accessible and engaging to all readers.

"I hope people who read my works will learn that nature influences us as much as we influence her. In so doing, I expect that people will recognize that we must become better stewards if we are to continue to reap cultural, ecologic, and economic benefits from our surroundings. If nothing else, I aspire to have readers of my work look carefully and thoughtfully at the birds that share our world—to recognize that we are all connected in a complex web of cultural, ecological, and evolutionary interactions."

BIOGRAPHICAL AND CRITICAL SOURCES:

PERIODICALS

BioScience, January, 1999, John L. Curnutt, review of *Avian Conservation: Research and Management,* p. 71.

Booklist, October 15, 2005, Nancy Bent, review of *In the Company of Crows and Ravens,* p. 15.
Library Journal, October 1, 2005, Robert Eagan, review of *In the Company of Crows and Ravens,* p. 106.
Wilson Bulletin, September, 1999, Robert W. Butler, review of *Avian Conservation,* p. 445.
Wilson Quarterly, autumn, 2005, Roxana Robinson, review of *In the Company of Crows and Ravens,* p. 119.

ONLINE

University of Washington Urban Ecology Department Web site, http://www.urbanecology.washington.edu/ (January 21, 2006), biographical information on John M. Marzluff.

*   *   *

MATHEWS, Lou 1946-

PERSONAL: Born in Glendale, CA, November 27, 1946; son of Ernesto Muller (a salesman and chemist) and Marjorie Peyton Mathews (a schoolteacher); married Alison McIlvaine Turner (a lawyer), December 21, 1983 (second marriage); children: Jennifer. *Education:* Attended Glendale Community College, 1968-70; University of California at Santa Cruz, B.A. (with honors), 1973; Vermont College, M.F.A., 1987.

ADDRESSES: Home—2801 Westshire Dr., Los Angeles, CA 90068. *Office*—UCLA Extension Writers' Program, 10995 Le Conte Ave., Rm. 440, Los Angeles, CA 90024.

CAREER: Writer, journalist, editor, and educator. *El Vaquero,* Glendale College, Glendale, CA, editor, 1968-70; *Glendale New Press,* Glendale, sportswriter, 1968-70; Bob's Big Boy Family Restaurants, Glendale, editor of national and local corporate house organs, 1968-70; *Sundaze,* Santa Cruz, CA, fiction editor, 1971-73; *Quarry West,* University of California at Santa Cruz, editor, 1977-80; *L.A. Style,* contributing editor, 1988-94, restaurant reviewer, 1992-94; *Westword,* University of California at Los Angeles, fiction editor, 1992-96, UCLA Extension Writers' Program, instructor, 1989—. Worked variously as a library page, telephone lineman, warehouseman, teamster, gas station attendant, sportswriter, fry cook, employment counselor, beer seller at Watsonville Raceway, loading dock swamper, and mechanic.

AWARDS, HONORS: Katherine Anne Porter Prize in Fiction, 1979; California Arts Commission fiction fellowship, 1989; Pushcart Prize, 1990-91; Teacher of the Year Award, UCLA Extension Writers' Program, 1992; National Endowment for the Arts fiction fellowship, 1992; Best Book Award, *Los Angeles Times,* 1999, for *L.A. Breakdown;* Recipient of scholarships for the Squaw Valley Writer's Conference, 1973, 1975, and Vermont College, 1985-87.

WRITINGS:

Valley Light, Poet and Printer Press (Bakersfield, CA), 1978.
Portales (Spanish language text), Houghton Mifflin (Boston, MA), 1987.
Just Like James (short stories), Sands Houghton (Los Angeles, CA), 1996.
L.A. Breakdown (novel), British Book Co. (Redondo Beach, CA), 1999.
The Muse in the Bottle: Great Writers Celebrate Drinking, Citadel Press/Kensington (New York, NY), 2002.

Short stories have appeared in anthologies, including *The Pushcart Prize XV,* Pushcart Press/W.W. Norton (New York, NY), 1991; *Love Stories for the Rest of Us/The Best of the Pushcart Prize,* Pushcart Press/ W.W. Norton (New York, NY), 1996; *L.A. Shorts,* Heyday Books (Berkeley, CA), 2000; *Dustup,* Sands Houghton (Los Angeles, CA), 2002; contributor of short stories to periodicals, including *Crazyhorse, Witness, Nimrod, Dustup, Big Moon, Quarry West, Portland Review, Fail Better, Splat Clock,* and *Sundaze;* contributor of articles to periodicals, including *L.A. Reader, L.A. Weekly, L.A. Style, Tin House, Los Angeles Times,* and *Mother Jones.*

PLAYS

Rancho Alisos, produced in Los Angeles, CA, 1996.
Captain Manners (radio play), produced at Glaxa Studios in Los Angeles, CA, 1996.

2x4, produced in Los Angeles, CA, 1997.
The Duke's Development, produced in Los Angeles, CA, 2000.

WORK IN PROGRESS: A novel of linked stories titled *Shaky Town,* a book about writing titled *Quotations from Chairman Lou,* and a play titled *Heal.*

SIDELIGHTS: Lou Mathews is the author of books and plays and received widespread public attention for his novel *L.A. Breakdown.* Set in Los Angeles, circa 1967, the novel is about the illegal and dangerous world of street racing. In the novel, the author describes a world that comes alive after dark and is peopled with a lost generation of young men and women who have left high school but have no thoughts of college. Drifting from one dead-end job to another, supplementing their income through thieving, doing the occasional stint in prison, and reluctantly—with the Vietnam war looming—entering the armed services when there is nothing else left. A *Publishers Weekly* contributor noted that the author "evocatively rendered" the American public's love of cars. The reviewer went on to call the novel a "snappy tale" and noted that the author's recreation of the street racing life "brings this world to life in vivid detail." Mark Rozzo, writing in the *Los Angeles Times Book Review,* called the novel "understated" and went on to comment that the author "deftly captures the mood of mid-'60s Los Angeles."

Mathews's full-length play, *The Duke's Development,* is set in 1640, twenty-four years after the death of Shakespeare, and focuses on an acting troupe hired to perform before a Duke at his castle. Unfortunately, the troupe soon finds itself fighting among themselves over the Duke's wishes to have only flashy, action-filled plays performed rather than the classics the troupe usually produces. Commenting on the play, the author told CA: "The idea expanded when I started really thinking of the parallels between the seventeenth century and the present. The dilemma for actors was the same: Art versus Money. Dukes were the studio heads of their time. That made me think of modern problems—the diminution of language, the rise of special effects, story analysis, test audiences, accounting, legal departments, agents. It was like taking dictation."

BIOGRAPHICAL AND CRITICAL SOURCES:

PERIODICALS

Los Angeles Times Book Review, August 1, 1999, Mark Rozzo, review of *L.A. Breakdown,* p. 10.

Publishers Weekly, August 16, 1999, review of *L.A. Breakdown,* p. 64.

*   *   *

MAURICE, Edward Beauclerk 1913-2003

PERSONAL: Born 1913, in England; died 2003.

CAREER: Bookseller. Worked in the Arctic for the Hudson's Bay Company. *Military service:* Served in the New Zealand Navy during World War II.

WRITINGS:

The Last Gentleman Adventurer: Coming of Age in the Arctic (autobiography), Houghton Mifflin (Boston, MA), 2005.

SIDELIGHTS: Edward Beauclerk Maurice was sixteen years old when he met a missionary from the Canadian Arctic, a visitor to Maurice's boarding school. He was fascinated by a film shown by the missionary, about life in the frozen North. His own family was in difficult circumstances following the death of his father, and soon, Maurice had found employment with the Hudson's Bay Company. Working at a trading post in the remote reaches of the Canadian Arctic, he became deeply involved in the lives of the native Inuits. He was so young that he was nicknamed "The Boy" by the locals. He became fluent in their language, and unlike many of his compatriots, he acquired a great respect for the Inuit culture. He eventually took an Inuit wife, and did his best to aid the people when they were stricken by an epidemic of a deadly influenza. Maurice lived among the Inuits for some ten years before leaving for military service in World War II; he later returned to England where he lived a quiet life as a bookseller for many decades.

Maurice recounted his own story in *The Last Gentleman Adventurer: Coming of Age in the Arctic,* which was published posthumously. A *Kirkus Reviews* writer called it "disarmingly captivating," noting that unlike most polar tales, which pit brave men against savage elements, this book focuses on the humanity of the hunters and their families. The stories, which capture a culture that is now virtually lost, are told "in remarkably clear and detailed prose," added the reviewer. A *Publishers Weekly* contributor also found the book "engrossing," and credited the author with relating his story in a "graceful style." The vividness and clarity of Maurice's writing was also praised by Andy Solomon, who wrote in the *Boston Globe:* "As on some da Vinci canvasses, we see no brush strokes here. We see a resourceful, compassionate young gentleman relating the adventure of a lifetime."

BIOGRAPHICAL AND CRITICAL SOURCES:

BOOKS

Maurice, Edward Beauclerk, *The Last Gentleman Adventurer: Coming of Age in the Arctic,* Houghton Mifflin (Boston, MA), 2005.

PERIODICALS

Boston Globe, January 8, 2006, Andy Solomon, review of *The Last Gentleman Adventurer.*
Entertainment Weekly, November 4, 2005, Joan Keener, review of *The Last Gentleman Adventurer,* p. 80.
Kirkus Reviews, September 1, 2005, review of *The Last Gentleman Adventurer,* p. 959.
Publishers Weekly, August 22, 2005, review of *The Last Gentleman Adventurer,* p. 47.*

*   *   *

MAURANA, Dyan
See MAZURANA, Dyan E.

*   *   *

MAZURANA, Dyan E.
(Dyan Mazurana)

PERSONAL: Female. *Education:* Earned Ph.D.

ADDRESSES: Office—Alan Shawn Feinstein International Famine Center, Friedman School of Nutrition Science and Policy, Tufts University, 126 Curtis St., Medford, MA 02155. *E-mail*—d. mazurana@tufts.edu.

CAREER: Harvard University, Kennedy School of Government, Cambridge, MA, research fellow, 2001-2002, visiting scholar, 2003-2004; Tufts University, Alan Shawn Feinstein International Famine Center, Medford, MA, senior research fellow and research director of Gender, Youth, and Community Program, 2002—. Works with various governments and international agencies to inform their policy on upholding the rights of women affected by armed conflict.

WRITINGS:

NONFICTION

(With Susan R. McKay) *Women and Peacebuilding,* International Centre for Human Rights and Democratic Development (Montreal, Quebec, Canada), 1999.

Women, Peace and Security: Study of the United Nations Secretary-General As Pursuant Security Council Resolution 1325, United Nations (New York, NY), 2002.

(With Susan McKay) *Where Are the Girls? Girls in Fighting Forces in Northern Uganda, Sierra Leone and Mozambique; Their Lives during and after the War,* International Centre for Human Rights and Democratic Development (Montreal, Quebec, Canada), 2004.

(With Elizabeth Stites and Neamat Nojumi) *Human Security and Livelihoods of Rural Afghans, 2002-2003,* Feinstein International Famine Center (Medford, MA), 2004.

(Editor, with Angela Raven-Roberts and Jane Parpart) *Gender, Conflict, and Peacekeeping,* Rowman & Littlefield (Lanham, MD), 2005.

Contributor to books, including *Documenting Women's Rights Violations in Armed Conflict Situations,* edited by Agnés Callamard, United Kingdom And International Center for Human Rights and Democratic Development (London, England), 2001.

SIDELIGHTS: Dyan E. Mazurana's areas of expertise include peacekeeping, women's human rights, and children involved in armed conflict. She has worked as an educator and a consultant with governments and various agencies to address issues such as human-rights abuses against women and girls during wars and postwar periods. Her work has taken her to Africa, the Balkans, and Afghanistan. In the book *Where Are the Girls? Girls Fighting Forces in Northern Uganda, Sierra Leone and Mozambique; Their Lives during and after the War,* Mazurana and coauthor Susan R. McKay present and analyze data regarding the use of children—particularly girls—in military forces. Studies show that in the period from 1995 to 2003, girls were used in government militias or armed opposition groups in fifty-five countries, and actually fought in armed conflicts in thirty-eight countries. One chapter focuses specifically on conflicts in Mozambique, Uganda, and Sierra Leone, while another examines the physical, emotional, and mental issues encountered by girls who fought in those three countries. The book concludes by suggesting ways to address the issues illuminated in the book. According to Shadia Abdel Rahim Mohammed in *Ahfad Journal,* the book is distinguished by "a good and clear style," and should raise awareness about the issues related to girls' involvement in armed conflict.

BIOGRAPHICAL AND CRITICAL SOURCES:

PERIODICALS

Ahfad Journal, June, 2004, Shadia Abdel Rahim Mohammed, review of *Where Are the Girls? Girls Fighting Forces in Northern Uganda, Sierra Leone and Mozambique; Their Lives during and after the War,* p. 77.

Choice, January, 2006, K. Staudt, review of *Gender, Conflict, and Peacekeeping.*

ONLINE

Alan Shawn Feinstein International Famine Center Web site, http://nutrition.tufts.edu/research/famine/ (January 21, 2006), biographical information about Dyan E. Mazurana.

*   *   *

McCLURE, Ken

PERSONAL: Born in Edinburgh, Scotland. *Education:* Edinburgh University, Ph.D.

ADDRESSES: Agent—c/o Author Mail, Allison & Busby, 13 Charlotte Mews, London W1T 4EJ, England. *E-mail*—info@kenmcclure.com.

CAREER: City Hospital, Edinburgh, Scotland, junior lab technician; writer, 2000—. Researcher and consultant, Medical Research Council of Great Britain.

WRITINGS:

NOVELS

Pestilence, Simon & Schuster (London, England), 1991.
Requiem, Simon & Schuster (London, England), 1992.
Crisis, Simon & Schuster (London, England), 1993.
Trauma, Simon & Schuster (London, England), 1995.
Chameleon, Pocket Books (London, England), 1995.
The Scorpion's Advance, Pocket Books (London, England), 1998.
Pandora's Helix, Pocket Books (London, England), 1998.
Donor, Simon & Schuster (London, England), 1998.
Resurrection, Simon & Schuster (London, England), 1999.
Tangled Web, Simon & Schuster (London, England), 2000.
Deception, Simon & Schuster (London, England), 2001.
Wildcard, Simon & Schuster (London, England), 2002.
The Gulf Conspiracy, Allison & Busby (London, England), 2004.
Eye of the Raven, Allison & Busby (London, England), 2005.
Past Lives, Allison & Busby (London, England), 2006.

McClure's work has been translated into twenty languages.

SIDELIGHTS: Ken McClure is an author of scientific thrillers that are popular in the United Kingdom. A native of Scotland, McClure earned a degree in molecular genetics after beginning his career modestly as a junior laboratory technician in an Edinburgh hospital. Extensive travel as part of his position with the Medical Research Council of Great Britain afforded him time to conceive plots and take notes, and beginning in 2000 he became a full-time author.

In the United Kingdom, McClure has been compared to Michael Crichton because both novelists use matters of scientific ethics to propel their plots. In McClure's case, these include an outbreak of smallpox in *Resurrection,* human cloning in *Tangled Web,* and the perils of genetically engineered plants in *Deception.* Ellie Barta-Moran, writing for *Booklist,* noted of *Resurrection,* "The smallpox virus may now be extinct, but good stories about it still thrive." In addition, Barta-Moran commented of *Tangled Web,* "McClure weaves his plot line skillfully."

Two of McClure's additional thrillers feature an unlikely investigator named Dr. Steven Dunbar, a trained scientific-medical specialist who sometimes finds his own life in danger as he seeks answers to crimes by applying medical forensics.

BIOGRAPHICAL AND CRITICAL SOURCES:

PERIODICALS

Booklist, February 15, 2000, Ellie Barta-Moran, review of *Resurrection,* p. 1083; June 1, 2000, Ellie Barta-Moran, review of *Tangled Web,* p. 1860.
Library Journal, July 1, 2005, Ann Kim, review of *Eye of the Raven,* p. 58.
Student BMJ, October, 2002, Helen Barratt, review of *Deception,* p. 394.

ONLINE

Ken McClure Home Page, http://www.kenmcclure.freeuk.com (January 6, 2006).
Reviewing the Evidence Web Site, http://www.reviewingtheevidence.com/ (January 6, 2006), Barbara Franchi, review of *The Gulf Conspiracy.**

*   *   *

McEWEN, Todd 1953-

PERSONAL: Born 1953, in CA; emigrated to Scotland, 1981; married Lucy Ellman (a writer). *Education:* Columbia University, graduated 1975.

ADDRESSES: Home—Edinburgh, Scotland. *Agent*—c/o Author Mail, Granta Books, 2/3 Hanover Yard, Noel Rd., London N1 8BE, England.

CAREER: Writer. Has worked in broadcasting, theater, and rare books. Former writer-in-residence in Aberdeen, Scotland.

WRITINGS:

Fisher's Hornpipe (novel), Harper & Row (New York, NY), 1983.
McX: A Romance of the Dour (novel), Grove Weidenfeld (New York, NY), 1990.
Arithmetic, Oxford University Press (London, England), 1998.
Who Sleeps with Katz (novel), Granta Books (London, England), 2003.

SIDELIGHTS: Todd McEwen is a novelist whose first comic novel, *Fisher's Hornpipe,* is set in Boston and Cambridge, Massachusetts. His second, *McX: A Romance of the Dour,* is set in his adopted home of Scotland. The protagonist, McX, is a working-class man whose life is spent visiting his favorite pubs and fish-and-chip eateries, a pursuit interrupted by a love affair. In a review of *McX,* in *Publishers Weekly,* Sybil Steinberg observed that "McEwen's prose is like [Franz] Kafka grafted onto [Samuel] Beckett."

Who Sleeps with Katz is set in New York around the holidays. After learning he has lung cancer, MacK walks around the city wondering which of the thousands of cigarettes he has smoked are to blame. He visits his favorite places with his companions, Mary-Ann and Isidor, the "Katz" of the title. As MacK wanders aimlessly about, often numbed by alcohol, he is succored by kind strangers as he contemplates the end of his life. John Sears reviewed the book for *Pop Matters* online, writing that "New York works hard as an environment in this novel. It offers both place and time, space and memory, to the characters who populate it, and is never reduced to those characters or their society but maintains an aloof, depersonalising distance, so that the city becomes both character and backdrop to the novel." Sears concluded that McEwen "has written in comic, intelligent and sometimes haunting prose a brilliant, convincing, human, emotionally raging portrait of a city and the people it makes, and who make it."

BIOGRAPHICAL AND CRITICAL SOURCES:

PERIODICALS

New York Times Book Review, Etelka Lehoczky, review of *Who Sleeps with Katz,* p. 28.
Publishers Weekly, June 8, 1990, Sybil Steinberg, review of *McX: A Romance of the Dour,* p. 46.
Spectator, April 28, 1990, Ross Clark, review of *McX,* p. 29.
Village Voice, December 10, 2003, review of *Who Sleeps with Katz,* p. 51.

ONLINE

Pop Matters, http://www.popmatters.com/ (March 7, 2006), John Sears, review of *Who Sleeps with Katz.**

*   *   *

McKAY, Susan 1942-

PERSONAL: Born 1942. *Education:* DePauw University, B.S., 1964; University of Colorado, M.S., 1965; University of Wyoming, Ph.D., 1978.

ADDRESSES: Office—Women's Studies Program, University of Wyoming, Ross Hall 422, Dept. 4297, 1000 E. University Ave., Laramie, WY 82071.

CAREER: Nurse, psychologist, and educator. University of Wyoming, Laramie, professor of women's studies and nursing.

MEMBER: American Psychological Association.

AWARDS, HONORS: W.K. Kellogg National fellow, 1983-86; Rockefeller Foundation scholar in residence, Bellagio, Italy, 1996; International Federation of University Women Peace Research Fellowship, Geneva, Switzerland, 1999; American Psychological Association fellow, 2002.

WRITINGS:

Assertive Childbirth: The Future Parents' Guide to a Positive Pregnancy, foreword by Charles Mahan, illustrated by Susan Duvall, Prentice-Hall (Englewood Cliffs, NJ), 1983.

(With Celeste R. Phillips) *Family-Centered Maternity Care: Implementation Strategies,* Aspen Systems (Rockville, MD), 1984.

(With Dyan E. Mazurana) *Women and Peacebuilding,* International Centre for Human Rights and Democratic Development (Montreal, Canada), 1999.

(With Dyan E. Mazurana) *Raising Women's Voices for Peacebuilding: Vision, Impact, and Limitations of Media Technologies,* Women, Ink (New York, NY), 2001.

The Courage Our Stories Tell: The Daily Lives and Maternal Child Health Care of Japanese American Women at Heart Mountain, Western History Publications (Powell, WY), 2002.

(With Dyan E. Mazurana) *Where Are the Girls?: Girls in Fighting Forces in Northern Uganda, Sierra Leone, and Mozambique: Their Lives during and after the War,* International Centre for Human Rights and Democratic Development (Montreal, Canada), 2004.

SIDELIGHTS: Susan McKay has nearly two decades of experience researching topics related to women in peacebuilding and armed conflict. McKay's *Women and Peacebuilding* was published in 2001 and written with Dyan E. Mazurana. The book examines how women from around the world work towards resolving conflict. Diana D'Souza, writing in the *Online Journal of Peace and Conflict Resolution,* praised the book's "solid contribution to conflict and peace studies." She stated: "For readers thirsty for solid information on women's peacebuilding, the material is gratifying."

McKay's 2004 publication, *Where Are the Girls?: Girls in Fighting Forces in Northern Uganda, Sierra Leone, and Mozambique: Their Lives during and after the War,* was also written with Mazurana. In this book, the pair analyze women or girls engaged in armed conflict in Northern Uganda, Sierra Leone, and Mozambique. Shadia Abdel Rahim Mohammed, reviewing the book in the *Ahfad Journal,* found that the book is "written in a good and clear style" and "raises the awareness of people."

BIOGRAPHICAL AND CRITICAL SOURCES:

PERIODICALS

Ahfad Journal, June, 2004, Shadia Abdel Rahim Mohammed, review of *Where Are the Girls?: Girls in*

Fighting Forces in Northern Uganda, Sierra Leone, and Mozambique: Their Lives during and after the War, p. 77.

ONLINE

International Centre for Human Rights and Democratic Development Web site, http://www.ichrdd.ca/ (February 24, 2006), author profile.

Online Journal of Peace and Conflict Resolution Web site, http://www.trinstitute.org/ojpcr/ (February 24, 2006), Diane D'Souza, review of *Women and Peacebuilding.*

University of Wyoming Web site, http://www.uwyo.edu/ (February 24, 2006), author profile.*

*　　*　　*

McKENDRY, Joe 1972-

PERSONAL: Born April 20, 1972, in Lowell, MA; son of Donald (a potter) and Judith (a teacher) McKendry; married Susan Hass (a marketing manager), August, 1999; children: Elsie, Owen. *Ethnicity:* "Caucasian." *Education:* Rhode Island School of Design, B.F.A.

ADDRESSES: Home—Boston, MA. *Agent*—c/o Author Mail, David. R. Godine, Publisher Inc., 9 Hamilton Pl., Boston, MA 02108-4715. *E-mail*—joemckendry@joemckendry.com.

CAREER: Freelance artist, author. Rhode Island School of Design, teacher; Massachusetts College of Art, teacher.

WRITINGS:

Beneath the Streets of Boston: Building America's First Subway, David R. Godine (Boston, MA), 2005.

SIDELIGHTS: An author and illustrator, Joe McKendry graduated from the Rhode Island School of Design and has stayed on there as a teacher of illustration. He made his publishing debut by offering readers a fascinating glimpse into the history of

America's first underground transit system in *Beneath the Streets of Boston: Building America's First Subway*. McKendry analyzes the traffic problems that plagued Boston's maze of streets during the late 1800s and prompted the development of an alternative form of public transportation. After a lengthy battle, the famous "T" system was built, sparking a longstanding transportation trend. McKendry follows the ongoing development of the city's subway system, highlighting both problem areas as well as accomplishments. "New England history buffs and those interested in the origins of mass transport will welcome this look at the beginnings of America's first subway," commented Nancy Menaldi-Scanlan in *School Library Journal*. A *Kirkus Reviews* critic referred to McKendry's book as "a stunning examination" of a challenging advance in transportation technology.

McKendry once commented: "During the creation of *Beneath the Streets of Boston* my goal was to present as simply as possible the story of how and why America's first subway came to be built. Research was gathered from turn-of-the-twentieth-century transit commission reports that detailed every facet of the subway's construction. To learn about the public's reaction the subway, I read newspaper articles or microfilm from important moments in the subways development (i.e., when particular parts of the tunnel were first opened to the public). Illustrations are watercolor paintings based on photographs primarily from the collection of *Historic New England*.

BIOGRAPHICAL AND CRITICAL SOURCES:

PERIODICALS

Booklist, June 1, 2005, Jennifer Mattson, review of *Beneath the Streets of Boston: Building America's First Subway,* p. 1802.
Boston Globe, June 5, 2005, Jennifer Schuessler, "The First Big Dig."
Horn Book, September-October, 2005, Margaret A. Bush, review of *Beneath the Streets of Boston,* p. 605.
Kirkus Reviews, June 1, 2005, review of *Beneath the Streets of Boston,* p. 640.
Publishers Weekly, July 19, 2004, Sally Lodge, "Climbing aboard the Subway," p. 92.
School Library Journal, September, 2005, Nancy Menaldi-Scanlan, review of *Beneath the Streets of Boston,* p. 226.

Trains, September, 2005, Kathi Kube, review of *Beneath the Streets of Boston,* p. 74.

ONLINE

Joe McKendry Home Page, http://joemckendry.com (April 11, 2006).

*   *   *

**McKENNA, Elizabeth Perle
    See PERLE, Liz**

*   *   *

McNALLY, Patrick S.

PERSONAL: Born in Detroit, MI. *Education:* University of Massachusetts at Amherst, B.A., 1989; State University of New York at Albany, Ph.D., 1995.

ADDRESSES: Agent—c/o Author Mail, Author Solutions, Inc., 1663 S. Liberty Dr., Bloomington, IN 47403. *E-mail*—patricksmcnally@aol.com.

CAREER: Historian and writer.

WRITINGS:

From Chappaquiddick to New York and Washington: Through Oklahoma City (nonfiction), Author Solutions (Bloomington, IN), 2004.

SIDELIGHTS: Patrick S. McNally told *CA:* "My formal academic training has been in mathematics. As a teenager I picked up an enthusiasm for voracious reading on the side, outside of any formal academic training, yet supplementing the latter.

"My book starts the process of tying together scattered threads which run from the Chappaquiddick 'accident' up to the bombings of the Murrah Building and World Trade Towers. Where the evidence indicates varying possibilities, this is pointed out, but without blandly burying the issue of 'what happened' under a philosophical cover. Although one may forecast various refinements and revisions in future analyses as evidence becomes sharply more clear, this book makes one of the clearest efforts yet in book format to lay down facts and analyses that may carry some long-term pertinence. Many other authors (Noam Chomsky being a case in point) who have reached the published book stage have frequently fallen into general socio-historical analyses about what the United States has been doing wrong in the Middle East for the last sixty years. While this has a general value in terms of broad background, it fails to point out the phony nature of the claims that two jet planes were able to level three World Trade Towers.

"Because this is a first attempt to begin placing the events of 9/11 in a real historical framework, the book goes back to earlier events as well. In some instances advantage is taken of relatively recent historical discoveries which are only beginning to receive publicity, such as the Mossad planning of the John F. Kennedy assassination, which Michael Collins Piper had begun investigating in the 1990s. The recently freed political prisoner Mordechai Vanunu only just declared his broad endorsement of the Piper thesis, but this may take some time to sink into public awareness. On the matter of Chappaquiddick, much more ambiguity still remains as to how it was done and who did the exact planning, but various scenarios are laid out which fit the real facts much better than the official story. With the initial bombing of the World Trade Center in 1993 and the later bombing of the Murrah Building, consistent tie-ins are made with the patterns which the spy agencies of Washington and Tel Aviv followed in the later 9/11 scenario."

BIOGRAPHICAL AND CRITICAL SOURCES:

ONLINE

Rense.com Web Site,, http://www.rense.com/general50/jfk.htm (March 29, 2004), Patrick S. McNally, "JFK—Murder Planned in Israel?"

*   *   *

MEIJER, Fik

PERSONAL: Male.

ADDRESSES: Agent—c/o Author Mail, Uitgeverij Verloren, Correspondentie, Postbus 1741, 1200 BS Hilversum, Amsterdam, The Netherlands.

CAREER: University of Amsterdam, Amsterdam, The Netherlands, professor of ancient history.

WRITINGS:

Wrakken, ankers en amforen: Archeologisch onderzoek in de Middellandse Zee, Strengholt (Naarden, The Netherlands), 1976.

A History of Seafaring in the Classical World, St. Martin's Press (New York, NY), 1986.

(Editor) A.B. Breebaart, *Clio and Antiquity: History and Historiography of the Greek and Roman World,* Verloren (Hilversum, The Netherlands), 1987.

Schipper, zeil de haven binnen, alles is al verkocht: Handel en transport in de oudheid, Ambo (Baarn, The Netherlands), 1990.

(With Onno van Nijf) *Trade, Transport, and Society in the Ancient World: A Sourcebook,* Routledge (New York, NY), 1992.

De oudheid van opzij: Oudhistorische notities, Ambo (Amsterdam, The Netherlands), 1997.

Paulus' zeereis naar Rome: Een reconstructie (title means "St. Paul's Voyage to Rome,"), Athenaeum-Polak & Van Gennep (Amsterdam, The Netherlands), 2000.

Keizers sterven niet in bed: Van Caesar tot Romulus Augustulus, 44 v.Chr.-476 n.Chr., Athenaeum-Polak & Van Gennep, 2002, translation by S.J. Leinbach published as *Emperors Don't Die in Bed,* Routledge (New York, NY), 2004.

Gladiatoren:Volksvermaak in het Colosseum, Athenaeum-Polak & Van Gennep (Amsterdam, The Netherlands), 2003, translation by Liz Waters published as *The Gladiators: History's Most Deadly Sport,* Thomas Dunne Books (New York, NY), 2005.

Vercingetorix: De mythe van Frankrijks oudste held, Athenaeum-Polak & Van Gennep (Amsterdam, The Netherlands), 2004.

Translator into Dutch, with Marius West, of Josephus Flavius's *Antiquities of the Jews* and *The Jewish War.*

SIDELIGHTS: Over a course of three decades, Fik Meijer has published volumes on maritime travel in ancient Greece and Rome, as well as books on Roman history. Some of his work has been translated into English, including *Emperors Don't Die in Bed* and *The Gladiators: History's Most Deadly Sport*. The latter title offers a detailed view of the grisly Roman sport of pitting people against animals—and against each other—in battles to the death. A *Publishers Weekly* reviewer felt that *The Gladiators* is a "superficial examination" that "fails to capture any of the excitement" of the mortal combat. Conversely, a *Kirkus Reviews* contributor liked Meijer's "unapologetic look at the blood-soaked rituals" that were part of life in Rome. The same critic praised *The Gladiators* as "a defiant, scholarly study."

BIOGRAPHICAL AND CRITICAL SOURCES:

PERIODICALS

Kirkus Reviews, October 1, 2005, review of *The Gladiators: History's Most Deadly Sport,* p. 1065.
Publishers Weekly, August 1, 2005, review of *The Gladiators,* p. 51.*

* * *

MEISEL, Joseph S. 1965-

PERSONAL: Born May 5, 1965, in Hanover, NH; son of Martin (a university professor) and Martha (Winkley) Meisel; married Felice Ramella (a baker), January 1, 1991; children: Luke Ramella. *Education:* Columbia University, A.B., 1988, A.M., 1992, Ph.D., 1999. *Hobbies and other interests:* Songwriting.

ADDRESSES: Office—Andrew W. Mellon Foundation, 140 E. 62nd St., New York, NY 10021. *E-mail*—jsm@ mellon.org.

CAREER: Writer. Columbia University, New York, NY, budget officer, 1989-92, 1994-99; Andrew W. Mellon Foundation, New York, NY, program officer, 1999—. Adjunct faculty member, Columbia University, 2001-02, and Bernard M. Baruch College of the City University of New York, 2004.

MEMBER: North American Conference on British Studies, North American Victorian Studies Association, American Historical Association, British Politics Group, Royal Historical Society (fellow).

AWARDS, HONORS: Residential fellow, St. Deiniol's Library, 1998.

WRITINGS:

Public Speech and the Culture of Public Life in the Age of Gladstone, Columbia University Press (New York, NY), 2001.

Also author of *Palmerston contre Disraeli: Humour et insulte à la Chambre des communes (milieu XIXe siècle).* Contributor to books, including *The Gladstone Umbrella: Papers Delivered at the Gladstone Centenary Conference, 1998,* edited by Peter Francis, Monad Press (Hawarden, England), 2001; *The Political Legacy of Margaret Thatcher,* edited by Stanislao G. Pugliese, Politico's Publishing (London, England), 2003; and *Palmerston Studies,* Volume 1, edited by Miles Taylor and David Brown, Hartley Institute, University of Southampton (Southampton, England). Contributor of articles and reviews to periodicals, including *History, Twentieth-Century British History, War, Literature, and the Arts,* and *Historical Research.*

WORK IN PROGRESS: Research on modern British history.

BIOGRAPHICAL AND CRITICAL SOURCES:

PERIODICALS

Albion, spring, 2003, Karen J. Musoff, review of *Public Speech and the Culture of Public Life in the Age of Gladstone,* p. 156.
Clio, fall, 2002, John Plotz, review of *Public Speech and the Culture of Public Life in the Age of Gladstone,* p. 110.

* * *

MERCER, Jeremy

PERSONAL: Male. *Education:* Carleton University, B.A.

ADDRESSES: Office—Kilometer Zero, Buster Burk, 12 rue Christiani, 75018 Paris, France. *Agent*—Kristin Lindstrom, 871 N. Greenbriar St., Arlington, VA 22205. *E-mail*—Jeremy@kilometerzero.org.

CAREER: Ottowa Citizen, Ottawa, Ontario, Canada, crime reporter, 1995-99; *Kilometer Zero* (magazine), Paris, France, founder and editor, beginning 2000, supervised Issues 1-5. Producer of performances, including *The Short Step* and *Venues.*

WRITINGS:

The Champagne Gang: High Times and Sweet Crimes, Warwick Publishing (Toronto, Ontario, Canada), 1998.
Money for Nothing: Ten Great Ways to Make Money Illegally, Warwick Publications (Toronto, Ontario, Canada), 1999.
Time Was Soft There: A Paris Sojourn at Shakespeare & Co., St. Martin's Press (New York, NY) 2005, published as *Books, Baguettes, and Bedbugs,* Orion (London, England), 2005.

Contributor to periodicals, including *Kilometer Zero, Saturday Night, Lola,* and *Quill & Quire.*

SIDELIGHTS: Jeremy Mercer spent four years working as a crime reporter for the *Ottawa Citizen* in Canada. During that time he produced two full-length books on criminal activities. After receiving what he perceived as a death threat from a subject of one of his newspaper stories, Mercer embarked for France. He lived in Paris until his money ran out, and then he decided to stay longer, at the famed bookstore Shakespeare & Co., where fledgling authors and artists can live temporarily free of charge. Mercer's experiences at the bookstore form the subject of *Time Was Soft There: A Paris Sojourn at Shakespeare & Co.*

To quote Jamie Engle in *Library Journal,* "Mercer tells an enchanting story" of his stay in the bookstore, including descriptions of the work he did there to defray his expenses, his relationship with the store's aging owner, and his interactions with the other residents. "Mercer is a genial, wide-eyed guide to the wild crew at the store," noted a *Kirkus Reviews* critic. The same critic found *Time Was Soft There* "catnip for book junkies." In *Publishers Weekly* a contributor called the book a "finely crafted memoir," and Elizabeth Dickie in *Booklist* concluded that Mercer's vignettes "will leave the reader wishing for such an idyllic sojourn."

Mercer told *CA:* "What first got me interested in writing was the general sensation as a young man that there was no other way to express everything I was thinking and feeling. Then, as my sense of political awarenesss grew, the desire to have stones to throw at the barricade. I am a firm believer in the power of nonfiction. *In Cold Blood, The Executioner's Song, Fast Food Nation, Nickel and Dimed*—these are the types of books I admire and love, the ones that tell brilliant true stories and affect change.

"I tend to slap ideas and phrases onto the screen and then spend hours massaging them until I feel they are less horrible. I am very thankful for deadlines as they force me to finish. Somebody once said of Alberto Giacometti that his sculptures had to be taken away from him or else he would have just kept whittling them down until there was nothing left. I think the same could happen to my books if I had too long to edit them. By the end, 100,000 words would be reduced to a paragraph of nouns.

"The most surprising thing I have learned as a writer is how much of the publishing game is marketing and how little of the publishing game is editing. I hope to spread ideas and inspire people to take action for what they believe in. I think one of the great ills of modern society is that too many people have become spectators: Watching television, letting elections go by without voting, doing nothing more than shaking their head from the car window as they watch another stand of oaks plowed under for the sake of a Wal-Mart. I want to be, in Socrates's words, a gadfly, rousing people from their docile slumber."

BIOGRAPHICAL AND CRITICAL SOURCES:

BOOKS

Mercer, Jeremy, *Time Was Soft There: A Paris Sojourn at Shakespeare & Co.,* St. Martin's Press (New York, NY), 2005.

PERIODICALS

Booklist, October 15, 2005, Elizabeth Dickie, review of *Time Was Soft There,* p. 12.

Independent (London, England), January 1, 2006, Olivia Cole, review of *Books, Baguettes, and Bedbugs.*

Kirkus Reviews, September 1, 2005, review of *Time Was Soft There,* p. 960.

Library Journal, October 1, 2005, Jamie Engle, review of *Time Was Soft There,* p. 75.

New Yorker, October 15, 2005, Elizabeth Dickie, review of *Time Was Soft There,* p. 12.

Publishers Weekly, August 22, 2005, review of *Time Was Soft There,* p. 46.

Sunday Times (London, England), December 11, 2005, Terence Blacker, review of *Books, Baguettes, and Bedbugs.*

ONLINE

Jeremy Mercer Home Page, http://www.jeremymercer. net (December 5, 2005).

* * *

MILLER, Brenda 1959-

PERSONAL: Born 1959. *Education:* University of Montana, M.F.A.; University of Utah, Ph.D.

ADDRESSES: Office—Western Washington University, Humanities 329, 516 High St., Bellingham, WA 98225. *E-mail*—Brenda.Miller@wwu.edu.

CAREER: Western Washington University, Bellingham, WA, currently associate professor of English; *Bellingham Review,* Bellingham, editor-in-chief. Has also worked as a massage therapist.

AWARDS, HONORS: Four Pushcart Prizes; creative writing fellowships from the Abraham Woursell Foundation, Ludwig Vogelstein Foundation, and Steffensen-Cannon Foundation.

WRITINGS:

Season of the Body: Essays, Sarabande Books (Louisville, KY), 2002.

(With Suzanne Paola) *Tell It Slant: Writing and Shaping Creative Nonfiction,* McGraw-Hill (Boston, MA), 2004.

Work represented in anthologies, including *The Beacon Best of 1999: Creative Writing by Women and Men of All Colors,* and *Storming Heaven's Gate: An Anthology of Spiritual Writings by Women.* Contributor to periodicals, including *Georgia Review, Prairie Schooner, Fourth Genre, Yoga Journal,* and the *Sun.*

SIDELIGHTS: English professor Brenda Miller's *Season of the Body: Essays* is a collection of observations on the physical body in which she reflects on her own life and relationships, Zen meditation, and Jewish heritage. Through her writings, the reader learns the sorrow of her sterility after suffering two ectopic pregnancies, her affection for her godson, and her experiences while caring for sick infants in a hospital. *Booklist* contributor Donna Seaman wrote that "Miller handles prose as though it were a living body." "In these autobiographical essays, Miller reminds readers of the mind-body connection," declared Pam Kingsbury in *Library Journal.*

Miller collaborated with Suzanne Paola in writing *Tell It Slant: Writing and Shaping Creative Nonfiction,* the main title of which is taken from a poem by Emily Dickinson. It is a volume of advice for those who would draw on their own lives to write and publish memoirs and personal essays. Steve Weinberg noted in the *Writer* that creative nonfiction that is based on personal experiences finds a smaller audience than does more journalistic writing. However, he added that "if the Miller-Paola regimen helps yield future Annie Dillards and Anne Lamotts, bravo."

BIOGRAPHICAL AND CRITICAL SOURCES:

PERIODICALS

Booklist, March 1, 2002, Donna Seaman, review of *Season of the Body: Essays,* p. 1085.

Kirkus Reviews, January 15, 2002, review of *Season of the Body,* p. 89

Library Journal, February 1, 2002, Pam Kingsbury, review of *Season of the Body,* p. 99.

Publishers Weekly, April 1, 2002, review of *Season of the Body,* p. 72.

Writer, November, 2005, Steve Weinberg, review of *Tell It Slant: Writing and Shaping Creative Nonfiction,* p. 46.

ONLINE

Women Writers, http://www.womenwriters.net/ (March 8, 2006), Lisa Johnson, review of *Season of the Body.*

*   *   *

MILLET, Richard 1953-

PERSONAL: Born 1953.

ADDRESSES: Agent—c/o Author Mail, Northwestern University Press, 629 Noyes St., Evanston, IL 60208-4210.

CAREER: Writer.

WRITINGS:

L'invention du corps de Saint Marc: roman (novel), P.O.L. (Paris, France), 1983.

L'innocence: roman (novel), P.O.L. (Paris, France), 1984.

Sept passions singulières: récits (fiction; title means "Seven Singular Passions"), P.O.L. (Paris, France), 1984.

Le sentiment de la langue: mélange, Champ Vallon (Paris, France), 1986.

Le plus haut miroir, Fata Morgana (Montpellier, France), 1986.

Beyrouth (travel), Champ Vallon (Paris, France), 1987.

L'angélus: récit, P.O.L. (Paris, France), 1988.

La chamber d'ivoire: récit, P.O.L. (Paris, France), 1989.

Laura Mendoza: récit, P.O.L. (Paris, France), 1991.

Accompagnement: lectures, P.O.L. (Paris, France), 1991.

(With Jacques Brault) *Recueil,* Champ Vallon (Seyssel, France), 1991.

L'écrivain Sirieix: récit, P.O.L. (Paris, France), 1992.

Le sentiment de la langue: I, II, III, Le Table Ronde (Paris, France), 1993.

Le chant des adolescents: récits, P.O.L. (Paris, France), 1993.

Coeur blanc: nouvelles (novellas), P.O.L. (Paris, France), 1994.

Un balcon à Beyrouth: récit, La Table Ronde (Paris, France), 1994.

La gloire des Pythre: roman (novel), P.O.L. (Paris, France), 1995.

(Editor and contributor, with Gérard Bocholier) *Pour saluer Robert Marteau* (criticism), Champ Vallon (Seyssel, France), 1996.

L'amour mendiant: notes sur le désir, P.O.L. (Paris, France), 1996.

L'amour des trois soeurs Piale: roman (novel), P.O.L. (Paris, France), 1997.

Cité perdue: Istanbul, 1967-1995, Fata Morgana (Saint-Clément-la-Rivière, France), 1998.

Lauve le pur: roman (novel), P.O.L. (Paris, France), 1999.

La voix d'alto: roman (novel), Gallimard (Paris, France), 2001.

Ma vie parmi les ombres: roman (novel; title means "My Life in the Shadows"), Gallimard (Paris, France), 2003.

Le renard dans le nom: récit, Gallimard (Paris, France), 2003.

Musique secrète, Gallimard (Paris, France), 2004.

Pour la musique contemporaine: chroniques discographiques, Fayard (Paris, France), 2004.

SIDELIGHTS: Richard Millet was named one of the "most penetrating and stylistically sophisticated French novelists born during the postwar years" by a contributor to the *France Magazine* Web site. The writer went on to note: "In his absorbing, pessimistic novels, Millet promulgates the Balzacian ideas that permanent love is a mirage, that a more glorious past is gone forever and that Western civilization is in decline."

In his novel *L'amour des trois soeurs Piale: roman,* the author tells the story of the three Piale sisters as it is related to an insurance salesman by the oldest, and now aged, sister. Much of the novel relates the love lives and tragedies of the sisters and others living on a remote plateau in France. "Key questions about the past are gradually answered as narrative viewpoints shift and the vivid characters . . . become even more complex," wrote John Taylor in the *Times Literary*

Supplement. Taylor went on to note: "Filled with evocative detail . . . the novel depicts the desperate inner urges and uncontrollable outer forces" that influence the characters' lives. Millet has also served as editor and contributor, with Gérard Bocholier, of *Pour saluer Robert Marteau,* a collection of essays honoring the French poet. Writing in the *French Review,* Glenn W. Fetzer called the essays in the volume "abundant, itinerant, and compelling."

BIOGRAPHICAL AND CRITICAL SOURCES:

PERIODICALS

Cahiers Jean Giraudoux, Volume 27, 1999, Sylviane Coyault, "Jean Giraudoux, Richard Millet et L'Institutrice," pp. 221-224.
French Review, December, 1998, Glenn W. Fetzer, review of *Pour saluer Robert Marteau* pp. 367-368.
Times Literary Supplement, May 1, 1998, John Taylor, review of *L'amour des trois soeurs Piale: roman,* p. 24.

ONLINE

France Magazine Web site, http://www.france magazine.org/ (March 4, 2006), "Leaving Home," profile of author's work.*

*   *   *

MILLIGAN, Bryce 1953-

PERSONAL: Born 1953, in Dallas, TX; son of J.B. (a consulting mechanic) and Maxine Carey (an elementary school teacher) Milligan; married Mary Guerrero (a librarian), May 24, 1975; children: Michael Bryce, Brigid Aileen. *Ethnicity:* "Irish, Choctaw, Norwegian, Cherokee." *Education:* University of North Texas, B.A., 1977; University of Texas at Austin, M.A. (language and linguistics), 1980. *Politics:* Democrat. *Religion:* "Catholic with pagan leanings." *Hobbies and other interests:* Restoration of antique instruments, limestone sculpture, study of ancient Near-Eastern languages; "I enjoy restoring antique guitars and occasionally making instruments. I have played music my entire life—cello, trumpet, flute, guitar, and other instruments, and I sculpt in both wood and stone. I am interested in astronomy . . . and in the history of science."

ADDRESSES: Home and office—627 E. Guenther, San Antonio, TX 78210. *E-mail*—milligan@wingspress.com.

CAREER: Guadalupe Cultural Arts Center, San Antonio, TX, director of literature program 1985-86, 1994-2000; North East School of Arts, San Antonio, director of creative writing program, 2000-02; Wings Press (publisher), San Antonio, owner, 1995—. Editor, *Pax: A Journal for Peace through Culture,* 1983-87; book critic for *San Antonio Express News,* 1983-87, and *San Antonio Light,* 1987-90; founding editor, *Vortex: A Critical Review,* 1986-90; coeditor, *Huehuetitlan* (journal), 1989-96.

MEMBER: PEN American Center, National Book Critics Circle, Texas Institute of Letters.

AWARDS, HONORS: Lone Star Award, Texas Library Association, 1991, for *With the Wind, Kevin Dolan;* Library Champion Award, San Antonio Public Library, 1998, for enhancement and involvement in San Antonio Public Library; Most Influential Teacher Award, North East School of the Arts, 2001; Bank Street College Best Book of the Year designation, 2002, for *Brigid's Cloak.*

WRITINGS:

FOR YOUNG ADULTS

With the Wind, Kevin Dolan, Corona (San Antonio, TX), 1987.
Battle of the Alamo: You Are There, illustrated by Charles Shaw, Texas Monthly Press (Austin, TX), 1990.
Comanche Captive: You Are There, illustrations by Charles Shaw, Texas Monthly Press (Austin, TX), 1990.
Lawmen: Stories of Men Who Tamed the West, illustrated by Charles Shaw, Disney Press (New York, NY), 1994.

The Mountain Men: Stories of Men Who Tamed the Wilderness, Disney Press (New York, NY), 1995.

FOR CHILDREN

Brigid's Cloak: An Ancient Irish Story, illustrated by Helen Cann, Eerdmans Publishing (Grand Rapids, MI), 2002.

The Prince of Ireland and the Three Magic Stallions, illustrated by Preston McDaniels, Holiday House (New York, NY), 2003.

POETRY; FOR ADULTS

Daysleepers & Other Poems, Corona (San Antonio, TX), 1984.

Litany Sung at Hell's Gate, M & A Editions (San Antonio, TX), 1990.

From inside the Tree (poetry and songs), Calberg Productions (San Antonio, TX), 1990.

Working the Stone, illustrated by Angela de Hoyos, Wings Press (Houston, TX), 1993.

Alms for Oblivion: A Poem in Seven Parts, Aark Arts (London, England), 2002.

Lost and Certain of It, Aark Arts (London, England), 2006.

OTHER

(Editor) Don Everett, *Albert Steves: A Paternal Portrait*, Watercress Press (San Antonio, TX), 1983.

(Editor) Kathleen Silber and Phyllis Speedlin, *Dear Birthmother*, Corona Publishing (San Antonio, TX), 1983.

(Editor) Cecilio Garcia-Camarillo, *And the Ground Spoke: Poems and Stories*, Guadalupe Cultural Arts Center (San Antonio, TX)1986.

(Editor) *Linking Roots: Writing by Six Women of Diverse Ethnic Origins*, M & A Editions (San Antonio, TX), 1993.

(Editor, with others) *American Journeys: The Hispanic American Experience* (CD ROM), Primary Source Media (Detroit, MI), 1995.

(Editor, with Angela de Hoyos and wife, Mary Guerrero Milligan) *Daughters of the Fifth Sun: A Collection of Latina Fiction and Poetry*, Riverhead Books (New York, NY), 1995.

(Editor) *This Promiscuous Light: Young Women Poets of San Antonio*, Wings Press (San Antonio, TX), 1996.

(Editor) *Corazón del Norte: Writing by North Texas Latinos*, Wings Press (San Antonio, TX), 1996.

(Editor, with Angela de Hoyos and Mary Guerrero Milligan) *¡Floricanto Sí!: A Collection of Latina Poetry*, Penguin Books (New York, NY), 1998.

Contributing editor to *Stone Drum*, 1988-93. Contributor to books, including *Texas Trees: A Friendly Guide*, by Paul W. Cox and Patty Leslie; *Sonnets to Human Beings and Other Selected Works*, edited by Ernesto Padilla; and *Writers at the Lake*, edited by Marylyn Croman. Contributor to periodicals, including *Albuquerque Journal*, *Chicago Tribune*, *Current*, *Dallas Morning News*, *Los Angeles Times*, *New York Times*, *Our Kids*, *Publishers Weekly*, and *San Antonio Kids*.

WORK IN PROGRESS: Princess, Priestess, Poet: Enheduanna of Ur, for Eerdmans Publishing, expected 2007. Currently researching Sumerian and cuneiform for young-adult novels to be published as a trilogy.

SIDELIGHTS: Bryce Milligan once commented: "I have been called a 'literary wizard,' a 'jack of all genres,' and 'a contemporary muse poet' (Edward Hirsch), among other things. The fact is, for most of my life I have always functioned in several endeavors (and often several genres) at once. I believe that I am naturally inclined to do so, and that my best writing is done while I am actively engaged in other more physical pursuits. I am interested in astronomy (my son is a professional astronomer) and in the history of science. My interests appear in my writing, which is in itself simply another way to explore them."

In *Daughters of the Fifth Sun: A Collection of Latina Fiction and Poetry*, Milligan served as editor, along with Angela de Hoyos and his wife, Mary Guerrero Milligan, of a collection of poems and fiction written by Latinas. The title includes a wealth of contemporary poets and authors, including Sandra Cisneros, Julia Alvarez, Ana Castillo, and Denise Chavez, among others. *Daughters of the Fifth Sun* extends to a far-reaching audience, both adults and young adults are meant to benefit from this collection of literatures. *USA Today* critic Steven G. Kellman noted that the collection includes a "distinctive combination of gender and ethnicity" and is a title that readers will treasure. On a similar note, Donna Seaman commented in *Booklist* that *Daughters of the Fifth Sun* is an "all-out celebration" of Latina writers and presents "a vibrant history of Latina literature."

Brigid's Cloak: An Ancient Irish Story focuses on the legendary tale of a much-loved Irish saint and her celebrated generosity. Critics have applauded Milligan for his narrative abilities in *Brigid's Cloak*. A *Publishers Weekly,* critic, for instance, noted that the story is "told with the gripping delivery of a well-seasoned storyteller," adding that Milligan "draws in readers" with his evocative use of words. The story of *Brigid's Cloak* begins when the infant Brigid is presented with a blue cloak by a Druid wizard who also blesses the young girl with magic. The magic bestowed onto Brigid presents itself many years later while she is tending to her flock of sheep. Somehow, Brigid is transported back in time into Jerusalem where she meets Mary and Joseph and witnesses the birth of Jesus. Brigid's renowned act of generosity occurs when she offers Mary her cloak, after which, Brigid returns to the present time and notices that her blue cloak is now adorned with ethereal stars. *Brigid's Cloak* also includes illustrations by Helen Cann, whose watercolor and mixed-media artwork was described by *Booklist* contributor Diane Foote as contributing "both authenticity and wonder to the tale." *Brigid's Cloak* was named a best-of-the-year book by both *Publishers Weekly* and Bank Street College.

Milligan acquaints young readers with an ancient Irish folktale that tells the story of a young prince who is sent on a quest to find three magic stallions owned by a giant in *The Prince of Ireland and the Three Magic Stallions.* A "geis" (curse) is placed on the prince of Ireland by his calculating stepmother who wants to be rid of the prince so that her own sons can rule Ireland. The prince can break the curse only if he succeeds in bringing back the three magic stallions. The story then follows the young prince and his two stepbrothers as they seek out and bargain with a giant named Sean O'Donal for the magical steeds. A critic for *Kirkus Reviewer* cited Milligan's "lilt of the language," while Jeanne Clancy Watkins noted in *School Library Journal* that Milligan's "poetic prose demands to be read aloud with a lilt and a brogue, and comely turns of phrase . . . beg readers to join in."

Milligan once commented: "My daughter is a published translator and scholar of comparative literature, which perhaps reflects my own life-long fascination with etymology, ancient languages and literatures from different times and places. In graduate school, it was my honor to study with Dr. Ruth Lehmann, a world-class interpreter of Old Irish and Anglo-Saxon, and with Dr. Winfred Lehmann, an internationally recognized scholar of Indo-European.

"After finishing my M.A., I settled in San Antonio, Texas, and became the weekly book critic for the *San Antonio Express-News* and the *San Antonio Light.* During this period I found and edited two literary magazines, *Pax: A Journal for Peace through Culture* and *Vortex: A Critical Review. . . .* My interest in contemporary Latina literature led me to edit the first major anthology of all-Latina writing, *Daughters of the Fifth Sun,* which spent three years on the New York Public Library's Best Books for the Teen Age list. I also edited the first Penguin anthology of Latina poetry, *¡Florricanto Sí!*

"In 1995, I purchased Wings Press. The press had published my book of poems, *Working the Stone,* and then went bankrupt. As the owner/publisher/editor/book designer, I enjoy having complete control over what and who I publish, and I very much enjoy the designing. Since 1995, Wings has published over one hundred titles, over half by women, mostly Latina, black, and Native American.

"My wife is a librarian, and we have shared many years reading aloud. "Sharing a life filled with mutual loves—children, books, the change of seasons—is what keeps me grounded and stable. Literature and writing are a great part of my life, but they are not everything. Creativity and craft are crucial, especially as they concern the idea of 'making.' Not much that is good in life just happens by accident. One makes a family, makes a song or poem, makes a book, makes a guitar, makes a garden, one even makes an old house continue to keep out the rain. This is why writers do not retire—to stop making is to stop living."

BIOGRAPHICAL AND CRITICAL SOURCES:

PERIODICALS

Booklist, September 15, 1995, Donna Seaman, review of *Daughters of the Fifth Sun: A Collection of Latina Fiction and Poetry,* p. 129; October 15, 2002, Diane Foote, *Brigid's Cloak: An Ancient Irish Story,* p. 408.

Kirkus Reviews, March 1, 2003, review of *The Prince of Ireland and the Three Magic Stallions,* p. 392.

Publishers Weekly, September 9, 2002, review of *Brigid's Cloak,* pp. 64-65.

School Library Journal, June, 2003, Jeanne Clancy Watkins, review of *The Prince of Ireland and the Three Magic Stallions,* p. 131.

USA Today, May, 1996, Steven G. Kellman, review of *Daughters of the Fifth Sun,* p. 80.

ONLINE

Wings Press Web site, http://www.wingspress.com/ (April 8, 2006), "Bryce Milligan."

*   *   *

MINGAY, G.E. 1923-2006
(Lee Lambert, Gordon Edmund Mingay)

OBITUARY NOTICE— See index for *CA* sketch: Born June 20, 1923, in Long Eaton, Derbyshire, England; died January 3, 2006. Historian, educator, and author. A professor emeritus at the University of Kent, Mingay was best known for his research and publications on agrarian history in the United Kingdom. He served in the Royal Naval Volunteer Reserve during World War II, during which he was commissioned as a cipher officer and was involved in D-Day operations support. Just after the war ended, he also served in Asia, leaving the service as a lieutenant commander in 1947. He then returned to England, paying for his education at Chatham Technical College through employment with the Kent education department. Next, he entered Nottingham University, where Mingay was convinced by one of his professors to focus on agrarian studies. He left the university with a Ph.D. in 1958 and taught at the London School of Economics as a lecturer in economic history until 1965. Mingay moved on to a better paying position at the University of Kent in 1965, where he was a reader in economic history and eventually professor of agrarian history from 1968 until his 1985 retirement. Best known for his writings on agrarian history, such as *English Landed Society in the Eighteenth Century* (1963), *Rural Life in Victorian England* (1976), and *A Social History of the English Countryside* (1990), Mingay also wrote biography and more general histories, such as *Arthur Young and His Times* (1975)

and *Parliamentary Enclosure in England: An Introduction to Its Causes, Incidence, and Impact, 1750-1850* (1997). While not teaching or writing, Mingay was a former editor of the *Agricultural Review* and was active in professional associations, including as a former president of the British Agricultural History Society. Interestingly, he also occasionally indulged in writing escapist thriller novels under the pen name of Lee Lambert. Among these are *The Guaymas Assignment* (1979), *Blonde for Danger* (1980), and *The Balinese Pearls* (1982).

OBITUARIES AND OTHER SOURCES:

PERIODICALS

Times (London, England), April 5, 2006, p. 58.

*   *   *

MINGAY, Gordon Edmund
See MINGAY, G.E.

*   *   *

MITHEN, Steven
See MITHEN, Steven J.

*   *   *

MITHEN, Steven J. 1960-
(Steven Mithen, Steven John Mithen)

PERSONAL: Born October 16, 1960, in Ashford, Kent, England; son of William and Pat Mithen; married; wife's name Susan; children: Hannah, Nicholas, Heather. *Education:* Sheffield University, B.A., 1983; York University, M.S., 1984; Cambridge University, Ph.D., 1988.

ADDRESSES: Office—School of Human and Environmental Sciences, University of Reading, Whiteknights, P.O. Box 227, Reading RG6 6AB, England. *E-mail*—s.j.mithen@reading.ac.uk.

CAREER: Trinity Hall, Cambridge, England, research fellow, 1987-91; McDonald Institute for Archeological Research, Cambridge, research associate, 1990-92; University of Reading, Reading, England, lecturer, 1992-96, reader, 1998-2000, professor of early history, 2000—, head of department.

MEMBER: British Academy (fellow), Society of Antiquaries of Scotland (fellow), Society of Antiquaries of London.

WRITINGS:

Thoughtful Foragers: A Study of Prehistoric Decision Making, Cambridge University Press (New York, NY), 1990.
The Prehistory of the Mind: A Search for the Origins of Art, Religion, and Science, Thames & Hudson (London, England), 1996.
(Editor and contributor) *Creativity in Human Evolution and Prehistory,* Routledge (New York, NY), 1998.
Hunter-Gatherer Landscape Archaeology, 2000.
After the Ice: A Global Human History, 20,000-5,000 B.C., Harvard University Press (Cambridge, MA), 2004.
The Singing Neanderthals: The Origins of Music, Language, Mind and Body, Weidenfeld & Nicolson (London, England), 2005.

Contributor to books, including *Evolutionary Aesthetics,* edited by E. Voland, Springer-Verlag, 2003; *Mesolithic Scotland: The Early Holocene Prehistory of Scotland and Its European Context,* edited by A. Saville, Society of Antiquaries of Scotland, 2004; *Theorizing Religions Past,* edited by H. Whitehouse and L.H. Martin, AltaMira Press, 2004; *Substance, Memory, Display: Archaeology and Art,* edited by C. Renfrew, E. DeMarrais, and C. Gosden, McDonald Institute for Archeological Research, 2004; and *The Seventy Great Inventions of the Ancient World,* Thames & Hudson, 2004. Contributor to professional journals, including the *Journal of the Royal Anthropological Institute, British Academy Review, Times Educational Supplement Teacher Magazine, Documenta Prahistorica, Planet Earth NERC,* and *New Scientist.*

SIDELIGHTS: A professor of early human history in England, Steven J. Mithen has become known for his books about the evolution of the human mind and its

psychology, and what is known as cognitive archeology, or the study of archeological findings and as evidence of how humans evolved intellectually over time. Since the 1990s, he has published a number of books that speculate on how the environment and evolution have molded the brain, affecting such human traits as language, reasoning, and the arts. Book reviewers and colleagues of Mithen's have often found his ideas stimulating.

In his *The Prehistory of the Mind: A Search for the Origins of Art, Religion, and Science,* Mithen further expounds upon the already established theory of modality—the idea that different types of cognition are maintained in separate areas of the brain and do not communicate with one another—and theorizes that the great leap in human evolution at the time of the rise of *Homo sapiens* came when the brain suddenly was able to integrate all these functions. This gave humans the ability to think in creative new ways that helped them to survive, as well as making art, imagination, and even religion possible. "Mithen's tale of separate intelligences evolving for millions of years in parallel, with the barriers between them finally crashing down, makes a fine narrative," reported T. Sambrook in the *Journal of the Royal Anthropological Institute.* "But on the whole natural selection has little regard for narratives and is more of a messy mosaic." Although Sambrook felt Mithen does not support his ideas with enough evidence, he admitted that the author offers "a startlingly new idea in human evolution, intelligently incorporating contemporary psychology." *Antiquity* contributor Jan F. Simek commented, "Overall, Mithen takes an interesting approach to the problem of the evolution of the human mind, but the details of his exposition detract greatly from his argument. He clearly has a standard to bear, that modern humans are a breed apart, and he chooses his data carefully to avoid contradicting this basic premise." Despite such qualms, a number of reviewers concluded that the book has a lot to offer, with Kent Anderson, for one, stating in a *School Arts* review that *The Prehistory of the Mind* "is a significant contribution from the discipline of archaeology and is worth reading."

Mithen wrote about the mysteries of intellectual evolution in his *The Singing Neanderthals: The Origins of Music, Language, Mind and Body.* Here, in contrast to noted psychologist Steven Pinker, Mithen posits that music, and the mind's ability to create songs, was not an accident that offers no evolutionary benefits for human survival. Rather, the author hypothesizes that music first developed out of *Homo sapiens*'s need to convey emotion by altering pitch in the voice, thus making communication more effective. The alteration in pitch eventually evolved into singing and music. While London *Observer* reviewer Peter Forbes pointed out that much of what Mithen relates is "unprovable conjecture," he added that the author provides "some suggestive insights" such as the "connection between music and walking upright," which has to do with the human ability to maintain a regular rhythm, something that chimpanzees cannot do. This ability then led to a discovery of the four-beat measure.

Although some of the scientific hypotheses Mithen has proposed in *The Prehistory of the Mind* and *The Singing Neanderthals* have been questioned, critics have consistently praised his more general discussion of human evolution and archeology in *After the Ice: A Global Human History, 20,000-5,000 B.C.* Here, the author creatively invents a fictional guide, nineteenth-century polymath James Lubbock, to lead readers around the world's many archeological finds that have helped scientists understand thousands of years of human history. Through his narrator, Mithen explains for the general reader how archeologists can examine ancient tools, bits of pottery, and other evidence to figure out how people once lived and how they intellectualized their world. *Booklist* contributor Gilbert Taylor praised *After the Ice* as "a successful marriage of fact and imagination." Anna Belfer-Cohen, writing in the *Journal of the Royal Anthropological Institute*, felt that the author's narrative technique can be "quite demanding, [but] one can enjoy it thoroughly and in the process gain fascinating insights as to how the human mind works."

BIOGRAPHICAL AND CRITICAL SOURCES:

PERIODICALS

American Antiquity, October, 1997, LeRoy McDermott, review of *The Prehistory of the Mind: A Search for the Origins of Art, Religion, and Science,* p. 760; October, 2000, Marcia-Anne Dobres, review of *Creativity in Human Evolution and Prehistory,* p. 768.
Antiquity, June, 1998, Jan F. Simek, review of *The Prehistory of the Mind,* p. 444; December, 1999, N. James, review of *Creativity in Human Evolution and Prehistory,* p. 924.

Booklist, September 1, 2004, Gilbert Taylor, review of *After the Ice: A Global Human History, 20,000-5,000 B.C.,* p. 42..
Current Anthropology, December, 1997, Raymond Corbey and Wil Roebroeks, review of *The Prehistory of the Mind,* p. 917.
Independent (London, England), February 19, 2006, Marek Kohn, review of *The Singing Neanderthals: The Origins of Music, Language, Mind and Body.*
Journal of the Royal Anthropological Institute, March, 1999, T. Sambrook, review of *The Prehistory of the Mind,* p. 107; September, 2004, Anna Belfer-Cohen, review of *After the Ice,* p. 714.
New Statesman, October 18, 1996, Christopher Badcock, review of *The Prehistory of the Mind,* p. 42.
New York Review of Books, May 28, 1998, Merlin Donald, Steven Mithen, and Howard Gardner, "*The Prehistory of the Mind:* An Exchange."
Observer (London, England), July 2, 2005, Peter Forbes, review of *The Singing Neanderthals.*
School Arts, December, 1997, Kent Anderson, review of *The Prehistory of the Mind,* p. 41.
Science News, March 5, 2005, review of *After the Ice,* p. 159.

* * *

MITHEN, Steven John
　See MITHEN, Steven J.

* * *

MONTAGU, Elizabeth 1917-2006

OBITUARY NOTICE— See index for *CA* sketch: Born July 4, 1917; died January 10, 2006. Author. The daughter of the Ninth Earl of Sandwich, Montagu wrote novels and short stories, and was perhaps best known for her 1955 book, *This Side of the Truth.* Trained in nursing, she served in that capacity during World War II at St. Thomas's Hospital in London. Leaving hospital work in 1946, she taught nursing at the Royal College of Nursing until 1950. Afterwards, she focused her attention on writing, producing the novels *Waiting for Camilla* (1953), *The Small Corner* (1955), and *This Side of the Truth.* She later translated the Carl Zuckmayer play *The Cold Light* (1958) and published a short story collection, *Change, and Other*

Stories (1966). Unfortunately, Montagu often suffered from writer's block, which she tried to alleviate by drinking alcohol. This resulted in an addiction that compromised her health and greatly limited her literary output. She completed no more books after her 1966 collection.

OBITUARIES AND OTHER SOURCES:

PERIODICALS

Times (London, England), February 10, 2006, p. 69.

*   *   *

MOREM, Susan

PERSONAL: Female.

ADDRESSES: *Office*—Premier Presentation, Inc., P.O. Box 41115, Minneapolis, MN 55441. *E-mail*—sue@ suemorem.com.

CAREER: Consultant, writer, and motivational speaker. Premier Presentation, Inc., Minneapolis, MN, president. Speaks at corporations and universities across the country.

WRITINGS:

How to Gain the Professional Edge: Achieve the Personal and Professional Image You Want, Better Books (Plymouth, MN), 1997, 2nd edition, 2005.
How to Get a Job and Keep It: Career and Life Skills You Need to Succeed, Ferguson Publishing (Chicago, IL), 2002.
101 Tips for Graduates: A Code of Conduct for Success and Happiness in Your Professional Life, Ferguson Publishing (New York, NY), 2005.

Author of weekly syndicated advice column.

WORK IN PROGRESS: *How to Get a Job and Keep It: Career and Life Skills You Need to Succeed,* 2nd edition, Ferguson Publishing (Chicago, IL), expected 2007.

SIDELIGHTS: Author Susan Morem has developed a successful career speaking and writing about how to succeed in the workplace. She is the president of Premier Presentation, Inc., a national training and consulting firm, and writes a weekly advice column about workplace issues. Morem is also the author of a number of books that give advice on succeeding in one's career, including 1997's *How to Gain the Professional Edge: Achieve the Personal and Professional Image You Want* and 2002's *How to Get a Job and Keep It: Career and Life Skills You Need to Succeed.*

In 2005 Morem published *101 Tips for Graduates: A Code of Conduct for Success and Happiness in Your Professional Life.* The book serves as an outline for recent high school and college graduates who are looking for guidance on how to succeed professionally. Divided into seven sections, the book contains bullet-pointed lists and tips on self-discipline, social skills, leadership, and communication.

Overall, critics responded positively to *101 Tips for Graduates.* Many readers found Morem's book to be a helpful and clearly written tool for people new to their careers. Morem provides readers with a "straightforward guide to help students adjust to the workplace," wrote one *Reference & Research Book News* contributor. Others enjoyed the author's abundance of hints and tips related to all aspects of leading a successful and happy life. Morem dispenses "tips on every subject from proofreading every document to following one's heart," observed Morgan Johnson-Doyle in a review for *School Library Journal.*

BIOGRAPHICAL AND CRITICAL SOURCES:

PERIODICALS

Reference & Research Book News, August, 2005, review of *101 Tips for Graduates: A Code of Conduct for Success and Happiness in Your Professional Life,* p. 118; August, 2005, review of *How to Gain the Professional Edge: Achieve the Personal and Professional Image You Want,* p. 118.
School Library Journal, August, 2005, Morgan Johnson-Doyle, review of *101 Tips for Graduates,* p. 146.

ONLINE

Susan Morem Home Page, http://www.suemorem.com (January 16, 2006).

* * *

MORGAN, Mary 1931-

PERSONAL: Born 1931, in United Kingdom; married; children: three.

ADDRESSES: Home—Seattle, WA. *Agent*—c/o Author Mail, St. Martin's Press, Publicity Dept., 175 5th Ave., New York, NY 10010. *E-mail*—Authormary14@cs.com.

CAREER: Writer and nurse. Served as a journalist, novelist, short story writer and monthly columnist. Also worked as an operating room nurse and midwife.

WRITINGS:

NOVELS

Willful Neglect, St. Martin's Press (New York, NY), 1997.
The House at the Edge of the Jungle, St. Martin's Press (New York, NY), 1999.
Deeper Waters, Thomas Dunne Books (New York, NY), 2002.
The Sound of Her Name, Thomas Dunne Books (New York, NY), 2005.

Author of a number of short stories and articles for a variety of publications, including the *Ladies' Home Journal, Ellery Queen's Mystery Magazine, Alfred Hitchcock's Mystery Magazine* and the *Seattle Post-Intelligencer.*

SIDELIGHTS: British-born author Mary Morgan started her career as a nurse and a midwife; it wasn't until she and her family moved to Seattle, Washington, that she began to pursue writing as a profession. Morgan started out writing professionally by selling short stories to general-interest publications

including the *Ladies' Home Journal* and the *Seattle Post Intelligencer* as well as to mystery journals like *Ellery Queen's Mystery Magazine.* It was this interest in writing mystery fiction that eventually led to Morgan's success as a novelist of mysteries.

In 1997, Morgan published her first novel, *Willful Neglect.* The story's main character is Noah Richards, a small-town lawyer who finds himself involved with a possible case of neglect when a young African-American boy mysteriously dies at the community hospital. The boy's family suspects that it was a matter of racism by the hospital's staff. Critics found *Willful Neglect* to be a strong and well-written novel overall. Many enjoyed the author's exploration of the psyches of her characters, and admired the intelligent and riveting development of the story line. Morgan's novel contains "sturdy prose," wrote Rex E. Klett in a review for the *Library Journal.* Other reviewers thought Morgan's novel would be an appealing addition to other literature of this genre. *Willful Neglect* is a "riveting read for fans of medical/legal mysteries," observed *Booklist* contributor William Beatty.

Morgan's second novel, 1999's *The House at the Edge of the Jungle,* focuses on brother and sister Isabel and Victor, who were evacuated from Malaya as young children before the Japanese invaded the country. In the process, the two were separated from their father and stepmother and grew up without knowing what happened to them. As an adult, Isabel convinces Victor to go back to Kuala Lumpur with her, where she hopes to uncover the mysterious disappearance of their family members.

Like Morgan's first novel, *The House at the Edge of the Jungle* was also met with positive reviews upon its release. For many critics, this was again a successful demonstration of the author's talents at developing a suspenseful and interesting story. The novel contains a "well-written, deftly structured story of cryptic family ties," wrote a *Publishers Weekly* contributor. For others, the novel's exotic setting and detailed descriptions of a different culture contributed to the book's appeal. *The House at the Edge of the Jungle* "will appeal to readers who enjoy foreign travel," noted Toni Hyde in a review for *Booklist.*

In 2002, Morgan published her third novel, *Deeper Waters.* This book returns to the story of Noah Richards, the main character of the author's first novel.

Here Noah has moved to a rental house on the ocean outside of Seattle, in an area Noah discovers is embroiled in a land-rights battle between developers and a local Indian tribe. Soon the murder of Quanda law student Jay Bishop near Noah's house cements Noah's involvement in solving the mystery of Jay's death and discovering the real story behind the land battle. Readers enjoyed Morgan's return to the character of Noah Richards, finding him to be an interesting and deeply developed protagonist. *Deeper Waters* continues the story of a "likable and believable hero," observed a *Kirkus Reviews* contributor. Critics also admired the book overall, finding the story line intriguing and complex, and clever in its use of the remote and alluring backdrop of Edward's Bay. Morgan's novel "deals with important themes in a beautiful setting," wrote Barbara Bibel in a review for *Booklist*.

BIOGRAPHICAL AND CRITICAL SOURCES:

PERIODICALS

Booklist, June 1, 1997, William Beatty, review of *Willful Neglect*, p. 1667; January 1, 1999, Toni Hyde, review of *The House at the Edge of the Jungle*, p. 833; May 15, 2002, Barbara Bibel, review of *Deeper Waters*, p. 1579.

Kirkus Reviews, April 15, 2002, review of *Deeper Waters*, p. 530; April 1, 2005, review of *The Sound of Her Name*, p. 379.

Library Journal, July 1997, Rex E. Klett, review of *Willful Neglect*, p. 131.

Publishers Weekly, August 11, 1997, review of *Willful Neglect*, p. 389; January 11, 1999, review of *The House at the Edge of the Jungle*, p. 58.

ONLINE

Mary Morgan Home Page, http://www.marymorgan.net (January 19, 2006).*

*   *   *

MORGAN, M. Gwyn 1937-

PERSONAL: Born 1937. *Education:* University of Exeter, B.A., 1959, Ph.D., 1962.

ADDRESSES: Office—History Department, University of Texas at Austin, 1 University Station B7000, Austin, TX 78712. *E-mail*—mgm@mail.utexas.edu.

CAREER: Educator and writer. University of Texas at Austin, professor of classics and history.

WRITINGS:

69 A.D.: The Year of Four Emperors, Oxford University Press (New York, NY), 2005.

SIDELIGHTS: Author M. Gwyn Morgan is a professor of classics and history. It is through this continued scholarship and study of ancient civilizations that Morgan wrote his first book, *69 A.D.: The Year of Four Emperors*. The book recounts one of the most politically chaotic years within the Roman Empire. During that timeframe four different men served as emperor—Galba, Otho, Vitellius, and Vespasian. Morgan takes the accounts of five ancient historians, including Tacitus, Suetonius, and Plutarch, and creates a cohesive story that strips away literary embellishments. The author's account is full of details about the events of that year, including Galba's march to Rome, Otho's suicide, Vitellius's extravagance, and the civil war between supporters of Otho and Vitellius.

Overall, *69 A.D.* was met with praise from critics and readers alike. For some reviewers, Morgan's ability to weave together the inconsistent and embellished stories of previous historians to create a more historically accurate account made the book an important addition to literature on the subject. Morgan's book "fills in the gaps left by previous accounts," wrote a *Kirkus Reviews* contributor. Others found the author's work to be a detailed and informative study of an important year in the history of the Roman Empire. Morgan creates a "superb portrait of this enigmatic and intriguing year," observed a reviewer for *Publishers Weekly*.

BIOGRAPHICAL AND CRITICAL SOURCES:

PERIODICALS

Kirkus Reviews, October 15, 2005, review of *69 A.D.: The Year of Four Emperors*, p. 1126.

Publishers Weekly, September 19, 2005, review of *69 A.D.,* p. 51.

ONLINE

University of Texas at Austin Web site, http://www. utexas.edu/ (January 16, 2006), biographical information about M. Gwyn Morgan.*

*   *   *

MORRISSEY, Robert 1947-
(Robert John Morrissey)

PERSONAL: Born September 7, 1947, in Boston, MA; son of Robert John (a university administrator) and Jane Mary (Gordon) Morrissey; married Helen Kenrich (marriage ended); married Marie-Claire Caravah; children: Julian, Laura, Paul, Daniele. *Ethnicity:* "Irish." *Education:* University of Massachusetts at Amherst, B.A., 1970; Sorbonne, University of Paris, M.A., 1971; attended Università per Stranieri, 1974, 1975; University of Chicago, Ph.D. (with honors), 1982.

ADDRESSES: Home—6116 S. Greenwood Ave., Chicago, IL 60637. *Office*—Department of Romance Languages and Literatures, University of Chicago, 1050 E. 59th St., Chicago, IL 60637.

CAREER: University of Chicago, Chicago, IL, instructor, 1978-81, assistant professor 1982-87, associate professor, 1987-97, professor of Romance languages and literatures, 1998—. Princeton University, visiting associate professor, 1988; École des Hautes Études en Sciences Sociales, guest research director, 1998; New York University, Andrew Delau Annual Lecturer, 1997; guest lecturer at other institutions, including University of Grenoble, University of Turin, Tulane University, University of Dallas, Stanford University, University of Montreal, and Duke University. Project for American and French Research on the Treasury of the French Language, director, 1978—; Chicago Group on Modern France, codirector, 1992—; conference organizer.

AWARDS, HONORS: Weinberg Fund fellow in Italy, 1973, and France, 1973-74; Lurcy Foundation, fellow in France, 1975-76, grant, 1982-83; National Endow-ment for the Humanities grants, 1978-79, 1990-93, 1997; Government of France, grant, 1983, *Centres d'excellence* award, 1993-97; Scaler Foundation grants, 1984-85, 1989-90, 1991-94; grant for Switzerland, American Council of Learned Societies, 1985; Packard Foundation grant, 1986-87; Mellon grant for Berlin and Paris, 1988; decorated chevalier, L'Ordre des Palmes Académiques, 1990; Florence Gould Foundation grants, 1994-96, 1996-2000; decorated chevalier, L'Ordre National du Mérite, 1997; Grand Prix d'Histoire Chateaubriand, 1997, for *L'Empereur à la barbe fleurie: Charlemagne dans la mythologie et l'histoire de France,*

WRITINGS:

La Rêverie jusqu'à Rousseau: Recherches sur un topos littéraire, French Forum (Lexington, KY), 1984.

L'Empereur à la barbe fleurie: Charlemagne dans la mythologie et l'histoire de France, Gallimard (Paris, France), 1997, translation by Catherine Tihanyi published as *Charlemagne and France: A Thousand Years of Mythology,* University of Notre Dame Press (Notre Dame, IN), 2003.

(Editor, with Denis Diderot and Jean d'Alembert) *L'Encyclopédie ou Dictionnaire raisonné des arts, des sciences et des métiers* (e-book), American and French Research on the Treasury of the French Language (Chicago, IL), 1998.

Contributor to books, including *La politique du texte,* Presses Universitaire de Lille (Paris, France), 1992; *Les Lieux de Mémoire: Les France; De l'archive à l'emblème,* edited by Pierre Nora, Gallimard (Paris, France), 1992; and *Home and Its Dislocations in Nineteeneth-Century France,* edited by Suzanne Nash, State University of New York Press (Albany, NY), 1993. Contributor of articles and reviews to French and American periodicals, including *French Forum, Scholarly Communication, Sociocriticism, Stanford French Review, French Review, Journal of Modern History,* and *Modern Philology.* Editor of special issue, *Substance,* 1988.

BIOGRAPHICAL AND CRITICAL SOURCES:

PERIODICALS

History: Review of New Books, fall, 2003, Felice Lifshitz, review of *L'Empereur à la barbe fleurie: Charlemagne dans la mythologie et l'histoire de France,* p. 23.

Journal of Modern History, December, 1999, David Ganz, review of *L'Empereur à la barbe fleurie,* p. 949.

Publishers Weekly, January 20, 2003, review of *L'Empereur à la barbe fleurie,* p. 66.

*   *   *

MORRISSEY, Robert John
     See MORRISSEY, Robert

*   *   *

MORRISSEY, Will 1951-

PERSONAL: Born July 1, 1951, in Long Branch, NJ. *Education:* Kenyon College, A.B. (summa cum laude), 1973; New School University, M.A., 1998, Ph.D., 2002.

ADDRESSES: Home—1 Cedar Ct., Hillsdale, MI 49242. *Office*—405 Delp Hall, Box 9, Hillsdale College, Hillsdale, MI 49242. *E-mail*—will.morrissey@ hillsdale.edu.

CAREER: Office of New Jersey State Senator S. Thomas Gagliano, legislative aide, 1981-89; New Jersey Transit Corp., assistant for communications in office of the executive director, 1989-90; Monmouth County Historical Commission, Freehold, NJ, executive director, 1996-2000; Hillsdale College, Hillsdale, MI, assistant professor of political science, 2000—. Guest speaker at George Mason University, University of Dallas, and Rutgers University. Rumson Planning Board, Rumson, NJ, secretary; consultant to Jersey Shore Partnership.

AWARDS, HONORS: Grant from U.S. Institute of Peace, 1990-93; citation for outstanding academic book, *Choice,* 1996, for *A Political Approach to Pacifism;* grant from Robert H. Horwitz Foundation.

WRITINGS:

Reflections on De Gaulle: Political Founding in Modernity, University Press of America (Lanham, MD), 1983, corrected edition, 2002.

Reflections on Malraux: Cultural Founding in Modernity, University Press of America (Lanham, MD), 1984.

(With Paul Eidelberg) *Our Culture "Left" or "Right,"* Edwin Mellen Press (Lewiston, NY), 1992.

A Political Approach to Pacifism, two volumes, Edwin Mellen Press (Lewiston, NY), 1996.

Culture in the Commercial Republic, University Press of America (Lanham, MD), 1996.

Contributor to books, including *The Moral Foundations of the American Republic,* edited by Robert H. Horwitz, University Press of Virginia (Charlottesville, VA), 1986; *Essays on the Closing of the American Mind,* edited by Robert L. Stone, Chicago Review Press (Chicago, IL), 1989; *Leo Strauss, the Straussians, and the American Republic,* edited by Kenneth L. Deutsch and John A. Murley, Rowman & Littlefield (Lanham, MD), 1999; and *The Moral of the Story: Literature and Public Ethics,* edited by Henry T. Edmondson III, Lexington Books (Lanham, MD), 2000. Contributor of articles and reviews to periodicals, including *Political Science Reviewer, St. John's Review, This World, Imprimis,* and *Social Science and Modern Society.* Assistant editor, *Interpretation: Journal of Political Philosophy.*

WORK IN PROGRESS: Self-Government and the American Founding: Presidents of Founding and Civil War.

*   *   *

MURKOFF, Heidi Eisenberg

PERSONAL: Married; children: two.

ADDRESSES: Office—The What to Expect Foundation, 144 W. 80th St., Ste. 5, New York, NY 10024.

CAREER: Cofounder of The What to Expect Foundation, New York, NY.

WRITINGS:

WITH MOTHER, ARLENE EISENBERG, AND SISTER, SANDEE EISENBERG HATHAWAY

The Special Guest Cookbook: Elegant Menus and Recipes for Those Who Are Allergic to Certain Foods, Bland Dieters/Calorie Counters,

Cholesterol Conscious, Diabetic/Hypoglycemic, Kosher/Milk Sensitive, Ovolacto Vegetarian, Pritikin Proselytes, Salt-Avoiding, Strictly Vegetarian, Beaufort Books (New York, NY), 1982.

What to Expect when You're Expecting, Workman Publishing (New York, NY), 1984, 3rd edition, 2002.

What to Eat when You're Expecting, Workman Publishing (New York, NY), 1986.

What to Expect the First Year, Workman Publishing (New York, NY), 1989, revised edition, 2003.

What to Expect the Toddler Years, Workman Publishing (New York, NY), 1994.

FOR CHILDREN; "WHAT TO EXPECT KIDS" SERIES

What to Expect at Bedtime, illustrated by Laura Rader, HarperFestival (New York, NY), 2000.

What to Expect when the Babysitter Comes, illustrated by Laura Rader, HarperFestival (New York, NY), 2000.

What to Expect when Mommy's Having a Baby, illustrated by Laura Rader, HarperFestival (New York, NY), 2000.

What to Expect when You Go to the Doctor, illustrated by Laura Rader, HarperFestival (New York, NY), 2000.

What to Expect when You Use the Potty, illustrated by Laura Rader, HarperFestival (New York, NY), 2000.

What to Expect when the New Baby Comes Home, illustrated by Laura Rader, HarperFestival (New York, NY), 2001.

What to Expect at Preschool, illustrated by Laura Rader, HarperFestival (New York, NY), 2001.

What to Expect at a Play Date, illustrated by Laura Rader, HarperFestival (New York, NY), 2001.

What to Expect when You Go to Kindergarten, illustrated by Laura Rader, HarperFestival (New York, NY), 2002.

What to Expect when You Go to the Dentist, illustrated by Laura Rader, HarperFestival (New York, NY), 2002.

OTHER

(With Sharon Mazel) *The What to Expect Baby-Sitter's Handbook,* Workman Publishing (New York, NY), 2003.

(With Sharon Mazel) *Eating Well when You're Expecting,* Workman Publishing, 2005.

Also author of *What to Expect Pregnancy Organizer,* Workman Publishing (New York, NY), and *Baby Basics: Your Month-by-Month Guide to a Healthy Pregnancy.* Contributing editor for *Baby Talk* and *Parenting.*

SIDELIGHTS: Heidi Eisenberg Murkoff developed a series of books for parents because when she was expecting her own first child, she was unable to find a positive book on pregnancy and birth. She collaborated with her writer-mother, Arlene Eisenberg, and her sister, nurse Sandee Eisenberg Hathaway, for the series that began with *What to Expect when You're Expecting.* The book informs new mothers on the physical, emotional, and psychological changes they can expect during pregnancy, as well as information about the development of the fetus. Furthermore, they advise readers on proper diet and exercise and choosing a doctor and describe labor and delivery. They also address the use of tobacco, alcohol, and drugs during pregnancy. Elise Goodman wrote in *Publishers Weekly* that the authors "seem to take a personal interest in the reader as they discuss early signs of pregnancy."

The writers supplement their first book by concentrating on the importance of diet in *What to Eat when You're Expecting.* Here they advise readers about proper nutrition postpartum and while breastfeeding, and they include information for women who are vegetarians or lactose intolerant. The authors followed this up with *What to Expect the First Year* and *What to Expect the Toddler Years. Newsweek* contributor Weston Kosova wrote that "what makes these books stand out are the long question-and-answer sections."

Following the success of her books for parents, Murkoff began an illustrated series for children in which Angus the Answer Dog answers the kinds of questions children ask when faced with new situations. Some of the topics include going to the doctor or dentist and starting preschool and kindergarten, as well as knowing *What to Expect when the New Baby Comes Home.* Kathy Broderick reviewed this title in *Booklist,* saying that it "succeeds on many levels, but most importantly, it allows a parent and child to have a reassuring conversation during a time of great change."

What to Expect when You're Expecting has been revised and reprinted several times. The third edition was published in 2002, the year following Arlene

Eisenberg's death. The clothes of the pregnant woman sitting in the rocking chair on the cover have changed and the newest information includes hints on working during pregnancy and alternative medicine. In an interview with Amy Dusek, published at *Atlanta Parent Online*, Murkoff noted that 150 pages have been added and said that "there's more information than ever. We've included dozens of new questions about cell phones, sushi, low-carb diets, spa treatments, sunless tanners, nursing after breast surgery, and much more, symptoms that we'd left out last time—such as clogged milk ducts and snoring—much more on second pregnancies and deliveries." The section about the father's role has been expanded, and Murkoff said that this edition includes "a kinder, gentler pregnancy diet." *Library Journal* contributor Barbara M. Bibel called the expanded edition "better than ever, still a classic, and a fitting memorial to Eisenberg."

Murkoff and Eisenberg founded The What to Expect Foundation, which promotes prenatal health for low-income women and which distributes *Baby Basics: Your Month-by-Month Guide to a Healthy Pregnancy*, a low-literacy pregnancy guide published in both English and Spanish for the clinics and organizations that serve them. Murkoff continues to manage the foundation, working with individuals, corporations, and other organizations who assist low-income families. She speaks to their needs through media appearances, and her promotional fees are used to fund the work of her foundation.

The What to Expect Foundation has partnered with other groups to create a Baby Basics program in Houston, Texas. Murkoff appeared in Houston with U.S. Surgeon General Richard H. Carmona, who praised the program and commented on the fact that a study has shown that one-third of English-speaking patients using public hospitals are unable to read and understand basic health materials. He emphasized that health literacy for expectant mothers is crucial to preventing birth defects and premature births. In his prepared remarks, published on Murkoff's Web site, Carmona said that "the health literacy activities that we're launching today reflect the strong commitment of The What to Expect Foundation to serving all families. With outstanding local partnerships, Baby Basics Houston will increase access to health information and improve Houstonians' health literacy. I am particularly impressed with the fact that Baby Basics focuses on minority and underserved communities. In 2005, it will touch the lives of every low-income expecting mother and baby in Houston and Harris County. You are all to be congratulated on these innovative efforts. Your work in the area of health literacy will resonate across Houston and beyond."

BIOGRAPHICAL AND CRITICAL SOURCES:

PERIODICALS

American Journal of Nursing, February, 1990, Charlene L. Stokamer, review of *What to Expect the First Year*, p. 104.

Booklist, July, 2001, Kathy Broderick, review of *What to Expect when the New Baby Comes Home*, p. 2020; November 15, 2001, Helen Rosenberg, review of *What to Expect when You Go to Preschool*, p. 578; June 1, 2002, Kathy Broderick, review of *What to Expect when You Go to the Dentist*, p. 1727.

Library Journal, April 1, 2002, Barbara M. Bibel, review of *What to Expect when You're Expecting*, p. 131.

Los Angeles Times, March 5, 1995, Elizabeth Mehren, "They're Experts on 'What to Expect,'" pp. E1-E4.

Newsweek, spring-summer, 1997, Weston Kosova, reviews of *What to Expect the First Year* and *What to Expect the Toddler Years*, p. 22.

New York Times, January 5, 1995, Janny Scott, "The Baby Makers."

Publishers Weekly, November 2, 1984, Elise Goodman, review of *What to Expect when You're Expecting*, p. 75; August 15, 1986, review of *What to Eat when You're Expecting*, pp. 73-74; April 28, 1989, review of *What to Expect the First Year*, p. 71; May 9, 2005, review of *Eating Well when You're Expecting*, p. 66.

School Library Journal, June, 2001, Martha Topol, review of *What to Expect when the New Baby Comes Home*, p. 140.

Whole Earth Review, spring, 1988, Cindy Fugett, review of *What to Expect when You're Expecting*, p. 91.

ONLINE

Atlanta Parent Online, http://www.atlantaparent.com/ (May, 2002), Amy Dusek, interview with Murkoff.

Heidi Eisenberg Murkoff Home Page, http://www.whattoexpect.org (July 9, 2005).*

MYCIO, Mary

PERSONAL: Female. *Education:* Hunter College, B.A.; New York University, J.D.

ADDRESSES: Home—Kiev, Ukraine. *Office*—IREX U-Media Legal Defense and Education Program, vul. Khreshchatyk 27A, Ste. 28, Kyiv 01001, Ukraine. *E-mail*—myciomary@yahoo.com.

CAREER: During early career, worked as a lawyer in Los Angeles, CA, and New York, NY; IREX U-Media Legal Defense and Education Program, Kyiv, Ukraine, director, 1998—; International Research and Exchanges Board, Washington, DC, head of Legal Defense and Education Project, 1999—; freelance journalist.

WRITINGS:

Wormwood Forest: A Natural History of Chernobyl, Joseph Henry Press (Washington, DC), 2005.

Contributor to periodicals, including *Newsday, Los Angeles Times, Omni, Jewish Monthly, European, Natural History, BBC Focus, Ukrainian Weekly,* and the *Kiev Post.*

SIDELIGHTS: When a nuclear power plant accident occurred in the former Soviet Union city of Chernobyl in 1986, millions of area residents were forced to evacuate for miles around. Twenty years later, the area is still largely abandoned by people, with the exception of a few government officials and squatters. Mary Mycio, an attorney and journalist, decided to investigate the area, planning to write an indictment of governmental bureaucracy that led to the disaster. Instead, as she relates in her first book, *Wormwood Forest: A Natural History of Chernobyl,* Mycio discovered that the area in and around Chernobyl was not at all what she had expected. Wild Przewalski's horses, elk, moose, wolves, and hundreds of species of birds were thriving there, apparently without mutations or other ill effects from the soil, plants, and water that were still irradiated with cesium and strontium isotopes. She also found the plant life to be doing well, and the few people who were living there also seemed to be surviving just fine. "In an objective and balanced assessment of the evacuation," remarked David R. Marples in the *St. Petersburg Times Online,* "she concludes that although the initial exodus was necessary and had an important impact on reducing radiation doses, the ones that took place more than a decade after the disaster did more harm than good because of the social and economic stresses involved."

Although Mycio does betray a concern for the high levels of radioactive strontium and cesium in the water, which are even more worrisome downstream from the disaster in supposedly safe areas, she is convinced that Chernobyl is making an amazing recovery, noting that the region has now become Europe's largest wildlife habitat. In addition, stated Marples, "Mycio is at her best when she focuses on the human element, providing poignant descriptions of the samosely, or voluntary settlers, who wandered back to their homes in the wake of the accident." A *Publishers Weekly* contributor concluded that "not all readers will share her cautious optimism, yet her verdict . . . is convincing."

BIOGRAPHICAL AND CRITICAL SOURCES:

PERIODICALS

Bulletin of the Atomic Scientists, January-February, 2006, Robert J. Baker, review of *Wormwood Forest: A Natural History of Chernobyl,* p. 59.
Library Journal, September 15, 2005, Eva Lautemann, review of *Wormwood Forest,* p. 87.
Nature, October 13, 2005, Brenda Howard, review of *Wormwood Forest,* p. 955.
Publishers Weekly, July 11, 2005, review of *Wormwood Forest,* p. 78.
Science News, October 15, 2005, review of *Wormwood Forest,* p. 255.

ONLINE

MosNews.com, http://www.mosnews.com/ (September 16, 2005), "U.S. Journalist in Hospital after Attack in Ukraine."
St. Petersburg Times Online, http://www.sptimes.ru/ (February 3, 2006), David R. Marples, "Man-made Eden," review of *Wormwood Forest.*
Wormwood Forest Web site, http://www.chernobyl.in.ua (April 18, 2006).

N

NÄASLUND, Göorel Kristina 1940-
(Göorel Kristina Carheden)

PERSONAL: Born 1940, in Röbäck, Sweden; married (divorced, c. 1970); partner's name Gullmar. *Education:* Degree in home economics; University of Minnesota, studied journalism; Karolinska Institutet, Ph.D. *Hobbies and other interests:* Skiing, cooking.

ADDRESSES: Home—Near Stockholm, Sweden. *Agent*—c/o Author Mail, Kärnhuset, Drottning Kristinas väg 19, 193 35 Sigtuna, Sweden. *E-mail*—gorel. kristina.naslund@psyk.ks.s.

CAREER: Psychologist, educator, pomologist, and writer. Established French cooking school and teacher of Swedish in Denver, CO, c. 1960s; *Expressen* (daily newspaper), Stockholm, Sweden, journalist beginning 1970; freelance writer; apple expert; currently psychologist in private practice.

WRITINGS:

(As Göorel Kristina Carheden) *Foods and Festivals, Swedish Style,* illustrated by Dick Sutphen, Dillon Press (Minneapolis, MN), 1968.
(Translator, as Göorel Kristina Carheden) *Swedish Cooking,* Inca Forlaget, 1971.
Vår Skona Grona Mat (for children), illustrated by Kristina Digman, Raben & Sjogren (Stockholm, Sweden), 1977, translated by Lauren Brown as *Our Apple Tree,* Roaring Brook Press (New Milford, CT), 2005.

Vår första svampbok, Raben & Sjogren (Stockholm, Sweden), 1998.
100 älskade äpplen, illustrated by Ingrid af Sandeberg, Kärnhuset (Sigtuna, Sweden), 2002.
Lilla äppelboken (for children), illustrated by Kristina Digman, Raben & Sjogren (Stockholm, Sweden), 2002.
Lilla vinterboken (for children), illustrated by Kristina Digman, Raben & Sjogren (Stockholm, Sweden), 2005.
Vem var det där?: en bok om ansiktsblindhet, Kärnhuset (Sigtuna, Sweden), 2006.

Author of numerous other books published in Swedish, including stories for children and books on cooking, psychology, and apples.

BIOGRAPHICAL AND CRITICAL SOURCES:

PERIODICALS

Booklist, August, 2005, Gillian Engberg, review of *Our Apple Tree,* p. 2035.
Children's Bookwatch, February, 2006, review of *Our Apple Tree.*
Kirkus Reviews, July 15, 2005, review of *Our Apple Tree,* p. 794.
School Library Journal, November, 2005, Genevieve Gallagher, review of *Our Apple Tree,* p. 118.

ONLINE

Kärnhuset Web site, http://www.karnhuset.com/ (May 29, 2006), "Göorel Kristina Näaslund."*

NEILLANDS, Robin 1935-2006
(Robin Hunter, Robin Hunter Neillands)

OBITUARY NOTICE— See index for *CA* sketch: Born December 3, 1935, in Glasgow, Scotland; died of prostate cancer, January 3, 2006. Publisher and author. Neillands was best known as a travel and military history writer. After his father was killed during World War II, he was raised by his grandmother. When he was older, he joined the 45 Commando Royal Marines in 1953, serving in the Middle East and in Cyprus; he then joined the Royal Marine Volunteer Reserve, where he served for twelve years. Afterwards, Neillands became a salesman, working for a biscuit maker, Huntley & Palmers, for a stationery supplier, and as an export manager for Pan Books. He then founded his own publishing company, Spur Books, which released travel guides. Neillands himself, who had traveled extensively with the military and while working for Pan Books, started producing travel guides and books about his own excursions. Among these are *Walking through Spain: From the Channel to Gibraltar* (1991), *Walking through Ireland: From Antrim to Kerry* (1993), and *Walking through Scotland: From the Borders to Cape Wrath* (1995). His love of travel also led him to found the Outdoor Travel Writers Guild and to serve as chair of the British Guild of Travel Writers from 1991 to 1993. Neillands, however, was also very interested in history, especially military history. Over the years, he produced such titles as *The Hundred Years War* (1990), *The Great Generals on the Western Front, 1914-1918* (1998), *Attrition: The War on the Western Front 1916* (2001) and *The Battle of Normandy* (2002). In addition to these titles, he occasionally wrote thrillers under the pseudonym Robin Hunter, including *The Fourth Angel* (1985), *Quarry's Contract* (1987), and *The London Connection* (1990); the first of these was adapted as a film starring Jeremy Irons. In later life, Neillands, who had never earned a college degree, went back to school. He finished a B.A. in history at the University of Reading in 2002, followed by a master's degree the next year. By this time, he was aware that he had prostate cancer, but he continued a grueling schedule of studies and writing until the end. In 2004, he released three more titles: *Eighth Army: From the Western Desert to the Alps, 1939-1945, The Old Contemptibles: The British Expeditionary Force, 1914,* and *Ulysses Grant.* His *The Death of Glory: The Western Front, 1915* was scheduled to be published in the spring of 2006.

OBITUARIES AND OTHER SOURCES:

PERIODICALS

Times (London, England), April 4, 2006, p. 55.

* * *

NEILLANDS, Robin Hunter
See NEILLANDS, Robin

* * *

NESSI, Pío Baroja y
See BAROJA, Pío

* * *

NEWCOMB, Robert 1951-

PERSONAL: Born 1951; married. *Education:* Earned a bachelor's degree from Colgate University. Also studied at the University of Southampton, England, through the American Institute for Foreign Study.

ADDRESSES: Agent—c/o Author Mail, Del Rey Publicity, Random House Publishing Group, 1745 Broadway, 18th Fl., New York, NY 10019.

CAREER: Novelist and business consultant. Served as chairman of an industry-related consulting firm before becoming a full-time writer.

WRITINGS:

"THE CHRONICLES OF BLOOD AND STONE" SERIES

The Fifth Sorceress, Del Rey/Ballantine Books (New York, NY), 2002.
The Gates of Dawn, Del Rey/Ballantine Books (New York, NY), 2003.
The Scrolls of the Ancients, Del Rey/Ballantine Books (New York, NY), 2004.

OTHER NOVELS

Savage Messiah (first novel in *"The Destinies of Blood and Stone"* series), Del Rey/Ballantine Books (New York, NY), 2006.

SIDELIGHTS: Author Robert Newcomb began his career in business, serving as the chairman of his own industry-related consulting group in New York. After he and his wife moved to Florida, Newcomb left consulting behind and began writing full time, specializing in fantasy novels.

In 2002, Newcomb published his first novel, *The Fifth Sorceress.* The book was the first in the author's "The Chronicles of Blood and Stone" series. The novel begins in the kingdom of Eutracia, where four sorceresses were convicted and exiled for their destructive quest for endowed blood. Endowed blood is the concept that individuals from a certain bloodline possess the ability to perform magic. Centuries later, the exiled sorceresses are plotting to kidnap Princess Shailiha. Shailiha's brother Tristan becomes the novel's protagonist as he struggles with his desire for adventure and his duties as prince and heir to the Eutracian throne.

Critics responded positively to *The Fifth Sorceress* overall. Many found Newcomb's prose to be strong and developed, with a story line that takes the reader on a well-crafted journey. Newcomb's first novel is a "well-written and compelling epic fantasy," wrote Jackie Cassada in a review for the *Library Journal.* Other readers liked the book's clean ending, and looked forward to reading more of Newcomb's novels. In *The Fifth Sorceress,* "the finish is neat, but it leaves you wanting more," observed a *Publishers Weekly* contributor.

Newcomb's next novel was 2003's *The Gates of Dawn.* This book finds the prince Tristan a fugitive, blamed for the death of his father. Tristan fights to show his countrymen that he was not responsible for the death and, at the same time, works to strengthen the country that has fallen apart around him. These misfortunes are heightened as the Paragon, the crystal harnessing the power of endowed blood, begins to lose its power. Tristan and others begin a quest to find out who is draining the stone and how to stop it.

Like its predecessor, *The Gates of Dawn* was also met with generally positive reviews. The book's unique story and refreshing approach to the fantasy genre were qualities that appealed to some readers. Newcomb's novel brings a "certain originality to this epic struggle between wizards and sorceresses," wrote a *Kirkus Reviews* contributor. Others thought the novel's plot and characters were rich with vivid detail. *The Gates of Dawn* is full of "lavish descriptions," commented Cassada in another *Library Journal* review.

In 2006, Newcomb published *Savage Messiah,* the first novel in his "The Destinies of Blood and Stone" series. This novel and series is set in the same world as Newcomb's previous series, and continues with many of the same characters as well. In this story The Orb of Vigors is causing destruction across the country, and Tristan is thought to be the one man who can repair the damage. Like Newcomb's other novels, this work is filled with wizards, puzzles, assassins, and mystery.

After its release, *Savage Messiah* garnered praise by critics and readers alike. For some readers, the book moved at a satisfyingly rapid pace and contained enough fantasy novel devices to keep the plot interesting. The book has "magic, intrigue, and plenty of action," wrote Cassada in a *Library Journal* review. For others, *Savage Messiah* was simply another welcome addition to the fantasy genre. Newcomb's book has a "breathless quality that makes for a fast and entertaining read," observed a *Kirkus Reviews* contributor.

BIOGRAPHICAL AND CRITICAL SOURCES:

PERIODICALS

Kirkus Reviews, May 1, 2002, review of *The Fifth Sorceress,* p. 626; June 15, 2003, review of *The Gates of Dawn,* p. 839; April 15, 2004, review of *The Scrolls of the Ancients,* p. 367; October 15, 2005, review of *Savage Messiah,* p. 1114.

Kliatt, November, 2002, Miles Klein, review of *The Fifth Sorceress,* p. 45.

Library Journal, August, 2002, Jackie Cassada, review of *The Fifth Sorceress,* p. 151; June 15, 2003, Jackie Cassada, review of *The Gates of Dawn,* p. 104; November 15, 2005, Jackie Cassada, review of *Savage Messiah,* p. 65.

Publishers Weekly, June 17, 2002, review of *The Fifth Sorceress,* p. 47; June 2, 2003, review of *The Gates of Dawn,* p. 39; October 31, 2005, review of *Savage Messiah,* p. 36.

ONLINE

Robert Newcomb Home Page, http://www.chroniclesof bloodandstone.com (January 23, 2006).

*   *   *

NICHOLSON, Deborah
See NICHOLSON, Deborah L.

*   *   *

NICHOLSON, Deborah L. 1961-
  (Deborah Nicholson)

PERSONAL: Born 1961, in Canada. *Education:* Attended college in Alberta, Canada. *Hobbies and other interests:* Volunteer work for local charities.

ADDRESSES: Home—Calgary, Alberta, Canada. *Agent*—Anne Dewe, Andrew Mann Ltd., 1 Old Compton St., London W1D 5JA, England. *E-mail*—debln@ shaw.ca.

CAREER: Centre for the Performing Arts, Calgary, Alberta, Canada, staff member for five years, became house manager for Theatre Calgary.

MEMBER: Writers' Union of Canada, Crime Writers of Canada, Mystery Writers Ink, British Crime Writers Association, Writers' Guild of Alberta.

WRITINGS:

"KATE CARPENTER" SERIES; MYSTERY NOVELS

House Report, Severn House (Sutton, England), 2004.
Evening the Score, Severn House (Sutton, England), 2004.

Sins of the Mother, Severn House (Sutton, England), 2005.
Flirting with Disaster, Severn House (Sutton, England), 2005.
Liar, Liar, Severn House (Sutton, England), 2006.

SIDELIGHTS: Having herself worked as a theater house manager in Calgary, Canada, mystery novelist Deborah L. Nicholson drew on this experience to create her series character, Kate Carpenter. The manager of the fictional Centenary Theatre in Calgary, Kate makes her debut in *House Report.* Although completely inexperienced with police procedures and detective work, Kate has read a lot of mystery novels, and so when a dead body turns up in her theater she takes it upon herself to start her own investigation. The victim has been bludgeoned with a hammer that has her boyfriend Norman "Cam" Caminsky's fingerprints on it, and when Kate learns that Cam's ex-wife has put out a restraining order against him, the evidence seems weighted against him. Of course, Kate believes Cam is innocent and sets out to find the real killer. "Unfortunately," stated a *Kirkus Reviews* contributor, "Kate's breeziness and self-regard undermine Nicholson's attempt to inject menace and obsession into a debut." In a *Booklist* review, however, Emily Melton maintained that the "writing is enthusiastic, the characters appealing, and the overall effect engaging."

In Nicholson's follow-up, *Evening the Score,* a piano competition has been scheduled at the Centenary. When Kate's former mentor and lover Stephan Bouchard shows up, Cam is naturally jealous, and this tension only gets worse when Stephan is named a suspect for yet another killing at the theater. While Melton, writing again in *Booklist,* felt that two unrelated murders at the same theater within about a month's time strained credibility, she enjoyed the "breezy writing style, intricate plots, and smart-mouthed, energetic heroine." Although a *Kirkus Reviews* contributor complained of the novel's "awkwardly constructed plot," the reviewer added that the "breezy first-person narrative . . . smoothes over the joints."

The crimes in *Sins of the Mother* and *Flirting with Disaster* do not occur at the Centenary. In the former mystery, Kate's cousin Carrie is accused of an attempted murder after leaving an abusive husband. This installment was praised by *Booklist* writer Melton for its "meaty plot, wry humor, deft writing, and an engaging heroine [that] make this a worthy successor" to the first two novels. *Flirting with Disaster* involves a serial killer known as the Bishop because of the chess pieces he leaves behind at the murder scenes. Much of the novel, however, involves Kate's complicated relationship with Cam, which seems to be falling apart when she refuses to go on a Caribbean cruise with him because of her work. When Cam moves out, Kate strikes up a relationship with another man, Doug, while rejecting a third, Jeff, who consequently starts threatening her.

Describing *Flirting with Disaster* as "DOA," a *Kirkus Reviews* critic complained that Nicholson spends too much time on Kate's relationships and not enough on the mystery. In a completely opposing view, Melton asserted in a *Booklist* article that this fourth novel in the series offers "nerve-tingling suspense . . . plenty of action, [and] memorable characters" in what is an "always-satisfying series."

BIOGRAPHICAL AND CRITICAL SOURCES:

PERIODICALS

Booklist, May 1, 2004, Emily Melton, review of *House Report,* p. 1515; October 15, 2004, Emily Melton, review of *Evening the Score,* p. 393; May 1, 2005, Emily Melton, review of *Sins of the Mother,* p. 1532; November 1, 2005, Emily Melton, review of *Flirting with Disaster,* p. 29.
Kirkus Reviews, May 1, 2004, review of *House Report,* p. 425; November 15, 2004, review of *Evening the Score,* p. 1071; November 1, 2005, review of *Flirting with Disaster,* p. 1165.
Midwest Book Review, July, 2005, review of *Sins of the Mother.*

ONLINE

AllReaders.com, http://www.allreaders.com/ (March 10, 2006), Marlene Robertson, review of *House Report.*
Deborah L. Nicholson Home Page, http://www.deborahnicholson.com (March 10, 2006).

*   *   *

NIELSEN, John

PERSONAL: Born in CA; children: three sons. *Education:* Graduated from Stanford University.

ADDRESSES: Home—Washington, DC. *Office*—National Public Radio, Science Desk, 635 Massachusetts Ave. N.W., Washington, DC 20001.

CAREER: During early career, worked as a journalist for newspapers, including the *Los Angeles Times, Orange County Register,* and *Salisbury Evening Post;* Massachusetts Institute of Technology, Boston, MA, former science journalism fellow; National Public Radio, Washington, DC, science correspondent and substitute news program host, 1990—. Guest lecturer at universities, including Princeton University, Yale University, and University of Utah.

AWARDS, HONORS: Science Writing Award, American Association for the Advancement of Science, 2005.

WRITINGS:

Condor: To the Brink and Back—The Life and Times of One Giant Bird, HarperCollins (New York, NY), 2005.

SIDELIGHTS: When John Nielsen was a boy growing up in Ventura County, California, condors were a fairly common site. Years later, after becoming a science journalist reporting on endangered species around the world, Nielsen decided to write about the endangered California condor. By the late 1980s, the species had diminished in numbers to only a couple dozen birds, and it was on the verge of extinction. While biologists debated whether the condors could best be protected in captivity or the wild, the numbers continued to dwindle until only twenty-seven were left. The situation became so perilous that the last wild condors were trapped and sheltered in facilities where they could be safely bred. By the time Nielsen published his book on the subject, *Condor: To the Brink and Back—The Life and Times of One Giant Bird,* about two hundred condors had been raised and some were released back into the wild. A *Publishers Weekly* contributor noted that the author seems to be most interested in describing the field work scientists conducted while studying the condor, as well as how they worked with the birds in captivity, writing that Nielsen "is most entranced by the hazards and pleasures of working with these birds." *Library Journal* contributor Henry T. Armistead concluded that *Condor* is a "dramatic conservation tale," while in *Booklist* Nancy Bent declared, "This is popular science writing at its peak."

BIOGRAPHICAL AND CRITICAL SOURCES:

PERIODICALS

Audubon, January-February, 2006, Todd Neale, review of *Condor: To the Brink and Back—The Life and Times of One Giant Bird,* p. 74.

Booklist, December 15, 2005, Nancy Bent, review of *Condor,* p. 10.

Kirkus Reviews, November 1, 2005, review of *Condor,* p. 1176.

Library Journal, December 1, 2005, Henry T. Armistead, review of *Condor,* p. 167.

Publishers Weekly, November 7, 2005, review of *Condor,* p. 64.

ONLINE

National Public Radio Web site, http://www.npr.org/ (March 13, 2006), biography of John Nielsen.*

*   *   *

NOLAN, Christopher 1970-

PERSONAL: Born July 30, 1970, in London, England; has dual citizenship in the United Kingdom and United States; married Emma Thomas (a film producer, production crew worker, and actress), 1997; children: three. *Education:* Attended University College London.

ADDRESSES: Agent—c/o Warner Brothers Studios, 3400 Riverside Dr., Burbank, CA 91522.

CAREER: Movie screenwriter, director, and producer. Has worked as maker of corporate training films. Director of films, including *Doodlebug,* 1997, *Following,* 1988, *Memento* 2000, *Insomnia,* 2002, *Batman Begins,* 2005, *The Exec,* 2006, and *The Prestige,* 2006; also directed television short *Tarantella,* PBS,

1989, and *Larceny,* 1996. Producer of films *Following,* 1998, and *The Prestige,* 2006; was also cinematographer and editor of *Following.*

AWARDS, HONORS: Silver Hitchcock award from Dinard British Film Festival, Best Director Award from Newport International Film Festival, Tiger Award from Rotterdam International Film Festival, and Black & White Award from Slamdance International Film Festival, all 1999, all for *Following;* CineLive Award and Critics Award, 2000; Jury Special Prize, Deauville Film Festival, 2000, ALFS award, London Critics Circle, 2001, for best British screenwriter of the year, Boston Society of Film Critics Award, 2001, for best screenplay, Los Angeles Film Critics Association Award, 2001, for best screenplay, Southeastern Film Critics Association Awards, 2001, for best original screenplay, Waldo Salt Screenwriting Award, Sundance Film Festival, 2001, Toronto Film Critics Association Award, 2001, for best screenplay, American Film Institute Award, 2002, for screenwriter of the year, Bram Stoker Award, 2002, for screenplay, Broadcast Film Critics Association Award, 2002, for best screenplay, Chicago Film Critics Award, 2002, for best screenplay, Russell Smith Award, Dallas-Fort Worth Film Critics Association, 2002, Edgar Allan Poe Award, 2002, for best motion picture, Florida Film Critics Award, 2002, for best screenplay, Independent Spirit Award, 2002, for best director and best screenplay, MTV Movie Award, 2002, for best new filmmaker, Online Film Critics Society Award, 2002, for best breakthrough filmmaker and best adapted screenplay, British Independent Film Award, best foreign independent film (English language), and Las Vegas Film Critics Society Awards, for best picture and best screenplay (original or adapted), all for *Memento;* ALFS award for best British Director of the Year, London Critics Circle, 2003, for *Insomnia.*

WRITINGS:

SCREENPLAYS; AND DIRECTOR

Doodlebug (short), Momac Films, 1997, collected in *Cinema 16: British Short Films,* Momac Films, 2003.

Following (also see below), Zeitgeist Films, 1998.

Memento (also see below; based on short story "Memento Mori" by Jonathan Nolan), Newmarket Films, 2000.

Memento & Following (screenplays), Faber & Faber (New York, NY), 2001.

(With David S. Goyer) *Batman Begins* (based on a story by Goyer and characters by Bob Kane), Warner Brothers, 2005.

Also author of unproduced screenplay *The Keys to the Street,* adapted from the novel of the same name by Ruth Rendell.

ADAPTATIONS: Batman Begins has been adapted into two young adult books: *Batman Begins: The Movie Storybook* by Benjamin Harper and *Training Bruce Wayne* by Holly Kowitt, both published by Scholastic, 2005.

WORK IN PROGRESS: Motion pictures, including *The Prestige,* directed by Nolan from a screenplay written with Jonathan Nolan, based on the novel by Christopher Priest, expected 2006; a sequel to *Batman Begins;* and *The Exec,* a futuristic drama.

SIDELIGHTS: Screenwriter-director Christopher Nolan, known for his dark dramas, reached new box-office heights with *Batman Begins* in 2005. The superhero film grossed 371 million dollars worldwide, more than twice its 150-million-dollar cost, making it one of the year's top moneymakers. It also received critical praise, and some film industry observers credited it with revitalizing the Batman franchise. This continued the upward trend of Nolan's career; before *Batman Begins,* he had directed well-received films such as *Memento,* which he also wrote, and *Insomnia,* a U.S. adaptation of a Norwegian film.

Nolan began making short films as a child and decided on a directing career by age twelve. His first feature-length film was 1998's *Following,* a low-budget effort starring his friend Jeremy Theobald as a would-be author who follows strangers around, ostensibly to gather ideas for his writings. One of the strangers is a criminal, and the writer becomes his accomplice. While the film had a limited release, it drew favorable attention from some critics. "Nolan is a talent who bears watching," commented Walter Addiego in the *San Francisco Examiner.* Meanwhile, in the *San Francisco Chronicle,* Mick LaSalle wrote: "That the movie succeeds as thoroughly as it does—getting deeper and creepier as it goes along—is evidence of a far-seeing creative imagination. Nolan is a compelling new talent."

Of his follow-up, *Memento, Variety* reviewer Lisa Nesselson observed: "Nolan avoids the sophomore slump with flying colors while deepening some of the themes so craftily explored in his debut effort." With a screenplay that Nolan based on a story by his brother Jonathan, the film tells the tale of a Los Angeles man, played by Guy Pearce, searching for his wife's murderer. His quest is made more difficult by his short-term memory loss. The movie, *Interview* contributor Ted Loos noted, shows Nolan's "modern approach to film noir," the genre of crime films popular in the late 1940s marked by morally compromised protagonists and a generally dark view of humanity. Nesselson also noticed the film noir aspects of *Memento,* saying it "has an impressive noir-in-the-sunshine feel." Loos termed the film a "must-see," while *Time* critic Richard Schickel deemed it "full of odd, hypnotic menace."

Nolan did not write his next directorial effort, *Insomnia,* which is also a remake, but he made it his own, according to some critics. It gave him a chance to work with some major stars, including Oscar winners Al Pacino, Hilary Swank, and Robin Williams. Like the Norwegian original, it deals with a murder investigation in a small town in the far northern latitudes during the summer, when the sun shines into the night. The U.S. version transplants the action from Norway to Alaska. Pacino plays a troubled detective called up from Los Angeles to help with the case and rendered sleepless by the midnight sun. Swank is a local police officer, and Williams is a suspect. *Variety* reviewer Todd McCarthy found the film "a gripping, highly dramatic thriller that more than confirms the distinctive talent of young Brit helmer Christopher Nolan." In *Time,* Schickel reported that Nolan "makes you feel the end-of-the-earth bleakness of his setting" and called the movie "thoughtful, quietly disturbing proof of a young director's gift."

Batman Begins offers a more serious view of the costumed crime-fighter than did the previous entry, 1997's campy *Batman & Robin,* directed by Joel Schumacher. Nolan's film explores Batman's origins, with wealthy youth Bruce Wayne deciding to adopt the Batman identity after witnessing the murder of his parents. Eventually, the formidable yet emotionally tortured superhero, played by Christian Bale, fights villains waging chemical warfare on his hometown, Gotham City. Several critics praised the film's dark tone. "That any filmmaker could now revive the comic book character and his retro-futuristic world of Gotham City is a minor miracle," wrote Kirk Honeycutt in the *Hollywood Reporter.* "But for Christopher Nolan to turn *Batman Begins* into such a smart, gritty, brooding, visceral experience is astonishing." *People* reviewer Leah Rozen dubbed the movie "compelling" and predicted it would "reinvigorate" the Batman film series, while *Christian Century* contributor Jason Byassee praised its handling of moral dilemmas and "its clever response to urban fears in the post-9/11 world." *Variety* commentator Todd McCarthy, however, found *Batman Begins* a bit too serious, stating: "There is talent and cleverness here, but not much excitement," and *New Yorker* critic David Denby saw "dull earnestness" in the screenplay. Nevertheless, the movie's overall success brought Nolan an assignment for the sequel and created high expectations for future Batman films. *Batman Begins,* related Ethan Alter in *Film Journal International,* "hints at even better things to come."

BIOGRAPHICAL AND CRITICAL SOURCES:

PERIODICALS

Australian Screen Education, summer, 2006, Richard Armstrong, "Somewhere in the Night: *Memento,*" p. 119.

Back Stage West, June 16, 2005, Jenelle Riley, "Never the Obvious: Christopher Nolan Cast a Wide Net to Snare His Batman Actors," p. 11.

Christian Century, July 26, 2005, Jason Byassee, "Fear Factor," p. 43.

Entertainment Weekly, January 21, 2005, preview of *Batman Begins,* p. 34; April 29, 2005, Daniel Fierman, "Bat Outta Hell," p. 30; October 21, 2005, Dalton Ross, "Dark Knight's Tale: Holy Boxed Sets, Batman! The Superhero Gets a Supersize Stack of New DVD Releases" p. 59.

Film Journal International, January, 2004, "Caine Summoned to Batcave," p. 52; July, 2005, Ethan Alter, review of *Batman Begins,* p. 99.

Hollywood Reporter, January 7, 2002, "The First Time: *Memento* Writer-Director Christopher Nolan," p. 12; May 13, 2002, Kirk Honeycutt, review of *Insomnia,* p. 8; May 28, 2002, Borys Kit, "Sleepless in Hollywood," p. 16; May 19, 2005, Chris Morris, "Dynamic Duo Score Big with *Batman* Teaming," p. 6; June 6, 2005, Kirk Honeycutt, review of *Batman Begins,* p. 14.

Interview, March, 2001, Ted Loos, interview with Christopher Nolan, p. 84, and review of *Memento,* p. 86.

Metro Magazine, winter, 2003, Steven Aoun, review of *Memento,* p. 265.

Narrative, January, 2005, William G. Little, "Surviving *Memento,*" p. 67.

Nation, June 10, 2002, Stewart Klawans, "Sleepless in Nightmute," p. 34.

Newsweek, June 3, 2002, David Ansen, "Going Sleepless in Alaska," p. 56; June 21, 2004, Devin Gordon, "Bat out of Hell," p. 64.

New Yorker, May 27, 2002, Anthony Lane, "Odd Couples"; June 13, 2005, David Denby, "Aiming Low," p. 187.

People, June 27, 2005, Leah Rozen, review of *Batman Begins,* p. 29.

Quadrant, October, 2002, Neil McDonald, review of *Insomnia,* p. 20.

San Francisco Chronicle, July 2, 1999, Mick LaSalle, "Creepy *Following* Does More with Less: Unusual Thriller a Promising Debut, p. C3.

San Francisco Examiner, April 24, 1998, Walter Addiego, "Playful Art-As-Movie Romp."

Science, June 1, 2001, Esther M. Sternberg, review of *Memento,* p. 1661.

Time, March 26, 2001, Richard Schickel, review of *Memento,* p. 73; May 27, 2002, Richard Schickel, "Sleepless in Alaska," p. 65; June 3, 2002, Jess Cagle, "Elegant Nightmares," p. 69.

Variety, September 18, 2000, Lisa Nesselson, review of *Memento,* p. 31; May 13, 2002, Todd McCarthy, "Nightless Pic Has Dark Soul," p. 23; April 17, 2003, Michael Fleming, "Nolan Wants Prestige," p. 1; June 6, 2005, McCarthy, review of *Batman Begins,* p. 46; October 24, 2005, Dave Lewis, review of *Batman Begins,* p. 30; December 6, 2005, Keith Collins, "Breaking Form: Filmmakers Tried on New Genres This Year," p. A14; February 27, 2006, "*Batman* Continues," p. 4.

W, December, 2000, Andrew Johnston, "Rise and Shine: Christopher Nolan, Filmmaker," p. 202.

ONLINE

BBC Web site, http://www.bbc.co.uk/ (October 16, 2000), David Wood, "Christopher Nolan: *Memento*—Style and Story."

Christopher Nolan Web site, http://www.christophernolan.net (April 27, 2006).

Groucho Reviews, http://www.grouchoreviews.com/ (May 3, 2005), interview with Christopher Nolan and Emma Thomas.

IGN.com, http://filmforce.ign.com/ (June 6, 2005), Jeff Otto, interview with Christopher Nolan.

Independent Feature Project Web site, http://www.ifp. org/ (June 1, 200), Michelle Bryant, "Christopher Nolan: Who Follows the Followers?"*

* * *

NORELL, Mark
See NORELL, Mark A.

* * *

NORELL, Mark A. 1957-
(Mark Norell)

PERSONAL: Born July 26, 1957, in St. Paul, MN. *Education:* California State University, Long Beach, B.S., 1980; San Diego State University, M.S., 1983; Yale University, Ph.D., 1988.

ADDRESSES: Home—New York, NY. *Office*—Division of Paleontology, American Museum of Natural History, Central Park W. at 79th St., New York, NY 10024-5192. *E-mail*—norell@amnh.org.

CAREER: Paleontologist, writer, and lecturer. American Museum of Natural History, New York, NY, curator and chairman of paleontology division. Has participated in several international scientific expeditions.

AWARDS, HONORS: New York City Leader of the Year award, *New York Times,* 1998; Distinguished Alumnus, California State University, Long Beach, 2000; Orbis Pictus award, National Council of Teachers, 2000, for *A Nest of Dinosaurs: The Story of Oviraptor;* Young Readers' Book of the Year award, *Scientific American,* for *Discovering Dinosaurs in the American Museum of Natural History;* Explorer's Club fellow; Willi Hennig Society fellow.

WRITINGS:

NONFICTION

(As Mark Norell) *All You Need to Know about Dinosaurs,* Sterling (New York, NY), 1991.

(With Lowell Dingus and Eugene S. Gaffney) *Discovering Dinosaurs in the American Museum of Natural History,* foreword by Angela Milner, Knopf (New York, NY), 1995, revised edition published as *Discovering Dinosaurs: Evolution, Extinction, and the Lessons of Prehistory,* University of California Press (Berkeley, CA), 2000.

(With Lowell Dingus) *Searching for Velociraptor,* HarperCollins (New York, NY), 1996.

(Consultant, with Philip J. Currie and Paul Sereno; as Mark Norell) Shelley Tanaka, *Graveyards of the Dinosaurs: What It's Like to Discover Prehistoric Creatures,* illustrated by Alan Barnard, Hyperion Books (New York, NY), 1998.

(With Lowell Dingus) *A Nest of Dinosaurs: The Story of Oviraptor* (young adult), illustrated by Mick Ellison, Doubleday (New York, NY), 1999.

(As Mark Norell) *Unearthing the Dragon: The Great Feathered Dinosaur Discovery,* photography and illustrations by Mick Ellison, Pi Press (New York, NY), 2005.

Also author of *Introduction to Tyrannosaurus, Introduction to Triceratops,* and *Introduction to Corythosaurus,* all Eyewitness Books (London, England), all 1993. Contributor to books, including *The Dinosaur Encyclopedia,* edited by G. Olshevsky, Publications International (Chicago, IL), 1990; *Imagining Dinosaur Imagery: The Science of Lost Worlds and Jurassic Art,* Academic Press (San Diego, CA), 2000.

Contributor to scientific journals, including *Science, Nature, Systematic Zoology, Journal of Herpetology, Trends in Ecology and Evolution, Journal of Vertebrate Paleontology, American Museum Novitiates, Cladistics, Scientific American,* and *Paleobiology.*

SIDELIGHTS: Paleontologist and museum curator Mark A. Norell has participated in several scientific expeditions in various countries, including Patagonia, Cuba, Chile, and Mongolia. Norell has made many significant discoveries during these expeditions and has even named dinosaurs such as the Apsaravis, Byronosaurus, and Achillonychus. In addition to his field work, Norell has also written several books about dinosaurs and related topics.

Norrell wrote *Discovering Dinosaurs in the American Museum of Natural History* with Lowell Dingus and Eugene S. Gaffney. The authors later revised the book and it was republished as *Discovering Dinosaurs: Evolution, Extinction, and the Lessons of Prehistory.* The original version is a guide to the Hall of Dinosaurs exhibit in the American Museum of Natural History; it contains descriptions of forty-one dinosaurs in a question-and-answer format. Reviewers applauded both the content and illustration of the book. Gilbert Taylor, writing in *Booklist,* described *Discovering Dinosaurs in the American Museum of Natural History* as "an appeal to replace imaginative speculation about the giant creatures with empirically convincing scientific information." A *Publishers Weekly* contributor called the first edition a "superb guide." The contributor further commented: "Handsomely illustrated . . . this volume takes us into a new world of dinosaurs."

In 1999 Norell published *A Nest of Dinosaurs: The Story of Oviraptor,* which he wrote with Lowell Dingus. In the book, the authors describe their field work in Mongolia, where they discovered the fossil of an Oviraptor perched over a nest of eggs. This discovery was significant because the Oviraptor was formerly believed to be a carnivorous dinosaur that stole eggs out of other dinosaurs' nests. The fossil that the authors found appeared to be parenting the eggs, not attacking them, thus changing the commonly held view of its behavior. Many critics responded favorably to the book. A *Horn Book* magazine reviewer pointed out the authors' skill in "explaining how one's best ideas can change in light of new evidence" which "allow[s] readers insight" into a constantly changing field. *School Library Journal* contributor Patricia Manning called the book "engrossing reading," while Marta Segal, writing in *Booklist,* concluded, "This book is a dream come true for children (or adults) fascinated by the creatures."

Norell followed *A Nest of Dinosaurs* with *Unearthing the Dragon: The Great Feathered Dinosaur Discovery.* The book is another account of Norell's field work; it documents his discovery of fossils indicating the existence of feathered dinosaurs in China. This discovery suggests that dinosaurs may be genetically closer to birds than previously believed. Critics enjoyed the personal insights provided by Norell. *Unearthing the Dragon* "provides both a personal story . . . and a scientific expose," commented Diane C. Donovan, a reviewer for *MBR Bookwatch.* Gloria Maxwell, writing in the *Library Journal,* held a similar opinion: "Scholars and dinosaur aficionados alike will enjoy Norell's personal account."

BIOGRAPHICAL AND CRITICAL SOURCES:

PERIODICALS

Booklist, May 15, 1995, Gilbert Taylor, review of *Discovering Dinosaurs in the American Museum of Natural History,* p. 1621; December 1, 1999, Marta Segal, review of *A Nest of Dinosaurs: The Story of Oviraptor,* p. 698.

Horn Book, January, 2000, review of *A Nest of Dinosaurs,* p. 101.

Library Journal, July 1, 2005, Gloria Maxwell, review of *Unearthing the Dragon: The Great Feathered Dinosaur Discovery,* p. 117.

MBR Bookwatch, October, 2005, Diane C. Donovan, review of *Unearthing the Dragon.*

Publishers Weekly, April 24, 1995, review of *Discovering Dinosaurs in the American Museum of Natural History,* p. 55.

School Library Journal, October, 2005, Patricia Manning, review of *A Nest of Dinosaurs,* p. 64.

ONLINE

American Museum of Natural History Web site, http://research.amnh.org/ (March 24, 2006), author biography and curriculum vitae.*

O

O'BRIEN, Martin

PERSONAL: Son of a naval officer and a headmistress; married; children: two daughters. *Education:* Attended Hertford College, Oxford.

ADDRESSES: Home—England. *Agent*—c/o Author Mail, Publicity Department, St. Martin's Press, 175 5th Ave., New York, NY 10010.

CAREER: During early career, worked as a copy subeditor; became travel editor for *Vogue* (magazine); travel and lifestyle writer for periodicals in the United States; screenplay writer and founder of a film production company.

WRITINGS:

All the Girls (travel), St. Martin's Press/Marek (New York, NY), 1982.
Jacquot and the Waterman (mystery novel), Headline Book Publishing (London, England), 2005, Thomas Dunne Books/St. Martin's Minotaur (New York, NY), 2006.

Also author of screenplays.

SIDELIGHTS: Martin O'Brien began his career as a travel and lifestyle journalist, but has more recently quit journalism to pursue writing mystery novels. His first book, *All the Girls,* is actually a quirky travel book about how O'Brien traveled the world and reported on various brothels. Over twenty years later, however, he went in an entirely different direction to complete his first mystery in a planned series, *Jacquot and the Waterman.* The main character is Chief Inspector Daniel Jacquot, a Marseilles police officer whose anguish over his recent breakup with his girlfriend, Boni, is now compounded by a disturbing case. A murderer known as the Waterman is drugging, raping, and drowning young women. The sensational case is making headlines in all the papers, and politicians are pressuring Jacquot's boss, who, in turn, puts the pressure on Jacquot to solve the case quickly.

Reviewers of *Jacquot and the Waterman* found much to praise in this police procedural, though some felt the ending is a bit flawed. Writing in *Booklist,* for example, Bill Ott reported that the novel has a "distinctly unsatisfying ending—almost as if O'Brien grew weary of the plot and decided to stop." A *Publishers Weekly* contributor similarly felt that the "biggest letdown" is "the identity of the Waterman," though as a whole the critic called the novel "an impressive debut." In her *Best Reviews* assessment, Harriet Klausner asserted that *Jacquot and the Waterman* "is a terrific French procedural starring a wonderful protagonist," while a *Kirkus Reviews* critic praised the "first-rate series hero."

BIOGRAPHICAL AND CRITICAL SOURCES:

PERIODICALS

Booklist, January 1, 2006, Bill Ott, review of *Jacquot and the Waterman,* p. 68.

Kirkus Reviews, November 1, 2005, review of *Jacquot and the Waterman,* p. 1165.

Library Journal, December 1, 2005, Michele Leber, "Mystery," review of *Jacquot and the Waterman,* p. 103.

Publishers Weekly, October 31, 2005, review of *Jacquot and the Waterman,* p. 35.

ONLINE

Advertiser Online, http://www.theadvertiser.news.com. au/ (January 21, 2006), review of *Jacquot and the Waterman.*

Best Reviews, http://thebestreviews.com/ (December 27, 2005), Harriet Klausner, review of *Jacquot and the Waterman.**

* * *

O'DONNELL, Pierce 1947-

PERSONAL: Born 1947, in Averill Park, NY; son of a liquor store owner and a librarian; married; wife's name Dawn; children: five. *Education:* Georgetown University, J.D.; Yale University, J.D.

ADDRESSES: Home—Montecito, CA. *Office*—O'Donnell Shaeffer Mortimer, LLP, 550 S. Hope St., Ste. 2000, Los Angeles, CA 90071.

CAREER: Clerk for Supreme Court Justice Byron R. White and for Ninth Circuit Court Judge Shirley M. Hufstedler; worked in a law firm in Los Angeles, CA; ran unsuccessfully as Democratic candidate for the U.S. Congress, 1980; O'Donnell & Gordon (law firm), former partner, beginning 1982; O'Donnell Shaeffer Mortimer LLP (law firm), Los Angeles, CA, currently partner. Former adjunct professor for Independent Film and Television Producers Program, University of California at Los Angeles; guest lecturer at universities, including Loyola University, University of Southern California, and Pepperdine University. Consultant, U.S. Senate Judiciary Committee on federal criminal law reform. Fellow, International Academy of Trial Lawyers, American College of Trial Lawyers, and American Board of Trial Advocates; member, American Institute of Law; member and former president, Economic Round Table of Los Angeles.

MEMBER: PEN.

AWARDS, HONORS: Named among the "100 Most Influential Lawyers in America," *National Law Journal.*

WRITINGS:

(With Michael J. Churgin and Dennis E. Curtis) *Toward a Just and Effective Sentencing System: Agenda for Legislative Reform,* foreword by Edward M. Kennedy, Praeger (New York, NY), 1977.

(With Dennis McDougal) *Fatal Subtraction: The Inside Story of Buchwald v. Paramount,* Doubleday (New York, NY), 1992, 2nd edition, Dove Books (West Hollywood, CA), 1996.

Dawn's Early Light (poetry), Rosebud (Chugiak, AK), 2001.

In Time of War: Hitler's Terrorist Attack on America, introduction by Anthony Lewis, New Press (New York, NY), 2005.

Also coauthor of screenplay *Home Team.* Contributor to periodicals and professional journals.

ADAPTATIONS: Fatal Subtraction was adapted to sound cassettes for Bantam Audio, 1992.

WORK IN PROGRESS: Funny You Asked about That.

SIDELIGHTS: Prominent California attorney Pierce O'Donnell has made a name for himself litigating cases involving large corporations and famous people. Among his clients have been companies such as Pfizer Inc., Miramax Films, DreamWorks SKG, Conoco Phillips, Bridgestone/Firestone, the National Broadcasting Company, Texaco, and Lockheed Martin Corp. He is best known for his work in the entertainment industry, first making a big name for himself when he represented writer Art Buchwald and agent/producer Alain Bernheim in a 1988 case against Paramount Pictures. Buchwald claimed that the movie studio had taken his and Bernheim's idea for the movie that became *Coming to America,* starring Eddie Murphy, and did not pay Buchwald a cent for it; also, Bernheim was denied the job of being the film's producer, as had been agreed. The case, in which the attorney portrayed Paramount as a sleazy company that manipulated accounting information to make it seem as though no profits were made on the film, made national headlines. It also became the subject of O'Donnell's book, *Fatal Subtraction: The Inside Story of Buchwald v. Paramount,* written with journalist Dennis McDougal.

In *Fatal Subtraction* the authors relate that the studio promised to pay Buchwald and Bernheim a fee and percentage of profits, but when Paramount declared that the movie lost eighteen million dollars, despite having about three hundred million dollars in sales, the plaintiffs were paid nothing. O'Donnell writes that this was typical of Hollywood studio practices, which he claims are insidiously designed to deny public profits no matter how well a film does. "He cites some of the outrageous large and small expenses figured in to create a loss situation," according to Fred Hift in *Video Age International.* Writing in the *American Business Law Journal,* Jordan H. Leibman explained that the most direct legal course of action would have been for the plaintiffs to sue Eddie Murphy, who took writing credit for the film. However, O'Donnell did not want the case to potentially turn on racism, so instead the attorney turned to "contract theory" for his case.

In the end, the plaintiffs received what was considered a meager compensatory settlement of a little over a million dollars. However, they won a moral victory in airing out what had been a longstanding point of contention between writers and artists against Hollywood's big studios: shady accounting practices designed to keep money in the hands of studio executives and movie stars. Many reviewers found *Fatal Subtraction* to be a compelling read. For example, Douglas Gomery wrote in *Cineaste* that "O'Donnell and McDougal paint a vivid 'David versus Goliath' narrative." Hift concluded, "This is an extraordinary, revelatory, briskly-written expose, surely among the most unusual ever penned about the wheelers and dealers in the film industry, and how they run their house of mirrors."

After the *Coming to America* case, O'Donnell established a strategy as a trial lawyer that he "has followed ever since," according to *Fortune* writer Tim Carvell: "He paints his clients as pawns in the hands of a large, arrogant opponent." Sometimes, however, the attorney has still been on the defense of large corporations, such as Metro-Goldwyn-Mayer (MGM). In a fight over the

ability to develop films featuring the character James Bond, Sony Pictures Entertainment was planning to make its own Bond Films. MGM sued, and, with O'Donnell on the case, won. O'Donnell manages his victories through his commanding understanding of how to exploit the media. The attorney, related Carvell, "has co-opted the techniques of persuasion that the studios have spent decades honing and has turned those techniques against their creators."

O'Donnell took up another controversial topic in *In Time of War: Hitler's Terrorist Attack on America.* The book is about how, in 1942, eight German-Americans planning sabotage were caught on American soil. Though the conspirators never carried out their plan—indeed, their own leader quickly turned them in—public outrage led to a quick trial. Six of the team were executed and the other two sent to prison. The trial had heavy political overtones, with President Franklin D. Roosevelt setting up a secret military tribunal for the prisoners that established a precedent that has been used by President George W. Bush against suspected terrorists since the September 11, 2001, attacks. Known as "Ex parte Quirin," the precedent was used against the Guatanamo Bay prisoners, and O'Donnell spends much of his book refuting the government's stand that it is a constitutional practice. A *Publishers Weekly* contributor called *In Time of War* "a passionate defense of the Bill of Rights." "This book addresses an important and emotional national issue," concluded Daniel K. Blewett in *Library Journal,* "and if we cannot even debate it, then the Constitution is dead."

O'Donnell's interest in politics eventually put him in legal trouble, however. In February 2006, he received three years of probation, heavy fines, and a ban on political fund-raising for making illegal contributions under an assumed name in 2000 and 2001 to Los Angeles Mayor James K. Hahn.

BIOGRAPHICAL AND CRITICAL SOURCES:

PERIODICALS

American Business Law Journal, November, 1993, Jordan H. Leibman, review of *Fatal Subtraction: The Inside Story of Buchwald v. Paramount,* pp. 535-552.

American Lawyer, August, 2005, Carlyn Kolker, review of *In Time of War: Hitler's Terrorist Attack on America,* p. 28.

Cineaste, fall, 1992, Douglas Gomery, review of *Fatal Subtraction,* p. 95.

Entertainment Weekly, August 28, 1992, Suzanne Ruta, review of *Fatal Subtraction,* p. 61.

Fortune, October 11, 1999, Tim Carvell, "Lights! Camera! Lawsuit! Hollywood Loves Courtroom Dramas. Pierce O'Donnell Knows How to Stage Them. His Target? Hollywood Itself," p. 189.

Library Journal, July 1, 2005, Daniel K. Blewett, review of *In Time of War,* p. 98.

Los Angeles Business Journal, February 19, 2001, "Profiles of the 50 Best-Compensated Lawyers in L.A.," p. 32.

Metropolitan News-Enterprise, February 3, 2006, "Pierce O'Donnell Fined, Banned from Fundraising after Pleading No Contest to Campaign Finance Charges," p. 1.

Mother Jones, November 13, 2005, "Radio: Bio of Attorney Pierce O'Donnell."

Publishers Weekly, June 8, 1992, review of *Fatal Subtraction,* p. 48; October 5, 1992, review of *Fatal Subtraction,* p. 29; May 23, 2005, review of *In Time of War,* p. 73.

Video Age International, October, 1992, Fred Hift, *Fatal Subtraction*—How Hollywood Really Does Business," p. 12.

ONLINE

O'Donnell Shaeffer Mortimer LLP Web site, http://www.oslaw.com/ (March 13, 2006), biography of Pierce O'Donnell.*

*   *   *

O'TATE, Ann
See COX, Ana Marie

*   *   *

OLSEN, Mark Andrew

PERSONAL: Married; wife's name Connie; children: three. *Education:* Graduate of Baylor University.

ADDRESSES: Home—Colorado Springs, CO. *Agent*—c/o Author Mail, Bethany House, 11400 Hampshire Ave. S., Minneapolis MN 55438.

CAREER: Writer, novelist, and screenwriter.

WRITINGS:

NOVELS

The Assignment, Bethany House (Minneapolis, MN), 2004.

(With Tommy Tenney) *Hadassah: One Night with the King,* Bethany House (Minneapolis, MN), 2004.

(With Tommy Tenney) *Hadassah: The Girl Who Became Queen Esther,* Bethany House (Minneapolis, MN), 2004.

(With Tommy Tenney) *The Hadassah Covenant,* Bethany House (Minneapolis, MN), 2005.

The Watchers, Bethany House (Minneapolis, MN), 2005.

SIDELIGHTS: In his first solo novel, *The Assignment,* Mark Andrew Olsen presents a spiritual thriller featuring a secret Catholic Church society called the Order of St. Lazare. The order's purpose is to find the "Restrainer," a person believed to have been alive since the time of Christ and who has the Divine task of holding off evil until a new age begins. When Father Stephen joins the Order of St. Lazare, he becomes involved in the hunt and, with other members of the order, traces the man to a tomb buried at Birkenau, the Polish concentration camp from World War II. However, an incarnation of Satan called the "Destroyer." is trying to thwart their efforts to reach him. Tamara Butler, writing in the *Library Journal,* commented that the "multifaceted plot of good and evil is a page-turner." A *Publishers Weekly* contributor noted that the author "knows how to raise the occasional goose bump."

Olsen has also collaborated with writer Tommy Tenney on a series of novels beginning with *Hadassah: One Night with the King.* The story revolves around a woman named Hadassah who is given a letter from the ancient queen of Persia, Esther. The letter has supposedly been passed down through generations of Hadassah's family and reveals Esther's life and times in detail. A *Publishers Weekly* contributor commented that "the authors reinvigorate an age-old story." The reviewer went on to note that the book has "a few surprise twists."

BIOGRAPHICAL AND CRITICAL SOURCES:

PERIODICALS

Library Journal, June 1, 2004, Tamara Butler, review of *The Assignment,* p. 116.
Publishers Weekly, November 10, 2003, review of *Hadassah: One Night with the King,* p. 41; May 10, 2004, review of *The Assignment,* p. 34.

ONLINE

FaithfulReader.com, http://www.faithfulreader.com/ (February 9, 2006), "Mark Andrew Olsen," interview with author.*

*   *   *

OLSON, Lynne 1952-

PERSONAL: Born 1952; married Stanley Cloud (a writer); children: Carly. *Education:* University of Arizona, graduated c. 1971.

ADDRESSES: *Home*—Washington, DC. *Agent*—c/o Author Mail, Knopf Publishing, 1745 Broadway, New York, NY 10019.

CAREER: Writer and journalist. Associated Press, reporter in Salt Lake City, UT, office, 1971, San Francisco, CA, office, 1972, New York, NY, office, Moscow correspondent, 1974-76, Washington, DC, office, 1976; *Baltimore Sun,* correspondent in Washington bureau, c. 1977-81; freelance writer, 1981—. Also assistant professor for five years at American University, Washington, DC.

AWARDS, HONORS: Christopher Award, 2002, for *Freedom's Daughters: The Unsung Heroines of the Civil Rights Movement from 1830 to 1970.*

WRITINGS:

(With husband, Stanley Cloud) *The Murrow Boys: Pioneers on the Front Lines of Broadcast Journalism,* Houghton Mifflin (Boston, MA), 1996.

Freedom's Daughters: The Unsung Heroines of the Civil Rights Movement from 1830 to 1970, Scribner (New York, NY), 2001.
(With Stanley Cloud) *A Question of Honor: The Kosciuszko Squadron; Forgotten Heroes of World War II,* Knopf (New York, NY), 2003, published as *For Your Freedom and Ours: The Kosciuszko Squadron: Forgotten Heroes of World War II,* William Heineman (London, England), 2003.

Contributor to periodicals, including *American Heritage, Smithsonian, Working Woman, Los Angeles Times Magazine, Ms., Elle, Glamour, Washington Journalism Review,* and *Baltimore* magazine.

SIDELIGHTS: Lynne Olson is a longtime journalist and freelance writer who has written historical/biographical books with her husband, Stanley Cloud, and a solo effort titled *Freedom's Daughters: The Unsung Heroines of the Civil Rights Movement from 1830 to 1970.* Considered the first comprehensive book about women's involvement in the civil rights movement, *Freedom's Daughters* recounts the activities of women from the days of slavery on through the modern movement for racial equality in America. Olson pays special attention to the meetings and relationships between white and black women, such as Eleanor Roosevelt, wife of President Franklin D. Roosevelt, and Pauli Murray, who led the first civil rights protest sit-in in 1944. The author points out that these relationships were vital to the movement since many of these women held leadership roles. Others discussed in the book include women such as Ida Mae Wells, a leader in the antilynching movement in the 1890s, and Rosa Parks, who sparked the Montgomery bus boycott when she refused to give up her seat on a bus to a white man. The author also delves into such organizations as the Student Nonviolent Coordinating Committee (SNCC), which played a important role in pushing for black voter registration in Mississippi. "Overall, Olson's analysis of SNCC and the Montgomery boycott superbly merges previous accounts of these events with current scholarship on SNCC," wrote Ann Short Chirhart in a review in the *Journal of Southern History.* The reviewer went on to note, "Clearly, many courageous women made the civil rights movement successful, and *Freedom's Daughters* makes a compelling addition to the movement's history."

Working with Cloud, Olson wrote *The Murrow Boys: Pioneers on the Front Lines of Broadcast Journalism.*

The book looks at the core crew of correspondents hired by legendary journalist Edward R. Murrow before and during World War II to help create the news bureau at the Columbia Broadcasting System, Inc. (CBS). In *A Question of Honor: The Kosciuszko Squadron; Forgotten Heroes of World War II,* which was published in England as *For Your Freedom and Ours: The Kosciuszko Squadron: Forgotten Heroes of World War II,* Olson and Cloud recount the mostly unrecognized and forgotten contributions made by Polish expatriates in the fight against Germany. As the title suggests, most of the book focuses on exploits of five Polish flyers who fled Poland after its invasion by Germany in World War II and went on to fly countless missions for the British Royal Air Force (RAF) and play a vital role in England's victory in the Battle of Britain in the process. As members of the Kosciuszko Squadron, RAF Squadron 303, which was named after American Revolutionary War hero Tadeusz Kosciuszko, these fliers "set records for aerial combat among the RAF for air-to-air kills against the Nazi air force," noted Kevin C.M. Benson in a review in *Armor.* Commenting on the book and the pilots in *Kliatt,* Raymond Puffer wrote, "Some had been in the outclassed Polish air force, others were civilians, but all were determined to fight against the Nazis, anytime and anywhere." Despite their dedication to the cause, however, the authors point out that these flyers earned little respect and were often mistreated. Puffer commented that their mistreatment "ranged from casual ingratitude to near-betrayal at the highest levels."

In a review of *A Question of Honor* in *Newsweek International,* Andrew Nagorski called the book "an impassioned, riveting account" of how these flyers and their home country of Poland were ultimately betrayed by the Allies after the war in an effort to appease the Soviet Union. Dale Farris wrote in the *Library Journal* that "the authors bring to life these courageous men as they struggled to reclaim their national heritage." Michael Karwowski, writing in the *Contemporary Review,* called the book "passionate and beautifully written." *Spectator* contributor Montagu Curzon commented, "Irksome as it is to read of Britain as traitor and coward, please swallow the pill and do so, because this is a tremendous story, grippingly told."

BIOGRAPHICAL AND CRITICAL SOURCES:

PERIODICALS

Armor, May-June, 2005, Kevin C.M. Benson, review of *A Question of Honor: The Kosciuszko Squadron; Forgotten Heroes of World War II,* p. 51.

Booklist, September 15, 2003, Gilbert Taylor, review of *A Question of Honor,* p. 198.
Contemporary Review, July, 2004, Michael Karwowski, review of *For Your Freedom and Ours: The Kosciuszko Squadron: Forgotten Heroes of World War II,* p. 53.
Journal of Southern History, August, 2003, Ann Short Chirhart, review of *Freedom's Daughters: The Unsung Heroines of the Civil Rights Movement from 1830 to 1970,* p. 744.
Kliaat, January, 2005, Raymond Puffer, review of *A Question of Honor,* p. 34.
Library Journal, August, 2003, Dale Farris, review of *A Question of Honor,* p. 104.
Newsweek International, October 6, 2003, Andrew Nagorski, review of *A Question of Honor,* p. 62.
Spectator, December 6, 2003, Montagu Curzon, review of *For Your Freedom and Ours,* p. 57.

ONLINE

A Question of Honor Web site, http://www.question ofhonor.com/ (January 17, 2005), biography of author.*

* * *

ORMESSON, Bruno Waldemar Francois-de-Paule Lefevre d'
    See D'ORMESSON, Jean

* * *

OSTOW, Micol 1976-

PERSONAL: Born April, 29, 1976. *Ethnicity:* "Puerto Rican and Jewish." *Education:* College graduate. *Hobbies and other interests:* Reading, running, watching inappropriate quantities of bad TV.

ADDRESSES: Home—New York, NY. *Agent*—c/o Author Mail, Simon Pulse/Simon & Schuster, 1230 Avenue of the Americas, New York, NY 10020.

CAREER: Writer and editor. Simon & Schuster, New York, NY, editor in trade nonfiction, then young-adult division. Creator of *Fireplace in a Box* and *Executive Desk Gong,* for Running Press, 2003.

WRITINGS:

FOR YOUNG ADULTS

(Compiler, with Steven Brizenoff) *The Quotable Slayer* (based on television series *Buffy the Vampire Slayer*), Simon Pulse (New York, NY), 2003.
30 Guys in 30 Days, Simon Pulse (New York, NY), 2005.
Changeling Places (based on television series *Charmed*), Simon Spotlight Entertainment (New York, NY), 2005.
Westminster Abby ("Students across the Seven Seas," series), Speak (New York, NY), 2005.
Ultimate Travel Games, Price, Stern, Sloan, 2006.
Emily Goldberg Learns to Salsa, Razorbill, 2006.

Also author (uncredited) of young-adult novels based on television series, including *American Dreams,* and for novel series, including "Fearless" and "Camp Confidential."

SIDELIGHTS: After graduating from college, Micol Ostow hired on with New York City publisher Simon & Schuster, and her job as editor eventually led to her second career as the author of young-adult novels. Describing her move to author as "a very organic" process in an online interview with *NYC24* contributor Catherine Shu, Ostow started as a ghostwriter for novels in popular ongoing series such as "Buffy the Vampire Slayer," "Charmed," and "Fearless," many based on television series and some published under house pseudonyms. From there, Ostow has begun to make her own name known to teen readers; her novels *30 Guys in 30 Days* and *Westminster Abby* appeared in 2005. Praising the first book as "tastefully written," *Kliatt* contributor Annette Wells added that older teens "will love this cleverly constructed novel" about a college freshman who decides to overcome her shyness by talking to a different guy each day for a month.

Part of the "Students across the Seven Seas" series, *Westminster Abby* centers around sixteen-year-old Abby, who has been sent to London for the summer by her parents as punishment for lying to them about her boyfriend James. While abroad, Abby meets up with a charming Brit named Ian and strikes up a fun relationship. A quandary arises when James appears in

London, hoping to win her back and rekindle their relationship despite the fact that he cheated on her: should she chose between Ian and James or opt for staying single? "This is as much a travel book as a romance, and for the most part, Ostow does a good job of fitting all the sights, sounds, and smells into the story," commented Ilene Cooper in a *Booklist* review of *Westminster Abby.* Catherine Ensley, writing in *School Library Journal,* also enjoyed the teen read, commenting that while "light in conflict," Ostow's story "will appeal to teens . . . whose lives are similarly sheltered and somewhat economically privileged."

BIOGRAPHICAL AND CRITICAL SOURCES:

PERIODICALS

Booklist, August, 2005, Ilene Cooper, review of *Westminster Abby,* p. 2016.
Kliatt, July, 2005, Annette Wells, review of *30 Guys in 30 Days,* p. 24.
School Library Journal, June, 2005, Catherine Ensley, review of *Westminster Abby,* p. 167.

ONLINE

NYC24 Web site, http://www.nyc24.org/ (April 11, 2005), Catherine Shu, "Confessions of an Undercover Author."*

* * *

OUELLETTE, Jennifer

PERSONAL: Female. *Hobbies and other interests:* Holds a black belt in jujitsu.

ADDRESSES: Home—Washington, DC. *Agent*—Mildred Marmur Associates, PMB 127, 2005 Palmer Ave., Larchmont, NY 10538.

CAREER: Writer and editor. Works as an associate editor and columnist for *APS News;* also writes science-related articles for a variety of periodicals and writes for the American Institute of Physics' television project, "Discoveries and Breakthroughs in Science."

MEMBER: National Association of Science Writers.

WRITINGS:

Black Bodies and Quantum Cats: Tales from the Annals of Physics, Penguin Books (New York, NY), 2005.

Contributor to periodicals, including *Discover* and *On Earth,* and to Web site journals, including *Salon.com.*

WORK IN PROGRESS: The Physics of the Buffyverse, for Penguin.

SIDELIGHTS: Jennifer Ouellette is a writer and editor who specializes in science. Her first book, *Black Bodies and Quantum Cats: Tales from the Annals of Physics,* is aimed at a mainstream audience unfamiliar with complex scientific issues; here, the author seeks to explain physical principles through pop culture references. To do so, she uses examples drawn from a wide range of interests, including the popular novel *The Da Vinci Code* and the movie *Dr. Strangelove.* For example, in one chapter Ouellette relates Einstein's theory of relativity to the film *Back to the Future.*

Black Bodies and Quantum Cats earned positive reviews from critics and readers alike. For some, the author's use of pop culture references and unusual pairings made for an enjoyable read. The book "makes physics and its history entertaining," wrote one *Science News* contributor. Others found that Ouellette's approachable writing style made it easy for general readers to understand the detailed scientific theories contained in the book. The author's prose "encourages generalists to give physics a try," observed Gilbert Taylor in *Booklist.*

BIOGRAPHICAL AND CRITICAL SOURCES:

PERIODICALS

Booklist, November 1, 2005, Gilbert Taylor, review of *Black Bodies and Quantum Cats: Tales from the Annals of Physics,* p. 9.
Library Journal, November 1, 2005, Marcia Franklin, review of *Black Bodies and Quantum Cats,* p. 110.
San Francisco Chronicle, December 22, 2005, Phillip Manning, review of *Black Bodies and Quantum Cats,* p. 1.
Science News, January 21, 2006, review of *Black Bodies and Quantum Cats,* p. 47.

ONLINE

Jennifer Ouellette Home Page, http://www.jennifer ouellette-writes.com (February 28, 2006).
Jennifer Ouellette Web log, Cocktail Party Physics, http://www.twistedphysics.typepad.com (April 18, 2006).

P

PALWICK, Susan

PERSONAL: Female. *Education:* Princeton University, A.B., 1982; Yale University, Ph.D., 1996.

ADDRESSES: *Office*—English Department/098, University of Nevada, Reno, Reno, NV 89557. *E-mail*—palwick@unr.nevada.edu.

CAREER: Writer and educator. University of Nevada, Reno, associate professor of English.

AWARDS, HONORS: Crawford Award for Best First Fantasy Novel, International Association for the Fantastic in the Arts, for *Flying in Place;* "Best Books of 2005" citation, *Library Journal,* for *The Necessary Beggar.*

WRITINGS:

FANTASY AND SCIENCE FICTION

Flying in Place, Tor (New York, NY), 1992.
The Necessary Beggar, Tor (New York, NY), 2005.

Contributor of short stories and creative nonfiction to the *Magazine of Fantasy and Science Fiction, Asimov's Science Fiction Magazine,* and the *Texas Review.* The author's work has been translated into Japanese.

WORK IN PROGRESS: *Shelter,* a novel.

SIDELIGHTS: Susan Palwick is an English professor and the author of fantasy fiction and science fiction. Writing on her Web page posting at the *University of Nevada, Reno* Web site, Palwick called her short stories mostly "contemporary retellings of fairy tales." Her longer fiction works, however, have garnered the most critical acclaim. Indeed, both of her first two novels have been recognized with awards.

Flying in Place tells the story of twelve-year-old Emma Gray. Emma is sexually abused by her father, a respected doctor, on an almost nightly basis. The assaults occur late at night while her oblivious mother, an English teacher, is sleeping. Emma's only means of protection and escape are her imaginary adventures with her long-dead sister, Ginny. In Emma's whimsies the girls go flying together and engage in other fantastical exploits. Reviewers of the novel predominantly remarked upon Palwick's delicate handling of a difficult topic. The "chilling and finely tuned" story "avoids pat solutions," noted a *Publishers Weekly* contributor. Harriet Klausner, writing in the *Baryon Online* magazine, noted that Palwick's characters are intentionally made flat in order to bring Emma's fantasy scenes into clearer focus. Klausner felt, however, that this results in a story that is "black and white with no gray." Nevertheless, Klausner called the book "thought provoking," and noted that the story "grips the reader."

Palwick's second novel, *The Necessary Beggar,* was released thirteen years after the initial publication of *Flying in Place.* The story is more overtly recognizable as science fiction. In the utopian city of Lemabantunk, located in the world of Gandiffri, a young man named Darroti falls in love with a woman serving as a holy beggar. When she is killed Darroti is wrongly accused, and subsequently convicted, of the crime. His punishment is that of banishment, and since his family refuses to part from him, they are all exiled to planet Earth, specifically to Reno, Nevada. When the family arrives through a portal at a refugee camp, they are forced to adjust from the utopian society they once knew to their decidedly more violent and chaotic new home. The book was praised widely by critics, especially as a subtle comment on the travails of immigrants. A *Publishers Weekly* reviewer called the book a "heart-wrenching . . . tragicomedy of cultural differences." Moreover, *Booklist* contributor Paula Luedtke concluded: "Palwick's beautifully crafted tale of exiles struggling to come to terms with a deeply troubled Earth is exquisite."

BIOGRAPHICAL AND CRITICAL SOURCES:

PERIODICALS

Booklist, October 1, 2005, Paula Luedtke, review of *The Necessary Beggar,* p. 43.
Library Journal, October 15, 2005, Jackie Cassada, review of *The Necessary Beggar,* p. 51.
Publishers Weekly, March 23, 1992, review of *Flying in Place,* p. 62; August 29, 2005, review of *The Necessary Beggar,* p. 38.

ONLINE

Baryon Online, http://www.baryon-online.com/ (March 24, 2006), Harriet Klausner, review of *Flying in Place.*
Romantic Times Book Club Online, http://www.romantictimes.com/ (March 24, 2006), Jen Talley Exum, review of *The Necessary Beggar.*
SF Reviews, http://www.sfreviews.net/ (March 24, 2006), T.M. Wagner, review of *The Necessary Beggar.*
University of Nevada, Reno Web site, http://www.unr.edu/ (March 24, 2006), author information and statement.*

*   *   *

PARKS, Adele

PERSONAL: Born in England; married (divorced, 2001); children: one son. *Education:* Studied English language and literature at Leicester University.

ADDRESSES: Agent—c/o Author Mail, Penguin Publicity, 80 Strand, London WC2R 0RL, England. *E-mail*—adele@adeleparks.com.

CAREER: Writer. Also worked in advertising and as an English teacher.

WRITINGS:

NOVELS

Playing Away, Pocket Books (New York, NY), 2000.
Game Over, Penguin Books (New York, NY), 2001.
Larger Than Life, Penguin Books (New York, NY), 2002.
The Other Woman's Shoes, Penguin Books (London, England), 2003, published as *Lust for Life,* Downtown Press (New York, NY), 2005.
Still Thinking of You (Even Though I Shouldn't Be), Penguin Books (London, England), 2004.
Husbands, Penguin Books (London, England), 2005.

SIDELIGHTS: Best-selling author Adele Parks debuted in 2000 with the first of her successful female characters looking for love in London. In *Playing Away,* Connie Green is a sexy, married management consultant who begins an adulterous relationship with a colleague she meets at a business convention. With husband Luke often away on business, Connie is bored until John Harding catches her attention and she is swept into a wild affair with disastrous consequences. One reviewer, writing for *Publishers Weekly,* felt that *Playing Away* is "initially humorous," but later "enervating" and "predictable." However, the same critic noted that "Parks is astute about male/female interactions" and "has cleverness to spare." Deborah Rysso of *Booklist* called the novel "compelling" and "fun."

In *Game Over,* Parks tells the story of Jocasta "Cas" Perry, a television producer who has just launched a successful new reality show in which couples who are ready to commit to marriage are tempted by ex-lovers. Cas herself has never been fond of commitment—that is, until she meets charming, upstanding Darren, who refuses to lure his former girlfriend away from her fiancée. Portraying the book as "a delightful romp," Kristine Huntley of *Booklist* noted that *Game Over* has "fun characters" and "a hilarious . . . premise." Writing for *Entertainment Weekly*, Allyssa Lee remarked, "There's some substance beneath that undeniably girlie cover."

Larger Than Life introduces readers to Georgina, who has been in love with Hugh since they met in college. Now, many years later, Hugh has left his wife and two children to be with Georgina, who soon finds herself filling the role of the pregnant "other woman." With a baby on the way and friends who do not understand her situation, Georgina is steadily growing uncertain as to whether Hugh is truly the man of her dreams. "It is a testimony to Parks's writing skills that her home-wrecker heroine retains our sympathy," observed Elizabeth Melette in *Library Journal*. Writing for *Booklist*, Patty Engelmann called *Larger Than Life* a "fun and funny ode to motherhood in modern London."

Parks's next novel, *The Other Woman's Shoes*, published in the United States as *Lust for Life*, is the story of two sisters, Martha and Eliza. Each sister thinks the other has the better life. Just as Eliza leaves her sexy but unmotivated musician-boyfriend and decides that older sister Martha has the stable life she wants, Martha's husband up and leaves, and Martha resolves to rid herself of her perfect-housewife persona. As the sisters essentially exchange lives, they must help each other find love and happiness. In a critique of the novel for *Kirkus Reviews*, one reviewer commented, "Throw in all the right ingredients—fashion, sex, and female empowerment—blend, and out comes this frothy, enjoyable read."

Parks's later novels are *Still Thinking of You (Even Though I Shouldn't Be)*, which focuses on four thirty-something college friends—Rich, Jason, Ted, and Lloyd—who meet at a French ski resort to celebrate Rich's recent engagement, and *Husbands*, which follows Bella Lawrence as she tries to find the right time to tell her new husband that she's still married to another man—who happens to be her best friend's new beau.

BIOGRAPHICAL AND CRITICAL SOURCES:

PERIODICALS

Booklist, June 1, 2000, Deborah Rysso, review of *Playing Away*, p. 1861; August, 2003, Patty Engelmann, review of *Larger Than Life*, p. 1957; March 15, 2004, Kristine Huntley, review of *Game Over*, p. 1266.

Entertainment Weekly, August 15, 2003, Sharon Tanenbaum, review of *Larger Than Life*, p. 83; March 19, 2004, Allyssa Lee, review of *Game Over*, p. 71.
Kirkus Reviews, September 1, 2005, review of *Lust for Life*, p. 938.
Library Journal, July, 2000, Joyce Smothers, review of *Playing Away*, p. 141; August, 2003, Elizabeth Melette, review of *Larger Than Life*, p. 134.
Publishers Weekly, May 29, 2000, review of *Playing Away*, p. 49.

ONLINE

Adele Parks Home Page, http://www.adeleparks.com (January 23, 2006).*

*   *   *

PASSET, Joanne E. 1954-

PERSONAL: Born September 10, 1954, in Upper Sandusky, OH; daughter of Norman F. (a farmer) and Almeda (a civil servant and homemaker; maiden name, Harrison) Passet. *Education:* Bluffton College, B.A., 1975; Bowling Green State University, M.A., 1979; Indiana University, M.L.S., 1980, Ph.D. (library science), 1988; University of Wisconsin—Madison, Ph.D. (history), 1999. *Politics:* Democrat.

ADDRESSES: Office—Indiana University East, 2325 Chester Blvd., Richmond, IN 47374. *E-mail*—jpasset@indiana.edu.

CAREER: Writer. Indiana University—Bloomington, librarian, 1982-88; University of California, Los Angeles, assistant professor of library and information science, 1988-90; Indiana University—Bloomington, assistant professor of library and information science, 1990-94; Bluffton College, Bluffton, OH, director of libraries, 1998-2000; Dominican University, River Forest, IL, associate professor of library and information science, 2000-01; Indiana University East, Richmond, assistant professor of history, 2001—.

MEMBER: Organization of American Historians, Communal Studies Association, Society for the History of Authorship, Reading, and Publishing, Rural

Women's Studies Association, Indiana Historical Society, Indiana Women's History Association, Indiana Association of Historians.

AWARDS, HONORS: Justin Winsor Prize, American Library Association, 1994; Martin Luther King, Jr. Award, Indiana University East, 2004.

WRITINGS:

(With Mary Niles Maack) *Aspirations and Mentoring in an Academic Environment,* Greenwood Press (Westport, CT), 1994.

Cultural Crusaders: Women Librarians in the American West, 1900-1917, University of New Mexico Press (Albuquerque, NM), 1994.

Sex Radicals and the Quest for Women's Equality, University of Illinois Press (Champaign, IL), 2004.

WORK IN PROGRESS: A biography of radical reformer Juliet H. Severance, M.D.

*   *   *

PEREZ, Lana
    See PEREZ, Marlene

*   *   *

PEREZ, Marlene
    (Lana Perez)

PERSONAL: Female.

ADDRESSES: Home—CA. *Agent*—c/o Author Mail, Roaring Brook Press, 2 Old New Milford Rd., Brookfield, CT 06804. *E-mail*—marlene@marleneperez.com.

CAREER: Writer.

AWARDS, HONORS: Quick Pick for Reluctant Readers citation, and Best Book for Young Adults nomination, both 2005, both for *Unexpected Development.*

WRITINGS:

Unexpected Development, Roaring Brook Press (Brookfield, CT), 2004.

UNDER PSEUDONYM LANA PEREZ

Bright Lights for Bella ("Star Sisterz" series), Mirrorstone (Renton, WA), 2005.

Figure in the Frost ("Knights of the Silver Dragon" series), Mirrorstone (Renton, WA), 2005.

Bella Goes Hollywood ("Star Sisterz" series), Mirrorstone (Renton, WA), 2006.

SIDELIGHTS: Marlene Perez made her publishing debut with the young-adult novel *Unexpected Development.* The Southern California-based writer became inspired to write the diary-style book after attending a conference in Los Angeles held by the Society of Children's Book Writers and Illustrators. During the day-long schedule of seminars and round tables, noted YA author Norma Fox Mazer discussed the obstacles presented by a writer's internal critic, and suggested ways of turning off one's internal editor and focusing on writing freely. Returning home, Perez sat down at her desk the very next day and started on the manuscript that would become *Unexpected Development.* In addition to this novel, she has published several books for role-playing game and book publisher Wizards of the Coast, all under the pen name Lana Perez. Part of the "Star Sisterz" series designed for pre-teens and featuring characters from a related game, *Bright Lights for Bella* and *Bella Goes Hollywood* follow the adventures of a fourteen-year-old as she struggles through the first year of high school and successfully resolves an assortment of dilemmas that many teens can relate to. In an online review for *BookLoons,* Ricki Marking-Camuto noted that Perez "has an uncanny ability to capture in her writing the way a young teenager thinks."

Unexpected Development follows seventeen-year-old Megan, a teen plagued by having overly large breasts. Made uncomfortable by the constant attention paid her double-D cleavage by ogling men, Megan begins to question the motive behind male attention, particularly after her boss at the pancake house where she works attempts to fondle her. Feeling doomed in romance due to being upstaged by her chest, Megan questions the seeming romantic possibilities that arise when her longtime crush, Jake Darrow, asks her out. Readers follow Megan as she weighs her options and accepts her chance at love in a novel that *Booklist* reviewer Hazel Rochman praised as a "wry" story in which Perez conveys a "rare honesty about body image, romance, and sex." "Perez is an author worth watching," commented Susan Riley in *School Library Journal,* while a *Publishers Weekly* critic concluded that "Meagan's appealing character will draw readers in, and will likely make the audience hope for more from this promising writer."

BIOGRAPHICAL AND CRITICAL SOURCES:

PERIODICALS

Booklist, November 15, 2004, Hazel Rochman, review of *Unexpected Development,* p. 598.
Bulletin of the Center for Children's Books, October, 2004, Deborah Stevenson, review of *Unexpected Development,* p. 95.
Journal of Adolescent & Adult Literacy, September, 2005, June Harris, review of *Unexpected Development,* p. 79.
Kirkus Reviews, September 1, 2004, review of *Unexpected Development,* p. 872.
Publishers Weekly, September 6, 2004, review of *Unexpected Development,* p. 64.
School Library Journal, October, 2004, Susan Riley, review of *Unexpected Development,* p. 175; November 25, 2005, Mary R. Hoffmann, review of *Unexpected Development,* p. 60.
Voice of Youth Advocates, December, 2004, review of *Unexpected Development,* p. 392.

ONLINE

BookLoons.com, http://www.bookloons.com/ (April 11, 2006), Ricki Marking-Camuto, review of *Bright Lights for Bella.*
Crescent Blues Online, http://www.crescentblues.com/ (April 11, 2006), Lynne Marie Pisano, review of *Unexpected Developments.*
Kidsreads.com, http://www.kidsreads.com/ (April 11, 2006), Paula Jolin, review of *Bright Lights for Bella.*
Marlene Perez Home Page, http://members.cox.net/ mardperez (April 11, 2006).*

PERLE, Liz
(Elizabeth Perle McKenna)

PERSONAL: Married first husband (divorced); married second husband; children: (first marriage) son; (second marriage) one; stepchildren: three.

ADDRESSES: Home—San Francisco, CA. *Office*—Common Sense Media, 1550 Bryant St., Ste. 555, San Francisco, CA 94103.

CAREER: Writer; editor and publisher for twenty years. Harper & Row, New York, NY, marketing department; Bantam Books, New York, marketing department and associate publisher; Prentice Hall Press, New York, publisher; Addison-Wesley, Boston, MA, vice president and publisher of general books; Hearst Book Group (William Morrow/Avon), New York, vice president and editorial director, 1991-93, publisher of general book division, 1993-94, vice president and publisher, 1994-95; Common Sense Media (nonpartisan media watchdog organization), San Francisco, CA, editor in chief.

WRITINGS:

NONFICTION

(As Elizabeth Perle McKenna) *When Work Doesn't Work Anymore: Women, Work and Identity,* Delacorte Press (New York, NY), 1997.
Money, a Memoir: Women, Emotions, and Cash, Holt (New York, NY), 2006.

SIDELIGHTS: Liz Perle worked in the publishing industry for twenty years before leaving the corporate world behind. She ultimately left her executive job as vice president and publisher of the Hearst Book Group (the parent company of prominent publishing houses William Morrow and Avon) because she felt that by defining herself through her job, she was denying herself happiness. In a panel discussion led by Barbara Jones and published in *Harper's* magazine, Perle stated that her corporate experience taught her that it "was more important to act right than be right. I had to look as if work was everything. Long hours are a requirement. Nothing, absolutely nothing, can appear to be more important than what you do." As a woman, and as a person, Perle went on to explain, "these rules don't make sense." Perle felt so strongly about these issues that she chronicled her decision to leave her career in *When Work Doesn't Work Anymore: Women, Work and Identity.*

In addition to sharing her own experiences in the book, Perle interviewed 200 working women and surveyed over 1,000 in order to illustrate that her encounters are not singular, but are instead part of a greater cultural phenomenon. Perle then argues that because women derive much of their identity from their work, they adhere to the demands of a "success culture," thus causing an imbalance between work and the rest of their lives. Perle goes so far as to advise women on how to reclaim that balance, namely by first recognizing that they are not their jobs, and by learning to redefine what they see as success. Indeed, a *Publishers Weekly* critic noted that Perle's approach is "so provocative and convincing . . . that it is likely to motivate many women to move from a culturally approved value system to a more personal one." Although *Time* contributor Jill Smolowe felt that "only well-paid women, like those in her survey, may be able to heed" this suggestion, Smolowe conceded that "such prescriptions for redefining worth and success are not abundantly simple, but they are abundantly sane."

Some time after Perle left her career, her husband decided to end their marriage. As a result, Perle lost her home, and she was left with only 1,500 dollars. Perle then found herself and her four-year-old son sleeping on a friend's couch. In an effort to make sense of this surprising turn of events, Perle wrote *Money, a Memoir: Women, Emotions, and Cash.* Much like her first book, Perle speaks of her own experiences and attempts to place them in a larger context based on the experiences of other women—a *Publishers Weekly* reviewer called the methodology a "sociological study-cum-memoir." Not surprisingly, Perle finds that women cheat themselves financially for several reasons, including not asking for an equitable salary at work, out of a fear of being resented or disliked. Indeed, Perle notes that many situations tied to women's finances are also tied to their emotions; take, for instance, retail therapy—the idea that spending money will make one feel good.

The book received somewhat mixed reviews. Although a *Kirkus Reviews* contributor noted that Perle's "memoir is frank and unflinching," the contributor also

felt that "it falters when she tries to apply her own experience with money to women in general." Nevertheless, commented Anne Fisher in *Fortune,* the author "tackles some intriguing and important questions." The *Publishers Weekly* reviewer similarly observed that *Money, a Memoir* "raises more questions than it answers," but went on to conclude that this is "part of its allure."

BIOGRAPHICAL AND CRITICAL SOURCES:

BOOKS

Perle, Liz, *Money, a Memoir: Women, Emotions, and Cash,* Holt (New York, NY), 2006.
Perle McKenna, Elizabeth, *When Work Doesn't Work Anymore: Women, Work and Identity,* Delacorte Press (New York, NY), 1997.

PERIODICALS

Fortune, February 20, 2006, Anne Fisher, review of *Money, a Memoir,* p. 140.
Harper's, December, 1997, Barbara Jacobs, "Giving Women the Business: On Winning, Losing, and Leaving the Corporate Game" (panel discussion), p. 47.
Kirkus Reviews, November 1, 2005, review of *Money, a Memoir,* p. 1177.
Library Journal, September 15, 1997, Barbara Hoffert, review of *When Work Doesn't Work Anymore,* p. 92.
New York Times, January 29, 2006, Ariel Levy, review of *Money, a Memoir.*
Publishers Weekly, June 16, 1997, review of *When Work Doesn't Work Anymore,* p. 51; June 30, 1997, Judy Quinn, "A Few Words with Elizabeth Perle McKenna," p. 18; October 31, 2005, review of *Money, a Memoir,* p. 41; December 19, 2005, Lynn Andriani, "Expense Account: Liz Perle's Memoir Is about What Money Can Do to Women" (profile and interview), p. 34.
Time, August 11, 1997, Jill Smolowe, review of *When Work Doesn't Work Anymore,* p. 56.
Women's Review of Books, February, 1998, Ann Withorn, review of *When Work Doesn't Work Anymore,* p. 15.

ONLINE

Common Sense Media Web site, http://www.commonsensemedia.org (March 27, 2006).

Money, a Memoir Web site, http://www.moneya
memoir.com (March 27, 2006).*

* * *

PHILLIPS, Scott

PERSONAL: Born in Wichita, KS; married; children:
a daughter.

ADDRESSES: Home—St. Louis, MO. *Agent*—Aragi,
Inc., 143 W. 27th St., Unit 4F, New York, NY 10001.
E-mail—scott@scottphillipsauthor.com.

CAREER: Writer. Worked as a translator and English
teacher in Paris France, a bookseller, and a feature
film screenwriter.

AWARDS, HONORS: Silver Medal for Best First Fiction, California Book Award, for *The Ice Harvest.*

WRITINGS:

NOVELS

The Ice Harvest, Ballantine Books (New York, NY),
2000.
The Walkaway, Ballantine Books (New York, NY),
2003.
Cottonwood, Ballantine Books (New York, NY), 2004.

Also author, with David Maisel, of the screenplay for
the film *Crosscut,* 1996.

ADAPTATIONS: The Ice Harvest was adapted for
film, Focus Features, 2005.

SIDELIGHTS: Scott Phillips has received widespread
recognition for his thrilling and funny debut crime
novel *The Ice Harvest.* The story focuses on a seedy
lawyer and mobster named Charlie Arglist who plans
to take off on Christmas Eve 1979 with money
belonging to a Wichita, Kansas, crime syndicate leader
named Bill Gerard. Arglist has been stealing money
from Gerard as part of his work for him running
"stripper" bars along with Arglist's partner, Vic

Cavenaugh. As the night progresses, Arglist becomes
caught up in an inebriated yuletide spirit that leads
him to a series of mishaps and the realization that he
is already running for his a life as the dead bodies
began to proliferate. "Newcomer Phillips's seedy
characters are skillfully developed, particularly the
semiremorseful Charlie," wrote a *Publishers Weekly*
contributor. Bob Lunn, writing in the *Library Journal,*
called the novel a "pitch-perfect foray into pulp fiction, witty and bitter."

In his next book, *The Walkaway,* Phillips once again
sets his noir thriller in Wichita and features Gunther
Fahnstiel, a retired cop who made a brief appearance
in *The Ice Harvest.* Living in a retirement home, the
confused Fahnstiel, who is losing his memory, suddenly has a flash of lucidity and takes off in search of
the money Arglist stole in *The Ice Harvest.* Soon on
Fahnstiel's trail are his wife, an ex-lover, a former colleague, and his son, all with agendas of their own.
"The expansive story . . . couldn't be more different
from the chilly anecdote to which it serves as both pre-
quel and sequel," wrote a *Kirkus Reviews* contributor,
who went on to refer to the novel and its predecessor
as "a pair of tours de force." Lunn, once again writing
in the *Library Journal,* commented, "When it comes
to present-day practitioners of noir, Phillips is one of
the best." A *Publishers Weekly* contributor commented
that the author "pens a story full of blood and bad attitude."

Phillips takes a new course in his novel *Cottonwood,*
which is set in frontier Kansas and San Francisco in
the latter part of the nineteenth century. The story
focuses on Bill Ogden over a period of nearly twenty
years. Bill, who knows both Greek and Latin, is a
seducer of women and becomes involved in a scheme
to bring cattle drovers to the area while cavorting with
Maggie, the wife of his partner, Marc Leval. Eventually a local gang called the "Bloody Benders"
interferes with their plans and the two partners have a
falling out. After Marc and Maggie leave town, Bill
ends up years later in San Francisco working as a
photographer, only to head back to Cottonwood,
Kansas, when he learns that Maggie has returned.
Writing in *Booklist,* Carrie Bissey commented that the
novel features the author's "brand of sly humor and
his skilled depictions of nasty human behavior." In a
review in *Entertainment Weekly,* Ben Spier noted that
the novel is "as starkly delineated and unsparing as an
antique tintype." A *Publishers Weekly* contributor

wrote, "Lively pacing and artful prose lend polish to Phillips's cheerfully grotesque chronicle of western antics."

BIOGRAPHICAL AND CRITICAL SOURCES:

PERIODICALS

Booklist, January 1, 2004, Carrie Bissey, review of *Cottonwood,* p. 826.

Entertainment Weekly, February 6, 2004, Ben Spier, review of *Cottonwood,* p. 155.

Kirkus Reviews, June 15, 2002, review of *The Walkaway,* p. 834; December 1, 2003, review of *Cottonwood,* p. 1378; December 15, 2004, review of *Cottonwood,* p. S4.

Library Journal, September 15, 2000, Bob Lunn, review of *The Ice Harvest,* p. 114; August, 2002, Bob Lunn, review of *The Walkaway,* p. 145.

New York Times, November 6, 2000, Janet Maslin, review of *The Ice Harvest,* p. E8; July 29, 2002, Janet Maslin, review of *The Walkaway,* p. B7.

New York Times Book Review, August 18, 2002, Marilyn Stasio, review of *The Walkaway,* p. 14; February 22, 2004, Marilyn Stasio, review of *Cottonwood,* p. 15.

Publishers Weekly, August 21, 2000, review of *The Ice Harvest,* p. 45; April 15, 2002, review of *The Walkaway,* p. 38; December 15, 2003, review of *Cottonwood,* p. 52.

Times Literary Supplement, June 14, 2002, Benjamin Markovits, review of *The Walkaway,* p. 21.

Tribune Books (Chicago, IL), November 26, 2000, review of *The Ice Harvest,* p. 2.

ONLINE

Bookreporter.com, http://www.bookreporter.com/ (September 19, 2004), Joe Hartlaub, review of *The Ice Harvest.*

Internet Movie Database, http://www.imdb.com/ (January 19, 2005), information on author's work in relation to movies.

Mystery Ink, http://www.mysteryinkonline.com/ (September 19, 2004), review of *The Ice Harvest.*

Noir Originals, http://www.allanguthrie.co.uk/ (April 14, 2003), James Lincoln Warren, interview with Phillips.

Scott Phillips Home Page, http://www.scottphillips author.com (September 19, 2004).

*   *   *

PITBLADO, Bonnie L. 1968-

PERSONAL: Born February 22, 1968, in Portland, OR; daughter of Colin B. (a professor of psychology) and Nancy V. (an economist) Pitblado; married Joseph B. Dulin (a risk management specialist), May 8, 2000; children: Ethan C. *Ethnicity:* "White, non-Hispanic." *Education:* Carleton College, B.A. (magna cum laude), 1990; University of Arizona, M.A., 1993, Ph. D., 1999.

ADDRESSES: Office—Department of Anthropology, 0730 Old Main Hill, Utah State University, Logan, UT 84322-0730; fax: 435-797-1240. *E-mail*—bpitblado@ hass.usu.edu.

CAREER: Writer, archaeologist, anthropologist, and educator. Western State College, Gunnison, CO, visiting professor, 2000-01, assistant professor of anthropology, 2001-02; Utah State University, Logan, assistant professor of anthropology, 2002—. Registered professional archaeologist; member of Utah Professional Archaeological Council, Colorado Council of Professional Archaeologists, and Center for the Study of the First Americans; Sierra Ancha Cliff Swelling Documentation Project, crew chief, 1995; worked as archaeological technician in Arizona, New Mexico, and Colorado, and at La Quina Neanderthal site in France; volunteer at Lehner Clovis site excavation and Lower Twin Mountain Folsom site excavation. Organizer of symposia; conference presenter.

MEMBER: American Anthropological Association, Society for American Archaeology (and its Women in Archaeology interest group and Geoarchaeology interest group), Plains Anthropological Society, Colorado Archaeological Society, Montana Archaeological Society, Wyoming Archaeological Society, Phi Beta Kappa, Sigma Xi.

AWARDS, HONORS: Telly Award for *Archaeology: Why It Rocks!;* grants from George C. Frison Anthropological Institute, Colorado Historical Society,

U.S. Bureau of Land Management, U.S. Forest Service, Marie Eccles Caine Foundation, and Institute of Museum and Library Services.

WRITINGS:

Late Paleoindian Occupation of the Southern Rocky Mountains, University Press of Colorado (Niwot, CO), 2003.

(With Beth Ann Camp, Stu Parkinson, and Dave Smellie) *Archaeology: Why It Rocks!* (juvenile; videotape with interactive CD-ROM), Media Services, Utah State University (Logan, UT), 2003.

Contributor to books, including *Climate Change in the Four Corners and Adjacent Regions: Implications for Environmental Restoration and Land Use Planning,* edited by W. Waugh, K. Petersen, and others, National Technical Information Service, (Springfield, VA), 1995; *River of Change: Prehistory of the Middle Little Colorado River Valley, Arizona,* edited by E. Charles Adams, Arizona State Museum (Tucson, AZ), 1996; and *Colorado Prehistory: A Context for the Southern Colorado River Basin,* edited by W.D. Lipe, M.D. Varien, and R.H. Wilshusen, Colorado Council of Professional Archaeologists (Denver, CO), 1999. Contributor of articles and reviews to journals, including *Plains Anthropologist, Southwestern Lore, Current Research in the Pleistocene, Journal of California and Great Basin Anthropology,* and *Mountain Geologist.*

WORK IN PROGRESS: Editing *Emerging Frontiers in Colorado Paleoindian Archaeology,* with Robert H. Brunswig; research on Paleoindian occupation of the southern Rocky Mountains.

SIDELIGHTS: Bonnie L. Pitblado told *CA:* "I write to communicate my research to other scholars, although I try to use language that everyone can understand. I love the English language—love words—and I try to use it well. My primary influences are those few archaeologists who write in an engaging fashion and treat their fellow researchers with civility and respect when discussing their work.

"Most of my research, and hence my writing, has been on the earliest human occupants of the Rocky Mountains, circa 10,000-7,500 years ago. My influence is the beauty and grandeur of the mountains themselves!;

"I am a methodical (sometimes I think plodding) writer. I start with the introduction and work my way through a manuscript in a highly linear fashion. I can't skip from section to section or manuscript to manuscript. If I start something, I finish it before I start something else."

BIOGRAPHICAL AND CRITICAL SOURCES:

ONLINE

Bonnie L. Pitblado Home Page, http://www.paleo indian.net (March 1, 2005).

*   *   *

POLITZER, Georges 1903-1942
(François Arouet)

PERSONAL: Born May 3, 1903, in Nagyvarad, Hungary; executed in Paris, France, May 23, 1942; married; wife's name Mai.

CAREER: Philosopher, writer, educator. Taught school in various places, including the cities of Moulins, Evreux, and Saint-Maur; also taught Workers' University; cofounder of *La Pensée;* founder of *L'Université Libre* and *La Pensée Libre,* c. 1940.

MEMBER: Teachers Union, French Communist Party (head of economic commission of the central committee).

WRITINGS:

Critique des fondements de la psychologie, Reider (Paris France), 1928, translation by Maurice Apprey published as *Critique of the Foundations of Psychology: The Psychology of Psychoanalysis,* Duquesne University Press (Pittsburgh, PA), 1994.

(As François Arouet) *La fin d'une parade philosophique: le Bergsonism,* Les Revues (Paris, France), 1929, reprinted under author's real name, J.J. Pauvert (Paris, France), 1969.

Les grands problèmes de la philosophie contemporaine, Bureau d'éditions (Paris, France), 1938.

Principes élémentaires de philosophie, Éditions Sociales (Paris, France), 1946, translation by Barbara L. Morris published as *Elementary Principles of Philosophy,* International Publishers (New York, NY), 1976.

Cours de philosophie, Éditions Sociales (Paris, France), 1946, translation by G.P. O'Day published as *An Elementary Course in Philosophy,* Curren Book Distributors (Sydney, Australia), 1950

Révolution et contre-revolution au XXe siècle, Éditions Sociales (Paris, France), 1947.

Bergsonisme: une mystification philosophique, Éditions Sociales (Paris, France), 1947.

La philosophie et les mythes (title means "The Philosophy and the Myths"), Éditions Sociales (Paris, France), 1969.

Les fondements de la psychologie, (title means "The Fundamentals of Psychology"), Éditions Sociales (Paris, France), 1969.

Ecrits (includes *La philosophie et les mythes* and *Les fondements de la psychologie*), edited by Jacques Debouzy, Editions Sociales (Paris, France), 1969.

Ecrits. II: les fondements de la psychologie (title means "The Fundamentals of Psychology"), Éditions Sociales (Paris, France), 1973.

Works published in several languages, including English, Polish, German, Kurdish, Turkish, Spanish, Italian, and Russian.

SIDELIGHTS: Hungarian Georges Politzer moved to France, where he gained fame as a leading Marxist theorist and psychologist. His first major work, *Critique des fondements de la psychologie,* sought to make psychology concrete and scientific. According to Terry Kupers in an essay for *Science and Society,* Politzer "designated the human Drama as the specific object for a scientific psychology. This Drama is the set of psychological facts that involve the subject as first person (Je) in acts that, while related to psychological processes that parallel them and to social and economic determinants that influence them, are themselves distinct as segments of the life of a particular individual." For Politzer, it was critical that psychology not be reduced to biology, physiology, or sociology. At the same time, he rejected nineteenth-century notions of purely interior life and Freudian unconscious. While greatly admiring Freud's theories of latent content and repression, Politzer thought the concept of an unconscious, where unacknowledged

thoughts reside, gave thoughts themselves too much reality. "Politzer's contribution to the development of a scientific psychology rests secure on the basis of [*Critique des fondements de la psychologie*], in which he insisted on rigor, an adequate definition of objects for a science, and a concrete study of the subject of the human drama," wrote Kupers.

In addition to his writings on psychology, Politzer also contributed to an introduction to *Principes élémentaires de philosophie,* which was translated into English as *Elementary Principles of Philosophy.* "A little classic in France since it first appeared in the days before World War II," according to *Science and Society* contributor Henry Mins, it provides a summary of Marxist philosophical foundations aimed at the layman, specifically the working man. While faulting it for some logical discrepancies, *Black Scholar* contributor Jack Carson, Jr., noted that the book's "general approach to the subject matter . . . is articulate, informative, and almost always correct."

Politzer was executed by the Nazis during their occupation of France in 1942.

BIOGRAPHICAL AND CRITICAL SOURCES:

PERIODICALS

Black Scholar, May-June, 1978, Jack Carson, Jr., review of *Elementary Principles of Philosophy,* pp. 42-44.

Science and Society, spring, 1973, Terry Kupers, "Historical Materialism and Scientific Psychology," pp. 81-90; summer, 1977, Henry Mins, review of *Elementary Principles of Philosophy,* p. 254.*

*   *   *

POPE, Hugh

PERSONAL: Male. *Education:* Attended the University of Oxford.

ADDRESSES: Agent—c/o Author Mail, Overlook Press, 1 Overlook Dr., Woodstock, NY 12498.

CAREER: Journalist and writer. Manages the *Wall Street Journal*'s Istanbul bureau. Has also worked for the *Los Angeles Times,* Reuters, and the BBC.

WRITINGS:

(With Nicole Pope) *Turkey Unveiled: Ataturk and After,* John Murray (London, England), 1997, also published as *Turkey Unveiled: A History of Modern Turkey,* Overlook Press (Woodstock, NY), 1998.

Sons of the Conquerors: The Rise of the Turkic World, Overlook Duckworth (New York, NY), 2005.

SIDELIGHTS: Hugh Pope is a writer and journalist who has written extensively about Turkey and the surrounding region as the Istanbul bureau chief for the *Wall Street Journal.* Pope has also worked as a reporter for other periodicals and news sources, including the *Los Angeles Times,* Reuters, and the BBC. He began his study of the Turkic region and cultures in college, as a student at the University of Oxford studying Arabic and Persian. Pope speaks fluent Turkish.

In 2005, Pope published *Sons of the Conquerors: The Rise of the Turkic World.* The book covers more than a decade of travels throughout the Turkic region, which includes the countries of Turkey, Azerbaijan, Turkmenistan, Uzbekistan, Kazakhstan, and the Kyrgyz Republic. The book is organized by what the author believes to be seven shared characteristics of the Turkic peoples, such as military vocation. Pope includes detailed information about Turkic culture that he has collected through interviews with both government officials and regular people.

Critics responded positively to *Sons of the Conquerors* overall. Many readers found the book to contain a wealth of information about the Turkic region, covering a wide range of topics and characteristics. Pope's book is "the most comprehensive work on the Turks today," wrote a reviewer for the *Economist.* Other readers found Pope to be an observant journalist, gleaning much inside knowledge and insight into the Turkic people. *Sons of the Conquerors* gives readers a "sensitive presentation of how Turks view themselves and their future," observed Gilbert Taylor in a review for *Booklist.*

BIOGRAPHICAL AND CRITICAL SOURCES:

PERIODICALS

Booklist, April 1, 2005, Gilbert Taylor, review of *Sons of the Conquerors: The Rise of the Turkic World,* p. 1340.
Economist, May 21, 2005, review of *Sons of the Conquerors,* p. 85.
For a Change, October-November, 1997, review of *Turkey Unveiled: Ataturk and After,* p. 20.
Kirkus Reviews, March 15, 2005, review of *Sons of the Conquerors,* p. 340.
Library Journal, June 1, 2005, Sean Michael Fleming, review of *Sons of the Conquerors,* p. 148.*

*   *   *

POWELL, Corey S. 1966-

PERSONAL: Born 1966.

ADDRESSES: *Home*—Brooklyn, NY. *Office*—Discover, 90 5th Ave., 11th Fl., New York, NY 10011.

CAREER: Writer, journalist, and editor. *Discover* magazine, New York, NY, editor and contributor; New York University, New York, NY, adjunct professor of science journalism. Previous positions include *Scientific American,* board of editors; *Physics Today*; and National Aeronautics and Space Administration (NASA) Goddard Space Flight Center, MD, gamma-ray telescope tester.

WRITINGS:

God in the Equation: How Einstein Became the Prophet of the New Religious Era, Free Press (New York, NY), 2002.

Has written for numerous publications, including *Scientific American, New York Times, San Francisco Chronicle,* and *Newsday.*

SIDELIGHTS: Longtime science writer and editor Corey S. Powell argues against the idea that science and religion are mutually exclusive in his first book, *God* in the Equation: How Einstein Became the Prophet of the New Religious Era. Referring to the new faith of "sci/religion," Powell delves into the world of physics from Einstein and beyond and reflects on his theory that famed physicist Albert Einstein paved a way for sci/religion that subsequent generations followed. These physicist's efforts focused on "framing models of the universe that reflect, a worshipful devotion to cosmic harmony," as noted by *Booklist* contributor Bryce Christensen. Powell also argues that Einstein is the "prophet" of this new religion because of his establishment of the theory of relativity, which combines certain aspects of both physics and metaphysics. In the book, the author explores such aspects of physics as dark energy and matter, which may be the unifying forces in the universe. The world of subatomic particles, the author contends, has a "mystical" connection and may provide the final clues for solving the puzzle of human consciousness.

In a review of *God in the Equation,* a *Kirkus Reviews* contributor wrote: "General, generous readers with an interest in science . . . will find this provocative, securely grounded in contemporary theories of physics, and at least worth pondering." Writing in *Science News,* another reviewer noted that the author "details many recent, startling revelations by cosmologists." A *Publishers Weekly* contributor wrote that Powell "convincingly shows the ways that science has molded itself into a new faith, and his book will surely generate controversy and skepticism."

BIOGRAPHICAL AND CRITICAL SOURCES:

PERIODICALS

Booklist, August, 2002, Bryce Christensen, review of *God in the Equation: How Einstein Became the Prophet of the New Religious Era,* p. 1894.
Kirkus Reviews, June 1, 2002, review of *God in the Equation,* p. 791.
Publishers Weekly, July 15, 2002, review of *God in the Equation,* p. 70.
Science News, October 5, 2002, review of *God in the Equation,* p. 223.

ONLINE

Discover Magazine Web site, http://www.discover.com/ (March 10, 2006), brief profile of author.

PRATT, Tim 1976-

PERSONAL: Born 1976; married Heather Shaw.

ADDRESSES: Home—Oakland, CA. *Agent*—c/o Author Mail, Night Shade Books, 1470 N.W. Saltzman Rd., Portland, OR 97229.

CAREER: Writer and poet. *Flytrap* (literary magazine), Oakland, CA, coeditor; *Locus* magazine, Oakland, CA, editor and book reviewer.

AWARDS, HONORS: Strange Horizons 2002 Reader's Choice Awards for Fiction, and Nebula Award nominee, 2003, both for *Little Gods;* Rhysling Award, long poem category, 2005, for "Soul Searching."

WRITINGS:

(With wife, Heather Shaw) *Living Together in Mythic Times* (chapbook), Tropism Press (Oakland, CA), 2001.
(With Heather Shaw) *Floodwater* (chapbook), Tropism Press (Oakland, CA), 2002.
(With Erin Donahoe) *Love: Sensual, Subversive, and Erotic Poetry and Art,* Vixen Press (San Francisco, CA), 2003.
Little Gods (short stories and poetry), Prime Books (Holicong, PA), 2003.
(With Heather Shaw) *Wintering Away* (chapbook), Tropism Press (Oakland, CA), 2003.
Pook's Original Miscellany (chapbook), Tropism Press (Oakland, CA), 2004.
The Strange Adventures of Rangergirl (novel), Bantam Spectra (New York, NY), 2005.
If There Were Wolves (poetry), Prime/Aegis, 2006.
Hart & Boot & Other Stories, Night Shade Books (Portland, OR), 2006.

Contributor of short stories to anthologies, including *TEL: Stories,* 2005; *The Best American Short Stories: 2005; The Year's Best Fantasy and Horror;* and *Twenty Epics,* 2006. Contributor of short stories to periodicals, including *Asimov's Science Fiction Magazine, Journal of Mythic Arts, Journal of Pulse-Pounding Narratives, Ultraverse, Realms of Fantasy, Polyphony, Third*

Alternative, Fortean Bureau, Intracities, Ideomancer, Abyss & Apex, Horrorfind, Far Sector, Slow Trains, Elysian Fiction, Twilight Showcase, and *Fantasy* magazine.

Contributor of poetry to periodicals, including *Asimov's Science Fiction Magazine, Strange Horizons, Snow Monkey, Chiaroscuro, Electric Wine, Recursive Angel, Modern Art Cave,* and *Jabberwocky.*

SIDELIGHTS: The author of fantasy, science fiction, and poetry, Tim Pratt has also collaborated with his wife, writer Heather Shaw, on several books, including *Floodwater,* which features solo efforts by both writers and a collaborative story. Commenting on Pratt's solo short story, "The Heart, a Chambered Nautilus," *Magazine of Fantasy and Science Fiction* contributor Charles De Lint noted that "the pleasure is in Pratt's language and in the payoff at the story's end." In his first solo collection, titled *Little Gods,* Pratt presents fifteen stories and four poems, including the Nebula-nominated title story. In a review in *Publishers Weekly,* a contributor commented that the author "is a writer to watch." Pratt's first novel, *The Strange Adventures of Rangergirl,* tells the story of Marzipan "Marzi" McCarty, who drops out of art school and becomes a writer of comics featuring the character of "Rangergirl" while working nights at a coffeehouse. When McCarty suspects that events in the real world are mirroring her comic stories, she discovers that she is the only one that can fight off impending disaster in the form of western villains coming from another dimension. Writing in *Booklist,* Regina Schroeder commented that "Marzi travels beyond the possible into a grand and magical western, indeed."

BIOGRAPHICAL AND CRITICAL SOURCES:

PERIODICALS

Booklist, November 15, 2005, Regina Schroeder, review of *The Strange Adventures of Rangergirl,* p. 33.

Kirkus Reviews, October 15, 2005, review of *The Strange Adventures of Rangergirl,* p. 1114.

Magazine of Fantasy and Science Fiction, June, 2003, Charles De Lint, review of *Floodwater,* p. 85.

Publishers Weekly, November 3, 2003, review of *Little Gods,* p. 59; October, 10, 2005, review of *The Strange Adventures of Rangergirl,* p. 41.

ONLINE

SFF Net, http://www.sff.net/ (January 19, 2005), "Tim Pratt's Bio."*

*   *   *

PRIOR, Robin

PERSONAL: Male.

ADDRESSES: Office—Australian Defense Force Academy, University of New South Wales, Canberra, Australian Capital Territory 2600, Australia. *E-mail*—r. prior@adfa.edu.au.

CAREER: Historian, educator, and writer. Australian Defense Force Academy, University of New South Wales, Canberra, Australia, associate professor and head of the School of Humanities and Social Sciences.

WRITINGS:

HISTORIES

Churchill's World Crisis As History, Croom Helm (London, England), 1983.

(With Trevor Wilson) *Command on the Western Front: The Military Career of Sir Henry Rawlinson, 1914-1918,* Basil Blackwell (Cambridge, MA), 1992, reprinted, Pen & Sword Books (Barnsley, South Yorkshire, England), 2004.

(With Trevor Wilson) *Passchendaele: The Untold Story,* Yale University Press (New Haven, CT), 1996, 2nd edition, 2002.

(With Trevor Wilson) *The First World War,* edited by John Keegan, Cassell (London, England), 1999, Smithsonian Books (Washington, DC), 2004.

(With Trevor Wilson) *The Somme,* Yale University Press (New Haven, CT), 2005.

Contributor to the *Oxford Companion to Australian Military History,* Oxford University Press (Melbourne, Australia), 1995.

SIDELIGHTS: Robin Prior is a historian whose primary interest is the military history of World War I, specifically concerning commanders and their competence and how technology impacted both the tactics and economics of the war. Prior has written several books with Trevor Wilson, including *Passchendaele: The Untold Story.* Drawing on previously unavailable material from a variety of sources, including documents from the Public Record Office in Kew and the Australian War Memorial, the authors provide new insight into one of the First World War's most legendary encounters. The Battle of Passchendaele in Flanders resulted in the deaths of approximately 275,000 Allied and 200,000 German soldiers. Writing in *History: Review of New Books,* Agnes F. Peterson noted that previous books about the battle have been written but that *Passchendaele* "makes its own contribution by concentrating on military plans and decisions rather than on human interest stories." Peterson added: "The text is clearly and succinctly written, and the arguments and explanations are persuasive, underpinned by excellent maps."

In their book *The First World War,* Prior and Trevor Wilson offer a look at the ground conflicts and battles on the European fronts. Writing in the *Library Journal,* James Tasato Mellone commented: "It is fitting at the close of the twentieth century that some thought be given to the initial calamity that set the century upon its destructive course." Prior is also a contributor to *The Oxford Companion to Australian Military History,* which *Journal of the Royal Australian Historical Society* contributor Ralph Sutton called "a valuable military history reference source."

Prior and Trevor Wilson focus on another historical battle in their book *The Somme.* In addition to writing about the infamous day of July 1, 1916, when 19,240 British soldiers died out of a total of 57,470 casualties, the authors explore the remaining months of battle as well. In their account, the authors make the case that the British effort to take the Somme was misconceived and did not stop the forward progress of the Germans into Romania. They further criticize the effort by noting that the British command could still have called off the battle, which continued to rage after that fateful day. Frederic Krome, writing in the *Library Journal,* pointed out that the authors go against the accepted historical account of soldiers being forced to march off to their doom, "replacing it with a picture of poor tactical coherence among the British commanders and faulty battle preparations." A *Contemporary Review* contributor wrote: "This is a magisterial piece of scholarship . . . presented in a clear, balanced and straightforward manner."

BIOGRAPHICAL AND CRITICAL SOURCES:

PERIODICALS

Contemorary Review, July, 2005, review of *The Somme,* p. 64.
History: Review of New Books, spring, 1997, Agnes F. Peterson, review of *Passchendaele: The Untold Story,* p. 123.
Journal of the Royal Australian Historical Society, June, 1998, Ralph Sutton, review of *The Oxford Companion to Australian Military History,* p. 97.
Library Journal, May 1, 2000, James Tasato Mellone, review of *The First World War,* p. 133; May 1, 2005, Frederic Krome, review of *The Somme,* p. 102.
Sabretache, September, 2005, Anthony Staunton, review of *The Somme,* p. 61.
Spectator, July 9, 2005, Alan Judd, review of *The Somme,* p. 37.

ONLINE

Australian Defense Force Academy, University of New South Wales Web site, http://www.unsw.adfa.edu.au/ (March 10, 2006), faculty profile of author.*

*　　*　　*

PUCHNER, Eric

PERSONAL: Married Katharine Noel (a novelist). *Education:* Attended Middlebury College and University of Arizona, Tucson.

ADDRESSES: Home—San Francisco, CA. *Agent*—Dorian Karchmar, William Morris Agency, 1325 Avenue of the Americas, New York, NY 10019. *E-mail*—eric@ericpuchner.com.

CAREER: Writer and educator. San Francisco State University, San Francisco, CA, taught English; Stanford University, Stanford, CA, faculty member, former Wallace Stegner and John L'Heureux Fellow; runs nonprofit training program for immigrants.

AWARDS, HONORS: Pushcart Prize and the Joseph Henry Jackson Award, both for *Music through the Floor.*

WRITINGS:

Music through the Floor: Stories, Scribner (New York, NY), 2005.

Contributor of stories to anthologies and periodicals, including the *Chicago Tribune, Zoetrope: All Story, Missouri Review, Glimmer Train,* and *Best New American Voices 2005.*

SIDELIGHTS: Eric Puchner contributed numerous short stories to top literary journals before his first collection of short fiction, *Music through the Floor: Stories,* was published in 2005. The collection features nine stories written from numerous perspectives, including adults, children, immigrants, and tourists. For example, in "Essay #3: Leda and the Swan," a teenage girl uses a homework assignment to reveal the emotional turmoil that she is experiencing. "Neon Tetras" is about a young boy who recognizes that his dad is attracted to a pretty, young salesclerk at a pet store. In another story, "Children of God," a young social worker who is a loner identifies with the two mentally retarded men that he is caring for, recognizing that they are also outsiders and discovering that, in their own way, they are also very brave. "Don't miss this introduction to a genuinely talented find," wrote a *Kirkus Reviews* contributor. Nicholas Fonseca, writing in *Entertainment Weekly,* called the collection a "wry, incisive book." In a review in *Booklist,* Donna Seaman was particularly impressed with the author's "insight into outsiders, fluency in pain and irony, and edgy humor." A *Publishers Weekly* contributor commented that "Puchner delivers emotional nuance with sure-handed prose."

BIOGRAPHICAL AND CRITICAL SOURCES:

PERIODICALS

Booklist, November 15, 2005, Donna Seaman, review of *Music through the Floor: Stories,* p. 28.

Entertainment Weekly, November 11, 2005, Nicholas Fonseca, review of *Music through the Floor,* p. 76.
Kirkus Reviews, September 15, 2005, review of *Music through the Floor,* p. 999.
Publishers Weekly, October 10, 2005, review of *Music through the Floor,* p. 37.

ONLINE

Eric Puchner Home Page, http://ericpuchner.com (January 19, 2006).*

*   *   *

PUNKE, Michael

PERSONAL: Male.

ADDRESSES: *Home*—MT. *Agent*—c/o Author Mail, Hyperion Editorial Department, 77 W. 66th St., 11th Fl., New York, NY 10023.

CAREER: Lawyer and writer. Former partner in a Washington, DC, law firm; worked on Capitol Hill and with the White House National Security Council.

WRITINGS:

The Revenant (novel), Carroll & Graf Publishers (New York, NY), 2002.
Fire and Brimstone: The North Butte Mining Disaster of 1917, Hyperion (New York, NY), 2006.

ADAPTATIONS: *The Revenant* is being adapted for film by Warner Bros.

SIDELIGHTS: In his first novel, *The Revenant,* Michael Punke recounts a fictionalized version of an historic frontiersman of the "Old West." Hugh Glass leaves Philadelphia as a teenager, spends time on the high seas with a pirate, and then heads to the West only to end up captured by Indians. He eventually escapes and ends up as a trapper with the Rocky Mountain Fur Company. During a trapping expedition, Glass is attacked by a bear and badly mauled. Two of his fellow trappers, John Fitzgerald and Jim Bridger, are left behind by the rest of the group to watch over him until he dies. Fitzgerald and Bridger eventually abandon him, but Glass unexpectedly survives. The novel then follows Glass as he sets out on a journey of epic proportions in pursuit of those he believes to have betrayed him. Along the way, he encounters and enlists the help of Indians and learns their way of life, as well as their survival and tracking skills in the wilderness. "A good adventure yarn, with plenty of historical atmosphere and local color," wrote a *Kirkus Reviews* contributor. A *Publishers Weekly* reviewer commented, "Told in simple expository language, this is a spellbinding tale of heroism and obsessive retribution."

BIOGRAPHICAL AND CRITICAL SOURCES:

PERIODICALS

Kirkus Reviews, April 15, 2002, review of *The Revenant*, p. 521.
Publishers Weekly, May 6, 2002, review of *The Revenant*, p. 31.*

*   *   *

PURVIS, Alston W. 1943-

PERSONAL: Born 1943; son of Melvin Purvis (a lawyer and law enforcement agent). *Education:* Virginia Commonwealth University, B.F.A.; Yale University, M.F.A.

ADDRESSES: Office—Boston University College of Fine Arts, 855 Commonwealth Ave., Boston, MA 02215. *E-mail*—apurvis@bu.edu.

CAREER: Graphic designer, translator, writer, and educator. Cooper Union, New York, NY, instructor, 1969-70; Royal Academy of Fine Arts, The Hague, Netherlands, associate professor, 1971-82; School of Visual Arts, New York, NY, director *ad interim,* 1998-2002; Boston University, Boston, MA, chairman of Graphic Design, c. 2002—; freelance graphic designer and translator for major galleries, corporations, and publishers. Also presented lectures at the American

Institute of Graphic Arts, the Wolfsonian Foundation at Florida International University, and elsewhere. *Exhibitions:* Solo and group exhibitions, including exhibitions in Amsterdam, Rotterdam, The Hague, London, New York, and Paris.

WRITINGS:

Dutch Graphic Design, 1918-1945, Van Nostrand Reinhold (New York, NY), 1992.
(With Martijn F. Le Coultre) *A Century of Posters,* Waanders (Zwolle, Netherlands), 2003.
(With Martijn F. Le Coultre) *Graphic Design 20th Century,* Princeton Architectural Press (New York, NY), 2003.
(With Philip B. Meggs) *Meggs' History of Graphic Design,* J. Wiley (Hoboken, NJ), 2005.
(With Alex Tresniowski) *The Vendetta: FBI Hero Melvin Purvis's War against Crime, and J. Edgar Hoover's War against Him,* Public Affairs Press (New York, NY), 2005.

Contributor of an essay to *Wendingen 1918-1932: A Journal for the Arts,* by Martijn F. Le Coultre, Princeton Architectural Press (New York, NY), 2001.

SIDELIGHTS: Alston W. Purvis has worked primarily as a graphic designer and educator and has authored or coauthored several graphic-design books. For example, in *A Century of Posters,* which he co-produced with Martijn F. Le Coultre, Purvis provides an introductory discussion of the history of posters, their changing styles, and the artists who produced them. The book also includes more than 400 illustrations of posters.

Although Purvis is known as an accomplished graphic designer, his father, Melvyn Purvis, achieved widespread national public acclaim in the 1930s and 1940s as a dedicated Federal Bureau of Investigation (FBI) agent who played a primary role in capturing some of the era's most notorious criminals, including John Dillinger. In *The Vendetta: FBI Hero Melvin Purvis's War against Crime, and J. Edgar Hoover's War against Him,* Purvis and collaborator Alex Tresniowski recount Purvis's father's career in the FBI and how then FBI director Hoover turned from an ardent supporter of Purvis to a jealous boss who tried to hamper the career of his one-time protégé even after the senior

Purvis left the FBI. A *Publishers Weekly* contributor called the book a "fascinating story." Deirdre Bray Root, writing in the *Library Journal*, noted that "this exciting story rings true." In a review in *Booklist*, Connie Fletcher called the book "gripping reading for true-crime fans."

BIOGRAPHICAL AND CRITICAL SOURCES:

PERIODICALS

Booklist, September 15, 2005, Connie Fletcher, *The Vendetta: FBI Hero Melvin Purvis's War against Crime, and J. Edgar Hoover's War against Him*, p. 12.

Library Journal, October 15, 2002, Anne Marie Lane, review of *A Century of Posters*, p. 69; October 1, 2005, Deirdre Bray Root, review of *The Vendetta*, p. 95.

Publishers Weekly, August 29, 2005, review of *The Vendetta*, p. 49.

ONLINE

South Dakota Public Broadcasting Web site, http://www.sdpb.org/ (April 29, 2003), Brian Bull, "Alston Purvis," radio interview with author.*

R

RANDALL, Lisa 1962-

PERSONAL: Born June 18, 1962; daughter of a sales representative (father) and primary schoolteacher (mother). *Education:* Harvard University, B.A., 1983, Ph.D., 1987.

ADDRESSES: Home—Cambridge, MA. *Office*—Harvard University, Department of Physics, 17 Oxford St., Cambridge, MA 02138. *E-mail*—randall@physics. harvard.edu.

CAREER: Theoretical physicist, educator, and writer. Harvard University, Cambridge, MA, teaching assistant, 1984, Adams House physics tutor, 1984-87, assistant senior tutor, 1985-87; University of California, Berkeley, CA, president's fellow, 1987-89; Lawrence Berkeley Laboratory, postdoctoral fellow, 1989-90; Massachusetts Institute of Technology (MIT), Cambridge, MA, assistant professor, 1991-95, associate professor, 1995-98, professor of physics, 1998-2001; Princeton University, Princeton, NJ, professor of physics, 1998-2000; Harvard University, Cambridge, MA, professor of theoretical physics, 2001—. Also Harvard Society of Fellows, junior fellow, 1990-91; Radcliffe Institute fellow, 2002; Radcliffe Institute Cosmology and Theoretical Astrophysics Cluster, chair, 2003; has served as associate editor of *Nuclear Physics,* 1999—, and editor of the *Annual Review of Nuclear and Particle Science,* 1997—, and the *Journal of High Energy Physics,* 1997-98, 2000—.

MEMBER: American Academy of Arts and Sciences, American Physical Society (fellow), Phi Beta Kappa.

AWARDS, HONORS: Westinghouse Science Talent Search winner; John Harvard Scholarship; Radcliffe Scholar; Elizabeth Cary Agassiz Scholar; Bell Labs Graduate Research Fellowship for Women, David J. Robbins Prize; National Science Foundation Young Investigator Award, Department of Energy Outstanding Junior Investigator Award, and Alfred P. Sloan Foundation Research Fellowship, all 1992; Premio Caterina Tomassoni e Felice Pietro Chisesi Award, University of Rome, La Sapienza, 2003; American Academy of Arts and Sciences (AAAS) Fellow, 2004; Klopsted Award, American Association of Physics Teachers, 2006.

WRITINGS:

Warped Passages: Unraveling the Mysteries of the Universe's Hidden Dimensions, Ecco (New York, NY), 2005.

Contributor to physics and science journals, including *Physical Review Letters* and *Nature,* and to mainstream periodicals, including the *New York Times* and the *Daily Telegraph.*

SIDELIGHTS: Lisa Randall is a theoretical physicist who studies particle physics and cosmology and conducts research into the fundamental nature of particles and forces. In her book *Warped Passages: Unraveling the Mysteries of the Universe's Hidden Dimensions,* the author explores her research into the theory that there are many more dimensions to the world than the three we perceive. Randall explains recent theories that include extra dimensions and brane-worlds that cannot be perceived from our perspective in the universe. She also provides a brief historical analysis of physics in the twentieth century and some of the major theories behind relativity and quantum mechanics.

In an article on the *Sunday Times* Web site, Sarah Baxter wrote: "There is . . . something beautiful and appealing about her research. Randall's hidden dimensions can be infinitesimally large or small in size, rolled and compressed like a hosepipe or warped like a distorting mirror at a funfair. A new universe—several, in fact—could fit alongside our own." Writing in *Booklist,* Gilbert Taylor noted the complexity of the topics but wrote that the author "writes as clearly as possible." A *Publishers Weekly* contributor commented that the author provides "much of the excitement of her field to life as she describes her quest to understand the structure of the universe." In a review in the *Library Journal,* Sara Rutter noted that the author's use of stories and other techniques make Randall "like an extraordinarily smart and lively college professor" who is imparting "the excitement of discovery." Writing in *Science News,* a reviewer noted that the author "provides an excellent primer to the most elusive and groundbreaking concepts of modern physics."

BIOGRAPHICAL AND CRITICAL SOURCES:

PERIODICALS

Booklist, September 1, 2005, Gilbert Taylor, review of *Warped Passages: Unraveling the Mysteries of the Universe's Hidden Dimensions,* p. 34.
Library Journal, September 1, 2005, Sara Rutter, review of *Warped Passages,* p. 174.
Newsweek, December 26, 2005, Jerry Adler, "Lisa Randall; Looking at the Earth's Tiniest Particles to Explain the Mysteries of the Cosmos," p. 86.
Publishers Weekly, July 11, 2005, review of *Warped Passages,* p. 73.
Science News, January 14, 2006, review of *Warped Passages,* p. 31.
SciTech Book News, December, 2005, review of *Warped Passages.*

ONLINE

Department of Physics, Harvard University Web site, http://www.physics.harvard.edu/ (March 11, 2006), faculty profile of author.

Morning News, http://www.themorningnews.org/ (March 11, 2006), Robert Birnbaum, "Birnbaum v. Lisa Randall," interview with author.
Sunday Times Online, http://www.timesonline.co.uk/ (June 19, 2005), Sarah Baxter, "Interview: Sarah Baxter meets Lisa Randall."*

*   *   *

REESE, James 1964-

PERSONAL: Born 1964, in Long Island, NY. *Education:* Attended University of Notre Dame; State University of New York at Stony Brook, M.A.

ADDRESSES: Home—FL. *Agent*—c/o Author Mail, HarperCollins Publishers, 10 E. 53rd St., 7th Fl., New York, NY 10022. *E-mail*—james@jamesreesebooks.com.

CAREER: Writer. Held various jobs in the nonprofit sector in the areas of the arts and the environment.

WRITINGS:

FICTION; "HERCULINE" TRILOGY

The Book of Shadows, William Morrow (New York, NY), 2002.
The Book of Spirits, William Morrow (New York, NY), 2005.

Also author of a play staged off-Broadway at the Actors Repertory Theatre in New York.

WORK IN PROGRESS: The concluding volume of "Herculine" trilogy.

SIDELIGHTS: James Reese is the author of books featuring the supernatural and with strong sexual content. In the first book of the "Herculine" trilogy, the heroine, Herculine, is an orphan in post-Revolutionary France who questions her true nature in terms of gender. She is eventually accused of being a witch and is rescued from a convent by a sorcerer who teaches her the ways of the occult so she can liberate two spirits, the lovers Father Louis and Madeleine de la Mettire, from their human forms. Herculine eventually succeeds in freeing the spirits, learning more about herself and the occult along the way until she recognizes her true identity and leaves Europe for the "New World" in the Americas. Michael Spinella, writing in *Booklist,* noted that the book is "rich in style and allusion, both literary and historical." A *Publishers Weekly* contributor called Reese "a star pupil in the Anne Rice school of dark sensuality."

In *The Book of Spirits,* Herculine is in early 1800s Virginia, where the protagonist becomes involved in the issue of slavery while further developing supernatural powers. In addition to his fictional characters, the author includes historical figures, from Indians such as Chief Osceola to Edgar Allan Poe's mother. In a review in *Booklist,* Debi Lewis wrote, "Part historical fiction, part supernatural tale, this is difficult to put down."

BIOGRAPHICAL AND CRITICAL SOURCES:

PERIODICALS

Booklist, February 1, 2002, Michael Spinella, review of *The Book of Shadows,* p. 924; July, 2005, Debi Lewis, review of *The Book of Spirits,* p. 1901.
Kirkus Reviews, January 1, 2002, review of *The Book of Shadows,* p. 15.
Library Journal, February 1, 2002, Laurel Bliss, review of *The Book of Shadows,* p. 133.
Publishers Weekly, February 4, 2002, review of *The Book of Shadows,* p. 51.

ONLINE

James Reese Home Page, http://www.jamesreese books.com (January 21, 2005).*

*   *   *

REGÀS, Rosa 1933-

PERSONAL: Born 1933, in Barcelona, Spain; married; children: five. *Education:* Attended college; graduated 1964.

ADDRESSES: Office—National Library of Spain, Paseo de Recoletos, 20, 28071 Madrid, Spain.

CAREER: Writer, publisher, and translator. Seix Barral (publisher), Barcelona, Spain, staff member, 1964-70; also worked for publishing house Edhasa during early career; founder and editor of Editorial La Gaya Ciencia (publisher), beginning 1983; founder and director of Revista Arquitecturas Bis y la Revista Cuadernos de la Gaya Ciencia; freelance translator for the United Nations, 1983-94; Ateneo Americano, Casa de América, Madrid, Spain, director, 1994-98; National Library of Spain, director, 2004—.

AWARDS, HONORS: Premio Nadal Prize, 1994, for *Azul;* Planeta Award, 2001, for *La Canción de Dorotea;* Sor Juana Inés de la Cruz Prize, for *Nosotras que nos gueremos tanto;* City of Barcelona Prize, for *Luna lunera.*

WRITINGS:

(Translator) Alan Coren, *Arthur el Solitario* (juvenile), illustrated by John Astrop, Altea (Madrid, Spain), 1986.
Ginebra, Ediciones Destino (Barcelona, Spain), 1988.
Memoria de Almator, Planeta (Barcelona, Spain), 1991.
Azul (novel; title means "Blue"), Ediciones Destino (Barcelona, Spain), 1994.
Viaje a la luz del Cham: Damasco, El Cham, un pedazo de tierra en el paraíso, Ediciones Destino (Barcelona, Spain), 1995.
Canciones de amor y de batalla: 1993-1995, El Pais/ Aguilar (Madrid, Spain) 1995.
Pobre corazón (title means "Poor Heart"), Ediciones Destino (Madrid, Spain), 1996.
(With Miquel Roca Junyent) *Los Nacionalismos en la España democrática: reflexiones 1996,* Ediciones Desinto (Barcelona, Spain), 1997.
Nosotras que nos gueremos tanto (novel; title means "We Who Love Each Other So Much"), Alfaguara (Madrid, Spain), 1997.
Genève: portait de ville par une Méditerranéenne, Les Editions Metropolis (Geneva, Switzerland), 1997.
(With Matias Briansó) *España: una nueva Mirada,* Lunwerg (Barcelona, Spain), 1997.
Desde el mar, Alianza (Madrid, Spain), 1997.

Sombras, nada más, Coordinacion de Difusion Cultural, Direccion de Literatura, UNAM, (Mexico, D.F.), 1998.

(With Gamel Woolsey) *Málaga en Llamas,* Temas de Hoy (Madrid, Spain), 1998.

Sangre de mi sangre: la aventura de los hijos, Temas de Hoy (Madrid, Spain), 1998.

(Selector and author of prologue) *Barcelona, un dia: un llibre de contes de la ciutat / presentación de Pasqual Maragall,* Grupo Santillana de Ediciones (Madrid, Spain), 1998.

Más canciones—1995-1998, Prames (Zaragoza, Spain), 1998.

Luna Lunera (novel; title means "Moony Moon"), Plaza & Janes (Barcelona, Spain), 1999.

(Editor and coordinator) *De Madrid—al cielo,* Muchnik Editores (Barcelona, Spain), 2000.

(Translator) Robert Louis Stevenson, *El extraño caso del Dr. Jekyll y Mr. Hyde,* Mondadori (Barcelona, Spain), 2000.

La Canción de Dorotea, (novel; title means "Dorothy's Song"), Planeta (Barcelona, Spain), 2001.

Lo que está en mi corazón (novel; title means "What Is in My Heart), Planeta (Barcelona, Spain), 2001.

Per un món millor, prologue by Josep Cuní, Ara Llibres (Barcelona, Spain), 2002.

Diario de una abuela de verano, Planeta (Barcelona, Spain), 2004.

Valor de la protesta: el compromiso con la vida, edited by Ignacio Fuentes, Icaria Editorial (Barcelona, Spain), 2004.

(With Pedro Molina Temboury) *Volcanes dormidos: un viaje por Centroamérica,* Ediciones B (Barcelona, Spain), 2005.

Viento armado, Planeta (Barcelona, Spain), 2006.

Contributor to books, including *El cuadro del mes,* Fundación Thyssen-Bornemisza (Madrid, Spain), 1997; *"Gauche divine,"* Ministerio de Educacion y Cultura/Lunwer Editores (Spain), 2000; *Cuentos de las dos orillas,* edited by José Monleón, Fundacion el Legado Andalusi (Granada, Spain), 2001; and *Inmenso prostíbulo: mujer y moralidad durante el franquismo,* edited by Assumpta Roura, Editorial Base (Barcelona, Spain), 2005; contributor to periodicals, including *El País* and *El Mundo.* Several of Regàs's works have been translated into Catalan.

SIDELIGHTS: Rosa Regàs is a well-known Spanish writer and novelist who won the prestigious 2001 Planeta Award, which includes a cash prize of over half a million dollars. Her Planet Award-winning novel, *La Canción de Dorotea* ("Dorothy's Song") focuses on a household torn apart after a university professor hires a caretaker for her sick father only to have a valuable ring turn up missing soon afterwards. In her novel *Azul* ("Blue") the author tells the story of Andrea and Martín. The married Andrea is having an affair with the younger Martín in a story that *World Literature Today* contributor David Ross Gerling compared to "*a novella rosa*" in that the story on the surface seems banal and unsophisticated. Actually, as Gerling pointed out, the novel showcases Regàs's ability to reveal the inner lives of both characters, even though their love affair is pedestrian in many ways and the characters eventually develop a growing dislike for each other, making them somewhat unsympathetic. In addition, the reviewer praised the author's descriptive passages, including those of the Mediterranean Sea and the Greek isles. Noting the novel's "insanely felicitous combination of high style and pulp fiction," Gerling went on to call the novel "amusingly manipulative, formidably well written, and not least of all, beautiful."

BIOGRAPHICAL AND CRITICAL SOURCES:

PERIODICALS

Library Journal, February 1, 2002, "Rosa Regàs Wins 2001 Planeta Award."

World Literature Today, spring, 1995, David Ross Gerling, review of *Azul,* p. 331.

ONLINE

Euroresidentes, http://www.euroresidentes.com/ (May 11, 2004), "Rosa Regas Next Director of the National Library of Spain."

Rosa Regàs Home Page, http://www.rosaregas.net (July 1, 2006).

OTHER

Catalan Novelist Rosa Regàs Reads from Her Work and Is Interviewed by Georgette Dorn (sound recording), Library of Congress, 2005.*

RHOADS, Colleen
   See COBLE, Colleen

*   *   *

RIVARD, Robert 1952-

PERSONAL: Born November 17, 1952, in Petoskey, MI; married Monika Maeckle (a media executive); children: Nicolas, Alexander. *Education:* University of Texas at San Antonio, bachelor's degree; graduated from Northwestern University, Kellogg Graduate School of Business.

ADDRESSES: Office—San Antonio Express-News, 400 3rd St., San Antonio, TX 78287-2171. *E-mail*—bob@robertrivard.com.

CAREER: Journalist. *Brownsville Herald,* Brownsville, TX, sports reporter, *Corpus Christi Caller Times,* Corpus Christi, TX, news reporter; 1970s; *Dallas Times Herald,* Dallas, TX, news reporter, c. 1980-83; *Newsweek* magazine, Central American bureau chief, became chief of correspondents, 1983-89; *San Antonio Light,* San Antonio, TX, reporter, 1989-93; *San Antonio Express-News,* San Antonio, reporter, 1993-94, managing editor, 1994-97, editor and senior vice president, news, 1997—. Board of directors, Inter-American Press Association.

MEMBER: American Society of Newspaper Editors.

AWARDS, HONORS: Distinguished Service Award for Foreign Correspondents, Society of Professional Journalists, 1982; Editor of the Year, *Editor & Publisher* magazine, 2000; Alumnus of the Year, University of Texas at San Antonio, 2000; Maria Moors Cabot Prize, Columbia University, 2002, for outstanding reporting on Latin America and contributions to better inter-American understanding.

WRITINGS:

Trail of Feathers: Searching for Philip True (nonfiction), Public Affairs Press (New York, NY), 2005.

SIDELIGHTS: Robert Rivard spent much of his career writing about Latin America and Latino immigrants to the United States. He covered civil wars in Central America in the 1980s and the war between Argentina and the United Kingdom over the Falkland Islands in 1982. He opened a news bureau in Central America for *Newsweek* and oversaw the founding of a Mexico news bureau for the *San Antonio Light,* a Texas newspaper. That paper eventually merged with the *San Antonio Express-News,* whose Mexico City bureau chief, Philip True, was murdered while researching a story in 1998. His murder and the investigation into it are the topic of Rivard's first book, *Trail of Feathers: Searching for Philip True.*

True disappeared in the Sierra Madre Mountains while reporting a story on the Huichol Indians (a tribe based in Western Mexico). Rivard was part of a search party that followed feathers from True's sleeping bag to find his body; he had been beaten and strangled. Two Huichol men were accused of the murder, but the legal case against them was complicated by lost evidence and their release by a judge at one point. They were finally convicted in 2004 but became fugitives before they could be imprisoned. Rivard's book portrays the misunderstanding that often occurs between U.S. residents and Mexicans, and the frustrations Rivard encountered in the Mexican court system. It also is a portrait of True, as an unconventional but dedicated journalist who loved Mexico.

Some critics thought Rivard especially good at depicting cross-cultural conflicts and praised other aspects of his work as well. "*Trail of Feathers* is tremendous for the way it digs into enormous issues of history, poverty, and bilateral misperceptions," commented Sam Quinones in the *Columbia Journalism Review.* "Moreover," Quinones concluded, "when it comes to editorial perseverance, Rivard is the gold standard." *Library Journal* contributor Deirdre Bray Root found the book "a fascinating look at an intriguing man and an alien culture," while a *Publishers Weekly* reviewer called it "engaging, compassionate, though sometimes long-winded." A *Kirkus Reviews* critic added that the work "displays the commitment of a professional journalist and the devotion of a friend."

BIOGRAPHICAL AND CRITICAL SOURCES:

PERIODICALS

Columbia Journalism Review, November-December, 2005, Sam Quinones, "Taking Justice: An Editor's Story of His Slain Reporter Reveals Much about Modern Mexico," p. 66.

Editor & Publisher, May 15, 2000, Mark Fitzgerald, "Rivard Pushes for True Facts," p. 5.

Kirkus Reviews, September 1, 2005, review of *Trail of Feathers: Searching for Philip True,* p. 962.

Library Journal, November 1, 2005, Deirdre Bray Root, review of *Trail of Feathers,* p. 99.

Publishers Weekly, August 1, 2005, review of *Trail of Feathers,* p. 130.

ONLINE

Robert Rivard Home Page, http://www.robertrivard. com (January 26, 2006).*

*   *   *

ROBBINS, Hollis

PERSONAL: Female. *Education:* Johns Hopkins University, B.A.; University of Colorado, Boulder, M.A.; Harvard University, Kennedy School of Government, master's degree; Princeton University, Ph.D.

ADDRESSES: Office—Millsaps College, Department of English, 1701 N. State St., Jackson, MS 39210.

CAREER: Educator, editor, and writer. Millsaps College, Jackson, MS, assistant professor of English.

WRITINGS:

(Editor, with Henry Louis Gates, Jr.) *In Search of Hannah Crafts: Critical Essays on "The Bondwoman's Narrative,"* Basic Civitas Books (New York, NY), 2004.

(Editor and author of introduction and notes, with Henry Louis Gates, Jr.) Harriet Beecher Stowe, *The Annotated Uncle Tom's Cabin,* W.W. Norton (New York, NY), 2006.

Also author of *Flushing Away Sentiment: Water Politics in Edith Wharton's The Custom of the Country.*

WORK IN PROGRESS: Coediting with Dr. Paula Garrett a collection of works by William Wells Brown.

SIDELIGHTS: Hollis Robbins is a college English professor who also has a degree in public policy and is interested in the relationship between bureaucratic and literary forms of writing. She is the editor, with Henry Louis Gates, Jr., of *In Search of Hannah Crafts: Critical Essays on "The Bondwoman's Narrative."* The book is a collection of essays or chapters focusing on the discovery by Gates and the eventual publication of *The Bondswoman's Narrative.* The novel was supposedly written by an escaped slave named Hannah Crafts and was not discovered until 2002. It may also hold the distinction of being the first novel written by an African-American woman. Among the issues addressed by the various authors are the literary influences on Crafts and the novel's place in the cannon of literature in general and African-American gothic literature in particular. Also part of the collection are essays focusing on the mystery surrounding Crafts's identity and the search to ascertain exactly who she was. Denise Simon, writing in the *Black Issues Book Review,* noted that "the heart of the book lies in the critical attention paid to Crafts's writing and its relation to the society in which she lived." Simon also wrote: "Gates and Robbins manage to present a full range of possibilities and perspectives." Writing in *Booklist,* Vanessa Bush commented that readers will enjoy the collection "for its penetrating look at issues regarding slavery and literature." In a review in the *Legacy: A Journal of American Women Writers,* Shirley Wilson Logan wrote: "One should not expect to come away with definitive answers to the questions that opened this review, but the careful reader will be challenged by some of the best thinking currently available on this fascinating, enigmatic tale."

BIOGRAPHICAL AND CRITICAL SOURCES:

PERIODICALS

Black Issues Book Review, May-June, 2004, Denise Simon, review of *In Search of Hannah Crafts: Critical Essays on "The Bondwoman's Narrative,"* p. 42.

Booklist, January 1, 2004, Vanessa Bush, review of *In Search of Hannah Crafts,* p. 808; January 1, 2005, review of *In Search of Hannah Crafts,* p. 766.

Legacy: A Journal of American Women Writers, June, 2005, Shirley Wilson Logan, review of *In Search of Hannah Crafts,* p. 209.

Reference & Research Book News, August, 2005, review of *In Search of Hannah Crafts,* p. 269.

ONLINE

Millsaps College, Department of English Web site, http://www.millsaps.edu/english/ (March 12, 2006), faculty profile of author.

Princeton University Web site, http://www.princeton.edu/ (March 12, 2006), brief profile of author's work.*

* * *

ROCHE, Mark W. 1956-
(Mark William Roche)

PERSONAL: Born August 29, 1956, in Weymouth, MA. *Education:* Studied in Bonn, West Germany (now Germany), 1976; Williams College, B.A. (magna cum laude), 1978; University of Tübingen, M.A., 1980; Princeton University, M.A., 1982, Ph.D., 1984. *Religion:* Roman Catholic.

ADDRESSES: Home—12418 Range Line Rd., Berrien Springs, MI 49003-9632. *Office*—College of Arts and Letters, 137 O'Shaughnessy Hall, University of Notre Dame, Notre Dame, IN 46556-5639; fax: 574-631-7743. *E-mail*—mroche@nd.edu.

CAREER: Writer, philosopher, and educator. Ohio State University, Columbus, assistant professor, 1984-90, associate professor of Germanic languages and literature, 1990-96, department chair, 1991-96; University of Notre Dame, Notre Dame, IN, Reverend Edmund P. Joyce, C.S.C. Professor of German Language and Literature and professor of philosophy, 1996—, department chair, 1996-97, I.A. O'Shaughnessy Dean of College of Arts and Letters, 1997—. Technical University of Dresden, visiting professor, 1994; Wake Forest University, distinguished visiting lecturer, 1995; guest lecturer at other institutions, including Michigan State University, Cornell University, University of Bielefeld, Rollins College, University of Louisville, Washington University, St. Louis, MO, and Sacred Heart University, Fairfield, CT; conference presenter; guest on media programs.

MEMBER: Phi Beta Kappa.

AWARDS, HONORS: Fulbright fellow, 1978-80; Max Kade fellow, 1981-82; Whiting fellow in the humanities, 1983-84; fellow of American Council of Learned Societies, 1985; grants from National Endowment for the Humanities and German Academic Exchange Service, 1991; Alexander von Humboldt fellow, 1997.

WRITINGS:

Dynamic Stillness: Philosophical Conceptions of Ruhe in Schiller, Hölderlin, Büchner, and Heine, Niemeyer (Tübingen, Germany), 1987.

Gottfried Benn's Static Poetry: Aesthetic and Intellectual-Historical Interpretations, University of North Carolina Press (Chapel Hill, NC), 1991.

Tragedy and Comedy: A Systematic Study and a Critique of Hegel, State University of New York Press (Albany, NY), 1998.

Die Moral der Kunst. Über Literatur und Ethik, Beck (Munich, Germany), 2002.

Why Literature Matters in the Twenty-first Century, Yale University Press (New Haven, CT), 2004.

Shorter works include *The Intellectual Appeal of Catholicism and the Idea of a Catholic University,* University of Notre Dame Press (Notre Dame, IN), 2003. Contributor to books, including *Inquiries into Values: The Inaugural Session of the International Society for Value Inquiry,* edited by Sander H. Lee, Edwin Mellen Press (Lewiston, NY), 1988; *Bertolt Brecht: Centenary Essays,* edited by Steve Giles and Rodney Livingstone, Rodopi (Amsterdam, Netherlands), 1998; *Literary Friendship, Literary Paternity: Essays in Honor of Stanley Corngold,* edited by Gerhard Richter, University of North Carolina Press (Chapel Hill, NC), 2002; *The Future of Religious Colleges,* edited by Paul J. Dovre, Eerdmans (Grand Rapids, MI), 2002; and *The New History of Germany Literature,* edited by David E. Wellbery, Harvard University Press (Cambridge, MA). Contributor of articles and reviews to academic journals, including *Journal of Value Inquiry, Journal of the Kafka Society of America, Clio: Journal of Literature, History, and the Philosophy of History, Post Script: Essays in Film and the Humanities, Modern Austrian Literature, Oxford German Studies, New Oxford Review, Revue Internationale de Philosophie,* and *Gottfried Benn Jahrbuch.* Associate editor, *Film and Philosophy,* 1997—.

BIOGRAPHICAL AND CRITICAL SOURCES:

PERIODICALS

Journal of English and Germanic Philology, April, 1995, Ruth Lorbe, review of *Gottfried Benn's*

Static Poetry: Aesthetic and Intellectual-Historical Interpretations, p. 303.

Modern Drama, summer, 2000, Jure Gantar, review of *Tragedy and Comedy: A Systematic Study and Critique of Hegel,* p. 314.

* * *

ROCHE, Mark William
See ROCHE, Mark W.

* * *

ROCHE, Maurice 1925-

PERSONAL: Born November 4, 1925, in Clermont-Ferrand, France; son of Gabriel Roche (engineer) and Louise Bonnefille. *Education:* Lycée du Parc à Lyon, Collège de Cusset, bachelor's degree.

ADDRESSES: Agent—c/o Author Mail, Les Impressions Nouvelles, Paris-Bruxelles, 12 reu du Président, 1050 Bruxelles, Belgium.

CAREER: Writer. Previously worked as a journalist, race-car test driver, composer for stage and concerts, and actor.

MEMBER: PEN Club (France).

WRITINGS:

Alfred de Vigny et l'ésotérisme, Éditions du Jardin de la France (Blois, France), 1948.

Art roman et renaissance au tombeau de Ronsard, Éditionis du Jardin de la France (Tours, France), 1950.

Balzac et la philosophe inconnu, Gibert-Clarey (Tours, France), 1951.

Goethe et Frédérique Brion, I.O.P. (Strasbourg, France), 1957.

Monteverdi (novel), Éditions du Seuil (Paris, France), 1959, reprinted, 1986.

Compact: roman (novel), Éditions du Seuil (Paris, France), 1966, published in English as *Compact,* Dalkey Archive Press (Elmwood Park, IL), 1988, original edition reprinted with original colors, La Petite Éole, 1996.

Circus: roman (novel), Éditions du Seuil (Paris, France), 1972.

(With Paolo Boni) *Ça!,* R.L.D. (Paris, France), 1973.

Codex: roman (novel), Éditions du Seuil (Paris, France), 1974.

Opéra bouffe: roman (novel; title means "Comic Opera"), Éditions du Seuil (Paris, France), 1975.

Mémoire: roman (novel), P. Belfond (Paris, France), 1976, reprinted, Tristam, 2000.

(With Raymond Federman) *The Voice in the Closet,* (includes *Echos* by Roche), Coda Press (Madison, WI), 1979, reprinted, Meyer & Meyer (Oxford, England), 2001.

(With Raymond Federman) *Echos* (includes *The Voice in the Closet* by Federman), Coda Press (Madison, WI), 1979.

Macabré: ou triumphe de haulte intelligence, Éditions du Seuil (Paris, France), 1979.

(With Arman) *Le traité du violon: Lithographies et Gravures Originales de Arman,* A. Rambert (Paris, France), 1979.

Maladie, mélodie: roman (novel), Éditions du Seuil (Paris, France), 1980.

Camar(a)de, Arthaud (Paris, France), 1981.

Écritures, Carte Blanche (Montmorency, France), 1985.

Je ne vais pas bien, mais il faut que j'y aille: roman (novel), Seuil (Paris, France), 1987.

Clauzel: Peinture (exposition publication), Galerie Annie Lagier (L'Isle-sur-la Sorgue, France), 1989.

Qui n'a pas vu Dieu n'a rien vu: zapping (novel), Éditions du Seuil (Paris, France), 1990.

Fidèles félidés, Cadex Éditionis (Saussines, France), 1992.

Grande humoresque opus 27 (fiction), Éditions du Seuil (Paris, France), 1997.

(With Edouard Glissant) *Un petit rien-du-tout tout neuf plié dans une feuille de persil,* Gallimard (Paris, France), 1997.

Pardonnez-moi, mon fils, Clémence Hiver Éditeur (Sauve, France), 1997.

Also author of *François Villon: fils du Loire,* [Tours, France], c. 1949. Contributor to *Sorbonne,* Editions Fata Morgana (Paris, France), 1968. Contributor to many journals and periodicals in France.

AUDIOBOOKS

Testament, Sontexte (Paris, France), 1979.

Eine Liebesgeschichte (fiction), Artalect (Paris, France), 1984.

SIDELIGHTS: French novelist Maurice Roche gained widespread attention with his 1966 debut novel *Compact: roman,* which was later published in English. Roche drew on his background as a musical composer to structure the novel with alternative narratives, each with a specific voice, tense, and typeface. The story revolves around a blind, dying man who uses his imagination and more to create erotic sensations as he deals with a doctor who seeks the man's tattooed skin. Mark Amerika, writing in the *American Book Review,* noted: "The text's interweavings make reading a literal blast." The story, he concluded, "opens you up to an alternate structure where everything is permitted." A *Publishers Weekly* contributor commented that the novel "is not for everyone, but should please fanciers of the literary underground." In a review for *Choice,* R. Runyon called the book "a difficult yet very significant work."

Mémoire: roman is a novel about a writer who is on sabbatical after getting a grant from the French government. The result of his work during that time is a book titled *Mémoire.* As the story tries to unfold, the reader encounters "incessant interruption of translations, phone calls, letters, . . . bodily processes and scatological metaphors," wrote James Leigh in the *French Review,* adding that the interruptions "force us to accept the text as disruption *per se.*" Leigh also noted that "not all will get the joke, it is a book that must be actively read."

Roche ruminates about life and especially death as he reflects on several macabre works of art in *Camar(a)-de.* M.A. Caws, writing in *World Literature Today,* noted: "It is Roche's vibrant imagination that holds all this together in page after page of sketch and counter-sketch."

BIOGRAPHICAL AND CRITICAL SOURCES:

BOOKS

Paris, Jean, *Maurice Roche* (includes selections of Roche's poems), Seghers (Paris, France), 1989.

PERIODICALS

American Book Review, September-October, 1989, Mark Amerika, review of *Compact: roman,* p. 13.

Choice, June, 1989, R. Runyon, review of *Compact,* p. 1688.

French Review, April, 1977, Dina Sherzer, review of *Opéra bouffe,* pp. 814-815; December, 1977, James Leigh, review of *Mémoire: roman,* pp. 335-336; May, 1989, Laurence Enjolras, review of *Je ne vais pas bien, mais il faut que j'y aille,* pp. 1100-1101.

Publishers Weekly, September 9, 1998, review of *Compact,* p. 120.

World Literature Today, winter, 1983, M.A. Caws, review of *Camar(a)de,* p. 68.*

*   *   *

ROCHEFORT, Christiane 1917-1998

PERSONAL: Born July 17, 1917, in Paris, France; died April 28, 1998; divorced. *Education:* Attended the Sorbonne.

CAREER: Writer. Worked as a model, actress, and journalist; Cannes Film Festival, press attaché, 1953-68.

AWARDS, HONORS: Nouvelle Vague prize, 1958; Prix du Roman Populiste, 1961, for *Les petits enfants du siècle;* Medicis Prize, 1988, for *La porte du fond: roman.*

WRITINGS:

Le repos du guerrier (novel), Grasset (Paris, France), 1958, translation by Lowell Bair published as *Warrior's Rest,* D. Mckay (New York, NY), 1962.

Les petits enfants du siècle (novel), Grasset (Paris, France), 1961, translation by Linda Asher published as *Children of Heaven,* D. McKay (New York, NY), 1962.

Les stance à Sophie (novel), Grasset (Paris, France), 1963, translation by Helen Eustis published as *Cats Don't Care for Money,* Cresset (London, England), 1966.

Une rose pour Morrison (novel; title means "A Rose for Morrison"), B. Grasset (Paris, France), 1966.

Printemps au parking (novel; title means "Spring in the Car Park"), B. Grasset (Paris, France), 1969.

Encore heureux qu'on va vers l'été (novel; title means "Once Again Happy That Summer Is Coming"), Grasset (Paris, France), 1975.

Les enfants d'abord (nonfiction; title means "Children First"), Grasset (Paris, France), 1976.

Journal de printemps: récit du livre, Éditions l'Étincelle (Montreal, Canada), 1977.

Ma vie revue et corrigée par l'auteur, introduction by Maurice Chavardès, Stock (Paris, France), 1978.

Quand tu vas chez les femmes (title means "How to Deal with Women"), Grassett (Paris, France), 1982.

Le monde est comme deux chevaux, Grasset (Paris, France), 1984.

La porte du fond: roman (novel; title means "The Far Door"), Grasset (Paris, France), 1988.

Conversations sans paroles: roman (novel; title means "Conversations without Words"), Grasset (Paris, France), 1997.

Adieu Andromède, Grasset (Paris, France), 1997.

Oeuvre romanesque (includes the novels *Le repos du guerrier,* and *Printemps au parking,* Grasset & Fasquelle (Paris, France), 2004.

Also author of *Cendresetor,* 1956; *C'est bizarre l'écriture,* 1970; *Archaos, ou, le jardin étincelant,* 1972, translation by Amos Kenan published as *Archaos, or The Glittering Garden,* 1974; translator of numerous books, including *John Lennon en flagrant Délire,* with Rachel Mizrahi, 1965; *Le cheval fini,* with Amos Kenan, 1966; and *Holocauste II,* with Amos Kenan, 1976.

ADAPTATIONS: Le repos du guerrier was adapted as the film *Love on a Pillow,* 1962.

SIDELIGHTS: Christiane Rochefort studied medicine, psychology, and ethnology at the Sorbonne and did not turn to writing until later in life. Her first novel was published when she was in her forties. A contributor to *Contemporary World Writers* noted that Rochefort's novels present a "diligent observation of the workings of society." The reviewer went on to comment: "What she has found increasingly necessary to condemn is the determination of present-day society to make the behaviour of its individual members conform to models which are presented as 'normal' and which exclude the exceptional." For example, the reviewer wrote that the author's novel *Le repos du guerrier,* which was published in English as *Warrior's Rest,* "questions the traditional conception of female sexuality." The story is based slightly on the fable of the lovers Orpheus and Eurydice and features a young French woman who falls in love with a former soldier who has become an alcoholic following the dropping of the atomic bomb on Hiroshima.

In *Les petits enfants du siècle,* published in English as *Children of Heaven,* the narrator's name is Josayne. The young girl's parents keep having children, a situation that the author uses to satirize French government efforts following the war to increase the country's birth rate by giving family allowances for each child born. Josayne grows up and finally meets her true love. As they look forward to marriage, however, the author warns that dreams and reality may be very different. A *Contemporary World Writers* contributor noted that the novel "illustrates the consequences of the material conditions of women's lives, including the generous French State child allowances that reduce women to childbearing machines." A contributor to *Women Writers Talking* wrote that the novel "has a perfectly linear structure, but time is handled deceptively: years can pass by in one sentence, whereas whole chapters may cover only a few hours. The love scenes at the end contain a section of puppetlike dialogue taken piecemeal from a trashy magazine, which renders a perfect cliché."

In *Encore heureux qu'on va vers l'été,* the author turns her attention to how the schooling that children receive is responsible for "corrupting children's natural goodness, independence, vision and eagerness to learn," as noted by *Times Literary Supplement* contributor Barbara Wright. The story revolves around three children who are part of a group that walk out of a class, but these three do not return and try to make it on their own. Wright commented: "Groups of children come together and separate; an underground civil war develops between the fierce but frightened Kafkaesque Authorities and the network of liberty-loving children and their adult sympathizers."

Rochefort keeps her focus on children in her nonfiction book *Les enfants d'abord,* which means "Children First." The book focuses on children as a social class of their own, and the author examines how society forces them to conform and eventually be exploited. M. Rumeau-Smith, writing in *World Literature Today,* noted: "The book is a penetrating, acrid and feverish essay."

La porte du fond: roman, or "The Far Door," is a novel about a little girl who undergoes abuse at the hands of her father as told by the girl some two decades later. Wright, commenting in the *Times Literary Supplement,* noted: "Rochefort shows her heroine as a survivor, but it is clear that as such she is in the tiniest of minorities." Wright also noted that "the whole story comes across as the sober truth." *French Review* contributor Robert J. Hartwig commented: "There is no trace of titillating sensationalism, facile psychologizing, whiny or man-hating feminism. On the other hand, the novel is profoundly interesting, psychological . . . and feminist." Commenting on the novel in the *Modern Language Review,* Margaret-Anne Hutton wrote: "By manipulating points of view and setting up parallel structures, Rochefort prompts us, as readers, to engage with the central issue of responsibility and consent, confronting us with our own prejudices and preconceptions."

BIOGRAPHICAL AND CRITICAL SOURCES:

BOOKS

Contemporary World Writers, 2nd edition, St. James Press (Detroit, MI), 1993.
Todd, Janet, editor, *Women Writers Talking,* Holmes & Meier (New York, NY), 1983.

PERIODICALS

Differences: A Journal of Feminist Cultural Studies, fall, 2001, Michael Lucey, "Sexuality, Politization, May 1968: Situating Christiane Rochefort's *Printemps au parking,*" pp. 33-68.
Forum for Modern Language Studies, July, 1995, Margaret-Anne Hutton, "'À la Guerre comme à la Guerre': A Reappraisal of Christiane Rochefort's *Le repos du guerrier,*" pp. 234-245.
French Review, December, 1990, Robert J. Hartwig, review of *La porte du fond: roman,* p. 390; March, 1994, Claudine Thiré, "*Les petits enfants du siècle,* ou, la thématique du quotidian," pp. 580-590.
Modern Language Review, April, 1995, Margaret-Anne Hutton, "Assuming Responsibility: Christiane Rochefort's Exploration of Child Sexual Abuse in *La porte du fond,*" pp. 333-344.

Spectator, December 10, 1998, Anita Broookner, "Prize-Winning Novels from France," p. 39.
Times Educational Supplement, August 25, 1978, Robert Béar, review of *Les petits enfants du siècle,* p. 14.
Times Literary Supplement, October 3, 1975, Barbara Wright, review of *Encore heureux qu'on va vers l'été,* p. 1152; January 27, 1989, Barbara Wright, review of *La porte du fond,* p. 88.
World Literature Today, summer, 1977, M. Rumeau-Smith, review of *Les enfants d'abord,* p. 415.

ONLINE

Matt & Andrej Koymasky Home Page, http://andrejkoymasky.com/ (February 3, 2006), brief biography of author.
Pegasos, http://www.kirjasto.sci.fi/ (March 4, 2006), "Christiane Rochefort (1917-1998)."
University of Sunderland Web site, http://www.sunderland.ac.uk/ (March 5, 2006), "Christiane Rochefort: *Les petits enfants du siècle.*"*

*   *   *

RODGERS, Marion Elizabeth 1958-

PERSONAL: Born 1958, in Santiago, Chile; married Jules Witcover (a columnist). *Education:* Graduate of Goucher College.

ADDRESSES: Home—Washington, DC. *Agent*—c/o Author Mail, Oxford University Press, 198 Madison Ave., New York, NY 10016.

CAREER: Writer.

AWARDS, HONORS: Book of the Year Gold Award for Biography, *Foreword* magazine, for *Mencken: The American Iconoclast.*

WRITINGS:

NONFICTION

(Editor) *Mencken and Sara: A Life in Letters; The Private Correspondence of H.L. Mencken and Sara Haardt,* McGraw-Hill (New York, NY), 1987.

(Editor) *The Impossible H.L. Mencken: A Selection of His Best Newspaper Stories,* Doubleday (New York, NY), 1991.

Mencken: The American Iconoclast, Oxford University Press (New York, NY), 2005.

SIDELIGHTS: Marion Elizabeth Rodgers has devoted much of her work to H.L. Mencken (1880-1956), one of the best-known American journalists of the first half of the twentieth century. As a newspaper columnist, he commented acerbically on American puritanism and other topics; as a magazine editor, he published promising authors who would become famous, such as F. Scott Fitzgerald and Langston Hughes. He was also a man with prejudices he fought as his life progressed, and was a devoted husband during his brief marriage.

Rodgers's books deal with all aspects of Mencken. His private life is the focus of an epistolary collection she edited, *Mencken and Sara: A Life in Letters; The Private Correspondence of H.L. Mencken and Sara Haardt.* Mencken met the much younger Haardt, an aspiring writer, in 1923; this book collects letters covering their entire relationship, which ended with her death in 1935, five years after they married. Several reviewers found the volume useful for a look at Mencken's gentler side. *National Review* contributor John C. Chalberg noted that Rodgers had "thoroughly annotated" the missives and provided an insightful introduction.

The Impossible H.L. Mencken: A Selection of His Best Newspaper Stories is "a fat and sassy anthology" of Mencken's columns for Baltimore newspapers and other journalistic works, according to *National Review* critic Terry Teachout. He deemed the collection valuable even though some pieces were available elsewhere, and others were not, in his opinion, among Mencken's most distinguished. A *Publishers Weekly* reviewer thought the book "carefully edited," adding that Rodgers's "useful introduction puts Mencken's career in perspective."

The public and the private Mencken come together in the biography *Mencken: The American Iconoclast.* Drawing on archival research and interviews, Rodgers covers his career as columnist, reporter, editor, and book author, portraying him as a prolific, brilliant man who had some serious flaws, such his bias against African Americans and Jews. Eventually, he tried to atone for his bigotry, seeking to bring black writers (including Hughes) to a wider audience and to call attention to the sufferings of Jews under Hitler. Several reviewers characterized the biography as comprehensive. Rodgers "does an excellent job of tying the strands together," remarked Joel W. Tscherne in *Library Journal.* A *Publishers Weekly* commentator called the book "meticulous," while to a *Kirkus Reviews* critic, it was "superb" and "the best Mencken biography to date."

Rodgers told *CA:* "My introduction to H.L. Mencken came by accident. In 1981, two weeks before my graduation from Goucher College, as I was researching the papers of alumna Sara Haardt, I literally tripped over a box of love letters between her and H.L. Mencken. Taped to the top of the collection was a stern command, written by Mencken, that it was not to be opened until that very year. To say that my life changed course at that moment would be an understatement. Suddenly, a door was swung open into Mencken's life through the tender route of romantic correspondence. During two decades, Mencken has pulled me through many happy adventures, both personal and professional. My editing two books of his work helped me appreciate Mencken's uncompromising prose and his relentless courage in his battles on behalf of individual freedom. This became the underlying theme of *Mencken.*

"Immediately after the publication of *Mencken and Sara,* while still in my twenties, I worked as a researcher for the prize-winning biographer Edmund Morris and his wife, author Sylvia Jukes Morris. The experience showed me how to organize and extract the essential from a multitude of primary sources and to form a narrative illuminating a subject's character. The tactile connection I get by handling one of Mencken's original letters—tracing his spidery signature or seeing the blot of beer foam that has smeared the ink—is the same feeling I get when I visit his house or walk along Charles Street in Baltimore. I want my readers to feel that they are there—smelling the brewing beer on Hollins Street, hearing the sound of Mencken pounding on his piano. Most of all, I want readers to sense the excitement Mencken inspired among his contemporaries, when he first burst on the American scene."

BIOGRAPHICAL AND CRITICAL SOURCES:

PERIODICALS

Chicago Tribune, February 8, 1987, Mark Harriss, review of *Mencken and Sara: A Life in Letters;*

The Private Correspondence of H.L. Mencken and Sara Haardt.

Kirkus Reviews, October 1, 2005, review of *Mencken: The American Iconoclast,* p. 1068.

Library Journal, October 15, 2005, Joel W. Tscherne, review of *Mencken,* p. 64.

National Review, October 9, 1987, John C. Chalberg, review of *Mencken and Sara,* p. 67; February 3, 1992, Terry Teachout, review of *The Impossible H.L. Mencken: A Selection of His Best Newspaper Stories,* p. 45.

New Yorker, February 24, 1992, John Updike, review of *The Impossible H.L. Mencken,* p. 98.

Publishers Weekly, September 27, 1991, review of *The Impossible H.L. Mencken,* p. 53; June 20, 2005, review of *Mencken,* p. 65.

Washington Post Book Review, February 5, 2006, Thomas Frank, review of *Mencken,* p. 2.

*   *   *

RUBIN, Jordan 1975(?)-
(Jordan S. Rubin)

PERSONAL: Born c. 1975; married; wife's name Nicki. *Education:* Holds a doctor of naturopathic medicine degree (NMD), credentials as a Certified Nutritional Consultant, and Ph.D. degrees from the People's University of the Americas School of Natural Medicine and the Academy of Natural Therapies.

ADDRESSES: Home—West Palm Beach, FL. *Office*—Garden of Life, 5500 Village Blvd., Ste. 202, West Palm Beach, FL 33407.

CAREER: Writer, nutritionist, entrepreneur, business executive, public speaker, and consultant. Garden of Life, founder and chief executive officer, 1998—. Frequent guest on television and radio talk shows.

WRITINGS:

Patient Heal Thyself: A Remarkable Health Program Combining Ancient Wisdom with Groundbreaking Clinical Research, Freedom Press (Topanga, CA), 2003.

(With Joseph Brasco) *Restoring Your Digestive Health: How the Guts and Glory Program Can Transform Your Life,* Twin Streams (New York, NY), 2003.

The Maker's Diet, Siloam (Lake Mary, FL), 2004.

The Maker's Diet Shopper's Guide, Siloam (Lake Mary, FL), 2005.

(With David Remedios) *The Great Physician's Rx for Health and Wellness,* Nelson Books (Nashville, TN), 2005.

SIDELIGHTS: Jordan Rubin is an author, nutritionist, consultant, and public speaker. In 1994, when he was nineteen, Rubin's health was severely threatened by the effects of Crohn's disease, a serious intestinal disease. He lost almost half his body weight and suffered from numerous other conditions, including immune system breakdown, anemia, diabetes, frequent infections, hair loss, fibromyalgia, and chronic depression. Conventional medicine was unable to help him, and hundreds of different types of alternative treatments failed to improve his condition. Finally, relief came when he encountered an unconventional nutritionist who "believed Jordan was ill because he was not eating the diet of the Bible," noted a writer on the *Maker's Diet* Web site. After he changed his lifestyle to reflect this change in diet, Rubin's health gradually began to improve until, some months later, he was free of symptoms and fully recovered from the disease that nearly took his life.

An entrepreneur and business owner, Rubin founded the nutritional company Garden of Life in 1998 to help him pass on his knowledge to others and to assist clients with achieving their nutritional goals. Rubin also began to write books explaining the dietary and nutritional systems that had saved him. In *The Maker's Diet,* for example, Rubin explains how one's health can be dramatically improved by following the simpler diet of those who lived during biblical times. "The overarching message is actually quite nonparochial: that we should eat the same foods consumed by more primitive people," namely, hormone-free, grass-fed animals; organic fruits, vegetables and grains; and raw, unpasteurized milk products," observed Shawn Donnelly in *Muscle & Fitness.* In an interview with Paul O'Donnell on the *Beliefnet* Web site, Rubin noted that the basis of the Maker's Diet is "to eat a healthy diet. There are two criteria for me to eat a food. Number one, it had to be created by God as a food. Number two, it needs to be consumed in the form that is compatible for the human body—in the form that God created it." Rubin suggests avoiding processed and refined foods, artificial sweeteners, hydrogenated oils, margarine, and other artificial foodstuffs. He suggests avoiding other types of food prohibited by the Bible, such pork and shellfish. Rubin also encourages followers of the diet to add whole food nutritional supplements to their diet. A reviewer in *Publishers Weekly* noted that "his approach is unique and provides a refreshing, holistic antidote to many of today's fad diets."

A number of Rubin's claims have been called controversial, and some critics have questioned his credibility, but he stands firmly behind the benefits he says are found in his nutritional programs. He told O'Donnell that a belief in God is not necessary to follow the Maker's Diet. However, Rubin also declared, "I believe that people that do are going to use this program above any other one."

Other of Rubin's books draw upon nutritional habits of the past in order to build a healthful diet in the present. *The Great Physician's Rx for Health and Wellness* takes up where *The Makers Diet* left off, providing a plan for a complete lifestyle makeover based on nutrition and hygiene precepts from the Bible. In *Patient Heal Thyself: A Remarkable Health Program Combining Ancient Wisdom with Groundbreaking Clinical Research,* Rubin explains the causes of several common diseases and includes advice on how to cure those diseases and reverse health problems. "Here [readers] will find a golden opportunity to learn how to begin to heal themselves," commented Paul A. Goldberg in the *Townsend Letter for Doctors and Patients. Restoring Your Digestive Health: How the Guts and Glory Program Can Transform Your Life* explores how diet and nutrition can help cure and reverse the effects of a number of digestive diseases. Reviewer Jule Klotter, writing in the *Townsend Letter for Doctors and Patients,* concluded that "even people who don't want to follow the full Guts and Glory Program can learn ways to enhance digestive health from this book."

BIOGRAPHICAL AND CRITICAL SOURCES:

PERIODICALS

Better Nutrition, August, 2003, "Powerful Healing," review of *Patient Heal Thyself: A Remarkable*

Health Program Combining Ancient Wisdom with Groundbreaking Clinical Research, p.16; June, 2004, "Whole Health," review of *The Maker's Diet,* p. 16.
Library Journal, October 1, 2005, Noemie Maxwell, review of *The Great Physician's Rx for Health and Wellness,* p. 102.
Muscle & Fitness, August, 2004, Shawn Donnelly, "Honor Thy Fodder: From the Last Supper to *New York Times* Bestseller, *The Maker's Diet* Shows Readers the Light of Eating Clean," p. 224.
Natural Health, September, 2003, Judy Bass, review of *Restoring Your Digestive Health: How the Guts and Glory Program Can Transform Your Life,* p. 88.
Newsweek, April 19, 2004, Arian Campo-Flores, "Diets: Now, Milk and Honey," review of *The Maker's Diet,* p. 14.
Publishers Weekly, April 26, 2004, review of *The Maker's Diet,* p. 62; September 12, 2005, review of *The Great Physician's Rx for Health and Wellness,* p. 63.
Townsend Letter for Doctors and Patients, August-September, 2003, Paul A. Goldberg, "Empowerment," review of *Patient Heal Thyself,* p. 159; July, 2004, Jule Klotter, "The Guts & Glory Program," review of *Restoring Your Digestive Health,* p. 127.

ONLINE

Beliefnet, http://www.beliefnet.com/ (January 23, 2006), Paul O'Donnell, "Eating from the Bible," interview with Jordan S. Rubin.
Maker's Diet, http://www.makersdiet.com/ (January 23, 2006), biography of Jordan S. Rubin.
NuvoBody, http://www.nuvobody.com/ (January 23, 2006), biography of Jordan S. Rubin.*

*   *   *

RUBIN, Jordan S.
See RUBIN, Jordan

*   *   *

RUBIN, William 1927-2006
(William Stanley Rubin)

OBITUARY NOTICE— See index for *CA* sketch: Born August 11, 1927, in New York, NY; died January 22, 2006, in Pound Ridge, NY. Art historian, museum curator, educator, and author. Rubin was an influential curator of painting and sculpture at the Museum of Modern Art. His interest in art stretched back to his time as a teenager at the Fieldstone School in New York City, where he was influenced by Victor D'Amico. D'Amico was director of education at the Museum of Modern Art at the time, and Rubin helped him on some projects at the museum. Rubin then enrolled at Columbia University. His education was interrupted by military service in Europe, but then he returned to complete an A.B. in 1949. This was followed by a master's degree in 1952 and a doctorate in 1959. His bachelor's degree was in Italian literature and language, but he contemplated a music career for a while, studying the subject at the University of Paris for a year. Next, he returned to Columbia for graduate studies in history before a class in medieval art persuaded him to return to his original passion. During the 1950s and much of the 1960s, Rubin taught art history at Sarah Lawrence College, as well as being a professor at the graduate school at the City University of New York from 1960 to 1968. It was at Sarah Lawrence that he became friends with Alfred Barr, director at the Museum of Modern Art at the time. Barr got Rubin involved with organizing small exhibitions, which eventually led to his taking the job as chief curator of painting and sculpture in 1968. The department Rubin led was the most prominent at the museum, and he soon became a dominant figure there. In 1973 he was made director of painting and sculpture, a post he held until 1988. During this time, he did much to acquire new modern works of art, including those by such prominent painters as Picasso, Miró, Cézanne, Matisse, and others, while removing some works he felt were less important. He also defined his division's emphasis on the historical narrative of modernism. While he was sometimes criticized for his evident ego, Rubin was also recognized for doing much to improve the museum's collection, especially after the Museum was expanded in 1984. In his last years, however, he was also chastised for some of his exhibitions, such as one featuring Oceanic and African art that critics felt did not adequately relate the pieces within their cultural context. In his final years at the Museum, Rubin became more and more critical of what he felt was a lack of the museum's interest in acquiring new works. He resigned in 1988. Afterwards, though, he continued to organize exhibitions on occasion; he was named a Chevalier of the French Legion of Honor in 1979, and an Officer in 1991, for his services to the art world. As a scholar, Rubin was also noted for his many books on art and art history. Among these are *Dada, Surrealism, and*

Their Heritage (1968), *Anthony Caro* (1975), and *Picasso and Braque: A Symposium* (1992), as well as a number of edited and coauthored titles.

OBITUARIES AND OTHER SOURCES:

PERIODICALS

Chicago Tribune, January 27, 2006, section 3, p. 7.
Los Angeles Times, January 26, 2006, p. B11.
New York Times, January 24, 2006, p. A19.
Times (London, England), January 27, 2006, p. 68.
Washington Post, January 25, 2006, p. B5.

*   *   *

RUBIN, William Stanley
See RUBIN, William

*   *   *

RUST, Elissa Minor 1977-

PERSONAL: Born 1977.

ADDRESSES: Home—Lake Oswego, OR. *Agent*—c/o Author Mail, Ohio University Press, Scott Quadrangle, 1 Ohio University, Athens, OH 45701-2979.

CAREER: Writer.

WRITINGS:

The Prisoner Pear: Stories from the Lake, Ohio University Press/Swallow Press (Athens, OH), 2005.

Contributor to periodicals, including *Baltimore Review, Orchid: A Literary Review, Honolulu Magazine,* and *Beacon Street Review.*

SIDELIGHTS: Short story writer Elissa Minor Rust's first fiction collection, *The Prisoner Pear: Stories from the Lake,* is an "intriguing, nicely polished debut collection of twelve stories," commented a *Kirkus Reviews* critic. Set in affluent areas of the Pacific Northwest, the stories are characterized by "solid, believable characters rendered in careful, deliberate prose," remarked a reviewer in *Publishers Weekly.*

In "Moon over Water," the moon rises and remains full for more than ninety consecutive days in the skies above Portland and western Oregon, causing increased growth and fertility for everything in nature, including human bodies. While the story's narrator, a mathematics professor, tries to figure out this amazing phenomenon, his students steadily drop out and head east, where the moon still goes through its familiar cycles. His wife and children, growing ever more obese, leave for the more comfortable surroundings of a relative's home in Denver. Though the unnatural moonrise threatens to shatter the life he knows, the narrator still works to enjoy the beauty of the event. In "Rich Girls," a working-class man signs up for a series of increasingly horrendous laboratory experiments, all for money to provide his wife and daughter a better lifestyle. Holly Martino, the protagonist of "Vital Organs," realizes that her kidneys are slowly vanishing—ceasing to exist—much to the dismay of her doctors. In the collection's title story, a young manager at UPS is emotionally torn over asking his well-to-do girlfriend to marry him, and looks for guidance in peculiar events that he interprets as personal signs and portents. The *Kirkus Reviews* contributor deemed Rust's work "thoughtful, surprising fiction."

BIOGRAPHICAL AND CRITICAL SOURCES:

PERIODICALS

Kirkus Reviews, October 15, 2005, review of *The Prisoner Pear: Stories from the Lake,* p. 1105.
Publishers Weekly, October 3, 2005, review of *The Prisoner Pear,* p. 48.*

*   *   *

RYLANDS, Jane Turner 1939-

PERSONAL: Born 1939; married Philip Rylands (museum director). *Education:* Graduated from the College of William and Mary.

ADDRESSES: Home—Venice, Italy. *Agent*—c/o Author Mail, Pantheon Books, 1745 Broadway, New York, NY 10019.

CAREER: Writer and educator. University of Maryland, European division, teacher of English for seventeen years.

WRITINGS:

SHORT STORIES

Venetian Stories, Pantheon Books (New York, NY), 2003.
Across the Bridge of Sighs: More Venetian Stories, Pantheon Books (New York, NY) 2005.

SIDELIGHTS: American expatriate Jane Turner Rylands has lived in Venice, Italy, for over thirty years and has written two short-story collections about her adopted home. The first, *Venetian Stories,* focuses on the city from the viewpoints of both visitors and natives. There are certain characters—such as Luigi, the postman—who feature in multiple stories, and this helps create a feeling of interconnectedness among the tales. *Booklist* reviewer Michael Spinella noted that the "carefully crafted and intertwined vignettes" are written in "magnificent prose." *Salon.com* contributor Charles Taylor was less enamored of *Venetian Stories,* observing that the collection feels "slight" in comparison to the work of other writers in the same genre. Taylor did, however, call the book "a pleasing diversion." Moreover, Ravi Shenoy, writing in a *Library Journal* review, voiced appreciation for Rylands's "keen observation" of her characters, and found the collection to be "wickedly funny." A *Kirkus Reviews* critic also praised the volume, calling it "charming" and "a smart and vivid debut."

Rylands followed *Venetian Stories* with *Across the Bridge of Sighs: More Venetian Stories,* a collection which "picks up masterfully" where Rylands's last effort left off, according to *Booklist* reviewer Frank Caso. This reviewer also found that the stories "provide a wonderful insight" into Venice. Shenoy, writing once more in the *Library Journal,* called the tales "simultaneously ironic and sympathetic," and again praised Rylands's "wicked humor." Additionally, a *Publishers Weekly* critic observed that the author "sometimes loses her characters in lofty prose," but felt that despite this the stories "prove entertaining" and ultimately twine together "with ease." A contributor to *Kirkus Reviews* noted that Rylands writes with a "simplicity" that comes from "experiencing a world in translation" by nature of being a foreigner, and thus regarded Rylands as "a singularly perceptive outsider." The contributor summed up *Across the Bridge of Sighs* as "elegant, worldly-wise and as captivating" as Venice itself.

BIOGRAPHICAL AND CRITICAL SOURCES:

PERIODICALS

Booklist, May 15, 2003, Michael Spinella, review of *Venetian Stories*, p. 1645; November 1, 2005, Frank Caso, review of *Across the Bridge of Sighs: More Venetian Stories*, p. 26.

Kirkus Reviews, April 1, 2003, review of *Venetian Stories*, p. 503; September 1, 2005, review of *Across the Bridge of Sighs*, p. 940.
Library Journal, June 1, 2003, Ravi Shenoy, review of *Venetian Stories*, p. 171; November 1, 2005, Ravi Shenoy, review of *Across the Bridge of Sighs*, p. 71.
Publishers Weekly, May 5, 2003, review of *Venetian Stories*, p. 198; September 12, 2005, review of *Across the Bridge of Sighs*, p. 40.
Town & Country, November, 2005, review of *Across the Bridge of Sighs*, p. 214.

ONLINE

Pantheon Books Web site, http://www.randomhouse.com/pantheon/ (March 28, 2006), brief biography of author.
Salon.com, http://www.salon.com/ (March 28, 2006), Charles Taylor, review of *Venetian Stories*.*

S

SALEEM, Hiner 1964-

PERSONAL: Born March 9, 1964, in Akrée, Iraqi Kurdistan.

ADDRESSES: Agent—c/o Author Mail, Farrar, Straus & Giroux, 19 Union Square W., New York, NY 10003.

CAREER: Writer, screenwriter, director, composer, producer, and filmmaker.

AWARDS, HONORS: Mannheim-Heidelberg International Film Festival Audience Award, 1998, for *Vive la mariée . . . et la libération du Kurdistan;* Venice Film Festival San Marco Prize, 2003, for *Vodka Lemon;* Mons International Festival of Love Films Grand Prize, 2004, for *Vodka Lemon.*

WRITINGS:

Le fusil de mon pere, Seuil (Paris, France), 2004, published as *My Father's Rifle: A Childhood in Kurdistan,* translated by Catherine Temerson, Farrar, Straus & Giroux (New York, NY), 2005.

SCREENPLAYS

(And director and composer) *Vive la mariée . . . et la libération du Kurdistan,* Les Films du Rivage, 1997.

(And director; English title, *Beyond Our Dreams*) *Passeurs de rêves,* UGC International, 2000.

(And director; television production) *Absolitude,* Mandala Productions, 2001.

(And director and actor) *Vodka Lemon,* Dulciné Films, 2003.

(And director, producer, and executive producer) *Kilomètre zéro,* Memento Films, 2005.

SIDELIGHTS: Hiner Saleem is an internationally known filmmaker, director, producer, screenwriter, and author. Born in Iraqi Kurdistan in 1964, Saleem left Iraq in the late 1970s and eventually settled in Paris, where he started making movies. *Beyond Our Dreams* is a "sprawling, tumultuous story told with fablelike simplicity," one that "sports both the virtues and limits of gentleness," commented Dennis Harvey in *Variety.* In the film, a young refugee couple, Dolovan and Zara flee turbulent Kurdistan for a hopeful better life in Paris. Accompanied by Zara's elderly parents, the pair travel across the freezing cold Caucasian Mountains toward a destination that is uncertain, but which they trust is better than the life they're leaving behind. Jolted from their home by the ethnic strife that enveloped Kurdistan, the couple experience further tragedy on the road as Zara's aged parents fall further and further behind in the harsh countryside and are finally lost. After a stay in a refugee commune in Armenia, Zara discovers that her father's suitcase is filled with money. Greedy predators descend on the two as they try to figure out how to proceed on their trek without visas. The pair are separated by the police, with Dolovan dodging arrest and Zara being robbed and abandoned in Ukraine. Desperately, Dolovan searches for Zara, hoping to reunite with her so that the two can continue their journey to Paris and a new, brighter future. "Always watchable, with a leisurely but confident pace," the story is "a vaguely mythic one, colored by streaks of absurdism, pathos and fairy-tale wish fulfillment," Harvey remarked.

Vodka Lemon, perhaps Saleem's best-known film, takes an absurdist look at a Kurdish community in Armenia, where no one seems to be at home and everyone is somewhere else, working to generate enough revenue to keep family and home together. A key character, never actually seen in the film, has gone to Paris to work and send money home to his father, Hamo, but never actually sends any. Even so, the agreeable Hamo manages to successfully court the widow who runs the concession stand where the vodka lemon is sold. Not all is cheerful in the movie, as violence and alcoholism are everyday occurrences, and the background landscape is perpetually covered in snow. "The temperature is icy but much warmth is generated by the characters' good humor and wry endurance of what fate has thrown their way," wrote reviewer Louis Menashe in *Cineaste.*

Saleem is also the author of *Le fusil de mon pere,* or *My Father's Rifle: A Childhood in Kurdistan.* The novel is an account, thinly fictionalized, of Saleem's childhood in the Kurdistan of the 1960s and 1970s. He tells of the close family life of the Kurdish communities of his childhood, but also describes the constant oppression the Kurds experienced at the hands of Turks, Iranians, and Iraqis. He describes how his father kept an ancient Czech rifle on hand in case he had to take up arms in support of the Kurdish military. Saleem tells how his family fought for independence with Kurdish troops, how the revolution was put down, and the life they experienced afterward in a refugee camp. After returning to their village, life took an even greater turn for the worse as Saddam Hussein's followers took over the village and increased their efforts to eliminate the Kurds. Even among the violence and oppression of the world around him, the young Saleem faced the same travails as any growing adolescent, and shows "what it's like to work through archetypal adolescent challenges during such terrifying upheaval," observed Gillian Engberg in *Booklist.* Eventually, the young Saleem realized that exile was his only hope if he was to have a future. A *Kirkus Reviews* critic called the book a "well-done but dispiriting memoir" that is "timely—and most depressing." Saleem "offers a haunting, sympathetic account of a young life amid the horrors of a war zone," commented a *Publishers Weekly* reviewer. Saleem "writes crisply, with economy and restraint," noted Daniel Sullivan in the *Weekly Standard,* "which allows him to treat several themes in his childhood completely and without sentimentality."

BIOGRAPHICAL AND CRITICAL SOURCES:

BOOKS

Saleem, Hiner, *My Father's Rifle: A Childhood in Kurdistan,* translated by Catherine Temerson, Farrar, Straus & Giroux (New York, NY), 2005.

PERIODICALS

Booklist, November 15, 2004, Gillian Engberg, review of *My Father's Rifle,* p. 550.

Cineaste, spring, 2005, Louis Menashe, review of *Vodka Lemon,* p. 80.

Daily Variety, May 24, 2005, Deborah Young, review of *Kilomètre zéro,* p. 18.

Hollywood Reporter, May 13, 2005, Duane Byrge, review of *Kilomètre zéro,* p. 9.

Kirkus Reviews, October 15, 2004, review of *My Father's Rifle,* p. 996.

Publishers Weekly, October 11, 2004, review of *My Father's Rifle,* p. 63.

Variety, September 25, 2000, Dennis Harvey, review of *Beyond Our Dreams,* p. 71.

Weekly Standard, January 24, 2005, Daniel Sullivan, review of *My Father's Rifle,* p. 35.

ONLINE

Farrar, Straus & Giroux Web site, http://www.fsgbooks.com/ (January 23, 2006), biography of Hiner Saleem.

Internet Movie Database, http://www.imdb.com/ (January 23, 2006).

SÁNCHEZ PIÑOL, Albert 1965-

PERSONAL: Born 1965, in Barcelona, Catalonia, Spain.

ADDRESSES: Home—Barcelona, Catalonia, Spain. *Agent*—c/o Author Mail, Farrar, Straus & Giroux, 19 Union Sq. W., New York, NY 10003.

CAREER: Anthropologist and writer.

AWARDS, HONORS: Ojo Critico Narrativa prize, 2003, for *La piel fría.*

WRITINGS:

Pallassos i monstres: la història tragicòmica de 8 dictadors africans (short stories), Edicions La Campana (Barcelona, Spain), 2000.
Les edats d'or, Proa (Barcelona, Spain), 2001.
La piel fría (novel), Edicions La Campana (Barcelona, Spain), 2002, translation by Cheryl Leah Morgan published as *Cold Skin,* Farrar, Straus & Giroux (New York, NY), 2005.

Also author of *Compagnie difficile,* Literalia, 2000. Contributor to many journals. Novel *La piel fría* has been translated into fifteen languages.

SIDELIGHTS: Anthropologist Albert Sánchez Piñol became an internationally renowned novelist with the publication in 2002 of *La piel fría.* Originally composed in Catalan, the author's native language, the English translation, *Cold Skin,* was released in 2005. The novel begins when an unnamed narrator is dropped off on a desolate Antarctic island to spend a year as a weather official, recording wind conditions. He intends to relieve the current weather official of his post, but when the narrator arrives, he finds no one on the island but a man named Gruner, the island's insane and hostile lighthouse keeper. On his first night, the narrator discovers the reason for his new companion's psychosis: every night, indigenous humanoid sea creatures emerge from the cold waters and attempt to wipe out the island's human inhabitants. The narrator and Gruner unwillingly become allies as they engage in a nightly fight for their lives against the terrible Sitauca, who have "eyes like eggs, pupils like needles, holes instead of noses, no eyebrows, no lips, [and] a huge mouth." Only one poses no threat: the submissive Aneris, a female Sitauca whom Gruner has trained and taken as a lover. The narrator is also lured into love by the tame creature, and he eventually attempts to befriend the Sitauca families, much to Gruner's scorn, which results in a violent end for one of the characters.

In *Library Journal,* reviewer Jack Shreve described *Cold Skin* as "a gripping and multifaceted allegory certain to be savored by many readers of intellectual fiction." *Booklist* contributor Debi Lewis called the book "a dizzying, surreal account," and went on to comment that though parts of the book are "heavy-handed, . . . it is still gruesomely riveting." One *Publishers Weekly* contributor likened the novel to an H.G. Wells tale, commenting that with its "elegant" sentences, the book "offers a tightly crafted allegory of human brutality both fascinating and repellent." In similar praise, a *Kirkus Reviews* contributor compared *Cold Skin* to a darker version of Robinson Crusoe, adding that, "for a novel that is as much parable as it is thriller, its impact is surprisingly emotional."

BIOGRAPHICAL AND CRITICAL SOURCES:

PERIODICALS

Booklist, September 1, 2005, Debi Lewis, review of *Cold Skin,* p. 66.
Entertainment Weekly, November 4, 2005, Gilbert Cruz, review of *Cold Skin,* p. 79; December 30, 2005, Jennifer Reese, "Literature of the Year," review of *Cold Skin,* p. 148.
Kirkus Reviews, September 1, 2005, review of *Cold Skin,* p. 939.
Library Journal, September 15, 2005, Jack Shreve, review of *Cold Skin,* p. 57.
New York Times Book Review, December 11, 2005, Marcel Theroux, "At the Bottom of the World," review of *Cold Skin,* p. 13.
Publishers Weekly, August 15, 2005, review of *Cold Skin,* p. 27.

ONLINE

Canongate Books Web site, http://www.canongate.net/ (January 23, 2006), "Albert Sánchez Piñol."

Esquire Online, http://www.esquire.com/ (November 30, 2005), Anna Godbersen, "Surreal World," review of *Cold Skin.**

* * *

SANDEL, Michael J.

PERSONAL: Married; children: two sons. *Education:* Graduated from Brandeis University (summa cum laude), 1975; Oxford University, D.Phil., 1981.

ADDRESSES: Home—Brookline, MA. *Office*—Department of Government, Harvard University, 1737 Cambridge St., Cambridge, MA 02138; fax: 617-495-0438. *E-mail*—msandel@gov.harvard.edu.

CAREER: Harvard University, Cambridge, MA, instructor in political philosophy, 1980-99, professor, 1999—, Anne T. and Robert M. Bass Professor of Government; Oxford University, visiting lecturer, 1998; Sorbonne, Paris, France, visiting professor, 2001; President's Council on Bioethics, council member, 2002-05. Has lectured to academic and general audiences in North America, Europe, Japan, India, and Australia.

AWARDS, HONORS: Rhodes Scholar; Phi Beta Kappa Teaching Prize, Harvard-Radcliffe, 1985; fellowships from Carnegie Corporation, National Endowment for the Humanities, Ford Foundation, and American Council of Learned Societies. Awarded three honorary degrees.

WRITINGS:

NONFICTION

Liberalism and the Limits of Justice, Cambridge University Press (New York, NY), 1982, 2nd edition, 1998.

(Editor) *Liberalism and Its Critics,* New York University Press (New York, NY), 1984.

Democracy's Discontent: America in Search of a Public Philosophy, Belknap Press (Cambridge, MA), 1996.

Public Philosophy: Essays on Morality in Politics, Harvard University Press (Cambridge, MA), 2005.

Contributor of numerous articles to scholarly journals, law reviews, and general publications, including *Atlantic Monthly, New Republic,* and *New York Times. Liberalism and the Limits of Justice* has been translated into seven languages.

SIDELIGHTS: Government and political philosophy professor Michael J. Sandel is well known as a strong intellectual opponent of liberal thought. Throughout his writings, including *Liberalism and the Limits of Justice* and *Liberalism and Its Critics,* he offers discourse critiquing the very basis of liberalism as a public philosophy. Sandel's third book, *Democracy's Discontent: America in Search of a Public Philosophy,* continues with this theme, focusing on "the manner in which liberalism and the conception of the person that it incorporates have played themselves out in the context of twentieth-century American politics and law," explained *Social Theory and Practice* contributor Paul Fairfield. Jerry F. Medler, writing in an *International Journal of Comparative Sociology* review, noted the duality of the book, pointing out the "analysis of the evolving expression of liberalism" paired with a discussion of the connection "between the changing U.S. political economy and the putative requirements of citizenship," and observed that there is little in the treatise to tie these elements together. Medler additionally suggested that although *Democracy's Discontent* "leads us to ponder life in a republican community, [Sandel's] presentation is far from persuasive." *Historian* critic Barbara Blumberg agreed somewhat, commenting that the author "overstates and romanticizes" the benefits of republican doctrine, but ultimately felt that "Sandel has written an important, provocative book."

In 2005 Sandel's collected essays were published as *Public Philosophy: Essays on Morality in Politics.* The book combines discussion of highly controversial topics—such as abortion and the scandals revealed during U.S. President Bill Clinton's years in office—with analysis of political philosophers such as Immanuel Kant. *Library Journal* contributor Scott Duimstra appreciated the history discussed in the book and found the commentary "thought-provoking." A *Publishers Weekly* reviewer felt that the compilation of essays, written at different times over the length of Sandel's career, made for "some repetition," and the critic questioned the effectiveness of juxtaposing a myriad of different writing styles in one volume. Ultimately, the reviewer concluded that *Public Philosophy* is "an effective, though sometimes lumpy, blend of the wonky and the philosophical."

BIOGRAPHICAL AND CRITICAL SOURCES:

PERIODICALS

American Journal of Sociology, May, 1997, Steven Tipton, review of *Democracy's Discontent: America in Search of a Public Philosophy,* p. 1729.

American Political Science Review, June, 1997, Susan Okin, review of *Democracy's Discontent,* p. 440.

Australian Journal of Political Science, March, 1998, Philip Petit, review of *Democracy's Discontent,* p. 153.

Christian Century, December 4, 1996, Christopher Beem, review of *Democracy's Discontent,* p. 1206.

Commentary, August, 1996, Wilfred M. McClay, review of *Democracy's Discontent,* p. 97.

Commonweal, November 22, 1996, R. Bruce Douglass, review of *Democracy's Discontent,* p. 26.

Ethics, April, 1997, William A. Galston, review of *Democracy's Discontent,* p. 509.

Foreign Affairs, March-April, 1996, Michael Lind, review of *Democracy's Discontent,* p. 135.

Historian, summer, 1998, Barbara Blumberg, review of *Democracy's Discontent,* p. 873.

Insight on the News, May 13, 1996, Ken Masugi, review of *Democracy's Discontent,* p. 31.

International Journal of Comparative Sociology, August, 1998, Jerry F. Medler, review of *Democracy's Discontent,* p. 331.

Journal of Church and State, autumn, 1997, Robert F. Drinan, review of *Democracy's Discontent,* pp. 803-804.

Journal of Public Administration Research and Theory, April, 1998, Gary Johnson, review of *Democracy's Discontent,* p. 291.

Library Journal, September 15, 2005, Scott Duimstra, review of *Public Philosophy: Essays on Morality in Politics,* p. 68.

Nation, May 6, 1996, Eric Foner, review of *Democracy's Discontent,* p. 34.

New Republic, April 1, 1996, Mary Ann Glendon, review of *Democracy's Discontent,* p. 39.

Political Theory, October, 1997, Eldon Eisenach, review of *Democracy's Discontent,* p. 761.

Publishers Weekly, September 26, 2005, review of *Public Philosophy,* p. 75.

Reason, February, 1997, James M. Buchanan, review of *Democracy's Discontent,* p. 59.

Review of Metaphysics, March, 1997, Roger Paden, review of *Democracy's Discontent,* p. 689.

Social Theory and Practice, spring, 1999, Paul Fairfield, review of *Democracy's Discontent,* p. 165.

U.S. News & World Report, April 29, 1996, John Leo, review of *Democracy's Discontent,* p. 23.

Wilson Quarterly, summer, 1996, Samuel H. Beer, review of *Democracy's Discontent,* p. 89.

Yale Law Journal, March, 1997, Mark V. Tushnet, review of *Democracy's Discontent,* pp. 1571-1610.

ONLINE

Harvard University, Department of Government Web site, http://www.gov.harvard.edu/ (March 28, 2006), profile of author.

President's Council on Bioethics Web site, http://www.bioethics.gov/ (March 28, 2006), brief biography of author.*

*   *   *

SANDS, Philippe 1960-
(Philippe Joseph Sands)

PERSONAL: Born October 17, 1960, in London, England; son of Alan and Ruth (Buchholz) Sands; married Natalia Marien Schiffrin, June 5, 1993; children: Leo, Lara. *Education:* Cambridge University, England, B.A., 1982, L.L.M., 1983.

ADDRESSES: Office—Faculty of Laws, University College London, Bentham House, Endsleigh Gardens, London WC1H 0EG, England. *E-mail*—p.sands@ucl.ac.uk.

CAREER: Lawyer, educator, editor, and writer. St. Catharine's College, Cambridge, England, research fellow, 1984-88; King's College, London, England, lecturer in law, 1988-93; London University School of Oriental and African Studies, lecturer in international law, 1993-97, reader in international law, 1997; Matrix Chambers, London, barrister; Foundation for International and Environmental Law and Development, London, cofounder, 1990, director, 1990-97; University of London, England, professor of international law, 2002—. New York University, New York, NY, visiting professor of law and director of the Centre on International Courts and Tribunals, University College, London, 1994; Soho Theatre Co., London, member of board of directors, 1996; Green Cross, London, 1995; has served as Specialist Adviser to the House of Lords Select Committee on Science and Technology.

WRITINGS:

(Editor and author of introduction) *Chernobyl, Law and Communication: Transboundary Nuclear Air Pollution, the Legal Materials,* Grotius Publications (Cambridge, England), 1988.

(Editor, with Joe Verhoeven and Maxwell Bruce) *The Antarctic Environment and International Law,* Graham & Trotman (London, England), 1992.

(Editor, with Richard Tarasofsky and Mary Weiss) *Documents in International Environment Law,* Manchester University Press (New York, NY), 1994, 2nd edition, edited with Paolo Galizzi, Cambridge University Press (New York, NY) 2004.

(Editor) *Greening International Law,* New Press (New York, NY), 1994.

(Editor, with Richard G. Tarasofsky) *Documents in European Community Environmental Law,* Manchester University Press (New York, NY), 1995.

(General editor, with Daniel Bethlehem and James Crawford) *International Environmental Law Reports,* edited by Cairo A.R. Robb, Cambridge University Press (New York, NY), 1999–2004.

(Editor, with Laurence Boisson de Chazournes) *International Law, the International Court of Justice, and Nuclear Weapons,* Cambridge University Press (New York, NY), 1999.

(Editor, with assistant editors Ruth Mackenzie and Yuval Shany) *Manual on International Courts and Tribunals,* Butterworths (London, England), 1999.

(Editor, with Richard L. Revesz and Richard B. Stewart) *Environmental Law, the Economy, and*

Sustainable Development: The United States, the European Union, and the International Community, Cambridge University Press (New York, NY), 2000.

(With Pierre Klein) *Bowett's Law of International Institutions,* Sweet & Maxwell (London, England), 2001.

(Editor) *From Nuremberg to the Hague: The Future of International Criminal Justice,* Cambridge University Press (New York, NY), 2003.

(Editor, with Mark Lattimer) *Justice for Crimes against Humanity,* Hart (Portland, OR), 2003.

Principles of International Environmental Law, 2nd edition, Cambridge University Press (New York, NY), 2003.

Lawless World: America and the Making and Breaking of Global Rules from FDR's Atlantic Charter to George W. Bush's Illegal War, Viking (New York, NY), 2005.

Articles on international, environmental and natural resources law have appeared in numerous publications.

SIDELIGHTS: Philippe Sands is an expert in international law and also has a strong interest in these laws as they pertain to governments and the environment. Sands has written or edited numerous books pertaining to these areas of interest. For example, he is editor of *From Nuremberg to the Hague: The Future of International Criminal Justice,* a collection of five essays covering topics such as the International Criminal Court's negotiation process and the relationship of current international law as it is traced back to the Nuremberg trials following World War II. Writing in the *Michigan Law Review,* Mark A. Drumbl noted, "The essays—concise and in places informal—carefully avoid legalese and arcania. Taken together, they cover an impressive spectrum of issues."

Sands is also the author of *Lawless World: America and the Making and Breaking of Global Rules from FDR's Atlantic Charter to George W. Bush's Illegal War.* The author primarily addresses the issue of the country's stance under the leadership of President Bush that the United States can pick and choose the international laws it wishes to obey. Sands also details how the U.S. Congress passed a law that essentially gave the U.S. president the ability to use any tactics available to free Americans arrested by the International Criminal Court. Writing in London's *Guardian,* Martin Jacques noted that the book is really about much more than the perception of the United States as a country unwilling to obey international law when it goes against its goals. Rather, Jacques noted that "it is far more important than that." He added, "In exploring the evolution of international law since the second world war, and the new American attitude of withdrawal and unilateralism, it goes to the very heart of the nature of the international order and its future." Jacques commented that the author "writes not as a dull international lawyer but as an astute observer of human situations." A *Kirkus Reviews* contributor commented, "Solid work. Those worried that the U.S. has become a rogue nation won't sleep any easier after reading this book." David Lakhdhir, writing in the *New York Law Journal,* commented that the author "thinks the United States (with British complicity) has gone seriously off course, and has written *Lawless World* as a wake-up call. In the process, he has written a highly readable, if disturbing, survey of the major current issues in international law."

BIOGRAPHICAL AND CRITICAL SOURCES:

PERIODICALS

Age (Melbourne, Australia), July 23, 2005, Julian Burnside, review of *Lawless World: America and the Making and Breaking of Global Rules from FDR's Atlantic Charter to George W. Bush's Illegal War.*

Arbitration International, November, 2005, review of *Lawless World,* p. 438.

Guardian (London, England), March 26, 2005, Martin Jacques, review of *Lawless World.*

Kirkus Reviews, August 15, 2005, review of *Lawless World,* p. 904.

Melbourne Journal of International Law, October, 2005, Phillippe Sands, "*Lawless World:* International Law after September 11, 2001 and Iraq," p. 437.

Michigan Law Review, May, 2005, Mark A. Drumbl, review of *From Nuremberg to the Hague: The Future of International Criminal Justice,* p. 1295.

New York Law Journal, October 26, 2005, David Lakhdhir, review of *Lawless World.*

Observer (London, England), March 6, 2005, John Kampfner, review of *Lawless World.*

Publishers Weekly, September 5, 2005, review of *Lawless World,* p. 50.

ONLINE

Matrix Chambers Web site, http://www.matrixlaw.co. uk/ (March 28, 2006), brief profile of author.

University College London Web site, http://www.ucl. ac.uk/ (March 28, 2006), faculty profile of author.

*   *   *

SANDS, Philippe Joseph
See SANDS, Philippe

*   *   *

SAUNT, Claudio 1967-

PERSONAL: Born October 18, 1967, in San Francisco, CA. *Education:* Columbia University, B.A., 1989; Duke University, M.A., 1991, Ph.D., 1996.

ADDRESSES: Office—Institute of Native American Studies, University of Georgia, Peabody Hall 1625, Athens, GA 30602. *E-mail*—csaunt@uga.edu.

CAREER: Historian, educator, and writer. St. Philip's Archaeological Project, Old Salem, NC, assistant director, 1993; Columbia University, New York, NY, lecturer, 1996-98; University of Georgia, Athens, assistant professor then associate professor of history, 1998—. Manuscript reviewer for journals, including *Journal of American History, Journal of Southern History, William and Mary Quarterly, American Indian Culture and Research Quarterly,* and *Journal of the Early Republic;* editorial board member of History Compass, an online collection of nine journals; member of the steering committee of the University of Georgia Institute of Native American Studies.

MEMBER: American Society for Ethnohistory, Southern Historical Association, Omohundro Institute of Early American History and Culture.

AWARDS, HONORS: National Endowment for the Humanities fellow, 1995; Mellon fellow, 1996-98; Bolton-Kinnaird Prize, 1998, for best journal article on Spanish borderlands history; Charles S. Sydnor Award for best book on Southern history, Southern Historical Association; and Wheeler-Voegelin Award for best book in ethnohistory, American Society of Ethnohistory, both 2000, both for *A New Order of Things: Property, Power, and the Transformation of the Creek Indians, 1733-1816*.

WRITINGS:

A New Order of Things: Property, Power, and the Transformation of the Creek Indians, 1733-1816, Cambridge University Press (New York, NY), 1999.

Black, White, and Indian: Race and the Unmaking of an American Family, Oxford University Press (New York, NY), 2005.

Contributor to numerous books, including *Dictionary of American History* and *Contact Points: North American Frontiers from the Mohawk Valley to the Mississippi, 1750-1830*, edited by Fredrick J. Teute and Andrew R.L. Cayton, University of North Carolina, 1998; contributor to periodicals, including *American Indian Quarterly, American Historical Review,* and *William and Mary Quarterly.*

SIDELIGHTS: Historian Claudio Saunt is primarily interested in the history of Native Americans, particularly tribes from the Southeast. In his first book, *A New Order of Things: Property, Power, and the Transformation of the Creek Indians, 1733-1816,* the author writes about the Creek Indians who once lived in the areas of Georgia and Alabama. Saunt outlines how the tribes became interested in commerce and the international trading of deer hides with the arrival of settlers. Relating how this new interest in commerce caused divisions in the tribe by introducing such concepts as personal wealth and unequal distribution of wealth among tribal members, the author focuses on one specific division between the rich and poor Creeks that led to a Creek civil war in 1812 called the Redstick War. "This book is based on an enormous amount of research, mostly in manuscript sources and much of it from Spanish archives," wrote Theda Perdue in the *Journal of Interdisciplinary History.* Perdue felt that because of Saunt's reliance on these primary sources, he provides illuminating detail about the Creeks of this time. Perdue also noted

that the author "masterfully weaves gender and race . . . into his compelling narrative of economic and political disparity." *Journal of Southern History* contributor Daniel K. Richter commented that the author has "a creative intellect, a fine eye for symbolic meaning, and an impressive body of research in long-neglected Spanish-language documents."

Black, White, and Indian: Race and the Unmaking of an American Family focuses on the Graysons, a Native American family whose ancestors include African slaves. Looking back on five generations of the Graysons, the author examines the family's interracial marriages. The author also reveals how some family members were split apart when the Creeks received U.S. citizenship in 1907 and the state designated some family members as white and some as black. "This is a fascinating look at a seldom-recognized aspect of American race relations," wrote Vernon Ford in *Booklist.*

BIOGRAPHICAL AND CRITICAL SOURCES:

PERIODICALS

Booklist, June 1, 2005, Vernon Ford, review of *Black, White, and Indian: Race and the Unmaking of an American Family,* p. 1746.

Journal of Interdisciplinary History, autumn, 2000, Theda Perdue, review of *A New Order of Things: Property, Power, and the Transformation of the Creek Indians, 1733-1816,* p. 287.

Journal of Southern History, August, 2002, Daniel K. Richter, review of *A New Order of Things,* p. 678.

ONLINE

University of Georgia Institute of Native American Studies Web site, http://www.uga.edu/inas/ (March 26, 2006), faculty profile of author.*

* * *

SAVAGE, Allan M.
See SAVAGE, Allan Maurice

SAVAGE, Allan Maurice 1946-
(Allan M. Savage)

PERSONAL: Born October 11, 1946, in Timmons, Ontario, Canada; son of Cecil (a laborer) and Gabrielle (Rondeau) Savage. *Ethnicity:* "Anglo-Saxon." *Education:* University of Toronto, B.A., 1974; St. Paul University, Ottawa, Ontario, Canada, B.Th., 1978; Heythrop College, London, postgraduate diploma in pastoral theology, 1978; Somerset Independent University, M.Th., 1989; University of South Africa, D.Th., 1996. *Religion:* Roman Catholic.

ADDRESSES: Home—292 Red River Rd., Thunder Bay, Ontario P7B 1A8, Canada. *E-mail*—savagea@ tbaytel.net.

CAREER: Roman Catholic Diocese of Thunder Bay, Thunder Bay, Ontario, Canada, priest, 1982—, and director of Adult Faith Office. University of Winnipeg, sessional lecturer in theology. Ontario Liturgical Conference, diocesan representative; Ontario Multifaith Council, board member.

MEMBER: Catholic Theological Association of Great Britain, American Catholic Philosophical Association.

WRITINGS:

A Phenomenological Understanding of Certain Liturgical Texts: The Anglican Collects for Advent and the Roman Catholic Collects for Lent, University Press of America (Lanham, MD), 2001.

(Under name Allan M. Savage; with Sheldon William Nicholl) *Faith, Hope, and Charity As Character Traits in Adler's Individual Psychology: With Related Essays in Spirituality and Phenomenology,* University Press of America (Lanham, MD), 2003.

Contributor of articles and reviews to periodicals, including *Canadian Journal of Adlerian Psychology, Quodlibet, Omni: Journal of Spiritual and Religious Care,* and *Explorations: Journal for Adventurous Thought.*

BIOGRAPHICAL AND CRITICAL SOURCES:

ONLINE

Personal Web Pages of Allan Savage, D.Th., http:// www.mentorcomputers.on.ca/savage (December 30, 2004).

SCHOFIELD, John A. 1948-

PERSONAL: Born August 23, 1948, in Wakefield, England; son of Jack (a civil servant) and Edna (a teacher; maiden name, Jones) Schofield. *Education:* Christ Church, Oxford, B.A., 1970; University of Edinburgh, M.Phil., 1973; University of London, Ph.D., 1979.

ADDRESSES: Office—Museum of London, London Wall, London EC2Y 5HN, England. *E-mail*—john@ jschd.demon.co.uk.

CAREER: Writer. Museum of London, London, England, archaeologist, 1974-98, curator of architecture, 1998—. City of London Archaeological Trust, secretary, 1991—.

MEMBER: Society of Antiquaries (fellow), Association of Diocesan and Cathedral Archaeologists (chair, 2000-05).

WRITINGS:

The Building of London from the Conquest to the Great Fire, British Museum Publications (London, England), 1984, 3rd edition, 2003.
(With A. Vince) *Medieval Towns,* Leicester University Press (Leicester, England), 1994, 2nd edition, 2003.
Medieval London Houses, Yale University Press (New Haven, CT), 1995, corrected edition, 2003.

Contributor of about forty articles to periodicals.

WORK IN PROGRESS: Archaeology of St Paul's Cathedral, Volume 1: *Excavation and Survey to 2004,* for Museum of London (London, England); *Holy Trinity Priory, London,* with R. Lea, Museum of London.

*   *   *

SCHRIFT, Shirley
See WINTERS, Shelley

*   *   *

SEMPLE, Andrea 1975-

PERSONAL: Born 1975, in England. *Education:* Attended University in Hull, England.

ADDRESSES: Home—Leeds, England. *Agent*—The Marsh Agency, 11 Dover St., London W1S 4LJ, England. *E-mail*—andrea@andreasemple.com.

CAREER: Writer. Worked variously as a manager for one of the world's largest nightclubs, in Ibiza, Spain; as a freelance journalist; and as publisher of *Writing Tips,* an e-newsletter.

WRITINGS:

(With Matt Haig) *The Internet Job Search Handbook,* How to Books (Oxford, England), 2001.

NOVELS

The Ex-Factor, Piatkus Books (London, England), 2002.
The Make-Up Girl, Piatkus Books (London, England, 2004.
The Man from Perfect, Piatkus Books (London, England), 2005.

Contributor to periodicals, including the *Guardian, Independent,* and *Eve.*

SIDELIGHTS: Novelist Andrea Semple was born and raised in England. She lived briefly in Ibiza, Spain, where she worked as part of the management team for a major nightclub, prior to returning to England. She has worked as a freelance journalist, her work appearing in such publications as the *Guardian, Eve,* and the *Independent.* Her first novel, *The Ex-Factor,* is a light, comedic work, following the adventures of Martha Seymore, an advice columnist for an English fashion magazine, who finds out her boyfriend is cheating on her. This failure of her own relationship forces Martha to question every bit of advice she has ever given in her column, and she goes off the deep end in her attempt to completely change her life. Aleksandra Kostovski, in a review for *Booklist,* compared Martha favorably to her fellow chick-lit heroine, Bridget Jones, stating that "readers will be pleased to find a character who's less self-deprecating and more self-assured."

Semple's follow-up novel, *The Make-Up Girl,* tells the story of Faith Wishart, a young woman who constantly invents the details of a fabulous life to convince her mother she is perfectly happy, when reality is far from her imaginings. In a review for *Library Journal,* Anika Fajardo found Semple's effort "an uneven read, at times engaging but generally predictable." However, Kostovski, again reviewing for *Booklist,* wrote that Semple is able to "replicate the quick-paced charm of her debut."

BIOGRAPHICAL AND CRITICAL SOURCES:

PERIODICALS

Booklist, September 15, 2004, Aleksandra Kostovski, review of *The Ex-Factor,* p. 228; October 15, 2005, Aleksandra Kostovski, review of *The Make-Up Girl,* p. 31.
Entertainment Weekly, November 11, 2005, Clarissa Cruz, Nina Willdorf, and Leah Greenblatt, "Chick Lit 101: Bad Boys, Cad Nauseum," review of *The Make-Up Girl,* p. 76.
Library Journal, October 1, 2005, Anika Fajardo, review of *The Make-Up Girl,* p. 68.

ONLINE

Andrea Semple Home page, http://www.andreasemple.com (January 25, 2006).

*   *   *

SHANKER, S.G.
    See SHANKER, Stuart G.

*   *   *

SHANKER, Stuart
    See SHANKER, Stuart G.

*   *   *

SHANKER, Stuart G.
    (S.G. Shanker, Stuart Shanker)

PERSONAL: Male. *Education:* University of Toronto, B.A., 1975, M.A., 1978; Oxford University, B.A., 1977, B.Phil., 1981, D.Phil., 1984.

ADDRESSES: Office—Milton & Ethel Harris Research Initiative, York University, HNES Bldg., Rm. 421, 4700 Keele St., Toronto, Ontario M3J 1P3, Canada. *E-mail*—shanker@yorku.ca.

CAREER: Psychologist, educator, and writer. York University, Toronto, Ontario, Canada, distinguished research professor of philosophy and psychology, director of the Milton and Ethel Harris Research Initiative. Also codirector of the Council of Human Development and chair for Canada of the Interdisciplinary Council of Learning and Developmental Disorders.

WRITINGS:

(Editor, as Stuart Shanker) *Ludwig Wittgenstein: Critical Assessments,* Croom Helm (Dover, NH), 1986.

(Editor, with John V. Canfield) *Wittgenstein's Intentions,* Garland (New York, NY), 1993.

(Editor) *Philosophy of Science, Logic, and Mathematics in the Twentieth Century,* Routledge (New York, NY), 1996.

(With Sue Savage-Rumbaugh and Talbot J. Taylor) *Apes, Language, and the Human Mind,* Oxford University Press (New York, NY), 1998.

Wittgenstein's Remarks on the Foundations of AI, Routledge (New York, NY), 1998.

(Editor, with David Bakhurst) *Jerome Bruner: Language, Culture, Self,* Sage (Thousand Oaks, CA), 2001.

(With Stanley Greenspan) *Toward a Psychology of Global Interdependency: A Framework for International Collaboration,* ICDL Press (Washington, DC), 2002.

(Editor, with David Kilfoyle) *Ludwig Wittgenstein: Critical Assessments,* Routledge (London, England), 2002.

(With Stanley I. Greenspan) *The First Idea: How Symbols, Language, and Intelligence Evolved from our Early Primate Ancestors to Modern Humans,* Da Capo Press (Cambridge, MA), 2004.

AS S.G. SHANKER

(Editor) *Philosophy in Britain Today,* State University of New York Press (Albany, NY), 1986.

(With V.A. Shanker) *A Wittgenstein Bibliography,* Croom Helm (London, England), 1986.

Wittgenstein and the Turning-Point in the Philosophy of Mathematics, State University of New York Press (Albany, NY), 1987.

(Editor, with G.H.R. Parkinson) *Routledge History of Philosophy,* ten volumes, Routledge (London, England), 1994–2000.

(Editor) *Gödel's Theorem in Focus,* Croom Helm (New York, NY), 1998.

Contributor to books, including *Wittgenstein and Quine,* edited by R.L. Arrington and H.J. Glock, Routledge (London, England), 1996.

SIDELIGHTS: Stuart G. Shanker is an expert in ape and child language development and has written extensively about these areas. In *Apes, Language, and the Human Mind,* which Shanker wrote with Sue Savage-Rumbaugh and Talbot J. Taylor, the authors focus on the issue of the ability of apes both to understand and use symbols. They discuss the history of research in this area and present their theory that new approaches in research are needed. "They suggest that a wholesale revision is necessary before science can truly understand the significance of ape abilities and performance," wrote Thomas Wynn in the *Quarterly Review of Biology,* adding that the book "is probably not for novice or casual readers" in this area.

Shanker collaborated with Stanley I. Greenspan to write *The First Idea: How Symbols, Language, and Intelligence Evolved from our Early Primate Ancestors to Modern Humans.* Shanker and Greenspan discuss cognitive development over the centuries, beginning with humans' early ancestors. They also explore the importance of an emotional connection between the mother, or other caregiver, and the infant as the basis for good cognitive development while rejecting the theory that language development is primarily a natural part of the human brain's biological "wiring." A *Publishers Weekly* contributor noted that the authors "maintain that symbolic thinking has been molded by cultural practices dating back to pre-human species." Writing in the *Quarterly Review of Biology,* A. Charles Catania commented that "in its breadth and illuminating details, this book will be a valuable resource for anyone interested in the origins of language." In a review in *Library Journal,* H. James Birx called *The First Idea* "a significant book on the crucial role that emotions play in the social development of human intelligence." A *Kirkus Reviews* contributor wrote that the authors present "a thorough, fairly readable study of cognitive development."

BIOGRAPHICAL AND CRITICAL SOURCES:

PERIODICALS

Booklist, September 15, 2004, Gilbert Taylor, review of *The First Idea: How Symbols, Language, and Intelligence Evolved from our Early Primate Ancestors to Modern Humans,* p. 181.

Kirkus Reviews, July 15, 2004, review of *The First Idea,* p. 671.

Library Bookwatch, January, 2005, review of *The First Idea.*

Library Journal, November 1, 2004, H. James Birx, review of *The First Idea,* p. 118.

Publishers Weekly, July 26, 2004, review of *The First Idea,* p. 46.

Quarterly Review of Biology, June, 1999, Thomas Wynn, review of *Apes, Language, and the Human Mind,* p. 249; September, 2005, A. Charles Catania, a review of *The First Idea,* p. 382.

ONLINE

Council of Human Development, http://www.councilhd.ca/ (March 26, 2006), brief profile of author.

Curled Up with a Good Book, http://www.curledup.com/ (March 26, 2006), Megan Kopp, review of *The First Idea.*

Milton & Ethel Harris Research Initiative (MEHRI) Web site, http://www.mehri.ca/ (April 18, 2006).

York University Department of Philosophy Web site, http://www.arts.yorku.ca/phil/ (March 26, 2006), faculty profile of author.

* * *

SHELTON, Connie 1951-
(Connie Lee Shelton)

PERSONAL: Born November 9, 1951, in Albuquerque, NM; daughter of Harold E. and Marilyn June Tidenberg; married Carl Daniel Shelton, July 24, 1993; children: Stephanie J. Quigley, Brandon S. March.

ADDRESSES: Home—Angel Fire, NM. *Office*—Columbine Publishing Group Inc, P.O. Box 416, Angel Fire, NM, 87710-0456. *Agent*—c/o Author Mail, Intrigue Press, 923 Williamson St., Madison, WI 53703.

CAREER: Writer. Pitney Bowes, Albuquerque, NM, collections supervisor, 1971-72; The March Company, Albuquerque, partner, 1974-90; Columbine Publishing Group, Angel Fire, NM, president, 1994.

MEMBER: Angel Fire Search and Rescue (secretary, 1995), Moreno Valley Arts Council (secretary, treasurer, 1995-96), Mystery Writers of America Rocky Mountain chapter (treasurer, 1998-2005), Small Publishers Association of America (director, 1998), Moreno Valley Writers Guild (board of directors, president, 1995—), Sisters in Crime, Publishers Marketing Association.

WRITINGS:

Deadly Gamble, Intrigue Press (Angel Fire, NM), 1995.

Publish Your Own Novel, Columbine Publishing Group (Angel Fire, NM), 1996.

Vacations Can Be Murder, Intrigue Press (Angel Fire, NM), 1996.

Partnerships Can Kill, Intrigue Press (Angel Fire, NM), 1997.

Small Towns Can Be Murder, Intrigue Press (Angel Fire, NM), 1998.

Memories Can Be Murder, Intrigue Press (Angel Fire, NM), 1999.

Honeymoons Can Be Murder, Intrigue Press (Philadelphia, PA), 2001.

Reunions Can Be Murder, Intrigue Press (Denver, CO), 2002.

Competition Can Be Murder: A Charlie Parker Mystery, Intrigue Press (Denver, CO), 2004.

Balloons Can Be Murder: A Charlie Parker Mystery, Intrigue Press (Boulder, CO), 2005.

SIDELIGHTS: Connie Shelton was born and raised in Albuquerque, New Mexico, and uses that area as the backdrop for her series of mysteries starring Charlie Parker, a combination certified public accountant and investigator. Shelton developed Parker in response to a longtime desire to create a female character with a man's name, similar to the detectives in mysteries by such successful writers as Sue Grafton and Sara Paretsky. In her original incarnation, Parker was a tough private investigator, similar to the heroines of those other authors' books, but Shelton eventually tamed the character into a softer, more vulnerable person, more in keeping with her own personal style. Although she created her other characters to be entirely original, or exhibiting traits of a variety of people she knows, Shelton admits that the character of Elsa Higgins is based strongly on her own grandmother. She attempts to keep the setting as accurate as possible, however, which sometimes proves difficult as she has since moved out of Albuquerque and only visits occasionally.

Shelton uses real-life experiences to inspire the plots of her mysteries, tapping into everything from a vacation in the Scottish highlands to her license as a hot-air balloon pilot and the miscarriages of two of her friends. In *Deadly Gamble,* Shelton's debut mystery, Parker, who normally leaves the investigating to her brother Ron, is forced to tackle a case on her own when he goes out of town. Stuart Miller, in a review for *Booklist,* dubbed Shelton's effort a "well-plotted debut mystery with a nice surprise ending and some excellent characterizations."

Vacations Can Be Murder takes Parker out of her home town and off to Hawaii, where she finds a dead body on the coast while taking a helicopter tour of Kauai. A contributor for *Publishers Weekly* enjoyed the narration but concluded that "this lightweight caper never quite gels into an engrossing mystery."

Returning from her trip to Hawaii, Parker is immediately embroiled in another mystery in *Partnerships Can Kill.* A high school friend approaches Parker when the friend's business partner suddenly dies, putting their previously successful restaurant into jeopardy. Although the man's death is ruled a suicide, Parker's friend asks her to look into things more closely, both due to her personal suspicions and because she cannot collect on their business insurance policy if the suicide verdict stands. In a review for *Publishers Weekly,* a contributor found that "Charlie is as methodical in her search for the killer as Shelton is in constructing this routine whodunit." Rex E. Klett, writing for *Library Journal,* called Shelton's effort "down-to-earth."

In *Small Towns Can Be Murder,* Parker finds herself looking into the death of a woman following a miscarriage, the circumstances made suspicious by the possibility that the woman suffered from spousal abuse. A contributor for *Publishers Weekly* found the novel of-

fered "little mystery or suspense," while Mary Frances Wilkins, in a review for *Booklist,* remarked that the book is "low key and grounded in daily life."

Charlie Parker has married her boyfriend, Drake, by the start of *Honeymoons Can Be Murder,* and she and her new husband are visiting Taos, New Mexico. In a trip that is part vacation and part work, Drake, a pilot, flies heli-skiers up to remote peaks. A friend of Drake's is accused of murder, and Parker sets out to discover the real killer. John Rowen, reviewing for *Booklist,* wrote that "the mystery here makes good use of the switched-identity gambit," and a reviewer for *Publishers Weekly* called the book a "solid effort."

Balloons Can Be Murder: A Charlie Parker Mystery incorporates the annual hot-air balloon festival in Albuquerque, New Mexico, with Shelton's own expertise as a balloon pilot. This mystery involves a new client of Parker and her brother, Rachel Fairfield. She is attempting to set a new altitude record but is receiving threatening notes to discourage her, followed by attempts on her life. Rex E. Klett, writing for *Library Journal,* called Shelton's work "a colorful addition to the series."

BIOGRAPHICAL AND CRITICAL SOURCES:

PERIODICALS

Booklist, January 15, 1995, Stuart Miller, review of *Deadly Gamble,* p. 900; April 15, 1998, Mary Frances Wilkens, review of *Small Towns Can Be Murder,* p. 1394; September 15, 1999, John Rowen, review of *Memories Can Be Murder,* p. 238; January 1, 2001, John Rowen, review of *Honeymoons Can Be Murder,* p. 926; March 15, 2004, Jenny McLarin, review of *Competition Can Be Murder: A Charlie Parker Mystery,* p. 1273.
Kirkus Reviews, September 15, 2005, review of *Balloons Can Be Murder: A Charlie Parker Mystery,* p. 1004.
Library Journal, May 1, 1997, Rex E. Klett, review of *Partnerships Can Kill,* p. 144; April 1, 1998, Rex E. Klett, review of *Small Towns Can Be Murder,* p. 129; December, 2002, Rex E. Klett, review of *Reunions Can Be Murder,* p. 183; November 1, 2005, Rex E. Klett, review of *Balloons Can Be Murder,* p. 56.

Publishers Weekly, September 11, 1995, review of Vacations Can Be Murder, p. 78; February 24, 1997, review of Partnerships Can Kill, p. 66; April 6, 1998, review of Small Towns Can Be Murder, p. 63; January 29, 2001, "February Publications," review of Honeymoons Can Be Murder, p. 69.

ONLINE

Connie Shelton Home Page, http://www.connieshelton. com (February 4, 2006).

* * *

SHELTON, Connie Lee
  See SHELTON, Connie

* * *

SHERRETT, James 1975-

PERSONAL: Born 1975, in Winnipeg, Manitoba, Canada. *Education:* Attended University of Manitoba.

ADDRESSES: Home—Vancouver, British Columbia, Canada. *Agent*—c/o Author Mail, Turnstone Press, 607-100 Arthur St., Winnipeg, Manitoba R3B 1H3, Canada. *E-mail*—james@upinontario.com.

CAREER: Writer. Jesse James Press, publisher and cofounder; worked variously as e-commerce and e-publishing director.

AWARDS, HONORS: Manitoba Literary Award, Heaven Chapbook of the Year, for *Up in Ontario,* 1996.

WRITINGS:

Up in Ontario, Turnstone Press (Winnipeg, Manitoba, Canada), 2003.

SIDELIGHTS: James Sherrett was born and raised in Winnipeg, Manitoba, Canada, a childhood that affected his choice of subjects on which to write. His memories include riding his bike through chilly mornings to school until the weather grew too cold, playing soccer and wearing cleats that allowed him to make sharp turns, participating in football and rugby, and of course, playing ice hockey. Although he was an indifferent student, he enjoyed English class because he could argue his opinions, and eventually he went on to study English at the University of Manitoba, where one of his major influences was writer Carol Shields. Sherrett's first novel, *Up in Ontario,* tells the story of Gilbert Dubois, a trapper and fishing guide in northwestern Ontario. Dubois marries, has a son, and eventually gets a divorce, but he and his son, Wade, bond over the years during a series of father/son hunting and fishing trips. A contributor for *Prairie Fire Online* remarked that "Sherrett's medium-long, meticulous descriptions are rendered in a simple, straightforward way that parallels the attitudes and behaviours of many people in the geographical district," and concluded that the book "is an exceptional debut." In a review for the *Winnipeg Free Press,* Corey Redekop wrote that "despite a lamentable tendency to speechifying near the end, Sherrett has produced an elegant elegy to the chasm that exists between us all."

BIOGRAPHICAL AND CRITICAL SOURCES:

PERIODICALS

Owen Sound Sun-Times (Owen Sound, Ontario, Canada), January 22, 2004, review of Up in Ontario.
Winnipeg Free Press, January 25, 2004, Corey Redekop, "Vacation for Mind and Soul," review of Up in Ontario.

ONLINE

Prairie Fire Online, http://www.prairiefire.ca/ (February 3, 2006), "James Sherrett."
Up in Ontario Home Page, http://www.upinontario. com (February 3, 2006).

* * *

SINGER, A.L.
  See LERANGIS, Peter

SINYARD, Neil 1945-
(Neil Richard Sinyard)

PERSONAL: Born September 2, 1945, in Hull, North Humberside, England; son of Richard (a decorator) and Florence Elsie (a homemaker; maiden name, Field) Sinyard; married Lesley Bonham (a homemaker); children: Nathalie, Jessica, Joel. *Ethnicity:* "White." *Education:* University of Hull, B.A. (with first-class honors); University of Manchester, M.A. *Politics:* "Lifelong Labour Party supporter." *Hobbies and other interests:* Music (mainly classical), football.

ADDRESSES: Home—42 Holderness Cres., Beverley HU17 0BE, England. *Office*—Department of English, University of Hull, Hull, Humberside HU6 7RX, England. *E-mail*—n.r.sinyard@hull.ac.uk.

CAREER: Writer and film critic. University of Hull, Hull, England, reader in film studies, 1989—.

AWARDS, HONORS: BP Arts Journalism Award, 1987; grants from Leverhulme Trust, 1990, and British Academy, 1998.

WRITINGS:

(With Adrian Turner) *Journey down Sunset Boulevard: The Films of Billy Wilder,* BCW, 1979.
Classic Movies, Hamlyn (London, England), 1985.
Directors: All-Time Greats, Gallery Books (New York, NY), 1985.
(General editor) *All-Time Box-Office Hits,* Gallery Books (New York, NY), 1985.
The Films of Richard Lester, Croom Helm (London, England), 1985.
Filming Literature: The Art of Screen Adaptation, Croom Helm (London, England), 1986.
The Films of Alfred Hitchcock, Admiral/Multimedia, 1986.
(With A. Goldau and H. Prinzler) *Zinnemann,* Verlag Filmland Presse (Munich, Germany), 1986.
The Films of Steven Spielberg, Hamlyn (London, England), 1987.
The Films of Woody Allen, Hamlyn (London, England), 1987.

The Best of Disney, W.H. Smith (London, England), 1988.
The Films of Mel Brooks, Hamlyn (London, England), 1988.
Marilyn, Magna Books, 1989.
Silent Movies, W.H. Smith (London, England), 1990.
The Films of Nicolas Roeg, Charles Letts (London, England), 1991.
Classic Movie Comedians, Bison (London, England), 1992.
Mel Gibson, Bison (London, England), 1992.
Children in the Movies, St. Martin's Press (New York, NY), 1992.
Clint Eastwood, Bison (London, England), 1995.
Jack Clayton, Manchester University Press (Manchester, England), 2000.
(Editor, with Ian MacKillop) *British Cinema of the 1950s: A Celebration,* Manchester University Press (Manchester, England), 2003.
Fred Zinnemann: Films of Character and Conscience, McFarland (Jefferson, NC), 2003.
Graham Greene: A Literary Life, Palgrave Macmillan (New York, NY), 2003.

Coeditor of "British Film Makers" series, Manchester University Press (Manchester, England), 2000—. Contributor to periodicals.

WORK IN PROGRESS: Books on Richard Lester and William Wyler; a book on Alfred Hitchcock and Bernard Herrmann.

SIDELIGHTS: Neil Sinyard told *CA:* "My primary motivation for writing is to communicate my love of someone's work to other people, hoping that there are people out there who feel the same or who will be stimulated. I've always felt the compulsion to write. As Graham Greene once said, 'I don't know what I'd do if I found I couldn't write another book.'

"I'm not aware of influences on my work as such, though I'm sure I unconsciously echo the style of people I admire—Billy Wilder, James Agee. I find myself quoting Leonard Bernstein a lot.

"My writing process involves long gestation and then intensive writing, generally at night. I write a first draft very roughly in longhand (I'm a one-finger typist, I'm afraid) and am often pleasantly surprised to find it close to the final version. When writing on Greene, I tried his method of 500 words a day, but it only worked in the final stage.

"I am inspired by a combination of suggestion and commission. I've been lucky in that a lot of my subjects have been labors of love: Wilder, Jack Clayton, Richard Lester, Hitchcock, Woody Allen, et cetera."

BIOGRAPHICAL AND CRITICAL SOURCES:

PERIODICALS

Contemporary Review, July, 2003, review of *British Cinema of the 1950s: A Celebration,* p. 63.

*   *   *

SINYARD, Neil Richard
See SINYARD, Neil

*   *   *

SMITH, Ursula 1934-

PERSONAL: Born January 3, 1934, in Santa Maria, CA; daughter of Jules (a physician) and Mary Loretta (a nurse; maiden name, Connolly) Bertero; married James Francis Smith (an insurance agent), July 19, 1958 (divorced, 1988); children: James, Jr., Joseph, Christopher, Ursula, Nora. *Education:* Lone Mountain College (now University of San Francisco), B.A., 1955; San Francisco State University, graduate studies, 1955-56.

ADDRESSES: Home—Middletown Springs, VT. *Office*—Linda Peavy/Ursula Smith, P.S., A Partnership, 169 Garron Rd., Middletown Springs, VT 05757. *E-mail*—ps@vermontel.net.

CAREER: Writer. Mission High School, San Francisco, CA, teacher of English, 1956-58; secretary and office manager for computer and real estate firms, Bozeman, MT, 1977-80; writer, 1980—. Gives readings, workshops, and presentations in women's history

and biography; formerly coeditor of Coalition for Western Women's History *Newsletter*; historical consultant for *Frontier House,* a Public Broadcasting Service documentary.

MEMBER: Editorial Freelancers Association, Western History Association.

AWARDS, HONORS: Paladin Award for best articles in *Montana, the Magazine of Western History,* with Linda Peavy, 1985, 2002; Notable Children's Trade Book in the field of social studies, National Council for Social Studies and the Children's Book Council, 1986, and Children's Book of the Year, Child Study Association of America, 1987, both for *Dreams into Deeds*; residency in nonfiction at Centrum, Port Townsend, WA, with Linda Peavy, 1988; National Endowment for the Humanities Fellowship, with Linda Peavy, 2003; recipient, with Linda Peavy, of Redd Center for Western Studies Independent Research Award and a Smithsonian Short-Term Visitors grant.

WRITINGS:

WITH LINDA PEAVY

Food, Nutrition & You, Scribner (New York, NY), 1982.
Women Who Changed Things, Scribner (New York, NY), 1983.
Dreams into Deeds: Nine Women Who Dared, Scribner (New York, NY), 1985.
Pamelia (three-act opera; music by Eric Funk), choral version produced at Carnegie Hall, New York, NY, 1989.
The Gold Rush Widows of Little Falls: A Story Drawn from the Letters of Pamelia and James Fergus, Minnesota Historical Society Press (St. Paul, MN), 1990.
Women in Waiting in the Westward Movement: Life on the Home Frontier, foreword by John Mack Faragher, University of Oklahoma Press (Norman, OK), 1994.
Pioneer Women: The Lives of Women on the Frontier, University of Oklahoma Press (Norman, OK), 1998.
Frontier Children, foreword by Elliott West, University of Oklahoma Press (Norman, OK), 1999.

(With Linda Peavy and Simon Shaw) *Frontier House,* photography by Audrey Hall, Atria Books (New York, NY), 2002.

Contributor to books, including *Native Athletes in Sport and Society,* edited by C. Richard King, University of Nebraska Press (Lincoln, NE), 2005; and *Portraits of Women in the American West,* edited by Dee Garceau-Hagen, Routledge (New York, NY), 2005. Also contributor to periodicals, with Linda Peavy, including *Nebraska Education News, Plainswoman, Cobblestone, Montana English Journal, Woman's Journal Advocate,* and *Montana, the Magazine of Western History*; contributor to the development of screenplays, dramatic scripts, and musical theater productions.

SIDELIGHTS: Ursula Smith, along with her partner Linda Peavy, has written a number of books focusing on the role of women in the history of the American West. Smith told CA: "Some truths are slow in coming. Swept as I was by the drama of the stories I read and heard in the history classes I took as a child and as a college student, it never occurred to me to question the accuracy of those texts. I was well over forty before I came to realize that half the story was missing. None of those books I had so enjoyed had given me the role models I needed in order to reach my fullest potential, for none of those books had told me about the women who shaped our past. I had grown up with the subtle message that everything worth writing about had been accomplished by men; women had done nothing worth remembering. I cannot overemphasize the impact that unstated message has had on countless young women.

"Convinced that future generations must not grow up with the same misconceptions, I have spent the last ten years of my life researching and writing the stories of women whose achievements were remarkable, yet unrecorded and largely unremembered. Writing these stories into history validates the lives of those women and somehow validates my own."

Among Smith and Peavy's most critically praised works are *The Gold Rush Widows of Little Falls: A Story Drawn from the Letters of Pamelia and James Fergus, Women in Waiting in the Westward Movement: Life on the Home Frontier,* and *Frontier Children. The Gold Rush Widows of Little Falls* concentrates on the town of Little Falls, Minnesota, and the many local women who were left behind while their husbands left for the gold fields of Colorado and Montana, hoping to strike it rich. Relying on the correspondence between a married couple in particular, and on other letters from women in that town, Smith and Peavy create a picture of the hard lives that women and their families suffered when husbands and fathers left home in search of a better life. Penny Kaganoff, writing in *Publishers Weekly,* called *The Gold Rush Widows of Little Falls* a "well-researched, highly readable study" and "a valuable addition to the history of the American West."

Smith and Peavy expand their focus in *Women in Waiting in the Westward Movement* to tell the stories of women throughout America who were left behind while their husbands headed west in search of gold or better farmland. Often left by their husbands for months or even years, the women raised their families, managed farms, survived fires and floods, and chronicled their daily lives in letters and diaries. A *Publishers Weekly* contributor noted that "the loneliness and fears of these all-but-abandoned women speak eloquently over the years." Renee H. Shea, writing in *Belles Lettres,* commented that "ultimately, what is most compelling about these women is not their hardships and loss but their grit, will, and, by various definitions, their triumphs."

Frontier Children contains some 200 photographs of children of the old West, both at work and at play, along with contemporary, firsthand accounts of their daily lives. The result is an honest, personal record of an aspect of western expansion often overlooked. Fred Egloff noted in *Booklist* that "all . . . facets of the frontier experience are examined in relation to how they affected . . . children." *Library Journal* contributor Daniel D. Liestman wrote, "Providing a unique window on a historical aspect of childhood, this book will appeal to a wide segment of readers."

BIOGRAPHICAL AND CRITICAL SOURCES:

PERIODICALS

Agricultural History, spring, 2001, Pamela Riney-Kehrberg, review of *Frontier Children,* p. 247.
American Historical Review, October, 1995, Peggy Pascoe, review of *Women in Waiting in the Westward Movement: Life on the Home Frontier,* p. 1304.

American Studies, spring, 1995, Renee M. Sentilles, review of *Women in Waiting in the Westward Movement,* p. 173.

Belles Lettres: A Review of Books by Women, spring, 1995, Renee H. Shea, review of *Women in Waiting in the Westward Movement,* p. 72.

Booklist, March 15, 1994, Denise Perry Donavin, review of *Women in Waiting in the Westward Movement,* p. 1325; April 15, 1996, Donna Seaman, review of *Pioneer Women: The Lives of Women on the Frontier,* p. 1418; October 1, 1999, Fred Egloff, review of *Frontier Children,* p. 341.

Choice, October, 1998, P.F. Field, review of *Pioneer Women,* p. 382.

Journal of American Culture, winter, 1998, Kathleen R. Winter, review of *Women in Waiting in the Westward Movement,* p. 102.

Journal of American History, June, 1995, Darlis A. Miller, review of *Women in Waiting in the Westward Movement,* p. 263.

Kliatt, July, 2003, Lind Piwowarczyk, review of *Frontier Children,* p. 49.

Library Journal, October 15, 1999, Daniel D. Liestman, review of *Frontier Children,* p. 84.

Pacific Historical Review, November, 1995, Glenda Riley, review of *Women in Waiting in the Westward Movement,* p. 607; May, 2001, Ruth B. Moynihan, review of *Frontier Children,* p. 324.

Pacific Northwest Quarterly, summer, 2000, LeRoy Ashby, review of *Frontier Children,* p. 164.

Publishers Weekly, April 6, 1990, Penny Kaganoff, review of *The Gold Rush Widows of Little Falls: A Story Drawn from the Letters of Pamelia and James Fergus,* p. 112; April 4, 1994, review of *Women in Waiting in the Westward Movement,* p. 68.

Southwestern Historical Quarterly, April, 2001, Tom Harvey, review of *Frontier Children,* p. 615.

Western Historical Quarterly, autumn, 2000, Peter F. Schmid, review of *Frontier Children,* p. 361.

Wild West, December, 2000, Chrys Ankeny, review of *Frontier Children,* p. 70.

Women's Studies, December, 1998, Thomas Hallock, review of *Pioneer Women,* p. 119.

ONLINE

Linda Peavy and Ursula Smith Home Page, http://peavyandsmith.com (March 13, 2006).

SONG, Yuwu 1958-

PERSONAL: Born October 1, 1958, in Beijing, China; son of Xuexun and Guolun (Zhao) Song. *Ethnicity:* "Chinese." *Education:* Luoyang Foreign Languages University, B.A., 1982; University of Texas at Austin, M.L.I.S., 1999; University of Alabama, Ph.D., 1999.

ADDRESSES: Home—3409 S. Rural Rd., No. 138, Tempe, AZ 85282. *Office*—University Libraries, Arizona State University, P.O. Box 871006, Tempe, AZ 85287.

CAREER: Arizona State University, Tempe, assistant librarian and instructor, 1999—. Also works as Internet Web designer.

WRITINGS:

Building Better Web Sites: A How-to-Do-It Manual for Librarians, Neal-Schuman Publishers (New York, NY), 2003.

(Editor) *Encyclopedia of Chinese-American Relations,* McFarland (Jefferson, NC), 2006.

WORK IN PROGRESS: Chinese Stamps, for McFarland, completion expected in 2006; *Chinese Filmography,* McFarland, 2006; *A Historical Dictionary of Sino-American Relations,* McFarland, 2006.

BIOGRAPHICAL AND CRITICAL SOURCES:

PERIODICALS

Booklist, December 1, 2003, Sean Kinder, review of *Building Better Web Sites: A How-to-Do-It Manual for Librarians,* p. 698.

*   *   *

SPATZ, Gregory 1964-

PERSONAL: Born 1964, in New York, NY; married second wife, Caridwen Irvine (a musician); children: two stepsons. *Education:* Haverford College, B.A.; University of New Hampshire, M.A.; University of Iowa Writers' Workshop, M.F.A.

ADDRESSES: Home—Spokane, WA. *Agent*—Peter Steinberg, Regal Literary, 1140 Broadway Penthouse, New York, NY 10001. *E-mail*—gspatz1@earthlink.net.

CAREER: Writer, educator, and musician. Eastern Washington University, Inland Northwest Center for Writers, Spokane, WA, director of the MFA program; John Reischman and the Jaybirds bluegrass band, violinist. Previously taught fiction at the University of Iowa, Iowa City, IA, and the University of Memphis, TN.

AWARDS, HONORS: Fellowships from the Michener-Copernicus Society of America, 1996, Bread Loaf Writers' Conference, 1996, and the Washington State Artist Trust, 1999, 2003; Mid-List Press First Series Award in short fiction, 2000; Washington State Book Award, 2003, for *Wonderful Tricks.*

WRITINGS:

FICTION

No One but Us, Algonquin Books of Chapel Hill (Chapel Hill, NC), 1995.
Wonderful Tricks: Stories, Mid-List Press (Minneapolis, MN), 2002.
Fiddler's Dream: A Novel, Southern Methodist University Press (Dallas, TX), 2006.

Short stories have appeared in literary journals and magazines, including the *New Yorker, Glimmer Train Stories, Iowa Review, Epoch, Indiana Review, Journal, Shenandoah,* and the *New England Review.*

SIDELIGHTS: Gregory Spatz is the author of novels and short stories. In his debut novel, *No One but Us,* the author tells the story of Charlie, who at the age of fifteen has an affair with his mother's best friend, Jolene, who is twenty-six. Eventually Jolene ends the relationship and moves away. Charlie grows up and is working as a sales clerk in Philadelphia when he learns from his mother that Jolene is living in San Francisco as a lesbian. Charlie, who is now in his twenties, and his girlfriend Angel travel across the country so Charlie can track down Jolene and talk with her about his guilt over the affair and how it has affected his life. A *Publishers Weekly* contributor com-

mented that the author's "story engages the reader with the compelling parallel voyages of self-discovery" that include Jolene's, Angel's and his mother's lives.

In his collection *Wonderful Tricks: Stories,* Spatz presents ten previously published short stories. "The loneliness and awkwardness of single parenting—for the adolescent child and the parent—figure prominently in Spatz's earnest, understated collection," noted a *Kirkus Reviews* contributor. A reviewer writing in *Publishers Weekly* commented that the author "explores the complicated, often bewildering emotions behind various forms of love." The reviewer also wrote that the author describes "his characters' inner lives in expressive but unadorned prose." Referring to them as "low-key stories" in a review in *Booklist,* Joanne Wilkinson also wrote that the stories are "filled with unexpected insight."

BIOGRAPHICAL AND CRITICAL SOURCES:

PERIODICALS

Booklist, August, 2002, Joanne Wilkinson, review of *Wonderful Tricks: Stories,* p. 1926.
Kirkus Reviews, July 15, 2002, review of *Wonderful Tricks,* p. 994.
Publishers Weekly, June 19, 1995, review of *No One but Us,* p. 48; September 2, 2002, review of *Wonderful Tricks,* p. 55.

ONLINE

Eastern Washington University Web site, http://www.ewu.edu/ (March 26, 2006), faculty profile of author.
Gregory Spatz Home Page, http://www.gregoryspatz.com (April 18, 2006).
Mid-list Press Web site, http://www.midlist.org/ (March 26, 2006), profile of author.
Spokesman-Review.com, http://www.spokesmanreview.com/ (February 3, 2004), Dan Webster, "Gregory Spatz," interview with author.

*   *   *

SPELVIN, George
See LERANGIS, Peter

SPIEGELMAN, Peter

PERSONAL: Born in New York, NY. *Education:* Vassar College, B.A.

ADDRESSES: Home—CT. *Agent*—c/o Author Mail, Knopf Publishing, 1745 Broadway, New York, NY 10019.

CAREER: Writer. Worked previously in financial services and banking software industries.

AWARDS, HONORS: Shamus Award for Best First Novel, for *Black Maps,* 2004.

WRITINGS:

SUBHEAD

Black Maps, Knopf (New York, NY), 2003.
Death's Little Helpers, Knopf (New York, NY), 2005.

SIDELIGHTS: Peter Spiegelman started his career in financial services and software, spending more than twenty years between a major Wall Street firm and a banking software company, before turning his attention toward fiction writing. He retired from business in 2001 and began working on his first novel, *Black Maps,* which was published in 2003. In 2004 the book won the Shamus Award for Best First Novel. Spiegelman capitalizes on his previous work experience in his story of John March, a policeman from the country who becomes a private investigator in the big city, after turning down a comfortable position leading the family-owned bank. March fails to escape the world of finance, however, as once he begins work as an investigator, he gets involved in a case concerning a bank under federal investigation and a banker who is being blackmailed. A contributor for *Kirkus Reviews* remarked that "March is a strong and fatalistic character with a flawless nose for bull," noting the novel is "not so much a who-dun-it as a who-didn't," and pronounced it "a provocative debut." Miles Klein, in a review for *Kliatt,* wrote that "the dialog here is absolutely crackling, the characters fascinating." In a review for *Publishers Weekly,* a contributor observed that "after a lengthy, but never boring, setup, Spiegelman's first novel pitches from one taut, suspenseful scene to another."

Spiegelman's follow-up novel, *Death's Little Helpers,* revisits John March as he delves into yet another financial mystery. When Gregory Danes, a financial analyst, disappears, his wife calls March in to determine what has happened to him. Danes has fallen on hard times at work, a fact that has his firm less than pleased. In fact, the Securities and Exchange Commission is looking into his accounts due to suspicion of insider trading. March soon discovers that other, less savory private investigators are also looking into Danes's whereabouts, and that they are willing to threaten March in order to throw him off the trail. A contributor for *Kirkus Reviews* noted that "Spiegelman's dialogue does at times descend to talkiness, . . . but his is a serious talent that rewards interest now with better around the corner." Roland Person, writing for *Library Journal,* remarked upon the positive effect on the book of Spiegelman's "considerable writing skill, complicated yet fair plots . . . and the developing character of March." Frank Sennett, writing for *Booklist,* dubbed this second March novel an "uneven but ultimately satisfying sequel," while Mark Harris, in a review for *Entertainment Weekly,* called Spiegelman's sophomore effort "a solidly crafted missing-persons mystery."

BIOGRAPHICAL AND CRITICAL SOURCES:

PERIODICALS

Booklist, May 1, 2005, Frank Sennett, review of *Death's Little Helpers,* p. 1537.
Entertainment Weekly, July 22, 2005, Mark Harris, review of *Death's Little Helpers,* p. 83.
Kirkus Reviews, August 1, 2003, review of *Black Maps,* p. 991; April 15, 2005, review of *Death's Little Helpers,* p. 448.
Kliatt, March, 2004, Miles Klein, review of *Black Maps,* p. 44.
Library Journal, June 1, 2003, Roland Person, review of *Black Maps,* p. 170; July 1, 2005, Roland Person, review of *Death's Little Helpers,* p. 59.
Publishers Weekly, August 12, 2002, "Sonny Mehta at Knopf Paid a 'Handsome' Six Figures for the Next Two Literary Thrillers by Peter Spiegelman

Starring P.I. John March to Agent Denise Marcil for North American Rights," p. 140; July 28, 2003, review of *Black Maps,* p. 83.

ONLINE

Peter Spielgelman Home Page, http://www.peter spiegelman.com (February 4, 2006).*

* * *

SPRENGLE, Artie
    See LERANGIS, Peter

* * *

STAMMERS, John

PERSONAL: Born in Islington, England. *Education:* King's College, London, England.

ADDRESSES: Home—Islington, England. *Agent*—c/o Author Mail, Pan Macmillan, 20 New Wharf Rd., London N1 9RR, England.

CAREER: Poet and educator. King's College, London, England, associate; also associated with two colleges of Cambridge University.

AWARDS, HONORS: Blue Nose Poetry competition winner, 1999, for "The Wolf Man"; Forward/ Waterstones Prize for Best First Collection and short-listed for Whitbread Poetry Award, both 2001, both for *Panoramic Lounge-Bar.*

WRITINGS:

POETRY

Panoramic Lounge-Bar, Picador (London, England), 2001.
Stolen Love Behaviour, Picador (London, England), 2005.

SIDELIGHTS: John Stammers is a London poet whose debut collection, *Panoramic Lounge-Bar,* received wide critical recognition for both its serious and more humorous poems. "John Stammers' first collection is peopled with the likes of Frank O'Hara, Gilbert and Sullivan, James Joyce, Roddy Lumsden, and Greta Garbo," commented Jane Holland in the *Poetry Review.* Holland went on to write, "His talent as a poet is real and unmistakable. . . . There is a sense in these poems that sleight-of-hand . . . is being used to divert us from the guiding intelligence behind the juggler behind the poet." Noting that while reading the poems she sometimes forgot that it is his first collection, Holland commented on the author's "sheer talent and technical expertise, outclassing other debuts around it with the ease and confidence of a born poet."

In his second collection of poems, *Stolen Love Behaviour,* the author writes about failed loves, urban landscapes, and various notable people, such as his poem "John Keats Walks Home Following a Night Spent Reading Homer with Cowden Clarke." "If his poems share a mood we might call that mood retrospect, reasonable bitterness, a tightly-controlled *esprit d'escalier,*" wrote Stephen Burt on the *Tower Poetry* Web site. Noting that "Stammers casts himself as a literary latecomer, a ghostly, witty commentator, whether at his own breakups or at other people's epiphanies," Burt added: "Stammers' long and information-dense lines, thick with fine-tuned emotion and cityscape detail, place him among older poets . . . whose repertoires include travel poetry and speculative linguistic investigation."

BIOGRAPHICAL AND CRITICAL SOURCES:

PERIODICALS

Poetry Review, Volume 91, number 2, summer, 2001, Jane Holland, review of *Panoramic Lounge-Bar.*

ONLINE

CliveJames.com, http://www.clivejames.com/ (March 27, 2006), brief biography of author.
John Stammers Home Page, http://www.pan macmillan.com/features2/johnstammers (March 14, 2006).

Pan Macmillan Web site, http://www.panmacmillan. com/ (March 14, 2006), brief profile of author.

Poetropical, http://www.poetropical.co.uk/ (March 27, 2006), brief profile of author.

Tower Poetry, http://www.towerpoetry.org.uk/ (March 27, 2006), Stephen Burt, review of *Stolen Love Behaviour.**

*   *   *

STEPHENS, Suzanne
   See KIRBY, Susan E.

*   *   *

STERLE, Francine 1952-
   (Francine M. Sterle)

PERSONAL: Born July 5, 1952, in Eveleth, MN; daughter of Frank and Anne (Rahne) Sterle; married Jonathan Speare (a clinical psychologist), July 20, 1984; children: Eleanor Speare, Benjamin Speare. *Education:* Bemidji State University, B.S., 1974, M.A., 1976; Warren Wilson College, M.F.A., 1991; attended Oxford University.

ADDRESSES: Home—4023 River Rd., Iron, MN 55751. *Agent*—c/o Author Mail, Tupelo Press, P.O. Box 539, Dorset, VT 05251. *E-mail*—fmsterle@ northlc.com.

CAREER: Writer, poet, and educator. Lake Superior Writers, mentor; poetry teacher in academic and community settings. Participant in the Bread Loaf Writers' Conference, Spoleto Writers' Workshop, and the Squaw Valley Community of Writers.

MEMBER: Academy of American Poets, Poetry Society of America, Associated Writing Programs.

AWARDS, HONORS: Loft-McKnight Foundation Award, The Loft, 1990, for poetry; Minnesota State Arts Board fellowship and Career Opportunity Grant, 1993, for poetry; Jerome Foundation Travel and Study Grant, 1997; Minnesota Editor's Prize, Tupelo Press, 2001, and Pushcart Prize nominee, both for *Every Bird Is One Bird;* residency fellowships from the Anderson Center for Interdisciplinary Studies, Leighton Studios at the Banff Centre for the Arts, and the Blacklock Nature Sanctuary.

WRITINGS:

POETRY

The White Bridge, Poetry Harbor, 1999.
Every Bird Is One Bird, Tupelo Press (Dorset, VT), 2001.
Nude in Winter, Tupelo Press (Dorset, VT), 2006.

Poems have appeared in literary journals, including the *North American Review, Nimrod, Beloit Poetry Journal, Zone 3, Birmingham Review, Cutbank, Wisconsin Review, Negative Capability, Visions International, Rosebud, California Quarterly,* and *Atlanta Review,* and in the anthologies *33 Minnesota Poets* and the *Cancer Poetry Project.*

SIDELIGHTS: Francine Sterle is a poet whose works are often about the world of nature, both as it is perceived on the outside and as the inner worlds that people sense. As the author noted in the *Midwest Quarterly,* "I am rooted in the landscape of northern Minnesota." She went on to write, "when I sit down to write, this is the world that enters me." For example, in Sterle's first book of poems, *The White Bridge,* the author writes a poem about a woman who is transformed into the ethereal body of an owl. In her poem "Habitat," Sterle writes about the "heavy air rolling from the uplands" and the creatures living in a marsh. In her *Midwest Quarterly* article, which included the poem "Habitat," the author wrote that structurally her poems are based "on simple configurations . . . in order to heighten the sense of primary seeing as well as to convey an instinctive, emotional involvement." In her second volume of poetry, *Every Bird Is One Bird,* Sterle presents her observations of the world around her through poems such as "Sparrow at My Window," a section of the longer poem "Two Women." Writing a review of *Every Bird Is One Bird* in the *Boston Review,* Catherine Daly commented, "Her sensible, compactly written lyrics build upon traditions of meditative and investigative poetry."

Sterle told *CA:* "*Nude in Winter* is a wide-ranging collection of poems that explore the intertwined lives of painter and painted and the powerful dynamic between desire and the disturbance it can yield. The canvas of poems stretches from the tormented self-portraits of Toulouse-Lautrec and Egon Schiele to the idealized depictions of Sassaferrato's madonna and Man Ray's nude, from Kahlo to Kollwitz, O'Keeffe to De Kooning. *Nude in Winter* is poised at the threshold between seer and seen and moves from the dark corners of experience to the sensual light of renewal."

BIOGRAPHICAL AND CRITICAL SOURCES:

PERIODICALS

Boston Review, October, 2003, Catherine Daly, review of *Every Bird Is One Bird,* p. 61.
Midwest Quarterly, Francine Sterle, "Habitat," p. 491.
Small Press Book Review, May, 1999, review of *The White Bridge,* p. 6; March, 2002, review of *Every Bird Is One Bird,* p. 12.

ONLINE

Francine Sterle Home Page, http://www.francinesterle. com (January 29, 2006).

*   *   *

STERLE, Francine M.
    See STERLE, Francine

*   *   *

STERNBERG, Jacques 1923-

PERSONAL: Born 1923, in Belgium.

ADDRESSES: Agent—c/o Author Mail, La Renaissance du Livre, Mons Expo, Avenue Thomas Edison, n°2, 7000 Mons, Belgium.

CAREER: Writer.

WRITINGS:

Le délit, Librairie Plon (Paris, France), 1954.

La sortie est au fond de l'espace: roman, (title means "The Way Out Is at the Bottom of Space"), Denoël (Paris, France), 1956.
Entre deux mondes incertains (stories; title means "Between Two Uncertain Worlds"), Denoël (Paris, France), 1957, reprinted, 1985.
L'employé: roman (novel), Les Editions de Minuit (Paris, France), 1958, reprinted, Editions Labor (Brussels, Belgium), 1989.
L'Architect, E. Losfeld (Paris, France), 1960.
Manuel du parfait petit secretaire commercial (fiction), illustrations by Soro, E. Losfeld (Paris, France), 1960.
La géometrie dans l'impossible (science fiction; title means "Impossible Geometrie"), Le Terrain Vague (Paris, France), 1960.
Un Siècle d'humour français, Les Productions de Paris (Paris, France), 1961.
Un jour ouvrable, E. Losfeld (Paris, France), 1961, reprinted, Nouvelles Editions Oswald (Paris, France), 1981.
La banlieue: roman (novel), Julliard (Paris, France), 1961, reprinted, Bibliothèque Marabout (Verviers, Belgium), 1976.
Un Siècle d'humour anglo-américain, Les Productions de Paris (Paris, France), 1962.
(Editor, with Jean Morin) Jonathan Swift, *Gulliver's Travels,* L'Ambassade du Livre (Paris, France), 1962.
(Adaptor) Denis Diderot, *Jacques le fataliste et son maître,* Petits-Fils de L. Danel (Loos-lez-Lille, France), 1963.
Les Chefs d'oeuvre du sourire, Éditions Planète (Paris, France), 1964.
(With Alex Grall) *Les Chefs d'oeuvre de l'érotisme,* Éditions Planète (Paris, France), 1964.
Toi, ma nuit, Editions Le Terrain Vague (Paris, France), 1965, translated as *Sexualis '95,* Berkley (New York, NY), 1967.
Les Chefs d'oeuvre de l'épouvante, Éditions Planète (Paris, France), 1965.
Les Chefs d'oeuvre du crime, Éditions Planète (Paris, France), 1965.
(With Maurice Toesca and Alex Grall) *Les Chefs d'oeuvre de l'amour sensual,* Éditions Planète (Paris, France), 1966.
(With Jacques Bergier and Alex Grall) *Les Chefs d'oeuvre du rire,* Éditions Planète (Paris, France), 1966.
Les Chefs d'oeuvre de la bande dessinée, rassemblés et présentés, Éditions Planète (Paris, France), 1967.

Les Chefs d'oeuvre du fantastique, Éditions Planète (Paris, France), 1967.

Les Chefs d'oeuvre de notre enfance, Éditions Planète (Paris, France), 1968.

C'est la guerre, Monsieur Gruber, pièce en un acte, Le Terrain Vague (Paris, France), 1968.

Les Chefs d'oeuvre du dessin d'humour, Éditions Planète (Paris, France), 1968.

(With Alain Resnais) *Je t'aime, je t'aime* (screenplay; title means "I Love You, I Love You"), Parc Film-Mag Bodard/Fox Europa, 1968, published as *Je t'aime, je t'aime: scénario et dialogues pour un fil d'Alain Resnais,* E. Losfeld (Paris, France), 1969.

Attention, planète habitée (science fiction; title means "Beware, Inhabited Planet"), E. Losfeld (Paris, France), 1969.

Les Chefs d'oeuvre de la science-fiction, Éditions Planète (Paris, France), 1970.

Univers zéro (science fiction), Gerard (Verviers, France), 1970.

(With Tristan Maya) *Les Chefs d'oeuvre de l'humour noir,* Éditions Planète (Paris, France), 1970.

Les charmes de la publicité, Denoël (Paris, France), 1971.

Chroniques de "France-soir" (nonfiction), E. Losfeld (Paris, France), 1971.

Un siècle de pin up, Éditions Planète (Paris, France), 1971.

Lettre aux gens malheureux et qui ont bien raison de l'être, E. Losfeld (Paris, France), 1972.

Futurs sans avenir: nouvelles (story collection), R. Laffont (Paris, France), 1971; translated as *Future without Future,* Seabury Press (New York, NY), 1973.

Le tour du monde en 300 gravures, Éditions Planète (Paris, France), 1972.

Kitsch (published in French as "Les Chefs d'oeuvre du kitsch"), edited by Mariana Henderson, St. Martin's Press (New York, NY), 1972.

Dictionnaire du mépris, Calmann-Levy (Paris, France), 1973.

A la dérive en dérvieur, Julliard (Paris, France), 1974.

Contes glacés (fiction; title means "Icy Tales"), Gerard (Verviers, Belgium), 1974, reprinted, Labor (Brussels, Belgium), 1998.

(With Henri Deuill) *Un Siècle de dessins contestataires,* Denoël (Paris, France), 1974.

Lettre ouverte aux Terriens, A. Michel (Paris, France), 1974.

(Compiler, with Pierre Chapelot) *Pin Up* (drawings), St. Martin's Press (New York, NY), 1974.

Sophie, la mer et la nuit: roman (novel; title means "Sophie, the Sea, the Night"), A. Michel (Paris, France), 1976.

Mémoires provisoires: ou, Comment rater tout ce que l'on réussit, Retz (Paris, France), 1977.

Le navigateur: roman (novel; title means "The Navigator"), A. Michel (Paris, France), 1977.

Vivre en survivant: demission, demerde, dérive, Tchou (Paris, France), 1977.

Mai 86: roman, (novel), A. Michel (Paris, France), 1978.

Topor, Seghers (Paris, France), 1978.

Agathe et Béatrice, Claire et Dorothée: roman, A. Michel (Paris, France), 1979.

Rever la mer: graveurs et illustrateurs du XIXe siècle, Gallimard (Paris, France), 1979.

Théâtre, C. Bourgois (Paris, France), 1979.

Suite pour Eveline sweet Evelin: roman (novel), A. Michel (Paris, France), 1980.

Ports en eaux-fortes: les ports du monde vus par les graveurs au 19e siècle, Editions Maritimes and d'outre-mer (Paris, France), 1980.

L'anonyme: roman, A. Michel (Paris, France), 1982.

Dictionnaire des idees revues, Denoël (Paris, France), 1985.

Les variations Sternberg: pour clavier de machine a ecrire sur deux themes de lettres commerciales, Pre aux Clercs (Paris, France), 1985.

Les pensées, preface by Bernard Tapie, Cherche midi (Paris, France), 1986.

188 contes à régler, illustrations by Roland Topor, Denoël (Paris, France), 1988.

Le shlemihl (novel), Julliard (Paris, France), 1989.

Histoires à dormir sans vous, Denoël (Paris, France), 1990.

Histoires à mourir de vous, Denoël (Paris, France), 1991.

Contes griffus, Denoël (Paris, France), 1993.

Dieu, moi et les autres: contes, Denoël (Paris, France), 1995.

Si loin de nulle part, Les Belles Lettres (Paris, France), 1998.

Le Coeur froid: roman (novel), C. Bourgois (Paris, France), 1972, reprinted, Gallimard (Paris, France), 2000.

Profession, mortel: fragments d'autobiographie, Belles lettres (Paris, France), 2000.

Oeuvres choisies: Fin de siècle, Un jour ouvrable, La banlieue, Le Délit (selected writings), Renaissance du livre (Tournai, Belgium), 2001.

Contributor of introductions or prefaces to books, including *Cami,* R. Julliard (Paris, France), 1964; *La moisson rouge,* by Dashiell Hammett, Culture, Arts, Loisirs (Paris, France), 1967; *La Vie secrète de Walter Mitty,* by James Thurber, Julliard (Paris, France), 1981; and *Une visite inopportune,* C. Bourgois (Paris, France, 1999); books published in several foreign languages, including English, Czech, German, and Japanese.

SIDELIGHTS: Several of French author Jacques Sternberg's writings, both nonfiction and speculative fiction, have been published in English translation, including *Sexualis '95, Kitsch, Pin Up,* and *Future without Future.*

Kitsch is the author's look at bad taste and schmaltz in the world as a part of popular culture seen in many places, including newspapers and advertisements. Calling the book "enjoyable" in a review in the *Library Journal,* Pat Goodfellow also noted that the author provides a "fascinating portrait of popular culture at is most brash and naïve."

Future without Future is a collection of seven science fiction stories and two novellas, including stories about a couple who do not realize they are living at the end of the world in 1999, a clerk who communicates with aliens, a vacation group lost in space, and an alien takeover of the Earth. A *Publishers Weekly* contributor noted, "The . . . short pieces are all skillful." Lynn Fell, writing in the *Librry Journal,* called the collection "grim glimpses of the future" and noted the author's "polished language and philosophical tone." Another reviewer writing for *Booklist* commented on Sternberg's "meditative style."

Mai 86: roman tells the story of a future world in which pollution has made the oceans a deadly place to swim and food is contaminated. The story, as told by the narrator, involves a people who try to survive by living apart from the masses, and who eventually revolt against an industrial society, which means the end of modern life with its polluting automobiles and factories. "The novel has . . . some power in so far as it extrapolates from trends present in contemporary industrial society and shows, often comically, what a nightmare could ensure from the total pollution of the globe," wrote Allen Thiher in the *French Review.*

Sternberg tells the story of a failure named Jacques in the novel *Le shlemihl,* taken from a Yiddish word for someone who does everything wrong. Starting with overbearing and overly critical parents, Jacques Sternberg, goes on to develop a full-blown neurosis that involves changing his name to Nathan so he doesn't sound so Jewish and a total self-absorption as a writer who is obsessed with fame. The novel covers the fictional Sternberg's life from birth to death. "Readers who like themes of a writer discovering his vocation will certainly enjoy *Le shlemihl,*" wrote Wendy Greenberg in the *French Review.* "If word play and Jewish humor are styles one appreciates, then Sternberg is a writer to read."

Sternberg also cowrote the screenplay for the 1968 film *Je t'aime, je t'aime,* a story about a man who travels via a time machine that can take him to the past for only one-minute intervals. Through the various "minutes" that the man spends in the past, the audience learns of the man's lover, who he thinks he may have murdered. "Although obsessed with time, memory, the past, the physical material of . . . [the film] is its love story and the daily lives of the couple involved in it," wrote Roger Greenspun in the *New York Times.*

BIOGRAPHICAL AND CRITICAL SOURCES:

BOOKS

Clute, John, and Peter Nichols, editors, *Encyclopedia of Science Fiction,* St. Martin's Press (New York, NY), 1993.

PERIODICALS

Booklist, June 1, 1974, review of *Future without Future,* p. 1082.
Choice, September, 1974, review of *Future without Future,* pp. 952-953.
French Review, May, 1979, Allen Thiher, review of *Mai 86: roman,* p. 954; February, 1991, Wendy Greenberg, review of *Le shlemihl,* p. 546.
Library Journal, July, 1973, Pat Goodfellow, review of *Kitsch,* p. 2075; February 1, 1974, Lynn Fell, review of *Future without Future,* p. 384.
New York Times, September 15, 1970, Roger Greenspun, review of *Je t'aime, je t'aime.*
Publishers Weekly, December 10, 1973, review of *Future without Future,* p. 31.*

STEVENSON, Harold W. 1924-2005
(Harold William Stevenson)

PERSONAL: Born November 19, 1924, in Dines, WY; died from pneumonia, July 8, 2005, in Palo Alto, CA; son of Merlin R. and Mildred M. (Stodick) Stevenson; married Nancy Guy, August 23, 1950; children; Peggy, Janet, Andrew, Patricia. *Education:* University of Colorado, B.A., 1947; Stanford University, M.A., 1948, Ph.D., 1951; University of Minnesota, D.S., 1996.

CAREER: Developmental psychologist, educator, and writer. Pomona College, Pomona, CA, assistant professor of psychology, 1950-53; University of Texas, Austin, began as assistant professor, became associate professor of psychology, 1953-59; University of Minnesota, Minneapolis, professor of child development and psychology, director of the Institute for Child Development, 1959-71; University of Michigan, Ann Arbor, professor of psychology and fellow of the Center for Human Growth and Development, 1971-2005, director of the program in child development and social policy, 1978-93.

Career-related activities include National Institute of Child Health and Human Development, committee member, 1964-67; Center for Advanced Studies in Behavioral Sciences, fellow, 1967-68, 1982-83, 1989-90; National Research Council, executive committee in the division of behavioral sciences, 1969-72; national Academy of Sciences-National Research Council, chairman of the advisory committee on child development, 1971-73; National Institute of Mental Health, member of the personality and cognition study section, 1975-79; Harvard University, member of the visiting committee at the Graduate School of Education, 1979-86; Tohoku Fukushi College, Japan, adjunct professor, 1989-2005; People's Republic of China, member of childhood development programs, Peking University, 1990-2005.

MEMBER: American Academy of the Arts and Sciences (fellow), National Academy of Education, American Psychological Association (president of the division of developmental psychology, 1964-65), Society for Research in Child Development (governing council, 1961-67, president, 1969-71, chairman of

long-range planning committee, 1971-74, social policy committee, 1977-85, international affairs committee, 1991-94), International Society for the Study of Behavioral Development (executive committee, 1972-77, president, 1987-91), Phi Beta Kappa, Sigma Xi.

AWARDS, HONORS: G. Stanley Hall Award, American Psychological Association, 1988; Distinguished Research Award, Society for Research in Child Development, 1993; J.M. Cattell Fellow Award in applied psychology, American Psychological Society, 1994; William James Fellow Award, 1995; Quest Award, American Federation of Teachers, 1995; Bronfenbrenner Award and Distinguished Scientist Award in Applications of Psychology, both American Psychological Association, both 1997.

WRITINGS:

(Editor, with Ira Iscoe) *Personality Development in Children,* University of Texas Press (Austin, TX), 1960.

(Editor, with others) *Child Psychology,* National Society for the Study of Education (Chicago, IL), 1963.

(Editor) *Concept of Developoment: A Report,* University of Chicago Press for the Society for Research in Child Development (Chicago, IL), 1966.

(Editor, with Eckhard H. Hess and Harriet L. Rheingold) *Early Behavior: Comparative and Developmental Approaches,* Wiley (New York, NY), 1967.

(Compiler) *Studies of Children's Learning: A Bibliography,* Psychonomic Journals (Goleta, CA), 1968.

Children's Learning, Appleton-Century-Crofts (New York, NY), 1972.

(Editor, with Daniel A. Wagner) *Cultural Perspectives on Child Development,* W.H. Freeman (San Francisco, CA), 1982.

(Editor, with Scott G. Paris and Gary M. Olson) *Learning and Motivation in the Classroom,* Lawrence Erlbaum Associates (Hillsdale, NJ), 1983.

(Editor, with Alberta E. Siegel) *Child Development Research and Social Policy,* University of Chicago Press (Chicago, IL), 1984.

(Editor and contributor, with Hiroshi Azuma and Kenji Hakuta) *Child Development and Education in Japan,* W.H. Freeman (New York, NY), 1986.

(Editor, with James W. Stigler and Shin-Ying Lee) *Mathematical Knowledge of Japanese, Chinese, and American Elementary School Children,* National Council of Teachers of Mathematics (Reston, VA), 1990.

(With James W. Stigler)*The Learning Gap: Why Our Schools Are Failing and What We Can Learn from Japanese and Chinese Education,* Summit Books (New York, NY), 1992.

Also author, with Nancy G. Stevenson, of *Social Interaction in an Interracial Nursery School;* contributor to numerous books, including *Interrelations and Correlates in Children's Learning and Problem Solving,* University of Chicago Press (Chicago, IL), 1968; *Schooling, Environment, and Cognitive Development: A Cross-Cultural Study,* University of Chicago Press (Chicago, IL), 1978; *Making the Grade in Mathematics: Elementary School Mathematics in the United States, Taiwan, and Japan,* National Council of Teachers of Mathematics (Reston, VA), 1990; *International Comparisons of Entrance and Exit Examinations: Japan, United Kingdom, France, and Germany,* U.S. Department of Education, Office of Educational Research and Improvement (Washington, DC), 1997.

SIDELIGHTS: Harold W. Stevenson was a developmental psychologist who conducted numerous cross-cultural studies focusing on education and school achievement and was most noted for his analysis of Asian schools that led to reforms in the United States. He was also the editor and author of books focusing child development and education, including *Child Development and Education in Japan,* which Stevenson contributed to and served as coeditor of with Hiroshi Azuma and Kenji Hakuta. The book's nineteen papers look at both the school systems and the cultural factors in Japan that have influenced child rearing and education. Stevenson's contributions focus on education and why Japanese children excel in the classroom as compared to American students, especially in the area of math. Writing in *Science,* Takie Sugiyama Lebra commented, "Those troubled by the problems of American education will gain new insight, if not solutions, from the cross-cultural material cogently presented."

Among the author's most notable books is *The Learning Gap: Why Our Schools Are Failing and What We Can Learn from Japanese and Chinese Education,* which Stevenson wrote with James W. Stigler. Based on comparative research conducted in Asian countries and the United States, the authors explore differences between the educational systems of countries like China, Japan, and Taiwan with the American system. They also discuss differences in cultural influences and psychological mindsets that also influence a child's education. For example, the authors report that one of the primary differences between Asian and American schoolchildren is that Asian parents and educational systems are more likely to emphasize individual effort as opposed to innate abilities. They also point out that there is a closer integration between school and home in Asia than America, which leads to students paying more attention to things like homework and being prepared for classes. Writing in *NEA Today,* Mark Simon commented that the book "offers a glimpse of what we'd know if the federal government were funding real educational research." A *Publishers Weekly* contributor called the book "timely, free of jargon and from 'culture-bashing.'"

BIOGRAPHICAL AND CRITICAL SOURCES:

PERIODICALS

Arithmetic Teacher, February, 1991, George Nattras, review of *Making the Grade in Mathematics: Elementary School Mathematics in the United States, Taiwan, and Japan,* p. 62; September, 1992, Rosamond Welchman-Tischler, review of *Mathematical Knowledge of Japanese, Chinese, and American Elementary School Children,* p. 57.

Bloomsbury Review, September, 1992, review of *The Learning Gap: Why Our Schools Are Failing and What We Can Learn from Japanese and Chinese Education,* p. 9.

Booklist, April 15, 1992, Stephanie Zvirin, review of *The Learning Gap,* p. 1490.

Choice, November, 1967, review of *Early Behavior: Comparative and Developmental Approaches,* p. 1054; September, 1972, review of *Studies of Children's Learning,* p. 886; November, 1986, review of *Child Development and Education in Japan,* p. 516.

Christian Science Monitor, May 11, 1992, Laurel Shaper Walters, review of *The Learning Gap,* p. 13.

Contemporary Sociology, January, 1988, Mary C. Brinton, review of *Child Development and Education in Japan,* p. 102; July, 1993, Merry I. White, review of *The Learning Gap,* p. 534.

Educational Leadership, November, 1973, review of *Children's Learning,* p. 182; November, 1986, review of *Child Development and Education in Japan,* p. 101.

Educational Studies, fall, 1987, review of *Child Development and Education in Japan,* p. 405.

Journal of Negro Education, summer, 1993, Reuben G. Pierce, review of *The Learning Gap,* p. 394.

Library Journal, May 1, 1992, Lois F. Roets, review of *The Learning Gap,* p. 96.

NEA Today, October, 1992, Mark Simon, review of *The Learning Gap,* p. 36.

New Republic, May 11, 1992, review of *The Learning Gap,* p. 47.

Public Interest, spring, 1992, Chester E. Finn, Jr., review of *The Learning Gap,* p. 106.

Publishers Weekly, March 9, 1992, review of *The Learning Gap,* p. 43.

Science Books & Films, September, 1987, review of *Child Development and Education in Japan,* p. 25.

Science, April 10, 1987, Takie Sugiyama Lebra, review of *Child Development and Education in Japan,* p. 205.

Times Educational Supplement, December 15, 1992, review of *The Learning Gap,* p. 21.

ONLINE

University of Michigan Center for Human Growth and Development Web site, http://www.chgd.umich.edu/ (January 29, 2006).

OBITUARIES

PERIODICALS

Los Angeles Times, July 22, 2005, p. B12.
Mercury News (San Jose, CA), July 21, 2005.
New York Times, July 16, 2005, p. B14.
Washington Post, July 23, 2005, p. B6.*

STEVENSON, Harold William
See STEVENSON, Harold W.

*   *   *

STIMPSON, Jeff

PERSONAL: Married; wife's name Jill; children: Alex, Edwin.

ADDRESSES: Home—New York, NY. *Agent*—c/o Author Mail, Academy Chicago Publishers, 363 W. Erie St., 7E, Chicago, IL 60610. *E-mail*—jeff@jeffslife.net.

CAREER: Journalist; has worked for the *Ithaca Journal,* Ithaca, NY, and Patuxent Publications, MD.

WRITINGS:

Alex: The Fathering of a Preemie (memoir), Academy Chicago Publishers (Chicago, IL), 2004.

SIDELIGHTS: Jeff Stimpson's *Alex: The Fathering of a Preemie,* described as being "breath-catchingly evocative of life's elemental grace and messy dignity" by a *Kirkus Reviews* contributor, is the story of his first son, who came into the world weighing twenty-one ounces. The memoir, which includes photographs, begins with Alex's birth in 1998 by caesarian section, prompted by fears that his growth after six and a half months in the womb was too slow and might progress better outside. Alex spent nearly all his first year in the hospital, attached to tubes that kept him alive. Stimpson describes the challenges he and his wife faced when their son finally came home, including Alex's mental and physical limitations and confrontations with their health insurance provider. The *Kirkus Reviews* contributor commented that "Stimpson writes in a quick and saturated voice fueled by the transience of Alex's condition."

Stimpson divides the book into sections by months, following Alex's progress until he is seven and entering kindergarten, by which time he has a younger brother. A *Publishers Weekly* reviewer concluded that the book is "a vivid picture of life in a preemie's family that will surely interest other parents of preemies." *Idaho State Journal* contributor Amy Christensen also approved of the book. She stated, "As rare as it is for a compelling parenting book to come along, it is even more unusual to find a text that would be worthy of recommendation to non-parents."

Stimpson told *CA:* "I couldn't say what first got me interested in writing for sure. I've been writing since I was about eight, seriously since age thirteen. To tell the truth, it was more like writing got interested in me.

"Writers I admire include Richard Yates, E.B. White, C.S. Forester, Barbara Tuchman, Shirley Jackson, and John Keegan. Among the classics, I especially like William Shakespeare, Herman Melville, and Victor Hugo.

"I work five days a week, the same time every day. My work usually consists of essays of 700 to 1,000 words, often concerning my children. I write snippets of ideas or observations, later building these into sentences and paragraphs that I embellish and rearrange into the final piece.

"The most surprising thing I have learned as a writer is the power that people still accord the published word."

BIOGRAPHICAL AND CRITICAL SOURCES:

BOOKS

Stimpson, Jeff, *Alex: The Fathering of a Preemie,* Academy Chicago Publishers (Chicago, IL), 2004.

PERIODICALS

Booklist, December 1, 2004, Vanessa Bush, review of *Alex,* p. 625.
Idaho State Journal, August, 2005, Amy Christensen, review of *Alex,* p. 28.
Kirkus Reviews, October 1, 2004, review of *Alex,* p. 952.

Library Journal, December 1, 2004, KellyJo Houtz, review of *Alex,* p. 144.
Publishers Weekly, November 8, 2004, review of *Alex,* p. 43.

ONLINE

Jeff Stimpson Home Page, http://www.jeffslife.net (January 11, 2006).

*　　*　　*

STRIEBER, Anne

PERSONAL: Married Whitley Strieber (a writer).

ADDRESSES: Home—San Antonio, TX. *Agent*—c/o Author Mail, St. Martin's Press, Publicity Dept., 175 5th Ave., New York, NY 10010.

WRITINGS:

(Editor, with husband, Whitley Strieber) *The Communion Letters* (nonfiction), HarperPrism (New York, NY), 1997.
An Invisible Woman (novel), Forge (New York, NY), 2004.
Little Town Lies (novel), Forge (New York, NY), 2005.

Collaborator with Whitley Strieber, on other books.

SIDELIGHTS: Anne Strieber often collaborates with her husband, Whitley Strieber, writing nonfiction works on topics that include alien encounters, but she also is the sole author of novels. In *An Invisible Woman,* Kealy Ryerson is a New York socialite married to a prosperous attorney. Soon after calling to tell her to take their children and run, her husband is killed along with his private-investigator associate and the district attorney. Unable to trust anyone, including her husband's colleagues, his clients, or the police, and unable to retrieve money from accounts mysteriously frozen, Kealy takes her teenaged children out of their private schools and flees. Her attempts to blend into a working-class community succeed. Without her makeup and upscale wardrobe, Kealy manages to become invisible, even to her former husband, the chief of police. A *Publishers Weekly* contributor commented that "a few of the characters defy stereotype, including mob boss Sal Bonacori and his wiseguy-wannabe son."

Strieber, who lives in San Antonio, sets her next novel, *Little Town Lies,* in the small eastern Texas town of Maryvale. Sally Hopkins is a burned-out social worker who leaves Houston to return home. Her Uncle Ed, the sheriff, has offered her a job as his receptionist but hopes that her background will help him unravel the clues to a rash of crimes that include animal torture, arson, and abuse. After Sally arrives, another crime is committed, this time murder. Eventually, Sally sorts them out with the help of state trooper Rob Farley.

Library Journal reviewer Rex E. Klett called *Little Town Lies* "solid and suspenseful work."

BIOGRAPHICAL AND CRITICAL SOURCES:

PERIODICALS

Kirkus Reviews, September 15, 2005, review of *Little Town Lies,* p. 1004.

Library Journal, January 1, 2005, Samantha J. Gust, review of *An Invisible Woman,* p. 101; November 1, 2005, Rex E. Klett, review of *Little Town Lies,* p. 55.

Publishers Weekly, October 11, 2004, review of *An Invisible Woman,* p. 56; August 8, 2005, review of *Little Town Lies,* p. 215.*

T

TANEN, Sloane A. 1970-

PERSONAL: Born June 9, 1970, in Los Angeles, CA; daughter of Ned (a film producer and studio executive) and Max (Kirman) Tanen; married Gary Taubes (a science writer), November 3, 2001. *Ethnicity:* "Caucasian." *Education:* Sarah Lawrence College, B.A., 1992; New York University, M.A. (literary theory), 1995; Columbia University, M.A. (art history), 1998. *Politics:* Democrat. *Religion:* Jewish.

ADDRESSES: Office—Greenwich Studios, 515 Greenwich St., Ste. 309, New York, NY 10013. *Agent*—Amy Williams, Collins McCormick, 10 Leonard St., New York, NY 10013. *E-mail*—tanens@aol.com.

CAREER: Writer. Painter, with work exhibited at galleries in New York, NY, Boston, MA, and Connecticut.

WRITINGS:

Bitter with Baggage Seeks Same: The Life and Times of Some Chickens (humor), photographs by Stefan Hagen, Bloomsbury (New York, NY), 2003.
Where Is Coco Going? (juvenile), photographs by Stefan Hagen, Bloomsbury (New York, NY), 2004.
Going for the Bronze: Still Bitter, More Baggage, Bloomsbury (New York, NY), 2005.

WORK IN PROGRESS: A children's book, completion expected in 2006.

BIOGRAPHICAL AND CRITICAL SOURCES:

PERIODICALS

Publishers Weekly, October 18, 2004, review of *Where Is Coco Going?,* p. 62.
School Library Journal, December, 2004, Laurie Edwards, review of *Where Is Coco Going?,* p. 123.

*   *   *

TATE, Elodia 1963-
(Elodia Evans, Elodia Tate-Evans)

PERSONAL: Given name is pronounced "e-low-dee-a"; born August 22, 1963, in Fort Stockton, TX; daughter of James (an auto mechanic) and Dora (in retail sales; maiden name, Pena) Tate; married Marvin Evans, April 4, 1987 (divorced January 31, 2004); children: Danae Tate, Devaun Evans, Dionne Evans, Derek Evans. *Ethnicity:* "Hispanic, Caucasian, Native American." *Politics:* Democrat. *Religion:* Christian.

ADDRESSES: Office—P.O. Box 578325, Modesto, CA 95357. *Agent*—Jeff Kleinman, Graybill & English, 1875 Connecticut Ave., Ste. 712, Washington, DC 20009.

CAREER: Expert Financial Services, Redwood City, CA, mortgage broker, 1984-88; Lamas Loan Group, Tracy, CA, loan officer, 1988-92; Adobe Mortgage,

Manteca/Modesto, CA, owner and mortgage broker, 1992-94; writer, health coach, and public speaker, Modesto, CA, 1995—; Modesto Magic Basketball Association.

WRITINGS:

(With Yolanda King) *Open My Eyes, Open My Soul: Celebrating Our Common Humanity,* foreword by Coretta Scott King, McGraw-Hill (New York, NY), 2003.

Contributor to books, including *Chicken Soup for the African American Soul.* Some writings appear under the names Elodia Evans or Elodia Tate-Evans.

WORK IN PROGRESS: Infinite Paths to Wellness: Stories and Resources to Offer Hope, Health, and Humor; research on alternative health.

SIDELIGHTS: Elodia Tate told *CA:* "I love storytelling to teach. I feel it is much better to tell a story than to preach. That way, the ones who hear the story with their hearts can do their own self-examination of the soul. I believe telling a story, either written or spoken, can change perceptions much more easily.

"I am Hispanic, Caucasian, and Native American, and my children are part African-American. However, I look more Caucasian, which allows me to be a 'fly on the wall' in certain environments and hear things that show me, even though we have come a long way, we still have a long way to go. That is my reason for reaching out to Yolanda King and writing *Open My Eyes, Open My Soul: Celebrating Our Common Humanity.*

"I had a health condition for years that was finally diagnosed as lupus/SLE. I took a natural approach, and the lupus has been in remission since 1995. That is what led to my interest in alternative medicine or natural health."

BIOGRAPHICAL AND CRITICAL SOURCES:

PERIODICALS

Black Issues Book Review, July-August, 2004, Lynette C. Velasco, review of *Open My Eyes, Open My Soul: Celebrating Our Common Humanity,* p. 31.

TATE-EVANS, Elodia
    See TATE, Elodia

*   *   *

TAYLOR, William L. 1931-

PERSONAL: Born October 4, 1931, in Brooklyn, NY; married Harriett Rosen; children: Lauren, Deborah, David. *Education:* Brooklyn College, B.A. (cum laude), 1952; Yale Law School, LL.B., 1954.

ADDRESSES: Office—Citizens' Commission on Civil Rights, 2000 M St. N.W., Ste. 400, Washington, DC 20036. *E-mail*—btaylor@cccr.org.

CAREER: Admitted to the bars of New York State, District of Columbia, and the U.S. Supreme Court; National Association for the Advancement of Colored People Legal Defense and Education Fund, attorney, 1954-58; Americans for Democratic Action, legislative representative, 1959-61; U.S. Commission on Civil Rights, general counsel, 1963-65, staff director, 1965-68; Center for National Policy Review, founder and director, 1970-86; in private practice, 1986—. Adjunct professor at Catholic University Law School and Georgetown Law School.

Affiliated with Metropolitan Washington Planning and Housing Association, 1976, and Puerto Rican Legal Defense Fund, 1976; Citizens's Commission on Civil Rights, acting chair; Leadership Conference on Civil Rights, vice chair, 1990s—; Leadership Conference on Civil Rights Education Fund, president; Poverty and Race Research Action Council, board and executive committee member. Also commencement speaker at Brooklyn College, 2001. *Military service:* U.S. Army, 1956-58.

AWARDS, HONORS: Yale Law School senior fellow, 1969-70; National Endowment for the Humanities grant, 1974; Thurgood Marshall Award, District of Columbia Bar, 1993; Hubert H. Humphrey Award, Leadership Conference on Civil Rights, 2001; honorary degree, Brooklyn College, 2001.

WRITINGS:

Hanging Together: Equality in an Urban Nation, Simon & Schuster (New York, NY), 1971.

Racial Segregation: Two Policy Views; Reports to the Ford Foundation, Ford Foundation (New York, NY), 1979.

(With Dianne M. Pichbe) *A Report on Shortchanging Children: The Impact of Fiscal Inequity on the Education of Students at Risk,* Committee on Education and Labor, U.S. House of Representatives, One Hundred First Congress, U.S. Government Printing Office (Washington, DC), 1990.

(Editor, with Karen McGill Arrington) *Voting Rights in America: Continuing the Quest for Full Participation,* Leadership Conference Education Fund, Joint Center for Political and Economic Studies (Washington, DC), 1992.

(Editor, with Susan M. Liss) *New Opportunities: Civil Rights at a Crossroads; Report of the Citizens' Commission on Civil Rights,* Citizens' Commission on Civil Rights (Washington, DC), 1993.

The Passion of My Times: An Advocate's Fifty-Year Journey in the Civil Rights Movement (memoir), Carroll & Graf (New York, NY), 2004.

A collection of Taylor's papers is held by the Library of Congress. Contributor of law reviews to periodicals, including the *Yale Law Journal, Columbia Law Review, New York University Law Review, North Carolina Law Review* and *Fordham Law Review.* Contributor of articles to the *New York Times, Washington Post,* and the *New York Review of Books.*

SIDELIGHTS: From the beginning of his career, William L. Taylor has been a civil rights advocate. He began his career as a staff attorney with the National Association for the Advancement of Colored People (NAACP) Legal Defense and Education Fund. During the 1960s, his work with the U.S. Commission on Civil Rights led to the enactment of civil rights laws. For sixteen years, Taylor was director of the Center for National Policy Review, the advocacy organization he founded that relied on private funding to conduct research. Taylor continues his work through organizations like the Citizens' Commission on Civil Rights and the Leadership Conference on Civil Rights. He worked for the reform of the Voting Rights Act of 1965, led coalitions that blocked the confirmation of Robert Bork to the Supreme Court in 1987, and was instrumental in the passage of the Civil Rights Act of 1991 and the National Voter Registration Act of 1993.

Taylor was lead counsel in several important school desegregation cases and helped write the brief that resulted in the Civil Rights Restoration Act of 1988 and desegregation in Little Rock, Arkansas, and he continues to be an advocate for poor and minority children. He writes of his long career in his memoir, *The Passion of My Times: An Advocate's Fifty-Year Journey in the Civil Rights Movement.* He also recalls his childhood as the son of Lithuanian immigrants and tells how he formed an interdenominational ball team in his Brooklyn neighborhood with the intent of surpassing the all-Jewish team. Taylor, who is Jewish, was a Dodger fan who was inspired to join the NAACP by his hero, Jackie Robinson. Taylor comments on the administration of George W. Bush and writes that former attorney general John Ashcroft "flat-out lied" about his opposition to segregation.

A *Publishers Weekly* reviewer noted that "what makes Taylor's book of special value, particularly to historians of the era, is that Taylor neither dramatizes nor romanticizes this work." A *Kirkus Reviews* contributor wrote that *The Passion of My Times* "is a "vivid and illuminating account of what it's taken, thus far, to get minority rights from the Constitution onto the street."

BIOGRAPHICAL AND CRITICAL SOURCES:

BOOKS

Taylor, William L., *The Passion of My Times: An Advocate's Fifty-Year Journey in the Civil Rights Movement,* Carroll & Graf (New York, NY), 2004.

PERIODICALS

Booklist, November 1, 2004, Vanessa Bush, review of *The Passion of My Times,* p. 449.

Kirkus Reviews, October 1, 2004, review of *The Passion of My Times,* p. 953.

Publishers Weekly, October 25, 2004, review of *The Passion of My Times,* p. 37.

*   *   *

TEMKO, Allan 1924-2006

OBITUARY NOTICE— See index for *CA* sketch: Born February 4, 1924, in New York, NY; died of congestive heart failure, January 25, 2006, in Orinda, CA. Critic, educator, and author. A longtime architecture critic for the *San Francisco Chronicle,* Temko was a

TENT

Pulitzer Prize-winning journalist whose critiques had an impact on many of the buildings in the Bay Area. He attended Columbia University, where he chanced to meet fellow student Jack Kerouac, who used Temko as the model for his character Roland Major in *On the Road.* Before completing his degree, America entered World War II, and Temko served in the U.S. Navy, seeing action in the Pacific Theater. After the war, he returned to school to complete his A.B. in 1947. For his graduate studies, Temko went to the University of Paris for several years, as well as the University of California at Berkeley. He then moved to France, where he lectured at the Sorbonne and the École des Arts et Metiers during the early 1950s. It was in Paris that he later said he gained an appreciation of architecture as art and as an expression of a civilized society. Returning to America in 1956, he was an assistant professor of journalism at the University of California at Berkeley until 1962, then a lecturer in city planning and social sciences there until 1970. Temko was also a professor of art at California State University, Hayward, during the 1970s, and a lecturer at Stanford from 1981 to 1982. He also guest lectured at such institutions as Princeton and Yale. It was his job as architecture critic at the *Chronicle,* however, that gained him the most attention. He took the job there in 1961, remaining in that role until he retired in 1993; he also served as art editor from 1979 to 1982. Temko was highly critical of some of the modern architecture that was changing San Francisco's skyline, and he also emphasized that buildings should not only be artistic but, when possible, environmentally friendly. Many of his comments were credited as having an influence on how some building plans were changed in San Francisco before they were built. When an earthquake there in 1989 destroyed many dilapidated buildings, he declared that it was a higher power that likely destroyed the worst structures there to make a statement. Winning the Pulitzer Prize in 1990 for his criticism work, Temko was the author of several books, including *Notre-Dame of Paris* (1955), *Eero Saarinen* (1962), and *No Way to Build a Ballpark: And Other Irreverent Essays on Architecture* (1993).

OBITUARIES AND OTHER SOURCES:

PERIODICALS

Chicago Tribune, January 27, 2006, section 3, p. 7.
Los Angeles Times, January 27, 2006, p. B11.

New York Times, January 27, 2006, p. A21.
Washington Post, January 29, 2006, p. C8.

* * *

TENT, Pam

PERSONAL: Female.

ADDRESSES: Home—San Francisco, CA. *Agent*—c/o Author Mail, Alyson Publications, P.O. Box 4371, Los Angeles, CA 90078. *E-mail*—pam@sweetpam.com.

CAREER: Cockettes (theatrical troupe), San Francisco, CA, cofounder and performer, 1970s. Worked as a singer in New York, NY; in film distribution in CA; and as an accountant in San Francisco, CA.

WRITINGS:

Midnight at the Palace: My Life As a Fabulous Cockette (memoir), Alyson Books (Los Angeles, CA), 2004.

SIDELIGHTS: Pam Tent, known as "Sweet Pam," was one of the founders of the Cockettes, a rollicking theatrical troupe that played to San Francisco audiences from 1969 to 1972. Tent was one of the females in the troupe. Other members, including Divine, who went on to enjoy a successful film career, were drag queens bedecked in wigs, feathers, and glitter. Female and male performers, both straight and gay, donned outrageous costumes and displayed a range of talent, coming together from the neighborhoods of "Baghdad by the Bay," to share their hedonism and to entertain audiences made up of kindred souls. In her memoir, *Midnight at the Palace: My Life As a Fabulous Cockette,* Tent brings the show to readers and describes the 1970s culture of sex, drugs, and rock-and-roll and the era that preceded commercialized radical theater and productions like *Oh! Calcutta.* A *Kirkus Reviews* contributor noted that Tent "carefully describes the Cockettes' free-style theater, its parodies of romance and success, the fun and absurdity of its political incorrectness."

Tent writes of the gender-bending shows that filled San Francisco's Palace Theater and of the celebrities who came to watch and listen, including Truman Capote and Andy Warhol. Tent, who lived with Dee Dee Ramone for a time, notes that as the troupe's reputation spread, the Cockettes were offered the New York engagement that was to be the beginning of their end. New York was not San Francisco, and the antics of the Cockettes caused many audience members, including well-known celebrities, to walk out during performances.

Tent used drugs and was sent to a psychiatric hospital for treatment. She also lost several friends to AIDS. Both experiences shaped her life. For a time she performed with two other Cockettes and soloed as a blues singer in New York. Eventually, she returned to California and worked in film production before becoming an accountant. She currently lives in the San Francisco Bay Area; the place where she made her mark in theater. Tent maintains an extensive Web site on Cockettes history, including photographs, posters, and reviews.

Kevin Riordan, who reviewed Tent's memoir in the *Lambda Book Report,* wrote that the "exploits of her ever-changing cast of characters are often amusing, even touching." A *Publishers Weekly* reviewer concluded by saying, "Tent deftly juggles a huge cast of characters while providing a nostalgic trip through San Francisco's gender-bending heyday."

BIOGRAPHICAL AND CRITICAL SOURCES:

BOOKS

Tent, Pam, *Midnight at the Palace: My Life As a Fabulous Cockette,* Alyson Books (Los Angeles, CA), 2004.

PERIODICALS

Booklist, November 15, 2004, Mike Tribby, review of *Midnight at the Palace,* p. 542.
Kirkus Reviews, October 1, 2004, review of *Midnight at the Palace,* p. 953.
Lambda Book Report, April-May, 2005, Kevin Riordan, "Let the Good Times Roll," review of *Midnight at the Palace,* p. 27.
Library Journal, April 1, 2005, Jim Van Buskirk, review of *Midnight at the Palace,* p. 64.

Publishers Weekly, October 25, 2004, review of *Midnight at the Palace,* p. 35.

ONLINE

Midnight at the Palace Web site, http://www.sweetpam.com (January 23, 2006), history of the Cockettes.*

*   *   *

THADEN, Barbara Z. 1955-
(Barbara Zembachs Thaden)

PERSONAL: Born July 3, 1955, in New York, NY; daughter of Arnold and Dace (Ozola) Zembachs; married David J. Thaden (a high school principal), August 15, 1981; children: Michael Tālis, Matthew Arne. *Ethnicity:* "Latvian." *Education:* Florida State University, B.S., M.S.; University of North Carolina at Chapel Hill, Ph.D. *Politics:* Democrat. *Religion:* Lutheran. *Hobbies and other interests:* Gardening.

ADDRESSES: Home—106 Saratoga Trail, Chapel Hill, NC 27516. *Office*—Department of English, St. Augustine's College, 1315 Oakwood Ave., Raleigh, NC 27610. *E-mail*—bzthaden@nc.rr.com.

CAREER: High school English teacher, 1978-85; technical writer, 1990-91, 1994; University of North Carolina at Greensboro, lecturer in English, 1994-96; St. Augustine's College, Raleigh, NC, associate professor of English, 1997—.

MEMBER: Modern Language Association of America.

AWARDS, HONORS: Ford Foundation fellow, 1989; Henry C. McBay research fellow, United Negro College Fund, 1999.

WRITINGS:

(Editor and contributor) *New Essays on the Maternal Voice in the Nineteenth Century,* Contemporary Research Press (Dallas, TX), 1995.

The Maternal Voice in Victorian Fiction: Rewriting the Patriarchal Family, Garland Publishing (New York, NY), 1997.

A Student Companion to Charlotte and Emily Brönte, Greenwood Press (Westport, CT), 2001.

Contributor to books, including *The Encyclopedia of Ethnic American Literature,* and *Women in Literature.* Contributor to periodicals, including *Dream International Quarterly, Apalachee Quarterly, College English, South Atlantic Review, Writing Instructor,* and *Dostoevsky Studies.*

WORK IN PROGRESS: Research on feminism, gnosticism, and Toni Morrison's *Paradise.*

SIDELIGHTS: Barbara Z. Thaden told *CA:* "As an associate professor of English at a historically black college, I am always looking for those works of fiction which are both supremely literary and wonderfully teachable. Jamaica Kincaid and Toni Morrison top my list of authors who grab students' attention and yet merit complex analysis. I am particularly interested in exploring the intersections of motherhood, patriarchy, colonialism, and religion. Kincaid's *Autobiography of My Mother* and Morrison's *Paradise* are novels perfect for analyzing these intersections."

BIOGRAPHICAL AND CRITICAL SOURCES:

PERIODICALS

School Library Journal, January, 2002, Pat Bender, review of *A Student Companion to Charlotte and Emily Brönte,* p. 168.

Victorian Studies, autumn, 1998, Carolyn Dever, review of *The Maternal Voice in Victorian Fiction: Rewriting the Patriarchal Family,* p. 176.

*   *   *

THADEN, Barbara Zembachs
See THADEN, Barbara Z.

*   *   *

THÉVENON, Patrick

PERSONAL: Male.

ADDRESSES: *Agent*—c/o Author Mail, Éditions Grasset & Fasquelle, 61, rue des Saints Pères, 75006 Paris, France.

CAREER: Writer.

WRITINGS:

A.A.: un roman-colleage conçu et réalisé, Tchou (Paris, France), 1967.

L'artefact (novel), Calmann-Lévy (Paris, France), 1977.

L'apathiste: sotie, Calmann-Lévy (Paris, France), 1978.

L'adonisant (novel), Calmann-Lévy (Paris, France), 1980.

Le fils puni et autres récits, Balland (Paris, France), 1981.

Le vice roi (novel; title means "The King of Vice"), Grasset (Paris, France), 1982.

Le Veilleur de jour: sotie, Grasset (Paris, France), 1983.

La vertu des simples (novel), Grasset (Paris, France), 1984.

L'air des cartes (novel), Grasset (Paris, France), 1985.

Le palais de la découverte: une intoxication alimentaire, Le Dillettante (Paris, France), 1985.

L'air des cimes (novel), Grasset (Paris, France), 1987.

SIDELIGHTS: In his first novel, *L'artefact,* Patrick Thévenon tells the story of Valentin Body, a young man dissatisfied with his own life and who begins to take on different personas. He even goes so far as to reshape his own body to the point where he undergoes a sex change operation and becomes "Valentine." The novel is essentially divided into three segments reflecting the protagonist's ability to overcome his predicament and rise to the level of a hero, to achieve a certain amount of stability, and then to eventually fall. *French Review* contributor Victor Carrabino noted that the author "experiments with the art of writing, and most of all with the creative process itself." The reviewer went on to comment that "he underlines the pain, the solitude and the joy that accompany the creative act."Carrabino called the book a "fascinating story."

Thévenon focuses on Pierre-Paul Jacquelin de la Roche, the "King of Vice," in his novel *Le vice roi.* The character is a wealthy sensualist devoted entirely to his own pleasures and cruelly contemptuous of the poor and the humble. He decides to take a sort of reverse pilgrimage, with each spot chosen as a place to practice and celebrate a particular cardinal sin. Jack Kolbert, writing in the *French Review,* commented that the author "has created a fascinating, most readable twentieth-century version of Husmans' *A rebours.*" Kolbert, who called the novel part travelogue, part moral novel, and part satire, also wrote, "The novel's chief virtue is that it is entertaining to read. At the same time, it transmits a very thoughtful message: even the king of vices will not escape ultimate sanctions."

BIOGRAPHICAL AND CRITICAL SOURCES:

PERIODICALS

French Review, March, 1979, Victor Carrabino, review of *L'artefact,* p. 676; February, 1984, Jack Kolbert, review of *Le vice roi,* pp. 420-421.*

*   *   *

THIERY, Herman
    See DAISNE, Johan

*   *   *

TIGHE, Carl

PERSONAL: Born in Birmingham, England.

ADDRESSES: Agent—c/o Author Mail, Gardners Books, 1 Whittle Dr., Willington Drove, Eastbourne, East Sussex BN23 6QH, England

CAREER: Derby University, Derby, Ireland, professor of creative writing and head of creative writing department; has also taught in Poland.

AWARDS, HONORS: City Life Writer of the Year Award, 2000, for *Pax: Variations;* Whitbread First Novel Award shortlist, 2001, and Authors Club Award, 2002, both for *Burning Worm;* All-London Drama Prize, for *A Whisper in the Wind.*

WRITINGS:

Gdansk: National Identity in the Polish-German Borderlands, Pluto Press (Concord, MA), 1990.
Rejoice! (short stories), Jonathan Cape (London, England), 1992.
The Politics of Literature: Poland, 1945-1989, University of Wales Press (Cardiff, Wales), 1999.
Pax: Variations (short stories), IMPress (Manchester, England), 2000.
Burning Worm (novel), Gardners Books (Eastbourne, East Sussex, England), 2001.
Writing and Responsibility, Routledge (New York, NY), 2005.

Also the author of radio plays and of stage play *A Whisper in the Wind.* Contributor to periodicals, including *Ambit* and *Metropolitan.*

ADAPTATIONS: A number of Tighe's plays and stories have been broadcast on BBC Radio 4, BBC Radio Wales, and other radio stations in the United Kingdom.

SIDELIGHTS: Carl Tighe is a short-story writer, novelist, playwright, and creative writing professor. He is also a scholar of Polish literature, and his fiction and nonfiction frequently address political and literary issues in Poland. *The Politics of Literature: Poland, 1945-1989* is an "elaborate study of the relationship between communism and literature in postwar Poland," according to Jerzy R. Krzyzanowski in *World Literature Today.* Topics covered include everything from the origins of Polish literary opposition and Communism to the conditions faced by professional writers in Poland and linguistic conflicts between writers and those who controlled the Communist ideology. Tighe also examines the works of Polish novelists, prose writers, journalists, and critics. Reviewer George Gomori noted in the *Journal of European Studies* that there is a lack of coverage of poets, philosophers, and playwrights. However, the critic maintained, all the writers included are "at one point practicing Marxists or at least Communist Party members," and therefore "the author's intention is to demonstrate the vital role that Left-leaning writers played in Poland's recent history." Unfortunately, Krzyzanowski felt that the book suffers from a number of "cavalier" comments and from several small, incorrect details that erode the overall credibility of the work; the reviewer observed that "many valuable observations lose their validity, overshadowed by statements and often by quoted facts that have no basis in reality." However, the book contains "some keen observations," and Tighe's profiles of a variety of Polish authors and their relation to politics "are informative and based on solid research," Krzyzanowski concluded.

Burning Worm, Tighe's debut novel, addresses the Solidarity years of early 1980s Poland "with wise playfulness," commented reviewer Nicholas Birns in the *Review of Contemporary Fiction.* Here, Polish professor S. Mroz writes about Eugene Hinks, an Irish author who draws parallels between the Polish and the Irish in that they are both rebellious, rural, and poor. However, the Hinks character does not rise above his circumstances, nor does he yearn to be a hero; instead, his main concern is simply to survive. Through his characters, Tighe examines what happens when people who have been consistently dominated finally have the chance to confront and experience freedom. "It is a remarkable work," attested Birns, "one that, though unabashedly inventive, is . . . ultimately out to capture the truth."

BIOGRAPHICAL AND CRITICAL SOURCES:

PERIODICALS

Bookseller, March 8, 2002, Benedicte Page, "Behind the Headlines," p. 12; April 26, 2002, "Tighe Wins Award," p. 37.
Journal of European Studies, March, 2001, George Gomori, review of *The Politics of Literature: Poland, 1945-1989,* p. 134.
Review of Contemporary Fiction, fall, 2002, Nicholas Birns, review of *Burning Worm,* p. 154.
World Literature Today, winter, 2000, Jerzy R. Krzyzanowski, review of *The Politics of Literature,* p. 195.*

*   *   *

TINGLE, Tim

PERSONAL: Male. *Education:* University of Texas, earned degree; currently attending graduate school at the University of Oklahoma.

ADDRESSES: Office—StoryTribe Publishing, 4417 Morningside Way, Canyon Lake, TX 78133. *E-mail*—timtingle@hotmail.com.

CAREER: Writer, entrepreneur, performer, musician, public speaker, and storyteller. New Canaan Farms (gourmet food manufacturer), San Marcos, TX, co-owner and operator, 1979-97; StoryTribe Publishing, Canyon Lake, TX, founder and publisher. Has worked as a marketing workshop presenter for the Texas Department of Agriculture, a touring storyteller in Germany for the U.S. Department of Defense, and as a performer at the Six Flags over Texas theme park. Has been a featured storyteller at numerous festivals, including the National Storytelling Festival, Minnesota Storytelling Festival, Keepers of the Word at Amherst College, Texas Storytelling Festival, Pete Seeger's Clearwater Revival Festival, and the Mississippi Storytelling Festival; teller-in-residence, International Storytelling Center, 2004.

AWARDS, HONORS: Named Contemporary Storyteller of the Year, Wordcraft Circle of Native American Writers and Storytellers, 2001; *Storytelling World* selection for year's best anthology, for *Texas Ghost Stories.*

WRITINGS:

Children of the Tracks and Other San Antonio Ghost Stories (sound recording), StoryTribe (Canyon Lake, TX) 1994.
Walking the Choctaw Road, Cinco Puntos Press (El Paso, TX), 2003.
(With Doc Moore) *Texas Ghost Stories: Fifty Favorites for the Telling,* Texas Tech University Press (Lubbock, TX), 2004.
(With Doc Moore) *Spooky Texas Tales,* illustrated by Gina Miller, Texas Tech University Press (Lubbock, TX), 2005.
Crossing Bok Chitto, illustrated by Jeane Rorex Bridges, Cinco Puntos Press (El Paso, TX), 2006.

Also author of *Grandma Spider Brings the Fire,* a collection of short stories on audiocassette. Contributor to periodicals, including *Storytelling World.*

ADAPTATIONS: Stories from *Walking the Choctaw Road* were adapted as the ballet *Trail of Tears: Walking the Choctaw Road* by Ballet Austin and the Polyanna Theatre Company.

WORK IN PROGRESS: Riding the Red Dirt Road, a collection of short stories, expected 2007.

SIDELIGHTS: Tim Tingle is best known as a professional storyteller and musician who has appeared at conferences and festivals throughout the United States and abroad. In 2003 he completed his tenth tour of Germany under the auspices of the U.S. Department of Defense. While there, he traveled to schools and performed for children of U.S. military personnel stationed in Germany. He is a frequent performer at schools and libraries, where he tells stories and promotes literacy. A member of the Choctaw Nation of Oklahoma, Tingle tells stories that reflect his Native American heritage, combining personal tales with historical events and traditional lore. His works have attracted the attention of Choctaw chief Gregory Pyle, who for four consecutive years requested a story from Tingle at the Annual State of the Nation Address at the Choctaw Labor Day Gathering. Tingle often complements his sessions with performances on the Native American flute, and frequently accompanies himself on a variety of gourd rattles and drums, thus "adding a haunting dimension to a concert," noted a biographer on the Tim Tingle Home Page.

Tingle's *Walking the Choctaw Road* consists of twelve stories, ranging from accounts of his father's experiences on the infamous Trail of Tears to traditional Choctaw folk tales and personal accounts of Tingle's modern-day experiences. In the story "Trail of Tears," a child carries along his mother's bones during the tragic days of the Native Americans' forced migration by U.S. troops. Other stories cover topics such as slave escapes, the morality of paying the price for one's own crimes, and Tingle's own experiences as an adolescent during the Vietnam War. Many of the stories provide lessons in traditional Choctaw culture, folk practices, and social values. The book also includes a glossary of Choctaw words, a bibliography of further readings on Choctaw history and tradition, and Tingle's lengthy introduction, which discusses Choctaw story sources, motifs, and historical events. A *Kirkus Reviews* contributor called Tingle a "superb storyteller," and noted that his "poetic language and a compelling but quiet voice honor the Native American traditions" present in the book. John Peters, writing in *Booklist,* commented that Tingle's "evocative language, expert pacing, and absorbing subject matter will rivet readers and listeners both."

BIOGRAPHICAL AND CRITICAL SOURCES:

PERIODICALS

Booklist, June 1, 2003, John Peters, review of *Walking the Choctaw Road,* p. 1758.
Childhood Education, winter, 2003, Irene A. Allen, review of *Walking the Choctaw Road,* p. 92.
Kirkus Reviews, June 1, 2003, review of *Walking the Choctaw Road,* p. 812.
Publishers Weekly, April 21, 2003, "Native American Connections," review of *Walking the Choctaw Road,* p. 65.
School Library Journal, March, 2005, Francisca Goldsmith, review of *Walking the Choctaw Road,* p. 89.

ONLINE

2 Young 2 Retire Web site, http://www.2young2retire. com/ (March 13, 2006), biography of Tim Tingle.
Educational Paperback Association Web site, http:// www.edupaperback.org/ (March 13, 2006), biography of Tim Tingle.
Tim Tingle Home Page, http://www.choctawstoryteller. com (March 13, 2006).*

*   *   *

TOKER, Leona 1950-

PERSONAL: Born August 14, 1950, in Vilnius, U.S. S.R. (now Lithuania); daughter of Aba (a professor of history) and Nedda (a professor of linguistics) Strazhas; married Gregory Zvi Toker (a physicist), 1972; children: Dana and Jonathan (twins). *Ethnicity:* "Jewish." *Education:* Vilnius University, M.A., 1973; Hebrew University of Jerusalem, Ph.D., 1981. *Politics:* "Not a member of any party." *Religion:* Jewish.

ADDRESSES: Office—Department of English, Hebrew University of Jerusalem, Jerusalem 91905, Israel. *E-mail*—toker@h2.hum.huji.ac.il.

CAREER: Schoolteacher, 1974-78; Hebrew University of Jerusalem, Jerusalem, Israel, professor of English, 1978—.

MEMBER: Council for Higher Education, Council of Editors of Learned Journals.

AWARDS, HONORS: Alexander von Humboldt fellowship.

WRITINGS:

Nabokov: The Mystery of Literary Structures, Cornell University Press (Ithaca, NY), 1989.
Eloquent Reticence: Withholding Information in Fictional Narrative, University Press of Kentucky (Lexington, KY), 1993.
(Editor, with Shlomith Rimmon-Kenan and Shuli Barzilai) *Rereading Texts, Rethinking Critical Presuppositions: Essays in Honour of H.M. Daleski,* Peter Lang (New York, NY), 1997.
Return from the Archipelago: Narratives of Gulag Survivors, Indiana University Press (Bloomington, IN), 2000.

BIOGRAPHICAL AND CRITICAL SOURCES:

PERIODICALS

Journal of English and Germanic Philology, April, 1994, Jeremy Hawthorn, review of *Eloquent Reticence: Withholding Information in Fictional Narrative,* p. 269.

*   *   *

TOURÉ 1971-

PERSONAL: Born March 20, 1971, in Boston, MA; married Rita Nakouzi, March 19, 2005. *Education:* Attended Emory University and Columbia University's graduate school of creative writing.

ADDRESSES: Home—New York, NY. *Office*—Black Entertainment Television, 1900 West Place N.E., Washington, DC 20018.

CAREER: Writer, novelist, journalist, editor, and television producer. Black Entertainment Television (BET), writer, host, and consulting producer, 2005—.

Frequent guest on television shows, including the *Today Show, O'Reilly Factor, Paula Zahn Now, Anderson Cooper 360°,* and *Topic A with Tina Brown.* Served as host of *Spoke N Heard* on MTV2.

AWARDS, HONORS: Zoetrope: All Story award for short story "A Hot Time at the Church of Kentucky Fried Souls and the Spectacular Final Sunday Sermon of the Right Revren Daddy Love."

WRITINGS:

The Portable Promised Land (short stories), Little, Brown (Boston, MA), 2002.
Soul City (novel), Little, Brown (New York, NY), 2004.
Never Drank the Kool-Aid (essays), Picador (New York, NY), 2006.

Contributor to books, including *The Best American Essays 1999,* edited by Robert Atwan and Edward Hoaglund, Houghton Mifflin (New York, NY), 1999; *Da Capo Best Music Writing 2004,* edited by Mickey Hart, Da Capo Press (New York, NY), 2004; and *Best American Erotica 2004,* edited by Susie Bright, Touchstone (New York, NY), 2004. Contributor to periodicals, including the *New Yorker, Rolling Stone, Playboy, Village Voice, Vibe, Tennis Magazine,* and the *New York Times.* Contributing editor, *Rolling Stone,* for ten years.

SIDELIGHTS: Television correspondent, commentator, producer, journalist, and editor Touré is also a novelist, short-story writer, and essayist. He has been a popular culture correspondent for the television network CNN, a frequent guest on other television news and commentary programs, and a producer for BET news. Regarding his one-word name, a biographer on the Touré home page noted, "Touré is his real name, the name his mother gave him when he was born, the name his parents consciously chose for him." In "the one-namedness there's a reference to the dislocation implicit in the African-American family name and a reach back to the unknown last names of Africa," the biographer wrote.

Touré's *The Portable Promised Land* is a short-story collection that is a "sharp celebration of black urban life, filled with characters at once surreal and familiar," observed *Library Journal* reviewer Ellen Flexman. With a combination of humor, social commentary, and magic realism, Touré approaches black culture and black stereotypes, allowing both to be "reclaimed and transformed to artfully address the politics and construction of race," stated Keir Graff in *Booklist*. The residents of Soul City populate the stories. In "Steviewondermobile," Huggy Bear Jackson drives the most tricked-out car in town, one that plays only the music of the soul-singing Wonder. Reverend Love preaches to his congregation inside a converted Kentucky Friend Chicken restaurant in "A Hot Time at the Church of Kentucky Fried Souls and the Spectacular Final Sunday Sermon of the Right Revren Daddy Love," until someone sets fire to the place in retaliation for the good reverend's repeated sexual misadventures. In "Blackmanwalking," young men learn the methods of the black man's strut at UCLA (the University at the Corner of Lenox Avenue in Harlem). In other tales, magical Air Jordan shoes give a youngster the ability to fly, and break-up ceremonies become as popular as wedding ceremonies. "More than anything," commented an *Antioch Review* critic, in this collection "there is an intensity of imagination rare in any writer." Touré "has blazed his own trail into fiction," commented Mondella Jones in the *Black Issues Book Review*. "The writing is fresh and exhilarating and serves as a breath of fresh air for readers looking for an alternative to mainstream fiction."

Touré revisits Soul City in his novel of the same name. This time, a hundred-foot afro pick stands as the city's landmark; a magical biscuit shop, where a DJ spins tunes and the baked goods are magically dabbed in heavenly butter, is the main meeting place; in their hug shop, a group of loving grandmothers heal the city's ailments better than doctors; a character named Fulcrum Negro travels back and forth to Heaven on a concealed pathway; and a ten-year-old boy preacher, the Revren Lil' Mo Love, delivers electrifying, and eclectic, sermons. In the main story, journalist Cadillac Jackson, a reporter for *Chocolate City Magazine*, arrives in Soul City to cover the mayoral election. While there, however, he falls in love with resident Mahogany Sunflower, the direct descendant of a family of black people who possessed the ability to fly. Touré "draws on his awareness of today's popular culture amusingly and smartly as very few writers have," commented Clarence V. Reynolds in the *Black Issues Book Review*. A *Publishers Weekly* reviewer remarked that "this charming and quirky fairy tale for grownups comes as a restful change." *Library Journal*

reviewer David A. Berona stated: "This is a cleverly written page-turner whose only disappointment is that it has to end."

Never Drank the Kool-Aid, a selection of Tourés essays, is a "varied collection of lucid, colorful pieces," according to a *Publishers Weekly* contributor. Many of the essays are personality profiles of hip-hop, rock, and R&B artists, including Prince, Wynton Marsalis, DMX, Lauryn Hill, and Eminem, as well as political figures such as Al Sharpton and sports stars such as Jennifer Capriati. The author explores the difficulties faced by a gay rapper; compares the structure of well-known rap collectives such as Wu-Tang Clan with traditional African family structure; and offers a deeply felt personal essay. A *Kirkus Reviews* contributor called the book "a wholly involving and piercingly intelligent examination of contemporary popular culture."

BIOGRAPHICAL AND CRITICAL SOURCES:

PERIODICALS

Antioch Review, winter, 2003, review of *The Portable Promised Land,* p. 186.

Black Issues Book Review, July-August, 2002, Mondella Jones, review of *The Portable Promised Land,* p. 36; September-October, 2004, Clarence V. Reynolds, review of *Soul City,* p. 50.

Booklist, June 1, 2002, Keir Graff, review of *The Portable Promised Land,* p. 1689; September 1, 2004, Vanessa Bush, review of *Soul City,* p. 66.

Daily Pennsylvanian, November 5, 2004, Courtney Edwards, "Writer Brings Novel to Life with Voice Impressions," profile of Touré.

Entertainment Weekly, September 3, 2004, Abby West, review of *Soul City,* p. 81.

Essence, November, 2004, Janice K. Bryant, review of *Soul City,* p. 138.

Kirkus Reviews, July 15, 2004, review of *Soul City,* p. 659; January 1, 2006, review of *Never Drank the Kool-Aid,* p. 35.

Library Journal, June 1, 2002, Ellen Flexman, review of *The Portable Promised Land,* p. 199; October 1, 2004, David A. Berona, review of *Soul City,* p. 74.

Publishers Weekly, May 27, 2002, review of *The Portable Promised Land,* p. 32; August 9, 2004, review of *Soul City,* p. 231; January 2, 2006, review of *Never Drank the Kool-Aid,* p. 48.

Review of Contemporary Fiction, spring, 2003, Rob Mawyer, review of *The Portable Promised Land,* p. 138.

Tribune Books (Chicago, IL), June 2, 2002, review of *The Portable Promised Land,* p. 5; June 29, 2003, review of *The Portable Promised Land,* p. 6.

ONLINE

BlackNews.com, http://www.blacknews.com/ (March 15, 2006), "Pop Culture Personality Touré Headed to BET News."

Touré Home Page, http://www.toure.com (March 13, 2006).*

*   *   *

TRANG, Corinne 1967-

PERSONAL: Born November 9, 1967, in Blois, France; daughter of Nhu Minh (in import-export food business) and Marie-Jeanne (Barbet) Trang; married Michael R. McDonough (an architect and author), September 28, 1996; children: Colette. *Ethnicity:* "Eurasian." *Education:* Attended St. John's University, 1987-90; Drexel University, B.S., 2003.

ADDRESSES: Home and office—Corinne Trang Studio, 131 Spring St., New York, NY 10012. *Agent*—Angela Miller, Miller Agency, 1 Sheridan Sq., Ste. 7B, New York, NY 10014. *E-mail*—web@corinnetrang. com.

CAREER: Food writer, food stylist, chef, food consultant and critic, and travel photographer. Meigher Communications, New York, NY, producing editor of magazines and cookbooks, 1996-98, director of *Saveur* test kitchen, 1997-98; cohost of a television pilot, *Melting Pot,* Food Network, 2000; guest chef at various establishments, including Le Colonial Restaurant, Philadelphia, PA, Yang Ming, Bryn Mawr, PA, Veruka, New York, NY, James Beard House, and Casa Malaparte Foundation in Italy; caterer of private parties; judge of culinary competitions. Drexel University, visiting faculty member, 2000—; Institute of Culinary Education, New York, NY, culinary instructor, 2003—; guest lecturer and critic at other institutions, including California College of Arts and Crafts, University of the Arts, Philadelphia, Rhode Island School of Design, University of Applied Sciences, Cologne, Germany, New York University, and Harvard University; public speaker at other venues; guest on radio and television programs, including *Martha Stewart Living, Home Matters, Cooking Live, The Early Show,* and *Feng Shui Revealed.* Member of James Beard Foundation.

MEMBER: International Association of Culinary Professionals, New York Women's Culinary Alliance.

AWARDS, HONORS: "Best of the Best Award," *Food and Wine* magazine, 1999, and *International Cookbook Revue* World Cookbook Awards, best Asian cookbook in the world and best Asian cookbook in English, 2000, all for *Authentic Vietnamese Cooking: Food from a Family Table.*

WRITINGS:

Authentic Vietnamese Cooking: Food from a Family Table, Simon & Schuster (New York, NY), 1999.

Essentials of Asian Cuisine: Fundamentals and Favorite Recipes, Simon & Schuster (New York, NY), 2003.

Contributor to books, including *Saveur Cooks Authentic French,* edited by Dorothy Kalins and others, Chronicle Books (San Francisco, CA), 1999; *Vegetables from Amaranth to Zucchini,* edited by Elizabeth Schneider, William Morrow (New York, NY), 2001; *The Encyclopedia of Food and Culture,* Thomson Gale (Detroit, MI), 2002; and *The New American Chef,* edited by Andrew Dornenburg and Karen Page, John Wiley (New York, NY), 2003. Contributor of articles and photographs to periodicals, including *Bottom Line Personal, Health, Cooking Light, Organic Style, Saveur, Moneysworth,* and *Food and Wine.*

WORK IN PROGRESS: Grilling with Asian Flavors, publication by Chronicle Books (San Francisco, CA) expected in 2006.

BIOGRAPHICAL AND CRITICAL SOURCES:

ONLINE

Corinne Trang Studio: Explore Asia's History, Culture, and Food, http://www.corinnetrang.com (April 2, 2005).

TREVOR, Doug
    See TREVOR, Douglas

*   *   *

TREVOR, Douglas
   (Doug Trevor)

PERSONAL: Married; children: two. *Education:* Princeton University, B.A. (magna cum laude), 1992; Université de Tours, France, Lettres Modernes, Licence, 1993; Harvard University, M.A., 1995, Ph.D., 1999.

ADDRESSES: Home—Iowa City, IA. *Office*—Department of English, University of Iowa, 308 English-Philosophy Bldg., Iowa City, IA 52242-1492. *E-mail*—Douglas-Trevor@uiowa.edu.

CAREER: Educator and author. University of Iowa, Iowa City, associate professor of English, faculty advisor to the general education program, 1999-2002, associate chair for undergraduate programs, 2005—, chair of the Undergraduate Steering Committee, 2005—. Has served as a member of various university committees.

MEMBER: Renaissance Society of America, Modern Language Association, Milton Society, Phi Beta Kappa.

AWARDS, HONORS: Francis LeMoyne Page Senior Thesis Award, Princeton University, 1992; graduate fellowship for study abroad, Rotary Foundation, 1992-93; research grants, Harvard Graduate Student Council, 1994, 1997; distinction in teaching, Harvard University, 1995, 1996; Chris O'Malley Prize in Short Fiction, University of Wisconsin, 1996, for "The Whores in Tours" (short story); doctoral summer research grant, Mellon Foundation, 1996; dissertation fellowship, Whiting Foundation, 1997-98; research grant, Newberry Library Consortium, 1999-2000; Old Gold Summer fellowship, University of Iowa, 2000, 2001; supplemental travel grants, University of Iowa, 2002, 2003; fellow, Obermann Center for Advanced Studies, University of Iowa, 2002; Sokolov Scholar in Fiction, Bread Loaf Writers' Conference, 2003; arts and humanities initiative grant, University of Iowa,

2003-04; David R.W.M. Keck Foundation and Andrew W. Mellon Foundation fellow, Huntington Library, 2004; Charles A. Ryskamp research fellowship, American Council of Learned Societies, 2004-05; John C. Gerber Teaching Prize, Department of English, University of Iowa, 2005; Iowa Short Fiction Award, 2005, for *The Thin Tear in the Fabric of Space;* Dean's Scholarship, University of Iowa, 2005-06; O. Henry Prize, 2006, for "Girls I Know."

WRITINGS:

(Editor, with Carla Mazzio) *Historicism, Psychoanalysis, and Early Modern Culture,* Routledge (New York, NY), 2000.
The Poetics of Melancholy in Early Modern England, Cambridge University Press (New York, NY), 2004.
The Thin Tear in the Fabric of Space (short stories), University of Iowa Press (Iowa City, IA), 2005.

Contributor to numerous collections, including *Reading the Early Modern Passions,* edited by Gail Kern Paster, Katherine Rowe, and Mary Floyd-Wilson, University of Pennsylvania Press, 2004; *The Best American Nonrequired Reading 2005* (anthology); and *Companion to Shakespeare's Sonnets,* edited by Michael Schoenfeldt, Blackwell Press, 2006. Contributor of short stories to literary journals, including the *Paris Review, Glimmer Train, New England Review,* and *Epoch.* Contributor of articles to journals and periodicals, including the *Sixteenth Century Journal, Modern Language Quarterly, Renaissance Quarterly,* and *Boston Book Review.* Served as fiction editor of the *Iowa Review,* 2000-04. Also serves as editorial advisor for *Shakespeare Yearbook* and a reviewer for *Shakespeare Quarterly, Renaissance Quarterly, Philological Quarterly,* and *Clio.*

SIDELIGHTS: Specializing in Renaissance literature, English professor Douglas Trevor has published a multitude of fiction and nonfiction works in periodicals, anthologies, and other collections. Trevor edited his first book, *Historicism, Psychoanalysis, and Early Modern Culture,* with Carla Mazzio. Part of the "Culture Work" series, the volume collects sixteen academic essays that attempt to determine whether people in early modern Europe understood the idea of "an inner self." In addition to Trevor and Mazzio, contributors include Anna Rosalin Jones, Peter Stally-brass, James R. Siemon, John Guillory, Eric Wilson, and Karen Newman, among others. Reviewer E. James Lieberman in *Library Journal* observed that the contributors to this work "write heady stuff" but went on to comment that readers "who enjoy brilliant speculation on rarefied ideas will be rewarded."

Following *Historicism, Psychoanalysis, and Early Modern Culture*, Trevor produced *The Poetics of Melancholy in Early Modern England*, which discusses the works of Edmund Spenser, John Donne, Robert Burton, and John Milton, and *The Thin Tear in the Fabric of Space*, a collection of short stories that earned the Iowa Short Fiction Award. Each protagonist in the collection attempts to deal with a loss, or "tear," in his or her life, such as the death of a loved one or self-annihilation. For example, in "Central Square," an alcoholic man spends time with a young Chilean woman who operates a coffee cart at the mall and helps awaken him to the reality that he is drinking himself to death. In "The Surprising Weight of the Body's Organs," a mother struggles to cope with her young son's death. In a critique of the collection for *Kirkus Reviews*, one contributor explained that the stories "trace the various facets of human loneliness" and are "about the difficulty of communicating in the face of loss." The contributor concluded by defining the stories in *The Thin Tear in the Fabric of Space* as "taut and rich." A reviewer for *Publishers Weekly* observed that "Trevor's writing has energy and his characters have authentic quirks."

BIOGRAPHICAL AND CRITICAL SOURCES:

PERIODICALS

Journal of Intercultural Studies, December, 2002, B. Ricardo Brown, review of *Historicism, Psychoanalysis, and Early Modern Culture,* p. 326.
Kirkus Reviews, September 1, 2005, review of *The Thin Tear in the Fabric of Space,* p. 941.
Library Journal, June 1, 2000, E. James Lieberman, review of *Historicism, Psychoanalysis, and Early Modern Culture,* p. 170.
Publishers Weekly, September 5, 2005, review of *The Thin Tear in the Fabric of Space,* p. 36.
Sixteenth Century Journal, winter, 2001, Allison Levy, review of *Historicism, Psychoanalysis, and Early Modern Culture,* p. 1218.

Times Literary Supplement, May 6, 2005, Katharine Craik, review of *The Poetics of Melancholy in Early Modern England,* p. 28.

ONLINE

University of Iowa Web site, http://www.uiowa.edu/ (January 23, 2006), biographical information on Trevor.

*   *   *

TRIOLET, Elsa 1896-1970
(Ella Iurievena Kagana, Daniel Laurent)

PERSONAL: Born Ella Iurievana Kagana, September 25, 1896, in Moscow, Russia; died June 16, 1970; immigrated to France, c. 1918; daughter of Yuri Kagan (a contract law lawyer) and Helena Youlievna (a pianist); married André Triolet (a French military attaché), 1918 (divorced); married Louis Aragon (a poet and writer), February 28, 1939. *Education:* Lycée Valitzki, Moscow, Russia, 1918.

CAREER: Writer. *Les Lettre Françaises,* journal of the intellectual Resistance during World War II, writer and editor. *Military service:* Served in the French Resistance during World War II.

AWARDS, HONORS: Médaille de la Résistance, Prix Goncourt, 1945, for *A Fine of Two Hundred Francs.*

WRITINGS:

Na Taiti, Ateney (Leningrad, Russia), 1925.
Zemlyanichka, Coopérative des Écrivains "Le Cercle," (Moscow, Russia) 1926, translation by Léon Robel published as *Fraise-des-bois,* with a preface by Louis Aragon, Gallimard (Paris, France), 1974, reprinted in 1997.
Zaschchitnyi tsvet, Fédération (Moscow, Russia), 1928, translation by Léon Robel published as *Camouflage,* Gallimard (Paris, France), 1976.
Bonsoir Thérèse, Éditions Denoël (Paris, France), 1938, Gallimard (Paris, France), 1978.

Maïakovski, poète russe, Éditions Sociales Inernationales (Paris, France), 1939, translation by John Rodker published as *Mayakovsky, Poet of Russia: Reminiscences from a Longer Work,* Hogarth (London, England), 1939.

Mille Regrets (stories; title means "A Thousand Regrets"), Denoël (Paris, France), 1941–43.

Le Cheval blanc (novel), Denoël (Paris, France), 1943, translation by Gerrie Thielens published as *The White Charger,* Rinehart (New York, NY), 1946, translation by Mervyn Savill published as *The White Horse,* Hutchinson (New York, NY), 1951.

(As Daniel Laurent) *Les Amants d'Avignon* (story; title means "The Lovers of Avignon"), Éditions de Minuit (Paris, France), 1943, translation published as *The Lovers of Avignon,* included in *A Fine of 200 Francs,* Reynal & Hitchcock (New York, NY), 1947.

(As Daniel Laurent) *Yvette,* Bibliothèque Française (Paris, France), 1943.

Qui est cet étranger qui n'est pas d'ici? ou Le mythe de la baronne Mélanie, Ides et Calendes (Paris, France), 1945, Éditions Denoël (Paris, France), 1997.

Ce n'était qu'un passage de ligne, Seghers (Paris, France), 1945.

Le premier accroc coûte deux francs (stories), Egloff (Paris, France), 1945, translation by Francis Golffing published as *A Fine of 200 Francs,* Reynal & Hitchock (New York, NY), 1947.

Personne ne m'aime (novel; title means "No One Loves Me"), Éditeurs Français Réunis (Paris, France), 1946.

(Translator) M. Iline, *Les montagnes et les hommes,* Éditions Hier et Aujourd'hui (Paris, France), 1946.

(With Raymon Peynet) *Dessins animés,* Bordas (Paris, France), 1947.

Les fantômes armés (novel; title means "Armed Ghosts"), Biliothèque Français (Paris, France), 1947, republished with *Personne ne m'aime,* as *Anne-Marie I-II,* 1952.

L'inspecteur des ruines (novel), Biliothèque Français, (Paris, France),1948, translation by Norman Cameron published as *The Inspector of Ruins,* Roy (New York, NY), 1953.

L'écrivain et le livre; ou, La suite dans les idées, Éditions Sociales (Paris, France), 1948.

(Translator) Ina Konstantinova, *La jeune fille de Kachine: Journal intime et letters,* Éditeurs Français Réunis (Paris, France), 1951.

(Translator, editor, and author of introduction) *Maïakovski: Vers et proses de 1913 à 1930,* Éditeurs Franççais Réunis (Paris, France), 1952.

Le cheval roux; ou, les intentions humaines (novel; title means "The Red Horse; or Human Intentions"), Éditeurs Français Réunis (Paris, France), 1953.

L'histoire d'Anton Tchekhov, sa vie, son oeuvre, Éditeurs Franççais Réunis (Paris, France), 1954.

(Translator) Anton Checkhov, *Théâtre,* two volumes, Éditeurs Français Réunis (Paris, France), 1954 1962.

(With Robert Doisneau) *Pour que Paris soit,* Éditions Cercle d'Art (Paris, France), 1956.

Le rendez-vous des étrangers (novel; title means "Meeting Point of Foreigners"), Gallimard (Paris, France), 1956.

Le monument (novel), Gallimard (Paris, France) 1957.

Elsa Triolet choisi par Aragon (collection), edited by Louis Aragon, Gallimard (Paris, France) 1960.

Les manigances: Journal d'une égoïste (novel; title means "Wangling: Journal of an Egoist"), 1962.

Oeuvres romanesques croisées d'Elsa Triolet et Aragon (collection; forty-two volumes), Laffont (Paris, France) 1964–74.

(Editor) *La poésie russe* (bilingual edition), Seghers (Paris, France), 1965.

Le grand jamais (novel; title means "It Will Never Happen"), Gallimard (Paris, France), 1965.

Écoutez-voir (novel; title means "Look and Listen"), Gallimard (Paris, France), 1968.

(Translator) Marina Tsvétaeva, *Marina Tsvétaeva,* Gallimard (Paris, France), 1968.

La mise en mots, Skira (Geneva, Switzerland), 1969.

Le rossignol se tait à l'aube (novel; title means "The Nightingale Falls Silent at Dawn"), Gallimard (Paris, France), 1970.

Proverbes d'Elsa, compiled by Jean Marcenac, preface by Edmonde Charles-Roux, Éditeurs Français Réunis (Paris, France), 1971.

(With Viktor Borisovich Shklovskii and Richard Sheldon) *Zoo; or, Letters Not about Love* (includes seven letters by author), translated by Richard Sheldon, Cornell University Press (Ithaca, NY) 1971.

Chroniques théâtrales: Les Lettres Françaises, 1948-1951 (criticism), edited by M. Lebre-Peytard, Gallimard (Paris, France), 1981.

Trois inédits, 1999.

Correspondance: 1921-1970, edited by Léon Robel, Gallimard (Paris, France), 2000.

"L'AGE DE NYLON" TRILOGY

Roses à crédit (title means "Roses on the Installment Plan"), Gallimard (Paris, France) 1958, reprinted, 1998.
Luna-Park, Gallimard (Paris, France) 1959.
L'âme (title means "The Soul"), Gallimard (Paris, France) 1963.

Contributor to books and collections, including *Trois inédits,* Société des amis de Louis Aragon et Elsa Triolet (Rambouillet, France), 1999; works have been translated in several languages, including Czech, Spanish, German, Russian, Portuguese, and Japanese.

SIDELIGHTS: French-émigré writer Elsa Triolet was a chronicler of her tumultuous times. In her novels she wrote about her childhood in Russia, her experiences with the French Resistance during World War II, and her disenchantment with politics during the postwar years. For several years she published theater reviews, and her translations of works by Russian poets and dramatists brought what would become classic works to wider audiences. She was also influential in her journalism and other work for the Resistance during World War II and as the wife of famous French poet and communist leader Louis Aragon, who composed five volumes of verse that each were inspired by Triolet in some way.

Born in Moscow, Triolet fled her homeland during the Russian Revolution and settled in Paris. Several people early encouraged Triolet to pursue a writing career. She and literary critic Viktor Shklovsky, a one-time suitor, had been corresponding regularly. Unknown to Triolet, Shklovsky published several of her letters to him in a work called *Zoo; or, Letters Not about Love,* so titled because Triolet had made Shklovsky, whose love was unrequited, promise that he not write love letters to her. When Shklovsky showed Russian novelist and dramatist Maxim Gorky the work, Gorky told him that the best part of the work was the series of letters by Triolet, known as "Alya" in the signed letters. When Shklovsky revealed Triolet's identity, Gorky encouraged her to write for publication.

In the late 1920s Triolet saw the publication of her first novels, which she wrote in Russian and were later translated into French. With *Na Taiti,* she recounts her experience of living in Tahiti. In the semiautobiographical *Zemlyanichka,* which was translated fifty years later as *Fraise-des-bois,* she describes the life of a middle-class Russian girl nicknamed Fraise-des-bois growing up before the 1917 Russian Revolution. Told in alternating third person by the governess and first person by the child, the story focuses on the girl's interior life. She is fraught with feelings of worthlessness, jealousy of an older sister, and fear of a future of suffering, loneliness, and death.

During 1938, Triolet published her first novel written originally in French. *Bonsoir Thérèse* contains five very different episodes dealing with a person called Thérèse, who appears in many forms: as a woman who leaves her husband, as the city of Paris, as a person trying to name a perfume, as a woman who in an epiphany sees herself as she truly is, and finally as a wife who kills her arms-trafficking husband and then commits suicide.

While France was occupied by the Nazis during World War II, Triolet was very active in the Resistance Movement and continued to write for a Resistance newspaper and produced two novels and numerous short stories, all designed to encourage other patriots. *Mille Regrets* contains eight of these stories. The novel *Le Cheval blanc,* translated into English as *The White Charger* and *The White Horse,* tells the episodic story of a young man named Michel Vigaud, who runs away from school to join the navy and wanders the world until the onset of World War II, when he dies in battle. Discussing the novel in *Comparative Literature Studies,* Lorene M. Birden noted that in writing the book Triolet likely drew from her knowledge of Russian oral epic literature.

Triolet also published several works under the pseudonym Daniel Laurent, including *Les amants d'Avignon,* which was published by an underground press during the war. It was later collected in *Le premier accroc coûte deux cents francs,* a collection of four novellas that was translated into English and published as *A Fine of 200 Francs.* In the story "Les amants," the author tells the tale of Juliette, a courier during the Resistance, and is one of Triolet's most anthologized works. "La vie privée d'Alexis Slavsky, artiste peintre," portrays how the war marred the ability of artists and intellectuals to create. The novellas "Notebooks Buried under a Peach Tree" and "A Fine of 200 Francs" complete the collection.

During the postwar years, Triolet published her darkest novels. She wrote the novels *Personne ne m'aime* and its sequel *les fantômes armés,* known collectively as *Anne-Marie I-II,* at the end of 1944 and early in 1945. Told in the third person by the narrator Anne-Marie and in the first person by Jenny, *Personne ne m'aime* revolves around thwarted Jenny's desire to find true love during World War II. Though she is a famous actress, she feels that no one loves her. In the end she develops breast cancer and commits suicide rather than suffer further. Anne-Marie, who has been the witness to Jenny's plight, becomes the central character of the second half of the book and is the primary protagonist in *Les fantômes armés*. Anne-Marie suffers a broken marriage, works for the Resistance, falls in love with another fighter who is later killed, and sees the Liberation. In the sequel, she tries to reassemble her life, becoming a photographer, but finding no place to fit in the mixed-up world of postwar politics and potential civil war between former collaborators and resistance fighters. According to a contributor to the *Dictionary of Literary Biography,* the second novel "sustains the suspense begun in the first book and develops at the same time a psychologically satisfying portrait of a thinker able to act in extraordinary situations and a truthful description of the intricate military and political circumstances of the Resistance movements."

In *The Inspector of Ruins,* Triolet tells the story of Antonin, who is a man adrift following his wife's death. As the narrator, Antonin tells of his wanderings in a genial tone, but his life turns out tragically. "Triolet showed an uncanny mastery in rendering the conditions in postwar Western Europe," wrote a *Dictionary of Literary Biography* contributor. The writer went on to note: "Many scenes are . . . highly dramatic, with a superb sense of the commonplace and of the exceptional. Most secondary characters in this novel are well developed, some of them memorably."

From 1948 to 1951, Triolet published theater reviews in the communist periodical *Lettres françaises,* which were later collected and republished in 1981 as the well-received *Chroniques théâtrales: Les Lettres Françaises, 1948-1951.* Among the writings are reviews of Parisian theaters and works by a number of noted French playwrights. Writing in *World Literature Today,* B.L. Knapp praised Triolet for her understanding of the "particular genius at work" and her "personal reactions, expressed in a continuously exciting and poetic style." *Times Literary Supplement* contributor John Weightman commented that the reviews "provide invaluable insights for the reader interested in the French theatre as a historical phenomenon." He added, "Without constituting great theatrical criticism her articles are full of surprises, and even have a sort of naïve freshness."

The author's works from the 1950s include translations of the two-volume plays of Anton Checkhov and the works of other notable writers. Although never an official member of the Communist Party, Triolet became disenchanted with the communist movement and quit the communist literary organization Conseil national des écrivains. In her 1957 novel *Le monument,* she portrays an Eastern European artist who has been commissioned to sculpt a larger-than-life statue of Stalin. When the statue mars the city vistas, the artist commits suicide. In this way, Triolet questioned the validity of social realism.

In 1959 Triolet published the first two volumes of her tenuously linked "Age de Nylon" trilogy. In *Roses à crédit,* Triolet satirizes the desire to attain material goods, portraying a young and intelligent woman who has grown up in poverty and who squanders her intelligence in amassing gadgets. *Luna-Park* tells of the discovery of a volume of letters in which the letter writer wrote about the desire to be part of the first voyage to the moon. Four years later *L'âme* appeared. This novel tells the story of a Nazi concentration camp survivor. A *Dictionary of Literary Biography* contributor described the book as "intellectually, politically, and morally . . . perhaps one of the finest French novels of the twentieth century."

During the 1960s, Triolet voiced her opposition to the persecution of Soviet authors such as Sakharov and Solzhenitsyn and the 1956 invasion of Czechoslovakia. In her novel *Le grand jamais* and its sequel *Écoutez-voir,* the author ponders the nature of historical truth. In the novels, the writer Régis, who considers historical truth a joke, dies and his widow, Madeleine, fights to prevent his followers from misrepresenting him. In the process, however, she discovers that even she does not really know her husband.

Troilet's work has suffered from neglect by critics and scholars. This neglect may be because she was misidentified as a communist by noncommunists and as being too unorthodox to suit the communist literary establishment.

BIOGRAPHICAL AND CRITICAL SOURCES:

BOOKS

Adereth, Max, *French Resistance Literature: The Example of Elsa Triolet and Louis Aragon*, Rodopi (Amsterdam, The Netherlands), 1990.

Adereth, Max, *Elsa Triolet and Louis Aragon: An Introduction to Their Interwoven Lives and Works*, Edwin Mellen (Lampeter, England), 1994.

Beaujour, Elizabeth Klosty, *Alien Tongues: Bilingual Russian Writers of the "First" Emigration*, Cornell University Press (Ithaca, NY), 1989.

Dictionary of Literary Biography, Volume 72: *French Novelists, 1930-1960*, Thomson Gale (Detroit, MI), 1988.

Desanti, Dominique, *Les Clés d'Elsa*, Ramsay (Paris, France), 1983.

Elsa Triolet (exhibition catalogue), Bibliothèque Nationale (Paris, France), 1972.

Holmes, Diana, *Ordinary Heroines: Resistance and Romance in the War Fiction of Elsa Triolet*, Berghahn (New York, NY), 1999.

Mackinnon, Lachlan, *The Lives of Elsa Triolet*, Chatto & Windus (London, England), 1988.

Madaule, Jacques, *Ce que dit Elsa*, Denoël (Paris, France), 1961.

Marcou, Lilly, *Elsa Triolet: Les Yeux et la mémoire*, Librairie Plon (Paris, France), 1994.

PERIODICALS

Arkansas Review, fall, 1994, Lorene M. Birden, "Verbal Repetition and Structure in the Works of Elsa Triolet," pp. 125-151.

Atlantic, September, 1949, Monica Stirling, "Elsa Triolet," pp. 76-78.

Atlantis, fall, 1988, Helena Lewis, "Elsa Triolet, et le parti communiste français and the Peace Movement in the Era of the Cold War," pp. 90-96.

Belles Letters, winter, 1993, Helena Lewis, "Elsa Triolet," pp. 32-36.

Comparative Literature Studies, summer, 1998, Lorene M. Birden, "Elsa Triolet's *Le Cheval blanc* As a French *Bylina*," pp. 255-277.

Economist, October 4, 1997, "Behind Their Men: French Muses," p. 90.

Kliatt, September, 1986, E. Barbra Boatner, review of *A Fine of 200 Francs*, p. 39.

French Cultural Studies, October, 1990, Margaret Atack, "Narratives of Disruption, 1940-1944," pp. 233-246; June, 1995, Susan E. Winer, "The Consommatrice of the 1950s in Elsa Triolet's *Roses à crédit*, pp. 123-144.

New York Times Book Review, August 17, 1986, Patricia T. O'Conner, review of *A Fine of 200 Francs*, p. 32.

Romantic Review, January-March, 2001, Dominique Jullien, "Aragon, Elsa Triolet: Love and Politics in the Cold War," p. 3.

Studies in Twentieth Century Literature, summer, 2001, Lorene M. Birden, "The 'Incongruous Stranger,' As Structural Element in the Novels of Elsa Triolet," pp. 322-349.

Times Literary Supplement, January 9, 1969, review of *Écoutez-voir*, p. 45; April 30, 1970, review of *Le rossignol se tait à l'aube*, p. 485; September 22, 1972, review of *Le cheval roux; ou, les intentions humaines*, p. 1086; October 9, 1981, John Weightman, review of *Chroniques théâtrales: Les Lettres Françaises, 1948-1951*, p. 1158.

Women's Review of Books, October, 1986, Sonya Michel, review of *A Fine of 200 Francs*, pp. 11-12.

World Literature Today, spring, 1977, B.H. Monter, review of *Camouflage*, p. 299; spring, 1982, B.L. Knapp, review of *Chroniques théâtrales*, pp. 307-308.

Yale French Studies, number 27, 1961, Konrad Bieber, "Ups and Downs in Elsa Triolet's Prose," pp. 81-85, Marie-Monique Pflaum-Vallin, "Elsa Triolet and Aragon: Back to Lilith," pp. 86-89.

ONLINE

Elsa Triolet, http://www2.ac-toulouse.fr/eco-triolet-toulouse (March 6, 2005), Web site devoted to author.

Louis Aragon-Elsa Triolet Equipe de Recherche Interdisciplinaire, http://www.louisaragon-elsatriolet.com (March 6, 2006), Web site devoted to the works of author and Louis Aragon.*

*   *   *

TUAOLO, Esera 1968-
(Esera Tavai Tuaolo)

PERSONAL: Born July 11, 1968, in Honolulu, HI; partner of Mitchell Wherley; children: Mitchell and Michele (twins). *Education:* Attended Oregon State University.

ADDRESSES: Home—Minneapolis, MN. *Agent*—c/o Author Mail, Sourcebooks, Inc., 1935 Brookdale Rd., Ste. 139, Naperville, IL 60563.

CAREER: Professional football player in National Football League, 1990-99, played for Atlanta Falcons, Carolina Panthers, Jacksonville Jaguars, Minnesota Vikings, and Green Bay Packers; currently a professional singer and actor.

WRITINGS:

(With John Rosengren) *Alone in the Trenches: My Life As a Gay Man in the NFL* (autobiography), Sourcebooks (Naperville, IL), 2006.

SIDELIGHTS: Former National Football League player Esera Tuaolo tells his personal story in *Alone in the Trenches: My Life As a Gay Man in the NFL*, written with John Rosengren. Tuaolo, an ethnic Samoan who was born in Hawaii and was a star player at Oregon State University, had a nine-year career in the NFL. He played for several teams over the years and made it to the 1998 Super Bowl, but during this time he lived in constant fear that his homosexuality would be discovered, resulting in his being ostracized or kicked out of the league. "Tuaolo began his coming-out journey after his sixth season in the NFL," reported Bruce C. Steele in an *Advocate* article. Tuaolo began reading *The David Kopay Story*, an autobiography from 1975 by the first professional football player to come out as a gay man. Tuaolo told Steele, "I saw myself going through the same thing. . . . I literally just started crying. All that hurt and anxiety came back." A few months later he met his partner, Mitchell Wherley.

With Wherley by his side, as well as the understanding of both his own and Wherley's parents, Tuaolo made it through his coming-out experience and now has a successful singing and acting career, a loving partner, and adopted twin children. Critics such as *Booklist* reviewer Wes Lukowsky praised Tuaolo's autobiography for its "admirable frankness." A *Publishers Weekly* writer also lauded the book, stating that it "communicates a warmth and openness that will appeal to both football fans and the gay community."

BIOGRAPHICAL AND CRITICAL SOURCES:

BOOKS

Tuaolo, Esera, and John Rosengren, *Alone in the Trenches: My Life As a Gay Man in the NFL*, Sourcebooks (Naperville, IL), 2006.

PERIODICALS

Advocate, November 26, 2002, Bruce C. Steele, "Tackling Football's Closet," p. 30.
Booklist, November 1, 2005, Wes Lukowsky, review of *Alone in the Trenches,* p. 12.
Library Journal, January 1, 2006, David Azzolina, review of *Alone in the Trenches,* p. 139.
Publishers Weekly, September 26, 2005, review of *Alone in the Trenches,* p. 71.

ONLINE

Esera Tuaolo Home Page, http://www.eseratuaolo.com (March 25, 2006).
ESPN Magazine Online, http://espn.go.com/magazine/ (October 30, 2002), Esera Tuaolo and Luke Cyphers, "Free and Clear," article about author.
Utopia Hawaii, http://www.utopiahawaii.com/ (March 14, 2006), "The Newest Addition to the Family," biography of Esera Tuaolo.*

*   *   *

TUAOLO, Esera Tavai
See TUAOLO, Esera

*   *   *

TUCCILLO, Liz

PERSONAL: Female.

ADDRESSES: Home—New York, NY. *Agent*—c/o Author Mail, Simon Spotlight Publicity Department, Simon & Schuster, Inc., 1230 Avenue of the Americas, New York, NY 10020.

CAREER: Sex and the City, Home Box Office (HBO), executive story editor; actress in films, including *Ed's Next Move,* 1996.

WRITINGS:

Fair Fight (play), produced in New York, NY, 1996.

Joe Fearless: A Fan Dance (play), produced in New York, NY, 2000.

Cheyenne: A Transwestern (one-act play), produced in New York NY, 2002.

Sex and the City (television series), HBO, 2002–2004.

(With Greg Behrendt) *He's Just Not That into You: The No-Excuses Truth to Understanding Guys* (self-help book), Simon Spotlight Entertainment (New York, NY), 2004.

(And producer) *Related* (television series), Warner Bros., 2005.

SIDELIGHTS: Liz Tuccillo contributed to every episode in the final two years of the popular television series *Sex and the City.* As a playwright, she counts among her productions *Joe Fearless: A Fan Dance,* a play about the world of basketball and the fans who love the sport. Watching the game between the K9s and the Breakers is Jo Donnelly, who is so obsessed with his team's performance that he alienates his wife, Linda, as well as other family members and friends. Elias Stimac reviewed the play in *Back Stage,* commenting that it "features plenty of courtside action, along with many moments of hilarity and humanity."

In the play *Cheyenne: A Transwestern,* Tuccillo defies stereotypes. The parts of the outlaws, the sheriff, and a mysterious stranger patterned after a Clint Eastwood character are played by women, while men wearing cutoff shorts and boots play the objects of their affection and lust. *Daily Variety* critic Joel Hirschhorn commented that "when Tuccillo's lines have bite," the play "succeeds in making a broader comment about modern role reversal."

Tuccillo and Greg Behrendt, a comedian who serves as a consultant for *Sex and the City,* collaborated in writing *He's Just Not That into You: The No-Excuses Truth to Understanding Guys,* a book intended to help women recognize when a man is not really interested and when it is time to get out of a relationship. According to the authors, among the signs to look for are the man not treating you well, not wanting to marry or being married already, not wanting a physical relationship, not calling or returning calls, and not making dates in advance. In addition to noting that women often rationalize poor behavior or think they are expecting too much, the authors emphasize that every woman deserves a man who loves her and treats her lovingly.

The book includes workbook assignments and "Dear Greg" letters and replies that make the authors' points. *Entertainment Weekly* reviewer Clarissa Cruz wrote that the success of the book "lies in the snappy back-and-forth between its authors." Behrendt is married and the father of two daughters. Jane S. Drabkin commented in *School Library Journal* that the messages contained in the book "can't be learned too early." New Line Cinema plans to produce a film based on the book, with Tuccillo and Behrendt writing the adaptation.

Tuccillo is also a writer for the television series *Related.* The story focuses on the four Sorelli sisters, who live in New York, and their widowed father, who has found a new love. *Variety* critic Laura Fries described the show as "the love child of *Friends* and *Sex and the City.*

BIOGRAPHICAL AND CRITICAL SOURCES:

PERIODICALS

Back Stage, July 21, 2000, Elias Stimac, review of *Joe Fearless: A Fan Dance,* p. 56.

Back Stage West, January 24, 2002, Paul Birchall, review of *Cheyenne: A Transwestern,* p. 7.

Crain's Detroit Business, November 1, 2004, Katie Merx, review of *He's Just Not That into You: The No-Excuses Truth to Understanding Guys,* p. 25.

Daily Variety, February 26, 2002, Joel Hirschhorn, review of *Cheyenne,* p. 18.

Entertainment Weekly, December 31, 2004, Clarissa Cruz, review of *He's Just Not That into You,* p. 90.

People, October 4, 2004, interview with Tuccillo and Behrendt, p. 61.

School Library Journal, April, 2005, Jane S. Drabkin, review of *He's Just Not That into You,* p. 163.

Variety, October 3, 2005, Laura Fries, review of *Related,* p. 62.*

*   *   *

TURCHIN, Peter 1957-

PERSONAL: Born 1957.

ADDRESSES: Office—University of Connecticut, 75 N. Eagleville Rd., U-43, Storrs, CT 06269-3043; fax: 860-486-6364 *E-mail*—peter.turchin@uconn.edu.

CAREER: Writer, ecologist, and educator. University of Connecticut, Storrs, professor of ecology and evolutionary biology and adjunct professor of mathematics, 1994—.

AWARDS, HONORS: Fulbright fellowship; Chancellor's Research and Excellence Award, University of Connecticut.

WRITINGS:

Quantitative Analysis of Movement: Measuring and Modeling Population Redistribution in Animals and Plants, Sinaur Associates (Sunderland, MA), 1998.

Complex Population Dynamics: A Theoretical/ Empirical Synthesis, Princeton University Press (Princeton, NJ), 2003.

Historical Dynamics: Why States Rise and Fall, Princeton University Press (Princeton, NJ), 2003.

War and Peace and War: The Life Cycles of Imperial Nations, Pi Press (New York, NY), 2006.

SIDELIGHTS: Peter Turchin is a writer, ecologist, and educator who studies topics such as the dynamics of natural populations, ecological mechanisms of population changes and fluctuations in mammals and insects, and the mechanistic basis of landscape ecology. He also conducts research in theoretical ecology and population dynamics and in the demographic and social dynamics of human populations. His research in these areas is reflected in books such as *Quantitative Analysis of Movement: Measuring and Modeling Population Redistribution in Animals and Plants,* which adds "a new dimension to traditional models of the dynamics of populations" by presenting "a quantitative analysis of movement at two scales: temporal and spatial," according to Jeannette Yen in the *Quarterly Review of Biology.* The book "provides, in one place, a nice compendium of the theory and practice of examining movement in plant and animal populations," reported *Ecology* contributor Steven L. Peck. Turchin offers detailed guidance on gathering and analyzing spatial data on the movement of animal and insect populations in what Peck called "a very fine addition to the literature."

Historical Dynamics: Why States Rise and Fall "is an extremely ambitious book and fascinating to read in parts," noted Kevin T. Kilty on the *Citizen Scientist* Web site. Here, Turchin asserts that any science, particularly disciplines such as history or sociology, cannot become mature sciences until they have evolved to the point where they incorporate mathematics. *Historical Dynamics* therefore, seeks to outline ways in which mathematics can be profitably applied to the study of history. He develops and applies quantitative models in two areas of vital importance to the development and failure of nations and states: "territorial expansion and contraction of agrarian states, and population growth and decline in relation to political stability," applied mainly to 1,400 years of European history from 500 to 1900 C.E., according to Rainer Kattel in *History: Review of New Books.* In the end, Kattel continued, "The author shows superb skill in explaining complex mathematical modeling in plain language, but he leaves readers wondering why create these models at all." As Kilty concluded, "Science matures through definitive experimentation and the testing of hypotheses." However, the use of mathematics does not in and of itself signal that a particular field has matured.

In *War and Peace and War: The Life Cycles of Imperial Nations,* Turchin applies the science of cliodynamics—the study of processes that change with time—to search for and find distinct patterns in the events of history. He "claims to have found the general mechanisms that cause empires to wax and wane—laws as true today as they were during the Roman or Ottoman Empires," remarked Philip Ball in the *Guardian.* By applying complex mathematical models and behavioral theories, Turchin "concludes that there are persistent cyclical historical patterns," related reviewer Jim Doyle in *Library Journal.* These patterns, according to Turchin, are readily identifiable and consistent in their repetition, and the seemingly chaotic nature of history can be explained by using these cliodynamic theories and patterns. Turchin "brings modern discoveries in psychology, experimental economics, evolutionary biology and even physics to bear on history," commented Mark Buchanan in the *New Scientist.* "This isn't just another arbitrary narrative." For example, on the frontiers of empires, where thoroughly alien populations are in close proximity and frequent conflict, individual concerns often give way to general social cooperation and solidarity among the harried populations existing at the empire's fringes. As these populations and societies cooperate, they flourish and grow, eventually becoming strong enough to overcome the empires that applied the initial stresses that spurred their growth. Turchin also notes that success will eventually beget decline, as competition for limited resources begins to undermine the solidarity of the culture, leading to collapse. Turchin's "ideas generate many fascinating discussions of a wide variety of historical episodes, rendered in lucid, vigorous prose," remarked a *Publishers Weekly* reviewer.

BIOGRAPHICAL AND CRITICAL SOURCES:

PERIODICALS

Ecology, June, 1999, Steven L. Peck, review of *Quantitative Analysis of Movement: Measuring and Modeling Population Redistribution in Animals and Plants,* p. 1451.

Guardian (London, England), August 25, 2005, Philip Ball, "Empire of the Sums," review of *War and Peace and War: The Life Cycles of Imperial Nations.*

History: Review of New Books, summer, 2004, Rainer Kattel, review of *Historical Dynamics: Why States Rise and Fall,* p. 168.

Library Journal, October 15, 2005, Jim Doyle, review of *War and Peace and War,* p. 70.

New Scientist, October 1, 2005, Mark Buchanan, "Legends of the Fall: Why Do Some Societies Build Great Empires Only to Have Them Crash and Burn?," review of *War and Peace and War,* p. 44.

Publishers Weekly, August 29, 2005, review of *War and Peace and War,* p. 48.

Quarterly Review of Biology, June, 1999, Jeannette Yen, review of *Quantitative Analysis of Movement,* p. 240; September, 2004, John M. Drake, "Life Sciences for the Twenty-first Century," review of *Complex Population Dynamics: A Theoretical/Empirical Synthesis,* p. 298.

ONLINE

Citizen Scientist, http://www.sas.org/TCS/ (March 11, 2005), Kevin T. Kilty, review of *Historical Dynamics.*

University of Connecticut Alumni Association Web site, http://www.uconnalumni.com/ (March 13, 2006), biography of Peter Turchin.*

V

VALIANTE, Gio 1971-
(Giovanni Valiante)

PERSONAL: Born April 11, 1971, in Naugatuck, CT; son of Fred (an accountant) and Joanne (a nurse practitioner) Valiante. *Education:* University of Florida, B.A., 1994, M.A., 1995; Emory University, Ph.D., 2001.

ADDRESSES: Office—Rollins College, 1000 Holt Ave., Ste. 2726, Winter Park, FL 32789. *E-mail*—gvaliante@rollins.edu.

CAREER: Elementary and middle school teacher, 1995-96; instructor with a community education program, 1996; Emory University, Atlanta, GA, instructor; Rollins College, Winter Park, FL, assistant professor. Consultant to *Golf Digest,* the Golf Channel, and the University of Florida.

MEMBER: American Educational Research Association, Southeastern Psychological Association, Georgia Educational Research Association, National Association for Invitational Education.

AWARDS, HONORS: Florida Educational Research Council grants, 1994; Harold E. Mitzel Award, Helen Dwight Reid Educational Foundation, 1997; National Academy of Education/Spenser Foundation postdoctoral fellow, 1998-99; first place, gender issues category, Southeastern Psychological Association Committee on Equality of Professional Opportunity; Critchfield Foundation, research grant for study of the psychology of pro golfers, 2001.

WRITINGS:

(With Mike Stachura) *Fearless Golf: Conquering the Mental Game,* Doubleday (New York, NY), 2005.

.

SIDELIGHTS: Gio Valiante is an educational and sports psychologist who grew up in Naugatuck, Connecticut, excelling at sports, including golf, and becoming president of his senior high school class. Valiante went on to earn a doctorate, and in 2001 he received a grant to travel with the Professional Golfers' Association of America (PGA) Tour to study the mental game of professional golfers. As a consequence, he has become a coach to a number of Tour players. *Sports Illustrated* writer Chris Lewis noted that "the root of Valiante's appeal to some golfers is the scientific basis of his instruction. Traditionally, golf psychology has been based on the synthesized wisdom of the game's great players. . . . Valiante is not without mantras—his signature line: Make fearless swings at precise targets—but he also draws on performance-enhancement research in biomechanics, neurology and ophthalmology."

Valiante has become a consultant expert on the psychology of golf and is the author, with Mike Stachura, of *Fearless Golf: Conquering the Mental Game.* The book includes anecdotes about great golfers like Ben Hogan and Jack Nicklaus, as well as contemporary top golfers. Valiante writes of the important role that overcoming tension-creating fear plays in perfecting the swing and how various golfers have overcome that fear. *Library Journal* reviewer Steve Silkunas commented that "Valiante is golf's equivalent of . . . Dr. Phil," the popular television psychologist. Silkunas concluded that *Fearless Golf* "is highly readable and offers insight for most golfers."

BIOGRAPHICAL AND CRITICAL SOURCES:

PERIODICALS

Library Journal, July 1, 2005, Steve Silkunas, review of *Fearless Golf: Conquering the Mental Game,* p. 93.
Sports Illustrated, January 31, 2005, Chris Lewis, "This Head Coach Is Hot," p. G4.

ONLINE

Bookreporter.com, http:www.bookreporter.com/ (July 15, 2005), Stuart Shiffman, review of *Fearless Golf.**

*   *   *

VALIANTE, Giovanni
    See VALIANTE, Gio

*   *   *

VALLVEY, Ángela 1964-

PERSONAL: Born 1964, in San Lorenzo, Ciudad Real, Spain.

ADDRESSES: Home—Spain. *Agent*—c/o Author Mail, Seven Stories Press, 140 Watts St., New York, NY 10013.

CAREER: Writer of poetry and juvenile and adult fiction.

AWARDS, HONORS: Jaén Poetry Award, Spain, 1998, for *El tamaño del universo;* Nadal Award, Spain, 2002, for *Los estados carenciales.*

WRITINGS:

El tamaño del universo (poems; title means "The Size of the Universe"), Hiperion (Madrid, Spain) 1998.
A la caza del ultimo hombre salvaje (novel), Emece Editores (Barcelona, Spain), 1999, reprinted, Siete Cuentos Editorial (New York, NY), 2001, translation by Margaret Jull Costa published as *Hunting the Last Wild Man,* Seven Stories Press (New York, NY), 2002.
Vias de extincion (novel), Emece Editores (Barcelona, Spain), 2000.
Los estados carenciales (novel; title means "The Deficient States"), Ediciones Destino (Barcelona, Spain), 2002.
No lo llames amor, Ediciones Destino (Barcelona, Spain), 2003.

Young adult fiction includes (translated) *The Sentimental Life of Bugs Bunny.*

SIDELIGHTS: Spanish writer Ángela Vallvey is the author of fiction for children and young adults, poetry, and adult fiction. Her first work to be translated for English audiences is the novel *A la caza del ultimo hombre salvaje.* A *Kirkus Reviews* contributor called the translation, *Hunting the Last Wild Man,* "a raucous debut." The protagonist, Candela, lives in an all-female household with her five sisters, mother, and aunt. Her youngest sister has recently returned home after discovering that her husband has been making porn films, casting himself in the lead roles. Candela works in comparative quiet in a mortuary, where she begins working on the body of Joaquin, a gypsy patriarch who is to be buried with his hat and cane. In preparing him, Candela makes a discovery that could change her life. The *Kirkus Reviews* writer concluded by describing the novel as "funny, fresh, and briskly written: a good story by a quick study."

Vallvey received the Nadal Award for her novel *Los estados carenciales.* The names of the main characters, Ulises and Penelope, are just one of the many indications in the novel of the author's admiration for classical literature. Penelope left her husband and her son, Telemaco, when the boy was a baby. She represents the contemporary Spanish woman who rejects the idea that a woman can find fulfillment only within marriage. *World Literature Today* contributor Luis Larios Vendrell noted that it is with the female characters that "Vallvey's craft becomes evident. Some of these scenes are really comical and reveal the advances achieved by Spanish women since 1975."

BIOGRAPHICAL AND CRITICAL SOURCES:

PERIODICALS

Kirkus Reviews, February 1, 2002, review of *Hunting the Last Wild Man,* p. 138.
Publishers Weekly, February 11, 2002, review of *Hunting the Last Wild Man,* p. 161.
World Literature Today, July-September, 2003, Luis Larios Vendrell, review of *Los estados carenciales,* p. 146.*

*   *   *

VANASSE, Deb 1957-
(Debra Lynn Lehmann)

PERSONAL: Born September 12, 1957, in St. Paul, MN; married; husband's name Tim; children: Lynx (son), Jessica. *Education:* Bemidji State University, B.A.; California State University at Dominguez Hills, master's degree. *Hobbies and other interests:* Reading, writing, traveling, music, dance.

ADDRESSES: Home—AK; winters in Baja, Mexico. *Agent*—c/o Author Mail, Sasquatch Books, 119 S. Main, Ste. 400, Seattle, WA 98104. *E-mail*—debv@gci.net.

CAREER: High school teacher in Nunapitchuk, AK, and other Alaskan villages; university instructor in Bethel, AK, and Fairbanks, AK, 1987-88; North Pole High School, educator, 1988-99; real estate broker.

WRITINGS:

YOUNG-ADULT NOVELS

A Distant Enemy, Lodestar Books (New York, NY), 1997.

Out of the Wilderness, Clarion Books (New York, NY), 1999.

PICTURE BOOKS

Alaska Animal Babies, photographs by Gavriel Jecan, Sasquatch Books (Seattle, WA), 2005.
Under Alaska's Midnight Sun, illustrated by Jeremiah Trammell, Sasquatch Books (Seattle, WA), 2005.
A Totem Tale, illustrated by Eric Brooks, Sasquatch Books (Seattle, WA), 2006.

SIDELIGHTS: Author Deb Vanasse has spent most of her adult life living in Alaska, much of it teaching high school and college in remote areas. As a result, the unique culture and environment of rural Alaska are key features of her work. Her first two books, *A Distant Enemy* and *Out of the Wilderness,* are young adult novels, but since then she has also published several picture books. "I could spend many years and many books attempting to capture the essence of Southwestern Alaska, an area so remote that few people get to experience it firsthand," Vanasse wrote on her home page.

Joseph, the protagonist of *A Distant Enemy,* is a half-Eskimo, half-white (kass'aq, in the Yup'ik Eskimo language) fourteen-year-old boy who lives in a small, remote Alaskan village. Joseph's kass'aq father abandoned the family to return to "civilization," and Joseph takes out his anger over this abandonment on every other kass'aq whom he encounters. These include the wildlife rangers, who enforce rules that restrict the Yup'ik from fishing, and his English teacher. That teacher, Mr. Townsend, and Joseph's grandfather try to help him, but Joseph still seems to be bent on allowing his rage to destroy him. *Booklist* reviewer Hazel Rochman commented that Vanasse "tries to do too much" in this book, but still praised "the strong sense of place and the drama of Joseph's personal conflict." A *Publishers Weekly* contributor also praised this aspect of the book, calling *A Distant Enemy* "a vivid portrait of modern Eskimo lifestyles, conflicts and fears . . . [and] a sensitive account of one teenager's coming of age."

Josh, the protagonist of *Out of the Wilderness,* has the opposite problem from Joseph: his father loves the Alaskan wilderness far too much. The man takes fifteen-year-old Josh and Josh's older half-brother, Nathan, out to a remote area, where they build a ten-foot-by-twenty-foot cabin with their own hands and survive by hunting, gathering, and building the things they need. Josh wants nothing more than to return to his friends and school, but Nathan and their father love this life. However, Nathan's passion for the wilderness causes him to take dangerous risks as he tries to get closer to nature, and it falls to Josh to save him. "Pragmatic Josh, intense Nathan, and the boys' guilt-ridden father are intriguingly drawn," Debbie Carton wrote in *Booklist,* and a *Publishers Weekly* reviewer deemed the book a "chilling winter's tale."

Under Alaska's Midnight Sun, one of Vanasse's first picture books, examines a unique aspect of life in Alaska: on the solstice (the longest day of the year) the sun never sets. A young girl struggles to stay awake to see the midnight sun, as she, her mother, and her baby brother walk out into the country to observe the animals also frolicking in the late-night sunshine. "The text is fresh and vivid," Carol L. MacKay wrote in *School Library Journal,* while according to *Booklist* reviewer Carolyn Phelan it "conveys [the girl's] excitement as well as her determination not to fall asleep before midnight."

BIOGRAPHICAL AND CRITICAL SOURCES:

PERIODICALS

ALAN Review, winter, 2000, Deb Vanasse, "On Taking Ourselves Too Seriously, and Other Tragic Mistakes."
Booklist, January 1, 1997, Hazel Rochman, review of *A Distant Enemy,* p. 846; March 15, 1999, Debbie Carton, review of *Out of the Wilderness,* p. 1330; May 1, 2005, Carolyn Phelan, review of *Under Alaska's Midnight Sun,* p. 1594.
Children's Bookwatch, September, 2005, review of *Under Alaska's Midnight Sun.*
Publishers Weekly, January 13, 1997, review of *A Distant Enemy,* p. 76; February 15, 1999, review of *Out of the Wilderness,* p. 108.
School Library Journal, August, 2005, Carol L. MacKay, review of *Under Alaska's Midnight Sun,* p. 107.

ONLINE

Deb Vanasse Home Page, http://www.debvanasse.com (April 8, 2006).

VANCE, Laura L. 1967-
(Laura Lee Vance)

PERSONAL: Born May 10, 1967, in Ellensburg, WA; daughter of LaDell (an engineer) and Beth (an artist) Vance; married Jennifer Anne Langton (an environmental scientist), January 7, 1988. *Education:* Western Washington University, B.A., 1989, M.A., 1991; Simon Fraser University, Ph.D., 1994.

ADDRESSES: Home—623 Hancock Dr., Americus, GA 31709. *Office*—Department of Sociology, Georgia Southwestern State University, 800 Wheatley St., Americus, GA 31709. *E-mail*—llv@canes.gsw.edu.

CAREER: Writer, sociologist, and educator. Georgia Southwestern State University, Americus, professor of sociology, 1994—.

WRITINGS:

Seventh-day Adventism in Crisis: Gender and Sectarian Change in an Emerging Religion, University of Illinois Press (Champaign, IL), 1999.

WORK IN PROGRESS: Research on intimate-partner violence in the rural South and on Mormon women.

BIOGRAPHICAL AND CRITICAL SOURCES:

PERIODICALS

American Journal of Sociology, November, 1999, John P. Bartowski, review of *Seventh-day Adventism in Crisis: Gender and Sectarian Change in an Emerging Religion,* p. 855.
Christian Century, September 22, 1999, Douglas Morgan, review of *Seventh-day Adventism in Crisis,* p. 907.
Church History, December, 2003, Rennie B. Schoepflin, review of *Seventh-day Adventism in Crisis,* p. 908.
Library Journal, April 15, 1999, Sandra Collins, review of *Seventh-day Adventism in Crisis,* p. 104.

VANCE, Laura Lee
    See VANCE, Laura L.

*   *   *

VanOOSTING, James 1951-

PERSONAL: Born 1951; son of Jean Reed; stepson of Robert Reed; married twice (divorced); married Dawn LaJuana Williams (a university dean), September 15, 2001. *Education:* Taylor University, graduated; Northwestern University, Ph.D.

ADDRESSES: Office—Fordham University, Rose Hill Campus, Bronx, NY 10458. *E-mail*—vanoosja@shu.edu.

CAREER: Educator and author. Southern Illinois University, Carbondale, professor of English for sixteen years, and department chair for eight years; Seton Hall University, NJ, dean of arts and sciences, beginning c. 1998. Visiting professor and St. Edmund Campion fellow, Fordham University, beginning 2005; visiting professor at University of California, San Diego, and Louisiana State University.

WRITINGS:

YOUNG-ADULT FICTION

Maxie's Ghost, Farrar, Straus (New York, NY), 1987.
Electing J.J., Farrar, Straus (New York, NY), 1990.
The Last Payback, HarperCollins (New York, NY), 1997.
Walking Mary, HarperCollins (New York, NY), 2005.

NONFICTION

Business Correspondence: Writer, Reader, and Text, Prentice-Hall (Englewood Cliffs, NJ), 1983.
The Business Report: Writer, Reader, and Text, Prentice-Hall (Englewood Cliffs, NJ), 1983.
The Business Speech: Writer, Reader, and Text, Prentice-Hall (Englewood Cliffs, NJ), 1985.
Practicing Business: Communication in the Workplace, Houghton Mifflin (Boston, MA), 1992.

(With Paul H. Gray) *Performance in Life and Literature,* Allyn & Bacon (Boston, MA), 1996.
And the Flesh Became Word: Reflections Theological and Aesthetic, Crossroad (New York, NY), 2005.

SIDELIGHTS: In addition to working as a college English professor, James VanOosting has written several novels for young-adult readers, among them *The Last Paycheck, Electing J.J.,* and *Walking Mary.* Narrated by twelve-year-old Dorothea "Dimple" Dorfman, *The Last Payback* focuses on a grief-stricken girl's desire for revenge immediately following the accidental death of her twin brother. Praising VanOosting for creating realistic characters, *Horn Book* reviewer Elizabeth S. Watson added that the novel's "intriguing plot and fast-paced dialogue" keep readers turning pages. In *Booklist* GraceAnne A. DeCandido also praised the work, calling *The Last Payback* "startling in its unsentimental, first-person approach." In praise of *Electing J.J.,* a humorous story about a middle-school newcomer who decides to run for town mayor of Framburg, Illinois and shake up stodgy town politics, a *Publishers Weekly* contributor deemed the novel "cleverly written and highly entertaining."

VanOosting tells what *School Library Journal* contributor Nancy P. Reeder called a "dark, disturbing tale of mental instability and sexual abuse" in his young-adult novel *Walking Mary. Walking Mary* draws readers back once again to Framburg, Illinois. This time they arrive during the 1940s and 1950s, as Pearl and Franklin Keenan are attempting to survive a harsh childhood under the sway of an abusive home and an authoritarian father. Almost drowning at age six, Pearl is pulled to safety by an elderly black woman known as Walking Mary; a poignant town fixture, the woman haunts the train station, awaiting the arrival of a beloved son who was actually killed during World War II. As a way of avoiding her own problems, Pearl becomes increasingly fascinated with Mary and takes up the habit of shadowing the woman, dressing in similar mourning black, and spending time at the train station. Although the two never speak, their lives ultimately reconnect during another tragic set of circumstances. In *Booklist* Frances Bradburn called VanOosting's story "quietly disturbing with undercurrents of foreboding" that will captivate readers, while a *Kirkus Reviews* critic praised the novel as a "wonderfully expressive" novel that "captures the magic and intensity of childhood" while also dealing in more serious themes.

BIOGRAPHICAL AND CRITICAL SOURCES:

PERIODICALS

Booklist, June 1, 1997, GraceAnne A. DeCandido, review of *The Last Payback,* p. 1706; August, 2005, Frances Bradburn, review of *Walking Mary,* p. 2017.

Bulletin of the Center for Children's Books, January, 1988, review of *Maxie's Ghost,* p. 104; June, 1997, review of *The Last Payback,* p. 377.

Horn Book, July-August, 1997, Elizabeth S. Watson, review of *The Last Payback,* p. 465.

Kirkus Reviews, April 15, 2005, review of *Walking Mary,* p. 484.

Kliatt, May, 2005, Janis Flint-Ferguson, review of *Walking Mary,* p. 19.

Publishers Weekly, October 30, 1987, review of *Maxie's Ghost,* p. 72; June 29, 1990, review of *Electing J.J.,* p. 102.

School Library Journal, January, 1988, Martha Rosen, review of *Maxie's Ghost,* p. 78; August, 1990, Joel Shoemaker, review of *Electing J.J.,* p. 150; July, 1997, Jana R. Fine, review of *The Last Payback,* p. 98; July, 2005, Nancy P. Reeder, review of *Walking Mary,* p. 110.

Voice of Youth Advocates, August, 2005, Susan Allen, review of *Walking Mary,* p. 227.*

* * *

VARGAS, Fred 1957-
(Frédérique Vargas)

PERSONAL: Born 1957, in France; children: a son.

ADDRESSES: Home—Paris, France. *Agent*—c/o Author Mail, Publicity Department, Simon & Schuster, Inc., 1230 Avenue of the Americas, New York, NY, 10020.

CAREER: Writer, archeologist, and historian.

WRITINGS:

Les jeux de l'amour et de la mort (novel; title means "The Games of Love and Death"), La Flèche (Sarthe, France), 1986.

L'homme aux cercle bleus (novel; title means "The Man with Blue Rings"), Hermé (Paris, France), 1991.

Ceux qui vont mourir te saluent (novel; title means "Those Who Are About to Die Salute You,"), V. Hamy (Paris, France), 1994.

Debout les morts (novel), V. Hamy (Paris, France), 1995, translation by Siân Reynolds published as *The Three Evangelists,* Harvill Secker (London, England), 2006.

Un peu plus loin sur la droite (novel), V. Hamy (Paris, France), 1996.

Sans feu ni lieu (novel; title means "Without Home or Hearth), V. Hamy (Paris, France), 1997.

L'homme à l'envers (novel), V. Hamy (Paris, France), 1999 translation by David Bellos published as *Seeking Whom He May Devour,* Vintage Books (New York, NY), 2006.

Les quatre fleuves (fiction, also printed in comic form), V. Hamy (Paris, France), 2000.

Pars vite et reviens tard, (novel; title means "Leave Quickly and Return Late"), V. Hamy (Paris, France), 2001, translation by David Bellos published as *Have Mercy on Us All,* Harvill (London, England), 2003, Simon & Schuster (New York, NY), 2005.

Petit traité de toutes vérités sur l'existence, V. Hamy (Paris, France), 2001.

Coule la Seine, illustrations by Baudoin, V. Hamy (Paris, France), 2002.

Critique de l'anxiété pure, V. Hamy (Paris, France), 2003.

Sous les vents de Neptune, V. Hamy (Paris, France), 2004.

Works have been published in foreign languages, including Spanish, Japanese, Greek, Italian, and German.

ADAPTATIONS: L'homme à l'envers has been adapted for film.

SIDELIGHTS: Fred Vargas researches the Middle Ages for an archeological institute and has written numerous detective novels, mostly while she has been on vacations. In *Ceux qui vont mourir te saluent,* which means "Those Who Are About to Die Salute You," the author presents a mystery that follows the death of Parisian art editor Henri Valhubert, who has been poisoned after going to Rome to appraise an unknown drawing by Michelangelo. *Debout les morts,* published in English as *The Three Evangelists,* focuses on the death of a woman who may be the singer Sophia Simeonides, who has disappeared after a mysterious tree appeared one day to be growing in her garden. On the case are the three evangelists, or historians, Mark, Luke, and Matthew. Writing for the *Tangled Web* online, a reviewer called *The Three Evangelists* a "tale of dusty research and police action . . . [that] makes us eager for more translations of Vargas's work."

Vargas tells the story of an ex-detective named Kehlweiler whose discovery of a bone in dog excrement leads him to investigate a possible murder in *Un peu plus loin sur la droite.* Kehlweiler, who was also in *Debout les morts,* returns in *Sans feu ni lieu,* which means "Without Home or Hearth." Along with his young helper Vandoosler and his assistants, the historians Mark, Luke, and Matthew, Kehlweiler sets out to solve a set of serial murders believed to be committed by a simpleton named Clement Vauquer, who is being sheltered by an ex-prostitute. Writing in the *French Review,* Davida Brautman noted, "Vargas recounts an ever-intriguing, plausible plot, replete with a sufficient number of interesting suspects, several good red herrings, and a dollop of humor to offset the seriousness of the crimes committed."

Have Mercy on Us All, originally published in French as *Pars vite et reviens tard,* features the recurring character of Adamsberg, a French policeman who this time is investigating the strange case of a seeming madman whose rants are actually prophesizing a coming plague that threatens Parisians. When three people are found strangled and made to look like victims of the plague, Adamsberg and his partner, Adrien Danglard, delve into the matter as the people of Paris panic, believing that a real plague is on the way. Bill Ott, writing in *Booklist,* called the novel a "beguiling mix of old and new" and noted that the author includes interesting facts about the plague and "a character-rich look at street life." A *Publishers Weekly* contributor called *Have Mercy on Us All* "a riveting blend of bio-thriller and historical cryptology," adding that the novel is an "exciting and careful whodunit." A *Kirkus Reviews* reviewer commented: "Captivating characters, historical oddities and clever plotting all add up to a scintillating tale."

BIOGRAPHICAL AND CRITICAL SOURCES:

BOOKS

Attack, M., and P. Powrie, editors, *Contemporary French Fiction by Women,* University of Manchester Press (Manchester, England), 1991.

PERIODICALS

Booklist, December 1, 2005, Bill Ott, review of *Have Mercy on Us All,* p. 29.
Entertainment Weekly, November 18, 2005, Whitney Pastorek, review of *Have Mercy on Us All,* p. 143.
French Review, December, 1999, Davida Brautman, review of *Sans feu ni lieu,* p. 386.
Guardian (London, England), November 18, 2004, "True Crime," interview with author.
Kirkus Reviews, October 1, 2005, review of *Have Mercy on Us All,* p. 1056.
Library Journal, July 1, 2005, Ann Kim, review of *Have Mercy on Us All,* p. 58; October 15, 2005, Ronnie H. Terpening, review of *Have Mercy on Us All,* p. 52.
New Scientist, July 31, 2004, Laura Spinney, "Riddle of Bones," interview with author, p. 46.
Publishers Weekly, October 3, 2005, review of *Have Mercy on Us All,* p. 49.

ONLINE

Grumpy Old Bookman, http://grumpyoldbookman. blogspot.com/ (January 16, 2006), review of *Have Mercy on Us All.*
Lire: le magazine littéraire, http://www.auteurs.net/ (March 6, 2006), Christine Ferniot, "Fred Vargas: Je veux travailler sur la peur de l'homme," interview with author.
Tangled Web, http://www.twbooks.co.uk/ (March 6, 2006), review of *The Three Evangelists.**

*   *   *

VARGAS, Frédérique
See VARGAS, Fred

VELDE, Rink van der 1932-2001

PERSONAL: Born June 18, 1932, in Ealsum, Netherlands; died February 17, 2001, in Drachten, Netherlands.

CAREER: Writer.

WRITINGS:

Joun healwei tolven (novel), Laverman (Drachten, Netherlands), 1962.

Forliezers (novel), Laverman (Drachten, Netherlands), 1964.

Beafeart nei Saint-Martin, Laverman (Drachten, Netherlands), 1965.

De Fûke, Laverman (Drachten, Netherlands), 1966, translated into English as *The Trap,* Permanent Press (Sag Harbor, NY), 1997.

Geiten, Griken en Gekken, Laverman (Drachten, Netherlands), 1967.

Rjochtdei, Laverman (Drachten, Netherlands), 1968.

Chamsyn, Laverman (Drachten, Netherlands), 1969.

Feroaring fan lucht, Friese Pers Boekerij (Leeuwarden/Ljouwert, Netherlands), 1971.

Pake Sytse, 1975.

Kruidenbitter: Kroegverhalen uit Friesland, Wereldbibliotheek (Amsterdam, Netherlands), 1975.

De houn sil om jim bylje, Friese Pers Boekerij (Leeuwarden/Ljouwert, Netherlands), 1978.

De Heidenen, Friese Pers Boekerij (Leeuwarden/Ljouwert, Netherlands), 1981.

Foekje, Friese Pers Boekerij (Leeuwarden/Ljouwert, Netherlands), 1982.

De ôfrekken, Friese Pers Boekerij (Leeuwarden/Ljouwert, Netherlands), 1982.

De lange jacht, Friese Pers Boekerij (Leeuwarden/Ljouwert, Netherlands), 1985.

De histoarje fam kammeraat Hallanski, Friese Pers Boekerij (Drachten, Netherlands), 1987.

Jan Hut, Friese Pers Boekerij (Leeuwarden/Ljouwert, Netherlands), 1989.

De nacht fan Belse Madam, Friese Pers Boekerij (Leeuwarden/Ljouwert, Netherlands), 1991.

Gjin lintsje foar Homme Veldstra, Friese Pers Boekerij (Leeuwarden/Ljouwert, Netherlands), 1993.

Rjochtdei op de Skieding, Friese Pers Boekerij (Leeuwarden/Ljouwert, Netherlands), 1993.

In fin mear as in bears, Friese Pers Boekerij (Leeuwarden/Ljouwert, Netherlands), 1995.

Smoarge grûn, Friese Pers Boekerij (Leeuwarden/Ljouwert, Netherlands), 1998.

Hepke, Friese Pers Boekerij (Leeuwarden/Ljouwert, Netherlands), 1999.

Alde Maaie (novel; title means "Old May"), Friese Pers Boekerij (Leeuwarden/Ljouwert, Netherlands), 2000.

(With Hylkje Goïnga and Hylke Speerstra) *Lowland Tales: Short Stories from Friesland,* translated by Henry J. Baron, Friese Pers Boekerij (Leeuwarden/Ljouwert, Netherlands), 2000.

It guozzeroer (novel; title means "The Goose Gun"), Friese Pers Boekerij (Leeuwarden/Ljouwert, Netherlands), 2001.

Also author of *De Kleine Kolonie,* 1960.

ADAPTATIONS: The Trap is being made into a Dutch film.

SIDELIGHTS: Frisian novelist and short-story writer Rink van der Velde's novel *Joun healwei tolven* was published in 1962. According to Henry J. Baron, writing in *World Literature Today,* van der Velde's typical protagonist is often "based on a roguish historical character." Although Baron contended that this works well for van der Velde, the "nonhero" in the novel *De nacht fan Belse Madam* challenges the reader's expectations. Rink van der Velde, nevertheless, became one of Friesland's most prolific and popular writers. Baron, once again writing in *World Literature Today,* applauded van der Velde's use of a "Columbo-like character" in *Gjin lintsje foar Homme Veldstra.* First appearing as a serial in a provincial paper, *Gjin lintsje foar Homme Veldstra,* according to Baron, "worked well as a serial and . . . as a novel." Baron complemented van der Velde for "bringing the reader into the . . . presence of a set of characters who amuse, delight and surprise."

The time of the Great Plague is the historical setting for van der Velde's novel *In fin mear as in bears.* The protagonist is a young boy, Salomon, who is "sent into exile by his father to save him." Baron, reviewing the novel for *World Literature Today,* noted that van der Velde "richly evokes the aura of the period and the region" and that "against that backdrop, [the protagonist] looms large as a kind of tragic hero with an instinct for righteousness bred in his bones."

Baron also commented in *World Literature Today* that at the center of van der Velde's novel *Hepke* is "the author himself." Baron wrote that "the author's storytelling voice never fails to gain and retain the reader's interest."

In his novel *De Fûke,* which was translated into English as *The Trap,* van der Velde tells the story of a fisherman and his wife who help hide Jews from the Germans in their remote cottage in the Netherlands province of Friesland. Dutch collaborators, however, eventually bring in the fisherman for questioning, and the story focuses on the fisherman's efforts to outwit his interrogators before they carry out the execution of his son, whom they claim to have captured. A *Publishers Weekly* contributor called the book "a gem of a novel with universal appeal." Writing in *Booklist,* Nancy Pearl and Henry J. Baron called the novel "a chilling reminder of human inhumanity."

The author brings back the detective character of Homme Veldstra from *Gjin lintsje foar Homme Veldstra* in his 1998 novel *Smoarge grûn.* This time the retired detective investigates the death of an old adversary that he respected and eventually became friends with before the man's untimely death in a sewage dump pond. Pointing out that the story is not really about solving the crime, *World Literature Today* contributor Baron noted, "The Homme stories never are. They are just as much about domestic small talk, the cost of living, changing times, and contemporary controversies." Baron went on to note that the novel "accomplishes its apparent purpose: to entertain the reader by intrigue and at the same time make the point that today's crimes make the transgressions of a past generation look like mere mischief."

Alde Maaie, which means "Old May," is a novel about Linse Pronk, a man who has dreams of taking over his town's bakery only to be sidetracked by World War II as he helps fight the German invasion of Holland. Pronk is eventually killed by one of his own countrymen after the Germans overrun the country, and his son Eabe sets out years later to learn the truth and eventually seek revenge. Baron, writing in *World Literature Today,* called the book "a first-rate story."

The author's last published work before his death, *It guozzeroer,* which means "The Goose Gun," focuses on the wartime exploits of Bavius Bouma, who keeps an old British muzzle loader in his room at a retirement home and eventually reveals the story of war and love that has led him to keep the relic by his side over the years. "The author's natural storytelling gift is amply demonstrated here," wrote Baron in *World Literature Today.* Baron went on to comment that "we have here simply a robust tale well told, with economy and suspense, with originality and authenticity."

BIOGRAPHICAL AND CRITICAL SOURCES:

PERIODICALS

Booklist, Nancy Pearl and Henry J. Baron, review of *The Trap,* p. 927.
Publishers Weekly, November 25, 1996, review of *The Trap,* p. 55.
World Literature Today, summer, 1992, Henry J. Baron, review of *De nacht fan Belse Madam,* p. 529; spring, 1994, Henry J. Baron, review of *Gjin lintsje foar Homme Veldstra,* p. 380; autumn, 1994, Henry J. Baron, review of *Rjochtdei op de Skieding,* pp. 831-832; spring, 1996, Henry J. Baron, review of *In fin mear as in bears,* pp. 419-420; autumn, 1999, Henry J. Baron, review of *Hepke,* p. 756; winter, 1999, Henry J. Baron, review of *Smoarge grûn,* p. 162; autumn, 2000, Henry J. Baron, review of *Alde maaie,* p. 864; summer-autumn, 2001, Henry J. Baron, review of *It guozzeroer,* p. 191.*

*   *   *

VINCENT, Isabel 1965-

PERSONAL: Born 1965.

ADDRESSES: Home—Toronto, Ontario, Canada. *Office*—c/o National Post, 300-1450 Don Mills Rd., Don Mills, Ontario M3B 3R5, Canada.

CAREER: Globe and Mail, Toronto, Ontario, Canada, began as reporter, Latin American Bureau Chief, 1991-95; *National Post,* Don Mills, Ontario, Canada, investigative reporter.

AWARDS, HONORS: Inter-American Press Association Citation, 1993, for coverage of Peru's Shining Path guerillas; National Newspaper Award finalist,

1994, for coverage of the drug wars in Rio de Janeiro, Brazil; Southam Fellowship and Canadian Association of Journalists' Award for excellence in investigative journalism, both for foreign reporting and *See No Evil: The Strange Case of Christine Lamont and David Spencer.*

WRITINGS:

See No Evil: The Strange Case of Christine Lamont and David Spencer, Reed Books Canada (Toronto, Ontario, Canada), 1995.
Hitler's Silent Partners: Swiss Banks, Nazi Gold, and the Pursuit of Justice, Morrow (New York, NY), 1997.
Bodies and Souls: The Tragic Plight of Three Jewish Women Forced into Prostitution in the Americas, 1860 to 1939, Morrow (New York, NY), 2005.

Contributor to periodicals, including *Marie Claire, Saturday Night, New Yorker, Independent, Daily Telegraph,* and other international publications.

SIDELIGHTS: Isabel Vincent is an award-winning multilingual journalist who was chosen as a finalist for Canada's National Newspaper Award, the equivalent of the American Pulitzer Prize, for her reporting on the drug wars in the shantytowns of Rio de Janeiro.

Vincent is the author of several nonfiction books, including *Hitler's Silent Partners: Swiss Banks, Nazi Gold, and the Pursuit of Justice,* an investigation into the fortunes that were deposited in Swiss and Swedish banks by European Jews threatened by the Nazis. Vincent also investigates whether these two countries secretly collaborated with the Germans, supplying them with resources to finance their war and reaping a windfall from the atrocities of World War II. Vincent's case study is the Hammersfelds, a family of Viennese Jews who have attempted to reclaim their assets. *Booklist* contributor Jay Freeman wrote that their efforts "add saving grace to what otherwise would be a depressing tale of greed and indifference to human suffering."

Bodies and Souls: The Tragic Plight of Three Jewish Women Forced into Prostitution in the Americas, 1860 to 1939 is Vincent's history of the sexual slavery of young Jewish women who were forced into prostitution by the Jewish gang known as Zwi Migdal. The gang ran brothels on several continents, including North America, and their base was in Buenos Aires, Argentina. Vincent follows the lives of three of the women the gang forced into prostitution, including Sophia Chamys, who was sent to Buenos Aires and locked in a house. The other Jewish residents of the city refused to acknowledge the women and would not give them proper burials when they died. Consequently, the prostitutes formed the Chesed Shel Ermess and purchased their own cemetery in 1916. In 1942, they bought a synagogue.

A *Kirkus Reviews* contributor described *Bodies and Souls* as "riveting and disturbing." A *Publishers Weekly* reviewer wrote that Vincent "demonstrates her strength as a writer and storyteller, which enables her to a least partially retrieve this all-but-lost world."

BIOGRAPHICAL AND CRITICAL SOURCES:

PERIODICALS

Booklist, October 15, 1997, Jay Freeman, review of *Hitler's Silent Partners: Swiss Banks, Nazi Gold, and the Pursuit of Justice,* p. 385.
Kirkus Reviews, September 1, 2005, review of *Bodies and Souls: The Tragic Plight of Three Jewish Women Forced into Prostitution in the Americas, 1860 to 1939,* p. 965.
Publishers Weekly, November 10, 1997, review of *Hitler's Silent Partners,* p. 67.*

*   *   *

VITEBSKY, Piers

PERSONAL: Male. *Education:* University of Cambridge, B.A., 1971, M.A., 1974; University of Oxford, diploma in social anthropology, 1972; attended Delhi School of Economics, 1977-79; School of Oriental and African Studies, London, Ph.D., 1982.

ADDRESSES: Home—England. *Office*—Scott Polar Research Institute, University of Cambridge, Lensfield Rd., Cambridge CB2 1ER, England. *E-mail*—pv100@cam.ac.uk.

CAREER: University of Cambridge, Scott Polar Research Institute, Cambridge, England, assistant director of research, 1986—.

WRITINGS:

Policy Dilemmas for Unirrigated Agriculture in Southeastern Sri Lanka: A Social Anthropologist's Report on Shifting and Semi-Permanent Cultivation in an Area of Moneragala District, Center of South Asian Studies, University of Cambridge (Cambridge, England), 1984.

Dialogues with the Dead: The Discussion of Mortality among the Sora of Eastern India, Cambridge University Press (Cambridge, England), 1993.

The Saami of Lapland, Wayland (Hove, England), 1993, reprinted, Thomson Learning (New York, NY), 1994.

The Shaman, Little, Brown (Boston, MA), 1995, published as *Shamanism,* University of Oklahoma Press (Norman, OK), 2001.

(With Caroline Humphrey) *Sacred Architecture,* Little, Brown (Boston, MA), 1997.

(With Tony Allan) *Triumph of the Hero: Greek and Roman Myth,* Duncan Baird (London, England), 1998.

(With Michael Kerrigan and Alan Lothian) *Epics of Early Civilization,* Duncan Baird (London, England), 1998.

(With Brian Leigh Molyneaux) *Sacred Earth, Sacred Stones,* Laurel Glen (San Diego, CA), 2001.

Reindeer People: Living with Animals and Spirits in Siberia (memoir), Houghton Mifflin (Boston, MA), 2005.

Author of documentary films, including *Siberia: After the Shaman,* Channel 4; *Arctic Aviators,* National Geographic; and *Flightpaths to the Gods,* BBC2. Contributor to periodicals, including *Natural History.*

SIDELIGHTS: Piers Vitebsky is an anthropologist who has carried out fieldwork in India since 1975 and the Siberian Arctic since 1988. *Dialogues with the Dead: The Discussion of Mortality among the Sora of Eastern India* is Vitebsky's study of a group of people he worked with during the 1970s, and then revisited in 1984 and 1992. The book presents their beliefs about death and the afterlife of the dead, who they refer to as sonum. K.I. Koppedrayer noted in the *International*

Journal of Comparative Sociology that "dialogues with the dead, mediated by funeral shamans—mainly women—in trance, are moving, complex, and densely packed with layers of social and personal meaning."

Sacred Earth, Sacred Stones is a revised version of the 1995 book *The Sacred Earth,* by Brian Leigh Molyneaux, whom Vitebsky joins for this edition. The volume examines twenty-five major sacred sites around the world, including Stonehenge, Machu Picchu, Teotihuacan, and Chichen Itza, but also less well-known sites. *Folklore* contributor Janet Bord noted that "apart from the sites, the book's subject-matter ranges across such topics as Creation, spirit paths, rock images, earth energy, spirituality, the ancestors, pilgrimages, sacred lakes, mandalas, ceremonial landscapes, shrines and temples, worship and ritual, the afterlife, and much more."

Vitebsky visited the Eveny tribe of northeastern Siberia for many years before writing *Reindeer People: Living with Animals and Spirits in Siberia.* It is a memoir and a study of life in a region where the temperature can fall to nearly minus one hundred degrees, so cold that boiling water thrown into the air will freeze before touching ground. In this environment, the relationship of the Eveny people with the animals that feed and warm them reaches back into prehistory. The animals are used for their meat and hides as well as for transportation and trade. In the past, the Eveny and their cousins, the Evenk, followed the animals as they migrated, and Vitebsky retraced those routes with some of the older hunters. Under the Soviets, the Eveny were forced to live in settlements, and while the wives maintained their villages and the children attended school, the men were often away for long periods managing the herds. Vitebsky documents the harm caused by the forced changes on the culture and the loss of self-esteem experienced by the reindeer herders.

Roger Took noted in *Geographical* that in spite of this history, the Eveny have retained their independence. Took wrote that it is this attribute "that has made significant intercourse particularly difficult for outsiders. It's much to Vitebsky's credit, therefore, that he has been able to glean so much natural and human detail, in addition to the purely anthropological and historical." A *Publishers Weekly* contributor wrote that Vitebsky's book "teems with strong personalities, perilous adventures and time-honored folkways."

"Gorgeously observed and evocative are his descriptions of living in the landscape," Anna Reid noted in the *Spectator*. A *Kirkus Reviews* contributor described *Reindeer People* as "extraordinary fieldnotes."

BIOGRAPHICAL AND CRITICAL SOURCES:

BOOKS

Vitebsky, Piers, *Reindeer People: Living with Animals and Spirits in Siberia,* Houghton Mifflin (Boston, MA), 2005.

PERIODICALS

Folklore, October, 2002, Janet Bord, review of *Sacred Earth, Sacred Stones,* p. 288.
Geographical, May, 2005, Roger Took, review of *Reindeer People,* p. 72.
International Journal of Comparative Sociology, November, 1998, K.I. Koppedrayer, review of *Dialogues with the Dead: The Discussion of Mortality among the Sora of Eastern India,* p. 419.
Journal of the Royal Anthropological Institute, June, 1995, Gananath Obeyesekere, review of *Dialogues with the Dead,* p. 458.
Kirkus Reviews, October 15, 2005, review of *Reindeer People,* p. 1128.
Library Journal, November 15, 2005, Dan Harms, review of *Reindeer People,* p. 74.
M2 Best Books, July 1, 2003, review of *Sacred Architecture.*
New Scientist, May 14, 2005, Nick Saunders, review of *Reindeer People,* p. 53.
People, December 5, 2005, Allison Lynn, review of *Reindeer People,* p. 55.
Publishers Weekly, October 24, 2005, review of *Reindeer People,* p. 51.
Spectator, April 23, 2005, Anna Reid, review of *Reindeer People,* p. 38.

ONLINE

Scott Polar Research Institute Web site, http://www.spri.cam.ac.uk/ (January 15, 2006).*

VOLTING, Dr. R.E.
    See LERANGIS, Peter

*   *   *

von MEHREN, Arthur T. 1922-2006
    (Arthur Taylor von Mehren)

OBITUARY NOTICE— See index for *CA* sketch: Born August 10, 1922, in Albert Lea, MN; died of pneumonia, January 16, 2006, in Cambridge, MA. Von Mehren was a former professor at Harvard University who was a scholar of international and comparative law. Graduating Phi Beta Kappa from Harvard in 1942, he earned his law degree there in 1945 and a Ph.D. in government the next year. He then studied in Zurich, Switzerland, and at the University of Paris, honing his language skills in German and French while also studying the laws of those countries. He returned home to join the Harvard faculty in 1946, becoming a full professor of law in 1953 and retiring as Story Professor of Law Emeritus in 1993. During his years at Harvard, von Mehren founded the Joseph Story Fellow program for young German academics, and in his early career there was chief of the Legislation Branch of the Legal Division for the U.S. Office of Military Government in Berlin. Considered a leader in international comparative law, he was a founder and former president of the American Society of Comparative Law, an advisor for the Private International Law for the U.S. Department of State, and an editor of the *American Journal of Comparative Law.* Von Mehren was the author, coauthor, or editor of numerous scholarly texts as well, including *The Civil Law System: Cases and Materials for the Comparative Study of Law* (1957; 2nd edition, 1976), *Law in the United States* (1988), *International Encyclopedia of Comparative Law* (1997), and *Law and Justice in a Multistate World* (2002).

OBITUARIES AND OTHER SOURCES:

PERIODICALS

New York Times, January 29, 2006, p. A26.

*   *   *

VON MEHREN, Arthur Taylor
    See VON MEHREN, Arthur T.

VORNBERGER, Cal 1950-
(Charles Calvin Vornberger)

PERSONAL: Born March 2, 1950, in Detroit, MI; son of Charles Calvin and Mary Arlene (Ruhl) Vornberger. *Education:* University of Michigan, B.A., 1972; Wayne State University, M.F.A., 1975. *Hobbies and other interests:* Photography.

ADDRESSES: Home—New York, NY. *Agent*—c/o Author Mail, Harry N. Abrams, Inc., 115 W. 18th St., New York, NY 10011. *E-mail*—cal@calvorn.com.

CAREER: Freelance art director, 1978-80; Modern Telecommunications, Inc., New York, NY, director of design, 1980-87; Tumble Interactive Media, Inc., founder and president, 1988-2000; EpicEdge, Austin, TX, chief creative officer, 2000. Instructor at the University of Texas, New York University, Hunter College, Pratt Institute, and Katharine Gibbs School; National Opera Institute, fellow.

WRITINGS:

Birds of Central Park, foreword by Marie Winn, Harry N. Abrams (New York, NY), 2005.

SIDELIGHTS: Cal Vornberger is an award-winning art director for film, stage, televison, corporate videos, music videos, political campaigns, and live events whose passion for his hobby developed into a new career as a travel photographer. It was cut short, however, with the events of September 11, 2001, that thereafter affected the travel industry. According to Rene Ebersole of *Audubon,* Vornberg, who can walk from his Manhattan apartment to Central Park in just a few minutes, took his camera to shoot autumn foliage when his attention was caught by a great egret fishing in Turtle Pond. He returned to the 843-acre park, which is an important stop for more than 200 species of migratory birds, and built a collection of bird photographs. "Initially he focused on bird portraits," noted Ebersole, "but he gradually became more interested in behaviors—cardinals courting, green heron fledglings braving their first flight, robins building their nests in the oddest of places."

One of Vornberger's photographs is of robins nested in a crevice of the Romeo and Juliet statue near the Delacorte Theater. That, along with another 174 color photographs, described as "stunning" by *Booklist* reviewer George Cohen, can be found in his book, *Birds of Central Park. Library Journal* contributor Howard Katz observed that "the robins appear spellbound as they gaze at the figure of Romeo bending over to plant a kiss on Juliet." The book includes seldom-seen birds Vornberger has captured on film, sometimes after receiving tips from other birdwatchers by cell phone. He devoted three years to the project. The volume is divided into four sections, one for each season, so that readers can quickly see when each species is likely to be observed. Also included is a fold-out pocket guide. Cohen concluded that "birdwatchers will be captivated."

BIOGRAPHICAL AND CRITICAL SOURCES:

PERIODICALS

Audubon, September-October, 2005, Rene Ebersole, "Robin, Robin, Wherefore Art Thou?," p. 52.
Booklist, October 15, 2005, George Cohen, review of *Birds of Central Park,* p. 15.
Library Journal, October 1, 2005, Howard Katz, review of *Birds of Central Park,* p. 107.
Science News, October 8, 2005, review of *Birds of Central Park,* p. 239.
Wisconsin Bookwatch, October, 2005, review of *Birds of Central Park.*

ONLINE

Cal Vornberger Home Page, http://www.calvorn.com (January 15, 2006).*

*   *   *

VORNBERGER, Charles Calvin
See VORNBERGER, Cal

W

WADE, Suzanne
See KIRBY, Susan E.

* * *

WAGNER, Matt 1961-

PERSONAL: Born 1961, in PA; married Barbara Schutz; two children.

ADDRESSES: Agent—c/o Author Mail, Dark Horse Comics, 10956 S.E. Main St., Milwaukee, OR 97222.

CAREER: Comic book creator, writer, and illustrator.

AWARDS, HONORS: Eisner Award, 1999, for best anthology, for collection *Grendel: Black, White, & Red,* and, with Tim Sale, best short story, "Devil's Advocate," from comic book *Grendel: Black, White, & Red,* number 1.

WRITINGS:

GRAPHIC NOVELS/COMIC BOOK COLLECTIONS

Mage: The Hero Discovered (three volumes), Donning Co. (Norfolk, VA), 1987, single-volume edition published by Image Comics (Berkeley, CA) 2004
(With others) *Grendel: Devil's Legacy,* Comico (Norristown, PA), 1988.

(With others) *Batman: Faces,* DC Comics (New York, NY), 1995.
(With others) *Batman: Riddler,* DC Comics (New York, NY), 1995.
Matt Wagner's Grendel Cycle, Dark Horse Comics (Milwaukee, OR), 1995.
(With others) *Sandman Mystery Theatre,* DC Comics (New York, NY),1995.
(With others) *Grendel Tales: Devils and Deaths,* Dark Horse Comics (Milwaukee, OR), 1996.
(With others) Matt Wagner's Grendel Tales: The Devil in Our Midst, Dark Horse Comics (Milwaukee, OR), 1998.
Mage: The Hero Defined (four volumes), Image Comics (Berkeley, CA), 1999.
(With others) *Neil Gaimon's Midnight Days,* Vertigo (New York, NY), 1999.
(With others) *Matt Wagner's Grendel Tales: Homecoming* Dark Horse Comics (Milwaukee, OR),2000.
(With Greg Rucka) *Grendel: Past Prime,* Dark Horse Comics (Milwaukee, OR), 2000.
(With others) *Doctor Mid-Nite,* DC Comics (New York, NY), 2000.
(With John K. Snyder III) *Doctor Mid-Nite,* book two, DC Comics (New York, NY), 2000.
(With others) *Grendel: Black, White, & Red,* Dark Horse Comics (Milwaukee, OR), 2000.
(With others) *Grendel Tales: The Devil May Care,* Dark Horse Comics (Milwaukee, OR), 2003.
(With Bernie Mireault) *Grendel: The Devil Inside,* Dark Horse Comics (Milwaukee, OR), 2004.
Superman/Batman/Wonder Woman: Trinity, DC Comics (New York, NY), 2004.
(With others) *Grendel: Red, White, & Black,* Dark Horse Comics (Milwaukee, OR), 2005.

(With others) *The Vamp: Sandman Mystery Theatre,* Volume 3, Vertigo (New York, NY), 2005.

Creator of comic book series, including *Mage* and *Grendel;* writer and/or artist for other comic series, including *Batman, Sandman Mystery Theatre, Dr. Mid-Nite, Ultimate Marvel Team-Up: Spider-Man and Wolverine,* and *Green Arrow.*

ADAPTATIONS: Mage was adapted into a screenplay by John Rogers, to be filmed by Spyglass Entertainment and Critical Mass Productions. John Wells Productions plans to film *Grendel,* with screenplay to be written by Carl Lund.

SIDELIGHTS: Matt Wagner's career in comic books has encompassed creating the *Mage* and *Grendel* series as well as writing or illustrating stories of established characters such as Batman, Superman, Spider-Man, Wolverine, and Wonder Woman. "I was first published as a creator-owned guy in the early 80's and then later, I went and did stuff for the big companies," Wagner told Adam Gallardo in an interview for the Dark Horse Comics Web site. "I find that balancing trick just perfectly easy. I guess part of that is I have found such reward, not only financially but creatively, from the two creator-owned series that I have."

The *Mage* series deals with an ordinary young man, Kevin Matchstick, who undergoes training with a wizard and emerges able to fight a variety of supernatural enemies. The series draws on the Arthurian legends to some degree. Comico published fifteen issues of *Mage,* which were then collected in three trade paperback volumes as *Mage: The Hero Discovered.* Wagner, who described the series to Gallardo as "a one-man show basically," drew critical praise for both his art and his words. Peter Coogan, reviewing the second volume for *Extrapolation,* noted that Wagner "used the archetypes of hero, wizard, and companion . . . to tell the tale of heroic discovery of self." Coogan added that Wagner's story "started out simply but grew more complex as he worked it out, and Wagner handled it masterfully. His art reflects his growth in understanding of his material and in his ability to present it. Wagner's artwork is pleasing to behold, because besides being beautiful, it tells the story, the true test of comics narrative. His panel composition can be complex, but is never muddled. His pages are

full but clear." Christy Tyson, critiquing the third volume in *Voice of Youth Advocates,* observed that "art and text combine to present a bold, dramatic contemporary world."

Wagner introduced the character of Grendel, a powerful assassin who takes the form of various people, in a supporting feature in the *Mage* series. Grendel's first alter ego was a wealthy, socially prominent, self-centered young man named Hunter Rose. The Hunter Rose stories are in some ways a commentary on the selfishness and aimlessness of modern young people. After Rose's death, Grendel had several other human identities, including that of Rose's granddaughter Christine Spar, and he also became a malevolent cosmic force not tied to one person. With a spin-off title devoted to Grendel, Wagner began collaborating with other artists and writers. "I thought the only way for me to grow and expand myself was to learn how other people see things," Wagner told Gallardo. Examples of collaboration include the trade paperbacks *Grendel: Black, White, & Red* and *Grendel: Red, White, & Black,* which feature stories, originally published in comics, written by Wagner and illustrated by himself and others using only the colors of the title. Some critics have praised the variety of artistic expression offered in these volumes. *Booklist* contributor Gordon Flagg, for instance, remarked on the "enjoyable diversity" of illustrators in the latter collection, which also provides an "alternative view" of Hunter Rose's story.

Wagner has also brought what some reviewers see as a distinctive approach to other creators' characters. *Superman/Batman/Wonder Woman: Trinity,* which he wrote and illustrated, provides "a fresh and satisfying take" on these heroes and their interactions, related Steve Raiteri in *Library Journal.* In *Booklist,* Flagg noted that this title features "sparse, thoughtful art and clear, elegant storytelling."Wagner, he added, has "a model style."

BIOGRAPHICAL AND CRITICAL SOURCES:

PERIODICALS

Booklist, September 1, 2004, Gordon Flagg, review of *Superman/Batman/Wonder Woman: Trinity,* p. 77; September 1, 2005, Flagg, review of *The*

Vamp: Sandman Mystery Theatre, Volume 3, p. 77; September 15, 2005, Flagg, review of *Grendel: Red, White, & Black,* p. 40.

Entertainment Weekly, April 1, 2005, Jeff Jensen, review of *Mage: The Hero Discovered,* one-volume edition, p. 73.

Extrapolation, winter, 1988, Peter Coogan, review of *Mage,* Volume 2, pp. 367-369.

Hollywood Reporter, January 5, 2004, "Wells Books Wagner Comic 'Grendel.'"

Library Journal, November 1, 2004, Steve Raiteri, review of *Superman/Batman/Wonder Woman,* p. 67.

Publishers Weekly, June 7, 2004, review of *Grendel: The Devil Inside,* p. 34.

School Library Journal, November, 2005, Melissa T. Jenvey, review of *The Vamp,* p. 180.

Voice of Youth Advocates, June, 1989, Christy Tyson, review of *Mage,* Volume 3, p. 120.

ONLINE

Comic Box, http://www.thecomicbox.com/ (July 1, 2006), Michael Nguyen, review of *Grendel: Black, White, & Red.*

Dark Horse Comics Web site, http://www.darkhorse.com/ (July 1, 2006), Adam Gallardo, interview with Matt Wagner.

Matt Wagner Home Page, http://www.mattwagner comics.com (July 1, 2006).

PopMatters, http://www.popmatters.com/ (July 1, 2006), Kevin Mathews, interview with Matt Wagner.

Shotgun Reviews, http://www.shotgunreviews.com/ (July 1, 2006), Troy Brownfield, interview with Matt Wagner.*

*   *   *

WAGNER, Ralph D. 1951-
(Alonzo Boardman)

PERSONAL: Born February 16, 1951, in New Brunswick, NJ; son of William James (a chemist) and Winifred (a library technician; maiden name, Belk) Wagner; married Susan Abbott (a teacher), February 5, 1983; children: William Abbott, Kevin Jacob. *Ethnicity:* "English-Canadian." *Education:* Middlebury Col-

lege, A.B., 1973; Rutgers University, M.L.S., 1975; University of Illinois, Ph.D., 2000. *Politics:* "Skeptical independent." *Religion:* Bahá'í.

ADDRESSES: Home—40 Taylor Ave., Westfield, MA 01085. *E-mail*—rdwagner@dinsdoc.com.

CAREER: Writer. U.S. Peace Corps, Washington, DC, volunteer librarian in Kinshasa, Congo, 1976-78; Northern Illinois University, DeKalb, business librarian, 1980-86; Western Illinois University, Macomb, acting library director, 1986-89; Eureka College, Eureka, IL, library director, 1989-91; Westfield State College, Westfield, MA, reference librarian, 1994-2001.

MEMBER: Mormon History Association.

WRITINGS:

A History of the Farmington Plan, Scarecrow Press (Lanham, MD), 2002.

Contributor to periodicals, including *American Libraries* and *Libraries and Culture: Journal of Library History.* Some writings appear under the pseudonym Alonzo Boardman.

WORK IN PROGRESS: Research on the sources and linguistics of the Book of Mormon, "by a non-Mormon with no hostility toward Mormonism."

SIDELIGHTS: Ralph D. Wagner told *CA:* "I believe that scholarly writing should be a pleasure to read, and the greatest compliment I have received from editors and reviewers is that my work is clear, free of jargon, and a good read."

*   *   *

WALLACE-MURPHY, Tim
(Timothy Wallace-Murphy)

PERSONAL: Male. *Education:* Studied medicine at University College, Dublin, Ireland.

ADDRESSES: Home—11 Dukes Rd., Totnes, Devon TQ9 5YA, England. *Agent*—c/o Author Mail, Red Wheel/Weiser/Conari, 65 Parker St., Ste. 7, Newburyport, MA 09150. *E-mail*—twallace-murphy@supanet. com.

CAREER: Lecturer, author, and psychologist. Cofounder of the European Templar Heritage Research Network (ETHRN).

WRITINGS:

An Illustrated Guidebook to Rosslyn Chapel, The Friends of Rosslyn (Edinburgh, Scotland), 1993.
The Templar Legacy and Masonic Inheritance within Rosslyn Chapel, The Friends of Rosslyn (Edinburgh, Scotland), 1994.
(With Trevor Ravenscroft) *The Mark of the Beast: The Continuing Story of the Spear of Destiny,* S. Weiser (York Beach, ME), 1997.
(With Marilyn Hopkins) *Rosslyn, Guardian of the Secrets of the Holy Grail,* Element (Boston, MA), 1999.
(With Marilyn Hopkins and Graham Simmans) *Rex Deus: The True Mystery of Rennes-le-Chateau,* Element (Boston, MA), 2000.
(With Marilyn Hopkins) *Templars in America: From the Crusades to the New World,* Weiser Books (Boston, MA), 2004.
(With Marilyn Hopkins) *Custodians of Truth: The Continuance of Rex Deus,* Weiser Books (Boston, MA), 2005.
Cracking the Symbol Code, Watkins Publishing, 2005.

WORK IN PROGRESS: The Enigma of the Freemasons, for The Disinformation Company; *What Islam Did for Us* and *The Knights Templar, the Myth and the Reality,* both for Watkins Publishing.

SIDELIGHTS: Perhaps Tim Wallace-Murphy's most controversial work is 2000's *Rex Deus: The True Mystery of Rennes-le-Chateau, written with Marilyn Hopkins and Graham Simmans.* In it, the authors explore the theory that Jesus Christ did not perish on the cross, but instead lived on to marry and have children with Mary Magdalene, who settled in France after his death. Direct descendants of this bloodline, who are rumored to have kept it pure to the present day, are referred to as Rex Deus, meaning "king God."

The Rex Deus did not originate with Jesus, the authors suggest, but can be traced further back to the twenty-four high priests of the Temple of Jerusalem. According to the authors, the Rex Deus were forced to keep the "true" teachings of Jesus secret for about two thousand years to avoid being persecuted by the Catholic Church, which desired to propagate its own fabricated version of the truth unhindered. The book explores the mystery of Rennes-le-Chateau and the physical and spiritual secrets that may be hidden within the French village. Wallace-Murphy and Marilyn Hopkins took the investigation of the subject further with *Custodians of Truth: The Continuance of Rex Deus.* One *Publishers Weekly* contributor felt that the book provides a "readable—if not fervent— overview of this controversial theory." Dina Komuves, contributor to the *Library Journal,* wrote that the book offers "more than enough viable detail to poke a few substantial holes into the credibility of strict fundamentalism."

BIOGRAPHICAL AND CRITICAL SOURCES:

PERIODICALS

Kindred Spirit (Devon, England), July-August, 2005, review of *Cracking the Symbol Code.*
Library Journal, October 1, 2005, Dina Komuves, review of *Custodians of Truth: The Continuance of Rex Deus,* p. 87.
Publishers Weekly, May 2, 2005, review of *Custodians of Truth,* p. 193.
Watkins Review (London, England), September, 2005, review of *Cracking the Symbol Code.*

ONLINE

Pagan News, http://www.pagannews.com/ (February 1, 2006), interview with Tim Wallace-Murphy and Marilyn Hopkins.

* * *

WALLACE-MURPHY, Timothy
See WALLACE-MURPHY, Tim

WALSH, Ann 1942-

PERSONAL: Born September 20, 1942, in Jasper, AL; became Canadian citizen; daughter of Alan Barrett (a speech therapist) and Margaret Elaine (a speech therapist) Clemons; married John F.D. Walsh (a French teacher), January 3, 1964; children: Katherine Margaret Ann, Megan Elizabeth Alva. *Education:* University of British Columbia, B.Ed., 1968. *Hobbies and other interests:* Amateur theatre, reading, the outdoors, literacy volunteer, travel.

ADDRESSES: Home—411 Winger Rd., Williams Lake, British Columbia V2G 3S6, Canada.

CAREER: Writer and elementary school teacher. Vancouver, British Columbia, Canada, and Williams Lake, British Columbia, Canada, elementary school teacher, 1964-78; community college instructor, 1979-89; full-time writer, 1990—. Adjudicator for Creative Writing Division of Cariboo Music Festival, 1988; has held various executive positions with the Williams Lake Players' Club. Member, Children's Literature Roundtable and Canadian Children's Book Centre.

MEMBER: Writers' Union of Canada (membership committee, 2000—), Canadian Society of Children's Authors, Illustrators & Performers, Canadian Children's Book Center, Federation of British Columbia Writers (regional representative, 1986—), Children's Writers and Illustrators of British Columbia, Williams Lake Writers' Group (founding member).

AWARDS, HONORS: Your Time, My Time was selected Best Canadian Children's Book, *Emergency Librarian,* 1984; *The Ghost of Soda Creek* was a Canadian Library Association notable book, 1990; *Your Time, My Time, Moses, Me and Murder!, The Ghost of Soda Creek, Shabash!, The Doctor's Apprentice, By the Skin of His Teeth,* and *Flower Power* have all been Canadian Children's Centre Our Choice selections.

WRITINGS:

YOUNG ADULT NOVELS

Your Time, My Time, Press Porcepic (Toronto, Ontario, Canada), 1984.

Moses, Me and Murder!, illustrated by C. Allen, Pacific Education Press (Vancouver, British Columbia, Canada), 1988.
The Ghost of Soda Creek, Press Porcepic (Toronto, Ontario, Canada), 1990.
Shabash!, Beach Holme (Vancouver, British Columbia, Canada), 1994.
The Doctor's Apprentice, Beach Holme (Vancouver, British Columbia, Canada), 1998.
By the Skin of His Teeth, Beach Holme (Vancouver, British Columbia, Canada), 2004.
Flower Power, Orca Books (Victoria, British Columbia, Canada), 2005.

PLAYS

The Making of a Hero (juvenile), first produced in Williams Lake, British Columbia, Canada, by Williams Lake Players' Club, 1979.
Banana Who? (juvenile), first produced in Williams Lake, British Columbia, Canada, by Williams Lake Players' Club, 1980.
The First of Sixty (playlet), 1989.

EDITOR

Winds through Time: An Anthology of Canadian Historical Young Adult Fiction, Beach Holme (Vancouver, British Columbia, Canada), 1998.
(And contributor) *Beginnings: Stories of Canada's Past,* Ronsdale Press (Vancouver, British Columbia, Canada), 2001.
Dark Times, Ronsdale Press (Vancouver, British Columbia, Canada), 2005.

Also author of poetry book *Across the Stillness,* Beach Holme (Vancouver, British Columbia, Canada), 1993. Contributor to books, including *Skelton at Sixty,* Porcupine's Quill (Erin, Ontario, Canada), 1986; *Hungry Poet's Cookbook,* Applezaba Press (Long Beach, CA), 1987; *The Skin of the Soul,* Paper Back Books, 1990; *B.C. Almanac Anthology,* Arsenal Pulp Press (Vancouver, British Columbia, Canada), 2000; and *Canadian Poems for Canadian Kids.*

Contributor of short stories and poetry to periodicals, including *Jack and Jill, Prairie Fire, Vancouver Sun, Bella, Canadian Short Stories, Hornby Collection,*

Woman to Woman, Quarry, Prairie Journal of Canadian Literature, Canadian Living, Interior Woman, and *Woman's World.*

SIDELIGHTS: A somewhat difficult childhood marked by frequent overseas moves was a significant influence on the eventual career path of American-born Canadian writer Ann Walsh. "My childhood," she once commented, "was spent in many different countries and eleven different schools by the time I reached grade six. . . . Some of my best friends as a child were the characters in the books I read voraciously. . . . I remember reading wherever we went and whatever we did. The constancy of my fictional friends, to whom I never had to bid goodbye, is perhaps, one of the main reasons that today I am a writer."

A prolific writer of fiction for children and young adults, Walsh published her first novel, *Your Time, My Time,* in 1984 and has since written several books as well as contributed short stories to numerous anthologies. Her particular niche is incorporating historical events and locales in her stories with the intent of educating as well as entertaining. Several *Resource Links* reviewers have lauded her ability to bring to life historical facts and characters. In a review of *The Doctor's Apprentice,* a book in the "Barkerville Mystery" series, Alyson Gillan commented: "Ann Walsh has given readers a strong novel with excellent values lessons for students from grades six to nine. She brings history alive in the pages." Another *Resource Links* contributor, Victoria Pennell, wrote that a later book in the series, *By the Skin of His Teeth,* is "an interesting read" that "provides insight into historical data and would prove useful in conjunction with studies of Canadian history."

As an editor, Walsh has also worked to share and promote historical fiction with readers. For example, her 1998 anthology, *Winds through Time: An Anthology of Canadian Historical Young Adult Fiction,* conveys an "overwhelming feeling . . . of satisfaction, that yes, this might help bring to life parts of Canadian history for young students," as Donna J. Johnson Alden attested in *Resource Links.*

Walsh told CA: "Five of my novels for young readers are set in Barkerville, once a rough and crowded gold rush town, which nestles among pine trees and mountains in the heart of the Cariboo Region. The gold and the miners who sought it [are gone], but the very air of the restored townsite is thick with history. Modern visitors often feel as if their presence is unwanted—as if the people who once lived in Barkerville are still there, hiding in the shadows, waiting patiently to reclaim their town. All of the people who created British Columbia have left their imprint on our province; from the First Nations people, to the gold miners, to the early settlers who felled trees and built houses in what is now downtown Vancouver. A writer must use imagination, sprinkled like fingerprint power, to raise those faint imprints left from earlier times; to discover who left them, and when and why, and which story needs to be told. The past is there, waiting, in our forests, rivers, mountains and even in the recipes which have been passed down to by those who have lived in this land before us."

BIOGRAPHICAL AND CRITICAL SOURCES:

PERIODICALS

Resource Links, October, 1998, Donna J. Johnson Alden, review of *Winds through Time: An Anthology of Canadian Historical Young Adult Fiction,* p. 20; February, 1999, Alyson Gillan, review of *The Doctor's Apprentice,* p. 29; June, 2005, Victoria Pennell, review of *By the Skin of His Teeth,* p. 35.

ONLINE

Canadian Society of Children's Authors, Illustrators and Performers Web site, http://www.canscaip.org/ (January 10, 2006), biographical information on Ann Walsh.

*   *   *

WALSH, Lawrence 1942-

PERSONAL: Born 1942; married; wife's name Suella (a teacher and writer).

ADDRESSES: Home—1803 Wornall Rd., Excelsior Springs, MO 64024. E-mail—landswalsh@prodigy.net.

CAREER: Bayer Corporation Quality Assurance Water Analysis Laboratory, former chemist; freelance writer. *Red Herring Mystery Magazine,* founding editor. Whispering Prairie Press, member of board of directors and president; Potpourri Publications, member of board, 1989-95, treasurer, 1993-95. Teacher at writing workshops and at libraries and schools, including Johnson County Community College, Maplewoods College. Judge for writing contests, including Longview College Scriptwriting Contest, 1991, and Kansas Coffin Awards, 1992.

MEMBER: Society of Children's Book Writers and Illustrators, Missouri Writers' Guild, Oklahoma Writers' Federation.

AWARDS, HONORS: Kansas Governor's Arts Award (with Suella Walsh), 1994.

WRITINGS:

(With wife, Suella Walsh) *The Unicorn and Other Children's Stories,* Potpourri Publications, 1993.
(With Suella Walsh) *They Would Never Be Friends,* Royal Fireworks Press (Unionville, NY), 1996.
(With Suella Walsh) *Through a Dark Tunnel,* Royal Fireworks Press (Unionville, NY), 2001.

Also author, with Suella Walsh, of books, including *Viewpoint in Fiction* for Potpourri Publications; *Running Scared, The Case of Erica's Weird Behavior* (uncredited), *Through a Dark Tunnel,* and *In the Middle of the Night,* for Royal Fireworks Press; and *Creating Fiction That Sells,* for Shannon River Press. Contributor to books, including *Chocolate for a Teen's Soul,* Simon & Schuster; and to periodicals, including *Highlights for Children, Writers' Journal, Buffalo Spree, Good Old Days, Byline, Mystery Forum, Friend, Potpourri, Missouri,* and *Missouri Life.*

*   *   *

WALSH, Suella

PERSONAL: Married Lawrence Walsh (a chemist and writer).

ADDRESSES: Home—1803 Wornall Rd., Excelsior Springs, MO 64024. *E-mail*—landswalsh@prodigy.net.

CAREER: Editor and author. Former elementary school teacher; freelance writer. Whispering Prairie Press, member of board of directors; Potpourri Publications, member of board, 1989-95, secretary, 1991-95. Teacher at writing workshops and at libraries and schools, including Johnson County Community College, Maplewoods College. Judge for writing contests, including Longview College Scriptwriting Contest, 1991, and Kansas Coffin Awards, 1992.

MEMBER: Society of Children's Book Writers and Illustrators, Missouri Writers' Guild, Oklahoma Writers' Federation.

AWARDS, HONORS: Kansas Governor's Arts Award (with Lawrence Walsh), 1994.

WRITINGS:

(With husband, Lawrence Walsh) *The Unicorn and Other Children's Stories,* Potpourri Publications, 1993.
(With Suella Walsh) *They Would Never Be Friends,* Royal Fireworks Press (Unionville, NY), 1996.
(With Suella Walsh) *Through a Dark Tunnel,* Royal Fireworks Press (Unionville, NY), 2001.

Also author, with Lawrence Walsh, of books, including *Viewpoint in Fiction* for Potpourri Publications; *Running Scared, The Case of Erica's Weird Behavior, Through a Dark Tunnel,* and *In the Middle of the Night,* for Royal Fireworks Press; and *Creating Fiction That Sells,* for Shannon River Press. Contributor to books, including *Chocolate for a Teen's Soul,* Simon & Schuster; and to periodicals, including *Highlights for Children, Writers' Journal, Buffalo Spree, Good Old Days, Byline, Mystery Forum, Friend, Potpourri, Missouri,* and *Missouri Life.* Former columnist.

*   *   *

WANG, Di 1956-

PERSONAL: Born June 20, 1956, in Chengdu, China; son of Guangyuan (a musician) and Yiaolin (an artist; maiden name, Wu) Wang; married Wei Li (an office manager), December 31, 1983; children: Ye. *Ethnicity:*

"Chinese." *Education:* Sichuan University, B.A., 1982, M.A. (history), 1985; Johns Hopkins University, M.A. (East Asian history), Ph.D., 1999.

ADDRESSES: Home—2904 Aztec Ct., College Station, TX 77845. *Office*—Department of History, Texas A&M University, College Station, TX 77843-4236. *E-mail*—di-wang@tamu.edu.

CAREER: Writer. Sichuan University, Chengdu, China, lecturer, 1985-87, associate professor, 1987-91; Texas A&M University, College Station, assistant professor, 1998-2004, associate professor of history, 2004—.

MEMBER: Chinese Historians in the United States (president).

AWARDS, HONORS: Grants from American Council of Learned Societies and National Endowment for the Humanities, 2002, Institute for International Research, Hopkins-Nanjing Center, Johns Hopkins University, 2004, and Japan Society for the Promotion of Science, 2004.

WRITINGS:

Kuachu fengbi de shijie: Changjiang shangyu guyu she hui yanjiu, 1644-1911 (title means "Striding Out of a Closed World: Social Transformation of the Upper Yangzi Region, 1644-1911"), Zhonghua Book (Beijing, China), 1993.
Street Culture in Chengdu: Public Space, Urban Commoners, and Local Politics, 1870-1930, Stanford University Press (Stanford, CA), 2003.

WORK IN PROGRESS: The Teahouses: Public Life in Twentieth-Century Chengdu, Volume 1: *The Teahouse: Small Business, Everyday Culture, and Public Politics in Chengdu, 1900-1950,* based on material in the Chengdu Municipal Archives.

BIOGRAPHICAL AND CRITICAL SOURCES:

PERIODICALS

Canadian Journal of History, August, 2004, Bill Sewell, review of *Street Culture in Chengdu: Public Space, Urban Commoners, and Local Politics, 1870-1930,* p. 421.

Pacific Affairs, summer, 2004, Michael Tsin, review of *Street Culture in Chengdu,* p. 325.

*   *   *

WASSERSTEIN, Wendy 1950-2006

OBITUARY NOTICE— See index for *CA* sketch: Born October 18, 1950, in New York, NY; died of lymphoma, January 30, 2006, in New York, NY. Actress and author. Wasserstein was a Tony Award and Pulitzer Prize-winning playwright best known for writing *The Heidi Chronicles.* Growing up the daughter of well-to-do Jewish parents, she initially intended to study either law or medicine for a career after leaving Mount Holyoke College, where she graduated with a degree in intellectual history in 1971. A writing course at Smith College during one summer changed her mind, however. She studied creative writing at the City College of New York, taking classes from such renowned figures as Joseph Heller and Israel Horvitz. In 1973, she had her first success with the play *Any Woman Can't,* which was produced Off-Broadway. Completing her master's degree that year, she then went to Yale, graduating with an M.F.A. in 1976. Finding a rather menial job delivering scripts for the Eugene O'Neill Theater, her next success came with her play *Uncommon Women and Others,* which was produced by Playwrights Horizons in 1977. Noticing that not many authors were writing scripts about the kinds of people she knew and had grown up with— middle-class, Jewish, liberal women—Wasserstein felt that someone should write plays about them. Her 1983 play, *Isn't It Romantic,* earned her a grant, which she used to travel to London and write her best-known work, *The Heidi Chronicles* (1988), which earned the Pulitzer Prize for drama and a Tony Award. The play, which chronicles the decades of the 1960s through the 1980s, was praised for offering a unique feminist view of those years. This was followed by another play with similar strong, female characters, *The Sisters Rosensweig,* which won the Outer Critics Circle Award and a Tony nomination, and was produced at the Lincoln Center in 1992. Her last plays include *Psyche in Love* (2004) and *Third* (2005). In addition to her dramas, Wasserstein also penned scripts for television, including an adaptation of her own work, *Uncommon Women and Others* (1978), a children's book titled *Pamela's First Musical* (1996), and the autobiographical *Shiksa Goddess; or, How I Spent My Forties* (2001). Her last publication was 2005's *Sloth.*

OBITUARIES AND OTHER SOURCES:

BOOKS

Wasserstein, Wendy, *Shiksa Goddess; or, How I Spent My Forties,* Knopf (New York, NY), 2001.

PERIODICALS

Chicago Tribune, January 31, 2006, section 1, pp. 1, 6.
Los Angeles Times, January 31, 2006, pp. A1, A14.
New York Times, January 31, 2006, pp. A1, A20.
Times (London, England), February 2, 2006, p. 61.
Washington Post, January 31, 2006, p. B6.

* * *

WATMAN, Max

PERSONAL: Married.

ADDRESSES: Home—Brooklyn, NY. *Office*—New York Sun, 105 Chambers St., New York, NY 10007. *Agent*—c/o Author Mail, Editorial Department, Ivan R. Dee, Publisher, 1332 N. Halsted St., Chicago, IL 60622-2694.

CAREER: Writer. *New York Sun,* turf correspondent. Also serves as the fiction chronicler for the *New Criterion* and an editor of the *Nebraska Review.*

WRITINGS:

Race Day: A Spot on the Rail with Max Watman, Ivan R. Dee (Chicago, IL), 2005.

Contributor of articles on horse racing to periodicals, including the *New York Times, Harper's, Wall Street Journal,* and *Parnassus.*

SIDELIGHTS: As the regular turf writer for the *New York Sun,* Max Watman has spent his fair share of time at the racetrack. In his first book, *Race Day: A*

Spot on the Rail with Max Watman, he gives others a chance to get acquainted with the histories, legacies, and rivalries of America's most famous horse-racing tracks and races.

Each chapter of *Race Day* discusses a specific racetrack, including the people behind its development, the horses that stretched for its finish line, and a description of one of the legendary races that made it famous. Among the tracks discussed in the collection are Arlington Park, Churchill Downs, Belmont Park, Hialeah (where Watman's grandfather often took him as a young boy), Pimlico, and Gulfstream. Watman's story begins in 1823 and ends in 2004 with Birdstone's win over Smarty Jones during the Belmont Stakes. Some of the stories in Watman's collection stem from his personal experiences at the races, and these, according to Amy Ford in the *Library Journal,* "are the best in the book, fresh and humorous." Writing for *Booklist,* Dennis Dodge noted that "each race makes for a good story, and Watman . . . is an amiable companion." A contributor to *Cindy Pierson Dulay's Horse-Races.net* termed Watman's book "a great tribute to American Thoroughbred racing," and concluded: "Any racing fan will enjoy this tour across the country and across history."

BIOGRAPHICAL AND CRITICAL SOURCES:

PERIODICALS

Booklist, June 1, 2005, Dennis Dodge, review of *Race Day: A Spot on the Rail with Max Watman,* p. 1741.
Library Journal, July 1, 2005, Amy Ford, review of *Race Day,* p. 93.

ONLINE

Cindy Pierson Dulay's Horse-Races.net, http://www.horse-races.net/ (February 1, 2006), review of *Race Day.**

* * *

WATSON, William E. 1962-

PERSONAL: Born October 25, 1962, in New York, NY; son of William (a musician) and Mary (a musician; maiden name, Tripician) Watson; married Debra Bartoletti (a nurse), May 30, 1987; children: Laura, William E., Jr., Margaret. *Ethnicity:* "Celtic-

American." *Education:* Eastern College, B.A., 1984; University of Pennsylvania, M.A., 1986, Ph.D., 1990. *Politics:* Republican. *Religion:* Roman Catholic.

ADDRESSES: *Office*—Department of History, Immaculata University, 1145 King Rd., Immaculata, PA 19345. *E-mail*—wwatson@immaculata.edu.

CAREER: Writer. Immaculata University, Immaculata, PA, associate professor of history, 1998—.

MEMBER: Society of Colonial Wars, Sons of the American Revolution, De Re Militari.

WRITINGS:

(With Alexander V. Riasanovsky) *Readings in Russian History,* Kendall-Hunt (Dubuque, IA), 1991.
The Collapse of Communism in the Soviet Union, Greenwood Press (Westport, CT), 1998.
Tricolor and Crescent, Praeger Publishers (Westport, CT), 2003.

Contributor to reference books. Contributor of articles and reviews to periodicals, including *Providence: Studies in Western Civilization, International Journal of Historical Studies, Pennsylvania Gazette, Pennsylvania Minuteman, America's Civil War, Naval History,* and *Canadian-American Slavic Studies.*

WORK IN PROGRESS: *The Ghosts of Duffy's Cut,* publication by Praeger Publishers (Westport, CT) expected in 2006; archival and archaeological research on the Duffy's Cut Mass Grave in Malvern, PA.

SIDELIGHTS: William E. Watson told *CA:* "Much of my research and writing is in the field of cross-cultural contact and conflict in history (medieval and modern). In my medieval fields, my work has focused on Frankish-Arab contacts through the era of the Crusades, in particular the period from Charles Martel through Charlemagne (especially the Battle of Tours), and Russo-Arab contacts, in particular the early medieval Arabic literature on the Rus and the Vikings in the East. In my modern fields I have focused on military history and on international relations in the period of World War II and the Cold War. I have an interest in the study of the rise and fall of empires over time—the causes and consequences of their places in history."

* * *

WEBBER, Desiree Morrison 1956-

PERSONAL: Born May 22, 1956, in La Mesa, CA; daughter of William (a metallurgist) and Juanita (a homemaker and secretary) Morrison; married Stephen Webber (a television producer), June 28, 1980; children: Clayton. *Ethnicity:* "Caucasian." *Education:* University of California, San Diego, B.A., 1982; University of Oklahoma, M.L.I.S., 1990.

ADDRESSES: *Agent*—c/o Author Mail, Eakin Press, P.O. Box 90159, Austin, TX 78709. *E-mail*—deswebber@yahoo.com.

CAREER: Librarian and writer. Moore Public Library, Moore, OK, head of children's services, 1990-97; Oklahoma Department of Libraries, Oklahoma City, public library consultant, 1997-2002; Mustang Public Library, Mustang, OK, director, 2002—.

MEMBER: Society of Children's Book Writers and Illustrators, American Library Association.

AWARDS, HONORS: Storytelling World award, International Reading Association, 1999, for *Travel the Globe: Multicultural Story Times;* Delta Kappa Gamma State Author Award, 2001, for *The Buffalo Train Ride;* Oklahoma Book Award finalist, 2004, for *Bone Head.*

WRITINGS:

CHILDREN'S NONFICTION

The Buffalo Train Ride, illustrations by Sandy Shropshire, Eakin Press (Austin, TX), 1999.
Bone Head: Story of the Longhorn, illustrated by Sandy Shropshire, Eakin Press (Austin, TX), 2003.

OTHER

Travel the Globe: Multicultural Story Times, illustrated by Sandy Shropshire, Libraries Unlimited (Englewood, CO), 1998.

The Kid's Book Club: Lively Reading and Activities for Grades 1-3, illustrated by Sandy Shropshire, Libraries Unlimited (Englewood, CO), 2001.

SIDELIGHTS: In addition to her work as a library administrator, Desiree Morrison Webber is the author of several storytelling guides for teachers and librarians, as well as *Bone Head: Story of the Longhorn* and *The Buffalo Train Ride,* two titles that reflect her research skills and her knowledge of the history of the American plain. In *Bone Head* Webber recounts the history of the often-overlooked Texas longhorn, and the reasons why this hardy breed was eclipsed by short-horned, more-easily domesticated cattle breeds by the end of the nineteenth century. John Sigwald, writing in *School Library Journal,* called the volume "thoroughly engaging," and added that "*Bone Head* evokes empathy for the cowhands and drovers who endured the elements, outlaws, and dangerous horns of stampede-prone cattle." Focusing on the same era, *The Buffalo Train Ride* follows the path of American bison toward extinction when their grazing lands were fenced in by increasing human settlement. The book focuses on the efforts of zoologist William Hornaday to preserve the species by creating the Wichita National Forest and Game Preserve as a home for the remaining buffalo at the turn of the twentieth century. In *School Library Journal* Coop Renner wrote that Webber's "unusual story is sure to interest animal lovers" and young ecology-minded readers.

Webber once commented: "As a librarian and a writer, I have written books for fellow educators and also for children in middle elementary. My professional books are written to help teachers and librarians to encourage young people to enjoy books and to use the library. Books that I write for children are nonfiction and, hopefully, are something interesting from which to read and learn.

"With co-workers, we jointly wrote *Travel the Globe: Multicultural Story Times,* which gives a series of story-hour programs for children aged four to eight. Each chapter covers a different country and includes stories, action rhymes, finger plays, activities, and crafts. Some of the stories are retellings of folk stories and some are original tales based on a country's traditions. For example, on visiting China, I wrote an original story about a young dragon who wants to swallow the sun. This is based on an ancient belief that solar eclipses were caused by dragons swallowing the sun. People would rush into the streets banging on pots and kettles to scare the dragon away. Apparently it was an effective method of scaring dragons because the sun always returned.

"After *Travel the Globe,* I wrote a children's nonfiction title about fifteen buffalo that ride a train from the Bronx Zoo to Oklahoma Territory, in 1907, to start the first federal bison preserve in the United States. The research for *The Buffalo Train Ride* took two years, plus one year of writing. I read diaries, letters, articles, books and a first-hand account of the rain ride by a Bronx Zoo employee.

"While working on *The Buffalo Train Ride,* a colleague, Sandra Shropshire, and I began a new program in the children's department of the Moore Public Library. We developed a young readers' book discussion group for children ages five to eight. Everyone conducted book discussion programs for children nine and older but what about discussing books with emerging readers. It was a great success and we learned that young children enjoyed sharing their opinions.

"After several years, Sandra and I wrote *The Kids' Book Club: Lively Reading and Activities for Grades 1-3.* It was our hope that other librarians would pick up the book and start a young readers' club at their libraries. Sandra and I found that the book club inspired children to read and drew them and their families to the library on a weekly basis. In addition, the reading club attracted both boys and girls, accomplished and unaccomplished readers.

"*Bone Head* is a children's nonfiction book about the near demise of the longhorn cattle breed. In my opinion, this animal carved out the Wild West. If not for the longhorns, there may never have been the American cowboys, chuck wagons or trail drives. *Bone Head* focuses on their colorful history to the near extinction of the breed before they, too, were also relocated to a federal preserve.

"I became interested in writing while attending college. I wrote articles for my college paper and sought out internships with weekly newspapers and, for a year, worked for a wire service that covered the San Diego City Council and the San Diego County Commissioners meetings. I thought I wanted to be a journalist but discovered that I enjoyed writing longer pieces. It gave me an opportunity to delve into the topic more and conduct further research.

I finished by undergraduate degree in communications at the University of California, San Diego, and then I later completed a master's degree in library and information sciences at the University of Oklahoma. Following that I became a children's librarian. This position inspired me not only to write for children but also to share ideas on getting children interested in books and in using the library. It is a pleasure to write something that you are interested in or inspired by.

"As someone with a full-time career, I had to write before and after hours. Each morning I woke up at four in the morning and worked for an hour and half to two hours before getting ready for work. In the evenings I tried to write for another hour. At first I thought I would never get anything accomplished just writing two or three hours each day, but I was like Aesop's turtle—slow and stead meets the goal."

BIOGRAPHICAL AND CRITICAL SOURCES:

PERIODICALS

Booklist, August, 1998, Julie Corsaro, review of *Travel the Globe: Multicultural Story Times,* p. 2021.
School Library Journal, February, 1999, Robin L. Gibson, "It's a Small, Small World," review of *Travel the Globe,* p. 41; May, 2002, Mary Lankford, review of *The Kids' Book Club: Lively Reading and Activities for Grades 1-3,* p. 183; March, 2000, Coop Renner, review of *The Buffalo Train Ride,* p. 262; February, 2004, John Sigwald, review of *Bone Head: Story of the Longhorn,* p. 171.

*   *   *

WEINBERG, Marjorie 1934-

PERSONAL: Born April 6, 1934, in Brooklyn, NY. *Education:* University of Michigan, B.A., 1956; Adelphi University, M.A., 1960; New York University, M.A., 1990.

ADDRESSES: Agent—c/o Author Mail, University of Nebraska Press, 233 N. 8th St., Lincoln, NE 68588-0255.

CAREER: Worked as speech and language pathologist; currently retired.

WRITINGS:

The Real Rosebud: The Triumph of a Lakota Woman, University of Nebraska Press (Lincoln, NE), 2004.

SIDELIGHTS: Marjorie Weinberg told *CA:* "In order to be able to write a book about the history of the prominent Yellow Robe Lakota Sioux family, going back several generations, I realized I needed firm academic footing. I enrolled at New York University for a graduate degree in cultural anthropology. Under the direction of Dr. Karen Blu, my thesis supervisor, I wrote about Rosebud Yellow Robe and the Jones Beach State Park Indian Village. When I had completed the manuscript for my book, she introduced me to a leading expert in the history of the Lakota, Dr. Ray De Maille. He read it with enthusiasm and recommended it to the University of Nebraska Press.

"The inspiration and motivation to write *The Real Rosebud: The Triumph of a Lakota Woman* came from Rosebud Yellow Robe herself. For our more than forty-year friendship, she had shared her wish to write the history of her family. I added to her wealth of family collections with research that I did over many years. Good luck had me locate correspondence between her parents and many outstanding people. One thing led to another, and with the cooperation of many members of her family I was able to complete the story.

"As Rosebud lay dying, I promised her I would write the story of her family. With the help of many good people, I was able to keep my promise."

BIOGRAPHICAL AND CRITICAL SOURCES:

PERIODICALS

Booklist, March 1, 2004, Deborah Donovan, review of *The Real Rosebud: The Triumph of a Lakota Woman,* p. p. 1131.

Women's Review of Books, May, 2004, Bethany Towne, review of *The Real Rosebud,* p. 24.

* * *

WEINSTEIN, Miriam 1946-

PERSONAL: Born November 3, 1946, in New York, NY; daughter of Saul and Sally (Barsky) Weinstein; married Peter Feinstein, 1973; children: Mirka, Elijah. *Education:* Brandeis University, B.A., 1967; Boston University, M.S., 1969. *Religion:* Jewish.

ADDRESSES: Agent—c/o Author Mail, Steerforth Press, 25 Lebanon St., Hanover, NH 03755.

CAREER: Writer and filmmaker.

WRITINGS:

Yiddish: A Nation of Words, Steerforth Press (South Royalton, VT), 2001.
(Editor) *Prophets and Dreamers: A Selection of Great Yiddish Literature,* Steerforth Press (South Royalton, VT), 2002.
The Surprising Power of Family Meals: How Eating Together Makes Us Smarter, Stronger, Healthier, and Happier, Steerforth Press (Hanover, NH), 2005.

Also contributor to newspapers and magazines.

SIDELIGHTS: Miriam Weinstein's books have dealt with topics as far ranging as the history of the Yiddish language and the benefits of family togetherness at meals. In *Yiddish: A Nation of Words,* she explores the language that European Jews developed from Hebrew, German, and other tongues, beginning in the Middle Ages, and took with them wherever they immigrated, producing important literature along the way. She also deals with the decline of Yiddish in the mid-twentieth century; many of its speakers died in the Holocaust, and others abandoned it because of persecution or assimilation. Weinstein notes that Yiddish remains culturally influential, and she hopes Jews will again embrace it to some degree.

Weinstein is not a scholar, several critics observed, but a capable generalist who has produced an appealing volume. The book is "engaging and clearly written," commented Sanford Pinsker in the *New Criterion,* who felt that Weinstein "knows what she is talking about" and displays "a cheerleader's passion." A *Publishers Weekly* reviewer called *Yiddish* "evocative, informative and accessible," while *Midstream* contributor Jack Fischel deemed it "a riveting account . . . that is both readable and minus the jargon of a more formal academic history." Fischel, though, dubbed Weinstein's optimism about the future of the language "wishful thinking." Pinsker also thought she does not fully acknowledge that "the end of the history she has so admirably written is that 'Yiddishland,' in any meaningful sense, is gone."

In *The Surprising Power of Family Meals: How Eating Together Makes Us Smarter, Stronger, Healthier, and Happier,* Weinstein lauds another possibly vanishing feature of our culture. Parents' jobs and children's activities often keep families from having meals together, which Weinstein believes is unfortunate because gathering for dinner promotes communication and strengthens relationships. It can even help children avoid serious problems, such as eating disorders and drug abuse, she writes, offering case studies as evidence. For families unable to share an evening meal regularly, she suggests developing other times for togetherness.

Critics generally saw much that was positive in Weinstein's book, although they also expressed reservations. Some of her conclusions about the benefits of familial dining are "open to argument," commented Jonathan Yardley in the *Washington Post,* but he found her basic point "absolutely right. Family matters." A *Publishers Weekly* contributor thought her topic more suited to magazines than a full-length book but still deemed the volume "stimulating" and "persuasive." *Booklist* reviewer Mark Knoblauch concluded that Weinstein is "careful not to overstate" potential results while making goals "attractive and attainable."

BIOGRAPHICAL AND CRITICAL SOURCES:

PERIODICALS

Booklist, September 15, 2005, Mark Knoblauch, review of *The Surprising Power of Family Meals: How Eating Together Makes Us Smarter, Stronger, Healthier, and Happier,* p. 14.

Kirkus Reviews, August 1, 2001, review of *Yiddish: A Nation of Words,* p. 1109.

Library Journal, October 15, 2001, Marianne Orme, review of *Yiddish,* p. 77; November 1, 2002, Gene Shaw, review of *Prophets and Dreamers: A Selection of Great Yiddish Literature,* p. 127; September 1, 2005, Ellen D. Gilbert, review of *The Surprising Power of Family Meals,* p. 164.

Midstream, November-December, 2002, Jack Fischel, "An Informative History," review of *Yiddish,* p. 39.

New Criterion, February, 2002, Sanford Pinsker, review of *Yiddish,* p. 74.

Publishers Weekly, September 3, 2001, review of *Yiddish,* p. 80; June 6, 2005, review of *The Surprising Power of Family Meals,* p. 47.

Washington Post, August 30, 2005, Jonathan Yardley, "The Ties That Bind at Mealtime," review of *The Surprising Power of Family Meals,* p. C8.

* * *

WEISBLAT, Tinky
(Tinky "Dakota" Weisblat)

PERSONAL: Born in Morristown, NJ; daughter of Abraham (an agricultural economist) and Janice (a teacher and antique dealer; maiden name, Hallett) Weisblat. *Ethnicity:* "White." *Education:* Mount Holyoke College, A.B.; University of Tennessee at Knoxville, M.S.; University of Texas at Austin, Ph.D., 1991. *Politics:* Democrat. *Religion:* "Sometimes Unitarian, sometimes Congregationalist."

ADDRESSES: Agent—c/o Author Mail, Merry Lion Press, 84 Middle Rd., Hawley, MA 01339. *E-mail*—tinky@merrylion.com.

CAREER: Paris en Films, Paris, France, worked as assistant to the vice president; singer and freelance journalist, 1991—. Museum of Television and Radio, senior editor of catalog, 2000-02.

MEMBER: International Association of Culinary Professionals.

WRITINGS:

The Pudding Hollow Cookbook, illustrated by Judith Russell, Merry Lion Press (Hawley, MA), 2004.

TV Diners, Merry Lion Press (Hawley, MA), in press.

Contributor of essays, articles and reviews to periodicals, including *American Quarterly, Boston Globe, Washington Post, Daily Hampshire Gazette, Berkshire Eagle, Shelburne Falls and West County News, Hartford Courant,* and *Velvet Light Trap.* Some writings appear under the name Tinky "Dakota" Weisblat.

WORK IN PROGRESS: Research for *The Green Emporium Cookbook,* with Michael Collins; research for *Food to Die For,* with Alice Kendrick.

SIDELIGHTS: Tinky Weisblat told *CA:* "In my writing I try to embody my contention that there is no authentic split between the public and the private or between the intellectual and the emotional. I tend to explore issues that interest me, from my home community to American popular culture, through the rubric of food writing.

"The emphasis on food came about originally by accident. With my freshly minted Ph.D. in American cultural history, I tried to find work as a film or television critic. To my surprise, I found that most newspapers and magazines were not interested in my scholarly credentials. I eventually discovered, however, that if I layered my academic interests into food writing, I could sell articles much more easily. Eventually I came to embrace food writing (if not the pounds it has often added to my waistline) as a structure that could actually help me do some of my most analytical and creative writing.

"*The Pudding Hollow Cookbook* is a loving tribute to the community in which I live. The idea for the book came from the illustrator, the late Judith Russell. A folk artist who spent much of her time at my mother's antique shop in nearby Shelburne Falls, Judy participated with me in the bicentennial pageant of my hometown, Hawley, Massachusetts, in 1992. In the pageant I portrayed Abigail Baker, who, according to legend, won a pudding contest in town in the late 1700s. The area of town in which she lived is still known as Pudding Hollow in tribute to Mrs. Baker's culinary expertise. Judy and I put out feelers to our rural neighbors, asking for recipes that would represent the friendly community in which we lived. The result, embellished by my prose and Judy's colorful paintings, is the cookbook. I don't think anything else I've written has been as beautiful or as heartfelt.

"My recent project, *TV Diners*, provides recipes and commentary associated with fifty classic American television programs and thus brings me back to my academic roots; my dissertation explored the on-and off-screen marriages of George Burns and Gracie Allen, Ozzie Nelson and Harriet Hilliard, and Lucille Ball and Desi Arnaz. I am nourishing my brain as well as my digestive system as I sit in front of my television set, looking for food but also for lively, intelligent ways to characterize these cultural products. This is a project that has inspired friends, relatives, and even strangers to help me. Interest in television, its significance, and its food-ways seems to cross boundaries of class and occupation. I look forward to a fun book and a lively, critical audience.

"If I were to give advice to an aspiring writer, it would be this. Write about your passions; write the way you talk; and be sure to have another creative outlet to complement your writing. My singing engagements give me the opportunity to make contact with my audience directly and to express myself physically and emotionally. I believe that they enhance my writing and are enhanced by it."

BIOGRAPHICAL AND CRITICAL SOURCES:

PERIODICALS

Booklist, May 15, 2004, Stephanie Zvirin, review of *The Pudding Hollow Cookbook*, p. 1587.

*   *   *

WEISBLAT, Tinky "Dakota"
See WEISBLAT, Tinky

*   *   *

WEISEL, Al

PERSONAL: Male.

ADDRESSES: Agent—c/o Author Mail, Touchstone Publicity Dept., Simon & Schuster, Inc., 1230 Avenue of the Americas, New York, NY 10020. *E-mail*—alw63@aol.com; rebels@livefastdieyoungbook.com.

CAREER: Freelance writer. CDNow, senior movies editor, 1999-2002. Former contributing editor for *Us Magazine*.

WRITINGS:

(With Lawrence Frascella) *Live Fast, Die Young: The Wild Ride of Making "Rebel without a Cause,"* Simon & Schuster (New York, NY), 2005.

Contributor to periodicals, including *Premiere* magazine, *Rolling Stone, Spin, Tracks, George, Travel & Leisure, Out, Washington Post, Time Out New York, Bulletin* (Australia), *New York Newsday,* and *Us Magazine*.

SIDELIGHTS: A prolific freelance writer, Al Weisel joined movie and theater critic Lawrence Frascella in creating his first book, *Live Fast, Die Young: The Wild Ride of Making "Rebel without a Cause."* Directed by Nicholas Ray in 1955, the movie *Rebel without a Cause* tackled tough issues for the time. Weisel and Frascella performed extensive research in studio archives and conducted interviews with accessible cast members to bring readers onto the set and into the minds of the cast and crew who participated in creating the landmark film. The authors detail how Ray drew from his own life in developing the dysfunctional relationship between Jim (played by James Dean) and his father.

In *Live Fast, Die Young,* Weisel and Frascella also reveal the origins of many of the film's famous symbols (including Dean's red jacket), the intricacies of the scriptwriting and casting for the movie, and the political dynamics of on-set affairs that dominated during production. The result of the authors' investigative work is a "well-researched study" and "riveting insider's account" that is "as dramatic and provocative as the movie," wrote Rosellen Brewer in the *Library Journal*. Expressing a similar high regard for the book, the *Kirkus Reviews* contributor maintained that *Live Fast, Die Young* is "at times more interesting than the movie itself."

BIOGRAPHICAL AND CRITICAL SOURCES:

PERIODICALS

Booklist, September 15, 2005, Gordon Flagg, review of *Live Fast, Die Young: The Wild Ride of Making "Rebel without a Cause,"* p. 17.

Kirkus Reviews, September 1, 2005, review of *Live Fast, Die Young,* p. 954.

Library Journal, October 1, 2005, Rosellen Brewer, review of *Live Fast, Die Young,* p. 77.

Publishers Weekly, August 29, 2005, review of *Live Fast, Die Young,* p. 46.

ONLINE

Al Weisel Home Page, http://home.nyc.rr.com/alweisel (January 16, 2006).*

*   *   *

WHITE, Jenny
    See WHITE, Jenny B.

*   *   *

WHITE, Jenny B. 1953-
    (Jenny White, Jenny Barbara White)

PERSONAL: Born 1953. *Education:* City University of New York, B.A.; Hacettepe University, Ankara, Turkey, M.A.; University of Texas, Austin, Ph.D.

ADDRESSES: Home—MA. *Office*—Department of Anthropology, Boston University, 232 Bay State Rd., Boston, MA 02215. *E-mail*—jbwhite@bu.edu.

CAREER: Educator and author. Boston University, associate professor of anthropology.

AWARDS, HONORS: Douglass Prize for best book in Europeanist anthropology, 2003, for *Islamist Mobilization in Turkey: A Study in Vernacular Politics.*

WRITINGS:

Money Makes Us Relatives: Women's Labor in Urban Turkey, University of Texas Press (Austin, TX), 1994, 2nd edition, Routledge (New York, NY), 2004.

Islamist Mobilization in Turkey: A Study in Vernacular Politics, University of Washington Press (Seattle, WA), 2002.

The Sultan's Seal (novel), W.W. Norton (New York, NY), 2006.

Also author of numerous articles about Islamic politics, women and Islam, family life, women's labor, small commodity production, and Turks in Germany.

WORK IN PROGRESS: A book about changing conceptions of Islam in Turkey.

SIDELIGHTS: Professor of anthropology Jenny B. White specializes in the regions of Turkey, the Middle East, and Germany, and has taught courses and written extensively on the anthropology, ethnicity, identity, and gender roles in these regions. First published in 1994 and fully revised in 2004, White's *Money Makes Us Relatives: Women's Labor in Urban Turkey* examines, according to Natasha Hall of the *Middle East Journal,* "why Turkey devalues women's work." White details how women in Turkey—specifically in Istanbul—spend as much as fifty hours per week creating goods to be sold throughout the world. In addition, she explains how women's labor influences their social networks. As Arlene Elowe MacLeod remarked in *Signs,* White's "research on the working-class woman and the ideological discourses shaping women's behavior in the Turkish context is a useful addition to the knowledge of gender roles and the intersection of developing world and capitalist economies."

In 2002, White released *Islamist Mobilization in Turkey: A Study in Vernacular Politics,* which, according to Christian Pond of *JMEWS: Journal of Middle East Women's Studies,* "examines how Islamist political parties in Turkey have been able to mobilize their constituencies and add to their growing political power and popularity." White believes that the Islamists' success is directly related to "vernacular politics," which she explains as their ability to use local networks and civic organizations to gain support. While Pond questioned a few of White's conclusions and felt that "there are a few aspects of the work that warrant further consideration," the reviewer considered the book "a wonderful and well-researched ethnography." Likewise, Quinn Mecham of the *Political Science Quarterly* found that "the book makes a profound contribution to our understanding of a localized political process in value-laden contexts."

White's first novel, *The Sultan's Seal,* is set in Turkey near the end of the Ottoman Empire. When a young Englishwoman who works for the sultan is found dead, magistrate Kamil Pasha launches an investigation into the murder and its possible connection to the murder of an English governess years earlier. *Booklist* reviewer Brad Hooper noted that the "impressive first novel rests securely on the author's background," while a *Publishers Weekly* critic found the book's writing to be "lyrical" and the characters "enchanting."

BIOGRAPHICAL AND CRITICAL SOURCES:

PERIODICALS

Booklist, November 15, 2005, Brad Hooper, review of *The Sultan's Seal,* p. 24.
JMEWS: Journal of Middle East Women's Studies, May, 2005, Christian Pond, review of *Islamist Mobilization in Turkey: A Study in Vernacular Politics,* p. 144.
Journal of the Royal Anthropological Institute, September, 1995, Lale Yalcin-Heckmann, review of *Money Makes Us Relatives: Women's Labor in Urban Turkey,* p. 670.
Kirkus Reviews, October 15, 2005, review of *The Sultan's Seal,* p. 1106.
Library Journal, December 1, 2005, Kathy Piehl, review of *The Sultan's Seal,* p. 117.
Middle East Journal, summer, 2003, Farha Ghannam, review of *Islamist Mobilization in Turkey,* p. 517; autumn, 2005, Natasha Hall, review of *Money Makes Us Relatives,* p. 702.
Political Science Quarterly, fall, 2003, Quinn Mecham, review of *Islamist Mobilization in Turkey,* p. 526.
Publishers Weekly, May 23, 2005, John F. Baker, "From Small Acorns," p. 14; October 10, 2005, review of *The Sultan's Seal,* p. 32.
Signs, spring, 1997, Arlene Elowe MacLeod, review of *Money Makes Us Relatives,* p. 757.

ONLINE

Boston University Web site, http://www.bu.edu/ (January 17, 2006), "Department of Anthropology Faculty."
Jenny B. White Home Page, http://www.jennywhite. net/ (July 11, 2006).

WHITE, Jenny Barbara
    See WHITE, Jenny B.

                    *   *   *

WILENTZ, Sean 1951-

PERSONAL: Born 1951. *Education:* Columbia University, B.A., 1972; Oxford University, Balliol College, B.A., 1974; Yale University, Ph.D., 1980.

ADDRESSES: Home—Princeton, NJ. *Office*— Princeton University, 134 Dickinson Hall, Rm. 129, Princeton, NJ 08544.

CAREER: Princeton University, Princeton, NJ, Dayton-Stockton Professor of History and director of American studies program.

AWARDS, HONORS: Albert J. Beveridge Award, American Historical Association, for *Chants Democratic: New York and the Rise of the American Working Class, 1788-1850.*

WRITINGS:

Chants Democratic: New York and the Rise of the American Working Class, 1788-1850, Oxford University Press (New York, NY), 1984, 20th anniversary edition, 2004.
(Editor) *Rites of Power: Symbolism, Ritual, and Politics since the Middle Ages,* University of Pennsylvania Press (Philadelphia, PA), 1985.
(Editor) *Major Problems in the Early Republic, 1787-1848: Documents and Essays,* D.C. Heath (Lexington, MA), 1992.
(Editor and author of introduction, with Michael Merrill) William Manning, *The Key of Liberty: The Life and Democratic Writings of William Manning, "a Laborer," 1747-1814,* Harvard University Press (Cambridge, MA), 1993.
(With Paul E. Johnson) *The Kingdom of Matthias: A Story of Sex and Salvation in 19th Century America,* Oxford University Press (New York, NY), 1994.
(Editor, with Greil Marcus) *The Rose & the Briar: Death, Love, and Liberty in the American Ballad,* W.W. Norton (New York, NY), 2005.

The Rise of American Democracy: Jefferson to Lincoln, W.W. Norton (New York, NY), 2005.

Andrew Jackson (biography), Times Books (New York, NY), 2005.

Contributor to periodicals, including the *New York Times, Los Angeles Times, New York Review of Books, London Review of Books, American Scholar, Le Monde,* and the *Nation,* and to Web site *Salon.com;* also author of liner notes for the *Bootleg Series, Volume 6: Bob Dylan Live 1964—Concert at Philharmonic Hall* by Bob Dylan. Contributing editor, *New Republic.*

ADAPTATIONS: The Rose & the Briar: Death, Love, and Liberty in the American Ballad was adapted as a sound recording, Columbia/Legacy (New York, NY), 2005.

SIDELIGHTS: Sean Wilentz is a professor of American social and political history, with a particular interest in the early years of the nation and in Jacksonian democracy. His work reflects these preoccupations, focusing primarily on late eighteenth-century and early nineteenth-century American politics and history. His first book, *Chants Democratic: New York and the Rise of the American Working Class, 1788-1850,* starts with the ratification of the Constitution and traces the development of the working class in New York City until the middle of the nineteenth century. Wilentz discusses how class distinctions developed along political lines, and not just economics, after the Revolution, as well as how industrialization during this time period affected the rise of working class people. New York City was particularly productive, with smaller scale industries such as clothing manufacturing and printing making up a large portion of available work. In an article for the *New Republic,* Herbert G. Gutman called Wilentz's effort "the best book yet written about the emergence of New York City's working class and a major contribution to American working-class history." Gutman went on to conclude that "no one has written more searchingly about how the rapid intrusion of market capitalism split artisan republican ideology and led working men and women to redefine their political and economic status by remaking older American beliefs."

In *The Key of Liberty: The Life and Democratic Writings of William Manning, "a Laborer," 1747-1814,* which Wilentz edited with Michael Merrill, readers are allowed to take a look into the mind of Revolution-era farmer William Manning, who defended Concord in 1775. Wilentz and Merrill provide an introduction and translation of sorts that shows the viewpoints commonly held by people regarding class around the time of the birth of the United States. Linda K. Kerber remarked in a review for the *Nation* that "they offer us Manning as evidence that class consciousness developed in the revolutionary era and that the struggle to build a plebeian democracy persisted long after the Revolution was over." She went on to note, however, that despite having knowledge of Manning's wife and family, Merrill and Wilentz fail to "inquire into the ways in which eighteenth-century laws of domestic relations—laws that even the most radical revolutionaries took care to keep in place—gave husbands control over their wives' persons and property and even, occasionally, adult sons control over their widowed mothers' persons and property," an oversight that reflects on the social and class structure of that time period.

The Kingdom of Matthias: A Story of Sex and Salvation in 19th Century America, by Wilentz and Paul E. Johnson, takes a very different look at American history and social structure than that of Wilentz's previous efforts. The book examines the rise of a small religious cult in New York City in the 1830s, the Kingdom of Matthias, which was led by Robert Matthews, a carpenter who set about creating a new religion with himself as its central figure. While the cult itself served as fodder for the tabloids of the day, it also was part of a major religious revival in the United States that saw the birth of the Mormons and the spread of Baptist and Methodist denominations. *Journal of Social History* contributor Perry Bush called the book "a marvelous tale that not only knits together some of the major interstices of the national scandal it became—salvation, sex, murder—but also reveals much about the sexual and economic underpinnings of nineteenth-century American evangelicalism." The critic added, however, that "at times the authors appear to squeeze the sources too hard, and cloud the account with isolated bits of tedium." On the other hand, *Nation* reviewer Michael P. Johnson considered the book "an elegant and provocative narrative, composed in ways that illuminate the odd angles at which their characters approached one another. It takes literary skill as well as historical mastery to stay responsible to the current of incurable loneliness that informs this and other American religious experiments."

With *The Rise of American Democracy: Jefferson to Lincoln,* Wilentz revisits the development of the

United States from the late eighteenth century to the mid-nineteenth century, offering a narrative history of the nation. His primary goal is to illustrate how the foundations of the country were not firmly entrenched in democratic principles, but how the seeds of the concept gradually spread until they formed the broader policies of the country that were challenged by and survived the Civil War. Malcolm Jones, in a review for *Newsweek*, found Wilentz's book to be "a magnificent chronicle, the life of an idea that, although it is mentioned nowhere in the Constitution, nevertheless slowly elbowed its way into the heart of American life." A contributor for the *Economist* called the volume "a dense, authoritative and well-written study. It has been ten years in the making, and brings together an impressive accrual of detail."

Continuing with his focus on the development of American democracy, Wilentz's biography *Andrew Jackson*, provides a history of Jackson's presidency and all of its controversies. *Library Journal* reviewer Bryan Craig declared the book "a great first read for students and general readers because of its affordability, new assessments, and writing style," while a contributor to *Kirkus Reviews* concluded that "Wilentz does a solid job of explaining the contributions of the Jackson presidency."

BIOGRAPHICAL AND CRITICAL SOURCES:

PERIODICALS

American Heritage, December, 1994, review of *The Kingdom of Matthias: A Story of Sex and Salvation in 19th Century America*, p. 126.

American Prospect, November, 2005, Alan Taylor, "Democratic Storytelling," review of *The Rise of American Democracy: Jefferson to Lincoln*, p. 42.

American Scholar, autumn, 2005, Richard E. Nicholls, "Power to the People: Winning the Revolution Did Not Assure Ordinary Americans a Role in Governing Themselves," review of *The Rise of American Democracy*, p. 134.

Artforum, December, 2004-January, 2005, Andrew Hultkrans, review of *The Rose & the Briar: Death, Love, and Liberty in the American Ballad*, p. 28.

Booklist, April 1, 1994, Brian McCombie, review of *The Kingdom of Matthias*, p. 1409; November 15, 2004, Ray Olson, review of *The Rose & the Briar*,

p. 542; September 15, 2005, Vanessa Bush, review of *The Rise of American Democracy*, p. 23; December 15, 2005, Ray Olson, review of *Andrew Jackson*, p. 16.

Choice, April, 2005, R.D. Cohen, review of *The Rose & the Briar*, p. 1410.

Economist, October 29, 2005, "The People's Road: American Democracy," review of *The Rise of American Democracy*, p. 89.

Journal of Social History, spring, 1997, Perry Bush, review of *The Kingdom of Matthias*, p. 739.

Kirkus Reviews, August 1, 2005, review of *The Rise of American Democracy*, p. 841; November 1, 2005, review of *Andrew Jackson*, p. 1180.

Library Journal, October 15, 2004, David Szatmary, review of *The Rose & the Briar*, p. 65; September 15, 2005, Steven Puro, review of *The Rise of American Democracy*, p. 76; December 1, 2005, Bryan Craig, review of *Andrew Jackson*, p. 142.

Nation, July 19, 1993, Linda K. Kerber, review of *The Key of Liberty: The Life and Democratic Writings of William Manning, "a Laborer," 1747-1814*, p. 108; November 14, 1994, Michael P. Johnson, review of *The Kingdom of Matthias*, p. 588.

National Review, November 7, 2005, Michael Knox Beran, "Telling No Tales," review of *The Rise of American Democracy*, p. 51.

New Republic, July 9, 1984, Herbert G. Gutman, review of *Chants Democratic: New York and the Rise of the American Working Class, 1788-1850*, p. 33; October 17, 1994, Lee Rust Brown, review of *The Kingdom of Matthias*, p. 52.

Newsweek, October 31, 2005, Malcolm Jones, "America from Tom to Abe: A Hip Historian's Take on How Democracy Took Root," p. 56.

New Yorker, December 6, 2004, review of *The Rose & the Briar*, p. 108; October 24, 2005, Jill Lepore, review of *The Rise of American Democracy*, p. 80.

New York Times Book Review, November 13, 2005, Gordon S. Wood, "A Constant Struggle," review of *The Rise of American Democracy*, pp. 10-11.

Publishers Weekly, April 18, 1994, review of *The Kingdom of Matthias*, p. 53; October 18, 2004, review of *The Rose & the Briar*, p. 58; August 1, 2005, review of *The Rise of American Democracy*, p. 57; October 31, 2005, review of *Andrew Jackson*, p. 42.

Sing Out!, spring, 2005, Michael Tearson, review of *The Rose & the Briar*, p. 107.

ONLINE

Princeton Packet Online, http://www.princetonpacket.com/ (March 15, 2006), information on author.

Princeton University History Department Web site, http://his.princeton.edu/ (March 15, 2006), author profile.*

*   *   *

WILLARD, Dale C.

PERSONAL: Married. *Education:* University of Oklahoma, B.A., 1959.

ADDRESSES: Home—Lafayette, CO. *Agent*—Stacey Glick, Dystel & Goderich Literary Management, One Union Square W., New York, NY 10003.

CAREER: Writer. Has worked variously as an engineer, a high school history teacher, a high school English teacher, and in educational films.

WRITINGS:

My Son, My Brother, My Friend: A Novel in Letters, InterVarsity Press (Downers Grove, IL), 1978, Cornerstone Press Chicago (Chicago, IL), 1995.
The Linnet's Tale, illustrated by James Noel Smith, Scribner (New York, NY), 2002.

SIDELIGHTS: Dale C. Willard's debut novel, *My Son, My Brother, My Friend: A Novel in Letters,* highlights the correspondence of four men. Through their letters, readers learn about their lives and desires. The book, originally published in 1978, was reprinted seventeen years later.

For his next literary undertaking, Willard crafted a "children's book" for adults. *The Linnet's Tale* takes place in the town of Tottensea Burrows, populated primarily by field mice and one linnet (or finch), named Waterford Hopstep, who fell out of a tree as a fledgling, was abandoned by his parents, and was raised by kindly mice. As the narrator of the story, Waterford introduces readers to an array of characters with unusual names: Merchanty Swift is a young, debonair mouse who performs an important heroic act; Mr. and Mrs. Fieldpea and their daughters, Almandine, Grenadine, and Incarnadine, own the town's bookstore; Opportune Baggs is the town inventor and creator of a Mousewriter machine. Dozens of other characters inhabit the quiet town—quiet, that is, until a feline moves in amidst the mice and pirate rats threaten the town's tranquility.

"You will want to live in Tottensea Burrows once you have read about it," remarked Mary Jessica Hammes in a review published on the *Online Athens* Web site. "The story is engaging and clever, filled with witty (not cumbersome) verbiage." A *Kirkus Reviews* contributor felt that *The Linnet's Tale* "should amuse the most childlike adults—and the most grown-up of children." In a review for *Booklist,* Michele Leber maintained: "These are endearing creatures, and their story is a charming one for all ages."

Willard explained to Hammes that the idea for the book came to him when he discovered a group of field mice eating from his dog's food dish. When Willard noticed the holes they had burrowed in his backyard, the author began concocting their imaginary world, and Tottensea Burrows was born. "It's an unusual story for adults," Willard told Hammes. "But I've always admired *The Wind in the Willows.*"

BIOGRAPHICAL AND CRITICAL SOURCES:

PERIODICALS

Booklist, March 15, 2002, Michele Leber, review of *The Linnet's Tale,* p. 1214.
Kirkus Reviews, January 15, 2002, review of *The Linnet's Tale,* p. 71.
Publishers Weekly, February 18, 2002, review of *The Linnet's Tale,* p. 74.

ONLINE

Online Athens Web site, http://www.onlineathens.com/ (May 13, 2002), Mary Jessica Hammes, "Charming Tale of Where the Wild Things Live," review of *The Linnet's Tale.*

*   *   *

WILSON, Dolores J.

PERSONAL: Born in Morgantown, WV.

ADDRESSES: Agent—c/o Author Mail, Medallion Press, 27825 N. Forest Garden Rd., Wauconda, IL 60084. *E-mail*—dj@doloresjwilson.com.

CAREER: Writer.

WRITINGS:

Big Hair and Flying Cows, Medallion Press (Palm Beach, FL), 2004.
Little Big Heart, Medallion Press (Palm Beach, FL), 2005.

WORK IN PROGRESS: Barking Goats and the Redneck Mafia, a new novel featuring Bertie Byrd.

SIDELIGHTS: "I like to make people smile, and if I can make them laugh out loud, that's even better," author Dolores J. Wilson revealed on her Web site. Perhaps that's why in her debut novel, *Big Hair and Flying Cows,* she created the fun, wacky denizens of Sweet Meadow, Georgia.

Big Hair and Flying Cows features Bertie Byrd, whose life could be described as anything but ordinary. Bertie works at her father's auto repair shop, drives a tow truck that the residents of Sweet Meadow treat as a taxi, gets visited by the senile (and often naked) old man who used to live in her house, and lately has been receiving notes from a stalker who calls himself "Jack." When Bertie goes to the courthouse to apply for a permit to park her tow truck in her driveway, she discovers that the official notices instructing her to do so were signed by a dead man. Writing for *School Library Journal,* Erin Dennington observed, "Although Wilson's debut novel can sometimes seem over-the-top, it's still a wonderful read." Conveying a similar sentiment, a reviewer for *Publishers Weekly* called *Big Hair and Flying Cows* "an affectionate chronicle of one woman's discovery that commitment, support, and trust are closer than she thought."

BIOGRAPHICAL AND CRITICAL SOURCES:

PERIODICALS

Publishers Weekly, February 28, 2005, review of *Big Hair and Flying Cows,* p. 42.

School Library Journal, August, 2005, Erin Dennington, review of *Big Hair and Flying Cows,* p. 152.

ONLINE

Dolores J. Wilson Home Page, http://www.doloresj wilson.com (February 5, 2006).

*   *   *

WINTER, Michael 1965-

PERSONAL: Born 1965, in England.

ADDRESSES: Home—Canada. *Agent*—c/o Author Mail, Bloomsbury USA, 175 5th Ave., New York, NY 10010.

CAREER: Writer.

AWARDS, HONORS: Newfoundland Arts and Letters Competition, three-time winner; Winterset Award, for *This All Happened: A Fictional Memoir;* Drummer General's Award, A Different Drummer Books, for *The Big Why.*

WRITINGS:

(Editor in chief) *Extremities: Fiction from the Burning Rock* (short stories), Killick Press (St. John's, Newfoundland, Canada), 1994.
Creaking in Their Skins (short stories), Quarry Press (Kingston, Ontario, Canada), 1994.
One Last Good Look (short stories), Porcupine's Quill (Erin, Ontario, Canada), 1999.
This All Happened: A Fictional Memoir (novel), House of Anansi Press (Toronto, Ontario, Canada), 2000.
The Big Why (novel), House of Anansi Press (Toronto, Ontario, Canada), 2004, Bloomsbury (New York, NY), 2006.

Contributor of short fiction to various periodicals, and to CBC Radio's *Between the Covers.*

SIDELIGHTS: English-born Michael Winter grew up in Newfoundland, Canada, an area that infuses the settings of much of his fiction. Two of his short-story collections, *Creaking in Their Skins* and *One Last Good Look,* follow the adventures of Gabriel English as he grows up in Newfoundland and eventually sets out to explore the world. The stories themselves offer a range of experiences and emotions, including love, the death of family members, sibling relationships, romantic failures, and enduring friendship. Gabriel English later reappears as the hero of Winter's first novel, *This All Happened: A Fictional Memoir,* a diary-style story that examines the development of a relationship over a one-year period while Gabriel writes a historical novel set in Newfoundland. A contributor for *Resource Links* remarked that "the actual story is highly crafted and a pleasure to read."

The Big Why, a fictional account of the year artist Rockwell Kent spent in Newfoundland with his family in 1914, is the historical novel that Gabriel English was supposedly writing during *This All Happened.* The novel traces Kent's departure from New York City in search of a change of scenery and his experiences during that period. *Library Journal* critic Leann Restaino called the book "a very slow-moving read," while a *Kirkus Reviews* contributor found it "a highly entertaining and ultimately profound novel of a quixotic man who reveres nature's awful beauty."

BIOGRAPHICAL AND CRITICAL SOURCES:

PERIODICALS

Entertainment Weekly, January 27, 2006, Michelle Kung, review of *The Big Why,* p. 89.
Kirkus Reviews, November 1, 2005, review of *The Big Why,* p. 1163.
Library Journal, December 1, 2005, Leann Restaino, review of *The Big Why,* p. 117.
Maclean's, October 4, 2004, Brian Bethune, "Lies, Secrets, Conundrums," review of *The Big Why,* p. 44.
Publishers Weekly, October 3, 2005, review of *The Big Why,* p. 47.
Resource Links, October, 2000, review of *This All Happened: A Fictional Memoir,* p. 48.

ONLINE

House of Anansi Press Web site, http://www.anansi.ca/ (March 15, 2006), brief biography of author.

Michael Winter's Web log, http://mhardywinter. blogspot.com (March 15, 2006).*

*   *   *

WINTERS, Shelley 1922(?)-2006
   (Shirley Schrift)

OBITUARY NOTICE— See index for *CA* sketch: Born August 18, 1922 (some sources say 1923 or 1920), in St. Louis, MO; died of heart failure, January 14, 2006, in Beverly Hills, CA. Actor and author. Winters, who won two Oscars for best supporting actress, became known in her later career for her gift for comedy and character acting. Getting into acting as a teenager, Winters tried out unsuccessfully for the role of Scarlet O'Hara in *Gone with the Wind.* The experience did encourage her acting ambitions, however. She graduated from New York's New Theater School and found work as a dress model and in summer stock theater. She took acting workshops at the New School after studies at Wayne State University and won a small part in the 1940 play *Conquest in April.* Her early career was a struggle and included finding work as an entertainer at hotels in the Catskills, in vaudeville, and in Off-Broadway plays. After appearing in the Broadway show *Rosalinda,* she was noticed by Columbia Studios head Harry Cohn, who signed her in 1942, but she only received small roles. While living in Hollywood, Winters shared an apartment with Marilyn Monroe, and in her memoirs she later credited herself for teaching Monroe how to pose seductively with her mouth slightly open, a look that became a Monroe trademark. Winters's first big movie break came with her supporting role in *A Double Life* (1947), in which she played a waitress who is murdered. Other notable parts came in such films as *The Great Gatsby* (1949) and *A Place in the Sun* (1951); the latter earned her an Academy Award nomination. Oscars for best supporting actress came with *The Diary of Anne Frank* (1959) and *A Patch of Blue* (1965). Winters embraced strong acting roles and enjoyed her growing reputation for her comical, bawdy characters, creating memorable parts such as in 1972's *The Poseidon Adventure,* in which she played a kindly, heroic, middle-aged woman who sacrifices her life for others; conversely, she played a bizarrely loveable yet murderous mother figure in the 1970 cult classic *Bloody Mama.* She also was notable in her television appearances, winning a Cannes Festival

International Television Award for best actress in 1965, and an Emmy Award in 1964 for best actress in *Two Is the Number.* After 1976's *Next Stop, Greenwich Village* and *The Tenant,* Winters appeared somewhat less often in movies. However, she still gained memorable roles in such films as *Heavy* (1995) and *Portrait of a Lady* (1996). She recorded her life story in two memoirs: *Shelley: Also Known As Shirley* (1980) and *Shelley II: The Middle of My Century* (1989).

OBITUARIES AND OTHER SOURCES:

BOOKS

Winters, Shelley, *Shelley: Also Known As Shirley,* Morrow (New York, NY), 1980.
Winters, Shelley, *Shelley II: The Middle of My Century,* Simon & Schuster (New York, NY), 1989.

PERIODICALS

Los Angeles Times, January 15, 2006, p. B12.
New York Times, January 16, 2006, p. A14.
Times (London, England), January 16, 2006, p. 51.
Washington Post, January 15, 2006, p. C9.

*   *   *

WITHAM, Larry 1952-
  (Larry A. Witham)

PERSONAL: Born in 1952.

ADDRESSES: Home—Burtonsville, MD. *Agent*—c/o Author Mail, Oxford University Press, 198 Madison Ave., New York, NY 10016.

CAREER: Journalist and author. Former reporter for the *Washington Times.*

AWARDS, HONORS: Cornell Award, Religion Newswriter's Association; Templeton Foundation award for articles on science and religion; three-time recipient of the Wilbur Award, Religion Communicators Council,

including: 2000, for "Seeking the Spirit: America's Churches in the 21st Century," and 2002, for "Pulpits in Peril: The Future of America's Clergy."

WRITINGS:

Rodzianko: An Orthodox Journey from Revolution to Millennium, 1917-1988, University Press of America (Lanham, MD), 1991.
The Negev Project: A Novel, Meridian Books (College Park, MD), 1994.
Dark Blossom: A Novel of East and West, Meridian Books (Burtonsville, MD), 1997.
(As Larry A. Witham) *Where Darwin Meets the Bible: Creationists and Evolutionists in America,* Oxford University Press (New York, NY), 2002.
By Design: Science and the Search for God, Encounter Books (San Francisco, CA), 2003.
The Measure of God: Our Century-Long Struggle to Reconcile Science and Religion, HarperSanFrancisco (San Francisco, CA), 2005.
(As Larry A. Witham) *Who Shall Lead Them?: The Future of Ministry in America,* Oxford University Press (New York, NY), 2005.

SIDELIGHTS: Journalist Larry Witham is best known for his writings on science and religion. In his *Where Darwin Meets the Bible: Creationists and Evolutionists in America,* Witham examines the age-old debate between creationists and evolutionists as to the origin of human beings. Witham also introduces a third theory, intelligent design, and explains how the lines between science and religion are often indistinct. In compiling the book, Witham conducted interviews with major names on all sides of the debate in an attempt to offer a neutral analysis of all theories, though he does predict that intelligent design will eventually overtake evolution as the most widely accepted scientific theory. The author also provides a wealth of biographical information on each of the debate's key players.

In a review of *Where Darwin Meets the Bible* for the *Christian Century,* religion and philosophy teacher Greg Peterson expressed the belief that Witham "brings together an impressive breadth of material" in the book, though Peterson also suggested that the author gives "little attention to what makes the intelligent design movement distinct from the earlier creation-science." However, Peterson ultimately acknowledged that "the book's most valuable contribution . . . is its detailed recording of the see-saw battle over the teaching and public funding of evolutionary and creationist viewpoints." *Science* contributor Kenneth R. Miller rendered the book "a virtual playbill that describes the principal actors in this modern passion play." Miller continued, "Any scientist tempted to believe that the major figures in the anti-evolution movement are half-hearted, insincere, or simply opportunistic in their assault against mainstream science would do well to read this book." One *Publishers Weekly* contributor commented on the author's "impeccable reportage, his erudite analysis, and his ability to synthesize complex and nuanced strains of thought," calling the book an "invaluable roadmap" to this controversy.

Witham's next book is a follow-up to *Where Darwin Meets the Bible. By Design: Science and the Search for God* further explores the relationship between intelligent design and religion. Witham explains how science and religion merge to form what has become known as "creation science." *World and I* contributor Gene Levinson felt that in this book, Witham "does an excellent job of describing the spectrum of beliefs over a broad range of subjects in nonjudgmental terms," and he "makes insightful connections between diverse specialties and disciplines and provides much-needed perspective." One *Publishers Weekly* contributor remarked, "Witham adeptly charts the course of the science and religion dialogue as the participants continue to search for common ground."

Near the end of the nineteenth century, a wealthy Scottish judge, Lord Gifford, donated his fortune to four Scottish universities in order to initiate a lecture series that would address the promotion and advancement of natural theology. Witham traces the history of this lecture series, the Gifford Lectures, in his *The Measure of God: Our Century-Long Struggle to Reconcile Science and Religion.* The book includes lecture summaries addressing topics in the fields of theology, psychology, sociology, philosophy, and history; profiles of some of the series's most renowned presenters; and synopses of historical and social ideas that have contributed to the advancement of theology. "Witham includes an impressive range of materials for a single volume," wrote a contributor to *Publishers Weekly,* who also termed the book "deeply researched and factually rich." In a *Library Journal* review,

Charles Seymour remarked that *The Measure of God* is "commendable for its engaging style, thorough research, and neutral stance."

Witham's next book, *Who Shall Lead Them?: The Future of Ministry in America,* considers some issues faced by modern Catholic and Protestant clergy. In it, Witham attempts to discover whether American clergy are in crisis, or if a readjustment of clerical roles is necessary in changing times. Witham examines the effect of modern issues on the clergy, such as the sex-abuse scandals in the Catholic Church, the introduction of homosexuals into the ministry, the evolution of the role of women in the ministry, the waning of resources that has made it necessary for some clerics to seek second jobs, and other challenging issues faced by the modern ministry. Witham draws on recent religious studies to make his points, and ponders how the ministry of the future will overcome these problems. In the *Wilson Quarterly,* reviewer Michele Dillon wrote that with this book, Witham "succeed[s] in providing a comprehensive, historically informed, and heavily empirical (if somewhat breathless) overview of the major concerns" surrounding the ministry of the new millennium. Expressing a similar opinion of the book, *Library Journal* contributor Augustine J. Curley described *Who Shall Lead Them?* as "insightful" and "valuable," stating that Witham "offers a balanced and nuanced view of several key aspects of contemporary ministry."

BIOGRAPHICAL AND CRITICAL SOURCES:

PERIODICALS

America, September 8, 2003, Howard J. Van Till, "What Kind of God?," review of *By Design: Science and the Search for God,* p. 24.

Booklist, March 15, 2003, Bryce Christensen, review of *By Design,* p. 1257.

Christian Century, February 24, 2004, Greg Peterson, review of *Where Darwin Meets the Bible: Creationists and Evolutionists in America,* p. 53; October 4, 2005, J. Nelson Kraybill, "Making Leaders," review of *Who Shall Lead Them?: The Future of Ministry in America,* p. 34.

Journal of Religion, April, 2004, Ronald L. Numbers, review of *Where Darwin Meets the Bible,* p. 291.

Library Journal, November 1, 2002, H. James Birx, review of *Where Darwin Meets the Bible,* p. 126; June 1, 2005, Augustine J. Curley, review of *Who*

Shall Lead Them?, p. 140; July 1, 2005, Charles Seymour, review of *The Measure of God: Our Century-Long Struggle to Reconcile Science and Religion,* p. 88.

Publishers Weekly, October 21, 2002, review of *Where Darwin Meets the Bible,* p. 65; March 10, 2003, review of *By Design,* p. 69; May 2, 2005, review of *Who Shall Lead Them?,* p. 192; July 11, 2005, review of *The Measure of God,* p. 86.

Science, January 31, 2003, Kenneth R. Miller, "The Emperor's New Design," review of *Where Darwin Meets the Bible,* p. 664.

Wilson Quarterly, autumn, 2005, Michele Dillon, review of *Who Shall Lead Them?,* p. 125.

World and I, October, 2003, Gene Levinson, review of *By Design,* p. 226.

ONLINE

Oxford University Press Web site, http://www.oup.com/ (February 5, 2006), "About the Author," description of *Who Shall Lead Them?**

*   *   *

WITHAM, Larry A.
    See WITHAM, Larry

*   *   *

WOOD, Ann 1970-

PERSONAL: Born 1970; children: Sam. *Education:* Attended Bennington College.

ADDRESSES: Home—Cape Cod, MA. *Agent*—c/o Author Mail, Leapfrog Press, P.O. Box 1495, Wellfleet, MA 02667.

CAREER: Writer. Currently a newspaper staff reporter.

AWARDS, HONORS: Award for arts and entertainment reporting, New England Press Association.

WRITINGS:

Bolt Risk (novel), Leapfrog Press (St. Paul, MN), 2005.

SIDELIGHTS: In a 2005 interview with Jillian Weise in the *Provincetown Banner,* author Ann Wood commented on contemporary fiction: "I think everybody is getting too academic and worried about pretty sentences instead of telling a good story. . . . I'm jealous of the pretty sentence guys, . . . but I don't write that way."

In a *Kirkus Reviews* critique of Wood's debut novel, *Bolt Risk,* a contributor described the author's writing style as "almost hypnotically spare prose." Written in the first person, the story begins with the narrator quitting her job as a personal assistant for a mediocre actress. She takes a job as an exotic dancer and meets Adam, a member of the rock band Z. After a short romance, they marry in the church of Satan, and Adam goes on tour, leaving the narrator alone to drink, smoke, dabble in drugs, and look for casual-sex partners. Eventually, the narrator's destructive behavior leads her to a mental institution, where she gains some introspection.

In *Publishers Weekly,* a reviewer acknowledged that the book contains "a genuine sentiment that speaks to alienated teenagers, world-weary hipsters and cynical survivors." Regarding the narrator of *Bolt Risk,* Wood acknowledged in the *Provincetown Banner* interview that "the difference between this and other girl books, is that she's angry like the guys are angry. And most girls want some kind of pity, want you to feel sorry for them, but she doesn't."

BIOGRAPHICAL AND CRITICAL SOURCES:

PERIODICALS

Kirkus Reviews, September 1, 2005, review of *Bolt Risk,* p. 942.

Provincetown Banner (Provincetown, MA), November 10, 2005, Jillian Weise, "Up and Coming Writer Gets Down and Dirty," interview with Ann Wood.

Publishers Weekly, August 29, 2005, review of *Bolt Risk,* p. 29.*

*   *   *

WYNNE, Ben 1961-
    (Benjamin R. Wynne)

PERSONAL: Born April 22, 1961, in Jackson, MS; son of George Ervin and Patricia Dear (Mullican) Wynne. *Ethnicity:* "Caucasian." *Education:* Millsaps

College, B.A., 1984; Mississippi College, M.A., 1995; University of Mississippi, Ph.D., 2000.

ADDRESSES: Agent—c/o Author Mail, Mercer University Press, 1400 Coleman Ave., Macon, GA 31207. *E-mail*—brw22@earthlink.net.

CAREER: Writer and historian.

MEMBER: American Historical Association, Organization of American Historians, Southern Historical Association.

WRITINGS:

A Hard Trip: A History of the 15th Mississippi Infantry, C.S.A., Mercer University Press (Macon, GA), 2003.

Contributor to books, including introduction to *Recollections and Letters of Robert E. Lee,* Barnes & Noble Books (New York, NY), 2004. Contributor to periodicals, including *Delta Sky* and *Americana.*

BIOGRAPHICAL AND CRITICAL SOURCES:

PERIODICALS

Journal of Southern History, November, 2004, Frank Allen Dennis, review of *A Hard Trip: A History of the 15th Mississippi Infantry, C.S.A.,* p. 929.

*   *   *

WYNNE, Benjamin R.
   See WYNNE, Ben

Y-Z

YAGHMAIAN, Behzad 1953-

PERSONAL: Born 1953, in Iran; immigrated to the United States. *Ethnicity:* Iranian.

ADDRESSES: *Home*—New York, NY. *Agent*—c/o Author Mail, Delacorte Press, 1745 Broadway, New York, NY 10019. *E-mail*—behzad.yaghmaian@gmail. com.

CAREER: Ramapo College, Ramapo, NJ, professor of political economy; *Neshat,* Iran, columnist, 1998-99; has also taught international political economics in Iran and Turkey.

WRITINGS:

Social Change in Iran: An Eyewitness Account of Dissent, Defiance, and New Movements for Rights, State University of New York Press (Albany, NY), 2002.
Embracing the Infidel: Stories of Muslim Migrants on the Journey West, Delacorte Press (New York, NY), 2005.

Contributor to journals.

SIDELIGHTS: Behzad Yaghmaian was born in Iran and later moved to the United States, where he studied international political economics. His primary focus is on globalization and the study of third-world nations, and he has published numerous academic articles on this subject. During the brief span of political opportunity in Iran from 1998 to 1999, Yaghmaian wrote a regular column for the newspaper *Neshat.* He has also served as a consultant for a documentary on Iran that was produced as a joint venture between PBS and Channel Four in England.

Yaghmaian's first book, *Social Change in Iran: An Eyewitness Account of Dissent, Defiance, and New Movements for Rights,* examines the cultural rift between the fundamentalist ideology and the new generation of Iranian youth. The book discusses the Islamic Republic and the results of the pressures for a free press and student rights. In a review for the *Middle East Journal,* Behrooz Ghamari-Tabrizi remarked that "although this book is fascinating reading, there are flaws in the author's understanding of the processes of change in Iran and in the way he conceptualizes them."

Embracing the Infidel: Stories of Muslim Migrants on the Journey West is the result of Yaghmaian's two-year journey across the Middle East and Europe as he followed migrants leaving Muslim countries for the West. Julia M. Klein, writing for *Mother Jones,* called the book an "intimate, horrifyingly vivid account of the plight of Muslim refugees." A contributor for *Kirkus Reviews* found the book to be "affecting, immediate and well written."

BIOGRAPHICAL AND CRITICAL SOURCES:

PERIODICALS

Booklist, November 1, 2005, Hazel Rochman, review of *Embracing the Infidel: Stories of Muslim Migrants on the Journey West,* p. 7.

Kirkus Reviews, November 1, 2005, review of *Embracing the Infidel,* p. 1180.

Library Journal, November 1, 2005, Lisa Klopfer, review of *Embracing the Infidel,* p. 102.

Middle East Journal, autumn, 2002, Behrooz Ghamari-Tabrizi, review of *Social Change in Iran: An Eyewitness Account of Dissent, Defiance, and New Movements for Rights,* p. 711.

Mother Jones, January-February, 2006, Julia M. Klein, review of *Embracing the Infidel,* p. 77.

ONLINE

Behzad Yaghmaian Home page, http://www.yaghmaian.com (March 15, 2006).

Ramapo College Web site, http://www.ramapo.edu/ (March 15, 2006), brief author biography.

* * *

YUSA, Michiko 1951-

PERSONAL: Born November 28, 1951, in Japan. *Ethnicity:* "Japanese." *Education:* International Christian University, Tokyo, Japan, B.A., 1974; University of California, Santa Barbara, M.A., 1977, Ph.D., 1983. *Hobbies and other interests:* Cooking, music, strolling.

ADDRESSES: Office—Western Washington University, 519 High St., Bellingham, WA 98225-9057. *E-mail*—yusa@wwu.edu.

CAREER: Writer and educator. Western Washington University, Bellingham, assistant professor, 1983-88, associate professor, 1988-94, professor, 1994—.

MEMBER: American Academy of Religion, Association for Asian Studies, Society for Asian and Comparative Philosophy.

WRITINGS:

(With Matsuo Soga) *Basic Kanji* (in Japanese), Taishukan (Tokyo, Japan), 1989.

Denki: Nishida Kitaro (in Japanese), Toeisha (Kyoto, Japan), 1998.

Japanese Religious Traditions, Prentice-Hall (Upper Saddle River, NJ), 2002.

Zen and Philosophy: An Intellectual Biography of Nishida Kitaro, University of Hawaii Press (Honolulu, HI), 2002.

(Editor, with Sarah Clark-Langager) *Isamu Noguchi and Skyviewing Sculpture,* Western Washington University (Bellingham, WA), 2004.

* * *

ZEILER, Thomas W. 1961(?)-

PERSONAL: Born c. 1961. *Education:* Emory University, B.A., 1983; University of Massachusetts—Amhurst, M.A., 1985, Ph.D., 1989.

ADDRESSES: Home—156 S. Rosemary St., Denver, CO 80230. *Office*—Department of History, 2334 UCB, University of Colorado at Boulder, Boulder, CO 80234-0234. *E-mail*—thomas.zeiler@colorado.edu.

CAREER: University of Colorado, Denver, visiting professor, 1991; University of Colorado, Boulder, lecturer, 1990-93, assistant professor, 1993-98, associate professor, 1998-2001, professor of history, 2001—. Member, Business History Conference; member, Department of State Advisory Committee on Historical Diplomatic Documentation, 2005—.

MEMBER: European Community Studies Association, Organization of American Historians, Society for Historians of American Foreign Relations, The Historical Society.

AWARDS, HONORS: Stuart L. Bernath Dissertation Fund Award, Society for Historians of American Foreign Relations, 1989; Teacher Recognition Award, Student Organization for Alumni Relations, University of Colorado at Boulder, 1996; Fulbright Senior fellowships, 1999, 2004-05; Stuart L. Bernath Lecture Prize, Society for Historians of American Foreign Relations, 2001; recipient of numerous research grants.

WRITINGS:

American Trade and Power in the 1960s, Columbia University Press (New York, NY), 1992.

Free Trade, Free World: The Advent of GATT, University of North Carolina Press (Chapel Hill, NC), 1999.

Dean Rusk: Defending the American Mission Abroad, Scholarly Resources (Wilmington, DE), 2000.

(With Alfred E. Eckes, Jr.) *Globalization and the American Century,* Cambridge University Press (New York, NY), 2003.

Unconditional Defeat: Japan, America, and the End of World War II, Scholarly Resources (Wilmington, DE), 2004.

Contributor to books, including *Government-Business Cooperation, 1945-1964: Volume 9: Corporatism in the Postwar Era,* edited by Robert F. Himmelberg, Garland Publishing, 1994; *The Encyclopedia of U.S. Foreign Relations,* Council on Foreign Relations, 1997; *Kennedy: The New Frontier Revisited,* edited by Mark White, St. Martin's Press, 1998; *American National Biography,* Volume 18, edited by John A. Garraty and Mark C. Carnes, Oxford University Press, 1999; *The Oxford Companion to American Military History,* edited by John Whiteclay Chambers II, Oxford University Press, 1999; and *The Oxford Companion to United States History,* Oxford University Press, 2000. Contributor to journals, including *Australian Economic History Review, American National Biography, Diplomatic History,* and *Business and Economic History.* Executive editor, *Diplomatic History: Journal of the Society for Historians of American Foreign Relations,* 2001—; editor-in-chief, *American Foreign Relations since 1600: A Guide to the Literature,* (ABC-Clio), 2004—. Member of editorial board, *H-Diplo* Listserve, 2001—, *Journal of International Sports History,* 2005—; associate editor, *Journal of Transatlantic Studies,* 2000—; board member, *Association of Transatlantic Studies,* 2000—.

WORK IN PROGRESS: *Global Games: The Spalding World Tour of 1888-1889* and *World War II: A Global History.*

SIDELIGHTS: History professor Thomas W. Zeiler has focused his research primarily on American political and military history, diplomatic history and international affairs, and global and world history. His first book, *American Trade and Power in the 1960s,* examines the less glamorous aspects of foreign trade policy during the Kennedy administration and beyond, forgoing the more frequently discussed Bay of Pigs, Cuban Missile Crisis, and Vietnam conflict for the 1962 Trade Expansion Act and the meetings leading to the General Agreement on Trade and Tariff (GATT). Nathan Godfried, writing for the *Journal of Interdisciplinary History,* stated that "the book's narrative proves informative, although it adds little to our understanding of why the United States lost economic power. Although occasionally provocative, the book's analysis remains problematic." On the other hand, *Canadian Journal of History* contributor Lawrence Aronsen remarked that "this book provides a useful corrective to earlier studies of the Kennedy administration that emphasized the president's inattention to the details of complicated policies and his inclination to follow narrowly defined American economic interests." Arsonsen concluded that it is "a first rate study of the trade policy of the Kennedy years."

Free Trade, Free World: The Advent of GATT examines the agreement more closely, providing a detailed history of the policies and discussions that led to it being put into operation. Forrest Capie stated in *Business History* that "while the book is well written there is a danger of the story being presented in overly dramatic terms," adding that "too much of the story reads as if the world began around the time of the study. This is a pity for it is an important subject and one from which business historians can learn and to which they can contribute." Although Gregory P. Marchildon also remarked on some flaws in his *Canadian Journal of History* assessment of *Free Trade, Free World,* he concluded: "Zeiler is to be commended for throwing much needed light on this very important episode in postwar history." The critic added, "Zeiler's book cannot be considered the definitive history of the birth of GATT. But he does provide a starting point for future historians of what, in retrospect, must be considered one of the pivotal institutions of the last fifty years."

Zeiler's *Dean Rusk: Defending the American Mission Abroad,* a part of the Scholarly Resources' "Biographies in American Foreign Policy" series, gives an overview of Dean Rusk's education and foreign policies; it then examines how that foreign policy affected the Vietnam War. Mary Carroll, writing for *Booklist,* recommended the volume "for readers interested in this important era in foreign policy."

BIOGRAPHICAL AND CRITICAL SOURCES:

PERIODICALS

Booklist, August, 1999, Mary Carroll, review of *Dean Rusk: Defending the American Mission Abroad,* p. 2016.

Business History, January, 2000, Forrest Capie, review of *Free Trade, Free World: The Advent of GATT,* p. 150.

Canadian Journal of History, August, 1993, Lawrence Aronsen, review of *American Trade and Power in the 1960s,* p. 372; August, 2000, Gregory P. Marchildon, review of *Free Trade, Free World,* p. 414.

Journal of Interdisciplinary History, winter, 1995, Nathan Godfried, review of *American Trade and Power in the 1960s,* p. 550.

ONLINE

H-Net.org, http://www.h-net.org/ (March 15, 2006), author profile.

University of Colorado Web site, http://www.colorado.edu/ (March 15, 2006), author's curriculum vitae.

University of North Carolina Press Web site, http://uncpress.unc.edu/ (March 15, 2006), information on author.*